COMING TO TERMS

American Plays & the Vietnam War

COMING TO TERMS
American Plays & the Vietnam War

Introduction by *James Reston, Jr.*

Theatre Communications Group, Inc.
New York • 1985

Coming to Terms is published by Theatre Communications Group, Inc., the national organization for the nonprofit professional theatre, 335 Lexington Ave., New York, NY 10017.

Designed by Soho Studio

Cover photograph of the Vietnam Veterans' Memorial by Charles Tasnadi, AP/Wide World Photos.

Manufactured in the United States of America

First Edition

Library of Congress Cataloging in Publication Data
Main entry under title:

Coming to terms.

Contents: Moonchildren / by Michael Weller
Botticelli / by Terrence McNally / How I got that
story / by Amlin Gray / Medal of honor rag / by
Tom Cole / [etc.]
1. Vietnamese Conflict, 1961-1975—Drama.
2. American drama—20th century. 3. War—Drama.
PS627.V53C6 1985   812'.54'080358   85-2846
ISBN 0-930452-44-5 (pbk.)

Contents

Introduction
by James Reston, Jr.

Memory, especially collective memory, is a subtle and in many ways fragile act. Normally, we think of it as the dominion of historians, as if they always have the last word. They deliver with their fat biographies, "The Life and Times of . . .," and their grand generalizations, "The Tragic Era . . .," and their trenchant analyses, "The Short and Long Range Causes of . . .," and it can sometimes be pretty dry stuff. Almost inevitably, such tracts recount in splendid detail the perambulations of men in power. Stock questions are asked of every historical epoch. What will HISTORY record? What will the historians think one hundred years later? How will reputations stand the "test of time"?

Vietnam will be different. For once, traditional historical method is inadequate. Facts and men in power are not at the core of this story, but rather the emotions of the generation which shouldered the profound consequences of this ill-conceived enterprise. The Vietnam generation, reacting to the decisions from on high, changed American society forever, and so the heart of the matter is emotional and cultural.

In the past several years we've heard quite a bit about the "lessons of Vietnam." Briefly, it became a point of argument in the campaign for the Democratic nomination in 1984 between Gary Hart and Walter Mondale. A spate of books, usually churned out by former policy makers and historians of public policy, have purported to address the issue. Even a label now exists—Vietnam revisionism—for this brand of scholarship. The problem has been bandied around as the United States flirts with "another Vietnam" in Central America.

And yet, for all the books, for all its mention in political debate, a sense of disquiet reigns. Vietnam is not yet, by any measure, a digested event of American history. It is a national experience that is still denied and repressed, not one which is folded into the sweep of our history and which we calmly acknowledge as the downside of American potentiality.

This is partly the failure of political leadership. Gerald Ford and Jimmy Carter were too weak as men and as leaders to educate the country on the resonance of the first American defeat in war. They needed to be the leaders of the Second Reconstruction of American history, comparable to the first after the American Civil War. If, after our first divisive war, America became a more racially equal society, then after Vietnam America needed to become a less militarist society. It did not happen. Instead, these presidents presided over amnesia and malaise. And in the great malaise, the victims were left to sort out their lives without help or respect or even acknowledgment.

Perhaps it is not entirely the politician's fault. Their silence or their half-hearted attempts at reconciliation, like their clemencies and pardon for Vietnam War resisters, were reflections of a national mood. For 10 years, the American people did not want to think about Vietnam. And since they did not want to think about it, politicians—and, yes, publishers and theatrical directors too—did not provide the public with food for thought. In effect, the whole culture together shut down on the subject.

Ronald Reagan changed all that. When his soldiers died in Lebanon and Grenada and El Salvador, and American patriotism again came to represent mainly anti-Communism; when Caspar Weinberger fashioned those empty phrases at the gravesites of Vietnam veterans, like "We never again will commit American boys to a war we don't intend to win," and Reagan himself declared Vietnam to have been a noble cause, the culture began to wake up from its long sleep. It was time to think again about the longest, costliest war in American history, for a Vietnam mythology was in the making.

But by the time it became fashionable to "think" about Vietnam, the nation had forgotten the total agony of the experience. If one reads the revisionist histories, it is as if Vietnam were only a question of whether Congress and domestic dissent shackled the military and didn't allow it to exercise its full measure of violence. If only we had bombed North Vietnam more and sooner, or picked some spot on the coast for another Inchon invasion early on, or invaded Cambodia when it would do some good. If only . . . if only: it is the standard refuge of losers. The lessons of Vietnam somehow got focused on policy questions to the exclusion of emotional and generational questions. The next time you enter a guerrilla war in a jungle, be sure. . . . What? . . . Sock it to the sanctuaries soon and hard! Deny the flow of arms from the outside! Then, by God, you'll show 'em you intend to win. . . . Such lessons are minor indeed, if they are lessons at all.

The real lessons lie in what happened to one generation of Americans. The Vietnam generation is unique in American history. The choices it faced, the manner in which it dealt with those choices, the problems it faced in the aftermath: that is the story of Vietnam. Only in dealing with that can the country come to terms with the war.

In 1985, this is far from an idle concern for some musty academic. For the Vietnam generation may not forever be unique. The truth is that at this moment there is not a sufficient appreciation of the Vietnam agony in our political community, in our culture, or in our youth, who are the candidates for the next Vietnam. We do not know it well enough to loathe it sufficiently. Without loathing, how can we prevent it from happening again? We have conveniently forgotten much of what is distasteful to remember. Memory is always that way, but this amnesia has consequences.

In my view, the most accurate, most profound memory of Vietnam lies in the arts. The novels, the plays, the painting and sculpture, the poetry—these all go to the emotional truth of the experience, and when they are good they are worth more than a mountain of books on the military campaigns or the chief political figures or the chapter-and-verse facts about the era. That is one more unique aspect of the Vietnam age. The playwright becomes more important than the historian, for in no other war of our history was the private word more important than the public pronouncements, the whispered intimacies between friends—whether dignitaries or the boys in the streets and trenches—more important than statements from lecterns or barricades or muddy foxholes. For such whisperings are seldom recorded. With the Vietnam experience, the history is the subtext.

But there is here also a question of the audience. We of the Vietnam generation, particularly the artists who have something to say about our experience, have the problem of how to get people to listen. Our message is not nice and jolly, although we may employ humor or satire or parody or the absurd to get it across. In the current mood of America, strong voices easily drown us out. These voices are not only loud but soothing, especially so since the country avoided the issue for a decade. It is flattering to be told now, if you are a Vietnam veteran, that yours was a noble cause, even though you never thought of it as a cause or as yours while you were enduring it. It is flattering to have memorials erected to your bravery and sacrifice, not only in Washington but in many state capitals. That veterans became passionate, almost hysterical, over whether their symbolic representation in a statue has a heroic or merely reflective air goes to their own internal conflicts within their own memory. Such internal conflicts are the very stuff of the stage.

The wall in Washington, after all, is not the only memorial which bears the names of the war dead. There is another memorial to the American soldier—smudged and nearly overgrown by the relentless jungle—in a village in Vietnam called My Lai. Upon its cement surface are the names of 504 Vietnamese dead. Over there, a different mythology is being created: that all

American soldiers were Lieutenant Calleys. The American soldier as devil competes with the American soldier as misunderstood, scorned, rediscovered and, finally, ennobled warrior. One does not have to travel halfway around the world to appreciate these competing images. They exist, dramatically and poignantly, within the soul of veterans and Vietnam avoiders alike.

The literature of Vietnam is now vast, and it is quite possible that before the final coming to terms is over, this war will compete even with the American Civil War in its literary output. If you want to know more about the "post-traumatic stress syndrome" that Emily Mann dramatizes so unflinchingly in *Still Life* and Steve Metcalfe highlights in that cruel line of *Strange Snow* where the sister speaks to her veteran brother of "generosity and love, feelings you've forgotten," there are reams of psychological tracts available. If you want to know more about those who said no, the dirges on the anti-war movement exist, but you will do far better to see a sprightly production of Michael Weller's wickedly funny and wonderful *Moonchildren*. If you want to delve into the latent violence the fear of Vietnam induced, the psychiatrists have looked at that too, of course, but it's all there in a much more arresting form in David Rabe's *Streamers*. Thick government studies have the statistics about how 80 percent of Vietnam veterans either disagreed with Vietnam policy or did not understand it, but as you regard the carnage on the stage at the end of *Streamers* and hear Richie say "I didn't even know what it was about exactly . . .," you will understand better what fighting and killing for no apparent reason means to the individual. In *Still Life*, you will learn that it means drugs, and divorce, and jail, and a loss of manhood. These are the social costs of fighting a war so adverse to the noble and radical principles upon which the country was founded.

The same dense studies show that the Vietnam veteran was distinguished not so much by the color of his skin as by his lack of education. Standards of leadership had to be lowered as in no other war in American history. The best, the brightest and the most cultured stayed away. Lieutenant Calley could never have been an American officer in any other war. In *Botticelli* Terrence McNally skillfully turns this situation upside down by giving us two wildly cultured grunts playing a parlor game outside a tunnel entrance in the jungle. Thus, the playwright teaches by inversion, a technique that artists can bring off best. Likewise it took an artist like Amlin Gray, in *How I Got That Story*, to make an essentially absurd war even more grotesquely absurd than it actually was, thereby making us laugh while we hurt. And by exploring the relation between madness and bravery and the hypocrisy of official honor, Tom Cole's *Medal of Honor Rag* will give you a powerful point of view for the next time the Pentagon hands out 8,000 medals.

In short, all the important lessons of Vietnam are here in this fine and varied collection of plays, in forms that enable the lessons to be felt and understood *totally* with the heart and soul, as well as with the mind. Such total understanding, with the total acceptance that understanding brings in its wake, is the only way that American culture will come to terms with the Vietnam memory.

The collection also demonstrates a point that many, even in the theatre, will not readily accept: that the stage has a special role in presenting living issues of the day. Its tools are beyond those of the historian and the journalist, for the stage is at home with the interior of things. In that sacred precinct, very often a deeper truth lies. The theatre is not at its best when it attempts to reproduce history or contemporary politics, but rather when it presents a *concept* of history against which the audience can test its own perceptions. The stage can humanize history and bring it alive, while professional historians and the television are dehumanizing. Such dehumanization is especially common with terrible events like Vietnam and Jonestown, where the public is shocked by the unthinkable.

The stage must recapture its proper confrontational role, making itself important not just by dealing with emotional issues of recollection and memory, but with issues that the society debates now, today. For the stage can pierce the shroud with which television covers our world. This book shows that playwrights are ready to apply their special gifts to the contemporary scene, to reclaim their special wisdom in relation to the affairs of today. It's up to the theatres to dare to let these voices be heard. Audiences, even in 1985, *will* respond.

Born in New York City in 1941, James Reston, Jr., a graduate of the University of North Carolina, spent three years in U.S. Army Intelligence. He is the author of two novels, several nonfiction books and two plays, *Sherman, the Peacemaker* and *Jonestown Express*. His latest book, *Sherman's March and Vietnam* (Macmillan), appeared earlier in 1985, after being excerpted in *The New Yorker*.

STREAMERS

David Rabe

About David Rabe

Born in Dubuque, Iowa in 1940, David Rabe was doing graduate work in theatre at Villanova University when he was drafted into the army. Assigned to a support group for hospitals, he spent 11 months in Vietnam. Returning to Villanova to complete his M.A., Rabe saw his first Vietnam play, *Sticks and Bones*, produced there in 1969. *The Basic Training of Pavlo Hummel* was premiered by Joseph Papp's New York Shakespeare Festival in May 1971; *Sticks and Bones* opened there less than six months later, and was subsequently moved to Broadway, winning the Tony Award for Best Play in 1972. Other plays by Rabe include *The Orphan, In the Boom Boom Room* and *Goose and Tom-Tom*, all first produced by Papp. Rabe's most recent play, *Hurlyburly*, was originally staged at Chicago's Goodman Theatre by Mike Nichols and then moved to Broadway, where as of early 1985 it is still running. Rabe also wrote the screenplay for *I'm Dancing as Fast as I Can*. In addition to his Tony, Rabe's many awards include an Obie for Distinguished Playwriting and the Dramatists Guild's Hull-Warriner Award.

Production History

Streamers opened at the Long Wharf Theatre in New Haven in January 1976, under the direction of Mike Nichols, and in April of that year was produced by Joseph Papp at Lincoln Center, with Nichols again directing. *Streamers* won the New York Drama Critics Circle Award as the best American play of 1976. Rabe wrote the screenplay for the Robert Altman film based on the play.

Characters

MARTIN
RICHIE
CARLYLE
BILLY
ROGER
COKES
ROONEY
M.P. LIEUTENANT
PFC HINSON (M.P.)
PFC CLARK (M.P.)
FOURTH M.P.

Time

The mid-1960s.

Place

An army barracks in Virginia.

MASTER SSU, MASTER YÜ, MASTER LI AND MASTER LAI

All at once Master Yü fell ill, and Master Ssu went to ask how he was. "Amazing!" exclaimed Master Yü. "Look, the Creator is making me all crookedy! My back sticks up like a hunchback's so that my vital organs are on top of me. My chin is hidden down around my navel, my shoulders are up above my head, and my pigtail points at the sky. It must be due to some dislocation of the forces of the yin and the yang. . . . "

"Do you resent it?" asked Master Ssu.

"Why, no," replied Master Yü. "What is there to resent . . .?"

Then suddenly Master Lai also fell ill. Gasping for breath, he lay at the point of death. His wife and children gathered round in a circle and wept. Master Li, who had come to find out how he was, said to them, "Shooooo! Get back! Don't disturb the process of change."

And he leaned against the doorway and chatted with Master Lai. "How marvelous the Creator is!" he exclaimed. "What is he going to make out of you next? Where is he going to send you? Will he make you into a rat's liver? Will he make you into a bug's arm?"

"A child obeys his father and mother and goes wherever he is told, east or west, south or north," said Master Lai. "And the yin and the yang— how much more are they to a man than father or mother! Now that they have brought me to the verge of death, how perverse it would be of me to refuse to obey them. . . . So now I think of heaven and earth as a great furnace and the Creator as a skilled smith. What place could he send me that would not be all right? I will go off peacefully to sleep, and then with a start I will wake up."

—CHUANG-TZU

They so mean around here, they steal your sweat.

—SONNY LISTON

The Play

Streamers

ACT ONE

The set is a large cadre room thrusting angularly toward the audience. The floor is wooden and brown. Brightly waxed in places, it is worn and dull in other sections. The back wall is brown and angled. There are two lights at the center of the ceiling. They hang covered by green metal shades. Against the back wall and to the stage right side are three wall lockers, side by side. Stage center in the back wall is the door, the only entrance to the room. It opens onto a hallway that runs off to the latrines, showers, other cadre rooms and larger barracks rooms. There are three bunks. BILLY's bunk is parallel to ROGER's bunk. They are upstage and on either side of the room, and face downstage. RICHIE's bunk is downstage and at a right angle to BILLY's bunk. At the foot of each bunk is a green wooden footlocker. There is a floor outlet near ROGER's bunk. HE uses it for his radio. A reading lamp is clamped onto the metal piping at the head of RICHIE's bunk. A wooden chair stands beside the wall lockers. Two mops hang in the stage left corner near a trash can.

It is dusk as the lights rise on the room. RICHIE is seated and bowed forward wearily on his bunk. HE wears his long-sleeved khaki summer dress uniform. Upstage behind him is MARTIN, a thin, dark young man, pacing, worried. A white towel stained red with blood is wrapped around his wrist. HE paces several steps and falters, stops. HE stands there.

RICHIE: Honest to God, Martin, I don't know what to say anymore. I don't know what to tell you.

MARTIN (*Beginning to pace again*): I mean it. I just can't stand it. Look at me.

RICHIE: I know.

MARTIN: I hate it.

RICHIE: We've got to make up a story. They'll ask you a hundred questions.

MARTIN: Do you know how I hate it?

RICHIE: Everybody does. Don't you think I hate it, too?

MARTIN: I enlisted, though. I enlisted and I hate it.

RICHIE: I enlisted, too.

MARTIN: I vomit every morning. I get the dry heaves. In the middle of every night. (HE *flops down on the corner of* BILLY*'s bed and sits there, slumped forward, shaking his head*)

RICHIE: You can stop that. You can.

MARTIN: No.

RICHIE: You're just scared. It's just fear.

MARTIN: They're all so mean; they're all so awful. I've got two years to go. Just thinking about it is going to make me sick. I thought it would be different from the way it is.

RICHIE: But you could have died, for God's sake. (HE *has turned now;* HE *is facing* MARTIN)

MARTIN: I just wanted out.

RICHIE: I might not have found you, though. I might not have come up here.

MARTIN: I don't care. I'd be out.

The door opens and a black man in filthy fatigues—they are grease-stained and dark with sweat—stands there. HE *is* CARLYLE, *looking about.* RICHIE, *seeing him, rises and moves toward him.*

RICHIE: No. Roger isn't here right now.

CARLYLE: Who isn't?

RICHIE: He isn't here.

CARLYLE: They tole me a black boy livin' in here. I don't see him. (HE *looks suspiciously about the room*)

RICHIE: That's what I'm saying. He isn't here. He'll be back later. You can come back later. His name is Roger.

MARTIN: I slit my wrist. (*Thrusting out the bloody, towel-wrapped wrist toward* CARLYLE)

RICHIE: Martin! Jesus!

MARTIN: I did.

RICHIE: He's kidding. He's kidding.

CARLYLE: What was his name? Martin? (HE *is confused and the confusion has made him angry.* HE *moves toward* MARTIN) You Martin?

MARTIN: Yes.

BILLY, *a white in his mid-twenties, blond and trim, appears in the door, whistling, carrying a slice of pie on a paper napkin. Sensing something,* HE *falters, looks at* CARLYLE, *then* RICHIE.

BILLY: Hey, what's goin' on?

CARLYLE (*Turning, leaving*): Nothin', man. Not a thing.

BILLY *looks questioningly at* RICHIE. *Then, after placing the piece of pie on the chair beside the door,* HE *crosses to his footlocker.*

RICHIE: He came in looking for Roger, but he didn't even know his name.

BILLY (*Sitting on his footlocker,* HE *starts taking off his shoes*): How come you weren't at dinner, Rich? I brought you a piece of pie. Hey, Martin.

MARTIN *thrusts out his towel-wrapped wrist.*

MARTIN: I cut my wrist, Billy.

RICHIE: Oh, for God's sake, Martin! (HE *whirls away*)

BILLY: Huh?

MARTIN: I did.

RICHIE: You are disgusting, Martin.

MARTIN: No. It's the truth. I did. I am not disgusting.

RICHIE: Well, maybe it isn't disgusting, but it certainly is disappointing.

BILLY: What are you guys talking about? (*Sitting there,* HE *really doesn't know what is going on*)

MARTIN: I cut my wrists, I slashed them, and Richie is pretending I didn't.

RICHIE: I am not. And you only cut one wrist and you didn't slash it.

MARTIN: I can't stand the army anymore, Billy. (HE *is moving now to petition* BILLY, *and* RICHIE *steps between them*)

RICHIE: Billy, listen to me. This is between Martin and me.

MARTIN: It's between me and the army, Richie.

RICHIE: (*Taking* MARTIN *by the shoulders as* BILLY *is now trying to get near* MARTIN): Let's just go outside and talk, Martin. You don't know what you're saying.

BILLY: Can I see? I mean, did he really do it?

RICHIE: No!

MARTIN: I did.

BILLY: That's awful. Jesus. Maybe you should go to the infirmary.

RICHIE: I washed it with peroxide. It's not deep. Just let us be. Please. He just needs to straighten out his thinking a little, that's all.

BILLY: Well, maybe I could help him?

MARTIN: Maybe he could.

RICHIE *is suddenly pushing at* MARTIN. RICHIE *is angry and exasperated.* HE *wants* MARTIN *out of the room.*

RICHIE: Get out of here, Martin. Billy, you do some push-ups or something.

Having been pushed toward the door, MARTIN *wanders out.*

BILLY: No.

RICHIE: I know what Martin needs. (HE *whirls and rushes into the hall after* MARTIN, *leaving* BILLY *scrambling to get his shoes on*)

BILLY: You're no doctor, are you? I just want to make sure he doesn't have to go to the infirmary, then I'll leave you alone. (*One shoe on,* HE *grabs up the second and runs out the door into the hall after them*) Martin! Martin, wait up!

Silence. The door has been left open. Fifteen or twenty seconds pass. Then someone is heard coming down the hall. HE *is singing "Get a Job" and trying to do the voices and harmonies of a vocal group.* ROGER, *a tall, well-built black in long-sleeved khakis, comes in the door.* HE *has a laundry bag over his shoulder, a pair of clean civilian trousers and a shirt on a hanger in his other hand. After dropping the bag on his bed,* HE *goes to his wall locker, where* HE *carefully hangs up the civilian clothes. Returning to the bed,* HE *picks up the laundry and then, as if struck,* HE *throws the bag down on the bed, tears off his tie and sits down angrily on the bed. For a moment, with his head in his hands,* HE *sits there. Then, resolutely,* HE *rises, takes up the position of attention, and simply topples forward, his hands leaping out to break his fall at the last instant and put him into the push-up position. Counting in a hissing, whispering voice,* HE *does ten push-ups before giving up and flopping onto his belly.* HE *simply doesn't have the will to do any more. Lying there,* HE *counts rapidly on.*

ROGER: Fourteen, fifteen. Twenty. Twenty-five.

BILLY, *shuffling dejectedly back in, sees* ROGER *lying there.* ROGER *springs to his feet, heads toward his footlocker, out of which* HE *takes an ashtray and a pack of cigarettes.*

You come in this area, you come in here marchin', boy: standin' tall.

BILLY, *having gone to his wall locker, is tossing a* Playboy *magazine onto his bunk.* HE *will also remove a towel, a Dopp kit and a can of foot powder.*

BILLY: I was marchin'.

ROGER: You call that marchin'?

BILLY: I was as tall as I am; I was marchin'—what do you want?

ROGER: Outa here, man; outa this goddamn typin'-terrors outfit and into some kinda real army. Or else out and free.

BILLY: So go; who's stoppin' you; get out. Go on.

ROGER: Ain't you a bitch.

BILLY: You and me more regular army than the goddamn sergeants around this place, you know that?

ROGER: I was you, Billy boy, I wouldn't be talkin' so sacrilegious so loud, or they be doin' you like they did the ole sarge.

BILLY: He'll get off.

ROGER: Sheee-it, he'll get off. (*Sitting down on the side of his bed and facing* BIL-LY, HE *lights up a cigarette.* BILLY *has arranged the towel, Dopp kit and foot powder on his own bed*) Don't you think L.B.J. want to have some sergeants in that Vietnam, man? In Disneyland, baby? Lord have mercy on the ole sarge. He goin' over there to be Mickey Mouse.

BILLY: Do him a lot of good. Make a man outa him.

ROGER: That's right, that's right. He said the same damn thing about himself and you, too, I do believe. You know what's the ole boy's MOS? His Military Occupation Specialty? Demolitions, baby. Expert is his name.

BILLY (*Taking off his shoes and beginning to work on a sore toe,* HE *hardly looks up*): You're kiddin' me.

ROGER: Do I jive?

BILLY: You mean that poor ole bastard who cannot light his own cigar for shakin' is supposed to go over there blowin' up bridges and shit? Do they wanna win this war or not, man?

ROGER: Ole sarge was over in Europe in the big one, Billy. Did all kinds a bad things.

BILLY (*Swinging his feet up onto the bed,* HE *sits, cutting the cuticles on his toes, powdering his feet*): Was he drinkin' since he got the word?

ROGER: Was he breathin', Billy? Was he breathin'?

BILLY: Well, at least he ain't cuttin' his fuckin' wrists.

> *Silence.* ROGER *looks at* BILLY, *who keeps on working.*

Man, that's the real damn army over there, ain't it? That ain't shinin' your belt buckle and standin' tall. And we might end up in it, man.

> *Silence.* ROGER, *rising, begins to sort his laundry.*

Roger . . . you ever ask yourself if you'd rather fight in a war where it was freezin' cold or one where there was awful snakes? You ever ask that question?

ROGER: Can't say I ever did.

BILLY: We used to ask it all the time. All the time. I mean, us kids sittin' out on the back porch tellin' ghost stories at night. 'Cause it was Korea time and the newspapers were fulla pictures of soldiers in snow with white frozen beards; they got these rags tied around their feet. And snakes. We hated snakes. Hated 'em. I mean, it's bad enough to be in the jungle duckin' bullets, but then you crawl right into a goddamn snake. That's awful. That's awful.

ROGER: It don't sound none too good.

BILLY: I got my draft notice, goddamn Vietnam didn't even exist. I mean, it

existed, but not as in a war we might be in. I started crawlin' around the
floor a this house where I was stayin' 'cause I'd dropped outa school, and
I was goin' "Bang, bang," pretendin'. Jesus.

ROGER (*Continuing with his laundry,* HE *tries to joke*): My first goddamn formation in basic, Billy, this NCO's up there jammin' away about how some
a us are goin' to be dyin' in the war. I'm sayin', "What war? What that
crazy man talkin' about?"

BILLY: Us, too. I couldn't believe it. I couldn't believe it. And now we got
three people goin' from here.

ROGER: Five.

> ROGER *and* BILLY *look at each other, and then turn away, each returning to*
> *his task.*

BILLY: It don't seem possible. I mean, people shootin' at you. Shootin' at you
to kill you. (*Slight pause*) It's somethin'.

ROGER: What did you decide you preferred?

BILLY: Huh?

ROGER: Did you decide you would prefer the snakes or would you prefer the
snow? 'Cause it look like it is going to be the snakes.

BILLY: I think I had pretty much made my mind up on the snow.

ROGER: Well, you just let 'em know that, Billy. Maybe they get one goin'
special just for you up in Alaska. You can go to the Klondike. Fightin' some
snowmen.

> RICHIE *bounds into the room and shuts the door as if to keep out something*
> *dreadful.* HE *looks at* ROGER *and* BILLY *and crosses to his wall locker, pulling*
> *off his tie as* HE *moves. Tossing the tie into the locker,* HE *begins unbuttoning*
> *the cuffs of his shirt.*

RICHIE: Hi, hi, hi, everybody. Billy, hello.

BILLY: Hey.

ROGER: What's happenin', Rich?

> *Moving to the chair beside the door,* RICHIE *picks up the pie* BILLY *left there.*
> HE *will place the pie atop the locker, and then, sitting,* HE *will remove his shoes*
> *and socks.*

RICHIE: I simply did this rather wonderful thing for a friend of mine, helped
him see himself in a clearer, more hopeful light—little room in his life for
hope? And I feel very good. Didn't Billy tell you?

ROGER: About what?

RICHIE: About Martin.

ROGER: No.

BILLY (*Looking up and speaking pointedly*): No.

    RICHIE *looks at* BILLY *and then at* ROGER. RICHIE *is truly confused.*

RICHIE: No? No?

BILLY: What do I wanna gossip about Martin for?

RICHIE (HE *really can't figure out what is going on with* BILLY. *Shoes and socks in hand,* HE *heads for his wall locker*): Who was planning to gossip? I mean, it did happen. We could talk about it. I mean, I wasn't hearing his goddamn confession. Oh, my sister told me Catholics were boring.

BILLY: Good thing I ain't one anymore.

RICHIE (*Taking off his shirt,* HE *moves toward* ROGER): It really wasn't anything, Roger, except Martin made this rather desperate, pathetic gesture for attention that seems to have brought to the surface Billy's more humane and protective side. (*Reaching out,* HE *tousles* BILLY*'s hair*)

BILLY: Man, I am gonna have to obliterate you.

RICHIE (*Tossing his shirt into his locker*): I don't know what you're so embarrassed about.

BILLY: I just think Martin's got enough trouble without me yappin' to everybody.

    RICHIE *has moved nearer* BILLY, *his manner playful and teasing.*

RICHIE: "Obliterate"? "Obliterate," did you say? Oh, Billy, you better say "shit," "ain't" and "motherfucker" real quick now or we'll all know just how far beyond the fourth grade you went.

ROGER (*Having moved to his locker, into which* HE *is placing his folded clothes*): You hear about the ole sarge, Richard?

BILLY (*Grinning*): You ain't . . . shit . . . motherfucker.

ROGER (*Laughing*): All right.

RICHIE (*Moving center and beginning to remove his trousers*): Billy, no, no. Wit is my domain. You're in charge of sweat and running around the block.

ROGER: You hear about the ole sarge?

RICHIE: What about the ole sarge? Oh, who cares? Let's go to a movie. Billy, wanna? Let's go. C'mon. (*Trousers off,* HE *hurries to his locker*)

BILLY: Sure. What's playin'?

RICHIE: I don't know. Can't remember. Something good, though.

    With a Playboy *magazine* HE *has taken from his locker,* ROGER *is settling down on his bunk, his back toward both* BILLY *and* RICHIE.

BILLY: You wanna go, Rog?

RICHIE (*In mock irritation*): Don't ask Roger! How are we going to kiss and hug and stuff if he's there?

BILLY: That ain't funny, man. (HE *is stretched out on his bunk, and* RICHIE *comes bounding over to flop down and lie beside him*)

RICHIE: And what time will you pick me up?

BILLY (HE *pushes at* RICHIE, *knocking him off the bed and onto the floor*): Well, you just fall down and wait, all right?

RICHIE: Can I help it if I love you? (*Leaping to his feet,* HE *will head to his locker, remove his shorts, put on a robe*)

ROGER: You gonna take a shower, Richard?

RICHIE: Cleanliness is nakedness, Roger.

ROGER: Is that right? I didn't know that. Not too many people know that. You may be the only person in the world who know that.

RICHIE: And godliness is in there somewhere, of course. (*Putting a towel around his neck,* HE *is gathering toiletries to carry to the shower*)

ROGER: You got your own way a lookin' at things, man. You cute.

RICHIE: That's right.

ROGER: You g'wan, have a good time in that shower.

RICHIE: Oh, I will.

BILLY (*Without looking up from his feet, which* HE *is powdering*): And don't drop your soap.

RICHIE: I will if I want to. (*Already out the door,* HE *slams it shut with a flourish*)

BILLY: Can you imagine bein' in combat with Richie—people blastin' away at you—he'd probably want to hold your hand.

ROGER: Ain't he somethin'?

BILLY: Who's zat?

ROGER: He's all right.

BILLY (*Rising,* HE *heads toward his wall locker, where he will put the powder and Dopp kit*): Sure he is, except he's livin' underwater.

Looking at BILLY, ROGER *senses something unnerving; it makes* ROGER *rise, and return his magazine to his footlocker.*

ROGER: I think we oughta do this area, man. I think we oughta do our area. Mop and buff this floor.

BILLY: You really don't think he means that shit he talks, do you?

ROGER: Huh? Awwww, man . . . Billy, no.

BILLY: I'd put money on it, Roger, and I ain't got much money.

BILLY *is trying to face* ROGER *with this, but* ROGER, *seated on his bed, has turned away.* HE *is unbuttoning his shirt.*

ROGER: Man, no, no. I'm tellin' you, lad, you listen to the ole Rog. You seen that picture a that little dolly he's got in his locker? He ain't swish, man, believe me—he's cool.

BILLY: It's just that ever since we been in this room, he's been different somehow. Somethin'.

ROGER: No, he ain't.

BILLY *turns to his bed, where* HE *carefully starts folding the towel. Then* HE *looks at* ROGER.

BILLY: You ever talk to any a these guys—queers, I mean? You ever sit down, just rap with one of 'em?

ROGER: Hell, no; what I wanna do that for? Shit, no.

BILLY (*Crossing to the trash can in the corner, where* HE *will shake the towel empty*): I mean, some of 'em are okay guys, just way up this bad alley, and you say to 'em, "I'm straight, be cool," they go their own way. But then there's these other ones, these bitches, man, and they're so crazy they think anybody can be had. Because they been had themselves. So you tell 'em you're straight and they just nod and smile. You ain't real to 'em. They can't see nothin' but themselves and these goddamn games they're always playin'. (*Having returned to his bunk,* HE *is putting on his shoes*) I mean, you can be decent about anything, Roger, you see what I'm sayin'? We're all just people, man, and some of us are hardly that. That's all I'm sayin'. (*There is a slight pause as* HE *sits there thinking. Then* HE *gets to his feet*) I'll go get some buckets and stuff so we can clean up, okay? This area's a mess. This area ain't standin' tall.

ROGER: That's good talk, lad; this area a midget you put it next to an area standin' tall.

BILLY: Got to be good fuckin' troopers.

ROGER: That's right, that's right. I know the meanin' of the words.

BILLY: I mean, I just think we all got to be honest with each other—you understand me?

ROGER: No, I don't understand you; one stupid fuckin' nigger like me—how's that gonna be?

BILLY: That's right; mock me, man. That's what I need. I'll go get the wax.

Out BILLY *goes, talking to himself and leaving the door open. For a moment* ROGER *sits, thinking, and then* HE *looks at* RICHIE's *locker and gets to his feet and walks to the locker.* HE *opens it and looks at the pinup hanging on the inside of the door.* HE *takes a step backward, looking.*

ROGER: Sheee-it.

Through the open door comes CARLYLE. ROGER *doesn't see him. And* CARLYLE *stands there looking at* ROGER *and the picture in the locker.*

CARLYLE: Boy . . . whose locker you lookin' into?

ROGER (HE *is startled, but recovers*): Hey, baby, what's happenin'?

CARLYLE: That ain't your locker, is what I'm askin', nigger. I mean, you ain't got no white goddamn woman hangin' on your wall.

ROGER: Oh, no—no, no.

CARLYLE: You don't wanna be lyin' to me, 'cause I got to turn you in you lyin' and you do got the body a some white goddamn woman hangin' there for you to peek at nobody around but you—you can be thinkin' about that sweet wet pussy an' maybe it hot an' maybe it cool.

ROGER: I could be thinkin' all that, except I know the penalty for lyin'.

CARLYLE: Thank God for that. (*Extending his hand, palm up*)

ROGER: That's right. This here the locker of a faggot. (*And* HE *slaps* CARLYLE's *hand, palm to palm*)

CARLYLE: Course it is; I see that; any damn body know that. (ROGER *crosses toward his bunk and* CARLYLE *swaggers about, pulling a pint of whiskey from his hip pocket*) You want a shot? Have you a little taste, my man.

ROGER: Naw.

CARLYLE: C'mon. C'mon. I think you a Tom you don't drink outa my bottle. (HE *thrusts the bottle toward* ROGER *and wipes a sweat- and grease-stained sleeve across his mouth*)

ROGER (*Taking the bottle*): Shit.

CARLYLE: That right. How do I know? I just got in. New boy in town. Somewhere over there; I dunno. They dump me in amongst a whole bunch a pale, boring motherfuckers. (HE *is exploring the room. Finding* BILLY's Playboy, HE *edges onto* BILLY's *bed and leafs nervously through the pages*) I just come in from P Company, man, and I been all over this place, don't see too damn many of us. This outfit look like it a little short on soul. I been walkin' all around, I tell you, and the number is small. Like one hand you can tabulate the lot of 'em. We got few brothers I been able to see, is what I'm sayin'. You and me and two cats down in the small bay. That's all I found. (*As* ROGER *is about to hand the bottle back,* CARLYLE, *almost angrily, waves him off*) No, no, you take another; take you a real taste.

ROGER: It ain't so bad here. We do all right.

CARLYLE (HE *moves, shutting the door. Suspiciously,* HE *approaches* ROGER): How about the white guys? They give you any sweat? What's the situation? No jive. I like to know what is goin' on within the situation before that situation get a chance to be closin' in on me.

ROGER (*Putting the bottle on the footlocker,* HE *sits down*): Man, I'm tellin' you, it ain't bad. They're just pale, most of 'em, you know. They can't help it; how they gonna help it? Some of 'em got little bit of soul, couple real good boys around this way. Get 'em little bit of Coppertone, they be straight, man.

CARLYLE: How about the NCOs? We got any brother NCO watchin' out for us or they all white, like I goddamn well KNOW all the officers are? Fuckin' officers always white, man; fuckin' snow cones and bars everywhere you look. (HE *cannot stay still.* HE *moves to his right, his left;* HE *sits,* HE *stands*)

ROGER: First sergeant's a black man.

CARLYLE: All right; good news. Hey, hey, you wanna go over the club with me, or maybe downtown? I got wheels. Let's be free. (*Now* HE *rushes at* ROGER) Let's be free.

ROGER: Naw . . .

CARLYLE: Ohhh, baby . . . ! (HE *is wildly pulling at* ROGER *to get him to the door*)

ROGER: Some other time. I gotta get the area straight. Me and the guy sleeps in here too are gonna shape the place up a little.

> ROGER *has pulled free, and* CARLYLE *cannot understand. It hurts him, depresses him.*

CARLYLE: You got a sweet deal here an' you wanna keep it, that right? (HE *paces about the room, opens a footlocker, looks inside*) How you rate you get a room like this for yourself—you and a couple guys?

ROGER: Spec 4. The three of us in here Spec 4.

CARLYLE: You get a room then, huh? (*And suddenly, without warning or transition,* HE *is angry*) Oh, man I hate this goddamn army. I hate this bastard army. I mean, I just got outa basic—off leave—you know? Back on the block for two weeks—and now here. They don't pull any a that petty shit, now, do they—that goddamn petty basic training bullshit? They do and I'm gonna be bustin' some head—my hand is gonna be upside all kinds a heads, 'cause I ain't gonna be able to endure it, man, not that kinda crap—understand? (*And again,* HE *is rushing at* ROGER) Hey, hey, oh, c'mon, let's get my wheels and make it, man, do me the favor.

ROGER: How'm I gonna? I got my obligations.

> *And* CARLYLE *spins away in anger.*

CARLYLE: Jesus, baby, can't you remember the outside? How long it been since you been on leave? It is so sweet out there, nigger; you got it all forgot. I had such a sweet, sweet time. They doin' dances, baby, make you wanna cry. I hate this damn army. (*The anger overwhelms him*) All these mother-actin' jacks givin' you jive about what you gotta do and what you can't do. I had a bad scene in basic—up the hill and down the hill; it ain't somethin' I enjoyed even a little. So they do me wrong here, Jim, they gonna be sorry. Some-damn-body! And this whole Vietnam THING—I do not dig it. (HE *falls on his knees before* ROGER. *It is a gesture that begins as a joke, a mockery. And then a real fear pulses through him to nearly fill the pose* HE *has taken*) Lord, Lord, don't let 'em touch me. Christ, what will I do, they DO! Whooooooooooooooo! And they pullin' guys outa here, too, ain't they? Pullin' 'em like weeds, man; throwin' 'em into the fire. It's shit, man.

ROGER: They got this ole sarge sleeps down the hall—just today they got him.

CARLYLE: Which ole sarge?

ROGER: He sleeps just down the hall. Little guy.

CARLYLE: Wino, right?

ROGER: Booze hound.

CARLYLE: Yeh; I seen him. They got him, huh?

ROGER: He's goin'; gotta be packin' his bags. And three other guys two days ago. And two guys last week.

CARLYLE (*Leaping up from* BILLY's *bed*): Ohhh, them bastards. And everybody just takes it. It ain't our war, brother. I'm tellin' you. That's what gets me, nigger. It ain't our war nohow because it ain't our country, and that's what burns my ass—that and everybody just sittin' and takin' it. They gonna be bustin' balls, man—kickin' and stompin'. Everybody here maybe one week from shippin' out to get blown clean away and, man, whata they doin'? They doin' what they told. That what they doin'. Like you? Shit! You gonna straighten up your goddamn area! Well, that ain't for me; I'm gettin' hat, and makin' it out where it's sweet and the people's livin'. I can't cut this jive here, man. I'm tellin' you. I can't cut it.

CARLYLE has moved toward ROGER, *and behind him now* RICHIE *enters, running, his hair wet, traces of shaving cream on his face. Toweling his hair,* HE *falters, seeing* CARLYLE. *Then* HE *crosses to his locker.* CARLYLE *grins at* ROGER, *looks at* RICHIE, *steps toward him and gives a little bow.*

My name is Carlyle; what is yours?

RICHIE: Richie.

CARLYLE (HE *turns toward* ROGER *to share his joke*): Hello. Where is Martin? That cute little Martin. (*And* RICHIE *has just taken off his robe as* CARLYLE *turns back*) You cute, too, Richie.

RICHIE: Martin doesn't live here. (*Hurriedly putting on underpants to cover his nakedness*)

CARLYLE (*Watching* RICHIE, HE *slowly turns toward* ROGER): You ain't gonna make it with me, man?

ROGER: Naw . . . like I tole you. I'll catch you later.

CARLYLE: That's sad, man; make me cry in my heart.

ROGER: You g'wan get your head smokin'. Stop on back.

CARLYLE: Okay, okay. Got to be one man one more time. (*On the move for the door, his hand extended palm up behind him, demanding the appropriate response*) Baby! Gimme! Gimme!

Lunging, ROGER *slaps the hand.*

ROGER: G'wan home! G'wan home!

CARLYLE: You gonna hear from me. (*And* HE *is gone out the door and down the hallway*)

ROGER: I can . . . and do . . . believe . . . that.

RICHIE, *putting on his T-shirt, watches* ROGER, *who stubs out his cigarette, then crosses to the trash can to empty the ashtray.*

RICHIE: Who was that?

ROGER: Man's new, Rich. Dunno his name more than that "Carlyle" he said. He's new—just outa basic.

RICHIE (*Powdering his thighs and under his arms*): Oh, my God . . .

> BILLY *enters, pushing a mop bucket with a wringer attached and carrying a container of wax.*

ROGER: Me and Billy's gonna straighten up the area. You wanna help?

RICHIE: Sure, sure; help, help.

BILLY (*Talking to* ROGER, *but turning to look at* RICHIE, *who is still putting powder under his arms*): I hadda steal the wax from Third Platoon.

ROGER: Good man.

BILLY (*Moving to* RICHIE, *joking, yet really irritated in some strange way*): What? Whata you doin', singin'? Look at that, Rog. He's got enough jazz there for an entire beauty parlor. (*Grabbing the can from* RICHIE's *hand*) What is this? Baby Powder! BABY POWDER!

RICHIE: I get rashes.

BILLY: Okay, okay, you get rashes, so what? They got powder for rashes that isn't baby powder.

RICHIE: It doesn't work as good; I've tried it. Have you tried it?

> *Grabbing* BILLY's *waist,* RICHIE *pulls him close.* BILLY *knocks* RICHIE's *hands away.*

BILLY: Man, I wish you could get yourself straight. I'll mop, too, Roger—okay? Then I'll put down the wax and you can spread it? (HE *has walked away from* RICHIE)

RICHIE: What about buffing?

ROGER: In the morning. (HE *is already busy mopping up near the door*)

RICHIE: What do you want me to do?

BILLY (*Grabbing up a mop,* HE *heads downstage to work*): Get inside your locker and shut the door and don't holler for help. Nobody'll know you're there; you'll stay there.

RICHIE: But I'm so pretty.

BILLY: NOW! (*Pointing to* ROGER. HE *wants to get this clear*) Tell that man you mean what you're sayin', Richie.

RICHIE: Mean what?

BILLY: That you really think you're pretty.

RICHIE: Of course I do; I am. Don't you think I am? Don't *you* think I am, Roger?

ROGER: I tole you—you fulla shit and you cute, man. Carlyle just tole you you cute, too.

RICHIE: Don't you think it's true, Billy?

BILLY: It's like I tole you, Rog.

RICHIE: What did you tell him?

BILLY: That you go down; that you go up and down like a yo-yo and you go blowin' all the trees like the wind.

> RICHIE *is stunned.* HE *looks at* ROGER, *and then* HE *turns and stares into his own locker. The* OTHERS *keep mopping.* RICHIE *takes out a towel, and putting it around his neck,* HE *walks to where* BILLY *is working.* HE *stands there, hurt, looking at* BILLY.

RICHIE: What the hell made you tell him I been down, Billy?

BILLY (*Still mopping*): It's in your eyes; I seen it.

RICHIE: What?

BILLY: You.

RICHIE: What is it, Billy, you think you're trying to say? You and all your wit and intelligence—your *humanity*.

BILLY: I said it, Rich; I said what I was tryin' to say.

RICHIE: *Did* you?

BILLY: I think I did.

RICHIE: *Do* you?

BILLY: Loud and clear, baby. (*Still mopping*)

ROGER: They got to put me in with the weirdos. Why is that, huh? How come the army *hate* me, do this shit to me—*know* what to do. (*Whimsical and then suddenly loud, angered, violent*) Now you guys put socks in your mouths, right now—get shut up—or I am gonna beat you to death with each other. Roger got work to do. To be doin' it!

RICHIE (*Turning to his bed,* HE *kneels upon it*): Roger, I think you're so innocent sometimes. Honestly, it's not such a terrible thing. Is it, Billy?

BILLY: How would I know? (HE *slams his mop into the bucket*) Oh, go fuck yourself.

RICHIE: Well, I can give it a try, if that's what you want. Can I think of you as I do?

BILLY (*Throwing down his mop*): GODDAMMIT! That's it! IT! (HE *exits, rushing into the hall and slamming the door behind him.* ROGER *looks at* RICHIE. *Neither quite knows what is going on. Suddenly the door bursts open and* BILLY *storms straight over to* RICHIE, *who still kneels on the bed*) Now I am gonna level with you. Are you gonna listen? You gonna hear what I say, Rich, and not what you think I'm sayin'? (RICHIE *turns away as if to rise, his manner flippant, disdainful*) No! Don't get cute; don't turn away cute. I wanna say somethin' straight out to you and I want you to hear it!

RICHIE: I'm all ears, goddammit! For what, however, I do not know, except some boring evasion.

BILLY: At least wait the hell till you hear me!

RICHIE (*In irritation*): Okay, okay! What?

BILLY: Now this is level, Rich; this is straight talk. (HE *is quiet, intense. This is difficult for him.* HE *seeks the exactly appropriate words of explanation*) No b.s. No tricks. What you do on the side, that's your business and I don't care about it. But if you don't cut the cute shit with me, I'm gonna turn you off. Completely. You ain't gonna get a good mornin' outa me, you understand, because it's gettin' bad around here. I mean, I know how you think—how you keep lookin' out and seein' yourself, and that's what I'm tryin' to tell you because that's all that's happenin', Rich. That's all there is to it when you look out at me and think there's some kind of approval or whatever you see in my eyes—you're just seein' yourself. And I'm talkin' the simple quiet truth to you, Rich. I swear I am.

BILLY *looks away from* RICHIE *now and tries to go back to the mopping. It is embarrassing for them all.* ROGER *has watched, has tried to keep working.* RICHIE *has flopped back on his bunk. There is a silence.*

RICHIE: How . . . do . . . you want me to be? I don't know how else to be.
BILLY: Ohhh, man, that ain't any part of it. (*The mop is clenched in his hands*)
RICHIE: Well, I don't come from the same kind of world as you do.
BILLY: Damn, Richie, you think Roger and I come off the same street?
ROGER: Shit . . .
RICHIE: All right. Okay. But I've just done what I wanted all my life. If I wanted to do something, I just did it. Honestly. I've never had to work or anything like that and I've always had nice clothing and money for cab fare. Money for whatever I wanted. Always. I'm not like you are.
ROGER: You ain't sayin' you really done that stuff, though, Rich.
RICHIE: What?
ROGER: That fag stuff.
RICHIE (HE *continues looking at* ROGER *and then* HE *looks away*): Yes.
ROGER: Do you even know what you're sayin', Richie? Do you even know what it means to be a fag?
RICHIE: Roger, of course I know what it is. I just told you I've done it. I thought you black people were supposed to understand all about suffering and human strangeness. I thought you had depth and vision from all your suffering. Has someone been misleading me? I just told you I did it. I know all about it. Everything. All the various positions.
ROGER: Yeh, so maybe you think you've tried it, but that don't make you it. I mean, we used to . . . in the old neighborhood, man, we had a couple dudes swung that way. But they was weird, man. There was this one little fella, he was a screamin' goddamn faggot . . . uh . . . (HE *considers* RICHIE, *wondering if perhaps* HE *has offended him*) Ohhh, ohhh, you ain't no screamin' goddamn faggot, Richie, no matter what you say. And the baddest man on the block was my boy Jerry Lemon. So one day Jerry's got the faggot

in one a them ole deserted stairways and he's bouncin' him off the walls. I'm just a little fella, see, and I'm watchin' the baddest man on the block do his thing. So he come bouncin' back into me instead of Jerry, and just when he hit, he gave his ass this little twitch, man, like he thought he was gonna turn me on. I'd never a thought that was possible, man, for a man to be twitchin' his ass on me, just like he thought he was a broad. Scared me to death. I took off runnin'. Oh, oh, that ole neighborhood put me into all kinds a crap. I did some sufferin', just like Richie says. Like this once, I'm swingin' on up the street after school, and outa this phone booth comes this man with a goddamned knife stickin' outa his gut. So he sees me and starts tryin' to pull his motherfuckin' coat out over the handle, like he's worried about how he looks, man. "I didn't know this was gonna happen," he says. And then he falls over. He was just all of a sudden dead, man; just all of a sudden dead. You ever seen anything like that, Billy? Any crap like that?

BILLY, *sitting on* ROGER's *bunk, is staring at* ROGER.

BILLY: You really seen that?
ROGER: Richie's a big-city boy.
RICHIE: Oh, no; never anything like that.
ROGER: "Momma, help me," I am screamin'. "Jesus, Momma, help me." Little fella, he don't know how to act, he sees somethin' like that.

For a moment THEY *are still, each thinking.*

BILLY: How long you think we got?
ROGER: What do you mean?

ROGER *is hanging up the mops;* BILLY *is now kneeling on* ROGER's *bunk.*

BILLY: Till they pack us up, man, ship us out.
ROGER: To the war, you mean? To Disneyland? Man, I dunno; that up to them IBMs. Them machines is figurin' that. Maybe tomorrow, maybe next week, maybe never.

The war—the threat of it—is the one thing THEY *share.*

RICHIE: I was reading they're planning to build it all up to more than five hundred thousand men over there. Americans. And they're going to keep it that way until they win.
BILLY: Be a great place to come back from, man, you know? I keep thinkin' about that. To have gone there, to have been there, to have seen it and lived.
ROGER (*Settling onto* BILLY's *bunk,* HE *lights a cigarette*): Well, what we got right here is a fool, gonna probably be one a them five hundred thousand, too. Do you know I cry at the goddamn anthem yet sometimes? The flag is

flyin' at a ball game, the ole Roger gets all wet in the eye. After all the shit been done to his black ass. But I don't know what I think about this war. I do not know.

BILLY: I'm tellin' you, Rog—I've been doin' a lot a readin' and I think it's right we go. I mean, it's just like when North Korea invaded South Korea or when Hitler invaded Poland and all those other countries. He just kept testin' everybody and when nobody said no to him, he got so committed he couldn't back out even if he wanted. And that's what this Ho Chi Minh is doin'. And all these other Communists. If we let 'em know somebody is gonna stand up against 'em, they'll back off, just like Hitler would have.

ROGER: There is folks, you know, who are sayin' L.B.J. is the Hitler, and not ole Ho Chi Minh at all.

RICHIE (*Talking as if this is the best news* HE's *heard in years*): Well, I don't know anything at all about all that, but I am certain I don't want to go—whatever is going on. I mean, those Vietcong don't just shoot you and blow you up, you know. My God, they've got these other awful things they do: putting elephant shit on these stakes in the ground and then you step on 'em and you got elephant shit in a wound in your foot. The infection is horrendous. And then there's these caves they hide in and when you go in after 'em, they've got these snakes that they've tied by their tails to the ceiling. So it's dark and the snake is furious from having been hung by its tail and you crawl right into them—your face. My God.

BILLY: They do not.

BILLY *knows* HE *has been caught;* THEY ALL *know it.*

RICHIE: I read it, Billy. They do.

BILLY (*Completely facetious, yet the fear is real*): That's bullshit, Richie.

ROGER: That's right, Richie. They maybe do that stuff with the elephant shit, but nobody's gonna tie a snake by its tail, let ole Billy walk into it.

BILLY: That's disgusting, man.

ROGER: Guess you better get ready for the Klondike, my man.

BILLY: That is probably the most disgusting thing I ever heard of. I DO NOT WANT TO GO! NOT TO NOWHERE WHERE THAT KINDA SHIT IS GOIN' ON! L.B.J. is Hitler; suddenly I see it all very clearly.

ROGER: Billy got him a hatred for snakes.

RICHIE: I hate them, too. They're hideous.

BILLY (*And now, as a kind of apology to* RICHIE, HE *continues his self-ridicule far into the extreme*): I mean, that is one of the most awful things I ever heard of any person doing. I mean, any person who would hang a snake by its tail in the dark of a cave in the hope that some other person might crawl into it and get bitten to death, that first person is somebody who oughta be shot. And I hope the five hundred thousand other guys that get sent over there kill 'em all—all them gooks—get 'em all driven back into Germany, where they belong. And in the meantime, I'll be holding the northern border against the snowmen.

ROGER (*Rising from* BILLY'*s bed*): And in the meantime before that, we better
be gettin' at the ole area here. Got to be strike troopers.

BILLY: Right.

RICHIE: Can I help?

ROGER: Sure. Be good. (*And* HE *crosses to his footlocker and takes out a radio*) Think
maybe I put on a little music, though it's gettin' late. We got time. Billy,
you think?

BILLY: Sure. (*Getting nervously to his feet*)

ROGER: Sure. All right. We can be doin' it to the music. (HE *plugs the radio into the floor outlet as* BILLY *bolts for the door*)

BILLY: I gotta go pee.

ROGER: You watch out for the snakes.

BILLY: It's the snowmen, man; the snowmen.

> BILLY *is gone and* "*Ruby,*" *sung by Ray Charles, comes from the radio. For
> a moment, as the music plays,* ROGER *watches* RICHIE *wander about the room,
> pouring little splashes of wax onto the floor. Then* RICHIE *moves to his bed and
> lies down, and* ROGER, *shaking his head, starts leisurely to spread the wax,
> with* RICHIE *watching.*

RICHIE: How come you and Billy take all this so seriously—you know.

ROGER: What?

RICHIE: This army nonsense. You're always shining your brass and keeping your
footlocker neat and your locker so neat. There's no point to any of it.

ROGER: We here, ain't we, Richie? We in the army. (*Still working the wax*)

RICHIE: There's no point to any of it. And doing those push-ups, the two of
you.

ROGER: We just see a lot a things the same way is all. Army ought to be a
serious business, even if sometimes it ain't.

RICHIE: You're lucky, you know, the two of you. Having each other for friends
the way you do. I never had that kind of friend ever. Not even when I
was little.

ROGER (*After a pause during which* HE, *working, sort of peeks at* RICHIE *every now
and then*): You ain't really inta that stuff, are you, Richie? (*It is a question
that is a statement*)

RICHIE (*Coyly* HE *looks at* ROGER): What stuff is that, Roger?

ROGER: That fag stuff, man. You know. You ain't really into it, are you? You
maybe messed in it a little is all—am I right?

RICHIE: I'm very weak, Roger. And by that I simply mean that if I have an
impulse to do something, I don't know how to deny myself. If I feel like
doing something, I just do it. I . . . will . . . admit to sometimes wishin'

I . . . was a little more like you . . . and Billy, even, but not to any severe extent.

ROGER: But that's such a bad scene, Rich. You don't want that. Nobody wants that. Nobody wants to be a punk. Not nobody. You wanna know what I think it is? You just got in with the wrong bunch. Am I right? You just got in with a bad bunch. That can happen. And that's what I think happened to you. I bet you never had a chance to really run with the boys before. I mean, regular normal guys like Billy and me. How'd you come in the army, huh, Richie? You get drafted?

RICHIE: No.

ROGER: That's my point, see. (HE *has stopped working.* HE *stands, leaning on the mop, looking at* RICHIE)

RICHIE: About four years ago, I went to this party. I was very young, and I went to this party with a friend who was older and . . . this "fag stuff," as you call it, was going on . . . so I did it.

ROGER: And then you come in the army to get away from it, right? Huh?

RICHIE: I don't know.

ROGER: Sure.

RICHIE: I don't know, Roger.

ROGER: Sure; sure. And now you're gettin' a chance to run with the boys for a little, you'll get yourself straightened around. I know it for a fact; I know that thing.

From off there is the sudden loud bellowing sound of SERGEANT ROONEY.

ROONEY (*Offstage*): THERE AIN'T BEEN NO SOLDIERS IN THIS CAMP BUT ME. I BEEN THE ONLY ONE—I BEEN THE ONLY ME!

And BILLY *comes dashing into the room.*

BILLY: Oh, boy.

ROGER: Guess who?

ROONEY (*Offstage*): FOR SO LONG I BEEN THE ONLY GODDAMN ONE!

BILLY (*Leaping onto his bed and covering his face with a* Playboy *magazine as* RICHIE *is trying to disappear under his sheets and blankets and* ROGER *is trying to get the wax put away so* HE *can get into his own bunk*): Hut who hee whor—he's got some yo-yo with him, Rog!

ROGER: Huh?

COKES *and* ROONEY *enter.* BOTH *are in fatigues and drunk and big-bellied.* THEY *are in their fifties, their hair whitish and cut short.* BOTH MEN *carry whiskey bottles, beer bottles.* COKES *is a little neater than* ROONEY, *his fatigue jacket tucked in and not so rumpled, and* HE *wears canvas-sided jungle boots.* ROONEY, *very disheveled, chomps on the stub of a big cigar.* THEY *swagger in, looking for fun, and stand there side by side.*

ROONEY: What kinda platoon I got here? You buncha shit sacks. Everybody look sharp. (*The* THREE BOYS *lie there, unmoving*) Off and on!

COKES: OFF AND ON! (HE *seems barely conscious, wavering as* HE *stands*)

ROGER: What's happenin', Sergeant?

ROONEY (*Shoving his bottle of whiskey at* ROGER, *who is sitting up*): Shut up, Moore! You want a belt? (*Splashing whiskey on* ROGER's *chest*)

ROGER: How can I say no?

COKES: My name is Cokes!

BILLY (*Rising to sit on the side of his bed*): How about me, too?

COKES: You wait your turn.

ROONEY (HE *looks at the three of them as if* THEY *are fools. Indicates* COKES *with a gesture*): Don't you see what I got here?

BILLY: Who do I follow for my turn?

ROONEY (*Suddenly, crazily petulant*): Don't you see what I got here? Everybody on their feet and at attention!

> BILLY *and* ROGER *climb from their bunks and stand at attention.* THEY *don't know what* ROONEY *is mad at.*

I mean it!

> RICHIE *bounds to the position of attention.*

This here is my friend, who in addition just come back from the war! The goddamn war! He been to it and he come back. (HE *is patting* COKES *gently, proudly*) The man's a fuckin' hero! (HE *hugs* COKES, *almost kissing him on the cheek*) He's always been a fuckin' hero.

> COKES, *embarrassed in his stupor, kind of wobbles a little from side to side.*

COKES: No-o-o-o-o-o . . . (*And* ROONEY *grabs him, starts pushing him toward* BILLY's *footlocker*)

ROONEY: Show 'em your boots, Cokes. Show 'em your jungle boots. (*With a long, clumsy step,* COKES *climbs onto the footlocker,* ROONEY *supporting him from behind and then bending to lift one of* COKES's *booted feet and display it for the boys*) Lookee that boot. That ain't no everyday goddamn army boot. That is a goddamn jungle boot! That green canvas is a jungle boot 'cause a the heat, and them little holes in the bottom are so the water can run out when you been walkin' in a lotta water like in a jungle swamp. (HE *is extremely proud of all this;* HE *looks at them*) The army ain't no goddamn fool. You see a man wearin' boots like that, you might as well see he's got a chestful a medals, 'cause he been to the war. He don't have no boots like that unless he been to the war! Which is where I'm goin' and all you slaphappy motherfuckers, too. Got to go kill some gooks. (HE *is nodding at them, smiling*) That's right.

COKES (*Bursting loudly from his stupor*): Gonna piss on 'em. Old booze. 'At's what I did. Piss in the rivers. Goddamn GIs secret weapon is old booze and he's pissin' it in all their runnin' water. Makes 'em yellow. Ahhhha ha, ha, ha! (HE *laughs and laughs, and* ROONEY *laughs, too, hugging* COKES)

ROONEY: Me and Cokesy been in so much shit together we oughta be brown. (*And then* HE *catches himself, looks at* ROGER) Don't take no offense at that, Moore. We been swimmin' in it. One Hundred and First Airborne, together. One-oh-one. Screamin' goddamn Eagles! (*Looking at each other, face to face, eyes glinting,* THEY *make sudden loud screaming-eagle sounds*) This ain't the army; you punks ain't in the army. You ain't ever seen the army. The army is Airborne! Airborne!

COKES (*Beginning to stomp his feet*): Airborne, Airborne! ALL THE WAY!

RICHIE, *amused and hoping for a drink, too, reaches out toward* ROONEY.

RICHIE: Sergeant, Sergeant, I can have a little drink, too.

ROONEY (*Looks at* RICHIE *and clutches the bottle*): Are you kiddin' me? You gotta be kiddin' me. (HE *looks to* ROGER) He's kiddin' me, ain't he, Moore? (*And then to* BILLY *and then to* COKES) Ain't he, Cokesy?

COKES *steps forward and down with a thump, taking charge for his bewildered friend.*

COKES: Don't you know you are tryin' to take the booze from the hand a the future goddamn Congressional Honor winner . . . Medal . . . ? (*And* HE *looks lovingly at* ROONEY. HE *beams*) Ole Rooney, Ole Rooney. (HE *hugs* ROONEY's *head*) He almost done it already.

And ROONEY, *overwhelmed, starts screaming "Aggggghhhhhhhhhh," a screaming-eagle sound, and making clawing eagle gestures at the air.* HE *jumps up and down, stomping his feet.* COKES *instantly joins in, stomping and jumping and yelling.*

ROONEY: Let's show these shit sacks how men are men jumpin' outa planes. Agggggghhhhhhhhhh. (*Stomping and yelling,* THEY *move in a circle,* ROONEY *followed by* COKES) A plane fulla yellin' stompin' men!

COKES: All yellin' stompin' men!

COKES *and* ROONEY *yell and stomp, making eagle sounds, and then* ROONEY *leaps up on* BILLY's *bed and runs the length of it until* HE *is on the footlocker,* COKES *still on the floor, stomping.* ROONEY *makes a gesture of hooking his rip cord to the line inside the plane.* THEY *yell louder and louder and* ROONEY *leaps high into the air, yelling "GERONIMO-O-O-O!" as* COKES *leaps onto the locker and then high into the air, bellowing "GERONIMO-O-O-O!"* THEY *stand side by side, their arms held up in the air as if grasping the shroud lines of open chutes.* THEY *seem to float there in silence.*

What a feelin' . . .

ROONEY: Beautiful feelin' . . .

For a moment more THEY *float there, adrift in the room, the sky, their memory.*
COKES *smiles at* ROONEY.

COKES: Remember that one guy, O'Flannigan . . . ?

ROONEY (*Nodding, smiling, remembering*): O'Flannigan . . .

COKES: He was this one guy . . . O'Flannigan . . . (HE *moves now toward the boys,* BILLY, ROGER *and* RICHIE, *who have gathered on* ROGER's *bed and footlocker.* ROONEY *follows several steps, then drifts backward onto* BILLY's *bed, where* HE *sits and then lies back, listening to* COKES) We was testing chutes where you could just pull a lever by your ribs here when you hit the ground—see—and the chute would come off you, because it was just after a whole bunch a guys· had been dragged to death in an unexpected and terrible wind at Fort Bragg. So they wanted you to be able to release the chute when you hit if there was a bad wind when you hit. So O'Flannigan was this kinda joker who had the goddamn sense a humor of a clown and nerves, I tell you, of steel, and he says he's gonna release the lever midair, then reach up, grab the lines and float on down, hanging. (*His hand paws at the air, seeking a rope that isn't there*) So I seen him pull the lever at five hundred feet and he reaches up to two fistfuls a air, the chute's twenty feet above him, and he went into the ground like a knife. (*The bottle, held high over his head, falls through the air to the bed,* ALL *watching it*)

BILLY: Geezus.

ROONEY (*Nodding gently*): Didn't get to sing the song, I bet.

COKES (*Standing, staring at the fallen bottle*): No way.

RICHIE: What song?

ROONEY (HE *rises up, mysteriously angry*): Shit sack! Shit sack!

RICHIE: What song, Sergeant Rooney?

ROONEY: "Beautiful streamer," shit sack.

COKES, *gone into another reverie, is staring skyward.*

COKES: I saw this one guy—never forget it. Never.

BILLY: That's Richie, Sergeant Rooney. He's a beautiful screamer.

RICHIE: He said "streamer," not "screamer," asshole.

COKES *is still in his reverie.*

COKES: This guy with his chute goin' straight up above him in a streamer, like a tulip, only white, you know. All twisted and never gonna open. Like a big icicle sticking straight up above him. He went right by me. We met eyes, sort of. He was lookin' real puzzled. He looks right at me. Then he looks up in the air at the chute, then down at the ground.

ROONEY: Did *he* sing it?

COKES: He didn't sing it. He started going like this. (HE *reaches desperately up-*

ward with both hands and begins to claw at the sky while his legs pump up and down) Like he was gonna climb right up the air.

RICHIE: Ohhhhh, Geezus.

BILLY: God.

ROONEY *has collapsed backward on* BILLY'*s bed and* HE *lies there and then* HE *rises.*

ROONEY: Cokes got the Silver Star for rollin' a barrel a oil down a hill in Korea into forty-seven chinky Chinese gooks who were climbin' up the hill and when he shot into it with his machine gun, it blew them all to grape jelly.

COKES, *rocking a little on his feet, begins to hum and then sing "Beautiful Streamer," to the tune of Stephen Foster's "Beautiful Dreamer."*

COKES: "Beautiful streamer, open for me . . . . The sky is above me . . . " (*And then the singing stops*) But the one I remember is this little guy in his spider hole, which is a hole in the ground with a lid over it. (*And* HE *is using* RICHIE'*s footlocker before him as the spider hole.* HE *has fixed on it, is moving toward it*) And he shot me in the ass as I was runnin' by, but the bullet hit me so hard (*His body kind of jerks and* HE *runs several steps*) it knocked me into this ditch where he couldn't see me. I got behind him. (*Now at the head of* RICHIE'*s bed,* HE *begins to creep along the side of the bed as if sneaking up on the footlocker*) Crawlin'. And I dropped a grenade into his hole. (HE *jams a whiskey bottle into the footlocker, then slams down the lid*) Then sat on the lid, him bouncin' and yellin' under me. Bouncin' and yellin' under the lid. I could hear him. Feel him. I just sat there.

Silence. ROONEY *waits, thinking, then leans forward.*

ROONEY: He was probably singin' it.

COKES (*Sitting there*): I think so.

ROONEY: You think we should let 'em hear it?

BILLY: We're good boys. We're good ole boys.

COKES (*Jerking himself to his feet,* HE *staggers sideways to join* ROONEY *on* BILLY'*s bed*): I don't care who hears it, I just wanna be singin' it.

ROONEY *rises;* HE *goes to the boys on* ROGER'*s bed and speaks to them carefully, as if lecturing people on something of great importance.*

ROONEY: You listen up; you just be listenin' up, 'cause if you hear it right you can maybe stop bein' shit sacks. This is what a man sings, he's goin' down through the air, his chute don't open.

Flopping back down on the bunk beside COKES, ROONEY *looks at* COKES *and then at the boys. The* TWO OLDER MEN *put their arms around each other and* THEY *begin to sing.*

ROONEY and COKES (*Singing*):   Beautiful streamer,
                                                     Open for me,
                                                     The sky is above me,
                                                     But no canopy.

BILLY (*Murmuring*): I don't believe it.

ROONEY and COKES: Counted ten thousand,
                                               pulled on the cord.
                                               My chute didn't open,
                                               I shouted, "Dear Lord."

                                               Beautiful streamer,
                                               This looks like the end,
                                               The earth is below me,
                                               My body won't bend.

                                               Just like a mother
                                               Watching o'er me,
                                               Beautiful streamer,
                                               Ohhhhh, open for me.

ROGER: Un-fuckin'-believable.
ROONEY (*Beaming with pride*): Ain't that a beauty.

   And then COKES *topples forward onto his face and flops limply to his side. The* THREE BOYS *leap to their feet.* ROONEY *lunges toward* COKES.

RICHIE: Sergeant!
ROONEY: Cokie! Cokie!
BILLY: Jesus.
ROGER: Hey!
COKES: Huh? Huh? (HE *sits up.* ROONEY *is kneeling beside him*)
ROONEY: Jesus, Cokie.
COKES: I been doin' that; I been doin' that. It don't mean nothin'.
ROONEY: No, no.
COKES (*Pushing at* ROONEY, *who is trying to help him get back to the bed.* ROONEY *agrees with everything* HE *is now saying and the noises* ROONEY *makes are little animal noises*): I told 'em when they wanted to send me back I ain't got no leukemia; they wanna check it. They think I got it. I don't think I got it. Rooney? Whata you think?
ROONEY: No.
COKES: My mother had it. She had it. Just 'cause she did and I been fallin' down.
ROONEY: It don't mean nothin'.

COKES (HE *lunges back and up onto the bed*): I tole 'em I fall down 'cause I'm drunk. I'm drunk all the time.

ROONEY: You'll be goin' back over there with me, is what I know, Cokie. (HE *is patting* COKES, *nodding, dusting him off*) That's what I know.

BILLY *comes up to them, almost seeming to want to be a part of the intimacy* THEY *are sharing.*

BILLY: That was somethin', Sergeant Cokes. Jesus.

ROONEY *whirls on* BILLY, *ferocious, pushing him.*

ROONEY: Get the fuck away, Wilson! Whata you know? Get the fuck away. You don't know shit. Get away! You don't know shit. (*And* HE *turns to* COKES, *who is standing up from the bed*) Me and Cokes are goin' to the war zone like we oughta. Gonna blow it to shit. (HE *is grabbing at* COKES, *who is laughing.* THEY *are both laughing.* ROONEY *whirls on the boys*) Ohhh, I'm gonna be so happy to be away from you assholes; you pussies. Not one regular army people among you possible. I swear it to my mother who is holy. You just be watchin' the papers for doin' darin' brave deeds. 'Cause we're old hands at it. Makin' shit disappear. Goddamn whooosh!

COKES: Whooosh!

ROONEY: Demnalitions. Me and . . . (*And then* HE *knows* HE *hasn't said it right*) Me and Cokie . . . . Demnal . . . . Demnali . . .

RICHIE (*Still sitting on* ROGER's *bed*): You can do it, Sergeant.

BILLY: Get it. (HE *stands by the lockers and* ROONEY *glares at him*)

ROGER: 'Cause you're cool with dynamite, is what you're tryin' to say.

ROONEY (*Charging at* ROGER, *bellowing*): Shut the fuck up, that's what you can do; and go to goddamn sleep. You buncha shit . . . sacks. Buncha mothers—know-it-all motherin' shit sacks—that's what you are.

COKES (*Shoulders back,* HE *is taking charge*): Just goin' to sleep is what you can do, 'cause Rooney and me fought it through two wars already and we can make it through this one more and leukemia that comes or doesn't come—who gives a shit? Not guys like us. We're goin' just pretty as pie. And it's lights-out time, ain't it, Rooney?

ROONEY: Past it, goddammit. So the lights are goin' out.

There is fear in the room, and the THREE BOYS *rush to their wall lockers, where* THEY *start to strip to their underwear, preparing for bed.* ROONEY *paces the room, watching them, glaring.*

Somebody's gotta teach you soldierin'. You hear me? Or you wanna go outside and march around awhile, huh? We can do that if you wanna. Huh? You tell me? Marchin' or sleepin'? What's it gonna be?

RICHIE (*Rushing to get into bed*): Flick out the ole lights, Sergeant; that's what we say.

BILLY (*Climbing into bed*): Put out the ole lights.

ROGER (*In bed and pulling up the covers*): Do it.

COKES: Shut up. (HE *rocks forward and back, trying to stand at attention.* HE *is saying good night*) And that's an order. Just shut up. I got grenades down the hall. I got a pistol. I know where to get nitro. You don't shut up, I'll blow . . . you . . . to . . . fuck. (*Making a military left face,* HE *stalks to the wall switch and turns the lights out.* ROONEY *is watching proudly, as* COKES *faces the boys again.* HE *looks at them*) That's right.

In the dark, there is only a spill of light from the hall coming in the open door. COKES *and* ROONEY *put their arms around each other and go out the door, leaving it partly open.* RICHIE, ROGER *and* BILLY *lie in their bunks, staring.* THEY *do not move.* THEY *lie there. The* SERGEANTS *seem to have vanished soundlessly once* THEY *went out the door. Light touches each of the boys as* THEY *lie there.*

ROGER (HE *does not move*): Lord have mercy, if that ain't a pair. If that ain't one pair a beauties.

BILLY: Oh, yeh. (HE *does not move*)

ROGER: Too much, man—too, too much.

RICHIE: They made me sad; but I loved them, sort of. Better than movies.

ROGER: Too much. Too, too much.

Silence.

BILLY: What time is it?

ROGER: Sleep time, men. Sleep time.

Silence.

BILLY: Right.

ROGER: They were somethin'. Too much.

BILLY: Too much.

RICHIE: Night.

ROGER: Night. (*Silence*) Night, Billy.

BILLY: Night.

RICHIE *stirs in his bed.* ROGER *turns onto his side.* BILLY *is motionless.*

I . . . had a buddy, Rog—and this is the whole thing, this is the whole point—a kid I grew up with, played ball with in high school, and he was a tough little cat, a real bad man sometimes. Used to have gangster pictures up in his room. Anyway, we got into this deal where we'd drive on down to the big city, man, you know, hit the bad spots, let some queer pick us up . . . sort of . . . long enough to buy us some good stuff. It was kinda the thing to do for a while, and we all did it, the whole gang of us.

So we'd let these cats pick us up, most of 'em old guys, and they were hurt-in' and happy as hell to have us, and we'd get a lot of free booze, maybe a meal, and we'd turn 'em on. Then pretty soon they'd ask us did we want to go over to their place. Sure, we'd say, and order one more drink, and then when we hit the street, we'd tell 'em to kiss off. We'd call 'em fag and queer and jazz like that and tell 'em to kiss off. And Frankie, the kid I'm tellin' you about, he had a mean streak in him and if they gave us a bad time at all, he'd put 'em down. That's the way he was. So that kinda jazz went on and on for sort of a long time and it was a good deal if we were low on cash or needed a laugh and it went on for a while. And then Frankie—one day he come up to me—and he says he was goin' home with the guy he was with. He said, what the hell, what did it matter? And he's sayin'—Frankie's sayin'—why don't I tag along? What the hell, he's sayin', what does it matter who does it to you, some broad or some old guy, you close your eyes, a mouth's a mouth, it don't matter—that's what he's sayin'. I tried to talk him out of it, but he wasn't hearin' anything I was sayin'. So the next day, see, he calls me up to tell me about it. Okay, okay, he says, it was a cool scene, he says; they played poker, a buck minimum, and he made a fortune. Frankie was eatin' it up, man. It was a pretty way to live, he says. So he stayed at it, and he had this nice little girl he was goin' with at the time. You know the way a real bad cat can sometimes do that— have a good little girl who's crazy about him and he is for her, too, and he's a different cat when he's with her?

ROGER: Uh-huh.

The hall light slants across BILLY's *face.*

BILLY: Well, that was him and Linda, and then one day he dropped her, he cut her loose. He was hooked, man. He was into it, with no way he knew out—you understand what I'm sayin'? He had got his ass hooked. He had never thought he would and then one day he woke up and he was on it. He just hadn't been told, that's the way I figure it; somebody didn't tell him somethin' he shoulda been told and he come to me wailin' one day, man, all broke up and wailin', my boy Frankie, my main man, and he was a fag. He was a faggot, black Roger, and I'm not lyin'. I am not lyin' to you.

ROGER: Damn.

BILLY: So that's the whole thing, man; that's the whole thing.

Silence. THEY *lie there.*

ROGER: Holy . . . Christ. Richie . . . you hear him? You hear what he said?

RICHIE: He's a storyteller.

ROGER: What you mean?

RICHIE: I mean, he's a storyteller, all right; he tells stories, all right.

ROGER: What are we into now? You wanna end up like that friend a his, or you don't believe what he said? Which are you sayin'?

The door bursts open. The sounds of machine guns and cannon are being made by someone, and CARLYLE, *drunk and playing, comes crawling in.* ROGER, RICHIE *and* BILLY *all pop up, startled, to look at him.*

Hey, hey, what's happenin'?

BILLY: Who's happenin'?

ROGER: You attackin' or you retreatin', man?

CARLYLE (*Looking up; big grin*): Hey, baby . . . ? (*Continues shooting, crawling. The* THREE BOYS *look at each other*)

ROGER: What's happenin', man? Whatcha doin'?

CARLYLE: I dunno, soul; I dunno. Practicin' my duties, my new abilities. (*Half sitting,* HE *flops onto his side, starts to crawl*) The low crawl, man; like I was taught in basic, that's what I'm doin'. You gotta know your shit, man, else you get your ass blown so far away you don't ever see it again. Oh, sure, you guys don't care. I know it. You got it made. You got it made. I don't got it made. You got a little home here, got friends, people to talk to. I got nothin'. You got jobs they probably ain't ever gonna ship you out, you got so important jobs. I got no job. They don't even wanna give me a job. I know it. They are gonna kill me. They are gonna send me over there to get me killed, goddammit. WHAT'S A MATTER WITH ALL YOU PEOPLE?

The anger explodes out of the grieving and ROGER *rushes to kneel beside* CARLYLE. HE *speaks gently, firmly.*

ROGER: Hey, man, get cool, get some cool; purchase some cool, man.

CARLYLE: Awwwww . . . (*Clumsily,* HE *turns away*)

ROGER: Just hang in there.

CARLYLE: I don't wanna be no DEAD man. I don't wanna be the one they all thinkin' is so stupid he's the only one'll go, they tell him; they don't even have to give him a job. I got thoughts, man, in my head; alla time, burnin', burnin' thoughts a understandin'.

ROGER: Don't you think we know that, man? It ain't the way you're sayin' it.

CARLYLE: It is.

ROGER: No. I mean, we all probably gonna go. We all probably gonna have to go.

CARLYLE: No-o-o-o-o.

ROGER: I mean it.

CARLYLE (*Suddenly* HE *nearly topples over*): I am very drunk. (*And* HE *looks up at* ROGER) You think so?

ROGER: I'm sayin' so. And I am sayin', "No sweat." No point.

CARLYLE *angrily pushes at* ROGER, *knocking him backward.*

CARLYLE: Awwwww, dammit, dammit, mother . . . shit . . . it . . . ohhhhhhh. (*Sliding to the floor, the rage and anguish softening into only breathing*) I mean it. I mean it. (*Silence.* HE *lies there*)

ROGER: What . . . a you doin' . . . ?

CARLYLE: Huh?

ROGER: I don't know what you're up to on our freshly mopped floor.

CARLYLE: Gonna go sleep—okay? No sweat . . . (*Suddenly very polite,* HE *is looking up*) Can I, soul? Izzit all right?

ROGER: Sure, man, sure, if you wanna, but why don't you go where you got a bed? Don't you like beds?

CARLYLE: Dunno where's zat. My bed. I can' fin' it. I can' fin' my own bed. I looked all over, but I can' fin' it anywhere. GONE! (*Slipping back down now,* HE *squirms to make a nest.* HE *hugs his bottle*)

ROGER (*Moving to his bunk, where* HE *grabs a blanket*): Okay, okay, man. But get on top a this, man. (HE *is spreading the blanket on the floor, trying to help* CARLYLE *get on it*) Make it softer. C'mon, c'mon . . . get on this.

BILLY *has risen with his own blanket, and is moving now to hand it to* ROGER.

BILLY: Cat's hurtin', Rog.

ROGER: Ohhhhh, yeh.

CARLYLE: Ohhhhh . . . it was so sweet at home . . . it was so sweet, baby; so-o-o-o good. They doin' dances make you wanna cry . . . . (*Hugging the blankets now,* HE *drifts in a kind of dream*)

ROGER: I know, man.

CARLYLE: So sweet . . . !

BILLY *is moving back to his own bed, where, quietly,* HE *sits.*

ROGER: I know, man.

CARLYLE: So sweet . . . !

ROGER: Yeh.

CARLYLE: How come I gotta be here?

On his way to the door to close it, ROGER *falters, looks at* CARLYLE, *then moves on toward the door.*

ROGER: I dunno, Jim.

BILLY *is sitting and watching, as* ROGER *goes on to the door, gently closes it and returns to his bed.*

BILLY: I know why he's gotta be here, Roger. You wanna know? Why don't you ask me?

ROGER: Okay. How come he gotta be here?

BILLY (*Smiling*): Freedom's frontier, man. That's why.

ROGER (*Settled on the edge of his bed and about to lie back*): Oh . . . yeh . . .

A distant bugle begins to play taps and RICHIE, *carrying a blanket, is approaching* CARLYLE. ROGER *settles back;* BILLY *is staring at* RICHIE; CARLYLE *does not stir; the bugle plays.*

Bet that ole sarge don't live a year, Billy. Fuckin' blow his own ass sky high.

RICHIE *has covered* CARLYLE. HE *pats* CARLYLE's *arm, and then straightens in order to return to his bed.*

BILLY: Richie . . . !

BILLY's *hissing voice freezes* RICHIE. HE *stands, and then* HE *starts again to move, and* BILLY's *voice comes again and* RICHIE *cannot move.*

Richie . . . how come you gotta keep doin' that stuff?

ROGER *looks at* BILLY, *staring at* RICHIE, *who stands still as a stone over the sleeping* CARLYLE.

How come?

ROGER: He dunno, man. Do you? You dunno, do you, Rich?

RICHIE: No.

CARLYLE (*From deep in his sleep and grieving*): It . . . was . . . so . . . pretty . . . !

RICHIE: No.

The lights are fading with the last soft notes of taps.

End of Act One

ACT TWO

Scene 1

Lights come up on the cadre room. It is late afternoon and BILLY *is lying on his stomach, his head at the foot of the bed, his chin resting on his hands.* HE *wears gym shorts and sweat socks; his T-shirt lies on the bed and his sneakers are on the floor.* ROGER *is at his footlocker, taking out a pair of sweat socks. His sneakers and his basketball are on his bed.* HE *is wearing his khakis.*

A silence passes, and then ROGER *closes his footlocker and sits on his bed, where* HE *starts lacing his sneakers, holding them on his lap.*

BILLY: Rog . . . you think I'm a busybody? In any way? (*Silence.* ROGER *laces his sneakers*) Roger?

ROGER: Huh? Uh-uh.

BILLY: Some people do. I mean, back home. (HE *rolls slightly to look at* ROGER) Or that I didn't know how to behave. Sort of.

ROGER: It's time we maybe get changed, don't you think? (HE *rises and goes to his locker.* HE *takes off his trousers, shoes and socks*)

BILLY: Yeh. I guess. I don't feel like it, though. I don't feel good, don't know why.

ROGER: Be good for you, man; be good for you. (*Pulling on his gym shorts,* HE *returns to his bed, carrying his shoes and socks*)

BILLY: Yeh. (HE *sits up on the edge of his bed.* ROGER, *sitting, is bowed over, putting on his socks*) I mean, a lot of people thought like I didn't know how to behave in a simple way. You know? That I overcomplicated everything. I didn't think so. Don't think so. I just thought I was seein' complications that were there but nobody else saw. (HE *is struggling now to put on his T-shirt.* HE *seems weary, almost weak*) I mean, Wisconsin's a funny place. All those clear-eyed people sayin' "Hello" and lookin' you straight in the eye. Everybody's good, you think, and happy and honest. And then there's all of a sudden a neighbor who goes mad as a hatter. I had a neighbor who came out of his house one morning with axes in both hands. He started then attackin' the cars that were driving up and down in front of his house. An' we all knew why he did it, sorta. (HE *pauses;* HE *thinks*) It made me wanna be a priest. I wanted to be a priest then. I was sixteen. Priests could help people. Could take away what hurt 'em. I wanted that, I thought. Somethin', huh?

ROGER (HE *has the basketball in his hands*): Yeh. But everybody's got feelin's like that sometimes.

BILLY: I don't know.

ROGER: You know, you oughta work on a little jump shot, my man. Get you some kinda fall-away jumper to go with that beauty of a hook. Make you tough out there.

BILLY: Can't fuckin' do it. Not my game. I mean, like that bar we go to. You think I could get a job there bartendin', maybe? I could learn the ropes. (HE *is watching* ROGER, *who has risen to walk to his locker*) You think I could get a job there off-duty hours?

ROGER (*Pulling his locker open to display the pinup on the inside of the door*): You don't want no job. It's that little black-haired waitress you wantin' to know.

BILLY: No, man. Not really.

ROGER: It's okay. She tough, man. (HE *begins to remove his uniform shirt.* HE *will put on an O.D. T-shirt to go to the gym*)

BILLY: I mean, not the way you're sayin' it, is all. Sure, there's somethin' about her. I don't know what. I ain't even spoke to her yet. But somethin'. I mean, what's she doin' there? When she's dancin', it's like she knows somethin'. She's degradin' herself, I sometimes feel. You think she is?

ROGER: Man, you don't even know the girl. She's workin'.

BILLY: I'd like to talk to her. Tell her stuff. Find out about her. Sometimes I'm thinkin' about her and it and I got a job there, I get to know her and she and I get to be real tight, man—close, you know. Maybe we screw, maybe we don't. It's nice . . . whatever.

ROGER: Sure. She a real fine-lookin' chippy, Billy. Got nice cakes. Nice little titties.

BILLY: I think she's smart, too. (ROGER *starts laughing so hard* HE *almost falls into his locker*) Oh, all I do is talk. "Yabba-yabba." I mean, my mom and dad are really terrific people. How'd they ever end up with somebody so weird as me?

ROGER (*Moves to* BILLY, *jostles him*): I'm tellin' you, the gym and a little ball is what you need. Little exercise. Little bumpin' into people. The soul is tellin' you.

BILLY *rises and goes to his locker, where* HE *starts putting on his sweat clothes.*

BILLY: I mean, Roger, you remember how we met in P Company? Both of us brand-new. You started talkin' to me. You just started talkin' to me and you didn't stop.

ROGER (*Hardly looking up*): Yeh.

BILLY: Did you see somethin' in me made you pick me?

ROGER: I was talkin' to everybody, man. For that whole day. Two whole days. You was just the first one to talk back friendly. Though you didn't say much, as I recall.

BILLY: The first white person, you mean. (*Wearing his sweat pants,* HE *is now at his bed, putting on his sneakers*)

ROGER: Yeh. I was tryin' to come outa myself a little. Do like the fuckin' headshrinker been tellin' me to stop them fuckin' headaches I was havin', you know. Now let us do fifteen or twenty push-ups and get over to that gymnasium, like I been sayin'. Then we can take our civvies with us—we can shower and change at the gym. (HE *crosses to* BILLY, *who flops down on his belly on the bed*)

BILLY: I don't know . . . I don't know what it is I'm feelin'. Sick like.

ROGER *forces* BILLY *up onto his feet and shoves him playfully downstage, where* THEY *both fall forward into the push-up position, side by side.*

ROGER: Do 'em, trooper. Do 'em. Get it.

ROGER *starts.* BILLY *joins in. After five,* ROGER *realizes that* BILLY *has his knees on the floor.* THEY *start again. This time,* BILLY *counts in double time.* THEY *start again. At about "seven,"* RICHIE *enters. Neither* BILLY *nor* ROGER *sees him.* THEY *keep going.*

ROGER and BILLY: . . . seven, eight, nine, ten . . .

RICHIE: No, no; no, no; no, no, no. That's not it; that's not it.

ROGER and BILLY (THEY *keep going, yelling the numbers louder and louder*): . . . eleven, twelve, thirteen . . .

RICHIE crosses to his locker and gets his bottle of cologne, and then returning to the center of the room to stare at them, HE stands there dabbing cologne on his face.

. . . fourteen, fifteen.

RICHIE: You'll never get it like that. You're so far apart and you're both humping at the same time. And all that counting. It's so unromantic.

ROGER (*Rising and moving to his bed to pick up the basketball*): We was exercisin', Richard. You heard a that?

RICHIE: Call it what you will, Roger.

With a flick of his wrist, ROGER tosses the basketball to BILLY.

Everybody has their own cute little pet names for it.

BILLY: Hey!

And BILLY tosses the ball at RICHIE, hitting him in the chest, sending the cologne bottle flying. RICHIE yelps, as BILLY retrieves the ball and, grabbing up his sweat jacket from the bed, heads for the door. ROGER, at his own locker, has taken out his suit bag of civilian clothes.

You missed.

RICHIE: Billy, Billy, Billy, please, please, the ruffian approach will not work with me. It impresses me not even one tiny little bit. All you've done is spill my cologne. (*HE bends to pick up the cologne from the floor*)

BILLY: That was my aim.

ROGER: See you.

BILLY is passing RICHIE. Suddenly RICHIE sprays BILLY with cologne, some of it getting on ROGER, as ROGER and BILLY, groaning and cursing at RICHIE, rush out the door.

RICHIE: Try the more delicate approach next time, Bill. (*Having crossed to the door, HE stands a moment, leaning against the frame. Then HE bounces to BILLY's bed, sings "He's just my Bill," and squirts cologne on the pillow. At his locker, HE deposits the cologne, takes off his shirt, shoes and socks. Removing a hard-cover copy of Pauline Kael's I Lost It at the Movies from the top shelf of the locker, HE bounds to the center of the room and tosses the book the rest of the way to the bed. Quite pleased with himself, HE fidgets, pats his stomach, then lowers himself into the push-up position, goes to his knees and stands up*) Am I out of my fucking mind? Those two are crazy. I'm not crazy.

RICHIE pivots and strides to his locker. With an ashtray, a pack of matches and a pack of cigarettes, HE hurries to his bed and makes himself comfortable to read, his head propped up on a pillow. Settling himself, HE *opens the book, finds his place, thinks a little, starts to read. For a moment* HE *lies there. And then* CARLYLE *steps into the room.* HE *comes through the doorway looking to his left and right.* HE *comes several steps into the room and looks at* RICHIE. RICHIE *sees him.* THEY *look at each other.*

CARLYLE: Ain't nobody here, man?

RICHIE: Hello, Carlyle. How are you today?

CARLYLE: Ain't nobody here? (HE *is nervous and angrily disappointed*)

RICHIE: Who do you want?

CARLYLE: Where's the black boy?

RICHIE: Roger? My God, why do you keep calling him that? Don't you know his name yet? Roger. Roger. (HE *thickens his voice at this, imitating someone very stupid.* CARLYLE *stares at him*)

CARLYLE: Yeh. Where is he?

RICHIE: I am not his keeper, you know. I am not his private secretary, you know.

CARLYLE: I do not know. I do not know. That is why I am asking. I come to see him. You are here. I ask you. I don't know. I mean, Carlyle made a fool outa himself comin' in here the other night, talkin' on and on like how he did. Lay on the floor. He remember. You remember? It all one hype, man; that all one hype. You know what I mean. That ain't the real Carlyle was in here. This one here and now the real Carlyle. Who the real Richie?

RICHIE: Well . . . the real Richie . . . has gone home. To Manhattan. I, however, am about to read this book. (*Which* HE *again starts to try to do*)

CARLYLE: Oh. Shit. Jus' you the only one here, then, huh?

RICHIE: So it would seem. (HE *looks at the air and then under the bed as if to find someone*) So it would seem. Did you hear about Martin?

CARLYLE: What happened to Martin? I ain't seen him.

RICHIE: They are shipping him home. Someone told about what he did to himself. I don't know who.

CARLYLE: Wasn't me. Not me. I keep that secret.

RICHIE: I'm sure you did. (*Rising, walking toward* CARLYLE *and the door, cigarette pack in hand*) You want the cigarette? Or don't you smoke? Or do you have to go right away? (*Closing the door*) There's a chill sometimes coming down the hall, I don't know from where. (*Crossing back to his bed and climbing in*) And I think I've got the start of a little cold. Did you want the cigarette?

CARLYLE *is staring at him. Then* HE *examines the door and looks again at* RICHIE. HE *stares at* RICHIE, *thinking, and then* HE *walks toward him.*

CARLYLE: You know what I bet? I been lookin' at you real close. It just a way

I got about me. And I bet if I was to hang my boy out in front of you, my big boy, man, you'd start wanting to touch him. Be beggin' and talkin' sweet to ole Carlyle. Am I right or wrong? (HE *leans over* RICHIE) What do you say?

RICHIE: Pardon?

CARLYLE: You heard me. Ohhh. I am so restless, I don't even understand it. My big black boy is what I was talkin' about. My thing, man; my rope, Jim. HEY, RICHIE! (*And* HE *lunges, then moves his fingers through* RICHIE's *hair*) How long you been a punk? Can you hear me? Am I clear? Do I talk funny? (HE *is leaning close*) Can you smell the gin on my mouth?

RICHIE: I mean, if you really came looking for Roger, he and Billy are gone to the gymnasium. They were—

CARLYLE: No. (HE *slides down on the bed, his arm placed over* RICHIE's *legs*) I got no athletic abilities. I got none. No moves. I don't know. HEY, RICHIE! (*Leaning close again*) I just got this question I asked. I got no answer.

RICHIE: I don't know . . . what . . . you mean.

CARLYLE: I heard me. I understood me. "How long you been a punk?" is the question I asked. Have you got a reply?

RICHIE (*Confused, irritated, but fascinated*): Not to that question.

CARLYLE: Who do if you don't? I don't. How'm I gonna? (*Suddenly there is a whistling in the hall, as if someone might enter, footsteps approaching, and* RICHIE *leaps to his feet and scurries away toward the door, tucking in his undershirt as* HE *goes*) Man, don't you wanna talk to me? Don't you wanna talk to ole Carlyle?

RICHIE: Not at the moment.

CARLYLE (HE *is rising, starting after* RICHIE, *who stands nervously near* ROGER's *bed*): I want to talk to you, man; why don't you want to talk to me? We can be friends. Talkin' back and forth, sharin' thoughts and bein' happy.

RICHIE: I don't think that's what you want.

CARLYLE (HE *is very near to* RICHIE): What do I want?

RICHIE: I mean, to talk to me. (*As if repulsed,* HE *crosses away. But it is hard to tell if the move is genuine or coy*)

CARLYLE: What am I doin'? I am talkin'. DON'T YOU TELL ME I AIN'T TALKIN' WHEN I AM TALKIN'! COURSE I AM. Bendin' over backwards. (*And pressing his hands against himself in his anger,* HE *has touched the grease on his shirt, the filth of his clothing, and this ignites the anger*) Do you know they still got me in that goddamn P Company? That goddamn transient company. It like they think I ain't got no notion what a home is. No nose for no home—like I ain't never had no home. I had a home. IT LIKE THEY THINK THERE AIN'T NO PLACE FOR ME IN THIS MOTHER ARMY BUT K.P. ALL SUDSY AND WRINKLED AND SWEATIN'. EVERY DAY SINCE I GOT TO THIS SHIT HOUSE,

MISTER! HOW MANY TIMES YOU BEEN ON K.P.? WHEN'S THE
LAST TIME YOU PULLED K.P.? (HE *has roared down to where* RICHIE *had
moved, the rage possessing him*)

RICHIE: I'm E.D.

CARLYLE: You E.D.? You E.D.? You Edie, are you? I didn't ask you what you
friends call you, I asked you when's the last time you had K.P.?

RICHIE (*Edging toward his bed.* HE *will go there, get and light a cigarette*): E.D. is
"Exempt from Duty."

CARLYLE (*Moving after* RICHIE): You ain't got no duties? What shit you talkin'
about? Everybody in this fuckin' army got duties. That what the fuckin'
army all about. You ain't got no duties, who got 'em?

RICHIE: Because of my job, Carlyle. I have a very special job. And my friends
don't call me Edie. (*Big smile*) They call me Irene.

CARLYLE: That mean what you sayin' is you kiss ass for somebody, don't it?
Good for you. (*Seemingly relaxed and gentle,* HE *settles down on* RICHIE's *bed.*
HE *seems playful and charming*) You know the other night I was sleepin' there.
You know.

RICHIE: Yes.

CARLYLE (*Gleefully, enormously pleased*): You remember that? How come you
remember that? You sweet.

RICHIE: We don't have people sleeping on our floor that often, Carlyle.

CARLYLE: But the way you crawl over in the night, gimme a big kiss on my
joint. That nice.

RICHIE (*Shocked,* HE *blinks*): What?

CARLYLE: Or did I dream that?

RICHIE (*Laughing in spite of himself*): My God, you're outrageous!

CARLYLE: Maybe you dreamed it.

RICHIE: What . . . ? No. I don't know.

CARLYLE: Maybe you did it, then; you didn't dream it.

RICHIE: How come you talk so much?

CARLYLE: I don't talk, man, who's gonna talk? YOU? (HE *is laughing and
amused, but there is an anger near the surface now, an ugliness*) That bore me
to death. I don't like nobody's voice but my own. I am so pretty. Don't
like nobody else face. (*And then viciously,* HE *spits out at* RICHIE) You goddamn face ugly fuckin' queer punk!

And RICHIE *jumps in confusion.*

RICHIE: What's the matter with you?

CARLYLE: You goddamn ugly punk face. YOU UGLY!

RICHIE: Nice mouth.

CARLYLE: That's right. That's right. And you got a weird mouth. Like to suck
joints.

RICHIE *storms to his locker, throwing the book inside.* HE *pivots, grabbing a towel, marching toward the door.*

Hey, you gonna jus' walk out on me? Where you goin'? You c'mon back. Hear?

RICHIE: That's my bed, for chrissake. (HE *lunges into the hall*)

CARLYLE: You'd best. (*Lying there,* HE *makes himself comfortable.* HE *takes a pint bottle from his back pocket*) You come back, Richie, I tell you a good joke. Make you laugh, make you cry. (HE *takes a big drink*) That's right. Ole Frank and Jesse, they got the stagecoach stopped, all the peoples lined up—Frank say, "All right, peoples, we gonna rape all the men and rob all the women." Jesse say, "Frank, no, no—that ain't it—we gonna . . . ." And this one little man yell real loud, "You shut up, Jesse; Frank knows what he's doin'. "

Loudly, HE *laughs and laughs.* BILLY *enters. Startled at the sight of* CARLYLE *there in* RICHIE's *bed,* BILLY *falters, as* CARLYLE *gestures toward him*)

Hey, man . . . ! Hey, you know, they send me over to that Vietnam, I be cool, 'cause I been dodgin' bullets and shit since I been old enough to get on pussy make it happy to know me. I can get on, I can do my job.

BILLY *looks weary and depressed. Languidly* HE *crosses to his bed.* HE *still wears his sweat clothes.* CARLYLE *studies him, then stares at the ceiling.*

Yeh. I was just layin' here thinkin' that and you come in and out it come, words to say my feelin'. That my problem. That the black man's problem altogether. You ever considered that? Too much feelin'. He too close to everything. He is, man; too close to his blood, to his body. It ain't that he don't have no good mind, but he BELIEVE in his body. Is . . . that Richie the only punk in this room, or is there more?

BILLY: What?

CARLYLE: The punk; is he the only punk? (*Carefully* HE *takes one of* RICHIE's *cigarettes and lights it*)

BILLY: He's all right.

CARLYLE: I ain't askin' about the quality of his talent, but is he the only one, is my question?

BILLY (HE *does not want to deal with this.* HE *sits there*): You get your orders yet?

CARLYLE: Orders for what?

BILLY: To tell you where you work.

CARLYLE: I'm P Company, man. I work in P Company. I do K.P. That all. Don't deserve no more. Do you know I been in this army three months and ten days and everybody still doin' the same shit and sayin' the same shit and wearin' the same green shitty clothes? I ain't been happy one day, and that a lotta goddamn misery back to back in this ole boy. Is that Richie a good punk? Huh? Is he? He takes care of you and Roger—that how come you in this room, the three of you?

BILLY: What?

CARLYLE (*Emphatically*): You and Roger are hittin' on Richie, right?

BILLY: He's not queer, if that's what you're sayin'. A little effeminate, but that's all, no more; if that's what you're sayin'.

CARLYLE: I'd like to get some of him myself if he a good punk, is what I'm sayin'. That's what I'm sayin'! You don't got no understandin' how a man can maybe be a little diplomatic about what he's sayin' sorta sideways, do you? Jesus.

BILLY: He don't do that stuff.

CARLYLE (*Lying there*): What stuff?

BILLY: Listen, man. I don't feel too good, you don't mind.

CARLYLE: What stuff?

BILLY: What you're thinkin'.

CARLYLE: What . . . am I thinkin'?

BILLY: You . . . know.

CARLYLE: Yes, I do. It in my head, that how come I know. But how do you know? I can see your heart, Billy boy, but you cannot see mine. I am unknown. You . . . are known.

BILLY (*As if* HE *is about to vomit, and fighting it*): You just . . . talk fast and keep movin', don't you? Don't ever stay still.

CARLYLE: Words to say my feelin', Billy boy.

RICHIE *steps into the room.* HE *sees* BILLY *and* CARLYLE, *and freezes.*

There he is. There he be.

RICHIE *moves to his locker to put away the towel.*

RICHIE: He's one of them who hasn't come down far out of the trees yet, Billy; believe me.

CARLYLE: You got rudeness in your voice, Richie—you got meanness I can hear about ole Carlyle. You tellin' me I oughta leave—is that what you think you're doin'? You don't want me here?

RICHIE: You come to see Roger, who isn't here, right? Man like you must have important matters to take care of all over the quad; I can't imagine a man like you not having extremely important things to do all over the world, as a matter of fact, Carlyle.

CARLYLE (HE *rises.* HE *begins to smooth the sheets and straighten the pillow.* HE *will put the pint bottle in his back pocket and cross near to* RICHIE): Ohhhh, listen—don't mind all the shit I say. I just talk bad, is all I do; I don't do bad. I got to have friends just like anybody else. I'm just bored and restless, that all; takin' it out on you two. I mean, I know Richie here ain't really no punk, not really. I was just talkin', just jivin' and entertainin' my own self.

Don't take me serious, not ever. I get on out and see you all later. (HE *moves for the door,* RICHIE *right behind him, almost ushering him*) You be cool, hear? Man don't do the jivin', he the one gettin' jived. That what my little brother Henry tell me and tell me.

Moving leisurely, CARLYLE *backs out the door and is gone.* RICHIE *shuts the door. There is a silence as* RICHIE *stands by the door.* BILLY *looks at him and then looks away.*

BILLY: I am gonna have to move myself outa here, Roger decides to adopt that sonofabitch.

RICHIE: He's an animal.

BILLY: Yeh, and on top a that, he's a rotten person.

RICHIE (HE *laughs nervously, crossing nearer to* BILLY): I think you're probably right. (*Still laughing a little,* HE *pats* BILLY*'s shoulder and* BILLY *freezes at the touch. Awkwardly* RICHIE *removes his hand and crosses to his bed. When* HE *has lain down,* BILLY *bends to take off his sneakers, then lies back on his pillow staring, thinking, and there is a silence.* RICHIE *does not move.* HE *lies there, struggling to prepare himself for something*) Hey . . . Billy? (*Very slight pause*) Billy?

BILLY: Yeh.

RICHIE: You know that story you told the other night?

BILLY: Yeh . . . ?

RICHIE: You know . . .

BILLY: What . . . about it?

RICHIE: Well, was it . . . about you? (*Pause*) I mean, was it . . . ABOUT you? Were you Frankie? (*This is difficult for him*) Are . . . you Frankie? Billy?

BILLY *is slowly sitting up.*

BILLY: You sonofabitch . . . !

RICHIE: Or was it really about somebody you knew . . . ?

BILLY (*Sitting, outraged and glaring*): You didn't hear me at all!

RICHIE: I'm just asking a simple question, Billy, that's all I'm doing.

BILLY: You are really sick. You know that? Your brain is really, truly rancid! Do you know there's a theory now it's genetic? That it's all a matter of genes and shit like that?

RICHIE: Everything is not so ungodly cryptic, Billy.

BILLY: You. You, man, and the rot it's makin' outa your feeble fuckin' brain.

ROGER, *dressed in civilian clothes, bursts in and* BILLY *leaps to his feet.*

ROGER: Hey, hey, anyone got a couple bucks he can loan me?

BILLY: Rog, where you been?

ROGER (*Throwing the basketball and his sweat clothes into his locker*): I need five. C'mon.

BILLY: Where you been? That asshole friend a yours was here.

ROGER: I know, I know. Can you gimme five?

RICHIE (HE *jumps to the floor and heads for his locker*): You want five. I got it. You want ten or more, even?

> BILLY, *watching* RICHIE, *turns, and nervously paces down right, where* HE *moves about, worried.*

BILLY: I mean, we gotta talk about him, man; we gotta talk about him.

ROGER (*As* RICHIE *is handing him two fives*): 'Cause we goin' to town together. I jus' run into him out on the quad, man, and he was feelin' real bad 'bout the way he acted, how you guys done him, he was fallin' down apologizin' all over the place.

BILLY (*As* RICHIE *marches back to his bed and sits down*): I mean, he's got a lotta weird ideas about us; I'm tellin' you.

ROGER: He's just a little fucked up in his head is all, but he ain't trouble. (HE *takes a pair of sunglasses from the locker and puts them on*)

BILLY: Who needs him? I mean, we don't need him.

ROGER: You gettin' too nervous, man. Nobody said anything about anybody needin' anybody. I been on the street all my life; he brings back home. I played me a little ball, Billy; took me a shower. I'm feelin' good! (HE *has moved down to* BILLY)

BILLY: I'm tellin' you there's something wrong with him, though.

ROGER (*Face to face with* BILLY, HE *is a little irritated*): Every black man in the world ain't like me, man; you get used to that idea. You get to know him, and you gonna like him. I'm tellin' you. You get to be laughin' just like me to hear him talk his shit. But you gotta relax.

RICHIE: I agree with Billy, Roger.

ROGER: Well, you guys got it all worked out and that's good, but I am goin' to town with him. Man's got wheels. Got a good head. You got any sense, you'll come with us.

BILLY: What are you talkin' about—come with you? I just tole you he's crazy.

ROGER: And I tole you you're wrong.

RICHIE: We weren't invited.

ROGER: I'm invitin' you.

RICHIE: No, I don't wanna.

ROGER (HE *moves to* RICHIE; *it seems* HE *really wants* RICHIE *to go*): You sure, Richie? C'mon.

RICHIE: No.

ROGER: Billy? He got wheels, we goin' in drinkin', see if gettin' our heads real bad don't just make us feel real good. You know what I mean. I got him right; you got him wrong.

BILLY: But what if I'm right?

ROGER: Billy, Billy, the man is waitin' on me. You know you wanna. Jesus. Bad cat like that gotta know the way. He been to D.C. before. Got cousins here. Got wheels for the weekend. You always talkin' how you don't do nothin'—you just talk it. Let's do it tonight—stop talkin'. Be cruisin' up and down the strip, leanin' out the window, bad as we wanna be. True cool is a car. We can flip a cigarette out the window—we can watch it bounce. Get us some chippies. You know we can. And if we don't, he knows a cathouse, it fulla cats.

BILLY: You serious?

RICHIE: You mean you're going to a whorehouse? That's disgusting.

BILLY: Listen who's talkin'. What do you want me to do? Stay here with you?

RICHIE: We could go to a movie or something.

ROGER: I am done with this talkin'. You goin', you stayin'? (HE *crosses to his locker, pulls into view a wide-brimmed black and shiny hat, and puts it on, cocking it at a sharp angle*)

BILLY: I don't know.

ROGER (*Stepping for the door*): I am goin'.

BILLY (*Turning,* HE *sees the hat*): I'm going. Okay! I'm going! Going, going, going! (*And* HE *runs to his locker*)

RICHIE: Oh, Billy, you'll be scared to death in a cathouse and you know it.

BILLY: BULLSHIT! (HE *is removing his sweat pants and putting on a pair of gray corduroy trousers*)

ROGER: Billy got him a lion-tamer 'tween his legs!

The door bangs open and CARLYLE *is there, still clad in his filthy fatigues, but wearing a going-to-town black knit cap on his head and carrying a bottle.*

CARLYLE: Man, what's goin' on? I been waitin' like throughout my fuckin' life.

ROGER: Billy's goin', too. He's gotta change.

CARLYLE: He goin', too! Hey! Beautiful! That beautiful! (*His grin is large, his laugh is loud*)

ROGER: Didn't I tell you, Billy?

CARLYLE: That beautiful, man; we all goin' to be friends!

RICHIE (*Sitting on his bed*): What about me, Carlyle?

CARLYLE *looks at* RICHIE, *and then at* ROGER *and then* HE *and* ROGER *begin to laugh.* CARLYLE *pokes* ROGER *and* THEY *laugh as* THEY *are leaving.* BILLY, *grabbing up his sneakers to follow, stops at the door, looking only briefly at* RICHIE. *Then* BILLY *goes and shuts the door. The lights are fading to black.*

Scene 2

In the dark, taps begins to play. And then slowly the lights rise, but the room remains dim. Only the lamp attached to RICHIE'*s bed burns and there is the glow and spill of the hallway coming through the transom.* BILLY, CARLYLE,

ROGER *and* RICHIE *are sprawled about the room.* BILLY, *lying on his stomach, has his head at the foot of his bed, a half-empty bottle of beer dangling in his hand.* HE *wears a blue oxford-cloth shirt and his sneakers lie beside his bed.* ROGER, *collapsed in his own bed, lies upon his back, his head also at the foot, a* Playboy *magazine covering his face and a half-empty bottle of beer in his hands, folded on his belly. Having removed his civilian shirt,* HE *wears a white T-shirt.* CARLYLE *is lying on his belly on* RICHIE's *bed, his head at the foot, and* HE *is facing out.* RICHIE *is sitting on the floor, resting against* ROGER's *footlocker.* HE *is wrapped in a blanket. Beside him is an unopened bottle of beer and a bottle opener.*

THEY *are all dreamy in the dimness as taps plays sadly on and then fades into silence.* NO ONE *moves.*

RICHIE: I don't know where it was, but it wasn't here. And we were all in it—it felt like—but we all had different faces. After you guys left, I only dozed for a few minutes, so it couldn't have been long. Roger laughed a lot and Billy was taller. I don't remember all the details exactly, and even though we were the ones in it, I know it was about my father. He was a big man. I was six. He was a very big man when I was six and he went away, but I remember him. He started drinking and staying home making model airplanes and boats and paintings by the numbers. We had money from Mom's family, so he was just home all the time. And then one day I was coming home from kindergarten, and as I was starting up the front walk he came out the door and he had these suitcases in his hands. He was leaving, see, sneaking out, and I'd caught him. We looked at each other and I just knew and I started crying. He yelled at me, "Don't you cry; don't you start crying." I tried to grab him and he pushed me down in the grass. And then he was gone. G-O-N-E.

BILLY: And that was it? That was it?

RICHIE: I remember hiding my eyes. I lay in the grass and hid my eyes and waited.

BILLY: He never came back?

RICHIE: No.

CARLYLE: Ain't that some shit. Now, I'm a jive-time street nigger. I knew where my daddy was all the while. He workin' in this butcher shop two blocks up the street. Ole Mom used to point him out. "There he go. That him—that your daddy." We'd see him on the street, "There he go."

ROGER: Man couldn't see his way to livin' with you—that what you're sayin'?

CARLYLE: Never saw the day.

ROGER: And still couldn't get his ass outa the neighborhood?

RICHIE *begins trying to open his bottle of beer.*

CARLYLE: Ain't that a bitch. Poor ole bastard just duck his head—Mom pointin' at him—he git this real goddamn hangdog look like he don't know who we talkin' about and he walk a little faster. Why the hell he never move away I don't know, unless he was crazy. But I don't think so. He come up to me once—I was playin'. "Boy," he says, "I ain't your daddy. I ain't. Your momma's crazy." "Don't you be callin' my momma crazy, Daddy," I tole him. Poor ole thing didn't know what to do.

RICHIE (*Giving up;* HE *can't get the beer open*): Somebody open this for me? I can't get this open.

BILLY *seems about to move to help, but* CARLYLE *is quicker, rising a little on the bunk and reaching.*

CARLYLE: Ole Carlyle get it.

RICHIE *slides along the floor until* HE *can place the bottle in* CARLYLE'*s outstretched hand.*

RICHIE: Then there was this once—there was this TV documentary about these bums in San Francisco, this TV guy interviewing all these bums, and just for maybe ten seconds while he was talkin' . . . (*Smiling,* CARLYLE *hands* RICHIE *the opened bottle*) to this one bum, there was this other one in the background jumpin' around like he thought he was dancin' and wavin' his hat, and even though there wasn't anything about him like my father and I didn't really ever see his face at all, I just kept thinkin': That's him. My dad. He thinks he's dancin'.

THEY *lie there in silence and suddenly, softly,* BILLY *giggles, and then* HE *giggles a little more and louder.*

BILLY: Jesus!

RICHIE: What?

BILLY: That's ridiculous, Richie; sayin' that, thinkin' that. If it didn't look like him, it wasn't him, but you gotta be makin' up a story.

CARLYLE (*Shifting now for a more comfortable position,* HE *moves his head to the pillow at the top of the bed*): Richie first saw me, he didn't like me much nohow, but he thought it over now, he changed his way a thinkin'. I can see that clear. We gonna be one big happy family.

RICHIE: Carlyle likes me, Billy; he thinks I'm pretty.

CARLYLE (*Sitting up a little to make his point clear*): No, I don't think you pretty. A broad is pretty. Punks ain't pretty. Punk—if he good-lookin'—is cute. You cute.

RICHIE: He's gonna steal me right away, little Billy. You're so slow, Bill. I prefer a man who's decisive. (HE *is lying down now on the floor at the foot of his bed*)

BILLY: You just keep at it, you're gonna have us all believin' you are just what you say you are.

RICHIE: Which is more than we can say for you.

Now ROGER *rises on his elbow to light a cigarette.*

BILLY: Jive, jive.

RICHIE: You're arrogant, Billy. So arrogant.

BILLY: What are you—on the rag?

RICHIE: Wouldn't it just bang your little balls if I were!

ROGER (*To* RICHIE): Hey, man. What's with you?

RICHIE: Stupidity offends me; lies and ignorance offend me.

BILLY: You know where we was? The three of us? All three of us, earlier on? To the wrong side of the tracks, Richard. One good black upside-down whorehouse where you get what you buy, no jive along with it—so if it's a lay you want and need, you go! Or don't they have faggot whorehouses?

ROGER: IF YOU GUYS DON'T CUT THIS SHIT OUT I'M GONNA BUST SOMEBODY'S HEAD! (*Angrily* HE *flops back on his bed. There is a silence as* THEY *all lie there*)

RICHIE: "Where we was," he says. Listen to him. "Where we was." And he's got more school, Carlyle, than you have fingers and . . . (HE *has lifted his foot onto the bed; it touches, presses,* CARLYLE's *foot*) toes. It's this pseudo-earthy quality he feigns—but inside he's all cashmere.

BILLY: That's a lie. (*Giggling,* HE *is staring at the floor*) I'm polyester, worsted and mohair.

RICHIE: You have a lot of school, Billy; don't say you don't.

BILLY: You said "fingers and toes"; you didn't say "a lot."

CARLYLE: I think people get dumber the more they put their butts into some schoolhouse door.

BILLY: It depends on what the hell you're talkin' about. (*Now* HE *looks at* CARLYLE, *and sees the feet touching*)

CARLYLE: I seen cats back on the block, they knew what was shakin'—then they got into all this school jive and, man, every year they went, they come back they didn't know nothin'.

BILLY *is staring at* RICHIE's *foot pressing and rubbing* CARLYLE's *foot.* RICHIE *sees* BILLY *looking.* BILLY *cannot believe what* HE *is seeing. It fills him with fear. The silence goes on and on.*

RICHIE: Billy, why don't you and Roger go for a walk?

BILLY: What? (HE *bolts to his knees.* HE *is frozen on his knees on the bed*)

RICHIE: Roger asked you to go downtown, you went, you had fun.

ROGER (*Having turned,* HE *knows almost instantly what is going on*): I asked you, too.

RICHIE: You asked me; you *begged* Billy. I said no. Billy said no. You took my ten dollars. You begged Billy. I'm asking you a favor now—go for a walk. Let Carlyle and me have some time.

Silence.

CARLYLE (HE *sits up, uneasy and wary*): That how you work it?

ROGER: Work what?

CARLYLE: Whosever turn it be.

BILLY: No, no, that ain't the way we work it, because we don't work it.

CARLYLE: See? See? There it is—that goddamn education showin' through. All them years in school. Man, didn't we have a good time tonight? You rode in my car. I showed you a good cathouse, all that sweet black pussy. Ain't we friends? Richie likes me. How come you don't like me?

BILLY: 'Cause if you really are doin' what I think you're doin', you're a fuckin' animal!

CARLYLE *leaps to his feet, hand snaking to his pocket to draw a weapon.*

ROGER: Billy, no.

BILLY: NO, WHAT?!

ROGER: Relax, man; no need. (HE *turns to* CARLYLE; *patiently, wearily,* HE *speaks*) Man, I tole you it ain't goin' on here. We both tole you it ain't goin' on here.

CARLYLE: Don't you jive me, nigger. You goin' for a walk like I'm askin', or not? I wanna get this clear.

ROGER: Man, we live here.

RICHIE: It's my house, too, Roger; I live here, too. (HE *bounds to his feet, flinging the blanket that has been covering him so it flies and lands on the floor near* ROGER'*s footlocker*)

ROGER: Don't I know that? Did I say somethin' to make you think I didn't know that?

Standing, RICHIE *is removing his trousers and throwing them down on his footlocker.*

RICHIE: Carlyle is my guest.

Sitting down on the side of his bed and facing out, RICHIE *puts his arms around* CARLYLE'*s thigh.* ROGER *jumps to his feet and grabs the blanket from the foot of his bed. Shaking it open,* HE *drops onto the bed, his head at the foot of the bed and facing off as* HE *covers himself.*

ROGER: Fine. He your friend. This your home. So that mean he can stay. It don't mean I gotta leave. I'll catch you all in the mornin'.

BILLY: Roger, what the hell are you doin'?

ROGER: What you better do, Billy. It's gettin' late. I'm goin' to sleep.

BILLY: What?

ROGER: Go to fucking bed, Billy. Get up in the rack, turn your back and look at the wall.

BILLY: You gotta be kiddin'.

ROGER: DO IT!

BILLY: Man . . . !

ROGER: Yeah . . . !

BILLY: You mean just . . .

ROGER: It been goin' on a long damn time, man. You ain't gonna put no stop to it.

CARLYLE: You . . . ain't . . . serious.

RICHIE (*Both* HE *and* CARLYLE *are staring at* ROGER *and then* BILLY, *who is staring at* ROGER): Well, I don't believe it. Of all the childish . . . infantile . . .

CARLYLE: Hey! (*Silence*) HEY! Even I got to say this is a little weird, but if this the way you do it . . . (*And* HE *turns toward* RICHIE *below him*) it the way I do it. I don't know.

RICHIE: With them right there? Are you kidding? My God, Carlyle, that'd be obscene. (*Pulling slightly away from* CARLYLE)

CARLYLE: Ohhh, man . . . they backs turned.

RICHIE: No.

CARLYLE: What I'm gonna do? (*Silence.* HE *looks at them, all three of them*) Don't you got no feelin' for how a man feel? I don't understand you two boys. Unless'n you a pair of motherfuckers. That what you are, you a pair of motherfuckers? You slits, man. DON'T YOU HEAR ME!? I DON'T UNDERSTAND THIS SITUATION HERE. I THOUGHT WE MADE A DEAL! (RICHIE *rises, starts to pull on his trousers.* CARLYLE *grabs him*) YOU GET ON YOUR KNEES, YOU PUNK, I MEAN NOW, AND YOU GONNA BE ON MY JOINT FAST OR YOU GONNA BE ONE BUSTED PUNK. AM I UNDERSTOOD? (HE *hurls* RICHIE *down to the floor*)

BILLY: I ain't gonna have this going on here; Roger, I can't.

ROGER: I been turnin' my back on one thing or another all my life.

RICHIE: Jealous, Billy?

BILLY (*Getting to his feet*): Just go out that door, the two of you. Go. Go on out in the bushes or out in some field. See if I follow you. See if I care. I'll be right here and I'll be sleepin', but it ain't gonna be done in my house. I don't have much in this goddamn army, but *here* is mine. (HE *stands beside his bed*)

CARLYLE: I WANT MY FUCKIN' NUT! HOW COME YOU SO UPTIGHT? HE WANTS ME! THIS BOY HERE WANTS ME! WHO YOU TO STOP IT?

ROGER (*Spinning to face* CARLYLE *and* RICHIE): *That's right,* Billy. Richie one a those people want to get fucked by niggers, man. It what he know was gonna happen all his life—can be his dream come true. Ain't that right, Richie! (*Jumping to his feet,* RICHIE *starts putting on his trousers*) Want to make it real in the world, how a nigger is an animal. Give 'em an inch, gonna take a mile. Ain't you some kinda fool, Richie? Hear me, Carlyle.

CARLYLE: Man, don't make me no nevermind what he think he's provin' an' shit, long as I get my nut. I KNOW I ain't no animal, don't have to prove it.

RICHIE (*Pulling at* CARLYLE's *arm, wanting to move him toward the door*): Let's go. Let's go outside. The hell with it.

But CARLYLE *tears himself free;* HE *squats furiously down on the bunk, his hands seizing it, his back to all of them.*

CARLYLE: Bull shit. Bullshit! I ain't goin' no-fuckin'-where—this jive ass ain't runnin' me. Is this you house or not? (HE *doesn't know what is going on;* HE *can hardly look at any of them*)

ROGER (*Bounding out of bed, hurling his pillow across the room*): I'm goin' to the fuckin' john, Billy. Hang it up, man; let 'em be.

BILLY: No.

ROGER: I'm smarter than you—do like I'm sayin'.

BILLY: It ain't right.

ROGER: Who gives a big rat's ass!

CARLYLE: Right on, bro! That boy know; he do. (HE *circles the bed toward them*) Hear him. Look into his eyes.

BILLY: This fuckin' army takin' everything else away from me, they ain't takin' more than they got. I see what I see—I don't run, don't hide.

ROGER (*Turning away from* BILLY, HE *stomps out the door, slamming it*): You fuckin' well better learn.

CARLYLE: That right. Time for more schoolin'. Lesson number one. (*Stealthily* HE *steps and snaps out the only light, the lamp clamped to* RICHIE's *bed*) You don't see what you see so well in the dark. It dark in the night. Black man got a black body—he disappear.

The darkness is so total THEY *are all no more than shadows.*

RICHIE: Not to the hands; not to the fingers. (*Moving from across the room toward* CARLYLE)

CARLYLE: You do like you talk, boy, you gonna make me happy.

BILLY, *nervously clutching his sneaker, is moving backward.*

BILLY: Who says the lights go out? Nobody goddamn asked me if the lights go out.

BILLY, *lunging to the wall switch, throws it. The overhead lights flash on, flooding the room with light.* CARLYLE *is seated on the edge of* RICHIE's *bed,* RICHIE *kneeling before him.*

CARLYLE: I DO, MOTHERFUCKER, I SAY! (*And the switchblade seems to leap from his pocket to his hand*) I SAY! CAN'T YOU LET PEOPLE BE?

BILLY *hurls his sneaker at the floor at* CARLYLE's *feet. Instantly* CARLYLE *is across the room, blocking* BILLY's *escape out the door.*

Goddamn you, boy! I'm gonna cut your ass, just to show you how it feel—and cuttin' can happen. This knife true.

RICHIE: Carlyle, now c'mon.

CARLYLE: Shut up, pussy.

RICHIE: Don't hurt him, for chrissake.

CARLYLE: Goddamn man throw a shoe at me, he don't walk around clean in the world thinkin' he can throw another. He get some shit come back at him.

BILLY doesn't know which way to go, and then CARLYLE, jabbing the knife at the air before BILLY's chest, has BILLY running backward, his eyes fixed on the moving blade. HE stumbles, having run into RICHIE's bed. HE sprawls backward and CARLYLE is over him.

No, no; no, no. Put you hand out there. Put it out. (*Slight pause;* BILLY *is terrified*) DO THE THING I'M TELLIN'! (BILLY *lets his hand rise in the air and* CARLYLE *grabs it, holds it*) That's it. That's good. See? See?

The knife flashes across BILLY's palm; the blood flows. BILLY winces, recoils, but CARLYLE's hand still clenches and holds.

BILLY: Motherfucker.

Again the knife darts, cutting, and BILLY yelps. RICHIE, on his knees beside them, turns away.

RICHIE: Oh, my God, what are you—

CARLYLE (*In his own sudden distress,* HE *flings the hand away*): That you blood. The blood inside you, you don't ever see it there. Take a look how easy it come out—and enough of it come out, you in the middle of the worst goddamn trouble you ever gonna see. And know I'm the man can deal that kinda trouble, easy as I smile. And I smile . . . easy. Yeah.

BILLY is curled in upon himself, holding the hand to his stomach as RICHIE now reaches tentatively and shyly out as if to console BILLY, who repulses the gesture. CARLYLE is angry and strangely depressed. Forlornly HE slumps onto BILLY's footlocker as BILLY staggers up to his wall locker and takes out a towel.

Bastard ruin my mood, Richie. He ruin my mood. Fightin' and lovin' real different in the feelin's I got. I see blood come outa somebody like that, it don't make me feel good—hurt me—hurt on somebody I thought was my friend. But I ain't supposed to see. One dumb nigger. No mind, he thinks, no heart, no feelings a gentleness. You see how that ain't true, Richie. Goddamn man threw a shoe at me. A lotta people woulda cut his heart out. I gotta make him know he throw shit, he get shit. But I don't hurt him bad, you see what I mean?

BILLY's back is to them, as HE stands hunched at his locker, and suddenly his voice, hissing, erupts.

BILLY: Jesus . . . H. . . . Christ . . . ! Do you know what I'm doin'? Do you know what I'm standin' here doin'? (HE *whirls now;* HE *holds a straight razor in his hand. A bloody towel is wrapped around the hurt hand.* CARLYLE *tenses, rises, seeing the razor*) I'm a twenty-four-year-old goddamn college graduate—intellectual goddamn scholar type—and I got a razor in my hand. I'm thinkin' about comin' up behind one black human being and I'm thinkin' nigger this and nigger that—I wanna cut his throat. THAT IS RIDICULOUS. I NEVER FACED ANYBODY IN MY LIFE WITH ANYTHING TO KILL THEM. YOU UNDERSTAND ME? I DON'T HAVE A GODDAMN THING ON THE LINE HERE!

The door opens and ROGER *rushes in, having heard the yelling.* BILLY *flings the razor into his locker.*

Look at me, Roger, look at me. I got a cut palm—I don't know what happened. Jesus Christ, I got sweat all over me when I think a what I was near to doin'. I swear it. I mean, do I think I need a reputation as a killer, a bad man with a knife? (HE *is wild with the energy of feeling free and with the anger at what these others almost made him do.* CARLYLE *slumps down on the footlocker;* HE *sits there*) Bullshit! I need shit! I got sweat all over me. I got the mile record in my hometown. I did four forty-two in high school and that's the goddamn record in Windsor County. I don't need approval from either one of the pair of you. (*And* HE *rushes at* RICHIE) You wanna be a goddamn swish—a goddamn faggot-queer—GO! Suckin' cocks and takin' it in the ass, the thing of which you dream—GO! AND YOU— (*Whirling on* CARLYLE) You wanna be a bad-assed animal, man, get it on—go—but I wash my hands. I am not human as you are. I put you down, I put you down—(HE *almost hurls himself at* RICHIE) you gay little piece of shit cake—SHIT CAKE. AND YOU—(*Hurt, confused,* RICHIE *turns away, nearly pressing his face into the bed beside which* HE *kneels, as* BILLY *has spun back to tower over the pulsing, weary* CARLYLE) you are your own goddamn fault, SAMBO! SAMBO! (*And the knife flashes up in* CARLYLE's *hand into* BILLY's *stomach, and* BILLY *yelps*) Ahhhhhhhhh. (*And pushes at the hand.* RICHIE *is still turned away*)

RICHIE: Well, fuck you, Billy.

BILLY (HE *backs off the knife*): Get away, get away.

RICHIE (*As* ROGER, *who could not see because* BILLY's *back is to him, is approaching* CARLYLE *and* BILLY *goes walking up toward the lockers as if* HE *knows where* HE *is going, as if* HE *is going to go out the door and to a movie, his hands holding his belly*): You're so-o messed up.

ROGER (*To* CARLYLE): Man, what's the matter with you?

CARLYLE: Don't nobody talk that weird shit to me, you understand?

ROGER: You jive, man. That's all you do—jive!

> BILLY, *striding swiftly, walks flat into the wall lockers;* HE *bounces, turns.* THEY *are all looking at him.*

RICHIE: Billy! Oh, Billy!

> ROGER *looks at* RICHIE.

BILLY: Ahhhhhhh. Ahhhhhhh.

> ROGER *looks at* CARLYLE *as if* HE *is about to scream, and beyond him,* BILLY *turns from the lockers, starts to walk again, now staggering and moving toward them.*

RICHIE: I think . . . he stabbed him. I think Carlyle stabbed Billy. Roger!

> ROGER *whirls to go to* BILLY, *who is staggering downstage and angled away, hands clenched over his belly.*

BILLY: Shut up! It's just a cut, it's just a cut. He cut my hand, he cut gut. (HE *collapses onto his knees just beyond* ROGER'*s footlocker*) It took the wind out of me, scared me, that's all. (*Fiercely* HE *tries to hide the wound and remain calm*)

ROGER: Man, are you all right?

> ROGER *moves to* BILLY, *who turns to hide the wound. Till now* NO ONE *is sure what happened.* RICHIE *only "thinks"* BILLY *has been stabbed.* BILLY *is pretending* HE *isn't hurt. As* BILLY *turns from* ROGER, HE *turns toward* RICHIE *and* RICHIE *sees the blood.* RICHIE *yelps and* THEY *all begin talking and yelling simultaneously.*

CARLYLE: You know what I was learnin', he was learnin' to talk all that weird shit, cuttin', baby, cuttin', the ways and means a shit, man, razors.

ROGER: You all right? Or what? He slit you?

BILLY: Just took the wind outa me, scared me.

RICHIE: Carlyle, you stabbed him; you stabbed him.

CARLYLE: Ohhhh, pussy, pussy, pussy, Carlyle know what he do.

ROGER (*Trying to lift* BILLY): Get up, okay? Get up on the bed.

BILLY (*Irritated, pulling free*): I am on the bed.

ROGER: What?

RICHIE: No, Billy, no, you're not.

BILLY: Shut up!

RICHIE: You're on the floor.

BILLY: I'm on the bed. I'm on the bed. (*Emphatically. And then* HE *looks at the floor*) What?

ROGER: Let me see what he did. (BILLY's *hands are clenched on the wound*) Billy, let me see where he got you.

BILLY (*Recoiling*): NO-O-O-O-O-O, you nigger!

ROGER (HE *leaps at Carlyle*): What did you do?

CARLYLE (*Hunching his shoulders, ducking his head*): Shut up.

ROGER: What did you do, nigger—you slit him or stick him? (*And then* HE *tries to get back to* BILLY) Billy, let me see.

BILLY (*Doubling over till his head hits the floor*): NO-O-O-O-O-O! Shit, shit, shit.

RICHIE (*Suddenly sobbing and yelling*): Oh, my God, my God, ohhhh, ohhhh, ohhhh. (*Bouncing on his knees on the bed*)

CARLYLE: FUCK IT, FUCK IT, I STUCK HIM. I TURNED IT. This mother army break my heart. I can't be out there where it pretty, don't wanna live! Wash me clean, shit face!

RICHIE: Ohhhh, ohhhhh, ohhhhhhhhhh. Carlyle stabbed Billy, oh, ohhhh, I never saw such a thing in my life. Ohhhhhh. (*As* ROGER *is trying gently, fearfully, to straighten* BILLY *up*) Don't die, Billy; don't die.

ROGER: Shut up and go find somebody to help. Richie, go!

RICHIE: Who? I'll go, I'll go. (*Scrambling off the bed*)

ROGER: I don't know. JESUS CHRIST! DO IT!

RICHIE: Okay. Okay. Billy, don't die. Don't die. (*Backing for the door,* HE *turns and runs*)

ROGER: The sarge, or C.Q.

BILLY (*Suddenly doubling over, vomiting blood.* RICHIE *is gone*): Ohhhhhhhhhh. Blood. Blood.

ROGER: Be still, be still.

BILLY (*Pulling at a blanket on the floor beside him*): I want to stand up. I'm . . . vomiting . . . (*Making no move to stand, only to cover himself*) blood. What does that mean?

ROGER (*Slowly standing*): I don't know.

BILLY: Yes, yes, I want to stand up. Give me blanket, blanket. (HE *rolls back and forth, fighting to get the blanket over him*)

ROGER: RIICCHHHIIIEEEE! (*As* BILLY *is furiously grappling with the blanket*) No, no. (HE *looks at* CARLYLE, *who is slumped over, muttering to himself.* ROGER *runs for the door*) Wait on, be tight, be cool.

BILLY: Cover me. Cover me.

At last BILLY *gets the blanket over his face. The dark makes him grow still.* HE *lies there beneath his blanket. Silence.* NO ONE *moves. And then* CARLYLE *senses the quiet;* HE *turns, looks. Slowly, wearily,* HE *rises and walks to where* BILLY *lies.* HE *stands over him, the knife hanging loosely from his left hand as* HE *reaches with his right to gently take the blanket and lift it slowly from* BILLY'*s face.* THEY *look at each other.* BILLY *reaches up and pats* CARLYLE'*s hand holding the blanket.*

I don't want to talk to you right now, Carlyle. All right? Where's Roger? Do you know where he is? (*Slight pause*) Don't stab me anymore, Carlyle, okay? I was dead wrong doin' what I did. I know that now. Carlyle, promise me you won't stab me anymore. I couldn't take it. Okay? I'm cold . . . my blood . . . is . . .

From off comes a voice.

ROONEY (*Offstage*): Cokesy? Cokesy wokesy? (*And* HE *staggers into the doorway, very drunk, a beer bottle in his hand*) Ollie-ollie oxen-freeee. (HE *looks at them.* CARLYLE *quickly, secretly, slips the knife into his pocket*) How you all doin'? Everybody drunk, huh? I los' my friend. (HE *is staggering sideways toward* BILLY'*s bunk, where* HE *finally drops down, sitting*) Who are you, soldier? (CARLYLE *has straightened, his head ducked down as* HE *is edging for the door*) Who are you, soldier?

And RICHIE, *running, comes roaring into the room.* HE *looks at* ROONEY *and cannot understand what is going on.* CARLYLE *is standing.* ROONEY *is just sitting there. What is going on?* RICHIE *moves along the lockers, trying to get behind* ROONEY, *his eyes never off* CARLYLE.

RICHIE: Ohhhhhh, Sergeant Rooney, I've been looking for you everywhere—where have you been? Carlyle stabbed Billy, he stabbed him.
ROONEY (*Sitting there*): What?
RICHIE: Carlyle stabbed Billy.
ROONEY: Who's Carlyle?
RICHIE: He's Carlyle. (*As* CARLYLE *seems about to advance, the knife again showing in his hand*) Carlyle, don't hurt anybody more!
ROONEY (*On his feet,* HE *is staggering toward the door*): You got a knife there? What's with the knife? What's goin' on here?

CARLYLE *steps as if to bolt for the door, but* ROONEY *is in the way, having inserted himself between* CARLYLE *and* RICHIE, *who has backed into the doorway.*

Wait! Now wait!
RICHIE (*As* CARLYLE *raises the knife*): Carlyle, don't! (HE *runs from the room*)
ROONEY: You watch your step, you understand. You see what I got here? (HE *lifts the beer bottle, waves it threateningly*) You watch your step, motherfucker. Relax. I mean, we can straighten all this out. We—(CARLYLE *lunges at* ROONEY, *who tenses*) I'm just askin' what's goin' on, that's all I'm doin'. No need to get all—(*And* CARLYLE *swipes at the air again;* ROONEY *recoils*) Motherfucker. Motherfucker. (HE *seems to be tensing, his body gathering itself*

for some mighty effort. And HE *throws his head back and gives the eagle yell)*
Eeeeeeeeeeeaaaaaaaaaaaaaaaaahhhhhh! Eeeeaaaaaaaaaaaaaahhhhhhhhhhhhhh!
(CARLYLE *jumps;* HE *looks left and right)* Goddammit, I'll cut you good. (HE
lunges to break the bottle on the edge of the wall lockers. The bottle shatters and
HE *yelps, dropping everything)* Ohhhhhhhh! Ohhhhhhhhhhhhhhh! (CARLYLE
bolts, running from the room) I hurt myself, I cut myself. I hurt my hand.
(*Holding the wounded hand,* HE *scurries to* BILLY's *bed, where* HE *sits on the edge,*
trying to wipe the blood away so HE *can see the wound)* I cut— (*Hearing a noise,*
HE *whirls, looks;* CARLYLE *is plummeting in the door and toward him.* ROONEY
stands) I hurt my hand, goddammit! (*The knife goes into* ROONEY's *belly.* HE
flails at CARLYLE) I HURT MY HAND! WHAT ARE YOU DOING?
WHAT ARE YOU DOING? WAIT! WAIT! (HE *turns away, falling to his*
knees, and the knife goes into him again and again) No fair. No fair!

ROGER, *running, skids into the room, headed for* BILLY, *and then* HE *sees*
CARLYLE *on* ROONEY, *the leaping knife.* ROGER *lunges, grabbing* CARLYLE,
pulling him to get him off ROONEY. CARLYLE *leaps free of* ROGER, *sending*
ROGER *flying backward. And then* CARLYLE *begins to circle* ROGER's *bed.* HE
is whimpering, wiping at the blood on his shirt as if to wipe it away. ROGER
backs away as CARLYLE *keeps waving the knife at him.* ROONEY *is crawling*
along the floor under BILLY's *bed and then* HE *stops crawling, lies there.*

CARLYLE: You don't tell nobody on me you saw me do this, I let you go, okay?
Ohhhhhhhhh. (*Rubbing, rubbing at the shirt*) Ohhhhhh, how'm I gonna
get back to the world now, I got all this mess to—
ROGER: What happened? That you—I don't understand that you did this! That
you did—
CARLYLE: YOU SHUT UP! Don't be talkin' all that weird shit to me—don't
you go talkin' all that weird shit!
ROGER: Nooooooooooooo!
CARLYLE: I'm Carlyle, man. You know me. You know me.

CARLYLE *turns,* HE *flees out the door.* ROGER, *alone, looks about the room.*
BILLY *is there.* ROGER *moves toward* BILLY, *who is shifting, undulating on his*
back.

BILLY: Carlyle, no; oh, Christ, don't stab me anymore. I'll die. I will—I'll die.
Don't make me die. I'll get my dog after you. I'LL GET MY DOG AFTER
YOU!

ROGER *is saying, "Oh, Billy, man, Billy."* HE *is trying to hold* BILLY. *Now*
HE *lifts* BILLY *into his arms.*

ROGER: Oh, Billy; oh, man. GODDAMMIT, BILLY!

A MILITARY POLICE LIEUTENANT *comes running in the door, his .45*
automatic drawn, and HE *levels it at* ROGER.

LIEUTENANT: Freeze, soldier! Not a quick move out of you. Just real slow, straighten your ass up.

ROGER has gone rigid; the LIEUTENANT is advancing on him. Tentatively ROGER turns, looks.

ROGER: Huh? No.

LIEUTENANT: Get your ass against the lockers.

ROGER: Sir, no. I—

LIEUTENANT (*Hurling ROGER away toward the wall lockers*): MOVE! (*Another M.P., PFC HINSON, comes in, followed by RICHIE, flushed and breathless*) Hinson, cover this bastard.

HINSON (*Drawing his .45 automatic, moving on ROGER*): Yes, sir.

The LIEUTENANT frisks ROGER, who is spread-eagled at the lockers.

RICHIE: What? Oh, sir, no, no. Roger, what's going on?

LIEUTENANT: I'll straighten this shit out.

ROGER: Tell 'em to get the gun off me, Richie.

LIEUTENANT: SHUT UP!

RICHIE: But, sir, sir, he didn't do it. Not him.

LIEUTENANT (*Fiercely HE shoves RICHIE out of the way*): I told you, all of you, to shut up. (*HE moves to ROONEY's body*) Jesus, God, this Sfc is cut to shit. He's cut to shit. (*HE hurries to BILLY's body*) This man is cut to shit.

CARLYLE appears in the doorway, his hands cuffed behind him, a third M.P., PFC CLARK, shoving him forward. CARLYLE seems shocked and cunning, his mind whirring.

CLARK: Sir, I got this guy on the street, runnin' like a streak a shit.

CLARK hurls the struggling CARLYLE forward and CARLYLE stumbles toward the head of RICHIE's bed as RICHIE, seeing him coming, hurries away along BILLY's bed and toward the wall lockers.

RICHIE: He did it! Him, him!

CARLYLE: What is going on here? I don't know what is going on here!

CLARK (*Club at the ready, HE stations himself beside CARLYLE*): He's got blood all over him, sir. All over him.

LIEUTENANT: What about the knife?

CLARK: No, sir. He must have thrown it away.

A FOURTH M.P. has entered to stand in the doorway, and HINSON, leaving ROGER, bends to examine ROONEY. HE will also kneel and look for life in BILLY.

LIEUTENANT: You throw it away, soldier?

CARLYLE: Oh, you thinkin' about how my sister got happened, too. Oh, you ain't so smart as you think you are! No way!

ROGER: Jesus God almighty.

LIEUTENANT: What happened here? I want to know what happened here.

HINSON (*Rising from* BILLY*'s body*): They're both dead, sir. Both of them.

LIEUTENANT (*Confidential, almost whispering*): I know they're both dead. That's what I'm talkin' about.

CARLYLE: Chicken blood, sir. Chicken blood and chicken hearts is what all over me. I was goin' on my way, these people jump out the bushes be pourin' it all over me. Chicken blood and chicken hearts. (*Thrusting his hands out at* CLARK) You goin' take these cuffs off me, boy?

LIEUTENANT: Sit him down, Clark. Sit him down and shut him up.

CARLYLE: This my house, sir. This my goddamn house.

CLARK *grabs* CARLYLE, *begins to move him.*

LIEUTENANT: I said to shut him up.

CLARK: Move it; move! (*Struggling to get* CARLYLE *over to* ROGER*'s footlocker as* HINSON *and the* FOURTH M.P. *exit*)

CARLYLE: I want these cuffs taken off my hands.

CLARK: You better do like you been told. You better sit and shut up!

CARLYLE: I'm gonna be thinkin' over here. I'm gonna be thinkin' it all over. I got plannin' to do. I'm gonna be thinkin' in my quietness; don't you be makin' no mistake.

CARLYLE *slumps over, muttering to himself.* HINSON *and the* FOURTH M.P. *return, carrying a stretcher.* THEY *cross to* BILLY, *chatting with each other about how to go about the lift.* THEY *will lift him;* THEY *will carry him out.*

LIEUTENANT (*To* RICHIE): You're Wilson?

RICHIE: No, sir. (*Indicating* BILLY) That's Wilson. I'm Douglas.

LIEUTENANT (*To* ROGER): And you're Moore. And you sleep here.

ROGER: Yes, sir.

RICHIE: Yes, sir. And Billy slept here and Sergeant Rooney was our platoon sergeant and Carlyle was a transient, sir. He was a transient from P Company.

LIEUTENANT (*Scrutinizing* ROGER): And you had nothing to do with this? (*To* RICHIE) He had nothing to do with this?

ROGER: No, sir, I didn't.

RICHIE: No, sir, he didn't. I didn't either. Carlyle went crazy and he got into a fight and it was awful. I didn't even know what it was about exactly.

LIEUTENANT: How'd the Sfc get involved?

RICHIE: Well, he came in, sir.

ROGER: I had to run off to call you, sir. I wasn't here.

RICHIE: Sergeant Rooney just came in—I don't know why—he heard all the yelling, I guess—and Carlyle went after him. Billy was already stabbed.

CARLYLE (*Rising, his manner that of a man who is taking charge*): All right now, you gotta be gettin' the fuck outa here. All of you. I have decided enough of the shit has been goin' on around here and I am tellin' you to be gettin' these motherfuckin' cuffs off me and you be gettin' me a bus ticket home. I am quittin' this jive-time army.

LIEUTENANT: You are doin' what?

CARLYLE: No, I ain't gonna be quiet. No way. I am quittin' this goddamn—

LIEUTENANT: You shut the hell up, soldier. I am ordering you.

CARLYLE: I don't understand you people! Don't you people understand when a man be talkin' English at you to say his mind? I have quit the army!

HINSON *returns.*

LIEUTENANT: Get him outa here!

RICHIE: What's the matter with him?

LIEUTENANT: Hinson! Clark!

HINSON *and* CLARK *move, grabbing* CARLYLE, *and* THEY *drag him, struggling, toward the door.*

CARLYLE: Oh, no. Oh, no. You ain't gonna be doin' me no more. I been tellin' you. To get away from me. I am stayin' here. This my place, not your place. You take these cuffs off me like I been tellin' you! My poor little sister Lin Sue understood what was goin' on here! She tole me! She knew! (HE *is howling in the hallway now*) You better be gettin' these cuffs off me!

Silence. ROGER, RICHIE *and the* LIEUTENANT *are all staring at the door. The* LIEUTENANT *turns, crosses to the foot of* ROGER*'s bed.*

LIEUTENANT: All right now. I will be getting to the bottom of this. You know I will be getting to the bottom of this. (HE *is taking two forms from his clipboard*)

RICHIE: Yes, sir.

HINSON *and the* FOURTH M.P. *return with another stretcher.* THEY *walk to* ROONEY, *talking to one another about how to lift him.* THEY *drag him from under the bed.* THEY *will roll him onto the stretcher, lift him and walk out.* ROGER *moves, watching them, down along the edge of* BILLY*'s bed.*

LIEUTENANT: Fill out these forms. I want your serial number, rank, your MOS, the NCOIC of your work. Any leave coming up will be canceled. Tomorrow at 0800 you will report to my office at the provost marshal's headquarters. You know where that is?

ROGER (*As the* TWO M.P.*'s are leaving with the stretcher and* ROONEY*'s body*): Yes, sir.

RICHIE: Yes, sir.

LIEUTENANT (*Crossing to* ROGER, HE *hands him two cards*): Be prepared to do some talking. Two perfectly trained and primed strong pieces of U.S. Army property got cut to shit up here. We are going to find out how and why. Is that clear?

RICHIE: Yes, sir.

ROGER: Yes, sir.

The LIEUTENANT *looks at each of them.* HE *surveys the room.* HE *marches out.*

RICHIE: Oh, my God. Oh. Oh.

RICHIE *runs to his bed and collapses, sitting hunched down at the foot.* HE *holds himself and rocks as if very cold.* ROGER, *quietly, is weeping.* HE *stands and then walks to his bed.* HE *puts down the two cards.* HE *moves purposefully up to the mops hanging on the wall in the corner.* HE *takes one down.* HE *moves with the mop and the bucket to* BILLY's *bed, where* ROONEY's *blood stains the floor.* HE *mops.* RICHIE, *in horror, is watching.*

What . . . are you doing?

ROGER: This area a mess, man. (*Dragging the bucket, carrying the mop,* HE *moves to the spot where* BILLY *had lain.* HE *begins to mop*)

RICHIE: That's Billy's blood, Roger. His blood.

ROGER: Is it?

RICHIE: I feel awful.

ROGER (HE *keeps mopping*): How come you made me waste all that time talkin' shit to you, Richie? All my time talkin' shit, and all the time you was a faggot, man; you really was. You shoulda jus' tole ole Roger. He don't care. All you gotta do is tell me.

RICHIE: I've been telling you. I did.

ROGER: Jive, man, jive!

RICHIE: No!

ROGER: You did bullshit all over us! ALL OVER US!

RICHIE: I just wanted to hold his hand, Billy's hand, to talk to him, go to the movies hand in hand like he would with a girl or I would with someone back home.

ROGER: But he didn't wanna; *he* didn't wanna.

Finished now, ROGER *drags the mop and bucket back toward the corner.* RICHIE *is sobbing;* HE *is at the edge of hysteria.*

RICHIE: He did.

ROGER: No, man.

RICHIE: He did. He did. It's not my fault.

ROGER *slams the bucket into the corner and rams the mop into the bucket. Furious,* HE *marches down to* RICHIE. *Behind him* SERGEANT COKES, *grinning and lifting a wine bottle, appears in the doorway.*

COKES: Hey! (RICHIE, *in despair, rolls onto his belly.* COKES *is very, very happy*) Hey! What a day, gen'l'men. How you all doin'?

ROGER (*Crossing up near the head of his own bed*): Hello, Sergeant Cokes.

COKES (*Affectionate and casual,* HE *moves near to* ROGER): How you all doin'? Where's ole Rooney? I lost him.

ROGER: What?

COKES: We had a hell of a day, ole Rooney and me, lemme tell you. We been playin' hide-and-go-seek, and I was hidin', and now I think maybe he started hidin' without tellin' me he was gonna and I can't find him and I thought maybe he was hidin' up here.

RICHIE: Sergeant, he—

ROGER: No. No, we ain't seen him.

COKES: I gotta find him. He knows how to react in a tough situation. He didn't come up here looking for me?

ROGER *moves around to the far side of his bed, turning his back to* COKES. *Sitting,* ROGER *takes out a cigarette, but* HE *does not light it.*

ROGER: We was goin' to sleep, Sarge. Got to get up early. You know the way this mother army is.

COKES (*Nodding, drifting backward,* HE *sits down on* BILLY's *bed*): You don't mind I sit here a little. Wait on him. Got a little wine. You can have some. (*Tilting his head way back,* HE *takes a big drink and then, looking straight ahead, corks the bottle with a whack of his hand*) We got back into the area—we had been downtown—he wanted to play hide-and-go-seek. I tole him okay, I was ready for that. He hid his eyes. So I run and hid in the bushes and then under this Jeep. 'Cause I thought it was better. I hid and I hid and I hid. He never did come. So finally, I got tired—I figured I'd give up, come lookin' for him. I was way over by the movie theater. I don't know how I got there. Anyway, I got back here and I figured maybe he come up here lookin' for me, figurin' I was hidin' up with you guys. You ain't seen him, huh?

ROGER: No, we ain't seen him. I tole you that, Sarge.

COKES: Oh.

RICHIE: Roger!

ROGER: He's drunk, Richie! He's blasted drunk! Got a brain turned to mush!

COKES (*In deep agreement*): That ain't no lie.

ROGER: Let it be for the night, Richie. Let him be for the night.

COKES: I still know what's goin' on, though. Never no worry about that. I always know what's goin' on. I always know. Don't matter what I drink or how much I drink. I always still know what's goin' on. But . . . I'll be goin' maybe and look for Rooney. (*But rising,* HE *wanders down center*) But . . . I mean, we could be doin' that forever. Him and me. Me under the Jeep. He wants to find me, he goes to the Jeep. I'm over here. He comes here. I'm gone. You know, maybe I'll just wait a little while more I'm here.

He'll find me then if he comes here. You guys want another drink. (*Turning, HE goes to BILLY's footlocker, where HE sits and takes another enormous guzzle of wine*) Jesus, what a goddamn day we had. Me and Rooney started drivin' and we was comin' to this intersection and out comes this goddamn Chevy. I try to get around her, but no dice. BINGO! I hit her in the left rear. She was furious. I didn't care. I gave her my name and number. My car had a headlight out, the fender bashed in. Rooney wouldn't stop laughin'. I didn't know what to do. So we went to D.C. to this private club I know. Had ten or more snorts and decided to get back here after playin' some snooker. That was fun. On the way, we picked up this kid from the engineering unit, hitchhiking. I'm starting to feel real clear-headed now. So I'm comin' around this corner and all of a sudden there's this car stopped dead in front of me. He's not blinkin' to turn or anything. I slam on the brakes, but it's like puddin' the way I slide into him. There's a big noise and we yell. Rooney starts laughin' like crazy and the kid jumps outa the back and says he's gonna take a fuckin' bus. The guy from the other car is swearin' at me. My car's still workin' fine, so I move it off to the side and tell him to do the same, while we wait for the cops. He says he wants his car right where it is and he had the right of way 'cause he was makin' a legal turn. So we're waitin' for the cops. Some cars go by. The guy's car is this big fuckin' Buick. Around the corner comes this little red Triumph. The driver's this blond kid got this blond girl next to him. You can see what's gonna happen. There's this fuckin' car sittin' there, nobody in it. So the Triumph goes crashin' into the back of the Buick with nobody in it. BIFF-BANG-BOOM. And everything stops. We're staring. It's all still. And then that fuckin' Buick kinda shudders and starts to move. With nobody in it. It starts to roll from the impact. And it rolls just far enough to get where the road starts a downgrade. It's driftin' to the right. It's driftin' to the shoulder and over it and onto this hill, where it's pickin' up speed 'cause the hill is steep and then it disappears over the side, and into the dark, just rollin' real quiet. Rooney falls over, he's laughin' so hard. I don't know what to do. In a minute the cops come and in another minute some guy comes runnin' up over the hill to tell us some other guy had got run over by this car with nobody in it. We didn't know what to think. This was fuckin' unbelievable to us. But we found out later from the cops that this wasn't true and some guy had got hit over the head with a bottle in a bar and when he staggered out the door it was just at the instant that this fuckin' Buick with nobody in it went by. Seein' this, the guy stops cold and turns around and just goes back into the bar. Rooney is screamin' at me how we been in four goddamn accidents and fights and how we have got out clean. So then we got everything all straightened out and we come back here to play hide-and-seek 'cause that's what ole Rooney wanted. (HE *is taking another drink, but finding the bottle empty*) Only now I can't find him. (*Near* RICHIE*'s footlocker stands a beer bottle and* COKES *begins to move toward it. Slowly* HE *bends and grasps the bottle;* HE *straightens, looking at it.* HE *drinks. And settles down on* RICHIE*'s footlocker*) I'll just sit a little.

RICHIE, *lying on his belly, shudders. The sobs burst out of him.* HE *is shaking.* COKES, *blinking, turns to study* RICHIE.

What's up? Hey, what're you cryin' about, soldier? Hey? (RICHIE *cannot help himself*) What's he cryin' about?

ROGER (*Disgustedly,* HE *sits there*): He's cryin' 'cause he's a queer.

COKES: Oh. You a queer, boy?

RICHIE: Yes, Sergeant.

COKES: Oh. (*Pause*) How long you been a queer?

ROGER: All his fuckin' life.

RICHIE: I don't know.

COKES (*Turning to scold* ROGER): Don't be yellin' mean at him. Boy, I tell you it's a real strange thing the way havin' leukemia gives you a lotta funny thoughts about things. Two months ago—or maybe even yesterday—I'da called a boy who was a queer a lotta awful names. But now I just wanna be figurin' things out. I mean, you ain't kiddin' me out about ole Rooney, are you, boys, 'cause of how I'm a sergeant and you're enlisted men, so you got some idea a vengeance on me? You ain't doin' that, are you, boys?

ROGER: No.

RICHIE: Ohhhh. Jesus. Ohhhh. I don't know what's hurtin' in me.

COKES: No, no, boy. You listen to me. You gonna be okay. There's a lotta worse things in this world than bein' a queer. I seen a lot of 'em, too. I mean, you could have leukemia. That's worse. That can kill you. I mean, it's okay. You listen to the ole sarge. I mean, maybe I was a queer, I wouldn't have leukemia. Who's to say? Lived a whole different life. Who's to say? I keep thinkin' there was maybe somethin' I coulda done different. Maybe not drunk so much. Or if I'd killed more gooks, or more krauts or more dinks. I was kindhearted sometimes. Or if I'd had a wife and I had some kids. Never had any. But my mother did and she died of it anyway. Gives you a whole funny different way a lookin' at things, I'll tell you. Ohhhhh, Rooney, Rooney. (*Slight pause*) Or if I'd let that little gook outa that spider hole he was in, I was sittin' on it. I'd let him out now, he was in there. (HE *rattles the footlocker lid under him*) Oh, how'm I ever gonna forget it? That funny little guy. I'm runnin' along, he pops up outa that hole. I'm never gonna forget him—how'm I ever gonna forget him? I see him and dive, goddamn bullet hits me in the side, I'm midair, everything's turnin' around. I go over the edge of this ditch and I'm crawlin' real fast. I lost my rifle. Can't find it. Then I come up behind him. He's half out of the hole. I bang him on top of his head, stuff him back into the hole with a grenade for company. Then I'm sittin' on the lid and it's made outa steel.

I can feel him in there, though, bangin' and yellin' under me, and his yelling I can hear is begging for me to let him out. It was like a goddamn Charlie Chaplin movie, everybody fallin' down and clumsy, and him in there yellin' and bangin' away, and I'm just sittin' there lookin' around. And he was Charlie Chaplin. I don't know who I was. And then he blew up. (*Pause*) Maybe I'll just get a little shut-eye right sittin' here while I'm waitin' for ole Rooney. We figure it out. All of it. You don't mind I just doze a little here, you boys?

ROGER: No.

RICHIE: No.

ROGER *rises and walks to the door.* HE *switches off the light and gently closes the door. The transom glows.* COKES *sits in a flower of light.* ROGER *crosses back to his bunk and settles in, sitting.*

COKES: Night, boys.

RICHIE: Night, Sergeant.

COKES *sits there, fingers entwined, trying to sleep.*

COKES: I mean, he was like Charlie Chaplin. And then he blew up.

ROGER (*Suddenly feeling very sad for this old man*): Sergeant . . . maybe you was Charlie Chaplin, too.

COKES: No. No. (*Pause*) No. I don't know who I was. Night.

ROGER: You think he was singin' it?

COKES: What?

ROGER: You think he was singin' it?

COKES: Oh, yeah. Oh, yeah; he was singin' it. (*Slight pause. Sitting on the footlocker,* HE *begins to sing a makeshift language imitating Korean, to the tune of "Beautiful Streamer."* HE *begins with an angry, mocking energy that slowly becomes a dream, a lullaby, a farewell, a lament*)

> Yo no som lo no
> Ung toe lo knee
> Ra so me la lo
> La see see oh doe.
>
> Doe no tee ta ta
> Too low see see
> Ra mae me lo lo
> Ah boo boo boo eee.
>
> Boo boo eee booo eeee
> La so lee lem
> Lem lo lee da ung
> Uhhh so ba booooo ohhhh.

Boo booo eee ung ba
Eee eee la looo
Lem lo lala la
Eeee oohhh ohhh ohhh ohhhhh.

In the silence, COKES *makes the soft, whispering sound of a child imitating an explosion, and his entwined fingers come apart. The dark figures of* RICHIE *and* ROGER *are near. The lingering light fades.*

END OF PLAY

BOTTICELLI

Terrence McNally

About Terrence McNally

Born in St. Petersburg, Florida in 1939 and raised in Corpus Christi, Texas, Terrence McNally is a Phi Beta Kappa graduate of Columbia University. Mc-Nally's first important play, *And Things That Go Bump in the Night*, premiered at The Guthrie Theater in Minneapolis in 1964; it opened on Broadway the following year. Other Broadway credits include *Noon, Bad Habits, The Ritz*, which was later adapted for film, and the 1984 musical *The Rink*, with a score by John Kander and Fred Ebb. Off Broadway productions include *Sweet Eros* and *Witness, Next, Where Has Tommy Flowers Gone?* and *Whiskey*. *The 5:48* and the recent *Mama Malone* were written for television. McNally has received two Guggenheim fellowships, an Obie award and a citation from the American Academy of Arts and Letters. Currently Vice President of the Dramatists Guild, he is a former winner of its Hull-Warriner Award.

Production History

Botticelli was first produced by Channel 13 in New York City in March 1968, directed by Glen Jordan. Its stage premiere was in August of that year, at the Berkshire Theatre Festival in Stockbridge, Massachusetts.

Playwright's Note

If the play is produced in an arena-type theatre, I would suggest the Man make his appearance through the audience. In a proscenium theatre, he might make his way down the center aisle with a follow spot on him. He must be center stage at the end of the play, a single light on his face.

Characters

WAYNE
STU
MAN

Time

An afternoon in the mid-1960s.

Place

A jungle in Vietnam.

The Play

Botticelli

Jungle foliage. Afternoon sun and shadows. Insect noises. Two soldiers, WAYNE *and* STU, *crouching with rifles.*

WAYNE: No, I'm not Marcel Proust.

STU: Proust was a stylist.

WAYNE: And he died *after* World War I.

STU: You sure?

WAYNE: 1922.

STU: Yeah?

WAYNE: November 4, 19—

STU: All right! (*Then*) What's up?

WAYNE (*Stiffening*): I thought I heard something. (*Relaxes*)

STU: Are you a . . . let's see . . . are you a Polish concert pianist who donated a large part of the proceeds from his concerts to the cause of Polish nationalism?

WAYNE: Oh, that's a real braincrusher, that one is!

STU: Well are you?

WAYNE: No I'm not Paderewski.

STU: Are you sure you're dead?

WAYNE: Oh brother!

STU: A dead European male in the arts beginning with P?

WAYNE: Why don't you write it down?

STU: Got it! You're a controversial Russian poet, novelist, dramatist and short-story writer.

WAYNE: Sorry. I'm not Pushkin.

STU: Pushkin wasn't considered controversial.

WAYNE: Who says?

STU: I do.

WAYNE: He was part Negro.

STU: What's controversial about that?

WAYNE: Dumas *père*?

STU: Don't change the subject. Controversial Russian writer. Come on. I've got you stumped, hunh? Look at you. Drew a blank. Hunh? Hunh?

WAYNE: I hope it's not Boris Pasternak you're crowing about.

STU: Drop dead, will you?

WAYNE: Then give up, hunh? (*Tenses*) Sshh! (*Relaxes*) Not yet.

STU: You'd think he'd starve in there by now.

WAYNE: Maybe he has. Why don't you go see?

STU: And get a grenade in the face. That tunnel could be half a mile long for all we know. He's buried in there like a groundhog. No, sir, I'm holding tight, staying right where I am, sergeant's orders. I got all the time in the world to wait for that bugger to stick his head out. (WAYNE *starts making cigarette*) Are you a . . .? I'm running dry. P's the hardest letter in the alphabet.

WAYNE: Wanna turn on?

STU: How much we got left?

WAYNE: If he's not out of there by tonight we're in trouble.

STU: Do you keep a diary?

WAYNE: Sure. Every night.

STU: No, who you are! Does he keep a diary?

WAYNE: I'm not Samuel Pepys.

STU: Smart-ass! (THEY *smoke*) Would you say this is the best part of the whole war?

WAYNE: What is?

STU: This. Pot.

WAYNE: No. I'd say Raquel Welch.

STU: Yeah.

WAYNE: What'd you think of her?

STU: I didn't.

WAYNE: Those goddam white leather boots up to here . . . and that yellow miniskirt . . .

STU: Hey, are you the outstanding English Baroque composer?

WAYNE: I'm not Henry Purcell. I thought Raquel Welch looked like a sexy . . . ostrich.

STU: Do the words "Rape of the Lock" mean anything to you?

WAYNE: No, and they don't mean anything to Alexander Pope either.

STU: Nuts!

WAYNE: Look, let me tell you who I am, hunh?

STU: No I said.

WAYNE: Brother, you're stubborn.

STU: And *you're* a Victorian playwright!

WAYNE: I'm not Arthur Wing Pinero.

STU: Sir.

WAYNE: Hunh?

STU: Sir Arthur Wing Pinero.

WAYNE: I know!

STU: You didn't say it.

WAYNE: I'd rather talk about Raquel Welch.

STU: Sure you would. You're getting stoned.

WAYNE: I'm not getting anything else.

STU: You still worrying about that letter from Susan?

WAYNE: Not since Raquel Welch I'm not.

STU: I bet.

WAYNE: Let her get a divorce. I don't care. Hell, the only mistake I made was thinking I had to marry her. I should've sent her to Puerto Rico. She could've had a vacation on me, too.

STU: Only you had scruples.

WAYNE: Leave me alone.

STU: Jesuit high school, Dominican college scruples.

WAYNE: God, you're insensitive. Wait'll *you* get married.

STU: Maybe I never will.

WAYNE: Yeah!

STU: I might not.

WAYNE: You'd marry the first girl who looked twice at you. Yours is one wedding I wouldn't want to miss. There's always Marlene Schroll.

STU: *As You Desire Me!*

WAYNE: What the—?

STU: You wrote *As You Desire Me.*

WAYNE: I'm not Luigi Pirandello.

STU: Okay, but simmer down, hunh?

WAYNE: It's a dumb game.

STU: Your idea.

WAYNE: I was trying to kill time.

STU: Well if we had something intelligent to discuss . . .

WAYNE: What's wrong with Raquel Welch?

STU: Nothing. She's the quintessence of intelligence.

WAYNE: I'm gonna bust you in the mouth. (*Pause*) I wish I'd burned my draft card.

STU: Are you a Russian composer?

WAYNE: I'm not Prokofiev.

STU: An Italian composer?

WAYNE: I'm not Puccini.

STU: An Italian composer?

WAYNE: I'm not Ponchielli.

STU: An Italian composer?

WAYNE: What are you, a record?

STU: An Italian composer?

WAYNE: All right, who?

STU: Pizzarella.

WAYNE: Go to hell.

STU: What's wrong with Pizzarella?

WAYNE: There's no Italian composer named Pizzarella.

STU: How do you know?

WAYNE: I know!

STU: Well maybe there is.

WAYNE: Yeah and you just made him up. Pizzarella. Look, if you're gonna play, play fair. Boy, you haven't changed since college. Even in charades you'd try to put something over.

STU: Like when?

WAYNE: Like when you did *The Brothers Karamazov*. Only you did it in Russian. How could anybody guess *The Brothers Karamazov* in a game of charades when *you* were doing it in Russian?

STU: It would've been too easy in English.

WAYNE: No wonder you never made the chess and bridge teams. Those are precise games. You don't muck with the rules in *them*. (*Pause*) Typical. Sulk now.

STU: I'm thinking.

WAYNE (*Rolls over on back, looks up at sky*): You know what I can't get over?

STU: Mmmmmm.

WAYNE: Poor Father Reilly.

STU: Yeah.

WAYNE: I mean just dropping dead like that. God, we were lucky having him for a teacher. And of all places to drop dead. He loved Rome the same way some men love women. I think he lived for his summer vacations. As much as he gave his students, his heart was always in Rome on the Spanish Steps or the Pincio. And I guess it was all those steps and hills that finally killed him. A great man.

STU: Wayne?

WAYNE: Yeah?

STU: An Italian composer?

WAYNE: You see this fist?

STU: I just thought of two more.

WAYNE: Real ones?

STU: Give up, you'll see.

WAYNE: If they're not, buddy . . . !

STU (*Looking at watch*): You've got fifteen seconds.

WAYNE: Unh . . . unh . . . unh . . . quit making me nervous . . . unh . . .

STU: Ten!

WAYNE: Palestrina!

STU: Who else?

WAYNE: Palestrina and . . . unh . . .

STU: Pizzarella?

WAYNE: Can it! Palestrina and . . .

STU: Five seconds.

WAYNE: Pergolesi. Giovanni Pergolesi! (*Burst of machine-gun fire,* THEY *both flatten out*) That dirty little . . . (*Aims, ready to fire*)

STU (*Terse whisper*): Homosexual Greek philosopher.

WAYNE: Brother, are you warped. I mean that's disgusting.

STU: Come on.

WAYNE: Plato wasn't homosexual.

STU: You were right there, climbing the Acropolis.

WAYNE: Your mind is really sick. A remark like that turns my stomach.

STU: Who made any remarks?

WAYNE: It's not even funny. (*Firing stops*) Where the hell is he? Come on, buster, stick your neck out. He's shooting to see if anybody's out here. We'll just have to sit tight.

STU: Apropos the Parthenon, did you by any chance supervise the rebuilding of it?

WAYNE: I'm not Phidias. What are we on now? Your Greek kick?

STU: You're a fine one to talk about *that*.

WAYNE: There's something crawling on you.

STU: Hey! What the hell is it? This country. Bugs in your shoes, bugs in your hair, bugs in your food. Look at him go. Eight legs . . . no, ten! . . . I guess those are wings . . . nice antennae . . . I used to be scared of bugs.

WAYNE: Do you have to have a conversation with him?

STU: Bon soir, bug. (*Crushes bug*)

WAYNE: I could never do that.

STU: Bugs have souls now, too?

WAYNE: Shut up about all that, will you?

STU: I don't suppose you're an Italian poet?

WAYNE: I'm not Petrarch, Einstein.

STU: It was just a wild guess.

WAYNE: You're never going to get me.

STU: I'm not going to give up either.

WAYNE: Stubborn, stubborn, stubborn!

STU: I'd lose all self-respect if I weren't.

WAYNE: Sshh.

STU: I mean the only reason to begin a game is to win it.

WAYNE: I said shut up!

The MAN *has come out of the tunnel.* HE's *young, emaciated.* HE *pauses at the entrance, quivering like a frightened rabbit. Spot on him.*

Look at the little bugger.

STU: Not so little through these sights.

WAYNE: Not yet! He has to come this way. Wait'll he's closer.

STU: You're not a French painter? A great master of the classical school?

WAYNE: I'm not Poussin.

STU: I've got another one. Impressionist.

WAYNE: French.

STU: Yeah.

WAYNE: I'm not Pissarro.

STU: I can't think of any more P's.

WAYNE: All right, *you* gave up, I'm—

STU: No!

MAN *has begun to move cautiously away from tunnel opening.*

WAYNE: Here he comes. Quiet now.

STU: Were you an Italian sculptor working with Giotto on the campanile in Florence.

WAYNE: I'm not Pisano. Get ready.

STU: Okay, and this is it, Wayne. Did you write a famous "Lives"?

WAYNE: I'm not Plutarch. Let's go.

MAN's *face contorts with pain as* HE *is cut down by a seemingly endless volley of gunfire.* HE *falls, twitches, finally lies still.* WAYNE *and* STU *approach.*

STU: Is he dead? I just asked!

WAYNE: Let's get back to camp.

STU: Okay, I give up. Who are you?

WAYNE: Pollaiuolo.

STU: Who?

WAYNE: Pollaiuolo. Antonio del Pollaiuolo.

STU: That's like Pizzarella.

WAYNE *and* STU *start moving off. Spot stays on* MAN's *face.*

WAYNE: Italian painter, sculptor and goldsmith. 1432-1498.

STU: Well I never heard of him.

WAYNE: Famous for his landscapes and the movement he put into the human body.

STU: Never heard of him.

WAYNE: He influenced Dürer, Signorelli and Verrocchio.

WAYNE and STU are just voices now.

STU: *Them* I've heard of.

WAYNE: Portrait of a Man? The Labors of Hercules? David? The Martyrdom of St. Sebastian? Tobias and the Angel?

STU: Never heard of him.

WAYNE: The tomb of Sixtus IV?

STU: Never heard of him.

WAYNE: Good God, he was a contemporary of Botticelli!

STU: Never heard of him.

WAYNE: Christ, you're dumb.

STU: I NEVER HEARD OF HIM.

Spot stays on MAN's face. Slow fade.

END OF PLAY

HOW I GOT
THAT STORY

Amlin Gray

About Amlin Gray

Born in New York City in 1946, Amlin Gray was drafted in 1966. A conscientious objector, he served as a medic in Vietnam. Trained as an actor after his army discharge, by the early 1970s Gray had taken up playwriting; his first two plays were presented at the O'Neill Theater Center in 1974 and 1976. He became a resident playwright at Milwaukee Repertory Theater in 1977, since which time 13 of his original plays, adaptations and translations have first been seen there. These include *Kingdom Come, Zones of the Spirit* and, most recently, an adaptation of *Christmas Carol*. Commissioned by Milwaukee's Theatre X, *The Fantod* was cited by the American Theatre Critics Association as one of nine outstanding new plays produced in regional theatre during the 1978-79 season. Gray has been the recipient of Guggenheim, Rockefeller and National Endowment for the Arts grants, and is a 1985 McKnight Fellow.

Production History

How I Got That Story was first presented by Milwaukee Repertory Theater in April 1979, under the direction of Sharon Ott. The play's New York premiere, directed by Carole Rothman, took place at The Second Stage in December 1980. In February 1982 the play re-opened Off Broadway, again under Rothman's direction.

Playwright's Note

Every sound effect in the play is made, live or on tape, by the Event actor. Where possible, the audience should be able to recognize his voice.

The setting is a wide, shallow space, as bare of props and set pieces as possible. This will help to characterize the Event as the Reporter sees it: broadly, shallowly, and in sharply isolated fragments.

The back wall should be textured in a range of shades from green to greenish brown, perhaps with collage materials (bamboo, scraps of Asian writing, etc.) blended in. The backdrop must serve alike for city scenes and scenes set in the countryside. To facilitate the Event's transformations, masked breaks should be provided in the back wall. Slides announcing the titles of the scenes, etc., appear on the back wall, as do photographs of the Event, as described.

A list of scenes follows:

Characters

THE REPORTER. An eager young man in his late 20s.

THE HISTORICAL EVENT. The actor playing this part appears at times as the entire Event, at other times as people who make up parts of the Event, as follows:

THE DEPUTY COORDINATOR

MR. KINGSLEY

AN AMBONESE PEDESTRIAN

A BONZE

MADAME ING

A STREET URCHIN

A G.I. IN MIMI'S FLAMBOYANT

LIEUTENANT THIBODEAUX (pronounced "TIH-buh-doe")

PFC PROCHASKA

A GUERRILLA

SERGEANT PEERS

LI (pronounced "Lee")

A CIVILIAN FLIGHT ANNOUNCER

AN AMERICAN PHOTOGRAPHER

AN AIR FORCE PILOT
AN AMBONESE PSYCHOLOGICAL WARFARE OFFICER
AN AMBONESE SOLDIER
A GUERRILLA INFORMATION OFFICER
OFFICER X
AN AMBONESE NUN

Time

The mid-1960s.

Place

Vietnam.

The Play

How I Got That Story

This play is dedicated to
SHARON OTT

ACT ONE

As the audience is just about getting settled, the EVENT *walks into the playing area, stands utterly impassive, and, his mouth moving minimally, begins to articulate a strange and Asian-sounding musical piece. If any stage light is on him, it goes out with the house lights.* HE *continues his instrumental-sounding version of the foreign melody in the darkness.*

Slide: HOW I GOT THAT STORY

Slide: starring

Slide: (Actor's name) as The Reporter

A light comes up as the slide goes off, showing the REPORTER *with pencil poised over his notepad, trying to locate the source of the elusive music. The light goes out.*

Slide: and

Slide: (Actor's name) as The Historical Event

A light comes up on the EVENT, *from whose passive presence music continues to issue.* HE *is now standing on his head.*

Slide: ACCREDITATION

Lights come up on the REPORTER. HE *is wearing a rumpled lightweight jacket with ink stains around the pockets.* HE *holds a somewhat crushed felt hat in one hand and speaks to the audience.*

REPORTER: Hello there. This is Am-bo Land. My new job with the Trans-PanGlobal Wire Service brought me here. It's not the safest place right now, but this is how I figure it. The last two years I've been reporting on the western part of East Dubuque. A lot goes on there. If you add it all up right, then you've got western East Dubuque. That's fine. But if you add up Am-bo Land, it's everyplace. It's *it*. It's what the world is like. If I just keep my eyes wide open I can understand the whole world. That's how I figure it. These are the Am-bo Land offices of TransPanGlobal. Good-sized outfit, hey? I'm here to pick up my accreditation card so I can work incountry. Spell that word without a hyphen.

VOICE: Next.

The REPORTER *walks over to a desk. The* DEPUTY COORDINATOR *is sitting behind it.*

COORDINATOR: May I help you?

REPORTER: I'm here to see Mr. Kingsley.

COORDINATOR: May I ask your business?

REPORTER: I'm just picking up my card so I can work incountry.

COORDINATOR: You'll see Mr. Kingsley.

REPORTER: Thank you.

COORDINATOR: Straight back, third door to the right, first left, and down the hall.

REPORTER: Thanks.

COORDINATOR: He's expecting you.

REPORTER: He is?

COORDINATOR: Yes.

REPORTER: How?

COORDINATOR: You said you work for TransPanGlobal?

REPORTER: Yes.

COORDINATOR: I'm sure you know, then, that our business is communication.

REPORTER: Thank you very much.

The REPORTER *moves off and into the maze of the* COORDINATOR'*s directions. When* HE *gets to* KINGSLEY'*s office,* KINGSLEY *is waiting for him.* KINGSLEY *stands up from his desk and shakes the* REPORTER'*s hand.*

KINGSLEY: I'm so happy to meet you. Please sit down. (HE *indicates a chair in front of his desk. The* REPORTER *sits*) Don't mind if I stare. It's one of the little pleasures of my job when a byline changes to a face. You look quite like your byline, I might say. I couldn't be more pleased.

REPORTER: Well, thank you.

KINGSLEY: I admire your work. Before I'd read two pages of the samples that you sent us, I said, "Bob"—please call me Bob, that's what I call myself—

REPORTER: Okay, Bob.

KINGSLEY: I said, "Bob, this is a man for TransPanGlobal. An impartial man. He views all sides and then he writes the truth as he believes it."

REPORTER: If I may, sir—

KINGSLEY: Bob.

REPORTER: Bob, I'm not sure I'd put it quite that way. I don't think belief is too much help to a reporter. What I try to do is *see*, then write the truth—Bob—as I *see* it.

KINGSLEY: My mistake. Poor choice of words. My meaning was, you don't allow some pietistic preconception to subvert your objectivity. You write what you see.

REPORTER: That's very nicely said, Bob. I'll subscribe to that.

KINGSLEY: On the other hand, you don't write *everything* you see.

REPORTER: I'm not quite sure I—

KINGSLEY: If your wife farts in church you don't run it on the human interest page.

REPORTER: I'm not married.

KINGSLEY: No, I know you're not. That was a figure of speech.

REPORTER (*"Go on"*): Okay.

KINGSLEY: To bring this down to cases. The Government of Madame Ing is fighting for its life. You probably know that the guerrillas don't confine themselves to Robert's Rules of Order. Madame Ing is forced, in kind, to bite and scratch a little. You may see a few examples. Some abridgement of the freedom of internal opposition. Some abridgement of the outer limbs of those involved. These things may rock you. Nothing wrong with that—as long as you keep one thing very firmly in mind. When we send out reports, the nearest terminal for them is the Imperial Palace. Madame Ing eats ticker tape like eel in fish sauce. That's the A-1 delicacy here, you'll have to try it. Can you handle chopsticks?

REPORTER: Yes, I—

KINGSLEY: Madame Ing is very sensitive to how she's viewed from overseas. Let's face it. When we applied for permission to set up an agency here, we didn't apply to the guerrillas. It's Ing who allowed us to come here, and it's Ing who has the power to send us back. (*Sliding a card across the desk to the* REPORTER) Let's have a signature.

REPORTER: What's this?

KINGSLEY: Your press card.

REPORTER (*Pleased*): Oh. (HE *signs*)

KINGSLEY (*Deftly seals the card in plastic*): You'll find this plastic proof against the rainy season, jungle rot . . . . I took a card like this intact right off the body of a newsman who had all but decomposed.

REPORTER: What happened to him?

KINGSLEY: Madame Ing expelled him but he didn't leave. The will of a developing government will find a way. (HE *hands the* REPORTER *his sealed card*) We're very glad you're with us.

Gray-out. KINGSLEY *disappears as the* REPORTER, *somewhat overloaded, retraces his steps through the maze of "corridors" and out onto the streets. His journey is accompanied by the sounds—made on tape, like all the sounds that follow, by the voice of the* EVENT—*of a ticker-tape machine, crossfading with the putt-beep-swish of Hondas.*

Slide: TIP

Lights full up on the REPORTER, *still a bit nonplussed as* HE *makes his way along the street.* HE *puts the press card in his hatband and the hat back on his head. The tape ends with a whooshing sound as a sudden wind blows the* REPORTER *to a standstill, makes him grab his hat.* HE *stands quite puzzled.*

REPORTER: That was odd. A sudden breeze, now nothing. (HE *wets his finger and holds it up; shrugs*) Oriental weather. (*Starts walking again*) I've heard that the guerrillas move so fast you feel a wind and don't see anything, but sitting in your pocket is a bomb. (*A moment's delay, then frantically* HE *pats his pockets from the chest down. Gives a sigh of relief. Then, registering something, returns to the first pocket that* HE *checked. Slowly* HE *draws out a neatly folded sheet of rice paper. Carefully* HE *opens it. It contains a single wooden match.* HE *reads the message on the paper*) "Han Sho Street and Perfume Boulevard in twenty minutes. A man will ask you for a light." (*Checking his watch*) Twenty minutes. That would be at two o'clock. What time is it now? (*Checking*) Twenty minutes of two! Excuse me, sir? (*A* MAN *in a conical reed hat has walked on*) Sir. Han Sho Street and Perfume Boulevard. Which way? (*The* AMBONESE PEDESTRIAN *snatches the* REPORTER's *hat off his head and runs*) Hey! Hey! (*A chase ensues, with the* MAN *appearing from unexpected places, then vanishing, the* REPORTER *farther and farther behind him. A continuation of the street-sounds tape accompanies the chase*) Hey, come back here! Stop! I need that! (*Finally the* MAN *strolls on with his reed hat in his hand and the* REPORTER's *on his head. Puffing, the* REPORTER *comes in sight*) Sir, it's not the hat I want. I won't begrudge you that. I know you probably live in very straitened circumstances. I just want the press card. (*The* MAN *points at an offstage sign*) Oh. Han Sho Street and Perfume Boulevard. (*The* MAN *holds out his own hat, bottom up. The* REPORTER *puts money in it. The* MAN *takes the* REPORTER's *hat from his head and flips it to its owner. Then the* MAN *ambles off, counting his money)* I made it. No one here though. (HE *takes the match out of his pocket and holds it awkwardly in front of him. After a moment)* I'll take the opportunity to absorb a little atmosphere. (*Writing in a little spiral notebook*) Busy intersection. People. Hondas. Over there a big pagoda. Lots of Buddhists in the windows, dressed in saffron robes. (*As* HE *goes on, the* BONZE— *in saffron robes—comes on, unseen by him. The* BONZE *is carrying a large red gasoline can)* All ages. Every window filled with faces. They're all looking over here in my direction. Not at me, though. I don't *think* at me. (*The* BONZE *has "poured" a pool of gasoline on the pavement)* I can smell their incense. (*The* BONZE *has set the can down and come up behind the* REPORTER. *The* REPORTER *spins around)* Oh! You startled me. (*Pause. The* BONZE *just stands there)* Are you my contact? (*Pause)* You're supposed to ask me something. (*The* BONZE *stands. The* REPORTER *starts to hold the match up again, to give the man a hint. The* BONZE *takes it)* That's not incense! That's gas!

In one resolute movement, the BONZE *walks back to the puddle of gas and sits down cross-legged in the middle of it.* HE *"empties" the rest of the can over his head.*

BONZE: Down with Madame Ing! Down with the repressive government of Am-bo Land! (HE *scrapes the match on the pavement and at once is "burning" [a red special and a piece of paper crackled in each hand can give the effect]. The* REPORTER *stands rooted with horror)*

REPORTER: Oh my god. He's burning. People up and down the street are watching. I am too. I'm watching. (*Quickly)* I'm not watching. I'm not here! I'm a reporter! I'm recording this! (HE *writes)* "The monk was sitting in the center of a column of fire. From time to time a light wind blew the flames away from his face. His face was twisted with the pain." The pain, my god—! (*To himself)* No! You're not here. You're just recording this. You look at it, you take the pencil, and you write it down. (*The* BONZE *topples sideways)* My god. (HE *forces his pencil to his pad and writes. Tape fades up: a low repeating chant in an Asian-sounding language)* "Charred black . . . black circle on the pavement . . . wisps of orange fabric drifted down the street."

The lights fade out. The chant continues in the darkness.

Slide: AUDIENCE

Lights come up on the REPORTER, *still shaken from his experience at the street corner.*

REPORTER: I went and talked this morning to the Reverend Father of the Han Sho Street Pagoda. Here. (HE *takes out his notebook)* I think I've got it clear

now. He explained to me that the—what's that? (HE *can't read his writing*)
—the immolation was a political act and a spiritual act at the same time.
There are six thousand monks in Am-bo Land. Of these six thousand, one
hundred and fifty have applied for permission to kill themselves. They wish
to demonstrate their faith. But the Reverend Father withholds permission
till the worldly motive—political protest—is sufficient by itself to justify the
act. (*Quoting*) "The spiritual act must be politically pure; the political act
must be spiritually pure." It's both at once. And so it's sort of—neither. . . .
If I'd had some sand or water—or I might have tried to damp the fire with
my jacket—but that would have been unethical. . . . I've got it all down
here, though. (*A gong sounds.* HE *starts*) The most amazing thing has happened! I'm about to talk to Madame Ing! She summoned me! Reporters
have waited years without getting an audience. I can't believe this is
happening.

The gong sounds again, a little louder. The REPORTER *walks awestruck into
the Presence.* MADAME ING *is seated, regally.*

ING: Here I sit and stand.
REPORTER: Um . . . yes. (*At a loss what to say*) I've seen you on the cover of
    Time magazine.
ING: Do not mention that loathsome publication in my presence.
REPORTER: But they named you "Woman of the Year."
ING: What year?
REPORTER: Why, last year.
ING: Why not this year?
REPORTER: They never give it to anyone twice in a row.
ING: In my country one must grow in honor as one grows in years. *Time*
    should have named me "Woman of the Decade," next year "Woman of
    the Century," and so on. I have summoned you.
REPORTER: I'm flabbergasted.
ING: I wish not to know what that word means.
REPORTER: To what do I owe the extraordinary honor of your summons?
ING: To your crime.
REPORTER: My crime?
ING: You bribed the monks of Han Sho Street Pagoda to set one of their fellows
    on fire.
REPORTER: What?
ING: They filled his veins with morphine till his blood was thin. They led him
    to the street and they set fire to him.
REPORTER: That's not true.
ING: Not true?
REPORTER: No. The man was alone. Nobody led him to the street.

ING: Then he was hypnotized.

REPORTER: He wasn't.

ING: How do you know?

REPORTER: Because I heard him speak.

ING: A man can speak under hypnosis.

REPORTER: Well, I'm sure he wasn't hypnotized.

ING: Men of the press are expected to have documentation for what they say. Do you have proof?

REPORTER: I saw him.

ING: Look at me. You see my face?

REPORTER: Yes . . . .

ING: Am I smiling?

REPORTER (*Peering as through darkness at her unreadable expression*): I don't know.

ING: The monk was hypnotized.

REPORTER: *You* have no proof.

ING: I know. You have admitted you do not know. Madame Ing has won that argument.

REPORTER: All right, then, let's just say that he was hypnotized. What makes you think I was behind it?

ING: I have proof.

REPORTER: What proof?

ING: Sheer logic. Highly valued in the West. Tell me what reason might this monk have had to light himself on fire?

REPORTER: Well, I've done a little work on that. His motives were political, exclusively—and therefore they were purely of the spirit. Only by being entirely the one and not at all the other could they be entirely the other and I really thought I had that.

ING: On his first day in my country, a reporter puts this barbecue on ticker tapes that go to every land. Is this not good for his career?

REPORTER: No—!

ING: No?

REPORTER: Well, yes—

ING: You are the one man with a motive for this foolishness.

REPORTER: I didn't do it.

ING: You have proof?

REPORTER: No—.

ING: I have shown you *my* proof. Madame Ing has won *that* argument. It is time to do my dance for you. (SHE *breaks toward a standing screen*)

REPORTER: Madame Ing, I hope you won't expel me.

ING: No. You may be wrong.

REPORTER: Wrong?

ING: You may *not* have bribed the monks to burn their friend. (*The gong sounds.*

SHE *passes behind the screen; emerges draped in a flowing costume*) I have an army and I have a private army. (*Dancing a prelude*) My private army is made up entirely of women.

REPORTER: Yes, I know.

ING (*Silencing him*): I speak to speak. I do not speak to give you information. Objections have been raised because I pay my women more than my regular army. But my women are all officers, down to the lowest private. Now I present the guerrilla chief. (SHE *assumes the posture of a bent-haunched, quavering man*) And this is the lowest of my Paramilitary Girls. (SHE *strikes the stance of a tall, fierce woman. In the dance that follows—a solo version of the entire Peking Opera—the Paramilitary Girl fights with the guerrilla and defeats him.* ING *withdraws behind her screen. Unseen,* SHE *uses a device to alter her voice— say a #10 can. Reverberant*) You find us inscrutable here in the East.

REPORTER: It's not just you. It's the Americans here too. I can't—

ING: Be patient. Soon you will understand even less. Your ignorance will be whipped with wind until it is pure as mist above the mountains. But you must await this time with patience—patient as the rocks. We will never be perfectly inscrutable to you till we have killed you and you do not know why. (*The gong sounds*)

REPORTER: Does that mean I go now?

Silence. The REPORTER *starts off as the lights fade out. Slides: on the back wall appear glimpses of parts of the face of the actor playing the* EVENT. *Each slide shows just a single feature. The slides are in exaggerated half-tone—broken into dots as if for reproduction—and thus suggestive of pictures in a newspaper. If the slides come from more than one projector, they should alternate arrhythmically.*

Slide: STRIP

The REPORTER *is standing on the sidewalk of the Strip.*

REPORTER: These people in power are a little hard to fathom. So I've come here, to the street they call the Strip. This is where the real people come, the normal, regular people. And what better place to look for the reality of this moment in history? Who better to talk to than the G.I.'s and the Government troops, the bar girls and the peddlers, people trying just to get along, to live their lives, to snatch a moment of pleasure or excitement in the midst of the horror and confusion of this war? (HE *starts to walk*) The bars have names like China Doll, Las Vegas, there's the Dragon Bar, that one's the Playboy. Up and down the street are skinny men in short sleeves selling local soda dyed bright red and blue. Little barefoot boys are selling dirty pictures. That is, I'm sure they're dirty. I assume they're dirty.

Filthy, probably. (A STREET URCHIN *has pattered on.* HE *thrusts three or four pictures at the* REPORTER, *arrayed like playing cards*) No thank you, I don't want to see them. No, but wait a minute. I should look. They're part of local color. (HE *pays the* BOY *and takes the pictures. Quickly joking to the audience*) Nope, they're black-and-white. (*Back to the pictures*) That's awful. Would you look at that? That's terrible. (*Putting the pictures in his pocket*) These are documents. These say it all. (*A* G.I. *passes the* REPORTER. HE *is looking very wired*) There's a G.I. going into that bar. I'm going to interview him. (*Reading the sign above the "door" the* G.I. *has gone through*) "Mimi's Flamboyant." Here I go—(HE *chokes off, coughing, fans the smoke away from his face. There is a blast of instrumental music—a tinny imitation of Western rock-and-roll, say, "Satisfaction"*) The music's so loud I can hardly see the people's faces. Where did my G.I. go? It's dark in here but all the girls are wearing sunglasses. The girls look very young. They're pretty. No, that's not objective. Stick to what's objective. But they are. (*The* G.I. *comes in from the back, carrying a drink.* HE *looks spent.* HE *sits down at a table*) Look, there's my G.I. now. Excuse me, soldier, can I talk to you?

G.I. (*Looks at* REPORTER *stonily*): About what?

REPORTER: All this.

G.I.: All what?

REPORTER: The whole thing.

G.I.: You in the army?

REPORTER: No.

G.I.: Then what in the fuck are you doin' over here?

REPORTER: It's my beat. I'm a reporter.

G.I.: A reporter? All right. Ask your questions.

REPORTER: What's it like?

G.I.: What's what like?

REPORTER: Combat.

G.I.: Scary.

REPORTER: Scary?

G.I.: What the fuck you think?

REPORTER: I figured it was scary.

G.I.: You're a fuckin' genius. Ask some more.

REPORTER: I don't think we've exhausted that subject yet.

G.I.: Naw, you got it figured, man. It's scary. You got that one fuckin' *down*.

REPORTER: Tell me some stories.

G.I.: Stories?

REPORTER: Anecdotes. Some things that happened.

G.I.: Only one thing happens, baby. You're out there in the jungle, right? The fuckin' boonies. Everything is green. And then the bullet comes. Your name is on it. That's the story.

REPORTER: Your name is on it?

G.I.: That's a rodge.

REPORTER: What if your name's not on it?

G.I.: Then it misses you and hits your buddy.

REPORTER: Do you have to duck?

G.I.: What?

REPORTER: Do you duck?

G.I.: Your mamma drop you on your head when you was little?

REPORTER: So you duck then?

G.I.: Man, you hug that ground like it was Raquel fuckin' Welch.

REPORTER: But if the bullet hasn't got your name, it isn't going to hit you.

G.I.: Right.

REPORTER: And if it's got your name—

G.I.: Man, if it's got your name, you can dig a hole and roll an APC on top of you, don't make no never mind.

REPORTER: Then why do you duck?

G.I.: Someone's shooting at your ass, you duck!

REPORTER: It still seems like a contradiction. Guess you've got to go out there and see it for yourself.

G.I.: Out where?

REPORTER: The boonies.

G.I.: Are you batshit?

REPORTER: Huh?

G.I.: You're going out there?

REPORTER: Yeah.

G.I.: What for?

REPORTER: I want to see. (*Showing his notebook*) I've got a job to do.

G.I.: You want to see. Tomorrow morning you wake up in your hotel room, you say, fine day, think I'll grab a chopper, go on out and hump the boonies. That ain't it, man. You can't want to go. Somebody got to make you go. Some mean old sergeant, damnfool captain got to tell you, soldier, grab your gear and get your ass out there and hump. You can't want to go.

REPORTER: I won't get out there if it's not by choice. I have to want to.

G.I.: I'm gonna tell you something, hombre. I'm gonna tell you once, so listen. You go out there if you're gonna, but you don't come near my unit. Do you read me? We get hit for sure. You're *bad luck*. You come close to my platoon, I'm gonna waste your ass. You'll never know what hit you. (*Exiting into the back*) Mama! Mamasan! Hey mama!

Blackout. Tape: the sound of helicopters in flight, then setting down—without, however, turning off their rotors.

Slide: FIELD

The REPORTER *in the field.* HE *has put a mottled green flak jacket over his shirt, and is wearing a tiger-fatigue hat with his accreditation card tucked in the camouflage band.* HE *speaks into the microphone of a cassette recorder that hangs off his hip.*

REPORTER: This is your correspondent in Am-bo Land, reporting from the field. I've gone out with an American reconnaissance platoon. The choppers dropped us in a clearing. We've regrouped behind the treeline.

Lights up on LIEUTENANT THIBODEAUX, *speaking to the troops.*

LIEUTENANT: Sweet Jesus fuckin' string my balls and hang me from a fuckin' tree, Christ fuckin' motherfuck god damn! Because this war has taught me two things, men. It's taught me how to kill and it's taught me how to swear. God fuckin' crap-eye son of a bee, and cunt my fuckin' jungle rot and hang me fuckin' upside-down and jangle my cojones. Joy roll! Fuckin²A! You hear me, men?

REPORTER: That's Lieutenant Thibodeaux. He's trying to help his troops achieve the right aggressive attitude.

LIEUTENANT: You hear me, men?

SOLDIERS (*On tape; with no trace of enthusiasm*): Yeah.

LIEUTENANT: Sound off like you got a pair! We're Airborne! Say it!

SOLDIERS: Airborne.

LIEUTENANT: Well, that's not outstanding, but it's better. Slip my disc and tie my tubes, god damn and fuckin' motherfuck!

REPORTER: He has to win the absolute confidence of the men in his command. If he's not able to, in combat, when he's giving them an order that requires them to risk their lives, it's possible that one of them may shoot him in the back. The soldiers call this "fragging."

LIEUTENANT: I won't lie to you. This is a dangerous mission. But I want you to know, men, I've been out there and I've come back. I've come back every god damn time. That's every motherloving asslick shitbrick pick your nose and fuck me time. I don't wear decorations in the field, but if any man here doesn't believe me he can come to my hootch when this thing is over and I'll show him my Sharpshooter's Badge with four bars and my two Good Conduct Medals. Suck my dick and kick my ass six ways from Sunday. Sing it with me. I wanna be an Airborne Ranger. I wanna be an Airborne Ranger. I wanna lead a life of danger.

SOLDIERS (*Barely audible*): I wanna lead a life of danger.

LIEUTENANT: 'Cause I fight out there beside my men. And here's one thing I promise you. If I give any of you men an order that requires you to lay down your life, it's because I'm wearing army green. I love this uniform. I love the army. Good luck, men. Let's move out!

The LIEUTENANT *turns and takes a step away. A shot rings out.* THIBODEAUX's *limbs sprawl outwards as the lights black out. Almost immediately, the lighs pick up the* REPORTER *in the same spot where* HE *stood at the beginning of the scene. Once more,* HE *speaks into his tape recorder.*

REPORTER: This is your correspondent in Am-bo Land, reporting from the field. Our mission was almost aborted by a circumstance the facts aren't quite all in on yet. We'll proceed with Sergeant Peers in charge. He's forming the platoon into a line. I'm supposed to walk at the end. The men say that'll give me the best view of everything that happens. (HE *walks in a circle, falling in behind the last soldier*—PFC PROCHASKA. PROCHASKA *carries an M-16 rifle.* THEY *hump the boonies during the following, the* REPORTER *carefully copying everything* PROCHASKA *does*) Excuse me? Soldier?

PFC (*Turning*): Yeah? Hey, stagger!

REPORTER: Stagger?

PFC: Don't walk in a line with me! Some sniper hits you gets me too.

REPORTER (*Sidestepping*): Check. Soldier?

PFC: Don't call me soldier. I got drafted. Call me Prochaska.

REPORTER: Check.

PFC: And keep it down.

REPORTER (*More quietly*): Is this your first patrol?

PFC: Do pigs shit ice cream?

REPORTER (*Not understanding*): No . . . (*Speaking furtively into his cassette recorder*) "Do pigs shit ice cream?" Look that up. (*To* PROCHASKA) What's the purpose—the objective—of this patrol?

PFC: Find the enemy.

REPORTER: Do you expect it to succeed?

PFC: I hope not.

REPORTER: Are you afraid?

PFC: Do cows have titties?

REPORTER: Yes . . . (*Into his recorder*) Check "Do cows have titties?" (*To* PROCHASKA) You don't think I'm bad luck, do you?

PFC: No, you good luck, brother.

REPORTER: Good luck? Super. Although it would defeat my entire purpose to affect the outcome of the mission in any way. But why am I good luck?

PFC: You're walking behind me.

REPORTER: Huh?

PFC: Go-rillas spring an ambush, the man in the back gets shot first.

REPORTER: Sure. That stands to reason.

PFC: You're not carrying a rifle either. They gonna take you for a medic.

REPORTER: What does that mean?

PFC: First they shoot the officer. Then they shoot the medic.

REPORTER: I thought they shot the man in back first.

PFC: Brother, either way . . .

REPORTER: I want to get this straight. Let's say for now that I'm not here, so you're the man in back. Good. Now the officer is Sergeant Peers, and there's the medic. Okay. So, the man in back and the officer get shot before the medic. But which of you gets shot first?

PFC: Man, we all get shot if you keep talking.

REPORTER: The sergeant is raising his hand. What does that mean?

PFC: Break time. You smoke?

REPORTER: No.

PFC: Save me your ciggies from your C's, okay?

REPORTER: Sure.

PFC: Don't sit near the radio. You do, they shoot you first. (HE *walks off. The* REPORTER *sits in place*)

REPORTER: When Pfc Prochaska said "C's," his reference was to C-rations, the G.I.'s meal-in-a-box. I'm about to open my first box of C's. (HE *takes a small box out of his pack. Reading*) "Meal, Combat, Individual." (HE *opens the box and finds a paper napkin on top; tucks it into his shirt like a bib. Then* HE *goes through the assorted tins and packets, reading their printed contents*) Cigarettes. (HE *puts the little four-pack of cigarettes aside for* PROCHASKA) Beans with Frankfurter Chunks in Tomato Sauce. Towel, Paper, Cleansing, Wet, Antiseptic. Interdental Stimulator. Cream substitute, Dry, Non-dairy. Chiclets. (HE *takes out a book of matches with an olive-drab cover*) "These matches are designed especially for damp climates. They will not light when wet."

While the REPORTER *has been busy with his C's, a* GUERRILLA *has appeared behind him, wearing foliage for camouflage.* HE *has watched the* REPORTER *for a moment, inhumanly still; then, with very small gestures to right and left, has closed in his fellow guerrillas—who are unseen—around the Americans for an ambush, and has vanished. Now the* REPORTER *fingers a small white wad.*

Toilet paper.

The ambush is sprung. The REPORTER *holds up his accreditation card. The firing is deafening, intolerably loud. It continues longer than its intensity would seem to allow, then quite suddenly it stops completely; all at once explodes again. The* REPORTER *low-crawls frantically away, nearly running into* SERGEANT PEERS, *who, having reached low ground, starts tuning in the field phone* HE *is carrying. It has a receiver like a regular telephone, leaving one of the* SERGEANT*'s ears free.*

SERGEANT (*To the* REPORTER): Cover my back.

REPORTER: What? Sergeant Peers, it's—(HE *was going to say "me"*)

SERGEANT: All behind my back's your field of fire.

REPORTER: I haven't got a weapon.

SERGEANT (*Looking at him for the first time*): Christ, it's that one. (HE *goes back to the radio*)

REPORTER: What happens now?

SERGEANT: I try and get my god damn channel.

REPORTER: Where's the radio man?

SERGEANT: Which piece of him?

REPORTER (*Taking out his notebook*): What was his name?

SERGEANT (*Into the radio*): HQ!

REPORTER: Was he a draftee or did he enlist?

SERGEANT: At ease, god damn it!

REPORTER: Sarge, I've got to get some facts. If I'm not getting facts there isn't any purpose to my being here.

SERGEANT: HQ!

REPORTER: I mean, consider for a moment what my situation is. I don't know anything I didn't know before I got here. What if I get killed? I don't know why that monk was burning, what my boss wants. . . . What's the word for this? Condition Red?

SERGEANT (*Into the phone*): HQ! We're pinned down. Our coordinates are 5730 by 9324.

REPORTER: What's your serial number?

SERGEANT: Will you shut the fuck up?

REPORTER: I'm not getting any news! If I'm not getting any news then what in Christ's name am I doing here? (*A grenade bursts.* HE *is hit in the rump*) I'm hit.

SERGEANT: Don't move. (HE *quickly checks the wound*) You're all right.

REPORTER: No I'm not all right. I'm hit.

SERGEANT: You're okay.

REPORTER: Is there blood?

SERGEANT: No sweat. You're gonna see that girl. (*Handing him a pressure dressing*) Here. Hold this on the wound.

REPORTER: It hurts! I'm going to die! They're going to kill me! Get me out of here! Christ Jesus, get me out of here!

A whistling.

SERGEANT: Here comes the artillery! Flatten!

With the SERGEANT'*s last word there comes a blackout, then a monstrous crashing, ten times louder than before. The barrage continues in the darkness.*

Slide: IMPRINTMENT

Lights come up on the REPORTER *in a hospital bed.* HE *is sleeping. There is a little cabinet next to the bed, with a phone on it. The* REPORTER's *field clothes are folded on a shelf underneath. His cassette recorder is on top. A knock comes at the door—a very soft one. The* REPORTER *doesn't register it, but* HE *stirs, rearranges himself for more sleep—sees the audience.*

REPORTER: Where am I? (HE *sits partway up and feels a rush of pain*) Ow! Excuse me. (*Discreetly,* HE *lifts the sheet and turns his hip; remembers*) Oh yeah. What day is this? The last thing I remember is the medic and the morphine. I should find out where I am. (HE *makes a move to get up; stops mid-motion*) I feel dizzy. (*The soft knock is repeated*) Come in? (LI *enters: a small, pretty Ambonese bar girl.* SHE *walks with little steps into the room*) Hello.

LI: You sleep?

REPORTER: No, I'm awake. Are you the nurse?

LI: My name Li. Bar girl. I work Coral Bar. You know?

REPORTER: Um—no, I've never been there.

LI: I come here too. Man downstairs who sometime let me in. Are you G.I.?

REPORTER: No.

LI: See? I know you not G.I. I like you better than G.I. (*Coming further into the room*) You very nice.

REPORTER (*Holding her off*): No, I'm not nice. I'm a reporter.

LI: Li not understand.

REPORTER: I'm someone who's not here—who's here but can't—do anything, except report.

LI (*Puzzled*): You like I go away?

REPORTER: No, you don't have to go away. . . .

LI: You lonely.

REPORTER: No I'm not. Not *lonely*. . .

LI: Yes, you lonely. I see.

REPORTER: I'm *alone*. It's a condition of the job.

LI: You tired.

REPORTER: Well, they've given me some medication. . . .

LI: You lie down.

REPORTER: I'm lying down.

LI: You lie down all the way—

REPORTER (*Escapes by jumping out of bed—*HE *is wearing blue institutional pajamas*): I've got a wonderful idea.

LI: No, where you go?

REPORTER: You sit down. Sit down on the bed. (*Going into the pockets of his field clothes*) Look, here's some money for your time. There's fifty *hoi*. Is that enough? I'm going to interview you.

LI (*Not knowing the word*): In-ter-view?

The REPORTER *has laid two small colored bills on the bed.* LI *picks them up and, somewhat uncertainly, sits down on the bed. The* REPORTER *sets up his tape recorder.*

REPORTER: I've been feeling, lately, quite confused. I think that maybe, if I just can try and understand one person who's involved in all this, then I might be onto something. Will you tell me your story?

LI: Oh, you like me tell you *story*. Now I see. I have G.I. friend teach me tell him your Jack and the Beanstalk. When I get to part where beanstalk grow I stop and he say "Fee Fi Fo Fum"—

REPORTER: Not that kind of story. Just your life. Where do you come from?

LI: Where you like I come from?

REPORTER: From wherever you were born.

LI: Okay. I try. (*Thinks a second, sizing the* REPORTER *up*) I was born in little village. I hate the guerrillas. Was so glad when many helicopters come all full of big Americans. Americans with big guns. You have gun?

REPORTER: No.

LI: Yes you do. I know you have gun.

REPORTER: No, I don't.

LI: Yes, great big huge big gun and shoot so straight—

REPORTER (*Turns off the tape*): No, no. That isn't what I want, Li. I just want your story. Nothing else.

LI: You shy.

REPORTER: It's just a question of professional procedure.

LI: You like woman to be like a man. I see now. Now I tell my story.

REPORTER: Wait. (HE *switches on his tape*) Go.

LI: I am spy. My name not Li at all.

REPORTER: What is it?

LI: My name *Gad Da Lai I Rang Toi Doung*. That mean Woman Who Love to Watch Foreigners Die. I hate Americans.

REPORTER: Now we're getting down to cases. I'll bet all you girls hate Americans.

LI (*Encouraged*): Yes. I love to kill them.

REPORTER: Have you killed very many?

LI: Every day I kill one or I no can sleep. I like to pull their veins out with my little white sharp teeth. This is only thing can make Li happy with a man.

REPORTER (*Getting drawn in*): Wow. That's *political*.

LI: I like to climb on top of you and bite you, chew your neck until your bones are in my teeth and then I crack them—

REPORTER: Stop! You're making this up too. Li, don't you understand. I want your real story. (LI *has found the light switch on the wall above the bed and turned it off*) Li, turn the lights back on.

LI: You tired.

REPORTER: I'm not tired, I just *feel* tired.

LI: You come here.

REPORTER: I'll bring the tape recorder and we'll talk some more.

LI: You like it in my country?

REPORTER (*Sitting on the bed*): No. I hate it. I don't understand what anybody's doing. I don't like it here at all.

LI: You like I turn lights on?

REPORTER: Yes.

LI: There. (*The lights are still off*)

REPORTER: There what?

LI: You no see lights? Then you have eyes closed.

REPORTER: No—

LI: I turn lights off again. (SHE *leaves them off*) You like that?

REPORTER: Are they on or off?

LI: You lie down.

REPORTER (*Does*): Do you wear sunglasses indoors? At Mimi's all the girls wear very dark dark glasses. Are you touching me? You're not supposed to touch me.

LI: I no touch you. (SHE *is touching him*)

REPORTER: I saw a man burn with a lot of people watching. I saw Ing dance. I was in the jungle and a piece of flying metal flew so fast you couldn't see it but it stopped inside my body. I'm in Am-bo Land. (*The phone rings*) The phone? (HE *picks it up*) Hello? (*Pause*) Mr. Kingsley, yes, hello! (*Pause*) You're here? Wait just a little second, Mr. Kingsley. (*Turning the lights on*) Li? (SHE *is gone. The* REPORTER *looks puzzled but relieved.* HE *takes the phone back up—interrupts his movement to make a quick check under the bed, but* LI *is truly gone. Into the phone*) I'm sorry, sir. . . . Hello?

KINGSLEY (*Bursts in, bearing flowers*): Hey there, how's the Purple Heart?

REPORTER: Hello, sir—

KINGSLEY (*Points a mock-stern finger at the* REPORTER): Sir?

REPORTER: Bob! Hello, Bob. You're so thoughtful to come visit me.

KINGSLEY (*Seeing the cassette recorder, which is still in the* REPORTER'*s lap*): I see you made a tape. You gonna pay the girl residuals? (*The* REPORTER *looks at the machine, then turns it off*) I got here half an hour ago and saw her coming in here. Figured this'd give you time enough. Hell, just in from the field most guys don't need but twenty seconds. (HE *plunks down the flowers on the cabinet*)

REPORTER: I was interviewing her.

KINGSLEY: Here's something else you'll need. (HE *takes a red-white-and-blue card out of his vest pocket and hands it to the* REPORTER)

REPORTER: What's this?

KINGSLEY: A business card.

REPORTER (*Looks at it*): It's just a number.

KINGSLEY: You hold on to that.

REPORTER (*Slips it in his shirt pocket*): Who is it?

KINGSLEY: Officer X.

REPORTER: Who's that?

KINGSLEY: He's probably lots of people. First-rate resource. He's got access to army supply lines. Got a couple of straws in the Ambonese milkshake too. You'll want a stereo system for starters. And an ice machine.

REPORTER: I don't need—

KINGSLEY: It's all on TransPanGlobal. X already has your name. Hey, you're our boy! We wouldn't want you cooped up here without a few amenities.

REPORTER: I've only got a flesh wound. I'll be out of here tomorrow, or today.

KINGSLEY: Today. Tomorrow.

REPORTER: Next day at the latest.

KINGSLEY: I guess you know you got off pretty easy.

REPORTER: Yes, I guess I did.

KINGSLEY: Good luck, huh?

REPORTER: Guess it was.

KINGSLEY: Good luck for you. Bad luck for TransPanGlobal.

REPORTER: How?

KINGSLEY: This thing has hit us right smack in the middle of a gore gap.

REPORTER: Gore gap?

KINGSLEY: Little guy from *Aujourd'hui* lost his esophagus last week. Two weeks ago some wop from *Benvenuto* got his ear blown off. We haven't had an injury for five months. God damn outlets don't believe you're really covering a war unless some blood flows with the ink. So let's say we announce your little contretemps the way it really happened. "On such-and-such a day our correspondent sallied forth to get the news. In the performance of his duty, he was wounded." (*As a questioner*) "Where?" "He took a little shrapnel." "Where?" "He took a little shrapnel in the ass." (*To the* REPORTER) Not too impressive. Let me ask you something. Why should we accept that you were wounded where you were and let the whole of TransPanGlobal look like shitheads—are you with me?—when a half a foot—six inches—from your perforated fanny is your spine?

REPORTER: My spine?

KINGSLEY: We're going to say the shrapnel lodged against your lower vertebrae. That's nothing that a brilliant surgeon, luck, and a short convalescence can't cure.

REPORTER: How short?

KINGSLEY: Three months.

REPORTER: Three months?

KINGSLEY: The spine's a very tricky area.

REPORTER: Why do you assume I'll go along with this?

KINGSLEY: We brought you here.

REPORTER: You brought me where?

KINGSLEY: To Am-bo Land.

REPORTER: That's supposed to make me grateful?

KINGSLEY: Don't you like it here?

REPORTER: What makes you even possibly imagine that I like it here?

KINGSLEY: By this point in their tour, we've found that most reporters have experienced imprintment.

REPORTER: What's—

KINGSLEY: Imprintment. A reporter goes to cover a country and the country covers him.

REPORTER: You think that Am-bo Land is covering me?

KINGSLEY: It's just a guess.

REPORTER: A guess.

KINGSLEY: That's all.

REPORTER: All right. I'm going to show you just how good a guess it is. (HE *gets out of bed*)

KINGSLEY: What are you doing?

REPORTER (*Getting his clothes out of the cabinet*): You see these socks? They're decomposing with the climate. Not the rain and mud. The *air.* The air is putrid in this country. When I go to put on clean socks in the morning they all smell as if some stranger took and *wore* them in the night. (HE *flings the socks away and starts to pull on his field clothes over his pajamas*) I can't *believe* you thought that Am-bo Land was covering me. It's true that I can't do my job, if that's the same thing. I can never tell what's going on. Nobody ever gives me any answers. If they do I'm asking stupid questions. That's not how my life is supposed to go! I won't accept that! I refuse! It doesn't rain here when it rains. It sweats. The palm leaves drip sweat even in the sunshine. Have you tried the beer? It's great. Tastes like the inside of a monkey's armpits.

KINGSLEY: Where are you going?

REPORTER: First I'm going to the airbase. That's four miles. From there, eleven thousand miles to East Dubuque.

KINGSLEY: You're leaving?

REPORTER: That's eleven thousand four miles. I'll be counting every centimeter.

KINGSLEY: What about the gore gap?

REPORTER: Blow your brains out. That'll fill it.

KINGSLEY: This is highly unprofessional. You know that.

REPORTER: No I don't. I don't know anything. I only know I'm going.

KINGSLEY: If you're going, I won't try to stop you.

REPORTER: Great. Goodbye. (*Limping slightly,* HE *starts out*)

KINGSLEY: You're sure you want to go?
REPORTER: I'm sure!
KINGSLEY: Enjoy your flight.
REPORTER: You bet I will! I'll savor every second.

The REPORTER *slams out. Blackout. Tape: A* CIVILIAN FLIGHT ANNOUNCER *speaks over an outdoor loudspeaker.*

FLIGHT ANNOUNCER (*In a voice that reeks routine*): Attention on the runway please. . . . Attention on the runway please. . . . Lone Star Airlines Flight 717 has completed its boarding procedure. . . . Clear the runway please. . . . Please clear the runway. . . . No more passengers may board at this time. . . . (*With a little more urgency*) Will the gentleman please clear the runway. . . . Flight 717 is taking off. . . . The gentleman is standing in the backblast. . . . Will the gentleman please limp a little faster, he is about to be cremated. . . .

Slide: PLANES

Simultaneously with the slide, the REPORTER *shouts from offstage.*

REPORTER: Okay! Okay!

Lights up on a black-and-yellow barrier with the legend, "DO NOT PASS BEYOND THIS POINT."

FLIGHT ANNOUNCER (*Still on tape*): Will the gimp in the pajama top accelerate his pace please . . . .
REPORTER (*Still offstage, but closer*): Yes, o-kay!
FLIGHT ANNOUNCER: Now will the moron kindly haul his ass behind the yellow barrier and await the next plane out at that location.
REPORTER (*Rushing on in total disarray*): Yes, all *right*! I'm here! I'm *here*!

The REPORTER *crawls under the barrier, ending up on the downstage side. The* PHOTOGRAPHER *hobbles on from the opposite direction.* HE *is missing an arm. One foot is in a huge cast. His clothes are multi-layered and multi-colored, and include a Clint Eastwood-style serape. Sundry cameras, lens cases, filter cases hang from straps around his neck and shoulders. A sign on his floppy field hat reads, "SAY CHEESE."*

PHOTOGRAPHER: Hey, man, I need a little help with something, can you help me out?
REPORTER (*Just sits on the asphalt, panting*): Damn it! *Damn* it!
PHOTOGRAPHER: Missed your plane, huh? That's a drag.
REPORTER: There's not another plane for seven hours.

PHOTOGRAPHER: There's one in fifteen minutes. That's the help I need.

REPORTER (*Pulls himself up by the barrier*): In fifteen minutes? Where?

PHOTOGRAPHER (*Pointing offstage*): Right over there. The Weasel. See? She's sleeping. But in fifteen minutes she'll be up there in the sky. It fucks your mind up.

REPORTER: That's a bomber.

PHOTOGRAPHER: Dig it.

REPORTER: I need a passenger plane.

PHOTOGRAPHER (*Enlightened*): You mean a plane to *go* somewhere. Okay, man. Not too zen, but. . . . Wanna help me out?

REPORTER: If I can.

PHOTOGRAPHER (*Extends his foot cast to be pulled off like a boot*): Here. Help me ditch this plaster, willya?

REPORTER: What's it on for?

PHOTOGRAPHER: German paper that I sometimes sell my snaps to wanted pictures of a minefield. Who knows why, right? Only, dig it man, the thing about a minefield is it looks like any other field. I mean like that's the whole idea, right? So I tramped a lot of paddies before I found one. Got an action shot, though. KRUUMP!

REPORTER: What happend to your arm?

PHOTOGRAPHER: Ooh that was righteous. It was nighttime. I was standing getting pictures of the tracer patterns. BAMMO! from behind! I got an incredible shot of that arm flying off. WHOOSH! Little bit underexposed, but something else, man. WHOOSH!

REPORTER: I think you ought to take my flight with me.

PHOTOGRAPHER: You wouldn't wanna leave if you could make these bomb runs.

REPORTER: I could make the bomb runs.

PHOTOGRAPHER: Nix. They just give seats to newsmen.

REPORTER: I'm a reporter.

PHOTOGRAPHER: Yeah? Well shit man, what you waiting for? Come help me get my foot up in the cockpit and then climb on in yourself.

REPORTER: No way. I've got a plane to catch.

PHOTOGRAPHER: These babies drop their goodies and they come right back. Takes half an hour.

REPORTER: They come back in half an hour?

PHOTOGRAPHER: Like a boomerang. Come on.

REPORTER: Not me.

PHOTOGRAPHER: I'm telling you, these flights are ab-*stract*.

REPORTER: Even if I wanted to, I couldn't.

PHOTOGRAPHER: Why not?

REPORTER: 'Cause they wouldn't let me on.

PHOTOGRAPHER: You're a reporter.

REPORTER: No I'm not. I was. I quit.

PHOTOGRAPHER: You quit?

REPORTER: That's right.

PHOTOGRAPHER: You give your card back?

REPORTER (*Lies*): —Yes.

PHOTOGRAPHER: You didn't, man. It's right there on your hat.

REPORTER (*Taking it out of the hatband*): I still have the card.

PHOTOGRAPHER: Come on! We're gonna miss the takeoff! It's outrageous, man, it pulls your smile till it's all the way back of your head! (HE *disappears*)

REPORTER (*Calling after him*): I'm not going to go. I'll help you load your cast in, but I'm not going to go.

PHOTOGRAPHER (*Off*): Come *on*, man!

REPORTER: Okay, but I'm only going to help you with your cast. . . .

The REPORTER *follows the* PHOTOGRAPHER *off. Blackout. Tape: an orientation by the* AIR FORCE PILOT, *crackling as if over earphones in a helmet.*

PILOT: I'm gonna tell you right off I don't want you here. I don't know why they let reporters on bomb runs and I'm damned if I'm gonna worry about you. This is a vertical mission. If they hit us while we're diving, I'll try to get the plane in a horizontal position, then I'll jump.

Slide: RUN

PILOT: That means there won't be any pilot, so you'll probably want to jump too.

Lights come up on the REPORTER *and the* PHOTOGRAPHER *seated in the plane.* THEY *are both wearing helmets. As the* PILOT *continues, the* REPORTER *tries to locate the devices* HE *mentions.*

There are two handles beside your seat. Move the one on the right first down then up. Your seat will eject you and your chute will open automatically. If the chute doesn't open you've got a spare, pull the cord on the front of your flight jacket. If that chute doesn't open you can lodge a complaint. Have a good flight and don't bother me.

The REPORTER *and the* PHOTOGRAPHER *lurch backwards in their seats as the plane takes off.*

PHOTOGRAPHER: Okay, man. When the pilot dives, you push a button on the left side of your helmet.

REPORTER: What does that do?

PHOTOGRAPHER: Try it, man. You see the nozzle there? Pure oxygen! (HE *takes a hit. The* REPORTER *follows suit*) You dive. The jungle gets closer and closer like it's flying up to slam you. You can see the tree that's going to hit you, then the leaves on the tree, then the veins on the leaves—and then the pilot pulls out and he starts to climb. The sky comes crushing down on you, your eyes go black, it's like you're being crushed by darkness. Then you level off and everything goes back to normal. Then you dive again. It's outa sight.

REPORTER: Can you see the victims on the ground?

PHOTOGRAPHER: Man, you can see their *faces*! You can see the little lights coming out of the end of their machine guns. Bullets flying up at just below the speed of sound, you screaming straight down toward 'em. Hit one and you cashed your checks!

REPORTER: One bullet couldn't bring a plane down.

PHOTOGRAPHER: Man, at that speed a stiff stream of piss could bring a plane down. Hey! We're diving!

REPORTER: Wait! I haven't got my background done! What's the pilot's hometown? I don't even know what the pilot's hometown is!

PHOTOGRAPHER: Wooo!

REPORTER: Stop the plane! I have to do an interview!

PHOTOGRAPHER: I thought you quit.

REPORTER: I did, but—(*The plane pitches sharply as it steepens its dive*) Oh-h-h—

PHOTOGRAPHER: Fifty meters in two seconds! Woo! This guy is good!

REPORTER: My stomach just went out with the exhaust fumes.

PHOTOGRAPHER: See that little man? Guerrilla. Look, he's waiting. Now he's lifting up his rifle.

REPORTER: Pull out!

PHOTOGRAPHER: The pilot let the bombs go. See? They're traveling down right next to us.

REPORTER: Those?

PHOTOGRAPHER: Uh-huh.

REPORTER: Those are bombs?

PHOTOGRAPHER: Yep.

REPORTER: If they slipped a half a foot they'd blow us up. They're getting closer!

PHOTOGRAPHER: Little man down there is firing!

REPORTER (*To the bomb outside his window*): Down there! Get him! We're your friends!

PHOTOGRAPHER: Yah! Little fucker hit the pilot! Good shot! Woo! (HE *starts snapping pictures*)

REPORTER: We're going to crash!

PHOTOGRAPHER: You bet your ass! We're going down!

REPORTER: Bail out!

PHOTOGRAPHER: You go. I'm staying. You don't think I'm gonna miss this!

REPORTER: Miss what?

PHOTOGRAPHER: When's the last time you saw shots of a plane crash taken *from the plane?*

REPORTER: I'm going! (HE *"bails out"*)

PHOTOGRAPHER: Great shot of your ass, Jim! Wooo!

The PHOTOGRAPHER *whoops and snaps pictures as the scream of the descent increases. The stage goes black as the crash is heard—a colossal explosion. House lights up for:*

Slide: INTERMISSION

ACT TWO

Slide: VILLAGE

Tape: the voice of the EVENT *renders the Ambonese national anthem, which is jerry-built and grandiose. As the lights come up, an* AMBONESE PSYCHOLOGICAL WARFARE OFFICER *is taking his place in front of a group of unseen villagers.* HE *carries a small table arrayed with assorted apparatus for the demonstration* HE *is about to perform. A small cassette player on the table is the source of the anthem.*

The REPORTER *is seated on the ground between us and the* OFFICER, *slightly off to one side.* HE *is dressed like a villager, in black-pajama pants, a conical hat, and sandals. By his feet is a small bundle.* HE *is sitting on his haunches Asian-style, quite relaxed and placid, waiting for the* OFFICER *to start. The* OFFICER *clicks off the cassette.*

OFFICER: Citizens of So Bin Village, you have done a hard day's work. The Government wishes to submit to you a presentation. (HE *arranges his apparatus, which includes a bowl of rice, a basin, chopsticks, a towel, and a quart jug of thick, fetid, poisonous-looking green liquid. While* HE *is thus employed, the* REPORTER *turns to the audience*)

REPORTER: I drifted in my parachute what seemed like miles and miles and I landed over there. I love this village. I've been here—I don't know how long. I think this is my third week. If I had to write a dateline, I'd be out of luck. I don't, though.

OFFICER (*Holding up the jug of green gunk*): This is defoliant. Our friends the Americans use it to improve the jungle so our enemy cannot use it for a hiding place. The enemy has told you that this harmless liquid poisons you and makes your babies come out of your stomachs with no arms and legs. This is not so. You will see for yourself when I have poured some defoliant in this bowl. (HE *does. Then "acting" stiffly*) My but it was hot today. My face is very dirty. I have need to wash my hands and face. (HE *does so, dipping and turning his hands in the green liquid, then splashing it on his face.* HE *looks as happy as the people in TV soap commercials*) Ah! That is refreshing! (HE *wipes himself dry*)

REPORTER (*To the audience*): A company of Government soldiers has been using this village as an outpost. They were here when I arrived. Today at dusk some transport choppers will be coming in to pick them up. I mean to pick *us* up. I'll catch a lift to the airbase, then a plane home. Home *America*. (*Bemusedly*) I don't know why I said that. Home where else?

OFFICER: Mm, my hard day's work has given me an appetite. I think that I will eat some rice. No fish sauce? Very well then, I will pour on some of this. (HE *pours defoliant over the bowl of rice and eats it with the chopsticks*)

REPORTER (*To the audience, referring to his squatting posture*): The villagers all sit this way. I started it because my wound reopened when I hit the ground. But after you get used to it, it's really very comfortable.

OFFICER (*Wiping his mouth*): My! That was good! But now my hearty meal has made me very thirsty. Ah! (HE *"discovers" the defoliant again and drinks the rest of it, straight from the jug; sets the empty on the table with a bang*) The guerrillas are liars. The Government speaks the truth. Goodbye. (HE *clicks the anthem back on and, to its accompaniment, walks off with his gear*)

REPORTER: It's very peaceful in this village. I've picked up bits and snatches of the language and I'm learning how to harvest rice. I spent the morning threshing. When you get the rhythm you can thresh all day. You slap the stalks against a board. The grains go sliding down and drop into a basket. That's all. Slap, slap, slap, slap. . . . Nothing to write about there. No hook. No angle. Slap, slap, slap. . . . (*A* GOVERNMENT SOLDIER *comes on.* HE *is tying the legs of a chicken with a cord that hangs from his belt*) There goes the last of the soldiers. I should go with him. Before I do, I want to show you what I've learned. (*To the* SOLDIER) *Tay dap moung.* (*Translating for the audience*) That means, "Stop please." (*To the* SOLDIER, *in a complimentary tone and with a gesture toward the chicken*) *Kin wau ran faun to bak im brong.* (*The* SOLDIER *stares at him in complete incomprehension. To the audience*) I understand the language better than I speak it. (*To the* SOLDIER *again, more slowly*) *Kin wau ran faun to bak im brong.*

SOLDIER: *Fop nah in gao breet? Rew ksawn ep lam?*

REPORTER (*To the* SOLDIER, *waving away his own words*): *Manh.* (*To the audience*) The trouble is that Ambonese has all these tones. You say the right sounds but the wrong tones and you've got a different meaning. Apparently I told him that his nose was like a bite of tree farm.

SOLDIER (*Challengingly*): *Op feo ting ko bi dang?*

REPORTER: Why? Because I *want* to speak your language. I want to *duc fi rop* what you are saying and to *fan bo doung* to you.

SOLDIER: *Ken hip yan geh wim parn ti brong, ip yuh rat.*

REPORTER (*To the audience*): He says his chicken speaks his language better, and it's dead. That's an Ambonese joke.

SOLDIER (*Indicating the* REPORTER'*s clothes*): *Fawn tip si bah?*

REPORTER: Am I a villager? Yes. Sure. Why not? *Meo.* I'm a villager. I'm happy here.

SOLDIER: *Prig paw yan tsi mah strak.*

REPORTER: You're not protecting me. I landed in a village you were occupying. *Nik kwan tap.* I wish you hadn't been here.

SOLDIER: *Wep ksi—*

REPORTER (*Cutting him off*): I'm not afraid of the guerrillas. *Manh kip.*

SOLDIER: *Manh kip?*

REPORTER: *Manh.* I'm not their enemy. In fact, I'd like to meet them. If you think I'm scared, you go ahead without me.

SOLDIER: *Sep?*

REPORTER: You go and catch your helicopter. I'm not leaving yet. *Ping dop.*

SOLDIER: *Ping dop?*

REPORTER: There'll be more troops through here. I can get a ride out anytime. America won't disappear. *Ping dop.* Go catch your helicopter. (*The* SOLDIER *shrugs and starts out*) Goodbye.

SOLDIER (*Turns*): *Dik ram vi clao brong.*

REPORTER (*Translating for himself*): "Now you'll enjoy your chicken." Good.

SOLDIER: *Wep ksi ren—*

REPORTER: Yes, the guerrillas—?

SOLDIER: *—vi clao—*

REPORTER: "—will enjoy—"

SOLDIER (*Points emphatically at the* REPORTER): *—seng.* (HE *goes off*)

REPORTER (*To the audience*): There'll be troops coming back to the village. I won't be here long. And the guerrillas—well, all right, if I surprise them, then it's dangerous. I won't though. Probably they almost know already that I've stayed behind. They'll know before they come. And so I'll have a chance to talk to them. They'll see I'm not their enemy. (HE *looks up at the sky*) It's getting dark now. (HE *crosses to his bundle and unwraps it*) I've been sleeping over here. Sometimes it's rained, and then I've made a lean-to with my parachute. Tonight, it looks like I can use it for a pillow. (HE *"fluffs up" his parachute—which is mottled shades of green—and stretches out*) I love the sky at night here. It's not a pretty sky, but it's alive. You can see the storms far off in all directions. The clouds are gray, and when the sheet lightning flashes behind them they look like flaps of dead skin, twitching. I know that that sounds ugly, but it's beautiful. (*A* GUERRILLA *comes in silently behind him*) The guerrillas can pretend they're animals. They talk to each other in the dark that way. They also can pretend they're trees and bushes, rocks and branches, vines. Sometimes they pretend they're nothing at all. That's when you know they're near. The world is never quite that still. You don't have to tell me. This time I know he's there.

Carefully but decisively, the REPORTER *stands up and turns to face the* GUERRILLA. *Blackout. Tape: jungle sounds—strange clicking, dripping, hissing of snakes, animal cries, etc.*

Slide: SELF-CRITICISM

A small, bare hut. The REPORTER *is sleeping on the floor. His head is covered by a black hood and his hands are tied behind his back. A* GUERRILLA IN-FORMATION OFFICER *comes in carrying a bowl of rice.*

GUERRILLA: Stand up, please.

REPORTER (*Coming awake*): What?

GUERRILLA: Please stand up.

REPORTER: It's hard with hands behind the back.

GUERRILLA: I will untie them.

REPORTER: That's all right. I'll make it. (*With some clumsiness,* HE *gets to his feet*) There I am.

GUERRILLA: I offered to untie your hands.

REPORTER: I'd just as soon you didn't. When you know that you can trust me, then untie my hands. I'd let you take the hood off.

GUERRILLA (*Takes the hood off*): Tell me why you think that we should trust you.

REPORTER: I'm no threat to you. I've never done you any harm.

GUERRILLA: No harm?

REPORTER: I guess I've wasted your munitions. Part of one of your grenades wound up imbedded in my derriere—my backside.

GUERRILLA: I speak French as well as English. You forget—the French were here before you.

REPORTER: Yes.

GUERRILLA: You told us that you came here as a newsman.

REPORTER: Right.

GUERRILLA: You worked within the system of our enemies and subject to their interests.

REPORTER: Partly subject.

GUERRILLA: Yet you say that you have never done us any harm.

REPORTER: All I found out as a reporter was I'd never find out anything.

GUERRILLA: Do we pardon an enemy sniper if his marksmanship is poor?

REPORTER: Yes, if he's quit the army.

GUERRILLA: Ah, yes. You are not a newsman now.

REPORTER: That's right.

GUERRILLA: What are you?

REPORTER: What am I? (*The* GUERRILLA *is silent*) I'm what you see.

GUERRILLA: What do you do?

REPORTER: I live.

GUERRILLA: You live?

REPORTER: That's all.

GUERRILLA: You live in Am-bo Land.

REPORTER: I'm here right now.

GUERRILLA: Why?

REPORTER: Why? You've got me prisoner.

GUERRILLA: If you were not a prisoner, you would not be here?

REPORTER: No.

GUERRILLA: Where would you be?

REPORTER: By this time, I'd be back in East Dubuque.

GUERRILLA: You were not leaving when we captured you.

REPORTER: I was, though. I was leaving soon.

GUERRILLA: Soon?

REPORTER: Yes.

GUERRILLA: When?

REPORTER: I don't know exactly. Sometime.

GUERRILLA: Sometime.

REPORTER: Yes.

GUERRILLA: You have no right to be here even for a minute. Not to draw one breath.

REPORTER: You have no right to tell me that. I'm here. It's where I am.

GUERRILLA: We are a spectacle to you. A land in turmoil.

REPORTER: I don't have to lie to you. Yes, that attracts me.

GUERRILLA: Yes. You love to see us kill each other.

REPORTER: No. I don't.

GUERRILLA: You said you didn't have to lie.

REPORTER: I'm not. It does—excite me that the stakes are life and death here. It makes everything—intense.

GUERRILLA: The stakes cannot be life and death unless some people die.

REPORTER: That's true. But I don't make them die. They're dying anyway.

GUERRILLA: You just watch.

REPORTER: That's right.

GUERRILLA: Your standpoint is aesthetic.

REPORTER: Yes, all right, yes.

GUERRILLA: You enjoy our situation here.

REPORTER: I'm filled with pain by things I see.

GUERRILLA: And yet you stay.

REPORTER: I'm here.

GUERRILLA: You are addicted.

REPORTER: Say I am, then! I'm addicted! Yes! I've said it! I'm addicted!

GUERRILLA: Your position in my country is morbid and decadent. It is corrupt, reactionary, and bourgeois. You have no right to live here.

REPORTER: This is where I live. You can't pass judgment.

GUERRILLA: I have not passed judgment. You are useless here. A man must give something in return for the food he eats and the living space he occupies. This is not a moral obligation but a practical necessity in a society where no one is to be exploited.

REPORTER: Am-bo Land isn't such a society, is it?

GUERRILLA: Not yet.

REPORTER: Well, I'm here right now. If you don't like that then I guess you'll have to kill me.

GUERRILLA: We would kill you as we pick the insects from the skin of a valuable animal.

REPORTER: Go ahead, then. If you're going to kill me, kill me.

GUERRILLA: We are not going to kill you.

REPORTER: Why not?

GUERRILLA: For a reason.

REPORTER: What's the reason?

GUERRILLA: We have told the leadership of TransPanGlobal Wire Service when and where to leave one hundred thousand dollars for your ransom.

REPORTER: Ransom? TransPanGlobal?

GUERRILLA: Yes.

REPORTER: But that's no good. I told you, I don't work there anymore.

GUERRILLA: Your former employers have not made the separation public. We have made our offer public. You will not be abandoned in the public view. It would not be good business.

REPORTER (*Truly frightened for the first time in the scene*): Wait. You have to think this out. A hundred thousand dollars is too much. It's much too much. You might get ten.

GUERRILLA: We have demanded one hundred.

REPORTER: They won't pay that. Take ten thousand. That's a lot to you.

GUERRILLA: It is. But we have made our offer.

REPORTER: Change it. You're just throwing away money. Tell them ten. They'll never pay a hundred thousand.

GUERRILLA: We never change a bargaining position we have once set down. This is worth much more than ten thousand dollars or a hundred thousand dollars.

REPORTER: Please—

GUERRILLA: Sit down.

REPORTER (*Obeys; then, quietly*): Please don't kill me.

GUERRILLA: Do not beg your life from me. The circumstances grant your life. Your employers will pay. You will live.

REPORTER: You sound so sure.

GUERRILLA: If we were not sure we would not waste this food on you. (HE *pushes the bowl of rice towards the* REPORTER)

REPORTER: How soon will I know?

GUERRILLA: Soon. Ten days.

REPORTER: That's not soon.

GUERRILLA: This war has lasted all my life. Ten days is soon. (*Untying the* REPORTER's *hands*) You will be fed on what our soldiers eat. You will think that we are starving you, but these are the rations on which we march toward our inevitable victory. Eat your rice. In three minutes I will tie you again.

The GUERRILLA *goes out. The* REPORTER *eats as best* HE *can. Blackout. Slides: the face of the* EVENT, *each frame now showing two of his features, in somewhat finer half-tone.*

Slide: RESCUE

Lights up on MR. KINGSLEY, *seated at his desk.* HE *is talking on the telephone.*

KINGSLEY: Sure they're going to bring him here, but hell, Dave, you don't really want to talk to him. Why put a crimp in your imagination? Make sure you don't contradict our bulletins. Beyond that, go to town. The sky's the limit. (*The* REPORTER *appears at the door*) Dave, I've got to sign off. Get to work on this right now, check? I'll be firing some more ideas your way as they occur to me. Over and out. (*The* REPORTER *wanders into the office.* HE *looks blown out.* HE *is still in his villager clothes*) So here you are. How far they bring you?

REPORTER: Three guerrillas brought me to the border of the City. Then they gambled with some sticks. One brought me here. He's gone.

KINGSLEY: You look all shot to shit. Sit down.

REPORTER (*Unthinkingly sits down on his haunches; then continues*): He had the longest knife I ever saw. Strapped here, across his back. It would have gone right through me. He took off his thongs and hid them in the underbrush and put on shoes. We started through the streets. He wasn't used to shoes. They came untied. He didn't know how to tie them. So he stood still and I tied them for him. All the time he had this knife. The longest knife I ever saw. (*Pause*) I'd have gone back out with him if he'd have let me.

KINGSLEY: How you fixed for cash?

REPORTER: I have some. (HE *takes some rumpled, pale bills of different colors out of his shirt*) Here.

KINGSLEY: I wasn't asking you to give it to me.

REPORTER: I owe it to you.

KINGSLEY: No you don't.

REPORTER: A hundred thousand dollars.

KINGSLEY: Just forget about it.

REPORTER: Am I supposed to work for you now? I can probably do some kind of work. I can't report the news.

KINGSLEY: We're square. We'll get our value for the hundred grand. You're a four-part feature. Maybe six if we can stretch it. We might try some kind of angle with a girl guerrilla. That's a thought. (HE *picks up the phone*) Get me Dave Feltzer again. (*To the* REPORTER) No, all we ask of you is don't give information to the rival press. We want a clean exclusive. We'll be signing your name to the story, by the way. Don't be surprised.

REPORTER: Why should I be surprised?

KINGSLEY: Well, when you read it.

REPORTER: I won't read it.

KINGSLEY: Okay. Want to catch the movie if you can. We're trying to interest Redford. (*Into the phone*) Yeah, hold on, Dave. (*To the* REPORTER) I think that's all then.

REPORTER: That's all? (*Pause.* KINGSLEY *just sits with the phone in his hand*) Okay. Goodbye, Bob. (HE *turns and leaves*)

KINGSLEY (*Into the phone*): Yeah Dave. Got a little brainstorm for the sequence in the punji pit. He's down there, right, he's got this bamboo sticking through his feet, and he looks up and sees an AK-47 clutched in little tapered fingers and the fingernails are painted red . . . .

Blackout. Tape: tinny Asian-Western rock-and-roll as in Act I, Scene 4 [STRIP]; this time a ballad—say, "Ruby Tuesday."

Slide: PROPOSAL

Lights up on LI*'s room at the Coral Bar. A bed, a doorway made of hanging beads, a screen.* LI *is behind the screen, dressing. The* REPORTER *is lying on the bed.* THEY *have just had sex. The* REPORTER *lies quietly a while before* HE *speaks.*

REPORTER: Li?

LI: Yes?

REPORTER: It's good here. It's so good with you.

LI (*Professionally*): It's good with you too.

REPORTER: When I look in your eyes, your eyes look back. I love that. That's so important to me.

LI: I love that too.

REPORTER: I love to be with you.

LI: I love to be with you too.

REPORTER: Do you love me, Li? You don't, I know.

LI: I love you. Love you best of all my men.

REPORTER: Do you know what? When I come here I pretend we short-time just because we both just want to. I pretend you wouldn't take my money only Mai Wah makes you take it.

LI: Mai Wah makes me or I no take money.

REPORTER: Would you short-time me for love?

LI: Yes.

REPORTER: Are you sure you would?

LI: Yes.

REPORTER: Are you absolutely sure?

LI: Yes.

REPORTER: Li, I don't have any money.

LI (*Emerging from behind the screen*): What you say?

REPORTER: I'm broke. No money.

LI: No. You joke with Li.

REPORTER: I had to see you and I didn't want to spoil it by telling you till after.

LI: I have to pay myself now. Mai Wah writes it down, who comes here, how much time. Now you no pay I have to pay myself.

REPORTER: I didn't know that.

LI: Now you know.

REPORTER: I paid a lot of times, Li. Maybe it's fair that you pay once.

LI: Get out of here.

REPORTER: Li—

LI: Next time I see money first, like you G.I. I thought you nice. You trick me. You get out of here.

REPORTER: Li, marry me.

LI: What you say?

REPORTER: I say I want us to get married.

LI: Now you really joke. You bad man.

REPORTER: I'm not joking, Li. I mean it.

LI: Yes? You marry me?

REPORTER: That's right.

LI: You take me to America?

REPORTER: America? No.

LI: Marry me, not take me to America? You leave me here?

REPORTER: I stay with you, Li. I'm not going to America.

LI: You lie. Sometime you go.

REPORTER: I'm never going to go. I'm going to stay here.

LI: No. America is good. Here no good. You marry me and take me to America.

REPORTER: If I wanted to go to America, I wouldn't want to marry you.

LI: Li just good enough for Am-bo Land. You have round-eye wife, go back to her. I know.

REPORTER: You're wrong, Li. I am never going back.

LI: You say then why you want to marry me.

REPORTER: You make me feel at home here and this country *is* my home. I want to sleep with you, wake up with you. I want to look at you and see you looking back.

LI: Where you live now?

REPORTER: Well, really nowhere just this minute. See, I haven't got a job right now—

LI: You go now.

REPORTER: Wait, Li—

LI: You come back, you show me money first. You owe me for three short-times because you stay so long.

REPORTER: Li, listen—

LI: No. You go away. Not be here when I come back.

> LI *goes out through the beaded curtain. Blackout. Tape: a distant foghorn.*

Slide: WORK

Dim lights up on the REPORTER. *It is dusk.* HE *is waiting for someone.* OF-FICER X *appears.* HE *wears a stateside class-A army overcoat with the bronze oak leaves of a major on the lapels.*

REPORTER: Officer X? Then you *are* an officer. I didn't know if that might be a code name.

X: What's with the gook suit?

REPORTER: It's just my clothes.

X: They've gotta go. Hawaiian shirts and shiny Harlem slacks is best for couriers. You have to blend in. Give me the card that Kingsley gave you. (*The* REPORTER *hands him the red-white-and-blue card from Act I, Scene 6* [IM-PRINTMENT]) You know the number?

REPORTER: No.

X (*Hands back the card*): Learn it. (*The* REPORTER *starts to put the card back in his pocket*) Learn it now. (*The* REPORTER *reads the card, trying to memorize the number. The effort of concentration is hard for him.* OFFICER X *takes the card back*) What's the number?

REPORTER (*With difficulty*): 7 . . . 38 . . . 472 . . . 4.

X: Again.

REPORTER: 738 . . . 47 . . . 24.

X (*Pockets the card*): Remember it. Don't write it down. Here. (HE *hands the* REPORTER *a packet wrapped in paper, tied with string*)

REPORTER: What is it?

X: Don't ask what, ask where.

REPORTER: Where?

X: Lin Cho District. Tan Hoi Street. Number 72.

REPORTER: Number 72 Tan Hoi Street.

X: Better put it under your shirt. But get an overcoat with inside pockets.

REPORTER (*Hiding the package as directed*): I can speak some Ambonese.

X: When we need that, we have interpreters. Be back here with the money in two hours. (*The* REPORTER *starts out*) Hold on. Do you have a weapon?

REPORTER: —Yes.

X: Let's see it. (*The* REPORTER *doesn't move.* X *takes out a handgun*) Here.

REPORTER: That's okay.

X: You'll pay me back in trade. Here, take it.

REPORTER: I don't need it.

X: Hell you don't.

REPORTER: I don't.

X: You've got to have it.

REPORTER: I don't want it.

X: I'll just ask you one more time. You gonna take the pistol? (*The* REPORTER *looks at it but doesn't answer*) Give me back the package.

REPORTER: I can get it where it's going.

X: Give it.

REPORTER: Number 72 Tan Hoi—

X: Nobody carries goods for me unless they're able to protect them.

REPORTER: I'll protect them.

X: If you won't use the gun, don't think I won't.

X *points the pistol at the* REPORTER. *The* REPORTER *gives him the packet.*

REPORTER: I can speak some Ambonese.

X: You told me. What's my number?

REPORTER: 7 . . . 7 . . . 38 . . . 738 . . . (*His face goes blank*)

X: Good. Don't remember it again.

X *leaves the way* HE *came. Blackout. Tape: babies crying.*

Slide: ORPHANAGE

The crying of the babies continues into the scene. Lights come up on an AM-BONESE NUN *tending children who are imagined to be in a long row of cribs between her and the audience. The* REPORTER *comes in left.*

REPORTER: Excuse me, Sister.

NUN: Yes?

REPORTER: The Mother Superior told me to come up here.

NUN: Yes?

REPORTER: I'm going to adopt a child.

NUN (*Scanning his garments; gently*): Adopt a child?

REPORTER: Yes.

NUN: Have you been interviewed?

REPORTER: Not yet. I have to get a bit more settled first. But the Mother Superior said I could come upstairs and if I chose a child she would keep it for me.

NUN: Ah. How old a child would you want?

REPORTER: He should probably not be very young. And tough. He should be tough. I don't have lots of money.

NUN: You said "he."

REPORTER: A girl would be all right. A girl would be nice.

NUN: It must be a girl. The Government has a law that only girls may be adopted. The boys are wards of the State. When they are older, they will go into the army.

REPORTER: Well, a girl is fine.

NUN (*Starting down the line with him, moving left*): This girl is healthy.

REPORTER: Hello. You're very pretty. You have cheek bones like a grownup, like your mommy must have had. Look. If I pull back my skin as tight as I can, I still don't have skin as tight as you. (HE *pulls his skin back toward his temples. One effect is that this gives him slanted eyes*) Why won't you look at me?

NUN: She is looking at you.

REPORTER: She doesn't trust me. (*To the child*) I won't hurt you. I just want to have a child of your country. Will you be my child? (*To the* NUN) She doesn't like me. Do you see that child down the line there? (*Pointing right*) That one's looking at me. Let's go talk to that child.

NUN: That section is boys. This way. (SHE *leads him to the next crib to the left*)

REPORTER: She's asleep but, look, her little fists are clenched. She wouldn't like me. I don't want to wake her up.

NUN: Here is another.

REPORTER (*To the third child*): Do you like me? I'll take care of you. I understand that you need food, and I'll try and be a friend to you. (*To the* NUN) She doesn't even hear my voice.

NUN: Here.

REPORTER: These aren't children! These are ancient people, shrunken down! Look at their eyes! They've looked at everything! They'll never look at me!

NUN: You're upsetting the children.

REPORTER (*Pointing toward the boys' section*): That child sees me. He's been looking at me since I came in the room. I want that child.

NUN: I've told you that you cannot have a boy—. Wait. Which child?

REPORTER: The one who's standing up and looking at me.

NUN: The child in green?

REPORTER: Yes.

NUN: You can have the child in green. The Government will not object to that. The boy is blind.

REPORTER: Blind?

NUN: Yes.

REPORTER: He isn't blind. He's looking at me.

NUN: He can't see you.

REPORTER: Yes he can.

NUN: He can't.

REPORTER: That child's the only one who sees me. How can he be blind?

NUN: He can't see.

REPORTER: He's looking at me! Can't you see? He's looking at me!

NUN: You'd better go now. Come back when you have made an application and have been approved. The boy will be here.

REPORTER: He's blind.

NUN: Yes.

REPORTER: I'm going to go now. (HE *doesn't move*)

NUN: Yes, please go now.

REPORTER: He's blind. (HE *starts out the way* HE *came*)

NUN: God be with you.

Blackout.

Slide: HOME

A street in the City. It is dead of night. The REPORTER *is walking along the street.* HE *is nearly stumbling from exhaustion. When the lights come up, it is as if—from the* REPORTER'S *point of view—they came up on the audience.* HE *looks at the audience quizzically.*

REPORTER: Hello. You look familiar. I believe I used to talk to you. Are you my readers? I'm doing very well. Last night I found a refrigerator carton that would shelter a whole family with their pigs and chickens. Next to it a trash pile I can live off for a week. If I can find my way back. I kind of get lost on these streets sometimes. (*Pause*) Sometimes I can stand like this and drift in all directions through the City, soaking up the sounds. . . . (*Sitting down on the pavement*) There's a firefight out there beyond the border of the City. Tracers from a helicopter gunship, see, they're streaming down like water from a hose. Green tracers coming up to meet them now, they climb up towards the ship and then they drop and their green fire goes out. They fall and hit some tree somewhere. The lumber industry is almost dead in Am-bo Land. A fact I read. The trees are all so full of metal that the lumber mills just break their sawblades. (*The lights take on bodiless whiteness*) Magnesium flares. They're floating down on little parachutes. I floated down like that once. Everything is turning silver and the shadows are growing and growing. The street looks like the surface of the moon. And listen.

The EVENT's *voice, on tape, has come softly on: elusive Asian music from the opening titles of the play. The* REPORTER *shuts his eyes. As the sounds continue,* HE *falls into a position almost too awkward to be sleep; a position that suggests a drunken stupor or a state of shock. The* EVENT *makes more sounds, blending them together almost soothingly: a helicopter passing overhead; distant mortar and automatic weapons fire; more Asian music, very lulling. From far along the street is heard the creaking sound of dolly wheels. The* PHOTOGRAPHER *comes on, now legless, propelling himself on a platform.*

PHOTOGRAPHER: Hey, is that a body, man? God damn, a Yankee dressed up like a gook. Yeah, that's a picture. Hold it. Smile, Charlie.

The PHOTOGRAPHER *takes a flash photo. Simultaneously with the flash, the stage goes black and the picture appears on the screen. It is the head and shoulders of a body in the same position as the* REPORTER's, *and dressed identically. The face is that of the* EVENT. *The picture holds for several seconds, then clicks off.*

Slide: HOW I GOT THAT STORY

END OF PLAY

MEDAL OF
HONOR RAG

Tom Cole

About Tom Cole

Born in 1933 in Paterson, New Jersey, Tom Cole took his undergraduate degree at Harvard, and, after studying Russian in army language school, returned to Harvard for a graduate degree in Slavic Languages and Literatures. The author of award-winning short stories and a novel, *An End to Chivalry*, Cole became a playwright with *Medal of Honor Rag*. His next play, *Fighting Bob*, was commissioned by Milwaukee Repertory Theater and produced Off Broadway in 1981. Cole's translations/adaptations of Gogol's *Dead Souls* and Ostrovsky's *The Forest* were also first staged by Milwaukee Rep. Since 1970 Cole has enjoyed an active association with film directors Irvin Kershner, Martin Rosen and Joyce Chopra, with whom he has worked on a long series of films both dramatic and documentary. Current projects include a screenplay of a Joyce Carol Oates story, *"Where Are You Going?,"* and both film and stage adaptations of Maxine Hong Kingston's *The Woman Warrior*. Cole has been the recipient of the Atlantic "First" Award, the Rosenthal Award of the National Institute of Arts and Letters, the CINE Golden Eagle and a playwriting fellowship from the National Endowment for the Arts.

Production History

Medal of Honor Rag was first presented by the Theatre Company of Boston in April 1975, under the direction of David Wheeler and Jan Egleson. The first New York production, directed by David Chambers, opened at the Theatre de Lys the following March. In April 1982 *Medal of Honor Rag* was telecast on PBS's *American Playhouse*, in a production directed by Lloyd Richards.

Playwright's Note

The characters in this play are fictional, but the events reported are all drawn from experiences and testimony of the period.

The words of Lyndon B. Johnson are excerpted from remarks made at a Congressional Medal of Honor award ceremony at the White House on November 19, 1968. A tape of the address is housed at the Lyndon B. Johnson Library in Austin, Texas.

Characters

DOCTOR, a white man in his early 40s, informal, hardworking, even overworked—the youngish doctor with simultaneous commitments to hospital, private patients, writing, family, research, teaching, public health, public issues, committees, special projects. White shirt and bow tie, soft jacket, somewhat weary. He is of European background,, but came to this country as a child. Possessor of a dry wit, which he is not averse to using for therapeutic purposes.

DALE JACKSON (D.J.), a black man two weeks before his 24th birthday, erect and even stiff in bearing, intelligent, handsome, restrained. An effect of power and great potential being held in for hidden reasons. Like the doctor, given to his own slants of humor as a way of dealing with people and, apparently, of holding them off.

HOSPITAL GUARD, a sergeant in uniform and on duty. White. An MP, on transitional assignment.

Time

April 23, 1971.

Place

Valley Forge Army Hospital, Pennsylvania.

The Play

Medal Of Honor Rag

An office, but not the doctor's own office. No signs of personal adaptation—looks more like an institutional space used by many different people, which is what it is. Rather small. A desk, a folding metal chair for the patient, a more comfortable chair for the doctor. Wastebasket. Ash tray.

With the lights still low, a squalid sound from a kazoo is heard, which flows into a rendition of the "Fixin' to Die Rag," by Country Joe and the Fish. A few verses: to bring back the mood of Vietnam. While the music plays, door opens stage rear and the DOCTOR *enters. Light pours in from the corridor, but the* DOCTOR *can't find the light switch in the room.* HE *feels about in half-light, then steps outside again, to find the switch there. Fluorescent overhead light comes on, and the* DOCTOR *putters about, hurriedly, in the office.* HE *rearranges the patient's chair. Takes several folders and a notepad out of his briefcase.*

The DOCTOR *studies one of the dossiers and then, after a beat, looks at his wristwatch. Takes out a cigarette, filter-holder, and match; puts cigarette into filter and filter in his mouth and lights the match. Holds the match and lets it burn without lighting the cigarette, while* HE *looks into the folder again. Puts match down, picks up pencil to make hurried notes in the dossier. Takes a small cassette recorder out of his briefcase, rummages for a cassette, checks its title, and puts it into recorder. Lights another match and this time lights*

122

the cigarette. Puts briefcase on floor beside the desk. Looks at watch, starts to make another note, takes a drag on cigarette.

Knock on door, and DALE JACKSON *enters, escorted by* HOSPITAL GUARD. D.J. *wears "hospital blue denims" and slippers or soft shoes.*

GUARD *places paper forms, in triplicate, on* DOCTOR'S *desk, points brusquely to place for signature. Holds out a ball-point pen to* DOCTOR. DOCTOR *signs, glancing at* D.J. GUARD *tears off one sheet for* DOCTOR, *retains others, and holds out his hand to reclaim his pen.* DOCTOR *hands back pen, abstractedly, and* GUARD *(in full sergeant's regalia) salutes him snappily. The* DOCTOR *looks at the* GUARD *as if* HE *were crazy. The* GUARD *still stands there, at attention.* D.J. *watches this. Finally, the doctor gets up halfway from his chair—a funny, inappropriate gesture—and waves at the man.*

DOCTOR: You can leave us alone.

GUARD (*Snappy salute*): Yes, sir! I'll report back for Sergeant Jackson on the hour, sir! (*About face, marches off*)

The DOCTOR *and* D.J. *look at each other.*

DOCTOR: Sergeant Jackson? (D.J. *nods*) Well, they seem to be keeping a pretty close eye on you.

D.J.: Where's the other doctor?

DOCTOR (*Settling back in his chair*): Sit down, please.

D.J.: They keep changing doctors.

DOCTOR: Would you rather see the other doctor?

D.J.: No, man . . . it's just that I have to keep telling the same story over and over again.

DOCTOR: Sometimes that's the only way to set things straight.

D.J.: You're not in the army, huh?

DOCTOR (*Twinkle*): How can you tell?

D.J.: Your salute is not of the snappiest.

DOCTOR: I came down from New York today. To see you.

D.J.: I must be a really bad case.

DOCTOR: You're a complicated case.

D.J.: Like they say, a special case. I am a special case. Did you know that?

DOCTOR: They keep a pretty close eye on you now.

D.J.: I went AWOL twice. From this hospital.

DOCTOR: Oh?

D.J.: But they'll never do anything to me.

DOCTOR: I understand.

D.J.: You understand, huh?

DOCTOR: I understand your situation.

D.J.: Yeah, well, mind telling me what it is?

DOCTOR: You don't need me to tell you that.

D.J.: So what *do* I need you for?

DOCTOR: I don't know—maybe *I* need *you.*

D.J.: That's a new one. That's one they haven't tried yet.

DOCTOR: Oh?

D.J.: Every doctor has his own tricks.

DOCTOR: Oh?

D.J.: That's one of yours.

DOCTOR: Oh? What's that?

D.J.: When it's your turn to talk, you get this look on your face—kind of like an old owl who's been constipated for about five hundred years, you know, and you say (*Imitation of* DOCTOR's *face*) "Oh?"

The DOCTOR *laughs at this, a little, but* HE *is watching* D.J. *very closely.* D.J. *speaks with sudden anger.*

Man, this is a *farce!* (HE *turns away—as if to "go AWOL" or to charge to the door—but* HE *gets immediate control of himself.* HE *is depressed*)

DOCTOR (*Calmly*): What should we do about it?

D.J.: Who's this "we"?

DOCTOR: Who else is there?

D.J.: We just going to keep asking each other questions?

DOCTOR: I don't know—what do you think?

D.J.: What do *you* think, man? *Do* you think?

DOCTOR: I listen.

D.J.: No, man, I mean, what do you think? You got that folder there. My life is in there. I'm getting near the end of the line with this stuff. I mean, sometimes I feel like there's not much time. You know? (HE *has wandered over to the desk, where* HE *proceeds to thumb through the folders on his case.* HE *does this with a studied casualness*)

DOCTOR: I'm aware of that.

D.J.: You some big-time specialist? (*Suddenly suspicious*)

DOCTOR: In a manner of speaking.

D.J.: What are you a specialist in?

DOCTOR: I do a lot of work with Vietnam veterans and their problems.

D.J.: Well I can *see* that, man. But what do you *specialize* in?

DOCTOR: I specialize in grief.

D.J. (*Laughs, embarrassed*): Shit. Come on.

DOCTOR (*As if taking a leap*): Impacted grief. That's the . . . special area I work in.

D.J. (*Disgusted*): I'm going to spend another hour in jive and riddles and double talk. Only it's not even an hour, right? It's, like, impacted.

DOCTOR: You know the word "impacted"?

D.J.: How dumb do you think I am?

DOCTOR: I don't think you're dumb at all. Matter of fact, the reverse. . . . (HE *has opened the dossier to a sheet, from which* HE *reads aloud*) "Subject is bright. His army G.T. rating is equivalent of 128 I.Q. In first interviews does not volunteer information. . . ." (*Smiles to* D.J., *who allows himself a small smile of recognition in return, then continues reading*) "He related he grew up in a Detroit ghetto and never knew his natural father. He sort of laughed when he said he was a 'good boy' and always did what was expected of him. Was an Explorer Scout and an altar boy. . . ."

D.J.: The other doctor talked a lot about depression.

DOCTOR: What did he say about it?

D.J.: He said I had it.

DOCTOR: Oh? And?

D.J.: He thought I oughta get rid of it. You know? (*The* DOCTOR *reacts*) Yeah, well he was the chief doctor here. The chief doctor for all the psychos in Valley Forge Army Hospital! See what I mean?

DOCTOR: Valley Forge.

D.J.: Yeah. . . .

DOCTOR: Why *don't* you get rid of it?

D.J. (*Animated*): Sometimes that's just what I want to do! Sometimes I want to throw it in their faces! (*Recollecting himself*) Now ain't that stupid? Like, whose face?

DOCTOR (HE *is keenly on the alert, but tries not to show it in the wrong way*): What do you want to throw in their faces?

D.J.: What are we talking about?

DOCTOR: What are you talking about?

D.J. *stares at him, won't or can't say anything. The* DOCTOR *continues gently, precisely.*

I was talking about depression. You said your doctor said you should try to get rid of it. I asked, simply, why *don't* you get rid of it?

D.J. *stares at him, still.* D.J. *is a man for whom it is painful to lose control.* HE *is held in, impassive.*

You meant the medal, didn't you, when you said, "throw it in their faces"?

D.J.: Well. That's why you're here, right? Because of the medal?

DOCTOR (*Gentle, persistent*): But I didn't bring it up. You did.

D.J.: You asked me why I don't get rid of it.

DOCTOR (*Repeating*): I was talking about depression.

D.J.: No. You meant the medal.

DOCTOR: *You* meant the medal. I never mentioned it. . . . Are you glad you have it?

D.J.: The depression?

DOCTOR: No. The medal.

D.J. (*Laughs*): Oh, man. . . . Oh, my. . . . Suppose I didn't have that medal. . . . You wouldn't be here, right? You wouldn't know me from a hole in the wall. I mean, I would be invisible to you. Like a hundred thousand other dudes that got themselves sent over there to be shot at by a lot of little Chinamen hiding up in the trees. I mean, you're some famous doctor, right? Because, you know, I'm a special case! Well I am, I am one big tidbit. I am what you call a "hot property" in this man's army. Yes, sir! I am an authentic hero, a showpiece. One look at me, enlistments go up two hundred percent. . . . I am a credit to my race. Did you know that? I am an honor to the city of Detroit, to say nothing of the state of Michigan, of which I am the only living Medal of Honor winner! I am a feather in the cap of the army, a flower in the lapel of the military—I mean, I am *quoting* to you, man! That is what they say at banquets, given in *my* honor! Yes, sir! And look at me! *Look at me!!* (*Pointing to himself in the clothing of a sick man, in an office of an army hospital*)

DOCTOR: I'm here because you're here.

D.J.: What?

DOCTOR: You ask, would I be here if you hadn't been given that medal. But if you hadn't been given that medal, you wouldn't be here, either. If my grandmother had wheels she'd be a trolley car. You know, it's a big *if*. . . .

D.J.: Yeah, but I'm saying a different *if*. If a trolley car didn't have wheels it still wouldn't be nobody's grandmother. It would just be a trolley car that couldn't go nowhere. Am I right?

DOCTOR (*After a pause*): You're right. . . . (*Brisk again*) Do you still have stomach pains?

D.J.: Yup.

DOCTOR: Nightmares?

D.J.: Yup.

DOCTOR: Same one?

D.J.: Yup.

DOCTOR (*Reads from folder*): "An anonymous soldier standing in front of him, the barrel of his AK-47 as big as a railroad tunnel, his finger on the trigger slowly pressing it."

D.J.: That's the one.

DOCTOR: Who is that anonymous soldier?

D.J.: You know who that is.

DOCTOR: No, I don't.

D.J.: Ain't you done your homework? (*Pointing to folder*)

DOCTOR: My memory is shaky. . . . Please?

D.J.: That's the dude who should have killed me.

DOCTOR: "Should have"?

D.J.: Would have.

DOCTOR: What happened?

D.J.: He misfired.

DOCTOR: And?

D.J.: And that's it.

DOCTOR: That's what?

D.J.: That's it, man. What do you want—a flag that pops out of his rifle and says "Bang"?

DOCTOR: They say you then beat him to death with the butt of your weapon. . . . In combat, near—Dakto.

D.J.: That's what they say.

DOCTOR: That is what they say.

D.J.: So I have heard.

DOCTOR: What else have you heard?

D.J.: That I showed "conspicuous gallantry."

DOCTOR: You're quoting to me?

D.J.: That is what they say, at banquets given in my honor.

DOCTOR: It's part of the citation. Is it not?

D.J. (*Quoting; far-away look*): Con-spicuous gallantry, above and beyond the call of duty. . . . (*With Texas accent*) "Ouah hearts and ouah hopes are turned to peace . . . as we assemble heah . . . in the East Room . . . this morning . . ."

DOCTOR: Lyndon B. Johnson?

D.J.: You got it.

DOCTOR: What did you feel?

D.J.: Nothing.

DOCTOR: But when he hung the medal around your neck, you were crying.

D.J.: See, you *done* your homework!

DOCTOR: Are you going to poke fun at me for the whole hour?

D.J.: Anything wrong with fun?

DOCTOR: Dale—

D.J.: D.J! People call me D.J. That's in the folder, too.

DOCTOR: D.J.

D.J.: Yes, Doctor?

DOCTOR: Do you want to listen to me for a moment?

D.J.: You said *you* was the one to listen.

DOCTOR: I can't listen if you won't tell me anything!

D.J.: I am *telling* you, man! If I knew what to tell to make me feel better, I woulda done it a long time ago. I ain't the doctor, I can't cure myself. . . . (*Pause*) Except one way, maybe.

DOCTOR (*Gently, after a beat*): What are you thinking of, right now?

D.J.: Nothing.

DOCTOR: No image? Nothing in your head?

D.J.: It doesn't have nothing to do with me.

DOCTOR: But *you* thought of it.

D.J.: It's about other guys, in The Nam. Stories we used to hear.

DOCTOR: Yes?

D.J.: "Standing up in a firefight. . . . " (*The* DOCTOR *waits*) We used to hear this . . . combat story. I wasn't in much combat, did you know that?

DOCTOR: Except for Dakto.

D.J.: Yeah. These guys, in their tenth or eleventh month—you know, we had to be there for 365 days on the button, right? Like, we got fed into one end of the computer and if we stayed lucky the computer would shit us back out again, one year later. These grunts—that's what we called the infantry . . .

DOCTOR: I know.

D.J.: I was in a tank, myself.

DOCTOR: What happened to these grunts you heard about?

D.J.: Ten months in the jungle, their feet are rotting, they seen torture, burnings, people being skinned alive—stories they're never going to tell no doctor, believe me. . . . Like, *you* never seen anything like that, right, so you can't comprehend this. . . . (*The* DOCTOR *starts to say something in rebuttal, but then waits*) You never seen your best friend's head blown right off his body so you can look right down in his neck-hole. You never seen somebody you loved, I'm telling you like I mean it, somebody you *loved* and you get there and it's nothing but a black lump, smells like a charcoal dinner, and that's your friend, right?—a black lump. You never seen anything like that, am I right?

DOCTOR (*Quietly*): If you say so.

D.J.: Well, *look* at you, man! Look at you, sitting there in your . . . suit!

DOCTOR: What's wrong with my suit?

D.J.: Ain't nothing wrong with your suit! . . . It's the man wearing the suit. That's what we are talking about!

DOCTOR: You were telling me a story. (HE *feels some satisfaction here—that D.J.'s feelings are beginning to pour out, even if obliquely—but tries not to show it*)

D.J.: A story?

DOCTOR (*Looking at words* HE *has jotted down*): About grunts . . . "standing up in a firefight."

D.J. (*Puzzled that* HE *was recalling this*): Oh. Yeah. So, they been through all these things, and they stayed alive so far, they kept their weapons clean, kept their heads down under cover, and then in the middle of a big firefight with 50-caliber rounds, tracers, all kinds of shit flying all over the place, they'll just stand up.

DOCTOR: They stand up?

D.J.: Yes, start firing into the trees, screaming at the enemy to come out and fight. . . . Maybe not screaming. Just standing straight up.

DOCTOR: And? (*Writing*)

D.J.: Get their heads blown off.

DOCTOR: Every time?

D.J.: Oh, man—*guaranteed!* You know how long you last standing up that way?

DOCTOR: A few seconds?

D.J.: You're a bright fella.

DOCTOR: So, why did they stand up?

D.J. (*Retreating again*): Yeah, why?

DOCTOR: Why do you think they stand up?

D.J.: I don't know. You're the doctor. You tell me.

DOCTOR: What made you think of it just now?

D.J.: I don't know.

DOCTOR: What do you feel about it?

D.J.: Nothing.

DOCTOR: Nothing. . . . (*Silence, for a moment.* HE *gets up, restless, takes a step or two—looks at* D.J., *who sits, immobilized*) D.J., I am going to tell you a few things. Right away.

D.J. (*Perking up*): You're breaking the rules, Doc.

DOCTOR: So be it—sometimes there is nothing else to do.

D.J.: I mean, how do you know I won't report you to your superior?

DOCTOR (*Smiling*): My superior?

D.J.: Don't shrinks have superiors? There must be a Shrink Headquarters somewhere. Probably in New York.

DOCTOR: Probably.

D.J.: So, I'll report that *you* did all the talking and made me—a psycho—take notes on everything you said. Here, man—(HE *sits down in the* DOCTOR's *place at desk, takes pad and pen, sets himself to write*) I'm ready. Tell me, how do you feel now that you're going to get busted into the ranks, emptying bedpans and suchlike? . . . Oh?

DOCTOR (HE *leans forward, to make his words take hold*): You see what's happening: we are playing games with each other. Because that's easy for you, and you are good at it. You could fill this hour, the week, the month that way until it really *is* too late! Do you understand that?

D.J.: Do you?

DOCTOR: How dumb do you think I am?

D.J. (*Trace of a smile*): I ain't decided yet. I don't have a folder on you with your scores in it.

DOCTOR: Yes. You're a very witty man, very quick—as long as the things we touch on don't really matter to you. But when they do, you go numb. You claim to feel nothing. Do you recognize what I'm saying?

D.J. (*Dull*): I don't know.

DOCTOR: Even your voice goes flat. Can you hear the sound of your own voice?

D.J. (*Flat*): I don't know.

DOCTOR: Do you see that?

D.J.: What?

DOCTOR: I merely *mentioned* the fact that you go numb—and you did! What do you think about that?

D.J.: Nothing.

DOCTOR: Nothing! You think nothing about the fact that you just go one-hundred-percent numb, like a stone, in response to everything that matters most in your own life? (HE *surreptitiously glances at his watch.* THEY *are well into the hour*)

D.J.: Well, now I *am* going to tell you something, man! (*Breaks out as if* HE *had been cornered*) I don't know why I'm in this hospital! I don't know why I'm in this room!

DOCTOR: Then why don't you leave it? We're not getting anywhere.

D.J. (*Mocking*): You mean I don't have to stay here till my hour's up?

DOCTOR: No. I'm not your Commanding Officer. So, go.

> D.J. *does start to go. But* HE *stops on the way to the door to return to the* DOC-TOR's *desk. There,* D.J. *picks up the various folders and drops them into the wastebasket.* HE *does the same thing, pointedly, with the* DOCTOR's *pen.* D.J. *stares at the* DOCTOR *for a moment, then walks to the door, opens it, and steps out into the corridor. The* DOCTOR *watches him, then heaves a sigh, leans on the desk to think about what has happened. But* D.J. *appears again at the door.*

D.J.: If I go out there, I'll be in the corridors. I hate the corridors. You ever walk the corridors of this place?

DOCTOR: Never had that pleasure.

D.J.: There's seven miles of them. Lined with basket cases. And I've walked them all, man. I've walked them all . . .

DOCTOR: So you're going to stay here with me just to keep out of the corridors for a while?

D.J.: That's right.

DOCTOR (*Not forcing the issue*): Fine. Make yourself comfortable.

> D.J. *smiles, goes to his chair, settles in, stretches, takes off his slippers, wiggles his toes, watches his bare feet as if they were amusing animals. Begins to do a musical beat on the chair, ignoring the* DOCTOR. *The* DOCTOR *calmly goes back to the wastebasket, extracts his folders and notebook, shakes the ashes off them.* HE *takes out his pen, taps it against the side of the basket, in counter-rhythm to* D.J.'s *beat, and blows the dust off. Then the* DOCTOR *settles comfortably at his desk, lights a cigarette, whistles a bit of the Mozart G-minor Symphony, begins to look through the folder as if to do some work on his own.*

Do you mind if I read a bit? To pass the time?

D.J. (*Cool*): Help yourself.

DOCTOR (*After a beat; musingly*): Here's an interesting story . . . a case study

I've been working on . . . trying to write it out for myself . . . about a certain man who was an unusual type for the world he came from. (*Reads from or refers to folder, as if in discussion of a neutral matter*) Rather gentle, and decent in manner . . . almost always easygoing and humorous. Noted for that. As a kid in a tough neighborhood, he had been trained by his mother to survive by combining the virtues of a Christian and a sprinter: he turned the other cheek and ran faster than anyone else. . . . (D.J. *is beginning to listen with interest*) This man was sent by his country to fight in a war. A war unlike any war he might have imagined. Brutal, without glory, without meaning, without good wishes for those who were sent to fight and without gratitude for those who returned. He was trained to kill people of another world in their own homes, in order to help them. How this would help them we do not really know. He was assigned to a tank and grew close with the others in the crew, as men always do in a war. He and his friends in that tank were relatively fortunate—for almost a year they lived through insufferable heat, insects, boredom, but were never drawn into heavy combat. Then one night he was given orders assigning him to a different tank. For what reason?

D.J.: There was no reason.

DOCTOR: There was no reason.

D.J.: It was the army.

DOCTOR: It was the army. The next day, his platoon of four M-48 tanks were driving along a road toward a place called Dakto, which meant nothing to him. Suddenly they were ambushed. First, by enemy rockets, which destroyed two of the tanks. Then, enemy soldiers came out of the woods to attack the two tanks still in commission. This man we were speaking of was in one of those tanks. But the tank with his old friends, the tank he would have been in—

D.J.: Should have been in.

DOCTOR: —the tank that he might have been in—that tank was on fire. It was about sixty feet away, and the crew he had spent eleven months and twenty-two days with in Vietnam was trapped inside it. . . . (D.J. *looks away, in pain*) He hoisted himself out and ran to the other tank. Speaking of standing up in a firefight. . . . Why he wasn't hit by the heavy crossfire we'll never know. He pulled out the first man he came to in the turret. The body was blackened, charred, but still alive. That was one of his friends.

D.J.: He kept making a noise to me, over and over again. Just kept making the same noise, but I couldn't find where his mouth was. . . .

DOCTOR: Then the tank's artillery shells exploded, killing everyone left inside. He saw the bodies of his other friends all burned and blasted, and then— for thirty minutes, armed first with a 45-caliber pistol and then with a submachine gun he hunted the Vietnamese on the ground, killing from ten to twenty enemy soldiers (no one knows for sure) . . . by himself. When he ran out of ammunition, he killed one with the stock of his submachine gun.

D.J.: He kept making this same noise to me . . . over and over.

DOCTOR (*After a pause*): When it was all over, it took three men and three shots of morphine to quiet him down. He was raving. He tried to kill the prisoners they had rounded up. They took him away to a hospital in Pleiku in a straitjacket. Twenty-four hours later he was released from that hospital, and within forty-eight hours he was home again in Detroit, with a medical discharge. . . .

D.J.: My mother didn't even know I was coming. . . .

DOCTOR: Go on.

D.J.(*Looking up*): You go on.

DOCTOR: That is the story.

D.J.: That's not the whole story.

DOCTOR: What happened when you got back to this country?

D.J.: What do you mean, what happened?

DOCTOR: One day you're in the jungle. These catastrophic things happen. Death, screaming, fire. Then suddenly you're sitting in a jet airplane, going home.

D.J.: They had *stewardesses* on that plane! D'you know that?

DOCTOR: Oh?

D.J.: *Stewardesses,* for shit's sake, man! They kept smiling at us.

DOCTOR: Did you smile back?

D.J. (*Straightforward*): I wanted to kill them.

DOCTOR: White girls?

D.J.: That's not the point.

DOCTOR: Are you sure?

D.J.: A white guy would have felt the same way I did. I . . . wanted to throw a hand grenade right in the middle of all those teeth.

DOCTOR: Do you think that was a bad feeling?

D.J.: Blowing up a girl's face, because she's smiling at me? Well, I'll tell you, man, it wasn't the way my mother brought me up to be. Not exactly.

DOCTOR: Neither was the war. Was it?

D.J.: Doc. Am I crazy?

DOCTOR: Maybe a little bit. But it's temporary. . . . It can be cured.

D.J.: *You* can cure me? (*Stares at the* DOCTOR)

DOCTOR: I didn't say that.

D.J.: Yeah, but you mean it, don't you?

DOCTOR: What was it like when you touched ground, in this country?

D.J.: You actually think that you can cure me!

DOCTOR: Did they have a Victory Parade for you?

D.J.: *Victory Parade?!*

DOCTOR: Soldiers always used to get parades, when they came home. Made them feel better.

D.J.: Victory Parades! Man. . . . (*Laughs at the insane wonder of the idea*)

DOCTOR: You mean there wasn't a band playing when you landed in the States?

D.J.: Man, let me tell you something—

DOCTOR: You didn't march together, with your unit?

D.J.: Unit? What unit?

DOCTOR: Well, the people you flew back with.

D.J.: I didn't know a soul in that plane, man! I didn't have no *unit*. Any unit I had, man, they're all burned to a crisp. How'm I supposed to march with that unit?—with a whiskbroom, pushing all these little black crumbs forward down the street, and everybody cheering, "There's Willie! See that little black crumb there? That's our Willie! No, no, that there crumb is my son, Georgie! Hi, Georgie. Glad to have you home, boy!"? Huh? . . . What are you talking about?! This wasn't World War Two, man, they sent us back one by one, when our number came up. I told you that!

DOCTOR: People were burned to a crisp in World War Two.

D.J.: Yeah, well there was a difference, because I *heard* about that war! When people came back from that war they *felt* like somebody. They were made to feel *good,* at least for a while.

DOCTOR: That's just what I was thinking.

D.J.: Then why didn't you just say it?

DOCTOR: I'd rather that you said it.

D.J.: Were you in that war?

DOCTOR: I remember it—very well.

D.J.: And you knew guys who had a parade with their unit.

DOCTOR: I did. Banners. Ticker tape.

D.J. (*Laughs at the thought*): Oh, man. How long ago was that?

DOCTOR: Where did you land?

D.J.: Seattle.

DOCTOR: Daytime? Night?

D.J.: Night.

A pause.

DOCTOR: Nothing?

D.J.: Nothing, man. Nothing.

Pause.

DOCTOR: I had one patient who got spat on, at the Seattle airport.

D.J.: Spat on?

DOCTOR: For not winning the war. He said an American Legionnaire, with a red face, apparently used to wait right at the gate . . . so he could spit on soldiers coming back, the moment they arrived.

D.J.: What are you telling me this for?

DOCTOR: Then, inside the terminal there was a group of young people screaming insults. White kids, with long hair. (*No reaction from* D.J. *The* DOCTOR
watches him carefully) Do you want to know why they were screaming insults?

D.J.: No, Doctor, I do not.

DOCTOR: For burning babies.

D.J.: I didn't burn no babies! (HE *begins to pace*. HE *is agitated. The* DOCTOR
watches, waits) The day I arrived, like, everything was disorganized. There
was a smaller plane took us to the nearest landing strip, know what I
mean?—and then you had to hitch a ride, or whatever, to find your own unit.

DOCTOR: Are you talking about Seattle?

D.J.: No, man. In The Nam. Like, my first day over there. My *first day*, mind
you! So, I hitched a ride on this truck. About six or seven guys in it, heading
toward Danang. I was a F.N.G., so I kept my mouth shut.

DOCTOR: F.N.G.?

D.J. (HE *pulls his chair up closer to the* DOCTOR's *desk, as if to confide in him, and*
HE *sits*): A F.N.G. is a Fucking New Guy. See? They all pick on you over
there, they hate you just because you're new. Like, nobody trusts you for
the simple fact that you never been through the miseries they been having.
At least, not yet. . . . Then you get friendly with your own little group,
see, your own three or four friends—the guys in my tank—and they mean
everything to you, they're like family—they're like everything you got in
this world—I—see, that was the—thing about—that was the. . . .

D.J. *suddenly can't go on*. HE *buries his face in his hands and is attacked by
a terrible grief—ambushed by it.* HE *tries to pull his hands away to speak again,
but it is impossible.* HE *sobs, or weeps, into his hands. The* DOCTOR *hesitates,
then goes around to the chair where* D.J. *sits, and stays there by him for a moment. The* DOCTOR *begins to lay a hand, lightly, on* D.J.'s *shoulder, so that*
D.J. *will not be completely alone with his grief. But* D.J. *breaks away, violently.*
HE *heads away, as if to escape. The* DOCTOR *moves to block another impetuous
exit, but* D.J. *had no clear intention.* HE *is frozen, sobbing. If his face is visible, it is painful to see. The* DOCTOR *watches him intently, almost like a hunter.*
HE *seems to be gauging his moment, when* D.J. *will be just in control enough
to hear what the* DOCTOR *is saying, but still vulnerable enough for a deep blow
to be struck. Finally* HE *speaks.*

DOCTOR: Is it the tank? (D.J. *cannot really answer*) Can you say it? (D.J. *almost begins
to speak, but the catch in his throat is still there.* HE *will break down again, if*
HE *speaks.* HE *shakes his head*) Do you want me to say it? (D.J. *cannot answer*)
You don't know why you are alive and they are dead. (D.J. *watches*) You
think you should be dead, too. (D.J. *listens, silent. At times* HE *tries to run
away from the words, but the* DOCTOR *stalks him*) Sometimes you feel that you
are really dead, already. You can't feel anything becasue it's too painful.

You dream about the rifle that should have killed you, with the barrel right in your face. You don't know why it didn't kill you, why just that rifle should have misfired. . . . (D.J. *hangs on these words*) And what about those orders that transferred you out of their tank? Why just that night? Why you? Why did the ambush come the next day? . . . There must be something magical about this, like the AK-47 that misfired for no reason. Perhaps you made all these things happen, just to save yourself. Perhaps it is all your fault, that your friends are dead. If you hadn't been transferred from their tank, then somehow they wouldn't have died. So you should die, too.

D.J. (*Bellowing*): I'm dead already!

DOCTOR (*Quieter*): Yes. You *feel*, sometimes, that you are dead already. You would like to die, to shut your eyes quietly on all this, and you don't know who you can tell about it. You keep it locked up like a terrible secret. . . . (D.J. *remains silent. The* DOCTOR's *words have the power to cause great pain in him. After a pause*) This is our work, D.J. This is what we have to do.

D.J.: I can't, man! I can't!

DOCTOR: You can. I know you can.

D.J. (*Stares at the* DOCTOR; *then speaks*): How do you know all this? From a book?

DOCTOR: I've been through it.

D.J.: *You* were in The Nam?

DOCTOR: No. But I had my own case of survivor guilt.

D.J.: That's jive and doubletalk! Don't start that shit with me.

DOCTOR: It's just shorthand to describe a complicated . . . sickness. It's the kind of thing that can make a man feel so bad that he thinks he wants to die.

D.J.: Where'd you get yours?

DOCTOR: You think it will help you to know that?

D.J.: Man, I take off my skin, and you just piss all over me! And . . .

DOCTOR: You want me to take my skin off, too. That's what you want?

D.J.: I want to get better! I don't want to be crazy!

DOCTOR: Yes. That's why I'm here, to—

D.J. (*Cutting him off*): You're not here!

DOCTOR: I'm not?

D.J.: There's something here. And it's wearing a bowtie. But I don't know *what* it is . . .

DOCTOR: Well, in this treatment, that's the way it works. Normally it's better that you *not* know about your doctor's personal—

D.J.: *Normally?!* Man, this ain't normally!

The DOCTOR *considers this, as a serious proposition. Historically, the abnormal war. The desperation of this man. And* HE *goes ahead, against his own reluctance.*

DOCTOR: All right. All right . . . I wasn't born here. I'm from Poland. I had a Jewish grandmother, but I was brought up as a regular kid. All right? . . . Life in Poland tends to get confusing. Either the Russians or Germans are always rolling in, flattening the villages and setting fire to people. You've got the picture? Anyway, World War Two came, the Nazis, the SS troops, and this time the Jewish kids were supposed to be killed—sent to Camps, gassed, starved, worked to death, beaten to death. That was the program . . . I didn't think of myself as Jewish. We didn't burn candles on Friday night, none of that. I wasn't Jewish. But my mother's mother was. So, to the Nazis I was Jewish. So, I should be dead now. I shouldn't be here. You're looking at someone who "should" be dead, like you. . . . See? (D.J. *nods.* HE *listens intensely*) They sent me to one of those Camps. But I was saved, by an accident. . . . You understand what I'm saying? Someone came along—a businessman—and he said he would buy some Jewish children, and the Nazis could use the money for armaments, or whatever. A deal. One gray morning—it was quite warm—they just lined us up, and started counting heads. When they got to the number the gentleman had paid for, they stopped. I got counted. The ones who didn't—my brother and sister and the others—they all died. But not me. For what reason? *There was no reason.* . . . So, that's it. Eventually, I ended up over here, I lied about my age, got into the army at the end of the war. I thought I wanted revenge. But now I know that I wanted to die, back over there. To get shot. But I failed. Came back, and I even marched in a Victory Parade, with my unit! So I was luckier than you, D.J. . . . But still, I didn't know why I hadn't died when everyone else did. I thought it must have been magic, and that it was my fault the others were dead—a kind of trade-off, you see, where my survival accounted for their deaths. My parents, everybody. I became quite sick. Depressed, dead-feeling . . .

D.J.: How did you get better?

DOCTOR: The same way you will.

D.J.: I thought you was going to cure me.

DOCTOR: No. Essentially, you are going to cure yourself.

D.J.: Wow. (*Shakes his head*)

DOCTOR: Others, men like you, have gone through such things, and they have gotten better. That might make you feel a little better, too, for a start.

D.J.: Yeah, misery loves company. Right?

DOCTOR: Nothing magical happened, D.J. None of this was your fault. (*Glances at his watch*)

D.J.: How much time we got left, Doc?

DOCTOR: Don't worry about the time. We have all the time we'll need.

D.J.: You're the one is always stealing a look at your watch!

DOCTOR: It's just a bad habit. Like picking my nose.

D.J.: I ain't seen you picking your nose.

DOCTOR: You will. You will.

D.J.: I guess that gives me a little something to look forward to, in my hospital stay.

DOCTOR (*Laughs*): I guess it does.

D.J.: A treat instead of a treatment. (*The* DOCTOR *is no longer amused.* HE *stares at* D.J., *expectantly.* D.J. *grows uneasy*) You want something from me.

DOCTOR: Mm. The truck.

D.J.: The truck?

DOCTOR: The story of the first—

D.J. (*Interrupting*): What truck?

DOCTOR: There was a truck.

D.J.: A truck . . . ?

DOCTOR: First day in Vietnam. F.N.G. You hitched a ride in a truck.

D.J.: Jesus.

DOCTOR: Don't feel like talking about it?

D.J.: No. I don't.

DOCTOR: That's as good a reason as any for telling me.

D.J. (*Reacts to this notion, but then goes along with it. Sits down again, as* HE *gets into the story*): Well, uh . . . we were riding along, in the truck. Real hot, you know, and nobody much was around . . . and we see there's a bunch of kids, maybe three, four of them crossing the road up ahead. . . . You know?

DOCTOR: How old were they?

D.J.: Well, it's hard to tell. Those people are all so *small*, you know?—I mean, all dried-up and tiny, man. . . . Maybe ten years old, twelve, I don't know. . . .

DOCTOR: And?

D.J.: Well, we see they're being pretty slow getting out of the road, so we got to swerve a little bit to miss them. . . . Not a lot, you know, but a little bit. This seems to make the guys in the back of the truck really mad. Like, somebody goes, "Little fuckers!" You know? . . . Then those kids, as soon as we pass, they start laughing at us, and give us the finger. Know what I mean? (HE *gives the* DOCTOR *the finger, to illustrate. The* DOCTOR *starts to laugh, but then puts his hand to his head, as if knowing what is to come*) Yeah. So I'm thinking to myself, "Now where did they learn to do that? That ain't some old oriental custom. They musta learned it from our guys." . . . Suddenly the guys on the truck start screaming for the driver to back up. So he jams on the brakes, and in this big cloud of dust he's grinding this thing in reverse as if he means to run those kids down, backwards. The kids start running away, of course, but one of 'em, maybe two, I don't know, they stop, you see, and give us the finger again, from the side of the road. And they're laughing. . . . So, uh . . . everybody on the truck opens fire. I mean, I couldn't believe it, they're like half a platoon, they got M-16s, automatic rifles, they're blasting away, it sounds like a pitched battle, they're pouring all this firepower into these kids. The kids are lying on the ground, they're dead about a hundred times over, and these guys are still firing rounds into their bodies, like they've gone crazy. And the kids' bodies are giving these little jumps into the air like rag dolls, and then they flop down again. . . .

DOCTOR (*Very quiet*): What happened then?

D.J.: They just sorta stopped, and me and these guys drove away. (*The DOCTOR waits*) I'm thinking to myself, you know, what *is* going on here? I must be out of tune. *My first day in the country,* and we ain't even reached the Combat Zone! I'm thinking, like, this is the enemy? Kids who make our trucks give a little jog in the road and give us the finger? I mean, come on, man! . . . And one guy, he sees I'm sort of staring back down the road, so he gives me like this, you know— (HE *simulates a jab of the elbow*) and he says, "See how we hose them li'l motherfuckers down, man?" Hose 'em down. You like that? . . . And they're all blowing smoke away from their muzzles and checking their weapons down, like they're a bunch of gunslingers, out of the Old West. . . . (HE *is shaking his head.* HE *still has trouble believing* HE *saw this*)

DOCTOR (*Measured*): Why do you think they did all that?

D.J.: I don't know. They went crazy, that's why!

DOCTOR: Went crazy. . . . Were all those soldiers white?

D.J.: I don't remember.

DOCTOR: What do you think?

D.J. (*A little dangerously*): I think some of them were white.

DOCTOR (*Waits.* D.J. *does not add anything*): And what did you do?

D.J.: What do you mean, what did I do?

DOCTOR: Well, did you report them to a superior officer?

D.J. (*Explodes*): *Superior officer?!* What superior officer? Their fucking lieutenant was *right there in the fucking truck,* he was the first one to open fire! I mean what are you talking about, man? Don't you know what is going on over there?

DOCTOR: Why get mad at me? I didn't shoot those children.

D.J. (*Confused, angry*): God *damn* . . . ! (*Glaring at the* DOCTOR) I mean, what are you accusing me of, man?

DOCTOR: I'm not accusing you of anything.

D.J.: Well, I'm asking you! What would you have done? You think you're so much smarter and better than me? You weren't there, man! That's why you can sit here and be the judge! Right? (*No reaction from the* DOCTOR, *except for a tic of nervousness under the extreme tension that has been created*) I mean, look at you sitting there in your suit, with that shit-eating grin on your face!

DOCTOR: You're getting mad at my suit again? You think my suit has caused these problems?

D.J. can't control his rage and frustration any longer. HE *blows up, grabs his chair—as the only object available—and swings it above his head as a weapon. The* DOCTOR *instinctively ducks away and shouts at* D.J. *to stop.*

Wait a minute! Sergeant! Stop that!

D.J. crashes the chair against the desk, or the floor. HE *cannot vent his physical aggression directly against the* DOCTOR. *After* D.J. *has torn up the room,* HE *stands, exhausted, confused, emptyhanded.*

Are you all right?

D.J. stares at the DOCTOR, *panting.* D.J. *moves away, into the silence of the room. The* DOCTOR *speaks neutrally.*

How did you feel about being a killer?
D.J.: *I didn't kill those kids, man!*
DOCTOR: I didn't say you did! Did I?

The DOCTOR *waits.* D.J. *glares at him, still full of rage and suspicion. But a deep point has been made, and* BOTH MEN *are aware of it. A pause.*

Did you ever tell people at home about any of this? About Dakto, about the truck?
D.J.: No. I didn't.
DOCTOR: Didn't they ask? Didn't anyone ever wonder why you came home early?
D.J.: Yeah, they asked.
DOCTOR: Who asked?
D.J.: My mother. Little kids, sometimes. My girl, Bea. . . .
DOCTOR: Sounds like everybody.
D.J.: No, not everybody. A lot of people didn't give a shit what happened.
DOCTOR: And you pretended you didn't give a shit, either?
D.J.: What do you want me to say, man?
DOCTOR: But what did you say when your mother or your friends asked you?
D.J.: You guess. You're the specialist.
DOCTOR (*After a pause*): All right, I will. You said, "Nothing happened. Nothing happened over there."
D.J.: Right on. Word for word.
DOCTOR: It's in the folder.
D.J.: Yeah, sure.
DOCTOR (*Takes words from report in the folder*): It also says you "lay up in your room a lot, staring at the ceiling. . . . " (HE *waits, to see if* D.J. *has anything to add*)
D.J.: Read. Read, man. I'm tired.

DOCTOR: Did you do that—did that happen to you right away?

D.J.: Right away . . . ? No. Well, at first I felt pretty good. Considering. . . . (*Trails off*) Considering, uh . . .

DOCTOR: Considering that you had just been heavily narcotized, tied up in a straitjacket, and shipped home in a semi-coma. After surviving a hell of death and horror, which by all odds should have left you dead yourself.

D.J.: Yeah. Considering that.

DOCTOR: You felt lucky that you had survived? At first?

D.J.: I just used to like going to bars with my cousin, William . . . my friends. I was glad to see my girl, Beatrice, and my mama. I joked around with them. I tried to be good to them . . . I shot baskets with the kids, down the block. Understand?

DOCTOR: Of course. And then what happened?

D.J.: It didn't last.

DOCTOR: And?

D.J.: I started laying up in my room. Staring at the ceiling.

DOCTOR: But what happened? What changed you?

D.J.: I don't remember.

DOCTOR: But you did go numb?

D.J.: You're talking me around in circles, Doc!

DOCTOR: I'm sorry. . . . This terrible delayed reaction, after a kind of relief—it seems so mysterious, but it's the common pattern for men who went through your kind of combat trauma . . .

D.J. (*With irony*): Well, I'm glad to hear that. But I sometimes began to suspect that my girl, Bea, might just prefer a man what can see and hear and think and feel things. And *do* things! You follow my meaning? A man what can walk and talk, stuff like that?

DOCTOR: Did you stop having sexual relations with her?

D.J.: Well, I have been trying to send you signals, man! You're none too quick on the pickup.

DOCTOR: Did she criticize you?

D.J.: Not about that. : . . . She wanted me to get a job, so we could get married.

DOCTOR: Well. The job situation must have been difficult in Detroit.

D.J.: Especially if you lay up in your room all day, staring at the ceiling. Funny thing about the city of Detroit—not too many people come up through your bedroom offering you a job, on most days. Did you know that?

DOCTOR: I've heard that, yes. . . . Did you stop getting out of bed altogether?

D.J.: No, I put my feet to the floor once in a while. Used to go on down to the V.A. and stand in line for my check.

DOCTOR: How did they treat you down there, at the Veterans' Office?

D.J.: Like shit.

DOCTOR: Did you know why you got treated that way?

D.J.: It wasn't just me personally, man.

DOCTOR: I know. But why?

D.J.: You know that a vet down the block from me flipped out last week—jumped up in the middle of his sleep and shot his woman in bed, because he thought she was the Vietcong laying there to ambush him? . . .

The DOCTOR *goes sharply on the alert at this, but waits for* D.J. *to continue.* D.J. *is profoundly uneasy about his own train of thought.*

Man, if I lose my cool again—just, freak out—what's to stop me from going up and down the streets of Detroit killing everything I see?

DOCTOR (*Concerned, quiet*): Do you actually think you could do that?

D.J.: How can you ask me that?

DOCTOR: I'm asking.

D.J. (*Charging at the* DOCTOR): Well what did I *do*—what did I get that medal for, man? For my good manners and gentle ways?

The DOCTOR *and* D.J. *stare at each other for a tense moment. The* DOCTOR *starts to fit up another cigarette and filter, but throws the filter away and lights up the cigarette.* HE *begins to pace restlessly.* D.J. *watches him. Then the* DOCTOR *abruptly turns back to* D.J.

DOCTOR: Tell me when you actually got the medal.

D.J.: You're making me nervous!

DOCTOR (*Keeps pacing*): As my grandmother used to say, "That should be the worst would ever happen to you."

D.J.: That's the grandmother, could have been a trolley car?

DOCTOR: *If* she had wheels.

D.J.: If she had wheels. Right.

During this colloquy—in which an ease, a trust seems to be forming between the men—the DOCTOR *has restrained himself, but* HE *is impatient now to pick up the thread.*

DOCTOR: Tell me when you actually got the medal!

D.J. (*This story is relatively easy for him to launch into;* HE *settles into his old chair in the course of telling it*): I been home eight, nine months. Then I get this call, they say it's some army office. They want to know if I'm clean—if I had any arrests since I been back, you know. I tell them I'm clean and just leave me alone. Then two MPs come to the door, in uniform, scare the shit out of my mama. They just tell her they want to find out a few things about me—whether I've been a good boy—whether I've been taking any drugs. She makes me roll up my sleeves right there (HE *does so for the* DOCTOR) to show—no tracks, see? When they leave, she is sure I've done something terrible, that I shouldn't be afraid to tell her, that she'll forgive me anything. And all I can do is sit there in the kitchen and laugh at her, which makes her mad, and even more sure I done something weird. . . . Well, about fifteen minutes later a colonel calls up from the Department of Defense in Washington, tells me they're going to give me the Congressional Medal of Honor, and could I come down to Washington right away, with my family, as President Lyndon B. Johnson hisself wants to hang it around my neck, with his own hands. He'll pay for the tickets, he says.

DOCTOR: So, another sudden ride on a jet plane.

D.J.: A goddamn *Honor Guard* meets us at the airport. Beatrice is peeing in her pants, my mother's with me, my cousin, William. . . . They got a dress-blue uniform waiting for me, just my size. Shoes, socks, everything. Escort, sirens. Yesterday afternoon for all they knew I was a junkie on the streets, today the President of the United States can't wait to see me. . . .

The DOCTOR *has picked up his cassette recorder while* D.J. *was finishing the story, and now* HE *clicks it on. The voice of Lyndon B. Johnson plays, from the award ceremony.*

VOICE OF L.B.J.: " . . . Secretary Resor . . . General Westmoreland. . . . Distinguished guests and members of the family. . . . Our hearts and our hopes are turned to peace as we assemble here in the East Room this morning. All our efforts are being bent in its pursuit. But in this company (*The* DOCTOR *points the recorder at* D.J.) we hear again, in our minds, the sounds of distant battle. . . .

The DOCTOR *turns the volume down, and the voice of L.B.J. drones quietly in the background, as* HE *waits for* D.J.*'s reaction.*

D.J.: Ain't that a lot of shit?

DOCTOR: You wept.

D.J.: I don't know, I kind of cracked up. The flashbulbs were popping in my eyes, my mother's hugging me, she's saying, "Honey, what are you crying about? You've made it back." It was *weird!*

The DOCTOR *has turned the volume up again to let a few more phrases from the presidential ceremony play, giving* D.J. *more time for reliving the moment.*

VOICE OF L.B.J.: "This room echoes once more to those words that describe the heights of bravery in war, above and beyond the call of duty. Five heroic sons of America come to us today from the tortured fields of Vietnam. They come to remind us that so long as that conflict continues our purpose and our hopes rest on the steadfast bravery of young men in battle. These five soldiers, in their separate moments of supreme testing, summoned a degree of courage that stirs wonder and respect and an overpowering pride in all of us. Through their spectacular courage they set themselves apart in a very select company . . . "

The DOCTOR *underlines these last words—"set themselves apart in a very select company"—with a gesture. Then* HE *flicks off the cassette recorder.*

D.J.: Weird, man.

DOCTOR: Why was it weird?

D.J.: I . . . I don't know?

DOCTOR: You *do* know!

D.J.: What are you driving at?

DOCTOR: What did you get that medal for? (*Repeating* D.J.*'s earlier words*) For your "good manners and gentle ways"?

D.J. (*Stares at the* DOCTOR. *The* DOCTOR *stares back*): I got that medal because I went totally out of my fucking skull and killed everything that crossed my sight! (*Pause*) They say I wanted to kill all the prisoners. *Me.*

DOCTOR: *You don't remember?*

D.J.: Nothing. . . . A few flashes, maybe. Those people are all so small. . . .

DOCTOR (HE *taps a finger on the cassette recorder, trying to recapture the specific moment* THEY *have been talking about—in the White House—but* HE *gradually gets caught up in the intense rush of his own thoughts*): So, your mother was hugging you, in the White House, for doing what she had trained you all your life not to do—for being a killer. And everybody was celebrating you for that. . . . And your dead friends from the tank, whom you had tried so hard to bury, came back again, to haunt you. You had to relive that story, that flash of combat when a man's life is changed forever, when he literally goes crazy, psychotic, in a world of no past and no future, compacted into a few seconds, a wild pounding of the heart, blinding light, explosions, terror, and his whole earlier life slides away from him through a . . . membrane as if lost forever, and all he can do is kill—all *that* was named, broadcast, printed on a banner and waved in your own face so you can never forget. . . . And you wonder why you wept, why you were confused, why you are here in this hospital? You wept for your dead friends, you wept for your dead self, for your whole life that slid away in the first fifteen seconds of that ambush on the road to Dakto. You were choking on your grief, a grief you couldn't share with anyone, and you became paralyzed by your guilt, and you still are, and you're going to be, until *you* decide to make your own journey back through that membrane into some acceptable reality. . . . Some real life, of your own. . . .

Both D.J. *and the* DOCTOR *seem momentarily stunned by the latter's outpouring.*

D.J.: I don't know how to do that, Doc.

DOCTOR: I will tell you. . . . (*Glances at watch, as if recollecting himself*) D.J., do you intend to stay in this hospital for a while?

D.J.: Why do you ask?

DOCTOR (*Reads from folder for an answer*): "Maalox and bland diet prescribed. G.I. series conducted. Results negative. Subject given thirty-day convalescent leave 16 October 1970. Absent Without Leave until 12 January 1971, when subject returned to Army hospital on own volition. Subsequent hearing recommended dismissal of AWOL charge and back pay reinstated . . . in cognizance of subject's outstanding record in Vietnam."

D.J.: Well, yeah, they can't do anything to me.

DOCTOR: Because of the medal?

D.J.: Because of the medal. . . .

DOCTOR (*After a beat*): I'm afraid we have only a few more minutes today. (*Scanning his appointments book*) I can come down the day after tomorrow, and I'd like to talk with you again. After that, if you want, I can see you three or four times a week.

D.J. (HE *automatically readies himself for the end of the hour*): Busy man like you? (*Light mockery*)

DOCTOR: Mm-hm. But I'd like to have you transferred up to New York. I can do that, if you'll make the request. . . . (HE *looks questioningly at* D.J.. D.J. *does not answer—nor does* HE *necessarily imply a "No"*) Well?

D.J.: We'll see.

DOCTOR: We'll see what?

D.J.: We'll see, when you come down again.

DOCTOR: Can I be sure you'll be here?

D.J.: You're looking for too many guarantees in life, man.

DOCTOR: No, I'm not. I'm looking for you to make a decision about yourself.

A knock at the door, and the HOSPITAL GUARD *immediately enters.*

You *can* get better, you know. . . .

GUARD: Reporting in for Sergeant Jackson, sir.

The DOCTOR *and* D.J. *look at each other.* D.J. *gets up, automatically, to go.*

DOCTOR (*To* GUARD): Will you wait outside for a moment? In the corridor?

GUARD: Will do, sir. May I ask, sir, how long?

DOCTOR: Not long. Until the interview is concluded.

GUARD: May I ask, sir, is the interview almost concluded?

DOCTOR: The interview is almost concluded. Just giving a summation.

GUARD: Will wait in corridor, sir, until conclusion of summation of interview. (HE *snaps to, gives salute. The* DOCTOR *waves him off, with his own facsimile of a salute. The* GUARD *wheels into an about-face and exits to station himself outside the door*)

D.J.: Attaboy.

DOCTOR: So?

D.J.: So?

DOCTOR: Do we have a deal?

D.J.: Hit me with the "summation."

DOCTOR (*Closes up his folder*): There is nothing to say that you don't already know. The only question is what to do about it. (D.J. *laughs*) It was a badly damaged self that you brought back to this country, and nothing has happened here, you see, to help you—

D.J. (*Cutting him off*): You're leaving a little something out, ain't you? Man, they gave me the Congressional Medal of Honor!

DOCTOR: So they did. And what happened?

D.J.: Well . . . I became a big hero!

DOCTOR: You became a big hero. . . . You appear on TV. The head of General Motors shakes your hand. You get married. You reenlist—reenlist!—travel around the state making recruiting speeches. You get a new car, a house with a big mortgage. Everybody gives you credit . . . for a while.

D.J.: Rags to riches, man.

DOCTOR: And then? (D.J. *makes a gesture of self-deprecation, meaning, more or less, "Here I am"*) Back to rags again.

D.J. (*Challenging*): But I got the medal! Didn't that medal save me from a lot of shit?

DOCTOR (*Beginning to pack up*): Did it ever occur to you that the medal, in some ways, might have made things worse?

D.J.: *Worse?* What are you talking about, man?

DOCTOR: Well, that's where we can begin our next session. . . . If you will simply commit yourself to being here. That's all I'm asking, you know.

D.J. (*Opening up the* DOCTOR'*s folder again*): No! I want to talk about it now. I mean, it sounds like you're just getting down to the nitty-gritty, am I right?

DOCTOR: It's all nitty-gritty, D.J. It's one layer of nitty-gritty after another, until you feel like living again. But we can't just extend this hour arbitrarily—

D.J.: Why not? Just tell the cowboy out there to take a walk. You got the rank here. . . .

DOCTOR: That's not the issue. Look, for one thing I'm a little tired, too. I got up at five this morning, and—

D.J.: Yeah. Well that should be the worst would ever happen to you!

DOCTOR: All right. Let's just say for now, that it's the rules of the game, by which we *both* can—

D.J. (*Pouncing on the word "game"*): So we *are* playing games! You hear?

DOCTOR: We're playing a game for your life!

D.J. (*Studies the* DOCTOR): What do you want from me, man?

DOCTOR: I want you to get better.

D.J.: No, you said you were going to tell me what I had to do.

DOCTOR: I said that?

D.J.: Yeah, you did—after a long speech about killing, when you got all excited. Probably, it slipped out, huh?

DOCTOR: Well, that gives us something else to look into, next time.

D.J. (*Sullen*): No, man. You want something from me. I been getting used to that . . . I think you're a star-fucker.

DOCTOR: A what?

D.J.: A star-fucker. Like, in the Rock world, or in the movies, these chicks who hang around close to the stars. They get their kicks, their thrills out of that.

DOCTOR: I'm not a "chick."

D.J.: But you're like one.

DOCTOR: Meaning?

D.J.: You come down here, you sniff me out. Because in your world, I'm probably a famous case. Because of my medal. Am I right?

DOCTOR (*Gets up, and starts to escort* D.J. *to the door*): I think we're back to where we started the hour. None of this will be easy, D.J., but I will be here the day after tomorrow, and as you say, we'll see what happens . . .

D.J. (*Interrupting*): You want to take that medal away from me, don't you?

DOCTOR (*A little stunned*): No. Why do you say that?

D.J.: Now be honest with me, man. Otherwise you're going to turn my head around backwards, for good. . . .

The DOCTOR *and* D.J. *look at each other for a long beat.*

DOCTOR: No, D.J., I don't want to take that medal, or anything else away from you. But when the time is ripe, when you are ready, you may not need it anymore. That's why *you* spoke, early this hour, of wanting to get rid of it, sometimes, and of "throwing it in their faces." You see, part of you already wants to throw it away, while—

D.J. (*Pulling away*): Throw it away!? (*Angrily*) You're the one who's crazy. You know what I'd be without that medal? I'd be just another invisible Nigger, waiting on line and getting shit on just for being there! I *told* you about that, man! You just don't *listen*!

DOCTOR: That's one of the very things that's driving you crazy.

D.J.: What is?

DOCTOR: That once again, in Detroit, you have been singled out from all the others.

D.J.: What are you talking about?

DOCTOR (*Pursuing* D.J.): You know what I'm talking about! It's the same story as the tank, all over again. Why are all the others suffering, on the streets, and only you have been spared? But you haven't been spared, and you *are* suffering. . . .

D.J.: So what are *you* doing? You going around telling every dude who has the Congressional Medal of Honor to just throw it away? You just dropping out of the sky into every hospital and nuthouse in the country, scrambling up the brains of everybody who—

DOCTOR (*Pouncing*): You think, then, that everybody with the Medal of Honor must be in some kind of hospital?

D.J.: Did I say that?

DOCTOR: You did. You let it slip out. . . . In some deep way, you agree with me.

D.J.: That what?

DOCTOR: That the medal can make a man sick—drive him into a hospital.

D.J.: The whole thing makes a man sick! There's a lot of sick vets who didn't get no Medal of Honor! And they're mainlining and getting beat up in the streets and sucking on the gin bottle, and they didn't get no Bronze Star, no nothing except maybe a Purple Heart and a *"less than honorable discharge"*—bad paper, man, you can't get a job, you can't get benefits, you can't get nothing if you got bad paper. Now you tell me, what does my medal have to do with *that?*

A knock on the door—on the words "bad paper, man"—and the GUARD *immediately enters. Poker-faced,* HE *listens to the end of* D.J.'s *tirade.*

GUARD: Has the summation been concluded, sir?

D.J.: God *damn.*

DOCTOR: Will you please wait just a minute?

GUARD: You'll have to contact chief of section, sir, about that.

D.J.(*Heated*): Didn't you hear the man? Now, fuck off!

DOCTOR: D.J.—

GUARD: Look, Sergeant. To him you're an important case, but to me you're just another nut.

D.J. (*Makes a threatening move at the* GUARD): Just another nut. Okay. . .

The GUARD *prepares to subdue* D.J. *with his club, if necessary. In no time, a serious scuffle is ready to break out.*

DOCTOR (*Throwing himself between them*): Will both of you stop this! That's an order!

GUARD: Sorry about that, sir. (*Returns to parade rest; stares stonily ahead*)

D.J.: I'll bet you are.

The DOCTOR *looks from one to the other of these near-combatants.* D.J. *is still simmering, with his back to him.*

DOCTOR: D.J. Do you watch TV here?

D.J.: Some.

DOCTOR: The news?

D.J.: Not if I can help it.

DOCTOR: You didn't see it? The other night?

D.J.: What?

DOCTOR: The medals . . . (*Watching* D.J. *closely*) Vietnam vets. Heroes? In wheelchairs, some of them; on crutches? At the Capitol steps? Washington? Throwing their medals away? A kind of miracle-scene, like the old—

D.J. (*Breaking in*): And that's what you want me to do! Hop right on down there and toss it up—

DOCTOR: You saw it?

D.J.: *I didn't see nothing!*

DOCTOR: Some of those men . . . I happen to know some of those men. . . .

D.J.: You cured them?

DOCTOR: They're curing themselves. And they're a lot like you. (D.J. *watches, noncommittal*) . . . But they refuse to stay isolated. They meet, in therapy groups, which they started. Up in New York. "Rap sessions" . . . a new kind of unit, you might say. . . . Everybody tells his story. You see? They're people who have been through the same fires you have, who were *there*, whom you can trust. . . .

D.J. (*After a pause*): Doc, those dudes on TV are all white.

DOCTOR: You *have* been watching them.

D.J.: Yup, and I'm going to tell you something. You got your reasons for wanting to see no more war, right?—and no more warriors. I dig that, for your sake. But a lot of folks don't want the black veteran to throw down *his* weapons so soon. Know what I mean? Like, we are supposed to be preparing ourselves for another war, right back here. Vietnam was just our basic training, see? I'm telling this to both of you, y'see, so you won't be too surprised when it comes.

> The GUARD *looks to the* DOCTOR *for instructions.*

DOCTOR (*To* D.J.): Why are you saying this right now?

D.J.: I want you to have something to think about, for the next session. Give us a good starting point. . . .

DOCTOR: Still poking fun at me?

D.J. (HE *waits a moment, then smiles and gives the* DOCTOR *a pat on the arm*): Don't you worry, Doc. I'll be seeing you. You just sit down now, and write your notes. In the folder.

> D.J. *walks to the door, where the* GUARD *momentarily blocks him, in order to give a last, official salute to the* DOCTOR. *The* DOCTOR *gives a half-despairing wave as* D.J. *watches.* D.J. *turns to the door, stops, and gives the* GUARD *an imperious cue to open the knob and make way for him. The* GUARD *does so, grudgingly. It is a minor, private triumph for* D.J. THE TWO *exit. The* DOCTOR *reflects for a moment, at his desk. Then, showing his weariness,* HE *packs up his belongings, gives the room a last look, and prepares to leave. Light on stage is reduced until* HE *is alone in the light with darkness around him. The feeling must be of a change in time. The* DOCTOR *steps forward out of the confines of the room, to the edge of the apron, and addresses the audience.*

DOCTOR: When I drove down again from New York, two days later, Dale Jackson did not appear for his hour of therapy. He was in fact AWOL, back in Detroit. He intended to do something about his money troubles. His wife was in a hospital for minor surgery, and he had been unable to pay the deposit. There were numerous protectors he might have gone to in the city for help—people who would not have allowed a Medal of Honor winner to sink into scandalous debt. But he went to none of them, this time. His wife was disturbed about the bill. This was on the evening of April 30. He promised her that he would come back to the hospital that night with a check, and also with her hair curlers and bathrobe. As he was leaving, he said, "Ain't you going to give me a kiss goodbye?" And he put his thumb in his mouth like a little boy, which made her laugh. He asked some friends to drive him to a place where he claimed he could get some money, and asked them to park—in a white section of town. He walked down the block, entered a grocery store and told the manager he was holding it up. He took out a pistol, but never fired a shot while the manager emptied his own gun, at point-blank range, into D.J.'s body. Death came, a few hours later, in Detroit General Hospital, of five gunshot wounds. His body went on a last unexpected jet airplane ride to Arlington National Cemetery, where he was given a hero's burial with an eight-man Army Honor Guard. I wrote to his mother about him, about what a remarkable human being even I could see he was, in only sixty minutes with him. She wrote back: "Sometimes I wonder if Dale tired of this life and needed someone else to pull the trigger." In her living room she keeps a large color photograph of him, in uniform, with the Congressional Medal of Honor around his neck.

Lights slow-fade down to darkness, as the DOCTOR *walks off. Blackout; and then lights up as the* DOCTOR, DALE JACKSON *and the* GUARD *converge, stand side-by-side, and bow to the audience.*

END OF PLAY

MOONCHILDREN

Michael Weller

About Michael Weller

Born in New York in 1942, Michael Weller studied music composition at Brandeis before taking his graduate degree in theatre at the University of Manchester in England. He taught, acted, wrote and directed in England, Italy and Germany for a number of years before returning to the States. *Moonchildren* is the first play of what may be thought of as a Weller trilogy about growing up in America; the middle play, *Fishing*, was premiered by the New York Shakespeare Festival in 1975 and revived by New York's Second Stage in 1981. *Loose Ends*, the third play, opened at Arena Stage in Washington, D.C. and then moved to New York's Circle in the Square in 1979. Originally a one-act, *Split* evolved into *At Home (Split, Part 1)* and *Abroad (Split, Part 2)*, and was so presented by Second Stage in 1980. Weller's most recent play, *The Ballad of Soapy Smith*, was originally produced by Seattle Repertory Theatre before playing at New York's Public Theatre in 1984. Weller is the author of the screenplays for two Milos Forman films, *Hair* and *Ragtime*.

Production History

Moonchildren premiered under the title *Cancer* at the Royal Court Theatre in London in September 1970, in a production co-directed by Roger Hendricks Simon and Peter Gill. The American premiere took place at Arena Stage in November 1970, under the direction of Alan Schneider. Schneider's production opened on Broadway in February 1972.

Characters

MIKE
COOTIE
NORMAN
RUTH
DICK
KATHY
BOB
RALPH
WILLIS

LUCKY
SHELLY
BREAM
EFFING
MURRAY
COOTIE'S FATHER
MILKMAN

Time

1965-66.

Place

A student apartment in an American university town.

The Play

Moonchildren

Scene 1

The stage is dark. You can't see anything.

MIKE: I heard something. She definitely made a noise.

RUTH: Shut up.

MIKE: I'm telling you, I know the noise they make. That was it.

RUTH: For crissakes, be quiet. You keep talking and she'll know we're here.

COOTIE: I was just thinking. I read somewhere about how they can see in the dark.

RUTH: I never read that.

COOTIE: No shit, I read they got these hundreds of thousands of millions of tiny, submicroscopic, photosensitive cells in each eyeball, so when it gets dark they can just turn on these cells and see like it was daytime.

MIKE: He's right, Ruth. Hey, Cootie, you're right. I remember reading that in a back issue of the *Vertebrate Review*.

COOTIE: That's it, that's the one. Special eyeball issue.

MIKE: Yeah, yeah. July.

RUTH: You guys must be pretty stupid if you believe that. What do you think they have whiskers for? The whole point of whiskers in the first place is so you can get around in the dark. That's why they stick out so far, so you don't bump into things. Chairs and refrigerators and that.

MIKE: Hey, shhhh. I think she's starting.

154

RUTH: Well, you're the one that got me going about whiskers in the first place, so don't tell me shhhh.

MIKE: O.K., O.K., I'm sorry, O.K.?

RUTH: So shut up if she's starting.

COOTIE (*Pause*): How many kittens can they have at any one session?

MIKE: There's a recorded case of thirty-eight.

RUTH: Shhhh, for chrissakes.

COOTIE: What I want to know is how are we gonna see her when she starts giving birth?

RUTH: Jesus, how stupid can you get? We'll turn on the light.

COOTIE: Yeah, but the whole thing is how do we know when to turn on the light? Like, what if we're too early?

MIKE: Or too late?

COOTIE: Yeah, what if we're too late?

MIKE: Or right in the middle . . .

COOTIE: Holy shit, yeah, what if we flip on the old lights when she's halfway through a severe uterine contraction? She'll go apeshit and clamp up and kill the kitten. And if the kitty gets really lucky and wriggles free, it'll grow up into a pretty fucked-up animal.

MIKE: We're sowing the seeds of a neurotic adult cathood . . .

COOTIE: . . . doo-wah, doo-wah . . .

RUTH: Hey, shut up, you guys, willya? Willya shut up?

COOTIE: We're just pointing out that's a shitty way to start life.

RUTH: I know the noise, all right?

MIKE: I think there's probably a more scientific way to watch a cat give birth.

RUTH: Everybody shut the fuck up.

A long pause.

NORMAN: How much longer are you guys gonna have the lights out?

COOTIE: Jesus Christ, Norman, why do you have to go creeping up like that? We forgot you were even in here.

NORMAN: I'm not creeping up. I'm just sitting here. Maybe you didn't notice when you came in, but I was reading this book. I mean, I thought you were only gonna have the lights out for maybe a few minutes or something, but you've already been in here for about an hour and . . . I really can't read very well with the lights off. I mean . . . you know . . .

COOTIE: Norman, you can't rush a cat when it's giving birth. You try to rush a cat in those circumstances and you come smack up against nature.

MIKE: Norman . . .

NORMAN: What?

MIKE: Don't fight nature, Norman.

NORMAN: I'm not. I'm just trying to read this book.

COOTIE (*Pause*): Is it a good book?

RUTH: For chrissakes, what's the matter with everyone?

NORMAN: I don't know. It's a pretty good book. I don't follow all of it. It's written in a funny kind of way, so you forget a lot of it right after you've read it. A lot of guys in the mathematics department say it's pretty good. I don't know though.

RUTH: Hey, Norman, can't you go to your room if you want to read?

NORMAN: I don't want to.

MIKE: Why not, Norman?

COOTIE: Yeah, why do you want to creep around in here being all spooky and everything when you could just go to your room and read, huh?

NORMAN: I don't know.

COOTIE: We may be in here for hours and hours, Norman. Maybe even all night. The whole operation from initial labor to the biting off of the umbilical cord could very easily take an entire night. (*Pause*) Norman?

NORMAN: All night, huh?

COOTIE: You never know.

RUTH: Brother, you try to get a few guys to shut up for a little while . . .

MIKE (*Loud*): C'mon, c'mon, hey, everybody, let's have a little quiet around here. I don't want to see anyone panic and lose their heads and start running in all different directions knocking down passersby and trampling on innocent women and children.

RUTH: I swear to Christ, Mike, if you don't shut up I'll kill you.

MIKE: O.K.

At this point, the hall door opens and the kitchen is lit up a little. DICK *is standing in the doorway trying to see into the dark, where* NORMAN *is sitting at a round kitchen table with a book by him, and* RUTH, MIKE *and* COOTIE *are crouched around a cardboard carton with a hole in it.* NORMAN *grabs up his book to take advantage of the crack of light.* DICK *just stands there.* RUTH *and* COOTIE *speak on top of each other.*

RUTH: Hey, c'mon, shut the door, Dick.

COOTIE: Shut the fucking door.

MIKE (*After a pause*): We'd really like you to shut the door, Richard.

DICK *shuts the door and everything goes black. A moment later it all lights up again because* DICK *has just opened the icebox and it's the kind that has an automatic light inside. So now we see* DICK *squatting in front of the icebox while the* OTHERS *watch him, except for* NORMAN, *who's really trying like mad to read. You can see the kitchen pretty clearly now. The icebox is very old, dating from the time when electricity was replacing the iceman. It's just a box on legs with one of those barrel-shaped coolers with vents on top. You maybe can't see it yet, but on the door of the icebox there's a large inscription that reads "GOD IS COOL." Stacked neatly against one wall are 816 empty two-*

quart milk bottles, layer upon layer with planks between each level. It's a deliberate construction. There's a huge copper stack heater in one corner by the sink, and it has a safety valve at the top with a copper tube coming out of it and snaking into the sink. The floor is vinyl, in imitation cork, alternating light and dark, but the conspicuous thing about this floor is that it's only half-finished. Where the cork tiles end there is a border of black tar, by now hard, and then wooden floor in broad plank. Around the kitchen table are six chairs, all from different sets. Various posters on the wall, but none as conspicuous as a map of Europe near where the telephone hangs. The sink is full of dirty dishes. There is a pad hanging by the icebox, and a pencil. Everyone uses the kitchen in a special way. So DICK *is squatting in front of the open icebox.*

RUTH: That's very cute, Richard.

MIKE: C'mon, shut the fucking icebox. We were in here first.

NORMAN: I was reading when you guys came in.

DICK *turns to them, looks, then turns back to the icebox.*

COOTIE: Dick, in my humble opinion you're a miserable cunt and a party pooper.

DICK (*Standing*): All right, now listen. This afternoon I went down to the Star Supermarket and got myself four dozen frozen hamburgers. Now that's forty-eight hamburgers, and I only had two of them for dinner tonight.

RUTH: And you never washed up.

MIKE: Hey, Dick, are those Star hamburgers any good?

DICK: Listen, I should have forty-six hamburgers, and when I counted just now there was only forty-three. Three hamburgers in one night. And for your information I've been keeping track of my hamburgers since the beginning of the semester. There's almost fifty hamburgers I can't account for.

COOTIE: Jesus, Dick, you should have said something before this.

MIKE: Yeah, Dick, you had all them hamburger thefts on your mind, you should have let it out. It's no good keeping quiet about something like that.

DICK: Look, I'm not about to make a stink about a couple of hamburgers here and there, but, Jesus Christ, almost sixty of them. I'm putting it down on common stock and we're gonna all pay for it. (HE *turns on the light*)

RUTH: Dick, willya turn out the light, please?

DICK: I'm sorry, but I've lost too many hamburgers. I'm putting down for four dozen. (HE *goes to the pad on the wall and makes an entry*)

RUTH: Now willya turn the light out?

DICK (*Examining list*): Shit, who put peanut butter down on common stock?

MIKE: I did. I got a jar of chunky last Thursday and when I opened it on Saturday somebody'd already been in there. I didn't eat all that chunky myself.

DICK: Well, I never had your peanut butter. I'm not paying for it.

MIKE: Well, I never had any of your goddamn sixty hamburgers either.

COOTIE: I think I may have had some of that chunky peanut butter. Could you describe your jar of chunky in detail?

MIKE: Elegant little glass jar, beige interior . . .

KATHY *enters through the front door, as opposed to the hall door. The hall door leads to everyone's rooms.*

KATHY: Oh, boy, look out for Bob. (SHE *starts across the kitchen to the hall door.* SHE *carries lots of books in a green canvas waterproof book bag slung over her shoulder*)

RUTH: What's wrong with Bob?

KATHY: He's in a really shitty mood. I've seen the guy act weird before. This is, I don't know, pretty bad, I guess.

MIKE: Where is he?

COOTIE: Yeah, where's Bob?

MIKE: Good old Bob.

COOTIE: Where's good old Bob?

KATHY: And fuck you too. I'm serious.

NORMAN (*Looking up from his book*): Boy, I really can't absorb very much with everyone talking.

KATHY: We were just sitting there, you know, in Hum 105, and that prick Johnson started in about the old cosmic equation again.

NORMAN: What's the cosmic equation?

RUTH: So why'd that upset Bob?

KATHY: I don't know. That's the thing . . .

DICK: I bet Bob's responsible for some of my hamburgers. I notice you and him never go shopping for dinner.

KATHY: It's really weird the way he sort of . . . well, like today, you know . . . I'm not kidding, he might be cracking up or something.

BOB *enters through the front door, carrying his books.* HE *looks all right.* EVERYONE *stares at him.*

RUTH: Hi, Bob.

MIKE: Hi, Bob.

COOTIE: Hi, Bob.

NORMAN: Hello, Bob.

BOB (*Pause*): Hi, Mike, hi, Ruth, hi, Cootie; hello, Norman. (*Pause*) Hi, Dick.

DICK: Listen, do you know anything about . . . ?

BOB: No, I haven't touched your fucking hamburgers.

DICK: Well, someone has.

MIKE: How you been, good old Bob?

COOTIE: How's the old liver and the old pancreas and the old pituitary and the . . .

BOB: Is there any mail?

COOTIE: There's this really big package from Beirut. It took four guys to get it up the stairs.

MIKE: We think it's a harp.

RUTH: There's a letter in your room.

BOB *looks at them quizzically, then goes down the hall.* KATHY *follows him.*

RUTH: I think Kathy's right. There's definitely something wrong with Bob.

DICK: Yeah, he's out of his fucking mind, that's what's wrong with him.

RUTH: You can talk.

MIKE: Hey, c'mon, c'mon, let's have a little order around here . . .

RUTH: Stop fucking around. You heard what Kathy said. Something's troubling Bob.

MIKE: So what?

COOTIE: Yeah, fuck Bob.

MIKE: Fuck good old Bob.

NORMAN: Maybe he's worried about the future. (ALL *look at him*) I mean, you know, maybe he's worried about it. I mean, I don't know him all that well. Just, you know, maybe he's worried about what he's gonna do when, you know, after he graduates and everything.

DICK: He ought to be worried.

MIKE: You bet your ass he oughta be. Same goes for all of you guys. You oughta be worried, Dick. Cootie, you oughta be worried. I oughta be worried. I am. I'm fucking petrified. You watch what happens at the graduation ceremony. There's gonna be this line of green military buses two miles long parked on the road outside and they're gonna pick us up and take us to Vietnam and we'll be walking around one day in the depths of the rain forest looking out for wily enemy snipers and carnivorous insects and tropical snakes that can eat a whole moose in one gulp and earthworms sixteen feet long and then one day when we least expect it this wily sniper'll leap out from behind a blade of grass and powie. Right in the head. I'm worried.

DICK: Anyone that can spell can get out of Vietnam.

NORMAN: I'm in graduate school. They can't get me.

DICK: Norman, you couldn't buy your way into the army.

NORMAN: I wouldn't go.

MIKE: Why wouldn't you go, Norman?

NORMAN: Huh?

COOTIE: Yeah, think of the army. What about them? They need good mathematics graduate students out there in the marshes of Quac Thop Chew Hoy Ben Van Pho Quay Gup Trin.

NORMAN: I don't agree with the war.

MIKE: Well, for God sakes, then, let's stop it.

NORMAN: I had my medical and everything. I passed. I could've pretended I was insane or something.

DICK: Pretended?

RUTH: Hey, doesn't anyone here give a shit about Bob?

MIKE: Hey, c'mon, everyone that gives a shit raise your hand. (COOTIE, MIKE, DICK *and* NORMAN *raise their hands*) See, we all give a shit. So what should we do?

RUTH: Well, I don't know. Maybe we ought to try and find out what's troubling him.

DICK: Maybe he doesn't want us to know. Just maybe.

COOTIE: Yeah, what if he's teetering on the brink of a complete schizophrenic withdrawal and the only thing keeping him sane is knowing we don't know what's troubling him.

MIKE: It's our duty as classmates and favorite turds to leave him alone.

RUTH: Maybe something's wrong between him and Kathy.

DICK: Like what?

RUTH: I don't know. That's what I'm asking.

DICK: He doesn't give a shit about her. Not really. She's just a good lay, that's all.

RUTH: How would you know, Dick?

NORMAN: I thought they were in love.

DICK: Jesus, Norman, where the hell is your head at?

NORMAN: Huh?

MIKE: Define the problem, then solve it.

COOTIE: Yeah, what's troubling good old Bob?

MIKE: I think we oughta all go to bed tonight with notebooks under our pillows, and when we get a well-focused and comprehensive idea about the central dilemma of Bob's existence we oughta write it down in clear, concise sentences, with particular attention to grammar and punctuation.

COOTIE: Yeah, then we can meet in here tomorrow and pool our insights.

MIKE: That's a really great plan.

RUTH: I'd really like to know what's troubling him.

DICK: I'd really like to know who the fuck is eating my hamburgers.

NORMAN: Why don't you talk to him?

RUTH: What?

NORMAN: I mean, you know—Bob. If you want to find out what's troubling him, probably the best thing to do is talk to him and say, What's troubling you, or something like that, and then if he wants to tell you he can and if he doesn't feel like talking about it . . . then . . . well, you know . . . .

RUTH: Yeah, maybe I'll do that.

NORMAN (*Pause*): Yeah, that's what I'd do if I wanted to know. I mean, I'm not saying I wouldn't like to know what's troubling him. I'd really like to know if you find out, but I . . .

> MIKE *has been kneeling by the cat box and peering into it.*

MIKE: Jesus Christ. Jesus H. fucking Christ.

NORMAN: What's wrong?

MIKE: She wasn't even in there.

COOTIE: What! All that time we were looking at an empty box and she wasn't even in there?

MIKE: She must've slipped out while we had our backs turned.

COOTIE: Sneaky little beastie.

MIKE: Cootie, you don't understand. She might be out there in the road right now.

COOTIE: Right now.

MIKE: With all the traffic.

COOTIE: Oh, Christ, and all those architects driving home drunk from seeing their mistresses . . .

MIKE: And trying to figure out what to tell the little woman. I mean, she's been waiting up all night in a chartreuse quilted sleeping gown with curlers in her hair . . .

COOTIE: Worrying about the kiddies. Three boys, twenty-seven girls. They all got appendicitis . . .

MIKE: Simultaneously. And when she called the kindly family doctor he was away in Cuba . . .

COOTIE: Doing research for his forthcoming book . . .

MIKE: "Chapter Eight: Peritonitis and Social Democracy."

COOTIE: Jesus, I hope we're not too late. (HE *and* MIKE *rush off down the hall*)

DICK: Hey, Norman, are these your bananas?

NORMAN: You can have one. I don't mind.

DICK *takes one and puts the others back in the icebox.* COOTIE *sticks his head in around the hall door.*

COOTIE: You coming, Ruth?

RUTH: No.

COOTIE: Your heart is full of bitterness and hate, Ruth. (*His head disappears again*)

DICK: You done the essay for Phil 720?

RUTH: No.

DICK: It's due tomorrow.

RUTH: Yeah?

DICK: Yeah.

NORMAN: Is that a good course, Philosophy 720?

RUTH: Nope. Professor Quinn is an albino dwarf queer with halitosis and he smokes too much.

DICK: He does not.

RUTH: Three packs of Pall Mall a day is too much. He's gonna die of cancer.

DICK: He's a genius.

RUTH: You have a thing about queers.

DICK: Fuck off, Ruth.

RUTH: You started it.

RUTH *goes into hall.* DICK *stands and eats his banana, chewing slowly.* NORMAN *tries to read but* DICK's *presence distracts him.*

DICK: How come you're reading that book?

NORMAN: I don't know. It's supposed to be pretty good.

DICK: What are you gonna do when you finish it?

NORMAN (*Thinks*): I'll start another one.

DICK: Yeah, but what happens when you forget this one. I mean, it'll be as if you hadn't even read it, so what's the point?

NORMAN: Oh, I don't know. I happen to believe you learn things even when you don't know it. Like, if you're reading something right now . . . I mean, I am reading something right now and maybe I'll forget it in a while . . . I mean, I'm forgetting a lot of it already, but I happen to believe I'm being altered in lots of ways I may not be aware of because of . . . well, you know, books and experiences. (*Pause*) Life.

DICK: That's what you believe, huh?

NORMAN: Um, yes, I believe that.

MIKE *and* COOTIE *enter, wearing heavy winter parkas and boots.* THEY *look like trappers.*

COOTIE: Boy, if we're too late I hate to think of all the dead cats we'll have on our conscience.

MIKE: You gonna help, Dick?

DICK: Fuck off.

MIKE: How about you, Norman, aren't you gonna do your bit for the world of cats?

NORMAN: I'm just in the middle of this chapter. (MIKE *and* COOTIE *shake their heads in disapproval and rush out.* NORMAN *tries to read again as* DICK *eats the banana, watching him*) Hey, it's really hard to read, you know, when someone's watching you and everything.

DICK: Don't you ever get the feeling you're really irrelevant?

NORMAN: I don't think so.

DICK (*In one breath*): I mean, you go into the mathematics department every day and sit there looking out the window and thinking about cars and women and every now and then a couple of numbers come into your head and there's all these Chinese guys running around solving all the problems worth solving while you sit there wondering what the hell you're doing.

NORMAN: No, it's not like that. Well, you know, it's not that simple. I mean . . . (*Pause*) I guess it's a lot like that. Are you doing anything relevant?

DICK: You can't get more relevant than Far Eastern studies. Ask me anything about the Far East and I'll tell you the answer. That's where everything's happening. China, Vietnam, Japan, Korea. You name it.

NORMAN: I guess I ought to know more about those things. I don't know, I keep thinking there's a lot of things I should know about.

DICK: The thing is, Norman, the way I see it, you're already deeply committed to the system. You take away black ghettos, stop the war in Vietnam, distribute the wealth equally throughout the country, and you wouldn't be in graduate school.

NORMAN: How come?

DICK: You see, you don't know anything about what makes it all work, do you? (HE *throws the banana peel into the cat box*)

NORMAN: Hey, you shouldn't throw that in there.

DICK: Why not?

NORMAN: Well, I mean, that's the box for the cat. Maybe she won't want to have kittens on a banana peel.

DICK: Norman, how long have you been living here?

NORMAN: Well, you know, about three months. A little longer maybe. About three months and two weeks altogether.

DICK: Have you ever seen a cat around here?

NORMAN: Well, I don't know. I'm out a lot of the time.

DICK: Norman, there is no fucking cat. We haven't got a cat. Boy, for a graduate student you got a lot to learn. (HE *starts out but turns to look* NORMAN *over a last time*) Jesus.

Then DICK's *gone down the hall.* NORMAN *kneels by the cat box and examines it as some muffled piano chords fill the silence. It's* BOB *playing a lazy, rich, drifting progression, moody-Bill-Evans-style.* KATHY *walks through the kitchen in a man's robe carrying a towel.* SHE *lights the stack heater. From inside the hall we hear* DICK's *voice yelling.*

DICK (*Offstage*): STOP PLAYING THAT FUCKING NOISE. I'M TRYING TO READ. HEY, BOB.

KATHY (*Goes to the hall door and yells down*): Mind your own goddamn business, Richard. (*A door slams, and the music, which had stopped momentarily, starts again, but louder.* SHE *turns*) Hey, listen, Norman. If you're gonna be in here for a while could you do me a favor and make sure no one turns off the water heater, 'cause I'm just taking a shower. And if you get a chance, could you put on some coffee, 'cause I'll be coming out in about ten minutes and I'd like a cup when I come out. O.K.?

NORMAN: Do you have any books on Vietnam?

KATHY (*Pause*): Yeah. A few.

NORMAN: Are they good books?

KATHY: Well, you know, some are, some aren't. Why?

NORMAN: I just, you know, wondered, that's all. (KATHY *watches* NORMAN *go to the stove and fumble around with the coffee percolator.* SHE *shrugs and goes out. We hear the bathroom door close and, moments later, the sound of a shower running*) Actually, I've been thinking I'd like to read some books about Vietnam. I mean it's been going on all this time. I don't know, though. I've never read any books about it. Maybe if I could read one book, then I'd know a little more about it and I could decide if I wanted to read another. Would it be O.K. if I borrowed one of your books to start with? I'd give it back as soon as I finished it. (HE *looks around and sees* HE's *alone.* HE *goes out the door. We hear the bathroom door opening and a yell*)

KATHY (*Offstage*): Goddammit, Norman, what are you doing in here?

NORMAN (*Offstage*): I was wondering if you'd lend me . . .

KATHY (*Offstage*): Hey, get the hell out of here, I'm taking a shower.

A door slams.

NORMAN (*Offstage*): I just wanted to know if it was O.K. for me to borrow one of those books about Vietnam.

KATHY (*Offstage*): Well, Jesus Christ, can't you wait till I'm done?

NORMAN (*Offstage*): Oh . . . yeah, I'm sorry. (*Pause*) Is that all right with you?

KATHY (*Offstage*): Hey, don't stand around out there. You can borrow as many goddamn books as you want, only get away from the door, 'cause it just so happens I don't like a lot of people standing around outside the bathroom door while I'm washing.

NORMAN *comes back into the kitchen.* HE *fixes a little more of the coffee, then goes to the hall door and yells down the hallway.*

NORMAN: I'll just make the coffee first, and when you're finished in there I'll come down to your room with you and get the book. Hey, listen, if you decide to have your coffee in here, could you go down to your room first and bring the book in with you? Yes, that's probably better. Hey, is that O.K.? (*Pause*) Hey, is that O.K.?

No answer. NORMAN *is left baffled, as the lights dim and* BOB's *piano chords keep going and going.*

Scene 2

It's a few days later. NORMAN *is reading.* RUTH *is making sandwiches, and* COOTIE *and* MIKE *are rolling up a banner.*

COOTIE: I don't know about the wording.

MIKE: I think it's pretty good wording.

COOTIE: I'm not too happy about it.

MIKE: You're unhappy about the wording.

COOTIE: Well, I'm not, you know, cut up about it or anything, but I'm definitely not as happy as I could be about it.

MIKE: Ruthie, we need an impartial third voice over here.

RUTH: Who wants orange marmalade?

MIKE: I'd like an orange marmalade.

COOTIE: I want two orange marmalade and one chunky peanut butter, please.

RUTH: How 'bout you, Norman?

COOTIE: And I wouldn't mind a chunky peanut butter and orange marmalade mixed.

RUTH: Hey, Norman, do you want sandwiches or not?

COOTIE: You gotta have sandwiches handy if you're coming, Norman. On your average march you'll find you get through a good two peanut butter and jellies before you even get to where you're supposed to demonstrate, and then after circling round and yelling militant slogans at the monument or park or poison gas plant or nuclear missile establishment for a couple hours, you're just about ready for another peanut butter and jelly.

MIKE: Or cream cheese and olives.

COOTIE: Bacon, lettuce, and tomato. I mean, I know you meet a lotta pretty groovy people at these marches, but you can't count on them having extra sandwiches for a new acquaintance.

RUTH: Hey, Norman, willya please tell me if you're coming with us or not?

NORMAN (*Unfriendly*): I'm going with Dick.

COOTIE: You're lucky there. You'll get hamburger on toasted roll if you go with Dick. He takes sterno and cooks right out there in the middle of lines of charging cops and tear gas and mace and everything.

DICK *enters*.

MIKE: Hey, Dick, you better hurry up and get dressed for the march.

COOTIE: Yeah, Dick, you don't want to be late or all the best ass'll be grabbed up.

DICK (*Indicating banner*): What's it say?

COOTIE: "Buy Government Bonds."

RUTH: You want some of our peanut butter and marmalade?

MIKE: What's this about giving away all our peanut butter and marmalade all of a sudden? He wouldn't give us any of his lousy hamburgers. We had to pay for those hamburgers on common stock.

DICK: Where's Kathy and Bob?

MIKE: Yeah, where's good old Bob? (*Yells*) HEY, YOU GUYS, ARE YOU COMING?

KATHY (*Offstage*): Yeah, hold on a minute, willya?

MIKE: They're coming.

COOTIE: Hey, Norman, I been watching you pretty closely for the last few days and I have this definite impression you've been displaying hostility toward me, Mike, and Ruth, in that order.

NORMAN: I'm just reading this book . . .

COOTIE: Don't be negative, Norman. You're trying to pretend I hadn't noticed your emotions. You happen to be up against a disciple of Freud, Jung, Adler, Pavlov, Skinner, and the honorable L. Ron Hubbard, to mention but a few. It just so happens I can detect subatomic trace particles of hostility within a six-mile radius of anywhere I am.

MIKE: It's no use contradicting him, Norman. If he says he can feel hostility, that's it. I mean, even I can feel it and I'm only moderately sensitive to hostility up to about a hundred eighty yards.

NORMAN: I'm not feeling hostile . . .

COOTIE: You're not only feeling it, you're dying to tell us about it. That's a basic axiom of hostility.

NORMAN: Oh, boy, you guys.

DICK: Leave him alone.

COOTIE: Dick, that's the worst thing you can do. I know you think you're being a good shit and everything, but if the guy is riddled with hostility and he doesn't get it out of his system, it's gonna go haywire and zing all around inside his body till he's twenty-eight years old and then he'll get cancer.

RUTH: You know, we're gonna be really late if those guys don't hurry up . . .

MIKE: That reminds me of a guy I was reading about. He got so pent up with hostility his head fell right down inside his body, no shit, that's what I was reading, right down between his shoulders.

COOTIE: Fell?

MIKE: Yeah, straight down till all you could see was these two little eyeballs peeping out over his collarbone.

COOTIE: Mike.

MIKE: What, Mel?

COOTIE (Pause): Fell?

MIKE (Pause): Sank?

COOTIE: Subsided.

MIKE: Right.

COOTIE: In fact, as I remember it, his head eventually disappeared completely.

MIKE: Don't rush me, I'm coming to that. Now, Norman, I want you to pay very close attention because this case is a lesson in itself. You see, everybody used to warn this particular guy to loosen up and maybe see an analyst, but the guy refused on the grounds that it would cost too much, and that turned out to be really stupid economy, because with his head inside him like that he couldn't see anything and he had to hire a guy, full time, seven days a week, to lead him around. The guy was so tight with his money he tried to solve the problem by rigging up this ingenious system of mirrors, like a periscope, but the natural movements of his body kept knocking the mirrors out of alignment, so in addition to the guy that led him around, he had to hire another guy, full time, seven days a week, to keep readjusting the mirrors. You can imagine the expense involved.

COOTIE: There was a very fine article about that guy in the *Hostility Journal*, spring number. Did you happen to catch that article, Norman?

MIKE: Did it tell about what happened to him?

COOTIE: Well, it was one of those stories in two parts, and wouldn't you know it, that's just when my subscription ran out.

MIKE: Oh, well, you missed the best part. You see, when his head got down as . . . *subsided* as far as his stomach . . .

COOTIE: . . . thank you . . .

MIKE: . . . he went and hired a topnotch transplant surgeon to replace his belly button with a flexible, clear plastic window so he could see where he was going.

COOTIE: Jumpin' Jehoshaphat!

MIKE: And I'm happy to announce, the operation was a complete success.

COOTIE: Fantastic! No problems with rejection or anything?

MIKE: Nope. The Dow Chemical Company set up a ten-man, two-woman research team and they developed a type of clear plastic window that matched the guy's antibodies perfectly. In a matter of weeks, the guy was able to live a completely normal life again, skin diving, stamp collecting, a lot of political work. He could even go to the movies when he felt like it, but he had to sit up on the back of the seat and it caused a lot of hard feelings with the people sitting directly behind him. But that's the great thing about the average moviegoing audience; they respected his infirmity.

COOTIE: Fuck a duck!

MIKE: Shut up, sonny boy, I ain't finished yet.

COOTIE: There's more?

MIKE: Yeah, you see, the really incredible thing was when the guy woke up one morning and realized his head was still sinking . . .

COOTIE: . . . subsiding . . .

MIKE: . . . and he went to this doctor to check it out. He was just walking along, you know, and when he got to this corner to stop for a red light a dog peed on his leg, and when he bent forward to see what was making his pants wet a guy up on some scaffolding right behind dropped a pipe wrench on his back, and the impact of this wrench, plus the slightly inclined position of the guy's upper body, knocked his head back into place.

COOTIE: Hot diggity!

MIKE: Well, the guy went apeshit, jumping all over the place, singing songs right out there on the streets . . . and that's just when it all had to happen. This poor guy, after all his suffering, was finally looking forward to a happy and produtive life . . .

COOTIE: Oh, shit, yeah, I remember now. The poor son of a bitch.

MIKE: Yeah, you 'member, he was just standing out there in the street stopping traffic in both directions, tears of humble gratitude streaming down his cheeks and some stupid . . . (HE *sees* KATHY *and* BOB *standing in the hallway door ready for the march*) . . . oh, hi, Bob, hi, Kathy.

RUTH: Hey, do you guys want some of our peanut butter and marmalade?

BOB: I've got an announcement.

COOTIE: We used to have a nearsighted canary . . .

RUTH: Listen, I gotta make these sandwiches and we're gonna end up short if I don't get some cooperation around here.

COOTIE: Hey, Norman hasn't even got a banner. Norman, aren't you gonna bring a banner?

BOB: Mel, willya please shut up? I'm trying to tell you guys something.

COOTIE: Well, fuck you, I'm talking to Norman. You want him to get all the way down to the demonstration and they disqualify him 'cause he doesn't have a banner.

RUTH: Everyone is gonna fucking well eat whatever I make.

DICK: You want some help?

RUTH: Look, it's not like I don't know how to make sandwiches . . .

MIKE: Hey, everyone, c'mon, c'mon, let's have a little order around here. Everybody stay where you are and don't panic. O.K., Bob, I think we got everything under control now.

BOB: Thank you.

MIKE: That's O.K., Bob.

BOB: I've just got this . . .

MIKE: Bob?

BOB: What?

MIKE: Anytime.

BOB: What?

MIKE: Anytime you want a little peace and quiet so you can make an announcement without a lot of people talking over you, just ask me and I'll do what I can for you.

BOB: Thank you, Mike.

MIKE: That's O.K., Bob, you're a good shit.

BOB (*Hesitates, trying to find words to frame his vague thoughts. When* HE *speaks, it is halting*): Look . . . I just thought maybe it was about time somebody around here . . .

MIKE: Do you want some water or anything?

RUTH: Oh, for chrissake, shut up, Mike.

COOTIE (*Cooling things*): Yeah, shut yer mouth, sonny boy, yer creatin' a public nuisance.

RUTH: Go on, Bob.

BOB: No, no, look, all I want to say is . . . Norman, if there is one way to remain irrelevant and ineffective it's to sit with your nose buried in a book while life is raging all around you. (NORMAN *looks up and closes his book*) Thank you. O.K. Announcement . . . (HE *walks around the room, again trying to think of how to put it. As* HE *starts to speak* . . .)

MIKE: Earthquakes in Singapore . . . ?

RUTH (*Incredible rage*): SHUT UP!

BOB: Never mind.

MIKE: Sorry. I'm sorry.

KATHY: What's wrong, Bob?

BOB: Really, nothing, nothing at all. I just had this stupid thought the other day in humanities. Johnson was saying something idiotic, as usual, and I just started to watch him carefully for the first time talking to us, you know, thirty kids who think he's a prick, and I realized that he probably thinks all of us are pricks . . . and I just started to wonder what we're all doing. You know what I mean? What the fuck are we all doing, seriously, tell me, I'd really like to know . . . in twenty-five words or less . . . . No, no, sorry, come on, carnival time. Let's go marching.

KATHY: I found the letter, Bob.

BOB: What letter? (KATHY *takes an official letter out of her bag*) Kathy, where did you get that? Come on, give it here.

KATHY: We're supposed to be like all together in here. If you can't say it yourself, I'll say it for you.

BOB *is momentarily confused, then realizes that* KATHY *thinks* HE *was trying to tell everyone about the letter.* HE *finds the situation absurd, annoying and funny.*

BOB: Kathy, that letter has nothing to do with anything and it's none of your business and would you please give it back?

KATHY *hands the letter to* RUTH. RUTH *reads.*

RUTH: Oh fuck.

RUTH *hands the letter on.* EACH *reads in turn. It ends in* MIKE*'s hands.* BOB *waits impatiently as the letter makes its round.* HE*'s embarrassed and then begins to find it funny that* EVERYONE, *especially* KATHY, *has construed the letter as his problem.* MIKE *is by now looking quite seriously at him.*

BOB (*Laughing it off*): It's just for the physical. I mean, I'm not dead yet.

As BOB *says this, something amusing passes through his mind and* HE *stops talking.* MIKE *is looking at the letter again. The* OTHERS *watch* BOB.

MIKE: They misspelled your name?

BOB (*Comes out of his brief daydream*): Huh?

MIKE: Jobert.

BOB (*Amused*): Oh, yeah.

MIKE: Jobert Rettie. Dear Jobert Rettie. Hi, Jobert.

BOB: Hi, Jike.

MIKE: Good old Jobert.

COOTIE: How ya feelin', good old Jobert?

BOB: Dead, how 'bout you?

MIKE (*Sees what's happening and comes to the rescue. Pause*): Hi, Jel.

COOTIE: Hi, Jike.

MIKE: Hi, Jorman.

NORMAN: Huh?

MIKE: Hi, Jorman.

NORMAN: Oh, hi.

MIKE: Hi, Jathy, hi Jick.

DICK: Fuck off.

MIKE: Juck off? Why should I juck off, Jick?

> The doorbell rings. COOTIE *rushes over and answers it. At the door, a young* man [RALPH] *in a suit and tie and horn-rimmed glasses, with an attache case,* which HE *has concealed just out of sight behind the doorframe.*

COOTIE: Hi, Jister.

MIKE: Ask him his name, Jel.

COOTIE: What's your name?

RALPH: Ralph.

COOTIE: Hi, Jalph, I'm Jel and that's Jathy, Jorman, Jike, Jick, and Job, and we're just on our way down to City Hall to beat the shit out of some cops. Wanna come?

RALPH (*Pauses momentarily, then launches his pitch*): I'm from the University of Buffalo and I'm in the neighborhood doing market research. You don't mind my asking you a few questions, do you? (*As* HE *says this last,* HE *reaches down, takes up his concealed attache case, bends his head like making ready for a dive, and advances swiftly but deliberately into the middle of the room. This swift movement, plus the running patter, is designed to force the average housewife to back away and give ground, but since* COOTIE *merely steps aside when* RALPH *bends down for his attache case, we are treated to the entire technique out of context.* RALPH *ends up in the middle of the room still bent over, motionless.* HE *looks up and around and straightens himself, laughing nervously at* EVERYONE *watching him*) Do all you people live here?

MIKE: No, we're just using the place for a few days. This is a fantastic coincidence because the guy that lives here just went away for a few days to do a series of special guest lectures at the University of Buffalo.

RALPH: Really? No kidding? That's some coincidence, huh? That's really a fantastic coincidence. Well, ahhh, here's what I'd like to do. I'd like to interview one of you people. I'll choose one of you at random and everybody else can listen and if the guy I choose has a particular opinion that differs significantly from what the rest of you believe, we'll just stop and take a consensus, O.K.? Hey, you guys all work, don't you? I mean, you're not students or anything?

COOTIE: We mostly hold various government jobs.

RALPH: I see. Are any of you married?

RUTH: I'm married to him [MIKE] and she's married to him [KATHY *and* BOB].

BOB: Actually, we're getting a divorce.

RALPH: Oh, I'm very sorry.

BOB (*Very sincerely to* RALPH): No, please. It's just, I've been dying for a while, nothing serious, you know, but now I've decided I'm definitely dead, you see, so I'll have to change my name. It's a legal technicality. We'll marry again under my new name. Jobert. (*Pause*) Job.

RALPH: Oh . . . well . . . that's certainly very unusual. Now this is going to get a little difficult, really. I've got to improvise some of these questions because the standard form is pretty rigid, like, you know, it asks things about your children's opinions and that would hardly apply in a case like . . .

MIKE: I have several kids by a former marriage.

RUTH: Hey, how come you never told me about that?

MIKE: If you remember, dear, we did discuss it.

RALPH: Can I just edge in here, I mean, ha-ha, I don't want to interrupt a little marital tiff or anything, but, ha-ha, you know. (*To* NORMAN) And how about you sir, do you have any children?

NORMAN: I don't have any children. I'm not married.

RALPH: Well, sir, I would guess, am I right, I would guess that you are the oldest person staying here. I only mean that in the sense of responsibility. Am I right?

MIKE: The guy that actually lives here is older, but he's not here right now.

RALPH: No, he's lecturing, right? I remember, ha-ha. Now I'd just like to ask you the following question. Have you ever heard of a teaching program called the World Volumes Encyclopedia?

DICK: Hey, are you selling encyclopedias?

RUTH: Hey, yeah, are you trying to sell us a set of encyclopedias?

RALPH: I'd like to make it very clear that I am not authorized to sell any product, I'm merely doing market research.

MIKE: Jesus Christ, he's not even selling the fucking things. You go and write to the central offices and you wait for a whole year to hear from them and when they finally decide to send a guy around he's not even authorized to sell you a set. I'm not hanging around here listening to a guy that isn't even authorized to sell the World Volumes Encyclopedia while millions of women and children are dying out there in Vietnam.

MIKE *grabs the banner and starts huzzahing as* OTHERS *follow him out the door.* DICK *and* NORMAN *stay behind with* RALPH, *who is yelling after them.*

RALPH: Hey, hey, listen, I can sell you a set if you want one. (HE *turns to* DICK *and* NORMAN) Hey, do you guys really want to buy a set of encyclopedias? I can sell you a set. I got a number of deals and there's a special discount for government employees.

DICK (*To* NORMAN): You going?

NORMAN: Yes, I've been reading a lot about it lately.

DICK: You want to come with me?

NORMAN: Well, yeah, if you don't have any other plans.

DICK: O.K., hold on a minute. (HE *goes out the hall door*)

RALPH: Hey, who are all you people?

NORMAN: We just live here.

RALPH: I go to college. I don't really come from Buffalo. I live in town. I'm trying to earn some money in my spare time. Are you guys really government employees?

NORMAN: I'm a graduate student.

RALPH: Yeah, well, I didn't want to say anything, but I didn't really think you guys were government employees. What are you studying?

NORMAN: Mathematics.

RALPH: I wanted to study mathematics. My father said he wouldn't pay so I'm studying law. Boy, do I hate law. I'm living at home. Do you guys all live here together?

NORMAN: Yes.

RALPH: And . . . and the girls, too?

NORMAN: Yes.

RALPH: Oh, boy, what a life, huh? I'm gonna get me a car pretty soon. I'm saving up. The thing is, I'm not really doing too well selling encyclopedias. I can't pull it off. I wish I could figure out why. I've been thinking about it and I think maybe it's because I can't give the sales pitch credibility. That's pretty bad if I'm gonna be a lawyer because a lot of the time you have to defend people you know are guilty. The thing is, these encyclopedias are really shitty. (HE *blushes*) Sorry. I mean, you know, they're not very good.

DICK *reenters.* HE *is carefully groomed, dressed in a pea jacket and well-laundered jeans.* HE *wears a large, orange Dayglo peace button.*

DICK: You ready?

RALPH: You going out?

DICK: Listen, if you're gonna eat anything, lay off the hamburgers, O.K.?

DICK *and* NORMAN *start out.*

NORMAN: I don't see why he has to go saying he's dead. I mean, that's only for him to have a physical. It's pretty easy to fail a physical. I've heard of guys that pretend . . .

DICK *and* NORMAN *are gone.*

RALPH (*Alone, looks at the open door*): Hey!

Blackout.

Scene 3

A few hours later. KATHY *is sitting in the kitchen, upset.* RUTH *comes in the front door.* SHE *has just returned from the march.*

RUTH: Bob here?

KATHY: No.

RUTH: Hey, what's wrong. You want some coffee?

KATHY: Please. (RUTH *takes off her coat and starts making coffee*) How was it?

RUTH: Weren't you there?

KATHY: No.

RUTH: I thought you and Bob were coming. You were on the bus and everything. I got lost when the cops charged. Boy, they really got some of those guys. Fucking pigs.

KATHY: When we got there he said he didn't feel like marching.

RUTH: Why not?

KATHY: Oh, Ruthie, I don't know. I don't know anything anymore. You devote two years to a guy and what does he give you? He never even told me about the letter. Drafted, and he didn't even tell me.

RUTH: He's not drafted. The letter's for the physical. All he has to do is act queer. They're not gonna take a queer musician.

KATHY: That's what I told him on the bus. He wouldn't even listen until I called him Job.

RUTH: What?

KATHY: He said he was dead. "Bob is dead."

RUTH: Bullshit, he's putting you on.

KATHY: That's what I mean. Me. He's even putting me on. Ungrateful bastard. The things I've done for him, Ruthie. Shit, I sound just like my mother. You know what I mean. I'm not complaining, but you know, you get tired of giving all the time and nothing's coming back. You know what I told him? I said he was the first guy I ever had an orgasm with. I mean, it really made him feel good. Now I gotta live with it. How can you explain something like that.

RUTH: Hey, no shitting around, did he really say he was gonna join?

KATHY: Ruthie, I'm telling you, he's serious. You know what he told me? He thinks the whole antiwar movement is a goddamn farce. I mean, Jesus, I really thought we were relating on that one. It's not like I'm asking the guy to go burn himself or anything but, I mean, he knows how I feel about the war and he's just doing it to be shitty. There's something behind it, I know that. He's like reaching out, trying to relate to me on the personal level by rejecting me but, like, I don't know how to break through. He says he's gonna study engineering in the army and then when he gets out he's gonna get some kind of plastic job and marry a plastic wife and live in a plastic house in some plastic suburb and have two point seven children. Oh, shit, Ruth, it's all too much. He went to a cowboy film.

RUTH: Well, you know, that's how it is.

KATHY: But Ruth, it's not like a fantasy scene. I know the guy. He'll go through with it. I mean, he really thinks he's serious. He doesn't see it's all part of a communication thing between him and me.

RUTH: I don't know. Like, maybe he's really serious. Mike's got this thing about physics. His tutor says he's a genius. O.K., maybe he is, like what do I know about physics? The thing is, he's gonna end up working for his old man in the lumber business. It's all laid out from the start. You have to fit in.

KATHY: You don't want him to do that, do you? If the guy is into physics you've gotta really stand behind him and make it all happen for him.

RUTH: I don't know. You have some kids and everything. I mean it's not like you can't have a meaningful life if you get married and have kids.

KATHY: Wow, I don't believe you really mean that.

RUTH: Look, Kathy, I don't want Mike to saw wood for the rest of his life, but what can I do about it? Why shouldn't he get into wood? Like, what if he does physics for the rest of his life and he's a genius and ends up head of department at some asshole university; you find out one day he's being financed by the C.I.A.

KATHY: These guys. They think they don't need you, so you go away and they freak out. Mike is a really brilliant guy. I mean, we all know that. You could really do things for him if you tried. You should've seen Bob when I first met him.

RUTH: I did.

KATHY: He used to compose all this really shitty music and like when he did something good he didn't even know it. You had to keep telling him yes, it's good, it's really great. A whole year it took for him to believe it. He's writing some fantastic stuff now, ever since, you know, I told him he was the first guy.

RUTH: Yeah, and look at him now.

KATHY (Upset again): You think you're really relating like crazy and then, I don't know, it's a whole new scene. It's like you don't even know him anymore.

RUTH: Maybe you ought to stop relating so hard.

KATHY: You don't know him, Ruth. I really know the guy and he needs me.

RUTH: Yeah, but maybe you ought to lay off for a while.

MIKE *bursts in through the front door.*

MIKE: Holy shit, where were you?

RUTH: I got lost and came home.

MIKE: Christ, it was horrible. We got stopped by this line of cops. Me and Cootie were right up front so I told him we should get everyone to join hands and stand still. We're standing there and this one pig starts running toward Cootie and you know how he gets when he sees pigs and he always gets diarrhea. I don't know, he should have said something, but he got the urge so bad he started to run, you know, trying to find a toilet, and this dumb pig thought he was trying to resist arrest.

KATHY: Is he all right?

MIKE: They took him to the hospital. He's, I don't know, they said he'll be all right. He got it in the back.

COOTIE *walks in.*

COOTIE: Boy, what a shitty march. You had to go and get separated with all the eats. I could've really used a marmalade and chunky peanut butter.

RUTH: Hey, did you know, Bob really wants to join the army? He's not even gonna try and get out. He didn't even go to the march.

COOTIE: He didn't miss much.

KATHY: He went to a goddamn cowboy film.

COOTIE: Hey, is that the one with Kirk Douglas and Gina Lollobrigida and Curt Jurgens and Orson Welles and Tom Courtenay and . . .

KATHY: You guys are really something. You don't give a shit what happens to him. I thought we were, like, all together here. Smug bastards. I'll tell you something.

COOTIE: What's that, Kathy?

KATHY: You're no better than the people fighting this war. (SHE *storms out of the room down the hall)*

MIKE: She's pretty cut up, huh?

RUTH: She thinks he's serious.

MIKE: Isn't he?

COOTIE *starts jumping and singing, punctuating each note with a leap.* HE *snarls the song.*

COOTIE: We shall over cu—u—um,
　　　　We shall over cu—u—um,
　　　　We shall overcome some day—ay-ay-ay-ay
　　　　Oh, oh, oh, deep in my heart
　　　　I do believe.
　　　　We shall over . . .

MIKE: Shut up, Mel.

COOTIE: If Bob's really serious, we gotta stop the war quick so he doesn't get sent over there to get killed by an antipersonnel bullet.

DICK *comes in, livid.*

DICK: Fucking Norman is fucking out of his fucking mind. That's the last time I ever take him with me. (HE *takes a bottle of milk from the icebox, kills it, and places it on the stack*)

MIKE: Hey, what's the matter, Dick, didn't you get yourself some left-wing ass?

COOTIE: Don't be ashamed, sonny. If she's waiting out there in the hallway, bring her in and show us the goods.

DICK: Norman had a fucking gun with him. He took a fucking revolver to the march.

MIKE: Is he a good shot?

DICK: I'm not shitting around. We're sitting on the bus and he's telling me he's reading Ho Chi Minh on guerrilla war and he doesn't think marches are effective. So he says he's gonna use the marchers like an indigenous population and start a guerrilla war against the cops. I mean, I thought he was just fucking around. You know Norman. Then he pulls out this fucking revolver right there on the bus, people looking and everything, and he says he's gonna get a few cops and would I help him create a diversion. He's out of his fucking mind.

MIKE: How many'd he get?

DICK: Fuck you.

COOTIE: He got the girl, huh?

DICK: Where's Kathy and Bob?

RUTH: Bob's not here.

DICK: Kathy here?

RUTH: Leave her alone. She's upset.

COOTIE: Yeah, I wouldn't try to lay her just yet, 'cause she's still going with Bob.

DICK *walks out down the hall.*

MIKE: That was a pretty stupid thing to say.

COOTIE: Just came out.

RUTH: Who cares? Everyone knows what dirty Dicky's up to. Except maybe Bob.

MIKE: And maybe Kathy.

RUTH: Kathy knows.

COOTIE: Do you think a guy could become a homosexual just by willpower? Could someone learn to like guys?

A knock on the front door.

RUTH: It's open.

In walks LUCKY, *the downstairs neighbor, led by* MR. WILLIS, *the landlord.*

WILLIS: Lucky tells me there's been a lotta noise up here. Is that right?

MIKE: Sorry, Mr. Willis, we had a little outburst up here. It's my fault. I just got a letter my sister had a baby.

COOTIE: We were celebrating.

WILLIS: That's all right, but keep it down. Lucky here was saying how you woke his wife up. She's a very ill person. I don't want any more complaints.

MIKE: Don't you worry about that, Mr. Willis, I'll take it on myself to keep this place really quiet.

LUCKY: Listen, I told you kids once before, and I'm not telling you again. You gotta get rid of those galvanized aluminum garbage cans in the yard and get plastic ones like everyone else.

RUTH (*Angry*): I don't see why we can't keep the ones . . .

MIKE: Ruth, now calm down, Ruth. I'm sorry, Lucky, but Ruth's pretty upset. Her father's fallen ill and they don't know for sure if it's . . . you know.

LUCKY: You got the galvanized aluminum ones out there. You'll have to get rid of the galvanized aluminum ones and get plastic.

WILLIS: I'll take care of the rest, Lucky. Thank you for bringing this particular grievance to my attention.

LUCKY: I'll give you till Monday, then I want to see plastic out there. (HE *leaves through front door*)

WILLIS: Whew, I hope I seen the last of that loony today. Nothin' but complaints day and night. The guy was born with a hair across his ass. So who's gonna give the landlord a little coffee?

RUTH *makes a move to get it.*

WILLIS: Thanks, sweetheart. Brother, what a day, what a stinker of a day. Where's Bobby?

MIKE: He's dead.

WILLIS: Dead? He's dead? You guys really kill me, you guys. You got a whole sense of humor like nothin' else. Dead, huh? Smart kid, Bobby. Hey, you been to the march?

COOTIE: Yep.

WILLIS: Great march. I watched it on Channel 8 in color. Brother, clothes you guys wear come out really good on color TV. You know, that guy Lucky can be a lotta trouble. He got a mind, like, you know, the size of a pinhead, you know what I mean? Just one sugar, sweetheart.

MIKE: You want the rent?

WILLIS: Rent, schment. I come to see how you guys are getting along and you talk to me about rent. How many landlords care, tell me that? One in a million, I can tellya. Hey, you decided whatya gonna do when you get out of college?

COOTIE: I'm gonna be a homosexual.

WILLIS: A homo. . . . You guys really slay me, you guys. What a sense of humor. You know, I'd give ten'a my other tenants for any one of you guys. You kids are the future of America, I mean that deeply, not too much milk, beautiful. Yeah, you kids live a great life up here. I got tenants complaining all the time about the way you kids carry on, and I'll tell ya something, you wanna know why they complain? 'Cause they'd give the last piece of hair on their heads to live like you kids are living.

RUTH: How's Mrs. Willis?

WILLIS: Huh? Oh, yeah, great, just great. Well, just between you and me and the wall she's gettin' to be a pain in the ass. She wants me to get rid of you, too. Why? I ask her. She don't like the way you live. O.K., I say, if you know so much, how do they live? She don't know and she don't wanna know. I try to tell her, you know, about the wild parties and stuff and taking drugs to have all new sensations in the body and the orgies with six or seven of you all at once. You should see her eyes light up. Same thing with all the tenants. When they hear what it's really like up here they go all funny. They'd pay me a hunnerd dollars to hear more, but they ain't got the nerve to ask. "Get rid of them." That's all I hear. Wamme to tell you something?

MIKE: If you got something to say you didn't ought to hold back.

WILLIS: Tremendous. You kids are tremendous. Listen. When the neighbors try to tellya about when they was young don't believe it. It's a lotta bull, and I should know. When we was young it was so boring you fell asleep when you was twenty and you never woke up again. You hear them stories Lucky tells about the war? Crap. He's sittin' down there holdin' his dick watchin' Doris Day on television. He'd give his left nut to know what's happenin' up here. This is the best cup of coffee I've had all day. I got a theory about it. It's when the head and the stomach don't talk to each other no more. That's when everything goes to hell. I'm gettin' so I don't know what I want half the time. I got these dreams, really crazy dreams. I got this one where I'm in a clearing, you know, it's right in the middle of the jungle and there's this tribe of Africans, I mean, like I don't know if they're Africans but they're livin' in the jungle and they're black so I figure they must be Africans. They got this skin. It's, you know, black, but really black. This maybe sounds kinda screwy, but it's really beautiful this skin. It's a dream, remember. I'm not sayin' black skin is beautiful, if you see what I mean. I'm in charge of the whole works in this jungle and I got it all organized so the men live in one hut and the women live in another hut and there's a big sort of square in between where nobody's

allowed after lights-out. They live like this all their life. There's no mar-
ryin' or anything. I'm a kind of witch doctor and I got this tribe believing . . . well, you know, they're just, like, Africans, and they don't know
you gotta have a man and a woman to make babies, and I got 'em thinkin'
you get babies when the moon shines down a girl's thing and hits the inside of her womb. And I got this whole ceremony where a girl comes to
me when she wants a baby and I tell her she gotta wait until it gets dark
and the moon comes up. Then I tie her to a plank, face up, and tilt the
plank so her thing is facing the moon and then I go to the hut with the
guys inside and get one of them to jerk off on a leaf, you know, one of
them tropical leafs that's really big. Then I roll this leaf up like it's a tube
and I sneak across the square holding this leaf in my hand all rolled up,
until I get to the girl. She's lying there in the moonlight all black and shiny
and her thing is opened right up 'cause she thinks . . . and I got this tube
full of jis in my hand, and I'm coming closer so I can smell everything
and . . . (*Comes out of it*) Jesus, what am I saying? I'm going crazy. It's just
a dream, what I'm telling you.

RUTH: That's the most beautiful thing I ever heard.

WILLIS: Listen, I got carried away. I didn't mean none of that.

MIKE: Mr. Willis, if you'd've had the opportunities we've had you'd've probably ended up one of the great poets of the century, and I mean that includes Rimbaud, Rilke, Williams, Pasternak, and Ginsberg.

COOTIE: And Whitman.

MIKE: Yes, Whitman included.

WILLIS: Oh, Jesus, you kids. I feel like I can tell you anything. Somebody
could've thought I was pretty screwy if I told them some of them things.

RUTH: How many landlords have poetry in their soul?

WILLIS: Yeah, yeah. Hey, I gotta run now. Listen, it's really great having you
guys around. If I could get some of them other tenants to come up here
and listen to you, the world would be a better place to live in, you know
what I mean?

MIKE: It would be a much better place.

COOTIE: A hundred percent better, at least.

RUTH: You're a beautiful person, Mr. Willis. Never be ashamed of it.

WILLIS: No, I ain't. I ain't ashamed of myself. Hey, you know what I was sayin'
before about all them complaints. I lost a lotta tenants on account of you.
I can't afford any more, so keep it quiet or I'll have to get rid of you.
Wonderful coffee, sweetheart. Seeya. (HE *leaves through front door*)

RUTH: I wonder how long before they put him away?

KATHY, *clothes a bit messed up, flounces into the kitchen and gets a glass of
water.* DICK *follows her as far as the kitchen, as if* HE *was trying to stop her,*

but when HE *gets to the doorframe* HE *stops, feeling the tension in the room.*
HE *tries to button his shirt casually, not sure whether* HE *wants the others*
to know what just happened between him and KATHY.

COOTIE: Hi, Dick, how's it hanging?

KATHY *stiffens at the sink.* DICK *turns and goes down the hall out of sight.*

MIKE: I still can't figure out what to get good old Bob for Christmas.

Before KATHY *can reply, the doorbell rings.* NO ONE *moves.*

COOTIE: Whose turn is it?
KATHY: You're a miserable bastard.
COOTIE: What'd I say? We're just playing a chess tournament.
KATHY: Listen, this is my scene, mine. You guys stay out of it. O.K., Ruth!
RUTH: It's her scene, guys, you stay out of it.
COOTIE: Roger.
MIKE: Sam.
COOTIE: Larry.
MIKE: Richard.
COOTIE: What's Richard getting Bob for Christmas?

The doorbell rings again, and MIKE *jumps up to get it.* SHELLY'*s standing there.*

MIKE: Hello there, I don't know you.
SHELLY: Hi. Does Norman live here?
MIKE: Does anyone here know a Norman?
SHELLY: He said he lived here. I met him at the march today. He said to come
    here and wait for him. I been standing out in the hall 'cause, like, I heard
    someone talking and I didn't want to disturb anyone and then this guy
    just came out so I figured, well, it's now-or-never kind of thing. I'm Shelly.
RUTH: Come on in. I'm Ruth.
SHELLY: Oh, good, then Norman does live here because I wasn't sure when
    he gave me the address. Sometimes you meet a guy at a march and he'll
    like give you an address and you end up waiting for a few days and he never
    shows. Did that ever happen to you? It's happened to me a lot of times.
KATHY: Listen everyone, I'm serious, I don't want him to know. I'll tell him
    when the time's right.
RUTH: It's your scene.

KATHY *exits down the hall.* SHELLY, *meanwhile, goes under the table and sits*
down on the floor.

SHELLY: I'm sorry about this. If you want to laugh go ahead, I'm used to it.
    It's just I've got this thing at the moment where I keep sitting under tables
    and I figured I'd better do it right away instead of pretending for a while

I didn't sit under tables. I mean, sitting under the table is "me" at the moment, so why hide it? Have you ever done it?

RUTH: Want some coffee, Shelly?

SHELLY: I'm a vegetarian.

MIKE: Coffee's made from vegetables.

SHELLY: I don't drink coffee, thanks. I'll just wait for Norman.

COOTIE: Where's Norman?

SHELLY: Well, he was arrested for carrying a concealed weapon, but he said it's O.K. because he has a permit. He's really a total-action freak, and he's very committed to the whole peace thing.

COOTIE: Oh.

MIKE: Well now . . .

COOTIE: How about that?

Fade-out.

Scene 4

NORMAN *is trying to read.* SHELLY *is under the table blowing bubbles.* MIKE *and* COOTIE *are playing chess.*

MIKE: I still think you should've said something, Norman. I mean it's got nothing to do with putting you on. If Dick said we didn't have a cat, all right, I mean he's got a right to think that but, I mean, it's really irresponsible of him to go running all over the place saying we don't.

NORMAN: Well, you turned off the lights that time when you came in. I was trying to read.

MIKE: Yeah, but that was the nitty-gritty, no-nonsense, down-to-earth needs of the moment because a cat just won't give birth with the lights on.

NORMAN: Dick says you don't have a cat.

MIKE: Will you listen to what I'm trying to tell you?

COOTIE: You can't move there.

MIKE: Why not?

COOTIE: Mate in thirty-four.

MIKE: Shit, I didn't see that. O.K., your game. (HE *and* COOTIE *start rearranging the pieces*)

COOTIE: Yeah, you see, Dick gets these things and he'll tell you, like, we don't have a cat or something like that. We would've explained if you'd just come out and asked instead of getting all hostile and paranoid and thinking we were putting you on.

SHELLY: Wow, bubbles are really something else. I think they're maybe divine.

MIKE: Bubbles are divine, Shelly.

COOTIE: So's Bogart.

SHELLY: Oh, Bogart, wow.

COOTIE: You're pretty happy, aren't you, Shelly?

SHELLY: Oh . . . yeah. Like, it's the right foods. And being under the table.

MIKE: You gotta watch the paranoid thing, Norman.

NORMAN: You were putting me on about the cat.

MIKE: See, you got this very paranoid thing about the cat.

NORMAN: I have not . . .

COOTIE: And the worst thing is how you get all defensive about it every time we bring it up. We're not denying your validity to doubt, Norman. We're not rejecting you as a human being. It's just you have a very paranoid personality because your father's a cop and that means you grew up in a very paranoid atmosphere.

SHELLY: Wow, your father's a cop?

NORMAN: Well, you know . . .

SHELLY: You never told me that. I think that's really great. My brother always wanted to be a cop.

COOTIE: My uncle's a cop.

MIKE: Yeah, that's right, our uncle's a cop.

NORMAN: That's what I mean, you see . . .

MIKE: What do you mean?

NORMAN: Well, I mean, you've got to go making fun of my father being a cop.

MIKE: Look, Norman, it just so happens our uncle is a cop and why the hell should you be the only one around here with a cop in the family. You see, you got paranoid again, thinking we're putting you on. I mean, we could do the same thing. How do we know your father's a cop? We don't. We trust you.

COOTIE: Yeah, and if you'd've been more outer-directed maybe you'd've seen you have a lot in common with us. A lot more than you ever expected.

MIKE: Then maybe we could've prevented that whole tragic episode with the gun.

NORMAN: Yeah, well, I don't know about you guys.

MIKE: You're not trying to say it wasn't a tragic episode?

COOTIE: It was an abortion of academic freedom, pure and simple.

MIKE: Hear! Hear!

COOTIE: I mean, when they can kick mathematics graduate students out of school just for trying to murder a few cops . . . . And, by the way, Norman, I've heard that your being kicked out of school was the doing of the Dean of Admissions, a man who is known far and wide to be cornholing his widowed sister in the eye-sockets regularly . . .

MIKE: And without love.

COOTIE: And when the moon comes up he ties her to this plank . . .

MIKE: Mel . . .

COOTIE: So put that in yer pipe and smoke it. And don't try to tell us you enjoy having to schlepp down to the Hays Bick every night to wash dishes for a dollar ten an hour.

NORMAN: Oh, I don't know.

SHELLY: Hey, are you guys brothers?

MIKE: Now there, look at that, Norman. Shelly's wondering about the relationship between Mel and me, and instead of being all paranoid about it and going crazy wondering, she comes right out and asks.

SHELLY: Hey, are you?

COOTIE: Yeah, we're brothers.

SHELLY: Wow, I didn't know that either. I keep learning all these things about you guys.

MIKE: See, everything's cool now. Everybody trusts each other. That's what it's all about.

NORMAN: Well, I mean, with washing dishes I get more time to read. I've been thinking a lot and I guess it's like Dick said. I was pretty irrelevant before. Mathematics is pretty irrelevant no matter how you look at it, and bad mathematics is about as irrelevant as you can get.

SHELLY: I left school after the first month. I'm not saying I'm really relevant, yet, but like, some of my friends in school are really into bad scenes. School is evil. You can't find out where it's at when you're studying all the time to fit your head into exams. I'm getting to where I can read recipes all day and really get something out of it.

NORMAN: Yeah. I'm learning all this stuff about Vietnam. It's really something. I mean, I'm getting to the point where maybe I can do something really relevant about it.

MIKE: I wouldn't call the gun business relevant.

NORMAN: I was still in school when I thought of that.

SHELLY: Norman's got this fantastic idea.

NORMAN: Well, I haven't thought it all out yet . . .

SHELLY: No, Norman-baby, don't like close all up. It's the most relevant thing I ever heard of.

COOTIE: Jesus, Norman, how long have you been walking around with this idea all locked up inside you?

NORMAN: I didn't get it all at once. It sort of came in stages, but I think it's about right.

COOTIE: Man, you're gonna go crazy if you keep everything inside like that.

SHELLY: Tell them the idea, Norman.

NORMAN: Well, you see . . . (*Pause*) I'm gonna set myself on fire as a protest against the war. (COOTIE *and* MIKE *look at him and exchange brief glances*) I've thought about it a lot. I mean, I've read I guess about a hundred books about the war and the more you read the more you see it's no one thing you can put your finger on. It's right in the middle of the whole system, like Dick said. I shouldn't've tried to kill those policemen, but I didn't know then they were part of the system like everything else. No one's got the right to take anyone else's life, that's what I've decided. But I've still got the right to take my own life for something I believe in.

SHELLY: I'm gonna burn with Norman. We're gonna burn together. We've thought it all through and, like, if he burns himself alone that's just one person. Everyone'll say he's insane, but if two of us do it . . . wow. Two people. What are they gonna say if two of us do it?

MIKE (*Pause*): Three of us.

COOTIE: Four of us.

MIKE: You, too, huh?

COOTIE: It's the only way.

NORMAN: Hey, wait a minute. I've read a lot about the whole subject and I really know why I'm gonna do it. I'm not just doing it for fun or anything. You can't just jump into it.

MIKE: Listen, Norman, you don't have to believe this if you don't want to but it's the truth, on my honor. Me and Cootie talked about the exact same thing a year ago. We were all ready to burn ourselves . . .

COOTIE: It was more than a year ago.

MIKE: More than a year?

COOTIE: Almost a year and a half.

MIKE: That's right, a year and a half, boy, time really goes quick . . .

COOTIE: It sure does . . .

MIKE: The thing is, we decided against it because we figured two isn't enough.

COOTIE: You know how the papers can lie. "Brothers Burn!"

MIKE: Yeah, "Hippie Brothers in Suicide Pact." That kind of shit.

COOTIE: But think of it. With four of us!

NORMAN: You really want to do it?

MIKE: It's the only way.

NORMAN: I mean, I wasn't sure yet. I hadn't made up my mind definitely. I was still looking for another way.

SHELLY: No, Norman-baby, it's the only relevant gesture. Like you said.

A long pause while NORMAN *thinks.*

NORMAN: O.K.!

COOTIE: After the Christmas vacation.

MIKE: No, no, after graduation. We'll study like mad and get fantastic grades and graduate with honors so they can't say we were cracking up or anything.

COOTIE: Yeah, we'll get Phi Beta Kappa. I'd like to see them say we're insane when two Phi Beta Kappas go up in flames with the son of a policeman and the daughter of a. . . . Hey, what does your father do?

SHELLY: Well, it's kind of funny. I mean, he's a pretty weird head in his way. He's got, like, six or seven jobs at any one time.

COOTIE: That's O.K. Daughter of a weird head with six or seven jobs at any given time. That covers the whole spectrum.

NORMAN: What does your father do? I mean, I know your uncle's a policeman because I trust you, but you never said what your father did. I was curious. Like if they bring our fathers into it what'll they say about you?

COOTIE: He's a trapper.

SHELLY: Wow, that's really something else. Like, a fur trapper?

MIKE: Furs and hides, you know. Rabbit and mink and muskrat and beaver and elk and reindeer and seal. Some otter. Penguin.

SHELLY: Wow, penguin.

COOTIE: Well, you know, he works the Great Northwest Territory up to the mouth of the St. Lawrence Seaway and over to the Aleutians.

SHELLY: Boy, this'll really blow everyone's mind.

MIKE: Yeah, this'll make everyone think twice, all right.

COOTIE: You know, we can't tell anyone about this. If word gets out they'll send squads of police around here and we'll get arrested and put under psychiatric observation and we'll get subjected to a battery of tests that make you look nuts no matter how you answer.

NORMAN: I won't say anything.

SHELLY: Oh, wow, like you don't even have to worry about me.

NORMAN: I didn't even know there were any trappers left.

A knock on the door.

MIKE: Come in.

VOICE: C'mon, c'mon, open up in there.

MIKE *opens the door and finds two cops standing there.* BREAM *is elderly and* EFFING *is young.*

BREAM: You live here?

MIKE: Yes, sir.

BREAM: Look, you know what I mean, you and who else.

MIKE: Well, there's me and my brother Cootie . . . um, Mel, and there's Norman, Dick, Bob, Kathy, and Ruth.

BREAM: Kathy and Ruth, huh? Those are girls' names.

MIKE: Kathy and Ruth are both girls, sir.

BREAM: Don't block the doorway. (MIKE *stands aside as* BREAM *and* EFFING *enter.* EFFING *wanders around the room, inspecting.* BREAM *indicates* SHELLY) Which one's she? You Kathy or Ruth?

SHELLY: I'm Shelly.

BREAM: Shelly, huh? You didn't say nothin' about no Shelly.

MIKE: She doesn't live here, sir.

BREAM: Visiting?

SHELLY: I'm with Norman.

BREAM: You're Norman, huh?

NORMAN: She's my girlfriend.

BREAM: Good, we got that straight.

EFFING: Hey, Bream, this here's a map of Europe.

BREAM: Yeah. Now listen. There's been a complaint from the people across there. I know you kids are students and you probably think you own the goddamn country, but I got some news for you. There's laws around here and you gotta obey them just like everyone else.

MIKE: We appreciate that, sir.

EFFING: Hey, Bream, look at all them milk bottles.

BREAM: Yeah. Now listen. I don't want to hear any more complaints about you guys. I'm a reasonable man, which is something you can get verified by askin' anyone on the force, but when I gotta put up with a lotta stupid complaints I can cause trouble and I mean real trouble, with a capital T.

EFFING: Hey, look at all them dishes in the sink, Bream.

BREAM: Yeah.

NORMAN: What was the complaint?

BREAM: What do you mean, what was the complaint? The complaint was guys and girls parading around in here bare-ass. Now look, I'm not the kind of dumb cop that goes around throwing his weight everywhere to prove he's some kind of big shot. I don't need to, you follow me. I know what I know and I know what I don't know, and one of the things I know I don't know is what the hell the kids are up to nowadays, but O.K. That's my problem. If you wanna run around naked that's O.K. by me, and I hope you kids take note of the fact that I'm winking one eye when it comes to the law about cohabitation.

MIKE: We appreciate that fact, sir. It was the first thing we noticed.

COOTIE: I sure appreciate it. I think I can speak for Norman and Shelly, and if any of the other guys were here they'd appreciate it a lot.

MIKE: I mean it's not as if we underestimate the life of a cop. For chrissakes, I mean, our uncle's a cop. His father's a cop. A lot of us around here are pretty close to the world of cops.

BREAM: You got cops in the family?

EFFING: Hey, Bream, look at this heater.

BREAM: Yeah.

MIKE: It's not like we don't know what you guys have to put up with. It can be a pretty crappy job.

BREAM: I don't know . . .

MIKE: I'm not saying it doesn't have its rewards. My uncle's life is full of rewards. His father's life is very meaningful.

BREAM: Yeah, that's what I mean.

COOTIE *gets up and starts to leave the room.*

EFFING: Hey, Bream, the kid's leaving the room.

COOTIE: I got a call from nature.

BREAM: That's legit. You go ahead, kid.

COOTIE *goes out the front door.*

EFFING: Hey, Bream, the kid says he's going to the euphemism and what if he's got some stuff on him or something. He can flush it down and come back clean.

BREAM: He's O.K.

EFFING: Jesus, Bream. Sir.

BREAM: The guy's new on the job. He don't know the score yet.

MIKE: You know how some people exaggerate. I mean, look what they say in the papers about you guys. Maybe, like after a shower we'll come in here to get an anchovy snack or chocolate milk or something, and we forget to put something on . . .

EFFING: Look at that, Bream, the girl keeps sitting under there . . .

BREAM: Goddammit, Effing, who's in charge around here?

EFFING: But she's sitting under there . . .

BREAM: Did we come here to investigate a complaint about a girl sitting under the table?

EFFING: No, sir, but . . .

BREAM: The girl happens to be well within her rights as a taxpaying citizen of the community to sit under any table she wants, and until we get complaints about her sitting under there, we leave her alone. Understand?

EFFING: Yeah, yeah, yeah . . .

SHELLY: Thanks.

BREAM: That's O.K., lady. The kid's a rookie. They give us pros a bad name. Now let me tell you something about the people complaining about you. They look in here and see you guys bare-assed and they're complaining because they're so sick of looking at each other they gotta go spying on you. We know about them people. They're strict Roman Catholics. Twelve kids in four rooms. The old man can't keep it in his pants for ten minutes running. So they got troubles, right, and everyone that's got troubles wants to give troubles to someone else. So they make a complaint, and that's well within their rights as law-abiding citizens of this community. I got enough troubles without their goddamn complaints. I got enough to do watching the Vietnam freaks and the niggers and the loonies going up on buildings with high-power rifles picking off everyone down below. Let me give you some good advice. Get curtains. They got some fiberglass curtains at Woolworth's, you can't tell them from real cotton. Twelve dollars and fifty cents a pair and they come in eight colors, plain and patterned. You get some curtain rods for a dollar sixty-nine apiece and for a total of twenty-eight dollars and thirty-eight cents you save yourself from a lot of crazy neighbors. If you can't afford twenty-eight dollars and thirty-eight cents, get some gingham, thirty-nine cents a yard at Penney's. Measure your windows and allow a foot extra at each end. All you gotta do is take up a three-inch hem at each end, fold it over once, and hand-stitch. A couple of curtain rings and you're in business. Can you remember that, or d'you want me to write it down?

SHELLY: Hey, yeah, would you do that?

BREAM takes out a notebook and starts to write. EFFING is nervous.

EFFING: The kid's been gone a long time.

BREAM: I got eyes, Effing.

EFFING: Yeah, yeah, yeah, O.K.

BREAM (*Writing*): So, what are you kids gonna do with yourselves? (*Pause*) Am I being nosy or something?

MIKE: No, I mean, there's a lot of opportunities all over the place. We're not jumping into anything without we've looked the whole thing over.

BREAM: Smart kids. Boy, that's really something. Cop sending his kid to college. They must pay him pretty good, huh?

NORMAN: I guess so.

BREAM: Yeah, what's he a sergeant . . . lieutenant or something?

NORMAN: He's Chief of Police for Erie County.

BREAM (*Whistles*): Whew! Pretty good. That shut me up O.K. Chief of Police. Oh, boy, that's really something.

NORMAN: It's just his job, you know.

BREAM: Look, ah, here's your instructions. I want them up by Wednesday. Any complaints after that and all of you guys'll be in court, father or no father, you understand me? This ain't Erie County.

MIKE: Yes, sir.

NORMAN: O.K.

COOTIE (*Returns and stands in the door. There's a pause*): That's better.

Scene 5

RUTH is scraping some cat food into a bowl. A cat comes in and eats. RUTH keeps glancing at her watch.

RUTH: Kitty-kitty-kitty-kitty-kitty. Chomp, chomp. Good girl. Make a lot of milk for the kitties.

KATHY comes in from the hall and throws herself down on a chair.

KATHY: Oh, Jesus, Ruth, how am I ever gonna tell him?

RUTH: Who?

KATHY: Bob, for chrissakes. Who else?

RUTH: Well, how should I know?

KATHY: I never slept with Dick. I know you got the idea I did, but it's not true. He never got all the way . . . .

RUTH: . . . O.K. . . .

KATHY: . . . Yet. (*Pause*) I'm not saying I wouldn't like to.

RUTH: So go ahead.

KATHY: Well, don't try to pretend it doesn't mean anything to you. You know as well as I do it'll kill Bob if he ever finds out I'm even thinking of sleeping with Dick.

RUTH: That's how it goes.

KATHY: Ruthie, look, we've know each other since freshman year. I can tell when you're thinking something. This is really a big decision I've gotta make. What am I gonna do about Bob? I mean, it feels like maybe we're you know, finished, but I like the guy. I really like him a lot and I respect his music. But I know he could never relate to me as a friend. It's gotta be tied up with sex. I mean, Richard really seems to dig me, but I don't know. He's pretty together. He's not the kind of guy you could really do something big for. Not like Bob.

RUTH: Oh, for shit's sake, Kathy, Dick is a fucking parasite.

KATHY: That's not fair, Ruth.

RUTH: Fair! Do you know what that guy's doing to get into graduate school? You ever heard of Professor Roper in the Eastern Studies department?

KATHY: He's Dick's adviser.

RUTH: Yeah, and he also happens to be queer as a three-dollar bill, and Dick is fucking his wife to keep her quiet so good old Roper can suck cock with all those graduate students from Thailand or Malaya, or whatever the hell they are.

KATHY: Who said?

RUTH: Who said? For chrissakes, Kathy, the whole goddam school knows about it. "Dirty Dicky."

KATHY: That's why?

RUTH: Yeah, what else? I mean, the guy washes eight times a day.

KATHY: Oh, man, how long have you guys known about this? I mean, why didn't anyone ever tell me? You can't just let him screw up his future like that. Hasn't anyone tried to do anything about it?

RUTH: Like tell him Mrs. Roper's got clap?

KATHY: Ruthie, the guy must be really suffering.

RUTH: Oh, shit, Kathy, let's not have the big savior thing.

KATHY: That's not very funny.

RUTH: Look, we're all gonna graduate pretty soon, and we're all gonna go away, and probably we'll never see each other again except maybe like at

Christmas or something. So why don't you worry about yourself and never mind about Dick and Bob. They'll be O.K.

KATHY: Boy, you sure have changed, Ruth. I don't know. You sure have changed.

BOB *comes through front door carrying books.*

BOB: I don't believe it. It's incredible. You know what happened today in counterpoint class? Remember I was telling you about Eric Shatz?

RUTH: . . . Three armpits . . . ?

BOB: The very one.

KATHY (*Nicely*): Bob . . .

BOB, *who has gone to the icebox to steal some of* DICK*'s hamburgers, stops short in whatever gesture* HE *is holding, only for a moment though, just long enough to cut* KATHY. *When* HE *resumes his story,* HE *is talking only to* RUTH, *who is wrapping a Christmas present.*

BOB: Today Shatz turned in this perfect, spotless, clean counterpoint exercise. I mean, for someone as filthy as Shatz, that's a miracle. They say his high-school yearbook voted him "The Most Likely to Attract Infectious Disease." (HE *has the hamburgers out by now.* KATHY, *being all nice, takes the hamburgers from him indicating that* SHE*'ll cook.* HE *goes away from her and sits with* RUTH) He picks his nose and squeezes his pimples right there in class, and his counterpoint exercises have to be seen to be believed. He writes them in pencil, and if he makes a mistake or something, he spits on his eraser and rubs the paper about a hundred times . . . per note, so by the time he hands it to Professor Bolin, it's just this gray sludge with lots of little black things swimming around on it. Anyway, about a week ago, when Shatz handed over his work, Professor Bolin put on a pair of gloves before he'd take it, so Shatz must've got the message and this week when Bolin called for homework, Shatz set this beautiful, clean exercise down on the piano. We couldn't believe it. Boilin just sat there staring at it, and we all sat staring at Bolin, and after about ten minutes, no shit, it took that long, Bolin turned to us and said, "Free will is an illusion." Isn't that too much?

KATHY: Bob, can I talk to you . . . ?

BOB (*Ignores her*): The thing is, Bolin's got a Ph.D. He's also written two books and a couple of hundred symphonies and string quartets and they say he taught himself twenty-two languages in four hours or something . . .

KATHY: Please, Bob, I want to talk to you . . .

BOB: And another thing, Bolin's wife got drunk at a faculty party for the music department last year and she yelled, "Fuck Schönberg, I wanna dance," and then she went and laid the only black professor in the school, which all goes to show that when Bolin tells you free will is an illusion . . . you better believe it.

KATHY (*Pointed*): Bob, I would like to talk to you . . .

BOB: Hey, Ruth, did I ever tell you the one about the guy that died and came back to life as Job?

KATHY: Oh, don't start that shit again.

BOB: Again? It started over a month ago. I mean, even Bolin caught on after two lessons. Of course, he still makes me walk around the music building every time I put down parallel fifths, but that's how it goes, life is trying at the best of times, every cloud has a silver lining, a stitch in time saves nine . . .

RUTH (*Looks at her watch*): I've gotta go.

BOB: Did I say something?

RUTH: No. Kathy wants to talk to you about sleeping with Dick.

KATHY: Ruth . . . bitch!

> RUTH *goes out the front door, grabbing her coat on the way.*

BOB (*Pause*): Meanwhile, back at the ranch. . . . You'll never believe this, but when I came in just now, I didn't expect that. Bedbugs, maybe. Thermonuclear war . . .

KATHY: She had no right.

BOB: I'm trying to think of something appropriate to say, like "Name the first one after me." That's Job. J-O-B. Job.

KATHY: Please, Bob, can I say something . . . ?

BOB: Do you have trouble pronouncing the name Job?

KATHY: Jesus Christ, you're impossible.

BOB: Ah, yes, but I exist, nonetheless.

KATHY: You've just cut me right out. You're not even trying to relate to me anymore. (*Pause*) Well, you're not.

BOB: No, Kathy. The fact is, I like you a lot. I, um, sort of love you, if you know what I mean.

KATHY: I don't really want to sleep with Dick.

BOB: Then don't.

KATHY: It's just, he tried to get me that night after the demonstration.

BOB: I know. He told me.

KATHY: That shit.

BOB: I thought it was pretty good of him.

KATHY: He never got into me, you know.

BOB: That's nice.

KATHY: Oh, Bob. I'm sorry.

BOB: If Bob were around I'm sure he'd forgive you.

KATHY: What'll we do?

BOB: What do you mean? Like study or something?

KATHY: Bob, how does it stand? Is it . . . it's over, isn't it?

BOB: Between us, you mean?

KATHY: Yes.

BOB: If that's what you want.

KATHY: Of course I don't want it. I love you a lot.

BOB: O.K., so let's study for Phil 720.

KATHY: Oh, for chrissakes, show some emotion. I don't know where I'm at with you half the time.

BOB: Look, what's the big hang-up? If you want to stay with me, O.K. If you want to move into Dick's room, go ahead. If you don't know for sure, stay one night with me and one night with him till you start feeling a definite preference for one of us . . .

KATHY: Jesus Christ, Bob, what's the matter with you?

BOB: I'm Job. Bob's dead.

KATHY (*Is in a furious slow burn.* SHE *stands and goes toward the hall door*): All right . . . all right . . .

Before KATHY *can exit a knock on the door stops her. A game. Who's going to open the door?* BOB *picks up a book and starts reading. Another knock.* KATHY *sighs.* SHE *'s above these silly games.* SHE *opens the door on a middle-aged man in well-cut coat. A businessman from head to foot. This is* MURRAY, BOB*'s uncle.*

MURRAY: Hi. Does Bob Rettie live here?

BOB (*Looks up from his book*): Murray!!

MURRAY: Can I come in?

BOB: What the hell are you doing here?

MURRAY: Guy flies a couple thousand miles to see his nephew, maybe he can come in, huh?

BOB: Yeah, yeah. Come in, come in . . . sit down . . . .

MURRAY: Hey, I bet you're surprised to see me, huh? Maybe a little happy.

BOB: Yeah, I mean I haven't seen you for a couple thousand years or something.

MURRAY (*To* KATHY): It's longer than that since he wrote.

BOB: Oh, ah, that's Kathy. My uncle.

MURRAY: How do you do.

KATHY: Hi.

MURRAY: You drink a lot of milk, huh?

BOB: Yeah.

THEY *laugh*.

MURRAY: Where'd you get that goddamn icebox?

BOB: Oh, you know . . .

MURRAY: Is this the way you been living? Bobby boy, why didn't you tell me. Write a letter, say Murray I need a little cash, I'd've sent you some money for a decent refrigerator.

BOB: Murray, we're living O.K.

MURRAY: So. I'm sorry for breathing. Did I interrupt something?

BOB: No. Nothing at all.

MURRAY: Are you two . . . ah . . .

BOB: Yeah—Murray, look, sit down, take your coat off. . . .

MURRAY: Hey, Bobby, Bobby-boy. You got long hair. . . .

BOB: Yeah, it keeps growing.

MURRAY: Still proud, huh? (*To* KATHY) Just like his mother . . . . (HE *looks at the two of them and shrugs*) Well what can I say . . . ?

KATHY: Look, I think I'll . . .

BOB: How long you in town for?

MURRAY: Oh, you know. Business.

KATHY: Excuse me, I'm gonna . . .

BOB: How's the kids?

MURRAY: Oh, fine, fine, keep asking about you.

BOB: Auntie Stella?

MURRAY: Oh. You know. We got a new house . . .

BOB: Great. Where you going, Kathy?

KATHY (*Has been edging toward the door. Quietly*): I'll be in Dick's room if you want me. (SHE *exits*)

MURRAY: Is she O.K.?

BOB (*Flat*): Yeah. It's her time of the month, you know.

MURRAY: Say no more. You don't have to tell me about that. Nice girl. Very nice. (*Laughs*) So . . .

BOB: Come through New York?

MURRAY: Yeah, you know, passed through.

BOB: You passed through New York, huh?

MURRAY (*Uneasy*): Yeah, sure, you know . . .

BOB: D'you see Mom?

MURRAY: Yeah, yeah, sure. She'd maybe like a letter every now and then. Your own mother.

BOB: It's not like that, Murray. When I see her, I see her.

MURRAY (*Shiver*): Jesus Christ. (HE *drinks*)

BOB: You O.K.?

MURRAY: Sit down, Bobby-boy.

BOB: I'm O.K. like this.

MURRAY: I got something to tell you, you should maybe be sitting down when I tell you.

BOB *sits.* MURRAY *pulls his chair close and takes* BOB*'s head in his hands.* BOB *is stiff.*

MURRAY: Bobby-boy, oh, Bobby. I'd like to see more of you. Me and the family. You maybe come out and visit, huh?

BOB (*Flat*): What's happened, Murray?

MURRAY: How am I supposed to tell you?

Pause.

BOB (*Long pause*): Cancer? (MURRAY *nods*) How long's she got?

MURRAY: A week, two weeks. I don't know. Any time now.

BOB: Those operations . . . kidney trouble. Oh, shit, why didn't someone tell me?

MURRAY: You got your studies, we should worry you to death?

BOB (*Flat*): Fuck you all.

MURRAY: I thought . . . I thought maybe you and me fly to New York tonight.

BOB: Yeah, get in there quick for the payoff. That'll be just great.

MURRAY: She doesn't know yet.

BOB: Yeah. "Hi, Mom, I just came flying in with Murray a couple of weeks before Christmas vacation to see you for no good reason." You think she won't guess?

MURRAY: She doesn't have to. We can always tell her something.

BOB: You planning to keep it from her, too? I bet it's the first thing she thought of. Two years. She had that first operation two years ago. She's been dying for two years and I didn't even fucking know it.

MURRAY: I don't want to hurt anybody.

BOB (*Pause*): I'll pack some stuff. No, you stay here. I want to be alone.

BOB *goes down the hall.* MURRAY *sits. Very short pause, then* MIKE *and* COOTIE *burst in through the front door, laden with Christmas presents.* THEY *see* MURRAY, *cross the kitchen to the hall door, exit, and start arguing loudly just outside in the hallway. After a moment* THEY *reenter,* MIKE *leading. Deferential.*

MIKE: Me and my friend were wondering if you could settle a little argument for us.

MURRAY: What?

MIKE: Were you or weren't you the guy behind the bar in *Key Largo*, starring Humphrey Bogart and Edward G. Robinson?

MURRAY: I'm Bob's uncle.

MIKE (*To* COOTIE): He's Bob's uncle.

COOTIE: Are you a for-real uncle?

MURRAY (*Confused*): Yeah, yeah, I'm his uncle.

COOTIE: Maternal or paternal.

MURRAY: I'm related to Bob through his mother. She was . . . she's my sister.

MIKE: That means you and him have different names.

MURRAY: Yeah, he's a Rettie, I'm a Golden.

MIKE: That's a pretty convincing story, mister.

COOTIE: Most of the pieces fit pretty good.

MIKE *and* COOTIE *start toward the hall.* SHELLY *comes in the front door.*

SHELLY: Hi, everyone.

MIKE: Hiya, Shelly.

COOTIE: Good old Shelly, hiya.

MIKE *and* COOTIE *are gone down the hall.*

SHELLY: Hey . . . excuse me, do you know if Norman's here?

MURRAY: I don't know who Norman is.

SHELLY: One of the guys here. I mean, like he lives here. You someone's father?

MURRAY: I'm Bob's uncle.

SHELLY: Bob? Oh, yeah, Job. (SHE *sits under the table*) I'm waiting for Norman. Hey, are you, like, a for-real uncle?

MURRAY: You kids keep asking that.

SHELLY: You don't think of him with an uncle.

MURRAY: Look, if you don't want me to stay in here, I'll go and help Bob.

SHELLY: No, you stay here. Like, I enjoy company. Hey, is he here?

MURRAY: I'm afraid I don't know your friend Norman.

SHELLY: I mean Job. Your nephew.

MURRAY: Yes, he's here. I'm waiting for him.

SHELLY: He's, like, in here somewhere? Inside the apartment?

MURRAY: Yes. Look, you want to go down and ask him about Norman, go ahead.

SHELLY: Is he in the toilet?

MURRAY: He's in his room.

SHELLY: Wow, that's like really weird.

MURRAY: He's just packing, that's all.

SHELLY: Yeah, but I mean, if you're his for-real uncle, how come you're like sitting in here when he's down there?

MURRAY: Look, he . . . (*Weeping softly*) . . . I don't know.

SHELLY: Hey, you're really crying like crazy. What's the matter? I thought you were, like, waiting for him to come back here, you know, to the apartment or something. I just wanted to know because I'm waiting for Norman to come back so I thought we could maybe sit here together waiting and that would be something we had in common, then you told me he was in his room packing and everything and I thought that was sorta weird 'cause if you're like his for-real uncle you could just go down there and be with him. Why's he packing?

BOB (*Entering with bag*): O.K. I'm ready.

SHELLY: Hey, Job, you going away?

BOB: I'll be back in a few days.

SHELLY: Like, you mean, you're not just going home early for Christmas vacation?

BOB: No.

SHELLY: Oh. O.K. Hey, Merry Christmas, you guys.

BOB: Merry Christmas.

MURRAY: Merry Christmas.

DICK *comes in through the front door.* BOB *and* MURRAY *start out.* DICK *is baffled.*

DICK: Hey, you going?

BOB: Yeah. Kathy's in your room. (*Pause*) She doesn't like it from behind.

BOB *and* MURRAY *are gone.*

DICK: Where's he going?

SHELLY: I don't know, but the guy with him is his for-real uncle and he's a weird head.

KATHY *comes into the kitchen.*

KATHY: Hey, did Bob just go out?

SHELLY: Wow, he didn't even tell you?

DICK: He left with his uncle.

KATHY: Uncle?

SHELLY: Yeah, like it's his for-real uncle, I'm pretty sure.

KATHY: Jesus, why didn't he say something. I mean, I been waiting for him down there . . .

SHELLY: Well, the uncle said Job went down to his room to pack, and I mean, like if you were in there with him and he started putting a lot of socks and underwear and toilet stuff in a suitcase you should've got suspicious and asked him something, like where's he going.

KATHY: Look, I went to the bathroom, O.K.?

SHELLY: Ya didn't flush.

KATHY: Mind your own business, Shelly. What does he expect me to do? How can I make plans for the Christmas vacation if he just . . . shit, he could've said something. (DICK, *in a feeble attempt to avoid* KATHY*'s rage, tries to sneak out down the hallway*) And listen, you, you have a lot of nerve telling him about that night.

DICK: I didn't say anything.

KATHY: He said you told him.

DICK: Honest, Kathy, I never did.

KATHY (*Vague*): I'm really getting to hate this place. (SHE *starts down the hall.* DICK *starts after her*)

DICK: Kathy!

Before DICK *can get down the hall,* RUTH *rushes in through the front door, breathless.*

RUTH: Oh, wow, have I ever had the most fantastic experience! (DICK *goes down the hall, slamming the door.* SHE *yells*) You're a shit, Dick.

SHELLY: You seen Norman?

RUTH: Oh, hi, Shelly. Hey, let me tell you about what just happened to me. It really blew my mind.

From down the hall, we hear voices singing.

MIKE and COOTIE (*Singing, offstage*):
>We wish you a Merry Christmas
>We wish you a Merry Christmas
>We wish you a Merry Christmas
>We wish you a Merry Christmas
>We wish you a Merry Christmas
>We wish you a Merry Christmas
>We wish you a Merry Christmas
>We wish you a Merry Christmas
>And . . . (THEY *rush in from the hall dressed in Santa Claus costumes and end the song*)
> . . . a Happy New Year.

MIKE: We got a present for you, Ruth.

SHELLY: Hey, where'd you get those?

COOTIE: We're doing collections this year. Yep.

MIKE: You want to see the great old present we got ya?

RUTH: I was just gonna tell Shelly what happened when I went to see Quinn. You know Quinn, the albino dwarf . . .

MIKE: Oh, yeah, old Quinn.

COOTIE: Good old Quinn.

RUTH: Yeah, right. Well, I had to see him about homework for the Christmas vacation and, I mean, like, he was the last person I wanted to see. I always thought he was a vicious little bastard. I mean, he can be pretty shitty.

MIKE: They say he shot a man in Abilene.

COOTIE: In the back.

RUTH: Listen, willya? I went into his office and he's standing by the window, you know, three feet high and everything. I thought he was probably gonna ask why I wasn't doing any homework, and I had this whole speech worked out about how I thought he was a pretentious little snot and how I frankly didn't give a shit about philosophy and even less of a shit about him, if that's possible and . . . oh, you know, I was really going to kill him. Anyway, he told me to come over to the window, so I came over and we both stood there looking out. Snow everywhere, like, white wherever you looked and a lot of snow coming down like in those paperweights you shake up, and there's all these kids down below coming out of the building, all little lumps moving across the white in slow motion, and we're looking at them, just the two of us for, I don't know, about a minute or two, and then he just turns to me, like without any warning, and says this incredibly beautiful thing . . .

MIKE: Hey, don't you want to see the nifty present we got ya?

RUTH: Let me tell you what the guy said, willya?

MIKE: Right, you tell us what Quinn said, then we'll show you the present.

RUTH: Yeah.

MIKE: Will you look at the present first, then tell us what Quinn said?

RUTH: For Christ sake, stop fucking around and listen.

MIKE: All right, what did Quinn say?

COOTIE: I'd like to hear what Quinn said.

As RUTH *is about to speak,* KATHY *runs through from the hall and out the front door with a valise in hand.* DICK *shouts from offstage down the hall.*

DICK (*Offstage*): Kathy. (HE *enters and, on his way across the room and out the front door, buttons his overcoat*) Kathy!

RUTH'*s face shows worry as* SHE *watches this. Seconds after* DICK *exits,* SHE *takes her coat and follows, leaving* MIKE, COOTIE *and* SHELLY *alone. There is a pause.*

COOTIE: What was that all about?

MIKE: Things around here are getting a little out of control, Cootie.

COOTIE: You feel that way, huh?

MIKE: I do.

COOTIE: Well, what are we gonna do about it, movies or roller-skating?

MIKE: Cootie, sometimes you're really a dumb asshole.

COOTIE: But then again sometimes I'm not. (*Gets up and walks down the hall slowly*)

SHELLY: Hey!

MIKE *exits after* COOTIE, *leaving* SHELLY *alone. Slow fade.*

Scene 6

Most of the posters are down. A bare feeling. Around graduation. There's some letters on the table. RUTH, *alone, is reading her letter.* DICK *comes in from outside, dressed for warm weather, perhaps carrying a box.* HE *opens the icebox.*

DICK: Shit, nothing left.

RUTH: We cleaned it.

DICK: Anyone gone yet?

RUTH: No. Why don't you look at your grades?

DICK (*Opens letter*): Jesus.

RUTH: Bad?

DICK: Fucking awful.

RUTH: Do you graduate?

DICK: Yeah, just.

RUTH: They sent Kathy's grades here.

DICK: That was tactful.

RUTH: Maybe she'll be around to pick them up. I got into graduate school.

DICK: Great.

RUTH: Philosophy.

DICK: Philosophy?

RUTH: Yeah! (*Pause*) I mean, you know, why not? (DICK *starts toward the hall*) Hey, Dick, I don't get it. You know that day she left, just before Christmas . . . did you get into her?

DICK: How low can you stoop, Ruth?

RUTH: No, I mean, you know, just, she must've done something to fuck you up this bad.

DICK: Kathy did not fuck me up.

RUTH: Yeah, well, ever since she left you've been looking like really terrible. You never even studied for finals. I mean, you were the academic head around here. Hey, you did get her, didn't you, and I bet she told you you were the first guy that ever turned her on: (DICK *starts out again*) Did she? Oh, come off it, Dick, I just . . . I thought we were friends.

DICK: You know what that goddamn fucking little cunt told me? Just before she left? She told me I was screwing Roper's wife. Me, screwing Roper's wife.

RUTH: Well, you know Kathy.

DICK: She said everybody in the whole fucking school knew about it. It got back to Roper.

RUTH: Wow, I bet he was pretty pissed off, huh?

DICK: He was pretty good about it, considering. He pulled me in after a tutorial and gave me the old "Richard, my boy" speech. He thought I started the rumor. Me. Shit. "Richard, my boy, it's said you're doing unenviable things to my wife. My boy, that particular assignment has already been well seen to. It's not like you to claim credit for someone else's work." You ever tried to do a paper for someone who thinks you've been saying you're screwing his wife? Shit. Poor old fairy. Boy, what a fucking mess.

BOB *comes in the front door.*

RUTH: Hey, Bob, you got your grades.

BOB: Oh, yeah. (HE *looks*)

RUTH: How'd you do?

BOB: O.K. This for Kathy?

RUTH: Yeah. (BOB *starts to open* KATHY's *letter*) Hey, that's private property.

BOB: What the fuck's gotten into you all of a sudden. (*Reads*) A, A, A, A . . . B minus. B minus in Poetry 210. Man, she really went to pieces

without us. I hope she hasn't had a nervous breakdown or anything. Whew,
B minus.

A knock on the door. DICK *opens it. It's* LUCKY.

LUCKY: Listen. I just seen Mr. Willis. He wants you out by tomorrow night.

BOB: How ya been, Lucky?

LUCKY: What? Oh, yeah. Well, if you want a hand, you know where to find me.

RUTH: Thanks a lot, buddy.

LUCKY: Don't get fresh, girlie, don't give me lip. You can talk how you want
   when you're with your own kind, but you show some respect when you're
   with Lucky. Smart alecks. Think you know everything. You don't . . . you
   don't know . . . you don't know what it's like living downstairs. That's
   something I know about. I know about living downstairs. I live downstairs.
   You seen me . . . you seen me out there, sitting out there. Well, you seen
   me . . .

BOB: Yeah, yeah, lots of times.

LUCKY: All right. That's what I mean. I sit out there. I'm out there. I got my
   Budweiser. I got my pretzels. Oh, yeah . . . I'm not just sitting out there,
   you know. I'm watching. I'm keeping my eyes open. (HE*'s slowly going into a trance*) I see them cars go by, all them cars. Fords. I see Fords out there.
   Chevies. Lincolns. Oldsmobiles. Plymouths. I see the odd Cadillac, oh,
   yeah, don't worry about that. It's all up here. You think I'm just sitting
   there with my Budweiser and pretzels. Think you know it all, oh, yeah.

DICK: Don't worry, we took care of it.

LUCKY: Huh?

DICK: We did like you said. Got rid of those plastic garbage cans and got some
   galvanized aluminum.

LUCKY: All right, that's what I mean. Now, if you want any help, I'll tell you
   what you do. You come downstairs. O.K.? (As HE *goes, we see him look around
   and call "Kitty-kitty"*)

RUTH: Guess I'll pack. (*Gets up to leave.* DICK *starts taking down one of his posters*)

BOB: Where's everyone?

RUTH: Mike and Mel went out with Norman. They're meeting Shelly at the
   flicks. *Casablanca.* You should see the marks they got. They're both magna
   cum.

DICK: Magna cum. Sneaky bastards.

RUTH: Yep. (SHE *goes out down hall*)

DICK: You staying for graduation?

BOB: No, you?

DICK (*Shakes head no*): Hey, you really going into the army?

BOB: Yeah, as a hostage. I don't know. What are you doing?

DICK: Shit, I don't know.

BOB: Anything lined up for the summer?

DICK: Yeah, delivering milk. It's your friendly college graduate, Mrs. Miller. "Such a shame, the boy went to college." Maybe I'll get sterilized, save any kids having to go through all this. She really was a bitch, you know.

BOB: I guess so.

DICK: Guess so, shit, I hope she gets cancer of the tits and suffers like crazy while she's dying. Honest to Christ, she's the first person I ever met I could really kill.

BOB: Yeah.

DICK: Oh, great humility scene.

BOB: No, it's just, you know, that's how it goes.

DICK: You know something, Bob? You know what's wrong with you?

BOB: I been waiting all this time for someone to tell me. What's wrong with me, Dick?

DICK: You let her get your balls, Bob.

BOB: That was pretty careless, wasn't it?

DICK: No shit, Bob. I remember when you got stung by that bee in the humanities quadrangle. I always wondered about that. I mean, you're supposed to yell when something like that happens. You don't stand there wondering if you should say something. You really are dead, you know.

BOB: Yeah, well, that's what I was trying to tell everyone right before Christmas. I thought I might just try it out, you know, being dead. Didn't feel any different.

DICK: I don't get it.

BOB: No, it's a pretty weird thing.

DICK: I gotta pack.

BOB: Yeah.

DICK *leaves the room.* MIKE *and* COOTIE *burst in through the front door, panting heavily.*

MIKE: Oh, shit, man, we've really had it. Christ, how could the guy do it? I thought he was kidding.

RUTH (*Comes in with a small suitcase*): Hey, you guys better hurry up and pack. We gotta be out of here tomorrow.

COOTIE: Ruth, sit down, huh? Something pretty bad just happened. Seriously, no shitting around.

RUTH: Where's Norman?

COOTIE: Norman's . . . he just . . . oh, shit.

MIKE: He set himself on fire.

BOB: He what?

MIKE: All that stuff he was reading. He just . . . I don't know. He got this idea. Oh, fuck, how could the stupid bastard ever . . . shit.

RUTH: I thought you guys were going to see *Casablanca.*

MIKE: No, we had to tell you that. He had this plan. Honest to shit, we didn't know he was serious. Him and Shelly. We thought he's just . . . we went to the common and he took all his clothes off and poured gasoline all over himself.

COOTIE: We were just shitting around, Ruth. Honest. If we thought he was serious we'd've stopped him, you know.

MIKE: It was that fucking Shelly.

RUTH: You fucking stupid . . .

MIKE: I'm telling you, it wasn't our fault. He wouldn't have lit the match. I know he poured the gasoline, but he'd never've lit the match.

BOB: He's . . .

MIKE: Oh, shit, it was awful. He just sat there turning black. I didn't want to look, but I couldn't turn away. His skin just, Christ, it just fell away from his face and his blood . . . (*Puts head in hand*)

RUTH: Stupid fucking guys. You should've known. Where's Shelly?

COOTIE: She went crazy, Ruth. She just cracked up. We had to practically knock her out. She's O.K. now.

SHELLY *comes in the front door. Her eyes are closed and her fists clenched.* RUTH *runs to her, doesn't know what to do.*

RUTH: Shelly, oh, Shelly, Jesus . . .

SHELLY (*Teeth clenched*): Fucking guys.

NORMAN *comes in.* HE'*s soaking wet and carries a gasoline can.* MIKE *and* COOTIE *rise.*

MIKE: See, everything's cool now. Everybody trusts each other. That's what it's all about. (HE *smiles oddly at the others*)

COOTIE (*Registering it all*): Holy shit!

MIKE *and* COOTIE *leave the room.*

SHELLY (*Yells*): Creeps. (*To* RUTH) You got any first-aid stuff?

RUTH: Yeah. (SHE *gets a box from the pantry. It's a huge white box with a red cross on it, obviously stolen*)

BOB: Hey, what happened?

NORMAN (*Sits*): I'm all right.

SHELLY: Don't talk, Norman. Would you make him some coffee?

RUTH: Yeah. Those guys said you burned yourself.

NORMAN: No, I'm O.K.

RUTH *makes coffee while* SHELLY *ties a bandage around* NORMAN'*s wrist.*

SHELLY: Sorry if this hurts. Hey, Ruth, those guys are really bastards. They gotta learn you don't joke around sometimes.

BOB: Hey, were you really gonna burn yourself?

NORMAN: Well, you know . . .

SHELLY: We were all supposed to do it. All four of us. We waited all this time for them to graduate with good grades and everything. Six months almost. I mean, like, the war could've ended. Fucking creeps. They went and put water in the gasoline can.

NORMAN: I think I might be getting a cold.

SHELLY: We're making coffee, Norman. Keep cool.

BOB: Hey, were you really serious?

NORMAN: Well, I thought, you know, with the war and everything.

SHELLY: Water, shit.

NORMAN: Well, there was some gas in that can.

SHELLY: Fucking creeps.

NORMAN: I definitely smelled some gas when I poured it over me.

SHELLY: Hold still, Norman.

NORMAN: I mean, I knew there was something wrong when I kept holding the match to my wrist and nothing happened.

SHELLY: What do you mean, nothing happened? What's wrong with you, Norman? You call that burn on your wrist nothing? It's the worst burn I ever saw. We're lucky we didn't get arrested.

NORMAN: I've seen movies of the Buddhist monks setting themselves on fire. They usually go up pretty quick in the movies. I bet it hurts a lot. My wrist really hurts.

RUTH (*Brings* NORMAN *some coffee*): Listen, we have to be out of here by tomorrow.

NORMAN: All right.

RUTH: Well, what are you gonna do?

NORMAN: I haven't thought about it too much. I thought I was going to be dead by now. I hadn't planned beyond that.

RUTH: You got a place to stay?

SHELLY: He'll stay with me.

NORMAN: Yeah, O.K.

RUTH: We'll have to have a big cleanup in case Willis comes around.

NORMAN: I was thinking maybe I'll try to get back into graduate school. I'm getting sick of washing dishes.

> BOB *has been taking down his map of Europe from the wall.*

BOB: I think I'll go to Europe.

NORMAN: I'm not really angry at Mel and Mike. In a way I'm kind of glad I'm not dead.

SHELLY: I think those two guys are really evil.

> RUTH *goes down the hall.*

BOB: You ever been to France?

SHELLY: I went last summer.

BOB: What's it like?

SHELLY: Shitty. They're really uptight in France. I got busted in Calais. Two weeks in prison with the runs. That's no joke.

BOB: Maybe England.

NORMAN: I was in England once.

BOB: What's it like?

NORMAN: I went on a bicycle trip with the Youth Hostel Organization. My father sent me.

BOB: How was it?

NORMAN: It was O.K.

SHELLY: England's a lousy place.

NORMAN: I don't know. I met some nice people. I saw Buckingham Palace. The food's not very good, but it didn't rain much. I guess it was a pretty valuable experience. I remember thinking at the time my horizons were a lot wider after that trip. I don't remember why I thought that. Maybe I'll go back there one day.

BOB: Oh, well, there's always Italy or Greece.

SHELLY: If you go over there, check out Algeria. Algeria's really something else.

MR. WILLIS *opens the door.*

WILLIS: O.K. if I step in? Hey, what have you done to your hand?

NORMAN: It's just a burn.

WILLIS: Too bad, huh? Look, how's about if I see everyone for a minute? Everybody here?

BOB (*Yelling*): DICK, RUTH, MIKE, COOTIE, C'MERE A MINUTE. MR. WILLIS WANTS US.

WILLIS: Hey, hey, hey, you don't have to do that. You don't have to yell on account of me. (ALL *come in*) Hi, how's everybody? Gettin' ready for the big day? You gonna wear them long robes and everything, hey? All that fancy ceremony. Pretty good, huh? Listen, I just wanna give the place a quick once-over because I'll tell you why. I got this tenant moving in pretty soon, so I gotta be sure everything's O.K. Get rid of them milk bottles, that's the first thing, and I'll pick up the rent for this month, O.K.? How 'bout this floor, huh? You gonna finish it? Hey, I asked a question, who's supposed to be doing this floor?

BOB: I am, Mr. Willis.

WILLIS: So how come you leave it half-finished?

BOB: Sorry, I never got the time.

WILLIS: Well, you get it. I give you good money for them tiles, put me back a hunnered bucks. How many landlords you find'll do that?

BOB: Yeah, O.K.

WILLIS: By tomorrow night, understand? Now, let's have a little look round the place. (HE *goes down the hall followed by* BOB, RUTH, COOTIE *and* MIKE)

NORMAN: Mike. (MIKE *turns*) Listen, I just want to tell you, I'm not angry about what happened.

MIKE: What do you mean?

SHELLY: You're a real creep pulling a trick like that.

MIKE: That's what I get for saving his life?

SHELLY: It's none of your business. It's the existential right of every living person to take his own life.

MIKE: No one's stopping you now.

NORMAN: What I wanted to say is, if you and Mel are coming back next year to go to graduate school, maybe we can share a place. I mean, you know, I could come down here early and look around.

MIKE: You going home for the summer?

SHELLY: He's staying with me.

NORMAN: Yeah, well I might go home for a few weeks. Visit my folks. The best way is you write to my father, care of the Police Department, Erie County, and if I'm not at home he'll know where to forward it.

MIKE: Right. Me and Cootie'll be up in the great Northwest Territory helping Dad with the furs. If you don't hear from us, just go ahead and find a place for all of us, 'cause sometimes the mail gets delayed.

NORMAN: Don't worry, I'll get a place.

MIKE: Commissioner of Police, Erie County.

NORMAN: That's right.

MIKE *smiles at him, not without warmth. In come* COOTIE, RUTH, BOB, DICK *and* MR. WILLIS.

WILLIS: Not bad. I'll tellya what I'll do. I'll keep the fifty-dollar deposit for holes in the plaster and the broken window.

COOTIE: Hey, we didn't break that window. That was broken when we moved in.

WILLIS: That's not my problem, Cootie. I keep the fifty and if any of you guys got an objection, you want to take it up with me, let's have it. Look, I got a living to make like everybody else in town. Maybe you think I'm being a rotten guy, but you wait. You go out there in the world and you're gonna see things, you'll think old Willis was Snow White and the Seven Dwarfs all rolled into one. You're gonna see dishonesty, you're gonna see mean people, you see swindlers, killers, queers, you see guys trying to double-park on Saturday morning, you take my word. The thing I love about you kids is you're honest, you're direct. There's no shitting around with you. Yeah, I know it sounds corny, but I'm gonna miss having you guys around. You gotta save this poor fuckin' country, and excuse my language. There was a time, I can remember, when you paid your taxes and you knew your money was goin' into the right things. Good, wholesome things. Look at it nowadays. Two blocks away there's a house full of guys known all over the neighborhood to practice open homosexuality. Open homosexuality two blocks away, and there's kids playing right outside that house every day. I don't know. I'd go jump in the lake if it wasn't for you kids. I never knew anyone like you, and I been around, let me tellya. You know where you are, you know where you're going, and you know how to get there. That's never happened before in the history of this whole fucking country. God bless you kids, and good luck. I'll take a check for the rent.

COOTIE *starts "For He's a Jolly Good Fellow"; the* OTHERS *join in.*

GROUP (*Singing*):
> For he's a jolly good fellow,
> For he's a jolly good fellow,
> For he's a jolly good fellow,
> That nobody can deny.
> That nobody can deny.
> That nobody can deny.
> (*Etc., all the way through.* WILLIS *beams, entirely unaware of the spoof*)

Scene 7

The next afternoon. The kitchen is bare of furniture. The icebox is gone, only a few milk bottles left. Only one chair left. BOB *is laying the vinyl tiles.* COOTIE *comes into the room with his* FATHER. HE *grabs the last valise by the front door.*

COOTIE: Hey, Bob, I'm going.
BOB: Yeah, we'll see you.
COOTIE: Yeah.
MIKE (*Comes into the kitchen from the hall door*): You going?
COOTIE: Yeah. Oh, this is my father. That's Mike, that's Bob.
BOB: Hi.
MIKE: Hi.
FATHER: A pleasure.
MIKE: What?
FATHER: It's a pleasure meeting you.
MIKE: Oh, yeah, right.
COOTIE: Well, see you guys. Hey, what you doing next year?
BOB: Oh, I got a job in a department store.
COOTIE: Playing piano?
BOB: Harp.
COOTIE: Great. Well, see ya.
BOB: See ya.
MIKE: Yeah, see ya, Cootie.
FATHER: Nice meeting you boys.

COOTIE *leaves with his* FATHER.

MIKE: They don't look like each other. Good old Cootie. Where's Norman?
BOB: He left about an hour ago.
MIKE: Never said good-bye or anything.
BOB: You should've seen it, putting all his stuff in the back of a police car.
MIKE: What?
BOB: Yeah, his old man's Commissioner of Police, or something.
MIKE: I'll be fucked.

RUTH *comes in from the hall with two suitcases and sets them down by some other suitcases near the door.*

RUTH: I guess that's it. Where's Cootie?
MIKE: He just left with his dad.
RUTH: Some friend. No good-bye or anything.
MIKE: We'll see him next year.
RUTH: No we won't.

MIKE *and* RUTH *go down the hall for their last luggage.* DICK *and the* MILKMAN *enter through the front door with empty cartons.* THEY *load the remaining bottles.*

DICK: Hey, I wouldn't mind a little help here. I gotta catch a train.
MILKMAN: I don't understand you guys. You're supposed to be college graduates. Eight hundred and fifty-seven two-quart milk bottles. That's not the kind of thing a grown-up person does. You're supposed to be grown-ups. I don't get it.

The phone is ringing.

DICK: That's the last one.
MILKMAN: O.K. I just hope you guys don't think you can go through life hoarding milk bottles like this. I got enough to do without this. I got a regular route. (*To* DICK) Look, if you want to pick up a lot of bottles, put your fingers right down inside, you get more that way.
DICK: O.K. Hey, you guys, you're a lot of help.

MILKMAN *and* DICK *go out with their cartons.*

BOB (*Answering phone*): Hello, oh, yes, how are you? No, this is Bob. Bob Rettie. No, music. Yes, of course I remember you. No, he's not in right now.

MIKE *and* RUTH *have reentered, motioning* BOB *that* THEY *have to go.* HE *motions back that it's O.K.* HE *waves good-bye as* THEY *pick up their suitcases and begin to leave.*

RUTH: Hey, good luck.

BOB: Yeah, yeah, you too. See ya, Mike.

MIKE: See ya.

RUTH *and* MIKE *exit through front door.*

BOB (*Back to phone*): Sorry, Mrs. Roper, I was just saying good-bye to some people I . . . some friends of mine. I don't know if he'll be back or not. Can I leave a message? (*Pause*) Look, Mrs. Roper, I'm very sorry about that but there's nothing I can do if he's gone. I can tell him to call you if he comes back, Mrs. Roper, look, calm down. Listen, I'm hanging up now, all right? I gotta hang up now. Good-bye, Mrs. Roper.

BOB *hangs up and returns to the floor tiles.* DICK *comes in alone through front door.*

DICK: Boy, that guy was sure pissed off about the bottles. You should've seen the look on his face.

BOB: Hey, you know that guy you studied with, Professor Roper?

DICK (*Pause*): Yes.

BOB: His wife just called.

DICK: What'd she want?

BOB: She just . . . I don't know. Nothing, I guess. Pretty weird.

DICK: Yeah, pretty weird. (HE *puts on his coat and takes up his bags*)

BOB: Hey, Dick.

DICK: What?

THEY *look at each other.*

BOB: I don't know. See ya.

DICK: Yeah. (*As* HE *is leaving,* HE *sees* KATHY, *who is standing in the doorway*)

KATHY: Hi. Can I come in? (DICK *moves aside.* HE *and* BOB *stare at her. This makes her a little nervous*) Everyone gone?

DICK and BOB(*Together*): Yeah . . . (THEY *exchange a nervous glance*)

BOB: Except for me and Dick. We're still here. We're right in front of you, as a matter of fact. . . .

DICK: That's a nice coat she's wearing. That's a very nice coat, Kathy.

KATHY (*Knows something is going on but doesn't know what*): Thanks.

BOB: Hey, Dick. (DICK *leaves*) See ya. (*To himself*)

KATHY: Finishing the floor?

BOB: Evidently.

KATHY: Kind of late, isn't it? (*Pause*) Did they send my grades here?

BOB: Right there. You did really shitty.

KATHY (*Gets the letter*): Bob, listen . . . I'm sorry about . . . sounds pretty silly.

BOB: No, I accept your apology for whatever you think you did.

KATHY: I saw Ruth the other day. She said you've been . . . well, pretty bad this semester.

BOB: Did she say that?

KATHY: I wish I'd known . . . couldn't you have . . . you should have told me to stay.

BOB: Well, it slipped my mind. Sorry.

KATHY: You shouldn't be so ashamed of your feelings.

BOB: O.K.

KATHY: I'm serious. You've gotta learn to let go. Like your music. It's all squenched and tidy.

BOB: O.K. I'll work on that.

KATHY: Oh, Bob.

BOB: What?

KATHY: I really wish you'd've told me. I'd've come back. I never really related to Richard.

BOB: I'll tell him when I see him.

KATHY: Yeah, you're right. Why the hell should you be nice? Oh, well, good luck . . . and, you know, when you see your mother say hello for me.

BOB: O.K.

KATHY: How is she?

BOB: She's O.K. Sort of dead.

KATHY: I like her, Bob. You're lucky. She's, you know, she's a real person.

BOB: No, she's you know, a real corpse.

KATHY: All right, have it your way.

BOB: No, it's not what I wanted particularly. No, taken all in all, from various different angles, I'd've preferred it if she lived. I'm pretty sure of that.

KATHY (*Pause*): She's not really . . . ?

BOB: School's over.

KATHY: Bob, do you know what you're saying?

BOB: Kathy, please get the fuck out of here.

KATHY: But, I mean, Ruth never told me. . . . Didn't you tell anyone?

BOB: Yeah, I just told you.

KATHY: But, I mean . . . when . . . when did . . .

BOB: Christmas. No, no, it was the day after.

KATHY (*Sits*): Jesus, Bob, why didn't you tell anyone? I mean, how could you live for six months without telling someone?

BOB (*No emotion*): Oh, I don't know. A little cunning. A little fortitude. A little perseverance. (*Pause*) I couldn't believe it. Not the last time anyway. They put her in this room. I don't know what you call it. They bring everybody there just before they kick the bucket. They just sort of lie there looking at each other, wondering what the hell they got in common to talk about. I couldn't believe that anyone could look like she looked and still be alive. (*Pause*) She knew. I'm sure of that. (*Pause*) Once, I remember, she tried to tell me something. I mean this noise came out of somewhere around her mouth, like somebody running a stick over a fence or something, and I thought maybe she's trying to tell me something. So I leaned over to hear better and I caught a whiff of that breath. Like fried puke. And I was sick all over her. (*Pause. Brighter*) But you want to know something funny, and I mean this really is funny, so you can laugh if you like. There was this lady dying next to my mother and she kept talking about her daughter Susan. Well, Susan came to visit the day I puked on Mom. And you know what? It was only Susan Weinfeld, which doesn't mean anything to you, but she happens to have been the girl I spent a good many of my best months as a sophomore in high school trying to lay. In fact, her virginity almost cost me a B plus in history and here we were, six years later, staring at each other across two dying mothers. I want to tell you something, Kathy. She looked fantastic. And I could tell she was thinking the same thing about me. I mean that kind of scene doesn't happen every day. It was like . . . (*thinks*) . . . it was like how we were the first time. Maybe, just possibly, a little better. So we went out and had a coffee in Mister Donut and started groping each other like crazy under the counter, and I mean we just couldn't keep our hands off each other, so I suggested we get a cab down to my mother's place since, you know, there happened to be no one there at the moment. But the funniest thing was when we get down to Mom's place and you know all those stairs you have to go up and there's Susan all over me practically screaming for it and I start fumbling around with the keys in the lock and none of them would fit. I must've tried every key about fifty fucking times and none of them would fit. Boy, what a drag. (*Pause*) Oh, we got in all right. Finally. I had to go downstairs, through the Salvatores' apartment, out the window, up the fire escape, and through Mom's place, but when I opened the front door, guess what? There's poor old Susan asleep on the landing. She really looked cute. I hated to wake her up. Anyway, by the time we'd made coffee and talked and smoked about a million cigarettes each we didn't feel like it anymore. Not really. We did it anyway but, you know, just to be polite, just to make some sense out of the evening. It was, taken all in all, a pretty ordinary fuck. The next morning we made plans to meet again that night. We even joked about it, you know, about what a super-fucking good time we'd have, and if you ask me, we could've probably really gotten into something incredible if we'd tried again, but when I went to the hospital I found out good old Mom had croaked sometime during the night, and somehow, I still don't know why to this day . . . I never got in touch with Susan again. And vice versa. It's a funny thing, you know. At the funeral there were all these people. Friends of Mom's—I didn't know any of them. They were all crying like crazy and I . . . well . . . (*Pause*) I never even got to the burial. The car I was in broke down on the Merritt Parkway. Just as well. I didn't feel like seeing all those people. I'd sure love to have fucked Susan again, though.

KATHY: Bob . . . I . . .

BOB (*Abstract*): Anyway . . . I just didn't feel like telling anyone. I mean, I wasn't all that upset. I was a little upset, mostly because I thought I ought to be more upset, but as for your actual grief, well. Anything interesting happen to you this semester . . . Kathy? (KATHY *has risen*) Going? (KATHY *is going out the door*) Give my regards to that guy you're rescuing at the moment; what's-his-name? (KATHY *is gone.* HE *shrugs. The cat wanders in from the hallway*) Hey, cat, what are you doing hanging around here? All the humans gone west. (*Puts the cat outside and shuts the door.* HE *nudges the tiles with his toe and looks around at the empty room*) Hey, guys, guess what happened to me? I want to tell you about this really incredible thing that happened to me . . . (HE *is faltering now, choking slightly, but* HE *doesn't know* HE's *about to crack. His body is doing something strange, unfamiliar*) Hey, what's happening . . . (HE's *crying now*) Oh, fuck, come on, come on. Shit, no, no . . .

Fade.

END OF PLAY

STILL LIFE

Emily Mann

About Emily Mann

Born in Boston in 1952, Emily Mann received a B.A. from Harvard and an MFA from the University of Minnesota. Her first play, *Annulla Allen: Autobiography of a Survivor*, premiered at The Guthrie Theater's Guthrie 2 under her direction in 1977 and was later produced at Chicago's Goodman Theatre and on *Earplay*. Mann's most recent play, *Execution of Justice*, which depicts the trial of Dan White for the killing of George Moscone and Harvey Milk, was commissioned by the Eureka Theatre Company of San Francisco and first produced by Actors Theatre of Louisville, as co-winner of its 1984 Great American Play Contest. Mann's directorial credits include the BAM Theater Company's productions of *He and She* and *Oedipus the King*, the Guthrie's *The Glass Menagerie* and ATL's *A Weekend near Madison*, which subsequently ran Off Broadway. She has been the recipient of a CAPS grant, a Guggenheim fellowship and an NEA artistic associateship, and is a 1985 McKnight Fellow. In 1983 Mann received the Rosamond Gilder Award from the New Drama Forum for "outstanding creative achievement in the theatre."

Production History

Still Life premiered at the Goodman Studio Theatre in October 1980, and was then produced at American Place Theatre in New York in early 1981. The American Place production, under Mann's direction, won Obies for playwriting, direction and all three performances, as well as for best production. The play has subsequently been performed around the world—in Johannesburg, at the Avignon and Edinburgh festivals, in London and Paris, and in major regional theatres and universities throughout the United States.

Playwright's Note

Still Life is about three people I met in Minnesota during the summer of 1978. It is about violence in America. The Vietnam War is the backdrop to the violence at home. The play is dedicated to the casualties of the war—all of them.

   The play is a "documentary" because it is a distillation of interviews I conducted during that summer. I chose the documentary style to insure that the reality of the people and events described could not be denied. Perhaps one could argue about the accuracy of the people's interpretations of events, but one cannot deny that these are actual people describing actual events as they saw and understood them.

The play is also a personal document. A specialist in the brain and its perceptions said to me after seeing *Still Life* that the play is constructed as a traumatic memory. Each character struggles with his traumatic memory of events and the play as a whole is my traumatic memory of their accounts. The characters speak directly to the audience so that the audience can hear what I heard, experience what I experienced.

I have been obsessed with violence in our country since I came of age in the 1960s. I have no answer to the questions I raise in the play but I think the questions are worth asking. The play is a plea for examination and self-examination, an attempt at understanding our own violence and a hope that through understanding we can, as Nadine says, "come out on the other side."

Production Notes

The actors speak directly to the audience. The rhythms are of real people's speech, but may also at times have the sense of improvisation one finds with the best jazz musicians: the monologues should sometimes sound like extended riffs.

The play is written in three acts but this does not denote act breaks. Rather, the acts represent movements and the play should be performed without intermission. The ideal running time is one hour and 30 minutes.

Lyrics for "No More Genocide" by Holly Near

Verse 1
Why do we call them the enemy
This struggling nation that we're bombing 'cross the sea
we put in prison/now independent
Why do we want these people to die
Why do we say North and South
Oh why, Oh why, Oh why?

Chorus
Well, that's just a lie
One of the many and we've had plenty
I don't want more of the same
Genocide in my name
Genocide, no, no, no, no

No more genocide, no, no, no, no
No more genocide in my name

Verse 2:
Why are our history books so full of lies
When no word is spoken of why the Indian dies
Or that the Chicano loves the California land
Do our books all say it was discovered by white man.

Chorus

Verse 3:
Why are the weapons of the war so young
Why are there only older men around when it's done
Why are so many of our soldiers black or brown
Do we say it's because they're good at cutting yellow people down.

Chorus

Characters

MARK, an ex-marine, Vietnam veteran, husband, artist, lover, father.
CHERYL, his wife, mother of his children.
NADINE, his friend, artist, mother of three, divorcee, a woman with many jobs
and many lives, 10-15 years older than Mark and Cheryl.

Time

The present.

Place

The setting is a long table with ashtrays, water glasses, Mark's pictures and slides upon it. Behind it is a large screen for slide projection. The look is of a conference room or perhaps a trial room.

The director may also choose to place each character in a separate area, i.e. Cheryl in her living room (couch), Mark in his studio (framing table), Nadine at home or at a cafe table.

The Play

Still Life

ACT ONE

I

MARK *snaps on slide of* CHERYL: *young, fragile, thin, hair flowing, quintessentially innocent.*

MARK: This is a picture of my wife before.
(*Lights up on* CHERYL. *Six months pregnant, heavy, rigid*)
This is her now.
She's been through a lot.
(*Snaps on photographic portrait of himself. Face gentle. Halo of light around head*)
This is a portrait Nadine made of me.
(*Lights up on* NADINE)
This is Nadine.
(*Lights out on* NADINE. *Snaps on slide of marine boot and leg just below the knee*)
This is a picture of my foot.
I wanted a picture of it because if I ever lost it,
I wanted to remember what it looked like.
(HE *laughs. Fade out*)

II

CHERYL: If I thought about this too much I'd go crazy.
So I don't think about it much.
I'm not too good with the past.
Now, Mark, he remembers.
That's his problem.
I don't know whether it's 1972 or 1981.
Sometimes I think about divorce.
God, I don't know.
Divorce means a lot of nasty things
like it's over.
It says a lot like
Oh yeah. I been there. I'm a divorcee. . . . Geez.
You could go on forever about that thing.
I gave up on it. No.
You know, I wasn't willing to give up on it,
and I should have,
for my own damn good.

You look:
It's all over now,
it's everywhere.
There are so many men like him now.

You don't have to look far to see how
sucked in you can get.

You got a fifty-fifty chance.

III

NADINE: When I first met Mark, it was the big stuff.
Loss of ego, we shared everything.

The first two hours I spent with him and what I thought
then is what I think now, and I know just about everything
there is to know, possibly.

He told me about it *all* the first week I met him.
We were discussing alcoholism.
I'm very close to that myself.
He said that one of his major projects
was to face all the relationships he'd been in
where he'd violated someone.

His wife is one.

He's so honest he doesn't hide anything.

He told me he beat her very badly.
He doesn't know if he can recover that relationship.

I've met his wife.
I don't know her.
I sometimes even forget . . .

He's the greatest man I've ever known.
I'm still watching him.

We're racing. It's very wild.
No one's gaming.
There are no expectations.
You have a foundation for a lifelong relationship.
He can't disappoint me.

Men have been wonderful to me,
but I've never been treated like this.
All these—yes, all these men—
businessmen, politicians, artists, patriarchs—none of
them, no one has ever demonstrated this to me.

He's beyond consideration.
I have him under a microscope.
I can't be fooled.
I know what natural means.
I know when somebody's studying.
I've been around a long time.
I'm forty-three years old.
I'm not used to being treated like this.

I don't know. I'm being honored, cherished, cared about.

Maybe this is how everybody's treated and I've missed out.
(*Laughs*)

IV

MARK: My biggest question to myself all my life was

How I would act under combat?
That would be who I was as a man.

I read my Hemingway.
You know . . .

The point is,
you don't *need* to go through it.

I would break both my son's legs
before I let him go through it.

CHERYL: I'm telling you—
if I thought about this, I'd go crazy.
So I don't think about it.

MARK: (*To* CHERYL)
I know I did things to you, Cheryl.
But you took it.
I'm sorry.
How many times can I say I'm sorry to you?
(*To audience*)
I've, uh, I've, uh, hurt my wife.

NADINE: He is incredibly gentle. It's madness to be treated this way. I
don't need it. It's great without it.

CHERYL: He blames it all on the war . . . but I want to tell
you . . . don't let him.

MARK: My wife has come close to death a number of times, but
uh . . .

NADINE: Maybe he's in awe of me.

CHERYL: See, I read into things,
and I don't know if you're supposed to, but I do.
Maybe I'm too against his artist world,
but Mark just gets into trouble
when he's into that art world.

NADINE: (*Laughing*)
Maybe he's this way to his mother.

CHERYL: One day I went into the basement to take my clothes out of the
washer,
Jesus I have to clean out that basement,
and I came across this jar . . .

NADINE: Especially from a guy who's done all these dastardly deeds.

CHERYL: He had a naked picture of me in there,
cut out to the form,
tied to a stake with a string.
And there was all this broken glass,
and I know Mark.
Broken glass is a symbol of fire.
(*Thinking*)
What else did he have at the bottom?

NADINE: I accept everything he's done.

CHERYL: Yeah, there was a razor blade in there

and some old negatives of the blood stuff, I think.
I mean, that was so violent.
That jar to me, scared me.
That jar to me said:
Mark wants to kill me.
Literally kill me for what I've done.
He's burning me at the stake like Joan of Arc.
It just blew my mind.

NADINE: Those jars he makes are brilliant, humorous.
He's preserving the war.
I'm intrigued that people think he's violent.
I know all his stories.
He calls himself a time-bomb.
But so are you, aren't you?

MARK: I don't know what it would be for women.
What war is for men.
I've thought about it. A lot.
I saw women brutalized in the war.
I look at what I've done to my wife.

CHERYL: He keeps telling me: He's a murderer.
I gotta believe he can be a husband.

MARK: The truth of it is, it's different
from what we've heard about war before.

NADINE: He's just more angry than any of us.
He's been fighting for years.
Fighting the priests, fighting all of them.

MARK: I don't want this to come off as a combat story.

CHERYL: Well, a lot of things happened that I couldn't handle.

MARK: It's a tragedy is what it is. It happened to a lot of people.

CHERYL: But not too, you know, not anything
dangerous or anything like that—
just crazy things.

NADINE: I guess all my friends are angry.

CHERYL: But, uh, I don't know.
It's really hard for me to bring back those years.

NADINE: Mark's just been demonstrating it, by picking up weapons,
leading a group of men.

CHERYL: Really hard for me to bring back those years.

MARK: My brother . . .
He has a whole bunch of doubts now,
thinking, "Well I wonder what I'd do
if I were in a fight."
And you don't NEED to go through that shit.

It's BULLSHIT.
It just chews people up.

NADINE: Leading a whole group into group sex, vandalism, theft.
That's not uncommon in our culture.

MARK: You go into a VFW hall, that's all men talk about.
Their trips on the war.

NADINE: I don't know anyone who cares so much about his parents.
He's trying to save them.
Like he sent home this bone of a man he killed, from Nam.
It was this neat attempt to demand for them to listen,
about the war.

MARK: I can't talk to these guys.
There's just no communication.
But we just . . . know.
We look and we know.

NADINE: See, he's testing everyone all the time.
In very subtle ways.
He can't believe I'm not shocked.
I think that intrigues him.

CHERYL: Oh. I don't know.
I want it suppressed as fast as possible.

NADINE: He laughed at me once.
He'd just told a whole raft of stories.
He said: "Anyone who understands all this naughtiness
must have been pretty naughty themselves."
Which is a pretty simplistic way of saying we can all do it.

MARK: I thought:
If I gave *you* the information,
I couldn't wash my hands of the guilt,
because I did things over there.
We all did.

CHERYL: I would do anything to help suppress it.

MARK: (*Quietly to audience*)
We all did.

V

NADINE: You know what war is for women?
A friend of mine sent me this line:
I'd rather go into battle three times than give birth once.
She said Medea said that.
I stuck it on my refrigerator.
I showed it to Mark. He laughed for days.

MARK: When Cheryl, uh, my wife and I first met,
I'd just come back from Nam.
I was so frightened of her.
She had this long hair and she was really thin.
I just thought she was really, uh,
really American.

NADINE: Do you know I never talked with my husband
about being pregnant?
For nine months there was something going on down there
and we never mentioned it. Ever.

MARK: You know, it was like I couldn't talk to her.
I didn't know how to respond.

NADINE: We completely ignored it.
We were obsessed with names.
We kept talking constantly about what we would name it.
I gained fifty pounds. It was sheer ignorance.
I was a good Catholic girl
and no one talked about such things.
I never knew what that part of my body was doing.

CHERYL: It was my naivety.
I was so naive to the whole thing, that his craziness
had anything to do with where he'd been.
I mean, I was naive to the whole world
let alone somebody
who had just come back from there.

NADINE: When the labor started, we merrily got in the car
and went to the hospital.
They put me immediately into an operating room.
I didn't even know what dilation meant.
And I couldn't.
I could not dilate.

CHERYL: See, I'd hear a lot from his family.
I worked for his father as a dental assistant.
And it was all they talked about—Mark—so I had to meet the
     guy.

NADINE: I was in agony, they knocked me out.

CHERYL: And I saw, I mean, I'd open a drawer and I'd see
these pictures—

NADINE: My lungs filled up with fluid.

CHERYL: . . . dead men. Men hanging. Things like that.
Pictures Mark had sent back.

MARK: Yeah. I kept sending everything back.

NADINE: They had to give me a tracheotomy.

My trachea was too small.
They went running out of the operating room to get
the right equipment.
Everyone thought I was going to die.
CHERYL: Once he sent back a bone of a man he killed. To his mother.
MARK: To my brother, not my mother.
CHERYL: Boy, did that lady freak.
NADINE: My husband saw them burst out of the room in a panic.
He thought I was gone.
CHERYL: Now it doesn't take much for that lady to freak.
Very hyper. I think I'd've gone nuts.
I think I'd wanna take it
and hit him over the head with it.
You just don't do those things.
WHAT THE HECK IS HAPPENING TO YOU? I'd say.
They never asked that though.
I don't think they wanted to know
and I think they were afraid to ask.
MARK: I know. I really wanted them to ask.
CHERYL: I think they felt the sooner forgotten, the better off you'd be.
NADINE: I remember leaving my body.
MARK: I'll never forget that.
CHERYL: They didn't want to bring up a bad subject.
MARK: I came home from a war, walked in the door,
they don't say anything.
I asked for a cup of coffee,
and my mother starts bitching at me about drinking coffee.
NADINE: I looked down at myself on that operating table and felt so free.
CHERYL: Your mother couldn't deal with it.
NADINE: They gave me a C-section.
I don't remember anything else.
CHERYL: My memory's not as good as his.
It's like I put bad things in one half
and in time I erase them.
NADINE: I woke up in the hospital room with tubes in my throat,
stitches in my belly. I could barely breathe.
My husband was there. He said: Have you seen the baby?
WHAT BABY, I said.

Can you believe it?

CHERYL: That's why I say there's a lot of things, weird things,
that happened to us, and I just generally put them
under the title of weird things . . .

and try to forget it.
And to be specific, I'm real vague on a lot of things.
NADINE: I never knew they were in there
and so I guess I didn't want them to come out.
CHERYL: I mean, my whole life has turned around since then.
I mean, gosh, I got a kid and another one on the way.
And I'm thinking of climbing the social ladder.
I've got to start thinking about schools for them,
and I *mean* this, it's a completely
different life,
and I've had to . . .
I've WANTED to change anyway.

It's really hard to bring these things back out.

NADINE: For my second child, the same thing happened.
By the third time around
they had to drag me out of the car.
I thought they were taking me to my death for sure.
MARK: Cheryl is amazing.
Cheryl has always been like chief surgeon.
When the shrapnel came out of my head,
she would be the one to take it out.
CHERYL: It's no big deal.
NADINE: So when people ask me about the birth of my children,
I laugh.
MARK: Just like with Danny.
She delivered Danny herself.
NADINE: My children were EXTRACTED from me.
CHERYL: It's no big deal. Just like pulling teeth.
Once the head comes out, there's nothing to it.

VI

MARK: I want to tell you what a marine is.

NADINE: CHERYL:
I have so much to do.   See, I got kids now.
Just to keep going.
                                         I can't be looking into
Just to keep my kids going.   myself.
I don't sleep at all.   I've got to be looking
                                         out.

When my kids complain
about supper.

I just say:
I know it's crappy food.
Well, go upstairs
and throw it up.

I was in a cafe today.

I heard the funniest comment:

She must be married.
She spends so much money.

For the next five years
at least.

When I'm ready to look
in, look out.

God, don't get into the
kid routine. It'll do
it to you every time.

Because you're getting
their best interests
mixed up with *your* best
interests. And they
don't go together.

They go together because
it *should* be your best
interest, and *then their*
best interest. So what
are you gonna do to them
in the meantime?

You're talking head-trips.

VII

MARK: There was this whole trip that we were really special.
        And our training was really hard,
        like this whole Spartan attitude.
CHERYL: The war is the base of all our problems.
        He gets crazy talking about it
        and you can't get him to stop
        no matter what he's doing to the people around him.
MARK: And there was this whole thing too
        I told Nadine about that really knocked me out.
        There was this whole ethic:
        You do not leave your man behind on the field.
        I love that.
CHERYL: Well, he's usually talking more than they can handle.
NADINE: You know, we had two months of foreplay.
MARK: I came to a point in there:

Okay, you're here, there's no escape, you're going to get taken,
it's all right to commit suicide.
And it was as rational as that.

We came across a hit at night, we got ambushed,
it was a black guy walking point, and you know,
bang, bang, bang.
You walk into it. It was a surprise.

Well, they got this black guy.
And they took his body and we found him about a week
  later . . .

CHERYL: People start getting really uncomfortable,
   and you can see it in his eyes,
   the excitement.

NADINE: The first time I met Mark,
   I'd gone to his shop to buy supplies.
   I didn't think anything about him at first.
   (I've never been attracted to younger men.)
   But he seemed to know what he was doing.

CHERYL: It's almost like there's fire in his eyes.

MARK: And they had him tied to a palm tree,
   and his balls were in his mouth.
   They'd opened up his stomach and it had been pulled out.
   And I knew . . .

NADINE: I saw some of his work.

MARK: Nobody was going to do that to me.

NADINE: Some of the blood photography I think.

MARK: Better for me to rationalize suicide
   because I didn't want . . .
   that.
   I don't know.

CHERYL: It bothers me because it's better left forgotten.
   It's just stirring up clear water.

NADINE: We talked and I left. But I felt strange.

MARK: R.J. was my best friend over there.
   He and I got into a whole weird trip.
   We found ourselves competing against one another,
   setting up ambushes,
   getting people on *kills* and things,
   being the best at it we could.

NADINE: All of a sudden, he came out of the shop and said:
   "You want a cup of tea?"

I was in a hurry,
(I'm always in a hurry)
but I said, "Sure," and we went to a tea shop.
(*Laughs*)

MARK: R.J. is dead.
He got killed in a bank robbery in Chicago.
(He was one of the few friends of mine who survived the war.)

NADINE: Two hours later, we got up from the table.
I'm telling you, neither of us could stand up.
We were gasping for breath.

MARK: See, I got all these people involved
in a Far East smuggling scam when we got back,
and then it all fell apart
and we were waiting to get arrested.

The smack got stashed in this car that was being held
in a custody lot.
Everyone was afraid to go get it.
So I decided to get it.
I did this whole trip Thanksgiving weekend.
I crawled in there,
stole the tires off the car
that were loaded with the smack.
I had R.J. help me.
We were doing the war all over again.
That was the last time I saw him alive.

NADINE: We had said it *all* in two hours.
What I thought then is what I think now
and I think I know everything there is to know.

We must have looked pretty funny staggering out of there.

MARK: I heard from one guy on a regular basis, maybe once a year.
He was green to Vietnam.
We were getting into
some real heavy contact that Christmas.
It was late at night, the VC went to us
while we were sleeping.
They just threw grenades in on us.
The explosion came, I threw this kid in a bush.
All I did was grab him down,
and he got a medical out of there.
But he feels I saved his life.

NADINE: When we got out onto the street we said good-bye

but we both knew that our whole lives had changed.

CHERYL: I know he has other women. I don't know who they are.
At this point I don't really care.
I have a child to think about
and just getting by every day.

NADINE: We used to meet and talk.
We'd meet in the plaza and talk.
We'd go for rides in the car and talk.

CHERYL: See, lots of times people break up.
And then the man goes on to the next one.
And you hear the guy say:
"Oh, my wife was crazy." Or something like that.
"She couldn't take it."

NADINE: Sometimes we'd be driving,
we'd have to stop the car and get our breaths.
We were dizzy, we were gasping for breath,
just from being together.

CHERYL: But the important question to ask is: WHY is she crazy?

MARK: So he wants to see me.
I haven't been able to see him.

CHERYL: My brother is a prime example.
He nearly killed his wife a number of times.
She was a real high-strung person.
She snapped.
The family keeps saying, oh, poor Marge, she was so crazy.

MARK: He was only in the bush maybe five, six weeks,
but it did something to him.
He spent two years, he wrote me a letter,
in a mental institution.
I don't know.

I knew he knew what I knew.

CHERYL: My brother's now got one little girl
that SAW her little brother
get shot in the head by his mother . . .

MARK: I know who's been there.
And they know.

CHERYL: And then saw her mother come after her.

MARK: But in a sense we want to be as far away
from each other as possible.
It's become a *personal* thing. The guilt.
There IS the guilt.
It's getting off on having all that power every day.

Because it was so nice.
I mean, it was power . . .

NADINE: You know they're doing surveys now, medical research on this.

MARK: I had the power of life and death.

NADINE: They think something actually changes
in the blood or the lungs when you feel this way.

CHERYL: I'm sorry. They were married too long
for it just to have been Marge.

MARK: I'm sitting here now deep down thinking about it . . .

NADINE: You watch. Soon there'll be a science of love,
and there should be.

CHERYL: When someone goes so-called crazy in a marriage,
I always think:
IT TAKES TWO.

MARK: It's like the best dope you've ever had,
the best sex you've ever had.

NADINE: It was like dying,
and it was the most beautiful feeling of my life.

CHERYL: My brother's on to a new woman now.

MARK: You never find anything better.
And that's not something
you're supposed to feel good about.

CHERYL: If Mark and I split up, I pity the next one.

MARK: I haven't told you what a marine is yet.

CHERYL: Women should warn each other.

Pause.

NADINE: Everything Mark did was justified.
We've all done it.
Murdered someone we loved, or ourselves.

MARK: I mean, we were trained to do one thing.
That's the one thing about the marines.
We were trained to kill.

NADINE: This is hard to say.
I have been in the jungle so long,
that even with intimates, I protect myself.
But I know that Mark felt good killing.
When he told me that I didn't bat an eye.
I understand.

CHERYL: Look,
I think Mark and R.J. were close
only because they both got off on the war.
And I think they were the only two over there that did.

Doesn't it kill you when they get into this men-talk?
All men don't talk like that,
when they get together to reminisce.
They don't talk about getting laid and dope.
Imagine getting together with your best girlfriend
and talking about what it was like the night before in the sack.
That grosses me out.

NADINE: I judge everyone so harshly
that it is pretty ironic
that I'm not moved by anything he tells me.
I'm not changed. I'm not shocked.
I'm not offended. And he must see that.

MARK: I had the power of life and death.
I wrote home to my brother.
I wrote him, I told him.
I wrote:
I dug it. I enjoyed it.
I really enjoyed it.

NADINE: I understand because I'm *convinced*
that I am even angrier than Mark.
I went off in a different direction, that's all.

CHERYL: Now I don't think Mark and R.J. were rare.
I think the DEGREE is rare.
I mean men would not be going on fighting like this
for centuries if there wasn't something besides
having to do it for their country.
It has to be something like Mark says.
I mean he said it was like orgasm.
He said it was the best sex he ever had.
You know where he can take that remark.
But what better explanation can you want?
And believe me, that is Mark's definition of glory.
Orgasm is GLORY to Mark.

MARK: I talked with R.J. about it.
He got into a hit once at about 8:30 at night.
And there was this "person" . . .
laying down, wounded,
holding onto a grenade.
(It was a high contact.)
We watched R.J. walk over and he just shot . . .
the person . . .
in the face.

He knew it.

As incredibly civilized as we are in this room, these things go
    on.

NADINE: Until you know a lot of Catholics
you can't understand what hate means.
I mean I'm a . . . I was a Catholic.
And Catholics have every right to hate like they do.
It requires a whole lifetime
to undo what that training does to them.

MARK: It's getting hard to talk.
Obviously, I need to tell it,
but I don't want to be seen as . . .
a monster.

NADINE: Just start talking to Catholics
who allow themselves to talk.
It's unspeakable what's been done to Catholic youths.
Every aspect of their life from their table manners
to their sexuality. It's just terrible.

MARK: I'm just moving through society now.

Pause.

VIII

NADINE: I mean my definition of sophistication
is the inability to be surprised by anything.

MARK: I look at my face in a mirror,
I look at my hand, and I cannot believe . . .
I did these things.

CHERYL: Mark's hit me before.

MARK: See, I see the war now through my wife.
She's a casualty too.
She doesn't get benefits for combat duties.
The war busted me up, I busted up my wife . . .

CHERYL: He's hit me more than once.

MARK: I mean I've hit my wife.

NADINE: Have you ever been drunk for a long period of time?

MARK: But I was always drunk.

NADINE: Well, I have.

MARK: We were always drunk.
It would boil out,
the anger,
when we were drunk.

NADINE: I used to drink a lot

and did vicious things when I was drunk.
And until you're there,
you don't *know.*

MARK: When I was sober, I found out what I'd done to her.
It was . . . I just couldn't stop.

CHERYL: I was really into speed—oh, how many years ago?
I'm not good with the past.
I mean Mark knows dates and years.
God I don't know.

MARK: It's like . . .
I feel terrible about it.
The last time it happened
it was about a year ago now.
I made up my mind to quit drinking
because drinking's what's brought it on.

CHERYL: We got into some kind of argument about speed.
And he pushed me down the stairs.
He hit me a couple of times.

NADINE: Yeah it's there and it takes years.
My husband I were
grooving on our fights.
I mean really creative.
And five years ago we got down to the count.
Where we were batting each other around.
Okay, I hit my husband. A lot.
See, I'm capable of it.

MARK: I dropped out of AA.
I put the cork in the bottle myself.

NADINE: Okay—I really was drunk, really mad.
And I beat him up and do you know what he said to me?
He turned to me after he took it and he said:
I didn't know you cared that much.
It was the most incredible thing.
And he stood there and held his face
and took it
and turned around in a state of glory and said:
I didn't think you cared.
I'll never hit another person again.

CHERYL: I went to the hospital
'cause my ribs . . .
I think, I don't know.
I don't remember it real clearly.
It had something to do with speed.

The fact that I wasn't, I was,
I wasn't rational.
No, I must have really tore into him.
I mean I can be nasty.
So anyway that was hard because I couldn't go to work
for a couple of weeks.

NADINE: And I see Mark.
The fact that he beat his wife.
I understand it.
I don't like it.
But I understand it.

MARK: I've been sober so long now, it's terrifying.
See, I really got into photography while I was drunk.
Got involved in the art program at the U.
I mean I could be fine
and then the wrong thing would come up
and it would shut me off.

NADINE: Don't distance yourself from Mark.

MARK: I'd space out and start talking about the war.
See, most of these people
didn't have to deal with it.
They all dealt with the other side.

NADINE: I was "anti-war," I marched, I was "non-violent."
(*Laughs*)

MARK: I brought some photos.
This is a picture of some people who at one point in time
were in my unit. That is,
they were there at the time the photo was taken.
Some of them are dead, some of them made it home,
(*Pause*)
some of them are dead now.

NADINE: But I'm capable of it.

MARK: After I was there, I could never move with people
who were against the war in a real way.
It took a part of our life.
I knew what it was and they didn't.

NADINE: We all are.

MARK: They could get as pissed off as they wanted to
I didn't fight with them.
I didn't bitch with them.
I just shut up. Excuse me.
(*Looks at audience. Sees or thinks* HE *sees they're on the other side. Moment of murderous anger.* HE *shuts up and exits*)

IX

CHERYL: I'm scared knowing that I have to keep my mouth shut.
I don't know this for a fact, but I mean
I fantasize a lot.
I have to.
I've got nothing else to do.
See, I've got no real line of communication at all, on this issue.
If I ever told him I was scared for my life, he'd freak out.
If I ever said anything like that, how would he react?
Would he get angry?
What do you think? Do I want to take that chance?

I got too much to lose.
Before, you know, when we were just single together,
I had nothing to lose. I have a little boy here.
And if I ever caught Mark hurting me
or that little boy again, I'd kill him.
And I don't wanna be up for manslaughter.

Danny means more to me than Mark does.
Only because of what Mark does to me.
He doesn't realize it maybe, but he squelches me.

God, I'm scared.
I don't wanna be alone for the rest of my life
with two kids. And I can't rob my children of what
little father they could have.

NADINE: I've always understood
how people could hurt each other
with weapons.

If you've been hurt to the quick,
and a weapon's around, WHAP.

I signed my divorce papers because
last time he came over, I knew if
there'd been a gun around, I'd've
killed him.

MARK *reenters*.

X

MARK: I'm sorry.
I don't think you understand.

Sure, I was pissed off at myself that I let myself go.
Deep down inside I knew I could have stopped it.

I could just have said:
I won't do it.
Go back in the rear, just not go out,
let them put me in jail. I could have said:
"I got a toothache," gotten out of it.
They couldn't have forced me.
But it was this duty thing.
It was like:
YOU'RE UNDER ORDERS.
You have your orders, you have your job,
you've got to DO it.

Well, it was like crazy.
At night, you could do anything . . .
It was free-fire zones. It was dark, then
all of a sudden, everything would just burn loose.
It was beautiful. . . . You were given all this power to work out-
side the law.
We all dug it.

But I don't make any excuses for it.
I may even be trying to do that now.
I could have got out.
Everybody could've.
If EVERYBODY had said *no*,
it couldn't have happened.
There were times we'd say:
let's pack up and go, let's quit.
But jokingly.
We knew we were there.
But I think I knew then
we could have got out of it.

NADINE: Oh,
I'm worried about men.

MARK: See, there was a point, definitely, when I was
genuinely interested in trying to win the war.
It was my own area.
I wanted to do the best I could.
I mean I could have played it really low-key.
I could have avoided things, I could have made sure
we didn't move where we could have contacts.

NADINE: I worry about them a lot.
MARK: And I watched the younger guys.
        Maybe for six weeks there was nothing.
        He'd drift in space wondering what he'd do under fire.
        It only takes once.
        That's all it takes . . .
        and then you dig it.
NADINE: Men are stripped.
MARK: It's shooting fireworks off, the Fourth of July.
NADINE: We took away all their toys . . . their armor.

When I was younger, I'd see a man in uniform
and I'd think:
what a hunk.
Something would thrill in me.
Now we look at a man in uniform—
a Green Beret, a marine—
and we're embarrassed somehow.
We don't know who they are anymore.
What's a man? Where's the model?

All they had left was being Provider.
And now with the economics, they're losing it all.
My father is a farmer.
This year, my mother learned to plow.
I talked to my father on the phone the other night and I said:
Hey, Dad, I hear Mom's learning how to plow.
Well, sure, he said.
She's been a farmer's wife for forty, fifty years.
Yes. But she's just learning to plow now.
And there was a silence
and then he said:
That's a feminist issue I'd rather not discuss
at the moment.

So. We don't want them to be the Provider,
because we want to do that ourselves.
We don't want them to be heroes,
and we don't want them to be knights in shining armor, John
    Wayne—
so what's left for them to be, huh?

Oh, I'm worried about men.
They're not coming through.
(My husband)
How could I have ever gotten married?

They were programmed to fuck,
now they have to make love.
And they can't do it.
It all comes down to fucking versus loving.

We don't like them in the old way anymore.
And I don't think they like us, much.
Now that's a war, huh?

End of Act One

ACT TWO

I

MARK: This is the photo I showed you.
Of some guys in my unit.

We were south-southwest of Danang—
we were in that whole triangle, not too far
from where My Lai was.
Near the mountains, near the coast.

Everybody knew about My Lai.
But it wasn't different from what was going on.
I mean, the grunts did it all the time.

This fellow up there, that's Michele.
He ended up in the nuthouse,
that's the fellow I pulled out of the bush.
This is the machine gunner.
The kid was so good
he handled the gun like spraying paint.
This kid was from down South.
Smart kid.
He got hit in the head, with grenade shrapnel.
He's alive, but he got rapped in the head.
That was the end of the war for him.

NADINE: I don't know what it is with Mark.
I have a lot of charming friends
that are very quiet, like him—
but they don't have his power.

CHERYL: You know what Mark's power is:
He's got an imagination that just doesn't quit.

NADINE: It got to be coincidental when we'd been somewhere together

and someone said: You know your friend Mark,
I liked the way he was so quiet.

MARK: There were no two ways about it . . .

CHERYL: He's got an imagination that, that embarrasses me . . .

MARK: People who were into it really got a chance to know.

CHERYL: Because I am conservative.

MARK: You knew that you were killing something.
You actually knew it, you saw it, you had the body.
You didn't take wounded. That was it.
You just killed them.
And they did the same to you.

NADINE: (*Laughing*)
I told him his face is a dangerous weapon.
He ought to be real responsible with it.

CHERYL: All his jars . . .

NADINE: I think we'd only known each other for a week and I said:
You should really have a license for that face.

MARK: (That's my friend, that's R.J.)
My friend R.J. used to carry a machete.
I don't know why he never did it.
But he always wanted to cut somebody's head off.

NADINE: You know why they went crazy out there?
It's that totally negative religion.
It makes you fit to kill.
Those commandments . . .

MARK: He wanted to put it on a stick and put it in a village.

NADINE: Every one of them
"Thou shalt not."

MARK: It was an abuse of the dead.
We got very sacred about taking the dead.

NADINE: Take an infant and start him out on the whole world with
THOU SHALT NOT . . .
and you're perpetually in a state of guilt
or a state of revolt.

MARK: There's a whole Buddhist ceremony.
R.J., everybody—got pissed off.
He wanted to let them know.

CHERYL: But he's got an imagination . . .

MARK: I never saw our guys rape women. I heard about it.

CHERYL: And it's usually sexually orientated somehow.

MARK: But you never took prisoners, so you'd have to get
involved with them while they were dying
or you'd wait until they were dead.

CHERYL: Everything Mark does is sexually orientated.

MARK: The Vietnamese got into that.
            There was this one instance I told you about
            where R.J. shot the person in the face . . .
            it was a woman.
CHERYL: I don't know why we got together.
MARK: The Vietnamese carried that body back.
            It took them all night long to work that body over.
CHERYL: When I think back on it, he was weird, off the war.
MARK: It was their spoils.
            They could do what they wanted.
NADINE: So you send these guys out there
            all their lives they've been listening
            to nuns and priests
            and they start learning to kill.
MARK: (*Snaps on picture of him with medal. Full dress*)
            This is a picture of my first Purple Heart.
NADINE: Sure Mark felt great. I understand that.
            His senses were finally alive.
CHERYL: His Purple Hearts never got to me.
            I was never impressed with the fighting man,
            I don't think.
MARK: A lot of people bullshitted that war
            for a lot of Purple Hearts.
            I heard about a guy who was in the rear
            who went to a whorehouse.
            He got cut up or something like that.
            And he didn't want to pay the woman
            or something like that.
            He ended up with a Purple Heart.
CHERYL: Well, drugs helped, a lot.
            We didn't have much in common.
MARK: I don't know. We were out in the bush.
            To me, a Purple Heart meant it was something you got
            when you were wounded and you bled.
            You were hurt during a contact.
            I didn't feel anything getting it.
            But I wanted a picture of it.
CHERYL: I mean, I've got to get that basement cleaned out.
MARK: Actually, I was pissed off about getting that medal.
CHERYL: My little boy's getting curious.
MARK: There were South Vietnamese who were sent out with us,
                fought with us.
CHERYL: He goes down and sees some of that crap down there Mark's
                saved . . .

MARK: They didn't really give a shit.
CHERYL: Never throws anything away.
MARK: If things got too hot you could always
           count on them running.
           Jackasses.
CHERYL: Mark's a packrat . . .
MARK: (*Holds up a belt*)
           I'm a packrat. I never throw anything away.
           This belt is an artifact.
           I took it off of somebody I killed.
           It's an NVA belt.
           I sent it home. I think it was kind of a trophy.

           This is the man's blood.
           That's a bullet hole.
           This particular fellow had a belt of grenades
           that were strapped to his belt.
           See where the rust marks are?

CHERYL: Everything he's done,
           everything is sexually orientated in some way.
           Whether it's nakedness or violence—it's all
           sexually orientated.
           And I don't know where this comes from.
           (MARK *searches for more slides*)
           He can take those slides
           and you know where he can put 'em.
           Right up his butt.
           I mean he's just,
           he'll go down there
           and dig up old slides.
           I won't do that for him anymore.
           I will not,
           no way.
MARK: Here's a picture of me . . .
           (*Snaps on picture of him and some children*)
CHERYL: He asked if he can take pictures of Danny and I . . .
MARK: And some kids. God I LOVED those kids.
CHERYL: I think that's why I'm so against the artist world.
           I just can't handle his work a lot of it.
           It's because he's done that to me.
MARK: Everybody hated them.
           You couldn't trust 'em.

           The VC would send the kids in with a flag.

I never saw this, I heard about it,
the kid would come in asking for C-rations,
try to be your friend, and they'd be maybe wired
with explosives or something
and the kid'd blow up.
There was a whole lot of weirdness . . .

CHERYL: Mark's got this series of blood photographs.
He made me pose for them.
There's a kitchen knife sticking into me,
but all you can see is reddish-purplish blood.
It's about five feet high.
He had it hanging in the shop! In the street!
Boy, did I make him take it out of there.

MARK: I really dug kids. I don't know why.
(*More pictures of kids*)
I did a really bad number . . .
It went contrary, I think,
to everything I knew.
I'm not ready to talk about that yet.

CHERYL: You just don't show people those things.

MARK: These are some pictures of more or less dead bodies and things.
(*Snaps on pictures of mass graves, people half blown apart, gruesome
pictures of this particular war*)
I don't know if you want to see them.
(*Five slides. Last picture comes on of a man, eyes towards us, the bones
of his arm exposed, the flesh torn, eaten away. It is too horrible to
look at.* MARK *looks at the audience, or hears them*)
Oh, Jesus.
Yeah . . .
We have to be patient with each other.
(HE *snaps the pictures off*)

CHERYL: You know. I don't think . . .

MARK: You know, I get panicky
if there's any element of control taken away from me.
(I don't like to be alone in the dark.
I'm scared of it. I'm not armed.)

I don't like fireworks.
If I can control them fine.
I don't like them when I can't control them.

I've had bad dreams
when my wife's had to bring me back out.

Nothing like jumping her, though.
I've heard about vets killing their wives in their sleep.
But this is personal—for me,
the gun was always the instrument, or a grenade.
I never grabbed somebody and slowly killed them.
I've never choked them to death or anything.
I've never beaten anybody up, well . . .

I never killed
with my bare hands.

Pause.

II

CHERYL: You know, I don't think that
men ever really protected women
other than war time.

NADINE: Listen, nobody can do it for you.
Now maybe if I weren't cunning and conniving and
manipulative and courageous,
maybe I wouldn't be able to say that.

MARK: It's still an instinctive reaction to hit the ground.

NADINE: I'll do anything as the times change to protect my stake in life.

CHERYL: And war's the only time man really goes out and protects
woman.

MARK: You know—when I got back, I said I'd never work again.
That's what I said constantly, that'd I'd never work again, for
anyone.

NADINE: I have skills now.
I remember when I didn't have them.
I was still pretty mad, but I wasn't ready.

MARK: I was MAD.
I figured I was *owed* a living.

NADINE: I'm stepping out now, right?

CHERYL: I know my mother protected my father all through his life.
Held things from him, only because she knew it would hurt him.

MARK: And then I got in a position where I couldn't work because
after I got busted and went to prison, no one would hire me.

I did the whole drug thing from a real
thought-out point of view.
I was really highly decorated, awards,
I was wounded twice.
I really looked good.

CHERYL: That's where I get this blurting out when I'm drunk.

Because I'm like my mother—
That's the only time my mother would really let my
father know what's going on in this house.
(When he's not around seven days a week is when she's had a
  couple.)
Otherwise she was protecting him all the time.
Excuse me. I'm going to get another drink.
(SHE *exits*)

MARK: I knew I could get away with a lot.
I knew I could probably walk down the streets
and kill somebody and I'd probably get off.
Simply because of the war.
I was convinced of it.

NADINE: I could have ended my relationship
with my husband years ago.
I sometimes wonder why I didn't.
And I don't want to think it was because of the support.

MARK: I thought about killing people when I got back.

NADINE: I've been pulling my own weight
for about eight years now.
Prior to that, I was doing a tremendous amount of work
that in our society is not measurable.

CHERYL: (*Angry. Reenters*)
My house is not my home.
It's not mine.

NADINE: I kept a house.
I raised my children.

CHERYL: Now, if it were mine I'd be busy at work.

NADINE: I was a model mother.

CHERYL: I'd be painting the walls,
I would be wallpapering the bedroom.
I would be making improvements.
I would be . . . linoleum the floor.
I can't do it.
Because it's not mine.

MARK: I thought of killing people when I got back.
I went to a party with a lady, Cheryl, you know,
later we got married—
She was into seeing people who were into LSD.
And I had tried a little acid this night,
but I wasn't too fucked-up.
And we went to this party.

NADINE: I tried to explain to Mark
that Cheryl may not always want from him what she wants right

now:
looking for him to provide, looking for status.

CHERYL: And Mark will never be ready to have the responsibility
of his own home. Never. Never.

MARK: And there was this big guy.
I was with a friend of mine who tried to rip him off,
or something like that.
He said, the big guy said:
Get the fuck out of here
or I'll take this fucking baseball bat
and split your head wide open.

CHERYL: And I'm being stupid to ever want it from Mark.

MARK: I started to size up what my options were . . .

NADINE: (*Shaking her head*)
Looking for him to provide, looking for status.

MARK: In a split second, I knew I could have him.
He had a baseball bat,
but there was one of these long glass coke bottles.
I knew. . . . Okay, I grabbed that.
I moved toward him, to stick it in his face.
I mean, I killed him.
I mean in my mind.
I cut his throat and everything.

CHERYL: Because your own home means upkeep.
Means, if there's a drip in the ceiling
you gotta come home and take care of it.

NADINE: But between us, I can't understand why a woman her age,
an intelligent woman,
who's lived through the sixties and the seventies,
who's living now in a society where woman have finally been
given permission
to drive and progress and do what they're entitled to do
. . . I mean, how can she think that way?

MARK: My wife saw this and grabbed me.
I couldn't talk to anybody the rest of the night.
I sat and retained the tension and said:
"I want to kill him."
They had to drive me home.
It was only the third time I'd been out with my wife.

CHERYL: That fucking dog in the backyard
—excuse my French—
That dog is so bad. I mean,
there are cow-pies like this out there.
(*Demonstrates size*)

And when I was three months pregnant and alone here—
when Mark and I—
when I finally got Mark to get out of here—
I came back to live
because I just could not go on living at my girlfriend's,
eating their food and not having any money and
—and I came back here
and I had to clean up that yard.

MARK: It wasn't till the next day that I really got shook by it.
My wife said,
"Hey, cool your jets."
She'd say, "Hey, don't do things like that.
You're not over there anymore.
Settle down, it's all right."

CHERYL: I threw up in that backyard picking up dog piles.
That dog hasn't been bathed since I took her over to
this doggie place and paid twenty dollars
to have her bathed.
And that was six months ago. That dog has flies.

You open the back door
and you always get one fly from the fricking dog.
She's like garbage. She . . . she . . .

MARK: I think my wife's scared of me.
I really do.
She'd had this really straight upbringing.
Catholic.
Never had much . . . you know.
Her father was an alcoholic and her mother was too.
I came along and offered her
a certain amount of excitement.

CHERYL: My backyard last year was so gorgeous.
I had flowers.
I had tomatoes.
I had a whole area garden.
That creeping vine stuff all over.
I had everything.
This year I could not do it with that dog back there.

MARK: Just after I got back, I took her up to these races.
I had all this camera equipment.
I started running out on the field.
I started photographing these cars zipping by at
ninety miles an hour.

NADINE: What's important to me is my work.

It's important to Mark too.

MARK: She'd just gotten out of high school.
She was just, you know, *at that point.*
She was amazed at how I moved through space.

NADINE: We talk for hours about our work.

MARK: 'Cuz I didn't take anybody with me.

NADINE: We understand each other's work.

MARK: I moved down everybody's throats verbally.
First of all it was a physical thing.
I was loud.
Then I'd do these trips to outthink people.

NADINE: His jars are amazingly original. Artifacts of the war.
Very honest.

MARK: I'd do these trips.

NADINE: You should see the portrait Mark did of himself.

MARK: I had a lot of power, drugs,
I was manipulating large sums of money.

NADINE: He has a halo around his head.
(*Laughs*)

MARK: She became a real fan.

NADINE: And the face of a devil.

CHERYL: That dog grosses me out so bad.
That dog slimes all over the place.
My kid, I don't even let him out in the backyard.
He plays in the front.
That's why his bike's out front.
I'll take the chance of traffic before I'll let him out
to be slimed over by that dog.

NADINE: She decided to have that child.

MARK: Later on, it got into this whole thing.
We lived together and with this other couple.

NADINE: It's madness.
Everyone was against it.

MARK: It was a whole . . . I don't know whether I
directed it . . . but it became this *big* . . .
sexual thing . . . between us . . . between them . . .
between groups of other people . . .
It was really a fast kind of thing.
Because no one really gave a shit.

CHERYL: Oh, shut up!

NADINE: His theory is she's punishing him.

MARK: I don't know why I was really into being a stud.

NADINE: Now no man has ever been able to lead *me* into sexual abuse.

MARK: I wasn't that way before I left, so I don't know.

Maybe it was like I was trying to be like all the other people.

NADINE: See, she participated. She had the right to say no.

CHERYL: That dog jumps the fence, takes off.
I have to pay twenty dollars
to get her out of the dog pound.
She is costin' me so damn much money that I hate her.
She eats better than we do.
She eats better than we do.

NADINE: She must have thought it would be fun.
And wow! That was that whole decade
where a whole population of people that age thought that way.

CHERYL: My Danny is getting to the age where there's gotta be food.
I mean he's three years old.
He goes to the freezer he wants ice cream there.
He goes in the icebox there's gotta be pop.
I mean it's not like he's an infant anymore.

NADINE: Every foul thing I've ever done,
I'm not uncomfortable about it.
And I don't blame anyone in my life.

CHERYL: These things have to be there.
And it's not there.

NADINE: I don't blame anyone.
I'm sorry, maybe you have to be older
to look back and say that.

CHERYL: But there's always a bag of dogfood in the place.
Anyways I run out of dogfood,
Mark sends me right up to the store.
But I run out of milk I can always give him Kool-Aid
for two or three days.
Yeah—that's the way it is though.
We haven't been to the grocery store in six months
for anything over ten dollars worth of groceries at a time.
There is no money.

III

MARK: You'd really become an animal out there.
R.J. and I knew what we were doing.

That's why a lot of other kids really got into trouble.
They didn't know what they were doing.

We knew it, we dug it, we knew
we were very good.

IV

CHERYL: I'd turn off to him.
          Because I knew that it was hard for me to accept—
          you know what he . . . what happened and all that.
          And it was hard for me to live with, and him being
          drunk and *spreading* it around to others.
          (*To* MARK)
          How long has it been since anything like that happened?
MARK: Well, last July I hurt you.
CHERYL: Yeah, but Danny was what a year and half so everything was
          pretty . . .
MARK: He was exposed to it.
          My wife, uh, Cheryl, left one night.
CHERYL: Don't.
MARK: She left with, uh, she had a person come over and pick her up
          and take her away.
          I walked in on this.
          I was drunk. Danny was in her arms.
          I attacked this other man and . . .
          I did something to him.
          I don't know.
          What did I do to him?
          Something.
CHERYL: You smashed his car up with a sledge hammer.
MARK: I, uh, Dan saw all that.
CHERYL: He was only six months old though.
MARK: No. Dan I think he knows a lot more than we think.
          He saw me drunk and incapable of walking up the steps.
          Going to the bathroom
          half on the floor and half in the bowl.
          He's a sharp kid.
          Cheryl and I separated this spring.
          And he really knew what was going on.
NADINE: Christ, I hate this country.
          I hate all of it.
          I've never really said it before.
MARK: I come in and apologize when I think about the incidents
          that I've done in the past now that I'm sober,
          and I feel terribly guilty.
          I've exploited Cheryl as a person, sexually . . .
          it wasn't exactly rape, but . . .

CHERYL: I can't deal with *that* at all.
          But I find that if I can at least put it out of my mind it's easier.

          If I had to think about what he's done to me, I'd
          have been gone a long time ago.
NADINE: I have yet to be out of this country, by the way.
          And I'm criticizing it as if I think it's better everywhere else.
MARK: See, I wanted to get back into the society and
          I wanted to live so much life, but I couldn't.
          I was constantly experimenting.
CHERYL: It was awful . . .
          He'd pick fights with people on the streets.
          Just about anyone. It was like a rage.
          He'd just whomp on the guy.
          Not physically but he would become very obstinate,
          very mean and cruel. In bars, handling people . . .
          (*To* MARK)
          You have to be *nice* to people to have them accept you.
MARK: I don't know.
          I was afraid.
          I thought people were. . . uh . . . I mean
          I was kind of paranoid.
          I thought everybody knew . . .
          I thought everybody knew what I did over there,
          and that they were against me.
          I was scared. I felt guilty and a sense of . . .
CHERYL: I can't talk to you.
NADINE: He's trying to judge himself.
          One time we were together after a
          long period of incredible, sharing times.
          I said: "You're so wonderful."
          And he started to cry.
MARK: (*To* NADINE)
          I've done terrible things.
NADINE: (*To* MARK)
          I know.
          (*Long pause*)
          Christ, I hate this country.

          I can remember everything.
          Back to being two years old,
          and all these terrible things they taught us.
          I can't believe we obeyed them *all*.

MARK: (*Very quiet*)
    I had two cousins who went through Vietnam.
    One was a truck driver and got through it.
    My other cousin was in the army.
    His unit, about one hundred men were climbing up a hill.
    They were all killed except for him and another guy.
    And they were lying there.
    The VC were going around putting bullets
    into people's heads.
    Making sure they were dead.
    And he had to lay there wounded faking he was dead.
    He and I never talked.
    Ever.
    Someone else communicated his story to me,
    and I know he knows my story.

    Pause.

V

CHERYL: I feel so sorry for Margie, my brother's wife.
    I told you about.
    You wonder why there's so much more lesbianism around now?
    Look at the men!
    You can see where that's turned a lot of women the other way.
NADINE: He possibly is overpowering.
    I don't know. She was proud to be his woman.
    So he said frog, and they all jumped.
    Well, that's terrific.
    It cost him a lot
    to have that power where he abused it.
CHERYL: Christ!
    Mark pushed me into that, once, too.
    We were doing this smack deal,
    he brought this woman into our room.
    He wanted me to play with her.
    He wanted me to get it on with her, too.
    It just blew my mind.
    I mean it just blew me away.
NADINE: I know, I know, I know . . .
    But I see when he talks about his wife,
    I feel encouraged that there are men that can be that way.
    He has never, ever said an unkind word about her.

God, I mean it's incredibly civilized
the way he talks about her.
In fact, had he ever said anything foul about her,
it would have grated on me.
Maybe he just knows what I require.
But I have yet to hear him say
anything bad about anyone;
even those terrible people he had to deal with
in the jungle.

MARK: I saw my cousin at his dad's funeral last December.

CHERYL: Now it's so complex
every time I look . . .
Oh, God . . . every time I look
at a piece of furniture,
it reminds me of something.

MARK: Wherever we moved,
we knew where the other was.
Something radiates between us.

NADINE: I think he's quite superior.
I really do.
I think he's got it all figured out.

MARK: Our eyes will meet, but we can't touch.

NADINE: I think he's gonna make it.
(*Nervous*)
I wonder how you perceive him.

MARK: There's no difference between this war and World War II.
I'm convinced of that.

Maybe it was different in that it was the race thing.
(*Admitting*)
We referred to them as zips, or dinks, or gooks.
But I don't think I would have had any trouble shooting
   anything.

We weren't freaks out there.
Guys in World War II cracked up, too.

We're their children.

I would like to play you a song.

Music: "No More Genocide" by Holly Near. MARK *turns on tape
recorder.*

End of Act Two

ACT THREE

I

MARK: (*Snaps on slide of him and R.J.*)
            This is a picture of me and R.J.
            We look like a couple of bad-asses.
            It was hot. Shit, I miss him.
            We were so close.
            We talked about everything.
            We talked about how each of us lost our
            virginity, we talked about girls.

CHERYL: (*Agitated*)
            My girlfriend across the street told me
            how babies were made when I was ten years old.
            I just got sick. I hated it.

MARK: We talked about fights, getting back on the streets, drugs.

CHERYL: From that moment on,
            I had a model:
            I wanted kids . . .

MARK: We talked about getting laid . . .

CHERYL: But I didn't want the husband that went along with it.
            I still feel that way.

MARK: We talked about how we would be inseparable
            when we came home.
            We never would have, even if he hadn't died.
            We knew too much about each other.

CHERYL: And this spooks me because I said this
            when I was ten years old.

MARK: (*New slide*)
            This is the place, the Alamo.
            That's where the rocket came in and
            killed a man . . . uh . . .
            (*Indicates in the picture*)
            We got hit one night.
            Some several people were sleeping, this fellow . . .
            (*Picture of him*)
            A rocket came in and blew his head off.

NADINE: I said to Mark:
            "You're still pissed off because they let you go.
            Even assholes stopped their kids from going.
            Your good Catholic parents sent you to slaughter."

MARK: It was near dawn.

We moved his body out of there.
We put his body on a rice-paddy dike.
I watched him. He was dead and he was
very close to me and I don't know.

NADINE: His parents pushed him into going.
They believed all those terrible cliches.

MARK: I didn't want him to lay in that place where he died.
I didn't want him laying in the mud.
And I think I was talking to him.
I was crying, I don't know.

NADINE: Do you know, to this day his father
will not say the word Vietnam.

MARK: His dog came out and started . . .
The dog was eating him.
I just came out and fired at the dog.
I got him killed.
(*Snaps picture*)
Later, I took that picture.

NADINE: But his father talked to everyone but Mark about the war.
He's got his medals on his wall.

MARK: I don't know.
It became a sacred place. It was "the Alamo."
That's what we named it.
I shot the dog because it was desecrating.
The dog was eating our friend . . .
I would have done anything, if I could have,
if I could have kept flies off of him, even.

NADINE: His father's ashamed of himself.
When you let your son go to war
for all the wrong reasons,
you can't face your son.

MARK: (*Crying*)
I just wanted him . . .
He coulda gone home the next day.
The war was over for him.
I wanted him to get home.

Pause.

II

CHERYL: I want to go home.

NADINE: To the church, to my family.
The sixties are over.

NADINE: The sixties . . .
You know, a lot of us went through that whole
decade pretending to ourselves we were pacifists.

MARK: I wanted to get home so bad.

CHERYL: Well, I mean I'm gonna have another kid.
I'm gonna have to take him to the Cathedral to be
baptized 'cuz our wedding wasn't blessed.
It wasn't in a church.
We had to get married and we had to do it fast.
In South Dakota.
In the clothes we'd been in for three days.

NADINE: As if we didn't know what violence was.

MARK: You know, the biggest thing I had to adjust to
coming home was I didn't have my gun.

CHERYL: My dad had just died so I didn't really care.
My dad and I were really close.
He was the only one who mattered . . .

MARK: I mean, that gun was mine.

CHERYL: I don't know why I'm remembering all this
all of a sudden . . .

MARK: I knew every part of it.

NADINE: God, we hated those vets.

MARK: The barrel burned out of it.
You know, I had a new barrel put in,
but I mean that gun was mine.
I took that gun everywhere I went.
I just couldn't live without that gun.

NADINE: All that nonsense about long hair, flowers and love.

CHERYL: I mean, my family just dug my father's hole
and put him right in there.

NADINE: And the women were exempt!
They were all supposed to be Mother Earths making pots.

CHERYL: My brother's wife went nuts and shot her two-year-old son and
killed him.
I told you.
I mean—all the things we did to him.
He had to come and get me out of jail
at three in the morning and he's not—
he wasn't a strong man.
So my father just jumped into that bottle
and nobody could get him out of it.

NADINE: I think I knew then what I know now.
MARK: When I got on the plane coming home
I was so happy. I didn't miss my gun then.
It was my birthday.
NADINE: I don't know.
MARK: I turned twenty-one.
I did my birthday coming home.
NADINE: Oh, Jesus.
MARK: I did my birthday across the dateline.
I was incredibly happy.
We hit Okinawa.
R.J. was there.
We saw all these guys who were just going over.
NADINE: I only hope I would have done exactly what Mark did.
MARK: All these guys were asking us how it was.
We were really getting off on the fact
that we were done.
These guys were so green and fat.
We were brown, we were skinny.
We were animals.
NADINE: I think he survived
because he became an animal.
I hope I would have wanted to live that bad.
CHERYL: I used to stay up all night with my dad.
I was doing a lot of speed then
and I used to stay up all night with him and talk.
I'd be sewing or something like that at the kitchen table
and he'd be sittin' there drinking and bitching.
MARK: I don't know why I couldn't talk to my parents when I got
back.
NADINE: We just can't face that in ourselves.
MARK: I told my dad everything when I was over there.
CHERYL: My dad was an intelligent, common-sense-type man.
He had no college education, but judging characters . . .
NADINE: Oh, God.
CHERYL: Oh, God.
MARK: The only way I could cry was to write to my dad.
"God, Dad. I'm really scared. I'm really terrified."
CHERYL: Oh, God. He could pick out people.
MARK: When I sent somebody out and they got killed,
I could tell my dad.
CHERYL: My dad told me: Stay away from Mark.
MARK: I got into L.A. . . . , called:

"Hey, I'm back. I'm back."
My dad said: "Oh, great. We're so relieved.
I'm so happy." My mother cried, she was happy.
I said: "I'm going to buy a hamburger."

CHERYL: He told me: Mark can't communicate, his style of dress is weird,
      the war . . .

MARK: I just got on this stool going round and round.
"Hey, I'm back."
No one wanted anything to do with me.
Fuckin' yellow ribbons.
I thought I was tired.

NADINE: The problem now is knowing what to do with what we know.

CHERYL: My dad said:
I want you to forget him.
Just forget him.
Get out of this now, while you can.

MARK: I waited around until 3 A.M.,
caught a flight, got out here.
6:30 in the morning.
Beautiful, beautiful day.
Got my stuff, threw it over my shoulder,
and started walking.

CHERYL: I saw Mark occasionally, anyway.
Shortly after that, my dad had a stroke.
You know, my dad and I are identical.

MARK: I walked in the door and set everything down.
I was home.
My dad looked at me, my mom looked at me.
I sat down. Said:
Could I have some coffee?
That's when my mother started raggin' on me
about drinking coffee.
The whole thing broke down.

NADINE: Oh, God . . .

CHERYL: My sister had a baby when she was seventeen.
They put her in a home, you know, the whole route.
Shortly after that, I was five years younger than her,
I was just starting to date.

MARK: "Well," my mom said, "you better get some sleep.
I've got a lot to do."
I said: like I don't want to sleep.

I got incredibly drunk.

CHERYL: I remember—I'd come home from a date.

The only time I saw my father was late at night.
He would take a look at me and say:
Well, I hope you learned from your sister
that the only way to stay out of trouble
is to keep your legs crossed.

MARK: My mom and dad had to go out that night.
I thought, well, I'd sit down
and talk with them at dinner.
They were gone.

CHERYL: End of conversation.

MARK: We didn't see each other that day.
We never really did see each other.

CHERYL: I mean, he got his point across . . .
more or less.

MARK: I had no idea what was going on.
This was 1970.
My hair was short.
I got really crazed out on junk and stuff.
Then when I was totally avoiding going home
somewhere in that I wanted to . . .
I really wanted bad to . . .
communicate with a woman.

NADINE: You know, all Mark did was—
He brought the war back home
and none of us could look at it.

MARK: I wanted to fuck my brains out.

CHERYL: God, I was naive.
I was naive as they come.
And to sit here and say that now knowing what I know
and what I've been through
just gives me the creeps.

MARK: No one wanted anything to do with me.

NADINE: We couldn't look at ourselves. We still can't.

CHERYL: Because I am so far from being naive.
I mean, just the idea if I ever divorced Mark . . .
I don't think I could ever find anyone who
could handle my past.
I mean, I have a hard time relating to it myself.

III

NADINE: Oh, God.
I'm worried about us.

I keep this quiet little knowledge with me every day.
I don't tell my husband about it
I don't tell my kids,
or Mark.
Or anyone.
But something has fallen apart.
I'm having trouble being a mother.
How can you believe in sending your children to special classes
when you know it doesn't matter?
Oh,
I worry, I worry,
I worry one of my daughters
will be walking down the street
and get raped or mugged by someone who is angry or hungry.
I worry I have these three beautiful daughters (pieces of life)
who I have devoted my whole life to,
who I've put all my energy into—bringing up—raising—
and then somebody up there goes crazy one day
and pushes the "go" button and
phew! bang, finished, the end.
I worry that my daughters won't want to give birth
because of my bad birthing experience.
And I worry that they *will* want to give birth.

I worry that—
Well, one of my daughters does blame me
for the divorce
because I have protected them from knowing
what kind of man their father really is.

(I worry that I worry too much about all this
and I worry that I really don't worry enough about it all.)
I worry so much it makes me sick.

I work eighteen hours a day just to pay the bills.
This year, I work on the feminist caucus,
I do my portraits, run my magazine, organize civic events.
I hold two jobs and more.
I invited my dear, sweet, ninety-one-year-old uncle
to come die at my house.

I go to recitals, shopping, graduation,
I don't go through the ritual
of getting undressed at night.
I sleep with my shoes on.
My husband's alcoholism has ruined us.

(Forty-five thousand dollars in debt.)

I don't dare get angry anymore.
Can you imagine what would happen,
if I got angry?
My children . . .
(*Can't go on*)

MARK: My wife means so much to me.
          I don't want to jeopardize what she's giving to me.
          I don't want to jeopardize her.

          It's like the Marine Corps.
          Cheryl is like a comrade. She's walking wounded now.
          You don't leave a comrade on the field.

NADINE: It's all out of control.
MARK: Sometimes I think Nadine loses sight of things.
          Sometimes, I think she's way ahead of me.
NADINE: I don't know what I'm doing.
MARK: I can't talk to you about Nadine.
NADINE: Oh, men. I have to take care of them.
          And they're all cripples.
          It's so depressing.
MARK: It's like I know that I'm carrying a time bomb
          and there are times that I just don't know
          if I'll go off.
          I don't know that in the end
          I won't destroy myself.
NADINE: And yet, there's that little voice inside me
          that reminds me that even though it's hopeless
          I have little children that can't survive without me.
MARK: Maybe because I just can't comprehend war.
          War that's political enough in terms of
          what you have and what you get out of it.

NADINE: I guess I could possibly be the most
          vulnerable person of all of us.
          But I've also built up all these other devices
          which will overrule that.
MARK: I need to tell you what I did.
          My wife knows it.
          She's come through times
          when I got to the very edge of suicide.
          She's helped me through a couple of times
          that without her help . . .

I'd be dead.
Now, I've been very honest with Nadine
except when she asked me about suicide.
I couldn't tell her that.

NADINE: I couldn't even think about suicide.

IV
The Spaghetti Story

CHERYL: I hate to cook.
Probably because he likes to cook.
I hate to cook.
I don't know how to cook,
and I hate it.

Mark does this spaghetti dinner once a year.
Has he ever told you about that?
Holy Christ!

MARK: Excuse me.
(*Leaves*)

CHERYL: Every day before Thanksgiving
Mark does a spaghetti dinner, and this
is a traditional thing.
This is the one traditional bone Mark has in his body,
and I'd like to break it.

He has 20-45 people come to this thing.
He makes ravioli, lasagne, spaghetti, meatballs,
three different kinds of spaghetti sauce:
shrimp, plain, meat sauce.
Oh, he makes gnocchi! He makes his own noodles!
And it's good.
He's a damn good cook for Italian food.
But you can imagine what I go through
for three weeks for that party
to feed forty people.
Sit-down dinner.
He insists it's a sit-down dinner.

So here I am running around
with no time to cook with him.
I'm trying to get enough shit in my house
to feed forty people sit-down dinner.
We heated the porch last year

because we did not have enough room to seat forty people.
And I run around serving all these slobs,
and this is the first year he's really charged anyone.
And we lose on it every year.
I mean, we lose, first year we lost $300.
This dinner is a $500 deal.
I'm having a baby this November,
and if he thinks he's having
any kind of spaghetti dinner,
he can get his butt out of here.
I can't take it.

Pizzas! He makes homemade pizzas.
You should see my oven.
Oh my God! There's pizza-shit everywhere.
Baked on.
And when it's over with,
he just gets up and walks out.
He's just done.
The cleanup is no big deal to him.
He won't even help.
He rolls up the carpets for this dinner.
People get smashed!
He's got wine everywhere, red wine.
It has to be red so if it gets on my rugs,
my rugs are ruined and my couch is ruined.
I've just said it so many times I hate it.
He knows I hate it.

My brother brought over some speed
to get me through that night.
My brother, Jack, who is a capitalist—
intelligent—makes me sick.
Never got into drugs. Was too old.
Missed that whole scene.
But he now has speed occasionally
on his bad day, you know, drink, two drinks one night,
speed to get him through the day.
Business man.

He brought me some speed to get me through the night
'cause he knew what a basket case I'd be.

And then Mark goes and invites my family.
And they're the last people I want to see at this.
Sure, they love it.
I mean, they all sit around and they

stuff themselves to death.
I'm not kidding!
It is one big stuffing feast.

The first time, the first spaghetti dinner we had was
right after Danny was born.
Danny's baby book got torn up.
I had to start a whole new one.
Mark's crazy friends.
Drunk.
Broken dishes everywhere.
I'm not kidding.
It's just a disaster.

Spaghetti on the walls.
Spaghetti pots dropped in the kitchen.
Spaghetti all over the sink.

That's why I ask him.
I go: "Why?"
"It's traditional. I have to do this every year."
It was three years ago he started.
Tradition, my ass.

I'm telling you.
I mean, he wonders why I can't sleep with him sometimes.
Because I just work up such a hate for him inside that . . .
(MARK *reenters*)
I'm a perfectionist.
My house has to be this way,
and before I go to sleep,
I'll pick up after him.
I'm constantly picking up after him.
Christ Almighty!
In the morning, if he comes in late,
he's read the newspaper
and there's newspaper all over the room.
He *throws* it when he's done with it.
I've broken toes on his shoes.
I broke *this* toe on his shoe.
He always leaves his shoes right out in walking space.
Every morning I trip on
either his tennis or his good shoes.
Whichever pair he doesn't have on.
He's so inconsiderate of other people.
He's so selfish, he's so self-centered.

And this is what I tell him.
I'm just tired of it.
He's so selfish.
Because this spaghetti dinner just ruins me.
Baby or no baby,
it just completely ruins me.
And he's showing off his,
his wonderful cooking that he does once a year.
And I suppose this is why I hate cooking.

V

MARK: (*Shows us slide of wounded children*)
This is a picture of some kids who were hurt.
I used to take care of them,
change their bandages and shit.
I loved these kids.

Oh, God . . .

VI

CHERYL: What am I gonna do? I mean,
someday Danny's gonna have to see Mark
for what he is.
And that just scares the piss right out of me.
NADINE: How do you tell your children their father is an asshole?
CHERYL: I don't wanna be here when Mark tells Danny
about the war.
I don't trust him.
NADINE: How could I tell my children that their father is
in town and hasn't called?
CHERYL: I don't trust what he's gonna tell the kid.
And the way I wanna bring the kid up,
you can't tell him anything.
NADINE: You can't tell your kids
they can't have something they want
because their father has squandered their money.
CHERYL: You're just better off not saying anything.
NADINE: What'm I going to do,
tell them he's off somewhere getting drunk
and has forgotten all about them?
CHERYL: I'm just, you know,

when that sort of thing comes along,
I live from day to day.

NADINE: The counselors tell me and my lawyers tell me
that I should stop protecting them from him.
But it's hard enough, don't you think?
They hurt enough already.

CHERYL: Later on, you know—
there might not be a war going on.
I might not have to deal with that.
And maybe someday *I* can explain to him.

NADINE: One time I told them he was in town
because I couldn't find a way
to cover up the fact that I knew.
They were depressed for weeks.
I have to protect them.

CHERYL: (*Angry*)
See, why do I have to do all this????
And I do.
I find myself doing everything.
Covering for him . . .

NADINE: I don't protect Mark.
He doesn't need it.
He judges himself all the time,
he's devoted to his son.

CHERYL: Sure Mark plays with him.
But when it comes to discipline,
that kid's a little brat,
I mean he is.
And Mark's never around when it comes to discipline.

NADINE: He works hard at his shop. He is supporting his family.

CHERYL: He's never around.

NADINE: He is working his way back into society.
He's beginning to believe in himself
and do his work.

CHERYL: I'm past the sixties.
I want to go back to the Church.
And Mark just will not understand the importance of this for me.
I mean, when there's no father around,
the Church shows some order, you know.

NADINE: He told me he's discovering
who he always thought he was.
I think of him as an artist
and a lifelong friend.

VII

MARK: (*Holding the picture* HE *has framed of the children*)
            I'm terrified . . .
            I have a son . . .
            There's another child on the way . . .
            I'm terrified for what I did now . . .
CHERYL: The war is the base of all our problems.
MARK: It's guilt . . .
            it's a dumb thing . . .
            it makes no sense logically . . .
            but I'm afraid there's this karma I built up
            of hurting . . .
            there are children involved . . .
            like it's all going to balance out
            at the expense of my kids.
CHERYL: I get so scared when he says that.
            I mean, I never did anything.
MARK: There's no logic to it but it's there.
            I try . . .
            I'm really intense with my boy.

            I think what we're beginning to see here is
            that it was a different world I was in.
            I'd like to be real academic about this . . .
            closed case . . .
            but this is an ongoing struggle.

NADINE: Mark!

MARK: I don't know.
            I just don't know.
            Sometimes I look at a news story.
            I look at something someone goes to prison for here,
            I think about it.
            There's no difference.
            It's just a different place.
            This country had all these rules and regulations
            and then all of a sudden they removed these things.

            Then you came back and try to make your life
            in that society where you had to deal with them.
            You find that if you violate them,
            which I found,
            you go to jail,
            which I did.

I sit back here sometimes and watch the news,
watch my mother,
watch my father.
My parents watch the news and say:
"Oh my God somebody did that!
Somebody went in there . . . and started shooting . . .
and killed all those people.
They ought to execute him."
I look at them.
I want to say,
"Hell, what the fuck,
why didn't you ever listen . . .
You want to hear what I did?"
It's real confusion.
I'm guilty and I'm not guilty.
I still want to tell my folks.
I need to tell them what I did.

VIII

CHERYL: There was a time when a man would confess to me,
"I'm a jerk,"
at a private moment
and I would smile
sweetly
and try to comfort him.

Now I believe him.

IX
The Confession

MARK: I . . . I killed three children, a mother and father in cold blood.
(*Crying*)
CHERYL: Don't.
MARK: I killed three children, a mother and father . . .

Long pause.

NADINE: Mark.

MARK: I killed them with a pistol in front of a lot of people.

I demanded something from the parents and then
systematically destroyed them.
And that's . . .

that's the heaviest part of what I'm carrying around.
You know about it now, a few other people know about it,
my wife knows about it, Nadine knows about it,
and nobody else knows about it.
For the rest of my life . . .

I have a son . . .
He's going to die for what I've done.
This is what I'm carrying around;
that's what this logic is about with my children.

A friend hit a booby-trap.
And these people knew about it.
I knew they knew.
I knew that they were working with the VC infrastructure.
I demanded that they tell me.
They wouldn't say anything.
I just wanted them to confess before I killed them.
And they wouldn't.
So I killed their children
and then I killed them.

I was angry.
I was angry with all the power I had.
I couldn't beat them.
They beat me.
(*Crying*)

I lost friends in my unit . . .
I did wrong.
People in the unit watched me kill them.
Some of them tried to stop me.
I don't know.
I can't. . . . Oh, God . . .

A certain amount of stink
went all the way back to the rear.
I almost got into a certain amount of trouble.

It was all rationalized,
that there was a logic behind it.
But they knew.
And everybody who knew had a part in it.
There was enough evidence,
but it wasn't a very good image to put out
in terms of . . .
the marines overseas, so nothing happened.

I have a child . . .
a child who passed through the age
that the little child was.
My son . . . my son
wouldn't know the difference between a VC and a marine.

The children were so little.

I suppose I could find a rationalization.

All that a person can do is try and find words
to try and excuse me,
but I know it's the same damn thing
as lining Jews up.
It's no different
than what the Nazis did.
It's the same thing.

I know that I'm not alone.
I know that other people did it, too.
More people went through more hell than I did . . .
but they didn't do this.

I don't know . . .
I don't know . . .
if it's a terrible flaw of *mine*,
then I guess deep down I'm just everything that's bad.

I guess there is a rationale that says
anyone who wants to live that bad
and gets in that situation . . .
(*Long pause*)
but I should have done better.
I mean, I really strove to be good.
I had a whole set of values.
I had 'em and I didn't.
I don't know.

I want to come to the point
where I tell myself that I've punished myself enough.
In spite of it all,
I don't want to punish myself anymore.
I knew I would want to censor myself for you.

I didn't want you to say:
What kind of a nut, what kind of a bad person is he?
And yet, it's all right.
I'm not gonna lie.

My wife tries to censor me . . .

from people, from certain things.
I can't watch war shows.
I can't drive.
Certain things I can't deal with.
She has to deal with the situation,
us sitting around, a car backfires,
and I hit the deck.

She knows about the graveyards, and R.J. and the woman.
She lives with all this still hanging out.
I'm shell shocked.

X

NADINE: Well, I'm going to look forward to the rest of my life
because of what I know.
I can't wait to test myself.
See, I guess I've known what it is to feel hopeless
politically.
And I've known what it is to plunge
personally.
But Mark has become a conscience for me.
Through him—I've come to understand the violence
in myself . . . and in him, and in all of us.
And I think if we can stay aware of that,
hold on to that knowledge,
maybe we can protect ourselves
and come out on the other side.

MARK: (*Mumbling*)
I'm just a regular guy.
A lot of guys saw worse.

NADINE: If anything I'm on a continuum now.

MARK: See, I didn't want to see people
going through another era of
being so ignorant of the fact that war kills people.

NADINE: And I don't know if it's cynicism or just experience,
but I'm sure I'm never gonna plunge
in the old way again.
I'm not saying that trying to sound tough.
I know about that. I know all about that.

MARK: I feel protective of our children.
Once you're out there, you know there is no justice.
I don't want the children to die.

NADINE: But I have no old expectations anymore.
And when you have none,

you're really free.
And you don't ever plunge.
What do you plunge for?

MARK: It will happen again.

NADINE: I'm just going to work so hard because of what I know.
I do every day.
Did I tell you about not going to sleep at night
because I can't bear to stop thinking about it all?
I'm just going to be so busy for whatever's left.
(But I'm not mad at anyone.)
I don't blame anyone.
I've forgiven everyone.
God, I feel my house is in order at last.

MARK: I DEDICATE . . . this evening to my friends . . .
I'd like a roll call for my friends who died.

NADINE: There's one other thing.
When we all sit around together
with our friends
and we tell women
that no man can do it for you,
we all know it's true,
but I guess for some of us
it never works that way.
At this point in my life,
this curtain has dropped.

MARK: Anderson, Robert.

NADINE: And we see . . .

MARK: Dafoe, Mark.

NADINE: We need them—to be here, questioning themselves
and judging themselves—and us—like Mark.

MARK: Dawson, Mark.

NADINE: I love Mark.

MARK: Fogel, Barry.

NADINE: Well, . . . so . . .
The material has been turning over and over.

MARK: Grant, Tommy.

NADINE: Where is it at now?

MARK: Gunther, Bobby.

NADINE: You see.

MARK: Heinz, Jerry.

NADINE: What do you see, just a cast of characters?

MARK: Jastrow, Alan.

Lawrence, Gordon.
Mullen, Clifford.

Roll call continues through CHERYL'S *speech, ending with a conscious decision on* MARK'S *part to name R.J. among the casualties of Vietnam.*

XI

CHERYL: The men have it all.

MARK: Nelson, Raymond.

CHERYL: They've had it for the longest time.

MARK: Nedelski, Michael.

CHERYL: There's another thing I believe.
There's a lot more people
that are messed up because of the way we were brought up.

MARK: Nevin, Daniel.

CHERYL: Not brought up, but the things we've been through
since we were brought up.

MARK: O'Brien, Stephen.

CHERYL: So I think our generation,

MARK: Rodriguez, Daniel.

CHERYL: the hippie generation, shortly before and after,
are gonna be the ones that suffer.

MARK: Rogers, John.

CHERYL: Because ninety percent of the men never straightened out.

MARK: Ryan, John.

CHERYL: But what I also believe
is that for every woman that has her beliefs,
there's a man that matches.

MARK: Sawyer, Steven.

CHERYL: Whether you find him or not,
is, is like finding a needle in a haystack.
With our population,
I mean, that's the odds you have.

MARK: Simon, Jimmy.

CHERYL: And there's the Women's Libs.
And there's a man for them too.

MARK: Skanolon, John.

CHERYL: See, what we're doing is crossing.
We're meeting the men
that should be with the other ones.
And I truly believe that,
that there is an equal balance.
Even though our group is so fucked-up.
And we are.

MARK: Spaulding, Henry.

CHERYL: You'll look, you'll go in college campuses now

and it's completely back the way it was . . .
and it should stay there.

MARK: Stanton, Ray.

CHERYL: I don't wanna see that shit come back.
I didn't even get that involved in it.
I got involved in it in my own little niche.
But I didn't, you know, get into it
in the school matter.
I went two years and I had it up to here.
And sure I would like to have gone on to school,
but I was competing with Mark.
And I'm not,
I do not like competing with someone.

MARK: Vechhio, Michael.

CHERYL: I'm a happy-go-lucky person.
I used to be anyway, before I met Mark,
where you couldn't depress me on the worst day.
And I had a good day every day of my life.

MARK: Walker,
Pause.

CHERYL: And that is the way life was gonna be for me.

MARK: R.J.
Pause.

XII

MARK *points to his photograph of two grapefruits, an orange, a broken egg,
with a grenade in the center on a dark background. Also some fresh bread,
a fly on the fruit. From far away it looks like an ordinary still life.*

MARK: My unit got blown up.
It was a high contact.
We got hit very, very hard.
The Marine Corps sends you
this extra food, fresh fruit, bread,
a reward
when you've had a heavy loss.

What can I say?
I am still alive—my friends aren't.
It's a still life.
I didn't know what I was doing.

The WOMEN*'s eyes meet for the first time as lights go down.*

END OF PLAY

STRANGE SNOW

Stephen Metcalfe

About Stephen Metcalfe

Born in New Haven in 1953, Stephen Metcalfe attended college in Pennsylvania and moved to New York City in 1976. His one-act plays *Jacknife* and *Baseball Play* were staged at New York's Quaigh Theatre in 1980; his full-length play *Vikings* was produced by Manhattan Theatre Club that same year. *Vikings* was later seen at the Edinburgh Festival and heard on *Earplay*. *Half a Lifetime* was also produced, as a one-act, at MTC; the expanded full-length version was first staged by Michigan's BoarsHead Theater, which premiered Metcalfe's *White Linen*, a cowboy play with songs, in 1982. In 1984 *Loves and Hours* was produced by Cincinnati Playhouse in the Park, and Metcalfe's most recent play, *The Incredibly Famous Willy Rivers*, opened at New York's WPA Theatre in December. Metcalfe is the recipient of a 1982 CAPS grant and a 1984 playwriting fellowship from the National Endowment for the Arts.

Production History

Commissioned by Manhattan Theatre Club in 1980, *Strange Snow* opened there in January 1982, in a production directed by Thomas Bullard. The play has subsequently been staged at numerous theatres across the country.

Characters

MEGS
MARTHA
DAVE

Time

The present.

Place

Dave and Martha's home.

The Play

Strange Snow

ACT ONE

Scene 1

The lights come up on MEGS *on the porch, stage left.* HE *looks in the window for signs of life. Nothing.* HE *begins banging on the front door.*

MEGS: Rise and shine, you sweet bear! It's time! The fishy-wishies are waitin' for us like whores in heat! We're the drunkest sailors on the block! Hah!? Hah!? (*Nothing.* HE *comes off the porch, looks upstairs*) Wake up, you great fool! We're gonna dance on Charlie the Tuna's grave! (HE *does a quick dance. Waits. Nothing.* HE *comes onto the porch again.* HE *bangs on the door*) Davey!? You up or what, guy? Hello? Rise and shine! Bed is for lovers or invalids, huh? Davey? Yo, Davey! You awake!?

A light comes on in the stairwell. MARTHA *comes roaring down the stairs.* SHE *is carrying a golf club.* SHE *is in a robe and slippers.* SHE *wears glasses.*

MARTHA: Stop it! Stop that noise! Stop it! (SHE *glares at* MEGS *through the panes of glass in the door.* SHE *brandishes the golf club threateningly*) If I have to come out there, you'll be sorry. I know how to use this!

MEGS *stops banging.* HE *grins.*

277

MEGS: Well, hi there, little lady. Nice mornin', huh? Kinda cold for golf though. Dark too. You always go golfin' in your PJs? You got mud cleats in your slippers? (MARTHA *glares at him, turns, puts down the club, goes to the phone*) Who you callin'? You're gonna wake'm up.

MARTHA: I'm calling the police.

MEGS: Why you callin' the police, woman?

MARTHA: I suggest you run. The police will come and they'll arrest you.

MEGS: Why would they want to do that?

MARTHA: Hello? Yes, I'd like the police. (*For* MEGS's *benefit*) I'd like to report a disturbance.

MEGS: Hey, come on, I'm no disturbance. I'm a friend of Davey's!

MARTHA: David?

MEGS: Dave Flanagan. This is his place, ain't it?

MARTHA: David is in bed. At this hour most people are! You'd better have a very good reason for making such a racket.

MEGS (*Grinning*): I wake you?

MARTHA: Of course you woke me! You scared me to death!

MEGS: I'm a buddy a Davey's.

MARTHA: I've never seen you here before.

MEGS: I've never been invited. But I'm a friend. Honest.

Pause.

MARTHA: Yes, hello? Could you please send a squad car to . . .

MEGS: No, wait, listen! You must be Davey's sister, Martha!

Pause.

MARTHA: I don't know you.!

MEGS: I feel like I know you! Davey talked about you all the time. Said you're swell.

Pause.

MARTHA: Never mind.

MARTHA *hangs up the phone. Moves to the door, unlocks it, opens it a crack. MEGS sticks his head in, grins.*

MEGS: Joseph Megessey. Everybody calls me Megs.

MARTHA *frowns at* MEGS *as if there is a bad taste in her mouth.*

MARTHA: Megs.

MEGS: That's my name, don't wear it out.

MARTHA: It's a ridiculous name.

MEGS: Ain't it? (*Pause*) Your brother and me, see, we're goin' fishin'.

MARTHA: Fishing.

MEGS: Yeah. It's opening day!

MARTHA: Ridiculous. The sun's not even up.

MEGS: Exactly. See, those trout'll be so bleary-eyed, they'll think our nightcrawlers are filet mignon. They'll go for 'em. Pow! And you know what we'll do, Martha? We'll bring'm home here and cook'm up for your dinner. What a you think a that?

MARTHA *retreats from the door, letting* MEGS *in.*

MARTHA: I think you're a fool. (SHE *turns on lights in the living room*)

MEGS (*Following*): No-o! It's opening day! The luck is rolling off me in waves! Smell? Perfume, huh?

MARTHA: Don't come near me. You smell like dirt.

MEGS: No! Nightcrawlers! (HE *displays a plastic baggy filled with nightcrawlers*) Hey, Martha! You want to come?

MARTHA: What? Where?

MEGS: Fishin'! I bet there's a rainbow that long just waitin' with your name on it. M-A-R-T-H-A!

MARTHA: Ridiculous.

MEGS: No! Listen, what say you go on upstairs and give your brother a poke in the breadbasket. Get him on down here.

MARTHA (*Brushing past him to close the door that* HE *has left wide open*): I will not! I'll have you know I was up till two in the morning correcting papers!

MEGS: Hey, no you weren't! On a Friday night?

MARTHA: Every night!

MEGS: I bet you was out hullaballooin' under the moon. I bet you got home five minutes ago and you threw on that robe to fool me!

MARTHA: You're preposterous.

MEGS: Ya can't fool me, woman! You got moonburns on your cheeks like roses!

MARTHA: I do not!

MEGS: Do!

MARTHA: Be quiet!

MARTHA *tries to move past* MEGS *and* HE *sweeps her into his arms.*

MEGS: Opening day, Martha! (*And* HE *dances* MARTHA *around the furniture*) Grab your partner, dance your partner, swing your partner!

MARTHA (*Simultaneously*): How dare you! Stop! You can't just . . . I'm not dressed for . . . stop!

MEGS: Skip to the loo, my darlin'! (*And* HE *deposits* MARTHA *in a chair*) Thank you, ma'am! Ginger Rogers and Fred Astaire better look out, huh? Yeah . . . uh, you think Davey's up?

MARTHA: Joseph, I don't think David remembered he made a date to go fishing with you.

MEGS: Opening day?

MARTHA: He wasn't home when I went to bed at two.

MEGS: Naw, he musta remembered. (*Yelling up the stairs*) C'mon guy! I got my waders in the car! God, it's good to meet you, Martha. Davey, he talked about you all the time, said you're swell. Hey, has he ever mentioned me to you?

MARTHA: I'd of remembered it if he had.

MEGS (*Grinning*): Yeah. (MARTHA *yawns*) Would you look at me keeping you up? You oughta be in dreamland restin' up for good ole Saturday night. Don't worry about me. I'm fine. I'll sit right here and wait. Go. Go to bed. (HE *sits*. HE *"waits"*)

Pause.

MARTHA: I'll tell him you're here. He won't like it. (*Pause*) He hates being woken up. (*Pause.* SHE *starts to leave;* SHE *stops*) He throws alarm clocks through windows. (*No response.* SHE *goes upstairs. Pause.* SHE *comes back down and proceeds briskly to the door with the intention of asking* MEGS *to leave*) I'm not going to do it. He'll take it out on me the rest of the day.

There is the sound of a toilet flushing from upstairs.

MEGS: Somebody's up! I hear something flushing down the drain. Let's hope it's not last night's dinner. (*Calling up the stairs*) 'Bout time, dude! Let's get a move on! I'm borin' your poor sister to death!

MARTHA: Why don't I get coffee on? You'll probably both need it.

MEGS: Hey, I'm fine.

MARTHA: Let me put it this way: David is going to need it.

MEGS: Don't go to any trouble.

MARTHA: I assure you, I won't. I'm up. (*With a touch of sarcasm*) I'm an early riser.

And THEY *move into the kitchen.*

MEGS: Know something? Me too. Up with the milkman every day. Listen, you do coffee and then Davey and I'll go. I got food and drink in the car. I planned ahead. We are gonna eat better'n turkeys on the first a November. Osmosis, see. The trout are gonna feel it in the air that we're fat and happy and they're gonna be so jealous they'll be chompin' on air bubbles. Hey! Look at this! (HE *takes what appears to be a large, brightly colored dustball from his pocket.* HE *places it ceremoniously on the table*)

MARTHA: What is it?

MEGS: It's a fly. I tied it myself. Ya like it?

MARTHA: It's colorful.

MEGS: Oh, goddam, it is that, ain't it? I figure it'll either drive a fish mad with

passion or scare'm half to death. Lotta hair and all of it cowlicks. Sorta
like you, woman.

MARTHA (*Her hands go to her hair*): What? Oh . . . it's a mess, isn't it?

MEGS: Oh, no, Martha. It's fine. It's just fine . . . uh, I wonder what's keepin'
that big guy. Think I oughta go bounce on his belly?

MARTHA: I don't think that would be a wise idea. Joseph . . . there are beer
cans in the wastebasket. They're David's discards. From last night. Before
he went out.

MEGS (HE *nudges the wastebasket. Cans rattle*): From last night? Oh. He forgot,
didn't he!

MARTHA: I'm afraid so.

MEGS: Yeah. Well . . . it's OK. My fault. My dumb mistake.

MARTHA: Joseph . . .

MEGS: No! Davey's a busy guy, drivin' those trucks here and there and back
again. Who has time for fishin'? Hey, it's been real good to meet you,
Martha. I'm sorry I woke you. I'll let myself out. (HE *begins to exit*)

Pause.

MARTHA: Joseph? This is ridiculous but . . . he's had hangovers
before . . . DAVID!? DAVID! GET UP THIS MINUTE! YOU'RE GO-
ING FISHING!

MEGS: You think he heard?

MARTHA: I'm sure the whole neighborhood did. DAVID!

MEGS: GET YOUR BUTT IN GEAR, GUY! PULL ON YOUR DRAWERS
AND PUT SOME DOUBLE KNOTS IN YOUR SNEAKERS! WE GOTTA
CATCH A TROUT FOR MARTHA'S DINNER!

MARTHA: YOU'VE GOT TO CATCH A TROUT FOR MY DINNER!

MEGS: You like trout, do ya?

MARTHA: I've never had them.

MEGS: Well, I've never caught'm but there's a first time for everything.

MARTHA: I bet there's a recipe in one of the cookbooks.

MEGS: You fry'm! You dump'm in corn flour and then whip'm into bacon
grease and they come out brown and tasty.

MARTHA: If you catch them and *clean* them, I'll cook them.

MEGS: You will? You're on, Martha. There's one sittin' under a log waitin' for
us and know what? It has your name right across the rainbow.
M-A-R-T-H-A!! (*And* HE *sweeps* MARTHA *into his arms again*) Swing your partner. Dance your partner. Glide your partner round and round. Skip to the
loo, my darlin'!

MARTHA (*Simultaneously*): Joseph, put me down . . . you can't just . . . oh!

And MARTHA *breaks into helpless giggles.* DAVE *enters down to the bottom of the stairs.* HE *is in boxer shorts and is horribly hung over.* MARTHA *and* MEGS *stop at the sight of him.*

DAVE: What in hell is goin' on?

MEGS (*Grins; pause*): You're up! (*Pause*) Look at you! Wouldn't go off a high dive in those johns, guy!

DAVE: What do you two think you're doing?

MARTHA: You and Joseph are going fishing, David.

DAVE: You're out of your mind.

MEGS: It's opening day, guy.

DAVE: Rain check.

MARTHA: David, you made a date to go fishing. Joseph has the car loaded and ready to go.

DAVE: Joseph?

MEGS: I got beer, sandwiches. It's a great adventure, guy.

DAVE: We plan this?

MEGS: Hey, last week. McDonald's, remember? How you been, I said. Good, you said. We oughta get together, said me. Fine, said you. Fishing, said me, opening day. Opening day, said you. Hah?! Hah?!Guess what today is, guy!!

DAVE: I thought fishing season was in the fall.

MEGS: No, that's huntin'. Don't worry, we'll do that too when the time comes. Opening day, Davey!

DAVE: I can't.

MEGS: Opening day?

DAVE: Sorry.

MEGS: Rainbows this long.

DAVE: Not up to it.

MEGS: Sure you are, Davey. A big ole nightcrawler on a hook? That'll perk your ass up. I got one here so big those rainbows'll have to be careful he don't eat them.

And MEGS *proudly displays one to* DAVE, *who almost gets sick.*

DAVE: Yech.

MARTHA: Go take a shower. You'll feel better.

DAVE: I'm passing.

MARTHA: You're doing no such thing. Shower and get dressed. I'll make breakfast for you both.

DAVE: I don't want to go fishing, Martha.

MARTHA: You're going.

DAVE: I don't want to go fishing.

MARTHA: David, I want a trout. Fried in corn flour. There's one waiting with my name on it.

MEGS: Davey? Hey, Davey? C'mon, guy. It'll be a great time. There's frost in the air and wondrous strange snow on the ground. The trout streams are gurglin' and singing. Know what they're sayin'? Wake up, Davey. It's time. It's time. Openin' day with your ole buddy, Megs. Damn! Makes me want to paint my face and pretend I'm Hiawatha. Whoo-whoo-whoo-whoo! *Fish*-ing! *Fish*-ing! (HE *keeps up his noise till* DAVE *says OK*)

DAVE: Megs, I . . . I don't . . . ahhh! OK!! (*Exiting*) I must have a screw loose.

MEGS: Never doubted it for a minute.

DAVE: I'm sleeping in the car.

MEGS: You'll sleep, I'll drive. Hey! You're beautiful! Don't you ever forget that.

DAVE (*Offstage*): God.

MARTHA: He didn't look very beautiful to me. Not in those baggy drawers of his.

MEGS: Martha, you're too much, you know that? You are. Something. He was not gonna go and you talked him into it.

MARTHA: I didn't talk him into anything.

MEGS (*Putting his hands affectionately on* MARTHA*'s arms*): Ain't you modest. I saw.

MARTHA (*Coldly*): I was making coffee.

And MARTHA *enters the kitchen.* MEGS *follows.*

MEGS: Hey, y'know, Martha, instant's fine with me. I drink so much instant my stomach's freeze-dried.

MARTHA: I find instant coffee foul. You'll have to make do with ground for drip.

MEGS: Drip? We'll go for it! I'll pretend I fell asleep and woke up in Dunkin Donuts. Hey, you got any milk? (*And* HE *sticks his nose in* MARTHA*'s refrigerator*)

MARTHA (*Annoyed*): Yes, of course I've got milk.

MEGS (*Bringing it out*): Thank God for that. Powdered creamer? I hate that shit. It tastes like powdered mouseballs to me. (*Pause*) Oh goddam, listen to me talk. Give me a bar a soap and I'll wash my mouth out as far down as my tonsils. Maybe it'll learn me to talk like a human being in front of a lady.

MARTHA: A lady? Really . . . besides, I'm used to it. I teach high school students, mouths like spittoons.

MEGS: Rap'm smartly upside the head. That'll learn'm.

MARTHA: My major was in biology, not the martial arts.

MEGS: Well, you ever have any problems, you let me know. I'm not good for much but one thing I could do is put the fear a God into a bunch a young punks. They oughta be bringin' you apples and candy and havin' crushes on you and stuff.

MARTHA: That'll be the day. (*Pause*) You must of been a delightful student.

MEGS: Me? Oh no, I was never any good at school. I specialized in Phys Ed, auto shop and smokin' in the lavatories. I'da driven you crazy.

MARTHA: I doubt it. I've developed a high tolerance level.

MEGS: I woulda. I could never keep my mouth shut. Everybody'd be laughin'. Not with me, at me. I didn't care. I liked the attention. (*Pause*) Hey, you, Martha! I bet you was a hell of a student. (*Pause.* MARTHA *looks at him suspiciously*) Well, were ya?

MARTHA: Yes, I was. I was mad for it.

MEGS: No!

MARTHA (*Proudly*): I loved to study. Straight A's in every subject.

MEGS: You're something, Martha. It must be great to be so smart.

MARTHA (*Gloating*): Yes, it is.

MEGS: I was dumber'n paint. But I sure as hell woulda brought you apples and candy, Martha. You can bet your sweet ass on that! (*And without thinking,* HE *swats* MARTHA *on the rump*) Sorry.

MARTHA: What would you like for breakfast?

MEGS: Hey, anything. Everything. My eyes could be bigger'n basketballs, they still wouldn't be bigger than my stomach.

MARTHA: I like pancakes on Saturday mornings.

MEGS: I do too. I love'm. Give me pancakes and the roadrunner on TV and Saturday morning is complete.

MARTHA: I like sausage too.

MEGS: Squealers? Sausage goes good with pancakes.

MARTHA: You'll have that then?

MEGS: Sausage and pancakes?

MARTHA: Would you rather eggs?

MEGS: Hey, how 'bout all three?

MARTHA: Why didn't I think of that.

MEGS: Goddam, Martha! Eggs and pancakes and sausage, it feels like Easter or something. And do you know what we'll have to go with it? Beer! I got a couple a cases in the car.

MARTHA: For breakfast? That's horrible.

MEGS: Breakfast beer. It's the best kind. Martha, ain't you ever had a beer for breakfast?

MARTHA: Joseph, there are those of us who have never had a beer.

MEGS: No! Woman, you are in for a treat. You sip on a breakfast beer and first thing you know, the cobwebs go, your voice rises two octaves, and God almighty, the sun comes up inside you! I'll go get some! (*And* HE *runs out of the kitchen, through the living room and out the front door*)

MARTHA: Joseph, I hardly . . . all right.

MARTHA *begins to take things from the refrigerator.* DAVE, *dressed, comes down the stairs and into the kitchen.* HE *looks around.*

DAVE: He leave?

MARTHA: He went to the car to get beer.

DAVE: Good. I could use one.

MARTHA: David, it happens to be five in the morning.

DAVE: You better believe it.

MARTHA: The idea is nauseating. You can't drink beer.

DAVE: I can. What an asshole.

MARTHA: Sshh. He'll hear you.

DAVE: I was talking about me. I wish you hadn't sided with him, Martha. He was gonna leave.

MARTHA: He looked so hurt when he thought you might of forgotten.

DAVE: I had forgotten. Martha, why is it you're a hardass with everything but stray animals? Bring'm in, give'm a warm bowl of milk, who ends up cleaning the turds off the floor? Me.

MARTHA: Hardly. Besides, your friend doesn't qualify as an animal.

DAVE (*Preoccupied*): He's not my friend. He's just somebody I know. We were in Vietnam together.

MARTHA (*Interested*): Oh. (*Pause*) I like him.

DAVE: You don't know him, sis.

MARTHA: I'm entitled to my first impressions. He's endearing is what he is.

DAVE: Endearing? (HE *laughs*) God, Martha, what do you know about endearing? (HE *sips from the coffee* MARTHA *has brought him.* HE *makes a face*) I wish he'd hurry up with that beer.

MARTHA: I wouldn't think you could stomach it after all you had last night. I assume the empties were just the start.

DAVE: Come on. I work hard all week. I'm entitled to cut loose on the weekend. You ought to try it sometime. It'd do you good.

Pause.

MARTHA: I'd love to. You can take me with you tonight.

DAVE (*Again preoccupied*): Forget it.

MARTHA: Why not? All you ever do is go out with the boys. I'd think you might like a woman around for a change.

DAVE: Women we can use, a sister we don't need. Besides, I date.

MARTHA: I've seen the kind of woman you date. Their idea of contributing to a conversation is to snap their chewing gum. Don't you think you might like a point of view for a change?

DAVE: I want a point of view, I'll listen to the news.

MARTHA: I'll be silent then. Unresponsive, unobtrusive, the kind of women men like.

DAVE: How do you know what men like? (*Laughing*) God, Martha, you're too much, you know that? You've hardly been out with anybody in your whole life but you're the authority on the subject.

MARTHA: David? Piss up a rope.

DAVE (*Surprised*): What'd I say already?

MARTHA: Just . . . drink your juice.

> MEGS *rushes through the front door, through the living room and into the kitchen.* HE *is carrying two sixes of beer.* HE *puts them on the counter.*

MEGS: Beer! We got it! I had to chop it out of the ice chest with a screwdriver! Be careful, it's colder than Alaska. One for you, one for me, and the by-God coldest a the bunch for you, Martha. Blow on it first, otherwise your tongue'll stick to the can. (HE *holds out a beer to* MARTHA)

DAVE: Forget it, Megs. Martha doesn't drink beer.

MEGS: Oh. Well, hey, it is early. (*And* HE *flips it in the air, catches it and sets it down*)

DAVE: Any time of the day is too early for her.

MARTHA: David? (*And* SHE *picks up the can of beer*)

DAVE: Yeah?

MARTHA: To opening day. (SHE *opens it. Shaken, it sprays her. Undaunted,* SHE *takes a mammoth gulp*)

MEGS: To opening day, by damn!

> MARTHA *takes the can down from her lips. Her eyes are watering and* SHE *is breathless.*

DAVE (*Sarcastic*): How's it taste, sis?

MARTHA (*Raising the can in toast*): To trout! (SHE *takes an even bigger gulp*)

MEGS (*Impressed*): Are we gonna catch us the limit or what? Breakfast beer, Martha!

> Pause as MARTHA *struggles to hold it down.*

MARTHA (*Breathless but with a challenging look at* DAVE): I have a confession, Joseph. I think I like beer.

DAVE: Terrific.

MEGS: I should say so! Finish that one off, I'll crack you another one.

MARTHA: I'll take it upstairs. I'll have to get dressed if I'm coming with you.

DAVE: What?

MEGS: You're coming along, Martha?

MARTHA: You invited me.

MEGS: Oh, this is so great. The rainbows'll never know what hit'm.

MARTHA (*Slapping* DAVE *on the shoulder*): Yes, I'm sure they'll be jumping in my lap dying to hear my women's point of view. (SHE *starts to exit*)

DAVE: Forget it, Martha.

MARTHA: Joseph doesn't mind, do you, Joseph?

MEGS: Mind? I should say not. I'm happy you're coming, Martha. If I'da known you wanted to, I'da asked you twice.

MARTHA (*Exiting*): I'll get ready.

MEGS: And don't you worry about breakfast. We'll stop along the way is what we'll do. We'll eat enough pancakes to build a house. On me! A woman doesn't buy when I'm around.

DAVE (*Sarcastic*): Dress warm, sis.

MARTHA (*Offstage*): David?

DAVE: Yeah?

MARTHA (*Offstage*): Up a rope!

MEGS (*Laughing*): She's great, your sister. I like her. (HE *puts on a Boston Red Sox hat that* HE *pulls from his pocket. It is old and well worn*) Hah!? Hah!? Opening day and we're goin' for it.

DAVE: Let's not.

MEGS: Huh?

DAVE: Let's say we have Martha make us some breakfast, we'll shoot the shit awhile, and you hit the road and let me get some sleep 'cause let me tell you, Megs, I don't feel good.

MEGS: You didn't recognize the hat, did ya? I wear it for luck.

DAVE: Bad luck, huh?

MEGS: It's changed its ways. It didn't like it over there in Nam any better than we did. It's not mine, it's Bobby's.

DAVE: Didn't help ole Bobby much, did it?

MEGS: It's helpin' me.

DAVE: Listen, don't get started.

MEGS: Sorry.

Pause.

DAVE: So . . . don't see you around much, Megs.

MEGS: I been puttin' a lot of hours at the garage. Hey, sweet bear, I opened up my own garage.

DAVE: You quit drivin'?

MEGS: It was time. Time to give those whores a rest, huh?

DAVE: Tell me about it.

MEGS: Yeah, but you're still barrelassin' 'cross them amber waves a grain, ain'tcha?

DAVE: Got a cake run. Produce distribution. Suits me fine.

MEGS: You ride'm, I'll repair'm! Did you know they hide under rocks?

DAVE: Who?

MEGS: Trout, guy! The speckled little bastards, they hide under rocks! Now what kind of a life is that, huh?

DAVE: You ever caught a trout?

MEGS (*Sheepish*): No . . . but I been practicin'! I been casting in the backyard! I had that line singing through the air like a bullwhip! Till I got snagged.

Neighbor's sheet. Ripped the hell out it. Boy, was she pissed. Good fishermen file the barbs off their hooks.

DAVE: Come on. Who told you that?

MEGS: TV! The American Sportsman! Watch Don Meredith hunt anacondas with a bowie knife! Trout fishin'! You file off the barbs so they have a chance.

DAVE: Right. We gonna do that?

MEGS: No fuckin' way, Jose!! Don't tell Martha, stud, but I got a feelin' the only way I'm gonna catch a fish is to drain the pond. We'll see! We'll see! Damn! This trout fishin' is a good time!

DAVE: Great. Terrific.

MEGS: Y'know, I only wear Bobby's hat on special occasions.

DAVE: Megs . . .

MEGS: No, really! Like when one of my kids needs a home run.

DAVE: Kids? What kids?

MEGS: Hey, I coached little league this last summer. Peewees. We screamed and hollered and lost every game. They want me for this year too. They like me.

DAVE: You're just a likable guy. God . . . I gotta lie down.

DAVE *enters the living room.* HE *lies on the couch.* MEGS *follows.*

MEGS: A home run in the ninth!?

DAVE: What?

MEGS: You liked the Yankees, Bobby liked the Red Sox. You guys bet. Bobby won on Carl Yastrzemski's home run in the ninth.

DAVE: That's right. Five bucks we bet.

MEGS: He loved those Red Sox, huh? Ole Bobby? Crazy for'm. He wanted us all to go to Fenway Park, remember? Beer and hot dogs, huh? Scream till we're hoarse. We oughta do that sometime, sweet Davey. Baseball season's just around the corner.

DAVE: Forget it.

MEGS: It'd be fun.

DAVE: Forget it.

MEGS: How come?

Pause.

DAVE: Hold out your hands.

MEGS (*Hiding them*): Aw, Davey . . . I ain't put my fists through glass in a long time.

DAVE: I've heard that before.

MEGS: Look at me now, Davey, huh? Look at me. Fat and happy. I bet you never seen me looking so good, guy.

DAVE: You look the same as before. (*Sarcastic*) Guy.

MEGS (*With an edge*): And you. You look real good too. And you just *stagger*

into me in the parking lot of ole McDonaldland. Damn. Fate's a funny
thing. (*Pause*) So talk to me some, huh?

DAVE: Talk? About what? (*And* HE *rises, goes to the liquor cabinet, gets a bottle of
whiskey from underneath.* HE *takes a sip, offers it to* MEGS)

MEGS: Never touch it, stud. Be wasted on me. Be like puttin' ethyl alcohol
in a lawnmower. (HE *is at the trophy case.* HE *picks up a photo*) These your
folks, huh?

DAVE: Huh? Yeah.

MEGS: Nice-lookin' mom. Sorta like Martha.

DAVE: She moved to Florida about a year ago. She didn't like the cold. She
calls once a week and she and Martha gang up on me.

MEGS: Maybe too many memories of your dad around here too, huh?

DAVE: Maybe.

MEGS: Musta been tough, Davey. Musta been real tough. You come hobblin'
off the plane on those crutches a yours and they lay that on you.

DAVE: Yeah. I was pissed. It was my dad's gung-ho vet shit that got me to enlist
in the first place and I'd been fantasizing for months on how the first thing
I was gonna do was deck the son of a bitch. I felt cheated.

MEGS (*Picking up a photograph*): Hey, is this Martha? (DAVE *looks, laughs*) Whoo,
she's changed, stud. Blossomed. (*Picking up a plaque*) And would you look
at this? All League!

DAVE: Team captain.

MEGS (*Picking up another photo*): Goddam! Look at you! Nice tie, studhoss.
When's this?

DAVE: Senior year.

MEGS: Would ya look at them apple cheeks?

DAVE: Future fuckin' lawyers club.

MEGS: You was gonna be a lawyer, Davey?

DAVE: What?

MEGS: You know, was that what you was, like, plannin'? To be a lawyer? After?

DAVE: I was gonna be everything, man. You name it, I was gonna be it.

MEGS: Hey. Know what all this is, Davey? Memories. Stuff to show your kids.

DAVE: Come off it, man. It's a bad joke. Something out of Archie Comics.
(*Calls up the stairs*) Hey, Martha! Let's go if we're going to go!

MEGS (*Calls up to* MARTHA): Dress warm, woman! We want you to catch rainbows, not your death of cold! Hey, sweet Davey, you think maybe she likes
me?

DAVE: Come off it, man. You two are from different planets. Only reason she's
comin' along is to bust my ass.

MEGS: Oh. Yeah. I guess you're right. (*Pause*) Sun's coming up. Real pretty.
Remember the sunrises? Over there? They were beauties, huh? Yeah.
Remember what ole Bobby'd say? If it wasn't for the C-rations we could

pretend we was in Hawaii. Remember him sayin' that? I do. (*Pause*) Know
what I hated? The waiting.

DAVE: Yeah. They always had to let us know in advance when we'd be goin'
out.

MEGS: Me, I never got used to it. Made me want to piss my pants every time.
Only way I could bear it was to get up for it, y'know? Something set in.
It was like I was numb and speedin' at the same time.

DAVE: Christ, you listening to yourself?

MEGS: Just talkin'.

DAVE: What you're talking about! We're not there, we're here!

MEGS: Damn right! We're here and now and that's what counts. Talking
doesn't hurt, Davey. (*Pause*) Maybe you don't do it often enough.

DAVE: I was never there, Megs.

MEGS: I ain't followin' that.

DAVE: Look, as far as I'm concerned it never happened. It's done with,
understand?

MEGS: How come I'm standin' here then?

DAVE: You got me.

MEGS: How come I'm wearin' Bobby's lucky hat?

DAVE: Burn the fuckin' thing.

MEGS: It was Bobby's.

DAVE: Bury it with him. (*And* HE *suddenly knocks the hat from* MEGS*'s head. An
ugly silence*) Yeah . . . this trout fishing is a great time. (MEGS *picks up the
hat. Pause.* MEGS *begins picking up empty beer cans*) Hey listen . . . Megs . . .
leave that stuff. Martha'll do it.

MEGS: My pleasure, stud. (*And* MARTHA *comes down the stairs*) By God, woman,
look at you! Straight out of an L.L. Bean catalogue!! The fish are gonna
take one look at you and walk out of the water with their hands up!

MARTHA: Thank you.

DAVE: Better get your glasses on or you'll trip over them when they do.

MARTHA: I don't need them. I have on contact lenses.

DAVE: Contacts!?

MARTHA: I've had them. I'll take those, Joseph. They get under foot like
marbles, don't they?

> *And a hard look passes between* DAVE *and* MARTHA.

DAVE: Have another beer, sis. Where'd you get the clothes?

MARTHA: I took some of my classes on a field trip to a freshwater pond. I
couldn't very well collect samples in a skirt.

MEGS: Hell, no. Would I change a muffler in a three-piece suit? You look ter-
rific, Martha, just terrific. God, are we going to catch the limit or what?
Listen, I'll start the car. Opening day, ladies and gentlemen, opening day!
Look out, trout, we're on our way! (HE *grabs the beer and exits*)

Pause.

MARTHA: You're drinking.

DAVE: You want to try this too?

MARTHA: I'll pass, thank you. You ready?

DAVE: Who you trying to impress, Martha, huh? Contact lenses? You drinking beer? Give me a break.

MARTHA: What is wrong, David, with me having a good time for once?

DAVE (*Gesturing in* MEGS*'s direction*): You're that desperate?

MARTHA: He's nice.

DAVE: Or maybe he's just as desperate as you.

MARTHA (*Softly*): Fuck you, David.

DAVE: Ooh, Miss Peach! Nice mouth for a schoolteacher. You talk that way to your students?

MARTHA: No. (*Pause*) Go back to bed if you want to. I'm going fishing. (SHE *exits*)

DAVE: Go on. The two of you have a great time! Hell with you both! (*Pause. There is the sound of a car starting up, revving.* HE *runs to the door*) Martha!? I'm coming! (HE *grabs his jacket, a fatigue jacket.* HE *picks up the bottle.* HE *exits*) I wouldn't miss this for the world.

Lights to black.

Scene 2

MARTHA *enters through the kitchen door, stage right.* SHE *has a blanket around her. Her pants and shoes are wet. Her hair is damp.* SHE *is shivering with cold.*

MARTHA: Ohhh . . . (SHE *runs through the kitchen, into the living room and up the stairs*)

Pause.

MEGS: Martha! Hey, Martha!? (HE *enters through the kitchen door.* DAVE *is out cold over his shoulder.* DAVE *groans*) It's A-OK, sweet bear. I gotcha. My wits are weak but my back is strong. (HE *almost slips*) Whoops! Good Christ, guy, there's water on the floor. I almost took us both out. (DAVE *groans*) You gonna be sick again? You alive back there, hah? Hey, nobody ever said trout fishing was gonna be easy. Martha!!? (HE *enters the living room*) Whew, you are heavy, stud. We'll have to make room for you in the trophy case. Have you stuffed and we'll hang a little sign on you. This is what we brought back alive. Barely. Martha, where'd you go, woman!? Don't worry, stud, we'll follow the puddles, we'll find her. Let's get you settled, stud. (HE *puts* DAVE *on the couch*) It's OK, sweet bear, it's A-OK. Some of us, we didn't drink, we'd cut our wrists, huh? You don't have to explain. I know.

You know I know. Looking good, studhoss, looking real good. You and me, we paddled twenty miles a shit creek, huh? Yeah. With our bare hands, we did. Me, I don't forget that. I'm like an elephant, short on smarts, long on memory. You sleep, stud. Ole Megs is on watch. You sleep.

MEGS *takes off his jacket, drapes it over the sleeping* DAVE, *and sits.* MARTHA *enters in warm, dry clothes.*

MARTHA: I was so cold. Is he all right?

MEGS: He's in dreamland is all. His head's gonna feel like a bowling alley when he wakes up but he's fine.

MARTHA: He finished off the whole bottle, the poor fool.

MEGS: Guzzled it is what he did. Wasn't the first time, won't be the last. (HE' *begins to laugh*)

MARTHA: What?

MEGS: You. You was a bedraggled cat, woman. You looked like you been on the spin cycle of a washing machine for fourteen hours.

MARTHA: If you hadn't had that blanket in the car I'd of frozen to death.

MEGS: You were terrific, Martha.

MARTHA: Every trout for a hundred miles is probably hiding under a rock in a state of shock.

MEGS: Martha, your fish was gettin' away!

MARTHA: Yes, I know! But I never thought you'd push me right in after it!

MEGS: I got excited! I mean, I knew you wanted the brainless thing so badly. God . . . he was beautiful, huh, Martha? A real rainbow. Hey, if I'da known you was gonna throw down the pole and try haulin' him in hand over hand, I'da got you a drop line.

MARTHA: I was startled! I felt as though I'd stepped on a frog. I could feel him through the string.

MEGS: He felt you.

MARTHA: He was heavy.

MEGS: Woman, he was cousin to the Loch Ness monster! Enormous! You got him onto that bank and I thought, look out, Martha! That baby's gonna take your leg off!

MARTHA: No!

MEGS: Yes!!

MARTHA: Really?

MEGS: Hey, would I lie? It's a good thing he threw the hook. He was gettin' pissed!

MARTHA: No. He was desperate. My heart went out to him.

MEGS: You're something, Martha. You are. Didn't I tell you there'd be one waitin' with your name on it? M-A-R-T-H-A! It was a good time?

Pause.

MARTHA: It was a wonderful time, Joseph.

MEGS (*Softly*): Yeah? That's just great.

MARTHA: *You* are having some soup.

MEGS: *Soup* would be great.

MARTHA: Come on. To the kitchen. Sit. Split pea with ham. Homemade.

MEGS: You're kiddin'. By God, if food doesn't come out of a can, I usually have a hard time recognizing it.

MARTHA: I'll have you know I'm a very good cook.

MEGS: Well, goddam, we're a team 'cause I like to eat.

MARTHA: Do your girlfriends cook for you?

MEGS: Tell you the truth, Martha, most a the girls I know don't know a waffle iron from a frisbee. I been keepin' a kinda low profile in the girlfriend department. Got kinda tired of mud wrestlers and hog callers. What about you, Martha? You must have to fight'm off with tomahawks.

MARTHA: I'm sorry to inform you I've given up the fight.

MEGS: Come on, woman, you're built like a brick shithouse!

MARTHA: What?

MEGS: Oh, goddam. Me and my mouth again. Sorry, Martha, but you are. I noticed it straight off.

MARTHA: That's the most ridiculous thing I've ever heard.

MEGS: No.

MARTHA: I'm shapeless.

MEGS: Solid. You're sturdy. You're a battleship!

MARTHA: Agreed. With the face of an icebreaker.

MEGS: No-oh.

MARTHA: Yes.

MEGS: No— . . .

MARTHA: Stop contradicting me! I know what I am. Plain and unattractive.

MEGS: Martha, I saw the picture in there. You used to be.

MARTHA: You're very nice to try and convince me otherwise but I look in the mirror every morning. I live with what I see. The soup will be ready in a moment.

MEGS: Y'know, Martha, some people, they get awful ugly the minute they open their mouths. And other people, like you, Martha, they grow on you. The more you get to know'm, the better lookin' they get.

MARTHA: Very few share your opinion.

MEGS: Oh. You give'm a chance to?

MARTHA: Look, I'm not one of those pieces of fluff you see in men's magazines. Does that make me less a woman? It does not. (*Pause*) And I'm a fool because for some stupid reason I think it does. And so I buy contact lenses and clothes I can't really afford. You think I'd of learned by now. You think I'd of learned at the start. (*Pause*) The soup is almost hot. (*Pause*) David had to even get me a date for my high school formal. I was on the decorations committee, the tickets committee. I put together the whole thing. Nobody asked me to go. David rounded up his friends and told them one of them had to invite me or he'd beat them all up. I think perhaps they drew straws. I didn't know. Suddenly I was invited, that's all that mattered. I was so happy. Well, it was something that couldn't be kept quiet, David's blackmail. I heard rumors. I confronted David. He wouldn't admit what he'd done but I knew.

Pause.

MEGS: You go?

Pause.

MARTHA: I got very sick the night of the prom. A twenty-four hour thing. David meant well.
MEGS: I crashed mine. Yeah, I did. Just walked in wearin' a motorcycle jacket, steel-toed jack boots, and shades, stood there like a madman, grinnin' at all those tuxedos, hopin' somebody'd try to throw me out. I think perhaps I also was very sick on the night of the prom.
MARTHA: Wouldn't we have made a lovely couple.
MEGS: You'da gone with me?
MARTHA: What?
MEGS: If, y'know, I'da like, asked you, you'da gone with me?
MARTHA: Well . . . yes.
MEGS: Nah.
MARTHA: Yes.
MEGS: Nah.
MARTHA (*Angrily*): Why do you always contradict me? Yes, I would have gone with you.
MEGS: Well, goddam, woman! We'da had a great time!! I can see it! (HE *jumps up, moves to the kitchen door*) I come to pick you up. I knock on the door. (HE *exits out the door.* HE *knocks three times*)
MARTHA: What are you doing? What are you doing?
MEGS (*Opening the door, stepping in*): This ain't detention, Martha. It's the prom. Answer the door.
MARTHA: You're in.

MEGS *realizes that* HE *is.* HE *grins.* HE *shuts the door.* HE *does a slow spin as if showing off something.*

MEGS: Hah!? Hah!?
MARTHA: What?
MEGS: Your mom. She thinks I look very dashing in my tuxedo.
MARTHA: Oh, you do.

MEGS (*Whipping off his hat*): The corsage is as big as a goddam dogwood tree. (HE *tosses his hat into the refrigerator*) Your father comes over to shake hands. He smells my breath to see if I've been drinking. (HE *exhales*) I have!

MARTHA: He approves. And offers you an aperitif for the road.

MEGS: Too late! You make your entrance down the stairway! You look . . . terrific!

MARTHA: My gown is silk and gossamer.

MEGS: Yeah. And you look terrific. Your hair is just so. Hey! Know what it is?

MARTHA (*Breaking the spell*): Preposterous.

MEGS: No! It's beautiful.

MARTHA: My shoes?

MEGS: Listen, you could click your heels three times and they'd take you to Kansas.

MARTHA: Ridiculous.

MEGS: No! (HE *retrieves his hat from the refrigerator*) There is a moment of embarrassment as I try to pin on your corsage. I am timid.

MARTHA: Of the occasion?

MEGS: Of your gunboats!

MARTHA (*Giggling, slapping at* MEGS): Stop! (SHE *takes the hat and puts it on her head, the bill facing backwards*) I smile reassuringly. (SHE *does*)

MEGS: And the air is heavy with the portent of things to come! (*Offering his arm*) Shall we go?

MARTHA: The chariot awaits?

MEGS (HE *mimes opening a car door for* MARTHA): '57 Chevy, roars like a PT boat but smooth as glass. In accord with the occasion I have thrown all the empty beer cans in the back seat.

MARTHA: How thoughtful. We arrive?

MEGS: We knock'm dead. You're beautiful.

MARTHA (*Softly*): You're handsome.

MEGS: We dance! (HE *does a ferocious dance: a combination of the jerk and the swim.* HE *sings the instrumental lead to* "En-A-Gada-Da-Vida" *by the Iron Butterfly as* HE *dances.* HE *stops, grinning*) They play a slow one. (HE *begins to sing* "Michelle" *by the Beatles.* HE *opens his arms to* MARTHA. SHE *comes to him.* THEY *sway*) What a terrific dancer you are.

MARTHA (*Shyly*): And you.

MEGS: If I step on your feet you give me a shot to the kidneys, OK?

MEGS *pulls* MARTHA *very close, his hands going down around her waist.* SHE *stiffens.*

MARTHA: This is stupid.

MEGS: Just dancing. (*And* HE *holds* MARTHA *tighter still*)

MARTHA (*With a growing terror at* MEGS*'s embrace*): Please. Stop it. Get your hands off me!

MARTHA *struggles free from* MEGS, *rips the hat from her head, tosses it away from her, staggers to the stove. Pause.*

MEGS: That's the thing about shy people, Martha. They think everybody's looking. Nobody is. 'Cept me. (*Unable to hide his anger, his frustration, his hurt*) And I like what I see!

MARTHA: For God's sake, sit down. The soup is ready.

MEGS: That bad a dancer, huh? Yeah . . . (HE *moves to exit out the kitchen door and suddenly, almost without thinking,* HE *punches out one of the panes of glass in the door*) Oh God, I'm sorry . . .

MARTHA (*Simultaneously with* MEGS*'s last line*): Joseph! Your hand . . .

MEGS: I'll pay for it, I promise, oh, I'm so sorry, I'll pay for it.

And MEGS *is hiding his hands from* MARTHA. SHE *is trying to see if they're cut.*

MARTHA: I don't care about the glass! Is your hand cut!?

MEGS: No, they're fine! (*And* MARTHA *sees the scars on his hands. Embarrassed,* HE *tries to hide them.* SHE *won't let him*) My hands . . . they ain't so pretty . . . .

MARTHA: You've done it before . . . .

MEGS: Yeah . . . .

MARTHA: Why . . .

MEGS: I dunno why, Martha. I'm real sorry. Listen, you tell Davey so long for me. (HE *starts to leave, going into the living room, heading for the front door*)

MARTHA: Joseph? (MEGS *stops*) I'd have wanted you to take me to the prom.

Pause.

MEGS: Yeah?

MARTHA (*Softly*): Yes.

MEGS: Really?

MARTHA (*Softly*): Yes. (*Pause*) Will you sit and have soup with me?

Pause.

MEGS: Only 'cause you asked 'stead of ordered. (HE *enters the kitchen,* HE *sits.* MARTHA *puts a bowl filled with soup in front of him*) Look at this. China. (*Looking at the plate the bowl is on*) They match too. I almost got a set a tableware once. Every time you bought groceries at the store, they gave you a plate. I just didn't shop often enough.

MARTHA: Go on. Start.

MEGS: No, I'm waitin' for you. It'll stay hot. I hate eating alone. You eat alone much, Martha?

MARTHA *is getting crackers.*

MARTHA: Sometimes I eat with David. David, however, eats alone. (*Pause*) I usually correct papers while I eat.

MEGS: Sounds to me like you give out way too much homework, Martha. (*Pause*) Sure smells good.

MARTHA (*Sitting*): Thank you.

MEGS: Good as Campbell's, I bet. I haven't even tasted it yet and I like it.

MARTHA: Now you can.

MARTHA *puts her napkin in her lap.* MEGS *is on the verge of digging in but notices this.* HE *puts down his spoon and carefully unfolds his napkin, placing it in his lap.* HE *tastes his soup.* HE *tastes it again. Perplexed, yet again.* HE *grins.*

MEGS: Good.

MARTHA *smiles, pleased.* THEY *eat. Pause.*

MARTHA: David said you two were in Vietnam together.

MEGS: Basic right through we were.

MARTHA: He never talks about it.

MEGS: No? Me, I talk about it all the time. To myself when there's no one around to listen. You ever had an ugly melody in your head? You can't get rid of it no matter how hard you try to hum something else.

MARTHA: David gets furious if you even mention it. (*Pause*) Did you know David's friend, Bobby?

MEGS: He told you about ole Bobby? Ole Bobby, Martha, he was . . . . You take a guy who does something well, he practices, right? Well, ole Bobby, he could just look at it once and do it better right off. Yup. And was he smart? He knew things. But see, he knew'm from here (*Tapping his chest*) as well as from here (*Tapping his head*). Ole Bobby was our heart. A regular waterwalker. We loved him. Oh, but we was some trio, Bobby, your brother and me. They thought I was lucky. Davey did anyway. Used to. He was always goin' on about how I was a lucky dollar, a rabbit's foot . . . yeah, I ain't foolin'. Really! Lucky Megs! (*Pause*) That all kinda ended when we lost ole Bobby. It was when, y'know, Davey got hurt and me, I uh . . . I got in the way like I got a habit a doin'. Oh, I'll tell you, Martha. Your brother is one sweet bear but ole Bobby was worth him and me rolled together. (*Pause*) You wouldn't a liked me much when I got home. Crazy. I got in fights a lot, dumb ones, five against one where I got the piss kicked out a me. It was not a nice time. And what it got down to was . . . well . . . one night I was lyin' around, contemplatin' the rafters, wonderin' if they could take my weight, and like . . . don't laugh or nothin', please . . . I prayed. I felt better. What was done, was done, y'know? For some reason we'd lost ole Bobby. And it was up to me to make that reason a good one.

'Cause ole Bobby, he deserved that. I think I've liked myself a little bit more ever since then. (*Pause.* MARTHA *starts to take the bowls*) Hey, no way, Jose! Cook doesn't clean. My turn. (HE *takes the bowls to the sink*)

MARTHA: I think I'm going to cry.

MEGS: Huh?

MARTHA: You make me want to laugh and cry at the same time. I rarely do either one.

MEGS: Oh. Guess I oughta get goin', huh? Sure wish we'd caught some trout. (HE *starts to exit*)

MARTHA: You're coming for dinner anyway!

MEGS (*In disbelief*): I am?

MARTHA: Yes! I'm going to buy steaks and I'm going to make a nice salad and I'm going to put potatoes in the oven and . . . and . . . we'll have wine! I'll get a nice bottle of wine! And pie! I baked a pie this week and we'll put ice cream on it and . . . unless of course you have other plans.

MEGS: Are you kiddin' me?

MARTHA: Yes?

MEGS: Are you kiddin' me?

MARTHA: You'll come?

MEGS: Fuckin' A, I'll come! With fuckin' bells on! You'll pardon the expression. And listen, I'm buyin' the wine!

MARTHA: I don't know wine.

MEGS: Me neither, so what? We'll shoot in the best. Know why? 'Cause you and me, Martha, we deserve it! Goddam, I better get cracking! It's gonna take me a year in the shower to get cleaned up and even then I'd hedge my bets!

MARTHA: Eight o'clock?

MEGS: Eight o'clock is good.

MARTHA: I can be ready earlier.

MEGS: Seven-thirty is earlier.

MARTHA: How about seven?

MEGS: Goddam, woman! Why don't I just stay and watch you change!? Just kiddin', just kiddin'. Opening Day. It feels like Christmas. (HE *puts his lucky hat on* MARTHA) I'll be back.

MARTHA: Bye, Joseph.

MEGS: Joseph. You're too much, Martha. Something. M-A-R-T-H-A!

MEGS *exits out the front door, slamming it behind him.* MARTHA *rushes to the door and peers out watching him go.*

MARTHA: Oh my . . .

DAVE *has stirred at the sound of the slamming door.* HE *sits up on the couch, groggy. A moment.* MARTHA *turns.* SHE *and* DAVE *look at each other.* MARTHA *is suddenly aware* SHE *is wearing the hat.* SHE *quickly takes it off. Lights to black.*

End of Act One

ACT TWO

Scene 1

MARTHA *enters down the stairs into the living room.* SHE *is wearing a beautiful dress in a light pastel color, her hair is carefully brushed back.* SHE *wears a bit of makeup.* DAVE *enters right behind her.* HE *is unchanged, unshaven, and is smoking a cigarette.*

DAVE: What a ya mean you invited him over for dinner?

MARTHA: I thought I spoke English. Invite, a verb, to request the participation of. Dinner. That's a meal if memory serves me.

DAVE: I don't want to eat dinner with him.

MARTHA: Your participation has not been requested. If you'd like to, you may. Go out if you don't.

DAVE: I don't even want the guy in my house.

MARTHA: It's my house too. What shall we do? Call Mother in Florida and ask for a tie-breaking vote?

DAVE: What is this, Martha? Be kind to stranger week? You don't even know Megs.

MARTHA: That's why I invited him over. To get to know him.

DAVE: What you're going to find out, you don't need.

MARTHA: David, I am trying to tidy up. It is difficult with you pretending you're Mount St. Helen's, spewing ashes everywhere.

DAVE: Sis, want to know what he was in Vietnam? Jacknife. That's what he called himself. It's a truckdriving term, sis. It's when you take a big, beautiful eighteen-wheeler and you crash it, turn it to shit. Jacknife. 'Cause he crashed trucks. He was crazy. And Vietnam made him crazier. He's spent more time in the can on assault charges than you can believe.

MARTHA: He's been very nice.

DAVE: Nothing's happened to get him started. Push the right button and he's off. Berserk, Martha.

MARTHA: I'm sorry you don't like him, I do.

DAVE: You want to go out with someone? OK, I'll set you up. Plenty a guys owe me favors; it'll be no problem.

MARTHA: No, thank you.

DAVE: Martha . . .

MARTHA (*Exiting to the kitchen*): I have to put potatoes in the oven.

DAVE (*Following*): He's nothing but a mechanic, Martha. He owns a garage for Christsake.

MARTHA: And you drive a truck, David. I try not to hold it against you.

Pause.

DAVE: Steak. We were gonna have trout for dinner. What a laugh. I froze my ass off.

MARTHA: I should have thought you were too drunk to feel anything.

DAVE: Martha, listen, I have his number someplace. Call him and tell him something came up, the P.T.A.

MARTHA: Are you joining us?

DAVE: The fucking board of education wants to see you!

MARTHA: Do you want a potato!?

DAVE: Yes! (*Pause*) If Dad was alive, he wouldn't let a guy like this on the front porch.

MARTHA: Go out, David. Call up your friends, go to a bar and get drunk and hoarse screaming at the television.

DAVE: No way.

MARTHA: Then not another word if you're staying! Be what you usually are, a presence in the house that eats whatever's put in front of it and grunts when spoken to. I'd be better off living with a Saint Bernard!

DAVE: What is with you today?

MARTHA: What do you care, David? Really, why this sudden concern about who I see?

DAVE: Hey, you're my sister.

MARTHA: I thought I was your housekeeper, your cook. I don't know how long it's been since I heard you say, Martha, how are you? I've been invited to a party, come along. Let's get together and do something. How's the old love life, kid?

DAVE: What love life? You never go out.

MARTHA: Exactly.

DAVE: OK, I'm sorry. I'll take more interest from now on, I really will. Hey, we'll go to a movie. How's that sound? But Martha, forget Megs. The guy is not up to your standards.

MARTHA: Has anyone ever been? My so-called standards, David, are merely something I've hidden behind so I could salvage a little pride. (*Pause*) Do you remember that cruise I went on last Easter break?

DAVE: Yeah. You got a nice tan.

MARTHA: It was a swinging singles cruise, a man for every maid. It was a ship filled with depressed, lonely people and I went hoping I might meet . . . what . . . a kindred soul, someone I liked, who liked me, anyone. And I might have. If I could have left my standards at dockside. But I was frightened and so when I went on board my standards walked right up the gangplank behind me. I got a nice tan.

DAVE: Martha, what, you're pissed off you didn't get laid?

MARTHA: Wouldn't you have been?

DAVE: Yeah, but you?

MARTHA: Oh, I'm sorry. Shy, plain women don't desire. When they're in bed at night they keep their hands off themselves and don't fantasize. (*Pause*) David, how many times have you made love?

DAVE: Hey, come on, huh?

MARTHA: Really. Fifteen times? Fifty times? One hundred?

DAVE: Gimme a break.

MARTHA: Good God, David, look at me! I'm almost the perfect image of the virgin schoolmarm. Tending other people's children is supposed to make me feel chaste and noble and fulfilled. Bullshit. I feel helpless and very stupid. I'm not a nun. I wrote boys' names in my notebooks when I was young. I prayed that they'd pull my hair so I'd pay attention to them.

DAVE: Kids don't know shit.

MARTHA: Oh, David, they know. I watch them. Girls are always glancing about. Is anyone looking? Is a boy looking? They are. You call them to the blackboard and they struggle up, bent at the waist, pulling their sweaters down.

DAVE: God, Martha, you checkin' out their boners?

MARTHA: You're horrible. I'm just telling you that they know! When you see a boy walking a girl to class, his arm around her, his mouth close to her ear, you know they know. Why should it be too late for me? (*Pause*. DAVE *suddenly giggles*. SHE *looks at him*. HE *laughs*. SHE *is annoyed*) What?

DAVE: Uh . . . before. About being a virgin schoolmarm? You said almost. I mean, I never thought that you . . . uh, it never occurred to me that . . . (HE *laughs*) Who'd you get it on with? Anybody I know?

MARTHA: You just . . . that's none of your business.

DAVE: Yeah, it is. Come on. Please?

MARTHA: Go away.

DAVE: Martha, I'm curious. Martha? Mar-tha? (HE *is laughing openly now*)

MARTHA: Leave me alone.

DAVE: Loosen the strings, sis. Come on, gossip a little.

Pause.

MARTHA: William Green.

DAVE: Ichabod Crane? I don't believe it. (HE *laughs harder than ever*)

MARTHA: That's why it's so hard for people like me. People like you make fun of someone's rear end or waistline. You turn love into a beauty pageant. Stop laughing!

DAVE (*Trying to stop but not succeeding*): No! No! It's not 'cause a the way you look.

MARTHA: Oh!

DAVE: It's just that . . . I mean, you're not what you'd call experienced. Are you? (HE *laughs*) No! And him . . . he was a shy guy and well . . . (HE *laughs*) Laurel and Hardy! This is another fine mess you've got me into! (HE *laughs*)

MARTHA: Oh, David, I could have died. Neither of us knew what we were doing. We were like two cars that had hooked bumpers . . . both of us pushing and pulling at the wrong times. And he kept apologizing the whole time. I'm terribly sorry. I think he'd hoped I'd changed my mind. (THEY *laugh*) I don't know why I'm laughing . . . it was horrible. No passion. Guilt for him. Frustrated tears for me.

DAVE (*Tenderly*): I'm sorry, kiddo.

MARTHA: He asked me to marry him. He'd been in bed with me so he thought he should.

DAVE (*Considering this a moment*): Y'know, he wasn't such a bad guy.

MARTHA (*Bristling*): Meaning I won't get many chances? Meaning I'm not in any position to pick and choose?

DAVE: Here you go again.

MARTHA: I didn't sleep with him so he'd marry me. We'd have made each other miserable. (*Pause*) Are you having dinner with us?

DAVE: Sis, you make dinner for Megs, he'll latch onto you. He'll be calling, coming by, telling me all sorts of crazy stuff. We won't be able to get rid of him. You're making a mistake, Martha.

MARTHA: It's my mistake then.

DAVE: Jesus, Martha, why won't you listen to me?! Do you know anything about men? No! You'd have a hard time handling the most perfect son of a bitch in the world, let alone this guy! (*Pause*) All right. All right. You'll see. You'll be beggin' him to leave.

MARTHA: Go get cleaned up. You'll feel better.

Pause.

DAVE (*Softly*): Is it really so bad here, Martha?

MARTHA: It's not so bad.

DAVE: I love this place. Every good memory I have is here. (*Pause*) I like having you around here, Martha. (*Pause*) Listen, I'm gonna be more appreciative, you'll see.

MARTHA: The things I want, you can't give me, David.

DAVE: You're gonna leave?

MARTHA: Someday. (*Long pause*) Go get cleaned up.

DAVE: Yeah. I got any clean clothes anywhere?

MARTHA: In the dryer.

DAVE (*Preoccupied*): Get'm for me, huh?

> DAVE *exits upstairs.* MARTHA *puts the finishing touches on her table.* MEGS *comes to the front door.* HE *has flowers which* HE *hides behind his back.* HE *is carrying a large bag.*

MEGS (*Knocking*): Hello, it's me! Front door!

> MARTHA *scurries around, checking everything to make sure it's perfect.* SHE *checks her reflection in one of the windows.* SHE *hurries to the door, pauses, takes a deep breath, lets* MEGS *in.*

MARTHA: Well now.

MEGS: Just a packhorse, that's me. (HE *displays the flowers, surprising* MARTHA)

MARTHA: Oh, my.

MEGS: Like'm? I told the guy I was a white knight going to meet a fair damsel. Give me your best!

MARTHA: They're beautiful.

MEGS: Wait. Here.

MARTHA: No!

MEGS: Yes! Candy.

MARTHA: Ohh . . .

MEGS: Just a mad seducer, that's me. I got wine too. No idea what goes with what so I got one of every color: white, pink and blood red. And . . . this!

MARTHA: Brandy?

MEGS: If beer for breakfast is sunrise, brandy is sundown. (*And doing a quick "bump and grind,"* HE *takes off his overcoat.* HE *is wearing a very wellmade, dark three-piece suit, a white shirt, a tie*)

MARTHA: Look at you.

MEGS: It looked real good in the store window. I hardly ever get to wear it. I figured what the hell, prom night, y'know? (*Pause*) I'm real glad to be here, Martha.

> MARTHA *hesitates, then leans up and kisses* MEGS *on the cheek. Lights go to black.*

Scene 2

> MEGS *and* MARTHA *are in the kitchen. Dinner has been finished.* MEGS *has taken off his jacket, loosened his tie, rolled up his sleeves.* HE *sits at the table and sips wine.* MARTHA *is putting the finishing touches on cleanup.*

MEGS: Martha, I feel like I fell asleep and woke up in the Waldorf Astoria.

MARTHA: Go on.

MEGS: I do. Steaks I usually eat are so bad, you put'm down knowin' the restaurant's gotta make up for it by givin' you all the beer you can drink. (*Pause*) Come on, Martha, you sit down.

MARTHA: Joseph . . .

MEGS: Hush, hush, hush. Sit. Have another glass of this Parisian nectar. I'm finishing up here. I'm not taking no for an answer. These hands may finger-paint in axle grease by day but come nightfall they whisper messages to me. Clean us, Megs. Drown us in boraxo. Wash the bathtub or something. So I do. My hands like it.

MARTHA: You're a funny man.

MEGS: I am, ain't I? Aren't. Aren't I. Good wine?

MARTHA: Oh yes. I heartily approve. (*Giggling*) Listen to me. Such an expert. The tip of my nose has gone numb. I'll be swinging from the chandeliers next. Oh, I want to wrap the steak in tinfoil for you so you can take it home.

MEGS: Hey, no way, Jose! That's teacher's lunch for two days.

MARTHA: You're taking it.

MEGS: Oh, God, I'm being ordered again. How can I refuse?

MARTHA: You can't.

MEGS: Are you sure?

MARTHA: I try not to eat lunch. You saw my picture in there. The Hindenburg. My idea of an exceptional Saturday night used to be two pounds of fudge and thirty term papers. I've finally eliminated the two pounds of fudge.

MEGS: And from all the right places too.

Pause.

MARTHA: This will be in the refrigerator. Don't you forget it either. More wine?

MEGS: You?

MARTHA: Yes.

MEGS: Me too.

MARTHA: Why don't you take the wine in the living room and get comfortable. I'll be there in a moment.

MEGS *enters the living room.* MARTHA *prepares a tray for the brandy: a cloth, snifters.* MEGS *is at the trophy case looking at* MARTHA'*s picture when* DAVE *comes downstairs.*

MEGS: Hey, some dinner. Can your sister cook!

DAVE: Not bad.

MEGS: Come on, stud, your idea a cooking is to throw the meat in a pan, turn the flame on high and go and take a shower.

DAVE: Yeah . . . (HE *moves to the kitchen*)

MEGS: Hey! Listen, if she asks for my references, lie! Hah!? Hah!?

And MEGS *punches* DAVE *affectionately in the belly.* DAVE *enters the kitchen.* HE *gets a beer from the icebox.*

MARTHA: It's going very well, don't you think?

DAVE: Your steak was pretty good. A little rare for my taste.

MARTHA: You seemed to be enjoying yourself.

DAVE: I didn't think either of you knew I was here. This is great, Martha. Terrific, Martha. Look at you, Martha. And you eating it up. I didn't know who to laugh at.

MEGS: Hey, team captain, big number fifty, like Butkus!

DAVE: Enthusiastic, isn't he?

MARTHA: Positive. Optimistic. It's refreshing.

Pause.

DAVE: He's a loser.

Pause. And MARTHA *suddenly slams an open drawer shut with a loud bang.*

MARTHA: You're the loser, David. Ever since you came home. What is it like to aspire to nothing more than getting drunk on Saturday night?

DAVE: I aspire to be left the fuck alone!

MARTHA: By what? Life in general? Why even be a human being, David?

DAVE: Good question.

MARTHA: The idea of anyone finding anything, even for a moment, offends you, you selfish . . .

DAVE (*Overlapping*): I want you to see what he's like!

MARTHA: I know what he's like. He's gentle and he's kind and we're having a wonderful time. He likes me. You didn't have to threaten to beat him up if he didn't.

DAVE: What?

MARTHA: The time you got me the prom date!

DAVE: Oh, God . . .

MARTHA: That was done out of generosity and love, feelings you've forgotten about. You're willing to keep me in this house just so it won't be empty on the rare occasions you decide to come home! Well, I'm moving, David. I'm leaving! Like Mother! All the tears she shed! Did you really think all of them were for Poppa? Most of them were for you! YOU MIGHT AS WELL HAVE BEEN DEAD TOO!

DAVE: How'd you like a slap in the mouth?

MARTHA: I—dare—you! (*And picking up her tray* SHE *exits to the living room*)

DAVE: You're a shrew, Martha! You got the face of a football cleat and could use a series of shots for distemper! Him tellin' you different doesn't make it so! It doesn't make it so!

MEGS: You shouldn't, Davey.

DAVE: I shouldn't what!?

MEGS: Talk to someone who loves you like that, you shouldn't.

DAVE: I want you to tell me something, man . . .

MARTHA: You don't have to tell him anything, Joseph . . .

DAVE: He does! Just what are you doin', huh? You plannin' on being lucky for my sister!? Like you were for me? Like you were for Bobby?

MARTHA: Just leave, David.

DAVE: He knows what I'm talking about.

MEGS: What bugs you, man? That you thought I was lucky? Or that you was so piss-assed scared, you grabbed hold a that luck like it was rosary beads?

DAVE: I'd give anything to know why it's your face I'm staring at and not Bobby's.

MEGS: Get fucked.

DAVE: He loved it, Martha! He ate it up! Get some! Get some a them gooks! Bap-bap-bap-bap-bap-bap! Blow'm away! Nothin' confusin' about that, huh, Jacknife?

MEGS: It was heartbreaking the things I did. I'll live my whole life being sorry for'm.

DAVE: But you loved it! You never had it so good. It was logical to you. And you just had to carry Bobby and me right along with you.

MEGS: Not Bobby, man. Bobby understood.

DAVE: Bobby is dead! Man! When you gonna remember that!?

MEGS: You fuckin' jocks . . . (*And suddenly* HE *blows.* HE *is at the trophy case and with a sweep of his hand* HE *sends trophies careening into the wall*) You and your fucking jock dreams! I was a truckdriving numbnuts and they drafted me! But you!

DAVE: Yeah!?

MEGS: He enlisted. Mr. High School Hero enlisted! Went marchin' off thinkin' those piranha-eyed, cheesefaced motherfuckers was gonna tackle you 'stead a blow you away!!

DAVE: Jacknife set me straight!

MEGS: I stayed alive the only way I could! I rooted in what was happening around me like a pig in shit! And you ain't gonna blame me or make me feel guilty no more!

DAVE: Thirty feet off the ground in a chopper, Martha, and he's screaming like a rabid dog to get loose!

MEGS: Yeah! And you so close to lucky Megs, I thought you was tryin' to cornhole me, man! No way, Megs. I can't, Megs! Not in a million, Megs! NEVER HAPPEN!

DAVE (*Overlapping*): We shoulda stayed put, motherfucker. We should have stayed! But we went! 'Cause a you!

MEGS: I had to throw him out of the helicopter, Martha! Commanding officer was threatening to shoot him!

DAVE: Bullshit!

MEGS: You chickenshit. I heard you, Davey.

DAVE: You heard what?

MEGS: I heard. You was scared and tight and you landed wrong and your ankles broke. Bobby and I came back for you. I got hit 'cause a that. And I lay there in the mud with the blood pumpin' from my chest, blurp-blurp, and I heard you. No, Bobby! Don't go back for him! Fuck Megs! Jacknife is dead! Don't go back for him, Bobby! But Bobby did go back, huh, Davey? (DAVE *exits*) You can't walk away from that! Bobby did go back! Davey!? Bobby did! BOBBY DID! '(*Pause. Then softly, through tears*) Bobby did . . . (*Pause*) Maybe we never shoulda jumped outta that helicopter. Shoot away, sir. All of us, we don't give a fuck! Dead or alive, we're stayin' right here! No way we're goin' down into that shit! Hindsight.

Pause.

MARTHA (*Softly*): Joseph?
MEGS: Mmm?
MARTHA: Let's go out and do something wonderful.

Pause.

MEGS: Whatcha got in mind, you mad miss?

Pause.

MARTHA: I'd like to see your gas station. (*Pause*) And we'll go by my school after. I'll show you where I work. I have keys. I could show you my classroom. Charts on the wall . . . tick-tack-toe on the blackboard. (*Pause*) Shall I get my coat?

Pause.

MEGS: OK. (MARTHA *gets their coats.* SHE *puts her own on, helps him into his*) Sneakin' back into high school, Martha. If I don't feel notorious or something.

Pause.

MARTHA: I'll protect you, Joseph.

Lights to black as MARTHA *and* MEGS *exit out the front door.*

Scene 3

It is several hours later. MEGS *and* MARTHA *enter through the kitchen door. There is a somberness, a preoccupation to* MEGS *that* MARTHA *is trying desperately to fight.* MEGS *is carrying a case of soda in his arms.* HE *holds the door for* MARTHA.

MARTHA: Thank you. And thank you for the gasoline.

MEGS: Better you than the A-rabs, Martha.

MARTHA: I like my case of soda too. Thank you very much for that.

MEGS: You're welcome.

MARTHA: A whole case of white birch beer. What am I going to do with that? (*Pause*) I suppose I could bathe in it.

MEGS: You don't want it, Martha, I'll take it back.

MARTHA: Joseph, no, I'm teasing.

MEGS: Oh.

MARTHA: You tease me unmercifully and then you can't tell when you're being teased.

MEGS: Sorry.

MARTHA: Teasing, it shows you're cared for, doesn't it? (*Pause.* MEGS *doesn't respond.* SHE *continues softly*) I think it does. (*Pause*) Do you know what white birch beer is, Joseph?

MEGS: No.

MARTHA: I'll tell you if you'd like.

MEGS: Please.

MARTHA: Snow-covered trees in a bottle. (*Pause*) Joseph, what's the matter? You're with me and then you're not with me.

MEGS: Sorry.

MARTHA: You were hoping he'd be home, weren't you? He's not your friend, Joseph.

MEGS: I'm his friend.

Pause.

MARTHA: You're a lovely man. I mean that.

MEGS: No, you don't.

MARTHA: I do and you are.

MEGS: I got big bulgy eyes.

MARTHA: Well . . .

MEGS: And I am sorta losin' my hair.

MARTHA: That's a sign of virility, Joseph.

MEGS: Whoa.

MARTHA: You have a wonderful, open smile.

MEGS: I do not.

MARTHA: You do.

MEGS: You're just leadin' me on, woman, so's you can get into my panties.

MARTHA: Now you're teasing me.

MEGS: Hey, it shows you're cared for. (*Pause. It seems* THEY *are almost going to kiss*) Martha, let's go look for him.

MARTHA (*Desperately*): He's not worth your concern. (*Pause*) Please. Let's have our brandy.

MARTHA *moves to pour.* SHE *is stopped by the sound of* DAVE *entering. There is blood on his face and hands. His shirt is open and there is blood on his T-shirt. His eye is discolored and swollen.* HE *moves as if* HE *is in a daze. Long silence.*

DAVE (*Softly*): I . . . uh . . . I fell down.

MEGS: How's the ground look, stud?

Pause.

DAVE: Martha . . .

MARTHA: What? You want someone to tend your wounds? I'm sorry, David not tonight.

Pause. DAVE *wants to say something, cannot.*

MEGS: Want some ice for that eye, Davey?

DAVE (*Softly*): Martha, I'm sorry . . . .

Pause.

MEGS: Come on, guy, sit. Let's see what you look like under all that blood. Don't worry, it's clean. You know me, I have to wipe my nose, I use my sleeve. (HE *wipes at* DAVE*'s mouth*) Hold on. (*Pause*) How can she understand, stud? She doesn't know. She wasn't there. (*Pause*) Hey, we hardly beat you home, guy. Yeah, we been out. I showed Martha my garage. It's just a garage and all but I put a case a pop in her arms so it turned out OK. You want a birch beer, Davey? Good pop. (*Silence*) Maybe Martha'd make us some coffee. (MARTHA *doesn't move*) Then we went and saw Martha's classroom. Whoo, stud, beakers and specimens and microscopes. All we needed was a lightning bolt and we coulda created a monster. And we woulda nicknamed him Davey.

DAVE (*Softly*): Jacknife.

MEGS: That's my name, don't wear it out. That's what Bobby called me.

DAVE: 'Cause you drove the trucks.

MEGS: I did. Crashed a lot of the mothers too. (*Pause*) Why don't you tell Martha what your nickname was. I bet she'd like to know. (*Pause*) No? I will then. High School! 'Cause he loved high school. You was All League and you loved high school. Maybe too much, huh? Ole Bobby had a nickname for everything, didn't he? (*Pause*) Huh? Tell Martha how Bobby could make it seem like Boy Scouts sitting around the campfire. Couldn't he do that? (*Pause*) He could, Martha. (*Pause. It is as if* HE *is suddenly making a decision*) When I first got back, Davey, and was drivin', I'd see ole Bobby standin' at the side of the road with his thumb out. Isn't that something? It'd be late at night maybe and I'd be tired and I'd blink my eyes and there he'd be, standing there in his combat fatigues. Lotta people think they understand what that's like, don't they, studhoss. Well, God love'm for bad liars. They can only try. You and me, we know it like it was yesterday morning. Know what else, Davey? Sometimes I'd even pick ole Bobby up. (DAVE *groans softly*) You believe that? I swear, one time Bobby sat next to me from Pittsburgh, P-A, all the way to Hartford, Connecticut. Wasn't a bad conversation either. You ever do that? Pick'm up? Davey? Did ya? Davey, did you ever do that?

MARTHA: David, did you ever do that?

DAVE (*Softly*): Oh, God, Martha . . .

MEGS: You did, didn't you. What'ja think? Scare ya? Nah. Nothin' scary about ole Red Sock. That was Bobby's nickname, Martha. 'Cause he loved the Red Sox. Didn't he, Davey? Huh? Ole Bobby?

DAVE: He was gonna take us to Fenway Park . . . we were gonna cheer . . . oh, Bobby . . . you shoulda stayed put. You shouldn't have gone back. Bobby didn't help you, Megs.

MEGS: Died reaching down for me. Opened up like a rose in front a my eyes. Never knew what hit him.

DAVE: Christ almighty, if he'd stayed, he would of lived!

MEGS: Guy, how many nights have I stared at the ceiling thinkin' that very thought. But he didn't stay put. Wasn't in him to leave me any more'n it was to leave you!

DAVE: If I hadn't been scared, if I hadn't landed wrong . . .

MEGS: Guy, things happen for a reason!

DAVE: What fucking reason!?

MEGS: I ain't sure. I'm only workin' on it.

DAVE: Then how come you're doin' so much better than me!?

MEGS: Davey . . . I been blamin' myself for things I have no control over since first light. The way I look . . . way I talk . . . way I act . . . I was never no high school hero. I didn't have so far to fall.

DAVE (*So tired*): I just want to be left alone. I want Bobby to leave me alone.

MEGS: Embrace him, stud. Take him in your arms. You and me, we got enough shithole memories to last a lifetime. He ain't one of'm. He was our friend. Our heart. A waterwalker. Did we love him? (*Pause*) What were we gonna do, when we got back, no matter what? (*Pause*) Come on. Help me . . . no matter what.

DAVE: I dunno.

MEGS: Yeah, ya do. Come on. We were gonna . . . Davey!

DAVE: I dunno, go to Fenway Park!

MEGS: Best seats in the house, huh? Huh?

DAVE: Hot dogs and beer.

MEGS: And that green grass, fresh mowed.

DAVE: The sun beating down.

MEGS: Take off our shirts, huh? Soak up some rays!

DAVE: And we were gonna cheer. Cheer for Bobby's favorite team.

MEGS: Cheer so loud, they was gonna start cheerin' us back, yeah. And then?

DAVE: And then we were gonna . . . (HE *stops*)

MEGS: What, Davey? (*Pause*) What?

DAVE: Go fishing . . . opening day. (*A silence.* HE *settles back in his chair, exhausted.* MEGS *moves away, lost in his own thoughts now*) Martha?

MARTHA: Yes?

DAVE: I got in a fight tonight.

MARTHA: I know you did.

DAVE: With kids. The bar was filled with kids in high school letter sweaters, barely eighteen, if they were at all, and I dunno . . . I'd look at them, sis, and it was bringing tears to my eyes looking at them and finally I couldn't anymore and I started pushing one of them. He looked scared. But he pushed back and when he did I just sorta waded into all of them. And Christ, Martha . . . they didn't know how to fight . . . they didn't know how to fight at all. I don't know what to do. I think I might have hurt one of them. Maybe they're still there. Maybe I should go back and see if he's all right.

MARTHA: Maybe you should.

DAVE: I will. (HE *moves to the front door.* HE *stops and turns*) I blame people. I blame people so goddam much. (*Pause*) I'm so sorry, Martha.

MARTHA: I know you are.

> DAVE *turns to leave.* HE *sees Bobby's lucky hat hanging by the door. Pause.* HE *puts on the hat.* HE *turns and looks at* MEGS. *Pause.* HE *exits. Silence.* MEGS *moves to the window, watches* DAVE *go off into the night.*

MEGS: It's snowing. Awful late in the year. Real pretty. Last gasp. (*Pause*) It's hard. Martha, sweet Martha, it's so God-fuckin' hard to put the fatigues to sleep . . . (*Pause.* HE *moves to leave*)

MARTHA: You're leaving?

MEGS: Thought I would. Let things get back to normal.

MARTHA: Has normal been succeeding so well?

MEGS: Your brother loves you, Martha. Well . . .

MARTHA: We never had brandy, Joseph.

MEGS: You're right. We didn't.

MARTHA: One glass. We deserve it.

MEGS: Shoot it in. (MARTHA *pours.* THEY *drink*) Sundown. (HE *moves to leave*)

MARTHA (*In despair*): Stay? (*Pause*) We'll go upstairs.

MEGS: What's there?

MARTHA (*Inaudibly*): Bedrooms. (*Clearing her throat*) Bedrooms.

MEGS (*Not unkindly*): Who the fuck we kiddin', Martha?

MARTHA: Mission accomplished, is that it?

MEGS: A woman like you, a madman like me, who we kiddin' but ourselves?

MARTHA: You brought me flowers and candy and wine. We were having a wonderful time.

MEGS: One a the best I ever had, Martha, but . . .

MARTHA: It doesn't have to end. If I've been fooling myself, I can fool myself a little longer.

MEGS: I can't, Martha. (HE *exits. Silence. Very slowly, as if* SHE's *afraid* SHE *might break,* MARTHA *sits. Silence.* HE *returns in a rush, closing the door quickly behind him*) Y'know, I bet we woulda left that prom dance early!

MARTHA: Do you think?

MEGS: Yeah! We woulda gone off for dinner at a fancy restaurant! Partridge maybe!

MARTHA: Partridge?

MEGS: Can't have cheeseburgers, woman! And then maybe we woulda driven someplace. Someplace quiet. And parked. And then . . . who knows?! (*Pause. And the false bravado falls away. Softly*) Who knows . . . (*Pause*) I'm real nervous, Martha.

MARTHA: It's prom night. We've been kissing and hugging in the back of your '57 Chevy for hours. And we've had brandy. (*Pause*) Let's go upstairs. (SHE *takes his hand*) It's time.

As MEGS *and* MARTHA *go up the stairs, the lights go to black.*

END OF PLAY

Literature
Across Cultures

FOURTH EDITION

Sheena Gillespie

Terezinha Fonseca

Tony Pipolo

Queensborough Community College
City University of New York

PEARSON
Longman

New York   San Francisco   Boston
London   Toronto   Sydney   Tokyo   Singapore   Madrid
Mexico City   Munich   Paris   Cape Town   Hong Kong   Montreal

Vice President and Editor-in-Chief: *Joseph Terry*
Managing Editor: *Erika Berg*
Development Editor: *Barbara Santoro*
Executive Marketing Manager: *Ann Stypuloski*
Senior Supplements Editor: *Donna Campion*
Media Supplements Editor: *Nancy Garcia*
Production Manager: *Ellen MacElree*
Project Coordination, Text Design, and Electronic Page Makeup:
Stratford Publishing Services
Cover Designer/Manager: *Wendy Ann Fredericks*
Cover Art: *Jose Ortega/Stock Illustration Source, Inc.*
Senior Manufacturing Buyer: *Al Dorsey*
Printer and Binder: *Courier*
Cover Printer: *Coral Graphic Services*

For permission to use copyrighted material, grateful acknowledgment is made
to the copyright holders on pp. 1142–1146, which are hereby made part of this
copyright page.

Library of Congress Cataloging-in-Publication Data

Literature across cultures / [compiled by] Sheena Gillespie, Terezinha Fonseca,
Tony Pipolo.—4th ed.
    p.   cm.
Includes bibliographical references and index.
ISBN 0-321-17208-6
    1. Literature—Collections.   I. Gillespie, Sheena, 1938–   II. Fonseca,
Terezinha.   III. Pipolo, Tony.
  PN6014.G43 2005
  808'.8—dc22   2004004541

Please visit our Web site at http://www.ablongman.com

ISBN 0-321-17208-6

3   4   5   6   7   8   9   10   CRW   07   06

To President Eduardo J. Marti for his vision and commitment to community college pedagogy.
—Sheena Gillespie

To Aila de Oliveira Gomes, whose intellectual and spiritual vocation has inspired generations of Brazilian students.
—Terezinha Fonseca

To all the students whose lives and minds have touched mine and made teaching one of life's great learning experiences.
—Tony Pipolo

Contents

PART ONE *Origins and Insights* 37

PART FOUR   *Race and Difference*

POETRY

DRAMA

PART FIVE *Individualism and Community*   813

FICTION

ESSAYS

APPENDIX D *Critical Approaches:*
A Case Study of Hamlet   *1087*

Preface for Instructors

> No one can deny the persisting continuities of long traditions, sustained
> habitations, national languages, and cultural geographies, but there seems
> no reason except fear and prejudice to keep insisting on their separation
> and distinctiveness, as if that were all human life were about. Survival in
> fact is about connections between things.
>
> —Edward Said

Literature Across Cultures invites students and instructors to explore "connections
between things," particularly the literature of the past and present, in contexts that
go beyond traditional boundaries in an attempt to recognize, respect, and learn
from the increasing heterogeneity of contemporary human experience.

Like its predecessors, the fourth edition of *Literature Across Cultures* continues
to highlight its most distinguished and identifying feature: The promotion of a conversation with traditional, multicultural, and contemporary voices through a study
of thematic topics.

We believe that the book's main focus on political, sociocultural, and multicultural aspects of a literary debate that includes the dialectic of the self and society,
women's issues, the causes and effects of war and violence—as well as issues of class,
race, ethnicity, and sexual preference—has contributed to its strong identity and
uniqueness among thematic anthologies.

ORGANIZATION OF THE TEXT

Following the tradition of the previous editions, the fourth edition of *Literature
Across Cultures* is organized around an introduction, five thematic parts, and four
pedagogical appendices. The introduction addresses reading and writing of literature as a social act, highlighting the relevance of a classroom collaborative approach
to provide instructors and students with college models for peer audience and self-monitoring practices.

Each of the five thematic parts follows a similar progression, consisting of fiction, essays, poetry, drama, a film unit, discussion questions, part assignments, and
research topics. The poetry section groups poems in clusters of two or three to help
students explore the multicultural diversity of the poetic experience. Our choices of

reading selections were based on the rich literary and ethnic perspectives that works from different times and cultures present on issues related to people's origins, gender, race, class, war, sexuality, the self, and the community.

These vital issues were chosen to stimulate class discussion, to promote comprehensive responses to literature in reading and writing, and to develop critical and argumentative skills. The four appendices—A. An Introduction to the Elements of Fiction, Nonfiction, Poetry, and Drama; B. Writing a Research Paper; C. Researching Literary Sources; and D. Critical Approaches: A Case Study of *Hamlet*—provide a stimulating apparatus for understanding the literary genres, the research paper, the Internet, and literary criticism. The book also includes a diverse range of teaching resources for instructors and students.

ENDURING FEATURES

The fourth edition is built on the following features of the three previous editions:

- An emphasis on the **multicultural aspects of literature** leads students beyond their literary and cultural traditions.
- The presentation of **fiction, nonfiction, poetry, and drama** as cultural productions suggests ways of combining the study of literature with cultural perspectives and interpretations.
- A stimulating focus on **five thematic units** suggests different ways of understanding and responding to literary reading strategies.
- **Discussion questions, collaborative group questions, and research topics** introduce students to the writing process, presenting strategies for writing the research paper, and information on locating critical sources.
- The presentation of a **concise and proven pedagogical apparatus** motivates students to acquire the critical and analytical skills they need to read and write about literature.

Each of the foregoing features was created to provide instructors and students with a variety of strategies for a rewarding and stimulating teaching/learning experience.

NEW FEATURES OF THE FOURTH EDITION

The fourth edition of *Literature Across Cultures* incorporates many excellent critiques and suggestions from our reviewers and colleagues. These new features also reflect our commitment to making *Literature Across Cultures* pedagogically useful to college students in their readings of texts, in group work with their peers, and in their written responses.

Revised Introductions to the Reading Selections

The introductions to the five parts have been extensively revised to highlight the ethnicities of the authors, to update background information, and to intensify the relevance of the cultural contexts of the texts.

New and Revised Discussion Questions

The new and revised discussion questions following each short story, each cluster of poems, and each play are meant to assist students in making informed responses to the reading selections. Their aim is to suggest multiple possibilities for the production of meaning. Specifically, this fourth edition devises a progression from close textual analysis to critical thinking and include **Journal Entries** suggestions, **Textual Considerations** questions, and **Cultural Contexts** questions, which expose students not only to cultural interactions with the sociohistorical realities of the literary texts, but also to interactive engagement with their peers.

Film Angles

The purpose of a separate film unit for each section of the book is to demonstrate both thematic continuity with the literature selections and the specific ways in which films affect society, mirroring—in both positive and negative ways—the moral, political, and psychological conflicts within society. To a great extent, this cultural impact is created directly by the specific artistic, stylistic, and technological means unique to films. The film angles, therefore, were designed to challenge students and teachers to identify, analyze, and appreciate the many aspects of film language and how the themes of each unit are embodied and expressed not only through a film's screenplay and dialogue—its literary aspects—but through its audio and visual grammar.

In some sections, the film units can be used in conjunction with the literature selections. In Part One: Origins and Insights and Part Four: Race and Difference sections, for example, several film versions of *Hamlet* and *Othello* are discussed. In other sections, students are provided with an historical overview that considers how important subjects (e.g., gender, race, and war) have been treated in film history. This is followed by attention to specific films that exemplify each theme. The questions are designed to get students thinking about the nature of the film experience and how it compares to the reading of literature. Films were selected to reflect both popular and more serious tastes, to demonstrate that cultural attitudes toward subjects such as gender, race, war, sexual difference, and violence can be examined not only in "highbrow" art films but also in genre movies with mass appeal. Because film is a distinctive art form, students are introduced to its terminology. These terms, like those pertinent to dramatic and poetic forms, are defined in the glossary.

Performance Exercises

This edition presents a series of Performance Exercises—interactive, collaborative work that encourages peer responses to the interrelationship between students and the dramatic text.

Separation of Reading and Writing Apparatus

The Introduction now separates the strategies for reading and writing about litera-ture in order to emphasize the diversity of each process and increase the accessibil-ity of this topic to students. The Strategies for Reading Literature section highlights the importance of student response, close textual reading, cultural con-texts, and collaborative peer discussion. The Strategies for Writing about Litera-ture section provides step-by-step guidelines on how to generate ideas for a critical paper, write a first draft, and revise it.

New and Revised Topics

The new and revised writing topics at the end of each thematic section are meant to provide students with engaging assignments and relevant research topics.

Revised Appendices

This edition includes revised versions of the following appendices:

Appendix A: "An Introduction to the Elements of Fiction, Nonfiction, Poetry, and Drama"
- Explores the complexities of the literary genres
- Provides a list of revised and new topics—67 in all—that discuss literature as cultural productions and address currently relevant issues in twenty-first-century society

Appendix B: "Writing a Research Paper"
- Engages students in academic dialogue
- Features new, expanded guidelines on writing a literary research paper, locat-ing critical materials, drafting the paper, employing quotations, organizing information, and documenting literary research papers and essays according to MLA style
- Provides models of students' research papers

Appendix C: "Researching Literary Sources"
- Provides students with an effective summary of Internet research principles
- Includes guidelines on reliability of information, search engines, and online sources and encyclopedias; literary criticism research sites; author-focused sites and sample research on James Joyce; and electronic databases, subscrip-tion services, and online searches

Appendix D: "Critical Approaches: A Case Study of *Hamlet*"
- Includes a discussion of several approaches to the play, including psychoana-lytic, psychosocial, new critical, reader-response, feminist, and new historical perspectives
- Engages the play from various critical viewpoints

New, Revised Instructor's Manual

A revised Instructor's Manual includes

- Strategies for discussing literature in an interactive classroom
- Selected critical biographies
- Audio/visual teaching resources
- Internet resources organized according to author
- A sample syllabus
- Teaching suggestions
- Expanded discussion of film
- Expanded filmographies

ACKNOWLEDGMENTS

We are grateful to Erika Berg, our editor, who has guided us through the fourth edition of our textbook, and to Barbara Santoro, who has worked with us throughout the revision. Our special thanks go to Delia Mellis for her assistance with the biographical endnotes and James Kenney for his revision of Appendix B, "Writing a Research Paper" and Appendix C, "Researching Literary Sources." Dr. Ellen Higgens, Dr. Ruth Kirstein, and Professor Maria Eugenia Hincapie contributed with excellent suggestions. We acknowledge our gratitude to Kathy Howard, Patty Gorton, and Gladys DeBuccio for their generous assistance in the preparation of the manuscript, and to Isabel Pipolo for typing the instructor's manual. We also received many invaluable suggestions from our colleagues at Queensborough Community College, many of whom have used our text since the first edition. Finally, we would like to thank the following reviewers:

Liz Ann Báez Aguilar, San Antonio College; Maryam Barrie, Washtenaw Community College; Sheryl Dworak, Moraine Valley Community College; Professor Elizabeth Flores, College of Lake County; Professor Sue Fox, Albuquerque Tech and Vocational Institute; R.C. Goetter, Gloucester Community College; Professor Kathryn Hamilton, Columbus State University; Michael Hennessy, Texas State University; William Lawler, University of Wisconsin—Stevens Point; Linda Panczner, University of Toledo; Professor Jewell-Ann Parto, Western Piedmont Community College; Jim Roderick, Truckee Meadows Community College; Lillian Ruiz, Greenfield Community College; Georgeanna Sellers, High Point University; Professor James Sodon, St. Louis Community College; and Dorothy U. Syler, Northern Virginia Community College.

Preface for Students

People and their cultures perish in isolation, but they are born or reborn
in contact with other men and women, with men and women of another
culture, another creed, another race. If we do not recognize our humanity
in others, we will not recognize it in ourselves.

—Carlos Fuentes

As teachers and students of literature, we believe that one of the most effective ways
to understand peoples of other cultures, creeds, and races is through language; a
person's words are the windows through which we gain access to his or her world.
In this anthology, we invite you to travel with us to worlds beyond your own, to
engage in a conversation among cultures, to explore unfamiliar traditions, and to
evaluate human relationships in an attempt to understand better the meanings of
community in our own pluralistic society and the multicultural society of the
twenty-first century.

We hope that as you listen to these voices, past and present, you will feel compelled to enter the conversation, to add your own voice and your own words. You
will soon realize that literature will provide you with one of the most stimulating
channels to enrich your sense of self, expand your creative power, question your
own assumptions about the world, and challenge you to become an active member
of your society. In brief, by fostering your encounter with the human condition, the
study of literature will help you grow as a student and as a human being. As you
engage in dialogue with the selections, both in writing and in discussion with your
fellow students, you will experiment with new ways of looking at yourself and
enlarging the windows from which you view the world. The journey we invite you
to share will be challenging—many of the voices that you will encounter, both classical and contemporary, respond to the human capacity for learning and transmitting knowledge to succeeding generations through language and abstract thought
and to the way different cultures assimilate while retaining their separate identities.

In Part One, "Origins and Insights," you will encounter many cultural variations: the oral traditions and affinity with the worlds of nature and spirit of Native
Americans; the love of language and pride in their history of Hispanic Americans;
the emphasis on kinship and music in the literature of African Americans; the

generational conflicts of Asian Americans; the poignancy of family loyalty among Italian Americans.

In Part Two, "Gender and Identity," you will be invited to examine traditional cross-cultural concepts of masculinity and femininity and to evaluate the degree to which they have affected both men and women in their individual quests for identity. Some of the voices in this part will ask you to decide whether gender conflicts should be confronted or avoided. Other voices will pose possibilities for freeing both sexes from the confines of traditional roles so that both men and women may become more dynamic and fulfilled.

In Part Three, "War and Violence," you will evaluate older heroic myths of war from other cultures as well as newer sensibilities advocating compromise as the desirable outcome of political conflict. You may also speculate on the misuses of power in a global, pluralistic society. Primarily, you will be asked to consider whether the recognition of our shared humanity will enable us to look beyond violence to peace.

In Part Four, "Race and Difference," you will be asked to reexamine many of the racial stereotypes with which we all have grown up. Some of these voices from diverse ethnic groups will invite you to share the anguish and anger of exclusion; others will challenge your preconceptions about race, class, and sexual preference; and still others will ask whether differences should be silenced or articulated, respected or shunned.

In Part Five, "Individualism and Community," you will confront the conflict, experienced in every culture, between the needs and desires of our individual selves and the needs and desires of the community. Many voices in this part debate the issue of individual freedom versus social responsibility; others advocate that solo voices join in the discord and harmony of the human chorus.

As you converse with the voices in this anthology, both old and new, you will travel into uncharted territories—into real and imagined worlds where many of the familiar guideposts will no longer apply. But this is as it should be. Being part of the global village of the twenty-first century requires that your generation sharpen its definition of an educated person. By adding your voice to the cultural conversations in this anthology, you will begin that process, perhaps leaving the familiar in favor of the unfamiliar.

The fourth edition of *Literature Across Cultures* also provides you with new features, such as Performance Exercises and Film Angles, that will enrich your enjoyment of literature and help you make connections between literature and the dramatic and cinematographic arts.

Sheena Gillespie
Terezinha Fonseca
Tony Pipolo

INTRODUCTION

Reading and Writing as a Social Act

Why read literature? is the question many instructors pose during the first class session of Introduction to Literature. Writer and critic Robert Scholes suggests that because students, like writers, have stories to tell, "learning to read books—or pictures, or films—is not just a matter of learning to read and write the texts of our lives."

Why do writers read and write? Emily Dickinson, a nineteenth-century poet, viewed reading as a means of traveling to far-off places: "There is no Frigate like a Book." Jorge Luis Borges (1899–1986), a twentieth-century Latin American novelist, thought of reading as a way of revitalizing the self: "I have always come to life after coming to books." African American writer Toni Morrison (1931–   ), a Nobel Prize–winning author, believes in the power of narrative to help us understand ourselves and others: "Narrative is radical, creating us at the very moment it is being created." Morrison is particularly concerned that the writer's words and stories be the windows through which both writer and reader gain knowledge not only of the self, but also of the self in relation to people of other ethnic groups and cultures. In other words, writers write to be read; they write for you, their audience. They communicate their insights to you in the hope that you will recognize aspects of your own thoughts and experiences in their essays and stories.

Although many students express skepticism about finding meanings in the literature of the past, most acknowledge readily that human beings throughout history have had experiences in common. According to the novelist Albert Camus (1913–1960), "Every great work of art makes the human face more admirable and richer." His suggestion is that as we share in reading of the sufferings and joys of others, we better understand our own. The novelist James Baldwin (1924–1987) also reminds us of the continuity of human experiences in his short story "Sonny's Blues":

> For while the tale of how we suffer, and how we are delighted, and how we may triumph is never new, it always must be heard. There isn't any other tale to tell. It's the only light we've got in all this darkness.

1

We invite you to approach the reading of the texts in this anthology from the vantage points suggested by Camus and Baldwin. Perhaps thinking about fiction, poetry, and drama as expressions of human suffering, delight, and triumph will make it possible for you to understand Medea's anger at being abandoned by her husband in favor of a younger woman; to empathize with Hamlet's attempt to find his real identity; and to share in the triumph of a nineteenth-century New England housewife's revolt. You might even discover something about yourself. As the novelist Toni Morrison reminds us, interacting with literature is a dynamic process engaging both reader and writer: "The imagination that produces work which bears and invites rereading, which points to future readings as well as contemporary ones, implies a shareable world and an especially flexible language. Readers and writers both struggle to interpret and perform within a common language shareable imaginative worlds."

THE MEANING OF LITERATURE

What is literature? Traditionally set apart from other kinds of discourse, literature has been defined by the *Webster's Universal Unabridged Dictionary* as "all writings in prose or verse, especially those of an imaginative or critical character." Although this definition, like many others, has proved to be incomplete, it does highlight the presence of two major features of literature: its language and its imaginative character. When combined, these two elements produce a fictional world that reflects and evokes reality.

One story in this anthology can be used to illustrate this power of literature. The introduction to "The Sniper" transports us, not to the real world of urban guerrillas in Dublin, but to the fictional atmosphere of a Dublin that Liam O'Flaherty especially re-created as a unique literary experience:

> The long June twilight faded into night, Dublin lay enveloped in darkness but for the dim light of the moon that shone through fleecy clouds, casting a pale light as of approaching dawn over the streets and the dark waters of the Liffey. Around the beleaguered Four Courts the heavy guns roared. Here and there through the city, machine-guns and rifles broke the silence of the night, spasmodically, like dogs barking on lone farms. Republicans and Free Staters were waging civil war.
>
> —"The Sniper"

Although O'Flaherty might have modeled his portrayal of Dublin on a factual description of this Irish city caught in the civil war between the Republicans and Free Staters, his city, in strictly literary terms, is fictional. His text articulates imaginatively and creatively the significance of an actual historical event.

In O'Flaherty's text, atmosphere and imagery provide insights into events that we have not experienced directly. Characterization is another way literature can broaden our experience. You will observe, in other texts in this volume, how characters such as Antigone, Hamlet, Eveline, and Roselily have dramatized across the centuries some of the most terrifying and stimulating possibilities of human experience. In this sense, literature can be defined as the enactment of human possibilities, or as a vehicle that will help us to discover more about ourselves and the meaning we can make of life. For the French philosopher Jean-Paul Sartre (1905–1980), the function of literature is to search for the meaning of life and to speculate about the role of human beings in the world.

Perhaps the best way to define literature is in practice, encountering the literary experience face-to-face through the readings in this anthology. In the process, you may notice that a literary work leads you to encounter not one precise, correct reading but a range of meanings evoked by the interaction of the text with your own experience as a reader. For instance, *Hamlet*, a work that is widely discussed from different critical perspectives, illustrates the variety of meanings that Shakespeare's readers have produced in the process of interpreting this play. In fact, one appendix in this anthology is devoted to exploring some of these various critical approaches and responses, known as psychoanalytic, formalist, reader-response, feminist, and New Historical (see Appendix D, "Critical Approaches").

THE FUNCTION OF LITERATURE

Following the literary tradition that the Latin poet Horace (65–8 B.C.) established for poetry, some scholars emphasize "to instruct" or "to delight," or both, as the major functions of literature. Recent scholarly opinion indicates that another function of literature is to actively shape our culture. For example, some literary historians believe that human beings learned how to cultivate a romantic idea of love only after reading works of literature that portrayed love in this light rather than as a social or sexual arrangement between a man and a woman. Both ancient and modern approaches emphasize two of literature's major functions: to construct and articulate sociocultural realities and to involve you as the reader in an invigorating interaction with these realities.

When you address the questions we formulate under "Cultural Contexts" in this anthology, you will be asked to interact with your classmates, to take sides, to make decisions, and to add your voice to various cultural and political issues related to class, race, gender, war, and violence. Consider, for instance, Wilfred Owen's poem "Disabled," in which his portrait of a disabled veteran stimulates our involvement in the violence perpetuated by World War I. By presenting such a viewpoint, literature can empower us—it can promote our active engagement with the world through our encounter with the poem's disclosure of the reality of violence caused by war. Thus, literature can fulfill a major cultural function in society.

STRATEGIES FOR READING LITERATURE: A STEP-BY-STEP GUIDELINE

Reading literature is a process in which you, as a reader, should engage actively. To respond well to literature, you must take a critical approach that involves three major procedures: previewing, highlighting, and annotating.

Step 1: Previewing

Even before you read a text, preview it by asking yourself some questions about the title, the writer, and the type of writing you are encountering:

- What does the title suggest?
- Have I heard of this author before?
- Does my anthology provide any information about this text?
- What type of text is this—a poem, a story, or a play?
- What kind of structure does it possess—stanzas, paragraphs, acts, scenes?
- How is the text organized—by contrast, or by cause and effect?

Step 2: Highlighting

Read the text closely, and highlight—by underlining words or coloring them with a highlighting pen—the sections that particularly strike you from the point of view of style, structure, ideas, characterization, or any other key features you have observed as a reader. Notice, for example, in the following passage taken from James Joyce's short story "Eveline," the repetition of the verb form "used to" and some of its variants (here highlighted in bold type) that indicate repeated action in the past. Identifying such a pattern enables you to discern the strong emotional links that Eveline has with the past. From this you may infer her psychological inability to accept change as a possibility for the future.

> One time there **used to** be a field there in which they **used to** play every evening with other people's children. Then a man from Belfast bought the field and built houses in it—not like the little brown houses but bright brick houses with shining roofs. The children of the avenue **used to** play together in that field—the Devines, the Waters, the Dunns, little Keogh the cripple, she and her brothers and sisters. Ernest, however, never played: he was too grown up. Her father **used** often **to** hunt them in out of the field with his blackthorn stick; but **usually** little Keogh **used to** keep *nix* and call out when he saw her father coming. Still they seemed to have been rather happy then . . .

Step 3: Annotating

Annotating means making marginal notes on the book's pages, or using a pad or note cards. Once you reach this phase, you are also involved in the critical process of selecting and summarizing. After a second and third reading, your notes will eventually lead you to respond to the literary and cultural impact of the text by identifying its words, imagery, and themes. Responding actively to the text therefore becomes a challenge for you as a reader because you will interact with it and define its meanings on the basis of both the factual evidence that you find there and your own insights and experiences.

The following guided reading of Kate Chopin's "The Story of an Hour" should help you to understand what we mean by interaction between the reader and the text. After previewing, highlighting, and annotating the text, you might consider approaching your analysis of the "Textual Considerations" of "The Story of an Hour" as a detective trying to solve a crime. Arm yourself with a dictionary and the-saurus, and be on the alert for the many textual hints and clues that the writer has supplied for you. Pay close attention to the text, including the words we have high-lighted in bold type, by examining how the author uses nouns, adjectives, images, and symbols to construct plot and to build characterization.

GUIDED READING

Kate Chopin (1851–1904) The Story of an Hour

"The Story of an Hour"

1. Knowing that **Mrs. Mallard** was afflicted with a heart trouble, great care was taken to break to her as gently as possible the news of her husband's death.

2. It was her sister Josephine who told her, in broken sentences, veiled hints that revealed in half concealing. Her husband's friend Richards was there, too, near her. It was he who had been in the newspaper office when intelligence of the railroad disaster was received, with Brently Mallard's name leading the list of "killed." He had only taken the time to assure himself of its truth by a second telegram, and had hastened to forestall any less careful, less tender friend in bearing the sad message.

3. She did not hear the story as many women have heard the same, with a paralyzed inability to accept its signif-icance. She wept at once, with sudden, **wild abandonment**, in her sister's arms. When the storm of grief had spent itself she went to her room alone. She would have no one follow her.

Textual Considerations

■ *What kinds of expectations does the opening paragraph raise in the reader about the protagonist and the plot of the story? Have you noticed that the pro-tagonist is addressed as Mrs. Mallard and that the starting point of the story is "the news of her husband's death"?*

■ *Respond to Josephine's and Richards's attitude about breaking the news to Mrs. Mallard.*

■ *Focus on paragraph 3. What does the phrase "wild abandonment" suggest? Are you surprised by Mrs. Mallard's insistence on being left alone after hear-ing such bad news? Explain.*

4. There stood, facing the open window, a comfortable, roomy armchair. Into this she sank, pressed down by a physical exhaustion that haunted her body and seemed to reach into her soul.

■ *What examples do you find of images of freedom and repression in paragraphs 4 and 5? Comment on these examples.*

5. She could see in the open square before her house the **tops of trees that were all aquiver with the new spring life. The delicious breath of rain was in the air**. In the street below a peddler was crying his wares. The notes of a distant song which some one was singing reached her faintly, and countless sparrows were twittering in the eaves.

■ *Writers frequently use nature to open a symbolic level for the text. What is unusual about the text's emphasis on spring, given the events of the story thus far? What other aspects of nature emerge in paragraphs 5 and 6? What do they suggest about Mrs. Mallard's state of mind? What kind of expectations do they raise in the reader?*

6. There were patches of blue sky showing here and there through the clouds that had met and piled above the other in the west facing her window.

7. She sat with her head thrown back upon the cushion of the chair quite motionless, except when a sob came up into her throat and shook her, as a child who has cried itself to sleep continues to sob in its dreams.

■ *Characterize your response to paragraphs 7 and 8.*

8. She was **young**, with a **fair**, calm face, whose **lines bespoke repression** and even a certain strength. But now there was a dull stare in her eyes, whose gaze was fixed away off yonder on one of those patches of blue sky. It was not a **glance of reflection**, but rather indicated a **suspension of intelligent thought**.

■ *What new aspects of Mrs. Mallard's personality occur in paragraph 8? To what might "the lines of repression" be attributable? Consider the difference between a "glance of reflection" and a "suspension of intelligent thought."*

9. There was **something coming to her** and she was waiting for it, fearfully. What was it? She did not know; it was too subtle and elusive to name. But she felt it, creeping out of the sky, reaching toward her through the sounds, the scents, the color that filled the air.

■ *What dramatic pattern is the text shaping in terms of plot (events, to rising action), characterization (Mrs. Mallard's reaction), and your own response as a reader? Focus on paragraphs 9 and 10.*

10. Now her bosom rose and fell tumultuously. She was beginning to recognize this thing that was approaching to possess her, and she was striving to beat it back with her will—as powerless as her two white slender hands would have been.

11. When she abandoned herself a little word escaped her **slightly parted lips**. She said it over and over under her breath: "**Free,** free, free!" **The vacant stare** and the look of terror that had followed it went from her eyes. They stayed keen and bright. Her **pulses beat fast**, and the coursing **blood warmed** and relaxed every inch of her body.

■ *What does "the vacant stare" suggest? What does "the look of terror" convey? Contrast the descriptions of Mrs. Mallard's bodily responses in paragraphs 4 and 11. To what extent are these physical and psychological reversals gender based (characteristic of women more than men)?*

12. She did not stop to ask if it were not a **monstrous** joy that held her. A clear and exalted perception enabled her to dismiss the suggestion as trivial.

■ *Check your thesaurus for various connotations of "monstrous." Speculate about Chopin's description of Mrs. Mallard's joy as "monstrous" in paragraph 12.*

13. She knew that she would weep again when she saw the kind tender hands folded in death; the face that had never looked save with love upon her, fixed and gray and dead. But she saw beyond that **bitter moment a long procession of years to come** that would belong to her absolutely. And she opened and spread her arms out to them in welcome.

■ *Notice how Mrs. Mallard contrasts the "bitter moment" of the present with "a long procession of years to come." To what extent does this contrast suggest her desire to rewrite her personal history? To what extent does the world of closed windows and fixed gender identities versus the evocations of freedom and self-discovery create narrative suspense?*

14. There would be no one to live for during those coming years: **she would live for herself. There would be no powerful will bending her in** that blind persistence with which men and women believe they have a right to impose a private will upon a fellow-creature. A kind intention or a cruel intention made the act seem no less a crime as she looked upon it in that brief moment of illumination.

■ *Does Mrs. Mallard surprise you with her realistic portrait of male and female relations? What does this moment of illumination amount to?*

15. And yet she had loved him—sometimes. Often she had not. What did it matter! What could love, the unsolved mystery, count for in face of this possession of self-assertion which she suddenly recognized as the strongest impulse of her being!

■ *To what extent do you empathize with Mrs. Mallard's desire for autonomy and psychological space?*

16. "Free! Body and soul free!" she kept whispering.

■ *How do you characterize Mrs. Mallard's emotional outburst?*

17. Josephine was kneeling before the closed door with her lips to the keyhole, imploring for admission. "**Louise**, open the door! I beg; open the door—you will make yourself ill. What are you doing, Louise? For heaven's sake open the door."

■ *Explain why Chopin withholds the protagonist's first name until paragraph 17.*

18. "Go away. I am not making myself ill." No; she was drinking in the very elixir of life through that open window.

■ *Identify the two voices that interact in this paragraph.*

19. Her fancy was running riot along **those days ahead of her**. Spring days, and summer days, and all sorts of days that would be her own. She breathed a quick prayer that life might be long. It was only **yesterday she** had thought with a shudder that life might be long.

■ *React to the way the text juxtaposes the repression of the past and the possibilities of the future. Such a pattern culminates in paragraph 20 in the image that Mrs. Mallard "carried herself unwittingly like a goddess of Victory." To what extent does Chopin suggest that Mrs. Mallard's triumph will be transitory?*

20. She arose at length and opened the door to her sister's importunities. There was a feverish triumph in her eyes, and she carried herself unwittingly like a goddess of Victory. She clasped her sister's waist, and together they descended the stairs. Richards stood waiting for them at the bottom.

21. Some one was opening the front door with a **latchkey**. It was Brently Mallard who entered, a little travelstained, composedly carrying his **gripsack** and **umbrella**. He had been far from the scene of the accident, and did not even know there had been one. He stood amazed at Josephine's piercing cry: at Richards's quick motion to screen him from the view of his **wife**. But Richards was too late.

■ *Read this paragraph carefully. Comment on the images of "latchkey," "gripsack," and "umbrella." What significance do you attach to Louise being referred to as "his wife"? To what extent does Richard's in-*

pense or expectation does this paragraph create in the reader?

22. When the doctors came they said that she had died of heart dis-ease—**of joy that kills**.

ability to protect Mrs. Mallard destabilize the action of the story? What kind of sus-

■ *How do you account for the ironic turn of the last sentence? Is it appropriate that the doctors misread the true cause of Mrs. Mallard's death? Explain.*

Read "The Story of an Hour" again at least twice. More ideas will no doubt sur-face at each new reading, and you will react to more details concerning the arrange-ment of the events, Mrs. Mallard's reactions and expectations, and your own ability as a reader to produce more meanings in response to the text. As you deepen your understanding of the story, you will also become more aware of its cultural implica-tions. To assist your interaction with the cultural possibilities of Chopin's text, you may discuss gender-related questions such as the ones listed in the following "Cul-tural Contexts."

1. To what extent does "The Story of an Hour" reflect a feminist outlook on the roles of women? What evidence is there that the story is told from the perspective of a female narrator?
2. Consider what the text reveals about marriage as an institution. Is the concept of marriage that Chopin's text explores still applicable to contemporary gender rela-tions?
3. Are men and women today more liberated than they were a century ago? Discuss the differences you see between then and now in their socially defined roles and "fixed gender identities" (identities determined by gender and social roles).

The following are some literature students' responses to the two literary and cultural topics listed below.

1. Respond to Kate Chopin's use of nature imagery in "The Story of an Hour."
2. React to the new meanings "The Story of an Hour" evokes as you think about the issues of gender and identity. Does this text reaffirm traditional ideas about gender relations, or does it provoke readers to discover different truths about gender relations?

In their responses to topic one, Chopin's use of nature imagery, the students pre-viewed, highlighted, and annotated the text before they outlined how Chopin's sugges-tive use of imagery communicates Mrs. Mallard's new expectations about her future:

Kate Chopin uses a great deal of imagery in "The Story of an Hour." Her description of "the tops of trees that were all aquiver with the new spring life" in paragraph 5 is a good example of her use of a nature image to communicate Mrs. Mallard's new feeling toward life, blooming, and rebirth.

In paragraph 8, the image of "those patches of blue sky," showing that even though the dominant color of the sky might be gray it possesses "patches of blue," suggests that the color blue is also an indicator of new spring life. In spring the color of the sky is blue. However, it is important to realize that Chopin's reference to the clouds can function as a fore-shadowing, indicating that the blue sky is as far off as Mrs. Mallard's expectations of freedom.

—Danielle Lucas

Kate Chopin's reference to "the new spring life," "the notes of a dis-tant song," "the delicious breath of rain," and "sparrows twittering" obvi-ously suggests how Mrs. Mallard begins to respond to life. She is born again like new spring life, and she is ready to take in a new clean breath like "the delicious breath of rain." Her aspiration is to live her own life like the sparrow who is free to fly. Chopin uses the "patches of blue sky . . . through the clouds" as an image of a clearing in Mrs. Mallard's life. Gone is the husband with his "powerful will bending her in." There is a clearing of "blue sky" for her.

Chopin says that Mrs. Mallard drinks in the very "elixir of life through the open window." Such an image supports the idea that Chopin uses nature imagery to show the freedom that Mrs. Mallard has now acquired.

—Mary Ellen Hogan

Two other students, Mike Lonergan and Robert Longstreet, also covered the preliminary reading strategies before they analyzed the issue of gender and identity as part of the larger cultural network Chopin's text evokes:

"The Story of an Hour" by Kate Chopin reaffirms traditional ideas about gender relations with a riptide that illuminates the reader.

Mr. and Mrs. Mallard portray a typical married couple of the late 1800s. Brently Mallard, the husband, is the head of the household, while Louise Mallard, his wife, is his possession. To quote Emily Dickinson, Louise "rose to his requirement . . . to take the honorable work of women, and of wife" (Poem 172).

Like a typical wife of this era, Mrs. Mallard was supposed to obey her husband without any rebukes. Knowing nothing different, Mrs. Mallard accepted these social norms of her time.

However, Chopin's "The Story of an Hour" reveals the aged wrinkle in this status quo arrangement by showing how, subconsciously, Mrs. Mallard's inner self and soul were being repressed and sentenced to death by lack of use.

—Mike Lonergan

"The Story of an Hour" is not a story that reaffirms traditional ideas about gender relations. In fact, Kate Chopin's text does just the opposite. It shows that no matter what your gender is, you should never lose your identity. The story suggests that instead of ignoring the restrictions of gender relations or hiding from them, you should try to eliminate them.

—Robert Longstreet

STRATEGIES FOR WRITING ABOUT LITERATURE: A STEP-BY-STEP GUIDELINE

Even the best writers feel challenged and intimidated by public exposure of their texts. Geoffrey Chaucer (1343–1400), for instance, sent one of his books away with a plea for its favorable reception. Yet, although writing is in many ways a private activity, most of the writing you will do in your introductory course to literature will come out of a public context, in which your texts will be read, shared, critiqued, and evaluated by your peers and instructor. Often, too, you will have the chance to engage in group discussion and to record in written form the conclusions your group reaches about the interpretation of a text. On such occasions, your instructor will divide your class into small groups and ask you to compare your own interpretation of a text with those of your classmates. Finally, after the secretary of your group records the group's conclusions, your group will then proceed to revise and edit your writing. In such a collaborative context, writing becomes a social act.

The following texts show the results of some peer groups' invigorating discussions of Chopin's "The Story of an Hour." Notice that the discussion conducted by group one led the students to equate marriage with the loss of self:

The Mallards' marriage is the marriage of two to make up one. In fact, their marriage can be represented as $A + B = C$. As in the chemical reaction necessary to human survival, wherein a molecule of glucose must give up a portion of itself to become a part of a larger molecule (dehydration synthesis), so it is in marriage. One part of the self must be given up to form the sacred union of marriage. It is an unfortunate circumstance of marriage that identity and the self must be its sacrificial lamb.

Our group concluded that it is not possible to have a "successful" marriage without some loss of self. Mr. and Mrs. Mallard have just such a marriage: a "successful" one.

—Recorded by Karen Digirolano

Unlike group one, whose overall observations about the loss of self in marriage offer insight into the Mallards' marriage, group two analyzes the evidence that the text provides about the Mallards as husband and wife:

Mr. Mallard was a typical husband, who never thought twice about his wife's thoughts or wishes. Neither did he think about the imposition of his own will over hers. Their marriage seemed a typical one. Mrs. Mallard, in fact, even "loved him—sometimes." For all intents and purposes, Mrs. Mallard seemed to have been a dutiful wife.

When informed of the news that her husband was dead, she acted as any woman would at her loss. However, when alone in her room, Mrs. Mallard came to know a feeling foreign to her: "There would be no one to live for during those coming years: she would live for herself. There would be no powerful will bending her in." She found herself looking forward to "those days ahead of her" which would truly be hers and no one else's. She even "spread her arms out to them in welcome."

The doctors were wrong when they said that Mrs. Mallard died of "the joy that kills." The shock to her weak heart was of sadness. When she saw her husband, she realized that her freedom was lost—once again.

—Recorded by Rina Russo

Group three's analysis of Mrs. Mallard's life in the past, present, and future shows a sense of historical development:

When Mrs. Mallard moves away from the past and the present to think of the days ahead in the future, she is obviously elated. She prays to live a long life, whereas before her husband died she had prayed for a short one. Mrs. Mallard's first reactions show us that when her husband was alive, she had no optimistic outlook on the future. She only wanted to die.

After his death, she drinks from the elixir of the open window, or from all the freedom (the birds, the trees, and the blue sky) that she witnesses outside. Through all these revelations, we can see how Mrs. Mallard evaluates her life in the past, present, and future.

—Recorded by Mary Ellen Hogan

After exploring the text and conducting a heated discussion about the Mallards and their marriage, group four concluded that Mr. and Mrs. Mallard were victims of their historical time:

We got the impression that even though Mrs. Mallard had an identity of her own, she was above all Mr. Mallard's wife. Thus, it was their nineteenth-century marriage that held Mrs. Mallard back from being the individual she really was: "She was young with a calm face whose lines bespoke repression."

Our group concluded that Mr. Mallard, like most husbands of his time, did not know how his wife felt. He probably thought he was a good husband to his wife. In fact, she sometimes loved him and "she knew that she would weep again when she saw the kind, tender hands folded in death." Our conclusion is that Mr. and Mrs. Mallard both were victims of the time they lived in.

—Recorded by Damien Donohue

SAMPLE READING

Sherwood Anderson (1876–1941) *Hands*

Upon the half decayed veranda of a small frame house that stood near the edge of a ravine near the town of Winesburg, Ohio, a fat little old man walked nervously up and down. Across a long field that had been seeded for clover but that had produced only a dense crop of yellow mustard weeds, he could see the public highway along which went a wagon filled with berry pickers returning from the fields. The berry pickers, youths and maidens, laughed and shouted boisterously. A boy clad in a blue shirt leaped from the wagon and attempted to drag after him one of the maidens, who screamed and protested shrilly. The feet of the boy in the road kicked up a cloud of dust that floated across the face of the departing sun. Over the long field came a thin girlish voice. "Oh, you Wing Biddlebaum, comb your hair, it's falling into your eyes," commanded the voice to the man, who was bald and whose nervous little hands fiddled about the bare white forehead as though arranging a mass of tangled locks.

Wing Biddlebaum, forever frightened and beset by a ghostly band of doubts, did not think of himself as in any way a part of the life of the town where he had lived for twenty years. Among all the people of Winesburg but one had come close to him. With George Willard, son of Tom Willard, the proprietor of the New Willard House, he had formed something like a friendship. George Willard was the reporter on the *Winesburg Eagle* and sometimes in the evenings he walked out along the highway to Wing Biddlebaum's house. Now as the old man walked up and down on the veranda, his hands moving nervously about, he was hoping that George Willard would come and spend the evening with him. After the wagon containing the berry pickers had passed, he went across the field through the tall mustard weeds and climbing a rail fence peered anxiously along the road to the town. For a moment he stood thus, rubbing his hands together and looking up and down the road, and then, fear overcoming him, ran back to walk again upon the porch on his own house.

In the presence of George Willard, Wing Biddlebaum, who for twenty years had been the town mystery, lost something of his timidity, and his shadowy personality, submerged in a sea of doubts, came forth to look at the world. With the young reporter at his side, he ventured in the light of day into Main Street or strode up and down on the rickety front porch of his own house, talking excitedly. The voice that had been low and trembling became shrill and loud. The bent figure straightened. With a kind of wriggle, like a fish returned to the brook by the fisherman, Biddlebaum the silent began to talk, striving to put into words the ideas that had been accumulated by his mind during long years of silence.

Wing Biddlebaum talked much with his hands. The slender expressive fingers, forever active, forever striving to conceal themselves in his pockets or behind his back, came forth and became the piston rods of his machinery of expression.

The story of Wing Biddlebaum is a story of hands. Their restless activity, like unto the beating of the wings of an imprisoned bird, had given him his name. Some obscure poet of the town had thought of it. The hands alarmed their owner. He wanted to keep them hidden away and looked with amazement at the quiet inexpressive hands of other men who worked beside him in the fields, or passed, driving sleepy teams on country roads.

When he talked to George Willard, Wing Biddlebaum closed his fists and beat with them upon a table or on the walls of his house. The action made him more comfortable. If the desire to talk came to him when the two were walking in the fields, he sought out a stump or the top board of a fence and with his hands pounding busily talked with renewed ease.

The story of Wing Biddlebaum's hands is worth a book in itself. Sympathetically set forth it would tap many strange, beautiful qualities in obscure men. It is a job for a poet. In Winesburg the hands had attracted attention merely because of their activity. With them Wing Biddlebaum had picked as high as a hundred and forty quarts of strawberries in a day. They became his distinguishing feature, the source of his fame. Also they made more grotesque an already grotesque and elusive individuality. Winesburg was proud of the hands of Wing Biddlebaum in the same spirit in which it was proud of Banker White's new stone house and Wesley Moyer's bay stallion, Tony Tip, that had won the two-fifteen trot at the fall races in Cleveland.

As for George Willard, he had many times wanted to ask about the hands. At times an almost overwhelming curiosity had taken hold of him. He felt that there must be a reason for their strange activity and their inclination to keep hidden away and only a growing respect for Wing Biddlebaum kept him from blurting out the questions that were often in his mind.

Once he had been on the point of asking. The two were walking in the fields on a summer afternoon and had stopped to sit upon a grassy bank. All afternoon Wing Biddlebaum had talked as one inspired. By a fence he had stopped and beating like a giant woodpecker upon the top board had shouted at George Willard, condemning his tendency to be too much influenced by the people about him. "You are destroying yourself," he cried. "You have the inclination to be alone and to dream and you are afraid of dreams. You want to be like others in town here. You hear them talk and you try to imitate them."

On the grassy bank Wing Biddlebaum had tried again to drive his point home. His voice became soft and reminiscent, and with a sigh of contentment he launched into a long rambling talk, speaking as one lost in a dream.

Out of the dream Wing Biddlebaum made a picture for George Willard. In the picture men lived again in a kind of pastoral golden age. Across a green open country came clean-limbed young men, some afoot, some mounted upon horses. In crowds the young men came to gather about the feet of an old man who sat beneath a tree in a tiny garden and who talked to them.

Wing Biddlebaum became wholly inspired. For once he forgot the hands. Slowly they stole forth and lay upon George Willard's shoulders. Something new and bold came into the voice that talked. "You must try to forget all you have learned," said the old man. "You must begin to dream. From this time on you must shut your ears to the roaring of the voices."

Pausing in his speech, Wing Biddlebaum looked long and earnestly at George Willard. His eyes glowed. Again he raised the hands to caress the boy and then a look of horror swept over his face.

With a convulsive movement of his body, Wing Biddlebaum sprang to his feet and thrust his hands deep into his trousers pockets. Tears came to his eyes. "I must be getting along home. I can talk no more with you," he said nervously.

Without looking back, the old man had hurried down the hillside and across a meadow, leaving George Willard perplexed and frightened upon the grassy slope. With a shiver of dread the boy arose and went along the road toward town. "I'll not ask him about his hands," he thought, touched by the memory of the terror he had seen in the man's eyes. "There's something wrong, but I don't want to know what it is. His hands have something to do with his fear of me and of everyone."

And George Willard was right. Let us look briefly into the story of the hands. Perhaps our talking of them will arouse the poet who will tell the hidden wonder story of the influence for which the hands were but fluttering pennants of promise.

In his youth Wing Biddlebaum had been a school teacher in a town in Pennsylvania. He was not then known as Wing Biddlebaum, but went by the less euphonic name of Adolph Myers. As Adolph Myers he was much loved by the boys of his school.

Adolph Myers was meant by nature to be a teacher of youth. He was one of those rare, little-understood men who rule by a power so gentle that it passes as a lovable weakness. In their feeling for the boys under their charge such men are not unlike the finer sort of women in their love of men.

And yet that is but crudely stated. It needs the poet there. With the boys of his school, Adolph Myers had walked in the evening or had sat talking until dusk upon the schoolhouse steps lost in a kind of dream. Here and there went his hands, caressing the shoulders of the boys, playing about the tousled heads. As he talked his voice became soft and musical. There was a caress in that also. In a way the voice and the hands, the stroking of the shoulders and the touching of the hair were a part of the schoolmaster's effort to carry a dream into the young minds. By the caress that was in his fingers he expressed himself. He was one of those men in whom the force that creates life is diffused, not centralized. Under the caress of his hands doubt and disbelief went out of the minds of the boys and they began also to dream.

And then the tragedy. A half-witted boy of the school became enamored of the young master. In his bed at night he imagined unspeakable things and in the morning went forth to tell his dreams as facts. Strange, hideous accusations fell from his loose-hung lips. Through the Pennsylvania town went a shiver. Hidden, shadowy doubts that had been in men's minds concerning Adolph Myers were galvanized into beliefs.

The tragedy did not linger. Trembling lads were jerked out of bed and questioned. "He put his arms about me," said one. "His fingers were always playing in my hair," said another.

One afternoon a man of the town, Henry Bradford, who kept a saloon, came to the schoolhouse door. Calling Adolph Myers into the school yard he began to beat him with his fists. As his hard knuckles beat down into the frightened face of the schoolmaster, his wrath became more and more terrible. Screaming with dismay, the children ran here and there like disturbed insects. "I'll teach you to put your hands on my boy, you beast," roared the saloon keeper, who tired of beating the master, had begun to kick him about the yard.

Adolph Myers was driven from the Pennsylvania town in the night. With lanterns in their hands a dozen men came to the door of the house where he lived alone and commanded that he dress and come forth. It was raining and one of the men had a rope in his hands. They had intended to hang the schoolmaster, but something in his figure, so small, white, and pitiful, touched their hearts and they let him escape. As he ran away into the darkness they repented of their weakness and ran after him, swearing and throwing sticks and great balls of soft mud at the figure that screamed and ran faster and faster into the darkness.

For twenty years Adolph Myers had lived alone in Winesburg. He was but forty but looked sixty-five. The name of Biddlebaum he got from a box of goods seen at a freight station as he hurried through an eastern Ohio town. He had an aunt in Winesburg, a black-toothed old woman who raised chickens, and with her he lived until she died. He had been ill for a year after the experience in Pennsylvania, and after his recovery worked as a day laborer in the fields, going timidly about and striving to conceal his hands. Although he did not understand what had happened he felt that the hands must be to blame. Again and again the fathers of the boys talked of the hands. "Keep your hands to yourself," the saloon keeper had roared, dancing with fury in the schoolhouse yard.

Upon the veranda of his house by the ravine, Wing Biddlebaum continued to walk up and down until the sun had disappeared and the road beyond the field was lost in the grey shadows. Going into his house he cut slices of bread and spread honey upon them. When the rumble of the evening train that took away the express cars loaded with the day's harvest of berries had passed and restored the silence of the summer night, he went again to walk upon the veranda. In the darkness he could not see the hands and they became quiet. Although he still hungered for the presence of the boy, who was the medium through which he expressed his love of man, the hunger became again a part of his loneliness and his waiting. Lighting a lamp, Wing Biddlebaum washed the few dishes soiled by his simple meal and, setting up a folding cot by the screen door that led to the porch, prepared to undress for the night. A few stray white bread crumbs lay on the cleanly washed floor by the table; putting the lamp upon a low stool he began to pick up the crumbs, carrying them to his mouth one by one with unbelievable rapidity. In the dense blotch of light beneath the table, the kneeling figure looked like a priest engaged in some service of his church. The nervous expressive fingers, flashing in and out of the light, might well have been mistaken for the fingers of the devotee going swiftly through decade after decade of his rosary.

● ● ●

To help you achieve your goal of becoming an able writer, we provide six guidelines that student writer Yasuko Osahi followed as she completed an essay on a literary work. Yasuko's instructor asked her students to write about one of several short stories, using the theme "Individualism and the Community."

Yasuko chose to write her two-page essay on "Hands," by Sherwood Anderson, because she wanted to learn more about American life through reading the work of writers like Anderson. Besides providing her with the source of information she needed, Anderson's text also stimulated her imagination because of the similarities it evoked between the communities portrayed in "Hands" and her mother's community in a small village in Japan.

Yasuko also knew that her *audience* (made up of her classmates and her instructor) and the *purpose* of her essay (to communicate to her audience her critical observations about "Hands") would control the development of her essay. And because she would be writing for a college audience, Yasuko also knew that she must organize her paper by presenting evidence from Anderson's text and following the conventions used to write a literary essay. Because writing is an act of discovery, Yasuko initially used some warm-up techniques to discover and generate ideas about her topic.

Step 1: Generating Ideas

Brainstorming. First, Yasuko *brainstormed* her topic by jotting down on a piece of paper all the ideas that occurred to her from her reading of Anderson's story.

> Biddlebaum: lived in two places
> Pennsylvania and Winesburg, Ohio
> Biddlebaum changes his real name.
> New profession: berry picker
> Carries the past with him
> Afraid of people, but feels good with George Willard
> How does the town react to him?
> Do they see him as a threat to them?
> They don't fear Biddlebaum, but just make fun of him.
> Pennsylvania and his past life
> A victim of violence
> The townspeople: ruthless, no pity for individuals
> Almost killed him
> Why?
> Did they see Biddlebaum as a threat to them?
> Why did they fear him? Who is to be blamed?

Freewriting. Yasuko's notes show that first she recorded her emotional reactions to Anderson's story, bringing to her reading her personal experiences based on the images, associations and memories of community violence her mother had passed down to her. Notice that at this step of the writing process she engaged in freewriting. Even though she didn't show any concern for grammar, spelling, or organization, her freewriting was focused enough to help her recall ideas and experiences as they occurred. In this freewriting process, Yasuko also started to ask questions introduced by *what, why, when, where,* and *who.* Such questions indicated she had also started to probe the meaning of the story and move in the direction of a critical assessment of Anderson's text.

The freewriting technique Yasuko used to write her journal entry also helped her to relax. Occasionally, she got stuck, but she persisted until her writing gained momentum. She did not use all the ideas she wrote down in her journal, but the following entry shows that she learned how to associate ideas, how to communicate her reactions about her topic, and how to explore feelings and emotions.

> I like "Hands," but can't relate the story to "Individualism-Community." What does community really mean? The townspeople? Biddlebaum lived in two places. I'll start with the first one. Violent people, like those in my mother's village. You can't be different. A teacher. His real name was Adolph Myers. Myers, Myers, then Biddlebaum. A dreamer. Anderson says that his characters are "grotesque." Look up this word. Individualism. Biddlebaum gives us an example of individualism. I like the story, and I sympathize with Biddlebaum. The town's people see him as a threat. They fear him. Town's people and community. Community. Biddlebaum's community. Now I see the point. Biddlebaum's first community. Relationship: Biddlebaum-community. His second community. Somebody in class said that if you don't understand the end of the story, you'll miss the point. Bread. At the end he is just eating bread crumbs. Why?

Clustering. Since Yasuko responds well to visual aids and likes to relate them to writing, she used *clustering* to develop and connect ideas about her topic. (See diagram on next page.) She wrote down her topic in the middle of a page and circled it. Then she drew connecting lines that radiated from the main topic to subtopics— ideas or words that occurred to her. Next she circled the subtopics and continued to draw other connecting lines to expose further ideas and relationships among them.

In the clustering phase, Yasuko moved by association of ideas as she explored her topic and shaped it into a pattern of informal organization. Notice, however, that her clustering also suggests a connection between the title of the story and specific ideas and words connected with it. During this process, Yasuko kept the text of Anderson's story open before her and consulted it to refresh her mind about key words, names, and descriptions.

Developing a Rough Outline. Yasuko continued to explore her topic by associating ideas and classifying them in a *rough outline:*

> Biddlebaum: a teacher. Uses his hands to communicate. Dreams of ideal times.
> Pennsylvania community: people liars, brutes. Use violence. Biddlebaum as a threat? Do they fear him? Why?

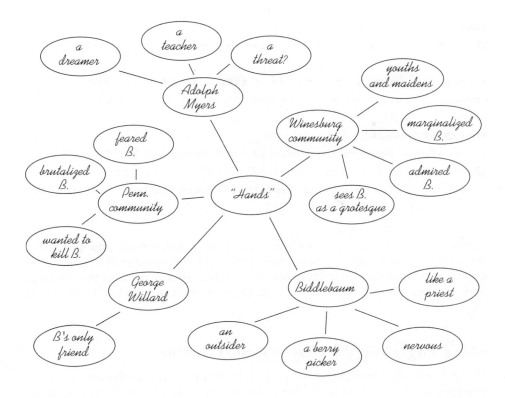

Winesburg community: isolated, new name, lonely, a grotesque, berry
   picker who sets a record. People don't fear him; just laugh at him;
   George Willard his only friend.
The real Biddlebaum is like a priest: above the laugh of the
   community.
Communities in "Hands" and Japanese communities. Similar in many
   ways. They hate people who threaten them because they are
   different.
Why can't we accept individuals who are different?

Step 2: Finding a Thesis

After examining the ideas in her brainstorming, journal entry, clustering, and rough outline, Yasuko noticed that her overall response to "Hands" was moving in the direction of one specific **thesis statement**, or central idea. Gradually, as the pattern she was pursuing emerged, she was able to reinforce her sense of purpose and audience and to write a thesis statement. To formulate her thesis statement, Yasuko wrote down her topic and then expressed her opinion or commented on the topic.

Topic:
The conflict between individualism and community in "Hands."
+
Student's comment, opinion, or attitude about the topic:
Communities use violence only when they are under threat.
=
Thesis statement:
The conflict between individualism and community in "Hands" shows that communities, like Biddlebaum's Pennsylvania community, use violence only against individuals who pose a threat to their stability.

Yasuko's thesis statement shows how she narrowed her topic and phrased it using language that is clear, precise, and specific. It is important to remember, however, that even though your thesis statement functions as a contract that you sign with your readers, you might have to change or revise it as you move from draft to essay.

Step 3: Organizing the Essay: A Formal Outline

When Yasuko developed her outline, she was already deeply involved in the cognitive process of critical thinking. She had engaged in the close reading and textual analysis of Anderson's story by studying its **character, plot, setting, theme, narrator, style, and tone.**

As the following outline shows, at this point Yasuko was ready to support her thesis statement on the basis of various ideas that she organized to build the body of her essay:

Thesis Statement
The conflict between individualism and community in "Hands" shows that communities, like Biddlebaum's Pennsylvania community, use violence only against individuals who pose a threat to their stability.

Supporting Ideas
  I. The Pennsylvania Community
     A. Biddlebaum as a threat to the community
        1. Biddlebaum: a real threat?
        2. The conflict between Biddlebaum and Pennsylvania community

      B. The community's reaction to Biddlebaum
         1. The community's disregard for individual rights
         2. The community's use of violence
  II. The Winesburg Community
     A. Biddlebaum as a member of the community
        1. Biddlebaum: a real member?
        2. Biddlebaum as an outsider
        3. Biddlebaum as a grotesque
     B. The community's reaction to Biddlebaum
        1. The community's view of Biddlebaum as a grotesque
        2. The community's acceptance of Biddlebaum
 III. The Real Biddlebaum
     A. Neither a threat nor a grotesque
     B. A holy man above his community

A formal outline like Yasuko's may be used as a preliminary form of planning before you write your first draft or during revision to check the organization of the draft. Either way, such an outline should serve as a guide, never a hindrance to making changes that improve your essay. Notice that in her outline Yasuko arranged the information in an order (Pennsylvania community, Winesburg community) that contrasts with the order (Winesburg, Pennsylvania) presented by Anderson in his short story. In her approach, Yasuko used a cause-and-effect pattern to show how the violent behavior of the Pennsylvania community accounts for the grotesque position that Biddlebaum occupies in Winesburg.

Yasuko's essay might be classified as an "analysis essay," or an essay that focuses on the study of one single element in relation to the whole. Her instructor might have considered other kinds of essays as well, such as the following examples:

1. A comparison-and-contrast essay discusses similarities and differences between elements in the same work or in different works.

    EXAMPLE: Compare and contrast the roles of the two communities in "Hands."

    or

    Compare and contrast the conflict between the individual and society in "Hands" and "Eveline."

2. A debate essay presents one or the other side of an argument.

    EXAMPLE: Take a position and explain whether individual rights should ever overshadow the claims of society. Support your arguments with examples from the texts discussed in class.

3. A reaction essay presents the reader's feelings and reactions about a work of literature or a literary issue.

   EXAMPLE: React to the statement that cities and places that are full of dislocated, grotesque people provide ideal settings for short stories. Use at least three of the texts discussed in class to support your arguments.

4. A combination essay combines several approaches. To write her analytical essay studying individualism and community in "Hands" (exploring one specific element in relation to the whole), Yasuko also used cause-and-effect (examination of the causes and the effects that are likely to result from them) as well as comparison and contrast (focus on the similarities and differences of two elements).

Step 4: Writing a Rough Draft with Peer Editing

At this point Yasuko kept writing and revising her essay until it was time to share her rough draft with some of her classmates. Notice that the writing Yasuko did so far was carried out in isolation, but she knew that this act of individual effort would culminate in a much anticipated social activity when she shared it with her classmates. Here is Yasuko's essay, followed by an evaluation form supplied by her instructor and filled out by her peer editors.

```
          Essay on Individualism and the Community
     The conflict between individualism and community in
"Hands" shows Biddlebaum's struggle against the two
communities in which he lived: the Pennsylvania community
and the Winesburg community. When viewed from this
perspective, this conflict also shows that communities
like Biddlebaum's Pennsylvania community use violence
only against individuals who pose a threat to their
stability. But what really happened in Pennsylvania was
that one day one of Biddlebaum's students acted in a
romantic way toward him, spreading rumors about his
potential homosexuality. Then the boys' parents got
together, and after making some inquiries about
Biddlebaum's habits, hastily concluded that he was a threat
to their youth. In my opinion, what happens to Biddlebaum
in Pennsylvania throws some light on how communities
respond to a potential threat against themselves.
     It is a dissatisfied member of the community who
leads his community in a hate-chase against Adolph Myers.
No one in the Pennsylvania community dared to raise a
voice in Biddlebaum's defense. Parents, in fact,
```

disregarded Biddlebaum's individual rights. Ironically, even though Biddlebaum's hands become the focal point of his downfall, it's through them that Biddlebaum manages to communicate his love of humanity. Led by its violent rage against Biddlebaum, the community beat, kicked, and almost killed him.

After leaving Pennsylvania, twenty years later we find Biddlebaum settled in another community, the community of Winesburg in Ohio. He decided to go to Winesburg because he had an aunt who lived there. That is when he changed his original name, Adolph Myers, to Biddlebaum, and made a living as a berry picker. After his aunt's death he lives completely alone. Biddlebaum was a berry picker who made only one friend, George Willard. In spite of their close relationship, there are times in which Biddlebaum and George do not feel comfortable with each other.

On one hand, the Winesburg community was proud of his ability to pick berries, but on the other hand, he was seen as weird and grotesque. However, the Winesburg community learns to accept Biddlebaum as a grotesque. This was shown in the opening paragraph of the story where Anderson presents Biddlebaum pacing up and down the veranda of his house.

Biddlebaum's mannerisms were made fun of by the youths and maidens, who managed to have a good laugh at his expense. At first the Winesburg community seems to react in a cruel way, but its reaction shows how Biddlebaum and his community unsettle each other.

From the point of view of the reader, who can see both communities, abusing and making fun of grotesque individuals like Biddlebaum made the Winesburg community feel confident and secure. However, unlike Biddlebaum's Winesburg community, his Pennsylvania community doesn't act in the same way. It is not violent. It is neither more sensitive nor enlightened than his Pennsylvania community. It would probably unleash the same kind of violence that his Pennsylvania community unleashed against him. The reason it didn't do so was that

Biddlebaum never became a threat to that community. He isolated himself and was very careful not to mingle with anyone except George Willard.

My mother had also told me some stories about her small village in the Far East--horror tales about sons and daughters who were severely punished until they learned that individuals don't belong to themselves but to their communities. Such stories showed that what was at stake was not only the preservation of values and traditions, but also the community's defense of themselves against any kind of threat posed by their members.

Peer Editing Evaluation Form

WRITER: Yasuko Osahi

PEER EDITORS: Mary Anne Saboya, Gaby Jackson, Michael Hughes, Tony Spindola

1. What does the writer want to say about the literary text in this paper? What aspects of the text does he or she focus on?

   The writer wants to explore the conflict of individualism and community in "Hands." She focuses on how Biddlebaum relates to the two communities: the Winesburg and the Pennsylvania communities.

2. What kind of audience does the writer seem to be addressing? Which aspects of the paper might especially strike the audience? Why? Consider the writer's choice of subject, depth of information, point of view, tone, and voice.

   Yasuko seems to be addressing her classmates and her instructors. Her thesis statement, "Communities use violence only against individuals who pose a threat to their stability," is powerful enough to strike her audience. Her choice of subject is good, but she needs to use more quotes to prove she is working close to the text. She also needs to soften the tone she uses in her essay.

3. What are the strengths of the paper? How might the paper be revised to better fulfill the writer's purpose and meaning?

   The strengths of the paper are Yasuko's choice of subject and her analysis of the two communities. Paragraphs 1, 3, and 4 need revision because at times she summarizes rather than interprets the story. Paragraphs 2 and 5 seem to go off track. Yasuko should rewrite them.

4. Have you noticed any words and sentences that do not work? How would you rephrase them?

We noticed that in paragraphs 4 and 5 she uses passive structures that are very vague. We would rephrase these sentences like this:

- *In the opening of the story, Anderson shows Biddlebaum pacing up and down the veranda of his house.*

- *The youths and maidens made fun of him and managed to laugh at his expense.*

5. Other comments

Select a title that appeals to your readers.

Step 5: Revising

After reading her peers' comments on her rough draft, Yasuko knew that she would have to revise her paper and rewrite most of its paragraphs. She focused on the suggestions her peers had made and read her essay again until she understood her peers' criticism that she should soften the tone of her essay and sharpen her critical focus.

Yasuko revised her paper and handed it in to her instructor. A few days later, her instructor returned it with some marginal comments and an overall evaluation:

Be more specific. See "Strategies for Revision" #10.2.

A powerful thesis statement. It shows psychological depth.

                    The Conflict of Individualism
                    and Community in "Hands"
           The conflict between individualism and
           community in "Hands" shows Biddlebaum's
           struggle against two of the communities in
           which he lived: the Pennsylvania community and
           Winesburg community. When viewed from this
           perspective, this conflict also shows that
           communities like Biddlebaum's Pennsylvania
           community *tend to* use violence only against individuals
           who pose a threat to their stability. But did
           Biddlebaum really pose a threat to the youth of
           the Pennsylvania community? Does Anderson's
           text present Biddlebaum as a homosexual who was
           corrupting the Pennsylvania youth? Why is it
           that Myer's Pennsylvania community reacted so

Isn't your opinion implied in the text? Have you considered the role of the narrator?

Is this community afraid of B.? What does the text suggest about that?

Isn't this ¶ out of place? Either delete or rewrite it.

violently against him, while his second community, the one in Winesburg, manages to establish a truce with him? In my opinion, what happens to Biddlebaum in Pennsylvania throws some light on how a community responds to a potential threat against itself.

a new ¶?

It is a dissatisfied member of the community who leads his community in a hate-chase against Adolph Myers. No one in the Pennsylvania community dared to raise a voice in Biddlebaum's defense. Parents, in fact, disregarded Biddlebaum's individual rights. Led by its violent rage against Biddlebaum, the community beat, kicked, and almost killed him.

Anderson's text also suggests that it may be fear or the spirit of preservation that controls the action that the Pennsylvania townspeople take against Biddlebaum. The community wanted to defend itself against the schoolteacher. The amount of violence it uses by "swearing and throwing sticks and great balls of soft mud" at him suggests that it feared Biddlebaum. If it got rid of him, it would also be able to eliminate the fear that he inspired. Once again the community would be able to restore its emotional balance.

Ironically, even though Biddlebaum's hands become the focal point of his tragedy, and Biddlebaum himself "felt that the hands must be to blame" (888), it is through them that Biddlebaum manages to inspire his students to dream.

To consider Biddlebaum's position in Winesburg, Ohio, we have to ask whether Biddlebaum has really become a member of his community. The fact that he is a berry picker who contributes to the Winesburg economy does not seem to count because Biddlebaum "did not think of himself as in any way a part of the life of the town where he had lived for twenty years" (885). He was still an outsider who contrasted with the other berry pickers. However, unlike his Pennsylvania community, Biddlebaum's Winesburg community learns to accept him as "grotesque." In fact, Anderson's text opens with a description of how Adolph Myers, now Biddlebaum, an old and eccentric individual who nervously paces up and down the veranda of his shabby house, contrasts with the "youths and maidens" of Winesburg, Ohio.

This argument merits development. What about a quote?

The fact that Biddlebaum and the "youths and maidens" unsettle each other seems to suggest that Biddlebaum will never become a real member of the Winesburg community. From the point of view of the reader, who can see both communities, abusing and making fun of grotesque individuals like Biddlebaum made the

Is there anything in text that suggests that? Use quotes.

Winesburg community feel confident and secure. However, unlike Biddlebaum's Winesburg community, his Pennsylvania community doesn't seem to act the same way. They are not violent. They are neither more sensitive nor more enlightened than his Pennsylvania community. They would probably unleash the same kind of violence that his Pennsylvania community unleashed against him. The reason they don't do so is that Biddlebaum never became a threat to the community. He isolated himself and was very careful not to mingle with anyone, except George Willard.

What about the ¶ on whom the real B. is? Check your outline.

My mother had also told me some stories about her small village in the Far East--horror tales about sons and daughters severely punished until they learned that individuals don't belong to themselves, but to their communities. Such stories showed that what was at stake was not

How does your conclusion tie in with "Hands?" ⎱ only the preservation of values and traditions, but also the community's defense of itself against any kind of threat posed by its members.

> Yasuko,
> Even though you've made same good points in your rough draft, your essay still needs a lot of work. Put it aside for a day or two, but during that time continue to read "Hands" to clarify your ideas.
>   Start your revision by reading your text aloud. Then develop your ¶/s more fully, use quotes to support your arguments, and follow the guidelines above.

After reading her instructor's comments, Yasuko rewrote and reorganized her paper. During this process, she revised her essay following the strategies for revision listed below, which her instructor had provided for the whole class.

STRATEGIES FOR REVISING THE DRAFT

Step 1: Responding to Content and Organization

The focus here should be the overall development of the essay. Concentrate on the title, thesis statement, supporting ideas, and organization.

- Is the title of your essay suggestive? Select a title that describes or announces the topic without restating the thesis statement. Make sure that your title appeals to the reader.
- Is the thesis clear and persuasive?
- Is your essay logically organized? Consider whether the opening paragraph introduces the topic. What about the conclusion? Does it summarizes the main ideas or offers an overall evaluation of the thesis?
- If necessary, rewrite your thesis statement and rearrange the major sections of your essay by adding, deleting, condensing, or changing the order of its various elements.

Step 2: Developing Paragraphs

- Relate each paragraph to the thesis of the essay.
- Make the main idea of each paragraph clear.
- Have a topic sentence for each paragraph.
- See that the parts of the paragraph relate to each other.
- Make your paragraph more interesting by using rhetorical questions, quotations, examples, and illustrations that will keep the reader's attention.
- To establish a clear context, when you write the first paragraph of your essay, identify the title, author, and characters in the work you are analyzing as if

you were writing not only for your classmates and instructor, but also for a broader audience. Notice the example below:

VAGUE: "Hands" portrays the tension that tend to arise between an individual and his community.

REVISED: "Hands," one of Sherwood Anderson's stories in *Winesburg, Ohio*, portrays the tension that arises between an individual, Biddlebaum, and his Winesburg community in Ohio.

Step 3: Checking for Purpose, Audience, and Tone

Ask yourself whether your essay fulfills its purpose to inform, entertain, persuade, or call its readers to action. Put yourself in the intended reader's place, and check your paper for clarity and precision of meaning.

- Who are your readers?
- Is your essay appropriate for your readers?
- Listen to the sound of the speaking voice of the text.
- What kind of attitude have you expressed in presenting your topic to your reader?
- Are you writing as if you were an authority on your subject?
- Is your writing too formal or too informal? Is it ironic, direct?
- What kind of language are you using to express this tone?

Step 4: Using Effective Language, Style, and Verbs

Remember that all literary interpretations begin with critical observations. Thus, to avoid laying out a plot summary—or retelling the story—strive to use verbs like the ones listed below, which will assist you in developing the critical focus you need to write a literary essay.

explore	portray	include
analyze	argue	highlight
mention	refer	discuss
demonstrate	suggest	examine
show	illustrate	explain
reveal	emphasize	express
present	use	chronicle
write	indicate	outline

EXAMPLE: In "Hands," Sherwood Anderson reveals how an individual becomes a potential threat to his community.

"Hands" explores the conflict between individualism and society on several levels.

Remember, however, that **purpose** and **audience** should always control your writing. Thus, if your presumed audience has not read the text, some plot summary would be necessary.

Whenever possible, try to infuse energy and conviction into your sentences by using the present tense and the active voice. The overuse of passive constructions—constructions with a subject that does not do the action or is acted upon—may weaken your sentences. For example,

PASSIVE: Biddlebaum's mannerisms are made fun of by the "youths and maidens" of Winesburg.

ACTIVE: The "youths and maidens" of Winesburg make fun of Biddlebaum.

PASSIVE: The conflict between the individual and society is explored in the opening of the story.

ACTIVE: The opening of "Hands" explores the conflict between individual and society.

STRATEGIES FOR PREPARING THE FINAL DRAFT

After revision, you may start to focus on the presentation of your essay. In this phase of the writing process, you should consider wordiness, redundancy, grammatical errors, mechanical problems (spelling, punctuation, capital letters, abbreviations), and the format required for preparing your manuscript. Bear in mind that the ear can detect flaws that the eye misses. Therefore, try reading your text aloud to catch mistakes that emerge not so much on the reader level of paragraph organization but on the more local level of the sentence or phrase.

See guidelines for title, margins, paging, and source citations in Appendix C, "Researching Literary Sources." If your school has a tutoring program, your instructor may ask you to revise your essay with the help of a writing tutor.

Writing the Final Draft

The final draft of Yasuko's essay on "Hands" follows.

- Do you consider her essay strong and effective enough?
- Would you suggest any further revision?

Osahi 1

Yasuko Osahi
Professor Jackson
English Composition II
May 21, 2005

The Conflict of Individualism
and Community in "Hands"

The conflict between individualism and community in Sherwood Anderson's short story "Hands"
shows the struggle of one individual--the protagonist, Wing Biddlebaum, or Adolph Myers--against two
main communities: the Pennsylvania community and the
Winesburg community. When viewed from this perspective, this conflict also shows that communities like
Biddlebaum's Pennsylvania community tend to use
violence against individuals who pose a threat to
their stability. But did Biddlebaum really pose a
threat to the youth of the Pennsylvania community?
Does Anderson's text present Biddlebaum as a homosexual who was corrupting the Pennsylvania youth? Why
is it that Myers's Pennsylvania community reacted so
violently against him, while his second community, the
one in Winesburg, manages to establish a truce with him?

The narrator's description of what happened in
Biddlebaum's Pennsylvania community throws much
light on how a community responds to a potential
threat against itself:

> With lanterns in their hands a dozen men
> came to the door of the house where he
> lived alone and commanded that he dress
> and come forth. It was raining and one of
> the men had a rope in his hands. They had
> intended to hang the schoolmaster, but
> something in his figure, so small, white,
> and pitiful, touched their hearts and
> they let him escape. (888)

Osahi 2

It is through the narrator's eyes that we see how any dissatisfied member of a community, like one of Biddlebaum's students, can lead his community in a hate-chase if he is clever enough to unleash some of the community's covert fears:

> A half-witted boy of the school became enamored of the young master. . . . Strange, hideous accusations fell from his loose-hung lips. Through the Pennsylvania town went a shiver. Hidden, shadowy doubts that had been in men's minds concerning Adolph Myers were galvanized into beliefs. (888)

Anderson's text also suggests that it may be fear or the spirit of preservation that controls the action that the Pennsylvania townspeople take against Biddlebaum. The community wanted to defend itself against the schoolteacher. The amount of violence it uses by "swearing and throwing sticks and great balls of soft mud" at him suggests that it feared Biddlebaum. If it got rid of him, it would also be able to eliminate the fear that his hands inspired. Once again the community would be able to restore its emotional balance. Ironically, even though Biddlebaum's "hands" became the focal point of his tragedy, and Biddlebaum himself "felt that the hands must be to blame" (888), it is through them that Biddlebaum manages to inspire his students to dream: "under the caress of his hands doubt and disbelief went out of the minds of the boys and they began also to dream" (888).

To consider Biddlebaum's position in Winesburg, Ohio, we have to ask whether Biddlebaum

Osahi 3

has really become a member of his community. The
fact that he is a berry picker who contributes to
the Winesburg economy does not seem to count
because Biddlebaum "did not think of himself as in
any way a part of the life of the town where he had
lived for twenty years" (885). He was still an outsider who contrasted with the other berry pickers.
However, unlike his Pennsylvania community,
Biddlebaum's Winesburg community learns to accept
him as a "grotesque." In fact, Anderson's text
opens with a description of how Adolph Myers, now
Biddlebaum, an old and eccentric individual who
nervously paces up and down the veranda of his
shabby house, contrasts with the "youths and
maidens" of Winesburg, Ohio. The fact that Biddlebaum and the "youths and maidens" unsettle each
other seems to suggest that Biddlebaum will never
become a real member of the Winesburg community.

From the point of view of the reader, who can
see the reality of both communities, the Winesburg
"youths and maidens" also seem to react in a cruel
way, by making fun of Biddlebaum's mannerisms and
by having a good laugh at his expense. However,
they don't seem to act out of fear. Their critique
of Biddlebaum seems to give them just the sense of
power they need to feel confident and secure about
themselves: "'Oh, you Wing Biddlebaum, comb your
hair, it's falling into your eyes,' commanded the
voice to the man, who was bald and whose nervous
little hands fiddled about the bare white forehead
as though arranging a mass of tangled locks" (885).
Biddlebaum, the weird and eccentric outsider, seems
to reaffirm the feelings that they belong in their

Osahi 4

own community. In some ways, the Winesburg community is neither better nor more civilized than Biddlebaum's Pennsylvania community. If driven by the fear of a potential threat to its stability, it might probably unleash the same kind of violence against people.

Neither community ever learns who Biddlebaum really is. Through Anderson's narrator, however, the reader gets a good glimpse of his real personality. The narrator stresses Biddlebaum's childlike innocence and his love of humanity. Last, but not least, the narrator also casts Biddlebaum in the figure of a holy man. The religious images at the end of the text presenting Biddlebaum "like a priest engaged in some service of his church" (889) suggest that Biddlebaum possesses the sensibility of a religious man--one that neither community would be able to appreciate.

"Hands" brought to my mind some of my mother's stories about her small village in Japan. Those horror tales portrayed sons and daughters who were severely punished when they refused to conform. For me, such tales also show that what was at stake, as much in my mother's village as in the communities in "Hands," was not only the preservation of traditional values, but also the communities' defense of themselves against individuals who are different and who pose a threat to their stability.

Osahi 5

Work Cited

Anderson, Sherwood. "Hands." <u>Literature Across Cultures</u>. Ed. Sheena Gillespie, Terezinha Fonseca, Antony Pipolo. 4th ed. New York: Pearson Longman, 2005.

PART ONE

ORIGINS AND INSIGHTS

Fiction

And the Soul Shall Dance, Wakako Yamauchi ◆ *Roman Fever*, Edith Wharton ◆ *First Confession*, Frank O'Connor ◆ *Father and I*, Pär Lagerkvist ◆ The Watch, *Elie Wiesel* ◆ The Sky Is Gray, *Ernest J. Gaines* ◆ *Young Goodman Brown*, Nathaniel Hawthorne

Essays

My People, Chief Seattle ◆ *The Allegory of the Cave*, Plato ◆ *Fraternity*, Garrett Hongo ◆ From *Imaginary Homelands*, Salman Rushdie

Poetry

The Negro Speaks of Rivers, Langston Hughes ◆ *First Light*, Linda Hogan ◆ *warm heart contains life*, Evangelina Vigil-Piñón ◆ *The Lamb*, William Blake ◆ *The Tyger*, William Blake ◆ *In the Tree House at Night*, James Dickey ◆ *Mid-term Break*, Seamus Heaney ◆ *During a Son's Dangerous Illness*, ◆ Denise Levertov ◆ *Lost Sister*, Cathy Song ◆ *The Possessive*, Sharon Olds ◆ *Breaking Tradition*, Janice Mirikitani ◆ *A Breeze Swept Through*, Luci Tapahonso ◆ *Fern Hill*, Dylan Thomas ◆ *If I could only live at the pitch that is near madness*, Richard Eberhart ◆ *Poem for My Father*, Eric Chock ◆ *The Gift*, Li-Young Lee ◆ *Fishermen*, James A. Emanuel ◆ *Frederick Douglass*, Robert Hayden ◆ *Tour 5*, Robert Hayden ◆ *Those Winter Sundays*, Robert Hayden ◆ *Runagate Runagate*, Robert Hayden

Drama

Oedipus Rex, Sophocles ◆ *Hamlet, Prince of Denmark*, William Shakespeare

The artist's imagination has always been captivated by the idea of the past and its relationship with the present. Stories from oral traditions of ancient cultures as well as our own evoke the power and mysteries of the past by portraying a time in which myths, fables, legends, and archetypes dictated the values of human actions within the community. As the Filipino-American writer Carlos Bulosan relates, ". . . when they started singing Philippine songs their voices were so sad, so full of yesterday and the haunting presence of familiar seas. . . ."

The ritual of storytelling was an integral part of Native American life, too—connecting, as contemporary writer Simon Ortiz reminds us, the people, the land, and the stories. "If anything is most vital, essential, and absolutely important in native cultural philosophy, it is this concept of interdependence: the fact that without land there is no life, and without a responsible social and cultural outlook by humans, no life-sustaining land is possible." Thus, as tribal members from the oldest to the youngest listened to, received, or retold stories about creation, nature, good and evil, war and peace, and life and death, they reflected on the myths and rituals of their cultural past and their relevance to the present and the future.

How can we reach and understand the past? What can we learn from it? Why are memories an important part of our private and communal selves? Some writers in Part One begin with what Toni Morrison calls "sites of memory"—places that have affected these writers' lives because of emotional or sensory associations with them. Contemporary Indian writer Salman Rushdie, now residing in the United States, refers in his *Imaginary Homelands* to his native Bombay as a city that reminds him that "the past is home, albeit a lost home in a lost city in the mists of lost time." The speaker in Dylan Thomas's poem "Fern Hill" also takes us back to the past and the Welsh landscapes and summer experiences that framed his childhood, while the protagonist of Wakako Yamauchi's story "And the Soul Shall Dance" associates the Imperial Valley of her Japanese American childhood with Mrs. Oka, a woman who shocked her neighbors by smoking cigarettes and drinking sake.

The past has been defined by various authors as a "foreign country," a "bucket of ashes," a "field of errors and ignorance," or a temporal continuum with the power to "delight and instruct." As you examine various aspects of the past in Part One texts, remember that we can try to understand our personal and historical pasts only with the aid of our memory and our imagination. As Lynne Sharon Schwartz reminds us, "Memory is something we reconstruct, something we create. Memory is a story we make up from snatches of the past."

People who have influenced our lives are often important catalysts in reconstructing and understanding our stories. Many texts in Part

One are concerned with the relationships among siblings and other family members. In his poem "In the Tree House at Night," James Dickey celebrates the spiritual presence of his now dead brother, and in their poems, Sharon Olds and Janice Mirikitani confront the reality of their adolescent daughters' transitions to adulthood. In "The Gift," Li-Young Lee recalls a tender moment with his father, while Eric Chock wrestles with his father's expectations for his son in "Poem for My Father."

Historical places such as Williamsburg, Ellis Island, and the Martin Luther King Jr. Memorial—or even photographs of a grandparent's birthplace—are also important sites of memory. They can motivate us to listen to the voices of the past or to search for our roots in an attempt to establish a dialogue with our past selves as we explore our own terrain further. To what extent is it important for us to try to understand our histories? Is it plausible to say that our identities and our individual lives are sometimes shaped by a fixed historical reality? Some of the writers in Part One speculate about these questions by examining the conditions under which people become particularly aware of historical identities. African American poet Robert Hayden celebrates the life and struggles of former slave Frederick Douglass in one poem, and in "Runagate Runagate" he reconstructs what it means to be a renegade caught in the grim historical reality that shaped the destiny of African slaves in the United States. In "The Watch," Holocaust survivor Elie Wiesel explores his protagonist's attempt to retrieve a watch that symbolizes the past—"the soul and memory of that time" of war and holocaust. "Once more," says the protagonist as he attempts to defy time and to retrieve the past, "I am the mitzvah child . . . I get ready to re-enact the scene my memory recalls."

Shakespeare's *Hamlet* offers us another example of how men and women can identify themselves with the past. One major question you will explore in the play is why the Danish prince wavers between remembering and forgetting the past that seems to link him and the political future of Denmark. What do people do when they realize that they carry the burden of the past with them or that the past can become an obstacle to their growth and to a redefinition of themselves? In Sophocles' *Oedipus Rex*, the protagonist's journey backwards into the past of blindness and transgression leads forward into the narrative present of self-knowledge, recognition, and revelation. In *Oedipus Rex*, the past also emerges as dramatic spectacle, controlling and shaping human destiny through the inexorable grip of the unconscious.

Native American Linda Hogan uses the metaphor of "First Light" to re-create the pristine beauty of her ancestral past, while Langston Hughes charts the historical and symbolic journey of his people from slavery to freedom in "The Negro Speaks of Rivers." In both texts we encounter yet another aspect of the past that voices the private and collective myths of the racial memory.

As you explore these and other texts from the sites of memory, consider them catalysts for your own recollections and discoveries of your personal and communal past, for as Oscar Wilde reminds us, "Memory is the diary that we carry about with us."

FICTION

Wakako Yamauchi

And the Soul Shall Dance

It's all right to talk about it now. Most of the principals are dead, except of course, me and my younger brother, and possibly Kiyoko Oka, who might be near forty-five now, because, yes, I'm sure of it, she was fourteen then. I was nine, and my brother about four, so he hardly counts at all. Kiyoko's mother is dead, my father is dead, my mother is dead, and her father could not have lasted all these years with his tremendous appetite for alcohol and pickled chilies—those little yellow ones, so hot they could make your mouth hurt; he'd eat them like peanuts and tears would surge from his bulging thyroid eyes in great waves and stream down the dark coarse terrain of his face.

My father farmed then in the desert basin resolutely named Imperial Valley, in the township called Westmoreland; twenty acres of tomatoes, ten of summer squash, or vice versa, and the Okas lived maybe a mile, mile and a half, across an alkaline road, a stretch of greasewood, tumbleweed and white sand, to the south of us. We didn't hobnob much with them, because you see, they were a childless couple and we were a family: father, mother, daughter, and son, and we went to the Buddhist church on Sundays where my mother taught Japanese, and the Okas kept pretty much to themselves. I don't mean they were unfriendly; Mr. Oka would sometimes walk over (he rarely drove) on rainy days, all dripping wet, short and squat under a soggy newspaper, pretending to need a plow-blade or a file, and he would spend the afternoon in our kitchen drinking sake and eating chilies with my father. As he got progressively drunker, his large mouth would draw down and with the stream of tears, he looked like a kindly weeping bullfrog.

Not only were they childless, impractical in an area where large families were looked upon as labor potentials, but there was a certain strangeness about them. I became aware of it the summer our bathhouse burned down, and my father didn't get right down to building another, and a Japanese without a bathhouse . . . well, Mr. Oka offered us the use of his. So every night that summer we drove to the Okas for our bath, and we came in frequent contact with Mrs. Oka, and this is where I found the strangeness.

Mrs. Oka was small and spare. Her clothes hung on her like loose skin and when she walked, the skirt about her legs gave her a sort of webbed look. She was pretty in spite of the boniness and the dull calico and the barren look; I know now that she couldn't have been over thirty. Her eyes were large and a little vacant, although once I saw them fill with tears; the time I insisted we take the old Victrola over and we played our Japanese records for her. Some of the songs were sad, and I imagined the nostalgia she felt, but my mother said the tears were probably from yawning or from the smoke of her cigarettes. I thought my mother resented her for not being more hospitable; indeed, never a cup of tea appeared before us, and between them the conversation of women was totally absent: the rise and fall of gentle voices, the arched eyebrows, the croon of polite surprise. But more than this, Mrs. Oka was *different*.

Obviously she was shy, but some nights she disappeared altogether. She would see us drive into her yard and then lurch from sight. She was gone all evening. Where could she have hidden in that two-roomed house—where in that silent dessert? Some nights she would wait out our visit with enormous forbearance, quietly pushing wisps of stray hair behind her ears and waving gnats away from her great moist eyes, and some nights she moved about with nervous agitation, her khaki canvas shoes slapping loudly as she walked. And sometimes there appeared to be welts and bruises on her usually smooth brown face, and she would sit solemnly, hands on lap, eyes large and intent on us. My mother hurried us home then: "Hurry, Masako, no need to wash well; hurry."

You see, being so poky, I was always last to bathe. I think the Okas bathed after we left because my mother often reminded me to keep the water clean. The routine was to lather outside the tub (there were buckets and pans and a small wooden stool), rinse off the soil and soap, and then soak in the tub of hot water and contemplate. Rivulets of perspiration would run down the scalp.

When my mother pushed me like this, I dispensed with ritual, rushed a bar of soap around me and splashed about a pan of water. So hastily toweled, my wet skin strapped the clothes to me, impeding my already clumsy progress. Outside, my mother would be murmuring her many apologies and my father, I knew, would be carrying my brother whose feet were already sandy. We would hurry home.

I thought Mrs. Oka might be insane and I asked my mother about it, but she shook her head and smiled with her mouth drawn down and said that Mrs. Oka loved her sake. This was unusual, yes, but there were other unusual women we knew. Mrs. Nagai was brought by her husband from a geisha house; Mrs. Tani was a militant Christian Scientist; Mrs. Abe, the midwife, was occult. My mother's statement explained much: sometimes Mrs. Oka was drunk and sometimes not. Her taste for liquor and cigarettes was a step in the realm of men; unusual for a Japanese wife, but at the time, in that place, and to me, Mrs. Oka loved her sake the way my father loved his, in the way of Mr. Oka, and the way I loved my candy. That her psychology may have demanded this anesthetic, that she lived with something unendurable, did not occur to me. Nor did I perceive the violence of emotions that the purple welts indicated—or the masochism that permitted her to display these wounds to us.

In spite of her masculine habits, Mrs. Oka was never less than a woman. She was no lady in the area of social amenities; but the feminine in her was innate and never left her. Even in her disgrace, she was a small broken sparrow, slightly floppy, too slowly enunciating her few words, too carefully rolling her Bull Durham, cocking her small head and moistening the ocher tissue. Her aberration was a protest of the life assigned her; it was obstinate, but unobserved, alas, unheeded. "Strange" was the only concession we granted her.

Toward the end of summer, my mother said we couldn't continue bathing at the Okas'; when winter set in we'd catch our death from the commuting and she'd always felt dreadful about our imposition on Mrs. Oka. So my father took the corrugated tin sheets he'd found on the highway and had been saving for some other use and built up our bathhouse again. Mr. Oka came to help.

While they raised the quivering tin walls, Mr. Oka began to talk. His voice was sharp and clear above the low thunder of the metal sheets.

He told my father he had been married in Japan previously to the present Mrs. Oka's older sister. He had a child by the marriage, Kiyoko, a girl. He had left the two to come to America intending to send for them soon, but shortly after his departure, his wife passed away from an obscure stomach ailment. At the time, the present Mrs. Oka was young and had foolishly become involved with a man of poor reputation. The family was anxious to part the lovers and conveniently arranged a marriage by proxy and sent him his dead wife's sister. Well that was all right, after all, they were kin, and it would be good for the child when she came to join them. But things didn't work out that way, year after year he postponed calling for his daughter, couldn't get the price of fare together, and the wife—ahhh, the wife, Mr. Oka's groan was lost in the rumble of his hammering.

He cleared his throat. The girl was now fourteen, he said, and begged to come to America to be with her own real family. Those relatives had forgotten the favor he'd done in accepting a slightly used bride, and now tormented his daughter for being forsaken. True, he'd not sent much money, but if they knew, if they only knew how it was here.

"Well," he sighed, "who could be blamed? It's only right she be with me anyway."

"That's right," my father said.

"Well, I sold the horse and some other things and managed to buy a third-class ticket on the Taiyo-Maru. Kiyoko will get here the first week of September." Mr. Oka glanced toward my father, but my father was peering into a bag of nails. "I'd be much obliged to you if your wife and little girl," he rolled his eyes toward me, "would take kindly to her. She'll be lonely."

Kiyoko-San came in September. I was surprised to see so very nearly a woman; short, robust, buxom: the female counterpart of her father; thyroid eyes and protruding teeth, straight black hair banded impudently into two bristly shucks, Cuban heels and white socks. Mr. Oka brought her proudly to us.

"Little Masako here," for the first time to my recollection, he touched me; he put his rough fat hand on the top of my head, "is very smart in school. She will help you with your school work, Kiyoko," he said.

I had so looked forward to Kiyoko-san's arrival. She would be my soul mate; in my mind I had conjured a girl of my own proportion: thin and tall, but with refinement and beauty I didn't yet possess that would surely someday come to the fore. My disappointment was keen and apparent. Kiyoko-san stepped forward shyly, then retreated with a short bow and small giggle, her fingers pressed to her mouth.

My mother took her away. They talked for a long time—about Japan, about enrollment in American school, the clothes Kiyoko-san would need, and where to look for the best values. As I watched them, it occurred to me that I had been deceived: this was not a child, this was a woman. The smile pressed behind her fingers, the way of her nod, so brief, like my mother when father scolded her: the face inscrutable, but something—maybe spirit—shrank visibly, like a piece of silk in water. I was disappointed; Kiyoko-san's soul was barricaded in her unenchanting appearance and the smile she fenced behind her fingers.

She started school from third grade, one below me, and as it turned out, she quickly passed me by. There wasn't much I could help her with except to drill her on pronunciation—the "L" and "R" sounds. Every morning walking to our rural school: land, leg, library, loan, lot; every afternoon returning home: ran, rabbit, rim, rinse, roll. That was the extent of our communication; friendly but uninteresting.

One particularly cold November night—the wind outside was icy; I was sitting on my bed, my brother's and mine, oiling the cracks in my chapped hands by lamplight—someone rapped urgently at our door. It was Kiyoko-san; she was hysterical, she wore no wrap, her teeth were chattering, and except for the thin straw zori, her feet were bare. My mother led her to the kitchen, started a pot of tea, and gestured to my brother and me to retire. I lay very still but because of my brother's restless tossing and my father's snoring, was unable to hear much. I was aware, though, that drunken and savage brawling had brought Kiyoko-san to us. Presently they came to the bedroom. I feigned sleep. My mother gave Kiyoko-san a gown and pushed me over to make room for her. My mother spoke firmly: "Tomorrow you will return to them; you must not leave them again. They are your people." I could almost feel Kiyoko-san's short nod.

All night long I lay cramped and still, afraid to intrude into her hulking back. Two or three times her icy feet jabbed into mine and quickly retreated. In the morning I found my mother's gown neatly folded on the spare pillow. Kiyoko-san's place in bed was cold.

She never came to weep at our house again but I know she cried: her eyes were often swollen and red. She stopped much of her giggling and routinely pressed her fingers to her mouth. Our daily pronunciation drill petered off from lack of interest. She walked silently with her shoulders hunched, grasping her books with both arms, and when I spoke to her in my halting Japanese, she absently corrected my prepositions.

Spring comes early in the Valley; in February the skies are clear though the air is still cold. By March, winds are vigorous and warm and wild flowers dot the desert floor, cockleburs are green and not yet tenacious, the sand is crusty underfoot, everywhere there is a smell of things growing and the first tomatoes are showing green and bald.

As the weather changed, Kiyoko-san became noticeably more cheerful, Mr. Oka, who hated so to drive, could often be seen steering his dusty old Ford over the road that passes our house, and Kiyoko-san sitting in front would sometimes wave gaily to us. Mrs. Oka was never with them. I thought of these trips as the westernizing of Kiyoko-san: with a permanent wave, her straight black hair became tangles of tiny frantic curls; between her textbooks she carried copies of *Modern Screen* and *Photoplay*, her clothes were gay with print and piping, and she bought a pair of brown suede shoes with alligator trim. I can see her now picking her way gingerly over the deceptive white peaks of alkaline crust.

At first my mother watched their coming and going with vicarious pleasure, "Probably off to a picture show; the stores are all closed at this hour," she might say. Later her eyes would get distant and she would muse, "They've left her home again; Mrs. Oka is alone again, the poor woman."

Now when Kiyoko-san passed by or came in with me on her way home, my mother would ask about Mrs. Oka—how is she, how does she occupy herself these rainy days, or these windy or warm or cool days. Often the answers were polite: "Thank you, we are fine," but sometimes Kiyoko-san's upper lip would pull over her teeth, and her voice would become very soft and she would say, "Drink, always drinking and fighting." And those times my mother would invariably say, "Endure, soon you will be marrying and going away."

Once a young truck driver delivered crates at the Oka farm and he dropped back to our place to tell my father that Mrs. Oka had lurched behind his truck while he was backing up, and very nearly let him kill her. Only the daughter pulling her away saved her, he said. Thoroughly unnerved, he stopped to rest himself and talk about it. Never, never, he said in wide-eyed wonder, had he seen a drunken Japanese woman. My father nodded gravely, "Yes, it's unusual," he said and drummed his knee with his fingers.

Evenings were longer now, and when my mother's migraines drove me from the house in unbearable self-pity, I would take walks in the desert. One night with the warm wind against me, the dune primrose and yellow poppies closed and fluttering, the greasewood swaying in languid orbit, I lay on the white sand beneath a shrub and tried to disappear.

A voice sweet and clear cut through the half-dark of the evening:

Red lips press against a glass
Drink the purple wine
      And the soul shall dance

Mrs. Oka appeared to be gathering flowers. Bending, plucking, standing, searching, she added to a small bouquet she clasped. She held them away; she looked at them slyly, lids lowered, demure, then in a sudden and sinuous movement, she broke into a stately dance. She stopped, gathered more flowers, and breathed deeply into them. Tossing her head, she laughed—softly, beautifully, from her dark throat. The picture of her imagined grandeur was lost to me, but the delusion that transformed the bouquet of tattered petals and sandy leaves, and the aloneness of a desert twilight into a fantasy that brought such joy and abandon made me stir with discomfort. The sound broke Mrs. Oka's dance. Her eyes grew large and her neck tense—like a cat on the prowl. She spied me in the bushes. A peculiar chill ran through me. Then abruptly and with childlike delight, she scattered the flowers around her and walked away singing:

Falling, falling, petals on a wind . . .

That was the last time I saw Mrs. Oka. She died before the spring harvest. It was pneumonia. I didn't attend the funeral, but my mother said it was sad. Mrs. Oka looked peaceful, and the minister expressed the irony of the long separation of Mother and Child and the short-lived reunion; hardly a year together, she said. We went to help Kiyoko-san address and stamp those black-bordered acknowledgments.

When harvest was over, Mr. Oka and Kiyoko-san moved out of the Valley. We never heard from them or saw them again, and I suppose in a large city, Mr. Oka found some sort of work, perhaps a janitor or dishwasher and Kiyoko-san grew up and found someone to marry.

[1974]

Journal Entry

Have you ever identified with the underdog or the outsider? If so, describe the experience and what you learned from it.

Textual Considerations

1. Masako characterizes Mrs. Oka as "different." Do you agree? What makes her different? How do the narrator's impressions of her change as the story develops?
2. What new aspects of Mrs. Oka's personality are revealed as the narrator watches her dance and sing at the end of the story?
3. Characterize the narrator's mother. What is her attitude toward Mrs. Oka? Is there any evidence that she is oppressed by her environment? Explain.
4. What is Kiyoko-san's role in the story? How does the narrator's mother relate to her? What part does she play in the narrator's life? Is she in any sense a **foil** to Masako? Cite evidence.
5. Describe the setting of Yamauchi's story and its many references to time elements. To what extent does place and time relate to the characters' identity and expectations?

Cultural Contexts

1. Discuss with your group the nature of the conflicts that emerge in the story. To what extent would your group classify them as cultural, as Mrs. Oka's inability to fit in her Japanese community, or as generational—illustrated by Mrs. Oka's relationship with her husband's daughter? Can your group reach a consensus about the nature of the conflicts?
2. What significance is there in Masako's decision, as the only Nisei (children of immigrant Japanese parents, second generation) to break the silence and tell Mrs. Oka's story? What makes her story worth telling? How do you interpret the last paragraph of the narrative?

Edith Wharton

Roman Fever

I

From the table at which they had been lunching two American ladies of ripe but well-cared-for middle age moved across the lofty terrace of the Roman restaurant and, leaning on its parapet, looked first at each other, and then down on the outspread glories of the Palatine and the Forum, with the same expression of vague but benevolent approval.

As they leaned there a girlish voice echoed up gaily from the stairs leading to the court below. "Well, come along, then," it cried, not to them but to an invisible companion, "and let's leave the young things to their knitting"; and a voice as fresh laughed back: "Oh, look here, Babs, not actually *knitting*—" "Well, I mean figuratively," rejoined the first. "After all, we haven't left our poor parents much else to do. . . ." and at that point the turn of the stairs engulfed the dialogue.

The two ladies looked at each other again, this time with a tinge of smiling embarrassment, and the smaller and paler one shook her head and colored slightly.

"Barbara!" she murmured, sending an unheard rebuke after the mocking voice in the stairway.

The other lady, who was fuller, and higher in color, with a small determined nose supported by vigorous black eyebrows, gave a good-humored laugh. "That's what our daughters think of us!"

Her companion replied by a deprecating gesture. "Not of us individually. We must remember that. It's just the collective modern idea of Mothers. And you see—" Half-guiltily she drew from her handsomely mounted black handbag a twist of crimson silk run through by two fine knitting needles. "One never knows," she murmured. "The new system has certainly given us a good deal of time to kill; and sometimes I get tired just looking—even at this." Her gesture was now addressed to the stupendous scene at their feet.

The dark lady laughed again, and they both relapsed upon the view, contemplating it in silence, with a sort of diffused serenity which might have been borrowed from the spring effulgence of the Roman skies. The luncheon hour was long past, and the two had their end of the vast terrace to themselves. At its opposite extremity a few groups, detained by a lingering look at the outspread city, were gathering up guidebooks and fumbling for tips. The last of them scattered, and the two ladies were alone on the air-washed height.

"Well, I don't see why we shouldn't just stay here," said Mrs. Slade, the lady of the high color and energetic brows. Two derelict basket chairs stood near and she pushed them into the angle of the parapet, and settled herself in one, her gaze upon the Palatine. "After all, it's still the most beautiful view in the world."

"It always will be, to me," assented her friend Mrs. Ansley, with so slight a stress on the "me" that Mrs. Slade, though she noticed it, wondered if it were not merely accidental, like the random underlinings of old-fashioned letter writers.

"Grace Ansley was always old-fashioned," she thought; and added aloud, with a retrospective smile: "It's a view we've both been familiar with for a good many years. When we first met here we were younger than our girls are now. You remember?"

"Oh, yes, I remember," murmured Mrs. Ansley, with the same undefinable stress. "There's that headwaiter wondering," she interpolated. She was evidently far less sure than her companion of herself and of her rights in the world.

"I'll cure him of wondering," said Mrs. Slade, stretching her hand toward a bag as discreetly opulent-looking as Mrs. Ansley's. Signing to the headwaiter, she explained that she and her friend were old lovers of Rome, and would like to spend the end of the afternoon looking down on the view—that is, if it did not disturb the service? The headwaiter, bowing over her gratuity, assured her that the ladies were most welcome, and would be still more so if they would condescend to remain for dinner. A full-moon night, they would remember. . . .

Mrs. Slade's black brows drew together, as though references to the moon were out of place and even unwelcome. But she smiled away her frown as the headwaiter retreated. "Well, why not? We might do worse. There's no knowing, I suppose, when the girls will be back. Do you even know back from *where*? I don't!"

Mrs. Ansley again colored slightly. "I think those young Italian aviators we met at the Embassy invited them to fly to Tarquinia for tea. I suppose they'll want to wait and fly back by moonlight."

"Moonlight—moonlight! What a part it still plays. Do you suppose they're as sentimental as we were?"

"I've come to the conclusion that I don't in the least know what they are," said Mrs. Ansley. "And perhaps we didn't know much more about each other."

"No; perhaps we didn't."

Her friend gave her a shy glance. "I never should have supposed you were sentimental, Alida."

"Well, perhaps I wasn't." Mrs. Slade drew her lids together in retrospect; and for a few moments the two ladies, who had been intimate since childhood, reflected how little they knew each other. Each one, of course, had a label ready to attach to the other's name; Mrs. Delphin Slade, for instance, would have told herself, or anyone who asked her, that Mrs. Horace Ansley, twenty-five years ago, had been exquisitely lovely—no, you wouldn't believe it, would you? . . . though, of course, still charming, distinguished. . . . Well, as a girl she had been exquisite; far more beautiful than her daughter Barbara, though certainly Babs, according to the new standards at any rate, was more effective—had more *edge*, as they say. Funny where she got it, with those two nullities as parents. Yes; Horace Ansley was—well, just the duplicate of his wife. Museum specimens of old New York. Good-looking, irreproachable, exemplary. Mrs. Slade and Mrs. Ansley had lived opposite each other—actually as well as figuratively—for years. When the drawing-room curtains in No. 20 East 73rd Street were renewed, No. 23, across the way, was always aware of it. And of all the movings, buyings, travels, anniversaries, illnesses—the tame chronicle of an estimable pair. Little of it escaped Mrs. Slade. But she had grown bored with it by the time her husband made his big *coup* in Wall Street, and when they bought in upper Park Avenue had already begun to think: "I'd rather live

opposite a speakeasy for a change; at least one might see it raided." The idea of seeing Grace raided was so amusing that (before the move) she launched it at a
woman's lunch. It made a hit, and went the rounds—she sometimes wondered if it
had crossed the street, and reached Mrs. Ansley. She hoped not, but didn't much
mind. Those were the days when respectability was at a discount, and it did the irreproachable no harm to laugh at them a little.

A few years later, and not many months apart, both ladies lost their husbands.
There was an appropriate exchange of wreaths and condolences, and a brief renewal
of intimacy in the half-shadow of their mourning; and now, after another interval,
they had run across each other in Rome, at the same hotel, each of them the modest
appendage of a salient daughter. The similarity of their lot had again drawn them
together, lending itself to mild jokes, and the mutual confession that, if in old days it
must have been tiring to "keep up" with daughters, it was now, at times, a little dull
not to.

No doubt, Mrs. Slade reflected, she felt her unemployment more than poor
Grace ever would. It was a big drop from being the wife of Delphin Slade to being
his widow. She had always regarded herself (with a certain conjugal pride) as his
equal in social gifts, as contributing her full share to the making of the exceptional
couple they were: but the difference after his death was irremediable. As the wife of
the famous corporation lawyer, always with an international case or two on hand,
every day brought its exciting and unexpected obligation: the impromptu entertaining of eminent colleagues from abroad, the hurried dashes on legal business to London, Paris or Rome, where the entertaining was so handsomely reciprocated; the
amusement of hearing in her wake: "What, that handsome woman with the good
clothes and the eyes is Mrs. Slade—*the* Slade's wife? Really? Generally the wives of
celebrities are such frumps."

Yes; being *the* Slade's widow was a dullish business after that. In living up to
such a husband all her faculties had been engaged; now she had only her daughter
to live up to, for the son who seemed to have inherited his father's gifts had died
suddenly in boyhood. She had fought through that agony because her husband was
there, to be helped and to help; now, after the father's death, the thought of the boy
had become unbearable. There was nothing left but to mother her daughter; and
dear Jenny was such a perfect daughter that she needed no excessive mothering.
"Now with Babs Ansley I don't know that I *should* be so quiet," Mrs. Slade sometimes half-enviously reflected; but Jenny, who was younger than her brilliant friend,
was that rare accident, an extremely pretty girl who somehow made youth and prettiness seem as safe as their absence. It was all perplexing—and to Mrs. Slade a little
boring. She wished that Jenny would fall in love—with the wrong man, even; that
she might have to be watched, out-maneuvered, rescued. And instead, it was Jenny
who watched her mother, kept her out of drafts, made sure that she had taken her
tonic. . . .

Mrs. Ansley was much less articulate than her friend, and her mental portrait of
Mrs. Slade was slighter, and drawn with fainter touches. "Alida Slade's awfully brilliant; but not as brilliant as she thinks," would have summed it up; though she
would have added, for the enlightenment of strangers, that Mrs. Slade had been an

extremely dashing girl; much more so than her daughter, who was pretty, of course, and clever in a way, but had none of her mother's—well, "vividness," someone had once called it. Mrs. Ansley would take up current words like this, and cite them in quotation marks, as unheard-of audacities. No; Jenny was not like her mother. Sometimes Mrs. Ansley thought Alida Slade was disappointed; on the whole she had had a sad life. Full of failures and mistakes; Mrs. Ansley had always been rather sorry for her. . . .

So these two ladies visualized each other, each through the wrong end of her little telescope.

II

For a long time they continued to sit side by side without speaking. It seemed as though, to both, there was a relief in laying down their somewhat futile activities in the presence of the vast Memento Mori which faced them. Mrs. Slade sat quite still, her eyes fixed on the golden slope of the Palace of the Caesars, and after a while Mrs. Ansley ceased to fidget with her bag, and she too sank into meditation. Like many intimate friends, the two ladies had never before had occasion to be silent together, and Mrs. Ansley was slightly embarrassed by what seemed, after so many years, a new stage in their intimacy, and one with which she did not yet know how to deal.

Suddenly the air was full of that deep clangor of bells which periodically covers Rome with a roof of silver. Mrs. Slade glanced at her wristwatch. "Five o'clock already," she said, as though surprised.

Mrs. Ansley suggested interrogatively: "There's bridge at the Embassy at five." For a long time Mrs. Slade did not answer. She appeared to be lost in contemplation, and Mrs. Ansley thought the remark had escaped her. But after a while she said, as if speaking out of a dream: "Bridge, did you say? Not unless you want to. . . . But I don't think I will, you know."

"Oh, no," Mrs. Ansley hastened to assure her. "I don't care to at all. It's so lovely here; and so full of old memories, as you say." She settled herself in her chair, and almost furtively drew forth her knitting. Mrs. Slade took sideway note of this activity, but her own beautifully cared-for hands remained motionless on her knee.

"I was just thinking," she said slowly, "what different things Rome stands for to each generation of travelers. To our grandmothers, Roman fever; to our mothers, sentimental dangers—how we used to be guarded!—to our daughters, no more dangers than the middle of Main Street. They don't know it—but how much they're missing!"

The long golden light was beginning to pale, and Mrs. Ansley lifted her knitting a little closer to her eyes. "Yes; how we were guarded!"

"I always used to think," Mrs. Slade continued, "that our mothers had a much more difficult job than our grandmothers. When Roman fever stalked the streets it must have been comparatively easy to gather in the girls at the danger hour; but when you and I were young, with such beauty calling us, and the spice of disobedience thrown in, and no worse risk than catching cold during the cool hour after sunset, the mothers used to be put to it to keep us in—didn't they?"

She turned again toward Mrs. Ansley, but the latter had reached a delicate point in her knitting. "One, two, three—slip two; yes, they must have been," she assented, without looking up.

Mrs. Slade's eyes rested on her with a deepened attention. "She can knit—in the face of *this*! How like her. . . ."

Mrs. Slade leaned back, brooding, her eyes ranging from the ruins which faced her to the long green hollow of the Forum, the fading glow of the church fronts beyond it, and the outlying immensity of the Colosseum. Suddenly she thought: "It's all very well to say that our girls have done away with sentiment and moonlight. But if Babs Ansley isn't out to catch that young aviator—the one who's a Marchese—then I don't know anything. And Jenny has no chance beside her. I know that too. I wonder if that's why Grace Ansley likes the two girls to go everywhere together? My poor Jenny as a foil—!" Mrs. Slade gave a hardly audible laugh, and at the sound Mrs. Ansley dropped her knitting.

"Yes—?"

"I—oh, nothing. I was only thinking how your Babs carries everything before her. That Campolieri boy is one of the best matches in Rome. Don't look so innocent, my dear—you know he is. And I was wondering, ever so respectfully, you understand . . . wondering how two such exemplary characters as you and Horace had managed to produce anything quite so dynamic." Mrs. Slade laughed again, with a touch of asperity.

Mrs. Ansley's hands lay inert across her needles. She looked straight out at the great accumulated wreckage of passion and splendor at her feet. But her small profile was almost expressionless. At length she said: "I think you overrate Babs, my dear."

Mrs. Slade's tone grew easier. "No; I don't. I appreciate her. And perhaps envy you. Oh, my girl's perfect; if I were a chronic invalid I'd—well, I think I'd rather be in Jenny's hands. There must be times . . . but there! I always wanted a brilliant daughter . . . and never quite understood why I got an angel instead."

Mrs. Ansley echoed her laugh in a faint murmur. "Babs is an angel too."

"Of course—of course! But she's got rainbow wings. Well, they're wandering by the sea with their young men; and here we sit . . . and it all brings back the past a little too acutely."

Mrs. Ansley had resumed her knitting. One might almost have imagined (if one had known her less well, Mrs. Slade reflected) that, for her also, too many memories rose from the lengthening shadows of those august ruins. But no; she was simply absorbed in her work. What was there for her to worry about? She knew that Babs would almost certainly come back engaged to the extremely eligible Campolieri. "And she'll sell the New York house, and settle down near them in Rome, and never be in their way . . . she's much too tactful. But she'll have an excellent cook, and just the right people in for bridge and cocktails . . . and a perfectly peaceful old age among her grandchildren."

Mrs. Slade broke off this prophetic flight with a recoil of self-disgust. There was no one of whom she had less right to think unkindly than of Grace Ansley. Would she never cure herself of envying her? Perhaps she had begun too long ago.

She stood up and leaned against the parapet, filling her troubled eyes with the tranquilizing magic of the hour. But instead of tranquilizing her the sight seemed to increase her exasperation. Her gaze turned toward the Colosseum. Already its golden flank was drowned in purple shadow, and above it the sky curved crystal clear, without light or color. It was the moment when afternoon and evening hang balanced in mid-heaven.

Mrs. Slade turned back and laid her hand on her friend's arm. The gesture was so abrupt that Mrs. Ansley looked up, startled.

"The sun's set. You're not afraid, my dear?"

"Afraid—?"

"Of Roman fever or pneumonia? I remember how ill you were that winter. As a girl you had a very delicate throat, hadn't you?"

"Oh, we're all right up here. Down below, in the Forum, it does get deathly cold, all of a sudden . . . but not here."

"Ah, of course you know because you had to be so careful." Mrs. Slade turned back to the parapet. She thought: "I must make one more effort not to hate her." Aloud she said: "Whenever I look at the Forum from up here, I remember that story about a great-aunt of yours, wasn't she? A dreadfully wicked great-aunt?"

"Oh, yes; great-aunt Harriet. The one who was supposed to have sent her young sister out to the Forum after sunset to gather a night-blooming flower for her album. All our great-aunts and grandmothers used to have albums of dried flowers."

Mrs. Slade nodded. "But she really sent her because they were in love with the same man—"

"Well, that was the family tradition. They said Aunt Harriet confessed it years afterward. At any rate, the poor little sister caught the fever and died. Mother used to frighten us with the story when we were children."

"And you frightened *me* with it, that winter when you and I were here as girls. The winter I was engaged to Delphin."

Mrs. Ansley gave a faint laugh. "Oh, did I? Really frightened you? I don't believe you're easily frightened."

"Not often; but I was then. I was easily frightened because I was too happy. I wonder if you know what that means?"

"I—yes . . ." Mrs. Ansley faltered.

"Well, I suppose that was why the story of your wicked aunt made such an impression on me. And I thought: 'There's no more Roman fever, but the Forum is deathly cold after sunset—especially after a hot day. And the Colosseum's even colder and damper'."

"The Colosseum—?"

"Yes. It wasn't easy to get in, after the gates were locked for the night. Far from easy. Still, in those days it could be managed; it *was* managed, often. Lovers met there who couldn't meet elsewhere. You knew that?"

"I—I dare say. I don't remember."

"You don't remember? You don't remember going to visit some ruins or other one evening, just after dark, and catching a bad chill? You were supposed to have gone to see the moon rise. People always said that expedition was what caused your illness."

There was a moment's silence; then Mrs. Ansley rejoined: "Did they? It was all so long ago."

"Yes. And you got well again—so it didn't matter. But I suppose it struck your friends—the reason given for your illness, I mean—because everybody knew you were so prudent on account of your throat, and your mother took such care of you. . . . You *had* been out late sight-seeing, hadn't you, that night?"

"Perhaps I had. The most prudent girls aren't always prudent. What made you think of it now?"

Mrs. Slade seemed to have no answer ready. But after a moment she broke out: "Because I simply can't bear it any longer—!"

Mrs. Ansley lifted her head quickly. Her eyes were wide and very pale. "Can't bear what?"

"Why—your not knowing that I've always known why you went."

"Why I went—?"

"Yes. You think I'm bluffing, don't you? Well, you went to meet the man I was engaged to—and I can repeat every word of the letter that took you there."

While Mrs. Slade spoke Mrs. Ansley had risen unsteadily to her feet. Her bag, her knitting and gloves, slid in a panic-stricken heap to the ground. She looked at Mrs. Slade as though she were looking at a ghost.

"No, no—don't," she faltered out.

"Why not? Listen, if you don't believe me. 'My one darling, things can't go on like this. I must see you alone. Come to the Colosseum immediately after dark tomorrow. There will be somebody to let you in. No one whom you need fear will suspect'—but perhaps you've forgotten what the letter said?"

Mrs. Ansley met the challenge with an unexpected composure. Steadying herself against the chair she looked at her friend, and replied: "No; I know it by heart too."

"And the signature? 'Only *your* D.S.' Was that it? I'm right, am I? That was the letter that took you out that evening after dark?"

Mrs. Ansley was still looking at her. It seemed to Mrs. Slade that a slow struggle was going on behind the voluntarily controlled mask of her small quiet face. "I shouldn't have thought she had herself so well in hand," Mrs. Slade reflected, almost resentfully. But at this moment Mrs. Ansley spoke. "I don't know how you knew. I burnt that letter at once."

"Yes; you would, naturally—you're so prudent!" The sneer was open now. "And if you burnt the letter you're wondering how on earth I know what was in it. That's it, isn't it?"

Mrs. Slade waited, but Mrs. Ansley did not speak.

"Well, my dear, I know what was in that letter because I wrote it!"

"You wrote it?"

"Yes."

The two women stood for a minute staring at each other in the last golden light. Then Mrs. Ansley dropped back into her chair. "Oh," she murmured, and covered her face with her hands.

Mrs. Slade waited nervously for another word or movement. None came, and at length she broke out: "I horrify you."

Mrs. Ansley's hands dropped to her knee. The face they uncovered was streaked with tears. "I wasn't thinking of you. I was thinking—it was the only letter I ever had from him!"

"And I wrote it. Yes; I wrote it! But I was the girl he was engaged to. Did you happen to remember that?"

Mrs. Ansley's head drooped again. "I'm not trying to excuse myself . . . I remembered. . . ."

"And still you went?"

"Still I went."

Mrs. Slade stood looking down on the small bowed figure at her side. The flame of her wrath had already sunk, and she wondered why she had ever thought there would be any satisfaction in inflicting so purposeless a wound on her friend. But she had to justify herself.

"You do understand? I found out—and I hated you, hated you. I knew you were in love with Delphin—and I was afraid; afraid of you, of your quiet ways, your sweetness . . . your . . . well, I wanted you out of the way, that's all. Just for a few weeks; just till I was sure of him. So in a blind fury I wrote that letter . . . I don't know why I'm telling you now."

"I suppose," said Mrs. Ansley slowly, "it's because you've always gone on hating me."

"Perhaps. Or because I wanted to get the whole thing off my mind." She paused. "I'm glad you destroyed the letter. Of course I never thought you'd die."

Mrs. Ansley relapsed into silence, and Mrs. Slade, leaning above her, was conscious of a strange sense of isolation, of being cut off from the warm current of human communion. "You think me a monster!"

"I don't know. . . . It was the only letter I had, and you say he didn't write it?"

"Ah, how you care for him still!"

"I cared for that memory," said Mrs. Ansley.

Mrs. Slade continued to look down on her. She seemed physically reduced by the blow—as if, when she got up, the wind might scatter her like a puff of dust. Mrs. Slade's jealousy suddenly leapt up again at the sight. All these years the woman had been living on that letter. How she must have loved him, to treasure the mere memory of its ashes! The letter of the man her friend was engaged to. Wasn't it she who was the monster?

"You tried your best to get him away from me, didn't you? But you failed; and I kept him. That's all."

"Yes. That's all."

"I wish now I hadn't told you. I'd no idea you'd feel about it as you do; I thought you'd be amused. It all happened so long ago, as you say; and you must do me the justice to remember that I had no reason to think you'd ever taken it seriously. How could I, when you were married to Horace Ansley two months afterward? As soon as you could get out of bed your mother rushed you off to Florence and married you. People were rather surprised—they wondered at its being done so quickly; but I thought I knew. I had an idea you did it out of *pique*—to be able to say you'd got ahead of Delphin and me. Girls have such silly reasons for doing the most serious things. And your marrying so soon convinced me that you'd never really cared."

"Yes. I suppose it would," Mrs. Ansley assented.

The clear heaven overhead was emptied of all its gold. Dusk spread over it, abruptly darkening the Seven Hills. Here and there lights began to twinkle through the foliage at their feet. Steps were coming and going on the deserted terrace—waiters looking out of the doorway at the head of the stairs, then reappearing with trays and napkins and flasks of wine. Tables were moved, chairs straightened. A feeble string of electric lights flickered out. Some vases of faded flowers were carried away, and brought back replenished. A stout lady in a dust coat suddenly appeared, asking in broken Italian if anyone had seen the elastic band which held together her tattered Baedeker. She poked with her stick under the table at which she had lunched, the waiters assisting.

The corner where Mrs. Slade and Mrs. Ansley sat was still shadowy and deserted. For a long time neither of them spoke. At length Mrs. Slade began again: "I suppose I did it as a sort of joke—"

"A joke?"

"Well, girls are ferocious sometimes, you know. Girls in love especially. And I remember laughing to myself all that evening at the idea that you were waiting around there in the dark, dodging out of sight, listening for every sound, trying to get in—Of course I was upset when I heard you were so ill afterward."

Mrs. Ansley had not moved for a long time. But now she turned slowly toward her companion. "But I didn't wait. He'd arranged everything. He was there. We were let in at once," she said.

Mrs. Slade sprang up from her leaning position. "Delphin there? They let you in?—Ah, now you're lying!" she burst out with violence.

Mrs. Ansley's voice grew clearer, and full of surprise. "But of course he was there. Naturally he came—"

"Came? How did he know he'd find you there? You must be raving!"

Mrs. Ansley hesitated, as though reflecting. "But I answered the letter. I told him I'd be there. So he came."

Mrs. Slade flung her hands up to her face. "Oh, God—you answered! I never thought of your answering. . . ."

"It's odd you never thought of it, if you wrote the letter."

"Yes. I was blind with rage."

Mrs. Ansley rose, and drew her fur scarf about her. "It is cold here. We'd better go . . . I'm sorry for you," she said, as she clasped the fur about her throat.

The unexpected words sent a pang through Mrs. Slade. "Yes; we'd better go." She gathered up her bag and cloak. "I don't know why you should be sorry for me," she muttered.

Mrs. Ansley stood looking away from her toward the dusky secret mass of the Colosseum. "Well—because I didn't have to wait that night."

Mrs. Slade gave an unquiet laugh. "Yes; I was beaten there. But I oughtn't to begrudge it to you, I suppose. At the end of all these years. After all, I had everything;

I had him for twenty-five years. And you had nothing but that one letter that he didn't write."

Mrs. Ansley was again silent. At length she turned toward the door of the terrace. She took a step, and turned back, facing her companion.

"I had Barbara," she said, and began to move ahead of Mrs. Slade toward the stairway.

[1936]

Journal Entry

Has any place affected you as Rome did the lives of Mrs. Slade and Mrs. Ansley? Describe the place and your emotional responses to it.

Textual Considerations

1. Analyze the implications of Wharton's choice of Rome as the "site of memory." Consider, for example, whether the events that occur there could have taken place elsewhere.
2. What are the literal and figurative meanings of the story's title?
3. Find as many examples as you can of foreshadowing, and analyze Wharton's use of this technique to prepare the reader for the ending.
4. Why is the Colosseum such an important element in the setting of Wharton's story? Does it matter that Mrs. Ansley looks at the Colosseum when she makes her final confession to Mrs. Slade?
5. Contrast the attitudes of the protagonists toward aging and widowhood. To what extent are they reconciled to their present? How have their pasts affected their attitudes toward the present?

Cultural Contexts

1. "Roman Fever" explores the urge that human beings sometimes feel to return to the past in an attempt to reconcile its contradictions with the present. Working with your group, make a list of the features and traits that Mrs. Slade uses to unravel the mysteries and enigmas of the past.
2. Discuss with members of your group the deep implications of the "metaphor of place." To what extent can a place—a historical or cultural site or a new country, for example—influence people's ability to act and make choices? Think of the role place has played in your lives.

Frank O'Connor

First Confession

All the trouble began when my grandfather died and my grandmother— my father's mother—came to live with us. Relations in the one house are a strain at the best of times, but, to make matters worse, my grandmother was a real old countrywoman and quite unsuited to the life in town. She had a fat, wrinkled face, and, to Mother's great indignation, went round the house in bare feet—the boots had her crippled, she said. For dinner she had a jug of porter and a pot of potatoes with—sometimes—a bit of salt fish, and she poured out the potatoes on the table and ate them slowly, with great relish, using her fingers by way of a fork.

Now, girls are supposed to be fastidious, but I was the one who suffered most from this. Nora, my sister, just sucked up to the old woman for the penny she got every Friday out of the old-age pension, a thing I could not do. I was too honest, that was my trouble; and when I was playing with Bill Connell, the sergeant-major's son, and saw my grandmother steering up the path with the jug of porter sticking out from beneath her shawl I was mortified. I made excuses not to let him come into the house, because I could never be sure what she would be up to when we went in.

When Mother was at work and my grandmother made the dinner I wouldn't touch it. Nora once tried to make me, but I hid under the table from her and took the bread-knife with me for protection. Nora let on to be very indignant (she wasn't, of course, but she knew Mother saw through her, so she sided with Gran) and came after me. I lashed out at her with the bread-knife, and after that she left me alone. I stayed there till Mother came in from work and made my dinner, but when Father came in later Nora said in a shocked voice: "Oh, Dadda, do you know what Jackie did at dinnertime?" Then, of course, it all came out; Father gave me a flaking; Mother interfered, and for days after that he didn't speak to me and Mother barely spoke to Nora. And all because of that old woman! God knows, I was heart-scalded.

Then, to crown my misfortunes, I had to make my first confession and communion. It was an old woman called Ryan who prepared us for these. She was about the one age with Gran; she was well-to-do, lived in a big house on Montenotte, wore a black cloak and bonnet, and came every day to school at three o'clock when we should have been going home, and talked to us of hell. She may have mentioned the other place as well, but that could only have been by accident, for hell had the first place in her heart.

She lit a candle, took out a new half-crown, and offered it to the first boy who would hold one finger—only one finger!—in the flame for five minutes by the school clock. Being always very ambitious I was tempted to volunteer, but I thought it might look greedy. Then she asked were we afraid of holding one finger—only one finger!—in a little candle flame for five minutes and not afraid of burning all over in roasting hot furnaces for all eternity. "All eternity! Just think of that! A whole lifetime goes by and it's nothing, not even a drop in the ocean of your sufferings." The woman was really interesting about hell, but my attention was all fixed on the half-crown. At the end of the lesson she put it back in her purse. It was a great disappointment; a religious woman like that, you wouldn't think she'd bother about a thing like a half-crown.

Another day she said she knew a priest who woke one night to find a fellow he didn't recognize leaning over the end of his bed. The priest was a bit frightened—naturally enough—but he asked the fellow what he wanted, and the fellow said in a deep, husky voice that he wanted to go to confession. The priest said it was an awkward time and wouldn't it do in the morning, but the fellow said that last time he went to confession, there was one sin he kept back, being ashamed to mention it,

and now it was always on his mind. Then the priest knew it was a bad case, because
the fellow was after making a bad confession and committing a mortal sin. He got
up to dress, and just then the cock crew in the yard outside, and—lo and behold!—
when the priest looked round there was no sign of the fellow, only a smell of burning timber, and when the priest looked at his bed didn't he see the print of two
hands burned in it? That was because the fellow had made a bad confession. This
story made a shocking impression on me.

But the worst of all was when she showed us how to examine our conscience.
Did we take the name of the Lord, our God, in vain? Did we honor our father and
our mother? (I asked her did this include grandmothers and she said it did.) Did we
love our neighbors as ourselves? Did we covet our neighbor's goods? (I thought of
the way I felt about the penny that Nora got every Friday.) I decided that, between
one thing and another, I must have broken the whole ten commandments, all on
account of that old woman, and so far as I could see, so long as she remained in the
house I had no hope of ever doing anything else.

I was scared to death of confession. The day the whole class went I let on to
have a toothache, hoping my absence wouldn't be noticed; but at three o'clock, just
as I was feeling safe, along comes a chap with a message from Mrs. Ryan that I was
to go to confession myself on Saturday and be at the chapel for communion with
the rest. To make it worse, Mother couldn't come with me and sent Nora instead.

Now, that girl had ways of tormenting me that Mother never knew of. She held
my hand as we went down the hill, smiling sadly and saying how sorry she was for
me, as if she were bringing me to the hospital for an operation.

"Oh, God help us!" she moaned. "Isn't it a terrible pity you weren't a good boy?
Oh, Jackie, my heart bleeds for you! How will you ever think of all your sins? Don't
forget you have to tell him about the time you kicked Gran on the shin."

"Lemme go!" I said, trying to drag myself free of her. "I don't want to go to
confession at all."

"But sure, you'll have to go to confession, Jackie," she replied in the same
regretful tone. "Sure, if you didn't, the parish priest would be up to the house, looking for you. 'Tisn't, God knows, that I'm not sorry for you. Do you remember the
time you tried to kill me with the bread-knife under the table? And the language
you used to me? I don't know what he'll do with you at all, Jackie. He might have to
send you up to the bishop."

I remember thinking bitterly that she didn't know the half of what I had to
tell—if I told it. I knew I couldn't tell it, and understood perfectly why the fellow in
Mrs. Ryan's story made a bad confession; it seemed to me a great shame that people
wouldn't stop criticizing him. I remember that steep hill down to the church, and
the sunlit hillsides beyond the valley of the river, which I saw in the gaps between
the houses like Adam's last glimpse of Paradise.

Then, when she had maneuvered me down the long flight of steps to the chapel
yard, Nora suddenly changed her tone. She became the raging malicious devil she
really was.

"There you are!" she said with a yelp of triumph, hurling me through the church
door. "And I hope he'll give you the penitential psalms, you dirty little caffler."

I knew then I was lost, given up to eternal justice. The door with the colored-glass panels swung shut behind me, the sunlight went out and gave place to deep shadow, and the wind whistled outside so that the silence within seemed to crackle like ice under my feet. Nora sat in front of me by the confession box. There were a couple of old women ahead of her, and then a miserable-looking poor devil came and wedged me in at the other side, so that I couldn't escape even if I had the courage. He joined his hands and rolled his eyes in the direction of the roof, muttering aspirations in an anguished tone, and I wondered had he a grandmother too. Only a grandmother could account for a fellow behaving in that heartbroken way, but he was better off than I, for he at least could go and confess his sins; while I would make a bad confession and then die in the night and be continually coming back and burning people's furniture.

Nora's turn came, and I heard the sound of something slamming and then her voice as if butter wouldn't melt in her mouth, and then another slam, and out she came. God, the hypocrisy of women! Her eyes were lowered, her head was bowed, and her hands were joined very low down on her stomach, and she walked up the aisle to the side altar looking like a saint. You never saw such an exhibition of devotion; and I remembered the devilish malice with which she had tormented me all the way from our door, and wondered were all religious people like that, really. It was my turn now. With the fear of damnation in my soul I went in, and the confessional door closed of itself behind me.

It was pitch-dark and I couldn't see priest or anything else. Then I really began to be frightened. In the darkness it was a matter between God and me, and He had all the odds. He knew what my intentions were before I even started; I had no chance. All I had ever been told about confession got mixed up in my mind, and I knelt to one wall and said: "Bless me, father, for I have sinned; this is my first confession." I waited for a few minutes, but nothing happened, so I tried it on the other wall. Nothing happened there either. He had me spotted all right.

It must have been then that I noticed the shelf at about one height with my head. It was really a place for grown-up people to rest their elbows, but in my distracted state I thought it was probably the place you were supposed to kneel. Of course, it was on the high side and not very deep, but I was always good at climbing and managed to get up all right. Staying up was the trouble. There was room only for my knees, and nothing you could get a grip on but a sort of wooden moulding a bit above it. I held on to the moulding and repeated the words a little louder, and this time something happened all right. A slide was slammed back; a little light entered the box, and a man's voice said: "Who's there?"

"'Tis me, father," I said for fear he mightn't see me and go away again. I couldn't see him at all. The place the voice came from was under the moulding, about level with my knees, so I took a good grip of the moulding and swung myself down till I saw the astonished face of a young priest looking up at me. He had to put his head on one side to see me, and I had to put mine on one side to see him, so we were more or less talking to one another upside-down. It struck me as a queer way of hearing confessions, but I didn't feel it my place to criticize.

"Bless me, father, for I have sinned; this is my first confession," I rattled off all in one breath, and swung myself down the least shade more to make it easier for him.

"What are you doing up there?" he shouted in an angry voice, and the strain the politeness was putting on my hold of the moulding, and the shock of being addressed in such an uncivil tone, were too much for me. I lost my grip, tumbled, and hit the door an unmerciful wallop before I found myself flat on my back in the middle of the aisle. The people who had been waiting stood up with their mouths open. The priest opened the door of the middle box and came out, pushing his biretta back from his forehead; he looked something terrible. Then Nora came scampering down the aisle.

"Oh, you dirty little caffler!" she cried. "I might have known you'd do it. I might have known you'd disgrace me. I can't leave you out of my sight for one minute."

Before I could even get to my feet to defend myself she bent down and gave me a clip across the ear. This reminded me that I was so stunned I had even forgotten to cry, so that people might think I wasn't hurt at all, when in fact I was probably maimed for life. I gave a roar out of me.

"What's all this about?" the priest hissed, getting angrier than ever and pushing Nora off me. "How dare you hit the child like that, you little vixen?"

"But I can't do my penance with him, father," Nora cried, cocking an outraged eye up at him.

"Well, go and do it, or I'll give you some more to do," he said, giving me a hand up. "Was it coming to confession you were, my poor man?" he asked me.

"'Twas, father," said I with a sob.

"Oh," he said respectfully, "a big hefty fellow like you must have terrible sins. Is this your first?"

"'Tis, father," said I.

"Worse and worse," he said gloomily. "The crimes of a lifetime. I don't know will I get rid of you at all today. You'd better wait now till I'm finished with these old ones. You can see by the looks of them they haven't much to tell."

"I will, father," I said with something approaching joy.

The relief of it was really enormous. Nora stuck out her tongue at me from behind his back, but I couldn't even be bothered retorting. I knew from the very moment that man opened his mouth that he was intelligent above the ordinary. When I had time to think, I saw how right I was. It only stood to reason that a fellow confessing after seven years would have more to tell than people that went every week. The crimes of a lifetime, exactly as he said. It was only what he expected, and the rest was the cackle of old women and girls with their talk of hell, the bishop, and the penitential psalms. That was all they knew. I started to make my examination of conscience, and barring the one bad business of my grandmother it didn't seem so bad.

The next time, the priest steered me into the confession box himself and left the shutter back the way I could see him get in and sit down at the further side of the grille from me.

"Well, now," he said, "what do they call you?"

"Jackie, father," said I.

"And what's a-trouble to you, Jackie?"

"Father," I said, feeling I might as well get it over while I had him in good humor, "I had it all arranged to kill my grandmother."

He seemed a bit shaken by that, all right, because he said nothing for quite a while.

"My goodness," he said at last, "that'd be a shocking thing to do. What put that into your head?"

"Father," I said, feeling very sorry for myself, "she's an awful woman."

"Is she?" he asked. "What way is she awful?"

"She takes porter, father," I said, knowing well from the way Mother talked of it that this was a mortal sin, and hoping it would make the priest take a more favorable view of my case.

"Oh, my!" he said, and I could see he was impressed.

"And snuff, father," said I.

"That's a bad case, sure enough, Jackie," he said.

"And she goes round in her bare feet, father," I went on in a rush of self-pity, "and she knows I don't like her, and she gives pennies to Nora and none to me, and my da sides with her and flakes me, and one night I was so heart-scalded I made up my mind I'd have to kill her."

"And what would you do with the body?" he asked with great interest.

"I was thinking I could chop that up and carry it away in a barrow I have," I said.

"Begor, Jackie," he said, "do you know you're a terrible child?"

"I know, father," I said, for I was just thinking the same thing myself. "I tried to kill Nora too with a bread-knife under the table, only I missed her."

"Is that the little girl that was beating you just now?" he asked.

"'Tis, father."

"Someone will go for her with a bread-knife one day, and he won't miss her," he said rather cryptically. "You must have great courage. Between ourselves, there's a lot of people I'd like to do the same to but I'd never have the nerve. Hanging is an awful death."

"Is it, father?" I said with the deepest interest—I was always very keen on hanging. "Did you ever see a fellow hanged?"

"Dozens of them," he said solemnly. "And they all died roaring."

"Jay!" I said.

"Oh, a horrible death!" he said with great satisfaction. "Lots of the fellows I saw killed their grandmothers too, but they all said 'twas never worth it."

He had me there for a full ten minutes talking, and then walked out the chapel yard with me. I was genuinely sorry to part with him, because he was the most entertaining character I'd ever met in the religious line. Outside, after the shadow of the church, the sunlight was like the roaring of waves on a beach; it dazzled me; and when the frozen silence melted and I heard the screech of trams on the road my heart soared. I knew now I wouldn't die in the night and come back, leaving marks on my mother's furniture. It would be a great worry to her, and the poor soul had enough.

Nora was sitting on the railing, waiting for me, and she put on a very sour puss when she saw the priest with me. She was mad jealous because a priest had never come out of the church with her.

"Well," she asked coldly, after he left me, "what did he give you?"

"Three Hail Marys," I said.

"Three Hail Marys," she repeated incredulously. "You mustn't have told him anything."

"I told him everything," I said confidently.

"About Gran and all?"

"About Gran and all."

(All she wanted was to be able to go home and say I'd made a bad confession.)

"Did you tell him you went for me with the bread-knife?" she asked with a frown.

"I did to be sure."

"And he only gave you three Hail Marys?"

"That's all."

She slowly got down from the railing with a baffled air. Clearly, this was beyond her. As we mounted the steps back to the main road she looked at me suspiciously.

"What are you sucking?" she asked.

"Bullseyes."

"Was it the priest gave them to you?"

"'Twas."

"Lord God," she wailed bitterly, "some people have all the luck! 'Tis no advantage to anybody trying to be good. I might just as well be a sinner like you."

[1951]

Journal Entry

What associations, memories, and emotions from your own experience with religion can you bring to your reading of this text?

Textual Considerations

1. The story, a recollection of a childhood experience, is told in the past tense from a first-person point of view. What are the advantages of this narrative technique? How might the story differ if Nora were to tell it? Explain.
2. Focus on O'Connor's use of humor. How does it affect the story's meaning? Cite two passages, and explain how the humor is achieved.
3. Characterize Jackie and speculate as to why he is obsessed with making a bad confession. How does this first experience affect his attitude toward the church?
4. Draw a character sketch of the priest. How old is he? Describe his personality traits. How does he react toward Nora and Jackie, the protagonist? Why does he give Jackie such a light penance?

5. Describe the confessional box. What atmosphere does it create? Why does it frighten Jackie but doesn't seem to frighten Nora? Explain.
6. Assume the persona of the protagonist and respond to his sister's statement, "I might just as well be a sinner like you."

Cultural Contexts

1. Evaluate the role of religion in the life of this community. Can your group relate to Jackie's fear of the confessional? Why or why not? To what extent have personal and communal attitudes toward religion changed since this story was written?
2. Discuss with your group the extent to which childhood memories affect people. To what extent are your childhood memories of family members similar to or different from one another's? How do childhood memories help to shape your sense of self?

Pär Lagerkvist

Father and I

When I was getting on toward ten, I remember, Father took me by the hand one Sunday afternoon, as we were to go out into the woods and listen to the birds singing. Waving good-bye to Mother, who had to stay at home and get the evening meal, we set off briskly in the warm sunshine. We didn't make any great to-do about this going to listen to the birds, as though it were something extra special or wonderful; we were sound, sensible people. Father and I, brought up with nature and used to it. There was nothing to make a fuss about. It was just that it was Sunday afternoon and Father was free. We walked along the railway line, where people were not allowed to go as a rule, but Father worked on the railway and so he had a right to. By doing this we could get straight into the woods, too, without going a round-about way.

Soon the bird song began and all the rest. There was a twittering of finches and willow warblers, thrushes and sparrows in the bushes, the hum that goes on all around you as soon as you enter a wood. The ground was white with wood anemones, the birches had just come out into leaf, and the spruces had fresh shoots; there were scents on all sides, and underfoot the mossy earth lay steaming in the sun. There was noise and movement everywhere; bumblebees came out of their holes, midges swarmed wherever it was marshy, and birds darted out of the bushes to catch them and back again as quickly.

All at once a train came rushing along and we had to go down on to the embankment. Father hailed the engine driver with two fingers to his Sunday hat and the driver saluted and extended his hand. It all happened quickly; then on we went, taking big strides so as to tread on the sleepers and not in the gravel, which was heavy going and rough on the shoes. The sleepers sweated tar in the heat, everything smelled, grease and meadowsweet, tar and heather by turns. The rails glinted in the sun. On either side of the line were telegraph poles, which sang as you passed them. Yes, it was a lovely day. The sky was quite clear, not a cloud to be seen, and there couldn't be any, either, on a day like this, from what Father said.

After a while we came to a field of oats to the right of the line, where a crofter we knew had a clearing. The oats had come up close and even. Father scanned them with an expert eye and I could see he was satisfied. I knew very little about such things, having been born in a town. Then we came to the bridge over a stream, which most of the time had no water to speak of but which now was in full spate. We held hands so as not to fall down between the sleepers. After that it is not long before you come to the platelayer's cottage lying embedded in greenery, apple trees and gooseberry bushes. We called in to see them and were offered milk, and saw their pig and hens and fruit trees in blossom; then we went on. We wanted to get to the river, for it was more beautiful there than anywhere else; there was something special about it, as farther upstream it flowed past where Father had lived as a child. We usually liked to come as far as this before we turned back, and today, too, we got there after a good walk. It was near the next station, but we didn't go so far. Father just looked to see that the semaphore was right—he thought of everything.

We stopped by the river, which murmured in the hot sun, broad and friendly. The shady trees hung along the banks and were reflected in the backwater. It was all fresh and light here; a soft breeze was blowing off the small lakes higher up. We climbed down the slope and walked a little way along the bank, Father pointing out the spots for fishing. He had sat here on the stones as a boy, waiting for perch all day long; often there wasn't even a bite, but it was a blissful life. Now he didn't have time. We hung about on the bank for a good while, making a noise, pushing out bits of bark for the current to take, throwing pebbles out into the water to see who could throw farthest; we were both gay and cheerful by nature, Father and I. At last we felt tired and that we had had enough, and we set off for home.

It was beginning to get dark. The woods were changed—it wasn't dark there yet, but almost. We quickened our steps. Mother would be getting anxious and waiting with supper. She was always afraid something was going to happen. But it hadn't; it had been a lovely day, nothing had happened that shouldn't. We were content with everything.

The twilight deepened. The trees were so funny. They stood listening to every step we took, as if they didn't know who we were. Under one of them was a glow-worm. It lay down there in the dark staring at us. I squeezed Father's hand, but he didn't see the strange glow, just walked on. Now it was quite dark. We came to the bridge over the stream. It roared down there in the depths, horribly, as though it wanted to swallow us up; the abyss yawned below us. We trod carefully on the sleepers, holding each other tightly by the hand so as not to fall in. I thought Father would carry me across, but he didn't say anything; he probably wanted me to be like him and think nothing of it.

We went on. Father was so calm as he walked there in the darkness, with even strides, not speaking, thinking to himself. I couldn't understand how he could be so calm when it was so murky. I looked all around me in fear. Nothing but darkness everywhere. I hardly dared take a deep breath, for then you got so much darkness inside you, and that was dangerous. I thought it meant you would soon die. I remember quite well that's what I thought then. The embankment sloped steeply down, as though into chasms black as night. The telegraph poles rose, ghostly, to the sky. Inside them was a hollow rumble, as though someone were talking deep down in the earth and the white porcelain caps sat huddled fearfully together listening to it. It was all horrible. Nothing was right, nothing real; it was all so weird.

Hugging close to Father, I whispered, "Father, why is it so horrible when it's dark?"

"No, my boy, it's not horrible," he said, taking me by the hand.

"Yes, Father, it is."

"No, my child, you mustn't think that. Not when we know there is a God."

I felt so lonely, forsaken. It was so strange that only I was afraid, not Father, that we didn't think the same. And strange that what he said didn't help me and stop me from being afraid. Not even what he said about God helped me. I thought he too was horrible. It was horrible that he was everywhere here in the darkness, down under the trees, in the telegraph poles which rumbled—that must be he— everywhere. And yet you could never see him.

We walked in silence, each with his own thoughts. My heart contracted, as though the darkness had got in and was beginning to squeeze it.

Then, as we were rounding a bend, we suddenly heard a mighty roar behind us! We were awakened out of our thoughts in alarm. Father pulled me down on to the embankment, down into the abyss, held me there. Then the train tore past, a black train. All the lights in the carriages were out, and it was going at frantic speed. What sort of train was it? There wasn't one due now! We gazed at it in terror. The fire blazed in the huge engine as they shovelled in coal; sparks whirled out into the night. It was terrible. The driver stood there in the light of the fire, pale, motionless, his features as though turned to stone. Father didn't recognize him, didn't know who he was. The man just stared straight ahead, as though intent on rushing into the darkness, far into the darkness that had no end.

Beside myself with dread, I stood there panting, gazing after the furious vision. It was swallowed up by the night. Father took me up on to the line; we hurried home. He said, "Strange, what train was that? And I didn't recognize the driver." Then we walked on in silence.

But my whole body was shaking. It was for me, for my sake. I sensed what it meant: it was the anguish that was to come, the unknown, all that Father knew nothing about, that he wouldn't be able to protect me against. That was how this world, this life, would be for me; not like Father's, where everything was secure and certain. It wasn't a real world, a real life. It just hurtled, blazing, into the darkness that had no end.

[1954]

Journal Entry

What images, memories, associations, or experiences with the word *father* can you bring to your reading of this text?

Textual Considerations

1. What qualities of the family males does the narrator stress in the first paragraph?
2. At what point does the son begin to feel that his father cannot protect him from the unknown? What foreshadows his fear?
3. What objects and experiences that formed part of their daytime walk are repeated at night? How do they differ?
4. How does the narrator's use of pronouns differ in the day and night sections of the story? How does this difference underline meaning?
5. Why doesn't the father react to the dark in the same way as the son? What is his reaction to the black train?

Cultural Contexts

1. Review the last paragraph of the story with the members of your group. What does the black train symbolize for the son? Is it temporary? Will he one day be as "secure and certain" as his father? Explain.
2. "Father and I" is a story about the rite of passage when a child becomes an adolescent and realizes that he or she can no longer depend on parents for protection. Are the two trains effective metaphors for what the narrator wants to convey? What other metaphors might he have used? Create a list of such metaphors with your group.

Elie Wiesel

The Watch

For my bar mitzvah, I remember, I had received a magnificent gold watch. It was the customary gift for the occasion, and was meant to remind each boy that henceforth he would be held responsible for his acts before the Torah and its timeless laws.

But I could not keep my gift. I had to part with it the very day my native town became the pride of the Hungarian nation by chasing from its confines every single one of its Jews. The glorious masters of our municipality were jubilant: they were rid of us, there would be no more kaftans on the streets. The local newspaper was brief and to the point: from now on, it would be possible to state one's place of residence without feeling shame.

The time was late April, 1944.

In the early morning hours of that particular day, after a sleepless night, the ghetto was changed into a cemetery and its residents into gravediggers. We were digging feverishly in the courtyard, the garden, the cellar, consigning to the earth, temporarily we thought, whatever remained of the belongings accumulated by several generations, the sorrow and reward of long years of toil.

My father took charge of the jewelry and valuable papers. His head bowed, he was silently digging near the barn. Not far away, my mother, crouched on the damp ground, was burying the silver candelabra she used only on Shabbat eve; she was moaning softly, and I avoided her eyes. My sisters burrowed near the cellar. The youngest, Tziporah, had chosen the garden, like myself. Solemnly shoveling, she declined my help. What did she have to hide? Her toys? Her school notebooks? As for me, my only possession was my watch. It meant a lot to me. And so I decided to bury it in a dark, deep hole, three paces away from the fence, under a poplar tree whose thick, strong foliage seemed to provide a reasonably secure shelter.

All of us expected to recover our treasures. On our return, the earth would give them back to us. Until then, until the end of the storm, they would be safe.

Yes, we were naïve. We could not foresee that the very same evening, before the last train had time to leave the station, an excited mob of well-informed friendly neighbors would be rushing through the ghetto's wide-open houses and courtyards, leaving not a stone or beam unturned, throwing themselves upon the loot.

Twenty years later, standing in our garden, in the middle of the night, I remember the first gift, also the last, I ever received from my parents. I am seized by an irrational, irresistible desire to see it, to see if it is still there in the same spot, and if defying all laws of probability, it has survived—like me—by accident, not knowing how or why. My curiosity becomes obsession. I think neither of my father's money nor of my mother's candlesticks. All that matters in this town is my gold watch and the sound of its ticking.

Despite the darkness, I easily find my way in the garden. Once more I am the bar mitzvah child; here is the barn, the fence, the tree. Nothing has changed. To my left, the path leading to the Slotvino Rebbe's house. The Rebbe, though, had changed: the burning bush burned itself out and there is nothing left, not even smoke. What could he possibly have hidden the day we went away? His phylacteries? His prayer shawl? The holy scrolls inherited from his famous ancestor Rebbe Meirl of Premishlan? No, probably not even that kind of treasure. He had taken everything along, convinced that he was thus protecting not only himself but his disciples as well. He was proved wrong, the wonder rabbi.

But I mustn't think of him, not now. The watch, I must think of the watch. Maybe it was spared. Let's see, three steps to the right. Stop. Two forward. I recognize the place. Instinctively, I get ready to re-enact the scene my memory recalls. I fall on my knees. What can I use to dig? There is a shovel in the barn; its door is never locked. But by groping around in the dark I risk stumbling and waking the people sleeping in the house. They would take me for a marauder, a thief, and hand me over to the police. They might even kill me. Never mind, I'll have to manage without a shovel. Or any other tool. I'll use my hands, my nails. But it is difficult; the soil is hard, frozen, it resists as if determined to keep its secret. Too bad, I'll punish it by being the stronger.

Feverishly, furiously, my hands claw the earth, impervious to cold, fatigue and pain. One scratch, then another. No matter. Continue. My nails inch ahead, my fingers dig in, I bear down, my every fiber participates in the task. Little by little the hole deepens. I must hurry. My forehead touches the ground. Almost. I break out in a cold sweat, I am drenched, delirious. Faster, faster. I shall rip the earth from end to end, but I must know. Nothing can stop or frighten me. I'll go to the bottom of my fear, to the bottom of night, but I will know.

What time is it? How long have I been here? Five minutes, five hours? Twenty years. This night was defying time. I was laboring to exhume not an object but time itself, the soul and memory of that time. Nothing could be more urgent, more vital.

Suddenly a shiver goes through me. A sharp sensation, like a bite. My fingers touch something hard, metallic, rectangular. So I have not been digging in vain. The garden is spinning around me, over me. I stand up to catch my breath. A moment later, I'm on my knees again. Cautiously, gently I take the box from its tomb. Here it is, in the palm of my hand: the last relic, the only remaining symbol of everything I had loved, of everything I had been. A voice inside me warns: Don't open it, it contains nothing but emptiness, throw it away and run. I cannot heed the warning; it is too late to turn back. I need to know, either way. A slight pressure of my thumb and the box opens. I stifle the cry rising in my throat: the watch is there. Quick, a match. And another. Fleetingly, I catch a glimpse of it. The pain is blinding: could this thing, this object, be my gift, my pride? My past? Covered with dirt and rust, crawling with worms, it is unrecognizable, revolting. Unable to move, wondering what to do, I remain staring at it with the disgust one feels for love betrayed or a body debased. I am angry with myself for having yielded to curiosity. But disappointment gives way to profound pity: the watch too lived through war and holocaust, the kind reserved for watches perhaps. In its way, it too is a survivor, a ghost infested with humiliating sores and obsolete memories. Suddenly I feel the urge to carry it to my lips, dirty as it is, to kiss and console it with my tears, as one might console a living being, a sick friend returning from far away and requiring much kindness and rest, especially rest.

I touch it, I caress it. What I feel, besides compassion, is a strange kind of gratitude. You see, the men I had believed to be immortal had vanished into fiery clouds. My teachers, my friends, my guides had all deserted me. While this thing, this nameless, lifeless thing had survived for the sole purpose of welcoming me on my return and providing an epilogue to my childhood. And there awakens in me a desire to confide in it, to tell it my adventures, and in exchange, listen to its own. What had happened in my absence: who had first taken possession of my house, my bed? Or rather, no; our confidences could wait for another time, another place: Paris, New York, Jerusalem. But first I would entrust it to the best jeweler in the world, so that the watch might recover its luster, its memory of the past.

It is growing late. The horizon is turning a deep red. I must go. The tenants will soon be waking, they will come down to the well for water. No time to lose. I stuff the watch into my pocket and cross the garden. I enter the courtyard. From under the porch a dog barks. And stops at once: he knows I am not a thief, anything but a thief. I open the gate. Halfway down the street I am overcome by violent remorse: I have just committed my first theft.

I turn around, retrace my steps through courtyard and garden. Again I find myself kneeling, as at Yom Kippur services, beneath the poplar. Holding my breath, my eyes refusing to cry, I place the watch back into its box, close the cover, and my first gift once more takes refuge deep inside the hole. Using both hands, I smoothly fill in the earth to remove all traces.

Breathless and with pounding heart, I reach the still deserted street. I stop and question the meaning of what I have just done. And find it inexplicable.

In retrospect, I tell myself that probably I simply wanted to leave behind me, underneath the silent soil, a reflection of my presence. Or that somehow I wanted to transform my watch into an instrument of delayed vengeance: one day, a child would play in the garden, dig near the tree and stumble upon a metal box. He would thus learn that his parents were usurpers, and that among the inhabitants of his town, once upon a time, there had been Jews and Jewish children, children robbed of their future.

The sun was rising and I was still walking through the empty streets and alleys. For a moment I thought I heard the chanting of schoolboys studying Talmud; I also thought I heard the invocations of Hasidim reciting morning prayers in thirty-three places at once. Yet above all these incantations, I heard distinctly, but as though coming from far away, the tick-tock of the watch I had just buried in accordance with Jewish custom. It was, after all, the very first gift that a Jewish child had once been given for his very first celebration.

Since that day, the town of my childhood has ceased being just another town. It has become the face of a watch.

[1964]

Journal Entry

Is there an object that you cherish as Wiesel did the gold watch? Describe why it has symbolic value for you.

Textual Considerations

1. What prompts Wiesel to dig up the watch twenty years later? What does he mean when he says that he was laboring to exhume "time itself, the soul and memory of that time"?
2. Discuss Wiesel's use of such literary devices as repetition, symbolism, and fragmented sentences to convey the narrator's attachment to his watch.
3. Identify the climactic scene in the text, and speculate on the meaning it carries for the narrator.
4. Except for the opening section of the essay, most of the narrative is written in the present tense. Where in the account of his return to his native town does Wiesel revert to the past tense? Why does he do so? What effect does he achieve?
5. Discuss whether the image of the neighbors looting the ghetto might have unconsciously influenced the protagonist to place the watch back inside the hole. What does this image, preceded by the expression "Yes, we were naïve," indicate about his attitude about human beings in the context of this story?

Cultural Contexts

1. Consider how "The Watch" explores the concept that human beings may personally be entrapped by a historical event. To what extent has the narrator in Wiesel's story come to terms with his historical past?
2. Discuss with your group the degree to which our personal past contributes to our present selves, and debate whether understanding our pasts is necessary for self-real-ization. Is it important to write about significant past experiences? What consensus did your group reach?

Ernest J. Gaines

The Sky Is Gray

1

Go'n be coming in a few minutes. Coming round that bend down there full speed. And I'm go'n get out my handkerchief and wave it down, and we go'n get on it and go.

I keep on looking for it, but Mama don't look that way no more. She's looking down the road where we just come from. It's a long old road, and far's you can don't see nothing but gravel. You got dry weeds on both sides, too, and you got trees on both sides, and fences on both sides, too. And you got cows in the pastures and they standing close together. And when we was coming out here to catch the bus I seen the smoke coming out of the cows's noses.

I look at my mama and I know what she's thinking. I been with Mama so much, just me and her, I know what she's thinking all the time. Right now it's home—Auntie and them. She's thinking if they got enough wood—if she left enough there to keep them warm till we get back. She's thinking if it go'n rain and if any of them have to go out in the rain. She's thinking 'bout the hog—if he go'n get out, and if Ty and Val be able to get him back in. She always worry like that when she leaves the house. She don't worry too much if she leave me there with the smaller ones, 'cause she know I'm go'n look after them and look after Auntie and everything else. I'm the oldest and she say I'm the man.

I look at my mama and I love my mama. She's wearing that black coat and that black hat and she's looking sad. I love my mama and I want to put my arm round her and tell her. But I'm not supposed to do that. She say that's weakness and that's cry-baby stuff, and she don't want no crybaby round her. She don't want you to be scared, either. 'Cause Ty's scared of ghosts and she's always whipping him. I'm scared of the dark, too, but I make 'tend I ain't. I make 'tend I ain't 'cause I'm the oldest, and I got to set a good sample for the rest. I can't ever be scared and I can't ever cry. And that's why I never said nothing 'bout my teeth. It's been hurting me and hurting me close to a month now, but I never said it. I didn't say it 'cause I didn't want act like a crybaby, and 'cause I know we didn't have enough money to go have it pulled. But, Lord, it been hurting me. And look like it wouldn't start till at night when you was trying to get yourself little sleep. Then soon's you shut your eyes—ummm-ummm, Lord, look like it go right down to your heartstring.

"Hurting, hanh?" Ty'd say.

I'd shake my head, but I wouldn't open my mouth for nothing. You open your mouth and let that wind in, and it almost kill you.

I'd just lay there and listen to them snore. Ty there, right 'side me, and Auntie and Val over by the fireplace. Val younger than me and Ty, and he sleeps with Auntie. Mama sleeps round the other side with Louis and Walker.

I'd just lay there and listen to them, and listen to that wind out there, and listen to that fire in the fireplace. Sometimes it'd stop long enough to let me get little rest. Sometimes it just hurt, hurt, hurt, Lord, have mercy.

2

Auntie knowed it was hurting me. I didn't tell nobody but Ty, 'cause we buddies and he ain't go'n tell anybody. But some kind of way Auntie found out. When she asked me, I told her no, nothing was wrong. But she knowed it all the time. She told me to mash up a piece of aspirin and wrap it in some cotton and jugg it down in that hole. I did it, but it didn't do no good. It stopped for a little while, and started right back again. Auntie wanted to tell Mama, but I told her, "Uh-uh." 'Cause I knowed we didn't have any money, and it just was go'n make her mad again. So Auntie told Monsieur Bayonne, and Monsieur Bayonne came over to the house and told me to kneel down 'side him on the fireplace. He put his finger in his mouth and made the Sign of the Cross on my jaw. The tip of Monsieur Bayonne's finger is some hard, cause he's always playing on that guitar. If we sit outside at night we can always hear Monsieur Bayonne playing on his guitar. Sometimes we leave him out there playing on the guitar.

Monsieur Bayonne made the Sign of the Cross over and over on my jaw, but that didn't do no good. Even when he prayed and told me to pray some, too, that tooth still hurt me.

"How you feeling?" he say.

"Same," I say.

He kept on praying and making the Sign of the Cross and I kept on praying, too.

"Still hurting?" he say.

"Yes, sir."

Monsieur Bayonne mashed harder and harder on my jaw. He mashed so hard he almost pushed me over on Ty. But then he stopped.

"What kind of prayers you praying, boy?" he say.

"Baptist," I say.

"Well, I'll be—no wonder that tooth still killing him. I'm going one way and he pulling the other. Boy, don't you know any Catholic prayers?"

"I know 'Hail Mary,'" I say.

"Then you better start saying it."

"Yes, sir."

He started mashing on my jaw again, and I could hear him praying at the same time. And, sure enough, after awhile it stopped hurting me.

Me and Ty went outside where Monsieur Bayonne's two hounds was and we started playing with them. "Let's go hunting," Ty say. "All right," I say; and we went on back in the pasture. Soon the hounds got on a trail, and me and Ty followed them all 'cross the pasture and then back in the woods, too. And then they cornered this little old rabbit and killed him, and me and Ty made them get back, and we picked up the rabbit and started on back home. But my tooth had started hurting me again. It was hurting me plenty now, but I wouldn't tell Monsieur Bayonne. That night I didn't sleep a bit, and first thing in the morning Auntie told me to go back and let Monsieur Bayonne pray over me some more. Monsieur Bayonne was in his kitchen making coffee when I got there. Soon's he seen me he knowed what was wrong.

"All right, kneel down there 'side that stove," he say. "And this time make sure you pray Catholic. I don't know nothing 'bout that Baptist, and I don't want know nothing 'bout him."

3

Last night Mama say, "Tomorrow we going to town."

"It ain't hurting me no more," I say. "I can eat anything on it."

"Tomorrow we going to town," she say.

And after she finished eating, she got up and went to bed. She always go to bed early now. 'Fore Daddy went in the Army, she used to stay up late. All of us sitting out on the gallery or round the fire. But now, look like soon's she finish eating she go to bed.

This morning when I woke up, her and Auntie was standing 'fore the fireplace. She say: "Enough to get there and get back. Dollar and a half to have it pulled. Twenty-five for me to go, twenty-five for him. Twenty-five for me to come back, twenty-five for him. Fifty cents left. Guess I get little piece of salt meat with that."

"Sure can use it," Auntie say. "White beans and no salt meat ain't white beans."

"I do the best I can," Mama say.

They was quiet after that, and I made 'tend I was still asleep.

"James, hit the floor," Auntie say.

I still made 'tend I was asleep. I didn't want them to know I was listening.

"All right," Auntie say, shaking me by the shoulder. "Come on. Today's the day."

I pushed the cover down to get out, and Ty grabbed it and pulled it back.

"You, too, Ty," Auntie said.

"I ain't getting no teef pulled," Ty say.

"Don't mean it ain't time to get up," Auntie say. "Hit it, Ty."

Ty got up grumbling.

"James, you hurry up and get in your clothes and eat your food," Auntie say. "What time y'all coming back?" she say to Mama.

"That 'leven o'clock bus," Mama say. "Got to get back in that field this evening."

"Get a move on you, James," Auntie say.

I went in the kitchen and washed my face, then I ate my breakfast. I was having bread and syrup. The bread was warm and hard and tasted good. And I tried to make it last a long time.

Ty came back there grumbling and mad at me.

"Got to get up," he say. "I ain't having no teefs pulled. What I got to be getting up for?"

Ty poured some syrup in his pan and got a piece of bread. He didn't wash his hands, neither his face, and I could see that white stuff in his eyes.

"You the one getting your teef pulled," he say. "What I got to get up for. I bet if I was getting a teef pulled, you wouldn't be getting up. Shucks; syrup again. I'm getting tired of this old syrup. Syrup, syrup, syrup. I'm go'n take with the sugar diabetes. I want me some bacon sometime."

"Go out in the field and work and you can have your bacon," Auntie say. She stood in the middle door looking at Ty. "You better be glad you got syrup. Some people ain't got that—hard's time is."

"Shucks," Ty say. "How can I be strong."

"I don't know too much 'bout your strength," Auntie say; "but I know where you go'n be hot at, you keep that grumbling up. James, get a move on you; your mama waiting."

I ate my last piece of bread and went in the front room. Mama was standing 'fore the fireplace warming her hands. I put on my coat and cap, and we left the house.

4

I look down there again, but it still ain't coming. I almost say, "It ain't coming yet," but I keep my mouth shut. 'Cause that's something else she don't like. She don't like for you to say something just for nothing. She can see it ain't coming. I can see it ain't coming, so why say it ain't coming. I don't say it, I turn and look at the river that's back of us. It's so cold the smoke's just raising up from the water. I see a bunch of pool-doos not too far out—just on the other side the lilies. I'm wondering if you can eat pool-doos. I ain't too sure, 'cause I ain't never ate none. But I done ate owls and blackbirds, and I done ate redbirds, too. I didn't want to kill the redbirds, but she made me kill them. They had two of them back there. One in my trap, one in Ty's trap. Me and Ty was go'n play with them and let them go, but she made me kill them 'cause we needed the food.

"I can't," I say. "I can't."

"Here," she say. "Take it."

"I can't," I say. "I can't. I can't kill him, Mama, please."

"Here," she say. "Take this fork, James."

"Please, Mama, I can't kill him," I say.

I could tell she was go'n hit me. I jerked back, but I didn't jerk back soon enough.

"Take it," she say.

I took it and reached in for him, but he kept on hopping to the back.

"I can't, Mama," I say. The water just kept on running down my face. "I can't," I say.

"Get him out of there," she say.

I reached in for him and he kept on hopping to the back. Then I reached in farther, and he pecked me on the hand.

"I can't, Mama," I say.

She slapped me again.

I reached in again, but he kept on hopping out my way. Then he hopped to one side and I reached there. The fork got him on the leg and I heard his leg pop. I pulled my hand out 'cause I had hurt him.

"Give it here," she say, and jerked the fork out of my hand.

She reached in and got the little bird right in the neck. I heard the fork go in his neck, and I heard it go in the ground. She brought him out and helt him right in front of me.

"That's one," she say. She shook him off and gived me the fork. "Get the other one."

"I can't, Mama," I say. "I'll do anything, but don't make me do that."

She went to the corner of the fence and broke the biggest switch over there she could find. I knelt 'side the trap, crying.

"Get him out of there," she say.

"I can't, Mama."

She started hitting me 'cross the back. I went down on the ground, crying.

"Get him," she say.

"Octavia?" Auntie say.

'Cause she had come out of the house and she was standing by the tree looking at us.

"Get him out of there," Mama say.

"Octavia," Auntie say, "explain to him. Explain to him. Just don't beat him. Explain to him."

But she hit me and hit me and hit me.

I'm still young—ain't no more than eight; but I know now; I know why I had to do it. (They was so little, though. They was so little. I 'member how I picked the feathers off them and cleaned them and helt them over the fire. Then we all ate them. Ain't had but a little bitty piece each, but we all had a little bitty piece, and everybody just looked at me 'cause they was so proud.) Suppose she had to go away? That's why I had to do it. Suppose she had to go away like Daddy went away? Then who was go'n look after us? They had to be somebody left to carry on. I didn't know it then, but I know it now. Auntie and Monsieur Bayonne talked to me and made me see.

5

Time I see it I get out my handkerchief and start waving. It's still 'way down there, but I keep waving anyhow. Then it come up and stop and me and Mama get on. Mama tell me go sit in the back while she pay. I do like she say, and the people look at me. When I pass the little sign that say "White" and "Colored," I start looking for a seat. I just see one of them back there, but I don't take it, 'cause I want my mama to sit down herself. She comes in the back and sit down, and I lean on the seat. They got seats in the front, but I know I can't sit there, 'cause I have to sit back of the sign. Anyhow, I don't want to sit there if my mama go'n sit back here.

They got a lady sitting 'side my mama and she looks at me and smiles little bit. I smile back, but I don't open my mouth, 'cause the wind'll get in and make that tooth ache. The lady take out a pack of gum and reach me a slice, but I shake my head. The lady just can't understand why a little boy'll turn down gum, and she reach me a slice again. This time I point to my jaw. The lady understands and smiles little bit, and I smile little bit, but I don't open my mouth, though.

They got a girl sitting 'cross from me. She got on a red overcoat and her hair's plaited in one big plait. First, I make 'tend I don't see her over there but then I start looking at her little bit. She make 'tend she don't see me, either, but I catch her looking that way. She got a cold, and every now and then she h'ist that little handkerchief to her nose. She ought to blow it, but she don't. Must think she's too much a lady or something.

Every time she h'ist that little handkerchief, the lady 'side her say something in her ear. She shakes her head and lays her hands in her lap again. Then I catch her kind of looking where I'm at. I smile at her little bit. But think she'll smile back? Uh-uh. She just turn up her little old nose and turn her head. Well, I show her both of us can turn us head. I turn mine too and look out at the river.

The river is gray. The sky is gray. They have pool-doos on the water. The water is wavy, and the pool-doos go up and down. The bus go round a turn, and you got plenty trees hiding the river. Then the bus go round another turn, and I can see the river again.

I look toward the front where all the white people sitting. Then I look at that little old gal again. I don't look right at her, 'cause I don't want all them people to know I love her. I just look at her little bit, like I'm looking out that window over there. But she knows I'm looking that way, and she kind of look at me, too. The lady sitting 'side her catch her this time, and she leans over and says something in her ear.

"I don't love him nothing," that little old gal says out loud.

Everybody back there hear her mouth, and all of them look at us and laugh.

"I don't love you, either," I say. "So you don't have to turn up your nose, Miss."

"You the one looking," she say.

"I wasn't looking at you," I say. "I was looking out that window, there."

"Out that window, my foot," she say. "I seen you. Everytime I turned round you was looking at me."

"You must of been looking yourself if you seen me all them times," I say.

"Shucks," she say, "I got me all kind of boyfriends."

"I got girlfriends, too," I say.

"Well, I just don't want you getting your hopes up," she say.

I don't say no more to that little old gal cause I don't want have to bust her in the mouth. I lean on the seat where Mama sitting, and I don't even look that way no more. When we get to Bayonne, she jugg her little old tongue out at me. I make 'tend I'm go'n hit her, and she duck down 'side her mama. And all the people laugh at us again.

6

Me and Mama get off and start walking in town. Bayonne is a little bitty town. Baton Rouge is a hundred times bigger than Bayonne. I went to Baton Rouge once—me, Ty, Mama, and Daddy. But that was 'way back yonder, 'fore Daddy went in the Army. I wonder when we go'n see him again. I wonder when. Look like he ain't ever coming back home. . . . Even the pavement all cracked in Bayonne. Got grass shooting right out the sidewalk. Got weeds in the ditch, too; just like they got at home.

It's some cold in Bayonne. Look like it's colder than it is home. The wind blows in my face, and I feel that stuff running down my nose. I sniff. Mama says use that handkerchief. I blow my nose and put it back.

We pass a school and I see them white children playing in the yard. Big old red school, and them children just running and playing. Then we pass a café, and I see a bunch of people in there eating. I wish I was in there 'cause I'm cold. Mama tells me keep my eyes in front where they belong.

We pass stores that's got dummies, and we pass another café, and then we pass a shoe shop, and that bald-head man in there fixing on a shoe. I look at him and I butt into that white lady, and Mama jerks me in front and tells me stay there.

We come up to the courthouse, and I see the flag waving there. This flag ain't like the one we got at school. This one here ain't got but a handful of stars. One at school got a big pile of stars—one for every state. We pass it and we turn and there it is—the dentist office. Me and Mama go in, and they got people sitting everywhere you look. They even got a little boy in there younger than me.

Me and Mama sit on that bench, and a white lady come in there and ask me what my name is. Mama tells her and the white lady goes on back. Then I hear somebody hollering in there. Soon's that little boy hear him hollering, he starts hollering too. His mama pats him and pats him, trying to make him hush up, but he ain't thinkin' 'bout his mama.

The man that was hollering in there comes out holding his jaw. He is a big old man and he's wearing overalls and a jumper.

"Got it, hanh?" another man asks him.

The man shakes his head—don't want open his mouth.

"Man, I thought they was killing you in there," the other man says. "Hollering like a pig under a gate."

The man don't say nothing. He just heads for the door, and the other man follows him.

"John Lee," the white lady says. "John Lee Williams."

The little boy juggs his head down in his mama's lap and holler more now. His mama tells him go with the nurse, but he ain't thinking 'bout his mama. His mama tells him again, but he don't even hear her. His mama picks him up and takes him in there, and even when the white lady shuts the door I can still hear little old John Lee.

"I often wonder why the Lord let a child like that suffer," a lady says to my mama. The lady's sitting right in front of us on another bench. She's got on a white dress and a black sweater. She must be a nurse or something herself, I reckon.

"Not us to question," a man says.

"Sometimes I don't know if we shouldn't," the lady says.

"I know definitely we shouldn't," the man says. The man looks like a preacher. He's big and fat and he's got on a black suit. He's got a gold chain, too.

"Why?" the lady says.

"Why anything?" the preacher says.

"Yes," the lady says. "Why anything?"

"Not us to question," the preacher says.

The lady looks at the preacher a little while and looks at Mama again.

"And look like it's the poor who suffers the most," she says. "I don't understand it."

"Best not to even try," the preacher says. "He works in mysterious ways— wonders to perform."

Right then little John Lee bust out hollering, and everybody turn they head to listen.

"He's not a good dentist," the lady says. "Dr. Robillard is much better. But more expensive. That's why most of the colored people come here. The white people go to Dr. Robillard. Y'all from Bayonne?"

"Down the river," my mama says. And that's all she go'n say, 'cause she don't talk much. But the lady keeps on looking at her, and so she says, "Near Morgan."

"I see," the lady says.

7

"That's the trouble with the black people in this country today," somebody else says. This one here's sitting on the same side me and Mama's sitting, and he is kind of sitting in front of that preacher. He looks like a teacher or somebody that goes to college. He's got on a suit, and he's got a book that he's been reading. "We don't question is exactly our problem," he says. "We should question and question and question—question everything."

The preacher just looks at him a long time. He done put a toothpick or something in his mouth, and he just keeps on turning it and turning it. You can see he don't like that boy with that book.

"Maybe you can explain what you mean," he says.

"I said what I meant," the boy says. "Question everything. Every stripe, every star, every word spoken. Everything."

"It 'pears to me that this young lady and I was talking 'bout God, young man," the preacher says.

"Question Him, too," the boy says.

"Wait," the preacher says. "Wait now."

"You heard me right," the boy says. "His existence as well as everything else. Everything."

The preacher just looks across the room at the boy. You can see he's getting madder and madder. But mad or no mad, the boy ain't thinking 'bout him. He looks at that preacher just's hard's the preacher looks at him.

"Is this what they coming to?" the preacher says. "Is that what we educating them for?"

"You're not educating me," the boy says. "I wash dishes at night so that I can go to school in the day. So even the words you spoke need questioning."

The preacher just looks at him and shakes his head.

"When I come in this room and seen you there with your book, I said to myself, 'Here's an intelligent man.' How wrong a person can be."

"Show me one reason to believe in the existence of a God," the boy says.

"My heart tells me," the preacher says.

"'My heart tells me,'" the boy says. "'My heart tells me.' Sure, 'My heart tells me.' And as long as you listen to what your heart tells you, you will have only what the white man gives you and nothing more. Me, I don't listen to my heart. The purpose of the heart is to pump blood throughout the body, and nothing else."

"Who's your paw, boy?" the preacher says.

"Why?"

"Who is he?"

"He's dead."

"And your mom?"

"She's in Charity Hospital with pneumonia. Half killed herself, working for nothing."

"And 'cause he's dead and she's sick, you mad at the world?"

"I'm not mad at the world. I'm questioning the world. I'm questioning it with cold logic, sir. What do words like Freedom, Liberty, God, White, Colored mean? I want to know. That's why *you* are sending us to school, to read and to ask questions. And because we ask these questions, you call us mad. No sir, it is not us who are mad."

"You keep saying 'us'?"

"'Us.' Yes—us. I'm not alone."

The preacher just shakes his head. Then he looks at everybody in the room—everybody. Some of the people look down at the floor, keep from looking at him. I kind of look 'way myself, but soon's I know he done turn his head, I look that way again.

"I'm sorry for you," he says to the boy.

"Why?" the boy says. "Why not be sorry for yourself? Why are you so much better off than I am? Why aren't you sorry for these other people in here? Why not be sorry for the lady who had to drag her child into the dentist office? Why not be sorry for the lady sitting on that bench over there? Be sorry for them. Not for me. Some way or the other I'm going to make it."

"No, I'm sorry for you," the preacher says.

"Of course, of course," the boy says, nodding his head. "You're sorry for me because I rock that pillar you're leaning on."

"You can't ever rock the pillar I'm leaning on, young man. It's stronger than anything man can ever do."

"You believe in God because a man told you to believe in God," the boy says. "A white man told you to believe in God. And why? To keep you ignorant so he can keep his feet on your neck."

"So now we the ignorant?" the preacher says.

"Yes," the boy says. "Yes." And he opens his book again.

The preacher just looks at him sitting there. The boy done forgot all about him. Everybody else make 'tend they done forgot the squabble, too.

Then I see that preacher getting up real slow. Preacher's great big old man and he got to brace himself to get up. He comes over where the boy is sitting. He just stands there a little while looking down at him, but the boy don't raise his head.

"Get up, boy," preacher says.

The boy looks up at him, then he shuts his book real slow and stands up. Preacher just hauls back and hit him in the face. The boy falls back 'gainst the wall, but he straightens himself up and looks right back at that preacher.

"You forgot the other cheek," he says.

The preacher hauls back and hit him again on the other side. But this time the boy braces himself and don't fall.

"That hasn't changed a thing," he says.

The preacher just looks at the boy. The preacher's breathing real hard like he just run up a big hill. The boy sits down and opens his book again.

"I feel sorry for you," the preacher says. "I never felt so sorry for a man before."

The boy makes 'tend he don't even hear that preacher. He keeps on reading his book. The preacher goes back and gets his hat off the chair.

"Excuse me," he says to us. "I'll come back some other time. Y'all, please excuse me."

And he looks at the boy and goes out the room. The boy h'ist his hand up to his mouth one time to wipe 'way some blood. All the rest of the time he keeps on reading. And nobody else in there say a word.

8

Little John Lee and his mama come out the dentist office, and the nurse calls somebody else in. Then little bit later they come out, and the nurse calls another name. But fast's she calls somebody in there, somebody else comes in the place where we sitting, and the room stays full.

The people coming in now, all of them wearing big coats. One of them says something 'bout sleeting, another one says he hope not. Another one says he think it ain't nothing but rain. 'Cause, he says, rain can get awful cold this time of year.

All round the room they talking. Some of them talking to people right by them, some of them talking to people clear 'cross the room, some of them talking to anybody'll listen. It's a little bitty room, no bigger than us kitchen, and I can see everybody in there. The little old room's full of smoke, 'cause you got two old men smoking pipes over by that side door. I think I feel my tooth thumping me some, and I hold my breath and wait. I wait and wait, but it don't thump me no more. Thank God for that.

I feel like going to sleep, and I lean back 'gainst the wall. But I'm scared to go to sleep. Scared 'cause the nurse might call my name and I won't hear her. And Mama might go to sleep, too, and she'll be mad if neither one of us heard the nurse.

I look up at Mama. I love my mama. I love my mama. And when cotton come I'm go'n get her a new coat. And I ain't go'n get a black coat, either. I think I'm go'n get her a red one.

"They got some books over there," I say. "Want read one of them?"

Mama looks at the books, but she don't answer me.

"You got yourself a little man there," the lady says.

Mama don't say nothing to the lady, but she must've smiled, 'cause I seen the lady smiling back. The lady looks at me a little while, like she's feeling sorry for me.

"You sure got that preacher out here in a hurry," she says to that boy.

The boy looks up at her and looks in his book again. When I grow up I want be just like him. I want clothes like that and I want to keep a book with me, too.

"You really don't believe in God?" the lady says.

"No," he says.

"But why?" the lady says.

"Because the wind is pink," he says.

"What?" the lady says.

The boy don't answer her no more. He just reads in his book.

"Talking 'bout the wind is pink," that old lady says. She's sitting on the same bench with the boy and she's trying to look in his face. The boy makes 'tend the old lady ain't even there. He just keeps on reading. "Wind is pink," she says again. "Eh, Lord, what children go'n be saying next?"

The lady 'cross from us bust out laughing.

"That's a good one," she says. "The wind is pink. Yes sir, that's a good one."

"Don't you believe the wind is pink?" the boy says. He keeps his head down in the book.

"Course I believe it, honey," the lady says. "Course I do." She looks at us and winks her eye. "And what color is grass, honey?"

"Grass? Grass is black."

She bust out laughing again. The boy looks at her.

"Don't you believe grass is black?" he says.

The lady quits her laughing and looks him. Everybody else looking at him, too. The place quiet, quiet.

"Grass is green, honey," the lady says. "It was green yesterday, it's green today, and it's go'n be green tomorrow."

"How do you know it's green?"

"I know because I know."

"You don't know it's green," the boy says. "You believe it's green because someone told you it was green. If someone had told you it was black you'd believe it was black."

"It's green," the lady says. "I know green when I see green."

"Prove it's green," the boy says.

"Sure, now," the lady says. "Don't tell me it's coming to that."

"It's coming to just that," the boy says. "Words mean nothing. One means no more than the other."

"That's what it all coming to?" the old lady says. That old lady got on a turban and she got on two sweaters. She got a green sweater under a black sweater. I can see the green sweater 'cause some of the buttons on the other sweater's missing.

"Yes ma'am," the boy says. "Words mean nothing. Action is the only thing. Doing. That's the only thing."

"Other words, you want the Lord to come down here and show Hisself to you?" she says.

"Exactly, ma'am," he says.

"You don't mean that, I'm sure?" she says.

"I do, ma'am," he says.

"Done, Jesus," the old lady says, shaking her head.

"I didn't go 'long with that preacher at first," the other lady says; "but now—I don't know. When a person say the grass is black, he's either a lunatic or something's wrong."

"Prove to me that it's green," the boy says.

"It's green because the people say it's green."

"Those same people say we're citizens of these United States," the boy says.

"I think I'm a citizen," the lady says.

"Citizens have certain rights," the boy says. "Name me one right that you have. One right, granted by the Constitution, that you can exercise in Bayonne."

The lady don't answer him. She just looks at him like she don't know what he's talking 'bout. I know I don't.

"Things changing," she says.

"Things are changing because some black men have begun to think with their brains and not their hearts," the boy says.

"You trying to say these people don't believe in God?"

"I'm sure some of them do. Maybe most of them do. But they don't believe that God is going to touch these white people's hearts and change things tomorrow. Things change through action. By no other way."

Everybody sit quiet and look at the boy. Nobody says a thing. Then the lady 'cross the room from me and Mama just shakes her head.

"Let's hope that not all your generation feel the same way you do," she says.

"Think what you please, it doesn't matter," the boy says. "But it will be men who listen to their heads and not their hearts who will see that your children have a better chance than you had."

"Let's hope they ain't all like you, though," the old lady says. "Done forgot the heart absolutely."

"Yes ma'am, I hope they aren't all like me," the boy says. "Unfortunately, I was born too late to believe in your God. Let's hope that the ones who come after will have your faith—if not in your God, then in something else, something definitely that they can lean on. I haven't anything. For me, the wind is pink, the grass is black."

9

The nurse comes in the room where we all sitting and waiting and says the doctor won't take no more patients till one o'clock this evening. My mama jumps up off the bench and goes up to the white lady.

"Nurse, I have to go back in the field this evening," she says.

"The doctor is treating his last patient now," the nurse says. "One o'clock this evening."

"Can I at least speak to the doctor?" my mama asks.

"I'm his nurse," the lady says.

"My little boy's sick," my mama says. "Right now his tooth almost killing him."

The nurse looks at me. She's trying to make up her mind if to let me come in. I look at her real pitiful. The tooth ain't hurting me at all, but Mama says it is, so I make 'tend for her sake.

"This evening," the nurse says, and goes on back in the office.

"Don't feel 'jected, honey," the lady says to Mama. "I been round them a long time—they take you when they want to. If you was white, that's something else; but we the wrong color."

Mama don't say nothing to the lady, and me and her go outside and stand 'gainst the wall. It's cold out there. I can feel that wind going through my coat. Some of the other people come out of the room and go up the street. Me and Mama stand there a little while and we start walking. I don't know where we going. When we come to the other street we just stand there.

"You don't have to make water, do you?" Mama says.

"No, ma'am," I say.

We go on up the street. Walking real slow. I can tell Mama don't know where she's going. When we come to a store we stand there and look at the dummies. I look at a little boy wearing a brown overcoat. He's got on brown shoes, too. I look at my old shoes and look at his'n again. You wait till summer, I say.

Me and Mama walk away. We come up to another store and we stop and look at them dummies, too. Then we go on again. We pass a café where the white people in there eating. Mama tells me keep my eyes in front where they belong, but I can't help from seeing them people eat. My stomach starts to growling 'cause I'm hungry. When I see people eating, I get hungry; when I see a coat, I get cold.

A man whistles at my mama when we go by a filling station. She makes 'tend she don't even see him. I look back and I feel like hitting him in the mouth. If I was bigger, I say; if I was bigger, you'd see.

We keep on going. I'm getting colder and colder, but I don't say nothing. I feel that stuff running down my nose and I sniff.

"That rag," Mama says.

I get it out and wipe my nose. I'm getting cold all over now—my face, my hands, my feet, everything. We pass another little café, but this'n for white people, too, and we can't go in there, either. So we just walk. I'm so cold now I'm 'bout ready to say it. If I knowed where we was going I wouldn't be so cold, but I don't know where we going. We go, we go, we go. We walk clean out of Bayonne. Then we cross the street and we come back. Same thing I seen when I got off the bus this morning. Same old trees, same old walk, same old weeds, same old cracked pave— same old everything.

I sniff again.

"That rag," Mama says.

I wipe my nose real fast and jugg that handkerchief back in my pocket 'fore my hand gets too cold. I raise my head and I can see David's hardware store. When we come up to it, we go in I don't know why, but I'm glad.

It's warm in there. It's so warm in there you don't ever want to leave. I look for the heater, and I see it over by them barrels. Three white men standing round the heater talking in Creole. One of them comes over to see what my mama want.

"Got any axe handles?" she says.

Me, Mama and the white man start to the back, but Mama stops me when we come up to the heater. She and the white man go on. I hold my hands over the heater and look at them. They go all the way to the back, and I see the white man pointing to the axe handles 'gainst the wall. Mama takes one of them and shakes it like she's trying to figure how much it weighs. Then she rubs her hand over it from one end to the other end. She turns it over and looks at the other side, then she shakes it again, and shakes her head and puts it back. She gets another one and she does it just like she did the first one, then she shakes her head. Then she gets a brown one and do it that, too. But she don't like this one, either. Then she gets another one, but 'fore she shakes it or anything, she looks at me. Look like she's trying to say something to me, but I don't know what it is. All I know is I done got warm now and I'm feeling right smart better. Mama shakes this axe handle just like she did the others, and shakes her head and says something to the white man. The white man just looks at his pile of axe handles, and when Mama pass him to come to the front, the white man just scratch his head and follows her. She tells me come on and we go on and start walking again.

We walk and walk, and no time at all I'm cold again. Look like I'm colder now 'cause I can still remember how good it was back there. My stomach growls and I suck it in to keep Mama from hearing it. She's walking right 'side me, and it growls so loud you can hear it a mile. But Mama don't say a word.

10

When we come up to the courthouse, I look at the clock. It's got quarter to twelve. Mean we got another hour and a quarter to be out here in the cold. We go and stand 'side a building. Something hits my cap and I look up at the sky. Sleet's falling.

I look at Mama standing there. I want stand close 'side her, but she don't like that. She say that's crybaby stuff. She say you got to stand for yourself, by yourself.

"Let's go back to that office," she says.

We cross the street. When we get to the dentist office I try to open the door, but I can't. I twist and twist, but I can't. Mama pushes me to the side and she twist the knob, but she can't open the door, either. She turns 'way from the door. I look at her, but I don't move and I don't say nothing. I done seen her like this before and I'm scared of her.

"You hungry?" she says. She says it like she's mad at me, like I'm the cause of everything.

"No, ma'am," I say.

"You want eat and walk back, or you rather don't eat and ride?"

"I ain't hungry," I say.

I ain't just hungry, but I'm cold, too. I'm so hungry and cold I want to cry. And look like I'm getting colder and colder. My feet done got numb. I try to work my toes, but I don't even feel them. Look like I'm go'n die. Look like I'm go'n stand right here and freeze to death. I think 'bout home. I think 'bout Val and Auntie and Ty and Louis and Walker. It's 'bout twelve o'clock and I know they eating dinner now. I can hear Ty making jokes. He done forgot 'bout getting up early this morning and right now he's probably making jokes. Always trying to make somebody laugh. I wish I was right there listening to him. Give anything in the world if I was home round the fire.

"Come on," Mama says.

We start walking again. My feet so numb I can't hardly feel them. We turn the corner and go on back up the street. The clock on the courthouse starts hitting for twelve.

The sleet's coming down plenty now. They hit the pave and bounce like rice. Oh, Lord; oh, Lord, I pray. Don't let me die, don't let me die, don't let me die, Lord.

11

Now I know where we going. We going back of town where the colored people eat. I don't care if I don't eat. I been hungry before. I can stand it. But I can't stand the cold.

I can see we go'n have a long walk. It's 'bout a mile down there. But I don't mind. I know when I get there I'm go'n warm myself. I think I can hold out. My hands numb in my pockets and my feet numb, too, but if I keep moving I can hold out. Just don't stop no more, that's all.

The sky's gray. The sleet keeps on falling. Falling like rain now—plenty, plenty. You can hear it hitting the pave. You can see it bouncing. Sometimes it bounces two times 'fore it settles.

We keep on going. We don't say nothing. We just keep on going, keep on going.

I wonder what Mama's thinking. I hope she ain't mad at me. When summer come I'm go'n pick plenty cotton and get her a coat. I'm go'n get her a red one.

I hope they'd make it summer all the time. I'd be glad if it was summer all the time—but it ain't. We got to have winter, too. Lord, I hate the winter. I guess everybody hate the winter.

I don't sniff this time. I get out my handkerchief and wipe my nose. My hands's so cold I can hardly hold the handkerchief.

I think we getting close, but we ain't there yet. I wonder where everybody is. Can't see a soul but us. Look like we the only two people moving round today. Must be too cold for the rest of the people to move round in.

I can hear my teeth. I hope they don't knock together too hard and make that bad one hurt. Lord, that's all I need, for that bad one to start off.

I hear a church bell somewhere. But today ain't Sunday. They must be ringing for a funeral or something.

I wonder what they doing at home. They must be eating. Monsieur Bayonne might be there with his guitar. One day Ty played with Monsieur Bayonne's guitar and broke one of the strings. Monsieur Bayonne was some mad with Ty. He say Ty wasn't go'n ever 'mount to nothing. Ty can go just like Monsieur Bayonne when he ain't there. Ty can make everybody laugh when he starts to mocking Monsieur Bayonne.

I used to like to be with Mama and Daddy. We used to be happy. But they took him in the Army. Now, nobody happy no more. . . . I be glad when Daddy comes home.

Monsieur Bayonne say it wasn't fair for them to take Daddy and give Mama nothing and give us nothing. Auntie say, "Shhh, Etienne. Don't let them hear you talk like that." Monsieur Bayonne say, "It's God truth. What they giving his children? They have to walk three and a half miles to school hot or cold. That's anything to give for a paw? She's got to work in the field rain or shine just to make ends meet. That's anything to give for a husband?" Auntie say, "Shhh, Etienne, shhh." "Yes, you right," Monsieur Bayonne say. "Best don't say it in front of them now. But one day they go'n find out. One day." "Yes, I suppose so," Auntie say. "Then what, Rose Mary?" Monsieur Bayonne say. "I don't know, Etienne," Auntie say. "All we can do is us job, and leave everything else in His hand . . ."

We getting closer, now. We getting closer. I can even see the railroad tracks.

We cross the tracks, and now I see the café. Just to get in there, I say. Just to get in there. Already I'm starting to feel little better.

12

We go in. Ahh, it's good. I look for the heater; there 'gainst the wall. One of them little brown ones. I just stand there and hold my hands over it. I can't open my hands too wide 'cause they almost froze.

Mama's standing right 'side me. She done unbuttoned her coat. Smoke rises out of the coat, and the coat smells like a wet dog.

I move to the side so Mama can have more room. She opens out her hands and rubs them together. I rub mine together, too, 'cause this keep them from hurting. If you let them warm too fast, they hurt you sure. But if you let them warm just little bit at a time, and you keep rubbing them, they be all right every time.

They got just two more people in the café. A lady back of the counter, and a man on this side the counter. They been watching us ever since we come in.

Mama gets out the handkerchief and count up the money. Both of us know how much money she's got there. Three dollars. No, she ain't got three dollars 'cause she had to pay us way up here. She ain't got but two dollars and a half left. Dollar and a half to get my tooth pulled, and fifty cents for us to go back on, and fifty cents worth of salt meat.

She stirs the money round with her finger. Most of the money is change 'cause I can hear it rubbing together. She stirs it and stirs it. Then she looks at the door. It's still sleeting. I can hear it hitting 'gainst the wall like rice.

"I ain't hungry, Mama," I say.

"Got to pay them something for they heat," she says.

She takes a quarter out the handkerchief and ties the handkerchief up again. She looks over her shoulder at the people, but she still don't move. I hope she don't spend the money. I don't want her spending it on me. I'm hungry, I'm almost starving I'm so hungry, but I don't want her spending the money on me.

She flips the quarter over like she's thinking. She's must be thinking 'bout us walking back home. Lord, I sure don't want walk home. If I thought it'd do any good to say something, I'd say it. But Mama makes up her own mind 'bout things.

She turns 'way from the heater right fast, like she better hurry up and spend the quarter 'fore she change her mind. I watch her go toward the counter. The man and the lady look at her. She tells the lady something and the lady walks away. The man keeps on looking at her. Her back's turned to the man, and she don't even know he's standing there.

The lady puts some cakes and a glass of milk on the counter. Then she pours up a cup of coffee and sets it 'side the other stuff. Mama pays her for the things and comes on back where I'm standing. She tells me sit down at the table 'gainst the wall.

The milk and the cakes's for me; the coffee's for Mama. I eat slow and I look at her. She's looking outside at the sleet. She's looking real sad. I say to myself, I'm go'n make all this up one day. You see, one day, I'm go'n make all this up. I want say it now; I want tell her how I feel right now; but Mama don't like for us to talk like that.

"I can't eat all this," I say.

They ain't got but just three little old cakes there. I'm so hungry right now, the Lord knows I can eat a hundred times three. But I want my mama to have one.

Mama don't even look my way. She knows I'm hungry, she knows I want it. I let it stay there a little while, then I get it and eat it. I eat just on my front teeth, though, 'cause if cake touch that back tooth I know what'll happen. Thank God it ain't hurt me at all today.

After I finish eating I see the man go to the juke box. He drops a nickel in it, then he just stand there a little while looking at the record. Mama tells me keep my eyes in front where they belong. I turn my head like she say, but then I hear the man coming toward us.

"Dance, pretty?" he says.

Mama gets up to dance with him. But 'fore you know it, she done grabbed the little man in the collar and done heaved him 'side the wall.

He hit the wall so hard he stop the juke box from playing.

"Some pimp," the lady back of the counter says. "Some pimp."

The little man jumps up off the floor and starts toward my mama. 'Fore you know it, Mama done sprung open her knife and she's waiting for him.

"Come on," she says. "Come on. I'll gut you from your neighbo to your throat. Come on."

I go up to the little man to hit him, but Mama makes me come and stand 'side her. The little man looks at me and Mama and goes on back to the counter.

"Some pimp," the lady back of the counter says. "Some pimp." She starts laughing and pointing at the little man. "Yes sir, you a pimp, all right. Yes sir-ree."

13

"Fasten that coat, let's go," Mama says.

"You don't have to leave," the lady says. Mama don't answer the lady, and we right out in the cold again. I'm warm right now—my hands, my ears, my feet—but I know this ain't go'n last too long. It done sleet so much now you got ice everywhere you look.

We cross the railroad tracks, and soon's we do, I get cold. That wind goes through this little old coat like it ain't even there. I got on a shirt and a sweater under the coat, but that wind don't pay them no mind. I look up and I can see we got a long way to go. I wonder if we go'n make it 'fore I get too cold.

We cross over to walk on the sidewalk. They got just one sidewalk back here, and it's over there.

After we go just a little piece, I smell bread cooking. I look, then I see a baker shop. When we get closer, I can smell it more better. I shut my eyes and make 'tend I'm eating. But I keep them shut too long and I butt up 'gainst a telephone post. Mama grabs me and see if I'm hurt. I ain't bleeding or nothing and she turns me loose.

I can feel I'm getting colder and colder, and I look up to see how far we still got to go. Uptown is 'way up yonder. A half mile more, I reckon. I try to think of something. They say think and you won't get cold. I think of that poem, "Annabel Lee." I ain't been to school in so long—this bad weather—I reckon they done passed "Annabel Lee" by now. But passed it or not, I'm sure Miss Walker go'n make me recite it when I get there. That woman don't never forget nothing. I ain't never seen nobody like that in my life.

I'm still getting cold. "Annabel Lee" or no "Annabel Lee," I'm still getting cold. But I can see we getting closer. We getting there gradually.

Soon's we turn the corner, I seen a little old white lady up in front of us. She's the only lady on the street. She's all in black and she's got a long black rag over her head.

"Stop," she says.

Me and Mama stop and look at her. She must be crazy to be out in all this bad weather. Ain't got but a few other people out there, and all of them's men.

"Y'all done ate?" she says.

"Just finish," Mama says.

"Y'all must be cold then?" she says.

"We headed for the dentist," Mama says. "We'll warm up when we get there."

"What dentist?" the old lady says. "Mr. Bassett?"

"Yes, ma'am," Mama says.

"Come on in," the old lady says. "I'll telephone him and tell him y'all coming."

Me and Mama follow the old lady in the store. It's a little bitty store, and it don't have much in there. The old lady takes off her head rag and folds it up.

"Helena?" somebody calls from the back.

"Yes, Alnest?" the old lady says.

"Did you see them?"

"They're here. Standing beside me."

"Good. Now you can stay inside."

The old lady looks at Mama. Mama's waiting to hear what she brought us in here for. I'm waiting for that, too.

"I saw y'all each time you went by," she says. "I came out to catch you, but you were gone."

"We went back of town," Mama says.

"Did you eat?"

"Yes, ma'am."

The old lady looks at Mama a long time, like she's thinking Mama might just be saying that. Mama looks right back at her. The old lady looks at me to see what I have to say. I don't say nothing. I sure ain't going 'gainst my mama.

"There's food in the kitchen," she says to Mama. "I've been keeping it warm."

Mama turns right around and starts for the door.

"Just a minute," the old lady says. Mama stops. "The boy'll have to work for it. It isn't free."

"We don't take no handout," Mama says.

"I'm not handing out anything," the old lady says. "I need my garbage moved to the front. Ernest has a bad cold and can't go out there."

"James'll move it for you," Mama says.

"Not unless you eat," the old lady says. "I'm old, but I have my pride, too, you know."

Mama can see she ain't go'n beat this old lady down, so she just shakes her head.

"All right," the old lady says. "Come into the kitchen."

She leads the way with that rag in her hand. The kitchen is a little bitty little old thing, too. The table and the stove just 'bout fill it up. They got a little room to the side. Somebody in there layin 'cross the bed cause I can see one of his feet. Must be the person she was talking to: Ernest or Alnest—something like that.

"Sit down," the old lady says to Mama. "Not you," she says to me. "You have to move the cans."

"Helena?" the man says in the other room.

"Yes, Alnest?" the old lady says.

"Are you going out there again?"

"I must show the boy where the garbage is, Alnest," the old lady says.

"Keep your shawl over your head," the old man says.

"You don't have to remind me, Alnest. Come, Boy," the old lady says.

We go out in the yard. Little old back yard ain't no bigger than the store or the kitchen. But it can sleet here just like it can sleet in any big back yard. And 'fore you know it, I'm trembling.

"There," the old lady says, pointing to the cans. I pick up one of the cans and set it right back down. The can's so light. I'm go'n see what's inside of it.

"Here," the old lady says. "Leave that can alone."

I look back at her standing there in the door. She's got that black rag wrapped round her shoulders, and she's pointing one of her little old fingers at me.

"Pick it up and carry it to the front," she says. I go by her with the can, and she's looking at me all the time. I'm sure the can's empty. I'm sure she could've carried it herself—maybe both of them at the same time. "Set it on the sidewalk by the door and come back for the other one," she says.

I go and come back, and Mama looks at me when I pass her. I get the other can and take it to the front. It don't feel a bit heavier than that first one. I tell myself I ain't go'n be nobody's fool, and I'm go'n look inside this can to see just what I been hauling. First, I look up the street, then down the street. Nobody coming. Then I look over my shoulder toward the door. That little old lady done slipped up there quiet's a mouse, watching me again. Look like she knowed what I was go'n do.

"Ehh, Lord," she says. "Children, children. Come in here, boy, and go wash your hands."

I follow her in the kitchen. She points toward the bathroom, and I go in there and wash up. Little bitty old bathroom, but it's clean, clean. I don't use any of her towels; I wipe my hands on my pants legs.

When I come back in the kitchen, the old lady done dished up the food. Rice, gravy, meat—and she even got some lettuce and tomato in a saucer. She even got a glass of milk and a piece of cake there, too. It looks so good, I almost start eating 'fore I say my blessing.

"Helena?" the old man says.

"Yes, Alnest?"

"Are they eating?"

"Yes," she says.

"Good," he says. "Now you'll stay inside."

The old lady goes in there where he is and I can hear them talking. I look at Mama. She's eating slow like she's thinking. I wonder what's the matter now. I reckon she's thinking 'bout home.

The old lady comes back in the kitchen.

"I talked to Dr. Bassett's nurse," she says. "Dr. Bassett will take you as soon as you get there."

"Thank you, ma'am," Mama says.

"Perfectly all right," the old lady says. "Which one is it?"

Mama nods toward me. The old lady looks at me real sad. I look sad, too.

"You're not afraid, are you?" she says.

"No, ma'am," I say.

"That's a good boy," the old lady says. "Nothing to be afraid of. Dr. Bassett will not hurt you."

When me and Mama get through eating, we thank the old lady again.

"Helena, are they leaving?" the old man says.

"Yes, Alnest."

"Tell them I say good-bye."

"They can hear you, Alnest."

"Good-bye both mother and son," the old man says. "And may God be with you."

Me and Mama tell the old man good-bye, and we follow the old lady in the front room. Mama opens the door to go out, but she stops and comes back in the store.

"You sell salt meat?" she says.

"Yes."

"Give me two bits worth."

"That isn't very much salt meat," the old lady says.

"That's all I have," Mama says.

The old lady goes back of the counter and cuts a big piece off the chunk. Then she wraps it up and puts it in a paper bag.

"Two bits," she says.

"That looks like awful lot of meat for a quarter," Mama says.

"Two bits," the old lady says. "I've been selling salt meat behind this counter twenty-five years. I think I know what I'm doing."

"You got a scale there," Mama says.

"What?" the old lady says.

"Weigh it," Mama says.

"What?" the old lady says. "Are you telling me how to run my business?"

"Thanks very much for the food," Mama says.

"Just a minute," the old lady says.

"James," Mama says to me. I move toward the door.

"Just one minute, I said," the old lady says.

Me and Mama stop again and look at her. The old lady takes the meat out of the bag and unwraps it and cuts 'bout half of it off. Then she wraps it up again and juggs it back in the bag and gives the bag to Mama. Mama lays the quarter on the counter.

"Your kindness will never be forgotten," she says. "James," she says to me.

We go out, and the old lady comes to the door to look at us. After we go a little piece I look back, and she's still there watching us.

The sleet's coming down heavy, heavy now, and I turn up my coat collar to keep my neck warm. My mama tells me turn it right back down.

"You not a bum," she says. "You a man."

[1963]

Journal Entry

Brainstorm on the word *mother*. What images, associations, memories does the word evoke? To what extent does the mother in "The Sky Is Gray" fulfill your criteria.

Textual Considerations

1. How does the author's choice of an eight-year-old child as narrator contribute to your understanding of the story's events? What, if any, are the limitations placed on the author by his use of a young boy to re-create the story?

2. The title "The Sky Is Gray" obviously describes the weather. What does the title refer to on a symbolic level? What other symbols are there, and how does the author use them to enhance theme?

3. To what extent does setting contribute to the understanding of the story? Include a description of the protagonist's home, its surroundings, the local bus, the town of Bayonne—its school, stores, café—and the dentist's office in your discussion of setting.

4. Why does the mother force James to kill the redbirds? What does this episode reveal about the way she is raising James? Why doesn't she communicate with her son? How does the redbird incident relate to the salt meat episode at the end of the story?
5. What does the episode of James and the little girl (part 5) add to the story? What aspects of the story would be omitted if Gaines had excluded it?
6. How do James and his mother react toward the bitter cold they feel on the streets of Bayonne? What personality traits emerge in their reaction to the cold weather?
7. What does the attitude of the black man at the colored café reveal about inner racism? What lesson does the mother teach James at the colored café?

Cultural Contexts

1. How does racial prejudice operate in the story? Does Gaines show it as white people's hatred of black people; as inner racism, hatred for people of your own race; or as people's dehumanizing attitude toward others? Interpret the symbolism connected with the white lady and her husband. Why do they help James and his mother? Explain.
2. What role does religion play in the story? What kind of religion do Monsieur Bayonne, the preacher, and the owners of the store practice? Explain. Working with your group, explain the meaning of the discussion between the young man and the preacher in the dentist's office. Consider also how their arguments affect James.

Nathaniel Hawthorne

Young Goodman Brown

Young Goodman[1] Brown came forth, at sunset, into the street at Salem village; but put his head back, after crossing the threshold, to exchange a parting kiss with his young wife. And Faith, as the wife was aptly named, thrust her pretty head into the street, letting the wind play with the pink ribbons of her cap while she called to Goodman Brown.

"Dearest heart," whispered she, softly and rather sadly, when her lips were close to his ear, "prithee put off your journey until sunrise and sleep in your own bed to-night. A lone woman is troubled with such dreams and such thoughts that she's afeared of herself sometimes. Pray tarry with me this night, dear husband, of all nights in the year."

"My love and my Faith," replied young Goodman Brown, "of all nights in the year, this one night must I tarry away from thee. My journey, as thou callest it, forth and back again, must needs be done 'twixt now and sunrise. What, my sweet, pretty wife, dost thou doubt me already, and we but three months married?"

---

[1] polite term of address for a man who ranks below gentleman.

"Then God bless you!" said Faith, with the pink ribbons; "and may you find all well when you come back."

"Amen!" cried Goodman Brown. "Say thy prayers, dear Faith, and go to bed at dusk, and no harm will come to thee."

So they parted; and the young man pursued his way until, being about to turn the corner by the meeting-house, he looked back and saw the head of Faith still peeping after him with a melancholy air, in spite of her pink ribbons.

"Poor little Faith!" thought he, for his heart smote him. "What a wretch am I to leave her on such an errand! She talks of dreams, too. Me-thought as she spoke there was trouble in her face, as if a dream had warned her what work is to be done to-night. But no, no; 'twould kill her to think it. Well, she's a blessed angel on earth; and after this one night, I'll cling to her skirts and follow her to heaven."

With this excellent resolve for the future, Goodman Brown felt himself justified in making more haste on his present evil purpose. He had taken a dreary road, darkened by all the gloomiest trees of the forest, which barely stood aside to let the narrow path creep through, and closed immediately behind. It was all as lonely as could be; and there is this peculiarity in such a solitude, that the traveller knows not who may be concealed by the innumerable trunks and the thick boughs overhead; so that with lonely footsteps he may yet be passing through an unseen multitude.

"There may be a devilish Indian behind every tree," said Goodman Brown, to himself and he glanced fearfully behind him as he added, "What if the devil himself should be at my very elbow!"

His head being turned back, he passed a crook of the road, and, looking forward again, beheld the figure of a man, in grave and decent attire, seated at the foot of an old tree. He arose at Goodman Brown's approach and walked onward side by side with him.

"You are late, Goodman Brown," said he. "The clock of the Old South was striking as I came through Boston, and that is full fifteen minutes agone."

"Faith kept me back a while," replied the young man, with a tremor in his voice, caused by the sudden appearance of his companion, though not wholly unexpected.

It was now deep dusk in the forest, and deepest in that part of it where these two were journeying. As nearly as could be discerned, the second traveller was about fifty years old, apparently in the same rank of life as Goodman Brown, and bearing a considerable resemblance to him, though perhaps more in expression than features. Still they might have been taken for father and son. And yet, though the elder person was as simply clad as the younger, and as simple in manner too, he had an indescribable air of one who knew the world, and who would not have felt abashed at the governor's dinner table, or in King William's[2] court, were it possible that his affairs should call him thither. But the only thing about him that could be fixed upon as remarkable was his staff, which bore the likeness of a great black snake, so curiously wrought that it might almost be seen to twist and wriggle itself

---

[2] William III, king of England from 1689 to 1702.

like a living serpent. This, of course, must have been an ocular deception, assisted by the uncertain light.

"Come, Goodman Brown," cried his fellow-traveller, "this is a dull pace for the beginning of a journey. Take my staff, if you are so soon weary."

"Friend," said the other, exchanging his slow pace for a full stop, "having kept covenant by meeting thee here, it is my purpose now to return whence I came. I have scruples touching the matter thou wot'st[3] of."

"Sayest thou so?" replied he of the serpent, smiling apart. "Let us walk on, nevertheless, reasoning as we go; and if I convince thee not thou shalt turn back. We are but a little way in the forest yet."

"Too far! too far!" exclaimed the goodman, unconsciously resuming his walk. "My father never went into the woods on such an errand, nor his father before him. We have been a race of honest men and good Christians since the days of the martyrs; and shall I be the first of the name of Brown that ever took this path and kept—"

"Such company, thou wouldst say," observed the elder person, interpreting his pause. "Well said, Goodman Brown! I have been as well acquainted with your family as with ever a one among the Puritans; and that's no trifle to say. I helped your grandfather, the constable, when he lashed the Quaker woman so smartly through the streets of Salem; and it was I that brought your father a pitch-pine knot, kindled at my own hearth, to set fire to an Indian village, in King Philip's war.[4] They were my good friends, both; and many a pleasant walk have we had along this path, and returned merrily after midnight. I would fain be friends with you for their sake."

"If it be as thou sayest," replied Goodman Brown, "I marvel they never spoke of these matters, or, verily, I marvel not, seeing that the least rumor of the sort would have driven them from New England. We are a people of prayer, and good works to boot, and abide no such wickedness."

"Wickedness or not," said the traveller with the twisted staff, "I have a very general acquaintance here in New England. The deacons of many a church have drunk the communion wine with me; the selectmen of divers towns make me their chairman; and a majority of the Great and General Court are firm supporters of my interest. The governor and I, too—But these are state secrets."

"Can this be so!" cried Goodman Brown, with a stare of amazement at his undisturbed companion. "Howbeit, I have nothing to do with the governor and council; they have their own ways, and are no rule for a simple husbandman[5] like me. But, were I to go on with thee, how should I meet the eye of that good old man, our minister, at Salem village? Oh, his voice would make me tremble both Sabbath day and lecture day!"

---

[3] Knowest.

[4] war waged between the Colonists (1675–1676) and the Wampanoag Indians, led by Metacomet, known as "King Philip."

[5] A common man; sometimes used specifically to denote a farmer.

Thus far the elder traveller had listened with due gravity; but now burst into a fit of irrepressible mirth, shaking himself so violently that his snake-like staff actually seemed to wriggle in sympathy.

"Ha! ha! ha!" shouted he again and again; then composing himself, "Well, go on, Goodman Brown, go on; but, prithee, don't kill me with laughing."

"Well, then, to end the matter at once," said Goodman Brown, considerably nettled, "there is my wife, Faith. It would break her dear little heart; and I'd rather break my own."

"Nay, if that be the case," answered the other, "e'en go thy ways, Goodman Brown. I would not for twenty old women like the one hobbling before us that Faith should come to any harm."

As he spoke he pointed his staff at a female figure on the path, in whom Goodman Brown recognized a very pious and exemplary dame, who had taught him his catechism in youth, and was still his moral and spiritual adviser, jointly with the minister and Deacon Gookin.

"A marvel, truly, that Goody[6] Cloyse should be so far in the wilderness at night fall," said he. "But with your leave, friend, I shall take a cut through the woods until we have left this Christian woman behind. Being a stranger to you, she might ask whom I was consorting with and whither I was going."

"Be it so," said his fellow-traveller. "Betake you the woods, and let me keep the path."

Accordingly the young man turned aside, but took care to watch his companion, who advanced softly along the road until he had come within a staff's length of the old dame. She, meanwhile, was making the best of her way, with singular speed for so aged a woman, and mumbling some indistinct words—a prayer, doubtless—as she went. The traveller put forth his staff and touched her withered neck with what seemed the serpent's tail.

"The devil!" screamed the pious old lady.

"Then Goody Cloyse knows her old friend?" observed the traveller, confronting her and leaning on his writhing stick.

"Ah, forsooth, and is it your worship indeed?" cried the good dame. "Yea, truly is it, and in the very image of my old gossip, Goodman Brown, the grandfather of the silly fellow that now is. But—would your worship believe it?—my broomstick hath strangely disappeared, stolen, as I suspect, by that unhanged witch, Goody Cory, and that, too, when I was all anointed with the juice of smallage and cinquefoil and wolf's bane—"

"Mingled with fine wheat and the fat of a new-born babe," said the shape of old Goodman Brown.

"Ah, your worship knows the recipe," cried the old lady, cackling aloud. "So, as I was saying, being all ready for the meeting, and no horse to ride on, I made up my mind to foot it; for they tell me there is a nice young man to be taken into communion to-night. But now your good worship will lend me your arm, and we shall be there in a twinkling."

---

[6] contraction of "Goodwife," a polite title for a married woman of humble rank.

"That can hardly be," answered her friend. "I may not spare you my arm, Goody Cloyse; but here is my staff, if you will."

So saying, he threw it down at her feet, where, perhaps, it assumed life, being one of the rods which its owner had formerly lent to the Egyptian magi. Of this fact, however, Goodman Brown could not take cognizance. He had cast up his eyes in astonishment, and, looking down again, beheld neither Goody Cloyse nor the serpentine staff but his fellow-traveller alone, who waited for him as calmly as if nothing had happened.

"That old woman taught me my catechism," said the young man; and there was a world of meaning in this simple comment.

They continued to walk onward, while the elder traveller exhorted his companion to make good speed and persevere in the path, discoursing so aptly that his arguments seemed rather to spring up in the bosom of his auditor than to be suggested by himself. As they went, he plucked a branch of maple to serve for a walking-stick, and began to strip it of the twigs and little boughs, which were wet with evening dew. The moment his fingers touched them they became strangely withered and dried up as with a week's sunshine. Thus the pair proceeded, at a good free pace, until suddenly, in a gloomy hollow of the road, Goodman Brown sat himself down on the stump of a tree and refused to go any farther.

"Friend," said he, stubbornly, "my mind is made up. Not another step will I budge on this errand. What if a wretched old woman do choose to go to the devil when I thought she was going to heaven: is that any reason why I should quit my dear Faith and go after her?"

"You will think better of this by and by," said his acquaintance, composedly. "Sit here and rest yourself a while; and when you feel like moving again, there is my staff to help you along."

Without more words, he threw his companion the maple stick, and was as speedily out of sight as if he had vanished into the deepening gloom. The young man sat a few moments by the roadside, applauding himself greatly, and thinking with how clear a conscience he should meet the minister in his morning walk, nor shrink from the eye of good old Deacon Gookin. And what calm sleep would be his that very night, which was to have been spent so wickedly, but so purely and sweetly now, in the arms of Faith! Amidst these pleasant and praiseworthy meditations, Goodman Brown heard the tramp of horses along the road, and deemed it advisable to conceal himself within the verge of the forest, conscious of the guilty purpose that had brought him thither, though now so happily turned from it.

On came the hoof-tramps and the voices of the riders, two grave old voices, conversing soberly as they drew near. These mingled sounds appeared to pass along the road, within a few yards of the young man's hiding-place; but, owing doubtless to the depth of the gloom at that particular spot, neither the travellers nor their steeds, were visible. Though their figures brushed the small boughs by the wayside, it could not be seen that they intercepted, even for a moment, the faint gleam from the strip of bright sky athwart which they must have passed. Goodman Brown alternately crouched and stood on tiptoe, pulling aside the branches and thrusting forth his head as far as he durst without discerning so much as a shadow. It vexed him the more, because he could have sworn, were such a thing possible, that he recognized the voices of the minister and Deacon Gookin, jogging along quietly as they were wont to do, when bound to some ordination or ecclesiastical council. While yet within hearing, one of the riders stopped to pluck a switch.

"Of the two, reverend sir," said the voice like the deacon's, "I had rather miss an ordination dinner than to-night's meeting. They tell me that some of our community are to be here from Falmouth and beyond, and others from Connecticut and Rhode Island, besides several of the Indian powwows, who, after their fashion, know almost as much deviltry as the best of us. Moreover, there is a goodly young woman to be taken into communion."

"Mighty well, Deacon Gookin!" replied the solemn old tones of the minister. "Spur up, or we shall be late. Nothing can be done, you know, until I get on the ground."

The hoofs clattered again; and the voices, talking so strangely in the empty air, passed on through the forest, where no church had ever been gathered or solitary Christian prayed. Whither, then, could these holy men be journeying so deep into the heathen wilderness? Young Goodman Brown caught hold of a tree for support, being ready to sink down on the ground, faint and overburdened with the heavy sickness of his heart. He looked up to the sky, doubting whether there really was a heaven above him. Yet, there was the blue arch, and the stars brightening in it.

"With heaven above, and Faith below, I will yet stand firm against the devil!" cried Goodman Brown.

While he still gazed upward into the deep arch of the firmament and had lifted his hands to pray, a cloud, though no wind was stirring, hurried across the zenith and hid the brightening stars. The blue sky was still visible, except directly overhead, where this black mass of cloud was sweeping swiftly northward. Aloft in the air, as if from the depths of the cloud, came a confused and doubtful sound of voices. Once the listener fancied that he could distinguish the accents of townspeople of his own, men and women, both pious and ungodly, many of whom he had met at the communion table, and had seen others rioting at the tavern. The next moment, so indistinct were the sounds, he doubted whether he had heard aught but the murmur of the old forest, whispering without a wind. Then came a stronger swell of those familiar tones, heard daily in the sunshine at Salem village, but never until now from a cloud of night. There was one voice, of a young woman, uttering lamentations, yet with an uncertain sorrow, and entreating for some favor, which, perhaps, it would grieve her to obtain; and all the unseen multitude, both saints and sinners, seemed to encourage her onward.

"Faith!" shouted Goodman Brown, in a voice of agony and desperation; and the echoes of the forest mocked him, crying, "Faith! Faith!" as if bewildered wretches were seeking her all through the wilderness.

The cry of grief, rage, and terror was yet piercing the night, when the unhappy husband held his breath for a response. There was a scream, drowned immediately in a louder murmur of voices, fading into far-off laughter, as the dark cloud swept away, leaving the clear and silent sky above Goodman Brown. But something fluttered lightly down through the air and caught on the branch of a tree. The young man seized it, and beheld a pink ribbon.

"My Faith is gone!" cried he, after one stupefied moment. "There is no good on earth; and sin is but a name. Come, devil; for to thee is this world given."

And, maddened with despair, so that he laughed loud and long, did Goodman Brown grasp his staff and set forth again, at such a rate that he seemed to fly along the forest path, rather than to walk or run. The road grew wilder and drearier and more faintly traced, and vanished at length, leaving him in the heart of the dark wilderness, still rushing onward with the instinct that guides mortal man to evil. The whole forest was peopled with frightful sounds—the creaking of the trees, the howling of wild beasts, and the yell of Indians; while sometimes the wind tolled like a distant church bell, and sometimes gave a broad roar around the traveller, as if all Nature were laughing him to scorn. But he was himself the chief horror of the scene, and shrank not from its other horrors.

"Ha! ha! ha!" roared Goodman Brown when the wind laughed at him. "Let us hear which will laugh loudest! Think not to frighten me with your deviltry! Come witch, come wizard, come Indian powwow, come devil himself, and here comes Goodman Brown. You may as well fear him as he fears you!"

In truth, all through the haunted forest there could be nothing more frightful than the figure of Goodman Brown. On he flew among the black pines, brandishing his staff with frenzied gestures, now giving vent to an inspiration of horrid blasphemy, and now shouting forth such laughter as set all the echoes of the forest laughing like demons around him. The fiend in his own shape is less hideous than when he rages in the breast of man. Thus sped the demoniac on his course, until, quivering among the trees, he saw a red light before him, as when the felled trunks and branches of a clearing have been set on fire, and throw up their lurid blaze against the sky, at the hour of midnight. He paused, in a lull of the tempest that had driven him onward, and heard the swell of what seemed a hymn, rolling solemnly from a distance with the weight of many voices. He knew the tune; it was a familiar one in the choir of the village meeting-house. The verse died heavily away, and was lengthened by a chorus, not of human voices, but of all the sounds of the benighted wilderness pealing in awful harmony together. Goodman Brown cried out; and his cry was lost to his own ear by its unison with the cry of the desert.

In the interval of silence he stole forward until the light glared full upon his eyes. At one extremity of an open space, hemmed in, by the dark wall of the forest, arose a rock, bearing some rude, natural resemblance either to an altar or a pulpit, and surrounded by four blazing pines, their tops aflame, their stems untouched, like candles at an evening meeting. The mass of foliage that had overgrown the summit of the rock was all on fire, blazing high into the night and fitfully illuminating the whole field. Each pendent twig and leafy festoon was in a blaze. As the red light arose and fell, a numerous congregation alternately shone forth, then disappeared in shadow, and again grew, as it were, out of the darkness, peopling the heart of the solitary woods at once.

"A grave and dark-clad company," quoth Goodman Brown.

In truth, they were such. Among them, quivering to-and-fro between gloom and splendor, appeared faces that would be seen next day at the council board of the province, and others which, Sabbath after Sabbath, looked devoutly heavenward, and benignantly over the crowded pews, from the holiest pulpits in the land. Some affirm that the lady of the governor was there. At least there were high dames well known to her, and wives of honored husbands, and widows, a great multitude, and ancient maidens, of excellent repute, and fair young girls, who trembled lest their mothers should espy them. Either the sudden gleams of light flashing over the obscure field bedazzled Goodman Brown, or he recognized a score of the church-members of Salem village famous for their especial sanctity. Good old Deacon Gookin had arrived, and waited at the skirts of that venerable saint, his revered pastor. But, irreverently consorting, with these grave, reputable, and pious people, these elders of the church, these chaste dames and dewy virgins, there were men of dissolute lives and women of spotted fame, wretches given over to all mean and filthy vice, and suspected even of horrid crimes. It was strange to see, that the good shrank not from the wicked, nor were the sinners abashed by the saints. Scattered also among their pale-faced enemies were the Indian priests, or powwows, who had often scared their native forest with more hideous incantations than any known to English witchcraft.

"But, where is Faith?" thought Goodman Brown; and, as hope came into his heart, he trembled.

Another verse of the hymn arose, a slow and mournful strain, such as the pious love, but joined to words which expressed all that our nature can conceive of sin, and darkly hinted at far more. Unfathomable to mere mortals is the lore of fiends. Verse after verse was sung; and still the chorus of the desert swelled between, like the deepest tone of a mighty organ; and, with the final peal of that dreadful anthem there came a sound, as if the roaring wind, the rushing streams, the howling beasts, and every other voice of the unconcerted wilderness were mingling and according with the voice of guilty man in homage to the prince of all. The four blazing pines threw up a loftier flame, and obscurely discovered shapes and visages of horror on the smoke wreaths above the impious assembly. At the same moment the fire on the rock shot redly forth and formed a glowing arch above its base, where now appeared a figure. With reverence be it spoken, the figure bore no slight similitude, both in garb and manner, to some grave divine of the New England churches.

"Bring forth the converts!" cried a voice that echoed through the field and rolled into the forest.

At the word, Goodman Brown stepped forth from the shadow of the trees and approached the congregation, with whom he felt a loathful brotherhood by the sympathy of all that was wicked in heart. He could have well nigh sworn that the shape of his own dead father beckoned him to advance, looking downward from a smoke wreath, while a woman, with dim features of despair, threw out her hand to warn him back. Was it his mother? But he had no power to retreat one step, nor to resist, even in thought, when the minister and good old Deacon Gookin seized his arms and led him to the blazing rock. Thither came also the slender form of a veiled female, led between Goody Cloyse, that pious teacher of the catechism, and Martha

Carrier,[7] who had received the devil's promise to be queen of hell. A rampant hag was she. And there stood the proselytes beneath the canopy of fire.

"Welcome, my children," said the dark figure, "to the communion of your race. Ye have found thus young your nature and your destiny. My children, look behind you!"

They turned; and flashing forth, as it were, in a sheet of flame, the fiend worshippers were seen; the smile of welcome gleamed darkly on every visage.

"There," resumed the sable form, "are all whom ye have reverenced from youth. Ye deemed them holier than yourselves, and shrank from your own sin, contrasting it with their lives of righteousness and prayerful aspirations heavenward. Yet here are they all in my worshipping assembly. This night it shall be granted you to know their secret deeds: how hoary-bearded elders of the church have whispered wanton words to the young maids of their households; how many a woman, eager for widow's weeds, has given her husband a drink at bedtime, and let him sleep his last sleep in her bosom; how beardless youths have made haste to inherit their fathers' wealth; and how fair damsels—blush not, sweet ones—have dug little graves in the garden, and bidden me, the sole guest, to an infant's funeral. By the sympathy of your human hearts for sin ye shall scent out all the places—whether in church, bed-chamber, street, field, or forest—where crime has been committed, and shall exult to behold the whole earth one stain of guilt, one mighty blood spot. Far more than this. It shall be yours to penetrate, in every bosom, the deep mystery of sin, the fountain of all wicked arts, and which inexhaustibly supplies more evil impulses than human power—than my power at its utmost—can make manifest in deeds. And now, my children, look upon each other."

They did so; and, by the blaze of the hell-kindled torches, the wretched man beheld his Faith, and the wife her husband, trembling before that unhallowed altar.

"Lo, there ye stand, my children," said the figure, in a deep and solemn tone, almost sad with its despairing awfulness, as if his once angelic nature could yet mourn for our miserable race. "Depending upon one another's hearts, ye had still hoped that virtue were not all a dream. Now are ye undeceived. Evil is the nature of mankind. Evil must be your only happiness. Welcome, again, my children, to the communion of your race."

"Welcome," repeated the fiend worshippers, in one cry of despair and triumph.

And there they stood, the only pair, as it seemed, who were yet hesitating on the verge of wickedness in this dark world. A basin was hollowed, naturally, in the rock. Did it contain water, reddened by the lurid light? or was it blood? or, perchance, a liquid flame? Herein did the shape of evil dip his hand and prepare to lay the mark of baptism upon their foreheads, that they might be partakers of the mystery of sin, more conscious of the secret guilt of others, both in deed and thought, than they could now be of their own. The husband cast one look at his pale wife, and Faith at him. What polluted wretches would the next glance show them to each other, shuddering alike at what they disclosed and what they saw!

---

[7] One of the women hanged for witchcraft in Salem in 1697.

"Faith! Faith!" cried the husband, "look up to heaven, and resist the wicked one."

Whether Faith obeyed he knew not. Hardly had he spoken when he found himself amid calm night and solitude, listening to a roar of the wind which died heavily away through the forest. He staggered against the rock, and felt it chill and damp; while a hanging twig, that had been all on fire, besprinkled his cheek with the coldest dew.

The next morning young Goodman Brown came slowly into the street of Salem village, staring around him like a bewildered man. The good old minister was taking a walk along the graveyard to get an appetite for breakfast and meditate his sermon, and bestowed a blessing, as he passed, on Goodman Brown. He shrank from the venerable saint as if to avoid an anathema. Old Deacon Gookin was at domestic worship, and the holy words of his prayer were heard through the open window. "What God doth the wizard pray to?" quoth Goodman Brown. Goody Cloyse, that excellent old Christian, stood in the early sunshine at her own lattice, catechizing a little girl who had brought her a pint of morning's milk. Goodman Brown snatched away the child as from the grasp of the fiend himself. Turning the corner by the meeting-house, he spied the head of Faith, with the pink ribbons, gazing anxiously forth, and bursting into such joy at sight of him that she skipped along the street and almost kissed her husband before the whole village. But Goodman Brown looked sternly and sadly into her face, and passed on without a greeting.

Had Goodman Brown fallen asleep in the forest and only dreamed a wild dream of a witch-meeting?

Be it so, if you will; but, alas! it was a dream of evil omen for young Goodman Brown. A stern, a sad, a darkly meditative, a distrustful, if not a desperate man did he become from the night of that fearful dream. On the Sabbath day, when the congregation were singing a holy psalm, he could not listen because an anthem of sin rushed loudly upon his ear and drowned all the blessed strain. When the minister spoke from the pulpit with power and fervid eloquence, and, with his hand on the open Bible, of the sacred truths of our religion, and of saint-like lives and triumphant deaths, and of future bliss or misery unutterable, then did Goodman Brown turn pale, dreading lest the roof should thunder down upon the gray blasphemer and his hearers. Often, awakening suddenly at midnight, he shrank from the bosom of Faith; and at morning or eventide, when the family knelt down at prayer, he scowled and muttered to himself, and gazed sternly at his wife, and turned away. And when he had lived long, and was borne to his grave a hoary corpse, followed by Faith, an aged woman, and children and grandchildren, a goodly procession, besides neighbors not a few, they carved no hopeful verse upon his tombstone, for his dying hour was gloom.

[1835]

Journal Entry

What do you know about Puritanism? Are there images you associate with pilgrims, witch trials, or religious beliefs? If necessary, consult a history text for a context in which to evaluate Hawthorne's story.

Textual Consideration

1. Setting plays an important thematic role in the story. Why is it important that the story begins and ends in Salem village?
2. Much of the story also takes place in the forest. Cite two or three events that are connected to the woods.
3. Why is it significant that the stranger whom Brown meets in the forest looks like Brown's father and also like Brown? Explain.
4. Discuss the symbolic meaning of young Goodman Brown's name. What function does it serve in the story?
5. Using evidence from the text, explain where Hawthorne casts doubts on the supernatural nature of the story.

Cultural Contexts

1. Consult the glossary for a definition of *allegory*. At what point in the story does the reader realize that "Young Goodman Brown" may be read as a moral allegory? Contrast the village of Salem with the forest from an allegorical point of view.
2. Explain how Hawthorne explores the portrait of Faith in the story. Discuss with members of your group the role she plays on the literal and allegorical levels of the story. How does her portrait of Brown differ from that of the narrator?

ESSAYS

My People

Yonder sky that has wept tears upon my people for centuries untold, and which to us appears changeless and eternal, may change. Today is fair. Tomorrow may be overcast with clouds. My words are like the stars that never change. Whatever Seattle says the great chief at Washington can rely upon with as much certainty as he can upon the return of the sun or the seasons. The White Chief says that Big Chief at Washington sends us greetings of friendship and goodwill. That is kind of him for we know he has little need of our friendship in return. His people are many. They are like the grass that covers vast prairies. My people are few. They resemble the scattering trees of a storm-swept plain. The great, and—I presume—good, White Chief sends us word that he wishes to buy our lands but is willing to allow us enough to live comfortably. This indeed appears just, even generous, for the Red Man no longer has rights that he need respect, and the offer may be wise also, as we are no longer in need of an extensive country. . . . I will not dwell on, nor mourn over, our untimely decay, nor reproach our paleface brothers with hastening it, as we too may have been somewhat to blame.

Youth is impulsive. When our young men grow angry at some real or imaginary wrong, and disfigure their face with black paint, it denotes that their hearts are black, and then they are often cruel and relentless, and our old men and old women are unable to restrain them. Thus it has ever been. Thus it was when the white men first began to push our forefathers further westward. But let us hope that the hostilities between us may never return. We would have everything to lose and nothing to gain. Revenge by young men is considered gain, even at the cost of their own lives, but old men who stay at home in times of war, and mothers who have sons to lose, know better.

Our good father at Washington—for I presume he is now our father as well as yours, since King George has moved his boundaries further north—our great good father, I say, sends us word that if we do as he desires he will protect us. His brave warriors will be to us a bristling wall of strength, and his wonderful ships of war will fill our harbors so that our ancient enemies far to the northward—the Hydas and Tsimpsians—will cease to frighten our women, children, and old men. Then in reality will he be our father and we his children. But can that ever be? Your God is not our God! Your God loves your people and hates mine. He folds his strong and protecting arms lovingly about the paleface and leads him by the hand as a father leads his infant son—but He has forsaken His red children—if they really are his. Our God, the Great Spirit, seems also to have forsaken us. Your God makes your people wax strong every day. Soon they will fill the land. Our people are ebbing away like a rapidly receding tide that will never return. The white man's God cannot love our people or He would protect them. They seem to be orphans who can look nowhere for help. How then can we be brothers? How can your God become our God and renew our prosperity and awaken in us dreams of returning greatness? If we have a common heavenly father He must be partial—for He came to his paleface children. We never saw Him. He gave you laws but He had no word for His red children whose teeming multitudes once filled this vast continent as stars fill the firmament. No; we are two distinct races with separate origins and separate destinies. There is little in common between us.

To us the ashes of our ancestors are sacred and their resting place is hallowed ground. You wander far from the graves of your ancestors and seemingly without regret. Your religion was written upon tables of stone by the iron finger of your God so that you could not forget. The Red Man could never comprehend nor remember it. Our religion is the traditions of our ancestors—the dreams of our old men, given them in solemn hours of night by the Great Spirit; and the visions of our sachems;[1] and it is written in the hearts of our people.

Your dead cease to love you and the land of their nativity as soon as they pass the portals of the tomb and wander way beyond the stars. They are soon forgotten and never return. Our dead never forget the beautiful world that gave them being.

Day and night cannot dwell together. The Red Man has ever fled the approach of the White Man, as the morning mist flees before the morning sun. However, your proposition seems fair and I think that my people will accept it and will retire to the reservation you offer them. Then we will dwell apart in peace, for the words of the Great White Chief seem to be the words of nature speaking to my people out of dense darkness.

It matters little where we pass the remnant of our days. They will not be many. A few more moons; a few more winters—and not one of the descendants of the mighty hosts that once moved over this broad land or lived in happy homes, protected by the Great Spirit, will remain to mourn over the graves of a people once more powerful and hopeful than yours. But why should I mourn at the untimely fate of my people? Tribe follows tribe, and nation follows nation, like the waves of the sea. It is the order of nature, and regret is useless. Your time of decay may be distant, but it will surely come, for even the White Man whose God walked and talked with him as friend with friend, cannot be exempt from the common destiny. We may be brothers after all. We will see.

We will ponder your proposition, and when we decide we will let you know. But should we accept it, I here and now make this condition that we will not be denied the privilege without molestation of visiting at any time the tombs of our ancestors, friends and children. Every part of this soil is sacred in the estimation of my people. Every hillside, every valley, every plain and grove, has been hallowed by some sad or happy event in days long vanished. . . . The very dust upon which you now stand responds more lovingly to their footsteps than to yours, because it is rich

---

[1] Tribal chiefs.

with the blood of our ancestors and our bare feet are conscious of the sympathetic touch. . . . Even the little children who lived here and rejoiced here for a brief season will love these somber solitudes and at eventide they greet shadowy returning spirits. And when the last Red Man shall have perished, and the memory of my tribe shall have become a myth among the White Men, these shores will swarm with the invisible dead of my tribe, and when your children's children think themselves alone in the field, the store, the shop, upon the highway, or in the silence of the pathless woods, they will not be alone. . . . At night when the streets of your cities and villages are silent and you think them deserted, they will throng with the returning hosts that once filled and still love this beautiful land. The White Man will never be alone.

Let him be just and deal kindly with my people, for the dead are not powerless. Dead, did I say? There is not death, only a change of worlds.

[c. 1855]

Journal Entry

Create contrasting lists of your associations with youth and age. How do they compare to Chief Seattle's?

Textual Considerations

1. Chief Seattle's speech contains many examples of figurative language, including "my words are like the stars that never change." What other metaphors and similes can you cite? How effective are they?
2. Is Chief Seattle seeking to inform or persuade his audience?
3. Who is Chief Seattle's intended audience? Explain.
4. Chief Seattle uses contrast and comparison at several points in his speech. What differences between the traditions of his people and "the White Man" are highlighted by this technique?
5. What other examples of comparison and contrast do you find in "My People"? Analyze their meaning from the thematic point of view.

Cultural Contexts

1. "There is not death, only a change of worlds." What does Chief Seattle's attitude toward death reveal about Native American religious beliefs? How does this philosophy of death compare to yours? Explain.
2. Working with your group, discuss the status of Native Americans in the last two centuries. What images of Native Americans are perpetuated by the media, including Hollywood movies? Discuss the image of Native Americans in the films *Dances with Wolves* or *Smoke Signals*.

Plato

The Allegory of the Cave

And now, I said, let me show in a figure how far our nature is enlightened or unenlightened: Behold! human beings living in an underground den, which has a mouth open towards the light and reaching all along the den; here they have been from their childhood, and have their legs and necks chained so that they cannot move, and can only see before them, being prevented by the chains from turning round their heads. Above and behind them a fire is blazing at a distance, and between the fire and the prisoners there is a raised way; and you will see, if you look, a low wall built along the way, like the screen which marionette players have in front of them, over which they show the puppets.

I see.

And do you see, I said, men passing along the wall carrying all sorts of vessels, and statues and figures of animals made of wood and stone and various materials, which appear over the wall? Some of them are talking, others silent.

You have shown me a strange image, and they are strange prisoners.

Like ourselves, I replied; and they see only their own shadows, or the shadows of one another, which the fire throws on the opposite wall of the cave?

True, he said; how could they see anything but the shadows if they were never allowed to move their heads?

And of the objects which are being carried in like manner they would only see the shadows?

Yes, he said.

And if they were able to converse with one another, would they not suppose that they were naming what was actually before them?

Very true.

And suppose further that the prison had an echo which came from the other side, would they not be sure to fancy when one of the passers-by spoke that the voice which they heard came from the passing shadow?

No question, he replied.

To them, I said, the truth would be literally nothing but the shadows of the images.

That is certain.

And now look again, and see what will naturally follow if the prisoners are released and disabused of their error. At first, when any of them is liberated and compelled suddenly to stand up and turn his neck round and walk and look towards the light, he will suffer sharp pains; the glare will distress him and he will be unable to see the realities of which in his former state he had seen the shadows; and then conceive some one saying to him, that what he saw before was an illusion, but that now, when he is approaching nearer to being and his eye is turned towards more real existence, he has a clearer vision—what will be his reply? And you may further imagine that his instructor is pointing to the objects as they pass and requiring him to name them—will he not be perplexed? Will he not fancy that the shadows which he formerly saw are truer than the objects which are now shown to him?

Far truer.

And if he is compelled to look straight at the light, will he not have a pain in his eyes which will make him turn away to take refuge in the objects of vision which he can see, and which he will conceive to be in reality clearer than the things which are now being shown to him?

True, he said.

And suppose once more, that he is reluctantly dragged up a steep and rugged ascent, and held fast until he is forced into the presence of the sun himself, is he not likely to be pained and irritated? When he approaches the light his eyes will be dazzled and he will not be able to see anything at all of what are now called realities.

Not all in a moment, he said.

He will require to grow accustomed to the sight of the upper world. And first he will see the shadows best, next the reflections of men and other objects in the water, and then the objects themselves; then he will gaze upon the light of the moon and the stars and the spangled heaven; and he will see the sky and the stars by night better than the sun or the light of the sun by day?

Certainly.

Last of all he will be able to see the sun, and not mere reflections of him in the water, but he will see him in his own proper place, and not in another; and he will contemplate him as he is.

Certainly.

He will then proceed to argue that this is he who gives the season and the years, and is the guardian of all that is in the visible world, and in a certain way the cause of all things which he and his fellows have been accustomed to behold.

Clearly, he said, he would first see the sun and then reason about him.

And when he remembered his old habitation, and the wisdom of the den and his fellow-prisoners, do you not suppose that he would felicitate himself on the change, and pity them?

Certainly, he would.

And if they were in the habit of conferring honors among themselves on those who were quickest to observe the passing shadows and to remark which of them went before, and which followed after, and which were together; and who were therefore best able to draw conclusions as to the future, do you think that he would care for such honors and glories, or envy the possessors of them? Would he not say with Homer,

Better to be the poor servant of a poor master,

and to endure anything, rather than think as they do and live after their manner?

Yes, he said, I think that he would rather suffer anything than entertain these false notions and live in this miserable manner.

Imagine once more, I said, such an one coming suddenly out of the sun to be replaced in his old situation; would he not be certain to have his eyes full of darkness?

To be sure, he said.

And if there were a contest, and he had to compete in measuring the shadows with the prisoners who had never moved out of the den, while his sight was still weak, and before his eyes had become steady (and the time which would be needed to acquire this new habit of sight might be very considerable) would he not be ridiculous? Men would say of him that up he went and down he came without his eyes; and that it was better not even to think of ascending; and if any one tried to loose another and lead him up to the light, let them only catch the offender, and they would put him to death.

No question, he said.

This entire allegory, I said, you may now append, dear Glaucon, to the previous argument; the prison-house is the world of sight, the light of the fire is the sun, and you will not misapprehend me if you interpret the journey upwards to be the ascent of the soul into the intellectual world according to my poor belief, which, at your desire, I have expressed—whether rightly or wrongly God knows. But, whether true or false, my opinion is that in the world of knowledge the idea of good appears last of all, and is seen only with an effort; and, when seen, is also inferred to be the universal author of all things beautiful and right, parent of light and of the lord of light in this visible world, and the immediate source of reason and truth in the intellectual; and that this is the power upon which he who would act rationally either in public or private life must have his eye fixed.

I agree, he said, as far as I am able to understand you.

Moreover, I said, you must not wonder that those who attain to this beatific vision are unwilling to descend to human affairs; for their souls are ever hastening into the upper world where they desire to dwell; which desire of theirs is very natural, if our allegory may be trusted.

Yes, very natural.

And is there anything surprising in one who passes from divine contemplations to the evil state of man, misbehaving himself in a ridiculous manner; if, while his eyes are blinking and before he has become accustomed to the surrounding darkness, he is compelled to fight in courts of law, or in other places, about the images or the shadows of images of justice, and is endeavouring to meet the conceptions of those who have never yet seen absolute justice?

Anything but surprising, he replied.

Any one who has common sense will remember that the bewilderments of the eyes are of two kinds, and arise from two causes, either from coming out of the light or from going into the light, which is true of the mind's eye, quite as much as of the bodily eye; and he who remembers this when he sees any one whose vision is perplexed and weak, will not be too ready to laugh; he will first ask whether that soul of man has come out of the brighter life, and is unable to see because unaccustomed to the dark, or having turned from darkness to the day is dazzled by excess of light. And he will count the one happy in his condition and state of being, and he will pity the other; or, if he have a mind to laugh at the soul which comes from below into the light, there will be more reason in this than in the laugh which greets him who returns from above out of the light into the den.

That, he said, is a very just distinction.

[c. 340 B.C.]

Journal Entry

Do you agree with Plato that human beings are often reluctant to confront unpleasant realities and prefer to fantasize and avoid them? What examples can you think of to support or refute his point of view?

Textual Considerations

1. An **allegory**, or **parable**, is a concrete story on one level and an explication of abstract, moral truths on another. Plato explains at the end what each part of history symbolizes on the moral level. What correspondences does he establish?
2. If we assume that the people in the cave represent humankind, why does Plato call them "prisoners"? Although Plato does not specify who placed the people in chains, who seems to be the jailer when the freed prisoner returns to free the others?
3. Plato equates making the "journey upwards" on the story level with gaining knowledge on the **abstract** level. Why, instead of making the ascent, would people prefer to remain in the cave with illusions of what is real? Do you agree with Plato's analysis of human nature here? Explain.
4. Plato's essay is presented as a dialogue between teacher and student. What contribution to structure and theme is made by the student's brief comments?
5. Review Plato's concluding paragraph. Is his final comment on the allegory necessary, or would you have been able to fit together his meaning without this ending? Explain.

Cultural Contexts

1. Plato says of the man who returns to the cave after seeing the sun that if the prisoners could lay hands on him, they would kill him. Are there historical or contemporary situations that fulfill this prediction?
2. Discuss with your group Plato's concept that human beings are often reluctant to confront reality. How does his viewpoint compare with Emily Dickinson's "Tell All the Truth but Tell It Slant" (Part Five)? What examples can you think of to support or refute Plato's thesis?

Garrett Hongo

Fraternity

It was high school in Gardena. I was in classes mostly with Japanese American kids—*kotonks*. Mainland Japanese, their ethnic pet name originated, during the war, with derisive Hawaiian GIs who thought of the sound of a coconut being hit with a hammer. Sansei *kotonks* were sons and daughters of the Nisei *kotonks* who had been sent off to the concentration camps during World War II. School was tepid, boring. We wanted cars, we wanted clothes, we wanted everything whites and blacks wanted to know about sex but were afraid to tell us. We "bee-essed" with the black kids in the school parking lot full of coastal fog before classes. We beat the white kids in math, in science, in typing. We ran track and elected cheerleaders. We *ruled*, we said. We were dumb, teeming with attitude and prejudice.

Bored, I took a creative writing class with an "academically mixed" bunch of students. There were Chicanos, whites, a black woman, and a troika of Japanese women who sat together on the other side of the room from me. They said nothing—*ever*—and wrote naturalistically correct *haiku*. Suddenly among boisterous non-Japanese, I enjoyed the gabbing, the bright foam of free talk that the teacher encouraged. An aging man in baggy pants that he wore with suspenders, he announced he was retiring at the end of the year and that he wanted no trouble, that he was going to read "Eee-bee White" during our hour of class every day, that we were welcome to read whatever we wanted so long as we gave him a list ahead of time, and that we could talk as much as we wanted so long as we left him alone. We could read, we could write, we could jive each other all class long. It was freedom. And I took advantage.

I sat next to a Chicano my age named Pacheco and behind a white girl a class younger than me named Regina. Behind us was a curly-headed white guy who played saxophone in the marching band. He'd been in academic classes with me, the only Caucasian among Japanese, a Korean, and a few Chinese. He was a joker, and I liked him, but usually stayed away—we didn't fraternize much across the races, though our school was supposed to be an experiment in integration.

Gardena H.S. wasn't so much a mix or blend as a mosaic. Along with a few whites and blacks, Japanese were in the tough, college-prep, "advanced placement" scholastic track. Most whites and blacks were in the regular curriculum of shop, business skills, and a minimum of academic courses. The "dumb Japs" were in there with them. And the Chicanos filled up what were called the *remedial* classes, all taught imperiously only in English, with no provision for language acquisition. We were a student body of about three thousand, and we walked edgily around each other, swaggering when we could, sliding the steel taps on our big black shoes along the concrete outdoor walkways when we wanted to attract a little attention, making a jest of our strut, a music in the rhythm of our walking. Blacks were bused in from Compton; the whites, Japanese, and Chicanos came from around the town. Girls seemed to me an ethnic group of their own too, giggling and forming social clubs, sponsoring dances, teaching some of us the steps.

Crazes of dress moved through our populations—for Chicanos: woolen Pendletons over thin undershirts and a crucifix; big low-top oxfords; khaki work trousers, starched and pressed; for the *bloods*: rayon and satin shirts in metallic "fly-ass" colors; pegged gabardine slacks; cheap moccasin-toed shoes from downtown shops in L.A.; and for us *Buddhas*: high-collar Kensingtons of pastel cloths, A tapered "Racer" slacks, and the same moccasin shoes as the bloods, who were our brothers. It was crazy. And *inviolable*. Dress and social behavior were a code one did not break for fear of ostracism and reprisal. Bad dressers were ridiculed. Offending speakers were beaten, tripped walking into the john, and set upon by gangs. They *wailed* on you if you fucked up. A girl was nothing except pride, an ornament of some guy's crude power and expertise in negotiating the intricacies of this inner-city semiotic of cultural display and hidden violence. I did not know girls.

I talked to Regina, saying "white girl" one time. She told me not to call her that, that she was *Portuguese* if anything, that I better *know* that white people were *always* something too. From vague memories of Hawaii, I reached for the few words in *Portuguese* that I knew, I asked her about the sweet bread her mother baked, about heavy donuts fried in oil and rolled in sugar. I said *bon dea* for "good day" to her. I read the books she talked about—Steinbeck, Kesey, Salinger, and Baldwin. Her mother brought paperbacks home from the salon she worked in, putting up other women's hair—*rich* women's. We made up our reading list from books her mother knew. I wanted desperately to impress her, so I began to write poetry too, imitating some melancholy rock and country-and-western lyrics. She invited me to her house after school. It was on the way, so I walked her home. It became a practice.

Her father was a big, diabetic man from Texas. With his shirt off, he showed me how he shot himself with insulin, poking the needle under the hairy red skin on his stomach, working it over the bulge of fat around his belly. He laughed a lot and shared his beer. There were other guys over too—white guys from the football team, a Filipino, and one other Japanese guy who played left tackle. They were tough, raucous, and talked easily, excitedly. I stood alone in the front yard one day, holding a soft drink in my hand, the barbecue party going on around me. Regina and her mother were baking bread inside. No one knew exactly what was going on, and I was still trying to pretend all was casual.

I took photographs of her. We had a picnic on the coast by the lighthouse near Marineland, on the bluffs over the Pacific. It was foggy, mist upon us and the tall, droopy grasses in the field we walked through, but we made do. She wrapped herself in the blanket she'd brought for us to sit on. We were in the tall grasses of the headlands far from the coast road. She posed. I changed lenses, dropping film canisters, other things. She waved to me, unbuttoning the blouse she was wearing, her body full of a fragrance. The warm, yeasty scent of her skin smelled like bread under bronze silk.

We couldn't be seen together—not at the private, car-club-sponsored Japanese dances out in the Crenshaw District, not at the whites-dominated dances after school in the high school gym. Whites did not see Buddhas, and Buddhas did not see bloods. We were to stay with our own—*that* was the code—though we mixed some in the lunch line, in a few classes, on the football field, and in gym. We segregated ourselves.

Regina and I went to the Chicano dances in El Monte. Pacheco introduced us to them. Regina, tanned Portuguese, passed for Chicana, so long as she kept her mouth shut and her lashes long. Pacheco showed her what skirts to wear, his quick hands fluttering through the crinolines and taffetas in her closet at home. He advised me to grow a mustache and let my black hair go long in the back, to slick it down with pomade and to fluff it up in front, then seal it all in hair spray. I bought brown Pendletons and blue navy-surplus bell-bottoms. I bought hard, steel-toed shoes. We learned trots and tangos. We learned *cuecas* and polkas. We *passed, ese,* and had a good time for a couple of months.

One day, Regina got hurt. She was stopped by one of the football players at the beach. She was stepping onto a bus when he came up behind her and grabbed her arm. She tried to twist away, and the arm snapped. She crumpled. Everyone ran. She rode in a friend's car to the hospital that day and had the arm set. She didn't call me.

I heard about it after school the next day, crossing the street against the light. It was summer, and I was taking classes while Regina spent her days at the beach. I'd see her weekdays, stopping at her house on the way home. I was going to her when, just outside the gates of our school, a guy I knew taunted me with the news. He was Japanese, and it was strange to hear him say anything about Regina. I hadn't realized anyone from my crowd knew about us.

I wanted to run the rest of the way to her house. I crossed over a rise of bare earth, then down to a bedded railway—a strip line so that scrap steel and aluminum could be shipped from the switching stations and railyards downtown to steel and aeronautical factories near our school. Brown hummocks rose above eye level and masked the track of crossties, steel rails, and the long bed of gravel. I was set upon there by a troop of Japanese boys. A crowd of them encircled me, taunting, then a single gangly fellow I recognized from gym class executed most of the blows. They beat me, grinding my face in the gravel, shouting epithets like *inu* ("dog"), *cow-fucker*, and *paddy-lover*.

I've seen hand-sized reef fish, in a ritual of spawning, leave their singular lairs, gathering in smallish, excitable schools—a critical mass—and, electrified by their circling assembly, suddenly burst the cluster apart with sequences of soloing, males alternating, pouncing above the finning group, clouding the crystalline waters above the circle with a roll of milt.

All spring and summer, I'd been immune, unaware of the enmity of the crowd. I hadn't realized that, in society, humiliation is a force more powerful than love. Love does not exist in society, but only between two, or among a family. A kid from Hawaii, I'd undergone no real initiation in shame or social victimization yet and maintained an arrogant season out of bounds, imagining I was exempt. It was humiliating to have been sent to Camp. The Japanese American community understood their public disgrace and lived modestly, with deep prohibitions. I was acting outside of this history. I could cross boundaries, I thought. But I was not yet initiated into the knowledge that we Japanese were *not* like anyone else, that we lived in a community of violent shame. I paid for my naïveté with a bashing I still feel today, with cuts that healed with scars I can still run my fingers along. I can still taste the blood, remember the split skin under the mustache on my upper lip, and feel the depth of an anger that must have been *historical, tribal,* arising from fears of dissolution and diaspora.

Separated societies police their own separations. I was hated one day, and with an intensity I could not have foreseen. I was lifted by my clothes, the hands of my schoolmates at the nape of my shirt collar and the back of the waistband of my trousers, and I was hurled against the scrawny trunk of a little jacaranda tree and beaten there, fists cracking against my arms as I tried to cover my face, thumping along my sides and back, booted feet flailing at my legs. I squirmed, crawled, cried out. And I wept. Out of fear and humiliation and a psychic wounding I understand only now. I was *hated*. I was high and needed lowering. My acts were canceled. Regina was canceled. Both by our own peoples, enacting parallel vengeances of their own, taking our bodies from us.

Our trystings were over, and, later that summer, Regina simply moved away. Her father was retiring, she said, and had found a nice trailer park up by Morro Bay. She wouldn't see me before she left. I had to surprise her at a Laundromat one Saturday. She gave me a paperback book. She laughed, made light of everything, but there was a complete *fear* of me that I felt from her, deeply, one I had not felt before—at least, it had never registered. *Race*. It is an exclusion, a punishment, imposed by the group. I've felt it often since. It is a fear of *fraternity*. A fraternity that is forbidden. I wept, but let her go.

[1995]

Journal Entry

What ideas, associations, experiences, emotions, or images of the word *fraternity* can you bring to your reading of Hongo's memoir?

Textual Considerations

1. In the first paragraph, Hongo describes his ethnic group. What portrait does he create?
2. "Gardena H.S. wasn't so much a mix or blend as a mosaic." What evidence supports this thesis?
3. "Dress and social behavior were a code one did not break for fear of ostracism and reprisal." What evidence here resonates with your own experiences in high school?
4. List the highlights of Hongo's relationship with Regina. Why does he devote so much space to this experience?
5. Hongo's brutal beating by his Japanese classmates was traumatic. Characterize your response to this incident.

Cultural Contexts

1. Hongo defines race as "an exclusion, a punishment" and "a fear of fraternity." Compare definitions of race in your group—using examples, as Hongo does, from your own experience. How do your definitions compare with his?
2. Discuss with your group Hongo's statement that "in society, humiliation is a force more powerful than love." How does his idea of community compare with yours? Have you ever been punished for "crossing boundaries"?

Salman Rushdie
From *Imaginary Homelands*

An old photograph in a cheap frame hangs on a wall of the room where I work. It's a picture dating from 1946 of a house into which, at the time of its taking, I had not yet been born. The house is rather peculiar—a three-storied gabled affair with tiled roofs and round towers in two corners, each wearing a pointy tiled hat. "The past is a foreign country," goes the famous opening sentence of L. P. Hartley's novel *The Go-Between*, "they do things differently there." But the photograph tells me to invert this idea; it reminds me that it's my present that is foreign, and that the past is home, albeit a lost home in a lost city in the mists of lost time.

A few years ago I revisited Bombay, which is my lost city, after an absence of something like half my life. Shortly after arriving, acting on an impulse, I opened the telephone directory and looked for my father's name. And, amazingly, there it was; his name, our old address, the unchanged telephone number, as if we had never gone away to the unmentionable country across the border. It was an eerie discovery. I felt as if I were being claimed, or informed that the facts of my faraway life were illusions, and that this continuity was the reality. Then I went to visit the house in the photograph and stood outside it, neither daring nor wishing to announce myself to its new owners. (I didn't want to see how they'd ruined the interior.) I was overwhelmed. The photograph had naturally been taken in black and white; and my memory, feeding on such images as this, had begun to see my childhood in the same way, monochromatically. The colors of my history had seeped out of my mind's eye; now my other two eyes were assaulted by colors, by the vividness of the red tiles, the yellow-edged green of cactus-leaves, the brilliance of bougainvillaea creeper. It is probably not too romantic to say that that was when my novel *Midnight's Children* was really born; when I realized how much I wanted to restore the past to myself, not in the faded grays of old family-album snapshots, but whole, in CinemaScope and glorious Technicolor.

Bombay is a city built by foreigners upon reclaimed land; I, who had been away so long that I almost qualified for the title, was gripped by the conviction that I, too, had a city and a history to reclaim.

It may be that writers in my position, exiles or emigrants or expatriates, are haunted by some sense of loss, some urge to reclaim, to look back, even at the risk of being mutated into pillars of salt. But if we do look back, we must also do so in the knowledge—which gives rise to profound uncertainties—that our physical alienation from India almost inevitably means that we will not be capable of reclaiming precisely the thing that was lost; that we will, in short, create fictions, not actual cities or villages, but invisible ones, imaginary homelands, Indias of the mind.

Writing my book in North London, looking out through my window onto a city scene totally unlike the ones I was imagining onto paper, I was constantly plagued by this problem, until I felt obliged to face it in the text, to make clear that (in spite of my original and I suppose somewhat Proustian ambition to unlock the gates of lost time so that the past reappeared as it actually had been, unaffected by the distortions of memory) what I was actually doing was a novel of memory and about memory, so that my India was just that: "my" India, a version and no more than one version of all the hundreds of millions of possible versions. I tried to make it as imaginatively true as I could, but imaginative truth is simultaneously honorable and suspect, and I knew that my India may only have been one to which I (who am no longer what I was, and who by quitting Bombay never became what perhaps I was meant to be) was, let us say, willing to admit I belonged.

This is why I made my narrator, Saleem, suspect in his narration; his mistakes are the mistakes of a fallible memory compounded by quirks of character and of circumstances and his vision is fragmentary. It may be that when the Indian writer who writes from outside India tries to reflect that world, he is obliged to deal in broken mirrors, some of whose fragments have been irretrievably lost.

But there is a paradox here. The broken mirror may actually be as valuable as the one which is supposedly unflawed. Let me again try and explain this from my own experience. Before beginning *Midnight's Children*, I spent many months trying simply to recall as much of the Bombay of the 1950s and 1960s as I could; and not only Bombay—Kashmir, too, and Delhi and Aligarh, which, in my book, I've moved to Agra to heighten a certain joke about the Taj Mahal. I was genuinely amazed by how much came back to me. I found myself remembering what clothes people had worn on certain days, and school scenes, and whole passages of Bombay dialogue verbatim, or so it seemed; I even remembered advertisements, film posters, the neon Jeep sign on Marine Drive, toothpaste ads for Binaca and for Kolynos, and a footbridge over the local railway line which bore, on one side, the legend "Esso puts a tiger in your tank" and, on the other, the curiously contradictory admonition: "Drive like Hell and you will get there." Old songs came back to me from nowhere. . . .

I knew that I had tapped a rich seam; but the point I want to make is that of course I'm not gifted with total recall, and it was precisely the partial nature of these memories, their fragmentation, that made them so evocative for me. The shards of memory acquired greater status, greater resonance, because they were *remains;* fragmentation made trivial things seem like symbols, and the mundane acquired numinous qualities. There is an obvious parallel here with archaeology. The broken pots of antiquity, from which the past can sometimes, but always provisionally, be reconstructed, are exciting to discover, even if they are pieces of the most quotidian objects.

It may be argued that the past is a country from which we have all emigrated, that its loss is part of our common humanity. Which seems to me self-evidently true; but I suggest that the writer who is out-of-country and even out-of-language may experience this loss in an intensified form. It is made more concrete for him by the physical fact of discontinuity, of his present being in a different place from his past, of his being "elsewhere." This may enable him to speak properly and concretely on a subject of universal significance and appeal.

But let me go further. The broken glass is not merely a mirror of nostalgia. It is also, I believe, a useful tool with which to work in the present.

John Fowles begins *Daniel Martin* with the words: "Whole sight: or all the rest is desolation." But human beings do not perceive things whole; we are not gods but wounded creatures, cracked lenses, capable only of fractured perceptions. Partial beings, in all the senses of that phrase. Meaning is a shaky edifice we build out of scraps, dogmas, childhood injuries, newspaper articles, chance remarks, old films, small victories, people hated, people loved; perhaps it is because our sense of what is the case is constricted from such inadequate materials that we defend it so fiercely, even to the death. The Fowles position seems to me a way of succumbing to the guru-illusion. Writers are no longer sages, dispensing the wisdom of the centuries. And those of us who have been forced by cultural displacement to accept the provisional nature of all truths, all certainties, have perhaps had modernism forced upon us. We can't lay claim to Olympus, and are thus released to describe our worlds in the way in which all of us, whether writers or not, perceive it from day to day. . . .

The Indian writer, looking back at India, does so through guilt-tinted spectacles. (I am of course, once more, talking about myself.) I am speaking now of those of us who emigrated . . . and I suspect that there are times when the move seems wrong to us all, when we seem, to ourselves, post-lapsarian men and women. We are Hindus who have crossed the black water; we are Muslims who eat pork. And as a result—as my use of the Christian notion of the Fall indicates—we are now partly of the West. Our identity is at once plural and partial. Sometimes we feel that we straddle two cultures; at other times, that we fall between two stools. But however ambiguous and shifting this ground may be, it is not an infertile territory for a writer to occupy. If literature is in part the business of finding new angles at which to enter reality, then once again our distance, our long geographical perspective, may provide us with such angles.

[1991]

Journal Entry

Rushdie describes Bombay as his "lost city." If you have such a place, write about a memory that conveys your emotional attachment to it.

Textual Considerations

1. Review the first paragraph of Rushdie's essay, and explain what the photograph represents to him.
2. Paragraph 7 begins, "But there is a paradox here. The broken mirror may actually be as valuable as the one which is supposedly unflawed." What is the meaning of the paradox to which Rushdie refers?
3. What points does Rushdie make concerning memory in paragraph 8? Review paragraphs 9–12 and explain.
4. What connections does Rushdie make between memory and the writer? Explain.

5. Identify some of the references Rushdie makes to literary works, including his own. To what extent do these references help to shape his theme of "lost time," "lost city," and "loss of self" in his text? How do they help him define his feelings about Bombay?

Cultural Contexts

1. Rushdie writes that all immigrants have an identity that is both "plural and partial." What does he mean? If you share his experience as an immigrant, explain how this experience has affected your identity.
2. Brainstorm with your group on your associations with homeland. Are these common motifs? How would you distinguish between real and imaginary homelands?

POETRY

Langston Hughes

The Negro Speaks of Rivers

I've known rivers:
I've known rivers ancient as the world and older than the flow of
    human blood in human veins.

My soul has grown deep like the rivers.

I bathed in the Euphrates when dawns were young.   5
I built my hut near the Congo and it lulled me to sleep.
I looked upon the Nile and raised the pyramids above it.

I heard the singing of the Mississippi when Abe Lincoln
    went down to New Orleans, and I've seen its muddy
    bosom turn all golden in the sunset.   10

I've known rivers:
Ancient, dusky rivers.

My soul has grown deep like the rivers.

[1926]

Linda Hogan

First Light

for Robin

In early morning
I forget I'm in this world
with crooked chiefs
who make federal deals.

117

In the first light   5
I remember who rewards me for living,
not bosses
but singing birds and blue sky.

I know I can bathe and stretch,
make jewelry and love   10
the witch and wise woman
living inside, needing to be silenced
and put at rest for work's long day.

In the first light
I offer cornmeal   15
and tobacco.
I say hello to those who came before me,
and to birds
under the eaves,
and budding plants.   20

I know the old ones are here.
And every morning I remember the song
about how buffalo left through a hole in the sky
and how the grandmothers look out from those holes
watching over us   25
from there and from there.

[1991]

Evangelina Vigil-Piñón

warm heart contains life

to our amás

warm heart contains life
heart's warmth
which penetrates through pen
lifeblood that reveals inner thoughts
subtly   5
like rustling leaves would secrets
to the winter wind
secrets collected
pressed between pages
to be kissed by lips red   10

protruding with warmth, desire
sometimes hurt, pain:

recuerdos°
like that autumn leaf you singled out
and saved   15
pressed in-between the memories of your mind
diary never written
but always remembered, felt
scripted en tu mente°
your daughters will never read it   20
but they'll inherit it
and they'll know it
when they look into your eyes
shining luz de amor, corazón°
unspoken, untold   25
keepsake for our treasure chests
que cargamos aquí adentro°
radiant with jewels
sculpted by sentimientos y penas
y bastante amor:°   30
> intuition tells us
> better having lived through pain
> than never having felt
> life's full intensity

[1982]

13 recuerdos: memories.   **19 en tu mente:** in your mind.   **24 luz de amor, corazón:** light of love, heart.   **27 que cargamos aquí adentro:** that we carry inside ourselves.   **30 sentimiento y penas y bastante amor:** feelings and sufferings and much love.

Journal Entry

What memories, associations, or images of heritage or ancestry can you bring to your reading of these texts?

Textual Considerations

1. Where are the rivers that Hughes mentions in "The Negro Speaks of Rivers"?
2. What historical incidents are part of the journey that the speaker in Hughes's poem imagines taking?
3. Why is the chronology of stanzas two and three significant in "The Negro Speaks of Rivers"?
4. In "First Light," how effective is Hogan's metaphor of "first light" in distinguishing between her ancestors and the "crooked chiefs" and "federal deals" of the present? To what do the latter two terms refer?

5. What lines in Hogan's "First Light" best communicate the security and strength she gets from her Native American heritage?
6. Characterize the relation between the past and the future in Vigil-Piñón's "warm heart contains life." To what extent does the speaker's bilingual text contribute to the poem's meaning? Explain.
7. Speculate on the thematic implications of the title of Vigil-Piñón's poem.
8. Compare and contrast the meaning of "rivers," "first light," and "warm hearts" in "The Negro Speaks of Rivers," "First Light," and "warm heart contains life." What do these images reveal about the speakers' attitudes toward their origins and the past?

Cultural Contexts

1. Hughes considers his racial history an enriching experience and Hogan uses the metaphor of first dawn to communicate the beauty and purity she associates with her ancestors. To what extent do you share their reverence for their ancestral pasts? Explain.
2. In a text she edited in 1983 entitled *Woman of Her Word: Hispanic Women Writers*, Vigil-Piñón describes the Latina writer: "As a person in the literature, the Latina is a woman of her word—*mujer de su palabra*. In this role, the Latina is self-sacrificing to her family as a mother and wife. She conveys values to her family members by way of example, and through the oral tradition, and, as such, she represents a tie to the cultural past." Discuss with your group how oral tradition functions in Vigil-Piñón's poem.

William Blake

The Lamb

Little Lamb, who made thee?
Dost thou know who made thee?
Gave thee life & bid thee feed,
By the stream & o'er the mead;
Gave thee clothing of delight,   5
Softest clothing wooly bright;
Gave thee such a tender voice,
Making all the vales rejoice!
Little Lamb I'll tell thee,
Little Lamb I'll tell thee!   10
He is calléd by thy name,

For he calls himself a Lamb:
He is meek & he is mild,
He became a little child:
I a child & thou a lamb,   15
We are calléd by his name.
Little Lamb God bless thee.
Little Lamb God bless thee.

[1789]

William Blake

The Tyger

Tyger! Tyger! burning bright
In the forests of the night,
What immortal hand or eye
Could frame thy fearful symmetry?

In what distant deeps or skies   5
Burnt the fire of thine eyes?
On what wings dare he aspire?
What the hand, dare seize the fire?

And what shoulder, & what art,
Could twist the sinews of thy heart?   10
And when thy heart began to beat,
What dread hand? & what dread feet?

What the hammer? what the chain?
In what furnace was thy brain?
What the anvil? what dread grasp   15
Dare its deadly terrors clasp?

[1794]

Journal Entry

Brainstorm on your associations with the words *lamb* and *tyger*.

Textual Considerations

1. To what extent does the second stanza of Blake's "The Tyger" answer the questions posed in the first stanza of "The Lamb?"
2. Explain the lamb's symbolic meaning in Blake's *The Lamb*.
3. What qualities of the tyger are suggested by the phrase "fearful symmetry"?
4. Identify words that evoke images of evil in "The Tyger."
5. What is the symbolic significance of the tyger?

Cultural Contexts

1. Respond to Blake's poems as two songs that complement each other. Blake's poems "The Lamb" and "The Tyger" belong to two different volumes entitled *Songs of Innocence* (1789) and *Songs of Experience* (1794). Compare and contrast how successfully Blake has expressed in the two poems what he calls "contrary sites of the Human Soul." Explain.
2. Speculate with members of your group as to why Blake answers the questions posed in "The Lamb" but not those in "The Tyger." How would you respond to those questions?

DICKEY AND HEANEY

James Dickey

In the Tree House at Night

And now the green household is dark.
The half-moon completely is shining
On the earth-lighted tops of the trees.
To be dead, a house must be still.
The floor and the walls wave me slowly; 5
I am deep in them over my head.
The needles and pine cones about me

Are full of small birds at their roundest,
Their fists without mercy gripping
Hard down through the tree to the roots 10
To sing back at light when they feel it.
We lie here like angels in bodies,
My brothers and I, one dead,
The other asleep from much living,

In mid-air huddled beside me. 15
Dark climbed to us here as we climbed
Up the nails I have hammered all day
Through the sprained, comic rungs of the ladder
Of broom handles, crate slats, and laths
Foot by foot up the trunk to the branches 20
Where we came out at last over lakes

Of leaves, of fields disencumbered of earth
That move with the moves of the spirit.
Each nail that sustains us I set here;
Each nail in the house is now steadied 25
By my dead brother's huge, freckled hand.
Through the years, he has pointed his hammer
Up into these limbs, and told us

That we must ascend, and all lie here.
Step after step he has brought me, 30
Embracing the trunk as his body,
Shaking its limbs with my heartbeat,
Till the pine cones danced without wind

And fell from the branches like apples.
In the arm-slender forks of our dwelling   35

I breathe my live brother's light hair.
The blanket around us becomes
As solid as stone, and it sways.
With all my heart, I close
The blue, timeless eye of my mind.   40
Wind springs, as my dead brother smiles
And touches the tree at the root;

A shudder of joy runs up
The trunk; the needles tingle;
One bird uncontrollably cries.   45
The wind changes round, and I stir
Within another's life. Whose life?
Who is dead? Whose presence is living?
When may I fall strangely to earth,

Who am nailed to this branch by a spirit?   50
Can two bodies make up a third?
To sing, must I feel the world's light?
My green, graceful bones fill the air
With sleeping birds. Alone, alone
And with them I move gently.   55
I move at the heart of the world.

[1961]

Seamus Heaney

Mid-term Break

I sat all morning in the college sick bay
Counting bells knelling classes to a close.
At two o'clock our neighbors drove me home.

In the porch I met my father crying—
He had always taken funerals in his stride—   5
And Big Jim Evans saying it was a hard blow.

The baby cooed and laughed and rocked the pram
When I came in, and I was embarrassed
By old men standing up to shake my hand

And tell me they were "sorry for my trouble,"   10
Whispers informed strangers I was the eldest,
Away at school, as my mother held my hand

In hers and coughed out angry tearless sighs.
At ten o'clock the ambulance arrived
With the corpse, stanched and bandaged by the nurses.   15

Next morning I went up into the room. Snowdrops
And candles soothed the bedside; I saw him
For the first time in six weeks. Paler now,

Wearing a poppy bruise on his left temple,
He lay in the four foot box as in his cot.   20
No gaudy scars, the bumper knocked him clear.

A four foot box, a foot for every year.

[1966]

Journal Entry

What experiences, images, or associations with the death of a sibling can you bring to your reading of these texts?

Textual Considerations

1. "To be dead, a house must be still." In Dickey's "In the Tree House at Night," does the speaker picture the tree house as dead or alive? What physical description of the tree house does the speaker include?
2. What role does the dead brother play in "In the Tree House at Night"? What emotions does the speaker reveal about his other brother?
3. How do the birds function symbolically in Dickey's poem? Why do they have to grip the root of the tree with their "fists" in order to "sing back at light"? What is the meaning of "light" throughout "In the Tree House at Night"?
4. What is Heaney's "Mid-term Break" about? How does the speaker's tone affect your understanding of the poem?
5. What images does the title "Mid-term Break" evoke?
6. What lines in "Mid-term Break" most contradict these images?
7. The speaker expresses his grief through understatement in "Mid-Term Break." What examples do you find most effective? How does the speaker's expression of grief compare and contrast with the speaker's feeling of dejection in "In the Tree House at Night"? Which one has most affected you?

Cultural Contexts

1. Review stanzas 4 and 5 of Dickey's poem with your group. What lines indicate that the tree house has a symbolic meaning? What connections does the poet establish between the tree house and his dead brother? Between the tree house and himself? What do the questions in the seventh and eighth stanzas contribute?
2. Discuss with members of your group the mourning rituals you are most familiar with. How do law and custom affect them? Whose attitude toward death reflects yours—Dickey's or Heaney's? Explain.

LEVERTOV AND SONG

Denise Levertov

During a Son's Dangerous Illness

You could die before me—
I've known it
always, the
dreaded worst, "unnatural" but
possible   5
in the play
of matter, matter and
growth and
fate.

My sister Philippa died   10
twelve years before I was born—
the perfect, laughing firstborn,
a gift to be cherished as my orphaned mother
had not been cherished. Suddenly:
death, a baby   15

cold and still.

Parent, child—death ignores
protocol, a sweep of its cape brushes
this one or that one at random

into the dust, it was   20
not even looking.
                       What becomes
of the past if the future
snaps off, brittle,
the present left as a jagged edge   25
opening on nothing?

Grief for the menaced world—lost rivers,
poisoned lakes—all creatures, perhaps
to be fireblasted
                       off the   30
whirling cinder we
love but not enough . . .
The grief I'd know if I

lived into
your unthinkable death   35
is a splinter
of that selfsame grief,
infinitely smaller but
the same in kind:
one   40
stretching the mind's fibers to touch
eternal nothingness,
the other
tasting in fear, the
desolation of   45
survival.

[1987]

Cathy Song

Lost Sister

1

In China,
even the peasants
named their first daughters
Jade—
the stone that in the far fields   5
could moisten the dry season,
could make men move mountains
for the healing green of the inner hills
glistening like slices of winter melon.

And the daughters were grateful: 10
they never left home.
To move freely was a luxury
stolen from them at birth.
Instead, they gathered patience,
learning to walk in shoes   15
the size of teacups,°
without breaking—
the arc of their movements
as dormant as the rooted willow,
as redundant as the farmyard hens.   20

But they traveled far
in surviving,
learning to stretch the family rice,
to quiet the demons,
the noisy stomachs.   25

2

There is a sister
across the ocean,
who relinquished her name,
diluting jade green
with the blue of the Pacific.   30
Rising with a tide of locusts,
she swarmed with others
to inundate another shore.
In America,
there are many roads   35
and women can stride along with men.

But in another wilderness,
the possibilities,
the loneliness,
can strangulate like jungle vines.   40
The meager provisions and sentiments
of once belonging—
fermented roots, Mah-Jongg° tiles and firecrackers—
set but a flimsy household
in a forest of nightless cities.   45
A giant snake rattles above,
spewing black clouds into your kitchen.
Dough-faced landlords
slip in and out of your keyholes,
making claims you don't understand,   50
tapping into your communication systems
of laundry lines and restaurant chains.

You find you need China:
your one fragile identification,
a jade link   55
handcuffed to your wrist.

You remember your mother
who walked for centuries,
footless—
and like her,   60

you have left no footprints,
but only because
there is an ocean in between,
the unremitting space of your rebellion.

[1987]

---

16 teacups: A reference to the practice of binding young girls' feet so that they remain small. This practice was common in China until the Communist revolution.   **43 Mah-Jongg:** Or mahjong, an ancient Chinese game played with dice and tiles.

Journal Entry

What memories, images, or associations of family can you bring to your reading of these texts?

Textual Considerations

1. In Levertov's poem, how does the son's illness in the present serve as a catalyst for the speaker's memories of her mother?
2. Explain the meaning of "death ignores protocol" in "During a Son's Dangerous Illness."
3. State the conflict at the heart of Song's poem.
4. In "Lost Sister," why do you think the speaker includes the tradition of footbinding in stanza one?
5. Why is the speaker ambivalent about her choice to travel across the ocean? What has she gained and lost?
6. How does she describe where she lives in the United States?
7. Explain why the lost sister and her mother have left no footprints.

Cultural Contexts

1. Review Song's biographical endnote and discuss with your group the following statement made by another Asian immigrant: "Oh Asia, that nets its children in ties of blood so binding that they cut the spirit." To what extent does this apply to Song's poem? Explain.
2. Analyze with your group the portraits of family members such as sisters, daughters, and others that emerge through personal and ancestral memories in the two poems. What do they reveal about the speaker's connection with the past? What emotions do they evoke?

OLDS, MIRIKITANI, AND TAPAHONSO

Sharon Olds

The Possessive

My daughter—as if I
owned her—that girl with the
hair wispy as a frayed bellpull

has been to the barber, that knife grinder,
and had the edge of her hair sharpened.   5

Each strand now cuts
both ways. The blade of new bangs
hangs over her red-brown eyes
like carbon steel.

        All the little   10
spliced ropes are sliced, the curtain of
dark paper-cuts veils the face that
started from next to nothing in my body—

My body. My daughter. I'll have to find
another word. In her bright helmet   15
she looks at me as if across a
great distance. Distant fires can be
glimpsed in the resin light of her eyes:

the watch fires of an enemy, a while before
the war starts.   20

[1980]

Janice Mirikitani

Breaking Tradition
for my Daughter

My daughter denies she is like me,
Her secretive eyes avoid mine.
   She reveals the hatreds of womanhood
   already veiled behind music and smoke and telephones.
I want to tell her about the empty room   5
   of myself.
   This room we lock ourselves in
   where whispers live like fungus,
   giggles about small breasts and cellulite,
   where we confine ourselves to jealousies,   10
   bedridden by menstruation.
   This waiting room where we feel our hands
   are useless, dead speechless clamps
   that need hospitals and forceps and kitchens
   and plugs and ironing boards to make them useful.   15
I deny I am like my mother. I remember why:
   She kept her room neat with silence,
   defiance smothered in requirements to be otonashii,
      passion and loudness wrapped in an obi,
      her steps confined to ceremony,   20
      the weight of her sacrifice she carried like
      a foetus. Guilt passed on in our bones.
I want to break tradition—unlock this room
   where women dress in the dark.
   Discover the lies my mother told me.   25
   The lies that we are small and powerless,
   that our possibilities must be compressed
   to the size of pearls, displayed only as
   passive chokers, charms around our neck.
Break Tradition.   30
   I want to tell my daughter of this room
   of myself
   filled with tears of violins,
   the light in my hands,
   poems about madness,   35
   the music of yellow guitars—
   sounds shaken from barbed wire and
   goodbyes and miracles of survival.
   This room of open window where daring ones escape.

My daughter denies she is like me   40
    her secretive eyes are walls of smoke
    and music and telephones,
    her pouting ruby lips, her skirts
    swaying to salsa, teena marie and the stones,
    her thighs displayed in carnavals of color.   45
    I do not know the contents of her room.
She mirrors my aging.
She is breaking tradition.

[1987]

Luci Tapahonso

A Breeze Swept Through
for my daughters, Lori Tazbah and Misty Dawn

The first born of dawn woman
slid out amid crimson fluid streaked with stratus clouds
    her body glistening August sunset pink
    light steam rising from her like rain on warm rocks
        (A sudden cool breeze swept through   5
        the kitchen and grandpa smiled then sang
        quietly knowing the moment.)
She came when the desert day cooled
and dusk began to move in
in that intricate changing of time   10
    she gasped and it flows from her now
    with every breath   with every breath
    she travels now
        sharing scarlet sunsets
        named for wild desert flowers   15
        her smile a blessing song.

And in mid-November
early morning darkness
after days of waiting pain
    the second one cried   wailing   20
    sucking first earth breath
    separating the heavy fog
    she cried and kicked   tiny brown limbs
    fierce movements as outside
    the mist lifted as   25

the sun is born again.
    (East of Acoma, a sandstone boulder
    split in two—a sharp, clean crack.)
    She is born of damp mist and early sun.
    She is born again   woman of dawn.   30
    She is born knowing the warm smoothness of rock.
    She is born knowing her own morning strength.

[1984]

Journal Entry

What experiences or knowledge of mother-daughter relationships can you bring to your reading of these texts?

Textual Considerations

1. Explain the thematic significance of the title of Olds's poem. What are your associations with the word *possessive*? Do you ever feel possessive about other people? Explain.
2. Identify images of war in "The Possessive." Why does the mother consider her daughter an enemy? Is the conflict resolved by the end of the poem? How?
3. How does the daughter in Mirikitani's poem express her rebellion?
4. Why doesn't the speaker in "Breaking Tradition" want to be like her mother?
5. Characterize the tone of the speaker in "Breaking Tradition."
6. What does the speaker mean by "she mirrors my aging" in "Breaking Traditions"?
7. Create a profile of both daughters in Tapahonso's poem.
8. Identify examples of visual and sensory images in Tapahonso's text and discuss their effectiveness in communicating meaning.

Cultural Contexts

1. To what extent are the texts by Olds and Mirikitani about breaking traditions? What traditions are being broken? By whom? How do you and your group members respond to their conflicts? Do adolescents always break traditions? Explain.
2. With members of your group, create a portrait of each of the mothers in the three poems. Which mother most appeals to you? Explain.

Dylan Thomas

Fern Hill

Now as I was young and easy under the apple boughs
About the lilting house and happy as the grass was green,
    The night above the dingle° starry,
      Time let me hail and climb
     Golden in the heydays of his eyes,   5
And honored among wagons I was prince of the apple towns
And once below a time I lordly had the trees and leaves
      Trail with daisies and barley
    Down the rivers of the windfall light.

And as I was green and carefree, famous among the barns   10
About the happy yard and singing as the farm was home,
    In the sun that is young once only,
      Time let me play and be
     Golden in the mercy of his means,
And green and golden I was huntsman and herdsman, the calves   15
Sang to my horn, the foxes on the hills barked clear and cold,
     And the sabbath rang slowly
    In the pebbles of the holy streams.

All the sun long it was running, it was lovely, the hay
Fields high as the house, the tunes from the chimneys, it was air   20
    And playing, lovely and watery
      And fire green as grass.
    And nightly under the simple stars
As I rode to sleep the owls were bearing the farm away,
All the moon long I heard, blessed among stables, the nightjars   25
    Flying with the ricks, and the horses
      Flashing into the dark.

And then to awake, and the farm, like a wanderer white
With the dew, come back, the cock on his shoulder: it was all
    Shining, it was Adam and maiden,   30
      The sky gathered again
    And the sun grew round that very day.
So it must have been after the birth of the simple light
In the first, spinning place, the spellbound horses walking warm

Out of the whinnying green stable   35
    On to the fields of praise.

And honored among foxes and pheasants by the gay house
Under the new made clouds and happy as the heart was long,
    In the sun born over and over,
        I ran my heedless ways,   40
    My wishes raced through the house high hay
And nothing I cared, at my sky blue trades, that time allows
In all his tuneful turning so few and such morning songs
    Before the children green and golden
        Follow him out of grace,   45

Nothing I cared, in the lamb white days, that time would take me
Up to the swallow thronged loft by the shadow of my hand,
    In the moon that is always rising,
        Nor that riding to sleep
    I should hear him fly with the high fields   50
And wake to the farm forever fled from the childless land.
Oh as I was young and easy in the mercy of his means,
        Time held me green and dying
    Though I sang in my chains like the sea.

[1946]

3 dingle: Wooded valley.

Richard Eberhart

If I could only live at the pitch that is near madness

If I could only live at the pitch that is near madness
When everything is as it was in my childhood
Violent, vivid, and of infinite possibility:
That the sun and the moon broke over my head.

Then I cast time out of the trees and fields,   5
Then I stood immaculate in the Ego;
Then I eyed the world with all delight,
Reality was the perfection of my sight.

And time has big handles on the hands,
Fields and trees a way of being themselves.   10
I saw battalions of the race of mankind
Standing stolid, demanding a moral answer.

I gave the moral answer and I died
And into a realm of complexity came
Where nothing is possible but necessity   15
And the truth wailing there like a red babe.

[1960]

Journal Entry

Write a short vignette focusing on a memorable moment in your childhood. Include as many sensory and visual images as you can recall to capture what makes it so significant.

Textual Considerations

1. How does Thomas's use of color reinforce meaning in "Fern Hill"? How do his references to music also contribute to the poem's meaning?
2. In stanza 4 the speaker compares his childhood to the garden of Eden. How does his comparison reinforce his concept of childhood innocence? How does it compare with the speaker's childhood in "Fern Hill"?
3. The speaker in "Fern Hill" sounds an ominous note for the first time in stanza 5. What foreshadowings of this danger can you find in earlier stanzas?
4. Explain the **paradox** in the last two lines of "Fern Hill."
5. Do you agree with Eberhart's description of childhood as "violent, vivid, and of infinite possibility"? Explain.
6. What further descriptions of childhood are added by each of the four lines in the second stanza of Eberhart's poem?
7. The third stanza contrasts with the first two. What has happened to time in line 9? To the fields and trees in line 10? What does he mean by a "moral answer" in line 12?

Cultural Contexts

1. The title of Thomas's poem refers to his aunt's house in Wales, where he obviously spent many carefree summers. Is there a "site of memory" that has shaped your historical past? Describe it to your group, and discuss the extent to which we are influenced by the landscapes of our pasts.
2. Eberhart equates adulthood with the "moral answer" and "the realm of complexity." Is he suggesting that in childhood people are more imaginative and more likely to think of possibilities as opposed to limitations? Discuss these ideas with members of your group and record your findings.

CHOCK, LEE, AND EMANUEL

Eric Chock

Poem for My Father

I lie dreaming
when my father comes to me and says,
I hope you write a book someday.
He thinks I waste my time,
but outside, he spends hours over stones, 5
gauging the size and shape a rock will take
to fill a space,
to make a wall of dreams around our home.
In the house he built with his own hands
I wish for the lure that catches all fish 10
or girls with hair like long moss in the river.
His thoughts are just as far and old
as the lava chips like flint off his hammer,
and he sees the mold of dreams
taking shape in his hands. 15
His eyes see across orchids on the wall,
into black rock, down to the sea,
and he remembers the harbor full of fish,
orchids in the hair of women thirty years before
he thought of me, this home, these stone walls. 20
Some rocks fit perfectly, slipping into place
with light taps of his hammer.
He thinks of me inside
and takes a big slice of stone,
and pounds it into the ground 25
to make the corner of the wall.
I cannot wake until I bring
the fish and the girl home.

[1989]

Li-Young Lee

The Gift

To pull the metal splinter from my palm
my father recited a story in a low voice.
I watched his lovely face and not the blade.
Before the story ended, he'd removed
the iron sliver I thought I'd die from.   5

I can't remember the tale,
but hear his voice still, a well
of dark water, a prayer.
And I recall his hands,
two measures of tenderness   10
he laid against my face,
the flames of discipline
he raised above my head.

Had you entered that afternoon
you would have thought you saw a man   15
planting something in a boy's palm,
a silver tear, a tiny flame.
Had you followed that boy
you would have arrived here,
where I bend over my wife's right hand.   20

Look how I shave her thumbnail down
so carefully she feels no pain.
Watch as I lift the splinter out.
I was seven when my father
took my hand like this,   25

and I did not hold that shard
between my fingers and think,
Metal that will bury me,
christen it Little Assassin,
Ore Going Deep for My Heart,   30
And I did not lift up my wound and cry,
Death visited here!
I did what a child does
when he's given something to keep.
I kissed my father.   35

[1986]

James A. Emanuel

Fishermen

When three, he fished these lakes,
Curled sleeping on a lip of rock,
Crib blankets tucked from ants and fishbone flies,
Twitching as the strike of bass and snarling reel
Uncoiled my shouts not quit   5
Till he jerked blinking up on all-fours,
Swaying with the winking leaves.
Strong awake, he shook his cane pole like a spoon
And dipped among the wagging perch
Till, tired, he drew his silver rubber blade   10
And poked the winding fins that tugged our string,
Or sprayed the dimpling minnows with his plastic gun,
Or, rainstruck, squirmed to my armpit in the poncho.

Ten years uncurled him, thinned him hard.
Now, far he casts his line into the wrinkled blue   15
And easy toes a rock, reel on his thigh
Till bone and crank cry out the strike
He takes with manchild chuckles, cunning
In his play of zigzag line and plunging silver.

Now fishing far from me, he strides through rain, shoulders   20
A spiny ridge of pines, and disappears
Near lakes that cannot be, while I must choose
To go or stay: bring blanket, blade, and gun,
Or stand a fisherman.

[1968]

Journal Entry

What associations, memories, or experiences do you have that relate to the bond between fathers and sons? To what extent are they reinforced or contradicted in the three poems?

Textual Considerations

1. How does the father in Chock's poem spend his days?
2. What are his dreams and memories? How do they affect his dreams for his son?
3. How does the speaker link past and present in Lee's "The Gift"?
4. What does Lee's poem make you see? Consider the images the speaker uses to describe his father's hands. Does he also reveal anything about his character? In which lines of the poem?

5. Why does the speaker include the scene with his wife? Would the poem's meaning change without it? Explain.
6. Compare and contrast the three fishing trips in Emanuel's poem.
7. Explain the significance of the last line of the poem.

Cultural Contexts

1. Assess the father/son relationship in each text. Which best reflects your experiences? Are conflicts between fathers and sons inevitable? Explain.
2. "Fishermen" is told from the point of view of the father, while the other two poems are narrated from the point of view of the sons. To what extent does that fact affect your responses to the texts? Explain.

Robert Hayden

Frederick Douglass°

When it is finally ours, this freedom, this liberty, this beautiful
and terrible thing, needful to man as air,
usable as earth; when it belongs at last to all,
when it is truly instinct, brain matter, diastole, systole,
reflex action; when it is finally won; when it is more   5
than the gaudy mumbo jumbo of politicians:
this man, this Douglass, this former slave, this Negro
beaten to his knees, exiled, visioning a world
where none is lonely, none hunted, alien,
this man, superb in love and logic, this man   10
shall be remembered. Oh, not with statues' rhetoric,
not with legends and poems and wreaths of bronze alone,
but with the lives grown out of his life, the lives
fleshing his dream of the beautiful, needful thing.

[1947]

Frederick Douglass: Born a slave, Douglass (1817–95) escaped and became an important spokes-man for the abolitionist movement and later for civil rights for African Americans.

Robert Hayden

Tour 5

The road winds down through autumn hills
in blazonry of farewell scarlet
and recessional gold,
past cedar groves, through static villages
whose names are all that's left   5
of Choctaw, Chickasaw.°

We stop a moment in a town
watched over by Confederate sentinels,

buy gas and ask directions of a rawboned man
whose eyes revile us as the enemy.   10

Shrill gorgon silence breathes behind
his taut civility
and in the ever-tautening air,
dark for us despite its Indian summer glow.
We drive on, following the route   15
of highwaymen and phantoms,

Of slaves and armies.
Children, wordless and remote,
wave at us from kindling porches.
And now the land is flat for miles,   20
the landscape lush, metallic, flayed,
its brightness harsh as bloodstained swords.

[1962]

6 **Choctaw, Chickasaw:** American Indian tribes, originally of Mississippi.

Robert Hayden

Those Winter Sundays

Sundays too my father got up early
and put his clothes on in the blueblack cold,
then with cracked hands that ached
from labor in the weekday weather made
banked fires blaze. No one ever thanked him.   5

I'd wake and hear the cold splintering, breaking.
When the rooms were warm, he'd call,
and slowly I would rise and dress,
fearing the chronic angers of that house,

Speaking indifferently to him,   10
who had driven out the cold
and polished my good shoes as well.
What did I know, what did I know
of love's austere and lonely offices?

[1962]

Robert Hayden

Runagate Runagate

I.

Runs falls rises stumbles on from darkness into darkness
and the darkness thicketed with shapes of terror
and the hunters pursuing and the hounds pursuing
and the night cold and the night long and the river
to cross and the jack-muh-lanterns beckoning beckoning   5
and blackness ahead and when shall I reach that somewhere
morning and keep on going and never turn back and keep on going

      Runagate
             Runagate
                    Runagate   10

Many thousands rise and go
many thousands crossing over

                        O mythic North
                 O star-shaped yonder Bible city

Some go weeping and some rejoicing   15
some in coffins and some in carriages
some in silks and some in shackles

      Rise and go or fare you well

No more auction block for me
no more driver's lash for me   20

        If you see my Pompey, 30 yrs of age,
        new breeches, plain stockings, negro shoes;
        if you see my Anna, likely young mulatto
        branded E on the right cheek, R on the left,
        catch them if you can and notify subscriber,   25
        Catch them if you can, but it won't be easy.
        They'll dart underground when you try to catch them,
        plunge into quicksand, whirlpools, mazes,
        turn into scorpions when you try to catch them.

And before I'll be a slave   30
I'll be buried in my grave

North star and bonanza gold
I'm bound for the freedom, freedom-bound
and oh Susyanna don't you cry for me

        Runagate   35

        Runagate

II.

Rises from their anguish and their power,

        Harriet Tubman,

        woman of earth, whipscarred,
        a summoning, a shining   40

        Mean to be free

And this was the way of it, brethren brethren,
way we journeyed from Can't to Can.

        Moon so bright and no place to hide,
        the cry up and the patterollers riding,   45
        hound dogs belling in bladed air.
        And fear starts a-murbling, Never make it,
        we'll never make it. *Hush that now,*
        and she's turned upon us, levelled pistol
        glinting in the moonlight: 50

        Dead folks can't jaybird-talk she says:
        you keep on going now or die, she says.

Wanted   Harriet Tubman   alias The General
alias Moses   Stealer of Slaves

In league with Garrison   Alcott   Emerson   55
Garrett   Douglass   Thoreau   John Brown

Armed and known to be Dangerous

Wanted   Reward   Dead or Alive

        Tell me, Ezekiel, oh tell me do you see
        mailed Jehovah coming to deliver me?   60

Hoot-owl calling in the ghosted air,
five times calling to the hants in the air.
Shadow of a face in the scary leaves,
shadow of a voice in the talking leaves:

Come ride-a my train   65

Oh that train, ghost-story train
through swamp and savanna movering movering,
over trestles of dew, through caves of the wish,
Midnight Special on a sabre track movering movering,
first stop Mercy and the last Hallelujah.   70

Come ride-a my train

Mean mean mean to be free.

[1985]

Journal Entry

Freewrite on your associations, images, or concepts of freedom. To what extent is freedom related to ethnicity? Explain.

Textual Considerations

1. According to Hayden, when and how will Douglass be remembered?
2. Research the origins of "mumbo jumbo" in line 6 of "Frederick Douglass." How does Hayden's use affect the poem's meaning?
3. What is the effect of delaying the subject of the first sentence until line 7 and the verb until line 11 in "Frederick Douglass"?
4. Does Hayden imply that there will come a time when freedom will belong to all? Do you agree? Why or why not?
5. Describe the effects of stopping for gas in "Tour 5."
6. Contrast the language of the first and last stanzas of "Tour 5." What is the effect on the poem's mood and meaning?
7. Characterize the father in "Those Winter Sundays." What is the effect of using *too* in the first line?
8. How does the son attempt to subdue the "chronic angers" of the house? How does the use of repetition in line 13 of "Those Winter Sundays" reinforce meaning?
9. What kind of relationship do father and son share in "Those Winter Sundays"? Explain the meaning of "offices" in the last line.
10. Consult a dictionary for the various meanings of **runagate**. What effect is gained by repeating it in the title, "Runagate Runagate"?
11. How do the visual effects in "Runagate Runagate" contribute to its sense of movement as the slaves attempt to escape to the North through the Underground Railroad?
12. What is the effect of juxtaposing the thoughts and feelings of the runagate with the slave owner's handbill providing reward for his capture?
13. If you are unfamiliar with Harriet Tubman or others mentioned in part II of "Runagate Runagate," research their contribution to the abolitionist movement.

Cultural Contexts

1. Construct with your group a brief narrative on the abolitionist movement based on your responses to question 13.
   To what extent does this statement apply to Hayden's poems in this anthology?
2. How does Frederick Douglass's idea expressed in his autobiography that "we have to do with the past only as it is useful for the present and the future" apply to the poem by Hayden? To what extent is the past always with us?

DRAMA

Sophocles

Oedipus Rex

CHARACTERS

OEDIPUS, *King of Thebes, supposed son of Polybos and Merope,*
  King and Queen of Corinth
IOKASTE, *wife of Oedipus and widow of the late King Laios*
KREON, *brother of Iokaste, a prince of Thebes*
TEIRESIAS, *a blind seer who serves Apollo*
PRIEST
MESSENGER, *from Corinth*
SHEPHERD, *former Servant of Laios*
SECOND MESSENGER, *from the palace*
CHORUS OF THEBAN ELDERS
CHORAGOS, *leader of the Chorus*
ANTIGONE *and* ISMENE, *young daughters of Oedipus and Iokaste.*
  They appear in the Exodos but do not speak.
Suppliants, Guards, Servants

SCENE. *Before the palace of* OEDIPUS, *King of Thebes. A central door and two
lateral doors open onto a platform which runs the length of the facade. On the
platform, right and left, are altars; and three steps lead down into the
orchestra, or chorus-ground. At the beginning of the action these steps are
crowded by suppliants who have brought branches and chaplets of olive leaves
and who sit in various attitudes of despair.* OEDIPUS *enters.*

PROLOGUE

OEDIPUS: My children, generations of the living
  In the line of Kadmos,° nursed at his ancient hearth:
  Why have you strewn yourselves before these altars
  In supplication, with your boughs and garlands?
  The breath of incense rises from the city   5
  With a sound of prayer and lamentation.
                              Children,
  I would not have you speak through messengers,

2. **Kadmos:** founder of Thebes, according to legend.

148

And therefore I have come myself to hear you—
I, Oedipus, who bear the famous name.
(*To a* PRIEST.) You, there, since you are eldest in the company,   10
Speak for them all, tell me what preys upon you,
Whether you come in dread, or crave some blessing:
Tell me, and never doubt that I will help you
In every way I can; I should be heartless
Were I not moved to find you suppliant here.   15
PRIEST: Great Oedipus, O powerful king of Thebes!
You see how all the ages of our people
Cling to your altar steps: here are boys
Who can barely stand alone, and here are priests
By weight of age, as I am a priest of God,   20
And young men chosen from those yet unmarried;
As for the others, all that multitude,
They wait with olive chaplets in the squares,
At the two shrines of Pallas,° and where Apollo°
Speaks in the glowing embers.
                                          Your own eyes   25
Must tell you: Thebes is tossed on a murdering sea
And cannot lift her head from the death surge.
A rust consumes the buds and fruits of the earth;
The herds are sick; children die unborn,
And labor is vain. The god of plague and pyre   30
Raids like detestable lightning through the city,
And all the house of Kadmos is laid waste,
All emptied, and all darkened: Death alone
Battens upon the misery of Thebes.

You are not one of the immortal gods, we know;   35
Yet we have come to you to make our prayer
As to the man surest in mortal ways
And wisest in the ways of God. You saved us
From the Sphinx,° that flinty singer, and the tribute
We paid to her so long; yet you were never   40
Better informed than we, nor could we teach you:
A god's touch, it seems, enabled you to help us.

Therefore, O mighty power, we turn to you:
Find us our safety, find us a remedy,

---

24. Pallas: Pallas Athena, Zeus's daughter; goddess of wisdom;   **24. Apollo:** Zeus's son, god of the sun, truth, and poetry.   **39. Sphinx:** a monster with the body of a lion, the wings of a bird, and the face of a woman. The Sphinx had challenged Thebes with a riddle, killing those who failed to solve it. When Oedipus answered correctly, the Sphinx killed herself.

Whether by counsel of the gods or of men. 45
A kin of wisdom tested in the past
Can act in a time of troubles, and act well.
Noblest of men, restore
Life to your city! Think how all men call you
Liberator for your boldness long ago; 50
Ah, when your years of kingship are remembered,
Let them not say *We rose, but later fell*—
Keep the State from going down in the storm!
Once, years ago, with happy augury,
You brought us fortune; be the same again! 55
No man questions your power to rule the land:
But rule over men, not over a dead city!
Ships are only hulls, high walls are nothing,
When no life moves in the empty passageways.

OEDIPUS: Poor children! You may be sure I know 60
All that you longed for in your coming here.
I know that you are deathly sick; and yet,
Sick as you are, not one is as sick as I.
Each of you suffers in himself alone
His anguish, not another's; but my spirit 65
Groans for the city, for myself, for you.

I was not sleeping, you are not waking me.
No, I have been in tears for a long while
And in my restless thought walked many ways.
In all my search I found one remedy, 70
And I have adopted it: I have sent Kreon,
Son of Menoikeus, brother of the queen,
To Delphi,° Apollo's place of revelation,
To learn there, if he can,
What act or pledge of mine may save the city. 75
I have counted the days, and now, this very day,
I am troubled, for he has overstayed his time.
What is he doing? He has been gone too long.
Yet whenever he comes back, I should do ill
Not to take any action the god orders. 80

PRIEST: It is a timely promise. At this instant
They tell me Kreon is here.

OEDIPUS: O Lord Apollo!
May his news be fair as his face is radiant!

PRIEST: Good news, I gather! he is crowned with bay,
The chaplet is thick with berries.

---

73. Delphi: location of the prophetic oracle, regarded as the keeper of religious truth.

OEDIPUS: We shall soon know;   85
  He is near enough to hear us now. (*Enter* KREON.) O prince:
  Brother: son of Menoikeus:
  What answer do you bring us from the god?
KREON: A strong one. I can tell you, great afflictions
  Will turn out well, if they are taken well.   90
OEDIPUS: What was the oracle? These vague words
  Leave me still hanging between hope and fear.
KREON: Is it your pleasure to hear me with all these
  Gathered around us? I am prepared to speak,
  But should we not go in?
OEDIPUS: Speak to them all,   95
  It is for them I suffer, more than for myself.
KREON: Then I will tell you what I heard at Delphi.
  In plain words
  The god commands us to expel from the land of Thebes
  An old defilement we are sheltering.   100
  It is a deathly thing, beyond cure;
  We must not let it feed upon us longer.
OEDIPUS: What defilement? How shall we rid ourselves of it?
KREON: By exile or death, blood for blood. It was
  Murder that brought the plague-wind on the city.   105
OEDIPUS: Murder of whom? Surely the god has named him?
KREON: My Lord: Laios once ruled this land,
  Before you came to govern us.
OEDIPUS: I know;
  I learned of him from others; I never saw him.
KREON: He was murdered; and Apollo commands us now   110
  To take revenge upon whoever killed him.
OEDIPUS: Upon whom? Where are they? Where shall we find a clue
  To solve that crime, after so many years?
KREON: Here in this land, he said. Search reveals
  Things that escape an inattentive man.   115
OEDIPUS: Tell me: Was Laios murdered in his house,
  Or in the fields, or in some foreign country?
KREON: He said he planned to make a pilgrimage.
  He did not come home again.
OEDIPUS: And was there no one,
  No witness, no companion, to tell what happened?   120
KREON: They were all killed but one, and he got away
  So frightened that he could remember one thing only.
OEDIPUS: What was that one thing? One may be the key
  To everything, if we resolve to use it.
KREON: He said that a band of highwaymen attacked them,   125
  Outnumbered them, and overwhelmed the king.

OEDIPUS: Strange, that a highwayman should be so daring—
    Unless some faction here bribed him to do it.
KREON: We thought of that. But after Laios' death
    New troubles arose and we had no avenger.   130
OEDIPUS: What troubles could prevent your hunting down the killers?
KREON: The riddling Sphinx's song
    Made us deaf to all mysteries but her own.
OEDIPUS: Then once more I must bring what is dark to light.
    It is most fitting that Apollo shows,   135
    As you do, this compunction for the dead.
    You shall see how I stand by you, as I should,
    Avenging this country and the god as well,
    And not as though it were for some distant friend,
    But for my own sake, to be rid of evil.   140
    Whoever killed King Laios might—who knows?—
    Lay violent hands even on me—and soon.
    I act for the murdered king in my own interest.

    Come, then, my children: leave the altar steps,
    Lift up your olive boughs!
                       One of you go   145
    And summon the people of Kadmos to gather here.
    I will do all that I can; you may tell them that.   (*Exit a* PAGE.)
    So, with the help of God,
    We shall be saved—or else indeed we are lost.
PRIEST: Let us rise, children. It was for this we came,   150
    And now the king has promised it.
    Phoibos° has sent us an oracle; may he descend
    Himself to save us and drive out the plague.

        (*Exeunt*° OEDIPUS *and* KREON *into the palace by the central door. The* PRIEST
        and the SUPPLIANTS *disperse right and left. After a short pause the* CHORUS
        enters the orchestra.)

    PARODOS

    STROPHE 1

CHORUS: What is God singing in his profound
    Delphi of gold and shadow?
    What oracle for Thebes, the Sunwhipped city?
    Fear unjoints me, the roots of my heart tremble.
    Now I remember, O Healer, your power, and wonder: 5
    Will you send doom like a sudden cloud, or weave it

---

152. Phoibos: Apollo.   **s.d. Exeunt:** Latin term meaning "they exit."

Like nightfall of the past?
Speak to me, tell me, O
Child of golden Hope, immortal Voice.

ANTISTROPHE 1

Let me pray to Athene, the immortal daughter of Zeus,   10
And to Artemis° her sister
Who keeps her famous throne in the market ring,
And to Apollo, archer from distant heaven—
O gods, descend! Like three streams leap against
The fires of our grief, the fires of darkness;   15
Be swift to bring us rest!
As in the old time from the brilliant house
Of air you stepped to save us, come again!

STROPHE 2

Now our afflictions have no end,
Now all our stricken host lies down   20
And no man fights off death with his mind;
The noble plowland bears no grain,
And groaning mothers cannot bear—
See, how our lives like birds take wing,
Like sparks that fly when a fire soars,   25
To the shore of the god of evening.

ANTISTROPHE 2

The plague burns on, it is pitiless,
Though pallid children laden with death
Lie unwept in the stony ways,
And old gray women by every path   30
Flock to the strand about the altars
There to strike their breasts and cry
Worship of Phoibos in wailing prayers:
Be kind, God's golden child!

STROPHE 3

There are no swords in this attack by fire,   35
No shields, but we are ringed with cries.
Send the besieger plunging from our homes
Into the vast sea-room of the Atlantic
Or into the waves that foam eastward of Thrace—

---

11. Artemis: goddess of the hunt.

For the day ravages what the night spares— 40
Destroy our enemy, lord of the thunder!
Let him be riven by lightning from heaven!

ANTISTROPHE 3

Phoibos Apollo, stretch the sun's bowstring,
That golden cord, until it sing for us,
Flashing arrows in heaven!
                             Artemis, Huntress, 45
Race with flaring lights upon our mountains!
O scarlet god,° O golden-banded brow,
O Theban Bacchos in a storm of Maenads,°

(*Enter* OEDIPUS, *center.*)

Whirl upon Death, that all the Undying hate!
Come with blinding torches, come in joy! 50

SCENE I

OEDIPUS: Is this your prayer? It may be answered. Come,
Listen to me, act as the crisis demands,
And you shall have relief from all these evils.

Until now I was a stranger to this tale,
As I had been a stranger to the crime. 5
Could I track down the murderer without a clue?
But now, friends,
As one who became a citizen after the murder,
I make this proclamation to all Thebans:
If any man knows by whose hand Laios, son of Labdakos, 10
Met his death, I direct that man to tell me everything,
No matter what he fears for having so long withheld it.
Let it stand as promised that no further trouble
Will come to him, but he may leave the land in safety.
Moreover: If anyone knows the murderer to be foreign, 15
Let him not keep silent: he shall have his reward from me.
However, if he does conceal it; if any man
Fearing for his friend or for himself disobeys this edict,
Hear what I propose to do:

I solemnly forbid the people of this country, 20
Where power and throne are mine, ever to receive that man

---

47. scarlet god: Bacchos, god of wine and revelry.   **48. Maenads:** female attendants of Bacchos.

Or speak to him, no matter who he is, or let him
Join in sacrifice, lustration, or in prayer.
I decree that he be driven from every house,
Being, as he is, corruption itself to us: the Delphic   25
Voice of Apollo has pronounced this revelation.
Thus I associate myself with the oracle
And take the side of the murdered king.

As for the criminal, I pray to God—
Whether it be a lurking thief, or one of a number—   30
I pray that that man's life be consumed in evil and wretchedness.
And as for me, this curse applies no less
If it should turn out that the culprit is my guest here,
Sharing my hearth.
                          You have heard the penalty.
I lay it on you now to attend to this   35
For my sake, for Apollo's, for the sick
Sterile city that heaven has abandoned.
Suppose the oracle had given you no command:
Should this defilement go uncleansed for ever?
You should have found the murderer: your king,   40
A noble king, had been destroyed!
                          Now I,
Having the power that he held before me,
Having his bed, begetting children there
Upon his wife, as he would have, had he lived—
Their son would have been my children's brother,   45
If Laios had had luck in fatherhood!
(And now his bad fortune has struck him down)—
I say I take the son's part, just as though
I were his son, to press the fight for him
And see it won! I'll find the hand that brought   50
Death to Labdakos' and Polydoros' child,
Heir of Kadmos' and Agenor's line.°
And as for those who fail me,
May the gods deny them the fruit of the earth,
Fruit of the womb, and may they rot utterly!   55
Let them be wretched as we are wretched, and worse!

For you, for loyal Thebans, and for all
Who find my actions right, I pray the favor
Of justice, and of all the immortal gods.
CHORAGOS: Since I am under oath, my lord, I swear   60
I did not do the murder, I cannot name

51–52. Labdakos, Polydoros, Kadmos, and **Agenor:** ancestors of Laios.

The murderer. Phoibos ordained the search;
Why did he not say who the culprit was?
OEDIPUS: An honest question. But no man in the world
   Can make the gods do more than the gods will.   65
CHORAGOS: There is an alternative, I think—
OEDIPUS: Tell me.
   Any or all, you must not fail to tell me.
CHORAGOS: A lord clairvoyant to the lord Apollo,
   As we all know, is the skilled Teiresias.
   One might learn much about this from him, Oedipus.   70
OEDIPUS: I am not wasting time:
   Kreon spoke of this, and I have sent for him—
   Twice, in fact; it is strange that he is not here.
CHORAGOS: The other matter—that old report—seems useless.
OEDIPUS: What was that? I am interested in all reports.   75
CHORAGOS: The king was said to have been killed by highwaymen.
OEDIPUS: I know. But we have no witnesses to that.
CHORAGOS: If the killer can feel a particle of dread,
   Your curse will bring him out of hiding!
OEDIPUS: No.
   The man who dared that act will fear no curse.   80

   (*Enter the blind seer* TEIRESIAS, *led by a* PAGE.)

CHORAGOS: But there is one man who may detect the criminal.
   This is Teiresias, this is the holy prophet
   In whom, alone of all men, truth was born.
OEDIPUS: Teiresias: seer: student of mysteries,
   Of all that's taught and all that no man tells,   85
   Secrets of Heaven and secrets of the earth:
   Blind though you are, you know the city lies
   Sick with plague; and from this plague, my lord,
   We find that you alone can guard or save us.

   Possibly you did not hear the messengers?   90
   Apollo, when we sent to him,
   Sent us back word that this great pestilence
   Would lift, but only if we established clearly
   The identity of those who murdered Laios.
   They must be killed or exiled.
                                   Can you use   95
   Birdflight° or any art of divination
   To purify yourself, and Thebes, and me
   From this contagion? We are in your hands.

---

96. Birdflight: the flight of birds was one sign used to predict the future.

There is no fairer duty
Than that of helping others in distress.   100
TEIRESIAS: How dreadful knowledge of the truth can be
    When there's no help in truth! I knew this well,
    But did not act on it; else I should not have come.
OEDIPUS: What is troubling you? Why are your eyes so cold?
TEIRESIAS: Let me go home. Bear your own fate, and I'll   105
    Bear mine. It is better so: trust what I say.
OEDIPUS: What you say is ungracious and unhelpful
    To your native country. Do not refuse to speak.
TEIRESIAS: When it comes to speech, your own is neither temperate
    Nor opportune. I wish to be more prudent.   110
OEDIPUS: In God's name, we all beg you—
TEIRESIAS: You are all ignorant.
    No; I will never tell you what I know.
    Now it is my misery; then, it would be yours.
OEDIPUS: What! You do know something, and will not tell us?
    You would betray us all and wreck the State?   115
TEIRESIAS: I do not intend to torture myself, for you.
    Why persist in asking? You will not persuade me.
OEDIPUS: What a wicked old man you are! You'd try a stone's
    Patience! Out with it! Have you no feeling at all?
TEIRESIAS: You call me unfeeling. If you could only see   120
    The nature of your own feelings . . .
OEDIPUS: Why,
    Who would not feel as I do? Who could endure
    Your arrogance toward the city?
TEIRESIAS: What does it matter?
    Whether I speak or not, it is bound to come.
OEDIPUS: Then, if "it" is bound to come, you are bound to tell me.   125
TEIRESIAS: No, I will not go on. Rage as you please.
OEDIPUS: Rage? Why not!
                                        And I'll tell you what I think:
    You planned it, you had it done, you all but
    Killed him with your own hands: if you had eyes,
    I'd say the crime was yours, and yours alone.   130
TEIRESIAS: So? I charge you, then,
    Abide by the proclamation you have made:
    From this day forth
    Never speak again to these men or to me;
    You yourself are the pollution of this country.   135
OEDIPUS: You dare say that! Can you possibly think you have
    Some way of going free, after such insolence?
TEIRESIAS: I have gone free. It is the truth sustains me.
OEDIPUS: Who taught you shamelessness? It was not your craft.

TEIRESIAS: You did. You made me speak. I did not want to.   140
OEDIPUS: Speak what? Let me hear it again more clearly.
TEIRESIAS: Was it not clear before? Are you tempting me?
OEDIPUS: I did not understand it. Say it again.
TEIRESIAS: I say that you are the murderer whom you seek.
OEDIPUS: Now twice you have spat out infamy. You'll pay for it!   145
TEIRESIAS: Would you care for more? Do you wish to be really angry?
OEDIPUS: Say what you will. Whatever you say is worthless.
TEIRESIAS: I say you live in hideous shame with those
   Most dear to you. You cannot see the evil.
OEDIPUS: Can you go on babbling like this for ever?   150
TEIRESIAS: I can, if there is power in truth.
OEDIPUS: There is:
   But not for you, not for you,
   You sightless, witless, senseless, mad old man!
TEIRESIAS: You are the madman. There is no one here
   Who will not curse you soon, as you curse me.   155
OEDIPUS: You child of total night! I would not touch you;
   Neither would any man who sees the sun.
TEIRESIAS: True: it is not from you my fate will come.
   That lies within Apollo's competence,
   As it is his concern.
OEDIPUS: Tell me, who made   160
   These fine discoveries? Kreon? or someone else?
TEIRESIAS: Kreon is no threat. You weave your own doom.
OEDIPUS: Wealth, power, craft of statemanship!
   Kingly position, everywhere admired!
   What savage envy is stored up against these,   165
   If Kreon, whom I trusted, Kreon my friend,
   For this great office which the city once
   Put in my hands unsought—if for this power
   Kreon desires in secret to destroy me!

He has bought this decrepit fortune-teller, this   170
Collector of dirty pennies, this prophet fraud—
Why, he is no more clairvoyant than I am!
                                   Tell us:
Has your mystic mummery ever approached the truth?
When that hellcat the Sphinx was performing here,
What help were you to these people?   175
Her magic was not for the first man who came along:
It demanded a real exorcist. Your birds—
What good were they? or the gods, for the matter of that?
But I came by,
Oedipus, the simple man, who knows nothing—   180

I thought it out for myself, no birds helped me!
And this is the man you think you can destroy,
That you may be close to Kreon when he's king!
Well, you and your friend Kreon, it seems to me,
Will suffer most. If you were not an old man,   185
You would have paid already for your plot.
CHORAGOS: We cannot see that his words or yours
Have been spoken except in anger, Oedipus,
And of anger we have no need. How to accomplish
The god's will best: that is what most concerns us.   190
TEIRESIAS: You are a king. But where argument's concerned
I am your man, as much a king as you.
I am not your servant, but Apollo's.
I have no need of Kreon or Kreon's name.

Listen to me. You mock my blindness, do you?   195
But I say that you, with both your eyes, are blind:
You cannot see the wretchedness of your life,
Nor in whose house you live, no, nor with whom.
Who are your father and mother? Can you tell me?
You do not even know the blind wrongs   200
That you have done them, on earth and in the world below.
But the double lash of your parents' curse will whip you
Out of this land some day, with only night
Upon your precious eyes.
Your cries then—where will they not be heard?   205
What fastness of Kithairon° will not echo them?
And that bridal-descant of yours—you'll know it then,
The song they sang when you came here to Thebes
And found your misguided berthing.
All this, and more, that you cannot guess at now,   210
Will bring you to yourself among your children.

Be angry, then. Curse Kreon. Curse my words.
I tell you, no man that walks upon the earth
Shall be rooted out more horribly than you.
OEDIPUS: Am I to bear this from him?—Damnation   215
Take you! Out of this place! Out of my sight!
TEIRESIAS: I would not have come at all if you had not asked me.
OEDIPUS: Could I have told that you'd talk nonsense, that
You'd come here to make a fool of yourself, and of me?
TEIRESIAS: A fool? Your parents thought me sane enough.   220
OEDIPUS: My parents again!—Wait: who were my parents?
TEIRESIAS: This day will give you a father and break your heart.

206. Kithairon: mountain where the infant Oedipus was left for dead.

OEDIPUS: Your infantile riddles! Your damned abracadabra!
TEIRESIAS: You were a great man once at solving riddles.
OEDIPUS: Mock me with that if you like; you will find it true.   225
TEIRESIAS: It was true enough. It brought about your ruin.
OEDIPUS: But if it saved this town?
TEIRESIAS (*to the* PAGE):   Boy, give me your hand.
OEDIPUS: Yes, boy; lead him away.
                                    —While you are here
       We can do nothing. Go; leave us in peace.
TEIRESIAS: I will go when I have said what I have to say.   230
       How can you hurt me? And I tell you again:
       The man you have been looking for all this time,
       The damned man, the murderer of Laios,
       That man is in Thebes. To your mind he is foreign-born,
       But it will soon be shown that he is a Theban,   235
       A revelation that will fail to please.
                                    A blind man,
       Who has his eyes now; a penniless man, who is rich now;
       And he will go tapping the strange earth with his staff.
       To the children with whom he lives now he will be
       Brother and father—the very same; to her   240
       Who bore him, son and husband—the very same
       Who came to his father's bed, wet with his father's blood.
       Enough. Go think that over.
       If later you find error in what I have said,
       You may say that I have no skill in prophecy.   245

                (*Exit* TEIRESIAS, *led by his* PAGE. OEDIPUS *goes into the palace.*)

ODE 1

STROPHE 1

CHORUS: The Delphic stone of prophecies
       Remembers ancient regicide
       And a still bloody hand.
       That killer's hour of flight has come.
       He must be stronger than riderless   5
       Coursers of untiring wind,
       For the son of Zeus° armed with his father's thunder
       Leaps in lightning after him;
       And the Furies° hold his track, the sad Furies.

---

7. son of Zeus: Apollo.   **9. Furies:** female spirits who avenged evil deeds.

ANTISTROPHE 1

Holy Parnassos° peak of snow   10
Flashes and blinds that secret man,
That all shall hunt him down:
Though he may roam the forest shade
Like a bull gone wild from pasture
To rage through grooms of stone.   15
Doom comes down on him; flight will not avail him;
For the world's heart calls him desolate,
And the immortal voices follow, forever follow.

STROPHE 2

But now a wilder thing is heard
From the old man skilled at hearing Fate in the wing-beat of a bird.   20
Bewildered as a blown bird, my soul hovers and cannot find
Foothold in this debate, or any reason or rest of mind.
But no man ever brought—none can bring
Proof of strife between Thebes' royal house,
Labdakos' line, and the son of Polybos°;   25
And never until now has any man brought word
Of Laios' dark death staining Oedipus the King.

ANTISTROPHE 2

Divine Zeus and Apollo hold
Perfect intelligence alone of all tales ever told;
And well though this diviner works, he works in his own night;   30
No man can judge that rough unknown or trust in second sight,
For wisdom changes hands among the wise.
Shall I believe my great lord criminal
At a raging word that a blind old man let fall?
I saw him, when the carrion woman° faced him of old,   35
Prove his heroic mind. These evil words are lies.

Scene II

KREON: Men of Thebes:
I am told that heavy accusations
Have been brought against me by King Oedipus.

I am not the kind of man to bear this tamely.

---

10. Parnassos: holy mountain, dwelling place of Zeus, king of the gods.   **25. Polybos:** Oedipus' adoptive father, king of Corinth.   **35. woman:** the Sphinx.

If in these present difficulties   5
He holds me accountable for any harm to him
Through anything I have said or done—why, then,
I do not value life in this dishonor.
It is not as though this rumor touched upon
Some private indiscretion. The matter is grave.   10
The fact is that I am being called disloyal
To the State, to my fellow citizens, to my friends.
CHORAGOS: He may have spoken in anger, not from his mind.
KREON: But did you not hear him say I was the one
Who seduced the old prophet into lying?   15
CHORAGOS: The thing was said; I do not know how seriously.
KREON: But you were watching him! Were his eyes steady?
Did he look like a man in his right mind?
CHORAGOS: I do not know.
I cannot judge the behavior of great men.
But here is the king himself.

(*Enter* OEDIPUS.)

OEDIPUS: So you dared come back.   20
Why? How brazen of you to come to my house,
You murderer!
                    Do you think I do not know
That you plotted to kill me, plotted to steal my throne?
Tell me, in God's name: am I coward, a fool,
That you should dream you could accomplish this?   25
A fool who could not see your slippery game?
A coward, not to fight back when I saw it?
You are the fool, Kreon, are you not? hoping
Without support or friends to get a throne?
Thrones may be won or bought: you could do neither.   30
KREON: Now listen to me. You have talked; let me talk, too.
You cannot judge unless you know the facts.
OEDIPUS: You speak well: there is one fact; but I find it hard
To learn from the deadliest enemy I have.
KREON: That above all I must dispute with you.   35
OEDIPUS: That above all I will not hear you deny.
KREON: If you think there is anything good in being stubborn
Against all reason, then I say you are wrong.
OEDIPUS: If you think a man can sin against his own kind
And not be punished for it, I say you are mad.   40
KREON: I agree. But tell me: what have I done to you?
OEDIPUS: You advised me to send for that wizard, did you not?
KREON: I did. I should do it again.
OEDIPUS: Very well. Now tell me:

How long has it been since Laios—
KREON: What of Laios?
OEDIPUS: Since he vanished in that onset by the road?   45
KREON: It was long ago, a long time.
OEDIPUS: And this prophet,
    Was he practicing here then?
KREON: He was; and with honor, as now.
OEDIPUS: Did he speak of me at that time?
KREON: He never did,
    At least, not when I was present.
OEDIPUS: But . . . the enquiry?
    I suppose you held one?
KREON: We did, but we learned nothing.   50
OEDIPUS: Why did the prophet not speak against me then?
KREON: I do not know; and I am the kind of man
    Who holds his tongue when he has no facts to go on.
OEDIPUS: There's one fact that you know, and you could tell it.
KREON: What fact is that? If I know it, you shall have it.   55
OEDIPUS: If he were not involved with you, he could not say
    That it was I who murdered Laios.
KREON: If he says that, you are the one that knows it!—
    But now it is my turn to question you.
OEDIPUS: Put your questions. I am no murderer.   60
KREON: First, then: You married my sister?
OEDIPUS: I married your sister.
KREON: And you rule the kingdom equally with her?
OEDIPUS: Everything that she wants she has from me.
KREON: And I am the third, equal to both of you?
OEDIPUS: That is why I call you a bad friend.   65
KREON: No. Reason it out, as I have done.
    Think of this first: would any sane man prefer
    Power, with all a king's anxieties,
    To that same power and the grace of sleep?
    Certainly not I.   70
    I have never longed for the king's power—only his rights.
    Would any wise man differ from me in this?
    As matters stand, I have my way in everything
    With your consent, and no responsibilities.
    If I were king, I should be a slave to policy.   75
    How could I desire a scepter more
    Than what is now mine—untroubled influence?
    No, I have not gone mad; I need no honors,
    Except those with the perquisites I have now.
    I am welcome everywhere; every man salutes me,   80
    And those who want your favor seek my ear,

Since I know how to manage what they ask.
Should I exchange this ease for that anxiety?
Besides, no sober mind is treasonable.
I hate anarchy   85
And never would deal with any man who likes it.
Test what I have said. Go to the priestess
At Delphi, ask if I quoted her correctly.
And as for this other thing: if I am found
Guilty of treason with Teiresias,   90
Then sentence me to death. You have my word
It is a sentence I should cast my vote for—
But not without evidence!
                          You do wrong
When you take good men for bad, bad men for good.
A true friend thrown aside—why, life itself   95
Is not more precious!
                      In time you will know this well:
For time, and time alone, will show the just man,
Though scoundrels are discovered in a day.
CHORAGOS: This is well said, and a prudent man would ponder it.
    Judgments too quickly formed are dangerous.   100
OEDIPUS: But is he not quick in his duplicity?
    And shall I not be quick to parry him?
    Would you have me stand still, hold my peace, and let
    This man win everything, through my inaction?
KREON: And you want—what is it, then? To banish me?   105
OEDIPUS: No, not exile. It is your death I want,
    So that all the world may see what treason means.
KREON: You will persist, then? You will not believe me?
OEDIPUS: How can I believe you?
KREON: Then you are a fool.
OEDIPUS: To save myself?
KREON: In justice, think of me.   110
OEDIPUS: You are evil incarnate.
KREON: But suppose that you are wrong?
OEDIPUS: Still I must rule.
KREON: But not if you rule badly.
OEDIPUS: O city, city!
KREON: It is my city, too!
CHORAGOS: Now, my lords, be still. I see the queen,
    Iokaste, coming from her palace chambers;   115
    And it is time she came, for the sake of you both.
    This dreadful quarrel can be resolved through her.

(*Enter* IOKASTE.)

IOKASTE: Poor foolish men, what wicked din is this?
   With Thebes sick to death, is it not shameful
   That you should rake some private quarrel up?   120
   (*To* OEDIPUS.) Come into the house.
                    —And you, Kreon, go now:
   Let us have no more of this tumult over nothing.
KREON: Nothing? No, sister: what your husband plans for me
   Is one of two great evils: exile or death.
OEDIPUS: He is right.
             Why, woman, I have caught him squarely   125
   Plotting against my life.
KREON: No! Let me die
   Accurst if ever I have wished you harm!
IOKASTE: Ah, believe it, Oedipus!
   In the name of the gods, respect this oath of his
   For my sake, for the sake of these people here!   130

      STROPHE 1

CHORAGOS: Open your mind to her, my lord. Be ruled by her, I beg you!
OEDIPUS: What would you have me do?
CHORAGOS: Respect Kreon's word. He has never spoken like a fool,
   And now he has sworn an oath.
OEDIPUS: You know what you ask?
CHORAGOS: I do.
OEDIPUS: Speak on, then.
CHORAGOS: A friend so sworn should not be baited so,   135
   In blind malice, and without proof.
OEDIPUS: You are aware, I hope, that what you say
   Means death for me, or exile at the least.

      STROPHE 2

CHORAGOS: No, I swear by Helios, first in heaven!
   May I die friendless and accurst,   140
   The worst of deaths, if ever I meant that!
   It is the withering fields
      That hurt my sick heart:
   Must we bear all these ills,
   And now your bad blood as well?   145
OEDIPUS: Then let him go. And let me die, if I must,
   Or be driven by him in shame from the land of Thebes.
   It is your unhappiness, and not his talk,
   That touches me.
           As for him—
   Wherever he goes, hatred will follow him.   150

KREON: Ugly in yielding, as you were ugly in rage!
  Natures like yours chiefly torment themselves.
OEDIPUS: Can you not go? Can you not leave me?
KREON: I can.
  You do not know me; but the city knows me,
  And in its eyes I am just, if not in yours.   (*Exit* KREON.)   155

ANTISTROPHE 1

CHORAGOS: Lady Iokaste, did you not ask the King to go to his chambers?
IOKASTE: First tell me what has happened.
CHORAGOS: There was suspicion without evidence; yet it rankled.
  As even false charges will.
IOKASTE: On both sides?
CHORAGOS: On both.
IOKASTE: But what was said?   160
CHORAGOS: Oh let it rest, let it be done with!
  Have we not suffered enough?
OEDIPUS: You see to what your decency has brought you:
  You have made difficulties where my heart saw none.

ANTISTROPHE 2

CHORAGOS: Oedipus, it is not once only I have told you—   165
  You must know I should count myself unwise
  To the point of madness, should I now forsake you—
      You, under whose hand,
        In the storm of another time,
        Our dear land sailed out free.   170
      But now stand fast at the helm!
IOKASTE: In God's name, Oedipus, inform your wife as well:
  Why are you so set in this hard anger?
OEDIPUS: I will tell you, for none of these men deserves
  My confidence as you do. It is Kreon's work,   175
  His treachery, his plotting against me.
IOKASTE: Go on, if you can make this clear to me.
OEDIPUS: He charges me with the murder of Laios.
IOKASTE: Has he some knowledge? Or does he speak from hearsay?
OEDIPUS: He would not commit himself to such a charge,   180
  But he has brought in that damnable soothsayer
  To tell his story.
IOKASTE: Set your mind at rest.
  If it is a question of soothsayers, I tell you
  That you will find no man whose craft gives knowledge
  Of the unknowable.
                    Here is my proof: 185

An oracle was reported to Laios once
(I will not say from Phoibos himself, but from
His appointed ministers, at any rate)
That his doom would be death at the hands of his own son—
His son, born of his flesh and of mine!   190

Now, you remember the story: Laios was killed
By marauding strangers where three highways meet;
But his child had not been three days in this world
Before the king had pierced the baby's ankles
And left him to die on a lonely mountainside.   195
Thus, Apollo never caused that child
To kill his father, and it was not Laios' fate
To die at the hands of his son, as he had feared.
This is what prophets and prophecies are worth!
Have no dread of them.
                              It is God himself   200
Who can show us what he wills, in his own way.
OEDIPUS: How strange a shadowy memory crossed my mind,
    Just now while you were speaking; it chilled my heart.
IOKASTE: What do you mean? What memory do you speak of?
OEDIPUS: If I understand you, Laios was killed   205
    At a place where three roads meet.
IOKASTE: So it was said;
    We have no later story.
OEDIPUS: Where did it happen?
IOKASTE: Phokis, it is called: at a place where the Theban Way
    Divides into the roads toward Delphi and Daulia.
OEDIPUS: When?
IOKASTE: We had the news not long before you came   210
    And proved the right to your succession here.
OEDIPUS: Ah, what net has God been weaving for me?
IOKASTE: Oedipus! Why does this trouble you?
OEDIPUS: Do not ask me yet.
    First, tell me how Laios looked, and tell me
    How old he was.
IOKASTE: He was tall, his hair just touched   215
    With white; his form was not unlike your own.
OEDIPUS: I think that I myself may be accurst
    By my own ignorant edict.
IOKASTE: You speak strangely.
    It makes me tremble to look at you, my king.
OEDIPUS: I am not sure that the blind man cannot see.   220
    But I should know better if you were to tell me—
IOKASTE: Anything—though I dread to hear you ask it.

OEDIPUS: Was the king lightly escorted, or did he ride
    With a large company, as a ruler should?
IOKASTE: There were five men with him in all: one was a herald;   225
    And a single chariot, which he was driving.
OEDIPUS: Alas, that makes it plain enough!
                                   But who—
    Who told you how it happened?
IOKASTE: A household servant,
    The only one to escape.
OEDIPUS: And is he still
    A servant of ours?
IOKASTE: No; for when he came back at last   230
    And found you enthroned in the place of the dead king,
    He came to me, touched my hand with his, and begged
    That I would send him away to the frontier district
    Where only the shepherds go—
    As far away from the city as I could send him.   235
    I granted his prayer; for although the man was a slave,
    He had earned more than this favor at my hands.
OEDIPUS: Can he be called back quickly?
IOKASTE: Easily.
    But why?
OEDIPUS: I have taken too much upon myself
    Without enquiry; therefore I wish to consult him.   240
IOKASTE: Then he shall come.
                 But am I not one also
    To whom you might confide these fears of yours?
OEDIPUS: That is your right; it will not be denied you,
    Now least of all; for I have reached a pitch
    Of wild foreboding. Is there anyone   245
    To whom I should sooner speak?

    Polybos of Corinth is my father.
    My mother is a Dorian: Merope.
    I grew up chief among the men of Corinth
    Until a strange thing happened—   250
    Not worth my passion, it may be, but strange.
    At a feast, a drunken man maundering in his cups
    Cries out that I am not my father's son!
    I contained myself that night, though I felt anger
    And a sinking heart. The next day I visited   255
    My father and mother, and questioned them. They stormed,
    Calling it all the slanderous rant of a fool;
    And this relieved me. Yet the suspicion
    Remained always aching in my mind;

I knew there was talk; I could not rest; 260
And finally, saying nothing to my parents,
I went to the shrine at Delphi.

The god dismissed my question without reply;
He spoke of other things.
　　　　　　　　Some were clear,
Full of wretchedness, dreadful, unbearable: 265
As, that I should lie with my own mother, breed
Children from whom all men would turn their eyes;
And that I should be my father's murderer.
I heard all this, and fled. And from that day
Corinth to me was only in the stars 270
Descending in that quarter of the sky,
As I wandered farther and farther on my way
To a land where I should never see the evil
Sung by the oracle. And I came to this country
Where, so you say, King Laios was killed. 275

I will tell you all that happened there, my lady.
There were three highways
Coming together at a place I passed;
And there a herald came towards me, and a chariot
Drawn by horses, with a man such as you describe 280
Seated in it. The groom leading the horses
Forced me off the road at his lord's command;
But as this charioteer lurched over towards me
I struck him in my rage. The old man saw me
And brought his double goad down upon my head 285
As I came abreast.
　　　　　　　He was paid back, and more!
Swinging my club in this right hand I knocked him
Out of his car, and he rolled on the ground.
　　　　　　　　　　I killed him.

I killed them all.
Now if that stranger and Laios were—kin, 290
Where is a man more miserable than I?
More hated by the gods? Citizen and alien alike
Must never shelter me or speak to me—
I must be shunned by all.
　　　　　　　And I myself
Pronounced this malediction upon myself! 295

Think of it: I have touched you with these hands,
These hands that killed your husband. What defilement!

Am I all evil, then? It must be so,
Since I must flee from Thebes, yet never again
See my own countrymen, my own country,   300
For fear of joining my mother in marriage
And killing Polybos, my father.
                                          Ah,
If I was created so, born to this fate,
Who could deny the savagery of God?
O holy majesty of heavenly powers!   305
May I never see that day! Never!
Rather let me vanish from the race of men
Than know the abomination destined me!

CHORAGOS: We too, my lord, have felt dismay at this.
But there is hope: you have yet to hear the shepherd.   310

OEDIPUS: Indeed, I fear no other hope is left me.

IOKASTE: What do you hope from him when he comes?

OEDIPUS: This much:
If his account of the murder tallies with yours,
Then I am cleared.

IOKASTE: What was it that I said
Of such importance?

OEDIPUS: Why, "marauders," you said,   315
Killed the king, according to this man's story.
If he maintains that still, if there were several,
Clearly the guilt is not mine: I was alone.
But if he says one man, singlehanded, did it,
Then the evidence all points to me.   320

IOKASTE: You may be sure that he said there were several;
And can he call back that story now? He cannot.
The whole city heard it as plainly as I.
But suppose he alters some detail of it:
He cannot ever show that Laios' death   325
Fulfilled the oracle: for Apollo said
My child was doomed to kill him; and my child—
Poor baby!—it was my child that died first.

No. From now on, where oracles are concerned,
I would not waste a second thought on any.   330

OEDIPUS: You may be right.
                                But come: let someone go
For the shepherd at once. This matter must be settled.

IOKASTE: I will send for him.
I would not wish to cross you in anything,
And surely not in this.—Let us go in.   (*Exeunt into the palace.*) 335

ODE 2

STROPHE 1

CHORUS: Let me be reverent in the ways of right,
Lowly the paths I journey on;
Let all my words and actions keep
The laws of the pure universe
From highest Heaven handed down.   5
For Heaven is their bright nurse,
Those generations of the realms of light;
Ah, never of mortal kind were they begot,
Nor are they slaves of memory, lost in sleep:
Their Father is greater than Time, and ages not.   10

ANTISTROPHE 1

The tyrant is a child of Pride
Who drinks from his great sickening cup
Recklessness and vanity,
Until from his high crest headlong
He plummets to the dust of hope.   15
That strong man is not strong.
But let no fair ambition be denied;
May God protect the wrestler for the State
In government, in comely policy,
Who will fear God, and on his ordinance wait.   20

STROPHE 2

Haughtiness and the high hand of disdain
Tempt and outrage God's holy law;
And any mortal who dares hold
No immortal Power in awe
Will be caught up in a net of pain: 25
The price for which his levity is sold.
Let each man take due earnings, then,
And keep his hands from holy things,
And from blasphemy stand apart—
Else the crackling blast of heaven   30
Blows on his head, and on his desperate heart.
Though fools will honor impious men,
In their cities no tragic poet sings.

ANTISTROPHE 2

Shall we lose faith in Delphi's obscurities,
We who have heard the world's core   35
Discredited, and the sacred wood
Of Zeus at Elis praised no more?
The deeds and the strange prophecies
Must make a pattern yet to be understood.
Zeus, if indeed you are lord of all,   40
Throned in light over night and day,
Mirror this in your endless mind:
Our masters call the oracle
Words on the wind, and the Delphic vision blind!
Their hearts no longer know Apollo,   45
And reverence for the gods has died away.

SCENE III

(*Enter* IOKASTE.)

IOKASTE: Princes of Thebes, it has occurred to me
To visit the altars of the gods, bearing
These branches as a suppliant, and this incense.
Our king is not himself: his noble soul
Is overwrought with fantasies of dread,   5
Else he would consider
The new prophecies in the light of the old.
He will listen to any voice that speaks disaster,
And my advice goes for nothing. (*She approaches the altar, right.*)
                              To you, then, Apollo,
Lycean lord, since you are nearest, I turn in prayer   10
Receive these offerings, and grant us deliverance
From defilement. Our hearts are heavy with fear
When we see our leader distracted, as helpless sailors
Are terrified by the confusion of their helmsman.

(*Enter* MESSENGER.)

MESSENGER: Friends, no doubt you can direct me: 15
Where shall I find the house of Oedipus,
Or, better still, where is the king himself?
CHORAGOS: It is this very place, stranger; he is inside.
This is his wife and mother of his children.
MESSENGER: I wish her happiness in a happy house,   20
Blest in all the fulfillment of her marriage.
IOKASTE: I wish as much for you: your courtesy
Deserves a like good fortune. But now, tell me:

Why have you come? What have you to say to us?
MESSENGER: Good news, my lady, for your house and your husband.   25
IOKASTE: What news? Who sent you here?
MESSENGER: I am from Corinth.
  The news I bring ought to mean joy for you,
  Though it may be you will find some grief in it.
IOKASTE: What is it? How can it touch us in both ways?
MESSENGER: The word is that the people of the Isthmus   30
  Intend to call Oedipus to be their king.
IOKASTE: But old King Polybos—is he not reigning still?
MESSENGER: No. Death holds him in his sepulchre.
IOKASTE: What are you saying? Polybos is dead?
MESSENGER: If I am not telling the truth, may I die myself.   35
IOKASTE (*to a* MAIDSERVANT):   Go in, go quickly; tell this to your master.
  O riddlers of God's will, where are you now!
  This was the man whom Oedipus, long ago,
  Feared so, fled so, in dread of destroying him—
  But it was another fate by which he died.   40

    (*Enter* OEDIPUS *center.*)

OEDIPUS: Dearest Iokaste, why have you sent for me?
IOKASTE: Listen to what this man says, and then tell me
  What has become of the solemn prophecies.
OEDIPUS: Who is this man? What is his news for me?
IOKASTE: He has come from Corinth to announce your father's death!   45
OEDIPUS: Is it true, stranger? Tell me in your own words.
MESSENGER: I cannot say it more clearly: the king is dead.
OEDIPUS: Was it by treason? Or by an attack of illness?
MESSENGER: A little thing brings old men to their rest.
OEDIPUS: It was sickness, then?
MESSENGER: Yes, and his many years.   50
OEDIPUS: Ah!
  Why should a man respect the Pythian hearth,° or
  Give heed to the birds that jangle above his head?
  They prophesied that I should kill Polybos,
  Kill my own father; but he is dead and buried,   55
  And I am here—I never touched him, never,
  Unless he died of grief for my departure,
  And thus, in a sense, through me. No. Polybos
  Has packed the oracles off with him underground.
  They are empty words.
IOKASTE: Had I not told you so?   60

---

51. Pythian hearth: Delphi; the alternative name came from the dragon Python, which once guarded Delphi until Apollo vanquished it.

OEDIPUS: You had; it was my faint heart that betrayed me.

IOKASTE: From now on never think of those things again.

OEDIPUS: And yet—must I not fear my mother's bed?

IOKASTE: Why should anyone in this world be afraid,
Since Fate rules us and nothing can be foreseen?   65
A man should live only for the present day.

Have no more fear of sleeping with your mother:
How many men, in dreams, have lain with their mothers!
No reasonable man is troubled by such things.

OEDIPUS: That is true; only—   70
If only my mother were not still alive!
But she is alive. I cannot help my dread.

IOKASTE: Yet this news of your father's death is wonderful.

OEDIPUS: Wonderful. But I fear the living woman.

MESSENGER: Tell me, who is this woman that you fear?   75

OEDIPUS: It is Merope, man; the wife of King Polybos.

MESSENGER: Merope? Why should you be afraid of her?

OEDIPUS: An oracle of the gods, a dreadful saying.

MESSENGER: Can you tell me about it or are you sworn to silence?

OEDIPUS: I can tell you, and I will.   80
Apollo said through his prophet that I was the man
Who should marry his own mother, shed his father's blood
With his own hands. And so, for all these years
I have kept clear of Corinth, and no harm has come—
Though it would have been sweet to see my parents again.   85

MESSENGER: And is this the fear that drove you out of Corinth?

OEDIPUS: Would you have me kill my father?

MESSENGER: As for that
You must be reassured by the news I gave you.

OEDIPUS: If you could reassure me, I would reward you.

MESSENGER: I had that in mind, I will confess: I thought   90
I could count on you when you returned to Corinth.

OEDIPUS: No: I will never go near my parents again.

MESSENGER: Ah, son, you still do not know what you are doing—

OEDIPUS: What do you mean? In the name of God tell me!

MESSENGER: —If these are your reasons for not going home.   95

OEDIPUS: I tell you, I fear the oracle may come true.

MESSENGER: And guilt may come upon you through your parents?

OEDIPUS: That is the dread that is always in my heart.

MESSENGER: Can you not see that all your fears are groundless?

OEDIPUS: Groundless? Am I not my parents' son?   100

MESSENGER: Polybos was not your father.

OEDIPUS: Not my father?

MESSENGER: No more your father than the man speaking to you.

OEDIPUS: But you are nothing to me!
MESSENGER: Neither was he.
OEDIPUS: Then why did he call me son?
MESSENGER: I will tell you:
  Long ago he had you from my hands, as a gift. 105
OEDIPUS: Then how could he love me so, if I was not his?
MESSENGER: He had no children, and his heart turned to you.
OEDIPUS: What of you? Did you buy me? Did you find me by chance?
MESSENGER: I came upon you in the woody vales of Kithairon.
OEDIPUS: And what were you doing there?
MESSENGER: Tending my flocks. 110
OEDIPUS: A wandering shepherd?
MESSENGER: But your savior, son, that day.
OEDIPUS: From what did you save me?
MESSENGER: Your ankles should tell you that.
OEDIPUS: Ah, stranger, why do you speak of that childhood pain?
MESSENGER: I pulled the skewer that pinned your feet together.
OEDIPUS: I have had the mark as long as I can remember. 115
MESSENGER: That was why you were given the name you bear.°
OEDIPUS: God! Was it my father or my mother who did it?
  Tell me!
MESSENGER: I do not know. The man who gave you to me
  Can tell you better than I.
OEDIPUS: It was not you that found me, but another? 120
MESSENGER: It was another shepherd gave you to me.
OEDIPUS: Who was he? Can you tell me who he was?
MESSENGER: I think he was said to be one of Laios' people.
OEDIPUS: You mean the Laios who was king here years ago?
MESSENGER: Yes; King Laios; and the man was one of his herdsmen. 125
OEDIPUS: Is he still alive? Can I see him?
MESSENGER: These men here
  Know best about such things.
OEDIPUS: Does anyone here
  Know this shepherd that he is talking about?
  Have you seen him in the fields, or in the town?
  If you have, tell me. It is time things were made plain. 130
CHORAGOS: I think the man he means is that same shepherd
  You have already asked to see. Iokaste perhaps
  Could tell you something.
OEDIPUS: Do you know anything
  About him, Lady? Is he the man we have summoned?
  Is that the man this shepherd means?
IOKASTE: Why think of him? 135

---

116. the name you bear: "Oedipus" translates as "the one with a swollen foot."

Forget this herdsman. Forget it all.
This talk is a waste of time.

OEDIPUS: How can you say that,
When the clues to my true birth are in my hands?

IOKASTE: For God's love, let us have no more questioning!
Is your life nothing to you? 140
My own is pain enough for me to bear.

OEDIPUS: You need not worry. Suppose my mother a slave,
And born of slaves: no baseness can touch you.

IOKASTE: Listen to me, I beg you: do not do this thing!

OEDIPUS: I will not listen; the truth must be made known. 145

IOKASTE: Everything that I say is for your own good!

OEDIPUS: My own good
Snaps my patience, then; I want none of it.

IOKASTE: You are fatally wrong! May you never learn who you are!

OEDIPUS: Go, one of you, and bring the shepherd here.
Let us leave this woman to brag of her royal name. 150

IOKASTE: Ah, miserable!
That is the only word I have for you now.
That is the only word I can ever have. *(Exit into the palace.)*

CHORAGOS: Why has she left us, Oedipus? Why has she gone
In such a passion of sorrow? I fear this silence: 155
Something dreadful may come of it.

OEDIPUS: Let it come!
However base my birth, I must know about it.
The Queen, like a woman, is perhaps ashamed
To think of my low origin. But I
Am a child of Luck; I cannot be dishonored. 160
Luck is my mother; the passing months, my brothers,
Have seen me rich and poor.
If this is so,
How could I wish that I were someone else?
How could I not be glad to know my birth?

ODE 3

STROPHE

CHORUS: If ever the coming time were known
To my heart's pondering,
Kithairon, now by Heaven I see the torches
At the festival of the next full moon,
And see the dance, and hear the choir sing 5
A grace to your gentle shade:
Mountain where Oedipus was found,
O mountain guard of a noble race!

May the god° who heals us lend his aid,
And let that glory come to pass   10
For our king's cradling-ground.

ANTISTROPHE

Of the nymphs that flower beyond the years,
Who bore you,° royal child,
To Pan° of the hills or the timberline Apollo,
Cold in delight where the upland clears,   15
Or Hermes° for whom Kyllene's° heights are piled?
Or flushed as evening cloud,
Great Dionysos,° roamer of mountains,
He—was it he who found you there,
And caught you up in his own proud   20
Arms from the sweet god-ravisher
Who laughed by the Muses'° fountains?

Scene IV

OEDIPUS: Sirs: though I do not know the man,
  I think I see him coming, this shepherd we want:
  He is old, like our friend here, and the men
  Bringing him seem to be servants of my house.
  But you can tell, if you have ever seen him.   5

(*Enter* SHEPHERD *escorted by* SERVANTS.)

CHORAGOS: I know him, he was Laios' man. You can trust him.
OEDIPUS: Tell me first, you from Corinth: is this the shepherd
  We were discussing?
MESSENGER: This is the very man.
OEDIPUS (*to* SHEPHERD):   Come here. No, look at me. You must answer
  Everything I ask.—You belonged to Laios?   10
SHEPHERD: Yes: born his slave, brought up in his house.
OEDIPUS: Tell me: what kind of work did you do for him?
SHEPHERD: I was a shepherd of his, most of my life.
OEDIPUS: Where mainly did you go for pasturage?
SHEPHERD: Sometimes Kithairon, sometimes the hills near-by.   15
OEDIPUS: Do you remember ever seeing this man out there?

9. god: Apollo. **13. Who bore you:** The Chorus wonders whether Oedipus might be the son of a nymph and a god: Pan, Apollo, Hermes, or Dionysus. **14. Pan:** God of nature; from the waist up, he is human, from the waist down, a goat. **16. Hermes:** Zeus's son, messenger of the gods; **16. Kyllene:** sacred mountain, the birthplace of Hermes. **18. Dionysos:** (Dionysus) god of wine, sometimes called Bacchos. **22. Muses:** nine goddesses, sisters, who are the patronesses of poetry, music, art, and the sciences.

SHEPHERD: What would he be doing there? This man?

OEDIPUS: This man standing here. Have you ever seen him before?

SHEPHERD: No. At least, not to my recollection.

MESSENGER: And that is not strange, my lord. But I'll refresh   20
His memory. He must remember when we two
Spent three whole seasons together, March to September,
On Kithairon or thereabouts. He had two flocks;
I had one. Each autumn I'd drive mine home
And he would go back with his to Laios' sheepfold.—   25
Is this not true, just as I have described it?

SHEPHERD: True, yes; but it was all so long ago.

MESSENGER: Well, then: do you remember back in those days,
That you gave me a baby boy to bring up as my own?

SHEPHERD: What if I did? What are you trying to say?   30

MESSENGER: King Oedipus was once that little child.

SHEPHERD: Damn you, hold your tongue!

OEDIPUS: No more of that!
It is your tongue needs watching, not this man's.

SHEPHERD: My king, my master, what is it I have done wrong?

OEDIPUS: You have not answered his question about the boy.   35

SHEPHERD: He does not know . . . He is only making trouble . . .

OEDIPUS: Come, speak plainly, or it will go hard with you.

SHEPHERD: In God's name, do not torture an old man!

OEDIPUS: Come here, one of you; bind his arms behind him.

SHEPHERD: Unhappy king! What more do you wish to learn?   40

OEDIPUS: Did you give this man the child he speaks of?

SHEPHERD: I did.
And I would to God I had died that very day.

OEDIPUS: You will die now unless you speak the truth.

SHEPHERD: Yet if I speak the truth, I am worse than dead.

OEDIPUS (*to* ATTENDANT):   He intends to draw it out, apparently—   45

SHEPHERD: No! I have told you already that I gave him the boy.

OEDIPUS: Where did you get him? From your house? From somewhere else?

SHEPHERD: Not from mine, no. A man gave him to me.

OEDIPUS: Is that man here? Whose house did he belong to?

SHEPHERD: For God's love, my king, do not ask me any more!   50

OEDIPUS: You are a dead man if I have to ask you again.

SHEPHERD: Then . . . Then the child was from the palace of Laios.

OEDIPUS: A slave child? or a child of his own line?

SHEPHERD: Ali, I am on the brink of dreadful speech!

OEDIPUS: And I of dreadful hearing. Yet I must hear.   55

SHEPHERD: If you must be told, then . . .
                                           They said it was Laios' child;
But it is your wife who can tell you about that.

OEDIPUS: My wife—Did she give it to you?

SHEPHERD: My lord she did.

OEDIPUS: Do you know why?

SHEPHERD: I was told to get rid of it.

OEDIPUS: Oh heartless mother!

SHEPHERD: But in dread of prophecies . . .   60

OEDIPUS: Tell me.

SHEPHERD: It was said that the boy would kill his own father.

OEDIPUS: Then why did you give him over to this old man?

SHEPHERD: I pitied the baby, my king,
And I thought that this man would take him far away
To his own country.
                He saved him—but for what a fate!   65
For if you are what this man says you are,
No man living is more wretched than Oedipus.

OEDIPUS: Ah God!
It was true!
        All the prophecies!
                —Now,
O Light, may I look on you for the last time!   70
I, Oedipus,
Oedipus, damned in his birth, in his marriage damned,
Damned in the blood he shed with his own hand!

(He rushes into the palace.)

ODE 4

STROPHE 1

CHORUS: Alas for the seed of men.
What measure shall I give these generations
That breathe on the void and are void
And exist and do not exist?
Who bears more weight of joy   5
Than mass of sunlight shifting in images,
Or who shall make his thought stay on
That down time drifts away?
Your splendor is all fallen.
O naked brow of wrath and tears,   10
O change of Oedipus!
I who saw your days call no man blest—
Your great days like ghosts gone.

ANTISTROPHE 1

That mind was a strong bow.
Deep, how deep you drew it then, hard archer,
At a dim fearful range,
And brought dear glory down!
You overcame the stranger°—   15
The virgin with her hooking lion claws—
And though death sang, stood like a tower
To make pale Thebes take heart.   20
Fortress against our sorrow!
True king, giver of laws,
Majestic Oedipus!
No prince in Thebes had ever such renown,   25
No prince won such grace of power.

STROPHE 2

And now of all men ever known
Most pitiful is this man's story:
His fortunes are most changed; his state
Fallen to a low slave's   30
Ground under bitter fate.
O Oedipus, most royal one!
The great door° that expelled you to the light
Gave at night—ah, gave night to your glory:
As to the father, to the fathering son.   35
All understood too late.
How could that queen whom Laios won,
The garden that he harrowed at his height,
Be silent when that act was done?

ANTISTROPHE 2

But all eyes fail before time's eye,   40
All actions come to justice there.
Though never willed, though far down the deep past,
Your bed, your dread sirings,
Are brought to book at last.
Child by Laios doomed to die,   45
Then doomed to lose that fortunate little death,
Would God you never took breath in this air
That with my wailing lips I take to cry:

18. stranger: the Sphinx. **33. door:** refers to the birth process.

For I weep the world's outcast.
I was blind, and now I can tell why: 50
Asleep, for you had given ease of breath
To Thebes, while the false years went by.

EXODOS°

(*Enter, from the palace,* SECOND MESSENGER.)

SECOND MESSENGER: Elders of Thebes, most honored in this land,
What horrors are yours to see and hear, what weight
Of sorrow to be endured, if, true to your birth,
You venerate the line of Labdakos!
I think neither Istros nor Phasis, those great rivers,   5
Could purify this place of all the evil
It shelters now, or soon must bring to light—
Evil not done unconsciously, but willed.
The greatest griefs are those we cause ourselves.

CHORAGOS: Surely, friend, we have grief enough already;   10
What new sorrow do you mean?
SECOND MESSENGER: The queen is dead.
CHORAGOS: O miserable queen! But at whose hand?
SECOND MESSENGER: Her own.
The full horror of what happened you cannot know,
For you did not see it; but I, who did, will tell you
As clearly as I can how she met her death.   15

When she had left us,
In passionate silence, passing through the court,
She ran to her apartment in the house,
Her hair clutched by the fingers of both hands.
She closed the doors behind her; then, by that bed   20
Where long ago the fatal son was conceived—
That son who should bring about his father's death—
We heard her call upon Laios, dead so many years,
And heard her wail for the double fruit of her marriage,
A husband by her husband, children by her child.   25
Exactly how she died I do not know:
For Oedipus burst in moaning and would not let us
Keep vigil to the end: it was by him
As he stormed about the room that our eyes were caught.
From one to another of us he went, begging a sword,   30

Exodos: final scene.

Hunting the wife who was not his wife, the mother
Whose womb had carried his own children and himself.
I do not know: it was none of us aided him,
But surely one of the gods was in control!
For with a dreadful cry   35
He hurled his weight, as though wrenched out of himself,
At the twin doors: the bolts gave, and he rushed in.
And there we saw her hanging, her body swaying
From the cruel cord she had noosed about her neck.
A great sob broke from him, heartbreaking to hear,   40
As he loosed the rope and lowered her to the ground.

I would blot out from my mind what happened next!
For the king ripped from her gown the golden brooches
That were her ornament, and raised them, and plunged them down
Straight into his own eyeballs, crying, "No more,   45
No more shall you look on the misery about me,
The horrors of my own doing! Too long you have known
The faces of those whom I should never have seen,
Too long been blind to those for whom I was searching!
From this hour, go in darkness!" And as he spoke,   50
He struck at his eyes—not once, but many times;
And the blood spattered his beard,
Bursting from his ruined sockets like red hail.
So from the unhappiness of two this evil has sprung,
A curse on the man and woman alike. The old   55
Happiness of the house of Labdakos
Was happiness enough: where is it today?
It is all wailing and ruin, disgrace, death—all
The misery of mankind that has a name—
And it is wholly and for ever theirs.   60
CHORAGOS: Is he in agony still? Is there no rest for him?
SECOND MESSENGER: He is calling for someone to open the doors wide
So that all the children of Kadmos may look upon
His father's murderer, his mother's—no,
I cannot say it!
        And then he will leave Thebes,   65
Self-exiled, in order that the curse
Which he himself pronounced may depart from the house.
He is weak, and there is none to lead him,
So terrible is his suffering.
        But you will see:
Look, the doors are opening; in a moment   70
You will see a thing that would crush a heart of stone.

(*The central door is opened,* OEDIPUS, *blinded, is led in.*)

CHORAGOS: Dreadful indeed for men to see.
  Never have my own eyes
  Looked on a sight so full of fear.

  Oedipus!   75
  What madness came upon you, what demon
  Leaped on your life with heavier
  Punishment than a mortal man can bear?
  No: I cannot even
  Look at you, poor ruined one.   80
  And I would speak, question, ponder,
  If I were able. No.
  You make me shudder.
OEDIPUS: God. God.
  Is there a sorrow greater?   85
  Where shall I find harbor in this world?
  My voice is hurled far on a dark wind.
  What has God done to me?—
CHORAGOS: Too terrible to think of, or to see.

          STROPHE 1

OEDIPUS: O cloud of night,   90
  Never to be turned away: night coming on,
  I cannot tell how: night like a shroud!
  My fair winds brought me here.
                         O God. Again
  The pain of the spikes where I had sight,
  The flooding pain   95
  Of memory, never to be gouged out.
CHORAGOS: This is not strange.
  You suffer it all twice over, remorse in pain,
  Pain in remorse.

          ANTISTROPHE 1

OEDIPUS: Ah dear friend   100
  Are you faithful even yet, you alone?
  Are you still standing near me, will you stay here,
  Patient, to care for the blind?
                         The blind man!
  Yet even blind I know who it is attends me,
  By the voice's tone—   105
  Though my new darkness hide the comforter.

CHORAGOS: Oh fearful act!
   What god was it drove you to rake black
   Night across your eyes?

STROPHE 2

OEDIPUS: Apollo. Apollo. Dear   110
   Children, the god was Apollo.
   He brought my sick, sick fate upon me.
   But the blinding hand was my own!
   How could I bear to see
   When all my sight was horror everywhere?   115
CHORAGOS: Everywhere; that is true.
OEDIPUS: And now what is left?
   Images? Love? A greeting even,
   Sweet to the senses? Is there anything?
   Ah, no, friends: lead me away.   120
   Lead me away from Thebes.
                   Lead the great wreck
   And hell of Oedipus, whom the gods hate.
CHORAGOS: Your misery, you are not blind to that.
   Would God you had never found it out!

ANTISTROPHE 2

OEDIPUS: Death take the man who unbound   125
   My feet on that hillside
   And delivered me from death to life! What life?
   If only I had died,
   This weight of monstrous doom
   Could not have dragged me and my darlings down.   130
CHORAGOS: I would have wished the same.
OEDIPUS: Oh never to have come here
   With my father's blood upon me! Never
   To have been the man they call his mother's husband!
   Oh accurst! Oh child of evil,   135
   To have entered that wretched bed—
                  the selfsame one!
   More primal than sin itself, this fell to me.
CHORAGOS: I do not know what words to offer you.
   You were better dead than alive and blind.
OEDIPUS: Do not counsel me any more. This punishment   140
   That I have laid upon myself is just.
   If I had eyes,
   I do not know how I could bear the sight

Of my father, when I came to the house of Death,
Or my mother: for I have sinned against them both   145
So vilely that I could not make my peace
By strangling my own life.
                 Or do you think my children,
Born as they were born, would be sweet to my eyes?
Ah never, never! Nor this town with its high walls,
Nor the holy images of the gods.
                      For I,   150
Thrice miserable!—Oedipus, noblest of all the line
Of Kadmos, have condemned myself to enjoy
These things no more, by my own malediction
Expelling that man whom the gods declared
To be a defilement in the house of Laios.   155
After exposing the rankness of my own guilt,
How could I look men frankly in the eyes?
No, I swear it,
If I could have stifled my hearing at its source,
I would have done it and made all this body   160
A tight cell of misery, blank to light and sound:
So I should have been safe in my dark mind
Beyond external evil.
             Ah Kithairon!
Why did you shelter me? When I was cast upon you,
Why did I not die? Then I should never   165
Have shown the world my execrable birth.

Ah Polybos! Corinth, city that I believed
The ancient seat of my ancestors: how fair
I seemed, your child! And all the while this evil
Was cancerous within me!
                For I am sick   170
In my own being, sick in my origin.
O three roads, dark ravine, woodland and way
Where three roads met; you, drinking my father's blood,
My own blood, spilled by my own hand: can you remember
The unspeakable things I did there, and the things   175
I went on from there to do?
              O marriage, marriage!
The act that engendered me, and again the act
Performed by the son in the same bed—
                   Ah, the net
Of incest, mingling fathers, brothers, sons,
With brides, wives, mothers: the last evil   180

That can be known by men: no tongue can say
How evil!
        No. For the love of God, conceal me
Somewhere far from Thebes; or kill me; or hurl me
Into the sea, away from men's eyes for ever.

Come, lead me. You need not fear to touch me.   185
Of all men, I alone can bear this guilt.

     (*Enter* KREON.)

CHORAGOS: Kreon is here now. As to what you ask,
  He may decide the course to take. He only
  Is left to protect the city in your place.
OEDIPUS: Alas, how can I speak to him? What right have I   190
  To beg his courtesy whom I have deeply wronged?
KREON: I have not come to mock you, Oedipus,
  Or to reproach you, either.
  (*To* ATTENDANTS.)   —You, standing there:
  If you have lost all respect for man's dignity,
  At least respect the flame of Lord Helios: 195
  Do not allow this pollution to show itself
  Openly here, an affront to the earth
  And Heaven's rain and the light of day. No, take him
  Into the house as quickly as you can.
  For it is proper   200
  That only the close kindred see his grief.
OEDIPUS: I pray you in God's name, since your courtesy
  Ignores my dark expectation, visiting
  With mercy this man of all men most execrable:
  Give me what I ask—for your good, not for mine.   205
KREON: And what is it that you turn to me begging for?
OEDIPUS: Drive me out of this country as quickly as may be
  To a place where no human voice can ever greet me.
KREON: I should have done that before now—only,
  God's will had not been wholly revealed to me.   210
OEDIPUS: But his command is plain: the parricide
  Must be destroyed. I am that evil man.
KREON: That is the sense of it, yes; but as things are,
  We had best discover clearly what is to be done.
OEDIPUS: You would learn more about a man like me?   215
KREON: You are ready now to listen to the god.
OEDIPUS: I will listen. But it is to you
  That I must turn for help. I beg you, hear me.

The woman is there—
Give her whatever funeral you think proper: 220

She is your sister.
　　　　　　—But let me go, Kreon!
Let me purge my father's Thebes of the pollution
Of my living here, and go out to the wild hills,
To Kithairon, that has won such fame with me,
The tomb my mother and father appointed for me,　　　　225
And let me die there, as they willed I should.
And yet I know
Death will not ever come to me through sickness
Or in any natural way: I have been preserved
For some unthinkable fate. But let that be.　　　　　230

As for my sons, you need not care for them.
They are men, they will find some way to live.
But my poor daughters, who have shared my table,
Who never before have been parted from their father—
Take care of them, Kreon; do this for me.　　　　　235

And will you let me touch them with my hands
A last time, and let us weep together?
Be kind, my lord,
Great prince, be kind!
　　　　　　　　Could I but touch them,
They would be mine again, as when I had my eyes.　　　240

(*Enter* ANTIGONE *and* ISMENE, *attended.*)

Ah, God!
Is it my dearest children I hear weeping?
Has Kreon pitied me and sent my daughters?
KREON:　Yes, Oedipus: I knew that they were dear to you
In the old days, and know you must love them still.　　　245
OEDIPUS:　May God bless you for this—and be a friendlier
Guardian to you than he has been to me!

Children, where are you?
Come quickly to my hands: they are your brother's—
Hands that have brought your father's once clear eyes　　　250
To this way of seeing—
　　　　　　　　Ah dearest ones,
I had neither sight nor knowledge then, your father
By the woman who was the source of his own life!
And I weep for you—having no strength to see you—,
I weep for you when I think of the bitterness　　　　255
That men will visit upon you all your lives.
What homes, what festivals can you attend
Without being forced to depart again in tears?

And when you come to marriageable age,
Where is the man, my daughters, who would dare   260
Risk the bane that lies on all my children?
Is there any evil wanting? Your father killed
His father; sowed the womb of her who bore him;
Engendered you at the fount of his own existence!
That is what they will say of you.

                              Then, whom   265
Can you ever marry? There are no bridegrooms for you,
And your lives must wither away in sterile dreaming.

O Kreon, son of Menoikeus!
You are the only father my daughters have,
Since we, their parents, are both of us gone for ever.   270
They are your own blood: you will not let them
Fall into beggary and loneliness;
You will keep them from the miseries that are mine!
Take pity on them; see, they are only children,
Friendless except for you. Promise me this,   275
Great prince, and give me your hand in token of it.

      (KREON *clasps his right hand.*)

Children.
I could say much, if you could understand me,
But as it is, I have only this prayer for you:
Live where you can, be as happy as you can—   280
Happier, please God, than God has made your father.

KREON: Enough. You have wept enough. Now go within.
OEDIPUS: I must; but it is hard.
KREON: Time eases all things.
OEDIPUS: You know my mind, then?
KREON: Say what you desire.
OEDIPUS: Send me from Thebes!
KREON: God grant that I may!   285
OEDIPUS: But since God hates me . . .
KREON: No, he will grant your wish.
OEDIPUS: You promise?
KREON: I cannot speak beyond my knowledge.
OEDIPUS: Then lead me in.
KREON: Come now, and leave your children.
OEDIPUS: No! Do not take them from me!
KREON: Think no longer
That you are in command here, but rather think   290
How, when you were, you served your own destruction.

(*Exeunt into the house all but the* CHORUS; *the* CHORAGOS *chants directly to the audience.*)

CHORAGOS: Men of Thebes: look upon Oedipus.

This is the king who solved the famous riddle
And towered up, most powerful of men.
No mortal eyes but looked on him with envy,   295
Yet in the end ruin swept over him.

Let every man in mankind's frailty
Consider his last day; and let none
Presume on his good fortune until he find
Life, at his death, a memory without pain.   300

[430 B.C.]

Journal Entry

Assume the persona of Iokaste and write a brief explanation of why you gave away your infant son.

Textual Considerations

1. Cite specific examples of Sophocles' use of dramatic **irony** throughout the play and discuss their thematic significance.
2. What are the functions of the chorus? What do they provide besides the spectacle of music, poetry, and dance? How effective is the chorus from the dramatic viewpoint?
3. What is the thematic significance of the plague as the background of the drama? Who inflicts the plague upon Thebes? Why?
4. Discuss the thematic relevance of the metaphor of blindness versus sight as well as its counterpart of darkness versus light. Include Oedipus's tug of war with Teiresias, as well as Oedipus's blinding of himself in your discussion. Explain why Oedipus's removal of his eyes takes place off stage.
5. What role does Iokaste play in *Oedipus Rex*? What position does she assume in relation to the oracle? To Oedipus's downfall? Explain.
6. To what extent can we explain Oedipus's character in terms of *hubris*, or human pride? Do you empathize with him? Why or why not?

Cultural Contexts

1. Does Sophocles present the play as ordained by divine forces? Is Oedipus responsible for his own downfall? Is he a victim of fate or a victim of his own unconscious? Read Freud's interpretation of this play (Appendix D) and discuss these issues with members of your group.
2. Sophocles' play culminates with the revelation that Oedipus has committed parricide and incest. Working with your group, attack or defend the thesis that by using his reason to destroy the Sphinx's savagery, Oedipus promotes humanism, progress, and social order.

Performance Exercises

PERFORMANCE EXPRESS (40 MINUTES)

To discuss the use of masks in performance, design full or half masks for Oedipus, Iokaste, Kreon, and Teiresias before this exercise is due. On the day of the performance, ask the masked actors to act out scenes 1, 2, and 3 in an improvisational and spontaneous style, and invite the whole class to react to the performance. How helpful is the use of a mask to amplify and hide emotions or show the character's real self? Do masks help the actors distance themselves from the audience? Could the actors have used their real faces as masks? What other acting resources did the masked actors have to develop in their performance? Explain.

PERFORMANCE PROJECTS

1. To learn about Greek theater production in the fifth century B.C., research through the Internet the production of *Oedipus Rex* with Tyrone Guthrie at Stratford, Canada, 1954. Then stage one scene of *Oedipus Rex* using classical costumes, and a chorus with chants and music. Notice that for the sake of clarity, most modern producers of ancient Greek drama distribute the lines of the chorus among the performers rather than having them speak in unison.
2. To test the dramatic effectiveness of ancient drama, act out one scene of *Oedipus Rex* in postmodern style. Decide on the use of costumes and the choices of time, place, and sets that evoke the tragic atmosphere of the play in the twentieth-first century. React to the possibility of using costumes connected with sets such as your college gym.

William Shakespeare
Hamlet, Prince of Denmark

CHARACTERS

CLAUDIUS, *King of Denmark*
HAMLET, *son to the late and nephew to the present king*
POLONIUS, *lord chamberlain*
HORATIO, *friend to Hamlet*
LAERTES, *son to Polonius*
VOLTIMAND ⎫
CORNELIUS ⎪
ROSENCRANTZ ⎬ *courtiers*
GUILDENSTERN ⎪
OSRIC ⎭
A GENTLEMAN
A PRIEST
MARCELLUS ⎫ *officers*
BERNARDO ⎭
FRANCISCO, *a soldier*
REYNALDO, *servant to Polonius*
PLAYERS
TWO CLOWNS, *grave-diggers*
FORTINBRAS, *Prince of Norway*
A CAPTAIN
ENGLISH AMBASSADORS
GERTRUDE, *Queen of Denmark, and mother to Hamlet*
OPHELIA, *daughter to Polonius*
GHOST *of Hamlet's father*
(LORDS, LADIES, OFFICERS, SOLDIERS, SAILORS, MESSENGERS, AND OTHER
    ATTENDANTS)

SCENE. Denmark.

ACT I

SCENE I

(*Elsinore. A platform° before the castle.*)

(*Enter* BERNARDO *and* FRANCISCO, *two sentinels.*)

BERNARDO: Who's there?
FRANCISCO: Nay, answer me°: stand, and unfold yourself.

I.i. s.d. platform: a level space on the battlements of the royal castle at Elsinore, a Danish seaport; now Helsingör.   **2. me:** this is emphatic, since Francisco is the sentry.

BERNARDO: Long live the king!°
FRANCISCO: Bernardo?
BERNARDO: He.   5
FRANCISCO: You come most carefully upon your hour.
BERNARDO: 'Tis now struck twelve; get thee to bed, Francisco.
FRANCISCO: For this relief much thanks: 'tis bitter cold,
    And I am sick at heart.
BERNARDO: Have you had quiet guard?
FRANCISCO: Not a mouse stirring.   10
BERNARDO: Well, good night.
    If you do meet Horatio and Marcellus,
    The rivals° of my watch, bid them make haste.

                    (*Enter* HORATIO *and* MARCELLUS.)

FRANCISCO: I think I hear them. Stand, ho! Who is there?
HORATIO: Friends to this ground.
MARCELLUS: And liegemen to the Dane.   15
FRANCISCO: Give you° good night.
MARCELLUS: O, farewell, honest soldier:
    Who hath reliev'd you?
FRANCISCO: Bernardo hath my place.
    Give you good night.   (*Exit* FRANCISCO.)
MARCELLUS: Holla! Bernardo!
BERNARDO: Say,
    What, is Horatio there?
HORATIO: A piece of him.
BERNARDO: Welcome, Horatio: welcome, good Marcellus.   20
MARCELLUS: What, has this thing appear'd again to-night?
BERNARDO: I have seen nothing.
MARCELLUS: Horatio says 'tis but our fantasy,
    And will not let belief take hold of him.
    Touching this dreaded sight, twice seen of us: 25
    Therefore I have entreated him along
    With us to watch the minutes of this night;
    That if again this apparition come,
    He may approve° our eyes and speak to it.
HORATIO: Tush, tush, 'twill not appear.
BERNARDO: Sit down awhile;   30
    And let us once again assail your ears,
    That are so fortified against our story
    What we have two nights seen.

---

3. Long live the king!: either a password or greeting; Horatio and Marcellus use a different one in line
15.   **13. rivals:** partners.   **16. Give you:** God give you.   **29. approve:** corroborate.

HORATIO: Well, sit we down,
   And let us hear Bernardo speak of this.
BERNARDO: Last night of all,   35
   When yond same star that's westward from the pole°
   Had made his course t' illume that part of heaven
   Where now it burns, Marcellus and myself,
   The bell then beating one,—

         (*Enter* GHOST.)

MARCELLUS: Peace, break thee off; look, where it comes again!   40
BERNARDO: In the same figure, like the king that's dead.
MARCELLUS: Thou art a scholar°; speak to it, Horatio.
BERNARDO: Looks 'a not like the king? mark it, Horatio.
HORATIO: Most like: it harrows° me with fear and wonder.
BERNARDO: It would be spoke to.°
MARCELLUS: Speak to it. Horatio.   45
HORATIO: What art thou that usurp'st this time of night,
   Together with that fair and warlike form
   In which the majesty of buried Denmark°
   Did sometimes march? by heaven I charge thee, speak!
MARCELLUS: It is offended.
BERNARDO: See it stalks away!   50
HORATIO: Stay! speak, speak! I charge thee, speak!   (*Exit* GHOST.)
MARCELLUS: 'Tis gone, and will not answer.
BERNARDO: How now, Horatio! you tremble and look pale:
   Is not this something more than fantasy?
   What think you on 't?   55
HORATIO: Before my God, I might not this believe
   Without the sensible and true avouch
   Of mine own eyes.
MARCELLUS: Is it not like the king?
HORATIO: As thou art to thyself:
   Such was the very armour he had on   60
   When he the ambitious Norway combated;
   So frown'd he once, when, in an angry parle,
   He smote° the sledded Polacks° on the ice.
   'Tis strange.
MARCELLUS: Thus twice before, and jump° at this dead hour,   65
   With martial stalk hath he gone by our watch.

---

36. pole: polestar.   **42. scholar:** exorcisms were performed in Latin, which Horatio as an educated man
would be able to speak.   **44. harrows:** lacerates the feelings.   **45. It . . . to:** a ghost could not speak
until spoken to.   **48. buried Denmark:** the buried king of Denmark.   **63. smote:** defeated.   **63.
sledded Polacks:** Polanders using sledges.   **65. jump:** exactly.

HORATIO: In what particular thought to work I know not;
    But in the gross and scope° of my opinion,
    This bodes some strange eruption to our state.
MARCELLUS: Good now,° sit down, and tell me, he that knows,   70
    Why this same strict and most observant watch
    So nightly toils° the subject° of the land,
    And why such daily cast° of brazen cannon,
    And foreign mart° for implements of war;
    Why such impress° of shipwrights, whose sore task   75
    Does not divide the Sunday from the week;
    What might be toward, that this sweaty haste
    Doth make the night joint-labourer with the day:
    Who is't that can inform me?
HORATIO: That can I;
    At least, the whisper goes so. Our last king,   80
    Whose image even but now appear'd to us,
    Was, as you know, by Fortinbras of Norway,
    Thereto prick'd on° by a most emulate° pride,
    Dar'd to the combat; in which our valiant Hamlet—
    For so this side of our known world esteem'd him—   85
    Did slay this Fortinbras; who, by a seal'd compact,
    Well ratified by law and heraldry,°
    Did forfeit, with his life, all those his lands
    Which he stood seiz'd° of, to the conqueror:
    Against the which, a moiety competent°   90
    Was gaged by our king; which had return'd
    To the inheritance of Fortinbras,
    Had he been vanquisher; as, by the same comart,°
    And carriage° of the article design'd,
    His fell to Hamlet. Now, sir, young Fortinbras,   95
    Of unimproved° mettle hot and full,°
    Hath in the skirts of Norway here and there
    Shark'd up° a list of lawless resolutes,°
    For food and diet,° to some enterprise
    That hath a stomach in't; which is no other—   100
    As it doth well appear unto our state—
    But to recover of us, by strong hand

---

68. gross and scope: general drift.   **70. Good now:** an expression denoting entreaty or expostulation.
72. toils: causes or makes to toil.   **72. subject:** people, subjects.   **73. cast:** casting, founding.
74. mart: buying and selling, traffic.   **75. impress:** impressment.   **83. prick'd on:** incited.   **83. emulate:** rivaling.   **87. law and heraldry:** heraldic law, governing combat.   **89. seiz'd:** possessed.   **90. moiety competent:** adequate or sufficient portion.   **93. comart:** joint bargain.   **94. carriage:** import, bearing.   **96. unimproved:** not turned to account.   **96. hot and full:** full of fight.   **98. Shark'd up:** got together in haphazard fashion.   **98. resolutes:** desperadoes.   **99. food and diet:** no pay but their keep.

And terms compulsatory, those foresaid lands
So by his father lost: and this, I take it,
Is the main motive of our preparations,   105
The source of this our watch and the chief head
Of this post-haste and romage° in the land.
BERNARDO: I think it be no other but e'en so:
Well may it sort° that this portentous figure
Comes armed through our watch; so like the king   110
That was and is the question of these wars.
HORATIO: A mote° it is to trouble the mind's eye.
In the most high and palmy state° of Rome,
A little ere the mightiest Julius fell,
The graves stood tenantless and the sheeted dead   115
Did squeak and gibber in the Roman streets:
As stars with trains of fire° and dews of blood,
Disasters° in the sun; and the moist star°
Upon whose influence Neptune's empire° stands
Was sick almost to doomsday with eclipse: 120
And even the like precurse° of fear'd events,
As harbingers preceding still the fates
And prologue to the omen coming on,
Have heaven and earth together demonstrated
Unto our climatures and countrymen.—   125

(*Enter* GHOST.)

But soft, behold! lo, where it comes again!
I'll cross° it, though it blast me. Stay, illusion!
If thou hast any sound, or use of voice,
Speak to me! (*It° spreads his arms.*)
If there be any good thing to be done,   130
That may to thee do ease and grace to me,
Speak to me!
If° thou art privy to thy country's fate,
Which, happily, foreknowing may avoid,
O, speak!   135
Or if thou hast uphoarded in thy life
Extorted treasure in the womb of earth,
For which, they say, you spirits oft walk in death, (*The cock crows.*)
Speak of it: stay, and speak! Stop it, Marcellus.

---

107. romage: bustle, commotion.   **109. sort:** suit.   **112. mote:** speck of dust.   **113. palmy state:** triumphant sovereignty.   **117. stars . . . fire:** i.e., comets.   **118. Disasters:** unfavorable aspects.   **118. moist star:** the moon, governing tides.   **119. Neptune's empire:** the sea.   **121. precurse:** heralding.   **127. cross:** meet, face, thus bringing down the evil influence on the person who crosses it.   **129. It:** the Ghost, or perhaps Horatio.   **133–139. If . . . :** in the following seven lines, Horatio recites the traditional reasons why ghosts might walk.

MARCELLUS: Shall I strike at it with my partisan?° 140
HORATIO: Do, if it will not stand.
BERNARDO: 'Tis here!
HORATIO: 'Tis here!
MARCELLUS: 'Tis gone! *(Exit* GHOST.*)*
   We do it wrong, being so majestical,
   To offer it the show of violence;
   For it is, as the air, invulnerable, 145
   And our vain blows malicious mockery.
BERNARDO: It was about to speak, when the cock crew.°
HORATIO: And then it started like a guilty thing
   Upon a fearful summons. I have heard,
   The cock, that is the trumpet to the morn, 150
   Doth with his lofty and shrill-sounding throat
   Awake the god of day; and, at his warning,
   Whether in sea or fire, in earth or air,
   Th' extravagant and erring° spirit hies
   To his confine°: and of the truth herein 155
   This present object made probation.°
MARCELLUS: It faded on the crowing of the cock.
   Some say that ever 'gainst° that season comes
   Wherein our Saviour's birth is celebrated,
   The bird of dawning singeth all night long: 160
   And then, they say, no spirit dare stir abroad;
   The nights are wholesome; then no planets strike,°
   No fairy takes, nor witch hath power to charm,
   So hallow'd and so gracious° is that time.
HORATIO: So have I heard and do in part believe it. 165
   But, look, the morn, in russet mantle clad,
   Walks o'er the dew of yon high eastward hill:
   Break we our watch up; and by my advice,
   Let us impart what we have seen to-night
   Unto young Hamlet; for, upon my life, 170
   This spirit, dumb to us, will speak to him.
   Do you consent we shall acquaint him with it,
   As needful in our loves, fitting our duty?
MARCELLUS: Let's do 't, I pray; and I this morning know
   Where we shall find him most conveniently. *(Exeunt.)* 175

---

140. partisan: long-handled spear with a blade having lateral projections. **147. cock crew:** according to traditional ghost lore, spirits returned to their confines at cockcrow. **154. extravagant and erring:** wandering. Both words mean the same thing. **155. confine:** place of confinement. **156. probation:** proof, trial. **158. 'gainst:** just before. **162. planets strike:** it was thought that planets were malignant and might strike travelers by night. **164. gracious:** full of goodness.

Scene II

(*A room of state in the castle.*)

(*Flourish. Enter* Claudius, *King of Denmark*, Gertrude *the Queen*, councilors, Polonius *and his Son* Laertes, Hamlet, *cum aliis*° [*including* Voltimand *and* Cornelius].)

KING: Though yet of Hamlet our dear brother's death
   The memory be green, and that it us befitted
   To bear our hearts in grief and our whole kingdom
   To be contracted in one brow of woe,
   Yet so far hath discretion fought with nature   5
   That we with wisest sorrow think on him,
   Together with remembrance of ourselves.
   Therefore our sometime sister, now our queen,
   Th' imperial jointress° to this warlike state,
   Have we, as 'twere with a defeated joy,—   10
   With an auspicious and a dropping eye,
   With mirth in funeral and with dirge in marriage,
   In equal scale weighing delight and dole,—
   Taken to wife: nor have we herein barr'd
   Your better wisdoms, which have freely gone   15
   With this affair along. For all, our thanks.
   Now follows, that° you know, young Fortinbras,
   Holding a weak supposal° of our worth,
   Or thinking by our late dear brother's death
   Our state to be disjoint° and out of frame,°   20
   Colleagued° with this dream of his advantage,°
   He hath not fail'd to pester us with message,
   Importing° the surrender of those lands
   Lost by his father, with all bands of law,
   To our most valiant brother. So much for him.   25
   Now for ourself and for this time of meeting:
   Thus much the business is: we have here writ
   To Norway, uncle of young Fortinbras,—
   Who, impotent and bed-rid, scarcely hears
   Of this his nephew's purpose,—to suppress   30
   His further gait° herein; in that the levies,
   The lists and full proportions, are all made

I.ii. s.d. **cum aliis:** with others.   **9. jointress:** woman possessed of a jointure, or, joint tenancy of an estate.   **17. that:** that which.   **18. weak supposal:** low estimate.   **20. disjoint:** distracted, out of joint. **20. frame:** order.   **21. Colleagued:** added to.   **21. dream . . . advantage:** visionary hope of success. **23. Importing:** purporting, pertaining to.   **31. gait:** proceeding.

Out of his subject°: and we here dispatch
You, good Cornelius, and you, Voltimand,
For bearers of this greeting to old Norway;   35
Giving to you no further personal power
To business with the king, more than the scope
Of these delated° articles allow.
Farewell, and let your haste commend your duty.

CORNELIUS: ⎫
VOLTIMAND: ⎭ In that and all things will we show our duty.   40

KING: We doubt it nothing: heartily farewell.

(*Exeunt* VOLTIMAND *and* CORNELIUS.)

And now, Laertes, what's the news with you?
You told us of some suit; what is't, Laertes?
You cannot speak of reason to the Dane,°
And lose your voice°: what wouldst thou beg, Laertes,   45
That shall not be my offer, not thy asking?
The head is not more native° to the heart,
The hand more instrumental° to the mouth,
Than is the throne of Denmark to thy father.
What wouldst thou have, Laertes?

LAERTES: My dread lord,   50
Your leave and favour to return to France;
From whence though willingly I came to Denmark,
To show my duty in your coronation,
Yet now, I must confess, that duty done,
My thoughts and wishes bend again toward France   55
And bow them to your gracious leave and pardon.°

KING: Have you your father's leave? What says Polonius?

POLONIUS: He hath, my lord, wrung from me my slow leave
By laboursome petition, and at last
Upon his will I seal'd my hard consent: 60
I do beseech you, give him leave to go.

KING: Take thy fair hour, Laertes; time be thine,
And thy best graces spend it at thy will!
But now, my cousin° Hamlet, and my son,—

HAMLET (*aside*):   A little more than kin, and less than kind!°   65

KING: How is it that the clouds still hang on you?

---

33. Out of his subject: at the expense of Norway's subjects (collectively).   **38. delated:** expressly
stated.   **44. the Dane:** Danish king.   **45. lose your voice:** speak in vain.   **47. native:** closely connected, related.   **48. instrumental:** serviceable.   **56. leave and pardon:** permission to depart.
64. cousin: any kin not of the immediate family.   **65. A little . . . kind:** i.e., my relation to you has
become more than kinship warrants; it has also become unnatural.

HAMLET: Not so, my lord; I am too much in the sun.°
QUEEN: Good Hamlet, cast thy nighted colour off,
  And let thine eye look like a friend on Denmark.
  Do not for ever with thy vailed lids   70
  Seek for thy noble father in the dust:
  Thou know'st 'tis common; all that lives must die,
  Passing through nature to eternity.
HAMLET: Ay, madam, it is common.°
QUEEN: If it be,
  Why seems it so particular with thee?   75
HAMLET: Seems, madam! nay, it is; I know not "seems."
  'Tis not alone my inky cloak, good mother,
  Nor customary suits° of solemn black,
  Nor windy suspiration° of forc'd breath,
  No, nor the fruitful river in the eye,   80
  Nor the dejected 'haviour of the visage,
  Together with all forms, moods, shapes of grief,
  That can denote me truly: these indeed seem,
  For they are actions that a man might play:
  But I have that within which passeth show;   85
  These but the trappings and the suits of woe.
KING: 'Tis sweet and commendable in your nature, Hamlet,
  To give these mourning duties to your father:
  But, you must know, your father lost a father;
  That father lost, lost his, and the survivor bound   90
  In filial obligation for some term
  To do obsequious° sorrow: but to persever
  In obstinate condolement° is a course
  Of impious stubbornness; 'tis unmanly grief;
  It shows a will most incorrect° to heaven,   95
  A heart unfortified, a mind impatient,
  An understanding simple and unschool'd:
  For what we know must be and is as common
  As any the most vulgar thing° to sense,
  Why should we in our peevish opposition   100
  Take it to heart? Fie! 'tis a fault to heaven,

---

67. I am . . . sun: the senses seem to be: I am too much out of doors, I am too much in the sun of your grace (ironical), I am too much of a son to you. Possibly an allusion to the proverb "Out of heaven's blessing into the warm sun"; i.e., Hamlet is out of house and home in being deprived of the kingship. **74. Ay . . . common:** i.e., it is common, but it hurts nevertheless; possibly a reference to the commonplace quality of the queen's remark.   **78. customary suits:** suits prescribed by custom for mourning. **79. windy suspiration:** heavy sighing.   **92. obsequious:** dutiful.   **93. condolement:** sorrowing. **95. incorrect:** untrained, uncorrected.   **99. vulgar thing:** common experience.

A fault against the dead, a fault to nature,
To reason most absurd; whose common theme
Is death of fathers, and who still hath cried,
From the first corse till he that died to-day,   105
"This must be so." We pray you, throw to earth
This unprevailing° woe, and think of us
As of a father: for let the world take note,
You are the most immediate° to our throne;
And with no less nobility° of love   110
Than that which dearest father bears his son,
Do I impart° toward you. For your intent
In going back to school in Wittenberg,°
It is most retrograde° to our desire:
And we beseech you, bend you° to remain   115
Here, in the cheer and comfort of our eye,
Our chiefest courtier, cousin, and our son.

QUEEN: Let not thy mother lose her prayers, Hamlet:
I pray thee, stay with us; go not to Wittenberg.

HAMLET: I shall in all my best obey you, madam.   120

KING: Why, 'tis a loving and a fair reply:
Be as ourself in Denmark. Madam, come;
This gentle and unforc'd accord of Hamlet
Sits smiling to my heart: in grace whereof,
No jocund health that Denmark drinks to-day,   125
But the great cannon to the clouds shall tell,
And the king's rouse° the heaven shall bruit again,°
Re-speaking earthly thunder. Come away.

(*Flourish. Exeunt all but* HAMLET.)

HAMLET: O, that this too too sullied flesh would melt,
Thaw and resolve itself into a dew!   130
Or that the Everlasting had not fix'd
His canon 'gainst self-slaughter! O God! God!
How weary, stale, flat and unprofitable,
Seem to me all the uses of this world!
Fie on't! ah fie! 'tis an unweeded garden,   135
That grows to seed; things rank and gross in nature
Possess it merely.° That it should come to this!
But two months dead: nay, not so much, not two:
So excellent a king; that was, to this,

---

107. unprevailing: unavailing.   **109. most immediate:** next in succession.   **110. nobility:** high
degree.   **112. impart:** the object is apparently love (1.110).   **113. Wittenberg:** famous German university founded in 1502.   **114. retrograde:** contrary.   **115. bend you:** incline yourself; imperative.
127. rouse: draft of liquor.   **127. bruit again:** echo.   **137. merely:** completely, entirely.

Hyperion° to a satyr; so loving to my mother 140
That he might not beteem° the winds of heaven
Visit her face too roughly. Heaven and earth!
Must I remember? why, she would hang on him,
As if increase of appetite had grown
By what it fed on: and yet, within a month— 145
Let me not think on't—Frailty, thy name is woman!—
A little month, or ere those shoes were old
With which she followed my poor father's body,
Like Niobe,° all tears:—why she, even she—
O God! a beast, that wants discourse of reason,° 150
Would have mourn'd longer—married with my uncle,
My father's brother, but no more like my father
Than I to Hercules: within a month:
Ere yet the salt of most unrighteous tears
Had left the flushing in her galled° eyes, 155
She married. O, most wicked speed, to post
With such dexterity° to incestuous sheets!
It is not nor it cannot come to good:
But break, my heart; for I must hold my tongue.

(*Enter* HORATIO, MARCELLUS, *and* BERNARDO.)

HORATIO: Hail to your lordship! 160
HAMLET: I am glad to see you well:
   Horatio!—or I do forget myself.
HORATIO: The same, my lord, and your poor servant ever.
HAMLET: Sir, my good friend; I'll change that name with you°:
   And what make you from Wittenberg, Horatio? 165
   Marcellus?
MARCELLUS: My good lord—
HAMLET: I am very glad to see you. Good even, sir.
   But what, in faith, make you from Wittenberg?
HORATIO: A truant disposition, good my lord. 170
HAMLET: I would not hear your enemy say so,
   Nor shall you do my ear that violence,
   To make it truster of your own report
   Against yourself: I know you are no truant.
   But what is your affair in Elsinore? 175
   We'll teach you to drink deep ere you depart.

---

140. Hyperion: God of the sun in the older regime of ancient gods. **141. beteem:** allow.
149. Niobe: Tantalus's daughter, who boasted that she had more sons and daughters than Leto; for this Apollo and Artemis slew her children. She was turned into stone by Zeus on Mount Sipylus. **150. discourse of reason:** process or faculty of reason. **155. galled:** irritated. **157. dexterity:** facility. **164. I'll . . . you:** I'll be your servant, you shall be my friend; also explained as "I'll exchange the name of friend with you."

HORATIO: My lord, I came to see your father's funeral.

HAMLET: I prithee, do not mock me, fellow-student;
I think it was to see my mother's wedding.

HORATIO: Indeed, my lord, it follow'd hard° upon.   180

HAMLET: Thrift, thrift, Horatio! the funeral bak'd meats°
Did coldly furnish forth the marriage tables.
Would I had met my dearest° foe in heaven
Or ever I had seen that day, Horatio!
My father!—methinks I see my father.   185

HORATIO: Where, my lord!

HAMLET: In my mind's eye, Horatio.

HORATIO: I saw him once; 'a° was a goodly king.

HAMLET: 'A was a man, take him for all in all,
I shall not look upon his like again.

HORATIO: My lord, I think I saw him yesternight.   190

HAMLET: Saw? who?

HORATIO: My lord, the king your father.

HAMLET: The king my father!

HORATIO: Season your admiration° for a while
With an attent ear, till I may deliver,
Upon the witness of these gentlemen,   195
This marvel to you.

HAMLET: For God's love, let me hear.

HORATIO: Two nights together had these gentlemen,
Marcellus and Bernardo, on their watch,
In the dead waste and middle of the night,
Been thus encount'red. A figure like your father,   200
Armed at point exactly, cap-a-pe,°
Appears before them, and with solemn march
Goes slow and stately by them: thrice he walk'd
By their oppress'd° and fear-surprised eyes,
Within his truncheon's° length; whilst they, distill'd°   205
Almost to jelly with the act° of fear,
Stand dumb and speak not to him. This to me
In dreadful secrecy impart they did;
And I with them the third night kept the watch;
Where, as they had deliver'd, both in time,   210
Form of the thing, each word made true and good,
The apparition comes: I knew your father;

---

180. hard: close.   **181. bak'd meats:** meat pies.   **183. dearest:** direst; the adjective *dear* in Shakespeare has two different origins: O.E. *deore*, "beloved," and O.E. *deor*, "fierce." *Dearest* is the superlative of the second.   **187. 'a:** he.   **193. Season your admiration:** restrain your astonishment.   **201. cap-a-pe:** from head to foot.   **204. oppress'd:** distressed.   **205. truncheon:** officer's staff.   **205. distill'd:** softened, weakened.   **206. act:** action.

These hands are not more like.

HAMLET: But where was this?

MARCELLUS: My lord, upon the platform where we watch'd.

HAMLET: Did you not speak to it?

HORATIO: My lord, I did;   215
But answer made it none: yet once methought
It lifted up it° head and did address
Itself to motion, like as it would speak;
But even then the morning cock crew loud,
And at the sound it shrunk in haste away,   220
And vanish'd from our sight.

HAMLET: 'Tis very strange.

HORATIO: As I do live, my honour'd lord, 'tis true;
And we did think it writ down in our duty
To let you know of it.

HAMLET: Indeed, indeed, sirs, but this troubles me.   225
Hold you the watch to-night?

MARCELLUS: ⎱
BERNARDO: ⎰   We do, my lord.

HAMLET: Arm'd, say you?

MARCELLUS: ⎱
BERNARDO: ⎰ Arm'd, my lord.

HAMLET: From top to toe?

MARCELLUS: ⎱
BERNARDO: ⎰   My lord, from head to foot.

HAMLET: Then saw you not his face?   230

HORATIO: O, yes, my lord; he wore his beaver° up.

HAMLET: What, look'd he frowningly?

HORATIO: A countenance more
In sorrow than in anger.

HAMLET: Pale or red?

HORATIO: Nay, very pale.

HAMLET: And fix'd his eyes upon you?

HORATIO: Most constantly.

HAMLET: I would I had been there.   235

HORATIO: It would have much amaz'd you.

HAMLET: Very like, very like. Stay'd it long?

HORATIO: While one with moderate haste might tell a hundred.

MARCELLUS: ⎱
BERNARDO: ⎰ Longer, longer.

HORATIO: Not when I saw't.

HAMLET: His beard was grizzled,—no?   240

HORATIO: It was, as I have seen it in his life,

---

217. it: its.   **231. beaver:** visor on the helmet.

A sable° silver'd.

HAMLET: I will watch to-night;
   Perchance 'twill walk again.

HORATIO: I warr'nt it will.

HAMLET: If it assume my noble father's person,
   I'll speak to it, though hell itself should gape   245
   And bid me hold my peace. I pray you all,
   If you have hitherto conceal'd this sight,
   Let it be tenable in your silence still;
   And whatsoever else shall hap to-night,
   Give it an understanding, but no tongue: 250
   I will requite your loves. So, fare you well:
   Upon the platform, 'twixt eleven and twelve,
   I'll visit you.

ALL: Our duty to your honour.

HAMLET: Your loves, as mine to you: farewell.   (*Exeunt all but* HAMLET.)
   My father's spirit in arms! all is not well;   255
   I doubt° some foul play: would the night were come!
   Till then sit still, my soul: foul deeds will rise,
   Though all the earth o'erwhelm them, to men's eyes.   *Exit.*

SCENE III

(*A room in* POLONIUS'*s house.*)

(*Enter* LAERTES *and* OPHELIA, *his Sister.*)

LAERTES: My necessaries are embark'd: farewell:
   And, sister, as the winds give benefit
   And convoy is assistant,° do not sleep,
   But let me hear from you.

OPHELIA: Do you doubt that?

LAERTES: For Hamlet and the trifling of his favour,   5
   Hold it a fashion° and a toy in blood,°
   A violet in the youth of primy° nature,
   Forward,° not permanent, sweet, not lasting,
   The perfume and suppliance of a minute°;
   No more.

OPHELIA: No more but so?

LAERTES: Think it no more: 10
   For nature, crescent,° does not grow alone

---

242. **sable:** black color. 256. **doubt:** fear. **I.iii. 3. convoy is assistant:** means of conveyance are available. **6. fashion:** custom, prevailing usage. **6. toy in blood:** passing amorous fancy. **7. primy:** in its prime. **8. Forward:** precocious. **9. suppliance of a minute:** diversion to fill up a minute. **11. crescent:** growing, waxing.

In thews° and bulk, but, as this temple° waxes,
The inward service of the mind and soul
Grows wide withal. Perhaps he loves you now,
And now no soil° nor cautel° doth besmirch   15
The virtue of his will: but you must fear,
His greatness weigh'd,° his will is not his own;
For he himself is subject to his birth:
He may not, as unvalued persons do,
Carve for himself; for on his choice depends   20
The safety and health of this whole state;
And therefore must his choice be circumscrib'd
Unto the voice and yielding° of that body
Whereof he is the head. Then if he says he loves you,
It fits your wisdom so far to believe it   25
As he in his particular act and place
May give his saying deed°; which is no further
Than the main voice of Denmark goes withal.
Then weigh what loss your honour may sustain,
If with too credent° ear you list his songs,   30
Or lose your heart, or your chaste treasure open
To his unmast'red° importunity.
Fear it, Ophelia, fear it, my dear sister,
And keep you in the rear of your affection,
Out of the shot and danger of desire.   35
The chariest° maid is prodigal enough,
If she unmask her beauty to the moon:
Virtue itself 'scapes not calumnious strokes:
The canker galls the infants of the spring,°
Too oft before their buttons° be disclos'd,°   40
And in the morn and liquid dew° of youth
Contagious blastments° are most imminent.
Be wary then; best safety lies in fear:
Youth to itself rebels, though none else near.
OPHELIA: I shall the effect of this good lesson keep,   45
As watchman to my heart. But, good my brother,
Do not, as some ungracious° pastors do,
Show me the steep and thorny way to heaven;
Whiles, like a puff'd° and reckless libertine,
Himself the primrose path of dalliance treads,   50

---

12. thews: bodily strength.   **12. temple:** body.   **15. soil:** blemish.   **15. cautel:** crafty device.   **17. greatness weigh'd:** high position considered.   **23. voice and yielding:** assent, approval.   **27. deed:** effect.   **30. credent:** credulous.   **32. unmast'red:** unrestrained.   **36. chariest:** most scrupulously modest.   **39. The canker . . . spring:** the cankerworm destroys the young plants of spring.   **40. buttons:** buds.   **40. disclos'd:** opened.   **41. liquid dew:** i.e., time when dew is fresh.   **42. blastments:** blights.   **47. ungracious:** graceless.   **49. puff'd:** bloated.

And recks° not his own rede.°

(*Enter* POLONIUS.)

LAERTES: O, fear me not.
   I stay too long: but here my father comes.
   A double° blessing is a double grace;
   Occasion° smiles upon a second leave.   55
POLONIUS: Yet here, Laertes? aboard, aboard, for shame!
   The wind sits in the shoulder of your sail,
   And you are stay'd for. There; my blessing with thee!
   And these few precepts° in thy memory
   Look thou character.° Give thy thoughts no tongue,   60
   Nor any unproportion'd° thought his act.
   Be thou familiar, but by no means vulgar.°
   Those friends thou hast, and their adoption tried,
   Grapple them to thy soul with hoops of steel;
   But do not dull thy palm with entertainment   65
   Of each new-hatch'd, unfledg'd° comrade. Beware
   Of entrance to a quarrel, but being in,
   Bear't that th' opposed may beware of thee.
   Give every man thy ear, but few thy voice;
   Take each man's censure, but reserve thy judgement.   70
   Costly thy habit as thy purse can buy,
   But not express'd in fancy°; rich, not gaudy;
   For the apparel oft proclaims the man,
   And they in France of the best rank and station
   Are of a most select and generous chief in that.°   75
   Neither a borrower nor a lender be;
   For loan oft loses both itself and friend,
   And borrowing dulleth edge of husbandry.°
   This above all: to thine own self be true,
   And it must follow, as the night the day,   80
   Thou canst not then be false to any man.
   Farewell: my blessing season° this in thee!
LAERTES: Most humbly do I take my leave, my lord.
POLONIUS: The time invites you; go; your servants tend.
LAERTES: Farewell, Ophelia; and remember well   85
   What I have said to you.
OPHELIA: 'Tis in my memory lock'd,

---

51. recks: heeds.   **51. rede:** counsel.   **54. double:** i.e., Laertes has already bade his father good-by.
55. Occasion: opportunity.   **59. precepts:** many parallels have been found to the series of maxims
which follows, one of the closer being that in Lyly's *Euphues*.   **60. character:** inscribe.
61. unproportion'd: inordinate.   **62. vulgar:** common.   **66. unfledg'd:** immature.   **72. express'd in
fancy:** fantastical in design.   **75. Are . . . that:** chief is usually taken as a substantive meaning "head,"
"eminence."   **78. husbandry:** thrift.   **82. season:** mature.

And you yourself shall keep the key of it.
LAERTES: Farewell.   (*Exit* LAERTES.)
POLONIUS: What is 't, Ophelia, he hath said to you?
OPHELIA: So please you, something touching the Lord Hamlet.   90
POLONIUS: Marry, well bethought:
  'Tis told me, he hath very oft of late
  Given private time to you; and you yourself
  Have of your audience been most free and bounteous:
  If it be so, as so't is put on° me.   95
  And that in way of caution, I must tell you,
  You do not understand yourself so clearly
  As it behooves my daughter and your honour.
  What is between you? give me up the truth.
OPHELIA: He hath, my lord, of late made many tenders°   100
  Of his affection to me.
POLONIUS: Affection! pooh! you speak like a green girl,
  Unsifted° in such perilous circumstance.
  Do you believe his tenders, as you call them?
OPHELIA: I do not know, my lord, what I should think.   105
POLONIUS: Marry, I will teach you: think yourself a baby;
  That you have ta'en these tenders° for true pay,
  Which are not sterling.° Tender° yourself more dearly;
  Or—not to crack the wind° of the poor phrase,
  Running it thus—you'll tender me a fool.°   110
OPHELIA: My lord, he hath importun'd me with love
  In honourable fashion.
POLONIUS: Ay, fashion° you may call it; go to, go to.
OPHELIA: And hath given countenance° to his speech, my lord,
  With almost all the holy vows of heaven.   115
POLONIUS: Ay, springes° to catch woodcocks.° I do know,
  When the blood burns, how prodigal the soul
  Lends the tongue vows: these blazes, daughter,
  Giving more light than heat, extinct in both,
  Even in their promise, as it is a-making,   120
  You must not take for fire. From this time
  Be somewhat scanter of your maiden presence;
  Set your entreatments° at a higher rate
  Than a command to parley.° For Lord Hamlet,
  Believe so much in him,° that he is young,   125

95. put on: impressed on.   **100, 104. tenders:** offers.   **103. Unsifted:** untried.   **107. tenders:** promises to pay.   **108. sterling:** legal currency.   **108. Tender:** hold.   **109. crack the wind:** i.e., run it until it is broken-winded.   **110. tender . . . fool:** show me a fool (for a daughter).   **113. fashion:** mere form, pretense.   **114. countenance:** credit, support.   **116. springes:** snares.   **116. woodcocks:** birds easily caught, type of stupidity.   **123. entreatments:** conversations, interviews.   **124. command to parley:** mere invitation to talk.   **125. so . . . him:** this much concerning him.

And with a larger tether may he walk
Than may be given you: in few,° Ophelia,
Do not believe his vows; for they are brokers°;
Not of that dye° which their investments° show,
But mere implorators of° unholy suits,   130
Breathing° like sanctified and pious bawds,
The better to beguile. This is for all;
I would not, in plain terms, from this time forth,
Have you so slander° any moment leisure,
As to give words or talk with the Lord Hamlet.   135
Look to 't, I charge you: come your ways.
OPHELIA: I shall obey, my lord.   (*Exeunt.*)

SCENE IV

(*The platform.*)

(*Enter* HAMLET, HORATIO, *and* MARCELLUS.)

HAMLET: The air bites shrewdly; it is very cold.
HORATIO: It is a nipping and an eager air.
HAMLET: What hour now?
HORATIO: I think it lacks of twelve.
MARCELLUS: No, it is struck.
HORATIO: Indeed? I heard it not: then it draws near the season   5
Wherein the spirit held his wont to walk.

(*A flourish of trumpets, and two pieces go off.*)

What does this mean, my lord?
HAMLET: The king doth wake° to-night and takes his rouse,°
Keeps wassail,° and the swagg'ring up-spring° reels°;
And, as he drains his draughts of Rhenish° down,   10
The kettle-drum and trumpet thus bray out
The triumph of his pledge.°
HORATIO: Is it a custom?
HAMLET: Ay, marry, is 't:
But to my mind, though I am native here
And to the manner born,° it is a custom   15
More honour'd in the breach than the observance.

---

127. in few: briefly.   **128. brokers:** go-betweens, procurers.   **129. dye:** color or sort.   **129. invest-ments:** clothes.   **130. implorators of:** solicitors of.   **131. Breathing:** speaking.   **134. slander:** bring disgrace or reproach upon.   **I.iv. 8. wake:** stay awake, hold revel.   **8. rouse:** carouse, drinking bout. **9. wassail:** carousal.   **9. up-spring:** last and wildest dance at German merry-makings.   **9. reels:** reels through.   **10. Rhenish:** rhine wine.   **12. triumph . . . pledge:** his glorious achievement as a drinker. **15. to . . . born:** destined by birth to be subject to the custom in question.

This heavy-headed revel east and west
Makes us traduc'd and tax'd of other nations:
They clepe° us drunkards, and with swinish phrase°
Soil our addition°; and indeed it takes   20
From our achievements, though perform'd at height,
The pith and marrow of our attribute.°
So, oft it chances in particular men,
That for some vicious mole of nature° in them,
As, in their birth—wherein they are not guilty,   25
Since nature cannot choose his origin—
By the o'ergrowth of some complexion,
Oft breaking down the pales° and forts of reason,
Or by some habit that too much o'er-leavens°
The form of plausive° manners, that these men,   30
Carrying, I say, the stamp of one defect,
Being nature's livery,° or fortune's star,°—
Their virtues else—be they as pure as grace,
As infinite as man may undergo—
Shall in the general censure take corruption   35
From that particular fault: the dram of eale°
Doth all the noble substance of a doubt
To his own scandal.°

                          (*Enter* GHOST.)

HORATIO: Look, my lord, it comes!
HAMLET: Angels and ministers of grace° defend us!
Be thou a spirit of health or goblin damn'd,   40
Bring with thee airs from heaven or blasts from hell,
Be thy intents wicked or charitable,
Thou com'st in such a questionable° shape
That I will speak to thee: I'll call thee Hamlet,
King, father, royal Dane: O, answer me!   45
Let me not burst in ignorance; but tell
Why thy canoniz'd° bones, hearsed° in death,
Have burst their cerements°; why the sepulchre,
Wherein we saw thee quietly interr'd,

---

19. clepe: call. **19. with swinish phrase:** by calling us swine. **20. addition:** reputation.
22. attribute: reputation. **24. mole of nature:** natural blemish in one's constitution. **28. pales:** palings (as of a fortification). **29. o'er-leavens:** induces a change throughout (as yeast works in bread).
30. plausive: pleasing. **32. nature's livery:** endowment from nature. **32. fortune's star:** the position in which one is placed by fortune, a reference to astrology. The two phrases are aspects of the same thing. **36. dram of eale:** has had various interpretations, the preferred one being probably, "a dram of evil." **36–38. the dram . . . scandal:** a famous crux. **39. ministers of grace:** messengers of God.
43. questionable: inviting question or conversation. **47. canoniz'd:** buried according to the canons of the church. **47. hearsed:** coffined. **48. cerements:** grave-clothes.

Hath op'd his ponderous and marble jaws,   50
To cast thee up again. What may this mean,
That thou, dead corse, again in complete steel
Revisits thus the glimpses of the moon,°
Making night hideous; and we fools of nature°
So horridly to shake our disposition   55
With thoughts beyond the reaches of our souls?
Say, why is this? wherefore? what should we do?

(GHOST *beckons* HAMLET.)

HORATIO: It beckons you to go away with it,
  As if it some impartment° did desire
  To you alone.
MARCELLUS: Look, with what courteous action   60
  It waves you to a more removed° ground:
  But do not go with it.
HORATIO: No, by no means.
HAMLET: It will not speak; then I will follow it.
HORATIO: Do not, my lord!
HAMLET: Why, what should be the fear?
  I do not set my life at a pin's fee;   65
  And for my soul, what can it do to that,
  Being a thing immortal as itself?
  It waves me forth again: I'll follow it.
HORATIO: What if it tempt you toward the flood, my lord,
  Or to the dreadful summit of the cliff   70
  That beetles o'er° his base into the sea,
  And there assume some other horrible form,
  Which might deprive your sovereignty of reason°
  And draw you into madness? think of it:
  The very place puts toys of desperation,°   75
  Without more motive, into every brain
  That looks so many fathoms to the sea
  And hears it roar beneath.
HAMLET: It waves me still.
  Go on; I'll follow thee.
MARCELLUS: You shall not go, my lord.
HAMLET: Hold off your hands!   80
HORATIO: Be rul'd; you shall not go.
HAMLET: My fate cries out,

---

53. glimpses of the moon: the earth by night.   **54. fools of nature:** mere men, limited to natural
knowledge.   **59. impartment:** communication.   **61. removed:** remote.   **71. beetles o'er:** overhangs
threateningly.   **73. deprive . . . reason:** take away the sovereignty of your reason. It was thought that
evil spirits would sometimes assume the form of departed spirits in order to work madness in a human
creature.   **75. toys of desperation:** freakish notions of suicide.

And makes each petty artere° in this body
As hardy as the Nemean lion's° nerve.°
Still am I call'd. Unhand me, gentlemen.
By heaven, I'll make a ghost of him that lets° me!   85
I say, away! Go on; I'll follow thee.   (*Exeunt* GHOST *and* HAMLET.)
HORATIO: He waxes desperate with imagination.
MARCELLUS: Let's follow; 'tis not fit thus to obey him.
HORATIO: Have after. To what issue° will this come?
MARCELLUS: Something is rotten in the state of Denmark.   90
HORATIO: Heaven will direct it.°
MARCELLUS: Nay, let's follow him.   (*Exeunt.*)

SCENE V

(*Another part of the platform.*)

(*Enter* GHOST *and* HAMLET.)

HAMLET: Whither wilt thou lead me? speak; I'll go no further.
GHOST: Mark me.
HAMLET: I will.
GHOST: My hour is almost come,
  When I to sulphurous and tormenting flames
  Must render up myself.
HAMLET: Alas, poor ghost!
GHOST: Pity me not, but lend thy serious hearing   5
  To what I shall unfold.
HAMLET: Speak; I am bound to hear.
GHOST: So art thou to revenge, when thou shalt hear.
HAMLET: What?
GHOST: I am thy father's spirit,
  Doom'd for a certain term to walk the night,   10
  And for the day confin'd to fast° in fires,
  Till the foul crimes done in my days of nature
  Are burnt and purg'd away. But that I am forbid
  To tell the secrets of my prison-house,
  I could a tale unfold whose lightest word   15
  Would harrow up thy soul, freeze thy young blood,
  Make thy two eyes, like stars, start from their spheres,°
  Thy knotted° and combined° locks to part

---

82. artere: artery.   **83. Nemean lion's:** Nemean lion was one of the monsters slain by Hercules.
83. nerve: sinew, tendon. The point is that the arteries which were carrying the spirits out into the body
were functioning and were as stiff and hard as the sinews of the lion.   **85. lets:** hinders.   **89. issue:** outcome.   **91. it:** i.e., the outcome.   **I.v. 11. fast:** probably, do without food. It has been sometimes taken
in the sense of doing general penance.   **17. spheres:** orbits.   **18. knotted:** perhaps intricately
arranged.   **18. combined:** tied, bound.

And each particular hair to stand an end,
Like quills upon the fretful porpentine°:   20
But this eternal blazon° must not be
To ears of flesh and blood. List, list, O, list!
If thou didst ever thy dear father love—
HAMLET: O God!
GHOST: Revenge his foul and most unnatural° murder.   25
HAMLET: Murder!
GHOST: Murder most foul, as in the best it is;
But this most foul, strange and unnatural.
HAMLET: Haste me to know't, that I, with wings as swift
As meditation or the thoughts of love,   30
May sweep to my revenge.
GHOST: I find thee apt;
And duller shouldst thou be than the fat weed°
That roots itself in ease on Lethe wharf,°
Wouldst thou not stir in this. Now, Hamlet, hear:
'Tis given out that, sleeping in my orchard,   35
A serpent stung me; so the whole ear of Denmark
Is by a forged process of my death
Rankly abus'd: but know, thou noble youth,
The serpent that did sting thy father's life
Now wears his crown.
HAMLET: O my prophetic soul!   40
My uncle!
GHOST: Ay, that incestuous, that adulterate° beast,
With witchcraft of his wit, with traitorous gifts,—
O wicked wit and gifts, that have the power
So to seduce!—won to his shameful lust   45
The will of my most seeming-virtuous queen:
O Hamlet, what a falling-off was there!
From me, whose love was of that dignity
That it went hand in hand even with the vow
I made to her in marriage, and to decline   50
Upon a wretch whose natural gifts were poor
To those of mine!
But virtue, as it never will be moved,
Though lewdness court it in a shape of heaven,
So lust, though to a radiant angel link'd,   55

---

20. porpentine: porcupine.   **21. eternal blazon:** promulgation or proclamation of eternity, revelation of the hereafter.   **25. unnatural:** i.e., pertaining to fratricide.   **32. fat weed:** many suggestions have been offered as to the particular plant intended, including asphodel; probably a general figure for plants growing along rotting wharves and piles.   **33. Lethe wharf:** bank of the river of forgetfulness in Hades. **42. adulterate:** adulterous.

Will sate itself in a celestial bed,
And prey on garbage.
But, soft! methinks I scent the morning air;
Brief let me be. Sleeping within my orchard,
My custom always of the afternoon,   60
Upon my secure° hour thy uncle stole,
With juice of cursed hebona° in a vial.
And in the porches of my ears did pour
The leperous° distilment; whose effect
Holds such an enmity with blood of man   65
That swift as quicksilver it courses through
The natural gates and alleys of the body,
And with a sudden vigour it doth posset°
And curd, like eager° droppings into milk,
The thin and wholesome blood: so did it mine;   70
And a most instant tetter bark'd about,
Most lazar-like,° with vile and loathsome crust,
All my smooth body.
Thus was I, sleeping, by a brother's hand
Of life, of crown, of queen, at once dispatch'd°:   75
Cut off even in the blossoms of my sin,
Unhous'led,° disappointed,° unanel'd,°
No reck'ning made, but sent to my account
With all my imperfections on my head:
O, horrible! O, horrible! most horrible!°   80
If thou hast nature in thee, bear it not;
Let not the royal bed of Denmark be
A couch for luxury° and damned incest.
But, howsomever thou pursues this act,
Taint not thy mind,° nor let thy soul contrive   85
Against thy mother aught: leave her to heaven
And to those thorns that in her bosom lodge,
To prick and sting her. Fare thee well at once!
The glow-worm shows the matin° to be near,
And 'gins to pale his uneffectual fire°:   90
Adieu, adieu, adieu! remember me.   (*Exit.*)
HAMLET: O all you host of heaven! O earth! what else?

---

61. secure: confident, unsuspicious. **62. hebona:** generally supposed to mean henbane, conjectured hemlock; ebenus, meaning "yew." **64. leperous:** causing leprosy. **68. posset:** coagulate, curdle. **69. eager:** sour, acid. **72. lazar-like:** leperlike. **75. dispatch'd:** suddenly bereft. **77. Unhous'led:** without having received the sacrament. **77. disappointed:** unready, without equipment for the last journey. **77. unanel'd:** without having received extreme unction. **80. O, . . . horrible:** many editors give this line to Hamlet; Garrick and Sir Henry Irving spoke it in that part. **83. luxury:** lechery. **85. Taint . . . mind:** probably, deprave not thy character, do nothing except in the pursuit of a natural revenge. **89. matin:** morning. **90. uneffectual fire:** cold light.

And shall I couple° hell? O, fie! Hold, hold, my heart;
And you, my sinews, grow not instant old,
But bear me stiffly up. Remember thee!   95
Ay, thou poor ghost, whiles memory holds a seat
In this distracted globe.° Remember thee!
Yea, from the table of my memory
I'll wipe away all trivial fond records,
All saws° of books, all forms, all pressures° past,   100
That youth and observation copied there;
And thy commandment all alone shall live
Within the book and volume of my brain,
Unmix'd with baser matter; yes, by heaven!
O most pernicious woman!   105
O villain, villain, smiling, damned villain!
My tables,°—meet it is I set it down,
That one may smile, and smile, and be a villain;
At least I am sure it may be so in Denmark: (*Writing.*)
So, uncle, there you are. Now to my word°;   110
It is "Adieu, adieu! remember me,"
I have sworn't.

              (*Enter* HORATIO *and* MARCELLUS.)

HORATIO: My lord, my lord—
MARCELLUS: Lord Hamlet,—
HORATIO: Heavens secure him!
HAMLET: So be it!
MARCELLUS: Hillo, ho, ho,° my lord!   115
HAMLET: Hillo, ho, ho, boy! come, bird, come.
MARCELLUS: How is't, my noble lord?
HORATIO: What news, my lord?
HAMLET: O, wonderful!
HORATIO: Good my lord, tell it.
HAMLET: No; you will reveal it.   120
HORATIO: Not I, my lord, by heaven.
MARCELLUS: Nor I, my lord.
HAMLET: How say you, then; would heart of man once think it?
    But you'll be secret?
HORATIO: }
MARCELLUS: }   Ay, by heaven, my lord.
HAMLET: There's ne'er a villain dwelling in all Denmark
    But he's an arrant° knave.   125

93. couple: add.   **97. distracted globe:** confused head.   **100. saws:** wise sayings.   **100. pressures:** impressions stamped.   **107. tables:** probably a small portable writing-tablet carried at the belt.   **110. word:** watchword.   **115. Hillo, ho, ho:** a falconer's call to a hawk in air.   **125. arrant:** thoroughgoing.

HORATIO: There needs no ghost, my lord, come from the grave
    To tell us this.
HAMLET: Why, right; you are in the right;
    And so, without more circumstance at all,
    I hold it fit that we shake hands and part:
    You, as your business and desire shall point you;   130
    For every man has business and desire,
    Such as it is; and for my own poor part,
    Look you, I'll go pray.
HORATIO: These are but wild and whirling words, my lord.
HAMLET: I am sorry they offend you, heartily;   135
    Yes, 'faith, heartily.
HORATIO: There's no offence, my lord.
HAMLET: Yes, by Saint Patrick,° but there is, Horatio,
    And much offence too. Touching this vision here,
    It is an honest° ghost, that let me tell you:
    For your desire to know what is between us,   140
    O'ermaster't as you may. And now, good friends,
    As you are friends, scholars and soldiers,
    Give me one poor request.
HORATIO: What is 't, my lord? we will.
HAMLET: Never make known what you have seen to-night.   145
HORATIO:
           } My lord, we will not.
MARCELLUS:
HAMLET: Nay, but swear 't.
HORATIO: In faith,
    My lord, not I.
MARCELLUS: Nor I, my lord, in faith.
HAMLET: Upon my sword.°
MARCELLUS: We have sworn, my lord, already.
HAMLET: Indeed, upon my sword, indeed. (GHOST *cries under the stage.*)   150
GHOST: Swear.
HAMLET: Ah, ha, boy! say'st thou so? art thou there, truepenny?°
    Come on—you hear this fellow in the cellarage—
    Consent to swear.
HORATIO: Propose the oath, my lord.
HAMLET: Never to speak of this that you have seen,   155
    Swear by my sword.
GHOST (*beneath*):   Swear.
HAMLET: Hic et ubique?° then we'll shift our ground.
    Come hither, gentlemen,
    And lay your hands again upon my sword: 160

---

137. Saint Patrick: St. Patrick was keeper of Purgatory and patron saint of all blunders and confusion.
139. honest: i.e., a real ghost and not an evil spirit.   **149. sword:** i.e., the hilt in the form of a cross.
152. truepenny: good old boy, or the like.   **158. Hic et ubique?:** here and everywhere?

Swear by my sword,
Never to speak of this that you have heard.

GHOST (*beneath*):   Swear by his sword.

HAMLET: Well said, old mole! canst work i' th' earth so fast?
A worthy pioner!° Once more remove, good friends.   165

HORATIO: O day and night, but this is wondrous strange!

HAMLET: And therefore as a stranger give it welcome.
There are more things in heaven and earth, Horatio,
Than are dreamt of in your philosophy.
But come;   170
Here, as before, never, so help you mercy,
How strange or odd soe'er I bear myself,
As I perchance hereafter shall think meet
To put an antic° disposition on,
That you, at such times seeing me, never shall,   175
With arms encumb'red° thus, or this head-shake,
Or by pronouncing of some doubtful phrase,
As "Well, well, we know," or "We could, an if we would,"
Or "If we list to speak," or "There be, an if they might,"
Or such ambiguous giving out,° to note°   180
That you know aught of me: this not to do,
So grace and mercy at your most need help you,
Swear.

GHOST (*beneath*):   Swear

HAMLET: Rest, rest, perturbed spirit! (*They swear.*) So, gentlemen,   185
With all my love I do commend me to you:
And what so poor a man as Hamlet is
May do, t' express his love and friending° to you,
God willing, shall not lack. Let us go in together;
And still your fingers on your lips, I pray.   190
The time is out of joint: O cursed spite,
That ever I was born to set it right!
Nay, come, let's go together.   (*Exeunt.*)

ACT II

SCENE I (*A room in* POLONIUS's *house.*)

(*Enter old* POLONIUS *with his man* [REYNALDO].)

POLONIUS: Give him this money and these notes, Reynaldo.

REYNALDO: I will, my lord.

---

165. pioner: digger, miner.   **174. antic:** fantastic.   **176. encumb'red:** folded or entwined.   **180. giving out:** profession of knowledge.   **180. to note:** to give a sign.   **188. friending:** friendliness.

POLONIUS: You shall do marvellous wisely, good Reynaldo,
  Before you visit him, to make inquire
  Of his behaviour.
REYNALDO: My lord, I did intend it.   5
POLONIUS: Marry, well said; very well said. Look you, sir,
  Inquire me first what Danskers° are in Paris;
  And how, and who, what means, and where they keep,°
  What company, at what expense; and finding
  By this encompassment° and drift° of question   10
  That they do know my son, come you more nearer
  Than your particular demands will touch it°:
  Take° you as 'twere, some distant knowledge of him;
  As thus, "I know his father and his friends;
  And in part him": do you mark this, Reynaldo?   15
REYNALDO: Ay, very well, my lord.
POLONIUS: "And in part him; but" you may say "not well:
  But, if't be he I mean, he's very wild;
  Addicted so and so": and there put on° him
  What forgeries° you please; marry, none so rank   20
  As may dishonour him; take heed of that;
  But, sir, such wanton,° wild and usual slips
  As are companions noted and most known
  To youth and liberty.
REYNALDO: As gaming, my lord.
POLONIUS: Ay, or drinking, fencing,° swearing, quarrelling,   25
  Drabbing°; you may go so far.
REYNALDO: My lord, that would dishonour him.
POLONIUS: 'Faith, no; as you may season it in the charge.
  You must not put another scandal on him,
  That he is open to incontinency°;   30
  That's not my meaning: but breathe his faults so quaintly°
  That they may seem the taints of liberty,°
  The flash and outbreak of a fiery mind,
  A savageness in unreclaimed° blood,
  Of general assault.°
REYNALDO: But, my good lord,—   35
POLONIUS: Wherefore should you do this?

II.i. **7. Danskers:** Danke was a common variant for "Denmark"; hence "Dane."   **8. keep:** dwell. **10. encompassment:** roundabout talking.   **10. drift:** gradual approach or course.   **11–12. come . . . it:** i.e., you will find out more this way than by asking pointed questions.   **13. Take:** assume, pretend. **19. put on:** impute to   **20. forgeries:** invented tales.   **22. wanton:** sportive, unrestrained.   **25. fencing:** indicative of the ill repute of professional fencers and fencing schools in Elizabethan times. **26. Drabbing:** associated with immoral women.   **30. incontinency:** habitual loose behavior.   **31. quaintly:** delicately, ingeniously.   **32. taints of liberty:** blemishes due to freedom.   **34. unreclaimed:** untamed.   **35. general assault:** tendency that assails all untrained youth.

REYNALDO: Ay, my lord,
  I would know that.
POLONIUS: Marry, sir, here's my drift;
  And, I believe, it is a fetch of wit°:
  You laying these slight sullies on my son,
  As 'twere a thing a little soil'd i' th' working,   40
  Mark you,
  Your party in converse, him you would sound,
  Having ever° seen in the prenominate° crimes
  The youth you breathe of guilty, be assur'd
  He closes with you in this consequence°;   45
  "Good sir," or so, or "friend," or "gentleman,"
  According to the phrase or the addition
  Of man and country.
REYNALDO: Very good, my lord.
POLONIUS: And then, sir, does 'a this—'a does—what was I about to say?
  By the mass, I was about to say something: where did I leave?   50
REYNALDO: At "closes in the consequence," at "friend or so," and "gentleman."
POLONIUS: At "closes in the consequence," ay, marry;
  He closes thus: "I know the gentleman;
  I saw him yesterday, or t' other day,
  Or then, or then; with such, or such; and, as you say,   55
  There was 'a gaming; there o'ertook in's rouse°;
  There falling out at tennis": or perchance,
  "I saw him enter such a house of sale,"
  Videlicet,° a brothel, or so forth.
  See you now;   60
  Your bait of falsehood takes this carp of truth:
  And thus do we of wisdom and of reach,°
  With windlasses° and with assays of bias,°
  By indirections° find directions° out:
  So by my former lecture° and advice,   65
  Shall you my son. You have me, have you not?
REYNALDO: My lord, I have.
POLONIUS: God bye ye°; fare ye well.
REYNALDO: Good my lord!
POLONIUS: Observe his inclination in yourself.°

---

38. fetch of wit: clever trick.   **43. ever:** at any time.   **43. prenominate:** before-mentioned.
45. closes . . . consequence: agrees with you in this conclusion.   **56. o'ertook in's rouse:** overcome
by drink.   **59. Videlicet:** namely.   **62. reach:** capacity, ability.   **63. windlasses:** i.e., circuitous paths.
63. assays of bias: attempts that resemble the course of the bowl, which, being weighted on one side,
has a curving motion.   **64. indirections:** devious courses.   **64. directions:** straight courses, i.e., the
truth.   **65. lecture:** admonition.   **67. bye ye:** be with you.   **69. Observe . . . yourself:** in your own
person, not by spies; or conform your own conduct to his inclination; or test him by studying yourself.

REYNALDO: I shall, my lord.   70
POLONIUS: And let him ply his music.°
REYNALDO: Well, my lord.
POLONIUS: Farewell!   (*Exit* REYNALDO.)

     (*Enter* OPHELIA.)

               How now, Ophelia! what's the matter?
OPHELIA: O, my lord, my lord, I have been so affrighted!
POLONIUS: With what, i' th' name of God?
OPHELIA: My lord, as I was sewing in my closet,°   75
   Lord Hamlet, with his doublet° all unbrac'd°;
   No hat upon his head; his stockings foul'd,
   Ungart'red, and down-gyved° to his ankle;
   Pale as his shirt; his knees knocking each other;
   And with a look so piteous in purport   80
   As if he had been loosed out of hell
   To speak of horrors,—he comes before me.
POLONIUS: Mad for thy love?
OPHELIA: My lord, I do not know;
   But truly, I do fear it.
POLONIUS: What said he?
OPHELIA: He took me by the wrist and held me hard;   85
   Then goes he to the length of all his arm;
   And, with his other hand thus o'er his brow,
   He falls to such perusal of my face
   As 'a would draw it. Long stay'd he so;
   At last, a little shaking of mine arm   90
   And thrice his head thus waving up and down,
   He rais'd a sigh so piteous and profound
   As it did seem to shatter all his bulk°
   And end his being: that done, he lets me go:
   And, with his head over his shoulder turn'd,   95
   He seem'd to find his way without his eyes;
   For out o'doors he went without their helps,
   And, to the last, bended their light on me.
POLONIUS: Come, go with me: I will go seek the king.
   This is the very ecstasy of love,   100
   Whose violent property° fordoes° itself
   And leads the will to desperate undertakings
   As oft as any passion under heaven
   That does afflict our natures. I am sorry.

---

71. ply his music: probably to be taken literally.   **75. closet:** private chamber.   **76. doublet:** close-fitting coat.   **76. unbrac'd:** unfastened.   **78. down-gyved:** fallen to the ankles (like gyves or fetters).   **93. bulk:** body.   **101. property:** nature.   **101. fordoes:** destroys.

What, have you given him any hard words of late?　　　　　　　　105
OPHELIA:　No, my good lord, but, as you did command,
　I did repel his letters and denied
　His access to me.
POLONIUS:　　　　That hath made him mad.
　I am sorry that with better heed and judgement
　I had not quoted° him: I fear'd he did but trifle,　　　　　　110
　And meant to wrack thee; but, beshrew my jealousy!°
　By heaven, it is as proper to our age
　To cast beyond° ourselves in our opinions
　As it is common for the younger sort
　To lack discretion. Come, go we to the king:　　　　　　　115
　This must be known; which, being kept close, might move
　More grief to hide than hate to utter love.°
　Come.　　　　　　　　　　　　　　　　　　(*Exeunt.*)

SCENE II

(*A room in the castle.*)

(*Flourish. Enter* KING *and* QUEEN, ROSENCRANTZ, *and* GUILDENSTERN
[*with others*].)

KING:　Welcome, dear Rosencrantz and Guildenstern!
　Moreover that° we much did long to see you,
　The need we have to use you did provoke
　Our hasty sending. Something have you heard
　Of Hamlet's transformation; so call it,　　　　　　　　　5
　Sith° nor th' exterior nor the inward man
　Resembles that it was. What it should be,
　More than his father's death, that thus hath put him
　So much from th' understanding of himself,
　I cannot dream of: I entreat you both,　　　　　　　　10
　That, being of so young days° brought up with him,
　And sith so neighbour'd to his youth and haviour,
　That you vouchsafe your rest° here in our court
　Some little time: so by your companies
　To draw him on to pleasures, and to gather,　　　　　　15
　So much as from occasion you may glean,
　Whether aught, to us unknown, afflicts him thus,

110. **quoted:** observed.　111. **beshrew my jealousy:** curse my suspicions.　113. **cast beyond:** over-shoot, miscalculate.　116–117. **might . . . love:** i.e., I might cause more grief to others by hiding the knowledge of Hamlet's love to Ophelia than hatred to me and mine by telling of it.　**II.ii. 2. Moreover that:** besides the fact that.　6. **Sith:** since.　11. **of . . . days:** from such early youth.　13. **vouchsafe your rest:** please to stay.

That, open'd, lies within our remedy.

QUEEN: Good gentlemen, he hath much talk'd of you;
And sure I am two men there are not living   20
To whom he more adheres. If it will please you
To show us so much gentry° and good will
As to expend your time with us awhile,
For the supply and profit° of our hope,
Your visitation shall receive such thanks   25
As fits a king's remembrance.

ROSENCRANTZ: Both your majesties
Might, by the sovereign power you have of us,
Put your dread pleasures more into command
Than to entreaty.

GUILDENSTERN: But we both obey,
And here give up ourselves, in the full bent°   30
To lay our service freely at your feet,
To be commanded.

KING: Thanks, Rosencrantz and gentle Guildenstern.

QUEEN: Thanks, Guildenstern and gentle Rosencrantz:
And I beseech you instantly to visit   35
My too much changed son. Go, some of you,
And bring these gentlemen where Hamlet is.

GUILDENSTERN: Heavens make our presence and our practices
Pleasant and helpful to him!

QUEEN: Ay, amen!

(*Exeunt* ROSENCRANTZ *and* GUILDENSTERN [*with some* ATTENDANTS].)

(*Enter* POLONIUS.)

POLONIUS: Th' ambassadors from Norway, my good lord,   40
Are joyfully return'd.

KING: Thou still hast been the father of good news.

POLONIUS: Have I, my lord? I assure my good liege,
I hold my duty, as I hold my soul,
Both to my God and to my gracious king: 45
And I do think, or else this brain of mine
Hunts not the trail of policy so sure
As it hath us'd to do, that I have found
The very cause of Hamlet's lunacy.

KING: O, speak of that; that do I long to hear.   50

POLONIUS: Give first admittance to th' ambassadors;
My news shall be the fruit to that great feast.

KING: Thyself do grace to them, and bring them in.   (*Exit* POLONIUS.)

---

22. gentry: courtesy.   **24. supply and profit:** aid and successful outcome.   **30. in . . . bent:** to the
utmost degree of our mental capacity.

He tells me, my dear Gertrude, he hath found
The head and source of all your son's distemper,   55
QUEEN: I doubt° it is no other but the main°;
His father's death, and our o'erhasty marriage.
KING: Well, we shall sift him.

(Enter AMBASSADORS VOLTIMAND and CORNELIUS, with POLONIUS.)

Welcome, my good friends!
Say, Voltimand, what from our brother Norway?
VOLTIMAND: Most fair return of greetings and desires.   60
Upon our first, he sent out to suppress
His nephew's levies; which to him appear'd
To be a preparation 'gainst the Polack;
But, better look'd into, he truly found
It was against your highness: whereat griev'd,   65
That so his sickness, age and impotence
Was falsely borne in hand,° sends out arrests
On Fortinbras; which he, in brief, obeys;
Receives rebuke from Norway, and in fine°
Makes vow before his uncle never more   70
To give th' assay° of arms against your majesty.
Whereon old Norway, overcome with joy,
Gives him three score thousand crowns in annual fee,
And his commission to employ those soldiers,
So levied as before, against the Polack: 75
With an entreaty, herein further shown, (*giving a paper.*)
That it might please you to give quiet pass
Through your dominions for this enterprise,
On such regards of safety and allowance°
As therein are set down.
KING: It likes° us well;   80
And at our more consider'd° time we'll read,
Answer, and think upon this business.
Meantime we thank you for your well-took labour:
Go to your rest; at night we'll feast together:
Most welcome home!   (*Exeunt* AMBASSADORS.)
POLONIUS: This business is well ended.   85
My liege, and madam, to expostulate
What majesty should be, what duty is,
Why day is day, night night, and time is time,

---

56. doubt: fear.   **56. main:** chief point, principal concern.   **67. borne in hand:** deluded.   **69. in fine:** in the end.   **71. assay:** assault, trial (of arms).   **79. safety and allowance:** pledges of safety to the country and terms of permission for the troops to pass.   **80. likes:** pleases.   **81. consider'd:** suitable for deliberation.

Were nothing but to waste night, day and time.
Therefore, since brevity is the soul of wit,° 90
And tediousness the limbs and outward flourishes,°
I will be brief: your noble son is mad:
Mad call I it; for, to define true madness
What is 't but to be nothing else but mad?
But let that go.
QUEEN: More matter, with less art. 95
POLONIUS: Madam, I swear I use no art at all.
That he is mad, 'tis true: 'tis true 'tis pity;
And pity 'tis 'tis true: a foolish figure°;
But farewell it, for I will use no art.
Mad let us grant him, then: and now remains 100
That we find out the cause of this effect,
Or rather say, the cause of this defect,
For this effect defective comes by cause:
Thus it remains, and the remainder thus.
Perpend.° 105
I have a daughter—have while she is mine—
Who, in her duty and obedience, mark,
Hath given me this: now gather, and surmise. (*Reads the letter.*)
"To the celestial and my soul's idol, the most beautified Ophelia,"—
That's an ill phrase, a vile phrase; "beautified" is a vile phrase: but you shall hear. 110
Thus: (*Reads.*)
"In her excellent white bosom, these, & c."
QUEEN: Came this from Hamlet to her?
POLONIUS: Good madam, stay awhile; I will be faithful. (*Reads.*)
                    "Doubt thou the stars are fire; 115
                    Doubt that the sun doth move;
                    Doubt truth to be a liar;
                    But never doubt I love.
"O dear Ophelia, I am ill at these numbers°; I have not art to reckon° my groans:
but that I love thee best, O most best, believe it. Adieu. 120
"Thine evermore, most dear lady, whilst this machine° is to him,

                                        HAMLET."

This, in obedience, hath my daughter shown me,
And more above,° hath his solicitings,
As they fell out° by time, by means° and place, 125
All given to mine ear.
KING: But how hath she
Receiv'd his love?

90. **wit:** sound sense or judgment.   91. **flourishes:** ostentation, embellishments   98. **figure:** figure of
speech.   105. **Perpend:** consider.   119. **ill . . . numbers:** unskilled at writing verses.   119. **reckon:**
number metrically, scan.   121. **machine:** bodily frame.   124. **more above:** moreover.   125. **fell out:**
occurred.   125. **means:** opportunities (of access).

POLONIUS: What do you think of me?
KING: As of a man faithful and honourable.
POLONIUS: I would fain prove so. But what might you think,
  When I had seen this hot love on the wing—   130
  As I perceiv'd it, I must tell you that,
  Before my daughter told me—what might you,
  Or my dear majesty your queen here, think,
  If I had play'd the desk or table-book,°
  Or given my heart a winking,° mute and dumb,   135
  Or look'd upon this love with idle sight;
  What might you think? No, I went round to work,
  And my young mistress thus I did bespeak°:
  "Lord Hamlet is a prince, out of thy star°;
  This must not be": and then I prescripts gave her,   140
  That she should lock herself from his resort,
  Admit no messengers, receive no tokens.
  Which done, she took the fruits of my advice;
  And he, repelled—a short tale to make—
  Fell into a sadness, then into a fast,   145
  Thence to a watch,° thence into a weakness,
  Thence to a lightness,° and, by this declension,°
  Into the madness wherein now he raves,
  And all we mourn for.
KING: Do you think 'tis this?
QUEEN: It may be, very like.   150
POLONIUS: Hath there been such a time—I would fain know that—
  That I have positively said "'Tis so,"
  When it prov'd otherwise?
KING: Not that I know.
POLONIUS (*pointing to his head and shoulder*):   Take this from this, if this be otherwise:
  If circumstances lead me, I will find   155
  Where truth is hid, though it were hid indeed
  Within the centre.°
KING: How may we try it further?
POLONIUS: You know, sometimes he walks four hours together
  Here in the lobby.   160
QUEEN: So he does indeed.
POLONIUS: At such a time I'll loose my daughter to him:
  Be you and I behind an arras° then;
  Mark the encounter: if he love her not

---

134. **play'd . . . table-book**: i.e., remained shut up, concealed this information.   135. **given . . . wink-ing**: given my heart a signal to keep silent.   138. **bespeak**: address.   139. **out . . . star**: above thee in position.   146. **watch**: state of sleeplessness.   147. **lightness**: lightheartedness.   147. **declension**: decline, deterioration.   157. **centre**: middle point of the earth.   163. **arras**: hanging, tapestry.

And be not from his reason fall'n thereon,° 165
Let me be no assistant for a state,
But keep a farm and carters.
KING: We will try it.

(*Enter* HAMLET [*reading on a book*].)

QUEEN: But, look, where sadly the poor wretch comes reading.
POLONIUS: Away, I do beseech you both, away: 170

(*Exeunt* KING *and* QUEEN [*with* ATTENDANTS].)

I'll board° him presently. O, give me leave.
How does my good Lord Hamlet?
HAMLET: Well, God-a-mercy.
POLONIUS: Do you know me, my lord?
HAMLET: Excellent well; you are a fishmonger.° 175
POLONIUS: Not I, my lord.
HAMLET: Then I would you were so honest a man.
POLONIUS: Honest, my lord!
HAMLET: Ay, sir; to be honest, as this world goes, is to be one man picked out of
ten thousand. 180
POLONIUS: That's very true, my lord.
HAMLET: For if the sun breed maggots in a dead dog, being a good kissing car-
rion,°—Have you a daughter?
POLONIUS: I have, my lord.
HAMLET: Let her not walk i' the sun°: conception° is a blessing: but as your daugh- 185
ter may conceive—Friend, look to 't.
POLONIUS (*aside*):   How say you by° that? Still harping on my daughter: yet he knew
me not at first; 'a said I was a fishmonger: 'a is far gone, far gone: and truly in
my youth I suffered much extremity for love; very near this. I'll speak to him
again. What do you read, my lord? 190
HAMLET: Words, words, words.
POLONIUS: What is the matter,° my lord?
HAMLET: Between who?°
POLONIUS: I mean, the matter that you read, my lord.
HAMLET: Slanders, sir: for the satirical rogue says here that old men have grey 195
beards, that their faces are wrinkled, their eyes purging° thick amber and
plum-tree gum and that they have a plentiful lack of wit, together with most
weak hams: all which, sir, though I most powerfully and potently believe, yet I
hold it not honesty° to have it thus set down, for yourself, sir, should be old as I
am, if like a crab you could go backward. 200

---

165. thereon: on that account.   **171. board:** accost.   **175. fishmonger:** an opprobrious expression meaning "bawd," "procurer."   **182–183. good kissing carrion:** i.e., a good piece of flesh for kissing (?).   **185. i' the sun:** in the sunshine of princely favors.   **185. conception:** quibble on "understanding" and "pregnancy."   **187. by:** concerning.   **192. matter:** substance.   **193. Between who?:** Hamlet deliberately takes matter as meaning "basis of dispute."   **196. purging:** discharging.   **199. honesty:** decency.

POLONIUS (*aside*):   Though this be madness, yet there is method in 't.—Will you walk out of the air, my lord?

HAMLET: Into my grave.

POLONIUS: Indeed, that's out of the air. (*Aside.*) How pregnant sometimes his replies are! a happiness° that often madness hits on, which reason and sanity 205
could not so prosperously° be delivered of. I will leave him, and suddenly contrive the means of meeting between him and my daughter.—My honourable lord, I will most humbly take my leave of you.

HAMLET: You cannot, sir, take from me any thing that I will more willingly part withal: except my life, except my life, except my life.   210

(*Enter* GUILDENSTERN *and* ROSENCRANTZ.)

POLONIUS: Fare you well, my lord.

HAMLET: These tedious old fools!

POLONIUS: You go to seek the Lord Hamlet; there he is.

ROSENCRANTZ (*to* POLONIUS):   God save you, sir!   (*Exit* POLONIUS.)

GUILDENSTERN: My honoured lord!   215

ROSENCRANTZ: My most dear lord!

HAMLET: My excellent good friends! How dost thou, Guildenstern? Ah, Rosencrantz! Good lads, how do ye both?

ROSENCRANTZ: As the indifferent° children of the earth.

GUILDENSTERN: Happy, in that we are not over-happy;   220
On Fortune's cap we are not the very button.

HAMLET: Nor the soles of her shoe?

ROSENCRANTZ: Neither, my lord.

HAMLET: Then you live about her waist, or in the middle of her favours?

GUILDENSTERN: 'Faith, her privates° we.   225

HAMLET: In the secret parts of Fortune? O, most true; she is a strumpet. What's the news?

ROSENCRANTZ: None, my lord, but that the world's grown honest.

HAMLET: Then is doomsday near: but your news is not true. Let me question more in particular: what have you, my good friends, deserved at the hands of For- 230
tune, that she sends you to prison hither?

GUILDENSTERN: Prison, my lord!

HAMLET: Denmark's a prison.

ROSENCRANTZ: Then is the world one.

HAMLET: A goodly one; in which there are many confines,° wards and dungeons,   235
Denmark being one o' the worst.

ROSENCRANTZ: We think not so, my lord.

HAMLET: Why, then, 'tis none to you; for there is nothing either good or bad, but thinking makes it so: to me it is a prison.

---

205. happiness: felicity of expression.   **206. prosperously:** successfully.   **219. indifferent:** ordinary.
225. privates: i.e., ordinary men (sexual pun on private parts).   **235. confines:** places of confinement.

ROSENCRANTZ: Why then, your ambition makes it one; 'tis too narrow for your   240
mind.

HAMLET: O God, I could be bounded in a nutshell and count myself a king of infinite space, were it not that I have bad dreams.

GUILDENSTERN: Which dreams indeed are ambition, for the very substance of the
ambitious° is merely the shadow of a dream.   245

HAMLET: A dream itself is but a shadow.

ROSENCRANTZ: Truly, and I hold ambition of so airy and light a quality that it is but
a shadow's shadow.

HAMLET: Then are our beggars bodies, and our monarchs and outstretched heroes
the beggars' shadows. Shall we to the court? for, by my fay,° I cannot reason.°   250

ROSENCRANTZ: } We'll wait upon° you.
GUILDENSTERN:

HAMLET: No such matter: I will not sort° you with the rest of my servants, for, to
speak to you like an honest man, I am most dreadfully attended.° But, in the
beaten way of friendship,° what make you at Elsinore?

ROSENCRANTZ: To visit you, my lord: no other occasion.   255

HAMLET: Beggar that I am, I am ever poor in thanks; but I thank you: and sure,
dear friends, my thanks are too dear a° halfpenny. Were you not sent for? Is it
your own inclining? Is it a free visitation? Come, come, deal justly with me:
come, come; nay, speak.

GUILDENSTERN: What should we say, my lord?   260

HAMLET: Why, any thing, but to the purpose. You were sent for; and there is a kind
of confession in your looks which your modesties have not craft enough to
colour: I know the good king and queen have sent for you.

ROSENCRANTZ: To what end, my lord?

HAMLET: That you must teach me. But let me conjure° you, by the rights of our   265
fellowship, by the consonancy of our youth,° by the obligation of our ever-
preserved love, and by what more dear a better proposer° could charge you
withal, be even and direct with me, whether you were sent for, or no?

ROSENCRANTZ (*aside to* GUILDENSTERN):   What say you?

HAMLET (*aside*):   Nay, then, I have an eye of you.—If you love me, hold not off.   270

GUILDENSTERN: My lord, we were sent for.

HAMLET: I will tell you why; so shall my anticipation prevent your discovery,° and
your secrecy to the king and queen moult no feather. I have of late—but
wherefore I know not—lost all my mirth, forgone all custom of exercises; and
indeed it goes so heavily with my disposition that this goodly frame, the earth,   275
seems to me a sterile promontory, this most excellent canopy, the air, look you,
this brave o'erhanging firmament, this majestical roof fretted° with golden fire,
why, it appeareth nothing to me but a foul and pestilent congregation of

---

244–45. very . . . ambitious: that seemingly most substantial thing which the ambitious pursue.
250. fay: faith.   **250. reason:** argue.   **251. wait upon:** accompany.   **252. sort:** class.   **253. dreadfully attended:** poorly provided with servants.   **254. in the . . . friendship:** as a matter of course
among friends.   **257. a:** i.e., at a.   **265. conjure:** adjure, entreat.   **266. consonancy of our youth:** the
fact that we are of the same age.   **267. better proposer:** one more skillful in finding proposals.
272. prevent your discovery: forestall your disclosure.   **277. fretted:** adorned.

vapours. What a piece of work is a man! how noble in reason! how infinite in
faculties!° in form and moving how express° and admirable! in action how like   280
an angel! in apprehension° how like a god! the beauty of the world! the
paragon of animals! And yet, to me, what is this quintessence° of dust? man
delights not me: no, nor woman neither, though by your smiling you seem to
say so.

ROSENCRANTZ: My lord, there was no such stuff in my thoughts.   285

HAMLET: Why did you laugh then, when I said "man delights not me"?

ROSENCRANTZ: To think, my lord, if you delight not in man, what lenten° entertainment the players shall receive from you: we coted° them on the way; and
hither are they coming, to offer you service.

HAMLET: He that plays the king shall be welcome; his majesty shall have tribute of   290
me; the adventurous knight shall use his foil and target°; the lover shall not
sigh gratis; the humorous man° shall end his part in peace; the clown shall
make those laugh whose lungs are tickle o' the sere°; and the lady shall say her
mind freely, or the blank verse shall halt for 't.° What players are they?

ROSENCRANTZ: Even those you were wont to take delight in, the tragedians of the   295
city.

HAMLET: How chances it they travel? their residence,° both in reputation and
profit, was better both ways.

ROSENCRANTZ: I think their inhibition° comes by the means of the late innovation.°

HAMLET: Do they hold the same estimation they did when I was in the city? are   300
they so followed?

ROSENCRANTZ: No, indeed, are they not.

HAMLET: How° comes it? do they grow rusty?

ROSENCRANTZ: Nay, their endeavour keeps in the wonted pace: but there is, sir, an
aery° of children, little eyases,° that cry out on the top of question,° and are   305
most tyrannically° clapped for 't: these are now the fashion, and so berattle° the
common stages°—so they call them—that many wearing rapiers° are afraid of
goose-quills° and dare scarce come thither.

---

280. faculties: capacity.   **280. express:** well-framed (?), exact (?).   **281. apprehension:** understanding.   **282. quintessence:** the fifth essence of ancient philosophy, supposed to be the substance of the
heavenly bodies and to be latent in all things.   **287. lenten:** meager.   **288. coted:** overtook and passed
beyond.   **291. foil and target:** sword and shield.   **292. humorous man:** actor who takes the part of
the humor characters.   **293. tickle o' the sere:** easy on the trigger.   **294. the lady . . . for 't:** the lady
(fond of talking) shall have opportunity to talk, blank verse or no blank verse.   **297. residence:** remaining in one place.   **299. inhibition:** formal prohibition (from acting plays in the city or, possibly, at
court).   **299. innovation:** the new fashion in satirical plays performed by boy actors in the "private"
theaters.   **306–321. How . . . load too:** the passage is the famous one dealing with the War of the
Theatres (1599–1602); namely, the rivalry between the children's companies and the adult actors.
305. aery: nest.   **305. eyases:** young hawks.   **305. cry . . . question:** speak in a high key dominating
conversation; clamor forth the height of controversy; probably "excel" (cf. line 459); perhaps intended to
decry leaders of the dramatic profession.   **306. tyrannically:** outrageously.   **306. berattle:** berate.
307. common stages: public theaters.   **307. many wearing rapiers:** many men of fashion, who were
afraid to patronize the common players for fear of being satirized by the poets who wrote for the children.   **308. goose-quills:** i.e., pens of satirists.

HAMLET: What, are they children? who maintains 'em? how are they escoted?° Will they pursue the quality° no longer than they can sing?° will they not say 310 afterwards, if they should grow themselves to common° players—as it is most like, if their means are no better—their writers do them wrong, to make them exclaim against their own succession?°

ROSENCRANTZ: 'Faith, there has been much to do on both sides; and the nation holds it no sin to tarre° them to controversy: there was, for a while, no money 315 bid for argument,° unless the poet and the players went to cuffs° in the question.°

HAMLET: Is't possible?

GUILDENSTERN: O, there has been much throwing about of brains.

HAMLET: Do the boys carry it away?°

ROSENCRANTZ: Ay, that they do, my lord; Hercules and his load° too. 320

HAMLET: It is not very strange; for my uncle is king of Denmark, and those that would make mows° at him while my father lived, give twenty, forty, fifty, a hundred ducats° a-piece for his picture in little.° 'Sblood, there is something in this more than natural, if philosophy could find it out.

(*A flourish* [*of trumpets within*].)

GUILDENSTERN: There are the players. 325

HAMLET: Gentlemen, you are welcome to Elsinore. Your hands, come then: the appurtenance of welcome is fashion and ceremony; let me comply° with you in this garb,° lest my extent° to the players, which, I tell you, must show fairly outwards, should more appear like entertainment than yours. You are welcome: but my uncle-father and aunt-mother are deceived. 330

GUILDENSTERN: In what, my dear lord?

HAMLET: I am but mad north-north-west°: when the wind is southerly I know a hawk from a handsaw.°

(*Enter* POLONIUS.)

POLONIUS: Well be with you, gentlemen!

HAMLET: Hark you, Guildenstern; and you too: at each ear a hearer: that great 335 baby you see there is not yet out of his swaddling-clouts.°

ROSENCRANTZ: Happily he is the second time come to them; for they say an old man is twice a child.

---

309. escoted: maintained.   **310. quality:** acting profession.   **310. no longer . . . sing:** i.e., until their voices change.   **311. common:** regular, adult.   **313. succession:** future careers.   **315. tarre:** set on (as dogs).   **316. argument:** probably, plot for a play.   **316. went to cuffs:** came to blows.   **316. question:** controversy.   **319. carry it away:** win the day.   **320. Hercules . . . load:** regarded as an allusion to the sign of the Globe Theatre, which was Hercules bearing the world on his shoulder.   **322. mows:** grimaces.   **323. ducats:** gold coins worth 9s. 4d.   **323. in little:** in miniature.   **327. comply:** observe the formalities of courtesy.   **328. garb:** manner.   **328. extent:** showing of kindness.   **332. I am . . . north-north-west:** I am only partly mad, i.e., in only one point of the compass.   **333. handsaw:** a proposed reading of hemshaw would mean "heron"; handsaw may be an early corruption of hernshaw. Another view regards hawk as the variant of hack, a tool of the pickax type, and handsaw as a saw operated by hand.   **336. swaddling-clouts:** clothes in which to wrap a newborn baby.

HAMLET: I will prophesy he comes to tell me of the players; mark it.—You say
right, sir: o' Monday morning°; 'twas then indeed.   340

POLONIUS: My lord, I have news to tell you.

HAMLET: My lord, I have news to tell you. When Roscius° was an actor in
Rome,—

POLONIUS: The actors are come hither, my lord.

HAMLET: Buz, buz!°   345

POLONIUS: Upon my honour,—

HAMLET: Then came each actor on his ass,—

POLONIUS: The best actors in the world, either for tragedy, comedy, history,
pastoral, pastoral-comical, historical-pastoral, tragical-historical, tragical-
comical-historical-pastoral, scene individable,° or poem unlimited°: Seneca°   350
cannot be too heavy, nor Plautus° too light. For the law of writ and the liberty,°
these are the only men.

HAMLET: O Jephthah, judge of Israel,° what a treasure hadst thou!

POLONIUS: What a treasure had he, my lord?

HAMLET: Why,   355
"One fair daughter, and no more,
The which he loved passing well."

POLONIUS (*aside*):   Still on my daughter.

HAMLET: Am I not i' the right, old Jephthah?

POLONIUS: If you call me Jephthah, my lord, I have a daughter that I love passing° 360
well.

HAMLET: Nay, that follows not.

POLONIUS: What follows, then, my lord?

HAMLET: Why,
"As by lot, God wot,"   365
and then, you know,
"It came to pass, as most like° it was,"—
the first row° of the pious chanson° will show you more; for look, where my
abridgement comes.°

(*Enter the* PLAYERS.)

You are welcome, masters; welcome, all. I am glad to see thee well. Welcome,   370
good friends. O, old friend! why, thy face is valanced° since I saw thee last:
comest thou to beard me in Denmark? What, my young lady and mistress!

---

340. o' Monday morning: said to mislead Polonius.   **342. Roscius:** a famous Roman actor.
345. Buz, buz: an interjection used at Oxford to denote stale news.   **350. scene individable:** a play
observing the unity of place.   **350. poem unlimited:** a play disregarding the unities of time and place.
350. Seneca: writer of Latin tragedies, model of early Elizabethan writers of tragedy.   **351. Plautus:**
writer of Latin comedy.   **351. law . . . liberty:** pieces written according to rules and without rules, i.e.,
"classical" and "romantic" dramas.   **353. Jephthah . . . Israel:** Jephthah had to sacrifice his daughter; see Judges 11.   **360. passing:** surpassingly.   **367. like:** probable.   **368. row:** stanza.   **368. chan-
son:** ballad.   **369. abridgement comes:** opportunity comes for cutting short the conversation.
371. valanced: fringed (with a beard).

By'r lady, your ladyship is nearer to heaven than when I saw you last, by the altitude of a chopine.° Pray God, your voice, like a piece of uncurrent° gold, be not cracked within the ring.° Masters, you are all welcome. We'll e'en to 't like 375 French falconers, fly at any thing we see: we'll have a speech straight: come, give us a taste of your quality; come, a passionate speech.

FIRST PLAYER: What speech, my good lord?

HAMLET: I heard thee speak me a speech once, but it was never acted; or, if it was, not above once; for the play, I remember, pleased not the million; 'twas caviar 380 to the general°: but it was—as I received it, and others, whose judgements in such matters cried in the top of° mine—an excellent play, well digested in the scenes, set down with as much modesty as cunning.° I remember, one said there were no sallets° in the lines to make the matter savoury, nor no matter in the phrase that might indict° the author of affectation; but called it an honest 385 method, as wholesome as sweet, and by very much more handsome than fine.° One speech in 't I chiefly loved: 'twas Æneas' tale to Dido°; and thereabout of it especially, where he speaks of Priam's slaughter: if it live in your memory, begin at this line: let me see, let me see—
"The rugged Pyrrhus°, like th' Hyrcanian beast,"°—   390
'tis not so:—it begins with Pyrrhus:—
"The rugged Pyrrhus, he whose sable arms,
Black as his purpose, did the night resemble
When he lay couched in the ominous horse,°
Hath now this dread and black complexion smear'd   395
With heraldry more dismal; head to foot
Now is he total gules°; horridly trick'd°
With blood of fathers, mothers, daughters, sons,
Bak'd and impasted° with the parching streets,
That lend a tyrannous and a damned light   400
To their lord's murder: roasted in wrath and fire,
And thus o'er-sized° with coagulate gore,
With eyes like carbuncles, the hellish Pyrrhus
Old grandsire Priam seeks."
So, proceed you.   405

---

374. chopine: kind of shoe raised by the thickness of the heel; worn in Italy, particularly at Venice. **374. uncurrent:** not passable as lawful coinage.   **375. cracked within the ring:** in the center of coins were rings enclosing the sovereign's head; if the coin was cracked within this ring, it was unfit for currency.   **381. caviar to the general:** not relished by the multitude.   **382. cried in the top of:** spoke with greater authority than.   **383. cunning:** skill.   **384. sallets:** salads: here, spicy improprieties. **385. indict:** convict.   **386. as wholesome . . . fine:** its beauty was not that of elaborate ornament, but that of order and proportion.   **387. Æneas' tale to Dido:** the lines recited by the player are imitated from Marlowe and Nashe's *Dido Queen of Carthage* (II.i. 214 ff.). They are written in such a way that the conventionality of the play within a play is raised above that of ordinary drama.   **390. Pyrrhus:** a Greek hero in the Trojan War.   **390. Hyrcanian beast:** the tiger; see Virgil, Aeneid, IV. 266.   **394. ominous horse:** Trojan horse.   **397. gules:** red, a heraldic term.   **397. trick'd:** spotted, smeared. **399. impasted:** made into a paste.   **402. o'er-sized:** covered as with size or glue.

POLONIUS: 'Fore God, my lord, well spoken, with good accent and good dis-
    cretion.

FIRST PLAYER: "Anon he finds him
    Striking too short at Greeks; his antique sword,
    Rebellious to his arm, lies where it falls,   410
    Repugnant° to command: Unequal match'd,
    Pyrrhus at Priam drives; in rage strikes wide;
    But with the whiff and wind of his fell sword
    Th' unnerved father falls. Then senseless Ilium,°
    Seeming to feel this blow, with flaming top   415
    Stoops to his base, and with a hideous crash
    Takes prisoner Pyrrhus' ear: for, lo! his sword
    Which was declining on the milky head
    Of reverend Priam, seem'd i' th' air to stick:
    So, as a painted tyrant,° Pyrrhus stood,   420
    And like a neutral to his will and matter,°
    Did nothing.
    But, as we often see, against° some storm,
    A silence in the heavens, the rack° stand still,
    The bold winds speechless and the orb below   425
    As hush as death, anon the dreadful thunder
    Doth rend the region,° so, after Pyrrhus' pause,
    Aroused vengeance sets him new a-work;
    And never did the Cyclops' hammers fall
    On Mars's armour forg'd for proof eterne°   430
    With less remorse than Pyrrhus' bleeding sword
    Now falls on Priam.
    Out, out, thou strumpet, Fortune! All you gods,
    In general synod,° take away her power;
    Break all the spokes and fellies° from her wheel,   435
    And bowl the round nave° down the hill of heaven,
    As low as to the fiends!"

POLONIUS: This is too long.

HAMLET: It shall to the barber's, with your beard. Prithee, say on: he's for a jig° or
    a tale of bawdry,° or he sleeps: say on: come to Hecuba.°   440

FIRST PLAYER: "But who, ah woe! had seen the mobled° queen—"

HAMLET: "The mobled queen?"

POLONIUS: That's good; "mobled queen" is good.

FIRST PLAYER: "Run barefoot up and down, threat'ning the flames

---

411. Repugnant: disobedient.   **414. Then senseless Ilium:** insensate Troy.   **420. painted tyrant:**
tyrant in a picture.   **421. matter:** task.   **423. against:** before.   **424. rack:** mass of clouds.   **427. region:**
assembly.   **430. proof eterne:** external resistance to assault.   **434. synod:** assembly.   **435. fellies:**
pieces of wood forming the rim of a wheel.   **436. nave:** hub.   **439. jig:** comic performance given at the
end or in an interval of a play.   **440. bawdry:** indecency.   **440. Hecuba:** wife of Priam, king of Troy.
441. mobled: muffled.

With bisson rheum°; a clout° upon that head 445
Where late the diadem stood, and for a robe,
About her lank and all o'er-teemed° loins,
A blanket, in the alarm of fear caught up;
Who this had seen, with tongue in venom steep'd
'Gainst Fortune's state would treason have pronounc'd°: 450
But if the gods themselves did see her then
When she saw Pyrrhus make malicious sport
In mincing with his sword her husband's limbs,
The instant burst of clamour that she made,
Unless things mortal move them not at all, 455
Would have made milch° the burning eyes of heaven,
And passion in the gods."

POLONIUS: Look, whe'r he has not turned° his colour and has tears in 's eyes.
  Prithee, no more.

HAMLET: 'Tis well; I'll have thee speak out the rest soon. Good my lord, will you 460
  see the players well bestowed? Do you hear, let them be well used; for they are
  the abstract° and brief chronicles of the time: after your death you were better
  have a bad epitaph than their ill report while you live.

POLONIUS: My lord, I will use them according to their desert.

HAMLET: God's bodykins,° man, much better: use every man after his desert, and 465
  who shall 'scape whipping? Use them after your own honour and dignity: the
  less they deserve, the more merit is in your bounty. Take them in.

POLONIUS: Come, sirs.

HAMLET: Follow him, friends: we'll hear a play tomorrow. (*Aside to* FIRST PLAYER.)
  Dost thou hear me, old friend; can you play the Murder of Gonzago? 470

FIRST PLAYER: Ay, my lord.

HAMLET: We'll ha 't to-morrow night. You could, for a need, study a speech of
  some dozen or sixteen lines,° which I would set down and insert in 't, could you
  not?

FIRST PLAYER: Ay, my lord. 475

  HAMLET: Very well. Follow that lord; and look you mock him not.—My good
  friends, I'll leave you till night: you are welcome to Elsinore.

(Exeunt POLONIUS and PLAYERS.)

ROSENCRANTZ: Good my lord!   (*Exeunt* [ROSENCRANTZ *and* GUILDENSTERN.])

HAMLET: Ay, so, God bye to you.—Now I am alone.
  O, what a rogue and peasant° slave am I! 480
  Is it not monstrous that this player here,
  But in a fiction, in a dream of passion,

---

445. bisson rheum: blinding tears.   **445. clout:** piece of cloth.   **447. o'er-teemed:** worn out with bearing children.   **450. pronounc'd:** proclaimed.   **456. milch:** moist with tears.   **458. turned:** changed.   **462. abstract:** summary account.   **465. bodykins:** diminutive form of the oath "by God's body."   **473. dozen or sixteen lines:** critics have amused themselves by trying to locate Hamlet's lines. Lucianus's speech III.ii. 226–231 is the best guess.   **480. peasant:** base.

Could force his soul so to his own conceit
That from her working all his visage wann'd,°
Tears in his eyes, distraction in 's aspect,   485
A broken voice, and his whole function suiting
With forms to his conceit?° and all for nothing!
For Hecuba!
What's Hecuba to him, or he to Hecuba,
That he should weep for her? What would he do,   490
Had he the motive and the cue for passion
That I have? He would drown the stage with tears
And cleave the general ear with horrid speech,
Make mad the guilty and appall the free,
Confound the ignorant, and amaze indeed   495
The very faculties of eyes and ears.
Yet I,
A dull and muddy-mettled° rascal, peak,°
Like John-a-dreams,° unpregnant of° my cause,
And can say nothing; no, not for a king.   500
Upon whose property° and most dear life
A damn'd defeat was made. Am I a coward?
Who calls me villain? breaks my pate across?
Plucks off my beard, and blows it in my face?
Tweaks me by the nose? gives me the lie i' th' throat, 505
As deep as to the lungs? who does me this?
Ha!
'Swounds, I should take it: for it cannot be
But I am pigeon-liver'd° and lack gall
To make oppression bitter, or ere this   510
I should have fatted all the region kites°
With this slave's offal: bloody, bawdy villain!
Remorseless, treacherous, lecherous, kindless° villain!
O, vengeance!
Why, what an ass am I! This is most brave,   515
That I, the son of a dear father murder'd,
Prompted to my revenge by heaven and hell,
Must, like a whore, unpack my heart with words,
And fall a-cursing, like a very drab,°
A stallion!°   520

---

484. wann'd: grew pale.   **486–487. his whole:** . . . **conceit:** his whole being responded with forms to suit his thought.   **498. muddy-mettled:** dull-spirited.   **498. peak:** mope, pine.   **499. John-a-dreams:** an expression occurring elsewhere in Elizabethan literature to indicate a dreamer. **499. unpregnant of:** not quickened by.   **501. property:** proprietorship (of crown and life).   **509. pigeon-liver'd:** the pigeon was supposed to secrete no gall; if Hamlet, so he says, had had gall, he would have felt the bitterness of oppression, and avenged it.   **511. region kites:** kites of the air.   **513. kindless:** unnatural.   **519. drab:** prostitute.   **520. stallion:** prostitute (male or female).

Fie upon 't! foh! About,° my brains! Hum, I have heard
That guilty creatures sitting at a play
Have by the very cunning of the scene
Been struck so to the soul that presently
They have proclaim'd their malefactions;   525
For murder, though it have no tongue, will speak
With most miraculous organ. I'll have these players
Play something like the murder of my father
Before mine uncle: I'll observe his looks:
I'll tent° him to the quick: if 'a do blench,°   530
I know my course. The spirit that I have seen
May be the devil°: and the devil hath power
T' assume a pleasing shape; yea, and perhaps
Out of my weakness and my melancholy,
As he is very potent with such spirits,°   535
Abuses me to damn me: I'll have grounds
More relative° than this°: the play's the thing
Wherein I'll catch the conscience of the king.

                                                                        Exit.

ACT III

SCENE I

(*A room in the castle.*)

(*Enter* KING, QUEEN, POLONIUS, OPHELIA, ROSENCRANTZ, GUILDENSTERN, LORDS.)

KING: And can you, by no drift of conference,°
  Get from him why he puts on this confusion,
  Grating so harshly all his days of quiet
  With turbulent and dangerous lunacy?
ROSENCRANTZ: He does confess he feels himself distracted;   5
  But from what cause 'a will by no means speak.
GUILDENSTERN: Nor do we find him forward° to be sounded,
  But, with a crafty madness, keeps aloof,
  When we would bring him on to some confession
  Of his true state.
QUEEN: Did he receive you well?   10
ROSENCRANTZ: Most like a gentleman.
GUILDENSTERN: But with much forcing of his disposition.°

---

521. About: about it, or turn thou right about.   **530. tent:** probe.   **530. blench:** quail, flinch.
532. May be the devil: Hamlet's suspicion is properly grounded in the belief of the time.   **535. spirits:**
humors.   **537. relative:** closely related, definite.   **537. this:** i.e., the ghost's story. **III.i. 1. drift of conference:** device of conversation.   **7. forward:** willing.   **12. forcing of his disposition:** i.e., against
his will.

ROSENCRANTZ: Niggard of question°; but, of our demands,
    Most free in his reply.
QUEEN: Did you assay° him
    To any pastime?   15
ROSENCRANTZ: Madam, it so fell out, that certain players
    We o'er-raught° on the way; of these we told him;
    And there did seem in him a kind of joy
    To hear of it: they are here about the court,
    And, as I think, they have already order   20
    This night to play before him.
POLONIUS: 'Tis most true:
    And he beseech'd me to entreat your majesties
    To hear and see the matter.
KING: With all my heart; and it doth much content me
    To hear him so inclin'd.   25
    Good gentlemen, give him a further edge,°
    And drive his purpose into these delights.
ROSENCRANTZ: We shall, my lord.   (*Exeunt* ROSENCRANTZ *and* GUILDENSTERN.)
KING: Sweet Gertrude, leave us too;
    For we have closely° sent for Hamlet hither,
    That he, as 'twere by accident, may here   30
    Affront° Ophelia:
    Her father and myself, lawful espials,°
    Will so bestow ourselves that, seeing, unseen,
    We may of their encounter frankly judge,
    And gather by him, as he is behav'd,   35
    If 't be th' affliction of his love or no
    That thus he suffers for.
QUEEN: I shall obey you.
    And for your part, Ophelia, I do wish
    That your good beauties be the happy cause
    Of Hamlet's wildness°: so shall I hope your virtues   40
    Will bring him to his wonted way again,
    To both your honours.
OPHELIA: Madam, I wish it may.   (*Exit* QUEEN.)
POLONIUS: Ophelia, walk you here. Gracious,° so please you,
    We will bestow ourselves. (*To* OPHELIA.) Read on this book;
    That show of such an exercise° may colour°   45
    Your loneliness. We are oft to blame in this,—

---

13. Niggard of question: sparing of conversation.   **14. assay:** try to win.   **17. o'er-raught:** overtook.
26. edge: incitement.   **29. closely:** secretly.   **31. Affront:** confront.   **32. lawful espials:** legitimate
spies.   **40. wildness:** madness.   **43. Gracious:** your grace (addressed to the king).   **45. exercise:** act
of devotion (the book she reads is one of devotion).   **45. colour:** give a plausible appearance to.

> 'Tis too much prov'd—that with devotion's visage
> And pious action we do sugar o'er
> The devil himself.

KING: (*Aside*) O, 'tis too true!
> How smart a lash that speech doth give my conscience!   50
> The harlot's cheek, beautied with plast'ring art,
> Is not more ugly to° the thing° that helps it
> Than is my deed to my most painted word:
> O heavy burthen!

POLONIUS: I hear him coming: let's withdraw, my lord.   55

(*Exeunt* KING *and* POLONIUS.)

(*Enter* HAMLET.)

HAMLET: To be, or not to be: that is the question:
> Whether 'tis nobler in the mind to suffer
> The slings and arrows of outrageous fortune,
> Or to take arms against a sea° of troubles,
> And by opposing end them? To die: to sleep;   60
> No more; and by a sleep to say we end
> The heart-ache and the thousand natural shocks
> That flesh is heir to, 'tis a consummation
> Devoutly to be wish'd. To die, to sleep;
> To sleep: perchance to dream: ay, there's the rub;   65
> For in that sleep of death what dreams may come
> When we have shuffled° off this mortal coil,°
> Must give us pause: there's the respect°
> That makes calamity of so long life°;
> For who would bear the whips and scorns of time,°   70
> Th' oppressor's wrong, the proud man's contumely,
> The pangs of despis'd° love, the law's delay,
> The insolence of office° and the spurns°
> That patient merit of th' unworthy takes,
> When he himself might his quietus° make   75
> With a bare bodkin?° who would fardels° bear,
> To grunt and sweat under a weary life,
> But that the dread of something after death,
> The undiscover'd country from whose bourn°

---

52. to: compared to.   **52. thing:** i.e., the cosmetic.   **59. sea:** the mixed metaphor of this speech has often been commented on; a later emendation, *siege* has sometimes been spoken on the stage.   **67. shuffled:** sloughed, cast.   **67. coil:** usually means "turmoil"; here, possibly "body" (conceived of as wound about the soul like rope); *clay, soil, veil,* have been suggested as emendations.   **68. respect:** consideration.   **69. of . . . life:** so long-lived.   **70. time:** the world.   **72. despis'd:** rejected.   **73. office:** office-holders.   **73. spurns:** insults.   **75. quietus:** acquittance; here, death.   **76. bare bodkin:** mere dagger; bare is sometimes understood as "unsheathed."   **76. fardels:** burdens.   **79. bourn:** boundary.

No traveller returns, puzzles the will 80
And makes us rather bear those ills we have
Than fly to others that we know not of?
Thus conscience° does make cowards of us all;
And thus the native hue° of resolution
Is sicklied o'er° with the pale cast° of thought, 85
And enterprises of great pitch° and moment°
With this regard° their currents° turn awry,
And lose the name of action—Soft you now!
The fair Ophelia! Nymph, in thy orisons°
Be all my sins rememb'red.

OPHELIA: Good my lord, 90
How does your honour for this many a day?

HAMLET: I humbly thank you; well, well, well.

OPHELIA: My lord, I have remembrances of yours,
That I have longed long to re-deliver;
I pray you, now receive them. 95

HAMLET: No, not I;
I never gave you aught.

OPHELIA: My honour'd lord, you know right well you did;
And, with them, words of so sweet breath compos'd
As made the things more rich: their perfume lost, 100
Take these again; for to the noble mind
Rich gifts wax poor when givers prove unkind.
There, my lord.

HAMLET: Ha, ha! are you honest?°

OPHELIA: My lord? 105

HAMLET: Are you fair?

OPHELIA: What means your lordship?

HAMLET: That if you be honest and fair, your honesty° should admit no discourse
to° your beauty.

OPHELIA: Could beauty, my lord, have better commerce° than with honesty? 110

HAMLET: Ay, truly; for the power of beauty will sooner transform honesty from
what it is to a bawd than the force of honesty can translate beauty into his likeness: this was sometime a paradox, but now the time° gives it proof. I did love
you once.

OPHELIA: Indeed, my lord, you made me believe so. 115

---

83. conscience: probably, inhibition by the faculty of reason restraining the will from doing wrong.
84. native hue: natural color; metaphor derived from the color of the face.   **85. sicklied o'er:** given a
sickly tinge.   **85. cast:** shade of color.   **86. pitch:** height (as of falcon's flight).   **86. moment:** importance.   **87. regard:** respect, consideration.   **87. currents:** courses.   **89. orisons:** prayers.   **104–9.**
are you honest . . . beauty: honest meaning "truthful" and "chaste" and fair meaning "just, honorable"
(line 106) and "beautiful" (line 108) are not mere quibbles; the speech has the irony of a double entendre.
108. your honesty: your chastity.   **109. discourse to:** familiar intercourse with.   **110. commerce:**
intercourse.   **113. the time:** the present age.

HAMLET: You should not have believed me; for virtue cannot so inoculate° our old stock but we shall relish of it°: I loved you not.

OPHELIA: I was the more deceived.

HAMLET: Get thee to a nunnery; why wouldst thou be a breeder of sinners? I am myself indifferent honest°; but yet I could accuse me of such things that it were   120
better my mother had not borne me: I am very proud, revengeful, ambitious, with more offences at my beck° than I have thoughts to put them in, imagination to give them shape, or time to act them in. What should such fellows as I do crawling between earth and heaven? We are arrant knaves, all; believe none of us. Go thy ways to a nunnery. Where's your father?   125

OPHELIA: At home, my lord.

HAMLET: Let the doors be shut upon him, that he may play the fool no where but in 's own house. Farewell.

OPHELIA: O, help him, you sweet heavens!

HAMLET: If thou dost marry, I'll give thee this plague for thy dowry: be thou as   130
chaste as ice, as pure as snow, thou shalt not escape calumny. Get thee to a nunnery, go: farewell. Or, if thou wilt needs marry, marry a fool; for wise men know well enough what monsters° you make of them. To a nunnery, go, and quickly too. Farewell.

OPHELIA: O heavenly powers, restore him!   135

HAMLET: I have heard of your° paintings too, well enough; God hath given you one face, and you make yourselves another: you jig,° you amble, and you lisp; you nick-name God's creatures, and make your wantonness your ignorance.° Go to, I'll no more on 't; it hath made me mad. I say, we will have no more marriage: those that are married already, all but one,° shall live; the rest shall keep   140
as they are. To a nunnery, go.   (*Exit.*)

OPHELIA: O, what a noble mind is here o'er-thrown!
The courtier's, soldier's, scholar's, eye, tongue, sword;
Th' expectancy and rose° of the fair state,
The glass of fashion and the mould of form,°   145
Th' observ'd of all observers,° quite, quite down!
And I, of ladies most deject and wretched,
That suck'd the honey of his music vows,
Now see that noble and most sovereign reason,
Like sweet bells jangled, out of time and harsh;   150
That unmatch'd form and feature of blown° youth
Blasted with ecstasy°: O, woe is me,

---

116. inoculate: graft (metaphorical).   **117. but . . . it:** i.e., that we do not still have about us a taste of the old stock, i.e., retain our sinfulness.   **120. indifferent honest:** moderately virtuous.   **122. beck:** command.
133. monsters: an allusion to the horns of a cuckold.   **136. your:** indefinite use.   **137. jig:** move with jerky motion; probably allusion to the jig, or song and dance, of the current stage.   **138. make . . . igno-rance:** i.e., excuse your wantonness on the ground of your ignorance.   **140. one:** i.e., the king.   **144. expectancy and rose:** source of hope.   **145. The glass . . . form:** the mirror of fashion and the pattern of courtly behavior.   **146. observ'd . . . observers:** i.e., the center of attention in the court.
151. blown: blooming.   **152. ecstasy:** madness.

T' have seen what I have seen, see what I see!

(*Enter* KING *and* POLONIUS.)

KING: Love! his affections do not that way tend;
    Nor what he spake, though it lack'd form a little,   155
    Was not like madness. There's something in his soul,
    O'er which his melancholy sits on brood;
    And I do doubt° the hatch and the disclose°
    Will be some danger: which for to prevent,
    I have in quick determination   160
    Thus set it down: he shall with speed to England,
    For the demand of our neglected tribute:
    Haply the seas and countries different
    With variable° objects shall expel
    This something-settled° matter in his heart,   165
    Whereon his brains still beating puts him thus
    From fashion of himself.° What think you on 't?
POLONIUS: It shall do well: but yet do I believe
    The origin and commencement of his grief
    Sprung from neglected love. How now, Ophelia!   170
    You need not tell us what Lord Hamlet said;
    We heard it all. My lord, do as you please;
    But, if you hold it fit, after the play
    Let his queen mother all alone entreat him
    To show his grief: let her be round° with him;   175
    And I'll be plac'd, so please you, in the ear
    Of all their conference. If she find him not,
    To England send him, or confine him where
    Your wisdom best shall think.
KING: It shall be so: 180
    Madness in great ones must not unwatch'd go.   (*Exeunt.*)

SCENE II

(*A hall in the castle.*)

(*Enter* HAMLET *and three of the* PLAYERS.)

HAMLET: Speak the speech, I pray you, as I pronounced it to you, trippingly on the
    tongue: but if you mouth it, as many of your° players do, I had as lief the town-
    crier spoke my lines. Nor do not saw the air too much with your hand, thus,
    but use all gently; for in the very torrent, tempest, and, as I may say, whirlwind

---

158. doubt: fear.   **158. disclose:** disclosure or revelation (by chipping of the shell).   **164. variable:**
various   **165. something-settled:** somewhat settled.   **167. From . . . himself:** out of his natural manner.   **175. round:** blunt.   **III.ii. 2. your:** indefinite use.

of your passion, you must acquire and beget a temperance that may give it 5
smoothness. O, it offends me to the soul to hear a robustious° periwig-pated°
fellow tear a passion to tatters, to very rags, to split the ears of the
groundlings,° who for the most part are capable of° nothing but inexplicable°
dumb-shows and noise: I would have such a fellow whipped for o'er-doing Ter-
magant°; it out-herods Herod°: pray you, avoid it.   10

FIRST PLAYER: I warrant your honour.

HAMLET: Be not too tame neither, but let your own discretion be your tutor: suit
the action to the word, the word to the action; with this special observance, that
you o'er-step not the modesty of nature: for any thing so overdone is from the
purpose of playing, whose end, both at the first and now, was and is, to hold, as 't 15
were, the mirror up to nature; to show virtue her own feature, scorn her own
image, and the very age and body of the time his form and pressure.° Now this
overdone, or come tardy off,° though it make the unskilful laugh, cannot but
make the judicious grieve; the censure of the which one° must in your allowance
o'erweigh a whole theatre of others. O, there be players that I have seen play, 20
and heard others praise, and that highly, not to speak it profanely, that, neither
having the accent of Christians nor the gait of Christian, pagan, nor man, have
so strutted and bellowed that I have thought some of nature's journeymen° had
made men and not made them well, they imitated humanity so abominably.

FIRST PLAYER: I hope we have reformed that indifferently° with us, sir.   25

HAMLET: O, reform it altogether. And let those that play your clowns speak no
more than is set down for them; for there be of° them that will themselves
laugh, to set on some quantity of barren° spectators to laugh too; though, in
the mean time, some necessary question of the play be then to be considered:
that's villanous, and shows a most pitiful ambition in the fool that uses it. Go, 30
make you ready.

(*Exeunt* PLAYERS.)

(*Enter* POLONIUS, GUILDENSTERN, *and* ROSENCRANTZ.)

How now, my lord! will the king hear this piece of work?

POLONIUS: And the queen too, and that presently.

HAMLET: Bid the players make haste.   (*Exit* POLONIUS.)
Will you two help to hasten them?   35

ROSENCRANTZ: }
GUILDENSTERN: }   We will, my lord.   (*Exeunt they two.*)

---

6. robustious: violent, boisterous.   **6. periwig-pated:** wearing a wig.   **8. groundlings:** those who
stood in the yard of the theater.   **8. capable of:** susceptible of being influenced by.   **8. inexplicable:** of
no significance worth explaining.   **10. Termagant:** a god of the Saracens; a character in the St.
Nicholas play, where one of his worshipers, leaving him in charge of goods, returns to find them stolen;
whereupon he beats the god (or idol), which howls vociferously.   **10. Herod:** Herod of Jewry; a character in The Slaughter of the Innocents and other cycle plays. The part was played with great noise and
fury.   **17. pressure:** stamp, impressed character.   **18. come tardy off:** inadequately done.   **19. the
censure . . . one:** the judgment of even one of whom.   **23. journeymen:** laborers not yet masters in
their trade.   **25. indifferently:** fairly, tolerably.   **27. of:** i.e., some among them.   **28. barren:** i.e., of wit.

HAMLET: What ho! Horatio!

(*Enter* HORATIO.)

HORATIO: Here, sweet lord, at your service.
HAMLET: Horatio, thou art e'en as just° a man
  As e'er my conversation cop'd withal.   40
HORATIO: O, my dear lord,—
HAMLET: Nay, do not think I flatter;
  For what advancement may I hope from thee
  That no revenue hast but thy good spirits,
  To feed and clothe thee? Why should the poor be flatter'd?
  No, let the candied tongue lick absurd pomp,   45
  And crook the pregnant° hinges of the knee
  Where thrift° may follow fawning. Dost thou hear?
  Since my dear soul was mistress of her choice
  And could of men distinguish her election,
  S' hath seal'd thee for herself; for thou hast been   50
  As one, in suff'ring all, that suffers nothing,
  A man that fortune's buffets and rewards
  Hast ta'en with equal thanks: and blest are those
  Whose blood and judgement are so well commeddled,
  That they are not a pipe for fortune's finger   55
  To sound what stop° she please. Give me that man
  That is not passion's slave, and I will wear him
  In my heart's core, ay, in my heart of heart,
  As I do thee.—Something too much of this.—
  There is a play to-night before the king;   60
  One scene of it comes near the circumstance
  Which I have told thee of my father's death:
  I prithee, when thou seest that act afoot,
  Even with the very comment of thy soul°
  Observe my uncle: if his occulted° guilt   65
  Do not itself unkennel in one speech,
  It is a damned° ghost that we have seen,
  And my imaginations are as foul
  As Vulcan's stithy.° Give him heedful note;
  For I mine eyes will rivet to his face,   70
  And after we will both our judgments join
  In censure of his seeming.°
HORATIO.   Well, my lord:

---

39. just: honest, honorable.   **46. pregnant:** pliant.   **47. thrift:** profit.   **56. stop:** hole in a wind instrument for controlling the sound.   **64. very . . . soul:** inward and sagacious criticism. **65. occulted:** hidden.   **67. damned:** in league with Satan.   **69. stithy:** smithy, place of stiths (anvils). **72. censure . . . seeming:** judgment of his appearance or behavior.

If 'a steal aught the whilst this play is playing,
And 'scape detecting, I will pay the theft. 75

> (*Enter trumpets and kettledrums,* KING, QUEEN, POLONIUS, OPHELIA,
> [ROSENCRANTZ, GUILDENSTERN, *and* OTHERS].)

HAMLET: They are coming to the play; I must be idle°: Get you a place.

KING: How fares our cousin Hamlet?

HAMLET: Excellent, i' faith; of the chameleon's dish°: I eat the air, promise-crammed: you cannot feed capons so.

KING: I have nothing with° this answer, Hamlet; these words are not mine.° 80

HAMLET: No, nor mine now. (*To* POLONIUS.) My lord, you played once i' the university, you say?

POLONIUS: That did I, my lord; and was accounted a good actor.

HAMLET: What did you enact?

POLONIUS: I did enact Julius Cæsar: I was killed i' the Capitol; Brutus killed me. 85

HAMLET: It was a brute part of him to kill so capital a calf there. Be the players ready?

ROSENCRANTZ: Ay, my lord; they stay upon your patience.

QUEEN: Come hither, my dear Hamlet, sit by me.

HAMLET: No, good mother, here's metal more attractive. 90

POLONIUS (*to the* KING): O, ho! do you mark that?

HAMLET: Lady, shall I lie in your lap? (*Lying down at* OPHELIA'*s feet.*)

OPHELIA: No, my lord.

HAMLET: I mean, my head upon your lap?

OPHELIA: Ay, my lord. 95

HAMLET: Do you think I meant country° matters?

OPHELIA: I think nothing, my lord.

HAMLET: That's a fair thought to lie between maids' legs.

OPHELIA: What is, my lord?

HAMLET: Nothing. 100

OPHELIA: You are merry, my lord.

HAMLET: Who, I?

OPHELIA: Ay, my lord.

HAMLET: O God, your only° jig-maker.° What should a man do but be merry? for look you, how cheerfully my mother looks, and my father died within's two 105 hours.

OPHELIA: Nay, 'tis twice two months, my lord.

HAMLET: So long? Nay then, let the devil wear black, for I'll have a suit of sables.°
O heavens! die two months ago, and not forgotten yet? Then there's hope a

---

76. idle: crazy, or not attending to anything serious. **78. chameleon's dish:** chameleons were supposed to feed on air. (Hamlet deliberately misinterprets the king's "fares" as "feeds.") **80. have . . . with:** make nothing of. **80. are not mine:** do not respond to what I ask. **96. country:** with a bawdy pun. **104. your only:** only your. **104. jig-maker:** composer of jigs (song and dance). **108. suit of sables:** garments trimmed with the fur of the sable, with a quibble on sable meaning "black."

great man's memory may outlive his life half a year: but, by 'r lady, 'a must build   110
churches, then; or else shall 'a suffer not thinking on,° with the hobbyhorse,
whose epitaph is "For, O, for, O, the hobbyhorse is forgot."°

(*The trumpets sound. Dumb show follows.*)

(*Enter a* King *and a* Queen [*very lovingly*]; *the* Queen *embracing him, and
he her.* [*She kneels, and makes show of protestation unto him.*] *He takes her
up, and declines his head upon her neck: he lies him down upon a bank of
flowers: she, seeing him asleep, leaves him. Anon comes in another man, takes
off his crown, kisses it, pours poison in the sleeper's ears, and leaves him. The*
Queen *returns; finds the* King *dead, makes passionate action. The* Poisoner,
*with some three or four come in again, seem to condole with her. The dead body
is carried away. The* Poisoner *woos the* Queen *with gifts: she seems harsh
awhile, but in the end accepts love.*)

(*Exeunt.*)

Ophelia:	What means this, my lord?
Hamlet:	Marry, this is miching mallecho°; it means mischief.
Ophelia:	Belike this show imports the argument of the play. 115

(*Enter* Prologue.)

Hamlet:	We shall know by this fellow: the players cannot keep counsel; they'll tell all.
Ophelia:	Will 'a tell us what this show meant?
Hamlet:	Ay, or any show that you'll show him: be not you ashamed to show, he'll not shame to tell you what it means. 120
Ophelia:	You are naught, you are naught°: I'll mark the play.
Prologue:	For us, and for our tragedy,
	Here stooping° to your clemency,
	We beg your hearing patiently. (*Exit.*)
Hamlet:	Is this a prologue, or the posy° of a ring? 125
Ophelia:	'Tis brief, my lord.
Hamlet:	As woman's love.

(*Enter* [*two Players as*] King *and* Queen.)

Player King:	Full thirty times hath Phoebus' cart gone round
	Neptune's salt wash° and Tellus'° orbed ground,
	And thirty dozen moons with borrowed° sheen 130
	About the world have times twelve thirties been,

---

111. suffer . . . on: undergo oblivion.   **112. "For . . . forgot":** verse of a song occurring also in *Love's Labour's Lost*, III.i.30; the hobbyhorse was a character in the Morris Dance.   **114. miching mallecho:** sneaking mischief.   **121. naught:** indecent.   **123. stooping:** bowing.   **125. posy:** motto.   **129. salt wash:** the sea.   **129. Tellus:** goddess of the earth (orbed ground).   **130. borrowed:** i.e., reflected.

Since love our hearts and Hymen° did our hands
Unite commutual° in most sacred bands.
PLAYER QUEEN: So many journeys may the sun and moon
Make us again count o'er ere love be done!   135
But, woe is me, you are so sick of late,
So far from cheer and from your former state,
That I distrust° you. Yet, though I distrust,
Discomfort you, my lord, it nothing must:
For women's fear and love holds quantity°;   140
In neither aught, or in extremity.
Now, what my love is, proof hath made you know;
And as my love is siz'd, my fear is so:
Where love is great, the littlest doubts are fear;
Where little fears grow great, great love grows there.   145
PLAYER KING: 'Faith, I must leave thee, love, and shortly too;
My operant° powers their functions leave° to do:
And thou shalt live in this fair world behind,
Honour'd, belov'd; and haply one as kind
For husband shalt thou—
PLAYER QUEEN: O, confound the rest!   150
Such love must needs be treason in my breast:
In second husband let me be accurst!
None wed the second but who kill'd the first.
HAMLET (*aside*):   Wormwood, wormwood.
PLAYER QUEEN: The instances that second marriage move   155
Are base respects of thrift, but none of love:
A second time I kill my husband dead,
When second husband kisses me in bed.
PLAYER KING: I do believe you think what now you speak;
But what we do determine oft we break.   160
Purpose is but the slave to memory,
Of violent birth, but poor validity:
Which now, like fruit unripe, sticks on the tree;
But fall, unshaken, when they mellow be.
Most necessary 'tis that we forget   165
To pay ourselves what to ourselves is debt:
What to ourselves in passion we propose,
The passion ending, doth the purpose lose.
The violence of either grief or joy
Their own enactures° with themselves destroy: 170
Where joy most revels, grief doth most lament;

---

132. Hymen: god of matrimony.   **133. commutual:** mutually.   **138. distrust:** am anxious about. **140. holds quantity:** keeps proportion between.   **147. operant:** active.   **147. leave:** cease.   **170. enactures:** fulfillments.

Grief joys, joy grieves, on slender accident.
This world is not for aye,° nor 'tis not strange
That even our loves should with our fortunes change;
For 'tis a question left us yet to prove,   175
Whether love lead fortune, or else fortune love.
The great man down, you mark his favourite flies;
The poor advanc'd makes friends of enemies.
And hitherto doth love on fortune tend;
For who° not needs shall never lack a friend,   180
And who in want a hollow friend doth try,
Directly seasons° him his enemy.
But, orderly to end where I begun,
Our wills and fates do so contrary run
That our devices still are overthrown;   185
Our thoughts are ours, their ends° none of our own:
So think thou wilt no second husband wed;
But die thy thoughts when thy first lord is dead.
PLAYER QUEEN: Nor earth to me give food, nor heaven light!
   Sport and repose lock from me day and night!   190
   To desperation turn my trust and hope!
   An anchor's° cheer° in prison be my scope!
   Each opposite° that blanks° the face of joy
   Meet what I would have well and it destroy!
   Both here and hence pursue me lasting strife,   195
   If, once a widow, ever I be wife!
HAMLET: If she should break it now!
PLAYER KING: 'Tis deeply sworn. Sweet, leave me here awhile;
   My spirits grow dull, and fain I would beguile
   The tedious day with sleep. (*Sleeps.*)
PLAYER QUEEN: Sleep rock thy brain;   200
   And never come mischance between us twain!   (*Exit.*)
HAMLET: Madam, how like you this play?
QUEEN: The lady doth protest too much, methinks.
HAMLET: O, but she'll keep her word.
KING: Have you heard the argument? Is there no offence in 't?   205
HAMLET: No, no, they do but jest, poison in jest; no offence i' the world.
KING: What do you call the play?
HAMLET: The Mouse-trap. Marry, how? Tropically.° This play is the image of a
   murder done in Vienna: Gonzago° is the duke's name; his wife, Baptista: you

173. **aye:** ever.   180. **who:** whoever.   182. **seasons:** matures, ripens.   186. **ends:** results.   192. **An anchor's:** an anchorite's.   192. **cheer:** fare; sometimes printed as *chair*.   193. **opposite:** adverse thing. 193. **blanks:** causes to *blanch* or grow pale.   208. **Tropically:** figuratively, *trapically* suggests a pun on *trap* in *Mouse-trap* (1.211).   209. **Gonzago:** in 1538 Luigi Gonzago murdered the Duke of Urbano by pouring poisoned lotion in his ears.

shall see anon; 't is a knavish piece of work: but what o' that? your majesty and   210
we that have free souls, it touches us not: let the galled jade° winch,° our with-
ers° are unwrung.°

    (*Enter* LUCIANUS.)

    This is one Lucianus, nephew to the king.
OPHELIA: You are as good as a chorus,° my lord.
HAMLET: I could interpret between you and your love, if I could see the puppets   215
    dallying.°
OPHELIA: You are keen, my lord, you are keen.
HAMLET: It would cost you a groaning to take off my edge.
OPHELIA: Still better, and worse.°
HAMLET: So you mistake° your husbands. Begin, murderer; pox,° leave thy   220
    damnable faces, and begin. Come: the croaking raven doth bellow for revenge.
LUCIANUS: Thoughts black, hands apt, drugs fit, and time agreeing;
    Confederate° season, else no creature seeing;
    Thou mixture rank, of midnight weeds collected,
    With Hecate's° ban° thrice blasted, thrice infected,   225
    Thy natural magic and dire property,
    On wholesome life usurp immediately.

    (*Pours the poison into the sleeper's ears.*)

HAMLET: 'A poisons him i' the garden for his estate. His name's Gonzago: the
    story is extant, and written in very choice Italian: you shall see anon how the
    murderer gets the love of Gonzago's wife.   230
OPHELIA: The king rises.
HAMLET: What, frighted with false fire!°
QUEEN: How fares my lord?
POLONIUS: Give o'er the play.
KING: Give me some light away!   235
POLONIUS: Lights, lights, lights!   (*Exeunt all but* HAMLET *and* HORATIO.)
HAMLET: Why, let the strucken deer go weep,
    The hart ungalled play;
  For some must watch, while some must sleep:
    Thus runs the world away.°   240

---

211. galled jade: horse whose hide is rubbed by saddle or harness.   **211. winch:** wince.   **212. with-
ers:** the part between the horse's shoulder blades.   **212. unwrung:** not wrung or twisted.   **214. chorus:** in many Elizabethan plays the action was explained by an actor known as the "chorus"; at a puppet
show the actor who explained the action was known as an "interpreter," as indicated by the lines following.   **215–218. dallying:** with sexual suggestion, continued in **keen** (sexually aroused), **groaning** (i.e.,
in pregnancy), and **edge** (i.e., sexual desire or impetuosity).   **219. Still . . . worse:** more keen, less
decorous.   **220. mistake:** err in taking.   **220. pox:** an imprecation.   **223. Confederate:** conspiring
(to assist the murderer).   **225. Hecate:** the goddess of witchcraft.   **225. ban:** curse.   **232. false fire:**
fireworks, or a blank discharge.   **237–240. Why . . . away:** probably from an old ballad, with allusion to
the popular belief that a wounded deer retires to weep and die. Cf. *As You Like It*, II, i. 66.

Would not this,° sir, and a forest of feathers°—if the rest of my fortunes turn
Turk with° me—with two Provincial roses° on my razed° shoes, get me a fellowship in a cry° of players,° sir?

HORATIO: Half a share.°

HAMLET: A whole one, I.   245
For thou dost know, O Damon dear,
   This realm dismantled° was
Of Jove himself; and now reigns here
   A very, very°—pajock.°

HORATIO: You might have rhymed.   250

HAMLET: O good Horatio, I'll take the ghost's word for a thousand pound.
   Didst perceive?

HORATIO: Very well, my lord.

HAMLET: Upon the talk of the poisoning?

HORATIO: I did very well note him.   255

HAMLET: Ah, ha! Come, some music! come, the recorders!°
For if the king like not the comedy,
Why then, belike, he likes it not, perdy.°
Come, some music!

(*Enter* ROSENCRANTZ *and* GUILDENSTERN.)

GUILDENSTERN: Good my lord, vouchsafe me a word with you.   260

HAMLET: Sir, a whole history.

GUILDENSTERN: The king, sir,—

HAMLET: Ay, sir, what of him?

GUILDENSTERN: Is in his retirement marvelous distempered.

HAMLET: With drink, sir?   265

GUILDENSTERN: No, my lord, rather with choler.°

HAMLET: Your wisdom should show itself more richer to signify this to his doctor;
   for, for me to put him to his purgation would perhaps plunge him into far more
   choler.

GUILDENSTERN: Good my lord, put your discourse into some frame° and start not   270
   so wildly from my affair.

HAMLET: I am tame, sir: pronounce.

---

241. this: i.e., the play.   **241. feathers:** allusion to the plumes which Elizabethan actors were fond of
wearing.   **242. turn Turk with:** go back on.   **242. two Provincial roses:** rosettes of ribbon like the
roses of Provins near Paris, or else the roses of Provence.   **242. razed:** cut, slashed (by way of ornament).   **243. cry:** pack (as of hounds).   **243. fellowship . . . players:** partnership in a theatrical company.   **244. Half a share:** allusion to the custom in dramatic companies of dividing the ownership into
a number of shares among the householders.   **247. dismantled:** stripped, divested.   **246–249. For . . .
very:** probably from an old ballad having to do with Damon and Pythias.   **249. pajock:** peacock (a bird
with a bad reputation). Possibly the word was patchock, diminutive of patch, clown.   **256. recorders:**
wind instruments of the flute kind.   **258. perdy:** corruption of par dieu.   **266. choler:** bilious disorder,
with quibble on the sense "anger."   **270. frame:** order.

GUILDENSTERN: The queen, your mother, in most great affliction of spirit, hath
    sent me to you.

HAMLET: You are welcome. 275

GUILDENSTERN: Nay, good my lord, this courtesy is not of the right breed. If it
    shall please you to make me a wholesome° answer, I will do your mother's com-
    mandment; if not, your pardon and my return shall be the end of my business.

HAMLET: Sir, I cannot.

GUILDENSTERN: What, my lord? 280

HAMLET: Make you a wholesome answer; my wit's diseased: but, sir, such answer as
    I can make, you shall command; or rather, as you say, my mother: therefore no
    more, but to the matter°: my mother, you say,—

ROSENCRANTZ: Then thus she says; your behaviour hath struck her into amaze-
    ment and admiration. 285

HAMLET: O wonderful son, that can so 'stonish a mother! But is there no sequel at
    the heels of this mother's admiration? Impart.

ROSENCRANTZ: She desires to speak with you in her closet, ere you go to bed.

HAMLET: We shall obey, were she ten times our mother. Have you any further
    trade with us? 290

ROSENCRANTZ: My lord, you once did love me.

HAMLET: And do still, by these pickers and stealers.°

ROSENCRANTZ: Good my lord, what is your cause of distemper? you do, surely, bar
    the door upon your own liberty, if you deny your griefs to your friend.

HAMLET: Sir, I lack advancement. 295

ROSENCRANTZ: How can that be, when you have the voice° of the king himself for
    your succession in Denmark?

HAMLET: Ay, sir, but "While the grass grows,"°—the proverb is something musty.

    (*Enter the* PLAYERS *with recorders.*)

    O, the recorders! let me see one. To withdraw° with you:—why do you go
    about to recover the wind° of me, as if you would drive me into a toil?° 300

GUILDENSTERN: O, my lord, if my duty be too bold, my love is too unmannerly.°

HAMLET: I do not well understand that. Will you play upon this pipe?

GUILDENSTERN: My lord, I cannot.

HAMLET: I pray you.

GUILDENSTERN: Believe me, I cannot. 305

HAMLET: I beseech you.

GUILDENSTERN: I know no touch of it, my lord.

---

277. wholesome: sensible.   **283. matter:** matter in hand.   **292. pickers and stealers:** hands, so
called from the catechism "to keep my hands from picking and stealing."   **296. voice:** support.   **298.
"While . . . grows":** the rest of the proverb is "the silly horse starves." Hamlet may be destroyed while
he is waiting for the succession to the kingdom.   **299. withdraw:** speak in private.   **300. recover the
wind:** get to the windward side.   **300. toil:** snare.   **301. if . . . unmannerly:** if I am using an unmannerly boldness, it is my love which occasions it.

HAMLET: 'Tis as easy as lying: govern these ventages° with your fingers and
thumb, give it breath with your mouth, and it will discourse most eloquent
music. Look you, these are the stops.   310
GUILDENSTERN: But these cannot I command to any utterance of harmony; I have
not the skill.
HAMLET: Why, look you now, how unworthy a thing you make of me! You would
play upon me; you would seem to know my stops; you would pluck out the
heart of my mystery; you would sound me from my lowest note to the top of   315
my compass°: and there is much music, excellent voice, in this little organ°; yet
cannot you make it speak. 'Sblood, do you think I am easier to be played on
than a pipe? Call me what instrument you will, though you can fret° me, you
cannot play upon me.

(*Enter* POLONIUS.)

God bless you, sir!   320
POLONIUS: My lord, the queen would speak with you, and presently.
HAMLET: Do you see yonder cloud that's almost in shape of a camel?
POLONIUS: By the mass, and 'tis like a camel, indeed.
HAMLET: Methinks it is like a weasel.
POLONIUS: It is backed like a weasel.   325
HAMLET: Or like a whale?
POLONIUS: Very like a whale.
HAMLET: Then I will come to my mother by and by. (*Aside.*) They fool me to the
top of my bent.°—I will come by and by.°
POLONIUS: I will say so.   (*Exit.*) 330
HAMLET: By and by is easily said.
Leave me, friends.   (*Exeunt all but* HAMLET.)
'Tis now the very witching time° of night,
When churchyards yawn and hell itself breathes out
Contagion to this world: now could I drink hot blood,   335
And do such bitter business as the day
Would quake to look on. Soft! now to my mother.
O heart, lose not thy nature; let not ever
The soul of Nero° enter this firm bosom:
Let me be cruel, not unnatural: 340
I will speak daggers to her, but use none;
My tongue and soul in this be hypocrites;

---

308. ventages: stops of the recorders.   **316. compass:** range of voice.   **316. organ:** musical instrument, i.e., the pipe.   **318. fret:** quibble on meaning "irritate" and the piece of wood, gut, or metal which
regulates the fingering.   **329. top of my bent:** limit of endurance, i.e., extent to which a bow may be
bent.   **329. by and by:** immediately.   **333. witching time:** i.e., time when spells are cast.   **339. Nero:**
murderer of his mother, Agrippina.

How in my words somever she be shent,°
To give them seals° never, my soul, consent!   (*Exit.*)

       SCENE III

       (*A room in the castle.*)

       (*Enter* KING, ROSENCRANTZ, *and* GUILDENSTERN.)

KING: I like him not, nor stands it safe with us
  To let his madness range. Therefore prepare you;
  I your commission will forthwith dispatch,°
  And he to England shall along with you:
  The terms° of our estate° may not endure   5
  Hazard so near us as doth hourly grow
  Out of his brows.°
GUILDENSTERN: We will ourselves provide:
  Most holy and religious fear it is
  To keep those many many bodies safe
  That live and feed upon your majesty.   10
ROSENCRANTZ: The single and peculiar° life is bound,
  With all the strength and armor of the mind,
  To keep itself from noyance°; but much more
  That spirit upon whose weal depend and rest
  The lives of many. The cess° of majesty   15
  Dies not alone; but, like a gulf,° doth draw
  What's near it with it: it is a massy wheel,
  Fix'd on the summit of the highest mount,
  To whose huge spokes ten thousand lesser things
  Are mortis'd and adjoin'd; which, when it falls,   20
  Each small annexment, petty consequence,
  Attends° the boist'rous ruin. Never alone
  Did the king sigh, but with a general groan.
KING: Arm° you, I pray you, to this speedy voyage;
  For we will fetters put about this fear,   25
  Which now goes too free-footed.
ROSENCRANTZ: We will haste us.
          (*Exeunt* GENTLEMEN [ROSENCRANTZ *and* GUILDENSTERN].)

       (*Enter* POLONIUS.)

POLONIUS: My lord, he's going to his mother's closet:

---

343. shent: rebuked.   **344. give them seals:** confirm with deeds. **III.iii. 3. dispatch:** prepare.
5. terms: condition, circumstances. **5. estate:** state. **7. brows:** effronteries. **11. single and peculiar:** individual and private. **13. noyance:** harm. **15. cess:** decease. **16. gulf:** whirlpool. **22. Attends:** participates in. **24. Arm:** prepare.

Behind the arras° I'll convey° myself,
To hear the process°; I'll warrant she'll tax him home°:
And, as you said, and wisely was it said,   30
'Tis meet that some more audience than a mother,
Since nature makes them partial, should o'erhear
The speech, of vantage.° Fare you well, my liege:
I'll call upon you ere you go to bed,
And tell you what I know.

KING: Thanks, dear my lord.   (*Exit* [POLONIUS].) 35
O, my offence is rank, it smells to heaven;
It hath the primal eldest curse° upon't,
A brother's murder. Pray can I not,
Though inclination be as sharp as will°:
My stronger guilt defeats my strong intent;   40
And, like a man to double business bound,
I stand in pause where I shall first begin,
And both neglect. What if this cursed hand
Were thicker than itself with brother's blood,
Is there not rain enough in the sweet heavens   45
To wash it white as snow? Whereto serves mercy
But to confront° the visage of offence?
And what's in prayer but this two-fold force,
To be forestalled° ere we come to fall,
Or pardon'd being down? Then I'll look up;   50
My fault is past. But, O, what form of prayer
Can serve my turn? "Forgive me my foul murder"?
That cannot be: since I am still possess'd
Of those effects for which I did the murder,
My crown, mine own ambition° and my queen.   55
May one be pardon'd and retain th' offence?°
In the corrupted currents° of this world
Offence's gilded hand° may shove by justice,
And oft 'tis seen the wicked prize° itself
Buys out the law: but 'tis not so above;   60
There is no shuffling,° there the action lies°
In his true nature; and we ourselves compell'd,
Even to the teeth and forehead° of our faults,

---

28. arras: screen of tapestry placed around the walls of household apartments.   **28. convey:** implication of secrecy; *convey* was often used to mean "steal."   **29. process:** proceedings.   **29. tax him home:** reprove him severely.   **33. of vantage:** from an advantageous place.   **37. primal eldest curse:** the curse of Cain, the first to kill his brother.   **39. sharp as will:** i.e., his desire is as strong as his determination.   **47. confront:** oppose directly.   **49. forestalled:** prevented.   **55. ambition:** i.e., realization of ambition.   **56. offence:** benefit accruing from offense.   **57. currents:** courses.   **58. gilded hand:** hand offering gold as a bribe.   **59. wicked prize:** prize won by wickedness.   **61. shuffling:** escape by trickery.   **61. lies:** is sustainable.   **63. teeth and forehead:** very face.

To give in evidence. What then? what rests?°
Try what repentance can: what can it not?   65
Yet what can it when one can not repent?
O wretched state! O bosom black as death!
O limed° soul, that, struggling to be free,
Art more engag'd!° Help, angels! Make assay!°
Bow, stubborn knees; and, heart with strings of steel,   70
Be soft as sinews of the new-born babe!
All may be well. (*He kneels.*)

    (*Enter* HAMLET.)

HAMLET: Now might I do it pat,° now he is praying;
And now I'll do 't. And so 'a goes to heaven;
And so am I reveng'd. That would be scann'd°:   75
A villain kills my father; and for that,
I, his sole son, do this same villain send
To heaven.
Why, this is hire and salary, not revenge.
'A took my father grossly, full of bread°;   80
With all his crimes broad blown,° as flush° as May;
And how his audit stands who knows save heaven?
But in our circumstance and course° of thought,
'Tis heavy with him: and am I then reveng'd,
To take him in the purging of his soul,   85
When he is fit and season'd for his passage?°
No!
Up, sword; and know thou a more horrid hent°:
When he is drunk asleep,° or in his rage,
Or in th' incestuous pleasure of his bed;   90
At game, a-swearing, or about some act
That has no relish of salvation in 't;
Then trip him, that his heels may kick at heaven,
And that his soul may be as damn'd and black
As hell, whereto it goes. My mother stays: 95
This physic° but prolongs thy sickly days.   (*Exit.*)
KING (*rising*):   My words fly up, my thoughts remain below:
Words without thoughts never to heaven go.   (*Exit.*)

---

64. rests: remains.   **68. limed:** caught as with birdlime.   **69. engag'd:** embedded.   **69. assay:** trial.
73. pat: opportunely.   **75. would be scann'd:** needs to be looked into   **80. full of bread:** enjoying his
worldly pleasures (see Ezekiel 16:49).   **81. broad blown:** in full bloom.   **81. flush:** lusty.   **83. in . . .
course:** as we see it in our mortal situation.   **86. fit . . . passage:** i.e., reconciled to heaven by forgiveness of his sins.   **88. heat:** seizing; or more probably, occasion of seizure.   **89. drunk asleep:** in a
drunken sleep.   **96. physic:** purging (by prayer).

Scene IV

(*The Queen's closet.*)

(*Enter* [Queen] Gertrude *and* Polonius.)

Polonius: 'A will come straight. Look you lay° home to him:
Tell him his pranks have been too broad° to bear with,
And that your grace hath screen'd and stood between
Much heat° and him. I'll sconce° me even here.
Pray you, be round° with him.   5
Hamlet (*within*):   Mother, mother, mother!
Queen: I'll warrant you,
Fear me not: withdraw, I hear him coming.

(Polonius *hides behind the arras.*)

(*Enter* Hamlet.)

Hamlet: Now, mother, what's the matter?
Queen: Hamlet, thou hast thy father much offended.
Hamlet: Mother, you have my father° much offended.   10
Queen: Come, come, you answer with an idle tongue.
Hamlet: Go, go, you question with a wicked tongue.
Queen: Why, how now, Hamlet!
Hamlet: What's the matter now?
Queen: Have you forgot me?
Hamlet: No, by the rood,° not so:
You are the queen, your husband's brother's wife;   15
And—would it were not so!—you are my mother.
Queen: Nay, then, I'll set those to you that can speak.
Hamlet: Come, come, and sit you down; you shall not budge;
You go not till I set you up a glass
Where you may see the inmost part of you.   20
Queen: What wilt thou do? thou wilt not murder me?
Help, help, ho!
Polonius (*behind*):   What, ho! help, help; help!
Hamlet (*drawing*):   How now! a rat? Dead, for a ducat, dead!

(*Makes a pass through the arras.*)

Polonius (*behind*):   O, I am slain! (*Falls and dies.*)   25
Queen: O me, what hast thou done?
Hamlet: Nay, I know not:

III.iv. 1. lay: thrust.   **2. broad:** unrestrained.   **4. Much heat:** i.e., the king's anger.   **4. sconce:** hide.
5. round: blunt.   **9–10. thy father . . . my father:** i.e., Claudius, the elder Hamlet.   **14. rood:** cross.

Is it the king?
QUEEN: O, what a rash and bloody deed is this!
HAMLET: A bloody deed! almost as bad, good mother,
As kill a king, and marry with his brother.   30
QUEEN: As kill a king!
HAMLET: Ay, lady, it was my word.

      (*Lifts up the arras and discovers* POLONIUS.)

Thou wretched, rash, intruding fool, farewell!
I took thee for thy better: take thy fortune;
Thou find'st to be too busy is some danger.
Leave wringing of your hands: peace! sit you down,   35
And let me wring your heart; for so I shall,
If it be made of penetrable stuff,
If damned custom have not braz'd° it so
That it be proof and bulwark against sense.
QUEEN: What have I done, that thou dar'st wag thy tongue   40
In noise so rude against me?
HAMLET: Such an act
That blurs the grace and blush of modesty,
Calls virtue hypocrite, takes off the rose
From the fair forehead of an innocent love
And sets a blister° there, makes marriage-vows   45
As false as dicers' oaths: O, such a deed
As from the body of contraction° plucks
The very soul, and sweet religion° makes
A rhapsody° of words: heaven's face does glow
O'er this solidity and compound mass   50
With heated visage, as against the doom
Is thought-sick at the act.°
QUEEN: Ay me, what act,
That roars so loud, and thunders in the index?°
HAMLET: Look here, upon this picture, and on this.
The counterfeit presentment° of two brothers.   55
See, what a grace was seated on this brow;
Hyperion's° curls; the front° of Jove himself;
An eye Mars, to threaten and command;
A station° like the herald Mercury
New-lightned on a heaven-kissing hill;   60

---

38. braz'd: brazened, hardened.   **45. sets a blister:** brands as a harlot.   **47. contraction:** the marriage
contract.   **48. religion:** religious vows.   **49. rhapsody:** senseless string.   **49–52. heaven's . . . act:**
heaven's face blushes to look down upon this world, compounded of the four elements, with hot face as
though the day of doom were near, and thought-sick at the deed (i.e., Gertrude's marriage).   **53. index:**
prelude or preface.   **55. counterfeit presentment:** portrayed representation.   **57. Hyperion's:** the
sun god's.   **57. front:** brow.   **59. station:** manner of standing.

A combination and form indeed,
Where every god did seem to set his seal,
To give the world assurance° of a man:
This was your husband. Look you now, what follows:
Here is your husband; like a mildew'd ear,°   65
Blasting his wholesome brother. Have you eyes?
Could you on this fair mountain leave to feed,
And batten° on this moor?° Ha! have you eyes?
You cannot call it love; for at your age
The hey-day° in the blood is tame, it's humble,   70
And waits upon the judgment: and what judgment
Would step from this to this? Sense, sure, you have,
Else could you not have motion,° but sure, that sense
Is apoplex'd° for madness would not err.
Nor sense to ecstasy was ne'er so thrall'd°   75
But it reserv'd some quantity of choice,°
To serve in such a difference. What devil was't
Tha thus hath cozen'd° you at hoodman-blind?°
Eyes without feeling, feeling without sight,
Ears without hands or eyes, smelling sans° all,   80
Or but a sickly part of one true sense
Could not so mope.°
O shame! where is thy blush? Rebellious hell,
If thou canst mutine° in a matron's bones.
To flaming youth let virtue be as wax,   85
And melt in her own fire: proclaim no shame
When the compulsive ardor gives the charge,°
Since frost itself as actively doth burn
And reason panders will.°

QUEEN: O Hamlet, speak no more:
Thou turn'st mine eyes into my very soul;   90
And there I see such black and grained° spots
As will not leave their tinct.

HAMLET: Nay, but to live
In the rank sweat of an enseamed° bed,

---

63. assurance: pledge, guarantee.   **65. mildew'd ear:** see Genesis 41:5–7.   **68. batten:** grow fat.
68. moor: barren upland.   **70. hey-day:** state of excitement.   **72–73. Sense . . . motion:** sense and
motion are functions of the middle or sensible soul, the possession of sense being the basis of motion.
74. apoplex'd: paralyzed; mental derangement was thus of three sorts: apoplexy, ecstasy, and diabolic
possession.   **75. thrall'd:** enslaved.   **76. quantity of choice:** fragment of the power to choose.
78. cozen'd: tricked, cheated.   **78. hoodman-blind:** blindman's buff.   **80. sans:** without.   **82. mope:**
be in a depressed, spiritless state, act aimlessly.   **84. mutine:** mutiny, rebel.   **87. gives the charge:**
delivers the attack.   **89. reason panders will:** the normal and proper situation was one in which reason
guided the will in the direction of good; here, reason is perverted and leads in the direction of evil.
91. grained: dyed in grain.   **93. enseamed:** loaded with grease, greased.

Stew'd in corruption, honeying and making love
Over the nasty sty,—
QUEEN: O, speak to me no more;   95
These words, like daggers, enter in mine ears;
No more, sweet Hamlet!
HAMLET: A murderer and a villain:
A slave that is not twentieth part the tithe
Of your precedent lord°; a vice of kings°;
A cutpurse of the empire and the rule,   100
That from a shelf the precious diadem stole,
And put it in his pocket!
QUEEN: No more!

(*Enter* GHOST.)

HAMLET: A king of shreds and patches,°—
Save me, and hover o'er me with your wings,
You heavenly guards! What would your gracious figure?   105
QUEEN: Alas, he's mad!
HAMLET: Do you not come your tardy son to chide,
That, laps'd in time and passion,° lets go by
Th' important° acting of your dread command?
O, say!   110
GHOST: Do not forget: this visitation
Is but to whet thy almost blunted purpose.
But, look, amazement° on thy mother sits:
O, step between her and her fighting soul:
Conceit in weakest bodies strongest works: 115
Speak to her, Hamlet.
HAMLET: How is it with you, lady?
QUEEN: Alas, how is 't with you,
That you do bend your eye on vacancy
And with th' incorporal° air do hold discourse?
Forth at your eyes your spirits wildly peep;   120
And, as the sleeping soldiers in th' alarm,
Your bedded° hair, like life in excrements,°
Start up, and stand an° end. O gentle son,
Upon the heat and flame of thy distemper
Sprinkle cool patience. Whereon do you look?   125

---

99. precedent lord: i.e., the elder Hamlet.   **99. vice of kings:** buffoon of kings; a reference to the Vice, or clown, of the morality plays and interludes.   **103. shreds and patches:** i.e., motley, the traditional costume of the Vice.   **108. laps'd . . . passion:** having suffered time to slip and passion to cool; also explained as "engrossed in casual events and lapsed into mere fruitless passion, so that he no longer entertains a rational purpose."   **109. important:** urgent.   **113. amazement:** frenzy, distraction.   **119. incorporal:** immaterial.   **122. bedded:** laid in smooth layers.   **122. excrements:** the hair was considered an excrement or voided part of the body.   **123. an:** on.

HAMLET: On him, on him! Look you, how pale he glares!
  His form and cause conjoin'd,° preaching to stones,
  Would make them capable.—Do not look upon me;
  Lest with this piteous action you convert
  My stern effects°: then what I have to do   130
  Will want true colour°; tears perchance for blood.
QUEEN: To whom do you speak this?
HAMLET: Do you see nothing there?
QUEEN: Nothing at all; yet all that is I see.
HAMLET: Nor did you nothing hear?
QUEEN: No, nothing but ourselves.
HAMLET: Why, look you there! look, how it steals away!   135
  My father, in his habit as he liv'd!
  Look, where he goes, even now, out at the portal!   (*Exit* GHOST.)
QUEEN: This is the very coinage of your brain:
  This bodiless creation ecstasy
  Is very cunning in.
HAMLET: Ecstasy!   140
  My pulse, as yours, doth temperately keep time,
  And makes as healthful music; it is not madness
  That I have utt'red: bring me to the test,
  And I the matter will re-word,° which madness
  Would gambol° from. Mother, for love of grace,   145
  Lay not that flattering unction° to your soul,
  That not your trespass, but my madness speaks:
  It will but skin and film the ulcerous place,
  Whiles rank corruption, mining° all within,
  Infects unseen. Confess yourself to heaven;   150
  Repent what's past; avoid what is to come°;
  And do not spread the compost° on the weeds,
  To make them ranker. Forgive me this my virtue°;
  For in the fatness° of these pursy° times
  Virtue itself of vice must pardon beg,   155
  Yea, curb° and woo for leave to do him good.
QUEEN: O Hamlet, thou hast cleft my heart in twain.
HAMLET: O, throw away the worser part of it,
  And live the purer with the other half.

---

127. **conjoin'd**: united.   129–30. **convert . . . effects**: divert me from my stern duty. For effects, possibly affects (affections of the mind).   131. **want true colour**: lack good reason so that (with a play on the normal sense of *colour*) I shall shed tears instead of blood.   144. **re-word**: repeat in words.   145. **gambol**: skip away.   146. **unction**: ointment used medicinally or as a rite; suggestion that forgiveness for sin may not be so easily achieved.   149. **mining**: working under the surface.   151. **what is to come**: i.e., the sins of the future.   152. **compost**: manure.   153. **this my virtue**: my virtuous talk in reproving you.   154. **fatness**: grossness.   154. **pursy**: short-winded, corpulent.   156. **curb**: bow, bend the knee.

Good night: but go not to my uncle's bed; 160
Assume a virtue, if you have it not.
That monster, custom, who all sense doth eat,
Of habits devil, is angel yet in this,
That to the use of actions fair and good
He likewise gives a frock or livery, 165
That aptly is put on. Refrain to-night,
And that shall lend a kind of easiness
To the next abstinence: the next more easy;
For use almost can change the stamp of nature,
And either . . . the devil, or throw him out° 170
With wondrous potency. Once more, good night:
And when you are desirous to be bless'd,°
I'll blessing beg of you. For this same lord, (*Pointing to* POLONIUS.)
I do repent: but heaven hath pleas'd it so,
To punish me with this and this with me, 175
That I must be their scourge and minister.
I will bestow him, and will answer well
The death I gave him. So, again, good night.
I must be cruel, only to be kind:
Thus bad begins and worse remains behind. 180
One word more, good lady.
QUEEN: What shall I do?
HAMLET: Not this, by no means, that I bid you do:
Let the bloat° king tempt you again to bed;
Pinch wanton on your cheek; call you his mouse;
And let him, for a pair of reechy° kisses, 185
Or paddling in your neck with his damn'd fingers,
Make you to ravel all this matter out,
That I essentially° am not in madness,
But mad in craft. 'Twere good you let him know;
For who, that's but a queen, fair, sober, wise, 190
Would from a paddock,° from a bat, a gib,°
Such dear concernings° hide? who would do so?
No, in despite of sense and secrecy,
Unpeg the basket on the house's top,
Let the birds fly, and like the famous ape,° 195
To try conclusions,° in the basket creep,

---

170. defective line usually emended by inserting *master* after *either*.   **172. be bless'd:** become blessed, i.e., repentant.   **183. bloat:** bloated.   **185. reechy:** dirty, filthy.   **188. essentially:** in my essential nature.   **191. paddock:** toad.   **191. gib:** tomcat.   **192. dear concernings:** important affairs.   **195. the famous ape:** a letter from Sir John Suckling seems to supply other details of the story, otherwise not identified: "It is the story of the jackanapes and the partridges; thou starest after a beauty till it be lost to thee, then let'st out another, and starest after that till it is gone too."   **196. conclusions:** experiments.

And break your own neck down.

QUEEN: Be thou assur'd, if words be made of breath,
And breath of life, I have no life to breathe
What thou hast said to me.   200

HAMLET: I must to England; you know that?

QUEEN: Alack,
I had forgot: 'tis so concluded on.

HAMLET: There's letters seal'd: and my two schoolfellows,
Whom I will trust as I will adders fang'd,
They bear the mandate; they must sweep my way,°   205
And marshal me to knavery. Let it work;
For 'tis the sport to have the enginer°
Hoist° with his own petar°: and 't shall go hard
But I will delve one yard below their mines,
And blow them at the moon: O, 'tis most sweet,   210
When in one line two crafts° directly meet.
This man shall set me packing°:
I'll lug the guts into the neighbour room.
Mother, good night. Indeed this counsellor
Is now most still, most secret and most grave,   215
Who was in life a foolish prating knave.
Come, sir, to draw° toward an end with you.
Good night, mother.

(Exeunt [severally; HAMLET *dragging in* POLONIUS].*)*

ACT IV

SCENE I

(A room in the castle)

(Enter KING *and* QUEEN, *with* ROSENCRANTZ *and* GUILDENSTERN.*)*

KING: There's matter in these sighs, these profound heaves;
You must translate: 'tis fit we understand them.
Where is your son?

QUEEN: Bestow this place on us a little while.

(Exeunt ROSENCRANTZ *and* GUILDENSTERN.*)*
Ah, mine own lord, what have I seen to-night!   5

---

205. sweep my way: clear my path.   **207. enginer:** constructor of military works, or possibly, artilleryman.   **208. Hoist:** blown up.   **208. petar:** defined as a small engine of war used to blow in a door or
make a breach, and as a case filled with explosive materials.   **211. two crafts:** two acts of guile, with
quibble on the sense of "two ships."   **212. set me packing:** set me to making schemes, and set me to
lugging (him), and, also, send me off in a hurry.   **217. draw:** come, with quibble on literal sense.

KING: What, Gertrude? How does Hamlet?
QUEEN: Mad as the sea and wind, when both contend
    Which is the mightier: in his lawless fit,
    Behind the arras hearing something stir,
    Whips out his rapier, cries, "A rat, a rat!"   10
    And, in this brainish° apprehension,° kills
    The unseen good old man.
KING: O heavy deed!
    It had been so with us, had we been there:
    His liberty is full of threats to all;
    To you yourself, to us, to every one.   15
    Alas, how shall this bloody deed be answer'd?
    It will be laid to us, whose providence°
    Should have kept short,° restrain'd and out of haunt,°
    This mad young man: but so much was our love,
    We would not understand what was most fit;   20
    But, like the owner of a foul disease,
    To keep it from divulging,° let it feed
    Even on the pith of life. Where is he gone?
QUEEN: To draw apart the body he hath kill'd:
    O'er whom his very madness, like some ore   25
    Among a mineral° of metals base,
    Shows itself pure; 'a weeps for what is done.
KING: O Gertrude, come away!
    The sun no sooner shall the mountains touch,
    But we will ship him hence: and this vile deed   30
    We must, with all our majesty and skill,
    Both countenance and excuse. Ho, Guildenstern!

        (*Enter* ROSENCRANTZ *and* GUILDENSTERN.)

    Friends both, go join you with some further aid:
    Hamlet in madness hath Polonius slain,
    And from his mother's closet hath he dragg'd him: 35
    Go seek him out; speak fair, and bring the body
    Into the chapel. I pray you, haste in this.
        (*Exeunt* ROSENCRANTZ *and* GUILDENSTERN.)
    Come, Gertrude, we'll call up our wisest friends;
    And let them know, both what we mean to do,
    And what's untimely done . . .°   40
    Whose whisper o'er the world's diameter,°

IV.i. **11. brainish:** headstrong, passionate.   **11. apprehension:** conception, imagination.   **17. providence:** foresight.   **18. short:** i.e., on a short tether.   **18. out of haunt:** secluded.   **22. divulging:** becoming evident.   **26. mineral:** mine.   **40.** defective line; some editors add: *so haply, slander*; others add: *for; haply, slander*; other conjectures.   **41. diameter:** extent from side to side.

As level° as the cannon to his blank,°
Transports his pois'ned shot, may miss our name,
And hit the woundless° air. O, come away!
My soul is full of discord and dismay.   (*Exeunt.*) 45

SCENE II

(*Another room in the castle.*)

(*Enter* HAMLET.)

HAMLET: Safely stowed.
ROSENCRANTZ ⎱ (*within*):   Hamlet! Lord Hamlet!
GUILDENSTERN ⎰
HAMLET: But soft, what noise? Who calls on Hamlet? O, here they come.

(*Enter* ROSENCRANTZ *and* GUILDENSTERN.)

ROSENCRANTZ: What have you done, my lord, with the dead body?
HAMLET: Compounded it with dust, whereto 'tis kin.
ROSENCRANTZ: Tell us where 'tis, that we may take it thence   5
   And bear it to the chapel.
HAMLET: Do not believe it.
ROSENCRANTZ: Believe what?
HAMLET: That I can keep your counsel° and not mine own. Besides, to be
   demanded of a sponge! What replication° should be made by the son of a king? 10
ROSENCRANTZ: Take you me for a sponge, my lord?
HAMLET: Ay, sir, that soaks up the king's countenance, his rewards, his authorities.°
   But such officers do the king best service in the end: he keeps them, like an ape
   an apple, in the corner of his jaw; first mouthed, to be last swallowed: when he
   needs what you have gleaned, it is but squeezing you, and, sponge, you shall be 15
   dry again.
ROSENCRANTZ: I understand you not, my lord.
HAMLET: I am glad of it: a knavish speech sleeps in a foolish ear.
ROSENCRANTZ: My lord, you must tell us where the body is, and go with us to the
   king.   20
HAMLET: The body is with the king, but the king is not with the body.° The king is
   a thing—

---

42. level: straight.   **42. blank:** white spot in the center of a target.   **44. woundless:** invulnerable.
IV.ii. 9. keep your counsel: Hamlet is aware of their treachery but says nothing about it.   **10. replication:** reply.   **12. authorities:** authoritative backing.   **21. The body . . . body:** there are many interpretations; possibly, "The body lies in death with the king, my father; but my father walks disembodied"; or "Claudius has the bodily possession of kingship, but kingliness, or justice of inheritance, is not with him."

GUILDENSTERN: A thing, my lord!
HAMLET: Of nothing: bring me to him. Hide fox, and all after.°   (*Exeunt.*)

SCENE III

(*Another room in the castle.*)

(*Enter* KING, *and two or three.*)

KING: I have sent to seek him, and to find the body.
   How dangerous is it that this man goes loose!
   Yet must not we put the strong law on him:
   He's lov'd of the distracted° multitude,
   Who like not in their judgement, but their eyes;   5
   And where 'tis so, th' offender's scourge° is weigh'd,°
   But never the offence. To bear all smooth and even,
   This sudden sending him away must seem
   Deliberate pause°: diseases desperate grown
   By desperate appliance are reliev'd,   10
   Or not at all.

             (*Enter* ROSENCRANTZ, [GUILDENSTERN,] *and all the rest.*)

                 How now! what hath befall'n?
ROSENCRANTZ: Where the dead body is bestow'd, my lord,
   We cannot get from him.
KING: But where is he?
ROSENCRANTZ: Without, my lord; guarded, to know your pleasure.
KING: Bring him before us.   15
ROSENCRANTZ: Ho! bring in the lord.

             (*They enter* [*with* HAMLET].)

KING: Now, Hamlet, where's Polonius?
HAMLET: At supper.
KING: At supper! where?
HAMLET: Not where he eats, but where 'a is eaten: a certain convocation of politic°   20
   worms° are e'en at him. Your worm is your only emperor for diet: we fat all
   creatures else to fat us, and we fat ourselves for maggots: your fat king and your
   lean beggar is but variable service,° two dishes, but to one table: that's the end.
KING: Alas, alas!

---

24. Hide . . . after: an old signal cry in the game of hide-and-seek.   **IV.iii. 4. distracted:** i.e., without power of forming logical judgments.   **6. scourge:** punishment.   **6. weigh'd:** taken into consideration. **9. Deliberate pause:** considered action.   **20–21. convocation . . . worms:** allusion to the Diet of Worms (1521).   **20. politic:** crafty.   **23. variable service:** a variety of dishes.

HAMLET: A man may fish with the worm that hath eat of a king, and eat of the fish   25
    that hath fed of that worm.

KING: What dost thou mean by this?

HAMLET: Nothing but to show you how a king may go a progress° through the
    guts of a beggar.

KING: Where is Polonius?   30

HAMLET: In heaven; send thither to see: if your messenger find him not there, seek
    him i' the other place yourself. But if indeed you find him not within this
    month, you shall nose him as you go up the stairs into the lobby.

KING (*to some* ATTENDANTS):   Go seek him there.

HAMLET: 'A will stay till you come.   (*Exeunt* ATTENDANTS.)   35

KING: Hamlet, this deed, for thine especial safety,—
    Which we do tender,° as we dearly grieve
    For that which thou hast done,—must send thee hence
    With fiery quickness: therefore prepare thyself;
    The bark is ready, and the wind at help,   40
    Th' associates tend, and everything is bent
    For England.

HAMLET: For England!

KING: Ay, Hamlet.

HAMLET: Good.

KING: So is it, if thou knew'st our purposes.

HAMLET: I see a cherub° that sees them. But, come; for England! Farewell, dear
    mother.   45

KING: Thy loving father, Hamlet.

HAMLET: My mother; father and mother is man and wife; man and wife is one
    flesh; and so, my mother. Come, for England!   (*Exit.*)

KING: Follow him at foot°; tempt him with speed aboard;
    Delay it not; I'll have him hence to-night: 50
    Away! for every thing is seal'd and done
    That else leans on th' affair: pray you, make haste.

    (*Exeunt all but the* KING.)

    And, England, if my love thou hold'st at aught—
    As my great power thereof may give thee sense,
    Since yet thy cicatrice° looks raw and red   55
    After the Danish sword, and thy free awe°
    Pays homage to us—thou mayst not coldly set
    Our sovereign process; which imports at full,
    By letters congruing to that effect,
    The present death of Hamlet. Do it, England;   60
    For like the hectic° in my blood he rages,

---

28. progress: royal journey of state.   **37. tender:** regard, hold dear.   **44. cherub:** cherubim are angels of knowledge.   **49. at foot:** close behind, at heel.   **55. cicatrice:** scar.   **56. free awe:** voluntary show of respect.   **61. hectic:** fever.

And thou must cure me; till I know 'tis done,
Howe'er my haps,° my joys were ne'er begun. *(Exit.)*

SCENE IV

(A plain in Denmark.)

(Enter FORTINBRAS *with his Army over the stage.)*

FORTINBRAS: Go, captain, from me greet the Danish king;
Tell him that, by his license,° Fortinbras
Craves the conveyance° of a promis'd march
Over his kingdom. You know the rendezvous.
If that his majesty would aught with us,   5
We shall express our duty in his eye°;
And let him know so.
CAPTAIN: I will do't, my lord.
FORTINBRAS: Go softly° on.   *(Exeunt all but* CAPTAIN.*)*

(Enter HAMLET, ROSENCRANTZ, [GUILDENSTERN,] *&c.)*

HAMLET: Good sir, whose powers are these?   10
CAPTAIN: They are of Norway, sir.
HAMLET: How purpos'd, sir, I pray you?
CAPTAIN: Against some part of Poland.
HAMLET: Who commands them, sir?
CAPTAIN: The nephew to old Norway, Fortinbras.   15
HAMLET: Goes it against the main° of Poland, sir,
Or for some frontier?
CAPTAIN: Truly to speak, and with no addition,
We go to gain a little patch of ground
That hath in it no profit but the name.   20
To pay five ducats, five, I would not farm it°;
Nor will it yield to Norway or the Pole
A ranker rate, should it be sold in fee.°
HAMLET: Why, then the Polack never will defend it.
CAPTAIN: Yes, it is already garrison'd.   25
HAMLET: Two thousand souls and twenty thousand ducats
Will not debate the question of this straw°;
This is th'imposthume° of much wealth and peace,
That inward breaks, and shows no cause without
Why the man dies. I humbly thank you, sir.   30

63. haps: fortunes.   **IV.iv. 2. license:** leave.   **3. conveyance:** escort, convey.   **6. in his eye:** in his presence.   **9. softly:** slowly.   **16. main:** country itself.   **21. farm it:** take a lease of it.   **23. fee:** fee simple.   **27. debate . . . straw:** settle this trifling matter.   **28. imposthume:** purulent abscess or swelling.

CAPTAIN: God be wi' you, sir.   (*Exit.*)
ROSENCRANTZ: Will 't please you go, my lord?
HAMLET: I'll be with you straight. Go a little before.
                                           (*Exeunt all except* HAMLET.)

How all occasions° do inform against° me,
And spur my dull revenge! What is a man,
If his chief good and market of his time°   35
Be but to sleep and feed? a beast, no more.
Sure, he that made us with such large discourse,
Looking before and after, gave us not
That capability and god-like reason
To fust° in us unus'd. Now, whether it be   40
Bestial oblivion, or some craven scruple
Of thinking too precisely on th' event,
A thought which, quarter'd, hath but one part wisdom
And ever three parts coward, I do not know
Why yet I live to say "This thing's to do";   45
Sith I have cause and will and strength and means
To do 't. Examples gross as earth exhort me:
Witness this army of such mass and charge
Led by a delicate and tender prince,
Whose spirit with divine ambition puff'd   50
Makes mouths at the invisible event,
Exposing what is mortal and unsure
To all that fortune, death and danger dare,
Even for an egg-shell. Rightly to be great
Is not to stir without great argument,   55
But greatly to find quarrel in a straw
When honour's at the stake. How stand I then,
That have a father kill'd, a mother stain'd,
Excitements of° my reason and my blood,
And let all sleep? while, to my shame, I see   60
The imminent death of twenty thousand men,
That, for a fantasy and trick° of fame,
Go to their graves like beds, fight for a plot°
Whereon the numbers cannot try the cause,
Which is not tomb enough and continent   65
To hide the slain? O, from this time forth,
My thoughts be bloody, or be nothing worth!   (*Exit.*)

---

33. occasions: incidents, events.   **33. inform against:** generally defined as "show," "betray" (i.e., his tardiness); more probably *inform* means "take shape," as in *Macbeth*, II.i.48.   **35. market of his time:** the best use he makes of his time, or, that for which he sells his time.   **40. fust:** grow moldy.   **59. Excitements of:** incentives to.   **62. trick:** toy, trifle,   **63. plot:** i.e., of ground.

Scene V

(*Elsinore. A room in the castle.*)

(*Enter* Horatio, [Queen] Gertrude, *and a* Gentleman.)

QUEEN: I will not speak with her.
GENTLEMAN: She is importunate, indeed distract;
  Her mood will needs be pitied.
QUEEN: What would she have?
GENTLEMAN: She speaks much of her father; says she hears
  There's tricks° i' th' world; and hems, and beats her heart°;   5
  Spurns enviously at straws°; speaks things in doubt,
  That carry but half sense: her speech is nothing,
  Yet the unshaped° use of it doth move
  The hearers to collection°; they yawn° at it,
  And botch° the words up fit to their own thoughts;   10
  Which, as her winks, and nods, and gestures yield° them,
  Indeed would make one think there might be thought,
  Though nothing sure, yet much unhappily.°
HORATIO: 'Twere good she were spoken with: for she may strew
  Dangerous conjectures in ill-breeding minds.°   15
QUEEN: Let her come in.   (*Exit* Gentleman.)
  (*Aside.*) To my sick soul, as sin's true nature is,
  Each toy seems prologue to some great amiss°:
  So full of artless jealousy is guilt,
  It spills itself in fearing to be spilt.°   20

(*Enter* Ophelia [*distracted*].)

OPHELIA: Where is the beauteous majesty of Denmark?
QUEEN: How now, Ophelia!
OPHELIA (*she sings*): How should I your true love know
    From another one?
  By his cockle hat° and staff,   25
    And his sandal shoon.°
QUEEN: Alas, sweet lady, what imports this song?

IV.v. **5. tricks:** deceptions. **5. heart:** i.e., breast. **6. Spurns . . . straws:** kicks spitefully at small objects in her path. **8. unshaped:** unformed, artless. **9. collection:** inference, a guess at some sort of meaning. **9. yawn:** wonder. **10. botch:** patch. **11. yield:** deliver, bring forth (her words). **13. much unhappily:** expressive of much unhappiness. **15. ill-breeding minds:** minds bent on mischief. **18. great amiss:** calamity, disaster. **19–20. So . . . split:** guilt is so full of suspicion that it unskillfully betrays itself in fearing to be betrayed. **25. cockle hat:** hat with cockleshell stuck in it as a sign that the wearer has been a pilgrim to the shrine of St. James of Compostella; the pilgrim's garb was a conventional disguise for lovers. **26. shoon:** shoes.

OPHELIA: Say you? nay, pray you mark.
   (*Song*) He is dead and gone, lady,   30
      He is dead and gone;
   At his head a grass-green turf,
      At his heels a stone.
   O, ho!
QUEEN: Nay, but, Ophelia—
OPHELIA: Pray you, mark   35
   (*Sings.*) White his shroud as the mountain snow,—

         (*Enter* KING.)

QUEEN: Alas, look here, my lord.
OPHELIA (*Song*):   Larded° all with flowers;
   Which bewept to the grave did not go
      With true-love showers.   40
KING: How do you, pretty lady?
OPHELIA: Well, God 'ild° you! They say the owl° was a baker's daughter. Lord, we
   know what we are, but know not what we may be. God be at your table!
KING: Conceit upon her father.
OPHELIA: Pray let's have no words of this; but when they ask you what it means, say   45
   you this:
   (*Song*) To-morrow is Saint Valentine's day.
      All in the morning betime,
   And I a maid at your window,
      To be your Valentine.°   50
   Then up he rose, and donn'd his clothes,
      And dupp'd° the chamber-door;
   Let in the maid, that out a maid
      Never departed more.
KING: Pretty Ophelia!   55
OPHELIA: Indeed, la, without an oath, I'll make an end on 't:
   (*Sings.*) By Gis° and by Saint Charity,
      Alack, and fie for shame!
   Young men will do 't, if they come to 't;
      By cock,° they are to blame.   60
   Quoth she, before you tumbled me,
      You promis'd me to wed.
   So would I ha' done, by yonder sun,
      An thou hadst not come to my bed.
KING: How long hath she been thus?   65

---

38. Larded: decorated.   **42. God 'ild:** god yield or reward.   **42. owl:** reference to a monkish legend
that a baker's daughter was turned into an owl for refusing bread to the Savior.   **50. Valentine:** this
song alludes to the belief that the first girl seen by a man on the morning of this day was his valentine or
true love.   **52. dupp'd:** opened.   **57. Gis:** Jesus.   **60. cock:** perversion of "God" in oaths.

OPHELIA: I hope all will be well. We must be patient: but I cannot choose but weep, to think they would lay him i' the cold ground. My brother shall know of it: and so I thank you for your good counsel. Come, my coach! Good night, ladies; good night, sweet ladies; good night, good night.   (*Exit.*)

KING: Follow her close; give her good watch, I pray you.   (*Exit* HORATIO.) 70
O, this is the poison of deep grief; it springs
All from her father's death. O Gertrude, Gertrude,
When sorrows come, they come not single spies,
But in battalions. First, her father slain:
Next your son gone; and he most violent author 75
Of his own just remove: the people muddied,
Thick and unwholesome in their thoughts and whispers,
For good Polonius' death; and we have done but greenly,°
In hugger-mugger° to inter him; poor Ophelia
Divided from herself and her fair judgement, 80
Without the which we are pictures, or mere beasts:
Last, and as much containing as all these,
Her brother is in secret come from France,
Feeds on his wonder, keeps himself in clouds,°
And wants not buzzers° to infect his ear 85
With pestilent speeches of his father's death;
Wherein necessity, of matter beggar'd,°
Will nothing stick° our person to arraign
In ear and ear.° O my dear Gertrude, this,
Like to a murd'ring-piece,° in many places 90
Gives me superfluous death. (*A noise within.*)

QUEEN: Alack, what noise is this?

KING: Where are my Switzers?° Let them guard the door.

(*Enter a* MESSENGER.)

What is the matter?

MESSENGER: Save yourself, my lord:
The ocean, overpeering° of his list,°
Eats not the flats with more impiteous haste 95
Than young Laertes, in a riotous head,
O'erbears your officers. The rabble call him lord;
And, as the world were now but to begin,
Antiquity forgot, custom not known,
The ratifiers and props of every word,° 100

---

78. greenly: foolishly. **79. hugger-mugger:** secret haste. **84. in clouds:** invisible. **85. buzzers:** gossipers. **87. of matter beggar'd:** unprovided with facts. **88. nothing stick:** not hesitate. **89. In ear and ear:** in everybody's ears. **90. murd'ring-piece:** small cannon or mortar; suggestion of numerous missiles fired. **92. Switzers:** Swiss guards, mercenaries. **94. overpeering:** overflowing. **94. list:** shore. **100. word:** promise.

They cry "Choose we: Laertes shall be king":
Caps, hands, and tongues, applaud it to the clouds:
"Laertes shall be king, Laertes king!" (*A noise within.*)

QUEEN: How cheerfully on the false trail they cry!
　　O, this is counter,° you false Danish dogs!　　　　　　　　　105

KING: The doors are broke.

(*Enter* LAERTES *with others.*)

LAERTES: Where is this king? Sirs, stand you all without.

DANES: No, let's come in.

LAERTES:　　　　　　　　　I pray you, give me leave.

DANES: We will, we will.　　　　　　(*They retire without the door.*)

LAERTES: I thank you: keep the door. O thou vile king,　　　110
　　Give me my father!

QUEEN:　　　　　　　Calmly, good Laertes.

LAERTES: That drop of blood that's calm proclaims me bastard,
　　Cries cuckold to my father, brands the harlot
　　Even here, between the chaste unsmirched brow
　　Of my true mother.　　　　　　　　　　　　　　　115

KING: What is the cause, Laertes,
　　That thy rebellion looks so giant-like?
　　Let him go, Gertrude; do not fear our person:
　　There's such divinity doth hedge a king,
　　That treason can but peep to° what it would,°　　　　　120
　　Acts little of his will. Tell me, Laertes,
　　Why thou art thus incens'd. Let him go, Gertrude.
　　Speak, man.

LAERTES: Where is my father?

KING:　　　　　　　　Dead.

QUEEN:　　　　　　　　　　But not by him.

KING: Let him demand his fill.　　　　　　　　　　　125

LAERTES: How came he dead? I'll not be juggled with:
　　To hell, allegiance! vows, to the blackest devil!
　　Conscience and grace, to the profoundest pit!
　　I dare damnation. To this point I stand,
　　That both the worlds I give to negligence,°　　　　　130
　　Let come what comes; only I'll be reveng'd
　　Most throughly° for my father.

KING:　　　　　　　　Who shall stay you?

LAERTES: My will,° not all the world's:

---

105. counter: a hunting term meaning to follow the trail in a direction opposite to that which the game has taken.　**120. peep to:** i.e., look at from afar off.　**120. would:** wishes to do.　**130. give to negligence:** he despises both the here and the hereafter.　**132. throughly:** thoroughly.　**133. My will:** he will not be stopped except by his own will.

And for my means, I'll husband them so well,
They shall go far with little.
KING: Good Laertes,   135
If you desire to know the certainty
Of your dear father, is 't writ in your revenge,
That, swoopstake,° you will draw both friend and foe,
Winner and loser?
LAERTES: None but his enemies.
KING: Will you know them then?   140
LAERTES: To his good friends thus wide I'll ope my arms;
And like the kind life-rend'ring pelican,°
Repast° them with my blood.
KING: Why, now you speak
Like a good child and a true gentleman.
That I am guiltless of your father's death,   145
And am most sensibly in grief for it,
It shall as level to your judgment 'pear
As day does to your eye.

       (*A noise within: "Let her come in."*)

LAERTES: How now! what noise is that?

       (*Enter* OPHELIA.)

O heat,° dry up my brains! tears seven times salt,   150
Burn out the sense and virtue of mine eye!
By heaven, thy madness shall be paid with weight,
Till our scale turn the beam. O rose of May!
Dear maid, kind sister, sweet Ophelia!
O heavens! is 't possible, a young maid's wits   155
Should be as mortal as an old man's life?
Nature is fine in love, and where 'tis fine,
It sends some precious instance of itself
After the thing it loves.
OPHELIA (*Song*):   They bore him barefac'd on the bier;   160
Hey non nonny, nonny, hey nonny;
And in his grave rain'd many a tear:—
Fare you well, my dove!
LAERTES: Hadst thou thy wits, and didst persuade revenge,
It could not move thus.   165
OPHELIA (*sings*):   You must sing a-down a-down,
An you call him a-down-a.

---

138. swoopstake: literally, drawing the whole stake at once, i.e., indiscriminately.   **142. pelican:** reference to the belief that the pelican feeds its young with its own blood.   **143. Repast:** feed.   **150. heat:** probably the heat generated by the passion of grief.

O, how the wheel° becomes it! It is the false steward,° that stole his master's
daughter.

LAERTES: This nothing's more than matter.   170

OPHELIA: There's rosemary,° that's for remembrance; pray you, love, remember:
and there is pansies,° that's for thoughts.

LAERTES: A document° in madness, thoughts and remembrance fitted.

OPHELIA: There's fennel° for you, and columbines°: there's rue° for you; and here's
some for me: we may call it herb of grace o' Sundays: O, you must wear your   175
rue with a difference. There's a daisy°: I would give you some violets,° but they
withered all when my father died: they say 'a made a good end,—
(*Sings.*) For bonny sweet Robin is all my joy.°

LAERTES: Thought° and affliction, passion, hell itself,
She turns to favour and to prettiness.   180

OPHELIA (*Song*):   And will 'a not come again?°
And will 'a not come again?
    No, no, he is dead:
    Go to thy death-bed:
He never will come again.   185
His beard was as white as snow,
All flaxen was his poll°:
    He is gone, he is gone,
    And we cast away° moan:
God ha' mercy on his soul!   190
And of all Christian souls, I pray God. God be wi' you.   (*Exit.*)

LAERTES: Do you see this, O God?

KING: Laertes, I must commune with your grief,
Or you deny me right.° Go but apart,
Make choice of whom your wisest friends you will,   195
And they shall hear and judge 'twixt you and me:
If by direct or by collateral° hand
They find us touch'd,° we will our kingdom give,
Our crown, our life, and all that we call ours,
To you in satisfaction; but if not,   200
Be you content to lend your patience to us,

---

168. wheel: spinning wheel as accompaniment to the song refrain.   **168–69. false steward . . . daughter:** the story is unknown.   **171. rosemary:** used as a symbol of remembrance both at weddings and at
funerals.   **172. pansies:** emblems of love and courtship. Cf. French *pensées*.   **173. document:** piece of
instruction or lesson.   **174. fennel:** emblem of flattery.   **174. columbines:** emblem of unchastity (?)
or ingratitude (?).   **174. rue:** emblem of repentance. It was usually mingled with holy water and then
known as herb of grace. Ophelia is probably playing on the two meanings of rue "repentant" and "even
for Ruth (pity)"; the former signification is for the queen, the latter for herself.   **176. daisy:** emblem of
dissembling, faithlessness.   **176. violets:** emblems of faithfulness.   **178. For . . . joy:** probably a line
from a Robin Hood ballad.   **179. Thought:** melancholy thought.   **181. And . . . again:** this song
appeared in the songbooks as "The Merry Milkmaids' Dumps."   **187. poll:** head.   **189. cast away:**
shipwrecked.   **194. right:** my rights.   **197. collateral:** indirect.   **198. touch'd:** implicated.

And we shall jointly labour with your soul
To give it due content.
LAERTES: Let this be so;
His means of death, his obscure funeral—
No trophy, sword, nor hatchment° o'er his bones,   205
No noble rite nor formal ostentation—
Cry to be heard, as 'twere from heaven to earth,
That I must call 't in question.
KING: So you shall;
And where th' offence is let the great axe fall.
I pray you, go with me.   (*Exeunt.*) 210

SCENE VI

(*Another room in the castle.*)

(*Enter* HORATIO *and others.*)

HORATIO: What are they that would speak with me?
GENTLEMAN: Sea-faring men, sir: they say they have letters for you.
HORATIO: Let them come in.   (*Exit* GENTLEMAN.)
I do not know from what part of the world
I should be greeted, if not from lord Hamlet.   5

(*Enter* SAILORS.)

FIRST SAILOR: God bless you, sir.
HORATIO: Let him bless thee too.
FIRST SAILOR: 'A shall sir, an 't please him. There's a letter for you, sir; it comes
from the ambassador that was bound for England; if your name be Horatio, as
I am let to know it is.   10
HORATIO (*reads*):   "Horatio, when thou shalt have overlooked this, give these fellows some means° to the king: they have letters for him. Ere we were two days
old at sea, a pirate of very warlike appointment gave us chase. Finding ourselves too slow of sail, we put on a compelled valour, and in the grapple I
boarded them: on the instant they got clear of our ship; so I alone became their 15
prisoner. They have dealt with me like thieves of mercy°: but they knew what
they did; I am to do a good turn for them. Let the king have the letters I have
sent; and repair thou to me with as much speed as thou wouldst fly death. I
have words to speak in thine ear will make thee dumb; yet are they much too
light for the bore° of the matter. These good fellows will bring thee where I 20
am. Rosencrantz and Guildenstern hold their course for England: of them I
have much to tell thee. Farewell.
"He that thou knowest thine, HAMLET."

---

205. hatchment: tablet displaying the armorial bearings of a deceased person. **IV.vi. 12. means:**
means of access. **16. thieves of mercy:** merciful thieves. **20. bore:** caliber, importance.

Come, I will give you way for these your letters;
And do 't the speedier, that you may direct me   25
To him from whom you brought them.   (*Exeunt.*)

Scene VII

(*Another room in the castle.*)

(*Enter* King *and* Laertes.)

King: Now must your conscience° my acquittance seal,
And you must put me in your heart for friend,
Sith you have heard, and with a knowing ear,
That he which hath your noble father slain
Pursued my life.
Laertes: It well appears: but tell me   5
Why you proceeded not against these feats,
So criminal and so capital° in nature,
As by your safety, wisdom, all things else,
You mainly° were stirr'd up.
King: O, for two special reasons;
Which may to you, perhaps, seem much unsinew'd,°   10
But yet to me th' are strong. The queen his mother
Lives almost by his looks; and for myself—
My virtue or my plague, be it either which—
She's so conjunctive° to my life and soul,
That, as the star moves not but in his sphere,°   15
I could not but by her. The other motive,
Why to a public count° I might not go,
Is the great love the general gender° bear him;
Who, dipping all his faults in their affection,
Would, like the spring° that turneth wood to stone,   20
Convert his gyves° to graces; so that my arrows,
Too slightly timber'd° for so loud° a wind,
Would have reverted to my bow again,
And not where I had aim'd them.
Laertes: And so have I a noble father lost;   25
A sister driven into desp'rate terms,°
Whose worth, if praises may go back° again,

IV.vii. 1. conscience: knowledge that this is true.   **7. capital:** punishable by death.   **9. mainly:** greatly.
10. unsinew'd: weak.   **14. conjunctive:** conformable (the next line suggesting planetary conjunction).
15. sphere: the hollow sphere in which, according to Ptolemaic astronomy, the planets were supposed
to move.   **17. count:** account, reckoning.   **18. general gender:** common people.   **20. spring:** i.e.,
one heavily charged with lime.   **21. gyves:** fetters; here, faults, or possibly, punishments inflicted (on
him).   **22. slightly timber'd:** light.   **22. loud:** strong.   **26. terms:** state, condition.   **27. go back:**
i.e., to Ophelia's former virtues.

Stood challenger on mount° of all the age°
For her perfections: but my revenge will come.
KING: Break not your sleeps for that: you must not think   30
That we are made of stuff so flat and dull
That we can let our beard be shook with danger
And think it pastime. You shortly shall hear more:
I lov'd your father, and we love ourself;
And that, I hope, will teach you to imagine—   35

(*Enter a* MESSENGER *with letters.*)

How now! what news?
MESSENGER: Letters, my lord, from Hamlet:
These to your majesty; this to the queen.°
KING: From Hamlet! who brought them?
MESSENGER: Sailors, my lord, they say; I saw them not:
They were given me by Claudio°; he receiv'd them   40
Of him that brought them.
KING: Laertes, you shall hear them.
Leave us.   (*Exit* MESSENGER.)
(*Reads:*) "High and mighty, You shall know I am set naked° on your kingdom. To-
morrow shall I beg leave to see your kingly eyes: when I shall, first asking your
pardon thereunto, recount the occasion of my sudden and more strange return.   45
          "HAMLET."

What should this mean? Are all the rest come back?
Or is it some abuse, and no such thing?
LAERTES: Know you the hand?
KING: 'Tis Hamlet's character. "Naked!"
And in a postscript here, he says "alone."   50
Can you devise° me?
LAERTES: I'm lost in it, my lord. But let him come;
It warms the very sickness in my heart,
That I shall live and tell him to his teeth,
"Thus didst thou."   55
KING: If it be so, Laertes—
As how should it be so? how otherwise?°—
Will you be rul'd by me?
LAERTES: Ay, my lord;
So you will not o'errule me to a peace.
KING: To thine own peace. If he be now return'd,

---

28. on mount: set up on high, mounted (on horseback).   **28. of all the age:** qualifies *challenger* and not
mount.   **37. to the queen:** one hears no more of the letter to the queen.   **40. Claudio:** this character
does not appear in the play.   **43. naked:** unprovided (with retinue).   **51. devise:** explain to.   **56. As . . .
otherwise?** how can this (Hamlet's return) be true? (yet) how otherwise than true (since we have the evidence of his letter)? Some editors read "How should it not be so," etc., making the words refer to
Laertes's desire to meet with Hamlet.

As checking at° his voyage, and that he means 60
No more to undertake it, I will work him
To an exploit, now ripe in my device,
Under the which he shall not choose but fall:
And for his death no wind of blame shall breathe,
But even his mother shall uncharge the practice° 65
And call it accident.

LAERTES: My lord, I will be rul'd;
The rather, if you could devise it so
That I might be the organ.°

KING: It falls right.
You have been talk'd of since your travel much,
And that in Hamlet's hearing, for a quality 70
Wherein, they say, you shine: your sum of parts
Did not together pluck such envy from him
As did that one, and that, in my regard,
Of the unworthiest siege.°

LAERTES: What part is that, my lord?

KING: A very riband in the cap of youth, 75
Yet needful too; for youth no less becomes
The light and careless livery that it wears
Than settled age his sables° and his weeds,
Importing health and graveness. Two months since,
Here was a gentleman of Normandy:— 80
I have seen myself, and serv'd against, the French,
And they can well° on horseback: but this gallant
Had witchcraft in 't; he grew unto his seat;
And to such wondrous doing brought his horse,
As had he been incorps'd and demi-natur'd° 85
With the brave beast: so far he topp'd° my thought,
That I, in forgery° of shapes and tricks,
Come short of what he did.

LAERTES: A Norman was 't?

KING: A Norman.

LAERTES: Upon my life, Lamord.° 90

KING: The very same.

LAERTES: I know him well: he is the brooch indeed
And gem of all the nation.

KING: He made confession° of you,
And gave you such a masterly report 95

---

60. checking at: used in falconry of a hawk's leaving the quarry to fly at a chance bird; turn aside.
65. uncharge the practice: acquit the stratagem of being a plot. **68. organ:** agent, instrument.
74. siege: rank. **78. sables:** rich garments. **82. can well:** are skilled. **85. incorps'd and demi-natur'd:** of one body and nearly of one nature (like the centaur). **86. topp'd:** surpassed. **87. forgery:** invention. **90. Lamord:** this refers possibly to Pietro Monte, instructor to Louis XII's master of the horse. **94. confession:** grudging admission of superiority.

For art and exercise° in your defence°
And for your rapier most especial,
That he cried out, 'twould be a sight indeed,
If one could match you: the scrimers° of their nation,
He swore, had neither motion, guard, nor eye,   100
If you oppos'd them. Sir, this report of his
Did Hamlet so envenom with his envy
That he could nothing do but wish and beg
Your sudden coming o'er, to play° with you.
Now, out of this,—
LAERTES: What out of this, my lord?   105
KING: Laertes, was your father dear to you?
  Or are you like the painting of a sorrow,
  A face without a heart?
LAERTES: Why ask you this?
KING: Not that I think you did not love your father;
  But that I know love is begun by time;   110
  And that I see, in passages of proof,°
  Time qualifies the spark and fire of it.
  There lives within the very flame of love
  A kind of wick or snuff that will abate it;
  And nothing is at a like goodness still;   115
  For goodness, growing to a plurisy,°
  Dies in his own too much°: that we would do,
  We should do when we would; for this "would" changes
  And hath abatements° and delays as many
  As there are tongues, are hands, are accidents°;   120
  And then this "should" is like a spendthrift° sigh,
  That hurts by easing. But, to the quick o' th' ulcer°:—
  Hamlet comes back: what would you undertake,
  To show yourself your father's son in deed
  More than in words?   125
LAERTES: To cut his throat i' th' church.
KING: No place, indeed, should murder sanctuarize°;
  Revenge should have no bounds. But, good Laertes,
  Will you do this, keep close within your chamber.
  Hamlet return'd shall know you are come home: 130
  We'll put on those shall praise your excellence
  And set a double varnish on the fame

---

96. art and exercise: skillful exercise. **96. defence:** science of defense in sword practice. **99. scrimers:** fencers. **104. play:** fence. **111. passages of proof:** proved instances. **116. plurisy:** excess, plethora. **117. in his own too much:** of its own excess. **119. abatements:** diminutions. **120. accidents:** occurrences, incidents. **121. spendthrift:** an allusion to the belief that each sigh cost the heart a drop of blood. **122. quick o' th' ulcer:** heart of the difficulty. **127. sanctuarize:** protect from punishment; allusion to the right of sanctuary with which certain religious places were invested.

The Frenchman gave you, bring you in fine together
And wager on your heads: he, being remiss,
Most generous and free from all contriving,   135
Will not peruse the foils; so that, with ease,
Or with a little shuffling, you may choose
A sword unbated,° and in a pass of practice°
Requite him for your father.
LAERTES: I will do 't:
And, for that purpose, I'll anoint my sword.   140
I bought an unction of a mountebank,°
So mortal that, but dip a knife in it,
Where it draws blood no cataplasm° so rare,
Collected from all simples° that have virtue
Under the moon,° can save the thing from death   145
That is but scratch'd withal: I'll touch my point
With this contagion, that, if I gall° him slightly,
It may be death.
KING: Let's further think of this;
Weigh what convenience both of time and means
May fit us to our shape°: if this should fail,   150
And that our drift look through our bad performance,°
'Twere better not assay'd: therefore this project
Should have a back or second, that might hold,
If this should blast in proof.° Soft! let me see:
We'll make a solemn wager on your cunnings°:   155
I ha 't:
When in your motion you are hot and dry—
As make your bouts more violent to that end—
And that he calls for drink, I'll have prepar'd him
A chalice° for the nonce, whereon but sipping,   160
If he by chance escape your venom'd stuck,°
Our purpose may hold there. But stay, what noise?

(*Enter* QUEEN.)

QUEEN: One woe doth tread upon another's heel,
So fast they follow: your sister's drown'd, Laertes.
LAERTES: Drown'd! O, where?   165
QUEEN: There is a willow° grows askant° the brook,
That shows his hoar° leaves in the glassy stream;

---

138. **unbated:** not blunted, having no button.   138. **pass of practice:** treacherous thrust.   141. **mountebank:** quack doctor.   143. **cataplasm:** plaster or poultice.   144. **simples:** herbs.   145. **Under the moon:** i.e., when collected by moonlight to add to their medicinal value.   147. **gall:** graze, wound.
150. **shape:** part we propose to act.   151. **drift . . . performance:** intention be disclosed by our bungling.   154. **blast in proof:** burst in the test (like a cannon).   155. **cunnings:** skills.   160. **chalice:** cup.   161. **stuck:** thrust (from *stoccado*).   166. **willow:** for its significance of forsaken love.
166. **askant:** aslant.   167. **hoar:** white (i.e., on the underside).

There with fantastic garlands did she make
Of crow-flowers,° nettles, daisies, and long purples°
That liberal° shepherds give a grosser name, 170
But our cold maids do dead men's fingers call them:
There, on the pendent boughs her crownet° weeds
Clamb'ring to hang, an envious sliver° broke;
When down her weedy° trophies and herself
Fell in the weeping brook. Her clothes spread wide; 175
And, mermaid-like, awhile they bore her up:
Which time she chanted snatches of old lauds°;
As one incapable° of her own distress,
Or like a creature native and indued°
Upon that element: but long it could not be 180
Till that her garments, heavy with their drink,
Pull'd the poor wretch from her melodious lay
To muddy death.
LAERTES: Alas, then, she is drown'd?
QUEEN: Drown'd, drown'd.
LAERTES: Too much of water hast thou, poor Ophelia, 185
And therefore I forbid my tears: but yet
It is our trick°; nature her custom holds,
Let shame say what it will: when these are gone,
The woman will be out.° Adieu, my lord:
I have a speech of fire, that fain would blaze, 190
But that this folly drowns it.   (*Exit.*)
KING: Let's follow, Gertrude:
How much I had to do to calm his rage!
Now fear I this will give it start again;
Therefore let's follow.   (*Exeunt.*)

ACT V

SCENE I

(*A churchyard.*)

(*Enter two* CLOWNS° [*with spades, &c*].)

FIRST CLOWN: Is she to be buried in Christian burial when she wilfully seeks her
   own salvation?

---

169. crow-flowers: buttercups.   **169. long purples:** early purple orchids.   **170. liberal:** probably, free-spoken.   **172. crownet:** coronet; made into a chaplet.   **173. sliver:** branch.   **174. weedy:** i.e., of plants.   **177. lauds:** hymns.   **178. incapable:** lacking capacity to apprehend.   **179. indued:** endowed with qualities fitting her for living in water.   **187. trick:** way.   **188–189. when . . . out:** when my tears are all shed, the woman in me will be satisfied.   **Vi.i. s.d. clowns:** the word *clown* was used to denote peasants as well as humorous characters; here applied to the rustic type of clown.

SECOND CLOWN: I tell thee she is; therefore make her grave straight°: the crowner°
hath sat on her, and finds it Christian burial.

FIRST CLOWN: How can that be, unless she drowned herself in her own defence?   5

SECOND CLOWN: Why, 'tis found so.

FIRST CLOWN: It must be "se offendendo"°; it cannot be else. For here lies the
point: if I drown myself wittingly,° it argues an act: and an act hath three
branches°; it is, to act, to do, and to perform: argal,° she drowned herself wittingly.   10

SECOND CLOWN: Nay, but hear you, goodman delver,°—

FIRST CLOWN: Give me leave. Here lies the water; good; here stands the man;
good: if the man go to this water, and drown himself, it is, will he, nill he, he
goes,—mark you that; but if the water come to him and drown him, he drowns
not himself: argal, he that is not guilty of his own death shortens not his own   15
life.

SECOND CLOWN: But is this law?

FIRST CLOWN: Ay, marry, is 't; crowner's quest° law.

SECOND CLOWN: Will you ha' the truth on 't? If this had not been a gentle-woman,
she should have been buried out o' Christian burial.   20

FIRST CLOWN: Why, there thou say'st°: and the more pity that great folk should
have countenance° in this world to drown or hang themselves, more than their
even° Christian. Come, my spade. There is no ancient gentlemen but gardeners, ditchers, and grave-makers: they hold up° Adam's profession.

SECOND CLOWN: Was he a gentleman?   25

FIRST CLOWN: 'A was the first that ever bore arms.

SECOND CLOWN: Why, he had none.

FIRST CLOWN: What, art a heathen? How dost thou understand the Scripture?
The Scripture says "Adam digged": could he dig without arms? I'll put
another question to thee: if thou answerest me not to the purpose, confess thy-   30
self°—

SECOND CLOWN: Go to.°

FIRST CLOWN: What is he that builds stronger than either the mason, the shipwright, or the carpenter?

SECOND CLOWN: The gallows-maker; for that frame outlives a thousand tenants.   35

FIRST CLOWN: I like thy wit well, in good faith: the gallows does well; but how does
it well? it does well to those that do ill: now thou dost ill to say the gallows is
built stronger than the church: argal, the gallows may do well to thee. To 't
again, come.

SECOND CLOWN: Who builds stronger than a mason, a shipwright, or a carpenter?   40

---

3. straight: straightway, immediately; some interpret "from east to west in a direct line, parallel with the
church." **3. crowner:** coroner. **7. "se offendendo"** for se defendendo, term used in verdicts of justifiable homicide. **8. wittingly:** intentionally. **8–9. three branches:** parody of legal phraseology.
9. argal: corruption of ergo, therefore. **11. delver:** digger. **18. quest:** inquest. **21. there thou
say'st:** that's right. **22. countenance:** privilege. **23. even:** fellow. **24. hold up:** maintain, continue.
30–31. confess thyself: "and be hanged" completes the proverb. **32. Go to:** perhaps, "begin," or
some other form of concession.

FIRST CLOWN: Ay, tell me that, and unyoke.°

SECOND CLOWN: Marry, now I can tell.

FIRST CLOWN: To 't.

SECOND CLOWN: Mass,° I cannot tell.

(*Enter* HAMLET *and* HORATIO [*at a distance*].)

FIRST CLOWN: Cudgel thy brains no more about it, for your dull ass will not mend   45
his pace with beating; and, when you are asked this question next, say "a grave-
maker": the houses he makes lasts till doomsday. Go, get thee in, and fetch me
a stoup° of liquor.   (*Exit* SECOND CLOWN.)

(*Song.* [*He digs.*])

In youth, when I did love, did love,
    Methought it was very sweet,   50
To contract—O—the time, for—a—my behove,°
    O, methought, there—a—was nothing—a—meet.

HAMLET: Has this fellow no feeling of his business, that 'a sings at gravemaking?

HORATIO: Custom hath made it in him a property of easiness.°

HAMLET: 'Tis e'en so: the hand of little employment hath the daintier sense.   55

FIRST CLOWN (*Song.*):   But age, with his stealing steps,
    Hath claw'd me in his clutch,
And hath shipped me into the land
    As if I had never been such. (*Throws up a skull.*)

HAMLET: That skull had a tongue in it, and could sing once: how the knave jowls°   60
it to the ground, as if 'twere Cain's jaw-bone,° that did the first murder! This
might be the pate of a politician,° which this ass now o'er-reaches°; one that
would circumvent God, might it not?

HORATIO: It might, my lord.

HAMLET: Or of a courtier; which could say "Good morrow, sweet lord! How dost   65
thou, sweet lord?" This might be my lord such-a-one, that praised my lord
such-a-one's horse, when he meant to beg it; might it not?

HORATIO: Ay, my lord.

HAMLET: Why, e'en so: and now my Lady Worm's; chapless,° and knocked about
the mazzard° with a sexton's spade: here's fine revolution, an we had the trick   70
to see 't. Did these bones cost no more the breeding, but to play at loggats°
with 'em? mine ache to think on 't.

FIRST CLOWN (*Song.*):   A pick-axe, and a spade, a spade,
    For and° a shrouding sheet:

---

41. unyoke: after this great effort you may unharness the team of your wits.   **44. Mass:** by the Mass.
48. stoup: two-quart measure.   **51. behove:** benefit.   **54. property of easiness:** a peculiarity that now
is easy.   **60. jowls:** dashes.   **61. Cain's jaw-bone:** allusion to the old tradition that Cain slew Abel with
the jawbone of an ass.   **62. politician:** schemer, plotter.   **62. o'er-reaches:** quibble on the literal sense
and the sense "circumvent."   **69. chapless:** having no lower jaw.   **70. mazzard:** head.   **71. loggats:** a
game in which six sticks are thrown to lie as near as possible to a stake fixed in the ground, or block of
wood on a floor.   **74. For and:** and moreover.

O, a pit of clay for to be made   75
    For such a guest is meet. (*Throws up another skull.*)

HAMLET: There's another: why may not that be the skull of a lawyer? Where be his
quiddities° now, his quillities,° his cases, his tenures,° and his tricks? why does
he suffer this mad knave now to knock him about the sconce° with a dirty
shovel, and will not tell him of his action of battery? Hum! This fellow might   80
be in 's time a great buyer of land, with his statutes, his recognizances,° his
fines, his double vouchers,° his recoveries°: is this the fine° of his fines, and the
recovery of his recoveries, to have his fine pate full of fine dirt? will his vouchers vouch him no more of his purchases, and double ones too, than the length
and breadth of a pair of indentures?° The very conveyances of his lands will   85
scarcely lie in this box; and must the inheritor° himself have no more, ha?

HORATIO: Not a jot more, my lord.

HAMLET: Is not parchment made of sheep-skins?

HORATIO: Ay, my lord, and of calf-skins° too.

HAMLET: They are sheep and calves which seek out assurance in that.° I will speak   90
to this fellow. Whose grave's this, sirrah?

FIRST CLOWN: Mine, sir.
    (*Sings.*) O, a pit of clay for to be made
    For such a guest is meet.

HAMLET: I think it be thine, indeed; for thou liest in 't.   95

FIRST CLOWN: You lie out on 't, sir, and therefore 't is not yours: for my part, I do
not lie in 't, yet it is mine.

HAMLET: Thou dost lie in 't, to be in 't and say it is thine: 'tis for the dead, not for
the quick; therefore thou liest.

FIRST CLOWN: 'Tis a quick lie, sir; 'twill away again, from me to you.   100

HAMLET: What man dost thou dig it for?

FIRST CLOWN: For no man, sir.

HAMLET: What woman, then?

FIRST CLOWN: For none, neither,

HAMLET: Who is to be buried in 't?   105

FIRST CLOWN: One that was a woman, sir; but, rest her soul, she's dead.

HAMLET: How absolute° the knave is! we must speak by the card,° or equivoca-
tion° will undo us. By the Lord, Horatio, these three years I have taken note of
it, the age is grown so picked° that the toe of the peasant comes so near the

---

78. quiddities: subtleties, quibbles.   **78. quillities:** verbal niceties, subtle distinctions.   **78. tenures:**
the holding of a piece of property or office or the conditions or period of such holding.   **79. sconce:**
head.   **81. statutes, recognizances:** legal terms connected with the transfer of land.   **82. vouchers:**
persons called on to warrant a tenant's title.   **82. recoveries:** process for transfer of entailed estate.
82. fine: the four uses of this word are as follows: (1) end, (2) legal process, (3) elegant, (4) small.
85. indentures: conveyances or contracts.   **86. inheritor:** possessor, owner.   **89. calf-skins:** parchments.   **90. assurance in that:** safety in legal parchments.   **107. absolute:** positive, decided.   **107. by
the card:** with precision, i.e., by the mariner's card on which the points of the compass were marked.
107–8. equivocation: ambiguity in the use of terms.   **109. picked:** refined, fastidious.

heel of the courtier, he galls° his kibe.° How long hast thou been a grave- 110
maker?

FIRST CLOWN: Of all the day i' the year, I came to 't that day that our last king
Hamlet overcame Fortinbras.

HAMLET: How long is that since?

FIRST CLOWN: Cannot you tell that? every fool can tell that: it was the very day that 115
young Hamlet was born; he that is mad, and sent into England.

HAMLET: Ay, marry, why was he sent into England?

FIRST CLOWN: Why, because 'a was mad: 'a shall recover his wits there; or, if 'a do
not, 'tis no great matter there.

HAMLET: Why? 120

FIRST CLOWN: 'Twill not be seen in him there; there the men are as mad as he.

HAMLET: How came he mad?

FIRST CLOWN: Very strangely, they say.

HAMLET: How strangely?

FIRST CLOWN: Faith, e'en with losing his wits. 125

HAMLET: Upon what ground?

FIRST CLOWN: Why, here in Denmark: I have been sexton here, man and boy,
thirty years.°

HAMLET: How long will a man lie i' the earth ere he rot?

FIRST CLOWN: Faith, i' a be not rotten before 'a die—as we have many pocky° 130
corses now-a-days, that will scarce hold the laying in—'a will last you some
eight year or nine year: a tanner will last you nine year.

HAMLET: Why he more than another?

FIRST CLOWN: Why, sir, his hide is so tanned with his trade, that 'a will keep out
water a great while; and your water is a sore decayer of your whoreson dead 135
body. Here's a skull now hath lain you i' th' earth three and twenty years.

HAMLET: Whose was it?

FIRST CLOWN: A whoreson mad fellow's it was: whose do you think it was?

HAMLET: Nay, I know not.

FIRST CLOWN: A pestilence on him for a mad rogue! 'a poured a flagon of Rhenish 140
on my head once. This same skull, sir, was Yorick's skull, the king's jester.

HAMLET: This?

FIRST CLOWN: E'en that.

HAMLET: Let me see. (*Takes the skull.*) Alas, poor Yorick! I knew him, Horatio: a
fellow of infinite jest, of most excellent fancy: he hath borne me on his back a 145
thousand times; and now, how abhorred in my imagination it is! my gorge rises
at it. Here hung those lips that I have kissed I know not how oft. Where
be your gibes now? your gambols? your songs? your flashes of merriment, that
were wont to set the table on a roar? Not one now, to mock your own grinning? quite chap-fallen? Now get you to my lady's chamber, and tell her, let her 150

---

110. galls: chafes. **110. kibe:** chilblain. **128. thirty years:** this statement with that in line 116 shows
Hamlet's age to be thirty years. **130. pocky:** rotten, diseased.

paint an inch thick, to this favour she must come; make her laugh at that.
Prithee, Horatio, tell me one thing.

HORATIO: What's that, my lord?

HAMLET: Dost thou think Alexander looked o' this fashion i' the earth?

HORATIO: E'en so.   155

HAMLET: And smelt so? pah! (*Puts down the skull.*)

HORATIO: E'en so, my lord.

HAMLET: To what base uses we may return, Horatio! Why may not imagination
trace the noble dust of Alexander, till'a find it stopping a bunghole?

HORATIO: 'Twere to consider too curiously,° to consider so.   160

HAMLET: No, faith, not a jot; but to follow him thither with modesty enough, and
likelihood to lead it: as thus: Alexander died, Alexander was buried, Alexander
returneth into dust; the dust is earth; of earth we make loam°; and why of that
loam, whereto he was converted, might they not stop a beer-barrel?

    Imperious° Cæsar, dead and turn'd to clay,   165
    Might stop a hole to keep the wind away:
    O, that that earth, which kept the world in awe,
    Should patch a wall t'expel the winter's flaw!°

But soft! but soft awhile! here comes the king.

    (*Enter* KING, QUEEN, LAERTES, *and the Corpse of* [OPHELIA, *in procession, with*
    PRIEST, LORDS, *etc.*].)

The queen, the courtiers: who is this they follow?   170
And with such maimed rites? This doth betoken
The corse they follow did with desp'rate hand
Fordo° it° own life: 'twas of some estate.
Couch° we awhile, and mark.   (*Retiring with* HORATIO.)

LAERTES: What ceremony else?

HAMLET: That is Laertes,   175
A very noble youth: mark.

LAERTES: What ceremony else?

FIRST PRIEST: Her obsequies have been as far enlarg'd°
As we have warranty: her death was doubtful;
And, but that great command o'ersways the order,   180
She should in ground unsanctified have lodg'd
Till the last trumpet; for charitable prayers,
Shards,° flints and pebbles should be thrown on her:
Yet here she is allow'd her virgin crants,°
Her maiden strewments° and the bringing home   185

---

160. curiously: minutely.   **163. loam:** clay paste for brickmaking.   **165. Imperious:** imperial.
168. flaw: gust of wind.   **173. Fordo:** destroy.   **173. it:** its.   **174. Couch:** hide, lurk.   **178. enlarg'd:**
extended, referring to the fact that suicides are not given full burial rites.   **183. Shards:** broken bits of
pottery.   **184. crants:** garlands customarily hung upon the biers of unmarried women.   **185. strew-
ments:** traditional strewing of flowers.

Of bell and burial.°
LAERTES: Must there no more be done?
FIRST PRIEST: No more be done:
We should profane the service of the dead
To sing a requiem and such rest to her
As to peace-parted° souls.   190
LAERTES: Lay her i' th' earth:
And from her fair and unpolluted flesh
May violets spring! I tell thee, churlish priest,
A minist'ring angel shall my sister be,
When thou liest howling.°
HAMLET: What, the fair Ophelia!   195
QUEEN: Sweets to the sweet: farewell! (*Scattering flowers.*)
I hop'd thou shouldst have been my Hamlet's wife;
I thought thy bride-bed to have deck'd, sweet maid,
And not have strew'd thy grave.
LAERTES: O, treble woe
Fall ten times treble on that cursed head,   200
Whose wicked deed thy most ingenious sense°
Depriv'd thee of! Hold off the earth awhile,
Till I have caught her once more in mine arms: (*Leaps into the grave.*)
Now pile your dust upon the quick and dead,
Till of this flat a mountain you have made,   205
T' o'ertop old Pelion,° or the skyish head
Of blue Olympus.
HAMLET: (*Advancing.*) What is he whose grief
Bears such an emphasis? whose phrase of sorrow
Conjures the wand'ring stars,° and makes them stand
Like wonder-wounded hearers? This is I,   210
Hamlet the Dane. (*Leaps into the grave.*)
LAERTES: The devil take thy soul! (*Grappling with him.*)
HAMLET: Thou pray'st not well,
I prithee, take thy fingers from my throat;
For, though I am not splenitive° and rash,   215
Yet have I in me something dangerous,
Which let thy wisdom fear: hold off thy hand.
KING: Pluck them asunder.
QUEEN: Hamlet, Hamlet!
ALL: Gentlemen,—

185–86. bringing . . . burial: the laying to rest of the body, to the sound of the bell.   **190. peace-parted:** allusion to the text "Lord, now lettest thy servant depart in peace."   **195. howling:** i.e., in hell.
201. ingenious sense: mind endowed with finest qualities.   **206. Pelion:** Olympus, Pelion, and Ossa are mountains in the north of Thessaly.   **209. wand'ring stars:** planets.   **215. splenitive:** quick-tempered.

HORATIO: Good my lord, be quiet.

(*The* ATTENDANTS *part them, and they come out of the grave.*)

HAMLET: Why, I will fight with him upon this theme   220
     Until my eyelids will no longer wag.°
QUEEN: O my son, what theme?
HAMLET: I lov'd Ophelia: forty thousand brothers
     Could not, with all their quantity° of love,
     Make up my sum. What wilt thou do for her?   225
KING: O, he is mad, Laertes.
QUEEN: For love of God, forbear° him.
HAMLET: 'Swounds,° show me what thou 'lt do:
     Woo 't° weep? woo 't fight? woo 't fast? woo 't tear thyself?
     Woo 't drink up eisel?° eat a crocodile?   230
     I'll do 't. Dost thou come here to whine?
     To outface me with leaping in her grave?
     Be buried quick with her, and so will I:
     And, if thou prate of mountains, let them throw
     Millions of acres on us, till our ground,   235
     Singeing his pate against the burning zone,°
     Make Ossa like a wart! Nay, an thou 'lt mouth,
     I'll rant as well as thou.
QUEEN: This is mere madness:
     And thus awhile the fit will work on him;   240
     Anon, as patient as the female dove.
     When that her golden couplets° are disclos'd,
     His silence will sit drooping.
HAMLET: Hear you, sir;
     What is the reason that you use me thus?   245
     I lov'd you ever: but it is no matter;
     Let Hercules himself do what he may,
     The cat will mew and dog will have his day.
KING: I pray thee, good Horatio, wait upon him.   (*Exit* HAMLET *and* HORATIO.)
     (*To* LAERTES.) Strengthen your patience in° our last night's speech;   250
     We'll put the matter to the present push.°
     Good Gertrude, set some watch over your son.
     This grave shall have a living° monument:

---

221. wag: move (not used ludicrously).   **224. quantity:** some suggest that the word is used in a deprecatory sense (little bits, fragments).   **227. forbear:** leave alone.   **228. 'Swounds:** oath, "God's wounds."   **229. Woo 't:** with thou.   **230. eisel:** vinegar. Some editors have taken this to be the name of a river, such as the Yssel, the Weissel, and the Nile.   **236. burning zone:** sun's orbit.   **242. golden couplets:** the pigeon lays two eggs; the young when hatched are covered with golden down.   **250. in:** by recalling.   **251. present push:** immediate test.   **253. living:** lasting; also refers (for Laertes' benefit) to the plot against Hamlet.

An hour of quiet shortly shall we see;
Till then, in patience our proceeding be. (*Exeunt.*) 255

SCENE II

(*A hall in the castle.*)

(*Enter* HAMLET *and* HORATIO.)

HAMLET: So much for this, sir: now shall you see the other:
You do remember all the circumstance?
HORATIO: Remember it, my lord!
HAMLET: Sir, in my heart there was a kind of fighting,
That would not let me sleep: methought I lay 5
Worse than the mutines° in the bilboes.° Rashly,°
And prais'd be rashness for it, let us know,
Our indiscretion sometime serves us well,
When our deep plots do pall°: and that should learn us
There's a divinity that shapes our ends, 10
Rough-hew° them how we will,—
HORATIO: That is most certain.
HAMLET: Up from my cabin,
My sea-gown° scarf'd about me, in the dark
Grop'd I to find out them; had my desire,
Finger'd° their packet, and in fine° withdrew 15
To mine own room again; making so bold,
My fears forgetting manners, to unseal
Their grand commission; where I found, Horatio,—
O royal knavery!—an exact command,
Larded° with many several sorts of reasons 20
Importing Denmark's health and England's too,
With, ho! such bugs° and goblins in my life,°
That, on the supervise,° no leisure bated,°
No, not to stay the grinding of the axe,
My head should be struck off.
HORATIO: Is 't possible? 25
HAMLET: Here's the commission: read it at more leisure.
But wilt thou hear me how I did proceed?

V.ii. 6. mutines: mutineers. **6. bilboes:** shackles. **6. Rashly:** goes with line 12. **9. pall:** fail. **11. Rough-hew:** shape roughly; it may mean "bungle." **13. sea-gown:** "A sea-gown, or a corase, high-collered, and short-sleeved gowne, reaching down to the mid-leg, and used most by seamen and saylors" (Cotgrave, quoted by Singer). **15. finger'd:** pilfered, filched. **15. in fine:** finally. **20. Larded:** enriched. **22. bugs:** bug-bears. **22. such . . . life:** such imaginary dangers if I were allowed to live. **23. supervise:** perusal. **23. leisure bated:** delay allowed.

HORATIO: I beseech you.

HAMLET: Being thus be-netted round with villanies,—
　　　Ere I could make a prologue to my brains,   30
　　　They had begun the play°—I sat me down,
　　　Devis'd a new commission, wrote it fair;
　　　I once did hold it, as our statists° do,
　　　A baseness to write fair° and labour'd much
　　　How to forget that learning, but, sir, now   35
　　　It did me yeoman's° service: wilt thou know
　　　Th' effect of what I wrote?

HORATIO: Ay, good my lord.

HAMLET: An earnest conjuration from the king,
　　　As England was his faithful tributary,
　　　As love between them like the palm might flourish,   40
　　　As peace should still her wheaten garland° wear
　　　And stand a comma° 'tween their amities,
　　　And many such-like 'As'es° of great charge,°
　　　That, on the view and knowing of these contents,
　　　Without debatement further, more or less,   45
　　　He should the bearers put to sudden death,
　　　Not shriving-time° allow'd.

HORATIO: How was this seal'd?

HAMLET: Why, even in that was heaven ordinant.°
　　　I had my father's signet in my purse,
　　　Which was the model of that Danish seal;   50
　　　Folded the writ up in the form of th' other,
　　　Subscrib'd it, gave 't th' impression, plac'd it safely,
　　　The changeling never known. Now, the next day
　　　Was our sea-fight; and what to this was sequent°
　　　Thou know'st already.   55

HORATIO: So Guildenstern and Rosencrantz go to 't.

HAMLET: Why, man, they did make love to this employment;
　　　They are not near my conscience; their defeat
　　　Does by their own insinuation° grow:
　　　'Tis dangerous when the baser nature comes   60
　　　Between the pass° and fell incensed° points
　　　Of mighty opposites.

HORATIO: Why, what a king is this!

30–31. prologue: . . . **play:** i.e., before I could begin to think, my mind had made its decision.   **33. statists:** statesmen.   **34. fair:** in a clear hand.   **36. yeoman's:** i.e., faithful.   **41. wheaten garland:** symbol of peace.   **42. comma:** smallest break or separation. Here amity begins and amity ends the period, and peace stands between like a dependent clause. The comma indicates continuity, link.   **43. 'As'es:** the "whereases" of a formal document, with play on the word ass.   **43. charge:** import, and burden.   **47. shriving-time:** time for absolution.   **48. ordinant:** directing.   **54. sequent:** subsequent.   **59. insinuation:** interference.   **61. pass:** thrust.   **61. fell incensed:** fiercely angered.

HAMLET: Does it not, think thee, stand° me now upon—
He that hath kill'd my king and whor'd my mother,
Popp'd in between th' election° and my hopes,   65
Thrown out his angle° for my proper life,
And with such coz'nage°—is 't not perfect conscience,
To quit° him with this arm? and is 't not to be damn'd,
To let this canker° of our nature come
In further evil?   70
HORATIO: It must be shortly known to him from England
What is the issue of the business there.
HAMLET: It will be short: the interim is mine;
And a man's life's no more than to say "One."
But I am very sorry, good Horatio,   75
That to Laertes I forgot myself;
For, by the image of my cause, I see
The portraiture of his: I'll court his favours:
But, sure, the bravery° of his grief did put me
Into a tow'ring passion.
HORATIO: Peace! who comes here?   80

         (*Enter a* COURTIER [OSRIC].)

OSRIC: Your lordship is right welcome back to Denmark.
HAMLET: I humbly thank you, sir. (*To* HORATIO.) Dost know this water-fly?°
HORATIO: No, my good lord.
HAMLET: Thy state is the more gracious; for 'tis a vice to know him. He hath much
    land, and fertile: let a beast be lord of beasts,° and his crib shall stand at the   85
    king's mess°: 'tis a chough°; but, as I say, spacious in the possession of dirt.
OSRIC: Sweet lord, if your lordship were at leisure, I should impart a thing to you
    from his majesty.
HAMLET: I will receive it, sir, with all diligence of spirit. Put your bonnet to his
    right use; 'tis for the head.   90
OSRIC: I thank you lordship, it is very hot.
HAMLET: No, believe me, 'tis very cold; the wind is northerly.
OSRIC: It is indifferent° cold, my lord, indeed.
HAMLET: But yet methinks it is very sultry and hot for my complexion.
OSRIC: Exceedingly, my lord; it is very sultry,—as 'twere,—I cannot tell how. But,   95
    my lord, his majesty bade me signify to you that 'a has laid a great wager on
    your head: sir, this is the matter,—

---

63. stand: become incumbent.   **65. election:** the Danish throne was filled by election.   **66. angle:**
fishing line.   **67. coz'nage:** trickery.   **68. quit:** repay.   **69. canker:** ulcer, or possibly the worm which
destroys buds and leaves.   **79. bravery:** bravado.   **82. water-fly:** vain or busily idle person.   **85. lord
of beasts:** cf Genesis 1:26, 28.   **85–86. his crib . . . mess:** he shall eat at the king's table, i.e., be one of
the group of persons (usually four) constituting a mess at a banquet.   **86. chough:** probably, chattering
jackdaw; also explained as chuff, provincial boor or churl.   **93. indifferent:** somewhat.

HAMLET: I beseech you, remember°—

(HAMLET *moves him to put on his hat.*)

OSRIC: Nay, good my lord; for mine ease,° in good faith. Sir, here is newly come to court Laertes; believe me, an absolute gentleman, full of most excellent differ-   100
ences, of very soft° society and great showing°: indeed, to speak feelingly° of him, he is the card° or calendar of gentry,° for you shall find in him the continent of what part a gentleman would see.

HAMLET: Sir, his definement° suffers no perdition° in you; though, I know, to divide him inventorially° would dozy° the arithmetic of memory, and yet but   105
yaw° neither, in respect of his quick sail. But, in the verity of extolment, I take him to be a soul of great article°; and his infusion° of such dearth and rareness,° as, to make true diction of him, his semblable° is his mirror; and who else would trace° him, his umbrage,° nothing more.

OSRIC: Your lordship speaks most infallibly of him.   110

HAMLET: The concernancy,° sir? why do we wrap the gentleman in our more rawer breath?°

OSRIC: Sir?

HORATIO (*aside to* HAMLET):   Is 't not possible to understand in another tongue?° You will do 't, sir, really.   115

HAMLET: What imports the nomination° of this gentleman?

OSRIC: Of Laertes?

HORATIO (*aside to* HAMLET):   His purse is empty already; all 's golden words are spent.

HAMLET: Of him, sir.

OSRIC: I know you are not ignorant—   120

HAMLET: I would you did, sir; yet, in faith, if you did, it would not much approve° me. Well, sir?

OSRIC: You are not ignorant of what excellence Laertes is—

HAMLET: I dare not confess that, lest I should compare with him in excellence; but to know a man well, were to know himself.°   125

OSRIC: I mean, sir, for his weapon; but in the imputation° laid on him by them, in his meed° he 's unfellowed.

HAMLET: What 's his weapon?

OSRIC: Rapier and dagger.

---

98. remember: i.e., remember thy courtesy; conventional phrase for "Be covered."   **99. mine ease:** conventional reply declining the invitation of "Remember thy courtesy."   **101. soft:** gentle.   **101. showing:** distinguished appearance.   **101. feelingly:** with just perception.   **102. card:** chart, map.   **102. gentry:** good breeding.   **104. definement:** definition.   **104. perdition:** loss, diminution.   **105. divide him inventorially:** i.e., enumerate his graces.   **105. dozy:** dizzy.   **106. yaw:** to move unsteadily (of a ship).   **107. article:** moment or importance.   **107. infusion:** infused temperament, character imparted by nature.   **107. dearth and rareness:** rarity.   **108. semblable:** true likeness.   **109. trace:** follow.   **109. umbrage:** shadow.   **111. concernancy:** import.   **112. breath:** speech.   **114. Is 't . . . tongue?:** i.e., can one converse with Osric only in this outlandish jargon?   **116. nomination:** naming.   **121. approve:** command.   **125. but . . . himself:** but to know a man as excellent were to know Laertes.   **126. imputation:** reputation.   **127. meed:** merit.

HAMLET: That's two of his weapons: but, well.   130
OSRIC: The king, sir, hath wagered with him six Barbary horses: against the which he
     has impawned,° as I take it, six French rapiers and poniards, with their assigns, as
     girdle, hangers,° and so: three of the carriages, in faith, are very dear to fancy,°
     very responsive° to the hilts, most delicate° carriages, and of very liberal conceit.°
HAMLET: What call you the carriages?   135
HORATIO (*aside to* HAMLET):   I knew you must be edified by the margent° ere you had
     done.
OSRIC: The carriages, sir, are the hangers.
HAMLET: The phrase would be more german° to the matter, if we could carry can-
     non by our sides: I would it might be hangers till then. But, on: six Barbary   140
     horses against six French swords, their assigns, and three liberal-conceited
     carriages; that's the French bet against the Danish. Why is this "impawned," as
     you call it?
OSRIC: The king, sir, hath laid, that in a dozen passes between yourself and him, he
     shall not exceed you three hits: he hath laid on twelve for nine; and it would   145
     come to immediate trial, if your lordship would vouchsafe the answer.
HAMLET: How if I answer "no"?
OSRIC: I mean, my lord, the opposition of your person in trial.
HAMLET: Sir, I will walk here in the hall: if it please his majesty, it is the breathing
     time° of day with me; let the foils be brought, the gentleman willing, and the   150
     king hold his purpose, I will win for him as I can; if not, I will gain nothing but
     my shame and the odd hits.
OSRIC: Shall I re-deliver you e'en so?
HAMLET: To this effect, sir; after what flourish your nature will.
OSRIC: I commend my duty to your lordship.   155
HAMLET: Yours, yours. (*Exit* OSRIC.) He does well to commend it himself; there are
     no tongues else for 's turn.
HORATIO: This lapwing° runs away with the shell on his head.
HAMLET: 'A did comply, sir, with his dug,° before 'a sucked it. Thus has hey—and
     many more of the same bevy that I know the drossy° age dotes on—only got   160
     the tune° of the time and out of an habit of encounter°; a kind of yesty° collec-
     tion, which carries them through and through the most fann'd and winnowed°
     opinions; and do but blow them to their trial, the bubbles are out.°

     (*Enter a* LORD.)

132. he has impawned: he has wagered.   **133. hangers:** straps on the sword belt from which the sword
hung.   **133. dear to fancy:** fancifully made.   **134. responsive:** probably, well balanced, corresponding
closely.   **134. delicate:** i.e., in workmanship.   **134. liberal conceit:** elaborate design.   **136. margent:**
margin of a book, place for explanatory notes.   **139. german:** germane, appropriate.   **149–50.**
breathing time: exercise period.   **158. lapwing:** peewit; noted for its wiliness in drawing a visitor away
from its nest and its supposed habit of running about when newly hatched with its head in the shell; possibly an allusion to Osric's hat.   **159. did comply . . . dug:** paid compliments to his mother's breast.
160. drossy: frivolous.   **161. tune:** temper, mood.   **161. habit of encounter:** demeanor of social
intercourse.   **161. yesty:** frothy.   **162. fann'd and winnowed:** select and refined   **163. blow . . . out:**
i.e., put them to the test, and their ignorance is exposed.

LORD: My lord, his majesty commended him to you by young Osric, who brings
    back to him, that you attend him in the hall: he sends to know if your pleasure   165
    hold to play with Laertes, or that you will take longer time.

HAMLET: I am constant to my purposes; they follow the king's pleasure: if his fit-
    ness speaks, mine is ready; now or whensoever, provided I be so able as now.

LORD: The king and queen and all are coming down.

HAMLET: In happy time,°   170

LORD: The queen desires you to use some gentle entertainment to Laertes before
    you fall to play.

HAMLET: She well instructs me.   (*Exit* LORD.)

HORATIO: You will lose this wager, my lord.

HAMLET: I do not think so; since he went into France, I have been in continual   175
    practice; I shall win at the odds. But thou wouldst not think how ill all 's here
    about my heart: but it is no matter.

HORATIO: Nay, good my lord,—

HAMLET: It is but foolery; but it is such a kind of gain-giving,° as would perhaps
    trouble a woman.   180

HORATIO: If your mind dislike any thing, obey it: I will forestall their repair hither,
    and say you are not fit.

HAMLET: Not a whit, we defy augury: there's a special providence in the fall of a
    sparrow. If it be now, 'tis not to come; if it be not to come, it will be now; if it be
    not now, yet it will come: the readiness is all°: since no man of aught he leaves   185
    knows, what is 't to leave betimes? Let be.

    (*A table prepared.* [*Enter*] *Trumpets, Drums, and Officers with cushions;*
    KING, QUEEN, [OSRIC,] *and all the State; foils, daggers,* [*and wine borne in;*]
    and LAERTES.)

KING: Come, Hamlet, come, and take this hand from me.

    (*The* KING *puts* LAERTES'*s hand into* HAMLET'*s.*)

HAMLET: Give me your pardon, sir: I have done you wrong;
    But pardon 't as you are a gentleman.
    This presence° knows,   190
    And you must needs have heard, how I am punish'd
    With a sore distraction. What I have done,
    That might your nature, honour and exception°
    Roughly awake, I here proclaim was madness.
    Was 't Hamlet wrong'd Laertes? Never Hamlet: 195
    If Hamlet from himself be ta'en away.
    And when he's not himself does wrong Laertes,
    Then Hamlet does it not, Hamlet denies it.
    Who does it, then? His madness: if 't be so,

---

170. in happy time: a phrase of courtesy.   **179. gain-giving:** misgiving.   **185. all:** all that matters.
190. presence: royal assembly.   **193. exception:** disapproval.

Hamlet is of the faction that is wrong'd;   200
His madness is poor Hamlet's enemy.
Sir, in this audience,
Let my disclaiming from a purpos'd evil
Free me so far in your most generous thoughts,
That I have shot mine arrow o'er the house,   205
And hurt my brother.
LAERTES: I am satisfied in nature,°
Whose motive, in this case, should stir me most
To my revenge: but in my terms of honour
I stand aloof; and will no reconcilement,
Till by some elder masters, of known honour,   210
I have a voice° and precedent of peace,
To keep my name ungor'd. But till that time,
I do receive your offer'd love like love,
And will not wrong it.
HAMLET: I embrace it freely;
And will this brother's wager frankly play.   215
Give us the foils. Come on.
LAERTES: Come, one for me.
HAMLET: I'll be your foil,° Laertes: in mine ignorance
Your skill shall, like a star i' th' darkest night,
Stick fiery off° indeed.
LAERTES: You mock me, sir.
HAMLET: No, by this hand.   220
KING: Give them the foils, young Osric. Cousin Hamlet,
You know the wager?
HAMLET: Very well, my lord;
Your grace has laid the odds o' th' weaker side.
KING: I do not fear it; I have seen you both;
But since he is better'd, we have therefore odds.   225
LAERTES: This is too heavy, let me see another.
HAMLET: This likes me well. These foils have all a length?

     (They prepare to play.)

OSRIC: Ay, my good lord.
KING: Set me the stoups of wine upon that table.
If Hamlet give the first or second hit,   230
Or quit in answer of the third exchange,
Let all the battlements their ordnance fire;

---

206. nature: i.e., he is personally satisfied, but his honor must be satisfied by the rules of the code of honor.   **211. voice:** authoritative pronouncement.   **217. foil:** quibble on the two senses: "background which sets something off," and "blunted rapier for fencing."   **219. Stick fiery off:** stand out brilliantly.

The king shall drink to Hamlet's better breath;
And in the cup an union° shall he throw,
Richer than that which four successive kings   235
In Denmark's crown have worn. Give me the cups;
And let the kettle° to the trumpet speak,
The trumpet to the cannoneer without,
The cannons to the heavens, the heavens to earth,
"Now the king drinks to Hamlet." Come begin: (*Trumpets the while.*)   240
And you, the judges, bear a wary eye.

HAMLET: Come on, sir.

LAERTES: Come, my lord. (*They play.*)

HAMLET: One.

LAERTES: No.

HAMLET: Judgment.

OSRIC: A hit, a very palpable hit.

        (*Drums, trumpets, and shot. Flourish. A piece goes off.*)

LAERTES: Well; again.

KING: Stay; give me drink. Hamlet, this pearl° is thine;
Here's to thy health. Give him the cup.   245

HAMLET: I'll play this bout first; set it by awhile.
Come. (*They play.*) Another hit; what say you?

LAERTES: A touch, a touch, I do confess 't.

KING: Our son shall win.

QUEEN: He's fat,° and scant of breath.
Here, Hamlet, take my napkin, rub thy brows: 250
The queen carouses° to thy fortune, Hamlet.

HAMLET: Good madam!

KING: Gertrude, do not drink.

QUEEN: I will, my lord; I pray you, pardon me. (*Drinks.*)

KING (*aside*):   It is the poison'd cup: it is too late.

HAMLET: I dare not drink yet, madam; by and by.   255

QUEEN: Come, let me wipe thy face.

LAERTES: My lord, I'll hit him now.

KING: I do not think 't.

LAERTES (*aside*):   And yet 'tis almost 'gainst my conscience.

HAMLET: Come, for the third, Laertes: you but dally;
I pray you, pass with your best violence;   260
I am afeard you make a wanton° of me.

LAERTES: Say you so? come on. (*They play.*)

---

234. **union:** pearl.   237. **kettle:** kettledrum.   244. **pearl:** i.e., the poison.   249. **fat:** not physically fit, out of training. Some earlier editors speculated that the term applied to the corpulence of Richard Burbage, who originally played the part, but the allusion now appears unlikely. "Fat" may also suggest "sweaty."   251. **carouses:** drinks a toast.   261. **wanton:** spoiled child.

OSRIC: Nothing, neither way.

LAERTES: Have at you now!

(LAERTES *wounds* HAMLET; *then, in scuffling, they change rapiers,*° *and* HAMLET *wounds* LAERTES.)

KING: Part them; they are incens'd.

HAMLET: Nay, come again.   (*The* QUEEN *falls.*)   265

OSRIC: Look to the queen there, ho!

HORATIO: They bleed on both sides. How is it, my lord?

OSRIC: How is 't, Laertes?

LAERTES: Why, as a woodcock° to mine own springe,° Osric;
    I am justly kill'd with mine own treachery.

HAMLET: How does the queen?

KING: She swounds° to see them bleed.   270

QUEEN: No, no, the drink, the drink,—O my dear Hamlet,—
    The drink, the drink! I am poison'd.   (*Dies.*)

HAMLET: O villany! Ho! let the door be lock'd:
    Treachery! Seek it out.   (LAERTES *falls.*)

LAERTES: It is here, Hamlet: Hamlet, thou art slain;   275
    No med'cine in the world can do thee good;
    In thee there is not half an hour of life;
    The treacherous instrument is in thy hand,
    Unbated° and envenom'd: the foul practice
    Hath turn'd itself on me; lo, here I lie,   280
    Never to rise again: thy mother's poison'd:
    I can no more: the king, the king's to blame.

HAMLET: The point envenom'd too!
    Then, venom, to thy work. (*Stabs the* KING.)

ALL: Treason! treason!   285

KING: O, yet defend me, friends; I am but hurt.

HAMLET: Here, thou incestuous, murd'rous, damned Dane.
    Drink off this potion. Is thy union here?
    Follow my mother.   (KING *dies.*)

LAERTES: He is justly serv'd;
    It is a poison temper'd° by himself.   290
    Exchange forgiveness with me, noble Hamlet:
    Mine and my father's death come not upon thee,
    Nor thine on me!   (*Dies.*)

HAMLET: Heaven make thee free of it! I follow thee.
    I am dead, Horatio. Wretched queen, adieu!   295

---

s.d. in scuffling, they change rapiers: according to a widespread stage tradition, Hamlet receives a scratch, realizes that Laertes's sword is unbated (not blunted), and accordingly forces an exchange. **268. woodcock:** as type of stupidity or as decoy.   **268. springe:** trap, snare.   **270. swounds:** swoons. **279. Unbated:** Not blunted with a button.   **290. temper'd:** mixed.

You that look pale and tremble at this chance,
That are but mutes° or audience to this act,
Had I but time—as this fell sergeant,° Death,
Is strict in his arrest—O, I could tell you—
But let it be. Horatio, I am dead;   300
Thou livest; report me and my cause aright
To the unsatisfied.

HORATIO: Never believe it:
I am more an antique Roman° than a Dane:
Here's yet some liquor left.

HAMLET: As th' art a man,
Give me the cup: let go, by heaven, I'll ha 't.   305
O God! Horatio, what a wounded name,
Things standing thus unknown, shall live behind me!
If thou didst ever hold me in thy heart,
Absent thee from felicity awhile,
And in this harsh world draw thy breath in pain,   310
To tell my story. (*A march afar off.*)
         What warlike noise is this?

OSRIC: Young Fortinbras, with conquest come from Poland,
To the ambassadors of England gives
This warlike volley.

HAMLET: O, I die, Horatio;
The potent poison quite o'er-crows° my spirit: 315
I cannot live to hear the news from England;
But I do prophesy th' election lights
On Fortinbras: he has my dying voice;
So tell him, with th' occurrents,° more and less,
Which have solicited.° The rest is silence.   (*Dies.*) 320

HORATIO: Now cracks a noble heart. Good night, sweet prince;
And flights of angels sing thee to thy rest!
Why does the drum come hither? (*March within.*)

(*Enter* FORTINBRAS, *with the* [*English*] AMBASSADORS [*and others*].)

FORTINBRAS: Where is this sight?

HORATIO: What is it you would see?
If aught of woe or wonder, cease your search.   325

FORTINBRAS: This quarry° cries on havoc.° O proud Death,
What feast is toward in thine eternal cell,
That thou so many princes at a shot

---

297. mutes: performers in a play who speak no words.   **298. sergeant:** sheriff's officer.   **303. Roman:** it was the Roman custom to follow masters in death.   **315. o'er-crows:** triumphs over.   **319. occurrents:** events, incidents.   **320. solicited:** moved, urged.   **326. quarry:** heap of dead.   **326. cries on:** havoc proclaims a general slaughter.

So bloodily hast struck?
FIRST AMBASSADOR: The sight is dismal;
And our affairs from England come too late: 330
The ears are senseless that should give us hearing,
To tell him his commandment is fulfill'd,
That Rosencrantz and Guildenstern are dead:
Where should we have our thanks?
HORATIO: Not from his mouth,°
Had it th' ability of life to thank you: 335
He never gave commandment for their death.
But since, so jump° upon this bloody question,°
You from the Polack wars, and you from England,
Are here arriv'd, give order that these bodies
High on a stage° be placed to the view;   340
And let me speak to th' yet unknowing world
How these things came about: so shall you hear
Of carnal, bloody, and unnatural acts,
Of accidental judgements, casual slaughters,
Of deaths put on by cunning and forc'd cause,   345
And, in this upshot, purposes mistook
Fall'n on th' inventors' heads: all this can I
Truly deliver.
FORTINBRAS: Let us haste to hear it,
And call the noblest to the audience.
For me, with sorrow I embrace my fortune: 350
I have some rights of memory° in this kingdom,
Which now to claim my vantage doth invite me.
HORATIO: Of that I shall have also cause to speak,
And from his mouth whose voice will draw on more°:
But let this same be presently perform'd,   355
Even while men's minds are wild; lest more mischance,
On° plots and errors, happen.
FORTINBRAS: Let four captains
Bear Hamlet, like a soldier, to the stage;
For he was likely, had he been put on,
To have prov'd most royal: and, for his passage,°   360
The soldiers' music and the rites of war
Speak loudly for him.
Take up the bodies: such a sight as this
Becomes the field,° but here shows much amiss.

---

334. his mouth: i.e., the king's. **337. jump:** precisely. **337. question:** dispute. **340. stage:** platform. **351. of memory:** traditional, remembered. **354. voice . . . more:** vote will influence still others. **357. On:** on account of, or possibly, on top of, in addition to. **360. passage:** death. **364. field:** i.e., of battle.

Go, bid the soldiers shoot.

365

(Exeunt [marching, bearing off the dead bodies; after which a peal of ordnance is shot off].)

[c. 1600]

Journal Entry

Is there a character in *Hamlet* with whom you identify? What is it about his or her personality or situation that interests you?

Textual Considerations

1. In act 2, Hamlet tries to discover the facts about Claudius's guilt while the king attempts to uncover the truth about Hamlet's madness. Explain what their plans have in common. How do they culminate in the "mousetrap," the play within the play? What purpose does the "mousetrap" serve? Explain.
2. Discuss the degree to which Hamlet's bitterness and sorrow are attributable to his mother's remarrying rather than to his father's death. What role does Gertrude play in King Hamlet's death? What arguments does Hamlet use against her when he confronts her in act 3, scene 4?
3. To what extent is Laertes a **foil** to Hamlet? Compare, for example, their responses to their fathers' murders. What do Hamlet's soliloquies reveal about his relationship with his father? Which of Hamlet's soliloquies do you find more interesting? Explain.
4. Investigate the dramatic impact of the play from its two extremes—the ghost's urge to disclose his story to Hamlet in act 1, scene 5, and Hamlet's plea for Horatio to tell his story in act 5, scene 2. What do these scenes reveal about Old Hamlet's and Hamlet's attitudes toward their origins? How effectively do these scenes enhance the dramatic action of the play?
5. Review Hamlet's interview with Ophelia in act 3, scene 1. Consider what his comments disclose about the motives and attitudes that prompt him to cast Ophelia, rather than Claudius, as his antagonist. Why does Ophelia commit suicide? What does Hamlet's letter to Ophelia reveal about him and his attitude toward women before his father's death?
6. Why does Hamlet delay in avenging his father's death? Discuss how Hamlet's act of remembering and forgetting the ghost—or his ambivalence toward the ghost's plea for revenge—informs his actions throughout the play.
7. Do you think *Hamlet* would lose much of its dramatic power if Shakespeare had cut out the role of Fortinbras? Speculate as to why some productions of *Hamlet* omit the Fortinbras role.

Cultural Contexts

1. What can we infer about Ophelia's and Gertrude's roles in *Hamlet*? Do these feminine characters merely fulfill the gender roles in the play, or do they also add to our understanding of Hamlet's character? Investigate also how Ophelia and Gertrude narrate the past, and how they establish a dramatic dialogue with the present and the

future. How do Hamlet's attacks on these characters and on women in general affect your response to the drama?

2. Explore the father-son relationship in *Hamlet*. In your discussion, debate with members of your group whether Hamlet, by inheriting the past and his father's designs, is also forced to inherit his father's moral law.

Performance Exercises

PERFORMANCE EXPRESS (45 MINUTES)

1. Following a long tradition established by actresses like Sarah Bernhardt (1844–1923) who played the role of Hamlet, select a female classmate and cast her in the role of Hamlet. Ask her to deliver an improvised and spontaneous version of the nursery scene (3.1.90–153) in which she interacts with Ophelia, who could be played by a woman or a man. Invite the whole class to discuss the dramatic effectiveness of this gender-reversal performance.

2. Peter Brooks, a British stage director, proposes the following performance exercise in his book *The Empty Space* (London: MacGibbon & Kee, 1968): "Take the two lines 'To be or not to be, That is the question' and give them to ten actors, one word each. The actors stand in a closed circle and endeavor to play the words one after the other trying to produce a living phrase. . . . When after long work the sentence suddenly flows, a thrilling freedom is experienced by everyone. They see in a flash the possibility of group playing, and the obstacles to it." Working with your group, follow Brooks's directions to deliver the same line above. Discuss your response to this exercise.

PERFORMANCE PROJECTS

1. British critic John Dover Wilson once stated that "we were never intended to reach the heart of Hamlet's mystery." Using Internet resources, read about John Gielgud's (1930s), Laurence Olivier's (1937), Michael Redgrave's (1950), and Richard Burton's (1964) performances of *Hamlet*. Then, working with your group, stage one key scene of *Hamlet* that clearly defines *your* approach to Hamlet's mysterious character. Does your group want to cast Hamlet as an idealist, a lunatic, or a neurotic or psychotic character? Which lines would you cut to suit your stage production? Decide on time period, costumes, props, and stage actions.

2. Discuss with your group the possibility of transferring the setting of *Hamlet* to the United State in the twenty-first century. Watch Ethan Hawke's and Campbell Scott's performances of *Hamlet* on video before you decide how you would stage one of the scenes of the play. Besides considering your Hamlet's physical appearance, dominant traits, and costumes, also decide whether you would lean toward a Freudian or a non-Freudian interpretation of the play. Explain your reasons. (See Appendix D on the Freudian interpretation of *Hamlet*.)

TOPICS FOR DISCUSSION
AND WRITING

Writing Topics

1. The understanding of parent by child and child by parent in this universally significant relationship is the focus of several relationships in Part One. Select two authors, and compare and contrast the portrayal of parents in the texts by Lagerkvist, Lee, and Chock or the role of parents in the poems by Levertov, Emanuel, or Tapahonso. What insights did the speakers gain through their recollections of family? To what extent are their relationships characterized by conflicting emotions?

2. A particular place evokes significant insights for the characters in "First Confession," "The Watch," and "Roman Fever." Analyze the interactions between people and places that make these insights possible.

3. Several short stories in Part One focus on the passage of time and the changes that occur in the lives of the characters. Using "First Confession," "The Watch," and/or "Young Goodman Brown," compare and contrast the attitudes that any two characters in two of the stories take toward the passage of time.

4. Hughes and Hayden focus on the heritage of African Americans. Analyze the interaction of past and present in any two poems by Hayden or Hughes. Include the role of setting in your analysis.

5. Rewrite Hamlet's dilemma from Horatio's point of view, and discuss the degree to which his view corresponds with your own.

6. Explore the mother-daughter relationships in "And the Soul Shall Dance," "The Possessive," and "Breaking Tradition." How are the mothers similar or different? To what extent do they conform to traditional roles? How have their character traits influenced the behavior and values of their daughters? What emotional ties were you aware of in the three texts?

7. The protagonists in "The Sky Is Gray," "The Watch," "And the Soul Shall Dance," and "Father and I" are involved in literal and symbolic journeys. Trace these journeys in any two of the texts, and analyze their emotional, physical, or psychological significance for the characters' lives.

8. "Fern Hill" and "In the Tree House at Night" capture the complexities of a relationship with places, particularly those that were part of our youth. Compare and contrast the role of nature in each text.

9. At the outset of the play *Oedipus Rex*, Oedipus as king is attempting to answer an objective question: Who murdered King Laios? As the drama progresses, however, Oedipus as an individual is confronted with the *subjective* question: Who am I? Explain what he learns about himself as he seeks to answer both questions.

10. How are the gods and their prophecies presented in *Oedipus Rex*? Does the fact that the oracle decreed that Oedipus will kill his father and marry his mother

absolve him of guilt for his actions? Write an analytical essay responding to these questions.

11. How does sexuality function in the protagonist's journey from innocence to experience in "Fraternity"? What is the connection between sexuality and innocence in Garrett Hongo's text?

12. Analyze Hamlet's psychological state at the outset of the drama. To what extent does his state of mind contribute to his actions later in the play?

13. Contrast portrayals of childhood with premonitions of adulthood in the texts by Eberhart, Thomas, Lagerkvist, or Yamauchi.

14. Analyze attitudes toward death in the texts by Dickey, Levertov, Heaney, or Chief Seattle, pointing out similarities and differences in their points of view. Limit yourself to these texts.

15. How do you confront death? Does your response to death conform to the viewpoints you inherited from your cultural tradition? Analyze the theme of death in two texts of your choice that reflect your own views of death.

Research Topics

1. Carry out a research project on your family history: Tape interviews with family members and collect old family photos, letters, diaries, memoirs, or any other family records that you might use as supporting evidence. Then check library sources, such as newspapers and magazines, to identify the major sociohistorical events that were part of your family's history. In writing the paper, consider assuming the personal voice of a family member and narrating your family history from his or her point of view.

2. *Oedipus Rex* and *Hamlet* have inspired diverse literary, psychological, and cultural responses. One of the most frequent interpretations of these plays concerns Sigmund Freud's psychoanalytic theory known as the Oedipus complex. To understand more about this theory, consult the references to psychoanalytic criticism in Appendix D, as well as sources such as Ernest Jones's *Hamlet and Oedipus* (New York: Norton, 1976) and Edmond Lowell's *Oedipus: The Ancient Legend and Its Later Analogues* (Baltimore: Johns Hopkins University Press, 1985). Applying Freud's theory to both dramas, write a research paper arguing whether the Oedipus complex helps explain the mental processes of the protagonists.

3. Many critics have argued that *Hamlet* belongs to the literary tradition of the revenge tragedy—a type of drama whose literary conventions demand suspense, violence, and revenge for a murder. Research the conventions of the revenge play, and demonstrate the extent to which you would or would not apply such conventions to *Hamlet*.

FILM ANGLES

ORIGINS AND INSIGHTS: THE FILM ANGLE

Since the themes of Part One—embodied in such varied works as "Young Goodman Brown," *Oedipus Rex*, and *Hamlet*—are among the most enduring in the history of literature, it is not surprising that they can also be found in films. Such films are based not only on literature (for example, there are several film versions of *Oedipus* and *Hamlet*) but also include those with original screenplays that deal with characters' quests for origins and insights into their lives. As in the case of Oedipus, this search often takes the form of characters' investigations into the past in an effort to determine their true identities or simply to better understand themselves. As the tragic fate of Oedipus attests, however, the insight gained from such a search does not always bring greater happiness.

Just as many of the themes found in literature can be found in films, certain narrative techniques are shared by the two media, although the forms they take are, of course, different. Films that tell stories, like novels and short stories, have narrative structures, plots, characters, dialogue, and specific points of view. Some films have dramatic "three-act" structures, like plays. Many films also have complex visual structures equivalent to imagery in poetry: The repetition of certain objects or colors or specific techniques can accumulate meaning by association, just as the repetition of such things in poems does. Although films are more visual than linguistic, they can also create **filmic metaphors** through the artful juxtaposition of images in which two gestures, objects, or actions are compared in a particular context.

FILM HISTORY AND GENRES

What kinds of movies can be examined profitably with regard to the themes of Part One? The range is wide, from recognized masterpieces such as *Citizen Kane* (d. Orson Welles, 1941) and biographical studies such as *Freud* (d. John Huston, 1962) and *The Miracle Worker* (d. Arthur Penn, 1962) to science fiction adventures such as *Back to the Future* (d. Robert Zemeckis, 1985) and *Big* (d. Penny Marshall, 1988) and horror classics such as *Psycho* (d. Alfred Hitchcock, 1960) and *The Shining* (d. Stanley Kubrick, 1980).

How does the type of movie—the **film genre** it belongs to—affect its treatment of these themes? A biographical drama, for example, often structures the narrative in light of a central fact about its real-life subject. The story line in *Freud* concerns how Sigmund Freud's investigation of the origins of his own sufferings led to his groundbreaking insights into the workings of the unconscious. Although such an approach may not provide a complete biographical portrait, using such a dramatic or thematic "hook" allows the filmmaker to organize the material toward a specific goal so that the protagonist is engaged in a quest for insights into his or her life. When a film is structured in this way, the viewer becomes actively involved in the quest as well, although one should remember that the structure—like the quest—is an artificial framework, not the "real life" of the biographical subject.

Popular films like *Back to the Future*, *Big*, *Terminator 2* (d. James Cameron, 1991), *Ghost World* (d. Terry Zwigoff, 2001), and *Donnie Darko* (d. Richard Kelly, 2001) belong to different genres—science fiction, teenage melodrama, supernatural—yet they are also examples, in one way or another, of the coming-of-age film. In this genre, young people undergo certain experiences and learn the difference between real and ideal parental figures in the process of growing up. It is worth noting that the universality of the themes of this part allows them to be incorporated in both a relatively realistic depiction of contemporary society, such as in *Ghost World*, and in futuristic fantasies such as *Back to the Future* and *Terminator 2*. In these and other films, the search for origins and insights is often disguised as an adventure. In Steven Spielberg's *Hook* (1991), for example—a reworking of the Peter Pan legend—a businessman in the real world must enter a fantasy world and rediscover his childhood in order to be a better father.

Questions to Consider

1. Look at a biographical film and try to identify the "hook"—the thematic premise that becomes the goal of the character's life and the central focus of the film. Does this key idea present the biographical subject too simplistically? Does the idea effectively organize the entire film? Would the film lose its coherence and be less appealing without it? Can you think of a better "hook" for the film?
2. Compare any two of the films mentioned (or others) that belong to different genres and consider how, in each case, the main character achieves his or her insights within the conventions of the genre.

CASE STUDIES

Citizen Kane

Sometimes the quest for origins or insights is initiated by a secondary character. In *Citizen Kane*, regarded as one of the greatest movies ever made, a newspaper reporter is assigned to investigate the meaning of "Rosebud," the last word uttered by the film's protagonist, Charles Foster Kane, before his death. The reporter interviews people who were close to Kane, but neither they nor he discovers who or what "Rosebud" is. The secret is revealed at the end of the film, but only to the audience, who must then weigh its significance in the light of what has been learned about the character throughout the film. The tracing of origins and gathering of insights, therefore, is the subject of the film, determining both its **flashback** narrative structure and its multiple **point of view.**

One of the film's many stylistic patterns is its consistent use of **deep-focus cinematography,** a way of filming that keeps all planes of action—foreground, middle ground, and background—and aspects of the **mise-en-scène** in sharp focus and in clear relation to each other. In *Citizen Kane*, this technique is repeatedly used to reveal the way the protagonist (Kane) relates to the significant people in his life. For example, in the important childhood scene in which Kane's mother sends him away to be raised by a banker, the boy Kane is seen through a window in the background playing outside in the snow while negotiations determining his future are being made by his parents and the banker in the foreground. This becomes a model **composition** in the film that both reiterates his childhood origins and provides continued insight into his character makeup. Examining a number of these shots is a productive way of learning how **visual motifs** produce and reinforce meaning in a film.

Questions to Consider

1. Although the character of Kane remains somewhat enigmatic, a compelling portrait of him can be drawn from the recollections of those who knew him. What features of Kane's personality help to fill in that portrait?
2. If Kane is emotionally immature and incapable of insight into his own character, as some characters suggest, does this explain why we aren't given his own point of view? If Kane were to have his own flashback, what do you think it would include? What would it exclude?
3. Locate and analyze several deep-focus shots in the film. What do they reveal about Kane's relationship with the other character(s) in the shot?

The Truman Show

Another variation on the themes in this part—of special relevance to the dominance of media in contemporary society—is *The Truman Show* (d. Peter Weir, 1998). The emerging consciousness of the main character involves the recognition that his entire life has been literally "programmed" by the media and is on view for millions of television addicts. Truman's determination to find the world beyond the fabricated one in which he lives is a heroic struggle that ends in a step into the unknown.

Questions to Consider

1. *The Truman Show* ends with the character's realization that the world he believed real is artificial. What is Truman's quest and when does it begin? How is he able to imagine another world?
2. Is Truman's quest and the film a metaphor for the limitations or false constructs about the world that all of us may have to confront at some point in our lives?

Hamlet

Language and Film

Shakespeare's plays have attracted filmmakers since the silent film era. Sound versions of Shakespeare often fail, however, because of the difficulty in finding film actors who can speak the Elizabethan language convincingly and because certain stage conventions, such as the soliloquy, do not transfer well to the screen. On stage the actor plays off a live audience and establishes an intimacy, whereas on screen the same actor, doing the same soliloquy, can seem artificial and remote. Innovative filmmakers have tried to solve these problems in a variety of ways—for example, by magnifying the actor's body language and physical features through close-ups, telegraphing small facial expressions and slight movements of the eyes that capture subtle nuances and convey feelings that might substitute for some of the language.

Some filmmakers reduce the language to a minimum, stressing narrative clarity over psychological and poetic depth. Others offset the language with contemporary settings and topical action; for example, Baz Luhrmann's *Romeo and Juliet* (1996) makes use of gang wars and ultra-hip set design. Still others eliminate the language altogether and adapt the story to contemporary tastes; the musical *West Side Story* (1960), also based on *Romeo and Juliet*, is a famous example.

In *Titus* (1999), her film version of Shakespeare's *Titus Andronicus*, director Julie Taymor uses all the technical resources of the cinema while "staging" the drama in a fictional fusion of several historical epochs that links the cruelties and tyrannies of ancient Rome (the play's setting) with those of Fascism in the twentieth century. The final scene is "set" in the Colosseum as a way of acknowledging the play as a violent spectacle. The result is a blend of theater and film that evades questions of realism and credibility because it unfolds within the theater of the imagination—an effective corollary to Shakespeare's wildly excessive text.

Even the most eloquent and successful film treatments by noted Shakespearean actors and directors—such as Laurence Olivier and Orson Welles—trim the language to avoid the film being inordinately long. Kenneth Branagh's complete *Hamlet* (1996) runs four hours. Although something is lost when lines and whole parts of soliloquies are cut, their meanings are often supplied through a film's "visual vocabulary."

One way filmmakers have solved the problem of the soliloquy is through the technique of **voice-over,** which preserves the intimate quality of an interior monologue. It is used in Olivier's *Hamlet*, in Grigory Kozintsev's Russian *Hamlet* of 1964, and in Michael Almeyrada's modern dress *Hamlet* of 2000. In the Olivier version, voice-over accentuates the character's isolation and loneliness and is often accompanied by close-ups of the actor's tormented face. In Kozintsev's film, we often hear Hamlet's inner thoughts while he is around other people—as in the scene with the visiting players—so that he seems to be commenting internally at the moment he witnesses something, rather than later, in retrospect. In each case, the filmmaker has found a way to incorporate the soliloquy into the film's world without sacrificing either intimacy or its privileged position in Shakespeare's text.

Question to Consider

1. Select a soliloquy from one of the film versions of *Hamlet* and examine carefully the way it is handled. Do you find the actor's delivery convincing? Has the soliloquy been shortened? What film techniques has the director used either to enliven the scene or to compensate for any cuts?

Hamlet on Film

Hamlet has been the subject of films since the early 1900s, and since 1990 there have been four film versions, including Branagh's period spectacle and Almeyrada's contemporary reading set in New York. Thanks to the technology of VHS and DVD, such famous stage performances as those of Richard Burton and Nicol Williamson from the 1960s and 1970s are also available for study.

The most curious silent film is the Danish-German production of 1920, based on historical sources as well as Shakespeare's play. Not only is Hamlet played by a woman, Asta Nielsen, but the character *is* a woman raised as a man because of political exigencies. This approach has fascinating implications for the character and the plot, culminating in the death scene when Horatio, while embracing the expiring "prince," suddenly realizes his friend's true sexual identity and love for him.

Laurence Olivier, one of the twentieth century's most honored actors, directed and starred in the first full-length film of *Hamlet*, which won the Academy Award for Best Picture of 1948. It can be productively compared to two more action-oriented costume versions, the first directed by Franco Zeffirelli in 1990, with Mel Gibson, and the second directed by and starring Kenneth Branagh in 1996. Because so many versions of *Hamlet* exist on VHS and DVD, students can examine the variable ways in which the character—perhaps the most psychologically and morally complex in all literature—can be interpreted. Just as critical and theoretical approaches shed light on different ways of looking at the play (see Appendix D in this book), seeing Hamlet portrayed by such different actors as Olivier, Branagh, and Gibson, along with Richard Burton, Nicol Williamson, Ethan Hawke, Kevin Kline, and Campbell Scott (the latter two in less available video versions) lets us *see* the many angles from which the character can be approached and appreciate the subtle differences of gestures and line readings that alter our understanding of the same text.

Question to Consider

1. Although the Asta Nielsen film had a narrative rationale for Hamlet's being played by a woman, in fact several noted actresses (e.g., Sarah Bernhardt) have played the prince as a man on stage. What impressions or behavioral or psychological aspects of Hamlet's character might lend themselves to this approach? Would it be possible for a woman to play Hamlet in a film in today's culture? Why or why not?

Scene Comparisons

Comparing the way two or more screen versions approach the same scene in the play not only illuminates the often contradictory potential meanings of the play, but is instructive in highlighting interpretive and ideological approaches and how they reflect certain critical fashions of the time. For example, an interpretation of Hamlet's behavior that once dominated dramatic criticism and stage performances was the Freudian approach (see Appendix D). Freudian psychoanalysis had perhaps its strongest hold on American culture between the late 1930s and the late 1950s, during which time novels and films were rife with psychological symbolism and frequent allusions to such concepts as the Oedipus complex.

Olivier's *Hamlet*, made in the midst of this period, manifests this influence—although since it was the *only* film version for decades, it was easy to forget that it was a specific reading of the play. Key scenes and speeches are composed and delivered in ways that make the Oedipal conflict central to the action and the primary cause of Hamlet's delay in avenging his father's murder. This approach is worked out in the film both through the use of the **subjective camera**, which renders Hamlet's key soliloquies truly introspective experiences (note the "To be or not to be" speech, for example), and through Olivier's sensitive performance, which emphasizes the prince's cultivated nature—his affinity with the arts and the best of human instincts—which makes the vengeful task before him seem all the more intolerable. In contrast to Olivier's subjective approach, Branagh's Hamlet is a more active, demonstrative character, even in the soliloquies, which often set against vast scenic backdrops that make them seem less interior meditations than public speeches.

Questions to Consider

1. Compare the bedroom scene between Hamlet and his mother in the Olivier film with the way it is handled in the Zeffirelli version, which also sees the character in Oedipal terms. In the Zeffirelli, Hamlet kisses his mother on the mouth. How does this gesture affect the scene and the appearance of his father's ghost? Since the

Oedipus complex is an unconscious phenomenon, how can it explain so literal a gesture? Discuss the implications of this treatment in comparison with Olivier's. Which version do you think is truest to the play? Which is the most effective? Why?

2. Examine the same soliloquy in both the Olivier and the Branagh versions. What similarities or differences can you identify? What seems to be the director's intention in each case? What do the differences in approach reveal about the character of Hamlet?

Hamlet in Modern Dress

The Olivier, Zeffirelli, and Branagh films are all period costume spectacles. Some filmmakers reject that approach and choose to modernize the play—a decision that must deal with a wholly different set of problems, not the least of which is having people who look and act just like people today but speak in Elizabethan verse. This approach, however, stresses the relevance of the play's conflicts and themes to contemporary society. In the Almeyrada film, Hamlet is the son of a businessman who has been murdered by his brother, who then takes over the company. Thus, the power struggles of royalty are replaced by the ambitions and rivalries of the corporate world in a modern metropolis.

Question to Consider

1. Study the Almeyrada film and consider the pros and cons of doing Hamlet in modern dress. The film uses many aspects of the contemporary world to give new twists and meanings to the text. In Ophelia's mad scene, for example, she scatters Polaroid photos instead of flowers. What other touches can you find, consistent with today's world, that give a modern edge to lines or ideas in the play?

Research Topics

1. *The Truman Show* raises serious questions about the manipulation of the media, especially television, and its influence on people's lives. Do you see any connection or thematic relationship between the film's fabrication of an entire world that the main character believes is "real" and the trend toward "reality" shows on television?

2. The films *Back to the Future*, *Big*, *The Shining*, and *Terminator 2* all manipulate time, suggesting that if we could see into the future or back into the past, we could change our lives. How do such fantasies affect the way insights are ordinarily achieved in life? What do they tell us about the conflicts and needs that are particular to childhood and adolescence and how to deal with them?

3. *Memento* (d. Christopher Nolan, 2001) also plays with time and narrative, so that the viewer continually wonders who and what can be trusted. How is the viewer's position analogous to that of the protagonist? Are we in a better position to gain insight into the character? How does the character's memory problem affect his ability to have any reliable insights? Does he ever learn where his problem originated? Is the film a metaphor for how people often forget or deny things that are unpleasant?

4. Does the protagonist of *Citizen Kane* share any character traits with Oedipus or Hamlet? In classic tragedy, as defined by Aristotle, the tragic hero must be a noble character with a tragic flaw (usually pride) who recognizes his errors in the end and accepts responsibility. Given these conditions, is the film a classic tragedy? Why or

why not? If Kane does not fit the description of a tragic figure, does this make it difficult for the viewer to sympathize with him?

5. What is the nature of the origins and insights in *Hamlet*? Does Hamlet's situation provoke his soul-searching? Do his speculations on the relationship between thought and action produce insights for the reader or viewer? How are these complex ideas effectively conveyed in any of the film versions?

6. One traditional interpretation of Hamlet's character stresses his procrastination—that is, his inability to take action against Claudius until circumstances push him to it at the end. This would suggest that he is a character more prone to thought than action. How can such a view be reconciled with such different film approaches as those of Olivier, Zeffirelli, and Branagh?

7. The Richard Burton, Nicol Williamson, and Kevin Kline *Hamlets* are actually recordings of live performances rather than true films. Examine one of these and consider what is gained or lost in retaining the limitations of the stage. Study a particular scene or soliloquy and compare it to the way the same scene or soliloquy is treated in one of the more cinematic versions discussed in this unit.

8. Compare any film version of *Hamlet* with the experience of reading the play. What are some of the obvious differences? If you read the play before seeing any version of it, what impressions of the character of Hamlet (or any others) did you bring to your viewing of the film? Did those impressions conflict with what you saw? Illustrate your response with specific examples. Were you inclined to revise your understanding or feelings about any of the characters as a result of seeing a film version of the play?

9. Examine and compare one or two soliloquies from two different film versions of *Hamlet*. How does each compare with the soliloquy in the play? Has the filmmaker made cuts in the soliloquy? Has he used mise-en-scène (e.g., setting and lighting) or film techniques (e.g., camera angles and camera movement) to prevent the scene from becoming static? Has the director's **editing** of the scene made the speech more dynamic? As a result of your examination, what have you learned (1) about the soliloquy and its importance in Shakespeare's plays and (2) about the differences between film and theater?

10. Compare Olivier's *Hamlet* with Branagh's by closely examining one or two identical scenes in each. Identify specific performative aspects—for example, voice, delivery, and body language—in each version that convey different impressions of the characters and the scenes. What specific cinematic elements—setting, lighting, framing of shots, editing, camera movements—has the director used in each version, and what effects do they have on the overall impression of the scene and the meanings we perceive?

PART TWO

GENDER AND IDENTITY

Fiction

Girl, Jamaica Kincaid ◆ *The Revolt of "Mother,"* Mary E. Wilkins Freeman ◆
A Respectable Woman, Kate Chopin ◆ *The Storm*, Kate Chopin ◆ *Roselily*, Alice
Walker ◆ *The Yellow Wallpaper*, Charlotte Perkins Gilman ◆ *Another Evening at
the Club*, Alifa Rifaat ◆ *Town and Country Lovers*, Nadine Gordimer

Essays

Professions for Women, Virginia Woolf ◆ *One Man's Kids*, Daniel Meier ◆ *The
Fraternal Bond as a Joking Relationship*, Peter Lyman ◆ *Sex, Lies and
Conversation: Why Is It So Hard for Men and Women to Talk to Each Other?*
Deborah Tannen

Poetry

Woman's Constancy, John Donne ◆ *The Sun Rising*, John Donne ◆ *For My Lover,
Returning to His Wife*, Anne Sexton ◆ *Adultery*, James Dickey ◆ *The Faithful
Wife*, Barbara L. Greenberg ◆ *Genesis*, Mahwash Shoaib ◆ *Ragazza*, Maryfrances
Wagner ◆ *Borders*, Pat Mora ◆ *Home Burial*, Robert Frost ◆ *The Harlem Dancer,*
Claude McKay ◆ *What Lips My Lips Have Kissed*, Edna St. Vincent Millay ◆
Colours, Yevgeny Yevtushenko ◆ *I Knew a Woman*, Theodore Roethke ◆ *My Last
Duchess*, Robert Browning ◆ *My Ex-Husband*, Gabriel Spera ◆ *To His Coy Mistress*,
Andrew Marvell ◆ *The Willing Mistress*, Aphra Behn ◆ *Bright Star,* John Keats ◆
*She Proves the Inconsistency of the Desires and Criticism of Men Who Accuse Women
of What They Themselves Cause*, Sor Juana Inés de la Cruz ◆ Sonnet 30 ◆ Sonnet
116 ◆ Sonnet 129 ◆ Sonnet 130, William Shakespeare

Drama

Medea, Euripides

The culturally diverse texts in Part Two invite you to join in conversation with writers from various cultures and traditions as they explore the degree to which gender has shaped individual and cultural identities from ancient times to the present. They ask, among other things, why various cultures have constructed different images of women at various points in their history—wide-ranging images such as goddess, rebel, warrior, sex object, mother, wife, and "other." Since many cultures are mainly patriarchal, the choice of female image no doubt projects a powerful representation of the male's own image. Many male and female writers included here ask you to evaluate the merit of sexual politics that promotes a male-dominated model of gender relationships.

Looking back, we discover several traditions that have created images of women to represent specific models of male-female relations. Major among these is the idealizing tradition, which portrays women as different and superior beings. For example, the Greek story of Pygmalion—the legendary sculptor who fell in love with the female statue he carved according to his own inspired view of beauty— illustrates an extreme idealization of the notion of women. Such an idealization often transforms a woman into a love object that men can use to escape immediate reality. Other idealizing traditions, such as platonic love and courtly love, also explore the Pygmalion model of gender relations. English romantic poet John Keats, in his sonnet "Bright Star" (1819), for example, evokes a romantic concept of women in the poet's transformation of his mistress into an image of permanence essential to his orderly view of the world. In contrast, English dramatist and poet William Shakespeare, in his sonnet "My Mistress' Eyes Are Nothing Like the Sun," playfully rejects the idealizing tradition; he views his lover more realistically, in keeping with the rational trend of Renaissance tradition.

The destructive effects of dominance in gender relationships are the focus of *Medea*, Euripides' classical play, written centuries ago but presenting emotional issues that resonate with contemporary audiences. The drama reinforces the myth of woman as "femme fatale" by dramatizing the story of a forsaken woman, driven by sexual jealousy and the loss of her husband to a younger woman, who resorts to extreme revenge to reestablish her sense of justice.

From a more radical point of view, Mexican poet Sor Juana Inés de la Cruz, an early feminist, challenges in "She Proves the Inconsistency . . ." the mystique of gender relations through the Christian focus, which polarizes the image of a woman into an "angel" or a "demon." The poet protests against the tradition that debased women in seventeenth-century Mexico, reflecting the cultural oppression of "raw erotic play," or the game of male power and dominance in which, if a woman says no, "she has no heart," and if she says yes, "she's a whore." To keep pace with the social evolution of "the modern woman," we should perhaps ask what has happened to the polar image of "virgin-whore" in our own day. To what extent have men and women been able to overcome the "raw erotic play" that has tended to shape male-female relations in terms of male power and dominance?

By the late nineteenth-century, "the woman question" had become a matter of public debate in Europe and the United States, as both male and female writers rebelled against the Victorian ideal of woman as "the angel in the house" and exposed the limitations of marriages in which traditional gender roles were obediently observed. In 1879, for example, Norwegian audiences were outraged by Henrik Ibsen's drama *A Doll House*, in which the protagonist, Nora, moves from negotiation to open confrontation with her husband and decides that finding her own identity as a person is more important than her roles of wife and even mother. British readers responded in a similar fashion to novelist George Gissing's sympathetic portrayal of women struggling to define themselves as educated persons in pursuit of economic independence in *The Odd Women* (1866), and in the United States, Southern writer Kate Chopin's novel *The Awakening* (1899) was banned a few months after publication because the author dared to focus explicitly on women's sexual pleasure and adultery. Although they were mainly condemned in their own time as immoral and irresponsible, contemporary critics view these writers as courageous pioneers who pointed the way to freeing men and women from the confinements of traditional gender roles.

Other texts focus on the complexities that men and women often encounter in trying to communicate their emotions to one another. Deborah Tannen, a professor of linguistics at Georgetown University, in her essay "Sex, Lies and Conversation: Why Is It So Hard for Men and Women to Talk to Each Other?" (1990), contrasts the ways men and women communicate with one another and the misunderstandings that occur when either partner fails to "listen" to the other. In her short story, "Another Evening at the Club," contemporary Egyptian writer Alifa Rifaat, despite opposition from her Muslim family, explores the extent to which feminine domesticity and financial dependence have restricted the identities of both genders.

Traditionally in literature and the arts, an older woman was viewed as a "wicked seductress" or an expert in the art of love. Now, however, relationships between older women and younger men are viewed more positively, as in such recent films as *Lovely and Amazing*, *Tadpole*, *Igby Goes Down*, and *Crush*. What is your response to the romantic possibility of this kind of relationship? How do you react to this gender pairing, which is opposite to the more traditional pairing of the older (often rich) man and the attractive younger woman? Do you think this model of gender relationship might eventually change the sexual politics of a male-dominated society?

The question of women's sexuality is the focus of several poets, including British feminist Aphra Behn (1640?–89), who—despite charges of indecency by her peers—freely discussed female sexual desires in her plays and poetry, including "The Willing Mistress." Also, contemporary American poet Anne Sexton grants her lover permission to return to his wife. In "The Faithful Wife," Barbara L. Greenberg fantasizes about a lover who is more exciting personally and sexually than her husband, and in "What Lips My Lips Have Kissed," Edna St. Vincent Millay contrasts the pleasure of summer days in the company of young lovers with the starkness and solitude of winter.

As you join the debate here between feminists and patriarchs in these and other texts from various cultures and traditions, you will be invited to speculate on questions such as the following: Are men rightly in charge of the family and the tribe? Should women be accorded the same personal, political, and economic rights as men? How have both men and women used traditional concepts of sexuality, femininity, and masculinity to manipulate each other? How have traditional societal and cultural expectations affected gender identity? What new possibilities are there for healthier gender relationships and more fulfilled individual selves? For despite the difficulties involve in forming relationships, one theme remains constant in all of these texts: We are social beings whose personal and cultural identities are rooted in our need for relatedness.

FICTION

‸‸‸

Jamaica Kincaid

Girl

Wash the white clothes on Monday and put them on the stone heap; wash the color clothes on Tuesday and put them on the clothesline to dry; don't walk barehead in the hot sun; cook pumpkin fritters in very hot sweet oil; soak your little cloths right after you take them off; when buying cotton to make yourself a nice blouse, be sure that it doesn't have gum on it, because that way it won't hold up well after a wash; soak salt fish overnight before you cook it; is it true that you sing benna[1] in Sunday school?; always eat your food in such a way that it won't turn someone else's stomach; on Sundays try to walk like a lady and not like the slut you are so bent on becoming; don't sing benna in Sunday school; you mustn't speak to wharf-rat boys, not even to give directions; don't eat fruits on the street—flies will follow you; *but I don't sing benna on Sundays at all and never in Sunday school;* this is how to sew on a button; this is how to make a buttonhole for the button you have just sewed on; this is how to hem a dress when you see the hem coming down and so to prevent yourself from looking like the slut I know you are so bent on becoming; this is how you iron your father's khaki shirt so that it doesn't have a crease; this is how you iron your father's khaki pants so that they don't have a crease; this is how you grow okra—far from the house, because okra tree harbors red ants; when you are growing dasheen,[2] make sure it gets plenty of water or else it makes your throat itch when you are eating it; this is how you sweep a corner; this is how you sweep a whole house; this is how you sweep a yard; this is how you smile to someone you don't like too much; this is how you smile to someone you don't like at all; this is how you smile to someone you like completely; this is how you set a table for tea; this is how you set a table for dinner; this is how you set a table for dinner with an important guest; this is how you set a table for lunch; this is how you set a table for breakfast; this is how to behave in the presence of men who don't know you very well, and this way they won't recognize immediately the slut I have warned you against becoming; be sure to wash every day, even if it is with your own spit; don't squat down to play marbles—you are not a boy, you know; don't pick people's flowers— you might catch something; don't throw stones at blackbirds, because it might not be a blackbird at all; this is how to make a bread pudding; this is how to make doukona;[3] this is how to make pepper pot;[4] this is how to make a good medicine for

[1] Calypso music.
[2] The edible rootstock of taro, a tropical plant.
[3] A spicy plantain pudding.
[4] A stew.

313

a cold; this is how to make a good medicine to throw away a child before it even becomes a child; this is how to catch a fish; this is how to throw back a fish you don't like, and that way something bad won't fall on you; this is how to bully a man; this is how a man bullies you; this is how to love a man, and if this doesn't work there are other ways, and if they don't work don't feel too bad about giving up; this is how to spit up in the air if you feel like it, and this is how to move quick so that it doesn't fall on you; this is how to make ends meet; always squeeze bread to make sure it's fresh; *but what if the baker won't let me feel the bread?*; you mean to say that after all you are really going to be the kind of woman who the baker won't let near the bread?

[1978]

Journal Entry

How do you respond to being nagged and lectured? Do you usually accept the advice offered in such situations? Explain.

Textual Considerations

1. What is your response to the speaker of the monologue in *Girl*? What topics does she cover in her harangue?
2. Is this conversation actually taking place in the present, or is the daughter remembering advice from earlier occasions? Cite evidence.
3. Using details from the text, create a description of the girl's life five years hence. What kind of adult will the girl become?
4. The daughter has only two lines in the story—one a protest and the other a question. What do her responses suggest about her willingness to accept or reject the advice?
5. Speculate about the kind of advice she should accept. Explain.

Cultural Contexts

1. "Benna" is the Caribbean equivalent to popular music in other cultures—such as calypso or rock and roll. Why does the mother warn her daughter against that kind of music? In your experience, is music a source of conflict between parents and children? Explain.
2. How do the several references to West Indian folk culture contribute to the theme? Working with your group, consider what the speaker implies about gender roles and gender relationships.

Mary E. Wilkins Freeman

The Revolt of "Mother"

"Father!"

"What is it?"

"What are them men diggin' over there in the field for?"

There was a sudden dropping and enlarging of the lower part of the old man's face, as if some heavy weight had settled therein; he shut his mouth tight, and went on harnessing the great bay mare. He hustled the collar on to her neck with a jerk.

"Father!"

The old man slapped the saddle upon the mare's back.

"Look here, father, I want to know what them men are diggin' over in the field for, an' I'm goin' to know."

"I wish you'd go into the house, mother, an' 'tend to your own affairs," the old man said then. He ran his words together, and his speech was almost as inarticulate as a growl.

But the woman understood; it was her most native tongue. "I ain't goin' into the house till you tell me what them men are doin' over there in the field," said she.

Then she stood waiting. She was a small woman, short and straight-waisted like a child in her brown cotton gown. Her forehead was mild and benevolent between the smooth curves of gray hair; there were meek downward lines about her nose and mouth; but her eyes, fixed upon the old man, looked as if the meekness had been the result of her own will, never of the will of another.

They were in the barn, standing before the wide open doors. The spring air, full of the smell of growing grass and unseen blossoms, came in their faces. The deep yard in front was littered with farm wagons and piles of wood; on the edges, close to the fence and the house, the grass was a vivid green, and there were some dandelions.

The old man glanced doggedly at his wife as he tightened the last buckles on the harness. She looked as immovable to him as one of the rocks in his pasture-land, bound to the earth with generations of blackberry vines. He slapped the reins over the horse, and started forth from the barn.

"*Father!*" said she.

The old man pulled up. "What is it?"

"I want to know what them men are diggin' over there in the field for."

"They're diggin' a cellar, I s'pose, if you've got to know."

"A cellar for what?"

"A barn."

"A barn? You ain't goin' to build a barn over there where we was goin' to have a house, father?"

The old man said not another word. He hurried the horse into the farm wagon, and clattered out of the yard, jouncing as sturdily on his seat as a boy.

The woman stood a moment looking after him, then she went out of the barn across a corner of the yard to the house. The house, standing at right angles with the great barn and a long reach of sheds and out-buildings, was infinitesimal compared with them. It was scarcely as commodious for people as the little boxes under the barn eaves were for doves.

A pretty girl's face, pink and delicate as a flower, was looking out of one of the house windows. She was watching three men who were digging over in the field which bounded the yard near the road line. She turned quietly when the woman entered.

"What are they digging for, mother?" said she. "Did he tell you?"

"They're diggin' for—a cellar for a new barn."

"Oh, mother, he ain't going to build another barn?"

"That's what he says."

A boy stood before the kitchen glass combing his hair. He combed slowly and painstakingly, arranging his brown hair in a smooth hillock over his forehead. He did not seem to pay any attention to the conversation.

"Sammy, did you know father was going to build a new barn?" asked the girl.

The boy combed assiduously.

"Sammy!"

He turned, and showed a face like his father's under his smooth crest of hair. "Yes, I s'pose I did," he said, reluctantly.

"How long have you known it?" asked his mother.

"'Bout three months, I guess."

"Why didn't you tell of it?"

"Didn't think 'twould do no good."

"I don't see what father wants another barn for," said the girl, in her sweet, slow voice. She turned again to the window, and stared out at the digging men in the field. Her tender, sweet face was full of a gentle distress. Her forehead was as bald and innocent as a baby's with the light hair strained back from it in a row of curl-papers. She was quite large, but her soft curls did not look as if they covered muscles.

Her mother looked sternly at the boy. "Is he goin' to buy more cows?" said she.

The boy did not reply; he was tying his shoes.

"Sammy, I want you to tell me if he's goin' to buy more cows."

"I s'pose he is."

"How many?"

"Four, I guess."

His mother said nothing more. She went into the pantry, and there was a clatter of dishes. The boy got his cap from a nail behind the door, took an old arithmetic from the shelf, and started for school. He was lightly built, but clumsy. He went out of the yard with a curious spring in the hips, that made his loose home-made jacket tilt up in the rear.

The girl went to the sink, and began to wash the dishes that were piled up there. Her mother came promptly out of the pantry, and shoved her aside. "You wipe 'em," said she; "I'll wash. There's a good many this mornin'."

The mother plunged her hands vigorously into the water, the girl wiped the plates slowly and dreamily. "Mother," said she, "don't you think it's too bad father's going to build that new barn, much as we need a decent house to live in?"

Her mother scrubbed a dish fiercely. "You ain't found out yet we're women-folks, Nanny Penn," said she. "You ain't seen enough of men-folks yet to. One of these days you'll find it out, an' then you'll know that we know only what men-folks think we do, so far as any use of it goes, an' how we'd ought to reckon men-folks in with Providence, an' not complain of what they do any more than we do of the weather."

"I don't care; I don't believe George is anything like that, anyhow," said Nanny. Her delicate face flushed pink, her lips pouted softly, as if she were going to cry.

"You wait an' see. I guess George Eastman ain't no better than other men. You hadn't ought to judge father, though. He can't help it, 'cause he don't look at things jest the way we do. An' we've been pretty comfortable here, after all. The roof don't leak—ain't never but once—that's one thing. Father's kept it shingled right up."

"I do wish we had a parlor."

"I guess it won't hurt George Eastman any to come to see you in a nice clean kitchen. I guess a good many girls don't have as good a place as this. Nobody's ever heard me complain."

"I ain't complained either, mother."

"Well, I don't think you'd better, a good father an' a good home as you've got. S'pose your father made you go out an' work for your livin'? Lots of girls have to that ain't no stronger an' better able to than you be."

Sarah Penn washed the frying-pan with a conclusive air. She scrubbed the outside of it as faithfully as the inside. She was a masterly keeper of her box of a house. Her one living-room never seemed to have in it any of the dust which the friction of life with inanimate matter produces. She swept, and there seemed to be no dirt to go before the broom; she cleaned, and one could see no difference. She was like an artist so perfect that he has apparently no art. To-day she got out a mixing bowl and a board, and rolled some pies, and there was no more flour upon her than upon her daughter who was doing finer work. Nanny was to be married in the fall, and she was sewing on some white cambric and embroidery. She sewed industriously while her mother cooked, her soft milk-white hands and wrists showed whiter than her delicate work.

"We must have the stove moved out in the shed before long," said Mrs. Penn. "Talk about not havin' things, it's been a real blessin' to be able to put a stove up in that shed in hot weather. Father did one good thing when he fixed that stove-pipe out there."

Sarah Penn's face as she rolled her pies had that expression of meek vigor which might have characterized one of the New Testament saints. She was making mince pies. Her husband, Adoniram Penn, liked them better than any other kind. She baked twice a week. Adoniram often liked a piece of pie between meals. She hurried this morning. It had been later than usual when she began, and she wanted to have a pie baked for dinner. However deep a resentment she might be forced to hold against her husband, she would never fail in sedulous attention to his wants.

Nobility of character manifests itself at loop-holes when it is not provided with large doors. Sarah Penn's showed itself to-day in flaky dishes of pastry. So she made the pies faithfully, while across the table she could see, when she glanced up from her work, the sight that rankled in her patient and steadfast soul—the digging of the cellar of the new barn in the place where Adoniram forty years ago had promised her their new house should stand.

The pies were done for dinner. Adoniram and Sammy were home a few minutes after twelve o'clock. The dinner was eaten with serious haste. There was never much conversation at the table in the Penn family. Adoniram asked a blessing, and they ate promptly, then rose up and went about their work.

Sammy went back to school, taking soft sly lopes out of the yard like a rabbit. He wanted a game of marbles before school, and feared his father would give him some chores to do. Adoniram hastened to the door and called after him, but he was out of sight.

"I don't see what you let him go for, Mother," said he. "I wanted him to help me unload that wood."

Adoniram went to work out in the yard unloading wood from the wagon. Sarah put away the dinner dishes, while Nanny took down her curl-papers and changed her dress. She was going down to the store to buy some more embroidery and thread.

When Nanny was gone, Mrs. Penn went to the door. "Father!" she called.

"Well, what is it!"

"I want to see you jest a minute."

"I can't leave this wood nohow. I've got to git it unloaded an' go for a load of gravel afore two o'clock. Sammy had ought to helped me. You hadn't ought to let him go to school so early."

"I want to see you jest a minute."

"I tell ye I can't, nohow, mother."

"Father, you come here." Sarah Penn stood in the door like a queen; she held her head as if it bore a crown; there was that patience which makes authority royal in her voice. Adoniram went.

Mrs. Penn led the way into the kitchen, and pointed to a chair. "Sit down, father," said she; "I've got somethin' I want to say to you."

He sat down heavily; his face was quite stolid, but he looked at her with restive eyes. "Well, what is it, mother?"

"I want to know what you're buildin' that new barn for, father?"

"I ain't got nothin' to say about it."

"It can't be you think you need another barn?"

"I tell ye I ain't got nothin' to say about it, mother, an' I ain't goin' to say nothin'."

"Be you goin' to buy more cows?"

Adoniram did not reply; he shut his mouth tight.

"I know you be, as well as I want to. Now, father, look here"—Sarah Penn had not sat down; she stood before her husband in the humble fashion of a Scripture woman— "I'm goin' to talk real plain to you; I never have sence I married you, but I'm goin' to now. I ain't never complained, an' I ain't goin' to complain now, but I'm goin' to talk plain. You see this room here, father; you look at it well. You see there ain't no carpet on the floor, an' you see the paper is all dirty, an' droppin' off the walls. We ain't had no new paper on it for ten year, an' then I put it on myself, an' it didn't cost but ninepence a roll. You see this room, father; it's all the one I've had to work in an' eat in an' sit in sence we was married. There ain't another woman in the whole town whose husband ain't got half the means you have but what's got better. It's all the room Nanny's got to have her company in; an' there ain't one of her mates but what's got better, an' their fathers not so able as hers is. It's all the room she'll have to be married in. What would you have thought, father, if we had had our weddin' in a room no better than this? I was married in my mother's parlor, with a carpet on the floor, an' stuffed furniture, an' a mahogany card-table. An' this is all the room my daughter will have to be married in. Look here, father!"

Sarah Penn went across the room as though it were a tragic stage. She flung open a door and disclosed a tiny bedroom, only large enough for a bed and bureau, with a path between. "There, father," said she—"there's all the room I've had to sleep in forty year. All my children were born there—the two that died, an' the two that's livin'. I was sick with a fever there."

She stepped into another door and opened it. It led into the small, ill-lighted pantry. "Here," said she, "is all the buttery I've got—every place I've got for my dishes, to set away my victuals in, an' to keep my milk-pans in. Father, I've been takin' care of the milk of six cows in this place, an' now you're goin' to build a new barn, an' keep more cows, an' give me more to do in it."

She threw open another door. A narrow crooked flight of stairs wound upward from it. "There, father," said she. "I want you to look at the stairs that go up to them two unfinished chambers that are all the places our son an' daughter have had to sleep in all their lives. There ain't a prettier girl in town nor a more ladylike one than Nanny, an' that's the place she has to sleep in. It ain't so good as your horse's stall; it ain't so warm an' tight."

Sarah Penn went back and stood before her husband. "Now, father," said she, "I want to know if you think you're doin' right an' accordin' to what you profess. Here, when we was married, forty year ago, you promised me faithful that we should have a new house built in that lot over in the field before the year was out. You said you had money enough, an' you wouldn't ask me to live in no such place as this. It is forty year now, an' you've been makin' more money, an' I've been savin' of it for you ever since, an' you ain't built no house yet. You've built sheds an' cow-houses an' one new barn, an' now you're goin' to build another. Father, I want to know if you think it's right. You're lodgin' your dumb beasts better than you are your own flesh an' blood. I want to know if you think it's right."

"I ain't got nothin' to say."

"You can't say nothin' without ownin' it ain't right, father. An' there's another thing—I ain't complained; I've got along forty year, an' I s'pose I should forty more, if it wa'n't for that—if we don't have another house. Nanny she can't live with us after she's married. She'll have to go somewheres else to live away from us, an' it don't seem as if I could have it so, noways, father. She wa'n't ever strong. She's got considerable color, but there wa'n't never any backbone to her. I've always took the heft of everything off her, an' she ain't fit to keep house an' do everything herself. She'll be all worn out inside of a year. Think of her doin' all the washin' an' ironin' an' bakin' with them soft white hands an' arms, an' sweepin'! I can't have it so, noways, father."

Mrs. Penn's face was burning; her mild eyes gleamed. She had pleaded her little cause like a Webster;[1] she had ranged from severity to pathos; but her opponent employed that obstinate silence which makes eloquence futile with mocking echoes. Adoniram arose clumsily.

"Father, ain't you got nothin' to say?" said Mrs. Penn.

"I've got to go off after that load of gravel. I can't stan' here talkin' all day."

"Father, won't you think it over, an' have a house built there instead of a barn?"

"I ain't got nothin' to say."

Adoniram shuffled out. Mrs. Penn went into her bedroom. When she came out, her eyes were red. She had a roll of unbleached cotton cloth. She spread it out on the kitchen table, and began cutting out some shirts for her husband. The men over in the field had a team to help them this afternoon; she could hear their halloos. She had a scanty pattern for the shirts; she had to plan and piece the sleeves.

Nanny came home with her embroidery, and sat down with her needlework. She had taken down her curl-papers, and there was a soft roll of fair hair like an aureole over her forehead; her face was as delicately fine and clear as porcelain. Suddenly she looked up, and the tender red flamed all over her face and neck. "Mother," said she.

"What say?"

"I've been thinking—I don't see how we're goin' to have any—wedding in this room. I'd be ashamed to have his folks come if we didn't have anybody else."

"Mebbe we can have some new paper before then; I can put it on. I guess you won't have no call to be ashamed of your belongin's."

"We might have the wedding in the new barn," said Nanny, with gentle pettishness. "Why, mother, what makes you look so?"

Mrs. Penn had started, and was staring at her with a curious expression. She turned again to her work, and spread out a pattern carefully on the cloth. "Nothin'," said she.

Presently Adoniram clattered out of the yard in his two-wheeled dump cart, standing as proudly upright as a Roman charioteer. Mrs. Penn opened the door and stood there a minute looking out; the halloos of the men sounded louder.

It seemed to her all through the spring months that she heard nothing but the halloos and the noises of saws and hammers. The new barn grew fast. It was a fine edifice for this little village. Men came on pleasant Sundays, in their meeting suits and clean shirt bosoms, and stood around it admiringly. Mrs. Penn did not speak of it, and Adoniram did not mention it to her, although sometimes, upon a return from inspecting it, he bore himself with injured dignity.

"It's a strange thing how your mother feels about the new barn," he said, confidentially, to Sammy one day.

Sammy only grunted after an odd fashion for a boy; he had learned it from his father.

The barn was all completed ready for use by the third week in July. Adoniram had planned to move his stock in on Wednesday; on Tuesday he received a letter

---

[1] Daniel Webster (1782–1852) was an American orator, lawyer, and statesman.

which changed his plans. He came in with it early in the morning. "Sammy's been to the post-office," said he, "an' I've got a letter from Hiram." Hiram was Mrs. Penn's brother, who lived in Vermont.

"Well," said Mrs. Penn, "what does he say about the folks?"

"I guess they're all right. He says he thinks if I come up country right off there's a chance to buy jest the kind of a horse I want." He stared reflectively out of the window at the new barn.

Mrs. Penn was making pies. She went on clapping the rolling-pin into the crust, although she was very pale, and her heart beat loudly.

"I dun' know but what I'd better go," said Adoniram. "I hate to go off jest now, right in the midst of hayin', but the ten-acre lot's cut, an' I guess Rufus an' the others can git along without me three or four days. I can't get a horse round here to suit me, nohow, an' I've got to have another for all that wood-haulin' in the fall. I told Hiram to watch out, an' if he got wind of a good horse to let me know. I guess I'd better go."

"I'll get your clean shirt an' collar," said Mrs. Penn calmly.

She laid out Adoniram's Sunday suit and his clean clothes on the bed in the little bedroom. She got his shaving-water and razor ready. At last she buttoned on his collar and fastened his black cravat.

Adoniram never wore his collar and cravat except on extra occasions. He held his head high, with a rasped dignity. When he was all ready, with his coat and hat brushed, and a lunch of pie and cheese in a paper bag, he hesitated on the threshold of the door. He looked at his wife, and his manner was defiantly apologetic. "*If* them cows come to-day, Sammy can drive 'em into the new barn," said he, "an' when they bring the hay up, they can pitch it in there."

"Well," replied Mrs. Penn.

Adoniram set his shaven face ahead and started. When he had cleared the door-step, he turned and looked back with a kind of nervous solemnity. "I shall be back by Saturday if nothin' happens," said he.

"Do be careful, father," returned his wife.

She stood at the door with Nanny at her elbow and watched him out of sight. Her eyes had a strange, doubtful expression in them; her peaceful forehead was contracted. She went in, and about her baking again. Nanny sat sewing. Her wedding-day was drawing nearer, and she was getting pale and thin with her steady sewing. Her mother kept glancing at her.

"Have you got that pain in your side this mornin'?" she asked.

"A little."

Mrs. Penn's face, as she worked, changed, her perplexed forehead smoothed, her eyes were steady, her lips firmly set. She formed a maxim for herself, although incoherently with her unlettered thoughts. "Unsolicited opportunities are the guide-posts of the Lord to the new roads of life," she repeated in effect, and she made up her mind to her course of action.

"S'posin' I *had* wrote to Hiram," she muttered once, when she was in the pantry— "s'posin' I had wrote, an' asked him if he knew of any horse? But I didn't, an' father's goin' wa'n't none of my doin'. It looks like a providence." Her voice rang out quite loud at the last.

"What are you talkin' about, mother?" called Nanny.

"Nothin'."

Mrs. Penn hurried her baking; at eleven o'clock it was all done. The load of hay from the west field came slowly down the cart track, and drew up at the new barn. Mrs. Penn ran out. "Stop!" she screamed—"stop!"

The men stopped and looked; Sammy upreared from the top of the load, and stared at his mother.

"Stop!" she cried out again. "Don't you put the hay in that barn; put it in the old one."

"Why, he said to put it in here," returned one of the haymakers, wonderingly. He was a young man, a neighbor's son, whom Adoniram hired by the year to help on the farm.

"Don't you put the hay in the new barn; there's room enough in the old one, ain't there?" said Mrs. Penn.

"Room enough," returned the hired man, in his thick, rustic tones. "Didn't need the new barn, nohow far as room's concerned. Well, I s'pose he changed his mind." He took hold of the horses' bridles.

Mrs. Penn went back to the house. Soon the kitchen windows were darkened, and a fragrance like warm honey came into the room.

Nanny laid down her work. "I thought father wanted them to put the hay into the new barn?" she said wonderingly.

"It's all right," replied her mother.

Sammy slid down from the load of hay, and came in to see if dinner was ready.

"I ain't goin' to get a regular dinner to-day, as long as father's gone," said his mother. "I've let the fire go out. You can have some bread an' milk an' pie. I thought we could get along." She set out some bowls of milk, some bread, and a pie on the kitchen table. "You'd better eat your dinner now," said she. "You might jest as well get through with it. I want you to help me afterward."

Nanny and Sammy stared at each other. There was something strange in their mother's manner. Mrs. Penn did not eat anything herself. She went into the pantry, and they heard her moving dishes while they ate. Presently she came out with a pile of plates. She got the clothes-basket out of the shed, and packed them in it. Nanny and Sammy watched. She brought out cups and saucers, and put them in with the plates.

"What you goin' to do, mother?" inquired Nanny, in a timid voice. A sense of something unusual made her tremble, as if it were a ghost. Sammy rolled his eyes over his pie.

"You'll see what I'm goin' to do," replied Mrs. Penn. "If you're through, Nanny, I want you to go upstairs an' pack up your things; an' I want you, Sammy, to help me take down the bed in the bedroom."

"Oh, mother, what for?" gasped Nanny.

"You'll see."

During the next few hours a feat was performed by this simple, pious New England mother which was equal in its way to Wolfe's storming of the Heights of

Abraham.[2] It took no more genius and audacity of bravery for Wolfe to cheer his wondering soldiers up those steep precipices, under the sleeping eyes of the enemy, than for Sarah Penn, at the head of her children, to move all their little household goods into the new barn while her husband was away.

Nanny and Sammy followed their mother's instructions without a murmur; indeed, they were overawed. There is a certain uncanny and superhuman quality about all such purely original undertakings as their mother's was to them. Nanny went back and forth with her light loads, and Sammy tugged with sober energy.

At five o'clock in the afternoon the little house in which the Penns had lived for forty years had emptied itself into the new barn.

Every builder builds somewhat for unknown purposes, and is in a measure a prophet. The architect of Adoniram Penn's barn, while he designed it for the comfort of four-footed animals, had planned better than he knew for the comfort of humans. Sarah Penn saw at a glance its possibilities. Those great box-stalls, with quilts hung before them, would make better bedrooms than the one she had occupied for forty years, and there was a tight carriage-room. The harness-room, with its chimney and shelves, would make a kitchen of her dreams. The great middle space would make a parlor, by-and-by, fit for a palace. Upstairs there was as much room as down. With partitions and windows, what a house would there be! Sarah looked at the row of stanchions before the allotted space for cows, and reflected that she would have her front entry there.

At six o'clock the stove was up in the harness-room, the kettle was boiling, and the table set for tea. It looked almost as home-like as the abandoned house across the yard had ever done. The young hired man milked, and Sarah directed him calmly to bring the milk to the new barn. He came gaping, dropping little blots of foam from the brimming pails on the grass. Before the next morning he had spread the story of Adoniram Penn's wife moving into the new barn all over the little village. Men assembled in the store and talked it over, women with shawls over their heads scuttled into each other's houses before their work was done. Any deviation from the ordinary course of life in this quiet town was enough to stop all progress in it. Everybody paused to look at the staid, independent figure on the side track. There was a difference of opinion with regard to her. Some held her to be insane; some, of a lawless and rebellious spirit.

Friday the minister went to see her. It was in the forenoon, and she was at the barn door shelling pease[3] for dinner. She looked up and returned his salutation with dignity, then she went on with her work. She did not invite him in. The saintly expression of her face remained fixed, but there was an angry flush over it.

The minister stood awkwardly before her, and talked. She handled the pease as if they were bullets. At last she looked up, and her eyes showed the spirit that her meek front had covered for a lifetime.

[2] James Wolfe (1727–1759) was a British general whose troops stormed the French army on the Plains of Abraham above Quebec.
[3] Old or variant spelling of "peas."

"There ain't no use talkin', Mr. Hersey," she said. "I've thought it all over an' over, an' I believe I'm doin' what's right. I've made it the subject of prayer, an' it's betwixt me an' the Lord an' Adoniram. There ain't no call for anybody else to worry about it."

"Well, of course, if you have brought it to the Lord in prayer, and feel satisfied that you are doing right, Mrs. Penn," said the minister, helplessly. His thin gray-bearded face was pathetic. He was a sickly man; his youthful confidence had cooled; he had to scourge himself up to some of his pastoral duties as relentlessly as a Catholic ascetic, and then he was prostrated by the smart.

"I think it's right jest as much as I think it was right for our forefathers to come over from the old country 'cause they didn't have what belonged to 'em," said Mrs. Penn. She arose. The barn threshold might have been Plymouth Rock from her bearing. "I don't doubt you mean well, Mr. Hersey," said she, "but there are things people hadn't ought to interfere with. I've been a member of the church for over forty year. I've got my own mind an' my own feet, an' I'm goin' to think my own thoughts an' go my own ways, an' nobody but the Lord is goin' to dictate to me unless I've a mind to have him. Won't you come in an' set down? How is Mis' Hersey?"

"She is well, I thank you," replied the minister. He added some more perplexed apologetic remarks; then he retreated.

He could expound the intricacies of every character study in the Scriptures, he was competent to grasp the Pilgrim Fathers and all historical innovators, but Sarah Penn was beyond him. He could deal with primal causes, but parallel ones worsted him. But, after all, although it was aside from his province, he wondered more how Adoniram Penn would deal with his wife than how the Lord would. Everybody shared the wonder. When Adoniram's four new cows arrived, Sarah ordered three to be put in the old barn, the other in the house shed where the cooking-stove had stood. That added to the excitement. It was whispered that all four cows were domiciled in the house.

Towards sunset on Saturday, when Adoniram was expected home, there was a knot of men in the road near the new barn. The hired man had milked, but he still hung around the premises. Sarah Penn had supper all ready. There were brown bread and baked beans and a custard pie; it was the supper that Adoniram loved on a Saturday night. She had on a clean calico, and she bore herself imperturbably. Nanny and Sammy kept close at her heels. Their eyes were large, and Nanny was full of nervous tremors. Still there was to them more pleasant excitement than anything else. An inborn confidence in their mother over their father asserted itself.

Sammy looked out of the harness-room window. "There he is," he announced, in an awed whisper. He and Nanny peeped around the casing. Mrs. Penn kept on about her work. The children watched Adoniram leave the new horse standing in the drive while he went to the house door. It was fastened. Then he went around to the shed. That door was seldom locked, even when the family was away. The thought how her father would be confronted by the cow flashed upon Nanny. There was a hysterical sob in her throat. Adoniram emerged from the shed and stood looking about in a dazed fashion. His lips moved; he was saying something, but they could not hear what it was. The hired man was peeping around a corner of the old barn, but nobody saw him.

Adoniram took the new horse by the bridle and led him across the yard to the new barn. Nanny and Sammy slunk close to their mother. The barn doors rolled back, and there stood Adoniram, with the long mild face of the great Canadian farm horse looking over his shoulder.

Nanny kept behind her mother, but Sammy stepped suddenly forward, and stood in front of her.

Adoniram stared at the group. "What on airth you all down here for?" said he. "What's the matter over to the house?"

"We've come here to live, father," said Sammy. His shrill voice quavered out bravely.

"What"—Adoniram sniffled—"what is it smells like cooking?" said he. He stepped forward and looked in the open door of the harness-room. Then he turned to his wife. His old bristling face was pale and frightened. "What on airth does this mean, mother?" he gasped.

"You come in here, father," said Sarah. She led the way, into the harness-room and shut the door. "Now, father," said she, "you needn't be scared. I ain't crazy. There ain't nothin' to be upset over. But we've come here to live, an' we're goin' to live here. We've got jest as good a right here as new horses an' cows. The house wa'n't fit for us to live in any longer, an' I made up my mind I wa'n't goin' to stay there. I've done my duty by you forty year, an' I'm goin' to do it now; but I'm goin' to live here. You've got to put in some windows and partitions; an' you'll have to buy some furniture."

"Why, mother!" the old man gasped.

"You'd better take your coat off an' get washed—there's the wash-basin—an' then we'll have supper."

"Why, mother!"

Sammy went past the window, leading the new horse to the old barn. The old man saw him, and shook his head speechlessly. He tried to take off his coat, but his arms seemed to lack the power. His wife helped him. She poured some water into the tin basin, and put in a piece of soap. She got the comb and brush, and smoothed his thin gray hair after he had washed. Then she put the beans, hot bread, and tea on the table. Sammy came in, and the family drew up. Adoniram sat looking dazedly at his plate, and they waited.

"Ain't you goin' to ask a blessin', father?" said Sarah.

And the old man bent his head and mumbled.

All through the meal he stopped eating at intervals, and stared furtively at his wife; but he ate well. The home food tasted good to him, and his old frame was too sturdily healthy to be affected by his mind. But after supper he went out, and sat down on the step of the smaller door at the right of the barn, through which he had meant his Jerseys to pass in stately file, but which Sarah designed for her front house door, and he leaned his head on his hands.

After the supper dishes were cleared away and the milk-pans washed, Sarah went out to him. The twilight was deepening. There was a clear green glow in the sky. Before them stretched the smooth level of field; in the distance was a cluster of hay-stacks like the huts of a village; the air was very cool and calm and sweet. The landscape might have been an ideal one of peace.

Sarah bent over and touched her husband on one of his thin, sinewy shoulders. "Father!"

The old man's shoulders heaved: he was weeping.

"Why, don't do so, father," said Sarah.

"I'll—put up the—partitions, an'—everything you—want, mother."

Sarah put her apron up to her face; she was overcome by her own triumph.

Adoniram was like a fortress whose walls had no active resistance, and went down the instant the right besieging tools were used. "Why, mother," he said, hoarsely, "I hadn't no idee you was so set on't as all this comes to."

[1891]

Journal Entry

How do both "mother" and "father" conform to and rebel against traditional gender roles? Do you identify with either character? Explain.

Textual Considerations

1. How does Freeman use the setting to contribute to the story's conflict? Identify location and details of the place and time of the action that contribute to the story's conflict.
2. How would you describe the relationship between the Penns? Does Freeman portray them by their works or their actions, or both? Explain.
3. To what extent is Nanny essential to the story? What is her function? Find examples and illustrations of feminine solidarity between Mrs. Penn and her daughter. Speculate on why the mother feels she must pass down to her daughter the feminine consciousness that "we know only what men-folks think we do."
4. Freeman uses expressions like "immovable as one of the works" or "meek vigor which might have characterized one of the New Testament Saints" to describe Mrs. Penn. Identify other expressions that sketch her physical and psychological portrait.
5. Explore the causes that motivate Mrs. Penn to break out of her socially defined role as an obedient wife. Include in your discussion the different ways in which she and her husband perceive the world. How effectively do they communicate with each other?

Cultural Contexts

1. To continue to examine the power of the patriarchal traditions that dictate Mrs. Penn's social confinement, as well as the dynamics of gender relations in their household, comment on the reaction of the male community to Mrs. Penn's "revolt." Include Minister Hersey in your discussion.
2. To better understand the interplay of gender and power in "The Revolt of 'Mother,'" speculate with members of your group about who really holds the power in the Penns' household. Is it the mother, who preserves the façade of patriarchal stability even though she revolts against her husband, or Adoniram, who, as the husband, is supposed to hold the real power?

Kate Chopin

A Respectable Woman

Mrs. Baroda was a little provoked to learn that her husband expected his friend, Gouvernail, up to spend a week or two on the plantation.

They had entertained a good deal during the winter; much of the time had also been passed in New Orleans in various forms of mild dissipation. She was looking forward to a period of unbroken rest, now, and undisturbed tête-à-tête with her husband, when he informed her that Gouvernail was coming up to stay a week or two.

This was a man she had heard much of but never seen. He had been her husband's college friend; was now a journalist, and in no sense a society man or "a man about town," which were, perhaps, some of the reasons she had never met him. But she had unconsciously formed an image of him in her mind. She pictured him tall, slim, cynical; with eye-glasses, and his hands in his pockets; and she did not like him. Gouvernail was slim enough, but he wasn't very tall nor very cynical; neither did he wear eye-glasses nor carry his hands in his pockets. And she rather liked him when he first presented himself.

But why she liked him she could not explain satisfactorily to herself when she partly attempted to do so. She could discover in him none of those brilliant and promising traits which Gaston, her husband, had often assured her that he possessed. On the contrary, he sat rather mute and receptive before her chatty eagerness to make him feel at home and in face of Gaston's frank and wordy hospitality. His manner was as courteous toward her as the most exacting woman could require; but he made no direct appeal to her approval or even esteem.

Once settled at the plantation he seemed to like to sit upon the wide portico in the shade of one of the big Corinthian pillars, smoking his cigar lazily and listening attentively to Gaston's experience as a sugar planter.

"This is what I call living," he would utter with deep satisfaction, as the air that swept across the sugar field caressed him with its warm and scented velvety touch. It pleased him also to get on familiar terms with the big dogs that came about him, rubbing themselves sociably against his legs. He did not care to fish, and displayed no eagerness to go out and kill grosbecs when Gaston proposed doing so.

Gouvernail's personality puzzled Mrs. Baroda, but she liked him. Indeed, he was a lovable, inoffensive fellow. After a few days, when she could understand him no better than at first, she gave over being puzzled and remained piqued. In this mood she left her husband and her guest, for the most part, alone together. Then finding that Gouvernail took no manner of exception to her action, she imposed her society upon him, accompanying him in his idle strolls to the mill and walks along the batture. She persistently sought to penetrate the reserve in which he had unconsciously enveloped himself.

"When is he going—your friend?" she one day asked her husband. "For my part, he tires me frightfully."

"Not for a week yet, dear. I can't understand; he gives you no trouble."

"No. I should like him better if he did: if he were more like others, and I had to plan somewhat for his comfort and enjoyment."

Gaston took his wife's pretty face between his hands and looked tenderly and laughingly into her troubled eyes. They were making a bit of toilet sociably together in Mrs. Baroda's dressing-room.

"You are full of surprises, ma belle," he said to her. "Even I can never count upon how you are going to act under given conditions." He kissed her and turned to fasten his cravat before the mirror.

"Here you are," he went on, "taking poor Gouvernail seriously and making a commotion over him, the last thing he would desire or expect."

"Commotion!" she hotly resented. "Nonsense! How can you say such a thing? Commotion, indeed! But, you know, you said he was clever."

"So he is. But the poor fellow is run down by overwork now. That's why I asked him here to take a rest."

"You used to say he was a man of ideas," she retorted, unconciliated. "I expected him to be interesting, at least. I'm going to the city in the morning to have my spring gowns fitted. Let me know when Mr. Gouvernail is gone; I shall be at my Aunt Octavie's."

That night she went and sat alone upon a bench that stood beneath a live oak tree at the edge of the gravel walk.

She had never known her thoughts or her intentions to be so confused. She could gather nothing from them but the feeling of a distinct necessity to quit her home in the morning.

Mrs. Baroda heard footsteps crunching the gravel; but could discern in the darkness only the approaching red point of a lighted cigar. She knew it was Gouvernail, for her husband did not smoke. She hoped to remain unnoticed, but her white gown revealed her to him. He threw away his cigar and seated himself upon the bench beside her; without a suspicion that she might object to his presence.

"Your husband told me to bring this to you, Mrs. Baroda," he said, handing her a filmy, white scarf with which she sometimes enveloped her head and shoulders. She accepted the scarf from him with a murmur of thanks, and let it lie in her lap.

He made some commonplace observation upon the baneful effect of the night air at that season. Then as his gaze reached out into the darkness, he murmured, half to himself:

"'Night of south winds—night of the large few stars!
Still nodding night—'"

She made no reply to this apostrophe to the night, which indeed, was not addressed to her.

Gouvernail was in no sense a diffident man, for he was not a self-conscious one. His periods of reserve were not constitutional, but the result of moods. Sitting there beside Mrs. Baroda, his silence melted for the time.

He talked freely and intimately in a low, hesitating drawl that was not unpleasant to hear. He talked of the old college days when he and Gaston had been a good deal to each other; of the days of keen and blind ambitions and large intentions. Now there was left with him, at least, a philosophic acquiescence to the existing order—only a desire to be permitted to exist, with now and then a little whiff of genuine life, such as he was breathing now.

Her mind only vaguely grasped what he was saying. Her physical being was for the moment predominant. She was not thinking of his words, only drinking in the tones of his voice. She wanted to reach out her hand in the darkness and touch him with the sensitive tips of her fingers upon the face or the lips. She wanted to draw close to him and whisper against his cheek—she did not care what—as she might have done if she had not been a respectable woman.

The stronger the impulse grew to bring herself near him, the further, in fact, did she draw away from him. As soon as she could so do without an appearance of too great rudeness, she rose and left him there alone.

Before she reached the house, Gouvernail had lighted a fresh cigar and ended his apostrophe to the night.

Mrs. Baroda was greatly tempted that night to tell her husband—who was also her friend—of this folly that had seized her. But she did not yield to the temptation. Beside being a respectable woman she was a very sensible one; and she knew there are some battles in life which a human being must fight alone.

When Gaston arose in the morning, his wife had already departed. She had taken an early morning train to the city. She did not return till Gouvernail was gone from under her roof.

There was some talk of having him back during the summer that followed. That is, Gaston greatly desired it; but this desire yielded to his wife's strenuous opposition.

However, before the year ended, she proposed, wholly from herself, to have Gouvernail visit them again. Her husband was surprised and delighted with the suggestion coming from her.

"I am glad, chère amie, to know that you have finally overcome your dislike for him; truly he did not deserve it."

"Oh," she told him, laughingly, after pressing a long, tender kiss upon his lips, "I have overcome everything! you will see. This time I shall be very nice to him."

[1894]

Kate Chopin

The Storm

I

The leaves were so still that even Bibi thought it was going to rain. Bobinôt, who was accustomed to converse on terms of perfect equality with his little son, called the child's attention to certain sombre clouds that were rolling with sinister intention from the west, accompanied by a sullen, threatening roar. They were at Friedheimer's store and decided to remain there till the storm had passed. They sat within the door on two empty kegs. Bibi was four years old and looked very wise.

"Mama'll be 'fraid, yes," he suggested with blinking eyes.

"She'll shut the house. Maybe she got Sylvie helpin' her this evenin'," Bobinôt responded reassuringly.

"No; she ent got Sylvie. Sylvie was helpin' her yistiday," piped Bibi.

Bobinôt arose and going across to the counter purchased a can of shrimps, of which Calixta was very fond. Then he returned to his perch on the keg and sat stolidly holding the can of shrimps while the storm burst. It shook the wooden store and seemed to be ripping great furrows in the distant field. Bibi laid his little hand on his father's knee and was not afraid.

II

Calixta, at home, felt no uneasiness for their safety. She sat at a side window sewing furiously on a sewing machine. She was greatly occupied and did not notice the approaching storm. But she felt very warm and often stopped to mop her face on which the perspiration gathered in beads. She unfastened her white sacque at the throat. It began to grow dark, and suddenly realizing the situation she got up hurriedly and went about closing windows and doors.

Out on the small front gallery she had hung Bobinôt's Sunday clothes to air and she hastened out to gather them before the rain fell. As she stepped outside, Alcée Laballière rode in at the gate. She had not seen him very often since her marriage, and never alone. She stood there with Bobinôt's coat in her hands, and the big rain drops began to fall. Alcée rode his horse under the shelter of a side projection where the chickens had huddled and there were plows and a harrow piled up in the corner.

"May I come and wait on your gallery till the storm is over, Calixta?" he asked.

"Come 'long in, M'sieur Alcée."

His voice and her own startled her as if from a trance, and she seized Bobinôt's—vest. Alcée, mounting to the porch, grabbed the trousers and snatched Bibi's braided jacket that was about to be carried away by a sudden gust of wind. He expressed an intention to remain outside, but it was soon apparent that he might as well have been out in the open: the water beat in upon the boards in driving sheets, and he went inside, closing the door after him. It was even necessary to put something beneath the door to keep the water out.

"My! what a rain! It's good two years sence it rain' like that," exclaimed Calixta as she rolled up a piece of bagging and Alcée helped her to thrust it beneath the crack.

She was a little fuller of figure than five years before when she married; but she had lost nothing of her vivacity. Her blue eyes still retained their melting quality; and her yellow hair, dishevelled by the wind and rain, kinked more stubbornly than ever about her ears and temples.

The rain beat upon the low, shingled roof with a force and clatter that threatened to break an entrance and deluge them there. They were in the dining room—the sitting room—the general utility room. Adjoining was her bed room, with Bibi's couch along side her own. The door stood open, and the room with its white, monumental bed, its closed shutters, looked dim and mysterious.

Alcée flung himself into a rocker and Calixta nervously began to gather up from the floor the lengths of a cotton sheet which she had been sewing.

"If this keeps up, *Dieu sait*[1] if the levees goin' to stan' it!" she exclaimed.

"What have you got to do with the levees?"

"I got enough to do! An' there's Bobinôt with Bibi out in that storm—if he only didn't left Friedheimer's!"

"Let us hope, Calixta, that Bobinôt's got sense enough to come in out of a cyclone."

She went and stood at the window with a greatly disturbed look on her face. She wiped the frame that was clouded with moisture. It was stiflingly hot. Alcée got up and joined her at the window, looking over her shoulder. The rain was coming down in sheets obscuring the view of far-off cabins and enveloping the distant wood in a gray mist. The playing of the lightning was incessant. A bolt struck a tall chinaberry tree at the edge of the field. It filled all visible space with a blinding glare and the crash seemed to invade the very boards they stood upon.

Calixta put her hands to her eyes, and with a cry, staggered backward. Alcée's arm encircled her, and for an instant he drew her close and spasmodically to him.

"*Bonté!*"[2] she cried, releasing herself from his encircling arm and retreating from the window, "the house'll go next! If I only knew w'ere Bibi was!" She would not compose herself; she would not be seated. Alcée clasped her shoulders and looked into her face. The contact of her warm palpitating body when he had unthinkingly drawn her into his arms, had aroused all the old-time infatuation and desire for her flesh.

"Calixta," he said, "don't be frightened. Nothing can happen. The house is too low to be struck, with so many tall trees standing about. There! aren't you going to be quiet? say, aren't you?" He pushed her hair back from her face that was warm and steaming. Her lips were as red and moist as pomegranate seed. Her white neck and a glimpse of her full, firm bosom disturbed him powerfully. As she glanced up at him the fear in her liquid blue eyes had given place to a drowsy gleam that unconsciously betrayed a sensuous desire. He looked down into her eyes and there

[1] God knows.
[2] "Goodness!"

was nothing for him to do but to gather her lips in a kiss. It reminded him of Assumption.

"Do you remember—in Assumption, Calixta?" he asked in a low voice broken by passion. Oh! she remembered; for in Assumption he had kissed her and kissed and kissed her; until his senses would well nigh fail, and to save her he would resort to a desperate flight. If she was not an immaculate dove in those days, she was still inviolate; a passionate creature whose very defenselessness had made her defense, against which his honor forbade him to prevail. Now—well, now—her lips seemed in a manner free to be tasted, as well as her round, white throat and her whiter breasts.

They did not heed the crashing torrents, and the roar of the elements made her laugh as she lay in his arms. She was a revelation in that dim, mysterious chamber; as white as the couch she lay upon. Her firm, elastic flesh that was knowing for the first time its birthright, was like a creamy lily that the sun invites to contribute its breath and perfume to the undying life of the world.

The generous abundance of her passion, without guile or trickery, was like a white flame which penetrated and found response in depths of his own sensuous nature that had never yet been reached.

When he touched her breasts they gave themselves up in quivering ecstasy, inviting his lips. Her mouth was a fountain of delight. And when he possessed her, they seemed to swoon together at the very borderland of life's mystery.

He stayed cushioned upon her, breathless, dazed, enervated, with his heart beating like a hammer upon her. With one hand she clasped his head, her lips lightly touching his forehead. The other hand stroked with a soothing rhythm his muscular shoulders.

The growl of the thunder was distant and passing away. The rain beat softly upon the shingles, inviting them to drowsiness and sleep. But they dared not yield.

The rain was over; and the sun was turning the glistening green world into a palace of gems. Calixta, on the gallery, watched Alcée ride away. He turned and smiled at her with a beaming face; and she lifted her pretty chin in the air and laughed aloud.

III

Bobinôt and Bibi, trudging home, stopped without at the cistern to make themselves presentable.

"My! Bibi, w'at will yo' mama say! You ought to be ashame'. You oughtn' put on those good pants. Look at 'em! An' that mud on yo' collar! How you got that mud on yo' collar, Bibi? I never saw such a boy!" Bibi was the picture of pathetic resignation. Bobinôt was the embodiment of serious solicitude as he strove to remove from his own person and his son's the signs of their tramp over heavy roads and through wet fields. He scraped the mud off Bibi's bare legs and feet with a stick and carefully removed all traces from his heavy brogans. Then, prepared for the worst—the meeting with an over-scrupulous housewife, they entered cautiously at the back door.

Calixta was preparing supper. She had set the table and was dripping coffee at the hearth. She sprang up as they came in.

"Oh, Bobinôt! You back! My! but I was uneasy. W'ere you been during the rain? An' Bibi? he ain't wet? he ain't hurt?" She had clasped Bibi and was kissing him effusively. Bobinôt's explanations and apologies which he had been composing all along the way, died on his lips as Calixta felt him to see if he were dry, and seemed to express nothing but satisfaction at their safe return.

"I brought you some shrimps, Calixta," offered Bobinôt, hauling the can from his ample side pocket and laying it on the table.

"Shrimps! Oh, Bobinôt! you too good fo' anything!" and she gave him a smacking kiss on the cheek that resounded. "*J'vous réponds*,[3] we'll have a feas' tonight! umph-umph!"

Bobinôt and Bibi began to relax and enjoy themselves, and when the three seated themselves at table they laughed much and so loud that anyone might have heard them as far away as Laballière's.

IV

Alcée Laballière wrote to his wife, Clarisse, that night. It was a loving letter, full of tender solicitude. He told her not to hurry back, but if she and the babies liked it at Biloxi, to stay a month longer. He was getting on nicely; and though he missed them, he was willing to bear the separation a while longer—realizing that their health and pleasure were the first things to be considered.

V

As for Clarisse, she was charmed upon receiving her husband's letter. She and the babies were doing well. The society was agreeable; many of her old friends and acquaintances were at the bay. And the first free breath since her marriage seemed to restore the pleasant liberty of her maiden days. Devoted as she was to her husband, their intimate conjugal life was something which she was more than willing to forego for a while.

So the storm passed and everyone was happy.

[1899]

Journal Entry

Chopin wrote both of these stories more than a century ago. How do your views on marital fidelity compare to hers? How do you account for the differences?

Textual Considerations

1. Create a profile of Mrs. Baroda in "A Respectable Woman." Is she a respectable woman? Why or why not? What is the husband's role in the story? What kind of marriage do they have?
2. What is your response to Gouvernail in "A Respectable Woman"? What evidence is there that he is attracted to Mrs. Baroda? Identify some of the romantic elements

---

[3] "I tell you."

Chopin explores to portray Gouvernail. How do they contrast with traits in Gaston's personality? What kind of appeal might they have exerted over Mrs. Borada?
3. What evidence does "The Storm" offer about the past relationship of Calixta and Alcée? Is it important for the reader to know about their past relationship? Explain your reasons.
4. How does Chopin use point of view to develop characterization in the first two sections of "The Storm"?
5. What is the symbolic significance of the storm? What chain of events does the storm set in motion? Pay particular attention to Chopin's use of language in "The Storm." Do her images reflect her attitude toward her characters? How? Does her choice of words imply empathy or judgment? Select evidence from the text to justify your point of view.
6. What is your response to the last sentence: "So the storm passed and everyone was happy." Do you agree with the conclusion of the story? How does this conclusion compare with the conclusion of "A Respectable Woman"? Explain.

Cultural Contexts

1. Chopin chose not to publish "The Storm" during her lifetime. How might readers in the 1890s have responded to her lack of condemnation of adultery or to the fact that both Calixta and Alcée enjoy their sexual encounter as equals? Working with your group, argue whether you accept or reject Calixta's and Alcée's attitude toward marriage and extramarital affairs.
2. The wives in "A Respectable Woman" and "The Storm" seem to experience some kind of awakening toward self-fulfillment. How would you characterize their sense of realization in each story? Would you define it as romantic, sexual, spiritual? Explain your viewpoint and defend your position to your group.

Alice Walker

Roselily

Dearly Beloved

She dreams; dragging herself across the world. A small girl in her mother's white robe and veil, knee raised waist high through a bowl of quicksand soup. The man who stands beside her is against this standing on the front porch of her house, being married to the sound of cars whizzing by on highway 61.

we are gathered here

Like cotton to be weighed. Her fingers at the last minute busily removing dry leaves and twigs. Aware it is a superficial sweep. She knows he blames Mississippi for the respectful way the men turn their heads up in the yard, the women stand waiting and knowledgeable, their children held from mischief by teachings from the wrong God. He glares beyond them to the occupants of the cars, white faces glued to promises beyond a country wedding, noses thrust forward like dogs on a track. For him they usurp the wedding.

in the sight of God

Yes, open house. That is what country black folks like. She dreams she does not already have three children. A squeeze around the flowers in her hands chokes off three and four and five years of breath. Instantly she is ashamed and frightened in her superstition. She looks for the first time at the preacher, forces humility into her eyes, as if she believes he is, in fact, a man of God. She can imagine God, a small black boy, timidly pulling the preacher's coattail.

to join this man and this woman

She thinks of ropes, chains, handcuffs, his religion. His place of worship. Where she will be required to sit apart with covered head. In Chicago, a word she hears when thinking of smoke, from his description of what a cinder was, which they never had in Panther Burn. She sees hovering over the heads of the clean neighbors in her front yard black specks falling, clinging, from the sky. But in Chicago. Respect, a chance to build. Her children at last from underneath the detrimental wheel. A chance to be on top. What a relief, she thinks. What a vision, a view, from up so high.

in holy matrimony.

Her fourth child she gave away to the child's father who had some money. Certainly a good job. Had gone to Harvard. Was a good man but weak because good language meant so much to him he could not live with Roselily. Could not abide TV in the living room, five beds in three rooms, no Bach except from four to six on Sunday afternoons. No chess at all. She does not forget to worry about her son among his father's people. She wonders if the New England climate will agree with him. If he will ever come down to Mississippi, as his father did, to try to right the country's wrongs. She wonders if he will be stronger than his father. His father cried off and on throughout her pregnancy. Went to skin and bones. Suffered nightmares, retching and falling out of bed. Tried to kill himself. Later told his wife he found the right baby through friends. Vouched for, the sterling qualities that would make up his character.

It is not her nature to blame. Still, she is not entirely thankful. She supposes New England, the North, to be quite different from what she knows. It seems right somehow to her that people who move there to live return home completely changed. She thinks of the air, the smoke, the cinders. Imagines cinders big as hailstones; heavy, weighing on the people. Wonders how pressure finds it way into the veins, roping the springs of laughter.

If there's anybody here that knows a reason why

But of course they know no reason why beyond what they daily have come to know. She thinks of the man who will be her husband, feels shut away from him because of the stiff severity of his plain black suit. His religion. A lifetime of black and white. Of veils. Covered head. It is as if her children are already gone from her. Not dead, but exalted on a pedestal, a stalk that has no roots. She wonders how to make new roots. It is beyond her. She wonders what one does with memories in a brand-new life. This had seemed easy, until she thought of it. "The reasons why . . . the people who" . . . she thinks, and does not wonder where the thought is from.

these two should not be joined

She thinks of her mother, who is dead. Dead, but still her mother. Joined. This is confusing. Of her father. A gray old man who sold wild mink, rabbit, fox skins to Sears, Roebuck. He stands in the yard, like a man waiting for a train. Her young sisters stand behind her in smooth green dresses, with flowers in their hands and hair. They giggle, she feels, at the absurdity of the wedding. They are ready for something new. She thinks the man beside her should marry one of them. She feels old. Yoked. An arm seems to reach out from behind her and snatch her backward. She thinks of cemeteries and the long sleep of grandparents mingling in the dirt. She believes that she believes in ghosts. In the soil giving back what it takes.

together

In the city. He sees her in a new way. This she knows, and is grateful. But is it new enough? She cannot always be a bride and virgin, wearing robes and veil. Even now her body itches to be free of satin and voile, organdy and lily of the valley. Memories crash against her. Memories of being bare to the sun. She wonders what it will be like. Not to have to go to a job. Not to work in a sewing plant. Not to worry about learning to sew straight seams in workingmen's overalls, jeans, and dress pants. Her place will be in the home, he has said, repeatedly, promising her rest she had prayed for. But now she wonders. When she is rested, what will she do? They will make babies—she thinks practically about her fine brown body, his strong black one. They will be inevitable. Her hands will be full. Full of what? Babies. She is not comforted.

let him speak

She wishes she had asked him to explain more of what he meant. But she was impatient. Impatient to be done with sewing. With doing everything for three children, alone. Impatient to leave the girls she had known since childhood, their children growing up, their husbands hanging around her, already old, seedy. Nothing about them that she wanted, or needed. The fathers of her children driving by, waving, not waving; reminders of times she would just as soon forget. Impatient to see the South Side, where they would live and build and be respectable and respected and free. Her husband would free her. A romantic hush. Proposal. Promises. A new life! Respectable, reclaimed, renewed. Free! In robe and veil.

or forever hold

She does not even know if she loves him. She loves his sobriety. His refusal to sing just because he knows the tune. She loves his pride. His blackness and his gray car. She loves his understanding of her *condition*. She thinks she loves the effort he will make to redo her into what he truly wants. His love of her makes her completely conscious of how unloved she was before. This is something; though it makes her unbearably sad. Melancholy. She blinks her eyes. Remembers she is finally being married, like other girls. Like other girls, women? Something strains upward behind her eyes. She thinks of the something as a rat trapped, concerned, scurrying to and fro in her head, peering through the windows of her eyes. She wants to live for once. But doesn't know quite what that means. Wonders if she has ever done it. If she ever will. The preacher is odious to her. She wants to strike him out of the way, out of her light, with the back of her hand. It seems to her he has always been standing in front of her, barring her way.

his peace.

The rest she does not hear. She feels a kiss, passionate, rousing, within the general pandemonium. Cars drive up blowing their horns. Firecrackers go off. Dogs come from under the house and begin to yelp and bark. Her husband's hand is like the clasp of an iron gate. People congratulate. Her children press against her. They look with awe and distaste mixed with hope at their new father. He stands curiously apart, in spite of the people crowding about to grasp his free hand. He smiles at them all but his eyes are as if turned inward. He knows they cannot understand that he is not a Christian. He will not explain himself. He feels different, he looks it. The old women thought he was like one of their sons except that he had somehow got away from them. Still a son, not a son. Changed.

She thinks how it will be later in the night in the silvery gray car. How they will spin through the darkness of Mississippi and in the morning be in Chicago, Illinois. She thinks of Lincoln, the president. That is all she knows about the place. She feels ignorant, *wrong*, backward. She presses her worried fingers into his palm. He is standing in front of her. In the crush of well-wishing people, he does not look back.

[1973]

Journal Entry

A rose is traditionally associated with sexual passion, while a lily connotes sexual purity. Is Roselily an appropriate name for Walker's protagonist? Why or why not?

Textual Considerations

1. What effects does Walker achieve by using the text of the marriage service to interrupt Roselily's thoughts? What do we learn about her past and her ambivalence about the future?
2. Characterize her husband by listing his faults and his virtues. What is his attitude toward marriage? How does he envision Roselily's role? What is her response?

3. Religion plays an important role in the story. Why does Roselily think of the preacher as someone who is always "barring her way"?
4. What is her husband's attitude toward *his* religion?
5. Roselily wants freedom, yet at the end of the ceremony, "her husband's hand is like the clasp of an iron gate." Cite and explain other images of entrapment.

Cultural Contexts

1. Contrasts form the basis of this story. How does Walker use differences in setting, characterization, religion, family, and community to heighten potential conflicts in the relationship? To what extent are Roselily's needs for freedom and respectability resolved?
2. Roselily reflects upon the father of her fourth child, who is white and who she met during the civil rights movement in the 1960s. Why does Walker focus on him? What do we know about him? How does Roselily feel about having given him the child? What is your group's response to her action?

Charlotte Perkins Gilman
The Yellow Wallpaper

It is very seldom that mere ordinary people like John and myself secure ancestral halls for the summer.

A colonial mansion, a hereditary estate, I would say a haunted house, and reach the height of romantic felicity—but that would be asking too much of fate!

Still I will proudly declare that there is something queer about it.

Else, why should it be let so cheaply? And why have stood so long untenanted?

John laughs at me, of course, but one expects that in marriage.

John is practical in the extreme. He has not patience with faith, an intense horror of superstition, and he scoffs openly at any talk of things not to be felt and seen and put down in figures.

John is a physician, and *perhaps*—(I would not say it to a living soul, of course, but this is dead paper and a great relief to my mind)—*perhaps* that is one reason I do not get well faster.

You see he does not believe I am sick!

And what can one do?

If a physician of high standing, and one's own husband, assures friends and relatives that there is really nothing the matter with one but temporary nervous depression—a slight hysterical tendency—what is one to do?

My brother is also a physician, and also of high standing, and he says the same thing.

So I take phosphates or phosphites—whichever it is, and tonics, and journeys, and air, and exercise, and am absolutely forbidden to "work" until I am well again.

Personally, I disagree with their ideas.

Personally, I believe that congenial work, with excitement and change, would do me good.

But what is one to do?

I did write for a while in spite of them, but it *does* exhaust me a good deal—having to be so sly about it, or else meet with heavy opposition.

I sometimes fancy that in my condition if I had less opposition and more society and stimulus—but John says the very worst thing I can do is to think about my condition, and I confess it always makes me feel bad.

So I will let it alone and talk about the house.

The most beautiful place! It is quite alone, standing well back from the road, quite three miles from the village. It makes me think of English places that you read about, for there are hedges and walls and gates that lock, and lots of separate little houses for the gardeners and people.

There is a *delicious* garden! I never saw such a garden—large and shady, full of box-bordered paths, and lined with long grape-covered arbors with seats under them.

There were greenhouses, too, but they are all broken now.

There was some legal trouble, I believe, something about the heirs and coheirs; anyhow, the place has been empty for years.

That spoils my ghostliness, I am afraid, but I don't care—there is something strange about the house—I can feel it.

I even said so to John one moonlight evening, but he said what I felt was a *draught*, and shut the window.

I get unreasonably angry with John sometimes. I'm sure I never used to be so sensitive. I think it is due to this nervous condition.

But John says if I feel so, I shall neglect proper self-control; so I take pains to control myself—before him, at least, and that makes me very tired.

I don't like our room a bit. I wanted one downstairs that opened on the piazza and had roses all over the window, and such pretty old-fashioned chintz hangings! But John would not hear of it.

He said there was only one window and not room for two beds, and no near room for him if he took another.

He is very careful and loving, and hardly lets me stir without special direction.

I have a schedule prescription for each hour in the day; he takes all care from me, and so I feel basely ungrateful not to value it more.

He said we came here solely on my account, that I was to have perfect rest and all the air I could get. "Your exercise depends on your strength, my dear," said he, "and your food somewhat on your appetite, but air you can absorb all the time." So we took the nursery at the top of the house.

It is a big, airy room, the whole floor nearly, with windows that look all ways, and air and sunshine galore. It was nursery first and then playroom and gymnasium, I should judge; for the windows are barred for little children, and there are rings and things in the walls.

The paint and paper look as if a boys' school had used it. It is stripped off—the paper—in great patches all around the head of my bed, about as far as I can reach, and in a great place on the other side of the room low down. I never saw a worse paper in my life.

One of those sprawling flamboyant patterns committing every artistic sin.

It is dull enough to confuse the eye in following, pronounced enough to constantly irritate and provoke study, and when you follow the lame uncertain curves for a little distance they suddenly commit suicide—plunge off at outrageous angles, destroy themselves in unheard of contradictions.

The color is repellent, almost revolting; a smoldering unclean yellow, strangely faded by the slow-turning sunlight.

It is a dull yet lurid orange in some places, a sickly sulphur tint in others.

No wonder the children hated it! I should hate it myself if I had to live in this room long.

There comes John, and I must put this away,—he hates to have me write a word.

We have been here two weeks, and I haven't felt like writing before, since that first day.

I am sitting by the window now, up in this atrocious nursery, and there is nothing to hinder my writing as much as I please, save lack of strength.

John is away all day, and even some nights when his cases are serious.

I am glad my case is not serious!

But these nervous troubles are dreadfully depressing.

John does not know how much I really suffer. He knows there is no *reason* to suffer, and that satisfies him.

Of course it is only nervousness. It does weigh on me so not to do my duty in any way!

I meant to be such a help to John, such a real rest and comfort, and here I am a comparative burden already!

Nobody would believe what an effort it is to do what little I am able,—to dress and entertain, and order things.

It is fortunate Mary is so good with the baby. Such a dear baby!

And yet I *cannot* be with him, it makes me so nervous.

I suppose John never was nervous in his life. He laughs at me so about this wall-paper!

At first he meant to repaper the room, but afterwards he said that I was letting it get the better of me, and that nothing was worse for a nervous patient than to give way to such fancies.

He said that after the wall-paper was changed it would be the heavy bedstead, and then the barred windows, and then that gate at the head of the stairs, and so on.

"You know the place is doing you good," he said, "and really, dear, I don't care to renovate the house just for a three months' rental."

"Then do let us go downstairs," I said, "there are such pretty rooms there."

Then he took me in his arms and called me a blessed little goose, and said he would go down to the cellar, if I wished, and have it whitewashed into the bargain.

But he is right enough about the beds and windows and things.

It is an airy and comfortable room as any one need wish, and, of course, I would not be so silly as to make him uncomfortable just for a whim.

I'm really getting quite fond of the big room, all but that horrid paper.

Out of one window I can see the garden, those mysterious deepshaded arbors, the riotous old-fashioned flowers, and bushes and gnarly trees.

Out of another I get a lovely view of the bay and a little private wharf belonging to the estate. There is a beautiful shaded lane that runs down there from the house. I always fancy I see people walking in these numerous paths and arbors, but John has cautioned me not to give way to fancy in the least. He says that with my imaginative power and habit of story-making, a nervous weakness like mine is sure to lead to all manner of excited fancies, and that I ought to use my will and good sense to check the tendency. So I try.

I think sometimes that if I were only well enough to write a little it would relieve the press of ideas and rest me.

But I find I get pretty tired when I try.

It is so discouraging not to have any advice and companionship about my work. When I get really well, John says we will ask Cousin Henry and Julia down for a long visit; but he says he would as soon put fireworks in my pillow-case as to let me have those stimulating people about now.

I wish I could get well faster.

But I must not think about that. This paper looks to me as if it *knew* what a vicious influence it had!

There is a recurrent spot where the pattern lolls like a broken neck and two bulbous eyes stare at you upside down.

I get positively angry with the impertinence of it and the everlastingness. Up and down and sideways they crawl, and those absurd, unblinking eyes are everywhere. There is one place where two breadths didn't match, and the eyes go all up and down the line, one a little higher than the other.

I never saw so much expression in an inanimate thing before, and we all know how much expression they have! I used to lie awake as a child and get more entertainment and terror out of blank walls and plain furniture than most children could find in a toy-store.

I remember what a kindly wink the knobs of our big, old bureau used to have, and there was one chair that always seemed like a strong friend.

I used to feel that if any of the other things looked too fierce I could always hop into that chair and be safe.

The furniture in this room is no worse than inharmonious, however, for we had to bring it all from downstairs. I suppose when this was used as a playroom they had to take the nursery things out, and no wonder! I never saw such ravages as the children have made here.

The wall-paper, as I said before, is torn off in spots, and it sticketh closer than a brother—they must have had perseverance as well as hatred.

Then the floor is scratched and gouged and splintered, the plaster itself is dug out here and there, and this great heavy bed which is all we found in the room, looks as if it had been through the wars.

But I don't mind it a bit—only the paper.

There comes John's sister. Such a dear girl as she is, and so careful of me! I must not let her find me writing.

She is a perfect and enthusiastic housekeeper, and hopes for no better profession. I verily believe she thinks it is the writing which made me sick!

But I can write when she is out, and see her a long way off from these windows.

There is one that commands the road, a lovely shaded winding road, and one that just looks off over the country. A lovely country, too, full of great elms and velvet meadows.

This wall-paper has a kind of sub-pattern in a different shade, a particularly irritating one, for you can only see it in certain lights, and not clearly then.

But in the places where it isn't faded and where the sun is just so—I can see a strange, provoking, formless sort of figure, that seems to skulk about behind that silly and conspicuous front design.

There's sister on the stairs!

Well, the Fourth of July is over! The people are all gone and I am tired out. John thought it might do me good to see a little company, so we just had mother and Nellie and the children down for a week.

Of course I didn't do a thing. Jennie sees to everything now.

But it tired me all the same.

John says if I don't pick up faster he shall send me to Weir Mitchell[1] in the fall.

But I don't want to go there at all. I had a friend who was in his hands once, and she says he is just like John and my brother, only more so!

Besides, it is such an undertaking to go so far.

I don't feel as if it was worth while to turn my hand over for anything, and I'm getting dreadfully fretful and querulous.

I cry at nothing, and cry most of the time.

Of course I don't when John is here, or anybody else, but when I am alone.

And I am alone a good deal just now. John is kept in town very often by serious cases, and Jennie is good and lets me alone when I want her to.

So I walk a little in the garden or down that lovely lane, sit on the porch under the roses, and lie down up here a good deal.

I'm getting really fond of the room in spite of the wall-paper. Perhaps *because* of the wall-paper.

It dwells in my mind so!

I lie here on this great immovable bed—it is nailed down, I believe—and follow that pattern about by the hour. It is as good as gymnastics, I assure you. I start, we'll say, at the bottom, down in the corner over there where it has not been touched, and I determine for the thousandth time that I *will* follow that pointless pattern to some sort of a conclusion.

I know a little of the principle of design, and I know this thing was not arranged on any laws of radiation, or alternation, or repetition, or symmetry, or anything else that I ever heard of.

It is repeated, of course, by the breadths, but not otherwise.

Looked at in one way each breadth stands alone, the bloated curves and flourishes—a kind of "debased Romanesque" with *delirium tremens*—go waddling up and down in isolated columns of fatuity.

---

[1] Dr. Silas Weir Mitchell, a renowned specialist in women's nervous diseases.

But, on the other hand, they connect diagonally, and the sprawling outlines run off in great slanting waves of optic horror, like a lot of wallowing seaweeds in full chase.

The whole thing goes horizontally, too, at least it seems so, and I exhaust myself in trying to distinguish the order of its going in that direction.

They have used a horizontal breadth for a frieze, and that adds wonderfully to the confusion.

There is one end of the room where it is almost intact, and there, when the crosslights fade and the low sun shines directly upon it, I can almost fancy radiation after all—the interminable grotesques seem to form around a common centre and rush off in headlong plunges of equal distraction.

It makes me tired to follow it. I will take a nap I guess.

I don't know why I should write this.

I don't want to.

I don't feel able.

And I know John would think it absurd. But I *must* say what I feel and think in some way—it is such a relief!

But the effort is getting to be greater than the relief.

Half the time now I am awfully lazy, and lie down ever so much.

John says I mustn't lose my strength, and has me take cod liver oil and lots of tonics and things, to say nothing of ale and wine and rare meat.

Dear John! He loves me very dearly, and hates to have me sick. I tried to have a real earnest reasonable talk with him the other day, and tell him how I wish he would let me go and make a visit to Cousin Henry and Julia.

But he said I wasn't able to go, nor able to stand it after I got there; and I did not make out a very good case for myself, for I was crying before I had finished.

It is getting to be a great effort for me to think straight. Just this nervous weakness I suppose.

And dear John gathered me up in his arms, and just carried me upstairs and laid me on the bed, and sat by me and read to me till it tired my head.

He said I was his darling and his comfort and all he had, and that I must take care of myself for his sake, and keep well.

He says no one but myself can help me out of it, that I must use my will and self-control and not let any silly fancies run away with me.

There's one comfort, the baby is well and happy, and does not have to occupy this nursery with the horrid wall-paper.

If we had not used it, that blessed child would have! What a fortunate escape! Why, I wouldn't have a child of mine, an impressionable little thing, live in such a room for worlds.

I never thought of it before, but it is lucky that John kept me here after all, I can stand it so much easier than a baby, you see.

Of course I never mention it to them any more—I am too wise,—but I keep watch of it all the same.

There are things in that paper that nobody knows but me, or ever will.

Behind that outside pattern the dim shapes get clearer every day.

It is always the same shape, only very numerous.

And it is like a woman stooping down and creeping about behind that pattern. I don't like it a bit. I wonder—I begin to think—I wish John would take me away from here!

It is so hard to talk with John about my case, because he is so wise, and because he loves me so.

But I tried it last night.

It was moonlight. The moon shines in all around just as the sun does.

I hate to see it sometimes, it creeps so slowly, and always comes in by one window or another.

John was asleep and I hated to waken him, so I kept still and watched the moonlight on that undulating wall-paper till I felt creepy.

The faint figure behind seemed to shake the pattern, just as if she wanted to get out.

I got up softly and went to feel and see if the paper *did* move, and when I came back John was awake.

"What is it, little girl?" he said. "Don't go walking about like that—you'll get cold."

I thought it was a good time to talk, so I told him that I really was not gaining here, and that I wished he would take me away.

"Why darling!" said he, "our lease will be up in three weeks, and I can't see how to leave before.

"The repairs are not done at home, and I cannot possibly leave town just now. Of course if you were in any danger, I could and would, but you really are better, dear, whether you can see it or not. I am a doctor, dear, and I know. You are gaining flesh and color, your appetite is better, I feel really much easier about you."

"I don't weigh a bit more," said I, "nor as much; and my appetite may be better in the evening when you are here, but it is worse in the morning when you are away!"

"Bless her little heart!" said he with a big hug, "she shall be as sick as she pleases! But now let's improve the shining hours by going to sleep, and talk about it in the morning!"

"And you won't go away?" I asked gloomily.

"Why, how can I, dear? It is only three weeks more and then we will take a nice little trip of a few days while Jennie is getting the house ready. Really dear you are better!"

"Better in body perhaps—" I began, and stopped short, for he sat up straight and looked at me with such a stern, reproachful look that I could not say another word.

"My darling," said he, "I beg of you, for my sake and for our child's sake, as well as for your own, that you will never for one instant let that idea enter your mind! There is nothing so dangerous, so fascinating, to a temperament like yours. It is a false and foolish fancy. Can you not trust me as a physician when I tell you so?"

So of course I said no more on that score, and we went to sleep before long. He thought I was asleep first, but I wasn't, and lay there for hours trying to decide whether that front pattern and the back pattern really did move together or separately.

On a pattern like this, by daylight, there is a lack of sequence, a defiance of law, that is a constant irritant to a normal mind.

The color is hideous enough, and unreliable enough, and infuriating enough, but the pattern is torturing.

You think you have mastered it, but just as you get well underway in following, it turns a back-somersault and there you are. It slaps you in the face, knocks you down, and tramples upon you. It is like a bad dream.

The outside pattern is a florid arabesque, reminding one of a fungus. If you can imagine a toadstool in joints, an interminable string of toadstools, budding and sprouting in endless convolutions—why, that is something like it.

That is, sometimes!

There is one marked peculiarity about this paper, a thing nobody seems to notice but myself, and that is that it changes as the light changes.

When the sun shoots in through the east window—I always watch for that first long, straight ray—it changes so quickly that I never can quite believe it.

That is why I watch it always.

By moonlight—the moon shines in all night when there is a moon—I wouldn't know it was the same paper.

At night in any kind of light, in twilight, candle light, lamplight, and worst of all by moonlight, it becomes bars! The outside pattern I mean, and the woman behind it is as plain as can be.

I didn't realize for a long time what the thing was that showed behind, that dim sub-pattern, but now I am quite sure it is a woman.

By daylight she is subdued, quiet. I fancy, it is the pattern that keeps her so still. It is so puzzling. It keeps me quiet by the hour.

I lie down ever so much now. John says it is good for me, and to sleep all I can.

Indeed he started the habit by making me lie down for an hour after each meal.

It is a very bad habit I am convinced, for you see I don't sleep.

And that cultivates deceit, for I don't tell them I'm awake—O no!

The fact is I am getting a little afraid of John.

He seems very queer sometimes, and even Jennie has an inexplicable look.

It strikes me occasionally, just as a scientific hypothesis,—that perhaps it is the paper!

I have watched John when he did not know I was looking, and come into the room suddenly on the most innocent excuses, and I've caught him several times *looking at the paper!* And Jennie too. I caught Jennie with her hand on it once.

She didn't know I was in the room, and when I asked her in a quiet, a very quiet voice, with the most restrained manner possible, what she was doing with the paper—she turned around as if she had been caught stealing, and looked quite angry—asked me why I should frighten her so!

Then she said that the paper stained everything it touched, that she had found yellow smooches on all my clothes and John's, and she wished we would be more careful!

Did not that sound innocent? But I know she was studying that pattern, and I am determined that nobody shall find it out but myself!

Life is very much more exciting now than it used to be. You see I have something more to expect, to look forward to, to watch. I really do eat better, and am more quiet than I was.

John is so pleased to see me improve! He laughed a little the other day, and said I seemed to be flourishing in spite of my wall-paper.

I turned it off with a laugh. I had no intention of telling him it was *because* of the wall-paper—he would make fun of me. He might even want to take me away.

I don't want to leave now until I have found it out. There is a week more, and I think that will be enough.

I'm feeling ever so much better! I don't sleep much at night, for it is so interesting to watch developments; but I sleep a good deal in the daytime.

In the daytime it is tiresome and perplexing.

There are always new shoots on the fungus, and new shades of yellow all over it. I cannot keep count of them, though I have tried conscientiously.

It is the strangest yellow, that wall-paper! It makes me think of all the yellow things I ever saw—not beautiful ones like buttercups, but old foul, bad yellow things.

But there is something else about that paper—the smell! I noticed it the moment we came into the room, but with so much air and sun it was not bad. Now we have had a week of fog and rain, and whether the windows are open or not, the smell is here.

It creeps all over the house.

I find it hovering in the dining-room, skulking in the parlor, hiding in the hall, lying in wait for me on the stairs.

It gets into my hair.

Even when I go to ride, if I turn my head suddenly and surprise it—there is that smell!

Such a peculiar odor, too! I have spent hours in trying to analyze it, to find what it smelled like.

It is not bad—at first, and very gentle, but quite the subtlest, most enduring odor I ever met.

In this damp weather it is awful, I wake up in the night and find it hanging over me.

It used to disturb me at first. I thought seriously of burning the house—to reach the smell.

But now I am used to it. The only thing I can think of that it is like is the *color* of the paper! A yellow smell.

There is a very funny mark on this wall, low down, near the mopboard. A streak that runs round the room. It goes behind every piece of furniture, except the bed, a long, straight, even *smooch*, as if it had been rubbed over and over.

I wonder how it was done and who did it, and what they did it for. Round and round and round—round and round and round—it makes me dizzy!

I really have discovered something at last.

Through watching so much at night, when it changes so, I have finally found out.

The front pattern *does* move—and no wonder! The woman behind shakes it!

Sometimes I think there are a great many women behind, and sometimes only one, and she crawls around fast, and her crawling shakes it all over.

Then in the very bright spots she keeps still, and in the very shady spots she just takes hold of the bars and shakes them hard.

And she is all the time trying to climb through. But nobody could climb through that pattern—it strangles so; I think that is why it has so many heads.

They get through, and then the pattern strangles them off and turns them upside down, and makes their eyes white!

If those heads were covered or taken off it would not be half so bad.

I think that woman gets out in the daytime!

And I'll tell you why—privately—I've seen her!

I can see her out of every one of my windows!

It is the same woman, I know, for she is always creeping, and most women do not creep by daylight.

I see her on that long road under the trees, creeping along, and when a carriage comes she hides under the blackberry vines.

I don't blame her a bit. It must be very humiliating to be caught creeping by daylight!

I always lock the door when I creep by daylight. I can't do it at night, for I know John would suspect something at once.

And John is so queer now, that I don't want to irritate him. I wish he would take another room! Besides, I don't want anybody to get that woman out at night but myself.

I often wonder if I could see her out of all the windows at once.

But, turn as fast as I can, I can only see out of one at one time.

And though I always see her, she *may* be able to creep faster than I can turn!

I have watched her sometimes away off in the open country, creeping as fast as a cloud shadow in a high wind.

If only that top pattern could be gotten off from the under one! I mean to try it, little by little.

I have found out another funny thing, but I shan't tell it this time! It does not do to trust people too much.

There are only two more days to get this paper off, and I believe John is beginning to notice. I don't like the look in his eyes.

And I heard him ask Jennie a lot of professional questions about me. She had a very good report to give.

She said I slept a good deal in the daytime.

John knows I don't sleep very well at night, for all I'm so quiet!

He asked me all sorts of questions, too, and pretended to be very loving and kind.

As if I couldn't see through him!

Still, I don't wonder he acts so, sleeping under this paper for three months.

It only interests me, but I feel sure John and Jennie are secretly affected by it.

Hurrah! This is the last day, but it is enough. John to stay in town over night, and won't be out until this evening.

Jennie wanted to sleep with me—the sly thing! but I told her I should undoubt-edly rest better for a night all alone.

That was clever, for really I wasn't alone a bit! As soon as it was moonlight and that poor thing began to crawl and shake the pattern, I got up and ran to help her.

I pulled and she shook, I shook and she pulled, and before morning we had peeled off yards of that paper.

A strip about as high as my head and half around the room.

And then when the sun came and that awful pattern began to laugh at me, I declared I would finish it to-day!

We go away to-morrow, and they are moving all my furniture down again to leave things as they were before.

Jennie looked at the wall in amazement, but I told her merrily that I did it out of pure spite at the vicious thing.

She laughed and said she wouldn't mind doing it herself, but I must not get tired.

How she betrayed herself that time!

But I am here, and no person touches this paper but me—not *alive!*

She tried to get me out of the room—it was too patent! But I said it was so quiet and empty and clean now that I believed I would lie down again and sleep all I could; and not to wake me even for dinner—I would call when I woke.

So now she is gone, and the servants are gone, and the things are gone, and there is nothing left but that great bedstead nailed down, with the canvas mattress we found on it.

We shall sleep downstairs to-night, and take the boat home to-morrow.

I quite enjoy the room, now it is bare again.

How those children did tear about here!

This bedstead is fairly gnawed!

But I must get to work.

I have locked the door and thrown the key down into the front path.

I don't want to go out, and I don't want to have anybody come in, till John comes.

I want to astonish him.

I've got a rope up here that even Jennie did not find. If that woman does get out, and tries to get away, I can tie her!

But I forgot I could not reach far without anything to stand on!

This bed will *not* move!

I tried to lift and push it until I was lame, and then I got so angry I bit off a little piece at one corner—but it hurt my teeth.

Then I peeled off all the paper I could reach standing on the floor. It sticks hor-ribly and the pattern just enjoys it! All those strangled heads and bulbous eyes and waddling fungus growths just shriek with derision!

I am getting angry enough to do something desperate. To jump out of the win-dow would be admirable exercise, but the bars are too strong even to try.

Besides I wouldn't do it. Of course not. I know well enough that a step like that is improper and might be misconstrued.

I don't like to *look* out of the windows even—there are so many of those creep-ing women, and they creep so fast.

I wonder if they all come out of that wall-paper as I did?

But I am securely fastened now by my well-hidden rope—you don't get *me* out in the road there!

I suppose I shall have to get back behind the pattern when it comes night, and that is hard!

It is so pleasant to be out in this great room and creep around as I please!

I don't want to go outside. I won't, even if Jennie asks me to.

For outside you have to creep on the ground, and everything is green instead of yellow.

But here I can creep smoothly on the floor, and my shoulder just fits in that long smooch around the wall, so I cannot lose my way.

Why there's John at the door!

It is no use, young man, you can't open it!

How he does call and pound!

Now he's crying for an axe.

It would be a shame to break down that beautiful door!

"John dear!" said I in the gentlest voice, "the key is down by the front steps, under a plantain leaf!"

That silenced him for a few moments.

Then he said—very quietly indeed, "Open the door, my darling!"

"I can't," said I. "The key is down by the front door under a plantain leaf!"

And then I said it again, several times, very gently and slowly, and said it so often that he had to go and see, and he got it of course, and came in. He stopped short by the door.

"What is the matter?" he cried. "For God's sake, what are you doing?"

I kept on creeping just the same, but I looked at him over my shoulder.

"I've got out at last," said I, "in spite of you and Jane. And I've pulled off most of the paper, so you can't put me back!"

Now why should that man have fainted? But he did, and right across my path by the wall, so that I had to creep over him every time!

[1891]

Journal Entry

Soon after Gilman's story was published in 1891, a Boston physician declared: "Such a story ought not to be written, . . . it was enough to drive anyone mad to read it" (*The Forerunner*, October 1913). Respond to the emotional impact of the story as a whole. What does the story say to you as a reader?

Textual Considerations

1. Prepare a profile of John, listing his good and bad points. Is he responsible for his wife's emotional state? Why or why not? To what extent do you agree with John that she should not write?

2. Analyze the connection between meaning and symbolism in the story. Consider, for example, the physical description of the bedroom, particularly the wallpaper. How does the narrator's description of it and feelings toward it change? Why is the color appropriate? What pattern does she discover, and what does it represent?

3. How does the author use stylistic changes to mirror the narrator's mental disintegration? Cite examples from the text.
4. Explain the narrator's statement "I've got out at last" in the next-to-last paragraph. To what extent is this true? Is there any sense in which madness can be liberating? Explain.
5. Gilman declared that her drive to write "The Yellow Wallpaper" was to save people from insanity. Do you think the story succeeds in fulfilling Gilman's wish? Cite evidence from the text to support your position.

Cultural Contexts

1. Discuss with your group the reasons for the current popularity of "The Yellow Wallpaper."
2. The rest cure prescribed by the narrator's doctor and physician-husband was standard treatment in Victorian medical theory for what is now known as postpartum depression. Discuss with your group how this "cure" might affect emotional depression and sense of identity.

Alifa Rifaat

Another Evening at the Club

In a state of tension, she awaited the return of her husband. At a loss to predict what would happen between them, she moved herself back and forth in the rocking chair on the wide wooden veranda that ran along the bank and occupied part of the river itself, its supports being fixed in the river bed, while around it grew grasses and reeds. As though to banish her apprehension, she passed her fingers across her hair. The specters of the eucalyptus trees ranged along the garden fence rocked before her gaze, with white egrets slumbering on their high branches like huge white flowers among the thin leaves.

The crescent moon rose from behind the eastern mountains and the peaks of the gently stirring waves glistened in its feeble rays, intermingled with threads of light leaking from the houses of Manfalout scattered along the opposite bank. The colored bulbs fixed to the trees in the garden of the club at the far end of the town stood out against the surrounding darkness. Somewhere over there her husband now sat, most likely engrossed in a game of chess.

It was only a few years ago that she had first laid eyes on him at her father's house, meeting his gaze that weighed up her beauty and priced it before offering the dowry. She had noted his eyes ranging over her as she presented him with the coffee in the Japanese cups that were kept safely locked away in the cupboard for important guests. Her mother had herself laid them out on the silver-plated tray with its elaborately embroidered spread. When the two men had taken their coffee, her father had looked up at her with a smile and had told her to sit down, and she had seated herself on the sofa facing them, drawing the end of her dress over her knees and looking through lowered lids at the man who might choose her as his wife. She had been glad to see that he was tall, well-built and clean-shaven except for a thin greying moustache. In particular she noticed the well-cut coat of English tweed and the silk shirt with gold links. She had felt herself blushing as she saw him returning her gaze. Then the man turned to her father and took out a gold case and offered him a cigarette.

"You really shouldn't, my dear sir," said her father, patting his chest with his left hand and extracting a cigarette with trembling fingers. Before he could bring out his box of matches Abboud Bey had produced his lighter.

"No, after you, my dear sir," said her father in embarrassment. Mingled with her sense of excitement at this man who gave out such an air of worldly self-confidence was a guilty shame at her father's inadequacy.

After lighting her father's cigarette Abboud Bey sat back, crossing his legs, and took out a cigarette for himself. He tapped it against the case before putting it in the corner of his mouth and lighting it, then blew out circles of smoke that followed each other across the room.

"It's a great honor for us, my son," said her father, smiling first at Abboud Bey, then at his daughter, at which Abboud Bey looked across at her and asked:

"And the beautiful little girl's still at secondary school?"

She lowered her head modestly and her father had answered:

"As from today she'll be staying at home in readiness for your happy life together. Allah permitting," and at a glance from her father she had hurried off to join her mother in the kitchen.

"You're a lucky girl," her mother had told her. "He's a real find. Any girl would be happy to have him. He's an Inspector of Irrigation though he's not yet forty. He earns a big salary and gets a fully furnished government house wherever he's posted, which will save us the expense of setting up a house—and I don't have to tell you what our situation is—and that's beside the house he owns in Alexandria where you'll be spending your holidays."

Samia had wondered to herself how such a splendid suitor had found his way to her door. Who had told him that Mr. Mahmoud Barakat, a mere clerk at the Court of Appeal, had a beautiful daughter of good reputation?

The days were then taken up with going the rounds of Cairo's shops and choosing clothes for the new grand life she would be living. This was made possible by her father borrowing on the security of his government pension. Abboud Bey, on his part, never visited her without bringing a present. For her birthday, just before they were married, he bought her an emerald ring that came in a plush box bearing the name of a well-known jeweler in Kasr el-Nil Street. On her wedding night, as he put a diamond bracelet round her wrist, he had reminded her that she was marrying someone with a brilliant career in front of him and that one of the most important things in life was the opinion of others, particularly one's equals and seniors. Though she was still only a young girl she must try to act with suitable dignity.

"Tell people you're from the well-known Barakat family and that your father was a judge," and he went up to her and gently patted her cheeks in a fatherly, reassuring gesture that he was often to repeat during their times together.

Then, yesterday evening, she had returned from the club somewhat lightheaded from the bottle of beer she had been required to drink on the occasion of someone's birthday. Her husband, noting the state she was in, hurriedly took her back home. She had undressed and put on her nightgown, leaving her jewelry on the dressing table, and was fast asleep seconds after getting into bed. The following morning, fully recovered, she slept late, then rang the bell as usual and had breakfast brought to her. It was only as she was putting her jewelry away in the wooden and mother-of-pearl box that she realized that her emerald ring was missing.

Could it have dropped from her finger at the club? In the car on the way back? No, she distinctly remembered it last thing at night, remembered the usual difficulty she had in getting it off her finger. She stripped the bed of its sheets, turned over the mattress, looked inside the pillow cases, crawled on hands and knees under the bed. The tray of breakfast lying on the small bedside table caught her eye and she remembered the young servant coming in that morning with it, remembered the noise of the tray being put down, the curtain being drawn, the tray then being lifted up again and placed on the bedside table. No one but the servant had entered the room. Should she call her and question her?

Eventually, having taken two aspirins, she decided to do nothing and await the return of her husband from work.

Directly he arrived she told him what had happened and he took her by the arm and seated her down beside him:

"Let's calm down and go over what happened."

She repeated, this time with further details, the whole story.

"And you've looked for it?"

"Everywhere. Every possible and impossible place in the bedroom and the bathroom. You see, I remember distinctly taking it off last night."

He grimaced at the thought of last night, then said:

"Anybody been in the room since Gazia when she brought in the breakfast?"

"Not a soul. I've even told Gazia not to do the room today."

"And you've not mentioned anything to her?"

"I thought I'd better leave it to you."

"Fine, go and tell her I want to speak to her. There's no point in your saying anything but I think it would be as well if you were present when I talk to her."

Five minutes later Gazia, the young servant girl they had recently employed, entered behind her mistress. Samia took herself to a far corner of the room while Gazia stood in front of Abboud Bey, her hands folded across her chest, her eyes lowered.

"Yes, sir?"

"Where's the ring?"

"What ring are you talking about, sir?"

"Now don't make out you don't know. The one with the green stone. It would be better for you if you hand it over and then nothing more need be said."

"May Allah blind me if I've set eyes on it."

He stood up and gave her a sudden slap on the face. The girl reeled back, put one hand to her cheek, then lowered it again to her chest and made no answer to any of Abboud's questions. Finally he said to her:

"You've got just fifteen seconds to say where you've hidden the ring or else, I swear to you, you're not going to have a good time of it."

As he lifted up his arm to look at his watch the girl flinched slightly but continued in her silence. When he went to the telephone Samia raised her head and saw that the girl's cheeks were wet with tears. Abboud Bey got through to the Superintendent of Police and told him briefly what had occurred.

"Of course I haven't got any actual proof but seeing that no one else entered the room, it's obvious she's pinched it. Anyway I'll leave the matter in your capable hands—I know your people have their ways and means."

He gave a short laugh, then listened for a while and said: "I'm really most grateful to you."

He put down the receiver and turned to Samia:

"That's it, my dear. There's nothing more to worry about. The Superintendent has promised me we'll get it back. The patrol car's on the way."

The following day, in the late afternoon, she'd been sitting in front of her dressing-table rearranging her jewelry in its box when an earring slipped from her grasp and fell to the floor. As she bent to pick it up she saw the emerald ring stuck between the leg of the table and the wall. Since that moment she had sat in a state of panic awaiting her husband's return from the club. She even felt tempted to walk down to the water's edge and throw it into the river so as to be rid of the unpleasantness that lay ahead.

At the sound of the screech of tires rounding the house to the garage, she slipped the ring onto her finger. As he entered she stood up and raised her hand to show him the ring. Quickly, trying to choose her words but knowing that she was expressing herself clumsily, she explained what an extraordinary thing it was that it should have lodged itself between the dressing-table and the wall, what an extraordinary coincidence she should have dropped the earring and so seen it, how she'd thought of ringing him at the club to tell him the good news but . . .

She stopped in mid-sentence when she saw his frown and added weakly: "I'm sorry. I can't think how it could have happened. What do we do now?"

He shrugged his shoulders as though in surprise.

"Are you asking me, my dear lady? Nothing of course."

"But they've been beating up the girl—you yourself said they'd not let her be till she confessed."

Unhurriedly, he sat himself down as though to consider this new aspect of the matter. Taking out his case, he tapped a cigarette against it in his accustomed manner, then moistened his lips, put the cigarette in place and lit it. The smoke rings hovered in the still air as he looked at his watch and said:

"In any case she's not got all that long before they let her go. They can't keep her for more than forty-eight hours without getting any evidence or a confession. It won't kill her to put up with things for a while longer. By now the whole town knows the servant stole the ring—or would you like me to tell everyone: 'Look, folks, the fact is that the wife got a bit tiddly on a couple sips of beer and the ring took off on its own and hid itself behind the dressing-table'? What do you think?"

"I know the situation's a bit awkward . . ."

"Awkward? It's downright ludicrous. Listen, there's nothing to be done but to give it to me and the next time I go down to Cairo I'll sell it and get something else in its place. We'd be the laughing-stock of the town."

He stretched out his hand and she found herself taking off the ring and placing it in the outstretched palm. She was careful that their eyes should not meet. For a moment she was on the point of protesting and in fact uttered a few words:

"I'd just like to say we could . . ."

Putting the ring away in his pocket, he bent over her and with both hands gently patted her on the cheeks. It was gesture she had long become used to, a gesture that promised her that this man who was her husband and the father of her child had also taken the place of her father who, as though assured that he had found her a suitable substitute, had followed up her marriage with his own funeral. The gesture told her more eloquently than any words that he was the man, she the woman, he the one who carried the responsibilities, made the decisions, she the one whose role it was to be beautiful, happy, carefree. Now, though, for the first time in their life together the gesture came like a slap in the face.

Directly he removed his hands her whole body was seized with an uncontrollable trembling. Frightened he would notice, she rose to her feet and walked with deliberate steps towards the large window. She leaned her forehead against the comforting cold surface and closed her eyes tightly for several seconds. When she opened them she noticed that the café lights strung between the trees on the opposite shore had been turned on and that there were men seated under them and a waiter moving among the tables. The dark shape of a boat momentarily blocked out the café scene; in the light from the hurricane lamp hanging from its bow she saw it cutting through several of those floating islands of Nile waterlilies that, rootless, are swept along with the current.

Suddenly she became aware of his presence alongside her.

"Why don't you go and change quickly while I take the car out? It's hot and it would be nice to have supper at the club."

"As you like. Why not?"

By the time she had turned round from the window she was smiling.

[1983]

Journal Entry

Rifaat is from Cairo, Egypt, where the tradition of arranged marriages is still observed. What knowledge or experience of such marriages can you bring to your reading of this text? Imagine yourself as the wife of the Inspector of Irrigation. How would your responses to your husband be similar to or different from Samia's?

Textual Considerations

1. To analyze "Another Evening at the Club" in terms of its narrative structure, consider Rifaat's use of **flashbacks** at several points in the story. Cite two or three examples and discuss their relation to the story's meaning.
2. Analyze how Rifaat uses the language of gazes, glances, slaps, and gestures to reinforce the story's theme. What evidence can you find of the influence of other cultures on the characters' beliefs and behavior? What examples do you find most effective?

3. Comment on the role of the servant girl. To what extent is she Samia's victim as well as Abboud Bey's?
4. Examine the bonds that tie the young wife to her husband. To what extent has marriage enhanced her sense of identity and autonomy? Explain how Samia's role as a wife upholds Abboud Bey's male identity.
5. What is the significance of the story's title? How does it relate to the concluding paragraph of the text? How do you respond to the title?

Cultural Contexts

1. Feminists, including the French writer Simone de Beauvoir, have suggested that men have occupied the position of subject, or actor, while women have occupied the position of marginalized object, or one acted upon. Identify and discuss with your group the cultural and economic forces that have contributed to a similar model of gender relations in Rifaat's text. Consider, too, how the wife's presence as object affects her husband's masculine identity.
2. Share with your classmates what you know about marriage traditions in different cultures. Then debate the merits of marriage customs centered on the "dowry" or the "sponsalia." Consider, too, the extent to which such traditions have affected Samia's and other women's views of themselves.

Nadine Gordimer

Town and Country Lovers

I

Dr. Franz-Josef von Leinsdorf is a geologist absorbed in his work; wrapped up in it, as the saying goes—year after year the experience of this work enfolds him, swaddling him away from the landscapes, the cities, and the people, wherever he lives: Peru, New Zealand, the United States. He's always been like that, his mother could confirm from their native Austria. There, even as a handsome small boy he presented only his profile to her: turned away to his bits of rock and stone. His few relaxations have not changed much since then. An occasional skiing trip, listening to music, reading poetry—Rainer Maria Rilke once stayed in his grandmother's hunting lodge in the forests of Styria and the boy was introduced to Rilke's poems while very young.

Layer upon layer, country after country, wherever his work takes him—and now he has been almost seven years in Africa. First the Côte d'Ivoire, and for the past five years, South Africa. The shortage of skilled manpower brought about his recruitment here. He has no interest in the politics of the countries he works in. His private preoccupation-within-the-preoccupation of his work has been research into underground watercourses, but the mining company that employs him in a senior though not executive capacity is interested only in mineral discovery. So he is much out in the field—which is the veld, here—seeking new gold, copper, platinum, and uranium deposits. When he is at home—on this particular job, in this particular country, this city—he lives in a two-roomed flat in a suburban block with a landscaped garden, and does his shopping at a supermarket conveniently across the street. He is not married—yet. That is how his colleagues, and the typists and secretaries at the mining company's head office, would define his situation. Both men and women would describe him as a good-looking man, in a foreign way, with the lower half of his face dark and middle-aged (his mouth is thin and curving, and no matter how close-shaven his beard shows like fine shot embedded in the skin round mouth and chin) and the upper half contradictorily young, with deep-set eyes (some would say grey, some black), thick eyelashes and brows. A tangled gaze: through which concentration and gleaming thoughtfulness perhaps appear as fire and languor. It is this that the women in the office mean when they remark he's not unattractive. Although the gaze seems to promise, he has never invited any one of them to go out with him. There is the general assumption he probably has a girl who's been picked for him, he's bespoken by one of his own kind, back home in Europe where he comes from. Many of these well-educated Europeans have no intention of becoming permanent immigrants; neither the remnant of white colonial life nor idealistic involvement with Black Africa appeals to them.

One advantage, at least, of living in underdeveloped or half-developed countries is that flats are serviced. All Dr. von Leinsdorf has to do for himself is buy his own supplies and cook an evening meal if he doesn't want to go to a restaurant. It is simply a matter of dropping in to the supermarket on his way from his car to his flat after work in the afternoon. He wheels a trolley up and down the shelves, and his simple needs are presented to him in the form of tins, packages, plastic-wrapped meat, cheeses, fruit and vegetables, tubes, bottles . . . At the cashier's counters where customers must converge and queue there are racks of small items uncategorized, for last-minute purchase. Here, as the coloured girl cashier punches the adding machine, he picks up cigarettes and perhaps a packet of salted nuts or a bar of nougat. Or razor-blades, when he remembers he's running short. One evening in winter he saw that the cardboard display was empty of the brand of blades he preferred, and he drew the cashier's attention to this. These young coloured girls are usually pretty unhelpful, taking money and punching their machines in a manner that asserts with the time-serving obstinacy of the half-literate the limit of any responsibility towards customers, but this one ran an alert glance over the selection of razor-blades, apologized that she was not allowed to leave her post, and said she would see that the stock was replenished "next time." A day or two later she recognized him, gravely, as he took his turn before her counter—"I ahssed them, but it's out of stock. You can't get it. I did ahss about it." He said this didn't matter. "When it comes in, I can keep a few packets for you." He thanked her.

He was away with the prospectors the whole of the next week. He arrived back in town just before nightfall on Friday, and was on his way from car to flat with his arms full of briefcase, suitcase, and canvas bags when someone stopped him by standing timidly in his path. He was about to dodge round unseeingly on the crowded pavement but she spoke. "We got the blades in now. I didn't see you in the shop this week, but I kept some for when you come. So . . ."

He recognized her. He had never seen her standing before, and she was wearing a coat. She was rather small and finely-made, for one of them. The coat was skimpy but no big backside jutted. The cold brought an apricot-graining of warm colour to her cheekbones, beneath which a very small face was quite delicately hollowed, and the skin was smooth, the subdued satiny colour of certain yellow wood. That crêpey hair, but worn drawn back flat and in a little knot pushed into one of the cheap wool chignons that (he recognized also) hung in the miscellany of small goods along with the razor-blades, at the supermarket. He said thanks, he was in a hurry, he'd only just got back from a trip—shifting the burdens he carried, to demonstrate. "Oh shame." She acknowledged his load. "But if you want I can run in and get it for you quickly. If you want."

He saw at once it was perfectly clear that all the girl meant was that she would go back to the supermarket, buy the blades, and bring the packet to him there where he stood, on the pavement. And it seemed that it was this certainty that made him say, in the kindly tone of assumption used for an obliging underling, "I live just across there— *Atlantis*—that flat building. Could you drop them by, for me—number seven-hundred-and-eighteen, seventh floor—"

She had not before been inside one of these big flat buildings near where she worked. She lived a bus- and train-ride away to the West of the city, but this side of the black townships, in a township for people her tint. There was a pool with ferns, not plastic, and even a little waterfall pumped electrically over rocks, in the entrance of the building *Atlantis;* she didn't wait for the lift marked GOODS but took the one meant for whites and a white woman with one of those sausage-dogs on a lead got in with her but did not pay her any attention. The corridors leading to the flats were nicely glassed-in, not draughty.

He wondered if he should give her a twenty-cent piece for her trouble—ten cents would be right for a black; but she said, "Oh no—please, here—" standing outside his open door and awkwardly pushing back at his hand the change from the money he'd given her for the razor-blades. She was smiling, for the first time, in the dignity of refusing a tip. It was difficult to know how to treat these people, in this country; to know what they expected. In spite of her embarrassing refusal of the coin, she stood there, completely unassuming, fists thrust down the pockets of her cheap coat against the cold she'd come in from, rather pretty thin legs neatly aligned, knee to knee, ankle to ankle.

"Would you like a cup of coffee or something?"

He couldn't very well take her into his study-cum-living-room and offer her a drink. She followed him to his kitchen, but at the sight of her pulling out the single chair to drink her cup of coffee at the kitchen table, he said, "No—bring it in here—" and led the way into the big room where, among his books and his papers, his files of scientific correspondence (and the cigar boxes of stamps from the envelopes), his racks of records, his specimens of minerals and rocks, he lived alone.

It was no trouble to her; she saved him the trips to the supermarket and brought him his groceries two or three times a week. All he had to do was to leave a list and the key under the doormat, and she would come up in her lunch-hour to collect them, returning to put his supplies in the flat after work. Sometimes he was home and sometimes not. He bought a box of chocolates and left it, with a note, for her to find; and that was acceptable, apparently, as a gratuity.

Her eyes went over everything in the flat although her body tried to conceal its sense of being out of place by remaining as still as possible, holding its contours in the chair offered her as a stranger's coat is set aside and remains exactly as left until the owner takes it up to go. "You collect?"

"Well, these are specimens—connected with my work."

"My brother used to collect. Miniatures. With brandy and whisky and that, in them. From all over. Different countries."

The second time she watched him grinding coffee for the cup he had offered her she said, "You always do that? Always when you make coffee?"

"But of course. It is no good, for you. Do I make it too strong?"

"Oh it's just I'm not used to it. We buy it ready—you know, it's in a bottle, you just add a bit to the milk or water."

He laughed, instructive: "That's not coffee, that's a synthetic flavouring. In my country we drink only real coffee, fresh, from the beans—you smell how good it is as it's being ground?"

She was stopped by the caretaker and asked what she wanted in the building? Heavy with the *bona fides* of groceries clutched to her body, she said she was working at number 718, on the seventh floor. The caretaker did not tell her not to use the whites' lift; after all, she was not black; her family was very light-skinned.

There was the item "grey button for trousers" on one of his shopping lists. She said as she unpacked the supermarket carrier, "Give me the pants, so long, then," and sat on his sofa that was always gritty with fragments of pipe tobacco, sewing in and out through the four holes of the button with firm, fluent movements of the right hand, gestures supplying the articulacy missing from her talk. She had a little yokel's, peasant's (he thought of it) gap between her two front teeth when she smiled that he didn't much like, but, face ellipsed to three-quarter angle, eyes cast down in concentration with soft lips almost closed, this didn't matter. He said, watching her sew, "You're a good girl"; and touched her.

She remade the bed every late afternoon when they left it and she dressed again before she went home. After a week there was a day when late afternoon became evening, and they were still in the bed.

"Can't you stay the night?"

"My mother," she said.

"Phone her. Make an excuse." He was a foreigner. He had been in the country five years, but he didn't understand that people don't usually have telephones in their houses, where she lived. She got up to dress. He didn't want that tender body to go out in the night cold and kept hindering her with the interruption of his hands; saying nothing. Before she put on her coat, when the body had already disappeared, he spoke, "But you must make some arrangement."

"Oh my mother!" Her face opened to fear and vacancy he could not read.

He was not entirely convinced the woman would think of her daughter as some pure and unsullied virgin . . . "Why?"

The girl said, "S'e'll be scared. S'e'll be scared we get caught."

"Don't tell her anything. Say I'm employing you." In this country he was working in now there were generally rooms on the roofs of flat buildings for tenants' servants. She said: "That's what I told the caretaker."

She ground fresh coffee beans every time he wanted a cup while he was working at night. She never attempted to cook anything until she had watched in silence while he did it the way he liked, and she learned to reproduce exactly the simple dishes he preferred. She handled his pieces of rock and stone, at first admiring the colours—"It'd make a beautiful ring or necklace, ay." Then he showed her the striations, the formation of each piece, and explained what each was, and how, in the long life of the earth, it had been formed. He named the mineral it yielded, and what that was used for. He worked at his papers, writing, writing, every night, so it did not matter that they could not go out together to public places. On Sundays she got into his car in the basement garage and they drove to the country and picnicked away up in the Magaliesberg, where there was no one. He read or poked about among the rocks; they climbed together, to the mountain pools. He taught her to swim. She had never seen the sea. She squealed and shrieked in the water, showing the gap between her teeth, as—it crossed his mind—she must do when among her own people. Occasionally he had to go out to dinner at the houses of colleagues from the mining company; she sewed and listened to the radio in the flat and he found her in the bed, warm and already asleep, by the time he came in. He made his way into her body without speaking; she made him welcome without a word. Once he put on evening dress for a dinner at his country's consulate; watching him brush one or two fallen hairs from the shoulders of the dark jacket that sat so well on him, she saw a huge room, all chandeliers and people dancing some dance from a costume film— stately, hand-to-hand. She supposed he was going to fetch, in her place in the car, a partner for the evening. They never kissed when either left the flat; he said, suddenly, kindly, pausing as he picked up cigarettes and keys, "Don't be lonely." And added, "Wouldn't you like to visit your family sometimes, when I have to go out?"

He had told her he was going home to his mother in the forests and mountains of his country near the Italian border (he showed her on the map) after Christmas. She had not told him how her mother, not knowing there was any other variety, assumed he was a medical doctor, so she had talked to her about the doctor's children and the doctor's wife who was a very kind lady, glad to have someone who could help out in the surgery as well as the flat.

She remarked wonderingly on his ability to work until midnight or later, after a day at work. She was so tired when she came home from her cash register at the supermarket that once dinner was eaten she could scarcely keep awake. He explained in a way she could understand that while the work she did was repetitive, undemanding of any real response from her intelligence, requiring little mental or physical effort and therefore unrewarding, his work was his greatest interest, it taxed his mental capacities to their limit, exercised all his concentration, and rewarded him constantly as much with the excitement of a problem presented as with the satisfaction of a problem solved. He said later, putting away his papers, speaking out of a silence: "Have you done other kinds of work?" She said, "I was in a clothing factory before. Sportbeau shirts; you know? But the pay's better in the shop."

Of course. Being a conscientious newspaper-reader in every country he lived in, he was aware that it was only recently that the retail consumer trade in this one had been allowed to employ coloureds as shop assistants; even punching a cash register represented advancement. With the continuing shortage of semi-skilled whites a girl like this might be able to edge a little farther into the white-collar category. He began to teach her to type. He was aware that her English was poor, even though, as a foreigner, in his ears her pronunciation did not offend, nor categorize her as it would in those of someone of his education whose mother tongue was English. He corrected her grammatical mistakes but missed the less obvious ones because of his own sometimes exotic English usage—she continued to use the singular pronoun "it" when what was required was the plural "they." Because he was a foreigner (although so clever, as she saw) she was less inhibited than she might have been by the words she knew she misspelled in her typing. While she sat at the typewriter she thought how one day she would type notes for him, as well as making coffee the way he liked it, and taking him inside her body without saying anything, and sitting (even if only through the empty streets of quiet Sundays) beside him in his car, like a wife.

On a summer night near Christmas—he had already bought and hidden a slightly showy but nevertheless good watch he thought she would like—there was a knocking at the door that brought her out of the bathroom and him to his feet, at his work-table. No one ever came to the flat at night; he had no friends intimate enough to drop in without warning. The summons was an imperious banging that did not pause and clearly would not stop until the door was opened.

She stood in the open bathroom doorway gazing at him across the passage into the living-room; her bare feet and shoulders were free of a big bath-towel. She said nothing, did not even whisper. The flat seemed to shake with the strong unhurried blows.

He made as if to go to the door, at last, but now she ran and clutched him by both arms. She shook her head wildly; her lips drew back but her teeth were clenched, she didn't speak. She pulled him into the bedroom, snatched some clothes from the clean laundry laid out on the bed, and got into the wall-cupboard, thrusting the key at his hand. Although his arms and calves felt weakly cold he was horrified, distastefully embarrassed at the sight of her pressed back crouching there under his suits and coat; it was horrible and ridiculous. *Come out!* he whispered. *No! Come out!* She hissed: *Where? Where can I go?*

Never mind! Get out of there!

He put out his hand to grasp her. At bay, she said with all the force of her terrible whisper, baring the gap in her teeth: *I'll throw myself out the window.*

She forced the key into his hand like the handle of a knife. He closed the door on her face and drove the key home in the lock, then dropped it among coins in his trouser pocket.

He unslotted the chain that was looped across the flat door. He turned the serrated knob of the Yale lock. The three policemen, two in plain clothes, stood there without impatience although they had been banging on the door for several minutes. The big dark one with an elaborate moustache held out in a hand wearing a plaited gilt ring some sort of identity card.

Dr. von Leinsdorf said quietly, the blood coming strangely back to legs and arms, "What is it?"

The sergeant told him they knew there was a coloured girl in the flat. They had had information; "I been watching this flat three months, I know."

"I am alone here." Dr. von Leinsdorf did not raise his voice.

"I know, I know who is here. Come—" And the sergeant and his two assistants went into the living-room, the kitchen, the bathroom (the sergeant picked up a bottle of after-shave cologne, seemed to study the French label), and the bedroom. The assistants removed the clean laundry that was laid upon the bed and then turned back the bedding, carrying the sheets over to be examined by the sergeant under the lamp. They talked to one another in Afrikaans, which the Doctor did not understand. The sergeant himself looked under the bed, and lifted the long curtains at the window. The wall-cupboard was of the kind that has no knobs; he saw that it was locked and began to ask in Afrikaans, then politely changed to English, "Give us the key."

Dr. von Leinsdorf said, "I'm sorry, I left it at my office—I always lock and take my keys with me in the mornings."

"It's no good, man, you better give me the key."

He smiled a little, reasonably. "It's on my office desk."

The assistants produced a screwdriver and he watched while they inserted it where the cupboard doors met, gave it quick, firm but not forceful leverage. He heard the lock give.

She had been naked, it was true, when they knocked. But now she was wearing a long-sleeved T-shirt with an appliquéd butterfly motif on one breast, and a pair of jeans. Her feet were still bare; she had managed, by feel, in the dark, to get into some of the clothing she had snatched from the bed, but she had no shoes. She had perhaps been weeping behind the cupboard door (her cheeks looked stained) but now her face was sullen and she was breathing heavily, her diaphragm contracting and expanding exaggeratedly and her breasts pushing against the cloth. It made her appear angry; it might simply have been that she was half-suffocated in the cupboard and needed oxygen. She did not look at Dr. von Leinsdorf. She would not reply to the sergeant's questions.

They were taken to the police station where they were at once separated and in turn led for examination by the district surgeon. The man's underwear was taken away and examined, as the sheets had been, for signs of his seed. When the girl was undressed, it was discovered that beneath her jeans she was wearing a pair of men's briefs with his name on the neatly-sewn laundry tag; in her haste, she had taken the wrong garment to her hiding-place.

Now she cried, standing there before the district surgeon in a man's underwear.

He courteously pretended not to notice. He handed briefs, jeans, and T-shirt round the door, and motioned her to lie on a white-sheeted high table where he placed her legs apart, resting in stirrups, and put into her where the other had made his way so warmly a cold hard instrument that expanded wider and wider. Her thighs and knees trembled uncontrollably while the doctor looked into her and touched her deep inside with more hard instruments, carrying wafers of gauze.

When she came out of the examining room back to the charge office, Dr. von Leinsdorf was not there; they must have taken him somewhere else. She spent what was left of the night in a cell, as he must be doing; but early in the morning she was released and taken home to her mother's house in the coloured township by a white man who explained he was the clerk of the lawyer who had been engaged for her by Dr. von Leinsdorf. Dr. von Leinsdorf, the clerk said, had also been bailed out that morning. He did not say when, or if she would see him again.

A statement made by the girl to the police was handed in to Court when she and the man appeared to meet charges of contravening the Immorality Act in a Johannesburg flat on the night of—December, 19—. *I lived with the white man in his flat. He had intercourse with me sometimes. He gave me tablets to take to prevent me becoming pregnant.*

Interviewed by the Sunday papers, the girl said, "I'm sorry for the sadness brought to my mother." She said she was one of nine children of a female laundry worker. She had left school in Standard Three because there was no money at home for gym clothes or a school blazer. She had worked as a machinist in a factory and a cashier in a supermarket. Dr. von Leinsdorf taught her to type his notes.

Dr. Franz-Josef von Leinsdorf, described as the grandson of a baroness, a cultured man engaged in international mineralogical research, said he accepted social distinctions between people but didn't think they should be legally imposed. "Even in my own country it's difficult for a person from a higher class to marry one from a lower class."

The two accused gave no evidence. They did not greet or speak to each other in Court. The Defence argued that the sergeant's evidence that they had been living together as man and wife was hearsay. (The woman with the dachshund, the caretaker?) The magistrate acquitted them because the State failed to prove carnal intercourse had taken place on the night of—December, 19—.

The girl's mother was quoted, with photograph, in the Sunday papers: "I won't let my daughter work as a servant for a white man again."

II

The farm children play together when they are small; but once the white children go away to school they soon don't play together any more, even in the holidays. Although most of the black children get some sort of schooling, they drop every year farther behind the grades passed by the white children; the childish vocabulary, the child's exploration of the adventurous possibilities of dam, koppies, mealie lands, and veld— there comes a time when the white children have surpassed these with the vocabulary of boarding-school and the possibilities of inter-school sports matches and the kind of adventures seen at the cinema. This usefully coincides with the age of twelve or thirteen; so that by the time early adolescence is reached, the black children are making, along with the bodily changes common to all, an easy transition to adult forms of address, beginning to call their old playmates *missis* and *baasie*—little master.

The trouble was Paulus Eysendyck did not seem to realize that Thebedi was now simply one of the crowd of farm children down at the kraal, recognizable in his sisters' old clothes. The first Christmas holidays after he had gone to boarding-school he brought home for Thebedi a painted box he had made in his wood-work class. He had to give it to her secretly because he had nothing for the other children at the kraal. And she gave him, before he went back to school, a bracelet she had made of thin brass wire and the grey-and-white beans of the castor-oil crop his father cultivated. (When they used to play together, she was the one who had taught Paulus how to make clay oxen for their toy spans.) There was a craze, even in the *platteland* towns like the one where he was at school, for boys to wear elephant-hair and other bracelets beside their watch-straps; his was admired, friends asked him to get similar ones for them. He said the natives made them on his father's farm and he would try.

When he was fifteen, six feet tall, and tramping round at school dances with the girls from the "sister" school in the same town; when he had learnt how to tease and flirt and fondle quite intimately these girls who were the daughters of prosperous farmers like his father; when he had even met one who, at a wedding he had attended with his parents on a nearby farm, had let him do with her in a locked storeroom what people did when they made love—when he was as far from his childhood as all this, he still brought home from a shop in town a red plastic belt and gilt hoop ear-rings for the black girl, Thebedi. She told her father the missus had given these to her as a reward for some work she had done—it was true she sometimes was called to help out in the farmhouse. She told the girls in the kraal that she had a sweetheart nobody knew about, far away, away on another farm, and they giggled, and teased, and admired her. There was a boy in the kraal called Njabulo who said he wished he could have brought her a belt and ear-rings.

When the farmer's son was home for the holidays she wandered far from the kraal and her companions. He went for walks alone. They had not arranged this; it was an urge each followed independently. He knew it was she, from a long way off. She knew that his dog would not bark at her. Down at the dried-up river-bed where five or six years ago the children had caught a leguaan one great day—a creature that combined ideally the size and ferocious aspect of the crocodile with the harm-lessness of the lizard—they squatted side by side on the earth bank. He told her traveller's tales: about school, about the punishments at school, particularly, exag-gerating both their nature and his indifference to them. He told her about the town of Middleburg, which she had never seen. She had nothing to tell but she prompted with many questions, like any good listener. While he talked he twisted and tugged at the roots of white stinkwood and Cape willow trees that looped out of the eroded earth around them. It had always been a good spot for children's games, down there hidden by the mesh of old, ant-eaten trees held in place by vigorous ones, wild asparagus bushing up between the trunks, and here and there prickly-pear cactus sunken-skinned and bristly, like an old man's face, keeping alive sapless until the next rainy season. She punctured the dry hide of a prickly-pear again and again with a sharp stick while she listened. She laughed a lot at what he told her, sometimes dropping her face on her knees, sharing amusement with the cool shady earth beneath her bare feet. She put on her pair of shoes—white sandals, thickly Blanco-ed against the farm dust—when he was on the farm, but these were taken off and laid aside, at the river-bed.

One summer afternoon when there was water flowing there and it was very hot she waded in as they used to do when they were children, her dress bunched modestly and tucked into the legs of her pants. The schoolgirls he went swimming with at dams or pools on neighbouring farms wore bikinis but the sight of their dazzling bellies and thighs in the sunlight had never made him feel what he felt now, when the girl came up the bank and sat beside him, the drops of water beading off her dark legs the only points of light in the earth-smelling, deep shade. They were not afraid of one another, they had known one another always; he did with her what he had done that time in the storeroom at the wedding, and this time it was so lovely, so lovely, he was surprised . . . and she was surprised by it, too—he could see in her dark face that was part of the shade, with her big dark eyes, shiny as soft water, watching him attentively: as she had when they used to huddle over their teams of mud oxen, as she had when he told her about detention weekends at school.

They went to the river-bed often through those summer holidays. They met just before the light went, as it does quite quickly, and each returned home with the dark— she to her mother's hut, he to the farmhouse—in time for the evening meal. He did not tell her about school or town any more. She did not ask questions any longer. He told her, each time, when they would meet again. Once or twice it was very early in the morning; the lowing of the cows being driven to graze came to them where they lay, dividing them with unspoken recognition of the sound read in their two pairs of eyes, opening so close to each other.

He was a popular boy at school. He was in the second, then the first soccer team. The head girl of the "sister" school was said to have a crush on him; he didn't particularly like her, but there was a pretty blonde who put up her long hair into a kind of doughnut with a black ribbon round it, whom he took to see films when the schoolboys and girls had a free Saturday afternoon. He had been driving tractors and other farm vehicles since he was ten years old, and as soon as he was eighteen he got a driver's licence and in the holidays, this last year of his school life, he took neighbours' daughters to dances and to the drive-in cinema that had just opened twenty kilometers from the farm. His sisters were married, by then; his parents often left him in charge of the farm over the weekend while they visited the young wives and grandchildren.

When Thebedi saw the farmer and his wife drive away on a Saturday afternoon, the boot of their Mercedes filled with fresh-killed poultry and vegetables from the garden that it was part of her father's work to tend, she knew that she must come not to the river-bed but up to the house. The house was an old one, thick-walled, dark against the heat. The kitchen was its lively thoroughfare, with servants, food supplies, begging cats and dogs, pots boiling over, washing being damped for ironing, and the big deep-freezer the missus had ordered from town, bearing a crocheted mat and a vase of plastic irises. But the dining-room with the bulging-legged heavy table was shut up in its rich, old smell of soup and tomato sauce. The sitting-room curtains were drawn and the T.V. set silent. The door of the parents' bedroom was locked and the empty rooms where the girls had slept had sheets of plastic spread over the beds. It was in one of these that she and the farmer's son stayed together whole nights—almost: she had to get away before the house servants, who knew her, came in at dawn. There was a risk someone would discover her or traces of her presence if he took her to his own bedroom, although she had looked into it many times when she was helping out in the house and knew well, there, the row of silver cups he had won at school.

When she was eighteen and the farmer's son nineteen and working with his father on the farm before entering a veterinary college, the young man Njabulo asked her father for her. Njabulo's parents met with hers and the money he was to pay in place of the cows it is customary to give a prospective bride's parents was settled upon. He had no cows to offer; he was a labourer on the Eysendyck farm, like her father. A bright youngster; old Eysendyck had taught him brick-laying and was using him for odd jobs in construction, around the place. She did not tell the farmer's son that her parents had arranged for her to marry. She did not tell him, either, before he left for his first term at the veterinary college, that she thought she was going to have a baby. Two months after her marriage to Njabulo, she gave birth to a daughter. There was no disgrace in that; among her people it is customary for a young man to make sure, before marriage, that the chosen girl is not barren, and Njabulo made love to her then. But the infant was very light and did not quickly grow darker as most African babies do. Already at birth there was on its head a quantity of straight, fine floss, like that which carries the seeds of certain weeds in the veld. The unfocused eyes it opened were grey flecked with yellow. Njabulo was the matt, opaque coffee-grounds colour that has always been called black; the colour of Thebedi's legs on which beaded water looked oyster-shell blue, the same colour as Thebedi's face, where the black eyes, with their interested gaze and clear whites, were so dominant.

Njabulo made no complaint. Out of his farm labourer's earnings he bought from the Indian store a cellophane-windowed pack containing a pink plastic bath, six napkins, a card of safety pins, a knitted jacket, cap and bootees, a dress, and a tin of Johnson's Baby Powder, for Thebedi's baby.

When it was two weeks old Paulus Eysendyck arrived home from the veterinary college for the holidays. He drank a glass of fresh, still-warm milk in the childhood familiarity of his mother's kitchen and heard her discussing with the old house-servant where they could get a reliable substitute to help out now that the girl Thebedi had had a baby. For the first time since he was a small boy he came right into the kraal. It was eleven o'clock in the morning. The men were at work in the lands. He looked about him, urgently; the women turned away, each not wanting to be the one approached to point out where Thebedi lived. Thebedi appeared, coming slowly from the hut Njabulo had built in white man's style, with a tin chimney, and a proper window with glass panes set in straight as walls made of unfired bricks would allow. She greeted him with hands brought together and a token movement representing the respectful bob with which she was accustomed to acknowledge she was in the presence of his father or mother. He lowered his head under the doorway of her home and went in. He said, "I want to see. Show me."

She had taken the bundle off her back before she came out into the light to face him. She moved between the iron bedstead made up with Njabulo's checked blankets and the small wooden table where the pink plastic bath stood among food and kitchen pots, and picked up the bundle from the snugly-blanketed grocer's box where it lay. The infant was asleep; she revealed the closed, pale, plump tiny face, with a bubble of spit at the corner of the mouth, the spidery pink hands stirring. She took off the woollen cap and the straight fine hair flew up after it in static electricity, showing gilded strands here and there. He said nothing. She was watching him as she had done when they were little, and the gang of children had trodden down a crop in their games or transgressed in some other way for which he, as the farmer's son, the white one among them, must intercede with the farmer. She disturbed the sleeping face by scratching or tickling gently at a cheek with one finger, and slowly the eyes opened, saw nothing, were still asleep, and then, awake, no longer narrowed, looked out at them, grey with yellowish flecks, his own hazel eyes.

He struggled for a moment with a grimace of tears, anger, and self-pity. She could not put out her hand to him. He said, "You haven't been near the house with it?"

She shook her head.

"Never?"

Again she shook her head.

"Don't take it out. Stay inside. Can't you take it away somewhere. You must give it to someone—"

She moved to the door with him.

He said, "I'll see what I will do. I don't know." And then he said: "I feel like killing myself."

Her eyes began to glow, to thicken with tears. For a moment there was the feeling between them that used to come when they were alone down at the river-bed.

He walked out.

Two days later, when his mother and father had left the farm for the day, he appeared again. The women were away on the lands, weeding, as they were employed to do as casual labour in the summer; only the very old remained, propped up on the ground outside the huts in the flies and the sun. Thebedi did not ask him in. The child had not been well; it had diarrhoea. He asked where its food was. She said, "The milk comes from me." He went into Njabulo's house, where the child lay; she did not follow but stayed outside the door and watched without seeing an old crone who had lost her mind, talking to herself, talking to the fowls who ignored her.

She thought she heard small grunts from the hut, the kind of infant grunt that indicates a full stomach, a deep sleep. After a time, long or short she did not know, he came out and walked away with plodding stride (his father's gait) out of sight, towards his father's house.

The baby was not fed during the night and although she kept telling Njabulo it was sleeping, he saw for himself in the morning that it was dead. He comforted her with words and caresses. She did not cry but simply sat, staring at the door. Her hands were cold as dead chickens' feet to his touch.

Njabulo buried the little baby where farm workers were buried, in the place in the veld the farmer had given them. Some of the mounds had been left to weather away unmarked, others were covered with stones and a few had fallen wooden crosses. He was going to make a cross but before it was finished the police came and dug up the grave and took away the dead baby: someone—one of the other labourers? their women?—had reported that the baby was almost white, that, strong and healthy, it had died suddenly after a visit by the farmer's son. Pathological tests on the infant corpse showed intestinal damage not always consistent with death by natural causes.

Thebedi went for the first time to the country town where Paulus had been to school, to give evidence at the preparatory examination into the charge of murder brought against him. She cried hysterically in the witness box, saying yes, yes (the gilt hoop ear-rings swung in her ears), she saw the accused pouring liquid into the baby's mouth. She said he had threatened to shoot her if she told anyone.

More than a year went by before, in that same town, the case was brought to trial. She came to Court with a new-born baby on her back. She wore gilt hoop ear-rings; she was calm; she said she had not seen what the white man did in the house.

Paulus Eysendyck said he had visited the hut but had not poisoned the child.

The Defence did not contest that there had been a love relationship between the accused and the girl, or that intercourse had taken place, but submitted there was no proof that the child was the accused's.

The judge told the accused there was strong suspicion against him but not enough proof that he had committed the crime. The Court could not accept the girl's evidence because it was clear she had committed perjury either at this trial or at the preparatory examination. There was the suggestion in the mind of the Court that she might be an accomplice in the crime; but, again, insufficient proof.

The judge commended the honourable behaviour of the husband (sitting in court in a brown-and-yellow-quartered golf cap bought for Sundays) who had not rejected his wife and had "even provided clothes for the unfortunate infant out of his slender means."

The verdict on the accused was "not guilty."

The young white man refused to accept the congratulations of press and public and left the Court with his mother's raincoat shielding his face from photographers. His father said to the press, "I will try and carry on as best I can to hold up my head in the district."

Interviewed by the Sunday papers, who spelled her name in a variety of ways, the black girl, speaking in her own language, was quoted beneath her photograph: "It was a thing of our childhood, we don't see each other anymore."

[1980]

Journal Entry

Gordimer was born in Johannesburg, South Africa, and has spent her artistic life protesting the laws of apartheid (the restrictive laws that governed blacks and those of mixed race). What knowledge or experience of apartheid can you bring to your reading of this text?

Textual Considerations

1. What does the first paragraph suggest about the doctor's ability to relate to people? How does his work affect his identity? How do his coworkers perceive him? To what extent is your response to him similar to or different from theirs?
2. Why is "the girl" not named in the story? Does her relationship with the geologist enhance her identity? How does their relationship change over the course of the story?
3. Comment on the role of the police in the story. Characterize your response to their treatment of the girl.
4. Describe Paulus and Thebedi's relationship as they were growing up. What causes it to change?
5. After seeing his baby for the first time, Paulus states that he feels like killing himself. Why does he later kill the baby?
6. Why does Thebedi give conflicting testimony during the investigation? To what extent are both she and Paulus personally responsible for their actions?
7. What role does Thebedi's husband play in the story? How do you respond to him?

Cultural Contexts

1. Why does Gordimer conclude both stories with a court scene? What is the effect of citing in each story the statement published in the Sunday newspaper? How do the published responses differ from the earlier accounts of the protagonists' relationships?
2. Discuss with your group how political repression and economics affect the lives of the characters. Are there parallels between the former system of apartheid in South Africa and race relations in the United States? Explain.

ESSAYS

Virginia Woolf

Professions for Women

When your secretary invited me to come here, she told me that your Society is concerned with the employment of women and she suggested that I might tell you something about my own professional experiences. It is true I am a woman; it is true I am employed, but what professional experiences have I had? It is difficult to say. My profession is literature; and in that profession there are fewer experiences for women than in any other, with the exception of the stage—fewer, I mean, that are peculiar to women. For the road was cut many years ago—by Fanny Burney, by Aphra Behn, by Harriet Martineau, by Jane Austen, by George Eliot—many famous women, and many more unknown and forgotten, have been before me, making the path smooth, and regulating my steps. Thus, when I came to write, there were very few material obstacles in my way. Writing was a reputable and harmless occupation. The family peace was not broken by the scratching of a pen. No demand was made upon the family purse. For ten and sixpence one can buy paper enough to write all the plays of Shakespeare—if one has a mind that way. Pianos and models, Paris, Vienna and Berlin, masters and mistresses, are not needed by a writer. The cheapness of writing paper is, of course, the reason why women have succeeded as writers before they have succeeded in the other professions.

But to tell you my story—it is a simple one. You have only got to figure to yourselves a girl in a bedroom with a pen in her hand. She had only to move that pen from left to right—from ten o'clock to one. Then it occurred to her to do what is simple and cheap enough after all—to slip a few of those pages into an envelope, fix a penny stamp in the corner, and drop the envelope in the red box at the corner. It was thus that I became a journalist; and my effort was rewarded on the first day of the following month—a very glorious day it was for me—by a letter from an editor containing a check for one pound ten shillings and sixpence. But to show you how little I deserve to be called a professional woman, how little I know of the struggles and difficulties of such lives, I have to admit that instead of spending that sum upon bread and butter, rent, shoes and stockings, or butcher's bills, I went out and bought a cat—a beautiful cat, a Persian cat, which very soon involved me in bitter disputes with my neighbors.

What could be easier than to write articles and to buy Persian cats with the profits? But wait a moment. Articles have to be about something. Mine, I seem to remember, was about a novel by a famous man. And while I was writing this review, I discovered that if I were going to review books I should need to do battle with a certain phantom. And the phantom was a woman, and when I came to know her better I called her after the heroine of a famous poem, The Angel in the House. It was she who used to come between me and my paper when I was writing reviews. It was she who bothered me and wasted my time and so tormented me that at last I killed her. You who come of a younger and happier generation may not have heard of her—you may not know what I mean by the Angel in the House. I will describe her as shortly as I can. She was intensely sympathetic. She was immensely charming. She was utterly unselfish. She excelled in the difficult arts of family life. She sacrificed herself daily. If there was chicken, she took the leg; if there was a draught she sat in it—in short she was so constituted that she never had a mind or a wish of her own but preferred to sympathize always with the minds and wishes of others. Above all—I need not say it—she was pure. Her purity was supposed to be her chief beauty—her blushes, her great grace. In those days—the last of Queen Victoria— every house had its Angel. And when I came to write I encountered her with the very first words. The shadow of her wings fell on my page; I heard the rustling of her skirts in the room. Directly, that is to say, I took my pen in hand to review that novel by a famous man, she slipped behind me and whispered: "My dear, you are a young woman. You are writing about a book that has been written by a man. Be sympathetic; be tender; flatter; deceive; use all the arts and wiles of our sex. Never let anybody guess that you have a mind of your own. Above all, be pure." And she made as if to guide my pen. I now record the one act for which I take some credit to myself, though the credit rightly belongs to some excellent ancestor of mine who left me a certain sum of money—shall we say five hundred pounds a year?—so that it was not necessary for me to depend solely on charm for my living. I turned upon her and caught her by the throat. I did my best to kill her. My excuse, if I were to be had up in a court of law, would be that I acted in self-defense. Had I not killed her she would have killed me. She would have plucked the heart out of my writing. For, as I found, directly I put pen to paper, you cannot review even a novel without having a mind of your own, without expressing what you think to be the truth about human relations, morality, sex. And all these questions, according to the Angel in the House, cannot be dealt with freely and openly by women; they must charm, they must conciliate, they must—to put it bluntly—tell lies if they are to succeed. Thus, whenever I felt the shadow of her wing or the radiance of her halo upon my page, I took up the inkpot and flung it at her. She died hard. Her fictitious nature was of great assistance to her. It is far harder to kill a phantom than a reality. She was always creeping back when I thought I had despatched her. Though I flatter myself that I killed her in the end, the struggle was severe; it took much time that had better have been spent upon learning Greek grammar; or in roaming the world in search of adventures. But it was a real experience; it was an experience that was bound to befall all women writers at that time. Killing the Angel in the House was part of the occupation of a woman writer.

But to continue my story. The Angel was dead; what then remained? You may say that what remained was a simple and common object—a young woman in a bedroom with an inkpot. In other words, now that she had rid herself of falsehood, that young woman had only to be herself. Ah, but what is "herself"? I mean, what is a woman? I assure you, I do not know. I do not believe that you know. I do not believe that anybody can know until she has expressed herself in all the arts and professions open to human skill. That indeed is one of the reasons why I have come here—out of respect for you, who are in process of showing us by your experiments what a woman is, who are in process of providing us, by your failures and successes, with that extremely important piece of information.

But to continue the story of my professional experiences. I made one pound ten and six by my first review; and I bought a Persian cat with the proceeds. Then I grew ambitious. A Persian cat is all very well, I said; but a Persian cat is not enough. I must have a motor car. And it was thus that I became a novelist—for it is a very strange thing that people will give you a motor car if you will tell them a story. It is a still stranger thing that there is nothing so delightful in the world as telling stories. It is far pleasanter than writing reviews of famous novels. And yet, if I am to obey your secretary and tell you my professional experiences as a novelist, I must tell you about a very strange experience that befell me as a novelist. And to understand it you must try first to imagine a novelist's state of mind. I hope I am not giving away professional secrets if I say that a novelist's chief desire is to be as unconscious as possible. He has to induce in himself a state of perpetual lethargy. He wants life to proceed with the utmost quiet and regularity. He wants to see the same faces, to read the same books, to do the same things day after day, month after month, while he is writing, so that nothing may break the illusion in which he is living—so that nothing may disturb or disquiet the mysterious nosings about, feelings round, darts, dashes and sudden discoveries of that very shy and illusive spirit, the imagination. I suspect that this state is the same both for men and women. Be that as it may, I want you to imagine me writing a novel in a state of trance. I want you to figure to your-selves a girl sitting with a pen in her hand, which for minutes, and indeed for hours, she never dips into the inkpot. The image that comes to my mind when I think of this girl is the image of a fisherman lying sunk in dreams on the verge of a deep lake with a rod held out over the water. She was letting her imagination sweep unchecked round every rock and cranny of the world that lies submerged in the depths of our unconscious being. Now came the experience, the experience that I believe to be far commoner with women writers than with men. The line raced through the girl's fingers. Her imagination had rushed away. It had sought the pools, the depths, the dark places where the largest fish slumber. And then there was a smash. There was an explosion. There was foam and confusion. The imagination had dashed itself against something hard. The girl was roused from her dream. She was indeed in a state of the most acute and difficult distress. To speak without figure she had thought of something, something about the body, about the passions which it was unfitting for her as a woman to say. Men, her reason told her, would be shocked. The consciousness of what men will say of a woman who speaks the truth about her passions had roused her from her artist's state of unconsciousness. She could write no more. The trance was over. Her imagination could work no longer. This I believe to be a very common experience with women writers—they are impeded by the extreme conventionality of the other sex. For though men sensibly allow them-selves great freedom in these respects, I doubt that they realize or can control the extreme severity with which they condemn such freedom in women.

These then were two very genuine experiences of my own. These were two of the adventures of my professional life. The first—killing the Angel in the House—I think I solved. She died. But the second, telling the truth about my own experiences as a body, I do not think I solved. I doubt that any woman has solved it yet. The obstacles against her are still immensely powerful—and yet they are very difficult to define. Outwardly, what is simpler than to write books? Outwardly, what obstacles are there for a woman rather than for a man? Inwardly, I think the case is very different; she has still many ghosts to fight, many prejudices to overcome. Indeed it will be a long time still, I think, before a woman can sit down to write a book without finding a phantom to be slain, a rock to be dashed against. And if this is so in literature, the freest of all professions for women, how is it in the new professions which you are now for the first time entering?

Those are the questions that I should like, had I time, to ask you. And indeed, if I have laid stress upon these professional experiences of mine, it is because I believe that they are, though in different forms, yours also. Even when the path is nominally open—when there is nothing to prevent a woman from being a doctor, a lawyer, a civil servant—there are many phantoms and obstacles, as I believe, looming in her way. To discuss and define them is I think of great value and importance; for thus only can the labor be shared, the difficulties be solved. But besides this, it is necessary also to discuss the ends and the aims for which we are fighting, for which we are doing battle with these formidable obstacles. Those aims cannot be taken for granted; they must be perpetually questioned and examined. The whole position, as I see it—here in this hall surrounded by women practising for the first time in history I know not how many different professions—is one of extraordinary interest and importance. You have won rooms of your own in the house hitherto exclusively owned by men. You are able, though not without great labor and effort, to pay the rent. You are earning your five hundred pounds a year. But this freedom is only a beginning; the room is your own, but it is still bare. It has to be furnished; it has to be decorated; it has to be shared. How are you going to furnish it, how are you going to decorate it? With whom are you going to share it, and upon what terms? These, I think, are questions of the utmost importance and interest. For the first time in history you are able to ask them; for the first time you are able to decide for yourselves what the answers should be. Willingly would I stay and discuss those questions and answers—but not tonight. My time is up; and I must cease.

[1931]

Journal Entry

Born in London of upper middle class parents, Woolf has emerged as one of the most important feminist writers and critics. Originally delivered as a talk in 1931, Woolf's "Professions for Women" raises questions that still resonate. What, for example, does having your own space mean to you? How will you decide "With whom are you going to share it, and upon what terms"?

Textual Considerations

1. What reasons does Woolf provide to support her thesis that "writing was a reputable and harmless occupation" for women?
2. What do Woolf's arguments suggest about a woman's place in her society?
3. What does the Angel in the House encourage Woolf to do? Is *angel* an appropriate term? Why or why not?
4. Consider Woolf's statement concerning the angel: "Had I not killed her she would have killed me." Is the angel still present today?
5. Do you agree that a woman must kill the angel to survive, both personally and professionally?

Cultural Contexts

1. Discuss with your group Woolf's concept that "it is far harder to kill a phantom than a reality." Why is this so? What forms do these phantoms take in contemporary culture?
2. How do you think Woolf's audience might have reacted to her speech? How would a postmodern female audience respond to her speech today? How do you respond? What cultural and economic tensions in Woolf's 1931 address have been resolved in your view? Which remain unresolved? Can your group reach a consensus?

Daniel Meier

One Man's Kids

I teach first graders. I live in a world of skinned knees, double-knotted shoelaces, riddles that I've heard a dozen times, stale birthday cakes, hurt feelings, wandering stories, and one lost shoe ("and if you don't find it my mother'll kill me"). My work is dominated by 6-year-olds.

It's 10:45, the middle of snack, and I'm helping Emily open her milk carton. She has already tried the other end without success, and now there's so much paint and ink on the carton from her fingers that I'm not sure she should drink it at all. But I open it. Then I turn to help Scott clean up some milk he has just spilled onto Rebecca's whale crossword puzzle.

While I wipe my milk- and paint-covered hands, Jenny wants to know if I've seen that funny book about penguins that I read in class. As I hunt for it in a messy pile of books, Jason wants to know if there is a new seating arrangement for lunch tables. I find the book, turn to answer Jason, then face Maya, who is fast approaching with a new knock-knock joke. After what seems like the 10th "Who's there?" I laugh and Maya is pleased.

Then Andrew wants to know how to spell "flukes" for his crossword. As I get to "u," I give a hand signal for Sarah to take away the snack. But just as Sarah is almost out the door, two children complain that "we haven't even had ours yet." I stop the snack mid-flight, complying with their request for graham crackers. I then return to Andrew, noticing that he has put "flu" for 9 Down, rather than 9 Across. It's now 10:50.

My work is not traditional male work. It's not a singular pursuit. There is not a large pile of paper to get through or one deal to transact. I don't have one area of expertise or knowledge. I don't have the singular power over language of a lawyer, the physical force of a construction worker, the command over fellow workers of a surgeon, the wheeling and dealing transitions of a businessman. My energy is not spent in pursuing, climbing, achieving, conquering, or cornering some goal or object.

My energy is spent in encouraging, supporting, consoling, and praising my children. In teaching, the inner rewards come from without. On any given day, quite apart from teaching reading and spelling, I bandage a cut, dry a tear, erase a frown, tape a torn doll, and locate a long-lost boot. The day is really won through matters of the heart. As my students groan, laugh, shudder, cry, exult, and wonder, I do too. I have to be soft around the edges.

A few years ago, when I was interviewing for an elementary-school teaching position, every principal told me with confidence that, as a male, I had an advantage over female applicants because of the lack of male teachers. But in the next breath, they asked with a hint of suspicion why I chose to work with young children. I told them that I wanted to observe and contribute to the intellectual growth of a maturing mind. What I really felt like saying, but didn't, was that I loved helping a child learn to write his name for the first time, finding someone a new friend, or sharing in the hilarity of reading about Winnie the Pooh getting so stuck in a hole that only his head and rear show.

I gave that answer to those principals, who were mostly male, because I thought they wanted a "male" response. This meant talking about intellectual matters. If I had taken a different course and talked about my interest in helping children in their emotional development, it would have been seen as closer to a "female" answer. I even altered my language, not once mentioning the word "love" to describe what I do indeed love about teaching. My answer worked; every principal nodded approvingly.

Some of the principals also asked what I saw myself doing later in my career. They wanted to know if I eventually wanted to go into educational administration. Becoming a dean of students or a principal has never been one of my goals, but they seemed to expect me, as a male, to want to climb higher on the career stepladder. So I mentioned that, at some point, I would be interested in working with teachers as a curriculum coordinator. Again, they nodded approvingly.

If those principals had been female instead of male, I wonder whether their questions, and my answers, would have been different. My guess is that they would have been.

At other times, when I'm at a party or a dinner and tell someone that I teach young children, I've found that men and women respond differently. Most men ask about the subjects I teach and the courses I took in my training. Then, unless they bring up an issue such as merit pay, the conversation stops. Most women, on the other hand, begin the conversation on a more immediate and personal level. They say things like "those kids must love having a male teacher" or "that age is just wonderful, you must love it." Then, more often than not, they'll talk about their own kids or ask me specific questions about what I do. We're then off and talking shop.

Possibly, men would have more to say to me, and I to them, if my job had more of the trappings and benefits of more traditional male jobs. But my job has no bonuses or promotions. No complimentary box seats at the ball park. No cab fare home. No drinking buddies after work. No briefcase. No suit. (Ties get stuck in paint jars.) No power lunches. (I eat peanut butter and jelly, chips, milk, and cookies with the kids.) No taking clients out for cocktails. The only place I take my kids is to the playground.

Although I could have pursued a career in law or business, as several of my friends did, I chose teaching instead. My job has benefits all its own. I'm able to bake cookies without getting them stuck together as they cool, buy cheap sewing materials, take out splinters, and search just the right trash cans for useful odds and ends. I'm sometimes called "Daddy" and even "Mommy" by my students, and if there's ever a lull in the conversation at a dinner party, I can always ask those assembled if they've heard the latest riddle about why the turkey crossed the road. (He thought he was a chicken.)

[1987]

Journal Entry

Can you imagine yourself in Meier's shoes? Why or why not?

Textual Considerations

1. What is your response to the essay's title? Discuss its significance.
2. What is the effect of Meier's introducing his pupils with incidents from his classroom experience?
3. Meier's essay was originally published in "About Men," in *The New York Times Magazine*. How might his intended audience respond to his essay?
4. What is your response to Meier's presentation of evidence or proof about the nobility of his profession?
5. Clarify Meier's purpose. Is he seeking only to inform his readers, or does he also wish to persuade? Cite evidence for your point of view.

Cultural Contexts

1. "My work is not traditional male work." How does the author define male work? How is it different from female work? What do these distinctions suggest about gender stereotypes in the workplace?

2. What does Meier's essay imply about society's attitude toward teaching children as a professional choice for a male? Do children need more male role models as teachers in elementary school? Can your group reach a consensus about these issues? Explain.

Peter Lyman

The Fraternal Bond as a Joking Relationship

One evening during dinner, forty-five fraternity men suddenly broke into the dining room of a nearby campus sorority, surrounded the thirty women residents, and forced them to watch while one pledge gave a speech on Freud's theory of penis envy as another demonstrated various techniques of masturbation with a rubber penis. The women sat silently staring downward at their plates listening for about ten minutes, until a woman law student who was the graduate resident in charge of the house walked in, surveyed the scene, and demanded, "Please leave immediately!" As she later described that moment, "There was a mocking roar from the men, 'It's tradition.' I said, 'That's no reason to do something like this, please leave!' And they left. I was surprised. Then the women in the house started to get angry. And the guy who made the penis envy speech came back and said to us, 'That was funny to me. If that's not funny to you I don't know what kind of sense of humor you have, but I'm sorry.'"

That night the women sat around the stairwell of their house discussing the event, some angry and others simply wanting to forget the whole thing. They finally decided to ask the university to require the men to discuss the event. When university officials threatened to take action, the men agreed to the meeting. I was asked by both the men and women involved to attend the discussion as a facilitator, and was given permission to write about the event as long as I concealed their identities.

In the women's view, the joke had not failed because of its subject; they considered sexual jokes to be a normal part of the erotic joking relationship between men and women. They criticized the emotional structure, the mixture of sexuality with aggression and the atmosphere of physical intimidation in the room. Although many of the men individually regretted the damage to their relationship with women friends in the group, they argued that the special group solidarity created by the initiation was a unique form of masculine friendship that justified the inconvenience caused the women.

Fraternal group bonding in everyday life frequently takes the form of *joking relationships*, in which men relate to each other by exchanging insults and jokes in order to create a feeling of solidarity that negotiates the latent tension and aggression they feel toward each other (Radcliffe-Brown, 1959). The humor of joking relationships is generally sexual and aggressive, and frequently consists of sexist or racist jokes. As Freud (1960:99) observed, the jokes men direct *toward* women are generally sexual, tend to be clever (like double entendres), and have a seductive purpose; but the jokes that men tell *about* women in the presence of other men tend to be sexist rather than intimate or erotic, and use hostile and aggressive rather than clever verbal forms. In this case study, joking relationships will be analyzed to uncover the emotional dynamics of fraternal groups and the impact of fraternal bonding upon relationships between men and women.

The Girls' Story

The women had frequently been the target of fraternity initiation rites in the past, and generally enjoyed this joking relationship with the men, if with a certain ambivalence. "There was the naked Christmas Carol event, they were singing 'We wish you a Merry Christmas,' and 'Bring on the hasty pudding' was the big line they liked to yell out. And they had five or six pledges who had to strip in front of the house and do naked jumping jacks on the lawn, after all the women in the house were lined up on the steps to watch." The women did not think these events were hostile because they had been invited to watch, and the men stood with them watching, suggesting that the pledges, not the women, were the targets of the joke. This defined the joke as sexual, not sexist, and part of the normal erotic joking relation between "guys and girls." Still, these jokes were ritual events, not real social relationships. One woman said, "We were just supposed to watch, and the guys were watching us watch. The men set the stage and the women are brought along to observe. They were the controlling force, then they jump into the car and take off."

At the meeting with the men, two of the women spoke for the group while eleven others sat silently in the center, surrounded by almost thirty men. The first woman began, "Your humor was pretty funny as long as it was sexual, but when it went beyond sexual to sexist, then it became painful. You were saying 'I'm better than you.' When you started using sex as a way of proving your superiority, it hurt me and made me angry."

The second woman said that the fraternity's raid had the tone of a rape. "I admit we knew you were coming over, and we were whispering about it. But it went too far, and I felt afraid to say anything. Why do men always think about women in terms of violating them, in sexual imagery? You have to understand that the combination of a sexual topic with the physical threat of all of you standing around terrified me. I couldn't move. You have to realize that when men combine sexuality and force, it's terrifying to women."

Many of the women began by saying, "I'm not a feminist, but . . . ," to reassure the men that although they felt angry, they hoped to reestablish the many individual friendships that had existed between men and women in the two groups. In part the issue was resolved when the women accepted the men's construction of the event as a joke, although a failed joke, transforming a discussion about sexuality and force into a debate about good and bad jokes.

For an aggressive joke to be funny, and most jokes must contain some hostility, the joke teller must send the audience a cue that says "this is meant as a joke." If accepted, the cue invokes special social rules that "frame" the hostile words that are typical of jokes, ensuring they will not be taken seriously. The men had implicitly sent such a cue when they stood *next* to the women during the naked jumping jacks. Verbal aggression mediated by the joke form will generally be without later consequences in the everyday world, and will be judged in terms of the formal intention of jokes, shared play and laughter.

In accepting construction of the event as "just a joke" the women absolved the men of responsibility for their actions by calling them "little boys." One woman said, "It's not wrong, they're just boys playing a prank. They're little boys, they don't know what they're doing. It was unpleasant, but we shouldn't make a big deal out of it." In appealing to the rules of the joke form (as in saying "That was funny to me, I don't know what kind of sense of humor you have"), the men sacrificed their personal friendships with the women in order to protect the feelings of fraternal solidarity it produced. In calling the men "little boys" the women were bending the rules of friendship, trying to preserve their relationships to the guys by playing a patient and nurturing role.

The Guys' Story

Aside from occasional roars of laughter, the men interrupted the women only once. When a woman began to say that the men had obviously intended to intimidate them, the men loudly protested that the women couldn't possibly judge their intentions, that they intended the whole event only as a joke, and the intention of a joke is, by definition, just fun.

At this point the two black men in the fraternity intervened to explain the rules of making joking relationships to the women. In a sense, they said, they agreed with the women, being the object of hostile jokes is painful. As they described it, the collective talk of the fraternity at meals and group events was entirely hostile joking, including many racist jokes. One said, "I'd had to listen to things in the house that I'd have hit someone for saying if I'd heard them outside." The guys roared with laughter, for the fraternal joking relation consisted almost entirely of aggressive words that were barely contained by the convention that joke tellers are not responsible for what they say.

One woman responded, "Maybe people should be hit for saying those things, maybe that's the right thing to do." But the black speaker was trying to explain the rules of male joke culture to the women. "If you'd just ignored us, it wouldn't have been any fun." To ignore a joke, even though it makes you feel hurt or angry, is to be cool, one of the primary masculine ideals of the group.

Another man tried to explain the failure of the joke in terms of the difference between the degree of "crudeness" appropriate "between guys" and between "guys and girls." He said, "As I was listening to the speech I was both embarrassed and amused. I was standing at the edge of the room, near the door, and when I looked at the guys I was laughing but when I looked at the girls I was embarrassed. I could see both sides at the same time. It was too crude for your sense of propriety. We have a different sense of crudeness you don't have. That's a cultural aspect of the difference between girls and guys."

The other men laughed as he mentioned "how crude we are at the house," and one of the black men added, "You wouldn't believe how crude it gets." Many of the men later said that although they individually found the jokes about women vulgar, the jokes were justified because they were necessary for the formation of the fraternal bond. These men thought that the mistake had been to reveal their crudeness to the women; this was "in bad taste."

In part the crudeness was a kind of "signifying" or "dozens," a ritual exchange of intimate insults that creates group solidarity. "If there's one theme that goes on it's the emphasis on being able to take a lot of ridicule, of shit, and not getting upset about it. Most of the interaction we have is verbally abusing each other, making disgusting references to your mother's sexuality, or the women you were seen with, or your sex organ, the size of your sex organ. And you aren't cool unless you can take it without trying to get back." Being cool is an important male value in other settings as well, like sports or work; the joking relationship is a kind of training that, in one guy's words, "teaches you how to keep in control of your emotions."

But the guys themselves would not have described their group as a joking relationship or fraternal bond, they called it friendship. One man said that he had found perhaps a dozen guys in the house who were special friends, "guys I could cry in front of." Another said, "I think the guys are very close, they would do nearly anything for each other, drive each other places, give each other money. I think when they have problems about school, their car, or something like that, they can talk to each other. I'm not sure they can talk to each other about women though." Although the image of crying in front of the other guys was mentioned as an example of the intimacy of the fraternal bond, no one could actually recall anyone in the group ever crying. In fact crying would be an admission of vulnerability which would violate the ideals of "strength" and "being cool."

The women interpreted the sexist jokes as a sign of vulnerability. "The thing that struck me the most about our meeting together," one said, "was when the men said they were afraid of trusting women, afraid of being seen as jerks." One of the guys added, "I think deep down all the guys would love to have satisfying relationships with women. I think they're scared of failing, of having to break away from the group they've become comfortable with. I think being in a fraternity, having close relationships with men is a replacement for having close relationships with women. It'd be painful for them because they'd probably fail." These men preferred to relate to women as a group at fraternity parties, where they could take women back to their rooms for quick sex without commitments.

Sexist jokes also had a social function, policing the boundaries of the group, making sure that guys didn't form serious relationships with girls and leave the fraternity (cf. Slater, 1963). "One of the guys just acquired a girlfriend a few weeks ago. He's someone I don't think has had a woman to be friends with, maybe ever, at least in a long time. Everybody has been ribbing him intensely the last few weeks. It's good natured in tone. Sitting at dinner they've invented a little song they sing to him. People yell questions about his girlfriend, the size of her vagina, does she have big breasts." Thus, in dealing with women, the group separated intimacy from sex, defining the male bond as intimate but not sexual (homosocial), and relationships with women as sexual but not intimate (heterosexual).

The Fraternal Bond in Men's Life Cycle

Men often speak of friendship as a group relationship, not a dyadic one, and men's friendships often grow from the experience of shared activities or risk, rather than from self-disclosing talk (cf. Rubin, 1983:130). J. Glenn Gray (1959:89–90) distinguishes the intimate form of friendship from the comradeship that develops from the shared experience of suffering and danger of men at war. In comradeship, he argues, the individual's sense of self is subordinated to a group identity, whereas friendship is based upon a specific feeling for another that heightens a sense of individuality.

In this case, the guys used joking relationships to suspend the ordinary rules and responsibilities of everyday life, placing the intimacy of the fraternal group in competition with heterosexual friendships. One of the men had been inexpressive as he listened to the discussion, but spoke about the fraternity in a voice filled with emotion: "The penis envy speech was a hilarious idea, great college fun. That's what I joined the fraternity for, a good time. College is a stage in my life to do crazy and humorous things. In ten years when I'm in the business world I won't be able to carry on like this [loud laughter from the men]. The initiation was intended to be humorous. We didn't think through how sensitive you women were going to be."

This speech gives the fraternal bond a specific place in the life cycle. The joking relationship is a ritual bond that creates a male group bond in the transition between boyhood and manhood: after the separation from the family where the authority of mothers limits fun, but before becoming subject to the authority of work. One man later commented on the transitional nature of the fraternal bond, "I think a lot of us are really scared of losing total control over our own lives. Having to sacrifice our individuality. I think we're scared of work in the same way we're scared of women." The jokes expressed hostility toward women because an intimate friendship with a woman was associated with "loss of control," namely the responsibility for work and family.

Most, but not all, of the guys in the fraternity were divided between their group identity and a sense of personal identity that was expressed in private friendships with women. Some of the guys, like one who could "see both sides" as he stood on the edge of the group during the initiation, had reached the point of leaving the fraternity because they couldn't reconcile the tension between his group identity and the sense of self that he felt in his friendships with women.

Ultimately the guys justified the penis envy joke because it created a special kind of male intimacy. But although the fraternal group was able to appropriate the guys' needs for intimacy and commitment it is not clear that it was able to satisfy those needs, because it defined strength as shared risk taking rather than a quality of individual character or personality. In Gray's terms, the guys were construct-ing comradeship through an erotic of shared activities with an element of risk, shared danger, or rule breaking such as sports, paramilitary games, wild parties, and hostile jokes. In these contexts, strength implied the substitution of a group identity for a personal code that might extend to commitment and care for others (cf. Bly 1982).

In the guys' world, aggression was identified with strength, and defined as loss of control only if it was angry. The fraternal bond was built upon an emotional bal-ance between aggression and anger, for life of the group centered upon the mobi-lization of aggressive energies in rule-governed activities, especially sports and games. In each arena, aggression was defined as strength (toughness) only when it was rule-governed (cool). Getting angry was called "losing control," and the guys thought they were most likely to lose control when they experienced themselves as personally dependent, that is, in relationships with women and at work. The sense of order within fraternal groups is based upon the belief that all members are equally dependant upon the rules, and that no *personal* dependence is created within the group. This is not true of the family or of relations with women, both of which are intimate, and, from the guys' point of view, are "out of control" because they are governed by emotional commitments.

The guys recognized the relationship between their male bond and the work world by claiming that "high officials of the University know about the way we act, and they understand what we are doing." Although this might be taken as evidence that the guys were internalizing their fathers' norms and thus inheriting the rights of patriarchy, the guys described their fathers as slaves to work and women, not as patriarchs. It is striking that the guys would not accept the notion that men have more power than women; to them it is not men who rule, but work and women that govern men.

[1987]

References

Bly, Robert. (1982) "What men really want: An interview with Keith Thompson." *New Age* 30–37, 50–51.

Freud, Sigmund. (1960) *Jokes and Their Relation to the Unconscious*. New York: W. W. Norton.

Gray, Glenn J. (1959) *The Warriors: Reflections on Men in Battle*. New York: Harper.

Radcliffe-Brown, Alfred. (1959) *Structure and Function in Primitive Society*. Glencoe: The Free Press.

Rubin, Lillian. (1983) *Intimate Strangers*. New York: Harper & Row.

Slater, Philip. (1963) "On Social Regression." *The American Sociological Review* 28:339–364.

Journal Entry

Respond to the concept that societal stereotypes of masculinity often result in men's masking their real emotions.

Textual Considerations

1. Summarize the incident that Lyman describes in the first part of the essay.
2. At the meeting Lyman attended, both groups expressed their views on the fraternity initiation incident. List the important differences between male and female attitudes toward joke culture that emerged from the discussion. With which responses do you agree or disagree? Explain.
3. What did the comments of the black fraternity members add to the debate?
4. To what extent did the responses of both male and female students conform to sexual stereotypes? Explain.
5. Make a list of the arguments you identify with in Lyman's text, and argue in their defense.
6. Comment on how Lyman's division of the text into three parts adds to its overall impact.

Cultural Contexts

1. What gender roles exist only in the United States? In some countries, for example, it is not unusual for men to express affection for one another or even to cry in public. Discuss how cultural experience affects gender stereotypes.
2. Working with your group, discuss male and female concepts of friendship. How are they similar? different? What are some of the implications of the differences you have noted? According to Lyman, how did the fraternity members distinguish between intimacy and friendship?

Deborah Tannen

Sex, Lies and Conversation: Why Is It So Hard for Men and Women to Talk to Each Other?

I was addressing a small gathering in a suburban Virginia living room—a women's group that had invited men to join them. Throughout the evening, one man had been particularly talkative, frequently offering ideas and anecdotes, while his wife sat silently beside him on the couch. Toward the end of the evening, I commented that women frequently complain that their husbands don't talk to them. This man quickly concurred. He gestured toward his wife and said, "She's the talker in our family." The room burst into laughter; the man looked puzzled and hurt. "It's true," he explained. "When I come home from work I have nothing to say. If she didn't keep the conversation going, we'd spend the whole evening in silence."

This episode crystallizes the irony that although American men tend to talk more than women in public situations, they often talk less at home. And this pattern is wreaking havoc with marriage.

The pattern was observed by political scientist Andrew Hacker in the late '70s. Sociologist Catherine Kohler Riessman reports in her new book *Divorce Talk* that most of the women she interviewed—but only a few of the men— gave lack of communication as the reason for their divorces. Given the current divorce rate of nearly 50 percent, that amounts to millions of cases in the United States every year—a virtual epidemic of failed conversation.

In my own research, complaints from women about their husbands most often focused not on tangible inequities such as having given up the chance for a career to accompany a husband to his, or doing far more than their share of daily life-support work like cleaning, cooking, social arrangements and errands. Instead, they focused on communication: "He doesn't listen to me," "He doesn't talk to me." I found, as Hacker observed years before, that most wives want their husbands to be, first and foremost, conversational partners, but few husbands share this expectation of their wives.

In short, the image that best represents the current crisis is the stereotypical cartoon scene of a man sitting at the breakfast table with a newspaper held up in front of his face, while a woman glares at the back of it, wanting to talk.

Linguistic Battle of the Sexes

How can women and men have such different impressions of communication in marriage? Why the widespread imbalance in their interests and expectations?

In the April [1990] issue of *American Psychologist*, Stanford University's Eleanor Maccoby reports the results of her own and others' research showing that children's development is most influenced by the social structure of peer interactions. Boys and girls tend to play with children of their own gender, and their sex-separate groups have different organizational structures and interactive norms.

I believe these systematic differences in childhood socialization make talk between women and men like cross-cultural communication, heir to all the attraction and pitfalls of that enticing but difficult enterprise. My research on men's and women's conversations uncovered patterns similar to those described for children's groups.

For women, as for girls, intimacy is the fabric of relationships, and talk is the thread from which it is woven. Little girls create and maintain friendships by exchanging secrets; similarly, women regard conversation as the cornerstone of friendship. So a woman expects her husband to be a new and improved version of a best friend. What is important is not the individual subjects that are discussed but the sense of closeness, of a life shared, that emerges when people tell their thoughts, feelings, and impressions.

Bonds between boys can be as intense as girls', but they are based less on talking, more on doing things together. Since they don't assume talk is the cement that binds a relationship, men don't know what kind of talk women want, and they don't miss it when it isn't there.

Boy's groups are larger, more inclusive, and more hierarchical, so boys must struggle to avoid the subordinate position in the group. This may play a role in women's complaints that men don't listen to them. Some men really don't like to listen, because being the listener makes them feel one-down, like a child listening to adults or an employee to a boss.

But often when women tell men, "You aren't listening," and the men protest, "I am," the men are right. The impression of not listening results from misalignment in the mechanics of conversation. The misalignment begins as soon as a man and a woman take physical positions. This became clear when I studied videotapes made by psychologist Paul Dorval of children and adults talking to their same-sex best friends. I found that at every age, the girls and women faced each other directly, their eyes anchored on each other's faces. At every age, the boys and men sat at angles to each other and looked elsewhere in the room, periodically glancing at each other. They were obviously attuned to each other, often mirroring each other's movements. But the tendency of men to face away can give women the impression they aren't listening even when they are. A young woman in college was frustrated: Whenever she told her boyfriend she wanted to talk to him, he would lie down on the floor, close his eyes, and put his arm over his face. This signaled to her, "He's taking a nap." But he insisted he was listening extra hard. Normally, he looks around the room, so he is easily distracted. Lying down and covering his eyes helped him concentrate on what she was saying.

Analogous to the physical alignment that women and men take in conversation is their topical alignment. The girls in my study tended to talk at length about one topic, but the boys tended to jump from topic to topic. The second-grade girls exchanged stories about people they knew. The second-grade boys teased, told jokes, noticed things in the room and talked about finding games to play. The sixth-grade girls talked about problems with a mutual friend. The sixth-grade boys talked about 55 different topics, none of which extended over more than a few turns.

Listening to Body Language

Switching topics is another habit that gives women the impression men aren't listening, especially if they switch to a topic about themselves. But the evidence of the 10th-grade boys in my study indicates otherwise. The 10th-grade boys sprawled across their chairs with bodies parallel and eyes straight ahead, rarely looking at each other. They looked as if they were riding in a car, staring out the windshield. But they were talking about their feelings. One boy was upset because a girl had told him he had a drinking problem, and the other was feeling alienated from all his friends.

Now, when a girl told a friend about a problem, the friend responded by asking probing questions and expressing agreement and understanding. But the boys dismissed each other's problems. Todd assured Richard that his drinking was "no big problem" because "sometimes you're funny when you're off your butt." And when Todd said he felt left out, Richard responded, "Why should you? You know more people than me."

Women perceive such responses as belittling and unsupportive. But the boys seemed satisfied with them. Whereas women reassure each other by implying, "You shouldn't feel bad because I've had similar experiences," men do so by implying, "You shouldn't feel bad because your problems aren't so bad."

There are even simpler reasons for women's impression that men don't listen. Linguist Lynette Hirschman found that women make more listener-noise, such as "mhm," "uhuh," and "yeah," to show "I'm with you." Men, she found, more often give silent attention. Women who expect a stream of listener-noise interpret silent attention as no attention at all.

Women's conversational habits are as frustrating to men as men's are to women. Men who expect silent attention interpret a stream of listener-noise as overreaction or impatience. Also, when women talk to each other in a close, comfortable setting, they often overlap, finish each other's sentences and anticipate what the other is about to say. This practice, which I call "participatory listenership," is often perceived by men as interruption, intrusion, and lack of attention.

A parallel difference caused a man to complain about his wife, "She just wants to talk about her own point of view. If I show her another view, she gets mad at me." When most women talk to each other, they assume a conversationalist's job is to express agreement and support. But many men see their conversational duty as pointing out the other side of an argument. This is heard as disloyalty by women, and refusal to offer the requisite support. It is not that women don't want to see other points of view, but that they prefer them phrased as suggestions and inquiries rather than as direct challenges.

In his book *Fighting for Life*, Walter Ong points out that men use "agonistic" or warlike, oppositional formats to do almost anything; thus discussion becomes debate, and conversation a competitive sport. In contrast, women see conversation as a ritual means of establishing rapport. If Jane tells a problem and June says she has a similar one, they walk away feeling closer to each other. But this attempt at establishing rapport can backfire when used with men. Men take too literally women's ritual "troubles talk," just as women mistake men's ritual challenges for real attack.

The Sounds of Silence

These differences begin to clarify why women and men have such different expectations about communication in marriage. For women, talk creates intimacy. Marriage is an orgy of closeness: you can tell your feelings and thoughts, and still be loved. Their greatest fear is being pushed away. But men live in a hierarchical world, where talk maintains independence and status. They are on guard to protect themselves from being put down and pushed around.

This explains the paradox of the talkative man who said of his silent wife, "She's the talker." In the public setting of a guest lecture, he felt challenged to show his intelligence and display his understanding of the lecture. But at home, where he has nothing to prove and no one to defend against, he is free to remain silent. For his wife, being home means she is free from the worry that something she says might offend someone, or spark disagreement, or appear to be showing off; at home she is free to talk.

The communication problems that endanger marriage can't be fixed by mechanical engineering. They require a new conceptual framework about the role of talk in human relationships. Many of the psychological explanations that have become second nature may not be helpful, because they tend to blame either women (for not being assertive enough) or men (for not being in touch with their feelings). A sociolinguistic approach by which male–female conversation is seen as cross-cultural communication allows us to understand the problem and forge solutions without blaming either party.

Once the problem is understood, improvement comes naturally, as it did to the young woman and her boyfriend who seemed to go to sleep when she wanted to talk. Previously, she had accused him of not listening, and he had refused to change his behavior, since that would be admitting fault. But then she learned about and explained to him the differences in women's and men's habitual ways of aligning themselves in conversation. The next time she told him she wanted to talk, he began, as usual, by lying down and covering his eyes. When the familiar negative reaction bubbled up, she reassured herself that he really was listening. But then he sat up and looked at her. Thrilled she asked why. He said, "You like me to look at you when we talk, so I'll try to do it." Once he saw their differences as cross-cultural rather than right and wrong, he independently altered his behavior.

Women who feel abandoned and deprived when their husbands won't listen to or report daily news may be happy to discover their husbands trying to adapt once they understand the place of small talk in women's relationships. But if their husbands don't adapt, the women may still be comforted that for men, this is not a failure of intimacy. Accepting the difference, the wives may look to their friends or family for that kind of talk. And husbands who can't provide it shouldn't feel their wives have made unreasonable demands. Some couples will still decide to divorce, but at least their decisions will be based on realistic expectations.

In these times of resurgent ethnic conflicts, the world desperately needs cross-cultural understanding. Like charity, successful cross-cultural communication should begin at home.

[1990]

Journal Entry

According to Tannen, "Women's conversational habits are as frustrating to men as men's are to women." Do you agree? Cite examples from your experience.

Textual Considerations

1. According to Tannen, the causes of communication difficulties between men and women are rooted in childhood patterns of socialization. What evidence does she provide to support her thesis?
2. How accurately does Tannen's hypothesis about communication between men and women reflect your own experience as a child and as an adult?
3. What solutions does Tannen offer to improve communication between the sexes?
4. What is your interpretation of and response to "cross-cultural communication"?
5. Is Tannen's purpose to inform, or does she also wish to persuade her readers? How do style and tone contribute to her purpose? Cite specific examples.

Cultural Contexts

1. Discuss the degree to which society and culture influence our concepts of masculinity and femininity. To what extent is it possible or desirable to go beyond stereotypical definitions?

2. With your group, discuss Tannen's question posed in the essay's title, and analyze carefully the components of sex, lies, and conversation. How do the responses for your generation compare to those cited in Tannen's research? How do you account for differences that exist?

POETRY

John Donne

Woman's Constancy

Now thou hast loved me one whole day,
To-morrow when thou leavest, what wilt thou say?
Wilt thou then antedate some new-made vow?
    Or say that now
We are not just those persons which we were?   5
Or that oaths made in reverential fear
Of Love, and his wrath, any may forswear?
Or, as true deaths true marriages untie,
So lovers' contracts, images of those,
Bind but till sleep, death's image, them unloose?   10
    Or, your own end to justify,
For having purposed change and falsehood, you
Can have no way but falsehood to be true?
Vain lunatic, against these 'scapes I could
    Dispute, and conquer, if I would;   15
    Which I abstain to do,
For by to-morrow I may think so too.

[1633]

John Donne

The Sun Rising

Busy old fool, unruly Sun,
  Why dost thou thus,
Through windows, and through curtains call on us?
Must to thy motions lovers' seasons run?
    Saucy pedantic wretch, go chide   5
    Late school boys and sour prentices,°
  Go tell Court-huntsmen, that the King will ride,
  Call country ants to harvest offices°;
Love, all alike, no season knows, nor clime,°
Nor hours, days, months, which are the rags of time.   10

    Thy beams, so reverend, and strong
    Why shouldst thou think?°
I could eclipse and cloud them with a wink,
But that I would not lose her sight so long;
    If her eyes have not blinded thine,   15
    Look, and tomorrow late, tell me,
  Whether both the Indias of spice and Mine°
Be where thou leftst them, or lie here with me.
Ask for those kings whom thou saw'st yesterday,
And thou shalt hear, All here in one bed lay.   20

    She'is° all States, and all Princes, I,
    Nothing else is.
Princes do but play us; compared to this,
All honor's mimic; all wealth alchemy.°
    Thou, sun, art half as happy'as° we,   25
    In that the world's contracted thus;
  Thine age asks ease, and since thy duties be
  To warm the world, that's done in warming us.
Shine here to us, and thou art everywhere;
This bed thy center° is, these walls, thy sphere.   30

[1633]

6 prentices: apprentices   **8 Call . . . offices:** i.e., notify the country's ants to carry out the duty of eating the harvest of grain and produce.   **9 clime:** climate   **11, 12 Thy beams . . . think?:** i.e., why shouldst thou think that thy beams are so reverend and strong?   **17 Indias of spice and Mine:** The India of "spice" is the East Indies; the India of "Mine" (gold) is the West Indies.   **21 She'is:** For scansion, these two words are to be considered one syllable ("shé's").   **24 all wealth alchemy:** i.e., all wealth is false because it has been created by alchemists.   **25 happy'as:** to be scanned as a trochee ("háppyàz").   **30 center:** the earth, around which the sun revolves (according to the Ptolemaic view of the solar system).

Journal Entry

What is your concept of the ideal gender relationship? How does it compare to Donne's view of the man-woman relationship in "Woman's Constancy" and "The Sun Rising"?

Textual Considerations

1. Describe the argumentative structure of "Woman's Constancy." Why does the speaker criticize his mistress for her supposed faithlessness? Identify the arguments the speaker uses to build the image of his mistress in this lyric meditation.
2. Where does the speaker change his tone throughout the text? Explain his mood or attitude in lines 14–17. Does he surprise the reader at the end of the poem?
3. How are the lovers in "Woman's Constancy" affected by time? How important are the speaker's references to "Now" (line 1), and "Tomorrow" (lines 2, 17)? Is time connected with any major theme of the lyric? Explain.
4. How effective is the speaker's image of the sun in "The Sun Rising"? Explain how he develops and expands this image. How does he use this image to create his ideal world of love?
5. Contrast the views of love expressed in "The Sun Rising" (lines 9–10) and "Woman's Constancy." How do they differ? What statements do these lyrics make about love, time, and the role of the mistress?

Cultural Contexts

1. Working with your group, try to identify some of today's popular love songs that use images of the cosmos, politics, and lovers' physical surroundings (like the bedroom in "The Sun Rising") to explore the theme of love.
2. How do today's love songs address the theme of love, including the dichotomy of the body and soul, sexuality, and the issue of time? How do they compare with John Donne's treatment of love in "Woman's Constancy" and "The Sun Rising"?

SEXTON AND DICKEY

Anne Sexton

For My Lover, Returning to His Wife

She is all there.
She was melted carefully down for you
and cast up from your childhood,
cast up from your one hundred favorite aggies.°

She has always been there, my darling.   5
She is, in fact, exquisite.
Fireworks in the dull middle of February
and as real as a cast-iron pot.

Let's face it, I have been momentary.
A luxury. A bright red sloop in the harbor.   10
My hair rising like smoke from the car window.
Littleneck clams out of season.

She is more than that. She is your have to have,
has grown you your practical your tropical growth.
This is not an experiment. She is all harmony.   15
She sees to oars and oarlocks for the dinghy,

has placed wild flowers at the window at breakfast,
sat by the potter's wheel at midday,
set forth three children under the moon,
three cherubs drawn by Michelangelo,   20

done this with her legs spread out
in the terrible months in the chapel.
If you glance up, the children are there
like delicate balloons resting on the ceiling.

She has also carried each one down the hall   25
after supper, their heads privately bent,
two legs protesting, person to person,
her face flushed with a song and their little sleep.

I give you back your heart.
I give you permission——   30

for the fuse inside her, throbbing
angrily in the dirt, for the bitch in her

and the burying of her wound——
for the burying of her small red wound alive——

for the pale flickering flare under her ribs,   35
for the drunken sailor who waits in her left pulse,
for the mother's knee, for the stockings,
for the garter belt, for the call——

the curious call
when you will burrow in arms and breasts   40
and tug at the orange ribbon in her hair
and answer the call, the curious call.

She is so naked and singular.
She is the sum of yourself and your dream.
Climb her like a monument, step after step.   45
She is solid.

As for me, I am a watercolor.
I wash off.

                                                                    [1967]

4 aggies: Colorful playing marbles.

James Dickey

Adultery

We have all been in rooms
We cannot die in, and they are odd places, and sad
Often Indians are standing eagle-armed on hills

In the sunrise   open wide to the Great Spirit
Or gliding in canoes   or cattle are browsing on the walls   5
Far away   gazing down with the eyes of our children

Not far away   or there are men driving
The last railspike, which has turned
Gold in their hands. Gigantic forepleasure lives

Among such scenes, and we are alone with it   10
At last. There is always some weeping
Between us   and someone is always checking

A wrist watch by the bed to see how much
Longer we have left. Nothing can come
Of this   nothing can come   15

Of us: of me with my grim techniques
Or you who have sealed your womb
With a ring of convulsive rubber:

Although we come together,
Nothing will come of us. But we would not give   20
It up, for death is beaten

By praying Indians   by distant cows   historical
Hammers   by hazardous meetings that bridge
A continent. One could never die here

Never die   never die   25
While crying. My lover, my dear one
I will see you next week

When I'm in town. I will call you
If I can. Please get hold of   please don't
Oh God, Please don't any more I can't bear . . . Listen: 30

We have done it again ˴ we are
Still living. Sit up and smile,
God bless you. Guilt is magical.

                                                        [1966]

Journal Entry

Brainstorm on your associations with adultery. Do you connect it with passion, desire, or love? Is guilt an element?

Textual Considerations

1. Discuss how Sexton's use of contrasting images of the wife and mistress contribute to the transience of the love affair the poem describes.
2. With whom do you empathize—the mistress or the wife—in "For My Lover, Returning to His Wife"? Cite evidence from the text to support your position. What does the poem reveal about the husband? What is your attitude toward him?
3. How does Dickey describe the "rooms we cannot die in" in "Adultery"? Characterize the scenes on the walls.
4. Why do the two lovers check their wrist watches in "Adultery"? If "nothing can come of this," why do they continue to meet?
5. How does the structure of "Adultery" help emphasize the speaker's ambivalent feelings? In what ways do both poems build to a climax? What change in rhythm occurs in the last three lines of Dickey's text? What is the effect of Sexton's contrasting images in the last six lines?

Cultural Contexts

1. Discuss the significance of the references to children in both poems. How do they contribute to the theme? What effect do they have on your attitudes to the affairs?
2. Working with your group, speculate about attitudes toward adultery. How do different cultures react toward this issue? How does your generation respond to marital infidelity? Is fidelity an intimate relationship or an unrealistic expectation, given the emphasis on sexuality in the present culture? Can your group reach a consensus on this issue?

Barbara L. Greenberg

The Faithful Wife

But if I *were* to have a lover, it would be someone
who could take nothing from you. I would, in conscience,
not dishonor you. He and I would eat at Howard Johnson's

which you and I do not enjoy. With him I would go
fishing because it is not your sport. He would wear blue   5
which is your worst color; he would have none of your virtues.

Not strong, not proud, not just, not provident, my lover
would blame me for his heart's distress, which you would never
think to do. He and I would drink too much and weep together

and I would bruise his face as I would not bruise your face   10
even in my dreams. Yes I would dance with him, but to a music
you and I would never choose to hear, and in a place

where you and I would never wish to be. He and I would speak
Spanish, which is not your tongue, and we would take
long walks in fields of burdock, to which you are allergic.   15

We would make love only in the morning. It would be
altogether different. I would know him with my other body,
the one that you have never asked to see.

[1979]

Mahwash Shoaib

Genesis

I.

The child of the sultan was born on a most
auspicious night. Nine months the nation had waited
with bated breath and when the time came, the
sultan ordered the chastest women of the land
to care for his wife. *She* didn't have to scream   5

that much, the harem would've made a fuss anyway.
Silks swirled and incandescent jewels shone

around her room, as the maids scurried past
sterner guards carrying items of need. Steam rising
from boiling water drew saffron hues from   10
the flickering torches and in the haze,
the panting, heaving women enacted the story of
centuries, spewing mild oaths. Her closest maids held her
clenched hands, and the midwife told her to push and
push, more, just a little while longer. And   15
she did, good woman that she was.

Prayers resounded outside the room and
the treasurer counted tinkling coins to be
dispatched at the happy news. With a final push, the
child was born and the maids quickly put him in   20
skeins of wool; he was bathed in rose water
and swathed in clothes of gold. A tray of coins
was passed over his head, blessed money to be given
to the poor. The men shouted from one turret to
another, "Sultana has borne a son!" The   25

sultan granted amnesty to many prisoners and
promised a pearl the size of an egg to the mother
of his son. Gifts of sonnets and gold piled up for
the new heir. The people of the moated city danced
for days, the royal feasts were remembered   30
for decades. And the royal historian wrote in his
private diary: "The wild oat is sown."

[1994]

Journal Entry

Imagine that you are the speaker's husband in "The Faithful Wife." Write a letter responding to your wife's criticism and arguing in defense of marriage as a healthy cultural institution.

Textual Considerations

1. What does Greenberg's poem reveal about the speaker's tone or attitude toward her husband? Prepare a profile of the husband to indicate how different he is from the lover the speaker fantasizes about.
2. Comment on Greenberg's use of humor in "The Faithful Wife." What poetic devices and techniques does she employ to provoke humor? How effective is she in using these poetic resources?

3. Discuss how the differences in the lengths of the stanzas, as well as sound effects and imagery, work stylistically and thematically in both poems.
4. Investigate the inferences of the last line of "Genesis" and the origin of the proverb: "The wild oat is sown." What do you think it contributes to the tone of the poem?
5. What is the symbolic significance of the titles of both poems? To what extent do they reflect the themes of the poems? Do they appeal to you? Why or why not?

Cultural Contexts

1. Greenberg is an American writer from Boston, while Shoaib is a native of Pakistan. To compare and contrast the two poems from the cultural viewpoint, speculate whether the speaker's liberated voice in "The Faithful Wife" fits in the context of "Genesis." What do the poems tell us about the position of women in each culture?
2. Argue about the poetic effectiveness of each poem in dealing with the theme of "beginnings." In your group's opinion, which poem is more successful in communicating the "genesis" of an event—"The Faithful Wife," which explores the theme of emotional intimacy and fantasy, or "Genesis," which explores beginnings from a historical perspective?

Maryfrances Wagner

Ragazza

A good Italian woman
will cover her dust-free house
with crocheted doilies,
bear dark-eyed sons,
know what to do   5
with artichokes and chick peas.
Her floors will shine.
She will serve tender brucaluni
in her perfect sauce,
make her own cannoli shells,   10
bake biscottas for every wedding.
Supper will be hot at six o'clock.
She will always wear dresses.
She will not balance the checkbook.
He can doze behind the paper   15
when she washes dishes.
Because she will never leave him,
he will forgive her bulging thighs.
Because he will never leave her,
she won't notice unfamiliar stains.   20

Italian men always know *ragazze*
who work the fields in Bivona.
For airfare one will come.
In time she will learn English.
In time they may learn to love.   25

[1983]

Pat Mora

Borders

My research suggests that men and women
may speak different languages that they
assume are the same. —Carol Gilligan

If we're so bright,
why didn't we notice?

I
The side-by-side translations
were the easy ones.
Our tongues tasted *luna*   5
chanting, chanting to the words
it touched; our lips circled
moon sighing its longing.
We knew: similar but different.

II
And we knew of grown-up talk,   10
how even in our own home
like became unlike,
how the child's singsong
                              I want, I want
burned our mouth   15
when we whispered in the dark.

III
But us? You and I
who've talked for years
tossing words back and forth
                              success, happiness   20

back and forth
over coffee, over wine
at parties, in bed
and I was sure you heard,
     understood,   25
though now I think of it
I can remember screaming
to be sure.

So who can hear
the words we speak   30
you and I, like but unlike,
and translate us to us
side by side?

[1986]

Robert Frost

Home Burial

He saw her from the bottom of the stairs
Before she saw him. She was starting down,
Looking back over her shoulder at some fear.
She took a doubtful step and then undid it
To raise herself and look again. He spoke   5
Advancing toward her: "What is it you see
From up there always?—for I want to know."
She turned and sank upon her skirts at that,
And her face changed from terrified to dull.
He said to gain time: "What is it you see?"   10
Mounting until she cowered under him.
"I will find out now—you must tell me, dear."
She, in her place, refused him any help,
With the least stiffening of her neck and silence.
She let him look, sure that he wouldn't see,   15
Blind creature; and awhile he didn't see.
But at last he murmured, "Oh," and again, "Oh."

"What is it—what?" she said.

                        "Just that I see."

"You don't," she challenged. "Tell me what it is."   20

"The wonder is I didn't see at once.
I never noticed it from here before.
I must be wonted to it—that's the reason.
The little graveyard where my people are!
So small the window frames the whole of it.   25
Not so much larger than a bedroom, is it?

There are three stones of slate and one of marble,
Broad-shouldered little slabs there in the sunlight
On the sidehill. We haven't to mind *those*.
But I understand: it is not the stones,   30
But the child's mound ——"

                         "Don't, don't, don't, don't," she cried.

She withdrew, shrinking from beneath his arm
That rested on the banister, and slid downstairs;
And turned on him with such a daunting look,   35
He said twice over before he knew himself:
"Can't a man speak of his own child he's lost?"

"Not you!—Oh, where's my hat? Oh, I don't need it!
I must get out of here. I must get air.—
I don't know rightly whether any man can."   40

"Amy! Don't go to someone else this time.
Listen to me. I won't come down the stairs."
He sat and fixed his chin between his fists.
"There's something I should like to ask you, dear."

"You don't know how to ask it."   45

                         "Help me, then."

Her fingers moved the latch for all reply.

"My words are nearly always an offense.
I don't know how to speak of anything
So as to please you. But I might be taught,   50
I should suppose. I can't say I see how.
A man must partly give up being a man
With womenfolk. We could have some arrangement
By which I'd bind myself to keep hands off
Anything special you're a-mind to name.   55
Though I don't like such things 'twixt those that love.
Two that don't love can't live together without them.
But two that do can't live together with them.
Don't carry it to someone else this time.
Tell me about it if it's something human.   60
Let me into your grief. I'm not so much
Unlike other folks as your standing there
Apart would make me out. Give me my chance.
I do think, though, you overdo it a little.
What was it brought you up to think it the thing   65

To take your mother-loss of a first child
So inconsolably—in the face of love.
You'd think his memory might be satisfied—"

"There you go sneering now!"

                                 "I'm not, I'm not!   70
You make me angry. I'll come down to you.
God, what a woman! And it's come to this,
A man can't speak of his own child that's dead."

"You can't because you don't know how to speak.
If you had any feelings, you that dug   75
With your own hand—how could you?—his little grave;
I saw you from that very window there,
Making the gravel leap and leap in air,
Leap up, like that, like that, and land so lightly
And roll back down the mound beside the hole.   80
I thought, Who is that man? I didn't know you.
And I crept down the stairs and up the stairs
To look again, and still your spade kept lifting.
Then you came in. I heard your rumbling voice
Out in the kitchen, and I don't know why,   85
But I went near to see with my own eyes.
You could sit there with the stains on your shoes
Of the fresh earth from your own baby's grave
And talk about your everyday concerns.
You had stood the spade up against the wall   90
Outside there in the entry, for I saw it."

"I shall laugh the worst laugh I ever laughed.
I'm cursed. God, if I don't believe I'm cursed."

"I can repeat the very words you were saying:
'Three foggy mornings and one rainy day   95
Will rot the best birch fence a man can build.'
Think of it, talk like that at such a time!
What had how long it takes a birch to rot
To do with what was in the darkened parlor?
You *couldn't* care! The nearest friends can go   100
With anyone to death, comes so far short
They might as well not try to go at all.
No, from the time when one is sick to death,
One is alone, and he dies more alone.
Friends make pretense of following to the grave,   105
But before one is in it, their minds are turned

And making the best of their way back to life
And living people, and things they understand.
But the world's evil. I won't have grief so
If I can change it. Oh, I won't, I won't!"   110

"There, you have said it all and you feel better.
You won't go now. You're crying. Close the door.
The heart's gone out of it: why keep it up?
Amy! There's someone coming down the road!"

"*You*—oh, you think the talk is all. I must go—   115
Somewhere out of this house. How can I make you—"

"If—you—do!" She was opening the door wider.
"Where do you mean to go? First tell me that.
I'll follow and bring you back by force. I *will!*—"

                                          [1930]

Journal Entry

Many linguists agree that indirectness is a characteristic of human communication. How does this concept apply to the texts by Wagner, Mora, and Frost?

Textual Considerations

1. Explain the significance of the titles of the poems by Wagner, Mora, and Frost. What does the title reveal about the theme of each poem and the speaker's attitude toward life? How do you respond to each of these poems? Would the poems evoke a different response if we changed their titles? Explain.
2. Identify the images that state the accomplishments of the "good Italian woman" in "Ragazza," and contrast them with what she will not do (lines 14, 17, and 20). Explain how language defines the ragazza's identity as a wife.
3. Discuss the speaker's concepts of personal identity in "Borders." How does the speaker develop this concept in stanzas I and II? Identify images that express this concept in the poem. How does language play a role in the speaker's identity as wife and mother?
4. Explain the dramatic situation of "Home Burial," citing in detail the events that lead to the confrontation on the stairs. According to Amy, why does her husband merit her anger?
5. To what extent does Amy succeed in being "heard" in "Home Burial"? Do you agree that the father feels the loss of the child less than the mother does? Explain.
6. Review the last lines of "Ragazza," "Borders," and "Home Burial." How effective are the speakers in communicating their moods? With whom do you empathize, and why?

Cultural Considerations

1. Apply Carol Gilligan's thesis (see p. 399) to "Borders." What does she mean by "different languages"? Review lines 50–55 of "Home Burial." What do these lines suggest about the husband's attitude toward his wife, toward communication within their relationship, and toward love? Characterize your response to the husband. How is Gilligan's thesis also relevant to "Home Burial"?

2. Working with your group, argue in favor of or against the conclusions of the three poems. What does each poem reveal about gender relations, sexuality, and cultural identity?

MCKAY AND MILLAY

Claude McKay

The Harlem Dancer

Applauding youths laughed with young prostitutes
And watched her perfect, half-clothed body sway;
Her voice was like the sound of blended flutes
Blown by black players upon a picnic day.
She sang and danced on gracefully and calm,   5
The light gauze hanging loose about her form;
To me she seemed a proudly-swaying palm
Grown lovelier for passing through a storm.
Upon her swarthy neck black shiny curls
Luxuriant fell; and tossing coins in praise,   10
The wine-flushed, bold-eyed boys, and even the girls,
Devoured her shape with eager, passionate gaze;
But looking at her falsely-smiling face,
I knew her self was not in that strange place.

[1917]

Edna St. Vincent Millay

What Lips My Lips Have Kissed

What lips my lips have kissed, and where, and why,
I have forgotten, and what arms have lain
Under my head till morning; but the rain
Is full of ghosts tonight, that tap and sigh
Upon the glass and listen for reply,   5
And in my heart there stirs a quiet pain
For unremembered lads that not again
Will turn to me at midnight with a cry.
Thus in the winter stands the lonely tree,
Nor knows what birds have vanished one by one,   10
Yet knows its boughs more silent than before:
I cannot say what loves have come and gone,
I only know that summer sang in me
A little while, that in me sings no more.

[1923]

Journal Entry

What knowledge of the Harlem Renaissance and the culture of the Jazz Age can you bring to your reading of these texts?

Textual Considerations

1. What words and images does the speaker use to contrast his perceptions of the dancer with those of her audience in McKay's poem?
2. What evidence does the speaker cite to justify his conclusion in the last line of "The Harlem Dancer"? Do you agree with his judgment? Why or why not? Is the speaker reliable, or does he romanticize the dancer's position?
3. State the theme of the first eight lines of Millay's poem. Do the speaker's gender and her inability to remember her individual lovers affect your response? How?
4. How effective is Millay's use of nature imagery to communicate meaning in the sonnet's sestet? Cite examples to justify your point of view.
5. How is the image of the tree in each poem consistent with the emotions each speaker expresses? Explain.

Cultural Contexts

1. What do both poems suggest about the relation between sexuality and identity and between sexuality and youth. To what extent is McKay's portrayal of gender relations relevant to today's society?
2. Working with your group, assess what you know about Harlem in the early 1920s, when it was the center of American jazz. How does "The Harlem Dancer" capture the experience of the Harlem Renaissance in the 1920s? Explain. What does "What Lips My Lips Have Kissed" suggest about the changing roles of women with respect to personal freedom and sexual identity in the 1920s?

Yevgeny Yevtushenko

Colours

When your face
appeared over my crumpled life
at first I understood
only the poverty of what I have.
Then its particular light   5
on woods, on rivers, on the sea,
became my beginning in the coloured world
in which I had not yet had my beginning.
I am so frightened, I am so frightened,
of the unexpected sunrise finishing,   10
of revelations
and tears and the excitement finishing,
I don't fight it, my love is this fear,
I nourish it who can nourish nothing,
love's slipshod watchman.   15
Fear hems me in.
I am conscious that these minutes are short
and that the colours in my eyes will vanish
when your face sets.

[1962]

Theodore Roethke

I Knew a Woman

I knew a woman, lovely in her bones,
When small birds sighed, she would sigh back at them;
Ah, when she moved, she moved more ways than one:
The shapes a bright container can contain!
Of her choice virtues only gods should speak,   5
Or English poets who grew up on Greek
(I'd have them sing in chorus, cheek to cheek).

How well her wishes went! She stroked my chin,
She taught me Turn, and Counter-turn, and Stand;
She taught me Touch, that undulant white skin;   10
I nibbled meekly from her proffered hand;
She was the sickle; I, poor I, the rake,
Coming behind her for her pretty sake
(But what prodigious mowing we did make).

Loves like a gander, and adores a goose: 15
Her full lips pursed, the errant note to seize;
She played it quick, she played it light and loose,
My eyes, they dazzled at her flowing knees;
Her several parts could keep a pure repose,
Or one hip quiver with a mobile nose   20
(She moved in circles, and those circles moved).

Let seed be grass, and grass turn into hay:
I'm martyr to a motion not my own;
What's freedom for? To know eternity.
I swear she cast a shadow white as stone.   25
But who would count eternity in days?
These old bones live to learn her wanton ways:
(I measure time by how a body sways).

[1954]

Journal Entry

How would you distinguish between the lover and the beloved in an intimate relationship? Is the lover more likely to fear the loss of the relationship? Explain.

Textual Considerations

1. On what metaphor is Yevtushenko's entire poem based? At what points does the comparison seem particularly appropriate?
2. Why is the speaker's life "crumpled" and impoverished in "Colours"? In what sense is it black and white, without color?
3. What aspect of the woman's physical being does the speaker emphasize throughout "I Knew a Woman"? Does his description ever go beyond the physical? Explain.
4. What is the effect of the imagery in lines 2, 4, 5–7, 12–14, 22, and 25 in "I Knew a Woman"?
5. Describe the relationship between the speaker and the woman in "Colours" and "I Knew a Woman." How does the speaker characterize himself in each of the poems?

Cultural Contexts

1. Roethke concludes his text by discussing eternity. How does he fuse the woman's physical presence with his discussion of the abstractions of freedom and eternity? Explain Yevtushenko's paradox of nourishing by one who can nourish nothing. Of what is he frightened? Why does he nourish his fear? Is his fear justified? Explain.
2. Would your group view the speakers in both poems as romantics? Does it surprise your group that the vulnerable person in each relationship is male? What gender stereotypes do the poems contradict? Summarize your group discussion.

Robert Browning

My Last Duchess

Ferrara

That's my last Duchess painted on the wall,
Looking as if she were alive; I call
That piece a wonder, now: Frà Pandolf's° hands
Worked busily a day, and there she stands.
Will't please you sit and look at her? I said   5
"Frà Pandolf" by design, for never read
Strangers like you that pictured countenance,
The depth and passion of its earnest glance,
But to myself they turned (since none puts by
The curtain I have drawn for you, but I)   10
And seemed as they would ask me, if they durst,
How such a glance came there; so, not the first
Are you to turn and ask thus. Sir, 'twas not
Her husband's presence only, called that spot
Of joy into the Duchess' cheek: perhaps   15
Frà Pandolf chanced to say "Her mantle laps
Over my Lady's wrist too much," or "Paint
Must never hope to reproduce the faint
Half-flush that dies along her throat": such stuff
Was courtesy, she thought, and cause enough   20
For calling up that spot of joy. She had
A heart—how shall I say?—too soon made glad,
Too easily impressed; she liked whate'er
She looked on, and her looks went everywhere.
Sir, 'twas all one! My favor at her breast,   25
The dropping of the daylight in the West,
The bough of cherries some officious fool
Broke in the orchard for her, the white mule
She rode with round the terrace—all and each
Would draw from her alike the approving speech,   30
Or blush, at least. She thanked men,—good; but thanked
Somehow—I know not how—as if she ranked
My gift of a nine-hundred-years-old name
With anybody's gift. Who'd stoop to blame
This sort of trifling? Even had you skill   35

In speech—(which I have not)—to make your will
Quite clear to such an one, and say, "Just this
Or that in you disgusts me; here you miss,
Or there exceed the mark"—and if she let
Herself be lessoned so, nor plainly set   40
Her wits to yours, forsooth, and made excuse,
—E'en then would be some stooping, and I choose
Never to stoop. Oh, Sir, she smiled, no doubt,
Whene'er I passed her; but who passed without
Much the same smile? This grew; I gave commands;   45
Then all smiles stopped together. There she stands
As if alive. Will't please you rise? We'll meet
The company below, then. I repeat,
The Count your Master's known munificence
Is ample warrant that no just pretence   50
Of mine for dowry will be disallowed;
Though his fair daughter's self, as I avowed
At starting, is my object. Nay, we'll go
Together down, Sir! Notice Neptune, though,
Taming a sea-horse, thought a rarity,   55
Which Claus of Innsbruck° cast in bronze for me.

[1842]

3 **Frá Pandolf's:** a fictitious artist.   **56 Claus of Innsbruck:** also a fictitious artist.

Gabriel Spera

My Ex-Husband

That's my ex-husband pictured on the shelf,
Smiling as if in love. I took it myself
With his Leica, and stuck it in that frame
We got for our wedding. Kind of a shame
To waste it on him, but what could I do?   5
(Since I haven't got a photograph of you.)
I know what's on your mind—you want to know
Whatever could have made me let him go—
He seems like any woman's perfect catch,
What with his ruddy cheeks, the neat mustache,   10
Those close-set, piercing eyes, that tilted grin.
But snapshots don't show what's beneath the skin!

Sure, he'd a certain charm, charisma, style,
That passionate, earnest glance he struck, meanwhile
Whispering the sweetest things, like, "Your lips   15
Are like plump rubies, eyes like diamond chips,"
Could flush the throat of any woman, not
Just mine. He knew the most romantic spots
In town, where waiters, who all knew his face,
Reserved an intimately dim-lit place   20
Half-hidden in a corner nook. Such stuff
Was all too well rehearsed, I soon enough
Found out. He had an attitude—how should
I put it—smooth, self-satisfied, too good
For the rest of the world, too easily   25
Impressed with his officious self. And he
Flirted—fine! but flirted somehow a bit
Too ardently, too blatantly, as if,
If someone ever noticed, no one cared
How slobbishly he carried on affairs.   30
Who'd lower herself to put up with shit
Like that? Even if you'd the patience—which
I have not—to go and see some counselor
And say, "My life's a living hell," or
"Everything he does disgusts, the lout!"—   35
And even if you'd somehow worked things out,
Took a long trip together, made amends,
Let things get back to normal, even then
You'd still be on the short end of the stick;
And I choose never ever to get stuck.   40
Oh, no doubt, it always made my limbs go
Woozy when he kissed me, but what bimbo
In the steno pool went without the same
Such kisses? So, I made some calls, filed some claims,
All kisses stopped together. There he grins,   45
Almost lovable. Shall we go? I'm in
The mood for Chez Pierre's, perhaps, tonight,
Though anything you'd like would be all right
As well, of course, though I'd prefer not to go
To any place with checkered tables. No,   50
We'll take my car. By the way, have I shown
You yet these lovely champagne flutes, hand blown,
Imported from Murano, Italy,
Which Claus got in the settlement for me!

[1992]

Journal Entry

What images, memories, experiences, or situations do you associate with jealousy? Why does it surface so often in gender relationships? Cite reasons.

Textual Considerations

1. What crime has the Duke's last Duchess committed in "My Last Duchess"?
2. Characterize the dramatic situation in "My Last Duchess." Consider the setting, the Duke's character, and the poem's final image of Neptune taming a sea-horse. What is the significance of the Neptune statue?
3. Discuss how Browning's use of dramatic irony in "My Last Duchess" results in our learning more about the Duke than he understands about himself. Consider, for example, his motivation for ordering the duchess's death. Cite evidence to show how the Duchess became a projection of the Duke's fears and insecurities.
4. How do you respond to Spera's parody of Browning's poem in "My Ex-Husband?" Do you think the parallels Spera draws in terms of tone and theme lead to a greater appreciation of Browning's "My Last Duchess"? Explain.
5. Why does Spera's speaker assume a female persona? Does gender reversal from Browning's male speaker to Spera's female voice add anything to the humorous tone of the poem? Explain.
6. Who is the speaker in "My Ex-Husband" addressing—her lover or her reader? Or is she engaging in a dialogue with herself? Cite evidence to support your point of view.

Cultural Contexts

1. Discuss the causes of the violence against spouses in Browning's and Spera's poems.
2. Working with your group, analyze the role of social class in each poem. Consider, for example, the extent to which the duchess was aware of class distinctions, and how her attitude toward other people affected the Duke. In "My Ex-Husband," focus on the role that Spera's updated setting plays in identifying the lovers' social class.

MARVELL AND BEHN

Andrew Marvell

To His Coy Mistress

Had we but world enough, and time,
This coyness, lady, were no crime.
We would sit down, and think which way
To walk, and pass our long love's day.
Thou by the Indian Ganges'° side   5
Shouldst rubies find; I by the tide
Of Humber° would complain. I would
Love you ten years before the flood,
And you should, if you please, refuse
Till the conversion of the Jews.   10
My vegetable love should grow
Vaster than empires and more slow;
An hundred years should go to praise
Thine eyes, and on thy forehead gaze;
Two hundred to adore each breast,   15
But thirty thousand to the rest;
An age at least to every part,
And the last age should show your heart.
For, lady, you deserve this state,
Nor would I love at lower rate.   20
      But at my back I always hear
Time's wingèd chariot hurrying near;
And yonder all before us lie
Deserts of vast eternity.

Thy beauty shall no more be found;   25
Nor, in thy marble vault, shall sound
My echoing song; then worms shall try
That long-preserved virginity,
And your quaint honor turn to dust,
And into ashes all my lust: 30
The grave's a fine and private place,
But none, I think, do there embrace.
      Now therefore, while the youthful hue
Sits on thy skin like morning dew
And while thy willing soul transpires   35

At every pore with instant fires,
Now let us sport us while we may,
And now, like amorous birds of prey,
Rather at once our time devour
Than languish in his slow-chapped power.   40
Let us roll all our strength and all
Our sweetness up into one ball,
And tear our pleasures with rough strife
Through the iron gates of life:
Thus, though we cannot make our sun   45
Stand still, yet we will make him run.

[1681]

5 Ganges: river in northern India.   **7 Humber:** estuary in northern England formed by the Ouse
and Trent rivers.

Aphra Behn

The Willing Mistress

Amyntas led me to a grove,
    Where all the trees did shade us;
The sun itself, though it had strove,
    It could not have betrayed us.
The place secured from human eyes   5
    No other fear allows
But when the winds that gently rise
    Do kiss the yielding boughs.

Down there we sat upon the moss,
    And did begin to play   10
A thousand amorous tricks, to pass
    The heat of all the day.
A many kisses did he give
    And I returned the same,
Which made me willing to receive   15
    That which I dare not name.

His charming eyes no aid required
    To tell their softening tale;
On her that was already fired
    'Twas easy to prevail.   20

He did but kiss and clasp me round,
　　Whilst those his thoughts expressed:

And laid me gently on the ground;
　　Ah who can guess the rest?

[1673]

Journal Entry

The rituals of courtship have long been associated with male leadership. How does Behn's text, written in 1673, reverse this tradition? How do you respond to her text?

Textual Considerations

1. How do you respond to the titles of the poems? What do they suggest about the images men create of women? Do these concepts of gender relationships seem out-of-date to you? Why or why not?
2. Explain what the image "I would/Love you ten years before the flood" in lines 7–8 of Marvell's poem suggests about the speaker's attitude toward time.
3. How do the images Marvell uses in the second and third sections of "To His Coy Mistress" mirror or contradict those in the first section?
4. How does the speaker in "To His Coy Mistress" characterize himself as a lover?
5. How does the speaker's gender and use of humor affect your response to "The Willing Mistress"?
6. Discuss female-male attitudes toward love in "To His Coy Mistress" and "The Willing Mistress."

Cultural Contexts

1. Aphra Behn, a seventeenth-century British writer, freely discussed female desire and issues concerning gender roles in her works. To what extent does she explore these issues in "The Willing Mistress"? Is it relevant that the lovers in the poem create a world of love ("a grove . . . secured from human eyes") separated from the outside world? Explain.
2. "To His Coy Mistress" is known as one of the most celebrated erotic poems in English literature. Working with your group, cite evidences of erotic elements in the poem.

KEATS AND DE LA CRUZ

John Keats

Bright Star

Bright star, would I were steadfast as thou art—
    Not in lone splendor hung aloft the night
And watching, with eternal lids apart,
    Like nature's patient, sleepless Eremite,°
The moving waters at their priestlike task   5
    Of pure ablution round earth's human shores,
Or gazing on the new soft fallen mask
    Of snow upon the mountains and the moors—
No—yet still steadfast, still unchangeable,
    Pillowed upon my fair love's ripening breast,   10
To feel forever its soft fall and swell,
    Awake forever in a sweet unrest,
Still, still to hear her tender-taken breath,
And so live ever—or else swoon to death.

[1819]

4 **Eremite:** hermit, devotee.

Sor Juana Inés de la Cruz

She Proves the Inconsistency of the Desires and Criticism of Men Who Accuse Women of What They Themselves Cause

Foolish men who accuse
women unreasonably,
you blame yet never see
you cause what you abuse.

You crawl before her, sad,   5
begging for a quick cure;

why ask her to be pure
when you have made her bad?

You combat her resistance
and then with gravity,   10
you call frivolity
the fruit of your intents.

In one heroic breath
your reason fails, like a wild
bogeyman made up by a child   15
who then is scared to death.

With idiotic pride
you hope to find your prize:
a regal whore like Thaïs°
and Lucretia° for a bride.   20

Has anyone ever seen
a stranger moral fervor:
you who dirty the mirror
regret it is not clean?

You treat favor and disdain   25
with the same shallow mock-
ing voice: love you and you squawk,
demur and you complain.

No answer at her door
will be a proper part: 30
say no—she has no heart,
say yes—and she's a whore.

Two levels to your game
in which *you* are the fool:
one you blame as cruel,   35
one who yields, you shame.

How can one not be bad
the way your love pretends
to be? Say no and she offends.
Consent and you are mad.   40

With all the fury and pain
your whims cause her, it's good
for her who has withstood
you. Now go and complain!

You let her grief take flight   45
and free her with new wings.

Then after sordid things
you say she's not upright.

Who is at fault in all
this errant passion? She   50
who falls for his pleas, or he
who pleads for her to fall?

Whose guilt is greater in
this raw erotic play?
The girl who sins for pay   55
or man who pays for sin?

So why be shocked or taunt
her for the steps you take?
Care for her as you make
her, or shape her as you want,   60

but do not come with pleas
and later throw them in
her face, screaming of sin
when you were at her knees.

You fight us from birth   65
with weapons of arrogance.
Between promise and pleading stance,
you are devil, flesh, and earth.

[1680]

---

19 Thaïs: an Athenian courtesan who was the mistress of Alexander the Great. **20 Lucretia:** daughter of Prefect of Kone who was raped by the son of King Tanquinius Superbus.

Journal Entry

What associations do you have with the romantic concept of woman as goddess? Is it outmoded in the postmodern age? Why or why not? How might such a concept affect the identify of both men and women?

Textual Considerations

1. The "Bright Star" is the North Star, a traditional symbol of permanence also used by other poets, such as Shakespeare. Compare and contrast the ways Keats uses this symbol in the octave and the sestet of the sonnet. Discuss the appeal of the image. What meanings does it suggest, and what emotions does it rouse in the reader?
2. Comment on the speaker's desire for steadfastness in lines 11, 12, and 14 of "Bright Star." What kind of permanence does the speaker aspire to? How central is the image of the star to express the speaker's romantic aspirations?
3. Summarize the key points of de la Cruz's arguments. To what extent do you agree or disagree with the logic and point of view she develops in the poem?

4. Describe the tone of de la Cruz's poem. Is the speaker sarcastic, angry, bitter, or objective? How does it compare with the tone of Keats's poem? Cite examples to support your answer.

5. Argue in favor of or against de la Cruz's statement that men "fight" women from birth "with weapons of arrogance."

6. Analyze the title of de la Cruz's poem. What does it reveal about the speaker? Does it seem to have been written by a catholic nun in seventeenth-century Mexico? Explain.

Cultural Contexts

1. How would you describe the effects of such stereotypes as goddess, madonna, or whore on women's identity? To what extent do these stereotypes promote a male-dominated model of gender relations? Explain.

2. Working with your group, discuss the degree to which Keats's romantic aspiration for the "fair love's ripening breast" of an idealized mistress in nineteenth-century England and de la Cruz's protest against the debasing view of women as demons and whores in seventeenth-century Mexico are relevant to women's position in society today.

William Shakespeare

30

When to the sessions of sweet silent thought
I summon up remembrance of things past,
I sigh the lack of many a thing I sought,
And with old woes new wail my dear time's waste.
Then can I drown an eye, unused to flow,　　　　　　5
For precious friends hid in death's dateless night,
And weep afresh love's long since cancelled woe,
And moan th'expense of many a vanished sight.
Then can I grieve at grievances foregone,
And heavily from woe to woe tell o'er　　　　　　　10
The sad account of fore-bemoanèd moan,
Which I new pay as if not paid before.
　　But if the while I think on thee, dear friend,
　　All losses are restored, and sorrows end.

[c. 1609]

William Shakespeare

116

Let me not to the marriage of true minds
Admit impediments. Love is not love
Which alters when it alterations find,
Or bends with the remover to remove.
O no, it is an ever-fixèd mark　　　　　　　　　　5
That looks on tempests and is never shaken;
It is the star to every wand'ring bark,
Whose worth's unknown, although his height be taken.
Love's not time's fool, though rosy lips and cheeks
Within his bending sickle's compass come.　　　　　10
Love alters not with his brief hours and weeks,

But bears it out ev'n to the edge of doom.
   If this be error and upon me proved,
   I never writ, nor no man ever loved.

[c. 1609]

William Shakespeare

129

Th'expense of spirit in a waste of shame
Is lust in action, and till action, lust
Is perjur'd, murd'rous, bloody, full of blame,
Savage, extreme, rude, cruel, not to trust,
Enjoy'd no sooner but despisèd straight,   5
Past reason hunted, and no sooner had,
Past reason hated as a swallowed bait
On purpose laid to make the taker mad:
[Mad] in pursuit and in possession so,
Had, having, and in quest to have, extreme,   10
A bliss in proof, and prov'd, [a] very woe,
Before, a joy propos'd, behind, a dream.
   All this the world well knows, yet none knows well
   To shun the heaven that leads men to this hell.

[c. 1609]

William Shakespeare

130

My mistress' eyes are nothing like the sun;
Coral is far more red than her lips' red;
If snow be white, why then her breasts are dun;
If hairs be wires, black wires grow on her head.
I have seen roses damasked,° red and white,   5
But no such roses see I in her cheeks;
And in some perfumes is there more delight
Than in the breath that from my mistress reeks.
I love to hear her speak, yet well I know
That music hath a far more pleasing sound;   10

I grant I never saw a goddess go°;
My mistress, when she walks, treads on the ground.
And yet, by heaven, I think my love as rare
As any she belied with false compare.

[c. 1609]

5 damasked: variegated.   **11 a goddess go**: walk.

Journal Entry

What is your definition of *true love*? How would you distinguish it from *falling in love* or *romantic love*? How do your definitions of love compare to those of Shakespeare?

Textual Considerations

1. Discuss the speaker's use of comparisons involving the past versus the present in sonnet 30. How do the losses the speaker suffered in the past (lines 6, 7, and 8) compare to what he gains in the present?
2. What is the theme of sonnet 116? Comment on the negative statements in lines 2, 4, and 9, and 11. What purpose do they serve to establish the theme of the sonnet? Explain.
3. Sonnet 116, stating the speaker's strong wish that true love might last forever, seems to be a favorite among Shakespeare's readers. Which of the four sonnets do you like best? Explain why, citing evidence from the text.
4. How does the speaker define "lust in action" in sonnet 129? How does he define lust before it becomes action and after it becomes action? What does the reversal in the sonnet's couplet (the last two lines of the poem) convey regarding the speaker's feeling about lust? To what extent do you agree or disagree with the speaker's point of view in this sonnet and in sonnets 30, 116, and 130?
5. Make a list of the eight major similes the speaker uses to describe his mistress's physical attributes in sonnet 130. What kind of portrait emerges in the sonnet? What does it reveal about the speaker's attitude toward his mistress?

Cultural Contexts

1. What does sonnet 130 reveal about Shakespeare's use of the convention of the literary mistress? What does it reveal about the idealization of women? What does it do to sustain or collapse this literary convention?
2. Working with your group, write a love sonnet in which you update the images that Shakespeare uses in sonnet 130. Start with a list of similes to portray your mistress's beauty; develop a theme, such as loss of love, aspirations toward true love, or sexual anxiety, for example; and aim at a fourteen-line poem. What does your poem reveal about cultural changes from Shakespeare's days to ours?

DRAMA

Euripides

Medea

Translated by Moses Hadas and John McLean

CHARACTERS

NURSE
CREON, *King of Corinth*
CHILDREN OF MEDEA
MEDEA
TUTOR
JASON
CHORUS, *Corinthian Women*
AEGEUS, *King of Athens*
MESSENGER

The scene represents the home of Medea at Corinth.

(*Enter* NURSE.)

NURSE: How I wish that the ship Argo[1] had never winged its way through the gray Clashing Rocks to the land of the Colchians! How I wish the pines had never been hewn down in the glens of Pelion, to put oars into the hands of the Heroes who went to fetch for Pelias the Golden Fleece! Then Medea my mistress would not have sailed to the towers of Iolcus, her heart pierced through and through with love for Jason, would not have prevailed on the daughters of Pelias to murder their father, would not now be dwelling here in Corinth with her husband and children. When she fled here she found favor with the citizens to whose land she had come and was herself a perfect partner in all things for Jason. (And therein lies a woman's best security, to avoid conflict with her husband.) But now there is nothing but enmity, a blight has come over their great love.

Jason has betrayed his own children and my mistress to sleep beside a royal bride, the daughter of Creon who rules this land, while Medea, luckless Medea, in her desolation invokes the promises he made, appeals to the pledges

---

[1] **Argo:** Jason's ship on the expedition of the Argonauts, sent by Pelias, king of Iolcus in Thessaly (Jason's uncle, who had usurped the throne), to Colchis on the Black Sea. The Symplegades were clashing rocks, one of the obstacles along the way. Pelion is a mountain in Thessaly. Medea was a princess of Colchis who fell in love with Jason and followed him back to Greece.

in which she put her deepest trust, and calls Heaven to witness the sorry recompense she has from Jason. Ever since she realized her husband's perfidy, she has been lying there prostrated, eating no food, her whole frame subdued to sorrow, wasting away with incessant weeping. She has not lifted an eye nor ever turned her face from the floor. The admonitions of her friends she receives with unhearing ears, like a rock or a wave of the sea. Only now and then she turns her white neck and talks to herself, in sorrow, of her dear father and her country and the home which she betrayed to come here with a husband who now holds her in contempt. Now she knows, from bitter experience, how sad a thing it is to lose one's fatherland. She hates her own children and has no pleasure at the sight of them. I fear she may form some new and horrible resolve. For hers is a dangerous mind, and she will not lie down to injury. I know her and she frightens me [lest she make her way stealthily into the palace where his couch is spread and drive a sharp sword into his vitals or even kill both the King and the bridegroom and then incur some greater misfortune.] She is cunning. Whoever crosses swords with her will not find victory easy, I tell you.

But here come the children, their playtime over. Little thought have they of their mother's troubles. Children do not like sad thoughts.

(*Enter* TUTOR, *with boys.*)

TUTOR: Ancient household chattel of my mistress, why are you standing here all alone at the gates, muttering darkly to yourself? What makes Medea want you to leave her alone?

NURSE: Aged escort of Jason's children, when their master's affairs go ill, good slaves find not only their misfortune but also their heart's grief. My sorrow has now become so great that a longing came over me to come out here and tell to earth and sky the story of my mistress's woes.

TUTOR: What? Is the poor lady not yet through with weeping?

NURSE: I wish I had your optimism. Why, her sorrow is only beginning, it's not yet at the turning point.

TUTOR: Poor foolish woman!—if one may speak thus of one's masters. Little she knows of the latest ills!

NURSE: What's that, old man? Don't grudge me your news.

TUTOR: It's nothing at all. I'm sorry I even said what I said.

NURSE: Please, I beg of you, don't keep it from a fellow slave. I'll keep it dark, if need be.

TUTOR: I had drawn near the checkerboards where the old men sit, beside the sacred water of Pirene, and there, when nobody thought I was listening, I heard somebody say that Creon the ruler of this land was planning to expel these children *and* their mother from Corinth. Whether the tale is true or not I do not know. I would wish it were not so.

NURSE: But will Jason ever allow his children to be so treated, even if he *is* at variance with their mother?

TUTOR: Old loves are weaker than new loves, and that man is no friend to this household.

NURSE: That's the end of us then, if we are to ship a second wave of trouble before we are rid of the first.

TUTOR: Meanwhile you keep quiet and don't say a word. This is no time for the mistress to be told.

NURSE: O children, do you hear what love your father bears you? Since he is my master, I do not wish him dead, but he is certainly proving enemy of those he should love.

TUTOR: Like the rest of the world. Are you only now learning that every man loves himself more than his neighbor? [Some justly, others for profit, as] now for a new bride their father hates these children.

NURSE: Inside, children, inside. It will be all right. (*To the* TUTOR.) And you keep them alone as much as you can, and don't let them near their mother when she's melancholy. I have already noticed her casting a baleful eye at them as if she would gladly do them mischief. She'll not recover from her rage, I know well, till the lightning of her fury has struck somebody to the ground. May it be enemies, not loved ones, that suffer!

MEDEA (*within*):   Oh! my grief! the misery of it all! Why can I not die?

NURSE: What did I tell you, dear children? Your mother's heart is troubled, her anger is roused. Hurry indoors, quick. Keep out of her sight, don't go near her. Beware of her fierce manner, her implacable temper. Hers is a selfwilled nature. Go now, get you inside, be quick. Soon, it is clear, her sorrow like a gathering cloud will burst in a tempest of fury. What deed will she do then, that impetuous, indomitable heart, poisoned by injustice?

(*Exeunt children with* TUTOR.)

MEDEA (*within*):   O misery! the things I have suffered, cause enough for deep lamentations! O you cursed sons of a hateful mother, a plague on you! And on your father! Ruin seize the whole household!

NURSE: Ah me, unhappy me! Why will you have your sons partake of their father's guilt? Why hate them? Ah children, your danger overwhelms me with anxiety. The souls of royalty are vindictive; they do not easily forget their resentment, possibly because being used to command they are seldom checked. It is better to be used to living among equals. For myself, at any rate, I ask not greatness but a safe old age. Moderation! Firstly, the very name of it is excellent; to practise it is easily the best thing for mortals. Excess avails to no good purpose for men, and if the gods are provoked, brings greater ruin on a house.

(*Enter* CHORUS.)

CHORUS: *I heard a voice, I heard a cry. It was the unhappy Colchian woman's. She is not yet calm. Pray tell us, old woman. From the court outside I heard her cries within. I do not rejoice, woman, in the griefs of this house. Dear, dear it is to me.*

NURSE: It is a home no more; the life has gone out of it. Its master a princess' bed enthralls, while the mistress in her chamber is pining to death, and her friends have no words to comfort her heart.

MEDEA (*within*): Oh! Would that a flaming bolt from Heaven might pierce my brain! What is the good of living any longer? O Misery! Let me give up this life I find so hateful. Let me seek lodging in the house of death.

CHORUS: *O Zeus, O Earth, O Light, hear what a sad lament the hapless wife intones. What is this yearning, rash woman, after that fearful bed? Will you hasten to the end that is Death? Pray not for that. If your husband worships a new bride, it is a common event; be not exasperated. Zeus will support your cause. Do not let grief for a lost husband waste away your life.*

MEDEA: (*within*) Great Zeus and Lady Themis, see you how I am treated, for all the strong oaths with which I bound my cursed husband? May I live to see him and his bride, palace and all, in one common destruction, for the wrongs that they inflict, unprovoked, on me! O father, O country, that I forsook so shamefully, killing my brother, my own!

NURSE: Hear what she says, how she cries out to Themis of Prayers and to Zeus whom mortals regard as the steward of oaths. With no small revenge will my mistress bate her rage.

CHORUS: *I wish she would come into our presence and hear the sound of the words we would speak. Then she might forget the resentment in her heart and change her purpose. May my zeal be ever at the service of my friends. But bring her here, make her come forth from the palace. Tell her that here too are friends. Make haste before she does any harm to those within. Furious is the surge of such a sorrow.*

NURSE: I shall do so, though I am not hopeful of persuading the mistress. But I freely present you with the gift of my labor. Yet she throws a baleful glare, like a lioness with cubs, at any servant who approaches her as if to speak. Blunderers and fools! that is the only proper name for the men of old who invented songs to bring the joy of life to feasts and banquets and festive boards, but never discovered a music of song or sounding lyre to dispel the weary sorrows of humanity, that bring death and fell havoc and destruction of homes. Yet what a boon to man, could these ills be cured by some! At sumptuous banquets why raise a useless strain? The food that is served and the satisfaction that comes to full men, that in itself is pleasure enough.

(*Exit* NURSE.)

CHORUS: *I hear a cry of grief and deep sorrow. In piercing accents of misery she proclaims her woes, her ill-starred marriage and her love betrayed. The victim of grievous wrongs, she calls on the daughter of Zeus, even Themis, Lady of Vows, who led her through the night by difficult straits across the briny sea to Hellas.*

(*Enter* MEDEA.)

MEDEA: Women of Corinth, do not criticize me, I come forth from the palace. Well I know that snobbery is a common charge, that may be levelled against recluse and busy man alike. And the former, by their choice of a quiet life, acquire an extra stigma: they are deficient in energy and spirit. There is no justice in the eyes of men; a man who has never harmed them they may hate at sight, without ever knowing anything about his essential nature. An alien, to be sure, should adapt himself to the citizens with whom he lives. Even the citizen is to be condemned if he is too selfwilled or too uncouth to avoid offending his fellows. So I . . . but this unexpected blow which has befallen me has broken my heart.

It's all over, my friends; I would gladly die. Life has lost its savor. The man who was everything to me, well he knows it, has turned out to be the basest of men. Of all creatures that feel and think, we women are the unhappiest species. In the first place, we must pay a great dowry to a husband who will be the tyrant of our bodies (that's a further aggravation of the evil); and there is another fearful hazard: whether we shall get a good man or a bad. For separations bring disgrace on the woman and it is not possible to renounce one's husband. Then, landed among strange habits and regulations unheard of in her own home, a woman needs second sight to know how best to handle her bedmate. And if we manage this well and have a husband who does not find the yoke of intercourse too galling, ours is a life to be envied. Otherwise, one is better dead. When the man wearies of the company of his wife, he goes outdoors and relieves the disgust of his heart [having recourse to some friend or the companions of his own age], but we women have only one person to turn to.

They say that we have a safe life at home, whereas men must go to war. Nonsense! I had rather fight three battles than bear one child. But be that as it may, you and I are not in the same case. You have your city here, your paternal homes; you know the delights of life and association with your loved ones. But I, homeless and forsaken, carried off from a foreign land, am being wronged by a husband, with neither mother nor brother nor kinsman with whom I might find refuge from the storms of misfortune. One little boon I crave of you, if I discover any ways and means of punishing my husband for these wrongs: your silence. Woman in most respects is a timid creature, with no heart for strife and aghast at the sight of steel; but wronged in love, there is no heart more murderous than hers.

LEADER: Do as you say, Medea, for just will be your vengeance. I do not wonder that you bemoan your fate. But I see Creon coming, the ruler of this land, bringing tidings of new plans.

(*Enter* CREON.)

CREON: You there, Medea, looking black with rage against your husband; I have proclaimed that you are to be driven forth in exile from this land, you and your two sons. Immediately. I am the absolute judge of the case, and I shall not go back to my palace till I have cast you over the frontier of the land.

MEDEA: Ah! Destruction, double destruction is my unhappy lot. My enemies are letting out every sail and there is no harbor into which I may flee from the menace of their attack. But ill-treated and all, Creon, still I shall put the question to you: Why are you sending me out of the country?

CREON: I am afraid of you—there's no need to hide behind a cloak of words—afraid you will do my child some irreparable injury. There's plenty logic in that fear. You are a wizard possessed of evil knowledge. You are stung by the loss of your husband's love. And I have heard of your threats—they told me of them— to injure bridegroom and bride and father of the bride. Therefore before anything happens to me, I shall take precautions. Better for me now to be hateful in your eyes than to relent and rue it greatly later.

MEDEA: Alas! Alas! Often ere now—this is not the first time—my reputation has hurt me and done me grievous wrong. If a man's really shrewd, he ought never to have his children taught too much. For over and above a name for uselessness that it will earn them, they incur the hostility and envy of their fellow men. Offer clever reforms to dullards, and you will be thought a useless fool yourself. And the reputed wiseacres, feeling your superiority, will dislike you intensely. I myself have met this fate. Because I have skill, some are jealous of me, others think me unsociable. But my wisdom does not go very far. However, you are afraid you may suffer something unpleasant at my hands, aren't you? Fear not, Creon; it is not my way to commit my crimes against kings. What wrong have you done me? You have only bestowed your daughter on the suitor of your choice. No, it is my husband I hate. You, I dare say, knew what you were doing in the matter. And now I don't grudge success to your scheme. Make your match, and good luck to you. But allow me to stay in this country. Though foully used, I shall keep my peace, submitting to my masters.

CREON: Your words are comforting to hear, but inside my heart there is a horrible fear that you are plotting some mischief, which makes me trust you even less than before. The hot-tempered woman, like the hot-tempered man, is easier to guard against than the cunning and silent. But off with you at once, make no speeches. My resolve is fixed; for all your skill you will not stay amongst us to hate me.

MEDEA: Please no, I beseech you, by your knees, by the young bride . . .

CREON: You are wasting your words; you will never convince me.

MEDEA: Will you drive me out and have no respect for my prayers?

CREON: Yes, for I love you less than I love my own family.

MEDEA: O fatherland, how strongly do I now remember you!

CREON: Yes, apart from my children, that is *my* dearest love.

MEDEA: Alas! the loves of men are a mighty evil.

CREON: In my opinion, that depends on the circumstances.

MEDEA: O Zeus, do not forget the author of this wickedness.

CREON: On your way, vain woman, and end my troubles.

MEDEA: The troubles are mine, I have no lack of troubles.

CREON: In a moment you will be thrust out by the hands of servants.

MEDEA: No, no, not that. But Creon I entreat you . . .

CREON: You seem to be bent on causing trouble, woman.

MEDEA: I shall go into exile. It is not *that* I beg you to grant me.

CREON: Why then are you clinging so violently to my hand?

MEDEA: Allow me to stay for this one day to complete my plans for departure and get together provision for my children, since their father prefers not to bother about his own sons. Have pity on them. You too are the father of children. It is natural that you should feel kindly. Stay or go, I care nothing for myself. It's them I weep for in their misfortune.

CREON: My mind is not tyrannical enough; mercy has often been my undoing. So now, though I know that it is a mistake, woman, you will have your request. But I give you warning: if tomorrow's divine sun sees you and your children inside the borders of this country, you die. True is the word I have spoken. [Stay, if you must, this one day. You'll not have time to do what I dread.]

(*Exit* CREON.)

CHORUS: *Hapless woman! overwhelmed by sorrow! Where will you turn? What stranger will afford you hospitality? God has steered you, Medea, into an unmanageable surge of troubles.*

MEDEA: Ill fortune's everywhere, who can gainsay it? But it is not yet as bad as that, never think so. There is still heavy weather ahead for the new bride and groom, and no little trouble for the maker of the match. Do you think I would ever have wheedled the king just now except to further my own plans? I would not even have spoken to him, nor touched him either. But he is such a fool that though he might have thwarted my plans by expelling me from the country he has allowed me to stay over for this one day, in which I shall make corpses of three of my enemies, father and daughter and my own husband.

My friends, I know several ways of causing their death, and I cannot decide which I should turn my hand to first. Shall I set fire to the bridal chamber or make my way in stealthily to where their bed is laid and drive a sword through their vitals? But there is one little difficulty. If I am caught entering the palace or devising my bonfire I shall be slain and my enemies shall laugh. Better take the direct way and the one for which I have the natural gift. Poison. Destroy them with poison. So be it.

But suppose them slain. What city will receive me? Whose hospitality will rescue me and afford me a land where I shall be safe from punishment, a home where I can live in security? It cannot be. I shall wait, therefore, a little longer and if any tower of safety shows up I shall carry out the murders in stealth and secrecy. However, if circumstances drive me to my wits' end, I shall take a sword in my own hands and face certain death to slay them. I shall not shirk the difficult adventure. No! by Queen Hecate[2] who has her abode in the recesses of my hearth—her I revere above all gods and have chosen to assist me—never shall any one of them torture my heart with impunity. I shall make their marriage a torment and grief to them. Bitterly shall they rue the match they have made and the exile they inflict on me.

But enough! Medea, use all your wiles; plot and devise. Onward to the dreadful moment. Now is the test of courage. Do you see how you are being

---

[2] **Hecate:** Greek goddess of mysterious origins who brought good luck to sailors.

treated? It is not right that the seed of Sisyphus[3] and Aeson should gloat over you, the daughter of a noble sire and descendant of the Sun. But you realize that. Moreover by our mere nature we women are helpless for good, but adept at contriving all manner of wickedness.

CHORUS: *Back to their sources flow the sacred rivers. The world and morality are turned upside-down. The hearts of men are treacherous; the sanctions of Heaven are undermined. The voice of time will change, and our glory will ring down the ages. Womankind will be honored. No longer will ill-sounding report attach to our sex.*

The strains of ancient minstrelsy will cease, that hymned our faithlessness. Would that Phoebus, Lord of Song, had put into woman's heart the inspired song of the lyre. Then I would have sung a song in answer to the tribe of males. History has much to tell of the relations of men with women.

You, Medea, in the mad passion of your heart sailed away from your father's home, threading your way through the twin rocks of the Euxine, to settle in a foreign land. Now, your bed empty, your lover lost, unhappy woman, you are being driven forth in dishonor into exile.

Gone is respect for oaths. Nowhere in all the breadth of Hellas is honor any more to be found; it has vanished into the clouds. Hapless one, you have no father's house to which you might fly for shelter from the gales of misfortune; and another woman, a princess, has charmed your husband away and stepped into your place.

(*Enter* JASON.)

JASON: Often and often ere now I have observed that an intractable nature is a curse almost impossible to deal with. So with you. When you might have stayed on in this land and in this house by submitting quietly to the wishes of your superiors, your forward tongue has got you expelled from the country. Not that your abuse troubles *me* at all. Keep on saying that Jason is a villain of the deepest dye. But for your insolence to royalty consider yourself more than fortunate that you are only being punished by exile. I was constantly mollifying the angry monarch and expressing the wish that you be allowed to stay. But in unabated folly you keep on reviling the king. That is why you are to be expelled.

But still, despite everything, I come here now with unwearied goodwill, to contrive on your behalf, Madam, that you and the children will not leave this country lacking money or anything else. Exile brings many hardships in its wake. And even if you do hate me, I could never think cruelly of you.

MEDEA: Rotten, heart-rotten, that is the word for you. Words, words, magnificent words. In reality a craven. You come to me, you come, my worst enemy! This isn't bravery, you know, this isn't valor, to come and face your victims. No! it's

---

[3] **Sisyphus:** In Greek mythology, a son of Aeolus and founder of the city of Ephyre, later Corinth. Sisyphus appears as a rogue and a trickster in numerous classical legends. He is best known for the punishment he received for revealing Zeus's rape of Aegina to her father, the river Asopus: in Hades he is condemned to roll a huge stone up a hill, only to have it roll down again each time.

the ugliest sore on the face of humanity, Shamelessness. But I thank you for coming. It will lighten the weight on my heart to tell your wickedness, and it will hurt you to hear it. I shall begin my tale at the very beginning.

I saved your life, as all know who embarked with you on the Argo, when you were sent to master with the yoke the fire-breathing bulls and to sow with dragon's teeth that acre of death. The dragon, too, with wreathed coils, that kept safe watch over the Golden Fleece and never slept—I slew it and raised for you the light of life again. Then, forsaking my father and my own dear ones, I came to Iolcus where Pelias reigned, came with you, more than fond and less than wise. On Pelias too I brought death, the most painful death there is, at the hands of his own children. Thus I have removed every danger from your path.

And after all those benefits at my hands, you basest of men, you have betrayed me and made a new marriage, though I have borne you children. If you were still childless, I could have understood this love of yours for a new wife. Gone now is all reliance on pledges. You puzzle me. Do you believe that the gods of the old days are no longer in office? Do you think that men are now living under a new dispensation? For surely you know that you have broken all your oaths to me. Ah my hand, which you so often grasped, and oh my knees, how all for nothing have we been defiled by this false man, who has disappointed all our hopes.

But come, I shall confide in you as though you were my friend, not that I expect to receive any benefit from you. But let that go. My questions will serve to underline your infamy. As things are now, where am I to turn? Home to my father? But when I came here with you, I betrayed my home and my country. To the wretched daughters of Pelias? They would surely give me a royal welcome to their home; I only murdered their father. For it is how it is. My loved ones at home have learned to hate me; the others, whom I need not have harmed, I have made enemies to oblige you. And so in return for these services you have made me envied among the women of Hellas! A wonderful, faithful husband I have in you, if I must be expelled from the country into exile, deserted by my friends, alone with my friendless children! A fine story to tell of the new bridegroom, that his children and the woman who saved his life are wandering about in aimless beggary! O Zeus, why O why have you given to mortals sure means of knowing gold from tinsel, yet men's exteriors show no mark by which to descry the rotten heart?

LEADER: Horrible and hard to heal is the anger of friend at strife with friend.

JASON: It looks as if I need no small skill in speech if, like a skilful steersman riding the storm with close-reefed sheets, I am to escape the howling gale of your verbosity, woman. Well, since you are making a mountain out of the favors you have done me, I'll tell *you* what I think. It was the goddess of Love and none other, mortal or immortal, who delivered me from the dangers of my quest. You have indeed much subtlety of wit, but it would be an invidious story to go into, how the inescapable shafts of Love compelled you to save my life. Still, I shall not put too fine a point on it. If you helped me in some way or other, good and well. But as I shall demonstrate, in the matter of my rescue you got more than you gave.

In the first place, you have your home in Greece, instead of in a barbarian land. You have learned the blessings of Law and Justice, instead of the Caprice of the Strong. And all the Greeks have realized your wisdom, and you have won great fame. If you had been living on the edges of the earth, nobody would ever have heard of you. May I have neither gold in my house nor skill to sing a sweeter song than Orpheus if my fortune is to be hid from the eyes of men. That, then, is my position in the matter of the fetching of the Fleece. (It was you who proposed the debate.)

There remains my wedding with the Princess, which you have cast in my teeth. In this connection I shall demonstrate, one, my wisdom; two, my rightness; three, my great service of love to you and my children. (Be quiet please.) When I emigrated here from the land of Iolcus, dragging behind me an unmanageable chain of troubles, what greater windfall could I have hit upon, I an exile, than a marriage with the king's daughter? Not that I was weary of your charms (that's the thought that galls you) or that I was smitten with longing for a fresh bride; still less that I wanted to outdo my neighbors in begetting numerous children. Those I have are enough, there I have no criticism to make. No! what I wanted, first and foremost, was a good home where we would lack for nothing (well I knew that the poor man is shunned and avoided by all his friends); and secondly, I wanted to bring up the children in a style worthy of my house, and, begetting other children to be brothers to the children born of you, to bring them all together and unite the families. Then my happiness would be complete. What do *you* want with more children? As for me, it will pay me to advance the children I have by means of those I intend to beget. Surely that is no bad plan? You yourself would admit it, if jealousy were not pricking you.

You women have actually come to believe that, lucky in love, you are lucky in all things, but let some mischance befall that love, and you will think the best of all possible worlds a most loathsome place. There ought to have been some other way for men to beget their children, dispensing with the assistance of women. Then there would be no trouble in the world.

LEADER: Jason, you arrange your arguments very skillfully. And yet in my opinion, like it or not, you have acted unjustly in betraying your wife.

MEDEA: Yes! I do hold many opinions that are not shared by the majority of people. In my opinion, for example, the plausible scoundrel is the worst type of scoundrel. Confident in his ability to trick out his wickedness with fair phrases he shrinks from no depth of villainy. But there is a limit to his cleverness. As there is also to yours. You may well drop that fine front with me, and all that rhetoric. One word will floor you. If you had been an honorable man, you would have sought my consent to the new match and not kept your plans secret from your own family.

JASON: And if I had announced to you my intention to marry, I am sure I would have found you a most enthusiastic accomplice. Why! even now you cannot bring yourself to master your heart's deep resentment.

MEDEA: That's not what griped you. No! your foreign wife was passing into an old age that did you little credit.

JASON: Accept my assurance, it was not for the sake of a woman that I made the match I have made. As I told you once already, I wanted to save you and to beget princes to be brothers to my own sons, thereby establishing our family.

MEDEA: May it never be mine . . . a happiness that hurts, a blessedness that frets my soul.

JASON: Do you know how to change your prayer to show better sense? "May I regard nothing useful as grievous, no good fortune as ill."

MEDEA: Insult me. *You* have a refuge, but I am helpless, faced with exile.

JASON: It was your own choice. Don't blame anyone else.

MEDEA: What did I do? Did I betray you and marry somebody else?

JASON: You heaped foul curses on the king.

MEDEA: And to your house also I shall prove a curse.

JASON: Look here, I do not intend to continue this discussion any further. If you want anything of mine to assist you or the children in your exile, just tell me. I am ready to give it with an ungrudging hand and to send letters of introduction to my foreign friends who will treat you well. If you reject this offer, woman, you will be a great fool. Forget your anger, and you will find it greatly to your advantage.

MEDEA: I would not use your friends on any terms or accept anything of yours. Do not offer it. The gifts of the wicked bring no profit.

JASON: At any rate, heaven be my witness that I am willing to render every assistance to you and the children. But you do not like what is good for you. Your obstinacy repulses your friends; it will only aggravate your suffering.

MEDEA: Be off with you. As you loiter outside here, you are burning with longing for the girl who has just been made your wife. Make the most of the union. Perhaps, god willing, you are making the kind of marriage you will some day wish unmade.

(Exit JASON.*)*

CHORUS: *Love may go too far and involve men in dishonor and disgrace. But if the goddess comes in just measure, there is none so rich in blessing. May you never launch at me, O Lady of Cyprus, your golden bow's passion-poisoned arrows, which no man can avoid.*

   May Moderation content me, the fairest gift of Heaven. Never may the Cyprian pierce my heart with longing for another's love and bring on me angry quarrelings and never-ending recriminations. May she have respect for harmonious unions and with discernment assort the matings of women.

   O Home and Fatherland, never, never, I pray, may I be cityless. It is an intolerable existence, hopeless, piteous, grievous. Let me die first, die and bring this life to a close. There is no sorrow that surpasses the loss of country.

   My eyes have seen it; not from hearsay do I speak. You have neither city nor friend to pity you in your most terrible trials. Perish, abhorred, the man who never brings himself to unbolt his heart in frankness to some honored friends! Never shall such a man be a friend of mine.

(*Enter* AEGEUS, *in traveler's dress.*)

AEGEUS: Medea, good health to you. A better prelude than that in addressing one's friends, no man knows.

MEDEA: Good health be yours also, wise Pandion's son, Aegeus. Where do you come from to visit this land?

AEGEUS: I have just left the ancient oracle of Phoebus.

MEDEA: What sent you to the earth's oracular hub?

AEGEUS: I was enquiring how I might get children.

MEDEA: In the name of Heaven, have you come thus far in life still childless?

AEGEUS: By some supernatural influence I am still without children.

MEDEA: Have you a wife or are you still unmarried?

AEGEUS: I have a wedded wife to share my bed.

MEDEA: Tell me, what did Phoebus tell you about offspring?

AEGEUS: His words were too cunning for a mere man to interpret.

MEDEA: Is it lawful to tell me the answer of the god?

AEGEUS: Surely. For, believe me, it requires a cunning mind to understand.

MEDEA: What then was the oracle? Tell me, if I may hear it.

AEGEUS: I am not to open the cock that projects from the skin . . .

MEDEA: Till you do what? Till you reach what land?

AEGEUS: Till I return to my ancestral hearth.

MEDEA: Then what errand brings your ship to this land?

AEGEUS: There is one Pittheus, king of Troezen . . .

MEDEA: The child of Pelops, as they say, and a most pious man.

AEGEUS: To him I will communicate the oracle of the god.

MEDEA: Yes, he is a cunning man and well-versed in such matters.

AEGEUS: Yes, and of all my comrades in arms the one I love most.

MEDEA: Well, good luck to you, and may you win your heart's desire.

AEGEUS: Why, what's the reason for those sad eyes, that wasted complexion?

MEDEA: Aegeus, I've got the basest husband in all the world.

AEGEUS: What do you mean? Tell me the reason of your despondency, tell me plainly.

MEDEA: Jason is wronging me; I never did him wrong.

AEGEUS: What has he done? Speak more bluntly.

MEDEA: He has another wife, to lord it over me in our home.

AEGEUS: You don't mean that he has done so callous, so shameful a deed!

MEDEA: Indeed he did. Me that used to be his darling he now despises.

AEGEUS: Has he fallen in love? Does he hate your embraces?

MEDEA: Yes, it's a grand passion! He was born to betray his loved ones.

AEGEUS: Let him go, then, since he is so base, as you say.

MEDEA: He became enamored of getting a king for a father-in-law.

AEGEUS: Who gave him the bride? Please finish your story.

MEDEA: Creon, the ruler of this Corinth.

AEGEUS: In that case, Madam, I can sympathize with your resentment.

MEDEA: My life is ruined. What is more, I am being expelled from the land.

AEGEUS: By whom? This new trouble is hard.

MEDEA: Creon is driving me out of Corinth into exile.

AEGEUS: And does Jason allow this? I don't like that either.

MEDEA: He says he does not, but he'll stand it. Oh! I beseech you by this beard, by these knees, a suppliant I entreat you, show pity, show pity for my misery. Do not stand by and see me driven forth to a lonely exile. Receive me into your land, into your home and the shelter of your hearth. So may the gods grant you the children you desire, to throw joy round your deathbed. You do not know what a lucky path you have taken to me. I shall put an end to your childlessness. I shall make you beget heirs of your blood. I know the magic potions that will do it.

AEGEUS: Many things make me eager to do this favor for you, Madam. Firstly, the gods, and secondly, the children that you promise will be born to me. In that matter I am quite at my wits' end. But here is how I stand. If you yourself come to Athens, I shall try to be your champion, as in duty bound. This warning, however, I must give you! I shall not consent to take you with me out of Corinth. If you yourself come to my palace, you will find a home and a sanctuary. Never will I surrender you to anybody. But your own efforts must get you away from this place. I wish to be free from blame in the eyes of my hosts also.

MEDEA: And so you shall. But just let me have a pledge for these services, and I shall have all I could desire of you.

AEGEUS: Do you not trust me? What is your difficulty?

MEDEA: I do trust you. But both the house of Pelias and Creon are my enemies. Bound by oaths, you would never hand me over to them if they tried to extradite me. But with an agreement of mere words, unfettered by any sacred pledge, you might be won over by their diplomatic advances to become *their* friend. For I have no influence or power, whereas they have the wealth of a royal palace.

AEGEUS: You take great precautions, Madam. Still, if you wish, I will not refuse to do your bidding. For me too it will be safer that way, if I have some excuse to offer to your enemies, and *you* will have more security. Dictate the oath.

MEDEA: Swear by the Floor of Earth, by the Sun my father's father, by the whole family of the gods, one and all——

AEGEUS: To do or not do what? Say on.

MEDEA: Never yourself to cast me out of your country and never, willingly, during your lifetime, to surrender me to any of my foes that desire to seize me.

AEGEUS: I swear by the Earth, by the holy majesty of the Sun, and by all the gods, to abide by the terms you propose.

MEDEA: Enough! And if you abide not by your oath, what punishment do you pray to receive?

AEGEUS: The doom of sacrilegious mortals.

MEDEA: Go and fare well. All is well. I shall arrive at your city as soon as possible, when I have done what I intend to do, and obtained my desire.

LEADER (*as* AEGEUS *departs*):   May Maia's son, the Lord of Journeys,[4] bring you safe to Athens, and may you achieve the desire that hurries you homeward; for you are a generous man in my esteem.

---

[4] **Maia's Son, the Lord of Journeys:** Mercury.

MEDEA: O Zeus and his Justice, O Light of the Sun! The time has come, my friends, when I shall sing songs of triumph over my enemies. I am on my way. Now I can hope that my foes will pay the penalty. Just as my plans were most storm-tossed at sea, this man has appeared, a veritable harbor, where I shall fix my moorings, when I get to the town and citadel of Pallas.

Now I shall tell you all my plans; what you hear will not be said in fun. I shall send one of my servants to ask Jason to come and see me. When he comes, I shall make my language submissive, tell him I approve of everything else and am quite contented [with his royal marriage and his betrayal of me, that I agree it is all for the best]; I shall only ask him to allow my children to remain. Not that I wish to leave them in a hostile land [for my enemies to insult]. No! I have a cunning plan to kill the princess. I shall send them with gifts to offer to the bride, to allow them to stay in the land—a dainty robe and a headdress of beaten gold. If she takes the finery and puts it on her, she will die in agony. She and anyone who touches her. So deadly are the poisons in which I shall steep my gifts.

But now I change my tone. It grieves me sorely, the horrible deed I must do next. I shall murder my children, these children of mine. No man shall take them away from me. Then when I have accomplished the utter overthrow of the house of Jason, I shall flee from the land, to escape the consequences of my own dear children's murder and my other accursed crimes. My friends, I cannot bear being laughed at by my enemies.

So be it. Tell me, what has life to offer them. They have no father, no home, no refuge from danger.

My mistake was in leaving my father's house, won over by the words of a Greek. But, as god is my ally, he shall pay for his crime. Never, if I can help it, shall he behold his sons again in this life. Never shall he beget children by his new bride. She must die by my poisons, die the death she deserves. Nobody shall despise *me* or think me weak or passive. Quite the contrary. I am a good friend, but a dangerous enemy. For that is the type the world delights to honor.

LEADER: You have confided your plan in me, and I should like to help you, but since I also would support the laws of mankind, I entreat you not to do this deed.

MEDEA: It is the only way. But I can sympathize with your sentiments. You have not been wronged like me.

LEADER: Surely you will not have the heart to destroy your own flesh and blood?

MEDEA: I shall. It will hurt my husband most that way.

LEADER: But it will make you the unhappiest woman in the world.

MEDEA: Let it. From now on all words are superfluous. (*To the* NURSE.) Go now, please, and fetch Jason. Whenever loyalty is wanted, I turn to you. Tell him nothing of my intentions, as you are a woman and a loyal servant of your mistress.

(*Exit* NURSE.)

CHORUS: *The people of Erechtheus have been favored of Heaven from the beginning. Children of the blessed gods are they, sprung from a hallowed land that no foeman's foot has trodden. Their food is glorious Wisdom. There the skies are always clear, and lightly do they walk in that land where once on a time blonde Harmony bore nine chaste daughters, the Muses of Pieria.*

Such is the tale, which tells also how Aphrodite sprinkled the land with water from the fair streams of Cephissus and breathed over it breezes soft and fragrant. Ever on her hair she wears a garland of sweet-smelling roses, and ever she sends the Loves to assist in the court of Wisdom. No good thing is wrought without their help.

How then shall that land of sacred rivers, that hospitable land receive you the slayer of your children? It would be sacrilege for you to live with them. Think. You are stabbing your children. Think. You are earning the name of murderess. By your knees we entreat you, by all the world holds sacred, do not murder your children.

Whence got you the hardihood to conceive such a plan? And in the horrible act, as you bring death on your own children, how will you steel your heart and hand? When you cast your eyes on them, your own children, will you not weep that you should be their murderess? When your own children fall at your feet and beg for mercy, you will never be able to dye your hands with their blood. Your heart will not stand it.

(*Enter* Jason, *followed by the* Nurse.)

JASON: I come at your bidding. Though you hate me, I shall not refuse you an audience. What new favor have you to ask of me, woman?

MEDEA: Jason, please forgive me for all I said. After all the services of love you have rendered me before, I can count on you to put up with my fits of temper. I have been arguing the matter out with myself. Wretched woman (thus I scolded myself), why am I so mad as to hate those that mean me well, to treat as enemies the rulers of this land and my husband who, in marrying a princess and getting brothers for my children, is only doing what is best for us all? What is the matter with me? Why am I still furious, when the gods are showering their blessings on me? Have I not children of my own? Am I forgetting that I am an exile from my native land, in sore need of friends? These reflections let me see how very foolish I have been and how groundless is my resentment. Now, I want to thank you. I think you are only doing the right thing in making this new match. I have been the fool. I ought to have entered into your designs, helped you to accomplish them, even stood by your nuptial couch and been glad to be of service to the new bride. But I am what I am . . . to say no worse, a woman. You ought not therefore to imitate me in my error or to compete with me in childishness. I beg your pardon, and confess that I was wrong then. But now I have taken better counsel, as you see.

Children, children, come here, leave the house, come out and greet your father as I do. Speak to him. Join your mother in making friends with him, forgetting our former hate. It's a truce; the quarrel is over. Take his right hand. Alas! my imagination sickens strangely. My children, will you stretch out loving arms like that in the long hereafter? My grief! How quick my tears are! My fears brim over. It is that long quarrel with your father, now done with, that fills my tender eyes with tears.

LEADER: From my eyes, too, the burning tears gush forth. May Sorrow's advance proceed no further.

JASON: That is the talk I like to hear, woman. The past I can forgive. It is only natural for your sex to show resentment when their husbands contract another marriage. But your heart has now changed for the better. It took time, to be sure, but you have now seen the light of reason. That's the action of a wise woman. As for you, my children, your father has not forgotten you. God willing, he has secured your perfect safety. I feel sure that you will yet occupy the first place here in Corinth, with your brothers. Merely grow up. Your father, and any friends he has in heaven, will see to the rest. May I see you, sturdy and strong, in the flower of your youth, triumphant over my enemies.

   You there, why wet your eyes with hot tears, and avert your pale cheek? Why are you not happy to hear me speak thus?

MEDEA: It's nothing. Just a thought about the children here.

JASON: Why all this weeping over the children? It's too much.

MEDEA: I am their mother. Just now when you were wishing them long life, a pang of sorrow came over me, in case things would not work out that way.

JASON: Cheer up, then. I shall see that they are all right.

MEDEA: Very well, I shall not doubt your word. Women are frail things and naturally apt to cry. But to return to the object of this conference, something has been said, something remains to be mentioned. Since it is their royal pleasure to expel me from the country—oh yes! it's the best thing for me too, I know well, not to stay on here in the way of you and the king; I am supposed to be their bitter enemy—*I* then shall go off into exile. But see that the children are reared by your own hand, ask Creon to let *them* stay.

JASON: I don't know if he will listen to me, but I shall try, as I ought.

MEDEA: At least you can get your wife to intercede with her father on their behalf.

JASON: Certainly, and I imagine I shall persuade her.

MEDEA: If she is a woman like the rest of us. In this task, I too shall play my part. I shall send the children with gifts for her, gifts far surpassing the things men make to-day [a fine robe, and a head-dress of beaten gold]. Be quick there. Let one of my maids bring the finery here. What joy will be hers, joys rather, joys innumerable, getting not only a hero like you for a husband, but also raiment which the Sun, my father's father, gave to his children. (MEDEA *takes the casket from a maid who has brought it, and hands it to the* CHILDREN.) Here, my children, take these wedding gifts in your hands. Carry them to the princess, the happy bride, and give them to her. They are not the kind of gifts she will despise.

JASON: Impetuous woman! Why leave yourself thus empty-handed? Do you think a royal palace lacks for raiment and gold? Keep these things for yourself, don't give them away. If my wife has any regard for me at all, she will prefer me to wealth, I'm sure.

MEDEA: Please let me. They say that gifts persuade even the gods, and gold is stronger than ten thousand words. Hers is the fortune of the hour; her now is god exalting. She has youth, and a king for a father. And to save my children from exile, I would give my very life, let alone gold.

   Away, my children, enter the rich palace and entreat your father's young wife, my mistress, to let you stay in Corinth. Give her the finery. That is most important. She must take these gifts in her hands. Go as fast as you can. Success attend your mission, and may you bring back to your mother the tidings she longs to hear.

(*Exeunt* CHILDREN *with* TUTOR *and* JASON.)

CHORUS: *Now are my hopes dead. The children are doomed. Already they are on the road to death. She will take it, the bride will take the golden diadem, and with it will take her ruin, luckless girl. With her own hands she will put the precious circlet of death on her blonde hair.*

The beauty of it, the heavenly sheen, will persuade her to put on the robe and the golden crown. It is in the halls of death that she will put on her bridal dress forthwith. Into that fearful trap she will fall. Death will be her portion, hapless girl. She cannot overleap her doom.

And you, poor man. Little luck your royal father-in-law is bringing you. Unwittingly, you are bringing death on your children, and on your wife an awful end. Ill-starred man, what a way you are from happiness.

And now I weep for your sorrow, hapless mother of these children. You will slaughter them to avenge the dishonor of your bed betrayed, criminally betrayed by your husband who now sleeps beside another bride.

(*Enter* CHILDREN *with their* TUTOR.)

TUTOR: Mistress, here are your children, reprieved from exile. Your gifts the royal bride took gladly in her hands. The children have made their peace with *her*. What's the matter? Why stand in such confusion, when fortune is smiling? [Why do you turn away your cheek? Why are you not glad to hear my message?]

MEDEA: Misery!

TUTOR: That note does not harmonize with the news I have brought.

MEDEA: Misery, and again Misery!

TUTOR: Have I unwittingly brought you bad news? I thought it was good. Was I mistaken?

MEDEA: Your message was . . . your message. It is not you I blame.

TUTOR: Why then are your eyes downcast and your tears flowing?

MEDEA: Of necessity, old man, of strong necessity. This is the gods' doing, and mine, in my folly.

TUTOR: Have courage. Some day your children will bring you too back home.

MEDEA: Ah me! Before that day I shall bring others to another home.

TUTOR: You are not the first woman to be separated from her children. We are mortals and must endure calamity with patience.

MEDEA: That I shall do. Now go inside and prepare their usual food for the children.

(*Exit* TUTOR.)

O my children, my children. For you indeed a city is assured, and a home in which, leaving me to my misery, you will dwell for ever, motherless. But I must go forth to exile in a strange land, before I have ever tasted the joy of seeing *your* happiness, before I have got you brides and bedecked your marriage beds and held aloft the bridal torches. Alas! my own self-will has brought me to misery. Was it all for nothing, my children, the rearing of you, and all the agonizing labor, all the fierce pangs I endured at your birth? Ah me, there was a time when I had strong hopes, fool as I was, that you would tend my old age and with your own hands dress my body for the grave, a fate that the world might envy. Now the sweet dream is gone. Deprived of you, I shall live a life of pain and sorrow. And you, in another world altogether will never again see your mother with your dear, dear eyes.

O the pain of it! Why do your eyes look at me, my children? Why smile at me that last smile? Ah! What can I do? My heart is water, women, at the sight of my children's bright faces. I could never do it. Goodbye to my former plans. I shall take my children away with me. Why should I hurt their father by *their* misfortunes, only to reap a double harvest of sorrow myself? No! I cannot do it. Goodbye to my plans.

And yet . . . what is the matter with me? Do I want to make myself a laughing-stock by letting my enemies off scot-free? I must go through with it. What a coward heart is mine, to admit those soft pleas. Come, my children, into the palace. Those that may not attend my sacrifices can see to it that they are absent. I shall not let my hand be unnerved.

Ah! Ah! Stop, my heart. Do not you commit this crime. Leave them alone, unhappy one, spare the children. Even if they live far from us, they will bring you joy. No! by the unforgetting dead in hell, it cannot be! I shall not leave my children for my enemies to insult. [In any case they must die. And if die they must, *I* shall slay them, who gave them birth.] My schemes are crowned with success. She shall not escape. Already the diadem is on her head; wrapped in the robe the royal bride is dying, I know it well. And now I am setting out on a most sorrowful road [and shall send these on one still more sorrowful]. I wish to speak to my children. Give your mother your hands, my children, give her your hands to kiss.

O dear, dear hand. O dear, dear mouth, dear shapes, dear noble faces, happiness be yours, but not here. Your father has stolen this world from you. How sweet to touch! The softness of their skin, the sweetness of their breath, my babies! Away, away, I cannot bear to see you any longer. (*Children retire within.*) My misery overwhelms me. O I *do* realize how terrible is the crime I am about, but passion overrules my resolutions, passion that causes most of the misery in the world.

CHORUS: *Often ere now I have grappled with subtle subjects and sounded depths of argument deeper than woman may plumb. But, you see, we also have a Muse who teaches us philosophy. It is a small class—perhaps you might find one in a thousand—the women that love the Muse.*

And I declare that in this world those who have had no experience of paternity are happier than the fathers of children. Without children a man does not know whether they are a blessing or a curse, and so he does not miss a joy he has never had and he escapes a multitude of sorrows. But them that have in their home young, growing

*children that they love, I see them consumed with anxiety, day in day out, how they are
to rear them properly, how they are to get a livelihood to leave to them. And, after all
that, whether the children for whom they toil are worth it or not, who can tell?*

*And now I shall tell you the last and crowning sorrow for all mortals. Suppose
they have found livelihood enough, their children have grown up, and turned out honest. Then, if it is fated that way, death carries their bodies away beneath the earth.
What then is the use, when the love of children brings from the gods this crowning sorrow to top the rest?*

MEDEA: My friends, all this time I have been waiting for something to happen,
watching to see what they will do in the royal palace. Now I see one of Jason's
attendants coming this way. His excited breathing shows that he has a tale of
strange evils to tell.

(*Enter* MESSENGER.)

MESSENGER: What a horrible deed of crime you have done, Medea. Flee, flee. Take
anything you can find, sea vessel or land carriage.

MEDEA: Tell me, what has happened that I should flee.

MESSENGER: The princess has just died. Her father Creon, too, killed by your
poisons.

MEDEA: Best of news! From this moment and for ever you are one of my friends
and benefactors.

MESSENGER: What's that? Are you sane and of sound mind, woman? You have
inflicted a foul outrage on a king's home, yet you rejoice at the word of it and
are not afraid.

MEDEA: I too have a reply that I might make to you. But take your time, my friend.
Speak on. How did they die? You would double my delight, if they died in agony.

MESSENGER: When your children, both your offspring, arrived with their father
and entered the bride's house, we rejoiced, we servants who had been grieved
by your troubles. Immediately a whisper ran from ear to ear that you and your
husband had patched up your earlier quarrel. And one kisses your children's
hands, another their yellow hair. I myself, in my delight, accompanied the children to the women's rooms. The mistress, whom we now respect in your place,
did not see the two boys at first, but cast a longing look at Jason. Then, however, resenting the entrance of the children, she covered her eyes with a veil
and averted her white cheek.

Your husband tried to allay the maiden's angry resentment, saying, "You
must not hate your friends. Won't you calm your temper, and turn your head
this way? You must consider your husband's friends your own. Won't you
accept the gifts and ask your father to recall their sentence of exile, for my
sake?" Well, when she saw the finery, she could not refrain, but promised her
husband everything, and before Jason and your children were far away from
the house she took the elaborate robes and put them on her. She placed the
golden diadem on her clustering locks and began to arrange her coiffure before
a shining mirror, smiling at her body's lifeless reflection. Then she arose from
her seat and walked through the rooms, stepping delicately with her fair white

feet, overjoyed with the gifts. Time and time again, standing erect, she gazes with all her eyes at her ankles.

But then ensued a fearful sight to see. Her color changed, she staggered, and ran back, her limbs all atremble, and only escaped falling by sinking upon her chair. An old attendant, thinking, I suppose, it was a panic fit, or something else of divine sending, raised a cry of prayer, until she sees a white froth drooling from her mouth, sees her rolling up the pupils of her eyes, and all the blood leaving her skin. Then, instead of a cry of prayer, she let out a scream of lamentation. Immediately one maid rushed to Creon's palace, another to the new bridegroom, to tell of the bride's misfortune. From end to end, the house echoed to hurrying steps. A quick walker, stepping out well, would have reached the end of the two hundred yard track, when the poor girl, lying there quiet, with closed eyes, gave a fearful groan and began to come to. A double plague assailed her. The golden diadem on her head emitted a strange flow of devouring fire, while the fine robes, the gifts of your children, were eating up the poor girl's white flesh. All aflame, she jumps from her seat and flees, shaking her head and hair this way and that, trying to throw off the crown. But the golden band held firmly, and after she had shaken her hair more violently, the fire began to blaze twice as fiercely. Overcome by the agony she falls on the ground, and none but her father could have recognized her. The position of her eyes could not be distinguished, nor the beauty of her face. The blood, clotted with fire, dripped from the crown of her head, and the flesh melted from her bones, like resin from a pinetree, as the poisons ate their unseen way. It was a fearful sight. All were afraid to touch the corpse, taught by what had happened to her.

But her father, unlucky man, rushed suddenly into the room, not knowing what had happened, and threw himself on the body. At once he groaned, and embracing his daughter's form he kissed it and cried, "My poor, poor child, what god has destroyed you so shamefully? Who is it deprives this aged tomb of his only child? Ah! let me join you in death, my child." Then, when he ceased his weeping and lamentation and sought to lift his aged frame upright, he stuck to the fine robes, like ivy to a laurel bush. His struggles were horrible. He would try to free a leg, but the girl's body stuck to his. And if he pulled violently, he tore his shrunken flesh off his bones. At last his life went out; doomed, he gave up the ghost. Side by side lie the two bodies, daughter and old father. Who would not weep at such a calamity?

It seems to me . . . I need not speak of what's in store for you; you yourself will see how well the punishment fits the crime. . . it's not the first time the thought has come, that the life of a man is a shadow. [I might assert with confidence that the mortals who pass for philosophers and subtle reasoners are most to be condemned.] No mortal man has lasting happiness. When the tide of fortune flows his way, one man may have more prosperity than another, but happiness never.

(*Exit* Messenger.)

LEADER: It seems that this day Fate is visiting his sins on Jason. Unfortunate daughter of Creon, we pity your calamity. The love of Jason has carried you through the gates of death.

MEDEA: My friends, I am resolved to act, and act quickly [to slay the children and depart from the land]. I can delay no longer, or my children will fall into the murderous hands of those that love them less than I do. In any case they must die. And if they must, I shall slay them, who gave them birth. Now, my heart, steel yourself. Why do we still hold back? The deed is terrible, but necessary. Come, my unhappy hand, seize the sword, seize it. Before you is a course of misery, life-long misery; on now to the starting post. No flinching now, no thinking of the children, the darling children, that call you mother. This day, this one short day, forget your children. You have all the future to mourn for them. Aye, to mourn. Though you mean to kill them, at least you loved them. Oh! I am a most unhappy woman.

(Exit MEDEA.*)*

CHORUS: *O Earth, O glorious radiance of the Sun, look and behold the accursed woman. Stop her before she lays her bloody, murderous hands on her children. Sprung are they from your golden race, O Sun, and it is a fearful thing that the blood of a god should be spilt by mortals. Nay, stop her, skyborn light, prevent her. Deliver the house from the misery of slaughter, and the curse of the unforgetting dead.*

Gone, gone for nothing, are your maternal pangs. For nothing did you bear these lovely boys, O woman, who made the inhospitable passage through the gray Clashing Rocks! Why let your spleen poison your heart? Why this murderlust, where love was? On the man that spills the blood of kinsmen the curse of heaven descends. Go where he may, it rings ever in his ears, bringing sorrows and tribulations on his house.

(The CHILDREN *are heard within.)*

Listen, listen. It is the cry of the children. O cruel, ill-starred woman.

ONE OF THE CHILDREN *(within):*   Ah me! What am I to do? Where can I escape my mother's murderous hands?

THE OTHER *(within):*   I know not, my dear, dear brother. She is killing us.

CHORUS: *Should we break in? Yes! I will save them from death.*

ONE OF THE CHILDREN *(within):*   Do, for god's sake. Save us. We need your help.

THE OTHER *(within):*   Yes, we are already in the toils of the sword.

CHORUS: *Heartless woman! Are you made of stone or steel? Will you slaughter the children, your own seed, slaughter them with your own hands?*

Only one woman, only one in the history of the world, laid murderous hands on her children, Ino whom the gods made mad, driven from home to a life of wandering by the wife of Zeus. Hapless girl, bent on that foul slaughter, she stepped over a precipice by the shore and fell headlong into the sea, killing herself and her two children together. What crime, more horrible still, may yet come to pass? O the loves of women, fraught with sorrow, how many ills ere now have you brought on mortals!

(Enter JASON, *attended.)*

JASON: You women there, standing in front of this house, is Medea still within, who wrought these dreadful deeds? Or has she made her escape? I tell you, she had better hide under the earth or take herself off on wings to the recesses of the sky, unless she wishes to give satisfaction to the family of the king. Does she think she can slay the rulers of the land and get safely away from this house? But I am not so anxious about her as I am about the children. The victims of her crimes will attend to her. It's my own children I am here to save, in case the relatives of the king do them some injury, in revenge for the foul murders their mother has committed.

LEADER: Jason, poor Jason, you do not know the sum of your sorrows, or you would not have said these words.

JASON: What is it? She does not want to kill me too, does she?

LEADER: Your children are dead, slain by their mother's hand.

JASON: For pity's sake, what do you mean? You have slain me, woman.

LEADER: Your children are dead, make no mistake.

JASON: Why, where did she slay them? Indoors or out here?

LEADER: Open the doors and you will see their bodies.

JASON: Quick, servants, loosen the bolts, undo the fastenings. Let me see the double horror, the dead bodies of my children, and the woman who . . . oh! let me punish her.

> MEDEA *appears aloft in a chariot drawn by winged dragons. She has the bodies of the* CHILDREN.

MEDEA: What's all this talk of battering and unbarring? Are you searching for the bodies and me who did the deed? Spare yourself the trouble. If you have anything to ask of me, speak if you will, but never shall you lay a hand on me. I have a magic chariot, given me by the Sun, my father's father, to protect me against my enemies.

JASON: You abominable thing! You most loathsomest woman, to the gods and me and all mankind. You had the heart to take the sword to your children, you their mother, leaving me childless. And you still behold the earth and the sun, you who have done this deed, you who have perpetrated this abominable outrage. My curses on you! At last I have come to my senses, the senses I lost when I brought you from your barbarian home and country to a home in Greece, an evil plague, treacherous alike to your father and the land that reared you. There is a fiend in you, whom the gods have launched against me. In your own home you had already slain your brother when you came aboard the Argo, that lovely ship. Such was your beginning. Then you married me and bore me children, whom you have now destroyed because I left your bed. No Greek woman would ever have done such a deed. Yet I saw fit to marry you, rather than any woman of Greece, a wife to hate me and destroy me, not a woman at all, but a tigress, with a disposition more savage than Tuscan Scylla.[5] But why all this?

---

[5] **Scylla:** the daughter of Hecate who was originally human but was turned into a monster by a rival in love. She survived by eating fish but also devoured sailors if their ships came near her cave.

Ten thousand reproaches could not sting you; your impudence is too engrained. The devil take you, shameless, abominable murderess of your children. I must bemoan my fate; no joy shall I have of my new marriage, and I shall never see alive the children I begot and reared and lost.

MEDEA: I might have made an elaborate rebuttal of the speech you have made, but Zeus the Father knows what you received at my hands and what you have done. You could not hope, nor your princess either, to scorn my love, make a fool of me, and live happily ever after. Nor was Creon, the matchmaker, to drive me out of the country with impunity. Go ahead, then. Call me tigress if you like, or Scylla that haunts the Tuscan coast. I don't mind, now I have got properly under your skin.

JASON: You too are suffering. You have your share of the sorrow.

MEDEA: True, but it's worth the grief, since you cannot scoff.

JASON: O children, what a wicked mother you got!

MEDEA: O children, your father's sins have caused your death.

JASON: Yet it was not *my* hand that slew them.

MEDEA: No, it was your lust, and your new marriage.

JASON: Because your love was scorned you actually thought it right to murder.

MEDEA: Do you think a woman considers that a small injury?

JASON: Good women do. But you are wholly vicious.

MEDEA: The children here are dead. That will sting you.

JASON: No! they live to bring fierce curses on your head.

MEDEA: The gods know who began it all.

JASON: They know, indeed, they know the abominable wickedness of your heart.

MEDEA: Hate me then. I despise your bitter words.

JASON: And I yours. But it is easy for us to be quit of each other.

MEDEA: How, pray? Certainly I am willing.

JASON: Allow me to bury these bodies and lament them.

MEDEA: Certainly not. I shall bury them with my own hands, taking them to the sanctuary of Hera of the Cape, where no enemy may violate their tombs and do them insult. Here in the land of Sisyphus we shall establish a solemn festival, and appoint rites for the future to expiate their impious murder. I myself shall go to the land of Erechtheus, to live with Aegeus, the son of Pandion. You, as is proper, will die the death you deserve, [struck on the head by a fragment of the Argo,] now you have seen the bitter fruits of your new marriage.

JASON: May you be slain by the Curse of your children, and Justice that avenges murder!

MEDEA: What god or power above will listen to you, the breaker of oaths, the treacherous guest?

JASON: Oh! abominable slayer of children.

MEDEA: Get along to the palace and bury your wife.

JASON: I go, bereft of my two sons.

MEDEA: You have nothing yet to bemoan. Wait till you are old.

JASON: My dear, dear children!

MEDEA: Yes, dear to their mother, not to you.

JASON: And yet you slew them.

MEDEA: I did, to hurt you.

JASON: Alas! my grief! I long to kiss their dear mouths.

MEDEA: Now you speak to them, now you greet them, but in the past you spurned them.

JASON: For god's sake, let me touch my children's soft skin.

MEDEA: No! You have gambled and lost.

JASON: O Zeus, do you hear how I am repelled, how I am wronged by this foul tigress, that slew her own children? But such lament as I may and can make, I hereby make. I call upon the gods. I invoke the powers above to bear me witness that you slew my children and now prevent me from embracing their bodies and giving them burial. Would that I had never begotten them, to live to see them slain at your hands.

CHORUS: *Zeus on Olympus hath a wide stewardship. Many things beyond expectation do the gods fulfil. That which was expected has not been accomplished; for that which was unexpected has god found the way. Such was the end of this story.*

(*Exeunt.*)

[431 B.C.]

Journal Entry

Is Medea a moral monster or a helpless victim of passion? Is Jason's infidelity the catalyst for her crime? Cite evidence to explain or justify Medea's and Jason's actions.

Textual Considerations

1. How would you characterize Jason, based on the portraits the nurse and Medea draw of him? What does the nurse's first speech reveal about Jason's mythological background? What contrast does she establish between Jason's roles in the past and the present? What does Medea's speech to the women of Corinth (page xx) reveal about Jason?

2. Identify images in Medea's memorable language that are especially effective in communicating her view of love, hate, and violence. Analyze what such a language reveals about Medea's magical power and her sense of self as a woman, lover, wife, and mother.

3. What does Medea's encounter with Creon reveal about male status in the play? Characterize Creon as a ruler. What makes him change his "fixed resolve" to exile Medea? What kinds of weapons does Medea use against Creon?

4. The chorus of Corinthian women plays an important role in *Medea*. What is the chorus's view of gender relationships? To what extent does it empathize with Medea? What is its attitude toward Jason, love, and gender relations?

5. To what extent do you consider Jason's decision to abandon Medea justifiable? Are his arguments convincing? Why or why not?

Cultural Considerations

1. Consider the psychological depth of *Medea* by applying to Medea's tragedy the definition of love as an irresistible passion that overpowers reason and eventually destroys itself.
2. The concept of preserving communal values emerges as an important aspect of ancient Greek culture. To what extent does Euripides present Jason and Medea as tearing apart the social fabric of the family and community? Does your group hold them accountable for their actions? Why or why not?

Performance Exercises

PERFORMANCE EXPRESS (45 MINUTES)

To create a dynamic group *ensemble*, cast one of your classmates as Medea and have her stand on a chair, surrounded by several other classmates who, sitting on the floor, will play the roles of Jason, Creon, the nurse, Aegeus, and Medea's children. Ask the actors sitting in the circle to question Medea about her origins, her skills as a sorcerer, her status as a barbarian in Corinth, the golden fleece myth, Jason's motives for deserting her, or any other plot or characterization issue.

PERFORMANCE PROJECTS

1. Use the Internet to carry out research on the style of acting in ancient Greece, focusing primarily on the use of masks and the choreography of the chorus. Then, working with your group, stage one of *Medea*'s key scenes in both ancient Greek and contemporary staging styles. Think about costumes, scenic designs, the use of masks, and the choreography of the chorus. What aspects of the play have been lost or highlighted in each staging? Think about the dramatic purpose of the scene you have selected and how you can best portray it.
2. In her speech to the chorus (pages 427–428), Medea delivers a manifesto about the status of women in ancient Greece. To stage this scene, cast one of your classmates in the role of a feminist Medea. Decide on the costume and scene design you would use to recreate this highly emotional character. Notice that your choices about Medea's costumes can help you evoke her status as a foreign barbarian, a formidable feminist, or a cold-blooded murderer.

TOPICS FOR DISCUSSION AND WRITING

Writing Topics

1. According to the French feminist Simone de Beauvoir in *The Second Sex*, "The word *love* has by no means the same sense for both sexes, and this is one of the most serious misunderstandings that divide them." Apply this thesis to any three texts in Part Two.

2. Several texts in this part portray a male vision of gender relationships as fragmented and commercialized. Apply this concept to the texts by Rifaat, Lyman, and Euripides.

3. Assume the role of therapist, and write an essay on your first session with Gilman's protagonist. Use examples of her viewpoint as the basis for your evaluation.

4. American linguist Deborah Tannen has observed that even though women usually start the conversation, it is men who control it. To what extent do you consider these linguistic differences a major factor in conversations between men and women?

5. Consider the functions that the myth of the perfect housewife or the cult of domesticity serves in society. In your discussion, consider the premise that such a myth, at its best, may fulfill women's highest aspirations and, at it worst, may contribute to women's low self-esteem. Use three texts from this part to support your arguments.

6. Analyze the sources of the woman's anger in "Home Burial," and write about the causes of her inability to accept that her husband also mourns their child's death. Review lines 92–93 and lines 100–105 before formulating your response.

7. Several authors representing diverse cultures focus on economics and gender. Compare and contrast the degree to which economics shapes gender relationships in "Another Evening at the Club" and "My Last Duchess."

8. Discuss the interplay of rationality and irrationality in "The Yellow Wallpaper" or *Medea*. Trace this theme in either text, pointing out its effects on the identity of the protagonist. Focus on the ironies and contradictions that the theme creates.

9. Apply to any three texts in this part the concept that women's worst enemy is the enemy inside themselves—in other words, their inability to change their own, ingrained psychological structure.

10. Several texts explore the issue of women's sexuality from different vantage points. Compare and contrast the attitudes toward this issue in the poems by Sexton, de la Cruz, Millay, and Greenberg.

11. To focus on changing aspects of masculinity, compare and contrast the condition of male power in the texts by Browning, Yevtushenko, and Marvell with indications of male powerlessness in the selection by Freeman. Analyze the cultural forces that shape male identity in each text.

12. Write an essay discussing attitudes toward sexual and marital fidelity in "A Respectable Woman" and "The Storm." What are the protagonists' positions in

relation to these issues? What do these texts reveal about societal commitment to marriage and fidelity in Chopin's time and in our time?

13. The tradition of the *mal marié* (badly married) is an important theme in several culturally diverse texts in Part Two. To investigate the claim that marriage bestows upon women a sense of fixed identity, analyze three texts, including "Raggaza" and "Roselily," that explore a married woman's sense of personal and societal alienation.

14. Compare and contrast the portrayals of husbands in the texts by Freeman, Chopin, and Rifaat. To what extent does each husband find fulfillment in his role? Cite evidence from the texts to support your point of view.

15. According to the French writer Charles Fourier, whenever men disgrace women, they end up degrading themselves. Choose two short stories from this part to illustrate your agreement or disagreement with Fourier's idea.

Research Topics

1. Several works in Part Two examine the history of women from different cultural viewpoints. To understand what these texts portray in light of the women's liberation movement, investigate the history of one of the following: Mary Wollstonecraft's *A Vindication of the Rights of Women* (1790), Olympe de Gourges's *Declaration of the Rights of Women and Female Citizens* (1791), the suffragette movement in nineteenth-century England, the movement of the American feminists in the 1970s, or the black women's movement in America in the last three decades. For sources, search under women—history, women—France, feminism, gender, American women and politics, African American women—history. You might also check:

   Krichmar, Albert. *The Women's Movement in the Seventies: An International English-Language Bibliography.*
   Sim, Janet. *The Progress of Afro-American Women: A Selected Bibliography and Resource Guide.*
   Williams, Ora. *American Black Women in the Arts and Social Sciences: A Bibliographic Survey, revised and expanded edition.*

2. Discuss the relation of violence and possessive love in Browning's "My Last Duchess," *Othello* (Part Four) and "A Rose for Emily" (Part Five). Read a critical essay on each text and cite the essays as your secondary sources of information.

3. The myth of the "warrior woman"—from the legend of the Amazons to Joan of Arc and from the writings of Cervantes and Spenser to the actions of modern guerrillas—explores the images of women who have appropriated the great deeds traditionally attributed to the world of men. Examine three works in this part, such as *Medea*, "The Revolt of 'Mother'" and "Professions for Women" that incorporate, in one way or another, the image of the rebellious warrior woman.

FILM ANGLES

GENDER AND IDENTITY: THE FILM ANGLE

The introduction to the literature section of Part Two speaks of "the different images of women at different points in their history . . . as wide-ranging as goddess, rebel, warrior, sex object, mother, wife, and 'other.'" Just as these images and the themes of the unit can be found in such varied works of literature as the Greek tragedy *Medea*, poems as different as "My Last Duchess" and "The Faithful Wife," and the short story "The Yellow Wallpaper," movies—both popular and elitist—are cultural products that assimilate and reflect attitudes toward women that are prevalent at different historical moments.

Gender and identity issues may be explicit, as they are in *Boys Don't Cry* (d. Kimberley Pierce, 1999) and *The Crying Game* (d. Neil Jordan, Great Britain, 1992), both of which explore the slippery boundaries between masculinity and femininity; or they may be implicit, affecting the conventions and formulas of genre movies in terms of the way they usually depict women, as in *Thelma and Louise* (d. Ridley Scott, 1991), *The Silence of the Lambs* (d. Jonathan Demme, 1991), and *Alien* (d. Ridley Scott, 1979) and its sequels.

In the following section and case studies, images of women range from the wives and mothers in *All That Heaven Allows, Far from Heaven,* and *The Hours,* to the goddesses and femmes fatales of **film noir** and the warrior in the *Alien* films. In studying these films, students should look for the many indirect, subtle ways in which important thematic points are made through such things as genre revisions and visual style. A close examination of the **mise-en-scène** of films—the way they are designed, framed, and composed—reveals many unstated ideas and clues as to how we should interpret the screenplay.

Question to Consider

1. Using a working definition of *gender* from the literature sections of Part Two, think of a recent film that might be examined from this perspective. How is male or female identity represented in the film? Does it conform to familiar stereotypes (e.g., men associated with aggressive behavior, women with passive behavior)? Or does it question such rigid definitions?

FILM HISTORY AND GENRES

From the 1920s through the 1950s, the dominant source of American filmmaking was Hollywood's studio system. When we speak of the classical Hollywood film, we mean the films that came out of this system and influenced generations of viewers long before the arrival of television. For the most part, the majority of movies that were produced in the studios were genre films: melodramas, horror or science fiction, musicals, romantic comedies, war films, and westerns.

Genre movies reach larger audiences and reflect popular taste and values. For this reason, genre studies are especially revealing of a society's attitudes about questions of gender at any specific historical moment. It follows that changes in the conventions and rules of genre movies understandably reflect changes in the social attitudes toward gender issues. Thus, scholars concerned about gender issues have reexamined Hollywood movies in terms of how genre conventions mirrored and reinforced the links between human behavior and prevailing social attitudes of any given time. Even genre movies that broke the rules—that is, by changing the formulas, disappointing audience expectations, and thereby questioning underlying values—shed light on the conflicts between social dictates and the desires and needs of the individual.

Melodrama

Perhaps the genre that most explicitly addressed the way gender roles functioned in society was the melodrama, sometimes derogatively referred to as the "soap opera." The appeal of the melodrama was so strong that it eventually became a fixture of daytime television and many popular evening programs.

The typical Hollywood melodrama tells a story of average people experiencing a crisis in their romantic lives, the resolution of which can be either happy or sad. Characters are generally ruled by one all-consuming wish, are engaged in a single, all-involving situation, and are governed by their emotions. Because they are rarely psychologically complex, the viewer can easily identify with their predicaments.

As men dominated the western, crime, war, horror, and science fiction genres, women were the privileged characters of the melodrama. Often, the central theme was the choice a women had to make between pursuing an independent career or accepting the social codes that mandated she could do so only at the expense of her "true" role as wife and mother—a dilemma faced by many women in American society during the 1930s, 1940s, and 1950s. Sacrificing one for the other was a constant theme in melodramas. In such classic examples as *Stella Dallas* (d. King Vidor, 1937), *Mildred Pierce* (d. Michael Curtiz, 1945), and *Letter from an Unknown Woman* (d. Max Ophuls, 1948), it is a woman's romantic prospects, career, personality, happiness, or misery that structures the narrative. In *Letter from an Unknown Woman*, the woman's centrality to the narrative is reinforced by the director's efforts to recreate the fictional world in accordance with her sensibility and point of view, letting her voice tell her story on the soundtrack while framing shots and using camera movements to express and imitate her emotional states.

Questions to Consider

1. Choose a scene from *Letter from an Unknown Woman* and discuss the means by which the director establishes and reinforces the woman's point of view. How effective are these techniques in helping the viewer enter into the woman's mind? Can a male viewer do this as easily as a female? Why or why not?
2. Recent melodramas include *The Bridges of Madison County* (d. Clint Eastwood, 1995) and *Far from Heaven* (d. Todd Haynes, 2002). Do these films conform to and/or modify the genre? What is the nature of the woman's dilemma in each case? Is the emphasis on her struggle to balance her emotional needs and her sense of social responsibility? How are these issues handled in the film?

Film Noir

Whereas women in melodramas were objects of idealization or pity, women in film noir were usually femmes fatales—deadly creatures who, like Clytemnestra or Medea of

Greek tragedy, lured men to their doom, even at the expense of their own lives and happiness, as retribution for sexual betrayal or rejection.

These films—like their Greek prototypes—involve crime and retribution. The femme fatale is the inverse image of the suffering woman in the melodrama. Classics of this form include *Double Indemnity* (d. Billy Wilder, 1944), *Leave Her to Heaven* (d. John Stahl, 1945), *The Postman Always Rings Twice* (d. Tay Garnett, 1946), and *The Lady from Shanghai* (d. Orson Welles, 1948).

In both the melodrama and film noir, the concept of the woman as goddess was prevalent. Although this was by no means a purely American phenomenon, the Hollywood studios were perhaps the primary manufacturers of this image. From the silent period, when such personalities as Greta Garbo created a sensation, the making and exploitation of the glamorous star was a staple of the Hollywood system. In some melodramas or *films noir*, this often involved a contradiction when actresses with glamorous star appeal (e.g., Joan Crawford, Bette Davis, or Lana Turner) played unglamorous housewives. Just as often, however, the glamorous star was equated with the femme fatale (e.g., Rita Hayworth in *The Lady from Shanghai*), complicating her appeal as well as the moral perspective of the film.

Questions to Consider

1. Popular examples of film noir in recent decades include *Body Heat* (1981, a remake of *Double Indemnity*), *Fatal Attraction* (d. Adrian Lyne, 1987), *Basic Instinct* (d. Paul Verhoeven, 1992), *Mulholland Drive* (d. David Lynch, 2001), and *Femme Fatale* (d. Brian de Palma, 2002)—all of which feature treacherous women who do not always pay for their crimes. Consider any of these films in conjunction with the story of Medea, who avenges herself on several people—and even murders her children—yet escapes "legal" punishment with the help of the gods.
2. Can this trend be tied to any contemporary attitudes toward strong women? Can it be seen as a backlash against feminist thinking and the challenges it posed to male-female relationships?
3. The phenomenon of the movie sex goddess goes back as far as the 1920s, with such female characters as "the vamp." Later examples of the type included such stars as Kim Novak and Marilyn Monroe. Is the "sex goddess" a remnant of the past, or are there actresses in today's films that are deliberately publicized to fit this category? If so, what does this say about today's attitudes and values about sexual stereotyping?

Action and Crime Films

Both *The Silence of the Lambs* and *Thelma and Louise* rework genre formulas. The former pits a young female FBI trainee, Clarice, against an awesome array of assertive male figures who challenge her self-esteem and identity in different ways: There is her dead father, who continues to shape her life and aspirations; the seasoned FBI agents, who challenge her confidence and courage; the psychotic mastermind Hannibal Lecter, who plays mind games that arouse her innermost fears; and finally, the serial killer, who is himself a confusion of genders.

Thelma and Louise takes two working class women whose weekend escape from nagging husband and job turns into an episodic journey across the American landscape that evokes both the western and the road movie, two genres usually dominated by men and masculine ideals. In both genres, the openness of space and the ruggedness of the terrain connote freedom from social constraint and the challenge of the wilderness, two images and themes associated with male characters not only in movies but in American literature (e.g., the novels of James Fenimore Cooper). In both film and literary traditions, the women of those genres are associated with the home, social constrictions, and civilization—the very things Thelma and Louise are trying to escape.

Question to Consider

1. Consider any crime thriller or science fiction film of recent years (e.g., *X-Men, The Matrix, Matrix Reloaded, Terminator 2, Terminator 3, Hulk*) and discuss the concept of role-playing. Is any distinction made between what men and women do vis-à-vis the action in the film? How is love interest integrated with the main action of the film?

CASE STUDIES

All That Heaven Allows

One of the finest examples of the melodrama—made by one of the genre's quintessential practitioners—Douglas Sirk's *All That Heaven Allows* has received extensive attention in the decades since its first release in 1956. It tells the story of a widow named Cary who falls in love with Ron, her young gardener, and must choose between her happiness and the hypocritical outrage the affair generates in her New England upper middle class social set and in her own children. Both groups express repugnance and disrespect, cheapening her affections by suggesting she is only attracted by "a good set of muscles." Film scholars have studied the film for its meticulous yet subtle rendering of a situation faced by many middle-aged women in American society, especially during the 1940s and 1950s, whose loneliness went unnoticed and whose potential for personal growth and happiness diminished every day. Even as a widow with her children grown, she was expected to be loyal to the memory of her dead husband and not tarnish the image of the sacrificing mother.

The woman's dilemma is well defined not only by the script but by the careful attention the director gives to the mise-en-scène. A constant visual motif, for example, is the way Cary is framed through various glass objects: windows, mirrors, and, at one critical point, a television screen. The sense of her being trapped within the very things in her home that constitute her comfortable middle class life is stressed repeatedly by these motifs as well as by the use of color and shadows.

So endearing is the film that two major filmmakers virtually remade it, adapting it to different cultural circumstances and times. German director Rainer Werner Fassbinder's *Ali: Fear Eats the Soul* (1974) is about a German working class widow who falls in love with a migrant Arab worker thirty years younger. Here, the shock effect is intensified by racial difference. More recently, Todd Haynes's *Far from Heaven* (2002; also discussed in Part Four's Film Angles) pays homage to Sirk's film while complicating the situation. The woman is younger and lives what seems to be an exemplary upper middle class life with a successful husband and two young children. When she discovers her husband's homosexuality, her life almost crumbles, and she takes comfort in her gardener, a widowed black man raising a young daughter.

Questions to Consider

1. How is the widow's situation initially presented in *All That Heaven Allows*? Do you get the impression that had the gardener not pursued her, she would have been content living the life she had? Why?
2. Describe the filmmaker's use of mirrors and windows in the Sirk film. What is the story context in each case? How does this framing device enrich our sense of Cary's situation and how she deals with it? How does the television scene fit into this imagery, and what does it add to our impressions?
3. How does Ron's association with nature function as a symbol in the film? What are the details of this association? What is the significance of the references to Thoreau's *Walden* in this context?
4. Look at either the Fassbinder or the Haynes film and compare it as a melodrama to the Sirk film. Sirk's film was made at the height of the melodrama's success in Hollywood, whereas the others are products of more culturally aware times in terms of gender issues. What details of either film's narrative or style reflect this knowledge? Do you think the other versions are better in any way? Why?

The *Alien* Series

The issues of gender and identity have affected other Hollywood genres as well. *Alien*, *Aliens* (d. James Cameron, 1986), and *Alien 3* (d. David Fincher, 1992), for example, demonstrate an important shift in the adventure, science fiction, and horror genres. The films contain and fuse features of these genres, in all three of which men had traditionally been the primary agents of action and women were in the more passive roles of homemaker, helper, or romantic interest.

The protagonist of the *Alien* films is Ripley, a woman whose evolution—from victor over the monster and lone survivor of the space mission in *Alien*, to warrior mother who battles the formidable "bad mother" Alien Queen in *Aliens*, to savior of the human race in *Alien 3*—was a groundbreaking development. By making the woman the heroine of genres in which men were traditionally the heroes and decision makers, the filmmakers radically revised the established formulas of action genres.

An important contributing element to the unity and success of the films is the presence of the same actress in all three. It is impossible to think of Ripley apart from Sigourney Weaver, whose ability to embody physical and psychological strength, maternal feelings, and heroic resolve in the course of the series allowed a character of depth and integrity to emerge convincingly. Ripley not only broke new ground in female incarnations; she is one of the most memorable and original screen creations of the last several decades.

Imagery and symbolism convey important ideas in the films. In *Alien*, the set design gives visual form to many implied but unstated associations between the human body and various artificial simulations. When the film opens, the camera explores a spaceship run entirely by machines while the crew sleeps in incubator-like cavities, dressed in loincloths resembling diapers. Connotations of nesting, birth, and infancy are evoked again on the alien spaceship, where the crew finds the eggs of the creatures in their prenatal state. The cavernous interior of the alien spaceship is even shaped like a huge womb. These links between the organic and nonorganic are epitomized by the alien creature itself, which is a fusion of the metallic and the biological and—with its phallic shape and ability to reproduce—has characteristics of both genders.

Questions to Consider

1. The *Alien* films propose that a woman can be both motherly and soldierly, aggressive and conciliatory, without compromising either function. What assumptions or expectations of the spectator are challenged by these facts? Can this challenge be applied to the way the spectator feels about male and female roles in society?

2. In *Alien* why do we see only parts of the creature, rather than a fully satisfying look at its whole body, until the very end of the movie? Apart from keeping the viewer in suspense, could there be some other reason the director forces us to imagine how the creature's parts ultimately cohere?

3. One reason for the characters' and the spectator's fear in *Alien* is that the creature can effectively conceal itself on the spaceship. What features allow it to do so? What physical aspects of the spaceship does it resemble? How does this relate to the film's overall themes?

4. How is the imagery in *Alien*—especially the allusions to the male and female body— related to the film's genre changes and to the questions of gender and identity?

5. Can you find image patterns in *Aliens* and *Alien 3* similar to the ones in *Alien*? What ideas or aspects of each film's story and theme can they be connected to?

The Hours

Perhaps no figure in literary history embodies the concerns raised by gender studies more importantly than Virginia Woolf, whose novel, *Mrs. Dalloway*, filmed in 1998, inspired Michael Cunningham's novel *The Hours*, made into a successful movie in 2002. *The Hours* relates Woolf's experience as she wrote the book to the lives of two American women—one an unhappy Los Angeles housewife in 1949, the other a contemporary lesbian New York editor. Bridging time periods and cultures, it is a literary tour de force, revealing a continuity of sensibility among women of diverse backgrounds.

The film *The Hours* (d. Stephen Daldry) expands the role of homosexuality subtly implied in *Mrs. Dalloway* by suggesting an affinity directly tied to sexual difference between the lonely novelist haunted by suicide and two of the characters in the other stories: the Los Angeles housewife who tries to kill herself following the surfacing of her repressed desires with a female neighbor and the homosexual writer dying of AIDS.

The thematic structure of *The Hours* relies considerably on framing and editing techniques to telegraph and underline the parallels and similarities the filmmaker wants to show among the three principal female characters. This is noticeable from the beginning, when the film cuts from a shot of Woolf to a shot of the editor making a similar gesture, each one shaking her head over a sink, or from a shot of the editor reaching for a vase that seems to be swept away by the husband of the housewife in the middle story (obviously a different vase). In such ways, the filmmaker sustains the sense of continuity among all three stories and time periods, investing them with a universal quality.

Point of view is another important technique in the film. Narrative voice-over is used, whereby the character of Virginia Woolf speaks aloud lines from *Mrs. Dalloway*, her novel in progress. Normally, such a technique is used when an entire film is being narrated from the point of view of a single character. Given the variance of time periods and places, however, Woolf cannot govern the point of view by speaking in the first person throughout. Nevertheless, she is the central or dominant *consciousness* of the film, the key figure in relation to whom we should understand and judge the others.

As in many films, language plays an important part in *The Hours* because it reflects the class and manners of the characters, many of whom are cultured, educated, and professionally successful. It is conceivable, however, that too refined a use of language can alienate or intimidate the average viewer.

Questions to Consider

1. Do you identify with any of the characters in *The Hours*? Which one? Which features of his or her personality and dilemma facilitate your capacity to identify?
2. Watch a brief scene that includes dialogue from the film. Listen carefully to the tones of the actors' voices and the rhythm of their speaking. What adjectives best describe the diction and speech patterns? What impressions do you form of the characters from these observations? Do they bear directly on gender and identity issues?
3. Are there techniques—visual, audio, or linguistic—that help to bridge the time periods and experiences of the three characters and reinforce the parallels in *The Hours*? How do they add to your appreciation or understanding of the film's themes?
4. In certain sequences from *The Hours*, we hear Woolf's voice over shots or scenes from the other stories—a film technique known as **audio-visual montage**. Select one of these passages and examine closely how the words relate especially to the situations in the other stories. What is the purpose and effect of this technique?

Research Topics

1. Select any classic example of a Hollywood genre—comedy, melodrama, western, crime, horror, musical, or science fiction—and discuss the ways in which it portrays gender roles. What changes in society's attitudes toward gender have occurred since the film was made? Try to re-imagine the same film by making changes in the story or treatment to accommodate the changes you have identified in today's society.
2. The melodramas *All That Heaven Allows* and *Far from Heaven*, made more than forty years apart, present different views of the same decade—the 1950s. Discuss the differences in subject matter, style, point of view, and theme that reflect the period in which each film was made. How is the female protagonist represented in each film? Is she more active than passive in either case? Is the resolution of the story in each case believable?
3. When literature is adapted to the screen, changes are often made because of a concern for how the public image of a star would be affected. (For example, the novel *Letter from an Unknown Woman* is a scathing account of the plight of a woman in turn-of-the-century Vienna who becomes a prostitute to support herself and her fatherless child; but the Hollywood film altered the story because it was thought that audiences would not accept a favorite star playing a prostitute.) Can you think of a film based on a novel that changed the conception or behavior of the female character? Why do you think this was done?
4. Do a close study of a film whose first-person narrator is a woman—for example, *Letter from an Unknown Woman, Mrs. Dalloway* (d. Marleen Gorris, Great Britain, 1998), *Clueless* (d. Amy Heckerling, 1995), or a recent film you've seen. What is the effect of the voice-over technique? Does the woman's voice always confirm and verify what we see, or is there sometimes a disparity between what the voice tells us and what we see? What is the function of this disparity?

5. Seek out one of the film versions of the Greek tragedy *Medea* and compare it with the play. Does the film capture the intensity of the drama? Analyze Medea's character as she appears in both play and film. What features are emphasized in the film version?

6. George Bernard Shaw's play *Pygmalion* was made into a film in 1938 and later into the musical *My Fair Lady*, which was filmed in 1964. Shaw satirized English class structure with a story of a linguistics professor who turns a guttersnipe into a "lady" by educating her outward manners and speech. Examine the play and its film incarnations in two ways: first, in terms of how it sheds light on social standards and on the disparity between a woman's public and private selves; and second, how it works as a contemporary version of the Greek myth of Pygmalion, a legendary king who fell in love with a statue of a beautiful woman who was brought to life by Aphrodite in answer to his prayers.

7. Alfred Hitchcock's *Vertigo* (1958) is a powerful psychological study of a man obsessed with turning a woman into the perfect embodiment of his ideal. Examine the film in terms of how it relates to the Pygmalion myth and speaks to one of the issues addressed by feminist studies concerning the "traditional" male's desire for the perfect woman.

8. Watch and study closely one of the following films—generally faithful to their literary sources—all of which focus on women and social attitudes toward marriage: *The Age of Innocence* (d. Martin Scorsese, 1993), *Portrait of a Lady* (d. Jane Campion, 1996), *Eyes Wide Shut* (d. Stanley Kubrick, Great Britain, 1999), and *The House of Mirth* (d. Terrence Davies, Great Britain, 2000). If possible, read the literary source as well. Then discuss the work in terms of how marriage is represented in the film. What is the principal female character's social position, and what is her view of marriage? Consider the time period that the film depicts. Are there any viewpoints in the film that you think are still viable today? Are there any ideas or situations in the film that you think might have been handled differently if the film had been made fifty years ago?

9. A number of foreign language films over the last decade have dealt openly with gender issues: *Raise the Red Lantern* (d. Zhang Yimou, Hong Kong, 1992), *Leila* (d. Dariush Mehrjui, Iran, 1997), *Kadosh* (d. Amos Gitai, Israel, 2000), *Y Tu Mama Tambien* (d. Alfonso Cuaron, Mexico, 2002), *Talk to Her* (d. Pedro Almodovar, Spain, 2002), and *Late Marriage* (d. Dover Kosashvili, Israel, 2002). Watch and examine two or three of these films and write an essay comparing the different views on women, marriage, and relationships that they represent.

PART THREE

WAR AND VIOLENCE

Fiction

A Mystery of Heroism, Stephen Crane ◆ *The Sniper*, Liam O'Flaherty ◆ *Silence*, Tadeusz Borowski ◆ *The Curse*, André Dubus ◆ *The Things They Carried*, Tim O'Brien ◆ *Like a Winding Sheet*, Ann Petry

Essays

A Brother's Murder, Brent Staples ◆ *Vietnam: What I Remember*, David W. Powell ◆ *Grant and Lee: A Study in Contrasts*, Bruce Catton ◆ *Not Just the Inner City: Well-to-Do Join Gangs*, Seth Mydans

Poetry

Reflection on the Vietnam War Memorial, Jeffrey Harrison ◆ *Facing It*, Yusef Komunyakaa ◆ *The Death of the Ball Turret Gunner*, Randall Jarrell ◆ *The Man He Killed*, Thomas Hardy ◆ *What Were They Like?*, Denise Levertov ◆ *Babiy Yar*, Yevgeny Yevtushenko ◆ *Prisons of Silence*, Janice Mirikitani ◆ *Disabled*, Wilfred Owen ◆ *Waking This Morning*, Muriel Rukeyser ◆ *The Dying Veteran*, Walt Whitman ◆ *The Artilleryman's Vision*, Walt Whitman ◆ *Concord Hymn*, Ralph Waldo Emerson ◆ *The Charge of the Light Brigade*, Alfred, Lord Tennyson ◆ *Idle Hands*, Gabriel Spera ◆ *Kindness*, Gabriel Spera ◆ *The Colonel*, Carolyn Forché ◆ *The Visitor*, Carolyn Forché ◆ The Memory of Elena, Carolyn Forché ◆ *As Children Together*, Carolyn Forché

Drama

Picnic on the Battlefield, Fernando Arrabal ◆ *The Conduct of Life*, Maria Irene Fornes

Why do nations go to war? What causes individuals to engage in violence? What is the relation between power and violence? Why do poets, artists, musicians, and filmmakers create images celebrating the glories of war? What causes so many people to prefer conflict and tension to stability and calm? According to German American social philosopher Hannah Arendt (1906–1975), a major cause of war throughout human history is the conflict between freedom and tyranny. Paul Fussell, an expert on modern warfare, laments: "The drift of modern history seems to imply that the power of the human mind to learn principles of human restraint and reform from modern wars is extremely limited. What people learn from wars seems to be this: the techniques for making each extremely efficient—that is, destructive and vicious." Even more ironic, in the name of freedom, innocent people are tortured, strangled, exiled, and murdered.

Why has the human imagination always been captivated by heroism and the horrors of war? And why do so few literary works celebrate the virtues and possibilities of peace? In his recent book, *War Is a Force That Gives Us Meaning*, Chris Hedges writes that "the myth of war is essential to justify the horrible sacrifices required in war, the destruction and death of innocents." In fact, ordinary people often bear a greater share of the human costs of war than do their leaders who initiate the conflicts. The writers of many of the texts in Part Three try to make sense of a world where violence is perpetrated not only by the horrors of war but also by the racial and ethnic conflicts erupting almost daily in cities throughout the United States and other countries of the world.

The texts in this part pose many questions about the nature and consequences of war and violence. Some, such as Walt Whitman's "The Dying Veteran," celebrate the glory and victory of war, whereas others, such as Wilfred Owen's "Disabled," portray the alienation and rejection experienced by returning veterans who were wounded physically and psychologically in the trench warfare of World War I. Another series of texts here explores the arbitrariness of war by attacking the tradition of the blind hatred of the enemy. Although Thomas Hardy and Denise Levertov belong to different historical moments, each of these poets, in "The Man He Killed" and "What Were They Like?" evokes war's irrationality by attempting to portray the enemy as a human being with a personal and cultural identity. "The Sniper," a story that dramatizes the suspense of an urban guerrilla episode during civil war in Ireland, brings the concern of the "myth of the enemy" even closer to home.

One of the most devastating aspects of World War II was Hitler's attempt to exterminate the Jewish people in the death camps of the Third Reich. In "Silence," by Tadeusz Borowski, you will enter the bizarre world of the concentration camp, a terrifying reminder of human depravity. And in Yevtushenko's "Babiy Yar," written to commemorate the massacre of some thirty-four thousand Jews from Kiev, who were rounded up, stripped, shot one by one, and then tossed into a mass grave, you will share the courageous attempts of the poet to identify with the "enemy"—the Jewish victims of Hitler's massacre. Other contemporary texts in Part Three focus on Latin America, re-creating conditions analogous to those of war: violence, torture, and dictatorship. During the 1980s alone, military right-wing forces took the lives of some eighty thousand people in El Salvador. In her drama The Conduct of Life, Maria Irene Fornes uses the political situations in various right-wing regimes as the backdrop, while poet Carolyn Forché, writing about her experiences as an American human rights advocate in El Salvador, uses her poetry of witness to remind us that the human spirit can sometimes transcend the tortured body.

The Vietnam War and its aftermath is the subject of several texts by Vietnam veterans, including Tim O'Brien, who—in his short story "The Things They Carried"—communicates the soldiers' attitudes toward their war experiences by describing what they are carrying in their pockets and on their shoulders. Poets Jeffrey Harrison and Yusef Komunyakaa record their responses to the Vietnam War Memorial designed by Asian American Maya Lin, while David W. Powell portrays the effects of post-traumatic stress disorder on Vietnam veterans.

It is generally acknowledged that alienation, apathy, and boredom often lead to violence and that violent actions are frequently the result of feeling powerless or excluded. The often gratuitous acts of violence we read about daily are the subjects of "The Curse, "Kindness," and "Idle Hands." Racial violence, also a daily occurrence, is explored in "A Brother's Murder" and "Like a Winding Sheet."

As you ponder the complexities of war and violence in these and other texts, you may find yourself reexamining your presuppositions about them and considering other solutions to conflict. It is difficult to improve on the wisdom of Chris Hedges: "The covenant of love is such that it recognizes both the fragility and the sanctity of the individual. It recognizes itself in the other. It alone can save us."

FICTION

Stephen Crane

A Mystery of Heroism

The dark uniforms of the men were so coated with dust from the incessant wrestling of the two armies that the regiment almost seemed a part of the clay bank which shielded them from the shells. On the top of the hill a battery was arguing in tremendous roars with some other guns, and to the eye of the infantry, the artillerymen, the guns, the caissons, the horses, were distinctly outlined upon the blue sky. When a piece was fired, a red streak as round as a log flashed low in the heavens, like a monstrous bolt of lightning. The men of the battery wore white duck trousers, which somehow emphasized their legs; and when they ran and crowded in little groups at the bidding of the shouting officers, it was more impressive than usual to the infantry.

Fred Collins, of A Company, was saying: "Thunder! I wisht I had a drink. Ain't there any water round here?" Then somebody yelled, "There goes th' bugler!"

As the eyes of half the regiment swept in one machinelike movement there was an instant's picture of a horse in a great convulsive leap of a death wound and a rider leaning back with a crooked arm and spread fingers before his face. On the ground was the crimson terror of an exploding shell, with fibres of flame that seemed like lances. A glittering bugle swung clear of the rider's back as fell headlong the horse and the man. In the air was an odour as from a conflagration.

Sometimes they of the infantry looked down at a fair little meadow which spread at their feet. Its long, green grass was rippling gently in a breeze. Beyond it was the gray form of a house half torn to pieces by shells and by the busy axes of soldiers who had pursued firewood. The line of an old fence was now dimly marked by long weeds and by an occasional post. A shell had blown the well-house to fragments. Little lines of gray smoke ribboning upward from some embers indicated the place where had stood the barn.

From beyond a curtain of green woods there came the sound of some stupendous scuffle, as if two animals of the size of islands were fighting. At a distance there were occasional appearances of swift-moving men, horses, batteries, flags, and with the crashing of infantry volleys were heard, often, wild and frenzied cheers. In the midst of it all Smith and Ferguson, two privates of A Company, were engaged in a heated discussion, which involved the greatest questions of the national existence.

The battery on the hill presently engaged in a frightful duel. The white legs of the gunners scampered this way and that way, and the officers redoubled their shouts. The guns, with their demeanours of stolidity and courage, were typical of something infinitely self-possessed in this clamour of death that swirled around the hill.

One of a "swing" team was suddenly smitten quivering to the ground, and his maddened brethren dragged his torn body in their struggle to escape from this turmoil and danger. A young soldier astride one of the leaders swore and fumed in his saddle, and furiously jerked at the bridle. An officer screamed out an order so violently that his voice broke and ended the sentence in a falsetto shriek.

The leading company of the infantry regiment was somewhat exposed, and the colonel ordered it moved more fully under the shelter of the hill. There was the clank of steel against steel.

A lieutenant of the battery rode down and passed them, holding his right arm carefully in his left hand. And it was as if this arm was not at all a part of him, but belonged to another man. His sober and reflective charger went slowly. The officer's face was grimy and perspiring, and his uniform was tousled as if he had been in direct grapple with an enemy. He smiled grimly when the men stared at him. He turned his horse toward the meadow.

Collins, of A Company, said: "I wisht I had a drink. I bet there's water in that there ol' well yonder!"

"Yes; but how you goin' to git it?"

For the little meadow which intervened was now suffering a terrible onslaught of shells. Its green and beautiful calm had vanished utterly. Brown earth was being flung in monstrous handfuls. And there was a massacre of the young blades of grass. They were being torn, burned, obliterated. Some curious fortune of the battle had made this gentle little meadow the object of the red hate of the shells, and each one as it exploded seemed like an imprecation in the face of a maiden.

The wounded officer who was riding across this expanse said to himself, "Why, they couldn't shoot any harder if the whole army was massed here!"

A shell struck the gray ruins of the house, and as, after the roar, the shattered wall fell in fragments, there was a noise which resembled the flapping of shutters during a wild gale of winter. Indeed, the infantry paused in the shelter of the bank appeared as men standing upon a shore contemplating a madness of the sea. The angel of calamity had under its glance the battery upon the hill. Fewer white-legged men laboured about the guns. A shell had smitten one of the pieces, and after the flare, the smoke, the dust, the wrath of this blow were gone, it was possible to see white legs stretched horizontally on the ground. And at that interval to the rear, where it is the business of battery horses to stand with their noses to the fight awaiting the command to drag their guns out of the destruction or into it or wheresoever these incomprehensible humans demanded with whip and spur—in this line of passive and dumb spectators, whose fluttering hearts yet would not let them forget the iron laws of man's control of them—in this rank of brute-soldiers there had been relentless and hideous carnage. From the ruck of bleeding and prostrate horses, the men of the infantry could see one animal raising its stricken body with its fore legs, and turning its nose with mystic and profound eloquence toward the sky.

Some comrades joked Collins about his thirst. "Well, if yeh want a drink so bad, why don't yeh go git it!"

"Well, I will in a minnet, if yeh don't shut up!"

A lieutenant of artillery floundered his horse straight down the hill with as great concern as it were level ground. As he galloped past the colonel of the infantry, he threw up his hand in swift salute. "We've got to get out of that," he roared angrily. He was a black-bearded officer, and his eyes, which resembled beads, sparkled like those of an insane man. His jumping horse sped along the column of infantry.

The fat major, standing carelessly with his sword held horizontally behind him and with his legs far apart, looked after the receding horseman and laughed. "He wants to get back with orders pretty quick, or there'll be no batt'ry left," he observed.

The wise young captain of the second company hazarded to the lieutenant colonel that the enemy's infantry would probably soon attack the hill, and the lieutenant colonel snubbed him.

A private in one of the rear companies looked out over the meadow, and then turned to a companion and said, "Look there, Jim!" It was the wounded officer from the battery, who some time before had started to ride across the meadow, supporting his right arm carefully with his left hand. This man had encountered a shell apparently at a time when no one perceived him, and he could now be seen lying face downward with a stirruped foot stretched across the body of his dead horse. A leg of the charger extended slantingly upward precisely as stiff as a stake. Around this motionless pair the shells still howled.

There was a quarrel in A Company. Collins was shaking his fist in the faces of some laughing comrades. "Dern yeh! I ain't afraid t' go. If yeh say much, I will go!"

"Oh course, yeh will! You'll run through that there medder, won't yeh?"

Collins said, in a terrible voice, "You see now!" At this ominous threat his comrades broke into renewed jeers.

Collins gave them a dark scowl and went to find his captain. The latter was conversing with the colonel of the regiment.

"Captain," said Collins, saluting and standing at attention—in those days all trousers bagged at the knees—"captain, I want t' get permission to go git some water from that there well over yonder!"

The colonel and the captain swung about simultaneously and stared across the meadow. The captain laughed. "You must be pretty thirsty, Collins?"

"Yes sir, I am."

"Well—ah," said the captain. After a moment he asked, "Can't you wait?"

"No, sir."

The colonel was watching Collins' face. "Look here, my lad," he said, in a pious sort of voice—"look here, my lad"—Collins was not a lad—"don't you think that's taking pretty big risks for a little drink of water?"

"I dunno," said Collins uncomfortably. Some of the resentment toward his companions, which perhaps had forced him into this affair, was beginning to fade. "I dunno whether 'tis."

The colonel and the captain contemplated him for a time.

"Well," said the captain finally.

"Well," said the colonel, "if you want to go, why, go."

Collins saluted. "Much obliged t' yeh."

As he moved away the colonel called after him. "Take some of the other boys' canteens with you an' hurry back now."

"Yes, sir, I will."

The colonel and the captain looked at each other then, for it had suddenly occurred that they could not for the life of them tell whether Collins wanted to go or whether he did not.

They turned to regard Collins, and as they perceived him surrounded by gesticulating comrades, the colonel said: "Well, by thunder! I guess he's going."

Collins appeared as a man dreaming. In the midst of the questions, the advice, the warnings, all the excited talk of his company mates, he maintained a curious silence.

They were very busy in preparing him for his ordeal. When they inspected him carefully it was somewhat like the examination that grooms give a horse before a race; and they were amazed, staggered by the whole affair. Their astonishment found vent in strange repetitions.

"Are yeh sure a-goin'?" they demanded again and again.

"Certainly I am," cried Collins, at last furiously.

He strode sullenly away from them. He was swinging five or six canteens by their cords. It seemed that his cap would not remain firmly on his head, and often he reached up and pulled it down over his brow.

There was a general movement in the compact column. The long animal-like thing moved slightly. Its four hundred eyes were turned upon the figure of Collins.

"Well, sir, if that ain't th' dernest thing! I never thought Fred Collins had the blood in him for that kind of business."

"What's he goin' to do, anyhow?"

"He's goin' to that well there after water."

"We ain't dyin' of thirst, are we? That's foolishness."

"Well, somebody put him up to it, an' he's doin' it."

"Say, he must be a desperate cuss."

When Collins faced the meadow and walked away from the regiment, he was vaguely conscious that a chasm, the deep valley of all prides, was suddenly between him and his comrades. It was provisional, but the provision was that he return as a victor. He had blindly been led by quaint emotions, and laid himself under an obligation to walk squarely up to the face of death.

But he was not sure that he wished to make a retraction, even if he could do so without shame. As a matter of truth, he was sure of very little. He was mainly surprised.

It seemed to him supernaturally strange that he had allowed his mind to manoeuver his body into such a situation. He understood that it might be called dramatically great.

However, he had no full appreciation of anything, excepting that he was actually conscious of being dazed. He could feel his dulled mind grouping after the form and colour of this incident. He wondered why he did not feel some keen agony of fear cutting his sense like a knife. He wondered at this, because human expression had said loudly for centuries that men should feel afraid of certain things, and that all men who did not feel this fear were phenomena— heroes.

He was, then, a hero. He suffered that disappointment which we would all have if we discovered that we were ourselves capable of those deeds which we most admire in history and legend. This, then, was a hero. After all, heroes were not much.

No, it could not be true. He was not a hero. Heroes had no shames in their lives, and, as for him, he remembered borrowing fifteen dollars from a friend and promising to pay it back the next day, and then avoiding that friend for ten months. When at home his mother had aroused him for the early labour of his life on the farm, it had often been his fashion to be irritable, childish, diabolical; and his mother had died since he had come to the war.

He saw that, in this matter of the well, the canteens, the shells, he was an intruder in the land of fine deeds.

He was now about thirty paces from his comrades. The regiment had just turned its many faces toward him.

From the forest of terrific noises there suddenly emerged a little uneven line of men. They fired fiercely and rapidly at distant foliage on which appeared little puffs of white smoke. The spatter of skirmish firing was added to the thunder of the guns on the hill. The little line of men ran forward. A colour sergeant fell flat with his flag as if he had slipped on ice. There was a hoarse cheering from this distant field.

Collins suddenly felt that two demon fingers were pressed into his ears. He could see nothing but flying arrows, flaming red. He lurched from the shock of this explosion, but he made a mad rush for the house, which he viewed as a man submerged to the neck in a boiling surf might view the shore. In the air, little pieces of shell howled and the earthquake explosions drove him insane with the menace of their roar. As he ran the canteens knocked together with a rhythmical tinkling.

As he neared the house, each detail of the scene became vivid to him. He was aware of some bricks of the vanished chimney lying on the sod. There was a door which hung by one hinge.

Rifle bullets called forth by the insistent skirmishers came from the far-off bank of foliage. They mingled with the shells and the pieces of shells until the air was torn in all directions by hootings, yells, howls. The sky was full of fiends who directed all their wild rage at his head.

When he came to the well, he flung himself face downward and peered into its darkness. There were furtive silver glintings some feet from the surface. He grabbed one of the canteens and, unfastening its cap, swung it down by the cord. The water flowed slowly in with an indolent gurgle.

And now as he lay with his face turned away he was suddenly smitten with the terror. It came upon his heart like the grasp of claws. All the power faded from his muscles. For an instant he was no more than a dead man.

The canteen filled with maddening slowness, in the manner of all bottles. Presently he recovered his strength and addressed a screaming oath to it. He leaned over until it seemed as if he intended to try to push water into it with his hands. His eyes as he gazed down into the well shone like two pieces of metal and in their expression was a great appeal and a great curse. The stupid water derided him.

There was the blaring thunder of a shell. Crimson light shone through the swift-boiling smoke and made a pink reflection on part of the wall of the well. Collins jerked out his arm and canteen with the same motion that a man would use in withdrawing his head from a furnace.

He scrambled erect and glared and hesitated. On the ground near him lay the old well bucket, with a length of rusty chain. He lowered it swiftly into the well. The bucket struck the water and then, turning lazily over, sank. When, with hand reaching tremblingly over hand, he hauled it out, it knocked often against the walls of the well and spilled some of its contents.

In running with a filled bucket, a man can adopt but one kind of gait. So through this terrible field over which screamed practical angels of death Collins ran in the manner of a farmer chased out of a dairy by a bull.

His face went staring white with anticipation—anticipation of a blow that would whirl him around and down. He would fall as he had seen other men fall, the life knocked out of them so suddenly that their knees were no more quick to touch the ground than their heads. He saw the long blue line of the regiment, but his comrades were standing looking at him from the edge of an impossible star. He was aware of some deep wheel ruts and hoofprints in the sod beneath his feet.

The artillery officer who had fallen in this meadow had been making groans in the teeth of the tempest of sound. These futile cries, wrenched from him by his agony, were heard only by shells, bullets. When wild-eyed Collins came running, this officer raised himself. His face contorted and blanched from pain, he was about to utter some great beseeching cry. But suddenly his face straightened and he called: "Say, young man, give me a drink of water, will you?"

Collins had no room amid his emotions for surprise. He was mad from the threats of destruction.

"I can't," he screamed, and in his reply was a full description of his quaking apprehension. His cap was gone and his hair was riotous. His clothes made it appear that he had been dragged over the ground by the heels. He ran on.

The officer's head sank down and one elbow crooked. His foot in its brass bound stirrup still stretched over the body of his horse and the other leg was under the steed.

But Collins turned. He came dashing back. His face had now turned gray and in his eyes was all terror. "Here it is! here it is!"

The officer was as a man gone in drink. His arm bent like a twig. His head drooped as if his neck were of willow. He was sinking to the ground, to lie face downward.

Collins grabbed him by the shoulder. "Here it is. Here's your drink. Turn over. Turn over, man, for God's sake!"

With Collins hauling at his shoulder, the officer twisted his body and fell with his face turned toward that region where lived the unspeakable noises of the swirling missiles. There was the faintest shadow of a smile on his lips as he looked at Collins. He gave a sigh, a little primitive breath like that from a child.

Collins tried to hold the bucket steady, but his shaking hands caused the water to splash all over the face of the dying man. Then he jerked it away and ran on.

The regiment gave him a welcoming roar. The grimed faces were wrinkled in laughter.

His captain waved the bucket away. "Give it to the men!"

The two genial, skylarking young lieutenants were the first to gain possession of it. They played over it in their fashion.

When one tried to drink the other teasingly knocked his elbow. "Don't, Billie! You'll make me spill it," said the one. The other laughed.

Suddenly there was an oath, the thud of wood on the ground, and a swift murmur of astonishment among the ranks. The two lieutenants glared at each other. The bucket lay on the ground empty.

[1896]

Journal Entry

Brainstorm on your associations with "heroism." Do you aspire to heroism? Why or why not?

Textual Considerations

1. In the opening paragraph, Crane contrasts the dark silhouettes on the hill of the artillerymen, the guns, the caissons, and the horses with the blue sky. He further contrasts the red streak from the fired ammunition with the white duck trousers of the battery men. At what other point in the story does Crane use color contrast to represent battle scenes? To what effect?
2. Irony is a key element in this text. Cite some particularly ironic actions in the narrative, and discuss their significance in relation to your understanding of the text's meaning and tone.
3. Reflect on the significance of the text's title. How does Crane define heroism—as an individual value or a social action dictated by circumstances? To what extent does Crane explain the "mystery"?
4. Speculate on the motives that trigger Collins' act of heroism.
5. Construct a profile of Fred Collins. Chart the stages in his feelings about his fellow soldiers, as well as his thoughts about heroism. Does he consider himself heroic? Why does he stop to give water to the dying lieutenant? Is this a heroic act? Explain.

Cultural Contexts

1. The "myth of war" is essential to justify the horrible sacrifices required in war—the destruction and the death of innocents. Debate this concept with your group. How does it apply to Crane's story? Summarize your finding.
2. Crane served as a war correspondent during the Spanish-American war and his war stories reflect his desire to shatter the beliefs of those who view war as heroic. Are there dangers in glorifying war? Explain.

Liam O'Flaherty

The Sniper

The long June twilight faded into night. Dublin lay enveloped in darkness but for the dim light of the moon that shone through fleecy clouds, casting a pale light as of approaching dawn over the streets and the dark waters of the Liffey. Around the beleaguered Four Courts the heavy guns roared. Here and there through the city, machine-guns and rifles broke the silence of the night, spasmodically, like dogs barking on lone farms. Republicans and Free Staters were waging civil war.

On a roof-top near O'Connell Bridge, a Republican sniper lay watching. Beside him lay his rifle and over his shoulders were slung a pair of field glasses. His face was the face of a student, thin and ascetic, but his eyes had the cold gleam of the fanatic. They were deep and thoughtful, the eyes of a man who is used to looking at death.

He was eating a sandwich hungrily. He had eaten nothing since morning. He had been too excited to eat. He finished the sandwich, and, taking a flask of whiskey from his pocket, he took a short draught. Then he returned the flask to his pocket. He paused for a moment, considering whether he should risk a smoke. It was dangerous. The flash might be seen in the darkness and there were enemies watching. He decided to take the risk.

Placing a cigarette between his lips, he struck a match. There was a flash and a bullet whizzed over his head. He dropped immediately. He had seen the flash. It came from the opposite side of the street.

He rolled over the roof to a chimney stack in the rear, and slowly drew himself up behind it, until his eyes were level with the top of the parapet. There was nothing to be seen—just the dim outline of the opposite housetop against the blue sky. His enemy was under cover.

Just then an armored car came across the bridge and advanced slowly up the street. It stopped on the opposite of the street, fifty yards ahead. The sniper could hear the dull panting of the motor. His heart beat faster. It was an enemy car. He wanted to fire, but he knew it was useless. His bullets would never pierce the steel that covered the gray monster.

Then round the corner of a side street came an old woman, her head covered by a tattered shawl. She began to talk to the man in the turret of the car. She was pointing to the roof where the sniper lay. An informer.

The turret opened. A man's head and shoulders appeared, looking toward the sniper. The sniper raised his rifle and fired. The head fell heavily on the turret wall. The woman darted toward the side street. The sniper fired again. The woman whirled round and fell with a shriek into the gutter.

Suddenly from the opposite roof a shot rang out and the sniper dropped his rifle with a curse. The rifle clattered to the roof. The sniper thought the noise would wake the dead. He stopped to pick the rifle up. He couldn't lift it. His forearm was dead.

"Christ," he muttered, "I'm hit."

Dropping flat onto the roof, he crawled back to the parapet. With his left hand he felt the injured right forearm. There was no pain—just a deadened sensation, as if the arm had been cut off.

Quickly he drew his knife from his pocket, opened it on the breast-work of the parapet, and ripped open the sleeve. There was a small hole where the bullet had entered. On the other side there was no hole. The bullet had lodged in the bone. It must have fractured it. He bent the arm below the wound. The arm bent back easily. He ground his teeth to overcome the pain.

Then taking out the field dressing, he ripped open the packet with his knife. He broke the neck of the iodine bottle and let the bitter fluid drip into the wound. A paroxysm of pain swept through him. He placed the cotton wadding over the wound and wrapped the dressing over it. He tied the ends with his teeth.

Then he lay against the parapet, and, closing his eyes, he made an effort of will to overcome the pain.

In the street beneath all was still. The armored car had retired speedily over the bridge, with the machine-gunner's head hanging lifelessly over the turret. The woman's corpse lay still in the gutter.

The sniper lay still for a long time nursing his wounded arm and planning escape. Morning must not find him wounded on the roof. The enemy on the opposite roof covered his escape. He must kill that enemy and he could not use his rifle. He had only a revolver to do it. Then he thought of a plan.

Taking off his cap, he placed it over the muzzle of his rifle. Then he pushed the rifle slowly over the parapet, until the cap was visible from the opposite side of the street. Almost immediately there was a report, and a bullet pierced the center of the cap. The sniper slanted the rifle forward. The cap slipped down into the street. Then catching the rifle in the middle, the sniper dropped his left hand over the roof and let it hang, lifelessly. After a few moments he let the rifle drop to the street. Then he sank to the roof, dragging his hand with him.

Crawling quickly to the left, he peered up at the corner of the roof. His ruse had succeeded. The other sniper, seeing the cap and rifle fall, thought he had killed his man. He was now standing before a row of chimney pots, looking across, with his head clearly silhouetted against the western sky.

The Republican sniper smiled and lifted his revolver above the edge of the parapet. The distance was about fifty yards—a hard shot in the dim light, and his right arm was paining him like a thousand devils. He took a steady aim. His hand trembled with eagerness. Pressing his lips together, he took a deep breath through his nostrils and fired. He was almost deafened with the report and his arm shook with the recoil.

Then when the smoke cleared he peered across and uttered a cry of joy. His enemy had been hit. He was reeling over the parapet in his death agony. He struggled to keep his feet, but he was slowly falling forward, as if in a dream. The rifle fell from his grasp, hit the parapet, fell over, bounded off the pole of a barber's shop beneath and then clattered on the pavement.

Then the dying man on the roof crumpled up and fell forward. The body turned over and over in space and hit the ground with a dull thud. Then it lay still.

The sniper looked at his enemy falling and he shuddered. The lust of battle died in him. He became bitten by remorse. The sweat stood out in beads on his forehead. Weakened by his wound and the long summer day of fasting and watching on the roof, he revolted from the sight of the shattered mass of his dead enemy. His teeth chattered, he began to gibber to himself, cursing the war, cursing himself, cursing everybody.

He looked at the smoking revolver in his hand, and with an oath he hurled it to the roof at his feet. The revolver went off with the concussion and the bullet whizzed past the sniper's head. He was frightened back to his senses by the shock. His nerves steadied. The cloud of fear scattered from his mind and he laughed.

Taking the whiskey flask from his pocket, he emptied it at a draught. He felt reckless under the influence of the spirit. He decided to leave the roof now and look for his company commander, to report. Everywhere around was quiet. There was not much danger in going through the streets. He picked up his revolver and put it in his pocket. Then he crawled down through the sky-light to the house underneath.

When the sniper reached the laneway on the street level, he felt a sudden curiosity as to the identity of the enemy sniper whom he had killed. He decided that he was a good shot, whoever he was. He wondered did he know him. Perhaps he had been in his own company before the split in the army. He decided to risk going over to have a look at him. He peered round the corner into O'Connell Street. In the upper part of the street there was heavy firing, but around here all was quiet.

The sniper darted across the street. A machine-gun tore up the ground around him with a hail of bullets, but he escaped. He threw himself face downward beside the corpse. The machine-gun stopped.

Then the sniper turned over the dead body and looked into his brother's face.

[1923]

Journal Entry

Under what circumstances, if any, can you imagine killing your brother?

Textual Considerations

1. Analyze the opening paragraph of the story to discuss setting and atmosphere. How does O'Flaherty use setting in the opening paragraph and throughout the story?
2. Observe O'Flaherty's frequent use of irony in "The Sniper," and analyze its effects on the story's meaning, style, and tone. Cite examples from the text.
3. Investigate the effects of the narrative **point of view** on the development of the story. To what extent does the narrator's stance affect your evaluation of the sniper? Is the sniper given a voice of his own in the story? Explain.

4. Chart the stages in the sniper's responses to his situation, and evaluate their plausibility. Argue whether he is a political "fanatic" as the text suggests, or whether the reader can detect glimpses of his humanity behind his political commitment as a sniper.

5. Identify some of the internal and external actions in the plot development of the story. How does O'Flaherty combine both actions? What role does the "old woman" play in the story? Explain the meaning of the narrator's final words about the woman.

Cultural Contexts

1. To what extent do you share the sniper's fanatic commitment to a political cause? Argue in favor of or against the position he takes to become a sniper. You may engage in an imaginary dialogue with him about his commitment.

2. Working with your group, examine how the violence of civil wars, like that of the war between the Republicans and the Free Staters in Ireland (1921), compare to the violence that results from war among nations. Can your group reach a consensus about whether young people today are willing to die for their country or their religion?

Tadeusz Borowski

Silence

At last they seized him inside the German barracks, just as he was about to climb over the window ledge. In absolute silence they pulled him down to the floor and panting with hate dragged him into a dark alley. Here, closely surrounded by a silent mob, they began tearing at him with greedy hands.

Suddenly from the camp gate a whispered warning was passed from one mouth to another. A company of soldiers, their bodies leaning forward, their rifles on the ready, came running down the camp's main road, weaving between the clusters of men in stripes standing in the way. The crowd scattered and vanished inside the blocks. In the packed, noisy barracks the prisoners were cooking food pilfered during the night from neighbouring farmers. In the bunks and in the passageways between them, they were grinding grain in small flour-mills, slicing meat on heavy slabs of wood, peeling potatoes and throwing the peels on to the floor. They were playing cards for stolen cigars, stirring batter for pancakes, gulping down hot soup, and lazily killing fleas. A stifling odour of sweat hung in the air, mingled with the smell of food, with smoke and with steam that liquefied along the ceiling beams and fell on the men, the bunks and the food in large, heavy drops, like autumn rain.

There was a stir at the door. A young American officer with a tin helmet on his head entered the block and looked with curiosity at the bunks and the tables. He wore a freshly pressed uniform; his revolver was hanging down, strapped in an open holster that dangled against his thigh. He was assisted by the translator who wore a yellow band reading "interpreter" on the sleeve of his civilian coat, and by the chairman of the Prisoners' Committee, dressed in a white summer coat, a pair of tuxedo trousers and tennis shoes. The men in the barracks fell silent. Leaning out of their bunks and lifting their eyes from the kettles, bowls and cups, they gazed attentively into the officer's face.

"Gentlemen," said the officer with a friendly smile, taking off his helmet—and the interpreter proceeded at once to translate sentence after sentence—"I know, of course, that after what you have gone through and after what you have seen, you must feel a deep hate for your tormentors. But we, the soldiers of America, and you, the people of Europe, have fought so that law should prevail over lawlessness. We must show our respect for the law. I assure you that the guilty will be punished, in this camp as well as in all the others. You have already seen, for example, that the S.S. men were made to bury the dead."

". . . right, we could use the lot at the back of the hospital. A few of them are still around," whispered one of the men in a bottom bunk.

". . . or one of the pits," whispered another. He sat straddling the bunk, his fingers firmly clutching the blanket.

"Shut up! Can't you wait a little longer? Now listen to what the American has to say," a third man, stretched across the foot of the same bunk, spoke in an angry whisper. The American officer was now hidden from their view behind the thick crowd gathered at the other end of the block.

"Comrades, our new Kommandant gives you his word of honour that all the criminals of the S.S. as well as among the prisoners will be punished," said the translator. The men in the bunks broke into applause and shouts. In smiles and gestures they tried to convey their friendly approval of the young man from across the ocean.

"And so the Kommandant requests," went on the translator, his voice turning somewhat hoarse, "that you try to be patient and do not commit lawless deeds, which may only lead to trouble, and please pass the sons of bitches over to the camp guards. How about it, men?"

The block answered with a prolonged shout. The American thanked the translator and wished the prisoners a good rest and an early reunion with their dear ones. Accompanied by a friendly hum of voices, he left the block and proceeded to the next.

Not until after he had visited all the blocks and returned with the soldiers to his headquarters did we pull our man off the bunk—where covered with blankets and half-smothered with the weight of our bodies he lay gagged, his face buried in the straw mattress—and dragged him on to the cement floor under the stove, where the entire block, grunting and growling with hatred, trampled him to death.

[1967]

Journal Entry

Respond to the setting of the concentration camp in "Silence." Imagine yourself in the place of the survivors.

Textual Considerations

1. Explore the thematic nuances of the story's title. Consider, for example, the effects of juxtaposing the silence of the concentration camp survivors with the speech of the young American officer through his interpreter.
2. Review the story carefully, and discuss how Borowski uses the physical appearance and language of the survivors to reinforce their psychic distance from the outside world.
3. How successful is "Silence" in portraying not only the narrator's realistic re-creation of a concentration camp but also his disillusionment and horror of war?
4. Analyze what "Silence" conveys about the survivors' need for revenge. Consider, too, what the text implies about the ability of the young American officer and other non-inmates to judge the actions of the inmates.
5. Use arguments from the text to support or challenge the thesis that in killing one of their former oppressors, the inmates in "Silence" perpetuate the violence that victimized them.

Cultural Contexts

1. Review Borowski's brief biography on page 1103 of this text. Then reread the story. What new insights did you discover? Can you imagine how you might behave in a place like Auschwitz? Use your journal entry to help you assess your viewpoint about this issue.
2. Working with your group, respond to the statement: "There is nothing one man will not do to another." Can you reach a consensus about this issue?

André Dubus

The Curse

Mitchell Hayes was forty-nine years old, but when the cops left him in the bar with Bob, the manager, he felt much older. He did not know what it was like to be very old, a shrunken and wrinkled man, but he assumed it was like this: fatigue beyond relieving by rest, by sleep. He also was not a small man. His weight moved up and down in the 170s, and he was five feet, ten inches tall. But now his body seemed short and thin. Bob stood at one end of the bar; he was a large, black-haired man, and there was nothing in front of him but an ashtray he was using. He looked at Mitchell at the cash register and said, "Forget it. You heard what Smitty said."

Mitchell looked away, at the front door. He had put the chairs upside down on the tables. He looked from the door past Bob to the empty space of floor at the rear; sometimes people danced there, to the jukebox. Opposite Bob, on the wall behind the bar, was a telephone; Mitchell looked at it. He had told Smitty there were five guys, and when he moved to the phone, one of them stepped around the corner of the bar and shoved him, one hand against Mitchell's chest, and it pushed him backward; he nearly fell. That was when they were getting rough with her at the bar. When they took her to the floor, Mitchell looked once toward her sounds, then looked down at the duckboard he stood on, or at the belly or chest of a young man in front of him.

He knew they were not drunk. They had been drinking before they came to his place, a loud popping of motorcycles outside, then walking into the empty bar, young and sunburned and carrying helmets and wearing thick leather jackets in August. They stood in front of Mitchell and drank drafts. When he took their first order, he thought they were on drugs, and later, watching them, he was certain. They were not relaxed in the way of most drinkers near closing time. Their eyes were quick, alert as wary animals, and they spoke loudly, with passion, but their passion was strange and disturbing, because they were only chatting, bantering. Mitchell knew nothing of the effects of drugs, so could not guess what was in their blood. He feared and hated drugs because of his work and because he was the stepfather of teenagers: a boy and a girl. He gave last call and served them and leaned against the counter behind him.

Then the door opened and the girl walked in from the night, a girl he had never seen, and she crossed the floor toward Mitchell. He stepped forward to tell her she had missed last call; but before he spoke, she asked for change for the cigarette machine. She was young—he guessed nineteen to twenty-one—and deeply tanned and had dark hair. She was sober and wore jeans and a dark-blue T-shirt. He gave her the quarters, but she was standing between two of the men and she did not get to the machine.

When it was over and she lay crying on the cleared circle of floor, he left the bar and picked up the jeans and T-shirt beside her and crouched and handed them to her. She did not look at him. She laid the clothes across her breasts and what Mitchell thought of now as her wound. He left her and dialed 911, then Bob's number. He woke up Bob. Then he picked up her sneakers from the floor and placed them beside her and squatted near her face, her crying. He wanted to speak to her and touch her, hold a hand or press her brow, but he could not.

The cruiser was there quickly, the siren coming east from town, then slowing and deepening as the car stopped outside. He was glad Smitty was one of them; he had gone to high school with Smitty. The other was Dave, and Mitchell knew him because it was a small town. When they saw the girl, Dave went out to the cruiser to call for an ambulance; and when he came back, he said two other cruisers had those scumbags and were taking them in. The girl was still crying and could not talk to Smitty and Dave. She was crying when a man and a woman lifted her onto a stretcher and rolled her out the door and she vanished forever in a siren.

Bob came in while Smitty and Dave were sitting at the bar drinking coffee and Smitty was writing his report; Mitchell stood behind the bar. Bob sat next to Dave as Mitchell said, "I could have stopped them, Smitty."

"That's our job," Smitty said. "You want to be in the hospital now?"

Mitchell did not answer. When Smitty and Dave left, he got a glass of Coke from the cobra and had a cigarette with Bob. They did not talk. Then Mitchell washed his glass and Bob's cup and they left, turning off the lights. Outside, Mitchell locked the front door, feeling the sudden night air after almost ten hours of air conditioning. When he had come to work, the day had been very hot, and now he thought it would not have happened in winter. They had stopped for a beer on their way somewhere from the beach; he had heard them say that. But the beach was not the reason. He did not know the reason, but he knew it would not have happened in winter. The night was cool, and now he could smell trees. He turned and looked at the road in front of the bar. Bob stood beside him on the small porch.

"If the regulars had been here . . ." Bob said.

He turned and with his hand resting on the wooden rail, he walked down the ramp to the ground. At his car, he stopped and looked over its roof at Mitchell.

"You take it easy," he said.

Mitchell nodded. When Bob got into his car and left, he went down the ramp and drove home to his house on a street that he thought was neither good nor bad. The houses were small, and there were old large houses used now as apartments for families. Most of the people had work, most of the mothers cared for their children and most of the children were clean and looked like they lived in homes, not caves like some he saw in town. He worried about the older kids, one group of them, anyway. They were idle. When he was a boy in a town farther up the Merrimack River, he and his friends committed every mischievous act he could recall on afternoons and nights when they were idle. His stepchildren were not part of that group. They had friends from the high school. The front-porch light was on for him and one in the kitchen at the rear of the house. He went in the front door and switched off the porch light and walked through the living and dining rooms to the kitchen. He got a can of beer from the refrigerator, turned out the light, and sat at the table. When he could see, he took a cigarette from Susan's pack in front of him.

Down the hall, he heard Susan move on the bed, then get up, and he hoped it wasn't for the bathroom but for him. He had met her eight years ago, when he had given up on ever marrying and having kids; then, one night, she came into the bar with two of her girlfriends from work. She made six dollars an hour going to homes of invalids, mostly what she called her little old ladies, and bathing them. She got the house from her marriage, and child support the guy paid for a few months till he left town and went south. She came barefoot down the hall and stood in the kitchen doorway and said, "Are you all right?"

"No."

She sat across from him, and he told her. Very soon, she held his hand. She was good. He knew if he had fought all five of them and was lying in pieces in the hospital bed, she would tell him he had done the right thing, as she was telling him now. He liked her strong hand on his. It was a professional hand, and he wanted from her something he had never wanted before: to lie in bed while she bathed him. When they went to bed, he did not think he would be able to sleep, but she knelt beside him and massaged his shoulders and rubbed his temples and pressed her hands on his forehead. He woke to the voices of Marty and Joyce in the kitchen. They had summer jobs, and always when they woke him, he went back to sleep till noon, but now he got up and dressed and went to the kitchen door. Susan was at the stove, her back to him, and Marty and Joyce were talking and smoking. He said, "Good morning," and stepped into the room.

"What are you doing up?" Joyce said.

She was a pretty girl with her mother's wide cheekbones, and Marty was a tall, good-looking boy, and Mitchell felt as old as he had before he slept. Susan was watching him. Then she poured him a cup of coffee and put it at his place and he sat. Marty said, "You getting up for the day?"

"Something happened last night. At the bar." They tried to conceal their excitement, but he saw it in their eyes. "I should have stopped it. I think I *could* have stopped it. That's the point. There were these five guys. They were on motorcycles, but they weren't bikers. Just punks. They came in late, when everybody else had gone home. It was a slow night, anyway. Everybody was at the beach."

"They rob you?" Marty asked.

"No. A girl came in. Young. Nice-looking. You know: just a girl, minding her business."

They nodded, and their eyes were apprehensive.

"She wanted cigarette change; that's all. Those guys were on dope. Coke or something. You know: They were flying in place."

"Did they rape her?" Joyce said.

"Yes, honey."

"The *fuck*ers."

Susan opened her mouth, then closed it, and Joyce reached quickly for Susan's pack of cigarettes. Mitchell held his lighter for her and said, "When they started getting rough with her at the bar, I went for the phone. One of them stopped me. He shoved me; that's all. I should have hit him with a bottle."

Marty reached over the table with his big hand and held Mitchell's shoulder.

"No, Mitch. Five guys that mean. And coked up or whatever. No way. You wouldn't be here this morning."

"I don't know. There was always a guy with me. But just one guy, taking turns."

"Great," Joyce said. Marty's hand was on Mitchell's left shoulder; she put hers on his right hand.

"They took her to the hospital," he said. "The guys are in jail."

"They are?" Joyce said.

"I called the cops. When they left."

"You'll be a good witness," Joyce said.

He looked at her proud face.

"At the trial," she said.

The day was hot, but that night, most of the regulars came to the bar. Some of the younger ones came on motorcycles. They were a good crowd: They all worked, except the retired ones, and no one ever bothered the women, not even the young ones with their summer tans. Everyone talked about it: Some had read the newspaper story, some had heard the story in town, and they wanted to hear it from Mitchell. He told it as often as they asked, but he did not finish it, because he was working hard and could not stay with any group of customers long enough.

He watched their faces. Not one of them, even the women, looked at him as if he had not cared enough for the girl or was a coward. Many of them even appeared sympathetic, making him feel for moments that he was a survivor of something horrible; and when that feeling left him, he was ashamed. He felt tired and old, making drinks and change, talking and moving up and down the bar. At the stool at the far end, Bob drank coffee; and whenever Mitchell looked at him, he smiled or nodded and once raised his right fist, with the thumb up.

Reggie was drinking too much. He did that two or three times a month, and Mitchell had to shut him off, and Reggie always took it humbly. He was a big, gentle man with a long brown beard. But tonight, shutting off Reggie demanded from Mitchell an act of will, and when the eleven-o'clock news came on the television and Reggie ordered another shot and a draft, Mitchell pretended not to hear him. He served the customers at the other end of the bar, where Bob was. He could hear Reggie calling, "Hey, Mitch; shot and a draft, Mitch."

Mitchell was close to Bob now. Bob said softly, "He's had enough."

Mitchell nodded and went to Reggie, leaned closer to him, so he could speak quietly, and said, "Sorry, Reggie. Time for coffee. I don't want you dead out there."

Reggie blinked at him.

"OK, Mitch." He pulled some bills from his pocket and put them on the bar. Mitchell glanced at them and saw at least a ten-dollar tip. When he ran up Reggie's tab, the change was $16.50, and he dropped the coins and shoved the bills into the beer mug beside the cash register. The mug was full of bills, as it was on most nights, and he kept his hand in there, pressing Reggie's into the others, and saw the sunburned young men holding her down on the floor and one kneeling between her legs, spread and held, and he heard their cheering voices and her screaming and groaning and finally weeping and weeping and weeping, until she was the siren crying, then fading into the night. From the floor behind him, far across the room, he felt her pain and terror and grief, then her curse upon him. The curse moved into his back and spread down and up his spine, into his stomach and legs and arms and shoulders until he quivered with it. He wished he were alone so he could kneel to receive it.

[1988]

Journal Entry

How is it possible to be a rape victim without being raped?

Textual Considerations

1. Analyze Mitchell's character. Do you think he did the right thing? Explain.
2. Do you agree with his family and friends that his intervention would have accomplished nothing? Why or why not?
3. How does the author's choice of an omniscient narrator affect the meaning and tone of the story?
4. Why do we find out so little about the girl?
5. Review the last paragraph. What does it reveal about Mitchell's psychological state? How does it reinforce the implications of the story's title?

Cultural Contexts

1. Dubus wrote this story while recovering from an automobile accident that occurred when he stopped to help a woman with a flat tire. He was hit by a car and lost a leg. What new meanings does this biographical information add to your understanding of the text?

2. Discuss with your group the effects of being a witness to violence. To what extent should people get involved? Is action or inaction more likely to result in some psychological suffering for the witness? How might you have responded in Mitchell's situation?

Tim O'Brien

The Things They Carried

First Lieutenant Jimmy Cross carried letters from a girl named Martha, a junior at Mount Sebastian College in New Jersey. They were not love letters, but Lieutenant Cross was hoping, so he kept them folded in plastic at the bottom of his rucksack. In the late afternoon, after a day's march, he would dig his foxhole, wash his hands under a canteen, unwrap the letters, hold them with the tips of his fingers, and spend the last hour of light pretending. He would imagine romantic camping trips into the White Mountains in New Hampshire. He would sometimes taste the envelope flaps, knowing her tongue had been there. More than anything, he wanted Martha to love him as he loved her, but the letters were mostly chatty, elusive on the matter of love. She was a virgin, he was almost sure. She was an English major at Mount Sebastian, and she wrote beautifully about her professors and roommates and midterm exams, about her respect for Chaucer and her great affection for Virginia Woolf. She often quoted lines of poetry; she never mentioned the war, except to say, Jimmy, take care of yourself. The letters weighed ten ounces. They were signed "Love, Martha," but Lieutenant Cross understood that "Love" was only a way of signing and did not mean what he sometimes pretended it meant. At dusk, he would carefully return the letters to his rucksack. Slowly, a bit distracted, he would get up and move among his men, checking the perimeter, then at full dark he would return to his hole and watch the night and wonder if Martha was a virgin.

The things they carried were largely determined by necessity. Among the necessities or near necessities were P-38 can openers, pocket knives, heat tabs, wrist watches, dog tags, mosquito repellent, chewing gum, candy, cigarettes, salt tablets, packets of Kool-Aid, lighters, matches, sewing kits, Military Payment Certificates, C rations, and two or three canteens of water. Together, these items weighed between fifteen and twenty pounds, depending upon a man's habits or rate of metabolism. Henry Dobbins, who was a big man, carried extra rations; he was especially fond of canned peaches in heavy syrup over pound cake. Dave Jensen, who practiced field hygiene, carried a toothbrush, dental floss, and several hotel-size bars of soap he'd stolen on R&R in Sydney, Australia. Ted Lavender, who was scared, carried tranquilizers until he was shot in the head outside the village of Than Khe in mid-April.

By necessity, and because it was SOP,[1] they all carried steel helmets that weighed five pounds including the liner and camouflage cover. They carried the standard fatigue jackets and trousers. Very few carried underwear. On their feet they carried jungle boots—2.1 pounds—and Dave Jensen carried three pairs of socks and a can of Dr. Scholl's foot powder as a precaution against trench foot. Until he was shot, Ted Lavender carried six or seven ounces of premium dope, which for him was a necessity. Mitchell Sanders, the RTO,[2] carried condoms. Norman Bowker carried a diary. Rat Kiley carried comic books. Kiowa, a devout Baptist, carried an illustrated New Testament that had been presented to him by his father, who taught Sunday school in Oklahoma City, Oklahoma. As a hedge against bad times, however, Kiowa also carried his grandmother's distrust of the white man, his grandfather's old hunting hatchet. Necessity dictated. Because the land was mined and booby-trapped, it was SOP for each man to carry a steel-centered, nylon-covered flak jacket, which weighed 6.7 pounds, but which on hot days seemed much heavier. Because you could die so quickly, each man carried at least one large compress bandage, usually in the helmet band for easy access. Because the nights were cold, and because the monsoons were wet, each carried a green plastic poncho that could be used as a raincoat or ground sheet or makeshift tent. With its quilted liner, the poncho weighed almost two pounds, but it was worth every ounce. In April, for instance, when Ted Lavender was shot, they used his poncho to wrap him up, then to carry him across the paddy, then to lift him into the chopper that took him away.

They were called legs or grunts.

To carry something was to "hump" it, as when Lieutenant Jimmy Cross humped his love for Martha up the hills and through the swamps. In its intransitive form, "to hump" meant "to walk," or "to march," but it implied burdens far beyond the intransitive.

Almost everyone humped photographs. In his wallet, Lieutenant Cross carried two photographs of Martha. The first was a Kodachrome snapshot signed "Love," though he knew better. She stood against a brick wall. Her eyes were gray and neutral, her lips slightly open as she stared straight-on at the camera. At night, sometimes, Lieutenant Cross wondered who had taken the picture, because he knew she had boyfriends, because he loved her so much, and because he could see the shadow of the picture taker spreading out against the brick wall. The second photograph had been clipped from the 1968 Mount Sebastian yearbook. It was an action shot—women's volleyball—and Martha was bent horizontal to the floor, reaching, the palms of her hands in sharp focus, the tongue taut, the expression frank and competitive. There was no visible sweat. She wore white gym shorts. Her legs, he thought, were almost certainly the legs of a virgin, dry and without hair, the left knee cocked and carrying her entire weight, which was just over one hundred pounds. Lieutenant Cross remembered touching that left knee. A dark theater, he remembered, and the movie was *Bonnie and Clyde*, and Martha wore a tweed skirt, and

---

[1] Standard operating procedure.
[2] Radiotelephone operator.

during the final scene, when he touched her knee, she turned and looked at him in a sad, sober way that made him pull his hand back, but he would always remember the feel of the tweed skirt and the knee beneath it and the sound of the gunfire that killed Bonnie and Clyde, how embarrassing it was, how slow and oppressive. He remembered kissing her good night at the dorm door. Right then, he thought, he should've done something brave. He should've carried her up the stairs to her room and tied her to the bed and touched that left knee all night long. He should've risked it. Whenever he looked at the photographs, he thought of new things he should've done.

What they carried was partly a function of rank, partly of field specialty.

As a first lieutenant and platoon leader, Jimmy Cross carried a compass, maps, code books, binoculars, and a .45-caliber pistol that weighed 2.9 pounds fully loaded. He carried a strobe light and the responsibility for the lives of his men.

As an RTO, Mitchell Sanders carried the PRC-25 radio, a killer, twenty-six pounds with its battery.

As a medic, Rat Kiley carried a canvas satchel filled with morphine and plasma and malaria tablets and surgical tape and comic books and all the things a medic must carry, including M&M's for especially bad wounds, for a total weight of nearly twenty pounds.

As a big man, therefore a machine gunner, Henry Dobbins carried the M-60, which weighed twenty-three pounds unloaded, but which was almost always loaded. In addition, Dobbins carried between ten and fifteen pounds of ammunition draped in belts across his chest and shoulders.

As PFCs or Spec 4s, most of them were common grunts and carried the standard M-16 gas-operated assault rifle. The weapon weighed 7.5 pounds unloaded, 8.2 pounds with its full twenty-round magazine. Depending on numerous factors, such as topography and psychology, the riflemen carried anywhere from twelve to twenty magazines, usually in cloth bandoliers, adding on another 8.4 pounds at minimum, fourteen pounds at maximum. When it was available, they also carried M-16 maintenance gear—rods and steel brushes and swabs and tubes of LSA oil— all of which weighed about a pound. Among the grunts, some carried the M-79 grenade launcher, 5.9 pounds unloaded, a reasonably light weapon except for the ammunition, which was heavy. A single round weighed ten ounces. The typical load was twenty-five rounds. But Ted Lavender, who was scared, carried thirty-four rounds when he was shot and killed outside Than Khe, and he went down under an exceptional burden, more than twenty pounds of ammunition, plus the flak jacket and helmet and rations and water and toilet paper and tranquilizers and all the rest, plus the unweighed fear. He was dead weight. There was no twitching or flopping. Kiowa, who saw it happen, said it was like watching a rock fall, or a big sandbag or something—just boom, then down—not like the movies where the dead guy rolls around and does fancy spins and goes ass over teakettle—not like that, Kiowa said, the poor bastard just flat-fuck fell. Boom. Down. Nothing else. It was a bright morning in mid-April. Lieutenant Cross felt the pain. He blamed himself. They stripped off Lavender's canteens and ammo, all the heavy things, and Rat Kiley said the obvious, the guy's dead, and Mitchell Sanders used his radio to report one U.S. KIA[3] and to request a chopper. Then they wrapped Lavender in his poncho. They carried him out to a dry paddy, established security, and sat smoking the dead man's dope until the chopper came. Lieutenant Cross kept to himself. He pictured Martha's smooth young face, thinking he loved her more than anything, more than his men, and now Ted Lavender was dead because he loved her so much and could not stop thinking about her. When the dust-off arrived, they carried Lavender aboard. Afterward they burned Than Khe. They marched until dusk, then dug their holes, and that night Kiowa kept explaining how you had to be there, how fast it was, how the poor guy just dropped like so much concrete. Boom-down, he said. Like cement.

In addition to the three standard weapons—the M-60, M-16, and M-79—they carried whatever presented itself, or whatever seemed appropriate as a means of killing or staying alive. They carried catch-as-catch-can. At various times, in various situations, they carried M-14s and CAR-15s and Swedish Ks and grease guns and captured AK-47s and Chi-Coms and RPGs and Simonov carbines and black-market Uzis and .38-caliber Smith & Wesson handguns and 66 mm LAWs and shotguns and silencers and blackjacks and bayonets and C-4 plastic explosives. Lee Strunk carried a slingshot; a weapon of last resort, he called it. Mitchell Sanders carried brass knuckles. Kiowa carried his grandfather's feathered hatchet. Every third or fourth man carried a Claymore antipersonnel mine—3.5 pounds with its firing device. They all carried fragmentation grenades—fourteen ounces each. They all carried at least one M-18 colored smoke grenade—twenty-four ounces. Some carried CS or teargas grenades. Some carried white-phosphorus grenades. They carried all they could bear, and then some, including a silent awe for the terrible power of the things they carried.

In the first week of April, before Lavender died, Lieutenant Jimmy Cross received a good-luck charm from Martha. It was a simple pebble, an ounce at most. Smooth to the touch, it was a milky-white color with flecks of orange and violet, oval-shaped, like a miniature egg. In the accompanying letter, Martha wrote that she had found the pebble on the Jersey shoreline, precisely where the land touched water at high tide, where things came together but also separated. It was this separate-but-together quality, she wrote, that had inspired her to pick up the pebble and to carry it in her breast pocket for several days, where it seemed weightless, and then to send it through the mail, by air, as a token of her truest feelings for him. Lieutenant Cross found this romantic. But he wondered what her truest feelings were, exactly, and what she meant by separate-but-together. He wondered how the tides and waves had come into play on that afternoon along the Jersey shoreline when Martha saw the pebble and bent down to rescue it from geology. He imagined bare feet. Martha was a poet, with the poet's sensibilities, and her feet would be brown and bare, the toenails unpainted, the eyes chilly and somber like the ocean in March, and though it was painful, he wondered who had been with her that

---

[3] Killed in action.

afternoon. He imagined a pair of shadows moving along the strip of sand where things came together but also separated. It was phantom jealousy, he knew, but he couldn't help himself. He loved her so much. On the march, through the hot days of early April, he carried the pebble in his mouth, turning it with his tongue, tasting sea salts and moisture. His mind wandered. He had difficulty keeping his attention on the war. On occasion he would yell at his men to spread out the column, to keep their eyes open, but then he would slip away into daydreams, just pretending, walking barefoot along the Jersey shore, with Martha, carrying nothing. He would feel himself rising. Sun and waves and gentle winds, all love and lightness.

What they carried varied by mission.

When a mission took them to the mountains, they carried mosquito netting, machetes, canvas tarps, and extra bug juice.

If a mission seemed especially hazardous, or if it involved a place they knew to be bad, they carried everything they could. In certain heavily mined AOs,[4] where the land was dense with Toe Poppers and Bouncing Betties, they took turns humping a twenty-eight-pound mine detector. With its headphones and big sensing plate, the equipment was a stress on the lower back and shoulders, awkward to handle, often useless because of the shrapnel in the earth, but they carried it anyway, partly for safety, partly for the illusion of safety.

On ambush, or other night missions, they carried peculiar little odds and ends. Kiowa always took along his New Testament and a pair of moccasins for silence. Dave Jensen carried night-sight vitamins high in carotin. Lee Strunk carried his slingshot; ammo, he claimed, would never be a problem. Rat Kiley carried brandy and M&M's. Until he was shot, Ted Lavender carried the starlight scope, which weighed 6.3 pounds with its aluminum carrying case. Henry Dobbins carried his girlfriend's pantyhose wrapped around his neck as a comforter. They all carried ghosts. When dark came, they would move out single file across the meadows and paddies to their ambush coordinates, where they would quietly set up the Claymores and lie down and spend the night waiting.

Other missions were more complicated and required special equipment. In mid-April, it was their mission to search out and destroy the elaborate tunnel complexes in the Than Khe area south of Chu Lai. To blow the tunnels, they carried one-pound blocks of pentrite high explosives, four blocks to a man, sixty-eight pounds in all. They carried wiring, detonators, and battery-powered crackers. Dave Jensen carried earplugs. Most often, before blowing the tunnels, they were ordered by higher command to search them, which was considered bad news, but by and large they just shrugged and carried out orders. Because he was a big man, Henry Dobbins was excused from tunnel duty. The others would draw numbers. Before Lavender died there were seventeen men in the platoon, and whoever drew the number seventeen would strip off his gear and crawl in head first with a flashlight and Lieutenant Cross's .45-caliber pistol. The rest of them would fan out as security. They would sit down or kneel, not facing the hole, listening to the ground

---

[4] Areas of operations.

beneath them, imagining cobwebs and ghosts, whatever was down there—the tunnel walls squeezing in—how the flashlight seemed impossibly heavy in the hand and how it was tunnel vision in the very strictest sense, compression in all ways, even time, and how you had to wiggle in—ass and elbows—a swallowed-up feeling—and how you found yourself worrying about odd things—will your flashlight go dead? Do rats carry rabies? If you screamed, how far would the sound carry? Would your buddies hear it? Would they have the courage to drag you out? In some respects, though not many, the waiting was worse than the tunnel itself. Imagination was a killer.

On April 16, when Lee Strunk drew the number seventeen, he laughed and muttered something and went down quickly. The morning was hot and very still. Not good, Kiowa said. He looked at the tunnel opening, then out across a dry paddy toward the village of Than Khe. Nothing moved. No clouds or birds or people. As they waited, the men smoked and drank Kool-Aid, not talking much, feeling sympathy for Lee Strunk but also feeling the luck of the draw. You win some, you lose some, said Mitchell Sanders, and sometimes you settle for a rain check. It was a tired line and no one laughed.

Henry Dobbins ate a tropical chocolate bar. Ted Lavender popped a tranquilizer and went off to pee.

After five minutes, Lieutenant Jimmy Cross moved to the tunnel, leaned down, and examined the darkness. Trouble, he thought—a cave-in maybe. And then suddenly, without willing it, he was thinking about Martha. The stresses and fractures, the quick collapse, the two of them buried alive under all that weight. Dense, crushing love. Kneeling watching the hole, he tried to concentrate on Lee Strunk and the war, all the dangers, but his love was too much for him, he felt paralyzed, he wanted to sleep inside her lungs and breathe her blood and be smothered. He wanted her to be a virgin and not a virgin, all at once. He wanted to know her. Intimate secrets—why poetry? Why so sad? Why the grayness in her eyes? Why so alone? Not lonely, just alone—riding her bike across campus or sitting off by herself in the cafeteria. Even dancing, she danced alone—and it was the aloneness that filled him with love. He remembered telling her that one evening. How she nodded and looked away. And how, later, when he kissed her, she received the kiss without returning it, her eyes wide open, not afraid, not a virgin's eyes, just flat and uninvolved.

Lieutenant Cross gazed at the tunnel. But he was not there. He was buried with Martha under the white sand at the Jersey shore. They were pressed together, and the pebble in his mouth was her tongue. He was smiling. Vaguely, he was aware of how quiet the day was, the sullen paddies, yet he could not bring himself to worry about matters of security. He was beyond that. He was just a kid at war, in love. He was twenty-two years old. He couldn't help it. A few moments later Lee Strunk crawled out of the tunnel. He came up grinning, filthy but alive. Lieutenant Cross nodded and closed his eyes while the others clapped Strunk on the back and made jokes about rising from the dead.

Worms, Rat Kiley said. Right out of the grave. Fuckin' zombie.

The men laughed. They all felt great relief.

Spook City, said Mitchell Sanders.

Lee Strunk made a funny ghost sound, a kind of moaning, yet very happy, and right then, when Strunk made that high happy moaning sound, when he went *Ahhooooo*, right then Ted Lavender was shot in the head on his way back from peeing. He lay with his mouth open. The teeth were broken. There was a swollen black bruise under his left eye. The cheekbone was gone. Oh shit, Rat Kiley said, the guy's dead. The guy's dead, he kept saying which seemed profound—the guy's dead. I mean really.

The things they carried were determined to some extent by superstition. Lieutenant Cross carried his good-luck pebble. Dave Jensen carried a rabbit's foot. Norman Bowker, otherwise a very gentle person, carried a thumb that had been presented to him as a gift by Mitchell Sanders. The thumb was dark brown, rubbery to the touch, and weighed four ounces at most. It had been cut from a VC corpse, a boy of fifteen or sixteen. They'd found him at the bottom of an irrigation ditch, badly burned, flies in his mouth and eyes. The boy wore black shorts and sandals. At the time of his death he had been carrying a pouch of rice, a rifle, and three magazines of ammunition.

You want my opinion, Mitchell Sanders said, there's a definite moral here.

He put his hand on the dead boy's wrist. He was quiet for a time, as if counting a pulse, then he patted the stomach, almost affectionately, and used Kiowa's hunting hatchet to remove the thumb.

Henry Dobbins asked what the moral was.

Moral?

You know. *Moral.*

Sanders wrapped the thumb in toilet paper and handed it across to Norman Bowker. There was no blood. Smiling, he kicked the boy's head, watched the flies scatter, and said, It's like with that old TV show—Paladin. Have gun, will travel.

Henry Dobbins thought about it.

Yeah, well, he finally said. I don't see no moral.

There it *is*, man.

Fuck off.

They carried USO stationery and pencils and pens. They carried Sterno, safety pins, trip flares, signal flares, spools of wire, razor blades, chewing tobacco, liberated joss sticks and statuettes of the smiling Buddha, candies, grease pencils, *The Stars and Stripes*, fingernail clippers, Psy Ops[5] leaflets, bush hats, bolos, and much more. Twice a week, when the resupply choppers came in, they carried hot chow in green Mermite cans and large canvas bags filled with iced beer and soda pop. They carried plastic water containers, each with a two-gallon capacity. Mitchell Sanders carried a set of starched tiger fatigues for special occasions. Henry Dobbins carried Black Flag insecticide. Dave Jensen carried empty sandbags that could be filled at night for added protection. Lee Strunk carried tanning lotion. Some things they carried in common. Taking turns, they carried the big PRC-77 scrambler radio,

---

[5] Psychological operations.

which weighed thirty pounds with its battery. They shared the weight of memory. They took up what others could no longer bear. Often, they carried each other, the wounded or weak. They carried infections. They carried chess sets, basketballs, Vietnamese-English dictionaries, insignia of rank, Bronze Stars and Purple Hearts, plastic cards imprinted with the Code of Conduct. They carried diseases, among them malaria and dysentery. They carried lice and ringworm and leeches and paddy algae and various rots and molds. They carried the land itself—Vietnam, the place, the soil—a powdery orange-red dust that covered their boots and fatigues and faces. They carried the sky. The whole atmosphere, they carried it, the humidity, the monsoons, the stink of fungus and decay, all of it, they carried gravity. They moved like mules. By daylight they took sniper fire, at night they were mortared, but it was not battle, it was just the endless march, village to village, without purpose, nothing won or lost. They marched for the sake of the march. They plodded along slowly, dumbly, leaning forward against the heat, unthinking, all blood and bone, simple grunts, soldiering with their legs, toiling up the hills and down into the paddies and across the rivers and up again and down, just humping, one step and then the next and then another, but no volition, no will, because it was automatic, it was anatomy, and the war was entirely a matter of posture and carriage, the hump was everything, a kind of inertia, a kind of emptiness, a dullness of desire and intellect and con-science and hope and human sensibility. Their principles were in their feet. Their calculations were biological. They had no sense of strategy or mission. They searched the villages without knowing what to look for, not caring, kicking over jars of rice, frisking children and old men, blowing tunnels, sometimes setting fires and sometimes not, then forming up and moving on to the next village, then other vil-lages, where it would always be the same. They carried their own lives. The pres-sures were enormous. In the heat of early afternoon, they would remove their helmets and flak jackets, walking bare, which was dangerous but which helped ease the strain. They would often discard things along the route of march. Purely for comfort, they would throw away rations, blow their Claymores and grenades, no matter, because by nightfall the resupply choppers would arrive with more of the same, then a day or two later still more, fresh watermelons and crates of ammuni-tion and sunglasses and woolen sweaters— the resources were stunning—sparklers for the Fourth of July, colored eggs for Easter. It was the great American war chest—the fruits of science, the smokestacks, the canneries, the arsenals at Hart-ford, the Minnesota forests, the machine shops, the vast fields of corn and wheat— they carried like freight trains; they carried it on their backs and shoulders—and for all the ambiguities of Vietnam, all the mysteries and unknowns, there was at least the single abiding certainty that they would never be at a loss for things to carry.

After the chopper took Lavender away, Lieutenant Jimmy Cross led his men into the village of Than Khe. They burned everything. They shot chickens and dogs, they trashed the village well, they called in artillery and watched the wreck-age, then they marched for several hours through the hot afternoon, and then at dusk, while Kiowa explained how Lavender died, Lieutenant Cross found himself trembling.

He tried not to cry. With his entrenching tool, which weighed five pounds, he began digging a hole in the earth.

He felt shame. He hated himself. He had loved Martha more than his men, and as a consequence Lavender was now dead, and this was something he would have to carry like a stone in his stomach for the rest of the war.

All he could do was dig. He used his entrenching tool like an ax, slashing, feeling both love and hate, and then later, when it was full dark, he sat at the bottom of his foxhole and wept. It went on for a long while. In part, he was grieving for Ted Lavender, but mostly it was for Martha, and for himself, because she belonged to another world, which was not quite real, and because she was a junior at Mount Sebastian College in New Jersey, a poet and a virgin and uninvolved, and because he realized she did not love him and never would.

Like cement, Kiowa whispered in the dark. I swear to God—boom-down. Not a word.

I've heard this, said Norman Bowker.

A pisser, you know? Still zipping himself up. Zapped while zipping.

All right, fine. That's enough.

Yeah, but you had to see it, the guy just—

I *heard*, man. Cement. So why not shut the fuck *up*?

Kiowa shook his head sadly and glanced over at the hole where Lieutenant Jimmy Cross sat watching the night. The air was thick and wet. A warm, dense fog had settled over the paddies and there was the stillness that precedes rain.

After a time Kiowa sighed.

One thing for sure, he said. The Lieutenant's in some deep hurt. I mean that crying jag—the way he was carrying on—it wasn't fake or anything, it was real heavy-duty hurt. The man cares.

Sure, Norman Bowker said.

Say what you want, the man does care.

We all got problems.

Not Lavender.

No, I guess not, Bowker said. Do me a favor, though.

Shut up?

That's a smart Indian. Shut up.

Shrugging, Kiowa pulled off his boots. He wanted to say more, just to lighten up his sleep, but instead he opened his New Testament and arranged it beneath his head as a pillow. The fog made things seem hollow and unattached. He tried not to think about Ted Lavender, but then he was thinking how fast it was, no drama, down and dead, and how it was hard to feel anything except surprise. It seemed un-Christian. He wished he could find some great sadness, or even anger, but the emotion wasn't there and he couldn't make it happen. Mostly he felt pleased to be alive. He liked the smell of the New Testament under his cheek, the leather and ink and paper and glue, whatever the chemicals were. He liked hearing the sounds of night. Even his fatigue, it felt fine, the stiff muscles and the prickly awareness of his own body, a floating feeling. He enjoyed not being dead. Lying there, Kiowa admired Lieutenant Jimmy Cross's capacity for grief. He wanted to share the man's pain, he wanted to care as Jimmy Cross cared. And yet when he closed his eyes, all he could think was Boom-down, and all he could feel was the pleasure of having his boots off and the fog curling in around him and the damp soil and the Bible smells and the plush comfort of night.

After a moment Norman Bowker sat up in the dark.

What the hell, he said. You want to talk, *talk*. Tell it to me.

Forget it.

No, man, go on. One thing I hate, it's a silent Indian.

For the most part they carried themselves with poise, a kind of dignity. Now and then, however, there were times of panic, when they squealed or wanted to squeal but couldn't, when they twitched and made moaning sounds and covered their heads and said Dear Jesus and flopped around on the earth and fired their weapons blindly and cringed and sobbed and begged for the noise to stop and went wild and made stupid promises to themselves and to God and to their mothers and fathers, hoping not to die. In different ways, it happened to all of them. Afterward, when the firing ended, they would blink and peek up. They would touch their bodies, feeling shame, then quickly hiding it. They would force themselves to stand. As if in slow motion, frame by frame, the world would take on the old logic—absolute silence, then the wind, then sunlight, then voices. It was the burden of being alive. Awkwardly, the men would reassemble themselves, first in private, then in groups, becoming soldiers again. They would repair the leaks in their eyes. They would check for casualties, call in dust-offs, light cigarettes, try to smile, clear their throats and spit and begin cleaning their weapons. After a time someone would shake his head and say, No lie, I almost shit my pants, and someone else would laugh, which meant it was bad, yes, but the guy had obviously not shit his pants, it wasn't that bad, and in any case nobody would ever do such a thing and then go ahead and talk about it. They would squint into the dense, oppressive sunlight. For a few moments, perhaps, they would fall silent, lighting a joint and tracking its passage from man to man, inhaling, holding in the humiliation. Scary stuff, one of them might say. But then someone else would grin or flick his eyebrows and say, Roger-dodger, almost cut me a new asshole, *almost*.

There were numerous such poses. Some carried themselves with a sort of wistful resignation, others with pride or stiff soldierly discipline or good humor or macho zeal. They were afraid of dying but they were even more afraid to show it.

They found jokes to tell.

They used a hard vocabulary to contain the terrible softness. *Greased*, they'd say. *Offed, lit up, zapped while zipping*. It wasn't cruelty, just stage presence. They were actors and the war came at them in 3-D. When someone died, it wasn't quite dying, because in a curious way it seemed scripted, and because they had their lines mostly memorized, irony mixed with tragedy, and because they called it by other names, as if to encyst and destroy the reality of death itself. They kicked corpses.

They cut off thumbs. They talked grunt lingo. They told stories about Ted Lavender's supply of tranquilizers, how the poor guy didn't feel a thing, how incredibly tranquil he was.

There's a moral here, said Mitchell Sanders.

They were waiting for Lavender's chopper, smoking the dead man's dope.

The moral's pretty obvious, Sanders said, and winked. Stay away from drugs. No joke, they'll ruin your day every time.

Cute, said Henry Dobbins.

Mind-blower, get it? Talk about wiggy—nothing left, just blood and brains.

They made themselves laugh.

There it is, they'd say, over and over, as if the repetition itself were an act of poise, a balance between crazy and almost crazy, knowing without going. There it is, which meant be cool, let it ride, because oh yeah, man, you can't change what can't be changed, there it is, there it absolutely and positively and fucking well *is*.

They were tough.

They carried all the emotional baggage of men who might die. Grief, terror, love, longing—these were intangibles, but the intangibles had their own mass and specific gravity, they had tangible weight. They carried shameful memories. They carried the common secret of cowardice barely restrained, the instinct to run or freeze or hide, and in many respects this was the heaviest burden of all, for it could never be put down, it required perfect balance and perfect posture. They carried their reputations. They carried the soldier's greatest fear, which was the fear of blushing. Men killed, and died, because they were embarrassed not to. It was what had brought them to the war in the first place, nothing positive, no dreams of glory or honor, just to avoid the blush of dishonor. They died so as not to die of embarrassment. They crawled into tunnels and walked point and advanced under fire. Each morning, despite the unknowns, they made their legs move. They endured. They kept humping. They did not submit to the obvious alternative, which was simply to close the eyes and fail. So easy, really. Go limp and tumble to the ground and let the muscles unwind and not speak and not budge until your buddies picked you up and lifted you into the chopper that would roar and dip its nose and carry you off to the world. A mere matter of falling, yet no one ever fell. It was not courage, exactly; the object was not valor. Rather, they were too frightened to be cowards.

By and large they carried these things inside, maintaining the masks of composure. They sneered at sick call. They spoke bitterly about guys who had found release by shooting off their own toes or fingers. Pussies, they'd say. Candyasses. It was fierce, mocking talk, with only a trace of envy or awe, but even so, the image played itself out behind their eyes.

They imagined the muzzle against flesh. They imagined the quick, sweet pain, then the evacuation to Japan, then a hospital with warm beds and cute geisha nurses.

They dreamed of freedom birds.

At night, on guard, staring into the dark, they were carried away by jumbo jets. They felt the rush of takeoff. *Gone!* they yelled. And then velocity, wings and engines, a smiling stewardess—but it was more than a plane, it was a real bird, a big sleek silver bird with feathers and talons and high screeching. They were flying. The weights fell off, there was nothing to bear. They laughed and held on tight, feeling the cold slap of wind and altitude soaring, thinking *It's over, I'm gone!*—they were naked, they were light and free—it was all lightness, bright and fast and buoyant, light as light, a helium buzz in the brain, a giddy bubbling in the lungs as they were taken up over the clouds and the war, beyond duty, beyond gravity and mortification and global entanglements—*Sin loi!*[6] they yelled, *I'm sorry, motherfuckers, but I'm out of it, I'm goofed, I'm on a space cruise, I'm gone!*—and it was a restful, disencumbered sensation, just riding the light waves, sailing that big silver freedom bird over the mountains and oceans, over America, over the farms and great sleeping cities and cemeteries and highways and the golden arches of McDonald's. It was flight, a kind of fleeing, a kind of falling, falling higher and higher, spinning off the edge of the earth and beyond the sun and through the vast, silent vacuum where there were no burdens and where everything weighed exactly nothing. *Gone!* they screamed, *I'm sorry but I'm gone!* And so at night, not quite dreaming, they gave themselves over to lightness, they were carried, they were purely borne.

On the morning after Ted Lavender died, First Lieutenant Jimmy Cross crouched at the bottom of his foxhole and burned Martha's letters. Then he burned the two photographs. There was a steady rain falling, which made it difficult, but he used heat tabs and Sterno to build a small fire, screening it with his body, holding the photographs over the tight blue flame with the tips of his fingers.

He realized it was only a gesture. Stupid, he thought. Sentimental, too, but mostly just stupid.

Lavender was dead. You couldn't burn the blame.

Besides, the letters were in his head. And even now, without photographs, Lieutenant Cross could see Martha playing volleyball in her white gym shorts and yellow T-shirt. He could see her moving in the rain.

When the fire died out, Lieutenant Cross pulled his poncho over his shoulders and ate breakfast from a can.

There was no great mystery, he decided.

In those burned letters Martha had never mentioned the war, except to say, Jimmy, take care of yourself. She wasn't involved. She signed the letters "Love," but it wasn't love, and all the fine lines and technicalities did not matter.

The morning came up wet and blurry. Everything seemed part of everything else, the fog and Martha and the deepening rain.

It was a war, after all.

Half smiling, Lieutenant Jimmy Cross took out his maps. He shook his head hard, as if to clear it, then bent forward and began planning the day's march. In ten minutes, or maybe twenty, he would rouse the men and they would pack up and head west, where the maps showed the country to be green and inviting. They

[6] "Sorry about that!"

would do what they had always done. The rain might add some weight, but otherwise it would be one more day layered upon all the other days.

He was realistic about it. There was that new hardness in his stomach.

No more fantasies, he told himself.

Henceforth, when he thought about Martha, it would be only to think that she belonged elsewhere. He would shut down the daydreams. This was not Mount Sebastian, it was another world, where there were no pretty poems or midterm exams, a place where men died because of carelessness and gross stupidity. Kiowa was right. Boom-down, and you were dead, never partly dead.

Briefly, in the rain, Lieutenant Cross saw Martha's gray eyes gazing back at him.

He understood.

It was very sad, he thought. The things men carried inside. The things men did or felt they had to do.

He almost nodded at her, but didn't.

Instead he went back to his maps. He was now determined to perform his duties firmly and without negligence. It wouldn't help Lavender, he knew that, but from this point on he would comport himself as a soldier. He would dispose of his good-luck pebble. Swallow it, maybe, or use Lee Strunk's slingshot, or just drop it along the trail. On the march he would impose strict field discipline. He would be careful to send out flank security, to prevent straggling or bunching up, to keep his troops moving at the proper pace and at the proper interval. He would insist on clean weapons. He would confiscate the remainder of Lavender's dope. Later in the day, perhaps, he would call the men together and speak to them plainly. He would accept the blame for what had happened to Ted Lavender. He would be a man about it. He would look them in the eyes, keeping his chin level, and he would issue the new SOPs in a calm, impersonal tone of voice, an officer's voice, leaving no room for argument or discussion. Commencing immediately, he'd tell them, they would no longer abandon equipment along the route of march. They would police up their acts. They would get their shit together, and keep it together, and maintain it neatly and in good working order.

He would not tolerate laxity. He would show strength, distancing himself.

Among the men there would be grumbling, of course, and maybe worse, because their days would seem longer and their loads heavier, but Lieutenant Cross reminded himself that his obligation was not to be loved but to lead. He would dispense with love; it was not now a factor. And if anyone quarreled or complained, he would simply tighten his lips and arrange his shoulders in the correct command posture. He might give a curt little nod. Or he might not. He might just shrug and say Carry on, then they would saddle up and form into a column and move out toward the villages of Than Khe.

[1986]

Journal Entry

Empty the contents of your backpack and write a journal entry on what they reveal about your personality.

Textual Considerations

1. How does the author use repetition to enhance theme? Consider, for example, the effect of the many references to Lavender's death and to Martha's letters.
2. Each man carries other things in addition to "necessities." Review the second paragraph. Cite examples of what they carry, and discuss what these things reveal about them. The men also carry psychological "things." What is suggested in the following examples?

   "They carried all they could bear, and then some, including a silent awe for the terrible power of the things they carried."
   "They all carried ghosts."
   "They carried all the emotional baggage of men who might die."

3. How does the author use variations in paragraph length to suggest the tedium of the soldiers' daily routines? Cite examples.
4. Why does Cross burn Martha's letter and photographs? What thematic roles does Martha play in the story?
5. What is the "moral" that Mitchell Sanders finds in the dead Vietcong boy in the irrigation ditch?

Cultural Contexts

1. Lieutenant Cross carried "the responsibility for the lives of his men." Did he feel responsible for Lavender's death? Do you think he was responsible for Lavender's death? How could Cross have prevented his death? How does Lavender's death affect the way Cross will command his troops in the future?
2. Using a dictionary and a thesaurus, list the various meanings and connotations of the word *carry*. Go through O'Brien's story with your group members, looking for examples that correspond to the meanings of *carry* on your lists. What multiple thematic roles does *carrying* play in the narrative?

Ann Petry

Like a Winding Sheet

He had planned to get up before Mae did and surprise her by fixing breakfast. Instead he went back to sleep and she got out of bed so quietly he didn't know she wasn't there beside him until he woke up and heard the queer soft gurgle of water running out of the sink in the bathroom.

He knew he ought to get up but instead he put his arms across his forehead to shut the afternoon sunlight out of his eyes, pulled his legs up close to his body, testing them to see if the ache was still in them.

Mae had finished in the bathroom. He could tell because she never closed the door when she was in there and now the sweet smell of talcum powder was drifting down the hall and into the bedroom. Then he heard her coming down the hall.

"Hi, babe," she said affectionately.

"Hum," he grunted, and moved his arms away from his head, opened one eye.

"It's a nice morning."

"Yeah," he rolled over and the sheet twisted around him, outlining his thighs, his chest. "You mean afternoon, don't ya?"

Mae looked at the twisted sheet and giggled. "Looks like a winding sheet," she said. "A shroud—." Laughter tangled with her words and she had to pause for a moment before she could continue. "You look like a huckleberry—in a winding sheet—"

"That's no way to talk. Early in the day like this," he protested.

He looked at his arms silhouetted against the white of the sheets. They were inky black by contrast and he had to smile in spite of himself and he lay there smiling and savouring the sweet sound of Mae's giggling.

"Early?" She pointed a finger at the alarm clock on the table near the bed, and giggled again. "It's almost four o'clock. And if you don't spring up out of there you're going to be late again."

"What do you mean 'again'?"

"Twice last week. Three times the week before. And once the week before and—"

"I can't get used to sleeping in the day time," he said fretfully. He pushed his legs out from under the covers experimentally. Some of the ache had gone out of them but they weren't really rested yet. "It's too light for good sleeping. And all that standing beats the hell out of my legs."

"After two years you oughtta be used to it," Mae said.

He watched her as she fixed her hair, powdered her face, slipping into a pair of blue denim overalls. She moved quickly and yet she didn't seem to hurry.

"You look like you'd had plenty of sleep," he said lazily. He had to get up but he kept putting the moment off, not wanting to move, yet he didn't dare let his legs go completely limp because if he did he'd go back to sleep. It was getting later and later but the thought of putting his weight on his legs kept him lying there.

When he finally got up he had to hurry and he gulped his breakfast so fast that he wondered if his stomach could possibly use food thrown at it at such a rate of speed. He was still wondering about it as he and Mae were putting their coats on in the hall.

Mae paused to look at the calendar. "It's the thirteenth," she said. Then a faint excitement in her voice. "Why it's Friday the thirteenth." She had one arm in her coat sleeve and she held it there while she stared at the calendar. "I oughtta stay home," she said. "I shouldn't go otta the house."

"Aw don't be a fool," he said. "To-day's payday. And payday is a good luck day everywhere, any way you look at it." And as she stood hesitating he said, "Aw, come on."

And he was late for work again because they spent fifteen minutes arguing before he could convince her she ought to go to work just the same. He had to talk persuasively, urging her gently and it took time. But he couldn't bring himself to talk to her roughly or threaten to strike her like a lot of men might have done. He wasn't made that way.

So when he reached the plant he was late and he had to wait to punch the time clock because the day shift workers were streaming out in long lines, in groups and bunches that impeded his progress.

Even now just starting his work-day his legs ached. He had to force himself to struggle past the out-going workers, punch the time clock, and get the little cart he pushed around all night because he kept toying with the idea of going home and getting back in bed.

He pushed the cart out on the concrete floor, thinking that if this was his plant he'd make a lot of changes in it. There were too many standing up jobs for one thing. He'd figure out some way most of 'em could be done sitting down and he'd put a lot more benches around. And this job he had—this job that forced him to walk ten hours a night, pushing this little cart, well, he'd turn it into a sittin'-down job. One of those little trucks they used around railroad stations would be good for a job like this. Guys sat on a seat and the thing moved easily, taking up little room and turning in hardly any space at all, like on a dime.

He pushed the cart near the foreman. He never could remember to refer to her as the forelady even in his mind. It was funny to have a woman for a boss in a plant like this one.

She was sore about something. He could tell by the way her face was red and her eyes were half shut until they were slits. Probably been out late and didn't get enough sleep. He avoided looking at her and hurried a little, head down, as he passed her though he couldn't resist stealing a glance at her out of the corner of his eyes. He saw the edge of the light colored slacks she wore and the tip end of a big tan shoe.

"Hey, Johnson!" the woman said.

The machines had started full blast. The whirr and the grinding made the building shake, made it impossible to hear conversations. The men and women at the machines talked to each other but looking at them from just a little distance away they appeared to be simply moving their lips because you couldn't hear what they were saying. Yet the woman's voice cut across the machine sounds—harsh, angry.

He turned his head slowly. "Good Evenin', Mrs. Scott," he said and waited.

"You're late again."

"That's right. My legs were bothering me."

The woman's face grew redder, angrier looking. "Half this shift comes in late," she said. "And you're the worst one of all. You're always late. Whatsa matter with ya?"

"It's my legs," he said. "Somehow they don't ever get rested. I don't seem to get used to sleeping days. And I just can't get started."

"Excuses. You guys always got excuses," her anger grew and spread. "Every guy comes in here late always has an excuse. His wife's sick or his grandmother died or somebody in the family had to go to the hospital," she paused, drew a deep breath. "And the niggers are the worse. I don't care what's wrong with your legs. You get in here on time. I'm sick of you niggers—"

"You got the right to get mad," he interrupted softly. "You got the right to cuss me four ways to Sunday but I ain't letting nobody call me a nigger."

He stepped closer to her. His fists were doubled. His lips were drawn back in a thin narrow line. A vein in his forehead stood out swollen, thick.

And the woman backed away from him, not hurriedly but slowly—two, three steps back.

"Aw, forget it," she said. "I didn't mean nothing by it. It slipped out. It was a accident." The red of her face deepened until the small blood vessels in her cheeks were purple. "Go on and get to work," she urged. And she took three more slow backward steps.

He stood motionless for a moment and then turned away from the red lipstick on her mouth that made him remember that the foreman was a woman. And he couldn't bring himself to hit a woman. He felt a curious tingling in his fingers and he looked down at his hands. They were clenched tight, hard, ready to smash some of those small purple veins in her face.

He pushed the cart ahead of him, walking slowly. When he turned his head, she was staring in his direction, mopping her forehead with a dark blue handkerchief. Their eyes met and then they both looked away.

He didn't glance in her direction again but moved past the long work benches, carefully collecting the finished parts, going slowly and steadily up and down, back and forth the length of the building and as he walked he forced himself to swallow his anger, get rid of it.

And he succeeded so that he was able to think about what had happened without getting upset about it. An hour went by but the tension stayed in his hands. They were clenched and knotted on the handles of the cart as though ready to aim a blow.

And he thought he should have hit her anyway, smacked her hard in the face, felt the soft flesh of her face give under the hardness of his hands. He tried to make his hands relax by offering them a description of what it would have been like to strike her because he had the queer feeling that his hands were not exactly a part of him any more—they had developed a separate life of their own over which he had no control. So he dwelt on the pleasure his hands would have felt—both of them cracking at her, first one and then the other. If he had done that his hands would have felt good now—relaxed, rested.

And he decided that even if he'd lost his job for it he should have let her have it and it would have been a long time, maybe the rest of her life before she called anybody else a nigger.

The only trouble was he couldn't hit a woman. A woman couldn't hit back the same way a man did. But it would have been a deeply satisfying thing to have cracked her narrow lips wide open with just one blow, beautifully timed and with all his weight in back of it. That way he would have gotten rid of all the energy and tension his anger had created in him. He kept remembering how his heart had started pumping blood so fast he had felt it tingle even in the tips of his fingers.

With the approach of night fatigue nibbled at him. The corners of his mouth dropped, the frown between his eyes deepened, his shoulders sagged; but his hands stayed tight and tense. As the hours dragged by he noticed that the women workers had started to snap and snarl at each other. He couldn't hear what they said because of the sound of machines but he could see the quick lip movements that sent words tumbling from the sides of their mouths. They gestured irritably with their hands and scowled as their mouths moved.

Their violent jerky motions told him that it was getting close on to quitting time but somehow he felt that the night still stretched ahead of him, composed of endless hours of steady walking on his aching legs. When the whistle finally blew he went on pushing the cart, unable to believe that it had sounded. The whirring of the machines died away to a murmur and he knew then that he'd really heard the whistle. He stood still for a moment filled with a relief that made him sigh.

Then he moved briskly, putting the cart in the store room, hurrying to take his place in the line forming before the paymaster. That was another thing he'd change, he thought. He'd have the pay envelopes handed to the people right at their benches so there wouldn't be ten or fifteen minutes lost waiting for the pay. He always got home about fifteen minutes late on payday. They did it better in the plant where Mae worked, brought the money right to them at their benches.

He stuck his pay envelope in his pants' pocket and followed the line of workers heading for the subway in a slow moving stream. He glanced up at the sky. It was a nice night, the sky looked packed full to running over with stars. And he thought if he and Mae would go right to bed when they got home from work they'd catch a few hours of darkness for sleeping. But they never did. They fooled around—cooking and eating and listening to the radio and he always stayed in a big chair in the living room and went almost but not quite to sleep and when they finally got to bed it was five or six in the morning and daylight was already seeping around the edges of the sky.

He walked slowly, putting off the movement when he would have to plunge into the crowd hurrying toward the subway. It was a long ride to Harlem and tonight the thought of it appalled him. He paused outside an all-night restaurant to kill time, so that some of the first rush of workers would be gone when he reached the subway.

The lights in the restaurant were brilliant, enticing. There was life and motion inside. And as he looked through the window he thought that everything within range of his eyes gleamed—the long imitation marble counter, the tall stools, the white porcelain topped tables and especially the big metal coffee urn right near the window. Steam issued from its top and a gas flame flickered under it—a lively, dancing, blue flame.

A lot of the workers from his shift—men and women—were lining up near the coffee urn. He watched them walk to the porcelain topped tables carrying steaming cups of coffee and he saw that just the smell of the coffee lessened the fatigue lines in their faces. After the first sip their faces softened, they smiled, they began to talk and laugh.

On a sudden impulse he shoved the door open and joined the line in front of the coffee urn. The line moved slowly. And as he stood there the smell of the coffee, the sound of the laughter and of the voices, helped dull the sharp ache in his legs.

He didn't pay any attention to the girl who was serving the coffee at the urn. He kept looking at the cups in the hands of the men who had been ahead of him. Each time a man stepped out of the line with one of the thick white cups the fragrant steam got in his nostrils. He saw that they walked carefully so as not to spill a single drop. There was a froth of bubbles at the top of each cup and he thought about how he would let the bubbles break against his lips before he actually took a big deep swallow.

Then it was his turn. "A cup of coffee," he said, just as he had heard the others say.

The girl looked past him, put her hands up to her head and gently lifted her hair away from the back of her neck, tossing her head back a little. "No more coffee for awhile," she said.

He wasn't certain he'd heard her correctly and he said, "What?" blankly.

"No more coffee for awhile," she repeated.

There was silence behind him and then uneasy movement. He thought someone would say something, ask why or protest, but there was only silence and then a faint shuffling sound as though the men standing behind him had simultaneously shifted their weight from one foot to the other.

He looked at her without saying anything. He felt his hands begin to tingle and the tingling went all the way down to his finger tips so that he glanced down at them. They were clenched tight, hard, into fists. Then he looked at the girl again. What he wanted to do was hit her so hard that the scarlet lipstick on her mouth would smear and spread over her nose, her chin, out toward her cheeks; so hard that she would never toss her head again and refuse a man a cup of coffee because he was black.

He estimated the distance across the counter and reached forward, balancing his weight on the balls of his feet, ready to let the blow go. And then his hands fell back down to his sides because he forced himself to lower them, to unclench them and make them dangle loose. The effort took his breath away because his hands fought against him. But he couldn't hit her. He couldn't even now bring himself to hit a woman, not even this one, who had refused him a cup of coffee with a toss of her head. He kept seeing the gesture with which she had lifted the length of her blonde hair from the back of her neck as expressive of her contempt for him.

When he went out the door he didn't look back. If he had he would have seen the flickering blue flame under the shiny coffee urn being extinguished. The line of men who had stood behind him lingered a moment to watch the people drinking coffee at the tables and then they left just as he had without having had the coffee they wanted so badly. The girl behind the counter poured water in the urn and swabbed it out and as she waited for the water to run out she lifted her hair gently from the back of her neck and tossed her head before she began making a fresh lot of coffee.

But he walked away without a backward look, his head down, his hands in his pockets, raging at himself and whatever it was inside of him that had forced him to stand quiet and still when he wanted to strike out.

The subway was crowded and he had to stand. He tried grasping an overhead strap and his hands were too tense to grip it. So he moved near the train door and stood there swaying back and forth with the rocking of the train. The roar of the train beat inside his head, making it ache and throb, and the pain in his legs clawed up into his groin so that he seemed to be bursting with pain and he told himself that it was due to all that anger-born energy that had piled up in him and not been used and so it had spread through him like a poison—from his feet and legs all the way up to his head.

Mae was in the house before he was. He knew she was home before he put the key in the door of the apartment. The radio was going. She had it turned up loud and she was singing along with it.

"Hello, Babe," she called out as soon as he opened the door.

He tried to say "hello" and it came out half a grunt and half sigh.

"You sure sound cheerful," she said.

She was in the bedroom and he went and leaned against the door jamb. The denim overalls she wore to work were carefully draped over the back of a chair by the bed. She was standing in front of the dresser, tying the sash of a yellow house-coat around her waist and chewing gum vigorously as she admired her reflection in the mirror over the dresser.

"Whatsa matter?" she said. "You get bawled out by the boss or somep'n?"

"Just tired," he said slowly. "For God's sake do you have to crack that gum like that?"

"You don't have to lissen to me," she said complacently. She patted a curl in place near the side of her head and then lifted her hair away from the back of her neck, ducking her head forward and then back.

He winced away from the gesture. "What you got to be always fooling with your hair for?" he protested.

"Say, what's the matter with you, anyway?" she turned away from the mirror to face him, put her hands on her hips. "You ain't been in the house two minutes and you're picking on me."

He didn't answer her because her eyes were angry and he didn't want to quarrel with her. They'd been married too long and got along too well and so he walked all the way into the room and sat down in the chair by the bed and stretched his legs out in front of him, putting his weight on the heels of his shoes, leaning way back in the chair, not saying anything.

"Lissen," she said sharply. "I've got to wear those overalls again tomorrow. You're going to get them all wrinkled up leaning against them like that."

He didn't move. He was too tired and his legs were throbbing now that he had sat down. Besides the overalls were already wrinkled and dirty, he thought. They couldn't help but be for she'd worn them all week. He leaned further back in the chair.

"Come on, get up," she ordered.

"Oh, what the hell," he said wearily and got up from the chair. "I'd just as soon live in a subway. There'd be just as much place to sit down."

He saw that her sense of humor was struggling with her anger. But her sense of humor won because she giggled.

"Aw, come on and eat," she said. There was a coaxing note in her voice. "You're nothing but a old hungry nigger trying to act tough and—" she paused to giggle and then continued, "You—"

He had always found her giggling pleasant and deliberately said things that might amuse her and then waited, listening for the delicate sound to emerge from her throat. This time he didn't even hear the giggle. He didn't let her finish what she was saying. She was standing close to him and that funny tingling started in his finger tips, went fast up his arms and sent his fist shooting straight for her face.

There was the smacking sound of soft flesh being struck by a hard object and it wasn't until she screamed that he realized he had hit her in the mouth—so hard that the dark red lipstick had blurred and spread over her full lips, reaching up toward the tip of her nose, down toward her chin, out toward her cheeks.

The knowledge that he had struck her seeped through him slowly and he was appalled but he couldn't drag his hands away from her face. He kept striking her and he thought with horror that something inside him was holding him, binding him to this act, wrapping and twisting about him so that he had to continue it. He had lost all control over his hands. And he groped for a phrase, a word, something to describe what this thing was like that was happening to him and he thought it was like being enmeshed in a winding sheet—that was it—like a winding sheet. And even as the thought formed in his mind his hands reached for her face again and yet again.

[1971]

Journal Entry

Imagine yourself as a juror in Johnson's domestic violence trial. Would you vote to acquit or convict? On what evidence?

Textual Considerations

1. Explain the meaning of Mae's statement in the beginning of the story, "You look like a huckleberry—in a winding sheet."
2. What further significance does the phrase "like a winding sheet" acquire when Johnson uses it at the end?
3. What is the effect of beginning the story with a nebulous "he" when the reader doesn't really discover who the "he" is until much later? Is the same effect also achieved by using "he" instead of "Johnson" so often throughout the text?

4. What is the author's attitude toward Mae? Toward Johnson? How do the descriptive phrases and the thought patterns help you determine these differing attitudes?
5. The story is organized in a chronological sequence, but how does Petry keep it moving forward without making the time structure obtrusive?

Cultural Contexts

1. What role does color play in the relationships between the characters in the story: Johnson and Mrs. Scott; Johnson and the girl at the coffee shop; Johnson and Mae?
2. Which is the primary cause of Johnson's behavior—his race or his social class? Working with your group, indicate whether Johnson is justified in releasing his frustrations on his wife? Can your group reach a consensus about this issue?

ESSAYS

Brent Staples

A Brother's Murder

It has been more than two years since my telephone rang with the news that my younger brother Blake—just 22 years old—had been murdered. The young man who killed him was only 24. Wearing a ski mask, he emerged from a car, fired six times at close range with a massive .44 Magnum, then fled. The two had once been inseparable friends. A senseless rivalry—beginning, I think, with an argument over a girlfriend—escalated from posturing, to threats, to violence, to murder. The way the two were living, death could have come to either of them from anywhere. In fact, the assailant had already survived multiple gunshot wounds from an incident much like the one in which my brother lost his life.

As I wept for Blake I felt wrenched backward into events and circumstances that had seemed light-years gone. Though a decade apart, we both were raised in Chester, Pennsylvania, an angry, heavily black, heavily poor, industrial city southwest of Philadelphia. There, in the 1960's, I was introduced to mortality, not by the old and failing, but by beautiful young men who lay wrecked after sudden explosions of violence. The first, I remember from my 14th year— Johnny, brash lover of fast cars, stabbed to death two doors from my house in a fight over a pool game. The next year, my teenage cousin, Wesley, whom I loved very much, was shot dead. The summers blur. Milton, an angry young neighbor, shot a crosstown rival, wounding him badly. William, another teen-age neighbor, took a shotgun blast to the shoulder in some urban drama and displayed his bandages proudly. His brother, Leonard, severely beaten, lost an eye and donned a black patch. It went on.

I recall not long before I left for college, two local Vietnam veterans—one from the Marines, one from the Army—arguing fiercely, nearly at blows about which outfit had done the most in the war. The most killing, they meant. Not much later, I read a magazine article that set that dispute in a context. In the story, a noncommissioned officer—a sergeant, I believe—said he would pass up any number of affluent, suburban-born recruits to get hard-core soldiers from the inner city. They jumped into the rice paddies with "their manhood on their sleeves," I believe he said. These two items—the veterans arguing and the sergeant's words—still characterize for me the circumstances under which black men in their teens and twenties kill one another with such frequency. With a touchy paranoia born of living battered lives, they are desperate to be real men. Killing is only *machismo* taken to the extreme. Incursions to be punished by death were many and minor, and they remain so: they include stepping on the wrong toe, literally; cheating in a drug deal; simply saying "I dare you" to someone holding a gun; crossing territorial lines in a gang dispute. My brother grew up to wear his manhood on his sleeve. And when he died,

502

he was in that group—black, male and in its teens and early twenties—that is far and away the most likely to murder or be murdered.

I left the East Coast after college, spent the mid- and late-1970s in Chicago as a graduate student, taught for a time, then became a journalist. Within ten years of leaving my hometown, I was overeducated and "upwardly mobile," ensconced on a quiet, tree-lined street where voices raised in anger were scarcely ever heard. The telephone, like some grim umbilical, kept me connected to the old world with news of deaths, imprisonings and misfortune. I felt emotionally beaten up. Perhaps to protect myself, I added a psychological dimension to the physical distance I had achieved. I rarely visited my hometown. I shut it out.

As I fled the past, so Blake embraced it. On Christmas of 1983, I traveled from Chicago to a black section of Roanoke, Virginia, where he then lived. The desolate public housing projects, the hopeless, idle young men crashing against one another— these reminded me of the embittered town we'd grown up in. It was a place where once I would have been comfortable, or at least sure of myself. Now, hearing of my brother's forays into crime, his scrapes with police and street thugs, I was scared, unsteady on foreign terrain.

I saw that Blake's romance with the street life and the hustler image had flow-ered dangerously. One evening that late December, standing in some Roanoke dive among drug dealers and grim, hair-trigger losers, I told him I feared for his life. He had affected the image of the tough he wanted to be. But behind the dark glasses and the swagger, I glimpsed the baby-faced toddler I'd once watched over. I nearly wept. I wanted desperately for him to live. The young think themselves immortal, and a dangerous light shone in his eyes as he spoke laughingly of making fools of the policemen who had raided his apartment looking for drugs. He cried out as I took his right hand. A line of stitches lay between the thumb and index finger. Kick-back from a shotgun, he explained, nothing serious. Gunplay had become part of his life.

I lacked the language simply to say: Thousands have lived this for you and died. I fought the urge to lift him bodily and shake him. This place and the way you are living smells of death to me, I said. Take some time away, I said. Let's go downtown tomorrow and buy a plane ticket anywhere, take a bus trip, anything to get away and cool things off. He took my alarm casually. We arranged to meet the following night—an appointment he would not keep. We embraced as though through glass. I drove away.

As I stood in my apartment in Chicago holding the receiver that evening in February 1984, I felt as though part of my soul had been cut away. I questioned myself then, and I still do. Did I not reach back soon enough or earnestly enough for him? For weeks I awoke crying from a recurrent dream in which I chased him, urgently trying to get him to read a document I had, as though reading it would protect him from what had happened in waking life. His eyes shining like black dia-monds, he smiled and danced just beyond my grasp. When I reached for him, I caught only the space where he had been.

[1986]

Journal Entry

What knowledge or experience of inner-city violence can you bring to your reading of Staples's text?

Textual Considerations

1. What do we learn about Blake's way of life from the essay's first paragraph?
2. How did the narrator escape the fate of the other young men in the ghetto? Does the fact that he did escape alter your opinion of those who didn't?
3. "As I fled the past, so Blake embraced it." How did this choice affect the brothers' relationship?
4. Staples uses several flashbacks in the essay. Identify examples, and discuss their impact on the essay's purpose.
5. Staples tries to maintain an objective tone. Are there points at which his tone becomes more personal? What examples can you cite? What is their effect?

Cultural Contexts

1. Respond to Staples's statement that he "was introduced to mortality, not by the old and failing, but by the beautiful young men who lay wrecked after sudden explosions of violence." Staples wrote this essay in 1986. Is his experience still relevant almost two decades later? Explain.
2. Discuss with your group Staples's reasons for including the argument between the Vietnam veterans. How does it add to your understanding of his thesis that "killing is only *machismo* taken to the extreme"? To what extent do you agree with this point of view?

David W. Powell

Vietnam: What I Remember[1]

The following events come to my conscious memory uninvited. I not only remember them vividly, I reexperience them with all my senses:

Froze with fright, standing up, the first time I was under fire

Watched two marines try to break open the skull of a dead Viet Cong with a large rock

Observed a marine intentionally shoot a girl four or six years of age

Watched the girl's grandfather carry her into our line of fire, sobbing

Had a lieutenant who delighted in sneaking up on me when I was on watch at night

Was offered a blood-soaked flak jacket and a helmet with a bullet hole through it as my first field equipment

[1] From "Patriotism Revisited," a memoir.

Had my boots rot off during an operation in the field
Observed two captured nurses being beaten and raped by marines
Rifle-butted a girl of twelve in the face when she would not move away
Strangled a captured Viet Cong for refusing to talk to an interpreter
Discovered brain matter on barbed wire I was stretching out
Observed a marine laugh as he stepped on the chest of a dead Viet Cong and watched blood squirt out of the enemy's wounds
Awoke to find a buffalo leech on my leg
Was abandoned under fire when a rocket jammed in my launcher
Was abandoned under fire when I was shot
Hit head and fell in open field. Watched my fellow marines run by me to seek cover for themselves
Received letter from wife telling me how much fun she and a girlfriend had on Friday nights when they went out to bars to dance
Watched fellow marine shoot himself in the foot to get evacuated
Heard same man cry in his sleep when he was returned to the company
Found marine boot with foot in it in a hedgerow
Almost run over by retreating U.S. tank
Saw Lt. Spivey hit a head-high booby trap
Nearly murdered villager for stealing my laundry
Watched Prestridge test his new M-16 by shooting a woman getting water from a nearby well
Identified Haas's remains
Exchanged letters with Haas's mother
Had an artillery canister fall six inches in front of my head
Was about to put on fresh boots when I discovered lice swimming in them
Saw seven-foot python climbing in ceiling just above my head
Bullets sounding like bees digging up ground all around me
Nearly trapped in Da Nang village my last night in Vietnam
Robbed by marines while I slept in Okinawa after tour was over
Circled over El Toro air base for two hours so that President Johnson could land and be photographed greeting returning veterans

Since my return I have held eighteen different jobs and have been unemployed for several six-month periods. This is a direct result of my Post Traumatic Stress Disorder, specifically a disdain for being told to do tasks I do not want to do; an exaggerated startle response, which is terribly embarrassing to me; and a lack of control over emotional flooding.

I divorced my first wife two years after I got out of the service. I divorced my second wife in 1982. I separated from a four year relationship in 1987. I have not had a significant relationship with a woman since then. I have no significant male or female friendships. I am aloof from my immediate family, who live in Tucson, Arizona.

[1994]

Journal Entry

What knowledge, experience, associations, or images of the Vietnam War can you bring to your reading of this text?

Textual Considerations

1. How does Powell's cataloging the events that come to his "conscious memory uninvited" develop the memoir's meaning?
2. Powell uses the verbs *observed* and *watched* several times. In these instances, what do these memories have in common?
3. What is the tone of the last two paragraphs? Explain.
4. How do the last two paragraphs differ thematically and stylistically from the rest of the memoir?
5. Identify specific lines in which the speaker collapses war myths, such as the myth of war as a great romantic adventure with *esprit de corps*, or soldiers' solidarity.

Cultural Contexts

1. To what extent does Powell's memoir support or challenge the image of the Vietnam veteran as an **antihero**?
2. Brainstorm with your group on your associations with patriotism. Was Powell's choice of title appropriate? Why do you think he chose it for his memoir?

Bruce Catton

Grant and Lee: A Study in Contrasts

When Ulysses S. Grant and Robert E. Lee met in the parlor of a modest house at Appomattox Court House, Virginia, on April 9, 1865, to work out the terms for the surrender of Lee's Army of Northern Virginia, a great chapter in American life came to a close, and a great new chapter began.

These men were bringing the Civil War to its virtual finish. To be sure, other armies had yet to surrender, and for a few days the fugitive Confederate government would struggle desperately and vainly, trying to find some way to go on living now that its chief support was gone. But in effect it was all over when Grant and Lee signed the papers. And the little room where they wrote out the terms was the scene of one of the poignant, dramatic contrasts in American history.

They were two strong men, these oddly different generals, and they represented the strengths of two conflicting currents that, through them, had come into final collision.

Back of Robert E. Lee was the notion that the old aristocratic concept might somehow survive and be dominant in American life.

Lee was tidewater Virginia, and in his background were family, culture, and tradition . . . the age of chivalry transplanted to a New World which was making its own legends and its own myths. He embodied a way of life that had come down through the age of knighthood and the English country squire. America was a land that was beginning all over again, dedicated to nothing much more complicated than the rather hazy belief that all men had equal rights and should have an equal chance in the world. In such a land Lee stood for the feeling that it was somehow of advantage to human society to have a pronounced inequality in the social structure. There should be a leisure class, backed by ownership of land; in turn, society itself should be keyed to the land as the chief source of wealth and influence. It would bring forth (according to this ideal) a class of men with a strong sense of obligation to the community; men who lived not to gain advantage for themselves, but to meet the solemn obligations which had been laid on them by the very fact that they were privileged. From them the country would get its leadership; to them it could look for the higher values—of thought, of conduct, of personal deportment—to give it strength and virtue.

Lee embodied the noblest elements of this aristocratic ideal. Through him, the landed nobility justified itself. For four years, the Southern states had fought a desperate war to uphold the ideals for which Lee stood. In the end, it almost seemed as if the Confederacy fought for Lee; as if he himself was the Confederacy . . . the best thing that the way of life for which the Confederacy stood could ever have to offer. He had passed into legend before Appomattox. Thousands of tired, underfed, poorly clothed Confederate soldiers, long since past the simple enthusiasm of the early days of the struggle, somehow considered Lee the symbol of everything for which they had been willing to die. But they could not quite put this feeling into words. If the Lost Cause, sanctified by so much heroism and so many deaths, had a living justification, its justification was General Lee.

Grant, the son of a tanner on the Western frontier, was everything Lee was not. He had come up the hard way and embodied nothing in particular except the eternal toughness and sinewy fiber of the men who grew up beyond the mountains. He was one of a body of men who owed reverence and obeisance to no one, who were self-reliant to a fault, who cared hardly anything for the past but who had a sharp eye for the future.

These frontier men were the precise opposites of the tidewater aristocrats. Back of them, in the great surge that had taken people over the Alleghenies and into the opening Western country, there was a deep, implicit dissatisfaction with a past that had settled into grooves. They stood for democracy, not from any reasoned conclusion about the proper ordering of human society, but simply because they had grown up in the middle of democracy and knew how it worked. Their society might have privileges, but they would be privileges each man had won for himself. Forms and patterns meant nothing. No man was born to anything, except perhaps to a chance to show how far he could rise. Life was competition.

Yet along with this feeling had come a deep sense of belonging to a national community. The Westerner who developed a farm, opened a shop, or set up in business as a trader, could hope to prosper only as his own community prospered—and his community ran from the Atlantic to the Pacific and from Canada down to Mexico. If the land was settled, with towns and highways and accessible markets, he could better himself. He saw his fate in terms of the nation's own destiny. As its horizons expanded, so did his. He had, in other words, an acute dollars-and-cents stake in the continued growth and development of his country.

And that, perhaps, is where the contrast between Grant and Lee becomes most striking. The Virginia aristocrat, inevitably, saw himself in relation to his own region. He lived in a static society which could endure almost anything except change. Instinctively, his first loyalty would go to the locality in which that society existed. He would fight to the limit of endurance to defend it, because in defending it he was defending everything that gave his own life its deepest meaning.

The Westerner, on the other hand, would fight with an equal tenacity for the broader concept of society. He fought so because everything he lived by was tied to growth, expansion, and a constantly widening horizon. What he lived by would survive or fall with the nation itself. He could not possibly stand by unmoved in the face of an attempt to destroy the Union. He would combat it with everything he had, because he could only see it as an effort to cut the ground out from under his feet.

So Grant and Lee were in complete contrast, representing two diametrically opposed elements in American life. Grant was the modern man emerging; beyond him, ready to come on the stage, was the great age of steel and machinery, of crowded cities and a restless burgeoning vitality. Lee might have ridden down from the old age of chivalry, lance in hand, silken banner fluttering over his head. Each man was the perfect champion of his cause, drawing both his strengths and his weaknesses from the people he led.

Yet it was not all contrast, after all. Different as they were—in background, in personality, in underlying aspiration—these two great soldiers had much in common. Under everything else, they were marvelous fighters. Furthermore, their fighting qualities were really very much alike.

Each man had, to begin with, the great virtue of utter tenacity and fidelity. Grant fought his way down the Mississippi Valley in spite of acute personal discouragement and profound military handicaps. Lee hung on in the trenches at Petersburg after hope itself had died. In each man there was an indomitable quality . . . the born fighter's refusal to give up as long as he can still remain on his feet and lift his two fists.

Daring and resourcefulness they had, too; the ability to think faster and move faster than the enemy. These were the qualities which gave Lee the dazzling campaigns of Second Manassas and Chancellorsville and won Vicksburg for Grant.

Lastly, and perhaps greatest of all, there was the ability, at the end, to turn quickly from war to peace once the fighting was over. Out of the way these two men behaved at Appomattox came the possibility of a peace of reconciliation. It was a possibility not wholly realized, in the years to come, but which did, in the end, help the two sections to become one nation again . . . after a war whose bitterness might have seemed to make such a reunion wholly impossible. No part of either man's life became him more than the part he played in this brief meeting in the McLean house at Appomattox. Their behavior there put all succeeding generations of Americans in their debt. Two great Americans, Grant and Lee—very different, yet under everything very much alike. Their encounter at Appomattox was one of the great moments of American history.

[1953]

Journal Entry

What knowledge of the issues involved in the U.S. Civil War do you bring to your understanding of this essay?

Textual Considerations

1. According to Catton, Grant and Lee had contrasting attitudes toward the past. What were they?
2. Focus on paragraphs 10 and 12. What is implicit in the author's associating Lee with a "static" society as opposed to Grant's concept of a "restless burgeoning vitality"?
3. In the latter part of the essay, Catton focuses on the similarities between the two men. Why does he state that their conduct was crucial to "all succeeding generations"?
4. Focus on paragraphs 3–13, and create an outline of Catton's rhetorical pattern of organization. Does he focus equally on the two men as he draws out their contrasting characteristics? Where does he contrast both in the same paragraph?
5. In paragraphs 13–16 Catton presents similarities between the two men. List them. Does the author remain objective throughout this comparison? Explain.

Cultural Contexts

1. Catton describes Lee as an aristocrat who believed in differences between social classes, whereas Grant embodied the ideal that America "was a land that was beginning all over again." With whose attitude do you agree? Are the values of both men implicit in your concept of the American dream?
2. Catton believes that history is shaped to a great extent by the personalities who dominate particular historical events. What examples can your group think of to support this point of view?

Seth Mydans

Not Just the Inner City: Well-to-Do Join Gangs

In suburban Hawthorne, social workers tell of the police officers who responded to a report of gang violence, only to let the instigators drive away in expensive cars, thinking they were a group of teenagers on their way to the beach.

In Tucson, Ariz., a white middle-class teenager wearing gang colors died, a victim of a drive-by shooting, as he stood with black and Hispanic members of the Bloods gang.

At Antelope Valley High School in Lancaster, Calif., about 50 miles north of Los Angeles, 200 students threw stones at a policeman who had been called to help enforce a ban on the gang outfits that have become a fad on some campuses.

Around the country, a growing number of well-to-do youths have begun flirting with gangs in a dalliance that can be as innocent as a fashion statement or as deadly as hard-core drug dealing and violence.

The phenomenon is emerging in a variety of forms. Some affluent white youths are joining established black or Hispanic gangs like the Crips and Bloods; others are forming what are sometimes called "copy-cat" or "mutant" or "yuppie" gangs.

The development seems to defy the usual socioeconomic explanations for the growth of gangs in inner cities, and it appears to have caught parents, teachers, and law-enforcement officers off guard.

Police experts and social workers offer an array of reasons: a misguided sense of the romance of gangs; pursuit of the easy money of drugs; self-defense against the spread of established hard-core gangs. And they note that well-to-do families in the suburbs can be as empty and loveless as poor families in the inner city, leaving young people searching for a sense of group identity.

Furthermore, "kids have always tried to shock their parents," said Marianne Diaz-Parton, a social worker who works with young gang members in the Los Angeles suburb of Lawndale, "and these days becoming a gang member is one way to do it."

A member of the South Bay Family gang in Hermosa Beach, a twenty-one-year-old surfer called Road Dog who said his family owned a chain of pharmacies, put it this way: "This is the nineties, man. We're the type of people who don't take no for an answer. If your mom says no to a kid in the nineties, the kid's just going to laugh." He and his friends shouted in appreciation as another gang member lifted his long hair to reveal a tattoo on a bare shoulder. "Mama tried."

Separating their gang identities from their home lives, the South Bay Family members give themselves nicknames that they carry in elaborate tattoos around the backs of their necks. They consented to interviews on the condition that only these gang names be used.

The gang's leader, who said he was the son of a bank vice president, flexed a bicep so the tattooed figure of a nearly naked woman moved suggestively. Voicing his own version of the basic street philosophy of gang solidarity, the leader, who is called Thumper, said, "If you want to be able to walk the mall, you have to know you've got your boys behind you."

From Cool to Dead

For young people who have not been hardened by the inner city, an attitude like this, if taken into the streets, can be dangerous, said Sgt. Wes McBride of the Los Angeles Sherriff's Department, who has gathered reports on the phenomenon from around the country.

"They start out thinking it's real cool to be a gang member," he said. "They are 'wannabes' with nothing happening around them to show them it's real dangerous, until they run afoul of real gang members, and then they end up dead."

In California's palm-fringed San Fernando Valley, said Manuel Velasquez, a social worker with Community Youth Gang Services, a private agency, "there are a lot of kids who have no business being in gangs who all of a sudden are going around acting like gang members."

"They play the part," he went on. "They vandalize. They do graffiti. They do all kinds of stuff. But when it comes down to the big stuff, it's: 'Wait a minute. That's enough for me. I want to change the rules.' And then they realize it's a little bit too late."

There are few statistics on middle-class involvement in gangs, and officials are reluctant to generalize about its extent or the form it is taking. But reports of middle-class gang activity come from places as disparate as Denver, Seattle, Tucson, Portland, Dallas, Phoenix, Chicago, Minneapolis, Omaha, and Honolulu.

Sgt. John Galea, until recently the head of the youth gang intelligence unit of the New York City Police Department, said that although there was no lack of youth violence in the city, organized street gangs as such were not a serious problem.

The South Bay Family, in Hermosa Beach, has evolved over the past five years from a group of bouncers for a rock band to a full-fledged street-wise, well-armed gang. But for the most part, white gangs, or white members of minority gangs, have just begun to be noticed in the past few months.

"Parents Are Totally Unaware"

"I think it's a new trend just since the latter part of 1989, and it's really interesting how it's getting out to suburban areas," said Dorothy Elmore, a gang intelligence officer for the Portland Police Bureau in Oregon. "We've got teachers calling up and saying: 'We've got some Bloods and Crips here. What's going on?'

"It's definitely coming from two-parent families, working class to middle class to upper middle class, predominantly white," she went on. "The parents are totally unaware of the kind of activity these kids are doing."

In Tucson, Sgt. Ron Zimmerling, who heads the Police Department's gang unit, said that "Kids from even our country-club areas were suddenly joining gangs."

After the drive-by shooting last summer in which a white teenager was killed, he said, he asked a black gang member about another white youth who had attached himself to the gang. "I don't know," the black member replied. "He just likes to hang out."

The phenomenon is better established but still relatively new in the Los Angeles area, the nation's gang capital.

"We have covered parties where I'm totally shocked at the mixture of people who are there," said Mrs. Diaz-Parton, of Community Youth Gang Services in Lawndale. "Your traditional Hispanic gang member is next to this disco-looking person who is next to a preppie guy who looks like he's getting straight A's on his way to college."

Bandannas and Baseball Caps

Irving G. Spergel, a sociology professor at the University of Chicago who studies gangs, emphasized that the phenomenon accounts for a very small part of the nation's gang problem, which is centered in inner cities. He said the four thousand to five thousand neo-Nazi skinhead groups around the country, which have their own style and ideology, were a separate and worrisome problem.

More trivial, but still troubling to school officials, is a trend toward gang fashions in some high schools and junior high schools. In Los Angeles, Phoenix, Tucson, and several California suburbs, students have staged demonstrations to protest bans on wearing certain colors, bandannas, jewelry, or baseball caps that can be a mark of gang membership.

Bare chests, tattoos, Budweiser beer, and a televised hockey game seemed to be the fashion one recent Saturday evening at an extremely noisy gathering of members of the South Bay Family in a small house in a middle-class neighborhood near the Pacific Coast Highway in Hermosa Beach. There were knives and a deer rifle in evidence, and some said they had pistols.

Asked about the gang's philosophy, Bam Bam, the son of a professor at the University of Southern California, shouted, "Right or wrong, your bros are your bros!"

"Another thing that goes good here is peace," said Road Dog loudly.

"Peace by force, man," shouted Porgy, who said his father was vice president of a plastics company.

"No drug dealing!" shouted Tomcat, the son of a stockbroker.

"Quit lying to him, man," said Little Smith. "There's drugs everywhere."

On a more reflective note, away from the crowd in a small back room, Porgy said: "There is no justification. We do what we do because we want to. I don't blame my mother. She did the best she could."

[1990]

Journal Entry

Brainstorm on your associations with gangs. What images, emotions, or ideas does the word *gang* evoke? Are gangs and violence synonymous in your experience?

Textual Considerations

1. Review the first section of Mydans's essay, and list the reasons cited for the growing popularity of gangs in suburbia.
2. Respond to Sgt. McBride's statement: "They are 'wannabes' with nothing happening around them to show them it's real dangerous, until they run afoul of real gang members, and then they end up dead."
3. Comment on the attitudes toward parents expressed by several gang members. Why are the parents "totally unaware of the kind of activity these kids are doing"?
4. Analyze Mydans's tone. Is it consistent with his purpose? Is he mainly trying to inform his audience? Explain.

5. To analyze the relation between fashion, identity, and politics, consider what Mydans's text reveals about gang centrality. Do you agree with students' protest demonstrations about the control of fashion? To what extent does fashion forge the gang's image and identity?

Cultural Contexts

1. Respond to Thumper's statement: "If you want to be able to walk the mall, you have to know you've got your boys behind you."
2. Are suburban gangs mainly making fashion statements, or are they potentially violent? What is your response to their bonding rituals? Write a summary of your group's responses to Mydans's essay.

POETRY

Jeffrey Harrison

Reflection on the Vietnam War Memorial

Here it is, the back porch of the dead.
You can see them milling around in there,
   screened in by their own names,
   looking at us in the same
vague and serious way we look at them.   5

An underground house, a roof of grass—
one version of the underworld. It's all
   we know of death, a world
   like our own (but darker, blurred)
inhabited by beings like ourselves.   10

The location of the name you're looking for
can be looked up in a book whose resemblance
   to a phone book seems to claim
   some contact can be made
through the simple act of finding a name.   15

As we touch the name the stone absorbs our grief.
It takes us in—we see ourselves inside it.
   And yet we feel it as a wall
   and realize the dead are all
just names now, the separation final.   20

[1987]

Yusef Komunyakaa

Facing It

My black face fades,
hiding inside the black granite.
I said I wouldn't,
dammit: No tears.
I'm stone. I'm flesh.   5
My clouded reflection eyes me
like a bird of prey, the profile of night
slanted against morning. I turn
this way—the stone lets me go.
I turn that way—I'm inside   10
the Vietnam Veterans Memorial
again, depending on the light
to make a difference.
I go down the 58,022 names,
half-expecting to find   15
my own in letters like smoke.
I touch the name Andrew Johnson;
I see the booby trap's white flash.
Names shimmer on a woman's blouse
but when she walks away   20
the names stay on the wall.
Brushstrokes flash, a red bird's
wings cutting across my stare.
The sky. A plane in the sky.
A white vet's image floats   25
closer to me, then his pale eyes
look through mine. I'm a window.
He's lost his right arm
inside the stone. In the black mirror
a woman's trying to erase names: 30
No, she's brushing a boy's hair.

[1988]

Journal Entry

You will need a picture of the Vietnam Memorial in Washington, D.C., in order to appreciate these poems. What functions do war memorials serve? Record your responses to any war memorial that you have visited in the United States or elsewhere.

Textual Considerations

1. In the first two stanzas of Harrison's text, the wall is portrayed as though it were transparent. What reactions to the wall does the speaker express in these lines? Compare his reactions to the reactions of the speaker in "Facing It."
2. What is the effect of comparing looking for the names on the memorial with looking up names in a phone book?
3. How is the wall portrayed in the last stanza of Harrison's poem? How does touching the names affect the speaker?
4. What lines in the beginning of "Facing It" best capture the speaker's emotional response to visiting the memorial?
5. Explain lines 15 and 16 of "Facing It." What happened to Andrew Johnson? How does the speaker know him?

Cultural Contexts

1. Discuss the thematic significance of the images in lines 19 through 30 of "Facing It." What might they be suggesting about the memorial and the dead veterans?
2. Why does the speaker in "Facing It" mention that 58,022 names appear on the memorial? To what extent did that affect your group's response to the text?

JARRELL AND HARDY

Randall Jarrell

The Death of the Ball Turret Gunner*

From my mother's sleep I fell into the State
And I hunched in its belly till my wet fur froze.°
Six miles from earth, loosed from its dream of life,
I woke to black flak° and the nightmare fighters.
When I died they washed me out of the turret with a hose.   5

[1945]

---

*Ball Turret Gunner: High-altitude bombers in World War II (1941–1945) contained a revolvable
gun turret both at the top and at the bottom, from which a machine-gunner could shoot at attacking
fighter planes. Gunners in these turrets were sometimes mutilated by the gunfire of attacking planes.
2 Froze: The stratospheric below-zero temperatures caused the moisture in the gunner's breath to
freeze as it contacted the collar of his flight jacket.   **4 flak:** the round, black explosions of antiaircraft
shells fired at bombers from the ground, an acronym of the German word *Fliergerabwehrkanone*.

Thomas Hardy

The Man He Killed

"Had he and I but met
  By some old ancient inn,
We should have sat us down to wet
  Right many a nipperkin!

"But ranged as infantry,   5
  And staring face to face,
I shot at him as he at me,
  And killed him in his place.

"I shot him dead because—
  Because he was my foe,   10
Just so: my foe of course he was;
  That's clear enough; although

"He thought he'd 'list, perhaps,
Off-hand like—just as I—
Was out of work—had sold his traps—   15
No other reason why.

"Yes; quaint and curious war is!
You shoot a fellow down
You'd treat if met where any bar is,
Or help to half-a-crown."   20

[1902]

Journal Entry

Brainstorm on your associations with war. What images, ideas, or emotions does the word *war* evoke? What experiences, your own or others, can you draw on?

Textual Considerations

1. How does the speaker in Jarrell's text connect sleeping and waking, dreams and nightmares, and life and death?
2. Who is the speaker in Jarrell's poem? In what has he been involved? How do you respond to the last line of the poem?
3. Who is the speaker in Hardy's poem? What story is he recalling? How does the poet use setting to enhance theme?
4. How does the sentence structure of Hardy's text convey the attitude of the speaker to his so-called foe?
5. What indications are there that the speaker is trying to clarify for himself his reasons for killing in Hardy's poem? Consider the repetition of "because" in lines 9 and 10 as well as the significance of "although" in line 12.

Cultural Contexts

1. Jarrell's text portrays the carnage that resulted from aerial combat during World War II, while Hardy's focuses on how war disrupts everyday human relationships. Discuss the effectiveness of these texts as antiwar poems.
2. Discuss with your group the effect of point of view on theme in both poems. Do you respond differently to Jarrell's text, lamenting the loss of a generation of young men, as opposed to the account of how the speaker killed his "enemy" in Hardy's text? Record your discussion.

LEVERTOV AND YEVTUSHENKO

Denise Levertov

What Were They Like?

1) Did the people of Vietnam
   use lanterns of stone?
2) Did they hold ceremonies
   to reverence the opening of buds?
3) Were they inclined to quiet laughter?   5
4) Did they use bone and ivory,
   jade and silver, for ornament?
5) Had they an epic poem?
6) Did they distinguish between speech and singing?

1) Sir, their light hearts turned to stone.   10
   It is not remembered whether in gardens
   stone lanterns illumined pleasant ways.
2) Perhaps they gathered once to delight in blossom,
   but after the children were killed
   there were no more buds.   15
3) Sir, laughter is bitter to the burned mouth.
4) A dream ago, perhaps. Ornament is for joy.
   All the bones were charred.
5) It is not remembered. Remember,
   most were peasants; their life   20
   was in rice and bamboo.
   When peaceful clouds were reflected in the paddies
   and the water buffalo stepped surely along terraces,
   maybe fathers told their sons old tales.
   When bombs smashed those mirrors   25
   there was time only to scream.
6) There is no echo yet
   of their speech which was like a song.
   It was reported their singing resembled
   the flight of moths in moonlight.   30
   Who can say? It is silent now.

[1966]

Yevgeny Yevtushenko

Babiy Yar

Over Babiy Yar
there are no memorials.
The steep hillside like a rough inscription.
I am frightened.
Today I am as old as the Jewish race.   5
I seem to myself a Jew at this moment.
I, wandering in Egypt.
I, crucified. I perishing.
Even today the mark of the nails.
I think also of Dreyfus. I am he.   10
The Philistine my judge and my accuser.
Cut off by bars and cornered,
ringed round, spat at, lied about;
the screaming ladies with the Brussels lace
poke me in the face with parasols.   15
I am also a boy in Belostok,
the dropping blood spreads across the floor,
the public-bar heroes are rioting
in an equal stench of garlic and of drink.
I have no strength, go spinning from a boot,   20
shriek useless prayers that they don't listen to;
with a cackle of "Thrash the kikes and save Russia!"
the corn-chandler is beating up my mother.
I seem to myself like Anna Frank
to be transparent as an April twig   25
and am in love, I have no need for words,
I need for us to look at one another.
How little we have to see or to smell
separated from foliage and the sky,
how much, how much in the dark room   30
gently embracing each other.
They're coming. Don't be afraid.
The booming and banging of the spring.
It's coming this way. Come to me.
Quickly, give me your lips.   35
They're battering in the door. Roar of the ice.

Over Babiy Yar
rustle of the wild grass.
The trees look threatening, look like judges.
And everything is one silent cry.   40

Taking my hat off
I feel myself slowly going grey.
And I am one silent cry
over the many thousands of the buried;
am every old man killed here, 45
every child killed here.
O my Russian people, I know you.
Your nature is international.
Foul hands rattle your clean name.
I know the goodness of my country. 50
How horrible it is that pompous title
the anti-semites calmly call themselves,
Society of the Russian People.
No part of me can ever forget it.
When the last anti-semite on the earth 55
is buried for ever
let the International ring out.
No Jewish blood runs among my blood,
but I am as bitterly and hardly hated
by every anti-semite 60
as if I were a Jew. By this
I am a Russian.

[1962]

Journal Entry

Levertov portrays the destruction of the Vietnamese people and their culture, while Yevtushenko is concerned with anti-Semitism and the genocide of Russian Jews. What contribution can you make to this conversation?

Textual Considerations

1. How does setting reinforce theme in Levertov's and Yevtushenko's texts?
2. What is the effect of Levertov's series of questions followed by a series of answers? Who might the questioner be? Is his or her occupation important?
3. In Levertov's poem, who is answering? Does his or her nationality matter? Characterize the attitude of the person answering the questions, the questions themselves, the people of Vietnam, and the war in this poem.
4. Yevtushenko uses literary techniques such as flashbacks, first-person narrator, and two relatively long stanzas to reinforce the meanings in "Babiy Yar." What aspects of this formal organization do you find most effective thematically? Explain.
5. In the latter part of "Babiy Yar," Yevtushenko addresses the Russian people. Characterize his attitude toward them. Does it surprise you that Yevtushenko's poem was originally banned in Russia because he was regarded as a traitor? Explain.

Cultural Contexts

1. In *Babiy Yar*, Yevtushenko refers to historical places and people. Review the poem and research the significance of his allusions to Dreyfus, Brussels, Belostok, and so on. Discuss what these references have in common.

2. Discuss with your group your responses to these protest poems. Should poetry be concerned with issues of war and violence? Under what circumstances can you imagine being involved in social protest?

MIRIKITANI AND OWEN

Janice Mirikitani

Prisons of Silence

1.
The strongest prisons are built
with walls of silence.

2.
Morning light falls between us
like a wall.
We have laid beside each other   5
as we have for years.
Before the war, when life
would clamor through our windows,
we woke joyfully to the work.

I keep those moments   10
like a living silent seed.

After day's work, I would
smell the damp soil in his hands,
his hands that felt the outlines
of my body in the velvet   15
night of summers.

I hold his warm hands to this
cold wall of flesh
as I have for years.

    3.
    Jap!   20
    Filthy Jap!

    Who lives within me?

    Abandoned homes, confiscated land,
    loyalty oaths, barbed wire prisons
    in a strange wasteland.   25

    Go home, Jap!
    Where is home?

    A country of betrayal.
    No one speaks to us.

We would not speak to each other.   30

We were accused.

Hands in our hair,
hands that spread our legs
and searched our thighs for secret weapons,
hands that knit barbed wire   35
to cripple our flight.

Giant hot hands flung me,
fluttering, speechless into
barbed wire, thorns in a broken wing.

The strongest prisons are built   40
with walls of silence.

4.

I watched him depart that day
from the tedious wall of wire,
the humps of barracks,
handsome in his uniform.   45

I would look each day for letters
from a wall of time,
waiting for approach of my deliverance
from a wall of dust.

I do not remember   50
reading about his death
only the wall of wind
that encased me, as I turned my head.

5.

U.S. Japs hailed as heroes!

I do not know the face of this country   55
it is inhabited by strangers
who call me obscene names.

Jap. Go home.
Where is home?

I am alone wandering   60
in this desert.
Where is home?
Who lives within me?

A stranger with a knife in her tongue
and broken wing,   65

mad from separations and losses cruel
as hunger.

Walls suffocate her as a tomb,
encasing history.

6.

I have kept myself contained   70
within these walls shaped to my body
and buried my rage.
I rebuilt my life
like a wall, unquestioning.
Obeyed their laws . . . their laws.   75

7.

All persons of Japanese ancestry
  filthy jap.
Both alien and non-alien
  japs are enemy aliens.
To be incarcerated   80
  for their own good
A military necessity
  The army to handle only the japs
Where is home?
A country of betrayal.   85

8.

This wall of silence crumbles
from the bigness of their crimes.
This silent wall
crushed by living memory.

He awakens from the tomb   90
I have made for myself
and unearths my rage.

I must speak.

9.

He faces me in this small
room of myself.
I find the windows   95
where light escapes.
From this cell of history
this mute grave,
we birth our rage.   100

We heal our tongues.

We listen to ourselves

     Korematsu, Hirabayashi, Yasui.

We ignite the syllables of our names.

We give testimony.   105

We hear the bigness of our sounds freed
like many clapping hands,
thundering for reparations.

We give testimony.

Our noise is dangerous.   110

10.
We beat our hands
like wings healed.

We soar
from these walls of silence.

                                                        [1987]

Wilfred Owen

Disabled

He sat in a wheeled chair, waiting for dark,
And shivered in his ghastly suit of grey,
Legless, sewn short at elbow. Through the park
Voices of boys rang saddening like a hymn,
Voices of play and pleasure after day,   5
Till gathering sleep had mothered them from him.

            ...

About this time Town used to swing so gay
When glow-lamps budded in the light blue trees,
And girls glanced lovelier as the air grew dim,—
In the old times, before he threw away his knees.   10
Now he will never feel again how slim
Girls' waists are, or how warm their subtle hands.
All of them touch him like some queer disease.

            ...

There was an artist silly for his face,
For it was younger than his youth, last year.   15

Now, he is old; his back will never brace;
He's lost his colour very far from here,
Poured it down shell-holes till the veins ran dry,
And half his lifetime lapsed in the hot race
And leap of purple spurted from his thigh.   20

...

One time he liked a blood-smear down his leg,
After the matches, carried shoulder-high.
It was after football, when he'd drunk a peg,
He thought he'd better join.—He wonders why.
Someone had said he'd look a god in kilts,   25
That's why; and maybe, too, to please his Meg,
Aye, that was it, to please the giddy jilts
He asked to join. He didn't have to beg;
Smiling they wrote his lie: aged nineteen years.
Germans he scarcely thought of; all their guilt,   30
And Austria's, did not move him. And no fears
Of Fear came yet. He thought of jewelled hilts
For daggers in plaid socks; of smart salutes;
And care of arms; and leave; and pay arrears;
Esprit de corps; and hints for young recruits.   35
And soon, he was drafted out with drums and cheers.

...

Some cheered him home, but not as crowds cheer Goal.
Only a solemn man who brought him fruits
Thanked him; and then enquired about his soul.

...

Now, he will spend a few sick years in institutes,   40
And do what things the rules consider wise,
And take whatever pity they may dole.
Tonight he noticed how the women's eyes
Passed from him to the strong men that were whole.
How cold and late it is! Why don't they come   45
And put him into bed? Why don't they come?

[1920]

Journal Entry

What knowledge of the merciless trench warfare of World War I or of the decision of the United States to relegate Americans of Japanese ancestry to prison camps after the Japanese attack on Pearl Harbor can you bring to your reading of these texts?

Textual Considerations

1. Review sections 3, 8, and 9 of "Prisons of Silence," and find examples from the poem to answer the following questions: What enables the victims to break through their silence? To what extent does their testimony make possible their transformation from victims to victors?
2. The narrator of "Prisons of Silence" frequently juxtaposes the discourses of silence and speech. Investigate the various relationships between silence and powerlessness and between speech and power in the poem.
3. Analyze the effects of Owen's juxtaposing images from the soldier's past and present life.
4. Characterize the tone of "Disabled." Is the speaker angry, bitter, resigned? How does tone reinforce theme?
5. How does society's attitude toward the soldier change after his injury? On what aspects of war and people's attitude toward war does the speaker comment?

Cultural Contexts

1. "Prisons of Silence" dramatizes the decision of the United States to relegate Americans of Japanese ancestry to prison camps after the Japanese attack on Pearl Harbor during World War II. Identify the images that most effectively chart the progression of their physical displacement and psychological alienation.
2. Examine the relationship between war and sex by analyzing the gender-related issues explored in lines 9–13, 25–28, and 43–44 of "Disabled." Debate with your group the extent to which the military uniform is still considered a magnet of sexual attraction.

RUKEYSER AND WHITMAN

Muriel Rukeyser

Waking This Morning

Waking this morning,
a violent woman in the violent day
Laughing.
       Past the line of memory
along the long body of your life,   5
in which move childhood, youth, your lifetime of touch,
eyes, lips, chest, belly, sex, legs, to the waves of the sheet.
I look past the little plant
on the city windowsill
to the tall towers bookshaped, crushed together in greed,   10
the river flashing flowing corroded,
the intricate harbor and the sea, the wars, the moon, the planets, all
      who people space

in the sun visible invisible.
African violets in the light
breathing, in a breathing universe.   I want strong peace, and delight, 15
the wild good.
I want to make my touch poems:
to find my morning, to find you entire
alive moving among the anti-touch people.

       I say across the waves of the air to you: 20
today once more
I will try to be non-violent
one more day
this morning, waking the world away
in the violent day.   25

                     [1973]

Walt Whitman

The Dying Veteran

(A Long Island incident—early part of the nineteenth century)

Amid these days of order, ease, prosperity,
Amid the current songs of beauty, peace, decorum,
I cast a reminiscence—(likely 'twill offend you,
I heard it in my boyhood;)—More than a generation since,
A queer old savage man, a fighter under Washington himself, 5
(Large, brave, cleanly, hot-blooded, no talker, rather spiritualistic,
Had fought in the ranks—fought well—had been all through the
    Revolutionary war,)
Lay dying—sons, daughters, church-deacons, lovingly tending him,
Sharping their sense, their ears, towards his murmuring, half-caught
    words:
"Let me return again to my war-days, 10
To the sights and scenes—to forming the line of battle,
To the scouts ahead reconnoitering,
To the cannons, the grim artillery,
To the galloping aids, carrying orders,
To the wounded, the fallen, the heat, the suspense, 15
The perfume strong, the smoke, the deafening noise;
Away with your life of peace!—your joys of peace!
Give me my old wild battle-life again!"

[1892]

Walt Whitman

The Artilleryman's Vision*

While my wife at my side lies slumbering, and the wars are over long,
And my head on the pillow rests at home, and the vacant midnight
    passes,
And through the stillness, through the dark, I hear, just hear, the breath
    of my infant,
There in the room as I wake from sleep this vision presses upon me;
The engagement opens there and then in fantasy unreal, 5
The skirmishers begin, they crawl cautiously ahead, I hear the irregular
    snap! snap!

I hear the sounds of the different missiles, the short *t-h-t! t-h-t!* of the
    rifle-balls,
I see the shells exploding leaving small white clouds, I hear the great
    shells shrieking as they pass,
The grape like the hum and whirr of wind through the trees,
    (tumultuous now the contest rages,)
All the scenes at the batteries rise in detail before me again,   10
The crashing and smoking, the pride of the men in their pieces,
The chief-gunner ranges and sights his piece and selects a fuse of the
    right time,
After firing I see him lean aside and look eagerly off to note the effect;
Elsewhere I hear the cry of a regiment charging, (the young colonel
    leads himself this time with brandish'd sword,)
I see the gaps cut by the enemy's volleys, (quickly fill'd up, no delay,)   15
I breathe the suffocating smoke, then the flat clouds hover low
    concealing all;
Now a strange lull for a few seconds, not a shot fired on either side,

Then resumed the chaos louder than ever, with eager calls and orders
of officers,
While from some distant part of the field the wind wafts to my ears a
    shout of applause, (some special success,)
And ever the sound of the cannon far or near, (rousing even in dreams a
    devilish exultation and all the old mad joy in the depths of my soul,)   20
And ever the hastening of infantry shifting positions, batteries, cavalry,
    moving hither and thither,
(The falling, dying, I heed not, the wounded dripping and red I heed
    not, some to the rear are hobbling,)
(Grime, heat, rush, aide-de-camps galloping by or on a full run,
With the patter of small arms, the warning *s-s-t* of the rifles, (these in
    my vision I hear or see,)
And bombs bursting in air, and at night the vari-color'd rockets.   25

[1886]

---

* **The Artilleryman's Vision:** First published as "The Veteran's Vision" in the 1865 edition of *Leaves of Grass* and with this title in the 1871 edition.

Journal Entry

Freewrite on your associations with the word *peace*. What visual images come to mind?
Are there colors, situations, or experiences that you link to the word?

Textual Considerations

1. What is the effect of the speaker's juxtaposing images of past and present and touch and antitouch in a poem about peace? Identify those you consider most effective in "Waking This Morning."
2. What is the speaker's attitude toward violence in Rukeyser's poem? Explain. Analyze the speaker's tone in the last stanza. What does it reveal about the speaker?
3. Identify images of peace in Whitman's "The Dying Veteran." What do they imply about the speaker's perspectives on peace? To what extent are they similar to yours?
4. Most of Whitman's lines in "The Dying Veteran" focus on images of war. What do they reveal about the experiences the veteran values so much?
5. Analyze the effect of repetition in the speaker's lines 11–15 of "The Dying Veteran." What do they add to the overall theme of the poem? What kinds of images do they highlight? What is their impact on the reader?.
6. Evaluate Whitman's use of visual imagery in "The Artilleryman's Vision." To what other sense does the poem appeal?
7. Explain the effects of the contrasting images of war, peace, and violence in Rukeyser's and Whitman's poems.

Cultural Contexts

1. Rukeyser's speaker focuses on the joys of peace while Whitman's dying veteran extols the thrills of war. With whose perspective do you agree? Why is it more difficult to write poems about peace?
2. Discuss with your group your responses to the veteran's postwar traumatic "vision" in "The Artilleryman's Vision." To what extent has he "survived" the war?

EMERSON AND TENNYSON

Ralph Waldo Emerson

Concord Hymn

> Sung at the Completion of the Battle
> Monument, July 4, 1837

By the rude bridge that arched the flood,
　Their flag to April's breeze unfurled,
Here once the embattled farmers stood
　And fired the shot heard round the world.

The foe long since in silence slept;　　　　　　　　　　　5
　Alike the conqueror silent sleeps;
And Time the ruined bridge has swept
Down the dark stream which seaward creeps.

On this green bank, by this soft stream,
　We set to-day a votive stone;　　　　　　　　　　　　10
That memory may their deed redeem,
　When, like our sires, our sons are gone.

Spirit, that made those heroes dare
　To die, and leave their children free,
Bid Time and Nature gently spare　　　　　　　　　　　15
　The shaft we raise to them and thee.

　　　　　　　　　　　　　　　　　　　　[1836]

Alfred, Lord Tennyson

The Charge of the Light Brigade

I
Half a league, half a league,
Half a league onward,
All in the valley of Death,
　Rode the six hundred.
"Forward, the Light Brigade!　　　　　　　　　　　　5

Charge for the guns!" he said.
Into the valley of Death
   Rode the six hundred.

II
"Forward, the Light Brigade!"
Was there a man dismay'd?   10
Not tho' the soldier knew
   Some one had blunder'd.
Theirs not to make reply,
Theirs not to reason why,
Theirs but to do and die.   15
Into the valley of Death
   Rode the six hundred.

III
Cannon to the right of them,
Cannon to the left of them,
Cannon in front of them   20
   Volley'd and thunder'd;
Storm'd at with shot and shell,
Boldly they rode and well,
Into the jaws of Death,
Into the mouth of hell   25
   Rode the six hundred.

IV
Flash'd all their sabres bare,
Flash'd as they turn'd in air
Sabring the gunners there,
Charging an army, while   30
   All the world wonder'd.
Plunged into the battery-smoke
Right thro' the line they broke;
Cossack and Russian
Reel'd from the sabre-stroke   35
   Shatter'd and sunder'd.
Then they rode back, but not,
   Not the six hundred.

V
Cannon to the right of them,
Cannon to the left of them,   40
Cannon behind them,
   Volley'd and thunder'd;
Storm'd at with shot and shell,

While horse and hero fell,
They that had fought so well 45
Came thro' the jaws of Death,
Back from the mouth of hell,
All that was left of them,
   Left of six hundred.

VI

When can their glory fade? 50
O the wild charge they made!
   All the world wonder'd.
Honour the charge they made!
Honour the Light Brigade,
   Noble six hundred! 55

[1854]

Journal Entry

What does patriotism, or love of country, mean to you? Compare and contrast your view of patriotism with the views of Emerson and Tennyson.

Textual Considerations

1. How does Emerson's use of alliteration contribute to the unity of the poem? What ideas does alliteration emphasize in lines 2, 5, 6, 8 and 11? Characterize the poem's tone.
2. Discuss the theme of Emerson's poem. What is the effect of waiting until the last stanza to introduce it? How does Emerson introduce it? Explain.
3. Consider how Tennyson explores the effects of sound and rhythm to convey the emotional intensity of the charge of the light brigade. Focus specifically on the patterns of rhythm and the phonic symbolism of the galloping of the horses in stanzas I and III.
4. How does the refrain of each stanza of "The Charge of the Light Brigade" contribute to the development of its dramatic action? What does it reveal about the light brigade's response to their commander's "blunder"?
5. Compare and contrast the last stanzas of the two poems. To whom are they addressed? How does Emerson's "those heroes dare/To die" compare with Tennyson's second-stanza "Theirs but to do and die"? Explain.

Cultural Contexts

1. To what extent is Tennyson's poem an expression of patriotism or a critique of Britain's attitude toward the Crimean War (1854–1856)? In your opinion, does "The Charge of the Light Brigade" display a prowar or an antiwar sensibility? Explain.
2. What is the purpose of war memorials for Emerson? Does your group think that the building of war memorials helps restore the intellectual and moral stamina of younger generations? What is the purpose of war memorials for your group? Is there a war memorial that has inspired your group? Describe it.

SPERA

Gabriel Spera

Idle Hands

We're shoveling the sheetrock, bricks, and planks
the builders couldn't use into a pocked
and rusted pickup, settling in the clay
outside the condos springing up around
what will be cul-de-sacs, when all at once   5
we see this snake come trickling through the gutter
licking slackly over tire treads sunk
from lumbering machines, and one of our
small crew, career odd-jobber, Keith, jumps up,
runs over, plants his steel-toed shoes, and hoists   10
his shovel, set to hack its head clean off—
but not yet, not before he watches it
recoil from where his shadow falls, almost
not smiling his first smile all day, and from
somebody else's mouth it seems I hear   15
my voice say, "Wait, it's just a garter snake,
it's harmless, just forget it, let it go."
And so he turns to me, his face the face
of someone stopped from beating something
he clearly feels he owns, he turns and says,   20
"S'that so? Well now, if you're so fucking sure
go pick it up. Go 'head, right now." I can't
begin to guess how many snakes I held
when I was younger, treadmilling my hands
beneath their waterfalling bodies, but   25
enough. Time was, I'd prowl through sagging barns
looking for them, and knew the bleached flat stones
where they'd be scrawled out, knew exactly where
to grab them to keep that trap of fishhook teeth
from clamping on my thumb, yet now I can't   30
be sure of anything, except how bad
Keith wants it dead, and not because he thinks
it's poisonous. Snakes I know, but hate
like Keith's is hard to figure. So I keep
my peace until he jabs, "Time's up," and watch   35

him work his shovel like a butter churn,
catching, scritching, shredding the luckless thing
in bows and ribbons into dirt.

[1992]

Gabriel Spera

Kindness

It's the small acts of kindness I take strength in, acts
of grace so beautiful and true, they make me weep
despite myself. Just take this story of the five
who went out cruising in the canyons after dark
and found a car parked on an empty stretch of road.   5
They smashed the windshield, slashed the tires, jammed the locks
and drove away—but then turned back to see if there
were anything inside the car worth taking. It's then
they find the owners, two young couples, early teens
who'd sneaked away from home to watch the stars come out   10
and kiss. They rush them, beat the boys, and drag the girls
into the brush. The one, her skirt half torn away,
pinned down, looks up and begs the stranger straddling her,
don't kill me, please, don't kill me. Shut your mouth, he says,
don't look me in the face, you'll be alright, and moves   15
a hand down to his belt. She turns her head, and says
as though to no one in the world, then kiss my cheek,
as a promise you won't kill me when it's done. And so
he pauses, perched above her, silent, though the dark
is queasy with the sound of muffled sobs, he stops   20
and kisses her wet cheek, and I, who've judged my kind
most harshly always, I with no good word for men,
can only hang my head to know the emptiness,
the pity, in this small and stunning act of grace.

[1992]

Journal Entry

What emotions, reactions, memories, or images of being in a situation in which you felt
powerless can you bring to your reading of these texts?

Textual Considerations

1. How does the speaker explore the dichotomy between town and nature in "Idle Hands"? Which images best evoke this contrast? What meaning would have been lost if the speaker had focused exclusively on one or the other?
2. Characterize Keith. How does his reaction to the snake mirror his attitude toward life in "Idle Hands"?
3. Explain the speaker's lines, "Snakes I know, but hate / like Keith's is hard to figure." Can you "figure" it? How do these lines reinforce the meaning of "Idle Hands"?
4. What is your response to the last five lines of "Kindness"? How is the poem's meaning enhanced by their phonic and rhythmic effects?
5. Analyze the speaker's roles in "Idle Hands" and "Kindness." When does their presence emerge most powerfully? What point of view do they express about the events in the poems?

Cultural Contexts

1. How does the snake function symbolically in "Idle Hands"? Is it important that the snake was harmless? Can you speculate on the origin of the title? Does the title help us better understand the poem? Explain.
2. Argue for or against the speaker's conclusion that the rapist's kiss on his victim's cheek becomes a "small and stunning act of grace." How does your group react to this provocative idea? Did you reach a consensus? Read the last two lines of the poem to fully understand the words that modify the poem's concluding statement.

Carolyn Forché

The Colonel

What you have heard is true. I was in his house. His wife carried a tray of coffee and sugar. His daughter filed her nails, his son went out for the night. There were daily papers, pet dogs, a pistol on the cushion beside him. The moon swung bare on its black cord over the house. On the television was a cop show. It was in English. Broken bottles were embedded in the 5 walls around the house to scoop the kneecaps from a man's legs or cut his hands to lace. On the windows there were gratings like those in liquor stores. We had dinner, rack of lamb, good wine, a gold bell was on the table for calling the maid. The maid brought green mangoes, salt, a type of bread. I was asked how I enjoyed the country. There was a brief commercial in 10 Spanish. His wife took everything away. There was some talk then of how difficult it had become to govern. The parrot said hello on the terrace. The colonel told it to shut up, and pushed himself from the table. My friend said to me with his eyes: say nothing. The colonel returned with a sack used to bring groceries home. He spilled many human ears on the table. They were 15 like dried peach halves. There is no other way to say this. He took one of them in his hands, shook it in our faces, dropped it into a water glass. It came alive there. I am tired of fooling around he said. As for the rights of anyone, tell your people they can go fuck themselves. He swept the ears to the floor with his arm and held the last of his wine in the air. Something for your 20 poetry, no? he said. Some of the ears on the floor caught this scrap of his voice. Some of the ears on the floor were pressed to the ground.

[1978]

Carolyn Forché

The Visitor

In Spanish he whispers there is no time left.
It is the sound of scythes arcing in wheat,
the ache of some field song in Salvador.
The wind along the prison, cautious
as Francisco's hands on the inside, touching 5
the walls as he walks, it is his wife's breath

slipping into his cell each night while he
imagines his hand to be hers. It is a small country.

There is nothing one man will not do to another.

[1979]

Carolyn Forché

The Memory of Elena

We spend our morning
in the flower stalls counting
the dark tongues of bells
that hang from the ropes waiting
for the silence of an hour.   5
We find a table, ask for *paella*,
cold soup and wine, where a calm
light trembles years behind us.

In Buenos Aires only three
years ago, it was the last time his hand   10
slipped into her dress, with pearls
cooling her throat and bells like
these, chipping at the night—

As she talks, the hollow
clopping of a horse, the sound   15
of bones touches together.
The *paella* comes, a bed of rice
and *camarones*, fingers and shells,
the lips of those whose lips
have been removed, mussels   20
the soft blue of a leg socket.

This is not *paella*, this is what
has become of those who remained
in Buenos Aires. This is the ring
of a rifle report on the stones,   25
her hand over his mouth,
her husband falling against her.

These are the flowers we bought
this morning, the dahlias tossed

on his grave and bells   30
waiting with their tongues cut out
for this particular silence.

[1977]

Carolyn Forché

As Children Together

Under the sloped snow
pinned all winter with Christmas
lights, we waited for your father
to whittle his soap cakes
away, finish the whisky,   5
your mother to carry her coffee
from room to room closing lights
cubed in the snow at our feet.
Holding each other's
coat sleeves we slid down   10
the roads in our tight
black dresses, past
crystal swamps and the death
face of each dark house,
over the golden ice   15
of tobacco spit, the blue
quiet of ponds, with town
glowing behind the blind
white hills and a scant
snow ticking in the stars.   20
You hummed *blanche comme
la neige*° and spoke of Montreal
where a québecoise could sing,
take any man's face
to her unfastened blouse   25
and wake to wine
on the bedside table.
I always believed this,
Victoria, that there might
be a way to get out.   30

You were ashamed of that house,
its round tins of surplus flour,

chipped beef and white beans,
relief checks and winter trips
that always ended in deer   35
tied stiff to the car rack,
the accordion breath of your uncles
down from the north, and what
you called the stupidity
of the Michigan French.   40

Your mirror grew ringed
with photos of servicemen
who had taken your breasts
in their hands, the buttons
of your blouses in their teeth,   45
who had given you the silk
tassles of their graduation,
jackets embroidered with dragons
from the Far East. You kept
the corks that had fired   50
from the bottles over their beds,
their letters with each city
blackened, envelopes of hair
from their shaved heads.

I am going to have it, you said.   55
Flowers wrapped in paper from carts
in Montreal, a plane lifting out
of Detroit, a satin bed, a table
cluttered with bottles of scent.

So standing in a platter of ice   60
outside a Catholic dance hall
you took their collars
in your fine chilled hands
and lied your age to adulthood.

I did not then have breasts of my own,   65
nor any letters from bootcamp
and when one of the men who had
gathered around you took my mouth
to his own there was nothing
other than the dance hall music   70
rising to the arms of iced trees.

I don't know where you are now, Victoria.
They say you have children, a trailer
in the snow near our town,

and the husband you found as a girl   75
returned from the Far East broken
cursing holy blood at the table
where nightly a pile of white shavings
is paid from the edge of his knife.

If you read this poem, write to me.   80
I have been to Paris since we parted.

[1980]

22 **blanche comme la neige:** white as the snow.

Journal Entry

The catalyst for Forché's poems was the two years she spent in El Salvador in the late 1970s. What knowledge of the atrocities of this dictatorship can you bring to your reading of these texts?

Textual Considerations

1. Forché refers to "The Colonel" as a "documentary poem." What stylistic aspects of the text suggest journalistic prose?
2. What portrait of the colonel emerges in the poem? How does Forché's ironic juxtaposition of domestic and violent images affect that portrayal? Cite three examples you find most effective.
3. Explain the meaning of the last line in "The Colonel."
4. The setting for "The Visitor" is the dark recesses of a Salvadoran prison. Cite images that best evoke the sense of individual tragedy and impending violence in Forché's other poems.
5. The speaker in "The Memory of Elena" addresses an imaginary listener to whom she shows several significant objects. What story emerges from the descriptions of the flowers and *paella*?
6. How does the juxtaposition of past and present in Elena's memories reinforce the horror of personal destruction caused by political dictatorships?
7. Forché's autobiographical poem "As Children Together" focuses on her own childhood and her friendship with Victoria. What portrait of Victoria emerges in the text?
8. What economic realities contribute to Victoria's inability to fulfill her dream to go to Montreal in "As Children Together"?

Cultural Contexts

1. React to Forché's conviction that "the twentieth-century human condition demands a poetry of witness." To what events might she be referring besides the dictatorship of El Salvador? Do you think it is essential that poets bear witness to atrocities? Explain.
2. Forché went to El Salvador as a journalist, poet, and human rights observer (1979–1980). She is committed to the concept that poetry should link the political and the personal, and that one function of the poet is to inform the audience of the horrors of the twentieth-century atrocities. With your group, share your journal entries on Forché's poems as well as your response to her concept of the poet's responsibility.

DRAMA

Fernando Arrabal

Picnic on the Battlefield

CHARACTERS

ZAPO, *a soldier*
MONSIEUR TÉPAN, *the soldier's father*
MADAME TÉPAN, *the soldier's mother*
ZÉPO, *an enemy soldier*
First Stretcher Bearer
Second Stretcher Bearer

A battlefield. The stage is covered with barbed wire and sandbags. The battle is at its height. Rifle shots, exploding bombs and machine guns can be heard.

  ZAPO is alone on the stage; flat on his stomach, hidden among the sandbags. He is very frightened. The sound of the fighting stops. Silence.

  ZAPO takes a ball of wool and some needles out of a canvas workbag and starts knitting a pullover, which is already quite far advanced. The field telephone, which is by his side, suddenly starts ringing.

ZAPO: Hallo, hallo . . . yes, Captain . . . yes, I'm the sentry of sector 47 . . . Nothing new, Captain . . . Excuse me, Captain, but when's the fighting going to start again? And what am I supposed to do with the hand-grenades? Do I chuck them in front of me or behind me? . . . Don't get me wrong. I didn't mean to annoy you . . . Captain, I really feel terribly lonely, couldn't you send me someone to keep me company? . . . even if it's only a nanny-goat? (*The CAPTAIN is obviously severely reprimanding him.*) Whatever you say, Captain, whatever you say. (*ZAPO hangs up. He mutters to himself. Silence. Enter MONSIEUR and MADAME TÉPAN carrying baskets as if they were going on a picnic. They address their son, who has his back turned and doesn't see them come in.*)

MONS. T (*ceremoniously*): Stand up, my son, and kiss your mother on the brow. (*ZAPO, surprised, gets up and kisses his mother very respectfully on the forehead. He is about to speak, but his father doesn't give him a chance.*) And now, kiss *me.*

ZAPO: But, dear Father and dear Mother, how did you dare to come all this way, to such a dangerous place? You must leave at once.

MONS. T: So you think you've got something to teach your father about war and danger, do you? All this is just a game to me. How many times—to take the first example that comes to mind—have I got off an underground train while it was still moving.

MME. T: We thought you must be bored, so we came to pay you a little visit. This war must be a bit tedious, after all.

ZAPO: It all depends.

MONS. T: I know exactly what happens. To start with you're attracted by the novelty of it all. It's fun to kill people, and throw hand-grenades about, and wear uniforms— you feel smart, but in the end you get bored stiff. You'd have found it much more interesting in my day. Wars were much more lively, much more highly colored. And then, the best thing was that there were horses, plenty of horses. It was a real pleasure; if the Captain ordered us to attack, there we all were immediately, on horseback, in our red uniforms. It was a sight to be seen. And then there were the charges at the gallop, sword in hand, and suddenly you found yourself face to face with the enemy, and he was equal to the occasion too—with his horses—there were always horses, lots of horses, with their well-rounded rumps—in his highly-polished boots, and his green uniform.

MME. T: No, no, the enemy uniform wasn't green. It was blue. I remember distinctly that it was blue.

MONS. T: I tell you it was green.

MME. T: When I was little, how many times did I go out to the balcony to watch the battle and say to the neighbour's little boy: "I bet you a gum-drop the blues win." And the blues were our enemies.

MONS. T: Oh, well, you must be right, then.

MME. T: I've always liked battles. As a child I always said that when I grew up I wanted to be a Colonel of dragoons. But my mother wouldn't hear of it, you know how she will stick to her principles at all costs.

MONS. T: Your mother's just a half-wit.

ZAPO: I'm sorry, but you really must go. You can't come into a war unless you're a soldier.

MONS. T: I don't give a damn, we came here to have a picnic with you in the country and to enjoy our Sunday.

MME. T: And I've prepared an excellent meal, too. Sausage, hard-boiled eggs— you know how you like them!—ham sandwiches, red wine, salad, and cakes.

ZAPO: All right, let's have it your way. But if the Captain comes he'll be absolutely furious. Because he isn't at all keen on us having visits when we're at the front. He never stops telling us: "Discipline and hand-grenades are what's wanted in war, not visits."

MONS. T: Don't worry, I'll have a few words to say to your Captain.

ZAPO: And what if we have to start fighting again?

MONS. T: You needn't think that'll frighten me, it won't be the first fighting I've seen. Now if only it was battles on horseback! Times have changed, you can't understand. (*Pause.*) We came by motor bike. No one said a word to us.

ZAPO: They must have thought you were the referees.

MONS. T: We had enough trouble getting through, though. What with all the tanks and jeeps.

MME. T: And do you remember the bottle-neck that cannon caused, just when we got here?

MONS. T: You mustn't be surprised at anything in wartime, everyone knows that.

MME. T: Good, let's start our meal.

MONS. T: You're quite right, I feel as hungry as a hunter. It's the smell of gunpowder.

MME. T: We'll sit on the rug while we're eating.

ZAPO: Can I bring my rifle with me?

MME. T: You leave your rifle alone. It's not good manners to bring your rifle to table with you. (*Pause.*) But you're absolutely filthy, my boy. How on earth did you get into such a state? Let's have a look at your hands.

ZAPO (*ashamed, holding out his hands*):   I had to crawl about on the ground during the manoeuvres.

MME. T: And what about your ears?

ZAPO: I washed them this morning.

MME. T: Well that's all right, then. And your teeth? (*He shows them.*) Very good. Who's going to give her little boy a great big kiss for cleaning his teeth so nicely? (*To her husband.*) Well, go on, kiss your son for cleaning his teeth so nicely. (M. TÉPAN *kisses his son.*) Because, you know, there's one thing I *will* not have, and that's making fighting a war an excuse for not washing.

ZAPO: Yes, mother. (*They eat.*)

MONS. T: Well, my boy, did you make a good score?

ZAPO: When?

MONS. T: In the last few days, of course.

ZAPO: Where?

MONS. T: At the moment, since you're fighting a war.

ZAPO: No, nothing much. I didn't make a good score. Hardly ever scored a bull.

MONS. T: Which are you best at shooting, enemy horses or soldiers?

ZAPO: No, not horses, there aren't any horses any more.

MONS. T: Well, soldiers then?

ZAPO: Could be.

MONS. T: Could be? Aren't you sure?

ZAPO: Well you see . . . I shoot without taking aim, (*pause*) and at the same time I say a Pater Noster for the chap I've shot.

MONS. T: You must be braver than that. Like your father.

MME. T: I'm going to put a record on. (*She puts a record on the gramophone—a pasodoble. All three are sitting on the ground, listening.*)

MONS. T: That really *is* music. Yes indeed, ole! (*The music continues. Enter an enemy soldier: ZÉPO. He is dressed like ZAPO. The only difference is the colour of their uniforms. ZÉPO is in green and ZAPO is in grey. ZÉPO listens to the music openmouthed. He is behind the family so they can't see him. The record ends. As he gets up ZAPO discovers ZÉPO. Both put their hands up. M. and MME. TÉPAN look at them in surprise.*) What's going on? (ZAPO *reacts—he hesitates. Finally, looking as if he's made up his mind, he points his rifle at ZÉPO.*)

ZAPO: Hands up! (ZÉPO *puts his hands up even higher, looking even more terrified. ZAPO doesn't know what to do. Suddenly he goes over quickly to ZÉPO and touches him gently on the shoulder, like a child playing a game of "tag".*) Got you! (*To his father, very pleased.*) There we are! A prisoner!

MONS. T: Fine. And now what're you going to do with him?

ZAPO: I don't know, but, well, could be—they might make me a corporal.

MONS. T: In the meantime, you'd better tie him up.

ZAPO: Tie him up? Why?

MONS. T: Prisoners always get tied up!

ZAPO: How?

MONS. T: Tie up his hands.

MME. T: Yes, there's no doubt about it, you must tie up his hands, I've always seen them do that.

ZAPO   Right. (*To his prisoner.*) Put your hands together, if you please.

ZÉPO: Don't hurt me too much.

ZAPO: I won't.

ZÉPO: Ow! You're hurting me.

MONS. T: Now, now, don't maltreat your prisoner.

MME. T: Is that the way I brought you up? How many times have I told you that we must be considerate of our fellow-men?

ZAPO: I didn't do it on purpose. (*To ZÉPO.*) And like that, does it hurt?

ZÉPO: No, it's all right like that.

MONS. T: Tell him straight out, say what you mean, don't mind us.

ZÉPO: It's all right like that.

MONS. T: Now his feet.

ZAPO: His feet as well, whatever next?

MONS. T: Didn't they teach you the rules?

ZAPO: Yes.

MONS. T: Well then!

ZAPO (*very politely, to ZÉPO*):   Would you be good enough to sit on the ground, please?

ZÉPO: Yes, but don't hurt me.

MME. T: You'll see, he'll take a dislike to you.

ZAPO: No he won't, no he won't. I'm not hurting you, am I?

ZÉPO: No, that's perfect.

ZAPO: Papa, why don't you take a photo of the prisoner on the ground and me with my foot on his stomach?

MONS. T: Oh, yes that'd look good.

ZÉPO: Oh no, not that!

MME. T: Say yes, don't be obstinate.

ZÉPO: No, I said no, and no it is.

MME. T: But just a little teeny weeny photo, what harm could that do you? And we could put it in the dining room, next to the life-saving certificate my husband won thirteen years ago.

ZÉPO: No—you won't shift me.

ZAPO: But why won't you let us?

ZÉPO: I'm engaged. And if she sees the photo one day, she'll say I don't know how to fight a war properly.

ZAPO: No she won't, all you'll need to say is that it isn't you, it's a panther.

MME. T: Come on, do say yes.

ZÉPO: All right then. But only to please you.

ZAPO: Lie down flat. (ZÉPO *lies down.* ZAPO *puts a foot on his stomach and grabs his rifle with a martial air.*)

MME. T: Stick your chest out a bit further.

ZAPO: Like this?

MME. T: Yes like that, and don't breathe.

MONS. T: Try to look like a hero.

ZAPO: What d'you mean, like a hero?

MONS. T: It's quite simple; try and look like the butcher does when he's boasting about his successes with the girls.

ZAPO: Like this?

MONS. T: Yes, like that.

MME. T: The most important thing is to puff your chest out and not breathe.

ZÉPO: Have you nearly finished?

MONS. T: Just be patient a moment. One . . . two . . . three.

ZAPO: I hope I'll come out well.

MME. T: Yes, you looked very martial.

MONS. T: You were fine.

MME. T: It makes me want to have my photo taken with you.

MONS. T: Now there's a good idea.

ZAPO: Right. I'll take it if you like.

MME. T: Give me your helmet to make me look like a soldier.

ZÉPO: I don't want any more photos. Even one's far too many.

ZAPO: Don't take it like that. After all, what harm can it do you?

ZÉPO: It's my last word.

MONS. T (*to his wife*):   Don't press the point, prisoners are always very sensitive. If we go on he'll get cross and spoil our fun.

ZAPO: Right, what're we going to do with him, then?

MME. T: We could invite him to lunch. What do you say?

MONS. T: I don't see why not.

ZAPO (*to* ZÉPO):   Well, will you have lunch with us, then?

ZÉPO: Er . . .

MONS. T: We brought a good bottle with us.

ZÉPO: Oh well, all right then.

MME. T: Make yourself at home, don't be afraid to ask for anything you want.

ZÉPO: All right.

MONS. T: And what about you, did you make a good score?

ZÉPO: When?

MONS. T: In the last few days, of course.

ZÉPO: Where?

MONS. T: At the moment, since you're fighting a war.

ZÉPO: No, nothing much. I didn't make a good score, hardly ever scored a bull.

MONS. T: Which are you best at shooting? Enemy horses or soldiers?

ZÉPO: No, not horses, they aren't any horses any more.

MONS. T: Well, soldiers, then?

ZÉPO: Could be.

MONS. T: Could be? Aren't you sure?

ZÉPO: Well you see . . . I shoot without taking aim, (*pause*) and at the same time I say an Ave Maria for the chap I've shot.

ZAPO: An Ave Maria? I'd have thought you'd have said a Pater Noster.

ZÉPO: No, always an Ave Maria. (*Pause*) It's shorter.

MONS. T: Come come, my dear fellow, you must be brave.

MME. T (*to* ZÉPO): We can untie you if you like.

ZÉPO: No, don't bother, it doesn't matter.

MONS. T: Don't start getting stand-offish with us now. If you'd like us to untie you, say so.

MME. T: Make yourself comfortable.

ZÉPO: Well, if that's how you feel, you can untie my feet, but it's only to please you.

MONS. T: Zapo, untie him. (ZAPO *unties him.*)

MME. T: Well, do you feel better?

ZÉPO: Yes, of course. I really am putting you to a lot of inconvenience.

MONS. T: Not at all, just make yourself at home. And if you'd like us to untie your hands you only have to say so.

ZÉPO: No, not my hands, I don't want to impose upon you.

MONS. T: No no, my dear chap, no no. I tell you, it's no trouble at all.

ZÉPO: Right . . . Well then, untie my hands too. But only for lunch, eh? I don't want you to think that you give me an inch and I take an ell.[1]

MONS. T: Untie his hands, son.

MME. T: Well, since our distinguished prisoner is so charming, we're going to have a marvelous day in the country.

ZÉPO: Don't call me your distinguished prisoner; just call me your prisoner.

MME. T: Won't that embarrass you?

ZÉPO: No, no, not at all.

MONS. T: Well, I must say you're modest. (*Noise of aeroplanes.*)

ZAPO: Aeroplanes. They're sure to be coming to bomb us. (ZAPO *and* ZÉPO *throw themselves on the sandbags and hide.*) (*To his parents.*) Take cover. The bombs will fall on you. (*The noise of the aeroplanes overpowers all the other noises. Bombs immediately start to fall. Shells explode very near the stage but not on it. A deafening noise.* ZAPO *and* ZÉPO *are cowering down between the sandbags.* M. TÉPAN *goes on talking calmly to his wife, and she answers in the same unruffled way. We can't hear what they are saying because of the bombing.* MME. TÉPAN *goes over to one of the baskets and takes an umbrella out of it. She opens it.* M. *and* MME. TÉPAN *shelter under it as if it were raining. They are standing up. They shift rhythmically from one foot to the other*

---

[1] **ell:** a unit of measure equal to 45 inches.

and talk about their personal affairs. The bombing continues. Finally the aeroplanes go away. Silence. M. Tépan stretches an arm outside the umbrella to make sure that nothing more is falling from the heavens.)

Mons. T (*to his wife*): You can shut your umbrella. (Mme. Tépan *does so. They both go over to their son and tap him lightly on the behind with the umbrella.*) Come on, out you come. The bombing's over. (Zapo *and* Zépo *come out of their hiding place.*)

Zapo: Didn't you get hit?

Mons. T: What d'you think could happen to your father? (*Proudly.*) Little bombs like that! Don't make me laugh! (*Enter, left, two Red Cross Soldiers. They are carrying a stretcher.*)

1st Stretcher Bearer: Any dead here?

Zapo: No, no one around these parts.

1st Stretcher Bearer: Are you sure you've looked properly?

Zapo: Sure.

1st Stretcher Bearer: And there isn't a single person dead?

Zapo: I've already told you there isn't.

1st Stretcher Bearer: No one wounded, even?

Zapo: Not even that.

2nd Stretcher Bearer (*to the* 1st S. B.): Well, now we're in a mess! (*To* Zapo *persuasively.*) Just look again, search everywhere, and see if you can't find us a stiff.

1st Stretcher Bearer: Don't keep on about it, they've told you quite clearly there aren't any.

2nd Stretcher Bearer: What a lousy trick!

Zapo: I'm terribly sorry. I promise you I didn't do it on purpose.

2nd Stretcher Bearer: That's what they all say. That no one's dead and that they didn't do it on purpose.

1st Stretcher Bearer: Oh, let the chap alone!

Mons. T (*obligingly*): We should be only too pleased to help you. At your service.

2nd Stretcher Bearer: Well, really, if things go on like this I don't know what the Captain will say to us.

Mons. T: But what's it all about?

2nd Stretcher Bearer: Quite simply that the others' wrists are aching with carting so many corpses and wounded men about, and that we haven't found any yet. And it's not because we haven't looked!

Mons. T: Well, yes, that really is annoying. (*To* Zapo.) Are you quite sure no one's dead?

Zapo: Obviously, Papa.

Mons. T: Have you looked under all the sandbags?

Zapo: Yes, Papa.

Mons. T (*angrily*): Well then, you might as well say straight out that you don't want to lift a finger to help these gentlemen, when they're so nice, too!

1st Stretcher Bearer: Don't be angry with him. Let him be. We must just hope we'll have more luck in another trench and that all the lot'll be dead.

Mons. T: I should be delighted.

MME. T: Me too. There's nothing I like more than people who put their hearts into their work.

MONS. T (*indignantly, addressing his remarks to the wings*):   Then is no one going to do anything for these gentlemen?

ZAPO: If it only rested with me, it'd already be done.

ZÉPO: I can say the same.

MONS. T: But look here, is neither of you even wounded?

ZAPO (*ashamed*):   No, not me.

MONS. T (*to* ZÉPO):   What about you?

ZÉPO (*ashamed*):   Me neither. I never have any luck.

MME. T (*pleased*):   Now I remember! This morning, when I was peeling the onions, I cut my finger. Will that do you?

MONS. T: Of course it will! (*Enthusiastically.*) They'll take you off at once!

1ST STRETCHER BEARER: No, that won't work. With ladies it doesn't work.

MONS. T: We're no further advanced, then.

1ST STRETCHER BEARER: Never mind.

2ND STRETCHER BEARER: We may be able to make up for it in the other trenches. (*They start to go off.*)

MONS. T: Don't worry! If we find a dead man we'll keep him for you! No fear of us giving him to anyone else!

2ND STRETCHER BEARER: Thank you very much, sir.

MONS. T: Quite all right, old chap, think nothing of it. (*The two stretcher bearers say goodbye. All four answer them. The stretcher bearers go out.*)

MME. T: That's what's so pleasant about spending a Sunday in the country. You always meet such nice people.

MONS. T (*pause*):   But why are you enemies?

MME. T: Your father is the only one who's capable of thinking such ideas; don't forget he's a former student of the Ecole Normale, *and* a philatelist.[2]

ZÉPO: I don't know, I'm not very well educated.

MME. T: Was it by birth, or did you become enemies afterwards?

ZÉPO: I don't know, I don't know anything about it.

MONS. T: Well then, how did you come to be in the war?

ZÉPO: One day, at home, I was just mending my mother's iron, a man came and asked me: "Are you Zépo?" "Yes." "Right, you must come to the war." And so I asked him: "But what war?" and he said: "Don't you read the papers then? You're just a peasant!" I told him I did read the papers but not the war bits. . . .

ZAPO: Just how it was with me—exactly how it was with me.

MONS. T: Yes, they came to fetch you too.

MME. T: No, it wasn't quite the same; that day you weren't mending an iron, you were mending the car.

MONS. T: I was talking about the rest of it. (*To* ZÉPO.) Go on, what happened then?

---

[2] **Ecole Normale . . . philatelist:** student of the Teacher's College and a stamp collector.

ZÉPO: Then I told him I had a fiancée and that if I didn't take her to the pictures on Sundays she wouldn't like it. He said that wasn't the least bit important.

ZAPO: Just how it was with me—exactly how it was with me.

ZÉPO: And then my father came down, and he said I couldn't go to the war because I didn't have a horse.

ZAPO: Just what my father said.

ZÉPO: The man said you didn't need a horse any more, and I asked him if I could take my fiancée with me. He said no. Then I asked whether I could take my aunt with me so that she could make me one of her custards on Thursdays; I'm very fond of them.

MME. T (*realizing that she'd forgotten it*):   Oh! The custard!

ZÉPO: He said no again.

ZAPO: Same as with me.

ZÉPO: And ever since then I've been alone in the trench nearly all the time.

MME. T: I think you and your distinguished prisoner might play together this afternoon, as you're so close to each other and so bored.

ZAPO: Oh no, Mother, I'm too afraid, he's an enemy.

MONS. T: Now now, you mustn't be afraid.

ZAPO: If you only knew what the General was saying about the enemy!

MME. T: What did he say?

ZAPO: He said the enemy are very nasty people. When they take prisoners they put little stones in their shoes so that it hurts them to walk.

MME. T: How awful! What barbarians!

MONS. T (*indignantly, to* ZÉPO):   And aren't you ashamed to belong to an army of criminals?

ZÉPO: I haven't done anything. I don't do anybody any harm.

MME. T: He was trying to take us in, pretending to be such a little saint!

MONS. T: We oughtn't to have untied him. You never know, we only need to turn our backs and he'll be putting a stone in our shoes.

ZÉPO: Don't be so nasty to me.

MONS. T: What'd you think we *should* be, then? I'm indignant. I know what I'll do. I'll go and find the Captain and ask him to let me fight in the war.

ZAPO: He won't let you, you're too old.

MONS. T: Then I'll buy myself a horse and a sword and come and fight on my own account.

MME. T: Bravo! If I were a man I'd do the same.

ZÉPO: Don't be like that with me, Madame. Anyway I'll tell you something—our General told us the same thing about you.

MME. T: How could he dare tell such a lie!

ZAPO: No—but the same thing really?

ZÉPO: Yes, the same thing.

MONS. T: Perhaps it was the same man who talked to you both?

MME. T: Well if it was the same man he might at least have said something different. That's a fine thing—saying the same thing to everyone!

MONS. T (*to* ZÉPO *in a different tone of voice*):   Another little drink?

MME. T: I hope you liked our lunch?

MONS. T: In any case, it was better than last Sunday.

ZÉPO: What happened?

MONS. T: Well, we went to the country and we put the food on the rug. While we'd got our backs turned a cow ate up all our lunch, and the napkins as well.

ZÉPO: What a greedy cow!

MONS. T: Yes, but afterwards, to get our own back, we ate the cow. (*They laugh.*)

ZAPO (*to* ZÉPO):   They couldn't have been very hungry after that!

MONS. T: Cheers! (*They all drink.*)

MME. T (*to* ZÉPO):   And what do you do to amuse yourself in the trench?

ZÉPO: I spend my time making flowers out of rags, to amuse myself. I get terribly bored.

MME. T: And what do you do with the flowers?

ZÉPO: At the beginning I used to send them to my fiancée, but one day she told me that the greenhouse and the cellar were already full of them and that she didn't know what to do with them any more, and she asked me, if I didn't mind, to send her something else.

MME. T: And what did you do?

ZÉPO: I go on making rag flowers to pass the time.

MME. T: Do you throw them away afterwards, then?

ZÉPO: No, I've found a way to use them now. I give one flower for each pal who dies. That way I know that even if I make an awful lot there'll never be enough.

MONS. T: That's a good solution you've hit on.

ZÉPO (*shyly*):   Yes.

ZAPO: Well, what I do is knit, so as not to get bored.

MME. T: But tell me, are all the soldiers as bored as you?

ZÉPO: It all depends on what they do to amuse themselves.

ZAPO: It's the same on our side.

MONS. T: Then let's stop the war.

ZÉPO: How?

MONS. T: It's very simple. (*To* ZAPO.) You just tell your pals that the enemy soldiers don't want to fight a war, and you (*to* ZÉPO) say the same to your comrades. And then everyone goes home.

ZAPO: Marvellous!

MME. T: And then you'll be able to finish mending the iron.

ZAPO: How is it that no one thought of such a good idea before?

MME. T: Your father is the only one who's capable of thinking such ideas; don't forget he's a former student of the Ecole Normale, *and* a philatelist.

ZÉPO: But what will the sergeant-majors and corporals do?

MONS. T: We'll give them some guitars and castanets to keep them quiet!

ZÉPO: Very good idea.

MONS. T: You see how easy it is. Everything's fixed.

ZÉPO: We shall have a tremendous success.

ZAPO: My pals will be terribly pleased.

MME. T: What d'you say to putting on the pasodoble we were playing just now, to celebrate?

ZÉPO: Perfect.

ZAPO: Yes, put the record on, Mother. (MME. TÉPAN *puts a record on. She turns the handle. She waits. Nothing can be heard.*)

MONS. T: I can't hear a thing.

MME. T: Oh, how silly of me! Instead of putting a record on I put on a beret. (*She puts the record on. A gay pasodoble is heard.* ZAPO *dances with* ZÉPO *and* MME. TÉPAN *with her husband. They are all very gay. The field telephone rings. None of the four hears it. They go on dancing busily. The telephone rings again. The dance continues.*

    The battle starts up again with a terrific din of bombs, shots and bursts of machine-gun fire. None of the four has seen anything and they go on dancing merrily. A burst of machine-gun fire mows them all down. They fall to the ground, stone dead. A shot must have grazed the gramophone; the record keeps repeating the same thing, like a scratched record. The music of the scratched record can be heard till the end of the play. The two STRETCHER BEARERS *enter left. They are carrying the empty stretcher.*)

SUDDEN CURTAIN

[1967]

Journal Entry

What images, ideas, or associations does the word *absurd* evoke for you? What elements of Arrabal's drama fit your lists? How would you define "theater of the absurd"?

Textual Considerations

1. Describe the phonic and visual images of war in the play. How does Arrabal convey them? Cite the impact of these effects and explain how they contribute to meaning.
2. What attitudes about war does the playwright convey by having Zépo and Zapo double and mirror each other? What role do the parents play in the drama? Contrast their views of war with those of Zépo and Zapo.
3. The sense of the absurdity of life in *Picnic on the Battlefield* is usually ascribed to the characters' inability to control their own lives. To examine how Arrabal communicates his view of the absurd to the audience, make a list of the contradictions, paradoxes, and contrast devices that dominate his characters' use of language.
4. How do you respond to the play's title and its ending? Why does Arrabal juxtapose *picnic* and *battlefield* in the play's title? Does the author foreshadow the end at an earlier point in the play? Cite evidence for your answer.
5. What role do the stretcher bearers play in *Picnic in the Battlefield*? Analyze the degree to which their presence advances or increases the dramatic action. What does their presence add to the war theme?

Cultural Contexts

1. Arrabal, who wrote this play when he was only fourteen, describes it as "panic the-ater." What aspects of *Picnic on the Battlefield* best fit his description?
2. Select examples of prowar or antiwar attitude in *Picnic on the Battlefield* to analyze the cultural conventions, war myths, and sensibilities that Monsieur and Madame Tépan, Zépo, Zapo, and the government officials exhibit regarding war. Discuss whether you and your classmates support these conventions and sensibilities.

Performance Exercises

PERFORMANCE EXPRESS (45 MINUTES)

. Select a comic dialogue from *Picnic on the Battlefield*—Zapo's imprisonment of Zépo and the dialogue that follows would be a good choice—and deliver it in a way that emphasizes the dehumanization of the characters. Invite the whole class to direct and advise the actors by suggesting facial movements, gestures, and voice qualities that highlight comic effects. Should the actors playing Zapo and Zépo be interchangeable in your staging of this scene? As costume designers, how would you dress them?

PERFORMANCE PROJECTS

1. Stage *Picnic on the Battlefield* in a way that would bring out the absurdity of its comic, one-dimensional characters and the wordplay of their disjointed dialogues. Consider the settings, props, costumes, and the phonic effects you would use in the stage direc-tions. What challenges do the roles of these "absurd" characters present to tradi-tional staging conventions?
2. To help you focus on *Picnic on the Battlefield* as a "theater of the absurd" play, use the Internet to access an English-language production of this play. Read about it, then stage Arrabal's play using sets, costumes, and music to evoke a twentieth-century war scenario. Discuss with your group which lines you would cut out to ensure the dra-matic impact you want your postmodern production to have on the audience.

Maria Irene Fornes

The Conduct of Life

CHARACTERS

ORLANDO, *an army lieutenant at*
the start of the play. A lieutenant
commander soon after.
LETICIA, *his wife, ten years his elder.*

ALEJO, *a lieutenant commander.*
Their friend.
NENA, *a destitute girl of twelve.*
OLIMPIA, *a servant.*

A Latin American country. The present.

The floor is divided in four horizontal planes. Downstage is the living room,
which is about ten feet deep. Center stage, eighteen inches high, is the dining
room, which is about ten feet deep. Further upstage, eighteen inches high, is a
hallway which is about four feet deep. At each end of the hallway there is a
door. The one to the right leads to the servants' quarters, the one to the left to
the basement. Upstage, three feet lower than the hallway (same level as the
living room), is the cellar, which is about sixteen feet deep. Most of the cellar is
occupied by two platforms which are eight feet wide, eight feet deep, and three
feet high. Upstage of the cellar are steps that lead up. Approximately ten feet
above the cellar is another level, extending from the extreme left to the
extreme right, which represents a warehouse. There is a door on the left of the
warehouse. On the left and the right of the living room there are archways
that lead to hallways or antechambers, the floors of these hallways are the same
level as the dining room. On the left and the right of the dining room there is a
second set of archways that lead to hallways or antechambers, the floors of
which are the same level as the hallways. All along the edge of each level there
is a step that leads to the next level. All floors and steps are black marble. In
the living room there are two chairs. One is to the left, next to a table with a
telephone. The other is to the right. In the dining room there are a large green
marble table and three chairs. On the cellar floor there is a mattress to the
right and a chair to the left. In the warehouse there is a table and a chair to
the left, and a chair and some boxes and crates to the right.

SCENE 1

ORLANDO *is doing jumping-jacks in the upper left corner of the dining room in*
the dark. A light, slowly, comes up on him. He wears military breeches held by
suspenders, and riding boots. He does jumping-jacks as long as it can be
endured. He stops, the center area starts to become visible. There is a chair
upstage of the table. There is a linen towel on the left side of the table. ORLANDO
dries his face with the towel and sits as he puts the towel around his neck.

ORLANDO: Thirty three and I'm still a lieutenant. In two years I'll receive a promotion or I'll leave the military. I promise I will not spend time feeling sorry for myself.—Instead I will study the situation and draw an effective plan of action. I must eliminate all obstacles.—I will make the acquaintance of people in high power. If I cannot achieve this on my own merit, I will marry a woman in high circles. Leticia must not be an obstacle.—Man must have an ideal, mine is to achieve maximum power. That is my destiny.—No other interest will deter me from this.—My sexual drive is detrimental to my ideals. I must no longer be overwhelmed by sexual passion or I will be degraded beyond hope of recovery. (*Lights fade to black.*)

SCENE 2

> ALEJO *sits to the right of the dining room table.* ORLANDO *stands to* ALEJO'S *left. He is now a lieutenant commander. He wears an army tunic, breeches, and boots.* LETICIA *stands to the left. She wears a dress that suggests 1940s fashion.*

LETICIA: What! Me go hunting! Do you think I'm going to shoot a deer, the most beautiful animal in the world? Do you think I'm going to destroy a deer? On the contrary. I would run in the field and scream and wave my arms like a mad woman and try to scare them away so the hunters could not reach them. I'd run in front of the bullets and let the mad hunters kill me—stand in the way of the bullets—stop the bullets with my body. I don't see how anyone can shoot a deer.

ORLANDO (*To* ALEJO.): Do you understand that? You, who are her friend, can you understand that? You don't think that is madness? She's mad. Tell her that—she'll think it's you who's mad. (*To* LETICIA.) Hunting is a sport! A skill! Don't talk about something you know nothing about. Must you have an opinion about every damn thing! Can't you keep your mouth shut when you don't know what you're talking about? (ORLANDO *exits right.*)

LETICIA: He told me that he didn't love me, and that his sole relationship with me was simply a marital one. What he means is that I am to keep this house, and he is to provide for it. That's what he said. That explains why he treats me the way he treats me. I never understood why he did, but now it's clear. He doesn't love me. I thought he loved me and that he stayed with me because he loved me and that's why I didn't understand his behavior. But now I know, because he told me that he sees me as a person who runs the house. I never understood that because I would have never—if he had said, "Would you marry me to run my house even if I don't love you." I would have never—I would have never believed what I was hearing. I would have never believed that these words were coming out of his mouth. Because I loved him. (ORLANDO *has entered.* LETICIA *sees him and exits left.* ORLANDO *enters and sits center.*)

ORLANDO: I didn't say any of that. I told her that she's not my heir. That's what I said. I told her that she's not in my will, and she will not receive a penny of my money if I die. That's what I said. I didn't say anything about running the house. I said she will not inherit a penny from me because I didn't want to be humiliated. She is capable of foolishness beyond anyone's imagination. Ask her what she would do if she were rich and could do anything she wants with her money. (LETICIA *enters.*)

LETICIA: I would distribute it among the poor.

ORLANDO: She has no respect for money.

LETICIA: That is not true. If I had money I would give it to those who need it. I know what money is, what money can do. It can feed people, it can put a roof over their heads. Money can do that. It can clothe them. What do you know about money? What does it mean to you? What do you do with money? Buy rifles? To shoot deer?

ORLANDO: You're foolish!—You're foolish! You're a foolish woman! (ORLANDO *exits. He speaks from offstage.*) Foolish. . . . Foolish. . . .

LETICIA: He has no respect for me. He is insensitive. He doesn't listen. You cannot reach him. He is deaf. He is an animal. Nothing touches him except sensuality. He responds to food, to the flesh. To music sometimes, if it is romantic. To the moon. He is romantic but he is not aware of what you are feeling. I can't change him—I'll tell you why I asked you to come. Because I want something from you—I want you to educate me. I want to study. I want to study so I am not an ignorant person. I want to go to the university. I want to be knowledge-able. I'm tired of being ignored. I want to study political science. Is political science what diplomats study? Is that what it is? You have to teach me elemental things because I never finished grammar school. I would have to study a great deal. A great deal so I could enter the university. I would have to go through all the subjects. I would like to be a woman who speaks in a group and have others listen.

ALEJO: Why do you want to worry about any of that? What's the use? Do you think you can change anything? Do you think anyone can change anything?

LETICIA: Why not? (*Pause.*) Do you think I'm crazy?—He can't help it.—Do you think I'm crazy?—Because I love him? (*He looks away from her. Lights fade to black.*)

SCENE 3

ORLANDO *enters the warehouse holding* NENA *close to him. She wears a gray over-large uniform. She is barefoot. She resists him. She is tearful and frightened. She pulls away and runs to the right wall. He follows her.*

ORLANDO (*Softly.*):   You called me a snake.

NENA: No, I didn't. (*He tries to reach her. She pushes his hands away from her.*) I was kidding.—I swear I was kidding.

He grabs her and pushes her against the wall. He pushes his pelvis against her. He moves to the chair dragging her with him. She crawls to the left, pushes the table aside and stands behind it. He walks around the table. She goes under it. He grabs her foot and pulls her out toward the down-stage side. He opens his fly and pushes his pelvis against her. Lights fade to black.

SCENE 4

OLIMPIA *is wiping crumbs off the dining room table. She wears a plain gray uniform.* LETICIA *sits to the left of the table facing front. She wears a dressing gown. She writes in a notebook. There is some silverware on the table.* OLIMPIA *has a speech defect.*

LETICIA: Let's do this.

OLIMPIA: O.K. (*She continues wiping the table.*)

LETICIA (*Still writing.*):   What are you doing?

OLIMPIA: I'm doing what I always do.

LETICIA: Let's do this.

OLIMPIA (*In a mumble.*):   As soon as I finish doing this. You can't just ask me to do what you want me to do, and interrupt what I'm doing. I don't stop from the time I wake up in the morning to the time I go to sleep. You can't interrupt me whenever you want, not if you want me to get to the end of my work. I wake up at 5:30. I wash. I put on my clothes and make my bed. I go to the kitchen. I get the milk and the bread from outside and I put them on the counter. I open the icebox. I put one bottle in and take the butter out. I leave the other bottle on the counter. I shut the refrigerator door. I take the pan that I use for water and put water in it. I know how much. I put the pan on the stove, light the stove, cover it. I take the top off the milk and pour it in the milk pan except for a little. (*Indicating with her finger.*) Like this. For the cat. I put the pan on the stove, light the stove. I put coffee in the thing. I know how much. I light the oven and put bread in it. I come here, get the tablecloth and I lay it on the table. I shout "Breakfast." I get the napkins. I take the cups, the saucers, and the silver out and set the table. I go to the kitchen. I put the tray on the counter, put the butter on the tray. The water and the milk are getting hot. I pick up the cat's dish. I wash it. I pour the milk I left in the bottle in the milk dish. I put it on the floor for the cat. I shout "Breakfast." The water boils. I pour it in the thing. When the milk boils I turn off the gas and cover the milk. I get the bread from the oven. I slice it down the middle and butter it. Then I cut it in pieces (*indicating*) this big. I set a piece aside for me. I put the rest of the bread in the bread dish and shout "Breakfast." I pour the coffee in the coffee pot and the milk in the milk pitcher, except I leave (*indicating*) this much for me. I put them on the tray and bring them here. If you're not in the dining room I call again. "Breakfast." I go to the kitchen, I fill the milk pan with water and let it soak. I pour my coffee, sit at the counter and eat my breakfast. I go upstairs to make your bed and clean your bathroom. I come down here to meet you and figure out what you want for lunch and dinner. And try to get you to think quickly so I can run to the market and get it bought before all the fresh stuff is bought up. Then, I start the day.

LETICIA: So?

OLIMPIA: So I need a steam pot.

LETICIA: What is a steam pot?

OLIMPIA: A pressure cooker.

LETICIA: And you want a steam pot? Don't you have enough pots?

OLIMPIA: No.

LETICIA: Why do you want a steam pot?

OLIMPIA: It cooks faster.

LETICIA: How much is it?

OLIMPIA: Expensive.

LETICIA: How much?

OLIMPIA: Twenty.

LETICIA: Too expensive. (OLIMPIA *throws the silver on the floor.* LETICIA *turns her eyes up to the ceiling.*) Why do you want one more pot?

OLIMPIA: I don't have a steam pot.

LETICIA: A pressure cooker.

OLIMPIA: A pressure cooker.

LETICIA: You have too many pots. (OLIMPIA *goes to the kitchen and returns with an aluminum pan. She shows it to* LETICIA.)

OLIMPIA: Look at this. (LETICIA *looks at it.*)

LETICIA: What? (OLIMPIA *hits the pan against the back of a chair, breaking off a piece of the bottom.*)

OLIMPIA: It's no good.

LETICIA: All right! (*She takes money from her pocket and gives it to* OLIMPIA.) Here. Buy it!—What are we having for lunch?

OLIMPIA: Fish.

LETICIA: I don't like fish.—What else?

OLIMPIA: Boiled plantains.

LETICIA: Make something I like.

OLIMPIA: Avocados. (LETICIA *gives a look of resentment to* OLIMPIA.)

LETICIA: Why can't you make something I like?

OLIMPIA: Avocados.

LETICIA: Something that needs cooking.

OLIMPIA: Bread pudding.

LETICIA: And for dinner?

OLIMPIA: Pot roast.

LETICIA: What else?

OLIMPIA: Rice.

LETICIA: What else?

OLIMPIA: Salad.

LETICIA: What kind?

OLIMPIA: Avocado.

LETICIA: Again. (OLIMPIA *looks at* LETICIA.)

OLIMPIA: You like avocados.

LETICIA: Not again.—Tomatoes. (OLIMPIA *mumbles.*) What's wrong with tomatoes besides that you don't like them? (OLIMPIA *mumbles.*) Get some. (OLIMPIA *mumbles.*) What does that mean? (OLIMPIA *doesn't answer.*) Buy tomatoes.— What else?

OLIMPIA: That's all.

LETICIA: We need a green.

OLIMPIA: Watercress.

LETICIA: What else?

OLIMPIA: Nothing.

LETICIA: For dessert.

OLIMPIA: Bread pudding.

LETICIA: Again.

OLIMPIA: Why not?

LETICIA: Make a flan.

OLIMPIA: No flan.

LETICIA: Why not?

OLIMPIA: No good.

LETICIA: Why no good!—Buy some fruit then.

OLIMPIA: What kind?

LETICIA: Pineapple. (OLIMPIA *shakes her head.*) Why not? (OLIMPIA *shakes her head.*) Mango.

OLIMPIA: No mango.

LETICIA: Buy some fruit! That's all. Don't forget bread. (LETICIA *hands* OLIMPIA *some bills.* OLIMPIA *holds it and waits for more.* LETICIA *hands her one more bill. Lights fade to black.*)

SCENE 5

The warehouse table is propped against the door. The chair on the left faces right. The door is pushed and the table falls to the floor. ORLANDO *enters. He wears an undershirt with short sleeves, breeches with suspenders and boots. He looks around the room for* NENA. *Believing she has escaped, he becomes still and downcast. He turns to the door and stands there for a moment. He takes a few steps to the right and stands there for a moment staring fixedly. He hears a sound from behind the boxes, walks to them and takes a box off.* NENA *is there. Her head is covered with a blanket. He pulls the blanket off.* NENA *is motionless and staring into space. He looks at her for a while, then walks to the chair and sits facing right staring into space. A few moments pass. Lights fade to black.*

SCENE 6

Leticia speaks on the telephone to Mona.

LETICIA: Since they moved him to the new department he's different. (*Brief pause.*) He's distracted. I don't know where he goes in his mind. He doesn't listen to me. He worries. When I talk to him he doesn't listen. He's thinking about the job. He says he worries. What is there to worry about? Do you think there is anything to worry about? (*Brief pause.*) What meeting? (*Brief pause.*) Oh, sure. When is it? (*Brief pause.*) At what time? What do you mean I knew? No one told me.—I don't remember. Would you pick me up? (*Brief pause.*) At one? Isn't one early? (*Brief pause.*) Orlando may still be home at one. Sometimes he's here a little longer than usual. After lunch he sits and smokes. Don't you think one thirty will give us enough time? (*Brief pause.*) No. I can't leave while he's smoking . . . I'd rather not. I'd rather wait till he leaves. (*Brief pause.*) . . . One thirty, then. Thank you, Mona. (*Brief pause.*) See you then. Bye. (Leticia *puts down the receiver and walks to stage right area.* Orlando's *voice is heard offstage left. He and* Alejo *enter halfway through the following speech.*)

ORLANDO: He made loud sounds not high-pitched like a horse. He sounded like a whale, like a wounded whale. He was pouring liquid from everywhere, his mouth, his nose, his eyes. He was not a horse by a sexual organ.—Helpless. A viscera.—Screaming. Making strange sounds. He collapsed on top of her. She wanted him off but he collapsed on top of her and stayed there on top of her. Like gum. He looked more like a whale than a horse. A seal. His muscles were soft. What does it feel like to be without shape like that. Without pride. She was indifferent. He stayed there for a while and then lifted himself off her and to the ground. (*Pause.*) He looked like a horse again.

LETICIA: Alejo, how are you? (Alejo *kisses* Leticia's *hand.*)

ORLANDO: (*As he walks to the living room. He sits left facing front.*) Alejo is staying for dinner.

LETICIA: Would you like some coffee?

ALEJO: Yes, thank you.

LETICIA: Would you like some coffee, Orlando?

ORLANDO: Yes, thank you.

LETICIA (*In a loud voice towards the kitchen.*):   Olimpia . . .

OLIMPIA: What?

LETICIA: Coffee . . . (Leticia *sits to the right of the table.* Alejo *sits center.*)

ALEJO: Have you heard?

LETICIA: Yes, he's dead and I'm glad he's dead. An evil man. I knew he'd be killed. Who killed him?

ALEJO: Someone who knew him.

LETICIA: What is there to gain? So he's murdered. Someone else will do the job. Nothing will change. To destroy them all is to say we destroy us all.

ALEJO: Do you think we're all rotten?

LETICIA: Yes.

ORLANDO: A bad germ?

LETICIA: Yes.

ORLANDO: In our hearts?

LETICIA: Yes.—In our eyes.

ORLANDO: You're silly.

LETICIA: We're blind. We can't see beyond an arm's reach. We don't believe our life will last beyond the day. We only know what we have in our hand to put in our mouth, to put in our stomach, and to put in our pocket. We take care of our pocket, but not of our country. We take care of our stomachs but not of our hungry. We are primitive. We don't believe in the future. Each night when the sun goes down we think that's the end of life—so we have one last fling. We don't think we have a future. We don't think we have a country. Ask anybody, "Do you have a country?" They'll say, "Yes." Ask them, "What is your country?" They'll say, "My bed, my dinner plate." But, things can change. They can. I have changed. You have changed. He has changed.

ALEJO: Look at me. I used to be an idealist. Now I don't have any feeling for anything. I used to be strong, healthy, I looked at the future with hope.

LETICIA: Now you don't?

ALEJO: Now I don't. I know what viciousness is.

ORLANDO: What is viciousness?

ALEJO: You.

ORLANDO: Me?

ALEJO: The way you tortured Felo.

ORLANDO: I never tortured Felo.

ALEJO: You did.

ORLANDO: Boys play that way. You did too.

ALEJO: I didn't.

ORLANDO: He was repulsive to us.

ALEJO: I never hurt him.

ORLANDO: Well, you never stopped me.

ALEJO: I didn't know how to stop you. I didn't know anyone could behave the way you did. It frightened me. It changed me. I became hopeless. (ORLANDO *walks to the dining room.*)

ORLANDO: You were always hopeless. (*He exits.* OLIMPIA *enters carrying three demitasse coffees on a tray. She places them on the table and exits.*)

ALEJO: I am sexually impotent. I have no feelings. Things pass through me which resemble feelings but I know they are not. I'm impotent.

LETICIA: Nonsense.

ALEJO: It's not nonsense. How can you say it's nonsense?—How can one live in a world that festers the way ours does and take any pleasure in life? (*Lights fade to black.*)

SCENE 7

NENA *and* ORLANDO *stand against the wall in the warehouse. She is fully dressed. He is barebreasted. He pushes his pelvis against her gently. His lips touch her face as he speaks. The words are inaudible to the audience. On the table there is a tin plate with food and a tin cup with milk.*

ORLANDO: Look this way. I'm going to do something to you. (*She makes a move away from him.*) Don't do that. Don't move away. (*As he slides his hand along her side.*) I just want to put my hand here like this. (*He puts his lips on hers softly and speaks at the same time.*) Don't hold your lips so tight. Make them soft. Let them loose. So I can do this. (*She whimpers.*) Don't cry. I won't hurt you. This is all I'm going to do to you. Just hold your lips soft. Be nice. Be a nice girl. (*He pushes against her and reaches an orgasm. He remains motionless for a moment, then steps away from her still leaning his hand on the wall.*) Go eat. I brought you food. (*She goes to the table. He sits on the floor and watches her eat. She eats voraciously. She looks at the milk.*) Drink it. It's milk. It's good for you. (*She drinks the milk, then continues eating. Lights fade to black.*)

SCENE 8

LETICIA *stands left of the dining room table. She speaks words she has memorized.* OLIMPIA *sits to the left of the table. She holds a book close to her eyes. Her head moves from left to right along the written words as she mumbles the sound of imaginary words. She continues doing this through the rest of the scene.*

LETICIA: The impact of war is felt particularly in the economic realm. The destruction of property, private as well as public may paralyze the country. Foreign investment is virtually . . . (*To* OLIMPIA.) Is that right? (*Pause.*) Is that right!

OLIMPIA: Wait a moment. (*She continues mumbling and moving her head.*)

LETICIA: What for? (*Pause.*) You can't read. (*Pause.*) You can't read!

OLIMPIA: Wait a moment. (*She continues mumbling and moving her head.*)

LETICIA: (*Slapping the book off* OLIMPIA's *hand.*) Why are you pretending you can read? (OLIMPIA *slaps* LETICIA's *hands. They slap each other's hands. Lights fade to black.*)

SCENE 9

ORLANDO *sits in the living room. He smokes. He faces front and is thoughtful.* LETICIA *and* OLIMPIA *are in the dining room.* LETICIA *wears a hat and jacket. She tries to put a leather strap through the loops of a suitcase. There is a smaller piece of luggage on the floor.*

LETICIA: This strap is too wide. It doesn't fit through the loop. (ORLANDO *doesn't reply.*) Is this the right strap? Is this the strap that came with this suitcase? Did the strap that came with the suitcase break? If so, where is it? And when did it break? Why doesn't this strap fit the suitcase and how did it get here. Did you buy this strap, Orlando?

ORLANDO: I may have.

LETICIA: It doesn't fit.

ORLANDO: Hm.

LETICIA: It doesn't fit through the loops.

ORLANDO: Just strap it outside the loops. (LETICIA *stands.* OLIMPIA *tries to put the strap through the loop.*)

LETICIA: No. You're supposed to put it through the loops. That's what the loops are for. What happened to the other strap?

ORLANDO: It broke.

LETICIA: How?

ORLANDO: I used it for something.

LETICIA: What! (*He looks at her.*) You should have gotten me one that fit. What did you use if for?—Look at that.

OLIMPIA: Strap it outside the loops.

LETICIA: That wouldn't look right.

ORLANDO: (*Going to look at the suitcase.*) Why do you need the straps?

LETICIA: Because they come with it.

ORLANDO: You don't need them.

LETICIA: And travel like this?

ORLANDO: Use another suitcase.

LETICIA: What other suitcase. I don't have another. (ORLANDO *looks at his watch.*)

ORLANDO: You're going to miss your plane.

LETICIA: I'm not going. I'm not travelling like this.

ORLANDO: Go without it. I'll send it to you.

LETICIA: You'll get new luggage, repack it and send it to me?—All right. (*She starts to exit left.*) It's nice to travel light. (*Off stage.*) Do I have everything?—Come, Olimpia.

> OLIMPIA *follows with the suitcases.* ORLANDO *takes the larger suitcase from* OLIMPIA. *She exits.* ORLANDO *goes up the hallway and exits through the left door. A moment later he enters holding* NENA *close to him. She is pale, dishevelled and has black circles around her eyes. She has a high fever and is almost unconscious. Her dress is torn and soiled. She is barefoot. He carries a new cotton dress on his arm. He takes her to the chair in the living room. He takes off the soiled dress and puts the new dress on her over a soiled slip.*

ORLANDO: That's nice. You look nice. (LETICIA'*s voice is heard. He hurriedly takes* NENA *out the door, closes it, and leans on it.*)

LETICIA: (*Off stage.*) It would take but a second. You run to the garage and get the little suitcase and I'll take out the things I need. (LETICIA *and* OLIMPIA *enter left.* OLIMPIA *exits right.*) Hurry. Hurry. It would take but a second. (*Seeing* ORLANDO.) Orlando, I came back because I couldn't leave without anything at all. I came to get a few things because I have a smaller suitcase where I can take a few things. (*She puts the suitcase on the table, opens it and takes out the things she mentions.*) A pair of shoes . . . (OLIMPIA *enters right with a small suitcase.*)

OLIMPIA: *Here.*

LETICIA:	OLIMPIA:
A nightgown,	A robe,
a robe,	a dress,
underwear,	a nightgown,
a dress,	underwear,
a sweater.	a sweater,
	a pair of shoes.

> LETICIA *closes the large suitcase.* OLIMPIA *closes the smaller suitcase.*

LETICIA (*Starting to exit.*):   Goodbye.

OLIMPIA (*Following* LETICIA.):   Goodbye.

ORLANDO: *Goodbye.*   (Lights fade to black.)

SCENE 10

NENA *is curled on the extreme right of the mattress.* ORLANDO *sits on the mattress using* NENA *as a back support.* ALEJO *sits on the chair. He holds a green paper in his hand.* OLIMPIA *sweeps the floor.*

ORLANDO: Tell them to check him. See if there's a scratch on him. There's not a scratch on that body. Why the fuss! Who was he and who's making a fuss? Why is he so important.

ALEJO: He was in deep. He knew names.

ORLANDO: I was never told that. But it wouldn't have mattered if they had because he died before I touched him.

ALEJO: You have to go to headquarters. They want you there.

ORLANDO: He came in screaming and he wouldn't stop. I had to wait for him to stop screaming before I could even pose a question to him. He wouldn't stop. I had put the poker to his neck to see if he would stop. Just to see if he would shut up. He just opened his eyes wide and started shaking and screamed even louder and fell over dead. Maybe he took something. I didn't do anything to him. If I didn't get anything from him it's because he died before I could get to him. He died of fear, not from anything I did to him. Tell them to do an autopsy. I'm telling you the truth. That's the truth. Why the fuss.

ALEJO (*Starting to put the paper in his pocket.*):   I'll tell them what you said.

ORLANDO: Let me see that. (ALEJO *takes it to him.* ORLANDO *looks at it and puts it back in* ALEJO's *hands.*) O.K. so it's a trap. So what side are you on? (*Pause.* ALEJO *says nothing.*) So what do they want? (*Pause.*) Who's going to question me? That's funny. That's very funny. They want to question me. They want to punch my eyes out? I knew something was wrong because they were getting nervous. Antonio was getting nervous. I went to him and I asked him if something was wrong. He said, no, nothing was wrong. But I could tell something was wrong. He looked at Velez and Velez looked back at him. They are stupid. They want to conceal something from me and they look at each other right in front of me, as if I'm blind, as if I can't tell that they are worried about something. As if there's something happening right in front of my nose but I'm blind and I can't see it. (*He grabs the paper from* ALEJO's *hand.*) You understand? (*He goes up the steps.*)

OLIMPIA: Like an alligator, big mouth and no brains. Lots of teeth but no brains. All tongue. (ORLANDO *enters through the left hallway door, and sits at the dining room table.* ALEJO *enters a few moments later. He stands to the right.*)

ORLANDO: What kind of way is this to treat me?—After what I've done for them?—Is this a way to treat me?—I'll come up . . . as soon as I can—I haven't been well.—O.K. I'll come up. I get depressed because things are bad and they are not going to improve. There's something malignant in the world.

Destructiveness, aggressiveness.—Greed. People take what is not theirs. There is greed. I am depressed, disillusioned . . . with life . . . with work . . . family. I don't see hope. (*He sits. He speaks more to himself than to* ALEJO.) Some people get a cut in a finger and die. Because their veins are right next to their skin. There are people who, if you punch them in their stomach the skin around the stomach bursts and the bowels fall out. Other people, you cut them open and you don't see any veins. You can't find their intestines. There are people who don't even bleed. There are people who bleed like pigs. There are people who have the nerves right on their skins. You touch them and they scream. They have their vital organs close to the surface. You hit them and they burst an organ. I didn't even touch this one and he died. He died of fear. (*Lights fade to black.*)

SCENE 11

NENA, ALEJO, *and* OLIMPIA *sit cross-legged on the mattress in the basement.* NENA *sits right*, ALEJO *center*, OLIMPIA *left.* NENA *and* OLIMPIA *play pattycake.* ORLANDO *enters. He goes close to them.*

ORLANDO: What are you doing?

OLIMPIA: I'm playing with her.

ORLANDO (*To* ALEJO.): What are you doing here? (ALEJO *looks at* ORLANDO *as a reply.* ORLANDO *speaks sarcastically.*) They're playing pattycake. (*He goes near* NENA.) So? (*Short pause.* NENA *giggles.*) Stop laughing! (NENA *is frightened.* OLIMPIA *holds her.*)

OLIMPIA: Why do you have to spoil everything. We were having a good time.

ORLANDO: Shut up! (NENA *whimpers.*) Stop whimpering. I can't stand your whimpering. I can't stand it. (*Timidly, she tries to speak words as she whimpers.*) Speak up. I can't hear you! She's crazy! Take her to the crazy house!

OLIMPIA: She's not crazy! She's a baby!

ORLANDO: She's not a baby! She's crazy! You think she's a baby? She's older than you think! How old do you think she is—Don't tell me that.

OLIMPIA: She's sick. Don't you see she's sick? Let her cry! (*To* NENA.) Cry!

ORLANDO: You drive me crazy too with your . . . (*He imitates her speech defect. She punches him repeatedly.*)

OLIMPIA: You drive me crazy! (*He pushes her off.*) You drive me crazy! You are a bastard! One day I'm going to kill you when you're asleep! I'm going to open you up and cut your entrails and feed them to the snakes. (*She tries to strangle him.*) I'm going to tear your heart out and feed it to the dogs! I'm going to cut your head open and have the cats eat your brain! (*Reaching for his fly.*) I'm going to cut your peepee and hang it on a tree and feed it to the birds!

ORLANDO: Get off me! I'm getting rid of you too! (*He starts to exit.*) I can't stand you!

OLIMPIA: Oh, yeah! I'm getting rid of you.

ORLANDO: I can't stand you!

OLIMPIA: I can't stand you!

ORLANDO: Meddler! (*To* ALEJO.) I can't stand you either.

OLIMPIA (*Going to the stairs.*):   Tell the boss! Tell her! She won't get rid of me! She'll get rid of you! What good are you! Tell her! (*She goes to* NENA.) Don't pay any attention to him. He's a coward.—You're pretty. (ORLANDO *enters through the hallway left door. He sits center at the dining room table and leans his head on it.* LETICIA *enters. He turns to look at her.*)

LETICIA: You didn't send it. (*Lights fade to black.*)

SCENE 12

LETICIA *sits next to the phone. She speaks to Mona in her mind.*

LETICIA: I walk through the house and I know where he's made love to her I think I hear his voice making love to her. Saying the same things he says to me, the same words.—(*There is a pause.*) There is someone here. He keeps someone here in the house. (*Pause.*) I don't dare look. (*Pause.*) No, there's nothing I can do. I can't do anything. (*She walks to the hallway. She hears footsteps. She moves rapidly to left and hides behind a pillar.* OLIMPIA *enters from right. She takes a few steps down the hallway. She carries a plate of food. She sees* LETICIA *and stops. She takes a few steps in various directions, then stops.*)

OLIMPIA: Here kitty, kitty. (LETICIA *walks to* OLIMPIA, *looks closely at the plate, then up at* OLIMPIA.)

LETICIA: What is it?

OLIMPIA: Food.

LETICIA: Who is it for? (OLIMPIA *turns her eyes away and doesn't answer.* LETICIA *decides to go to the cellar door. She stops halfway there.*) Who is it?

OLIMPIA: A cat. (LETICIA *opens the cellar door.*)

LETICIA: It's not a cat. I'm going down. (*She opens the door to the cellar and starts to go down.*) I want to see who is there.

ORLANDO (*Offstage from the cellar.*):   What is it you want? (*Lights fade to black.*)

SCENE 13

ORLANDO *leans back on the chair in the basement. His legs are outstretched. His eyes are bloodshot and leery. His tunic is open.* NENA *is curled on the floor.* ORLANDO *speaks quietly. He is deeply absorbed.*

ORLANDO: What I do to you is out of love. Out of want. It's not what you think. I wish you didn't have to be hurt. I don't do it out of hatred. It is not out of rage. It is love. It is a quiet feeling. It's a pleasure. It is quiet and it pierces my insides in the most internal way. It is my most private self. And this I give to you.—Don't be afraid.—It is a desire to destroy and to see things destroyed and to see the inside of them.—It's my nature. I must hide this from others. But I don't feel remorse. I was born this way and I must have this.—I need love. I wish you did not feel hurt and recoil from me. (*Lights fade to black.*)

SCENE 14

ORLANDO *sits to the right and* LETICIA *sits to the left of the table.*

LETICIA: Don't make her scream. (*There is a pause.*)

ORLANDO: You're crazy.

LETICIA: Don't I give you enough?

ORLANDO (*He's calm.*): Don't start.

LETICIA: How long is she going to be here?

ORLANDO: Not long.

LETICIA: Don't make her cry. (*He looks at her.*) I can't stand it. (*Pause.*) Why do you make her scream?

ORLANDO: I don't make her scream.

LETICIA: She screams.

ORLANDO: I can't help it. (*Pause.*)

LETICIA: I tell you I can't stand it. I'm going to ask Mona to come and stay with me.

ORLANDO: No.

LETICIA: I want someone here with me.

ORLANDO: I don't want her here.

LETICIA: Why not?

ORLANDO: I don't.

LETICIA: I need someone here with me.

ORLANDO: Not now.

LETICIA: When?

ORLANDO: Soon enough.—She's going to stay here for a while. She's going to work for us. She'll be a servant here.

LETICIA: . . . No.

ORLANDO: She's going to be a servant here. (*Lights fade to black.*)

SCENE 15

OLIMPIA *and* NENA *are sitting at the dining room table. They are separating stones and other matter from dry beans.*

NENA: I used to clean beans when I was in the home. And also string beans. I also pressed clothes. The days were long. Some girls did hand sewing. They spent the day doing that. I didn't like it. When I did that, the day was even longer and there were times when I couldn't move even if I tried. And they said I couldn't go there anymore, that I had to stay in the yard. I didn't mind sitting in the yard looking at the birds. I went to the laundryroom and watched the women work. They let me go in and sit there. And they showed me how to press. I like to press because my mind wanders and I find satisfaction. I can iron all day. I like the way the wrinkles come out and things look nice. It's a miracle isn't it? I could earn a living pressing clothes. And I could find my grandpa and take care of him.

OLIMPIA: Where is your grandpa?

NENA: I don't know. (*They work a little in silence.*) He sleeps in the streets. Because he's too old to remember where he lives. He needs a person to take care of him. And I can take care of him. But I don't know where he is.—He doesn't know where I am.—He doesn't know who he is. He's too old. He doesn't know anything about himself. He only knows how to beg. And he knows that, only because he's hungry. He walks around and begs for food. He forgets to go home. He lives in the camp for the homeless and he has his own box. It's not an ugly box like the others. It is a real box. I used to live there with him. He took me with him when my mother died till they took me to the home. It is a big box. It's big enough for two. I could sleep in the front where it's cold. And he could sleep in the back where it's warmer. And he could lean on me. The floor is hard for him because he's skinny and it's hard on his poor bones. He could sleep on top of me if that would make him feel comfortable. I wouldn't mind. Except that he may pee on me because he pees in his pants. He doesn't know not to. He is incontinent. He can't hold it. His box was a little smelly. But that doesn't matter because I could clean it. All I would need is some soap. I could get plenty of water from the public faucet. And I could borrow a brush. You know how clean I could get it? As clean as new. You know what I would do? I would make holes in the floor so the pee would go down to the ground. And you know what else I would do?

OLIMPIA: What?

NENA: I would get straw and put it on the floor for him and for me and it would make it comfortable and clean and warm. How do you like that? Just as I did for my goat.

OLIMPIA: You have a goat?

NENA: . . . I did.

OLIMPIA: What happened to him?

NENA: He died. They killed him and ate him. Just like they did Christ.

OLIMPIA: Nobody ate Christ.

NENA: . . . I thought they did. My goat was eaten though.—In the home we had clean sheets. But that doesn't help. You can't sleep on clean sheets, not if there isn't someone watching over you while you sleep. And since my ma died there just wasn't anyone watching over me. Except you.—Aren't you? In the home they said guardian angels watch your sleep, but I didn't see any there. There weren't any. One day I heard my grandpa calling me and I went to look for him. And I didn't find him. I got tired and I slept in the street, and I was hungry and I was crying. And then he came to me and he spoke to me very softly so as not to scare me and he said he would give me something to eat and he said he would help me look for my grandpa. And he put me in the back of his van . . . And he took me to a place. And he hurt me. I fought with him but I stopped fighting—because I couldn't fight anymore and he did things to me. And he locked me in. And sometimes he brought me food and sometimes he didn't. And he did things to me. And he beat me. And he hung me on the wall. And I got sick. And sometimes he brought me medicine. And then he said he had to take me somewhere. And he brought me here. And I am glad to be here because you are here. I only wish my grandpa were here too. He doesn't beat me so much anymore.

OLIMPIA: Why does he beat you? I hear him at night. He goes down the steps and I hear you cry. Why does he beat you?

NENA: Because I'm dirty.

OLIMPIA: You are not dirty.

NENA: I am. That's why he beats me. The dirt won't go away from inside me.—He comes downstairs when I'm sleeping and I hear him coming and it frightens me. And he takes the covers off me and I don't move because I'm frightened and because I feel cold and I think I'm going to die. And he puts his hand on me and he recites poetry. And he is almost naked. He wears a robe but he leaves it open and he feels himself as he recites. He touches himself and he touches his stomach and his breasts and his behind. He puts his fingers in my parts and he keeps reciting. Then he turns me on my stomach and puts himself inside me. And he says I belong to him. (*There is a pause.*) I want to conduct each day of my life in the best possible way. I should value the things I have. And I should value all those who are near me. And I should value the kindness that others bestow upon me. And if someone should treat me unkindly, I should not blind myself with rage, but I should see them and receive them, since maybe they are in worse pain than me. (*Light fades to black.*)

SCENE 16

LETICIA *speaks on the telephone with Mona. She speaks rapidly.*

LETICIA: He is violent. He has become more so. I sense it. I feel it in him.—I understand his thoughts. I know what he thinks.—I raised him. I practically did. He was a boy when I met him. I saw him grow. I was the first woman he loved. That's how young he was. I have to look after him, make sure he doesn't get into trouble. He's not wise. He's trusting. They are changing him.—He tortures people. I know he does. He tells me he doesn't but I know he does. I know it. How could I not. Sometimes he comes from headquarters and his hands are shaking. Why should he shake? What do they do there?—He should transfer. Why do that? He says he doesn't do it himself. That the officers don't do it. He says that people are not being tortured. That that is questionable.— Everybody knows it. How could he not know it when everybody knows it. Sometimes you see blood in the streets. Haven't you seen it? Why do they leave the bodies in the streets,—how evil, to frighten people? They tear their fingernails off and their poor hands are bloody and destroyed. And they mangle their genitals and expose them and they tear their eyes out and you can see the empty eyesockets in the skull. How awful, Mona. He musn't do it. I don't care if I don't have anything! What's money! I don't need a house as big as this! He's doing it for money! What other reason could he have! What other reason could he have!! He shouldn't do it. I cannot look at him without thinking of it. He's doing it. I know he's doing it.—Shhhh! I hear steps. I'll call you later. Bye, Mona. I'll talk to you. (*She hangs up the receiver. Lights fade to black.*)

SCENE 17

The living room. OLIMPIA *sits to the right,* NENA *to the left.*

OLIMPIA: I don't wear high heels because they hurt my feet. I used to have a pair but they hurt my feet and also (*Pointing to her calf.*) here in my legs. So I don't wear them anymore even if they were pretty. Did you ever wear high heels? (NENA *shakes her head.*) Do you have ingrown nails? (NENA *looks at her questioningly.*) Nails that grow twisted into the flesh. (NENA *shakes her head.*) I don't either. Do you have sugar in the blood? (NENA *shakes her head.*) My mother had sugar in the blood and that's what she died of but she lived to be eighty six which is very old even if she had many things wrong with her. She had glaucoma and high blood pressure. (LETICIA *enters and sits center at the table.* NENA *starts to get up.* OLIMPIA *signals her to be still.* LETICIA *is not concerned with them.*)

LETICIA: So, what are you talking about?

OLIMPIA: Ingrown nails. (NENA *turns to* LETICIA *to make sure she may remain seated there.* LETICIA *is involved with her own thoughts.* NENA *turns front. Lights fade to black.*)

SCENE 18

ORLANDO *is sleeping on the dining room table. The telephone rings. He speaks as someone having a nightmare.*

ORLANDO: Ah! Ah! Ah! Get off me! Get off! I said get off! (LETICIA *enters.*)

LETICIA: (*Going to him.*) Orlando! What's the matter! What are you doing here!

ORLANDO: Get off me! Ah! Ah! Ah! Get off me!

LETICIA: Why are you sleeping here! On the table. (*Holding him close to her.*) Wake up.

ORLANDO: Let go of me. (*He slaps her hands as she tries to reach him.*) Get away from me. (*He goes to the floor on his knees and staggers to the telephone.*) Yes. Yes. it's me.—You did?—So?—It's true then.—What's the name?—Yes, sure.—Thanks.—Sure. (*He hangs up the receiver. He turns to look at* LETICIA. *Lights fade to black.*)

SCENE 19

Two chairs are placed side by side facing front in the center of the living room. LETICIA *sits on the right.* ORLANDO *stands on the down left corner.* NENA *sits to the left of the dining room table facing front. She covers her face.* OLIMPIA *stands behind her, holding* NENA *and leaning her head on her.*

ORLANDO: Talk.

LETICIA: I can't talk like this.

ORLANDO: Why not?

LETICIA: In front of everyone.

ORLANDO: Why not?

LETICIA: It is personal. I don't need the whole world to know.

ORLANDO: Why not?

LETICIA: Because it's private. My life is private.

ORLANDO: Are you ashamed?

LETICIA: Yes. I am ashamed!

ORLANDO: What of . . . ? What of . . . ?—I want you to tell us—about your lover.

LETICIA: I don't have a lover. (*He grabs her by the hair.* OLIMPIA *holds on to* NENA *and hides her face.* NENA *covers her face.*)

ORLANDO: You have a lover.

LETICIA: That's a lie.

ORLANDO (*Moving closer to her.*):   It's not a lie. (*To* LETICIA.) Come on tell us. (*He pulls harder.*) What's his name? (*She emits a sound of pain. He pulls harder, leans toward her and speaks in a low tone.*) What's his name?

LETICIA: Albertico. (*He takes a moment to release her.*)

ORLANDO: Tell us about it. (*There is silence. He pulls her hair.*)

LETICIA: All right. (*He releases her.*)

ORLANDO: What's his name?

LETICIA: Albertico.

ORLANDO: Go on. (*Pause.*) Sit up! (*She does.*) Albertico what?

LETICIA: Estevez. (ORLANDO *sits next to her.*)

ORLANDO: Go on. (*Silence.*) Where did you first meet him?

LETICIA: At . . . I . . .

ORLANDO (*He grabs her by the hair.*):   In my office.

LETICIA: Yes.

ORLANDO: Don't lie.—When?

LETICIA: You know when.

ORLANDO: When! (*Silence.*) How did you meet him?

LETICIA: You introduced him to me. (*He lets her go.*)

ORLANDO: What else? (*Silence.*) Who is he!

LETICIA: He's a lieutenant.

ORLANDO (*He stands.*):   When did you meet with him?

LETICIA: Last week.

ORLANDO: When!

LETICIA: Last week.

ORLANDO: When!

LETICIA: Last week. I said last week.

ORLANDO: Where did you meet him?

LETICIA: . . . In a house of rendez-vous . . .

ORLANDO: How did you arrange it?

LETICIA: . . . I wrote to him . . . I

ORLANDO: Did he approach you?

LETICIA: No.

ORLANDO: Did he!

LETICIA: No.

ORLANDO (*He grabs her hair again.*):   He did! How!

LETICIA: I approached him.

ORLANDO: How!

LETICIA (*Aggressively.*):   I looked at him! I looked at him! I looked at him! (*He lets her go.*)

ORLANDO: When did you look at him?

LETICIA: Please stop. . . !

ORLANDO: Where! When!

LETICIA: In your office!

ORLANDO: When?

LETICIA: I asked him to meet me!

ORLANDO: What did he say?

LETICIA (*Aggressively.*):   He walked away. He walked away! He walked away! I asked him to meet me.

ORLANDO: What was he like?

LETICIA: . . . Oh . . .

ORLANDO: Was he tender? Was he tender to you!

> *She doesn't answer. He puts his hand inside her blouse. She lets out an excruciating scream. He lets her go and walks to the right of the dining room. She goes to the telephone table, opens the drawer, takes a gun and shoots* ORLANDO. ORLANDO *falls dead.* NENA *runs to downstage of the table.* LETICIA *is disconcerted then puts the revolver in* NENA'*s hand and steps away from her.*

LETICIA: Please . . .

> NENA *is in a state of terror and numb acceptance. She looks at the gun. Then, up. The lights fade.*

[1985]

Journal Entry

What knowledge, experience, associations, or images of dictatorships and political oppression can you bring to the reading of Fornes's play?

Textual Considerations

1. What does the first speech of the play reveal about Orlando's fashioning of himself as a torturer and a military man? Identify specific words and images that also imply the interplay of his sexual identity with military power. To what extent does Fornes present his male identity as a product of an oppressive military dictatorship?

2. Analyze the women in Fornes's play. How does Fornes portray them? How do they establish a sense of self in Orlando's politically oppressed household? How do they express their sense of power or powerlessness? Explain.

3. Describe some of the dramatic techniques Fornes has created for *The Conduct of Life*. Include devices related to action, characters, and stage direction in your discussion,

and explain how these techniques relate to the theme of subjugation, domination, and political empowerment.
4. How effective is Fornes in exploring male-female relations in the play? Discuss the theme of "dictatorship in the bedroom and in the country." How does Orlando's relation to Nena and Leticia reflect the theme of political dictatorship? Explain.
5. To what extent does language empower the characters in the play? Include Nena and Olimpia in your discussion.

Cultural Contexts

1. Fornes's play illuminates political and feminist issues in a Latin American country in the present. Does the play also suggest ideas that go beyond the political context of Orlando's household? Is the play strictly about violence, dictatorship, and politics, or does it also explore attitudes about the world, people, and the human condition? Which characters reveal an attitude toward life that appeals to your group? Explain why.
2. In a telephone interview on July 7, 1994, Fornes suggested this alternate ending to the play: "Leticia is disconcerted, then puts the revolver in Nena's hand, begging her to take responsibility for the shooting of Orlando." Does this conclusion work for you and your group? Why or why not?

Performance Exercises

PERFORMANCE EXPRESS (45 MINUTES)

Cast two members of your group in the roles of Orlando and Leticia and have them improvise Scene 19, Orlando's interrogation of his wife. Then cast two other members of your group in the roles of Orlando and a political prisoner under interrogation. Perform the two scenes for your class, and ask them to respond to the impact of these social-protest scenes. Which better reveals the fears of torture in the interrogation process?

PERFORMANCE PROJECTS

1. Stage *The Conduct of Life*, in a performance that presents images of oppression and subjugation as sequential flashes of a film projected on a screen. Use music, lighting, and costumes in a postmodern, unconventional performance of the play.
2. Rewrite an abridged version of *The Conduct of Life*, adding to it an updated version of a Greek chorus that analyzes and comments on the ongoing action. Perform your revised version of the play to your classmates, and discuss the dramatic focus of your production. To what extent does the strong speaking voice of the chorus affect the dramatic impact of the play?

TOPICS FOR DISCUSSION AND WRITING

Writing Topics

1. In "A Brother's Murder," Staples cites many examples of the violence and dangers inherent in ghetto life. Write an essay discussing the impressions that his brother's experiences made on you, including any stereotypes you had to modify as a result of reading about them. Clarify your purpose and meaning. Think of a provocative statement to begin your essay, and end with an effective conclusion.

2. Many sociologists have argued that the news media, particularly television, contribute to a romanticization of war, portraying it as high drama. How do the texts by Jarrell, Owen, Levertov, or Yevtushenko refute the media's point of view?

3. Plot and suspense are considered essential elements of a successful story, yet "The Things They Carried" is virtually plotless and offers little suspense. How does O'Brien compensate for the lack of a traditional plot? What elements does he use instead to capture the reader's interest? Why does he deemphasize plot in this story? To what effect?

4. The relationship between patriotism and heroism in the Civil War is the focus of the texts by Whitman (two poems), Crane, and Catton. Explore this theme in any three texts. With whose point of view are you most in agreement? Cite evidence you found convincing.

5. The Vietnam War and its aftermath is the subject of several texts in this part. Compare and contrast the portrayals of this theme. With whose perspective were you most in tune? Explain.

6. "The Sniper," "Silence," and "The Curse" make use of the literary convention of the surprise ending. Review the last paragraphs of the three stories, and write an analysis of the meanings they introduce or the ironies they reinforce.

7. Several texts explore the relationship between the discourses of speech and silence. To what extent do Levertov, Yevtushenko, and Forché make it possible for you to listen to the "voice of silence"? Write a postscript expressing what you "heard."

8. Apply the notion of physical and psychological violence in the stories by Dubus and Petry.

9. Antiheroism is the focus of the texts by Powell and Arrabal. With whose point of view are you most in agreement? Cite evidence you found most convincing.

10. According to the Russian American pacifist Emma Goldman, "Organized violence at the top . . . creates individual violence at the bottom." Test the validity of her hypothesis by applying it to any three texts in Part Three.

11. Consider the relationship of gender and violence in "Kindness," "The Curse," and "Like a Winding Sheet." What do the texts also imply about the interplay of sexuality and violence?

12. Write an essay discussing the idea that *Picnic on the Battlefield* portrays war as a private, social, and political game devoid of moral purpose. Argue whether Arrabal's play also explores other issues besides the war topic. Does *Picnic on the Battlefield* make statements about human beings? What kinds of statements? Cite evidence from the play.

13. Compare and contrast war images you encounter in such texts as "The Dying Veteran," *Picnic on the Battlefield*, "Concord Hymn," "Charge of the Light Brigade," and "The Things They Carried." How do they compare with the war images provided by network television? Limit yourself to three texts.

14. Write an essay analyzing the images of violence in Spera's poems. Is he raising issues about the causes of violence? What do his portrayals of violence suggest about our postmodern culture?

15. Write an essay discussing the interplay of sexuality and political power in *The Conduct of Life*. Explain how Orlando's sexual politics reflects and shapes his political life.

Research Topics

1. War songs such as "Lili Marlene," "For Johnny," "When This Bleeding War Is Over," and "Hymn of Hate"—and many others that emphasize either the patriotic view of war or various forms of war protest—became an important part of the tradition of the two world wars. Research some lyrics from World Wars I and II, the Vietnam War, the Persian Gulf War, or the current "war on terrorism" to write a documented paper analyzing their function as war poetry or war propaganda. Speculate on other functions they may have served.

2. Write a documented paper summarizing the history of women in World Wars I and II, the Vietnam War, the Persian Gulf War, or the current antiterrorist "war." Starting with the domestic view of women as lovers, mothers, and peacemakers, as well as the image of women as "stepdaughters" of war—nurses, doctors, ambulance drivers—move to the current view of women as actively engaged in war.

3. To investigate the relationship between race and war, write a documented paper on the history of African American soldiers. Examine the contributions they made to American history from the time of the Civil War to the time of the Vietnam War. You may need to rely on the testimonials of slaves, abolitionists, and veterans from the two world wars and the Vietnam War. Among other sources you might check:

McPherson, James M. *The Negro's Civil War: How American Blacks Felt and Acted During the War for the Union*. New York: Ballantine, rpt. 1991.

Wallace, Terry. *Bloods: An Oral History of the Vietnam War by Black Veterans*. New York: Random House, 1984.

FILM ANGLES

WAR AND VIOLENCE: THE FILM ANGLE

This unit, like the one on Race and Difference (Part Four), is divided into two sections because it deals with two subjects, not one. That is, although all wars are violent, not all violence is linked to war. As a perusal of any newspaper or news program on television would attest, violence occurs in every society, every day, in a variety of ways. A distinction between war and violence is evident in the literature selections of this part as well. Many focus on war, while the short story "The Curse" and several poems deal with social violence and its effects on the individual.

Do movies have anything new or significant to add to our knowledge and awareness of war and violence? Actually, more than any other theme in this book, war and violence have a long and intimate connection to film history. The words themselves conjure up concrete images in the mind and allude to actions—the heart and soul of motion pictures. Although it may be easy to understand why movies have represented war and violence, however, it is also true that, along with television, they have perpetuated the fascination Americans seem to have with violent subjects. Novelist Scott Turow remarked that "we need only glance at a TV screen to realize that murder remains an American preoccupation." This affinity between film and television media and violent subject matter is itself an important subject in need of investigation.

The very ease and directness with which movies deal with war and violence often make it difficult to grasp the moral perspective from which we judge the action in some films. Even if a filmmaker's point of view is highly critical of war or violence, that perspective is often lost or overshadowed by the powerful impressions induced by graphic images. This problem has caused many critics and censoring groups to accuse filmmakers who depict violent subject matter realistically of exploiting or glorifying war and violence, rather than denouncing them.

The first half-hour of Steven Spielberg's *Saving Private Ryan* (1998), for example, which recounts the allied invasion of Europe in World War II, is filled with images of bloodied limbs, dismemberment, and heads being blown off—in vivid color and close-ups. Yet neither Spielberg nor those who have written about the film would contend that the film glorifies war. Several key questions arise, then, concerning the moral perspective of films that deal with war or violence and how the viewer should incorporate brutal imagery in an overall understanding of a film's narrative and theme.

Questions to Consider

1. What purpose is served by graphic detail in a war film? Is the filmmaker justified because he aims for "greater realism"? Are the images designed to repel us and show how horrific war is? If so, is this aim consistent with the rest of the movie, which, in the case of *Saving Private Ryan*, seems to celebrate the heroism of American soldiers?
2. Think of a movie that contains realistic depictions of violent actions. What was your reaction to the violence? Do you think the way it was presented helped or hindered your appreciation and understanding of the film's theme?

578

WAR: HISTORY AND GENRE

The War Film

Many films, including such classics as *Gone with the Wind* (1939) and *Casablanca* (1947), include war as a backdrop to the characters' lives. Others, such as the Italian film *Life is Beautiful* (1997), focus on individuals or societies that are the victims of war. None of these belongs to the genre of the war film, per se, which emerged in the silent period as a response to World War I. As a genre, the war film treats war as a phenomenon that societies are forced to engage in from time to time in order to defend such things as freedom or to suppress a hostile leader or regime. Most of the war films of the 1940s and 1950s, depicting the fight against Hitler and Nazi Germany, are examples of the genre.

Not every war film was or is antiwar any more than every novel about war is against war. Neither James Jones's *From Here to Eternity* (made into a film in 1953) nor Norman Mailer's *The Naked and the Dead* (made into a film in 1958) is primarily against war. No doubt this is because both were set during World War II, generally considered a "just" war because it was fought against the spread of Nazism and Fascism in Europe. The typical war film treats going to war as an unfortunate necessity, but it generally does not take a critical stance against war. This is because such films often have a direct correlation to the sentiments in society that are contemporaneous to the war in question.

In films about World War II, for example, American soldiers, it was assumed, fought with the confidence that the enemy was clear and that their country was behind their efforts. The viewer was encouraged to identify with the soldier risking his life to rid the world of "evil" ideologies and the tyrants who enforce them. This identification factor is an important element in narrative filmmaking, in which the viewer is emotionally and psychologically bound to the principal character or characters and endorses the values he or they represent. In this sense, a typical war film that follows the rules of the genre is in accord with the audience's feelings and values.

In a typical example of the war film genre, therefore, the following features are usually found:

1. Soldiers in combat situations fight a clearly defined enemy.
2. The film usually has an unambiguous moral perspective.
3. The viewer easily identifies with the central protagonist(s).
4. There is a credible sense that the war is fought for a clear purpose, that the battles waged by fighting men serve this purpose, and that even the lives of soldiers are a justifiable sacrifice.
5. The film has narrative closure and a relatively cathartic effect, based on imminent victory or the success of a particular mission.

Question to Consider

1. Consider any war film you have seen in terms of how many of these genre features it contains.

The Antiwar Film

How is the natural agreement between the viewer and the model war film affected when a film takes a critical stance against war? This, too, has a long history, as far back as *All Quiet on the Western Front* (d. Lewis Milestone, 1930), based on a famous novel by Erich

Maria Remarque. Moreover, despite the general view that World War II was a "just" war, it has been less than gloriously presented in such films as *The Bridge on the River Kwai* (d. David Lean, Great Britain, 1957) and *The Thin Red Line* (d. Terrence Malick, 1998). More overtly antiwar films were made about the Vietnam War, consistent with the conflicted social attitudes about that war. *The Deer Hunter* (d. Michael Cimino, 1978) and *Platoon* (d. Oliver Stone, 1986) are among the most well known. An important indication that a film is taking a critical position toward war is that it problematizes or violates one or more of the standard rules or features of the genre, as listed earlier.

The question raised previously—namely, how do we determine what perspective or point of view a film takes toward its subject—is relevant in this context. It is generally easier to resolve this in a work of literature because it is the work of one author, who shapes the plot, develops the theme, selects the language, and controls the tone and mood of the piece. Whether blatant or subtle, ironic or nonjudgmental, the moral perspective is established by the intention of the author, whether his or her views are presented in the third person or channeled through a first-person narrator. In Liam O'Flaherty's story, "The Sniper," for example, the author adopts a deceptively simple and neutral tone, restricting our knowledge to the experience of the sniper, but it is exactly that control and tone that allows the surprise ending to resonate with such a powerful effect.

Films present us with a complex variation of the ruling voice of a narrative—its point of view. Because the medium uses means other than language to communicate, the filmmaker's intentions are often misunderstood. We see and hear much more than any one "voice" can control, which means we must pay as much attention to a film's audio and visual "texts" as we do to its screenplay and dialogue. The student must look closely at the director's other "writing" instruments—the images on the screen and the way they are framed, composed, lit, and filmed by the camera, what is known as a film's **mise-en-scène**—as equally powerful expressive instruments, embodying ideas that may or may not be put into words. To determine whether a film is antiwar, then, we need to examine not only how it departs from the basic conventions and rules of the genre but how it employs cinematic elements.

Questions to Consider

1. What characteristics of the classic genre war film are missing from *All Quiet on the Western Front, The Bridge on the River Kwai, The Deer Hunter, Platoon,* and *The Thin Red Line*? How does the absence of these features make any of these films antiwar?
2. What aspects of the mise-en-scène in any of these films can be interpreted as establishing or reinforcing an antiwar message?

CASE STUDY

Paths of Glory and *Full Metal Jacket*

The director Stanley Kubrick made two extraordinary war films—*Paths of Glory* (1957), set during World War I, and *Full Metal Jacket* (1987), set during the Vietnam War. A comparison of these two films and of their protagonists is an enlightening lesson in how the genre convention of providing a protagonist with whom the viewer can identify can make an important difference in how we understand the film and recognize its perspective.

Paths of Glory, based on a novel by Humphrey Cobb, focuses more on the corruption of the officers who run wars and the way the military system victimizes the soldiers in the trench. The clear moral perspective that allows us to judge this situation is provided by the protagonist, Colonel Dax, whose courage, integrity, and loyalty to his men are never in question. *Full Metal Jacket*, based on the novel *The Short-Timers* by ex-marine Gustav Hasford, follows the training of a group of marines from boot camp to their assignment in Vietnam. Contrary to the situation as presented in the earlier film, however, Kubrick makes it difficult for the viewer to identify with the protagonist, Joker, whose behavior and thinking is ambivalent and morally questionable.

Besides problematizing viewer identification, the film's mise-en-scène is an important key to Kubrick's intentions. Especially in the first half, many shots are designed and composed to underline the rigidity and uniformity of the basic training process. The recruits are often lined up symmetrically in a manner that stresses the need for group behavior and thinking at the expense of the individual.

Sound and music are also important elements in a movie. Kubrick always used music that belonged to the period in which the film was set. In *Full Metal Jacket*, many popular songs from the 1960s, some linked directly to the war, contribute to the ironic tone of the film. For example, the film's abrupt transition from the bloody climax of part one to the Vietnam section is accompanied by the song "These Boots Are Made for Walking," sung over a shot of a prostitute on the streets of Saigon. This use of what is called **audio-visual** montage can be a rich source of probing a film's multilayered meanings.

Questions to Consider

1. List the character features of Colonel Dax, the protagonist of *Paths of Glory*. Which of these features seem crucial to the viewer's ability to identify with the character?
2. Can Colonel Dax be considered antiwar? What are his views toward war? How does his character compare to that of other officers and soldiers in the film?
3. What are the features of the main protagonist in *Full Metal Jacket*? What does his nickname, Joker, convey about him? What other clues does Kubrick provide to show how Joker might reflect the moral, political, and social ambiguities that characterized the Vietnam War?
4. How do the compositions in *Full Metal Jacket* serve the director's overall point of view? Would a film with an uncritical view toward war or military training include similar kinds of shots? What other cinematic features can you identify in the film that convey an idea about how to interpret character behavior or action?
5. Examine the lyrics of "These Boots Are Made for Walking" and other songs in *Full Metal Jacket* and discuss how they interact directly with the images and scenes depicted in each case. What idea(s) emerges from this juxtaposition of music and image? What does it add to our understanding of the film and the director's point of view?

Research Topics

1. With the help of a VHS or DVD player, watch *Full Metal Jacket*, *The Thin Red Line*, or *Paths of Glory* several times and stop it at selected images to study the way the director has deliberately framed and composed images. See if you can detect patterns of such imagery, and interpret what those patterns reveal about the director's intentions and the meaning of the film.
2. Both *Saving Private Ryan* and *The Thin Red Line* deal with World War II from a contemporary perspective. How does each film represent the war? What role does the imagery play in each film?
3. Compare the first-person point of view in *Full Metal Jacket* or *The Thin Red Line* with a war story or novel in the first person in terms of how each guides our perceptions and feelings.

4. To examine the nature of the war film as a genre, study any two "classical Hollywood" war films from the list provided and see if you can identify the narrative elements and aspects of character they have in common. What does it tell you about how a genre works?

5. Both Tim O'Brien's short story in this book, "The Things They Carried," and Gustav Hasford's *The Short-timers*, the novel on which *Full Metal Jacket* is based, are narratives written by men who fought in Vietnam. The screenplay for the film was also cowritten by Hasford and Michael Herr, another Vietnam war veteran. Compare the O'Brien story to the Vietnam section of either the Hasford novel or the film in terms of how each depicts the experience of the soldier in that war.

6. Compare *Saving Private Ryan* and *Full Metal Jacket* as war films. How does each film fit or not fit the mold of the genre? If an identification figure is an essential component of the genre, how does the protagonist in each of these films function in this capacity? Does the specific war in each case have any bearing on the film's relationship to the genre or to your reactions?

7. Compare *Full Metal Jacket* with other films about the Vietnam War (e.g., *The Deer Hunter* or *Platoon*). Do they present similar views of that war? If not, how are they different? How would you describe the main characters in each work in terms of their ability to function as identification figures?

8. Watch the video of either *War Photographer* (d. Christian Frei, 2002) or *First Kill* (d. Coco Schrijber, Holland, 2002), or any other documentary on war, and compare the way such a film examines the subject with how a fictionalized war film does it. What differences in techniques can you discern between narrative films and documentaries? Without such conventions as a dramatic story line and character involvement, how does a documentary engage the viewer? Do we learn more about the subject of war from a documentary? Is the representation of violence more or less justified in a documentary than it is in a narrative film?

VIOLENCE: HISTORY AND GENRE

Unlike war, which is a specific event, violence is a behavioral phenomenon that can belong to many events—individual and group, private and social—and crosses all class, cultural, national, and racial lines. Many philosophers and psychologists—including Friedrich Nietzsche and Sigmund Freud—believe that violence is inherent in human nature and will always present a problem for the individual and for society as a whole.

Stanley Kubrick's *A Clockwork Orange* (1971), based on the novel by Anthony Burgess, seems to endorse this view by implying that in order to deal with violence, societies often resort to other forms of it. David Fincher's *Fight Club* (1999), based on the novel by Chuck Palahniuk, associates violence with men and suggests that it is connected to the primal instincts of the race. Its protagonist, enraged and bored with the world and his own failures, begins a "fight club," in which similarly disillusioned single men meet late at night for boxing matches in which they pummel each other brutally. The twist in the story concerns the identity of the main character and suggests that every man has a "double" who carries his deeply repressed rage. Unlike the character in *A Clockwork Orange*, however, the protagonist in *Fight Club* turns his aggression inward.

Question to Consider

1. Think of some recent films containing violence. How is it presented in each case? Can you detect a viewpoint that represents what the director wants you to think about the violence in each case? Does the film's viewpoint suggest that nothing can ultimately be done to eliminate violence and aggression? What does the film suggest about society's responsibility? Is it in some way the cause of violence? If so, is society responsible for finding a cure?

Violence has a long history in the movies and can be found in many genres other than war films, including westerns, crime and detective films, horror and science fiction thrillers, and ordinary melodramas. Even Tom and Jerry cartoons have come under fire for treating violence as a humorous activity without realistic consequences, thus providing a dangerous model for children. To talk about violence in movies, it is useful to distinguish between films that are about violent actions or situations—such as riots, serial killings, rape, or domestic violence—and films about other subjects that include violence and present it in a disturbing manner.

Some filmmakers have made the very issue of violence the theme of their films. In Sam Peckinpah's *Straw Dogs* (1971), the protagonist, a mild-mannered mathematician played by Dustin Hoffman, is forced to confront his avowed pacifism when he and his wife are assaulted by local thugs. Some critics interpreted this film, as well as Peckinpah's *The Wild Bunch* (1969), as **allegories** about the inherent violence of American society and the ongoing debate during the late 1960s and early 1970s between advocates of the Vietnam War, known as "hawks," and advocates of peace, known as "doves."

During this same period, Arthur Penn directed *Bonnie and Clyde* (1967), a film about bank robbers during the Great Depression. The film ends in a shocking bloodbath as the two lead characters are riddled with bullets. Historians now read this film as a displaced expression of the racism and violence underlying American society that also emerged during the civil rights movement and the Vietnam War.

Whereas a war film's graphic violence may be justified by the message the film conveys, other films that indulge in excessive violence are sometimes said to appeal to blood-thirsty viewers who enjoy spectacles of carnage. Accusations along this line were made against the grisly Colosseum combats in *Gladiator* (d. Ridley Scott, 2000), a costume epic in which men enslaved by the Roman empire are sent into the arena with the barest of weapons to defend themselves against impossible odds and an almost certain bloody death—all of it for the purpose of entertaining the emperor and the Roman citizens. The line between artistic edification and exploitation is often a thin one, and films like *Gladiator* reopen that debate.

Some filmmakers, for various reasons, and according to the taste and permissiveness of the times, leave the violence **off-screen** entirely, somewhat in the tradition of Greek tragedy, in which representations of violence on the stage were considered morally and aesthetically inappropriate. A subject like rape, for example, once considered too distressing to show on the screen, is only implied in *Johnny Belinda* (d. Jean Negulesco, 1948) but is depicted more graphically in *The Accused* (d. Jonathan Kaplan, 1988). Greater tolerance and changes in cultural and social attitudes over forty years no doubt have affected what is shown on the screen, but this does not preclude other reasons for the differences in the treatment of such subjects.

Finally, the depiction of violence not only may be justified but may illuminate an important dimension of a character's personality. In Martin Scorsese's *Raging Bull*

(1980), the protagonist—famous prizefighter Jake La Motta—uses the boxing ring to act out his anger and rage against others as well as to punish himself for that rage. The character is portrayed as so insecure and inarticulate that the bloody rituals of the boxing ring become his only form of expression. Although this does not excuse the violence, it places it in a meaningful though disturbing context.

Questions to Consider

1. Often, genre films like *The Wild Bunch* (a western) and *Bonnie and Clyde* (a crime drama) are indirect reflections of social and political realities occurring at the time they were made. Can you think of any genre films that you have seen over the past few years—crime, science fiction, or horror films—that can be interpreted in a similar way?
2. The rape scene is left out of Andre Dubus's story "The Curse," somewhat like actions that "occur" off-screen in a movie. Compare this to the treatment of the rape in *The Accused*. What are the artistic, narrative, psychological, and thematic reasons behind the treatment in each case? Do they seem justified to you?
3. Consider these conflicting views of *Gladiator*: (1) that the film's unrestrained violence is justified because it shows that the Roman Empire, though allegedly civilized, indulged in blood sports and was indifferent to the value of human life; and (2) that the excessive violence is just an excuse to show what special effects, digital filmmaking, and editing can achieve in the endless effort to gratify spectators who like bloody action.
4. Many social critics believe media violence has a direct relation to violence in society. Consider the series of teenage horror films and their sequels, sometimes referred to as "slasher" films—*Friday the 13th, Halloween, The Nightmare on Elm Street, Scream,* and *I Know What You Did Last Summer*—as examples of increasingly graphic violence on the screen. What does the popularity of such films—both in theaters and in VHS and DVD formats—say about American audiences and about the filmmakers who continue to gratify the appetite for such films? Are the films merely entertaining, or do they reflect an indifference to violence in society itself?

CASE STUDY

A Clockwork Orange

A Clockwork Orange created a scandal when it was released in 1971. It created such an outcry in Great Britain, where it was blamed as the cause of copycat crimes, that its director, Stanley Kubrick, withdrew it from distribution for over twenty-five years. Its shock effect had to do, in part, with the fact that, as presented, the viewer can neither identify with nor approve of either the individual who commits violence or the society that attempts to correct his behavior. Alex, the main character of a futuristic society, is a thuggish sociopath addicted to violence and criminal behavior. Upon his arrest and incarceration, he is subject to an experimental technique called the Lodovico method. He is constrained like a mental patient, his eyes pried and clipped open, and forced to watch endless acts of violence on a movie screen in the hope that he will develop conditioned reflexes that will suppress his own violent instincts.

The film raises disturbing ethical questions about the limits to which a society will go to protect itself in relation to the freedom of the individual. The viewer is presented with an impossible choice: Should the state be granted unlimited license to prevent crime by any means necessary, even at the expense of the individual? Or should we condemn such excessive measures in the name of libertarian values, even though this may give the perpetrators of violence license to trample on those very values?

No small part of the film's shock effect, still felt by audiences today, is the style in which everything is presented—a fusion of audio and visual excess that in itself does a kind of violence by assaulting the senses, rendering the action both hyper-real and sur-real. The exuberance with which Alex and his "droogs" brutalize others disturbed many viewers, who concluded that it meant the director endorsed such behavior. The same style, however, characterizes the Lodovico method, equating its sanitized form of brain-washing with a violence to the spirit every bit as brutal as the behavior it purports to cor-rect. All in all, the film can be understood as a dark social satire, mocking the extremes of liberalism as well as the abuses and follies of the society that tries to control them. Some viewers found, however, that the film's assault on the mind and the senses made it difficult to be entertained.

Questions to Consider

1. How would you characterize the violence in *A Clockwork Orange*? Does it seem to be an expression of youthful rebellion against a corrupt society, or is it mindless and ran-dom? Would your reactions to it be different in either case?

2. The end of the film implies that the Lodovico method ultimately fails. Does this sug-gest that it was the wrong method or that society simply lacks the ability to deal with Alex's kind of violence?

3. Although *A Clockwork Orange* takes place in the future, we have now arrived at that point. How does the film's vision of the future accord with the present state of society? How does it compare with other visions of the future you can think of in science fiction films?

4. The film, like the novel, is presented in the first person, from Alex's point of view. How does this affect the viewer's involvement and ability to identify? Are there any aspects of Alex's personality that redeem him in ethical or human terms?

5. Analyze a sequence from the film that illustrates the director's visual style. How does the mise-en-scène—set design, costumes, lighting, and use of color—contribute to this style and to the film's atmosphere?

6. The language in the film closely follows that in the Burgess novel, much of it made up of invented words and composites of familiar ones. What is the function and effect of this language? Can this language be seen as an expression or instrument of the individual's rebellious stance against society?

Research Topics

1. Consider one or more of the following films—*Unforgiven* (d. Clint Eastwood, 1992), *Gangs of New York* (d. Martin Scorsese, 2002), *Bloody Sunday* (d. Paul Greengrass, United Kingdom/Ireland, 2002), or *Mystic River* (d. Clint Eastwood, 2003)—in which the use of violence may be, as in the case of *Raging Bull*, both distressing and enlight-ening and in which an intelligent handling of it makes it less exploitative and more informative. Look at the film carefully and analyze specific examples that illustrate how the representation of violence is necessary to a full understanding of the film's themes. Are there limits to how far a filmmaker should go in achieving this goal?

2. Critics and censoring bodies argue that depictions of violence in movies and televi-sion help to create a permissive atmosphere in society, so that people accept violence as a legitimate means of dealing with anger and frustration against individuals who

have harmed them or against perceived injustices of society. Do some library research on this topic and evaluate the merits or flaws of this viewpoint. Use references to specific movies or television programs to support your points.

3. Choose one of the films discussed in this section that is based on a novel—*A Clockwork Orange* or *Fight Club*—and compare the movie to the novel, specifically in relation to the different ways in which violence is represented. Does a literary description of violence evoke similar emotions to a cinematic one? If not, what does this say about the way each medium affects the impact of violence? Does the very nature of film imply that it is difficult for a viewer to retain an objective viewpoint toward a depiction of graphic violence?

PART FOUR

RACE AND DIFFERENCE

Fiction

The Moment Before the Gun Went Off, Nadine Gordimer ◆ *The Smells of Home,* Sandip Roy ◆ *The Lesson,* Toni Cade Bambara ◆ *I Stand Here Ironing,* Tillie Olsen ◆ *Jasmine,* Bharati Mukherjee ◆ *Désirée's Baby,* Kate Chopin

Essays

Silent Dancing, Judith Ortiz Cofer ◆ *How I Learned to Read and Write,* Frederick Douglass ◆ *Borrowed Time: An AIDS Memoir,* Paul Monette ◆ *A Chinaman's Chance: Reflections on the American Dream,* Eric Liu

Poetry

I Hear America Singing, Walt Whitman ◆ *Poet Power,* Denise Levertov ◆ *Indian Boarding School: The Runaways,* Louise Erdrich ◆ *Public School No. 18: Paterson, New Jersey,* Maria Mazziotti Gillan ◆ *The Weary Blues,* Langston Hughes ◆ *Dream Variations,* Langston Hughes ◆ *Harlem (A Dream Deferred),* Langston Hughes ◆ *Telephone Conversation,* Wole Soyinka ◆ *On the Subway,* Sharon Olds ◆ *Chinese Fireworks Banned in Hawaii,* Eric Chock ◆ *Latero Story,* Tato Laviera ◆ *AIDS,* May Sarton ◆ *How to Watch Your Brother Die,* Michael Lassell ◆ *Cross Plains, Wisconsin,* Martín Espada ◆ *Federico's Ghost,* Martín Espada ◆ *Tony Went to the Bodega but He Didn't Buy Anything,* Martín Espada

Drama

Othello, the Moor of Venice, William Shakespeare ◆ *Kiss of the Spider Woman,* Manuel Puig

"Ours is the only nation to have a dream and give its name to one—the American Dream," wrote the literary critic Lionel Trilling more than fifty years ago. Although the United States continues to be a nation of immigrants in search of that dream, many groups have felt excluded from the right to equality promised in the Declaration of Independence of 1776. These groups are challenging the ideal of the "melting pot," which was first expressed in Hector St. Jean de Crevecoeur's 1781 statement that "individuals of all nations are melted down in a new race of men" and which has shaped the collective consciousness of North Americans for more than two centuries.

In a 1991 interview, the Asian American writer Bharati Mukherjee proposed that the metaphor of a "fusion chamber," in which elements interact but do not melt, has perhaps become a more appropriate metaphor to describe the new, multiracial democracy of the present time and the twenty-first century. The African America novelist Toni Morrison concurs: "We have to acknowledge that the thing we call 'literature' is pluralistic now just as society ought to be. The melting pot never worked." And in his 1999 commencement address at Hamilton College, professor and critic Henry Louis Gates Jr. told graduating students that, in his view, "Pluralism isn't supposed to be about leaping the boundaries, it's supposed to be about breaking those boundaries down, acknowledging the fluid and interactive nature of all our identities."

Much of the literature in Part Four portrays the irrationality of racism and the politics of exclusion and examines their effects on the groups that continue to challenge the myths of assimilation and justice for all. Walt Whitman's poem "I Hear America Singing" (1867), for instance, celebrates the delight of diversity in what Whitman envisions as a truly democratic America. In a strong epic voice, Whitman communicates to all Americans, regardless of class and race, the idealized vision of democracy engraved in the Declaration of Independence (1776) and the Gettysburg Address (1863). However, in the poems by Langston Hughes written over two decades, we hear the voices of exclusion. In "The Weary Blues," set in a bar in Harlem in the 1920s, the singer finds a catharsis in the blues songs of his people, in spite of his poverty and personal pain; and in "Dream Variations," the speaker sounds an optimistic note as he imagines himself flinging his arms wide and dancing in the sunlight. In "Harlem," however, written in the 1940s, the speaker sounds an ominous note as he explores the consequences of deferring the dreams of African Americans. In very few lines, Hughes presents possible responses to hope denied and ends with the possibility of explosion, foreshadowing the race riots of the 1960s.

Kate Chopin's "Désirée's Baby" brings students in touch with characters whose marital relations across racial lines end in a crude awareness of their ethnic heritage. On the wife's side, her oppressed female condition makes her the primary victim of a racist drama after the discovery of visible signs of color in her baby. On the husband's side, the reader can only speculate that his chance encounter with his own black identity will exacerbate the roots of his male-centered racism, leading to the only possible solution—ethnic self-hatred. Chopin's story articulates and historicizes issues related to ethnic origins, racial prejudice, and interracial marriage in the late nineteenth century that are still pertinent today.

The effects of economic inequities are poignantly recorded in Tillie Olsen's story, "I Stand Here Ironing," as the speaker reveals how a lifetime of poverty and drudgery limited her own choices as well as the decisions she made that adversely affected the life of her daughter. In "The Lesson," Toni Cade Bambara exposes the economic realities of ghetto life through a visit by a group of African American grade school children to an expensive toy store in Manhattan. One of them concluded: "This is not much of a democracy if you ask me. Equal chance to pursue happiness means an equal crack at the dough, don't it?"

Conflicts between ethnic identification and cultural assimilation are the focus of Tato Laviera's "Latero Story" and Judith Ortiz Cofer's "Silent Dancing," as the speakers reveal how bicultural and bilingual differences have affected their identities and have contributed to linguistic, geographical, and cultural displacement. In Maria Mazziotti Gillan's "Public School No. 18: Paterson, New Jersey," the Italian American speaker finally learns, as an adult, to find her own voice and an identity strong enough to confront and challenge the myth of Anglo-Saxon superiority, which was reinforced by the educational institutions she attended. In "Indian Boarding School: The Runaways," Native American writer Louise Erdrich powerfully portrays the presumptuous and insensitive attempts of members of the dominant cultures to impose their lifestyle and value system on a cultural minority.

Eric Liu offers a different perspective in his 1994 essay, "A Chinaman's Chance: Reflections on the American Dream," in which he urges his peers to share his faith in the "unique destiny" of the United States to absorb "hyphenates" like himself, who will contribute to "an ever more vibrant future for *all* Americans." Eric Chock, an Asian American of Hawaiian descent, disagrees, however, lamenting the passing of an important Chinese tradition of setting off fireworks during New Year festivities in his native state.

Cultural attitudes toward homosexuals and lesbians have also resulted in social and political exclusion, as revealed in the subjects of Sandip Roy's "The Smells of Home" and Manuel Puig's *Kiss of the Spider Woman.* Other texts address the issue of AIDS and explore new definitions of and meanings for the concept of love. Paul Monette's

"Borrowed Time: An AIDS Memoir" and Michael Lassell's "How to Watch Your Brother Die" focus on sexual preference and the gay community's capacity for grief, rage, and desire for connection.

As you read these and other texts in this part, consider how factors such as race, social class, and sexual preference have contributed to or detracted from your own position of privilege in contemporary society. You might also consider Gates's challenge in his commencement address as you forge your own identity in the more diverse and complex world of the twenty-first century:

> I don't say "express yourself," as Madonna might. I say: Students invent yourselves, and don't restrict yourself to off-the-rack models, either, because there isn't one way to be white or black, gay or straight, Hispanic or Asian, liberal or conservative, male or female. The stronger the sense you nurture of the contingent nature of all such identities, the less likely it is that you will be harmed by them, or in their name inflict harm upon others. One of my heroes, James Baldwin, put it this way: "Each of us helplessly and forever contains the other, male and female, female and male, white and black, black and white. We are a part of each other."

FICTION

Nadine Gordimer

The Moment Before the Gun Went Off

Marais Van der Vyver shot one of his farm laborers, dead. An accident, there are accidents with guns every day of the week—children playing a fatal game with a father's revolver in the cities where guns are domestic objects, nowadays, hunting mishaps like this one, in the country—but these won't be reported all over the world. Van der Vyver knows his will be. He knows that the story of the Afrikaner farmer—regional leader of the National Party and commandant of the local security commando—shooting a black man who worked for him will fit exactly *their* version of South Africa, it's made for them. They'll be able to use it in their boycott and divestment campaigns, it'll be another piece of evidence in their truth about the country. The papers at home will quote the story as it has appeared in the overseas press, and in the back and forth he and the black man will become those crudely drawn figures on anti-apartheid banners, units in statistics of white brutality against blacks quoted at the United Nations—he, whom they will gleefully be able to call "a leading member" of the ruling Party.

People in the farming community understand how he must feel. Bad enough to have killed a man, without helping the Party's, the government's, the country's enemies as well. They see the truth of that. They know, reading the Sunday papers, that when Van der Vyver is quoted saying he is "terribly shocked," he will "look after the wife and children," none of those Americans and English, and none of those people at home who want to destroy the white man's power will believe him. And how they will sneer when he even says of the farm boy (according to one paper, if you can trust any of those reporters), "He was my friend, I always took him hunting with me." Those city and overseas people don't know it's true: farmers usually have one particular black boy they like to take along with them in the lands; you could call it a kind of friend, yes, friends are not only your own white people, like yourself, whom you take into your house, pray with in church, and work with on the Party committee. But how can those others know that? They don't want to know it. They think all blacks are like the bigmouth agitators in town. And Van der Vyver's face in the photographs, strangely opened by distress—everyone in the district remembers Marais Van der Vyver as a little boy who would go away and hide himself if he caught you smiling at him, and everyone knows him now as a man who hides any change of expression round his mouth behind a thick, soft mustache, and in his eyes by always looking at some object in hand, a leaf or a crop fingered, pen or stone picked up, while concentrating on what he is saying, or while listening to you. It just

591

goes to show what shock can do; when you look at the newspaper photographs you feel like apologizing, as if you had stared in on some room where you should not be.

There will be an inquiry; there had better be, to stop the assumption of yet another case of brutality against farm workers, although there's nothing in doubt—an accident, and all the facts fully admitted by Van der Vyver. He made a statement when he arrived at the police station with the dead man in his *bakkie*. Captain Beetge knows him well, of course; he gave him brandy. He was shaking, this big, calm, clever son of Willem Van der Vyver, who inherited the old man's best farm. The black was stone dead, nothing to be done for him. Beetge will not tell anyone that after the brandy Van der Vyver wept. He sobbed, snot running onto his hands, like a dirty kid. The captain was ashamed for him, and walked out to give him a chance to recover himself.

Marais Van der Vyver left his house at three in the afternoon to cull a buck from the family of kudu he protects in the bush areas of his farm. He is interested in wildlife and sees it as the farmers' sacred duty to raise game as well as cattle. As usual, he called at his shed to pick up Lucas, a twenty-year-old farmhand who had shown mechanical aptitude and whom Van der Vyver himself had taught to maintain tractors and other farm machinery. He hooted, and Lucas followed the familiar routine, jumping onto the back of the truck. He liked to travel standing up there, spotting game before his employer did. He would lean forward, bracing against the cab below him.

Van der Vyver had a rifle and .30 caliber ammunition beside him in the cab. The rifle was one of his father's, because his own was at the gunsmith's in town. Since his father died (Beetge's sergeant wrote "passed on") no one had used the rifle, and so when he took it from a cupboard he was sure it was not loaded. His father had never allowed a loaded gun in the house, he himself had been taught since childhood never to ride with a loaded weapon in a vehicle. But this gun was loaded. On a dirt track, Lucas thumped his fist on the cab roof three times to signal: look left. Having seen the white-ripple-marked flank of a kudu, and its fine horns raking through disguising bush, Van der Vyver drove rather fast over a pothole. The jolt fired the rifle. Upright, it was pointing straight through the cab roof at the head of Lucas. The bullet pierced the roof and entered Lucas's brain by way of his throat.

That is the statement of what happened. Although a man of such standing in the district, Van der Vyver had to go through the ritual of swearing that it was the truth. It has gone on record, and will be there in the archive of the local police station as long as Van der Vyver lives, and beyond that, through the lives of his children, Magnus, Helena, and Karel—unless things in the country get worse, the example of black mobs in the town spreads to the rural areas and the place is burned down as many urban police stations have been. Because nothing the government can do will appease the agitators and the whites who encourage them. Nothing satisfies them, in the cities: blacks can sit and drink in white hotels now, the Immorality Act has gone, blacks can sleep with whites . . . It's not even a crime anymore.

Van der Vyver has a high, barbed security fence round his farmhouse and garden which his wife, Alida, thinks spoils completely the effect of her artificial stream with its tree ferns beneath the jacarandas. There is an aerial soaring like a flagpole in the backyard. All his vehicles, including the truck in which the black man died, have aerials that swing their whips when the driver hits a pothole: they are part of the security system the farmers in the district maintain, each farm in touch with every other by radio, twenty-four hours out of twenty-four. It has already happened that infiltrators from over the border have mined remote farm roads, killing white farmers and their families out on their own property for a Sunday picnic. The pothole could have set off a land mine, and Van der Vyver might have died with his farm boy. When neighbors use the communications system to call up and say they are sorry about "that business" with one of Van der Vyver's boys, there goes unsaid: it could have been worse.

It is obvious from the quality and fittings of the coffin that the farmer has provided money for the funeral. And an elaborate funeral means a great deal to blacks; look how they will deprive themselves of the little they have, in their lifetime, keeping up payments to a burial society so they won't go in boxwood to an unmarked grave. The young wife is pregnant (of course) and another little one, a boy wearing red shoes several sizes too large, leans under her jutting belly. He is too young to understand what has happened, what he is witnessing that day, but neither whines nor plays about; he is solemn without knowing why. Blacks expose small children to everything, they don't protect them from the sight of fear and pain the way whites do theirs. It is the young wife who rolls her head and cries like a child, sobbing on the breast of this relative and that. All present work for Van der Vyver or are the families of those who work; in the weeding and harvest seasons, the women and children work for him too, carried at sunrise to the fields, wrapped in their blankets, on a truck, singing. The dead man's mother is a woman who can't be more than in her late thirties (they start bearing children at puberty), but she is heavily mature in a black dress, standing between her own parents, who were already working for old Van der Vyver when Marais, like their daughter, was a child. The parents hold her as if she were a prisoner or a crazy woman to be restrained. But she says nothing, does nothing. She does not look up; she does not look at Van der Vyver, whose gun went off in the truck, she stares at the grave. Nothing will make her look up; there need be no fear that she will look up, at him. His wife, Alida, is beside him. To show the proper respect, as for any white funeral, she is wearing the navy blue and cream hat she wears to church this summer. She is always supportive, although he doesn't seem to notice it; this coldness and reserve—his mother says he didn't mix well as a child—she accepts for herself but regrets that it has prevented him from being nominated, as he should be, to stand as the Party's parliamentary candidate for the district. He does not let her clothing, or that of anyone else gathered closely, make contact with him. He, too, stares at the grave. The dead man's mother and he stare at the grave in communication like that between the black man outside and the white man inside the cab the moment before the gun went off.

The moment before the gun went off was a moment of high excitement shared through the roof of the cab, as the bullet was to pass, between the young black man outside and the white farmer inside the vehicle. There were such moments, without explanation, between them, although often around the farm the farmer would pass the young man without returning a greeting, as if he did not recognize him. When the bullet went off what Van der Vyver saw was the kudu stumble in fright at the report and gallop away. Then he heard the thud behind him, and past the window saw the young man fall out of the vehicle. He was sure he had leapt up and toppled—in fright, like the buck. The farmer was almost laughing with relief, ready to tease, as he opened his door, it did not seem possible that a bullet passing through the roof could have done harm.

The young man did not laugh with him at his own fright. The farmer carried him in his arms, to the truck. He was sure, sure he could not be dead. But the young black man's blood was all over the farmer's clothes, soaking against his flesh as he drove.

How will they ever know, when they file newspaper clippings, evidence, proof, when they look at the photographs and see his face—guilty! guilty! they are right!— how will they know, when the police stations burn with all the evidence of what has happened now, and what the law made a crime in the past? How could they know that *they do not know*. Anything. The young black callously shot through the negligence of the white man was not the farmer's boy; he was his son.

[1972]

Journal Entry

Choices can sometimes involve pain. Write a journal entry on a choice that you made involving pain—your own or others. What did you learn from the experience?

Textual Considerations

1. From whose point of view is the story told? How and why does the author put the reader in an awkward position?
2. How does Van der Vyver's wife view her husband's emotional state?
3. Why will the captain not tell anyone that Van der Vyver wept? How does Van der Vyver's weeping confirm or refute his wife's opinion of him?
4. What is ironic about the statement that "blacks can sleep with whites now"?
5. What important choices has Van der Vyver made in the past? What does he now face as a result?

Cultural Contexts

1. Gordimer's protagonist assumes financial responsibility for the family of the young man he shot accidentally. How does this affect your view of him? Would he have done this had the young man not also been his illegitimate son? Why or why not?
2. Analyze with your group the public and private lives of Van der Vyver. To what extent was his public life the result of a personal choice or a response to the political system of apartheid?

Sandip Roy

The Smells of Home

When she was seven years old Savitri's aunt visited from England. She brought her boxes of delicious chocolates filled with strawberries and hazelnuts and lots of pretty dresses. But what Savitri loved best was to bury her head in her aunt's suitcase and breathe in the fragrance of her clothes and cosmetics.

"Lavender, lilac, rosemary," she would whisper to herself making a daisychain of flowers she had never seen.

It was a scorchingly hot summer even by Delhi standards. In the afternoons her aunt would draw the blinds and take a nap. Savitri would tiptoe into the dark room and carefully open the suitcase. Then she would bury her head in the soft cottons and smooth silks and breathe deeply and surreptitiously. It was like a little corner of England trapped in there. She would feel herself falling through it and leaving the hot parched Delhi streets and the cruel blue Indian skies far behind. It smelled cool and fresh—so unlike the ripe kitchen smells that clung to her mother's sari—turmeric and sweat and stale talcum powder.

"Foxglove, primrose, daffodil."

She was now walking down a little cobbled street past houses like the picture on her tin of chocolates. She was going home to have scones and strawberries and cream. Her house had a pointed tiled roof and a chimney. And ivy on the walls or was it honeysuckle?

"Honeysuckle, bluebells, forget-me-not."

Crouched near the suitcase, like a little mouse, Savitri wished she could pack herself in with the soft nighties and synthetic saris. She imagined waking up and finding she was in England.

"Savi," her mother's shrill voice could be heard from downstairs. "Where is that girl? Savi, you haven't finished your rice. Come down or the cat will eat it up."

Savitri decided that when she grew up she would go to England.

Avinash was not quite from England. He was from New York. Well, not New York, New York but some small university town in the northern part of the state where he was just finishing his Ph.D. in Economics or something like that. It all sounded very difficult to Savitri. She liked to read Wordsworth and Keats. Not even Byron—there was something too hot and sunny about Byron, something sinewy and dangerous seemed to lurk beneath his poetry. For her Keats and Wordsworth had a watercolor feel about them which she found very soothing. Their colors were more muted. Savitri had never liked bright harsh colors—pinks and oranges and yellows.

"Look at that girl," her mother would say. "Only seventeen and dresses like a widow."

Avinash seemed the perfect match for her. Serious, academic and sober—he didn't wear hot pinks and sunny yellows either.

"My son," said his mother to Savitri's mother over a cup of tea, "has always been the top boy in his class. A model student his principal called him. Never one to wander the streets like these other roadside Romeos. That was why I never had the slightest fear of sending him to America. You know Mrs. Dutt, it's all about up-bringing and family. If you bring him up right, then why should you fear?"

Savitri's mother nodded wisely.

"Everyone told me," continued his mother, "See one day he'll call and an-nounce he wants to marry some American girl. But I said 'I trust my Avi. He would not break his mother's heart.' Arre, he is my only son. He knows his duty. Ever since his poor father died I have brought him up myself. It was not easy on a school-teacher's salary. But I had faith and see him now. Do you know he has had papers published in important journals. Why, my friend Sulata said to me, 'Look Bani, mark my words if your Avi does not get the Nobel Prize one day.'"

In the pause that ensued as all assembled digested this piece of information, Savitri's aunt jumped in.

"So how old is Avinash exactly?"

"Well," said his mother defensively, "he's thirty-three. But what's age in a man? My husband was eleven years older than me. I don't believe in all this same-age marriages that go on these days. You need some difference in age to maintain a bal-ance in the household. And tell me, how can you respect your husband if you are the same age as him?

"I've been telling him for so long now—get married, get married. But he keeps saying, 'First I must finish my Master's.' Then it was, 'Oh I must complete my Ph.D. and get a job, Ma. How will I have a family on a student's income?' So responsible, no? The day he got his professorship I said 'Enough Avi. Now I have to see you settled down with a good girl. Then only can I shut my eyes in peace.' He said 'But I don't have tenure yet' and I said '*Bas*. I will not listen anymore to your excuses.' We are not running after looks in my family," she said glancing at Savitri who was a little plain. "Good family and education is what we value. Avi's father was a renowned professor you know—he wrote three books. And I hear your Savitri has an M.A. in English Literature."

Avinash took Savitri out for dinner once. He was a thin quiet man with thin-ning hair and owlish glasses. He smelt faintly of lemony aftershave. They did not have much in common. She knew nothing about Economics, he had long forgotten his Wordsworth. They concentrated instead on the food and discussed the merits of the Tandoori chicken. When they exhausted that topic, they ate in silence listening to the ebb and flow of conversation at the tables around them.

"What was he like?" asked her mother.

"All right, I suppose," she answered. Though she had not found much in com-mon with him she had not found anything objectionable either. At least he did not wear those loud colorful shirts with big flowers that she had seen American tour-ists wear.

Only once she said, almost wistfully, "You know I really wanted to go to England."

Her father laughed and said, "Savi, Wordsworth's England is long dead. In your grandfather's time people would go to England for then England still had power and glory. Now it is truly a nation of shopkeepers. And most of the shopkeepers are Indian anyway. You are lucky, you are going to the richest country in the world."

"And such a brilliant husband," added her mother.

"And so courteous and well-mannered," added her aunt. "I hope my daughter is as lucky as you."

"Heather, daisy, larkspur," Savitri said under her breath, playing with the words as if they were prayer beads.

Savitri was amazed at how easily she left India behind. As the airplane left Delhi airport she looked out of the window at the lights of Delhi growing smaller and smaller. She had a sense of her past, her ties, her home all falling away behind her like an unraveling sari. "Perhaps," she thought sipping her Coca-Cola, "I was not meant to be Indian at all." She glanced over at Avinash, seated next to her, absorbed in the latest issue of *Time*. He glanced up at her and finding himself caught in her gaze looked away guiltily. Then he said quietly "How do you imagine America?"

"America—I don't know," she said wonderingly. "Big buildings, fast cars, movies."

"Washing machines," she added as an afterthought. "Lawnmowers, microwaves."

"You never thought of America as freedom?"

"Freedom?" she said perplexed. "No not really." Then she smiled slightly and said, "Maybe it was for you when you went there as a student. But I am going there as your wife."

"That's true," he replied.

"Are you afraid that now I am going with you, you will lose your freedom?" she asked half-teasingly.

"Who is really free anyway?" he answered without looking at her and returned to the magazine. She opened her mouth to speak but he seemed to have drawn curtains around himself.

Savitri hated America from the moment she stepped off that plane. The accents jarred her—they had none of the clean crispness of the BBC World Service programs she so loved and listened to on her father's prized short-wave radio. The freeways with their whizzing cars and many lanes terrified her. She could not imagine ever being able to drive on them. Yet Avinash had told her that if you didn't know how to drive here you were a prisoner. She was confused by all the machines she needed to handle and all the buttons she had to press whether to get money from the bank or to buy a roll of stamps. But most of all she missed having people to talk to.

Avinash spent long hours at school sometimes coming home after she had gone to bed. She would lie in the dark hearing the purr of the microwave as he warmed his dinner. Her mother always waited for her father to come home before she had dinner. But Savitri invariably got a headache if she let herself go hungry too long. She would leave his dinner on the table in front of the jar of Priya mango pickles. She would lie in bed and try and figure out what he was eating.

"He must be finished with the dal, he is probably on the chicken now." She would hear him open the refrigerator as he got some Coke. They needed to get more Coke and detergent and something else. She knitted her brows and tried to remember what. Soon she knew she would hear the tap running as he rinsed the dishes and then the clank of the dishes being loaded into the dishwasher. That was when she closed her eyes and turned on her side, away from his side of the bed. It was her way of punishing him for being late again. But he did not seem to mind. She would feel the bed as he climbed onto it. Then the sharp minty smell of toothpaste. In a little while she would hear his gentle easy breathing and she would lie awake angry, making grocery lists in her head.

Everyday she would run downstairs at two o'clock and check the mail. She had even come to know the postman. He always said, "Hi, how's it going?" But no one ever wrote to her. All she got were catalogs from department stores. She would spend the afternoon reading about furniture sales and installment plans to buy home entertainment systems. Apart from that all they seemed to get were bills and coupons from pizza-joints. She had written two letters home but had not gotten anything from India. Mail from India could take twenty days Avinash told her. Once she found a personal letter from India. In her excitement at seeing an Indian stamp she tore it open before she realized the letter was for Avinash. Though she did not read it he was very annoyed.

"I am your wife. We share the same bank account," she said.

"You don't understand," he replied, "letters are different. It could be, could be anything."

Savitri remembered the day she got her first letter. It had been raining all day— a fine dispiriting drizzle. She had wanted to walk down to the library but was stuck indoors since Avinash for some reason had left the umbrella in his office. Frustrated she had spent the whole day rearranging her spices. She had poured them into individual little spice-jars and then labeled the jars in her best handwriting. For a while she debated whether to write the Hindi names or the English ones—haldi, jeera, and dhania or turmeric, cumin, coriander? She finally decided on "Turmeric," "Cumin," "Coriander." But she did not know the word for methi so she left it blank. She smelt her hands—and suddenly remembered her mother cooking and then wiping her hands on her sari. Her old saris always had turmeric stains.

She wiped her hands on a paper towel and ran downstairs to get the mail. And there it was, a neat little envelope with Mrs. Mitra written on it in an almost childish uneven handwriting. She turned it over but there was no sender's name or address. The postmark was local. Puzzled she climbed up the stairs slowly trying to figure out who it was.

She put Avinash's mail on the dining table and pulled out the Kashmiri letter-cutter her friend Leena had given her and slit open the envelope. There was just one sheet in there—a yellow ruled sheet torn from a writing pad.

Dear Mrs. Mitra, (it said)

You don't know me but I have been dreading your arrival for months now. I have been your husband's lover for over two years now. I always knew I would have to keep it a secret but I didn't expect this. Avi said he is merely doing his duty and his mother would kill herself otherwise. Maybe that is so. I don't know too much about Indians. Avi never introduced me to his friends. I am no longer his lover. I couldn't bear the hypocrisy and I did not want to share. He thought we could carry on just as before except it would have to be at my place now. He can't understand why I would make such a fuss. After all, it had always been a secret from everyone else. Now we'd just keep it a secret from you too. Avi said, "It's not as if I promised to marry you or something." That's true, so why am I writing you this? Especially since I have broken up with him? I'd like to think I want to warn you and save you. But I think it's just my own vindictiveness and selfishness. I wanted to make him understand what he is doing to you and me. I wanted to hurt Avinash and the only way I knew how was through you. Forgive me if you can.

Sincerely,
John Elwood

She tore the letter up with shaking hands. Then she sat and put the pieces back together as if she could rearrange the words to say something else. Four times she lifted the receiver to call Avinash. Four times she put it down. She sat and stared at the neatly arranged spices and tried to remember the English for methi. Maybe she should just write methi. She wondered what would happen to her now. How much did a one-way fare to India cost? She sat and watched one television program after another letting the images drip meaninglessly in front of her. When Avinash came home she was already in bed.

"It's only nine o'clock," he said, "are you all right?"

She lay curled up on her side, her fists clenched in her mouth to prevent herself from screaming. She buried her face in the pillow and tried to summon up the old familiar smells of home.

"Turmeric, coriander, cumin," she whispered fiercely as if in exorcism.

But all she could smell was the happy lemon-lime spring-fresh smell of freshly laundered sheets. She buried herself deeper trying desperately to go home.

She felt him approaching the bed.

Mustard, poppyseed, methi. She was drawing a ring of spices to protect her.

She felt his hand on her forehead—cold and clammy. She shrank away from his touch.

Turmeric, coriander, methi.

Flies buzzing round her head.

Turmeric, coriander, methi.

Falling, falling, falling. . .

Her mother in the kitchen. . .

Her father reading the newspaper. . .

Old Sushila chopping the fish. . .

Haldi, dhania, methi

Haldi, dhania, methi. . .

[1996]

Journal Entry

The speaker in Roy's story recalls the many fragrances she associates with home. What memories of "smells" of home can you bring to your reading of this text?

Textual Considerations

1. Characterize Savitri. How does the author use visual, auditory, and sensory imagery to reveal Savitri's emotions to the reader?
2. Avinash's mother is sure that her son "would not break his mother's heart." To what extent do the events of the story contradict or affirm her point of view? What is your response to Avinash?
3. Identify and analyze the central conflict of the story.
4. What is your response to the story's ending? Where does the author use irony to foreshadow the contents of the letter?
5. How does Savitri change during the story?

Cultural Contexts

1. Avinash associates America with personal freedom, while Savitri relates it to big buildings, fast cars, movies, and microwaves. What kind of freedom might Avinash be seeking? Does he find it? Are Savitri's expectations more attainable? Why or why not?
2. The author of the story left Calcutta, India, to settle in San Francisco. Working with your group, analyze the roles that setting plays in the text. Consider, for example, the thematic significance of India, England, and the United States. Is this primarily a story about the immigrant experience? Explain.

Toni Cade Bambara

The Lesson

Back in the days when everyone was old and stupid or young and foolish and me and Sugar were the only ones just right, this lady moved on our block with nappy hair and proper speech and no makeup. And quite naturally we laughed at her, laughed the way we did at the junk man who went about his business like he was some big-time president and his sorry-ass horse his secretary. And we kinda hated her too, hated the way we did the winos who cluttered up our parks and pissed on our handball walls and stank up our hallways and stairs so you couldn't halfway play hide-and-seek without a goddamn gas mask. Miss Moore was her name. The only woman on the block with no first name. And she was black as hell, cept for her feet, which were fish-white and spooky. And she was always planning these boring-ass things for us to do, us being my cousin, mostly, who lived on the block cause we all moved North the same time and to the same apartment then spread out gradual to breathe. And our parents would yank our heads into some kinda shape and crisp up our clothes so we'd be presentable for travel with Miss Moore, who always looked like she was going to church, though she never did. Which is just one of the things the grownups talked about when they talked behind her back like a dog. But when she came calling with some sachet she'd sewed up or some gingerbread she'd made or some book, why then they'd all be too embarrassed to turn her down and we'd get handed over all spruced up. She'd been to college and said it was only right that she should take responsibility for the young ones' education, and she not even related by marriage or blood. So they'd go for it. Specially Aunt Gretchen. She was the main gofer in the family. You got some ole dumb shit foolishness you want somebody to go for, you send for Aunt Gretchen. She been screwed into the go-along for so long, it's a blood-deep natural thing with her. Which is how she got saddled with me and Sugar and Junior in the first place while our mothers were in a la-de-da apartment up the block having a good ole time.

So this one day Miss Moore rounds us all up at the mailbox and it's puredee hot and she's knockin herself out about arithmetic. And school suppose to let up in summer I heard, but she don't never let up. And the starch in my pinafore scratching the shit outta me and I'm really hating this nappy-head bitch and her goddamn college degree. I'd much rather go to the pool or to the show where it's cool. So me and Sugar leaning on the mailbox being surly, which is a Miss Moore word. And Flyboy checking out what everybody brought for lunch. And Fat Butt already wasting his peanut-butter-and-jelly sandwich like the pig he is. And Junebug punchin on Q.T.'s arm for potato chips. And Rosie Giraffe shifting from one hip to the other waiting for somebody to step on her foot or ask her if she from Georgia so she can kick ass, preferably Mercedes'. And Miss Moore asking us do we know what money is, like we a bunch of retards. I mean real money, she say, like it's only poker chips or monopoly papers we lay on the grocer. So right away I'm tired of this and say so. And would much rather snatch Sugar and go to the Sunset and terrorize the West Indian kids and take their hair ribbons and their money too. And Miss Moore files that remark away for next week's lesson on brotherhood, I can tell. And finally I say we oughta get to the subway cause it's cooler and besides we might meet some cute boys. Sugar done swiped her mama's lipstick, so we ready.

So we heading down the street and she's boring us silly about what things cost and what our parents make and how much goes for rent and how money ain't divided up right in this country. And then she gets to the part about we all poor and live in the slums, which I don't feature. And I'm ready to speak on that, but she steps out in the street and hails two cabs just like that. Then she hustles half the crew in with her and hands me a five-dollar bill and tells me to calculate 10 percent tip for the driver. And we're off. Me and Sugar and Junebug and Flyboy hangin out the window and hollering to everybody, putting lipstick on each other cause Flyboy a faggot anyway, and making farts with our sweaty armpits. But I'm mostly trying to figure how to spend this money. But they all fascinated with the meter ticking and Junebug starts laying bets as to how much it'll read when Flyboy can't hold his breath no more. Then Sugar lays bets as to how much it'll be when we get there. So I'm stuck. Don't nobody want to go for my plan, which is to jump out at the next light and run off to the first bar-b-que we can find. Then the driver tells us to get the hell out cause we there already. And the meter reads eighty-five cents. And I'm stalling to figure out the tip and Sugar say give him a dime. And I decide he don't need it bad as I do, so later for him. But then he tries to take off with Junebug foot still in the door so we talk about his mama something ferocious. Then we check out that we on Fifth Avenue and everybody dressed up in stockings. One lady in a fur coat, hot as it is. White folks crazy.

"This is the place," Miss Moore say, presenting it to us in the voice she uses at the museum. "Let's look in the windows before we go in."

"Can we steal?" Sugar asks very serious like she's getting the ground rules squared away before she plays. "I beg your pardon," say Miss Moore, and we fall out. So she leads us around the windows of the toy store and me and Sugar screamin, "This is mine, that's mine, I gotta have that, that was made for me, I was born for that," till Big Butt drowns us out.

"Hey, I'm goin to buy that there."

"That there? You don't even know what it is, stupid."

"I do so," he say punchin on Rosie Giraffe. "It's a microscope."

"Whatcha gonna do with a microscope, fool?"

"Look at things."

"Like what, Ronald?" ask Miss Moore. And Big Butt ain't got the first notion. So here go Miss Moore gabbing about the thousands of bacteria in a drop of water and the somethinorother in a speck of blood and the million and one living things in the air around us is invisible to the naked eye. And what she say that for? Junebug go to town on that "naked" and we rolling. Then Miss Moore ask what it cost. So we all jam into the window smudgin it up and the price tag say $300. So then she ask how long'd take for Big Butt and Junebug to save up their allowances. "Too long," I say. "Yeh," adds Sugar, "outgrown it by that time." And Miss Moore say no, you never outgrow learning instruments. "Why, even medical students and interns and," blah, blah, blah. And we ready to choke Big Butt for bringing it up in the first damn place.

"This here costs four hundred eighty dollars," says Rosie Giraffe. So we pile up all over her to see what she pointin out. My eyes tell me it's a chunk of glass cracked with something heavy, and different-color inks dripped into the splits, then the whole thing put into a oven or something. But for $480 it don't make sense.

"That's a paperweight made of semi-precious stones fused together under tremendous pressure," she explains slowly, with her hands doing the mining and all the factory work.

"So what's a paperweight?" asks Rosie Giraffe.

"To weigh paper with, dumbbell," say Flyboy, the wise man from the East.

"Not exactly," say Miss Moore, which is what she say when you warm or way off too. "It's to weigh paper down so it won't scatter and make your desk untidy." So right away me and Sugar curtsy to each other and then to Mercedes who is more the tidy type.

"We don't keep paper on top of the desk in my class," say Junebug, figuring Miss Moore crazy or lyin one.

"At home, then," she say. "Don't you have a calendar and pencil case and a blotter and a letter-opener on your desk at home where you do your homework?" And she know damn well what our homes look like cause she nosys around in them every chance she gets.

"I don't even have a desk," say Junebug. "Do we?"

"No. And I don't get no homework neither," says Big Butt.

"And I don't even have a home," say Flyboy like he do at school to keep the white folks off his back and sorry for him. Send this poor kid to camp posters, is his specialty.

"I do," says Mercedes. "I have a box of stationery on my desk and a picture of my cat. My godmother bought the stationery and the desk. There's a big rose on each sheet and the envelopes smell like roses."

"Who wants to know about your smelly-ass stationery," say Rosie Giraffe fore I can get my two cents in.

"It's important to have a work area all your own so that . . ."

"Will you look at this sailboat, please," say Flyboy, cuttin her off and pointin to the thing like it was his. So once again we tumble all over each other to gaze at this magnificent thing in the toy store which is just big enough to maybe sail two kittens across the pond if you strap them to the posts tight. We all start reciting the price tag like we in assembly. "Handcrafted sailboat of fiberglass at one thousand one hundred ninety-five dollars."

"Unbelievable," I hear myself say and am really stunned. I read it again for myself just in case the group recitation put me in a trance. Same thing. For some reason this pisses me off. We look at Miss Moore and she lookin at us, waiting for I dunno what.

"Who'd pay all that when you can buy a sailboat set for a quarter at Pop's, a tube of glue for a dime, and a ball of string for eight cents? It must have a motor and a whole lot else besides," I say. "My sailboat cost me about fifty cents."

"But will it take water?" say Mercedes with her smart ass.

"Took mine to Alley Pond Park once," say Flyboy. "String broke. Lost it. Pity."

"Sailed mine in Central Park and it keeled over and sank. Had to ask my father for another dollar."

"And you got the strap," laugh Big Butt. "The jerk didn't even have a string on it. My old man wailed on his behind."

Little Q.T. was staring hard at the sailboat and you could see he wanted it bad. But he too little and somebody'd just take it from him. So what the hell. "This boat for kids, Miss Moore?"

"Parents silly to buy something like that just to get all broke up," say Rosie Giraffe.

"That much money it should last forever," I figure.

"My father'd buy it for me if I wanted it."

"Your father, my ass," say Rosie Giraffe getting a chance to finally push Mercedes.

"Must be rich people shop here," say Q.T.

"You are a very bright boy," say Flyboy. "What was your first clue?" And he rap him on the head with the back of his knuckles, since Q.T. the only one he could get away with. Though Q.T. liable to come up behind you years later and get his licks in when you half expect it.

"What I want to know is," I says to Miss Moore though I never talk to her, I wouldn't give the bitch that satisfaction, "is how much a real boat costs? I figure a thousand'd get you a yacht any day."

"Why don't you check that out," she says, "and report back to the group?" Which really pains my ass. If you gonna mess up a perfectly good swim day least you could do is have some answers. "Let's go in," she say like she got something up her sleeve. Only she don't lead the way. So me and Sugar turn the corner to where the entrance is, but when we get there I kinda hang back. Not that I'm scared, what's there to be afraid of, just a toy store. But I feel funny, shame. But what I got to be shamed about? Got as much right to go in as anybody. But somehow I can't seem to get hold of the door, so I step away for Sugar to lead. But she hangs back too. And I look at her and she looks at me and this is ridiculous. I mean, damn, I have never ever been shy about doing nothing or going nowhere. But then Mercedes steps up and then Rosie Giraffe and Big Butt crowd in behind and shove, and next thing we all stuffed into the doorway with only Mercedes squeezing past us, smoothing out her jumper and walking right down the aisle. Then the rest of us tumble in like a glued-together jigsaw done all wrong. And people lookin at us. And it's like the time me and Sugar crashed into the Catholic church on a dare. But once we got in there and everything so hushed and holy and the candles and the bowin and the handkerchiefs on all the drooping heads, I just couldn't go through with the plan. Which was for me to run up to the altar and do a tap dance while Sugar played the nose flute and messed around in the holy water. And Sugar kept givin me the elbow. Then later teased me so bad I tied her up in the shower and turned it on and locked her in. And she'd be there till this day if Aunt Gretchen hadn't finally figured I was lyin about the boarder takin a shower.

Same thing in the store. We all walkin on tiptoe and hardly touchin the games and puzzles and things. And I watched Miss Moore who is steady watchin us like she waitin for a sign. Like Mama Drewery watches the sky and sniffs the air and takes note of just how much slant is in the bird formation. Then me and Sugar bump smack into each other, so busy gazing at the toys, specially the sailboat. But we don't laugh and go into our fat-lady bump-stomach routine. We just stare at that price tag. Then Sugar run a finger over the whole boat. And I'm jealous and want to hit her. Maybe not her, but I sure want to punch somebody in the mouth.

"Watcha bring us here for, Miss Moore?"

"You sound angry, Sylvia. Are you mad about something?" Givin me one of them grins like she tellin a grown-up joke that never turns out to be funny. And she's lookin very closely at me like maybe she planning to do my portrait from memory. I'm mad, but I won't give her that satisfaction. So I slouch around the store bein very bored and say, "Let's go."

Me and Sugar at the back of the train watchin the tracks whizzin by large then small then getting gobbled up in the dark. I'm thinkin about this tricky toy I saw in the store. A clown that somersaults on a bar then does chin-ups just cause you yank lightly at his leg. Cost $35. I could see me askin my mother for a $35 birthday clown. "You wanna who that costs what?" she'd say, cocking her head to the side to get a better view of the hole in my head. Thirty-five dollars could buy new bunk beds for Junior and Gretchen's boy. Thirty-five dollars and the whole household could go visit Granddaddy Nelson in the country. Thirty-five dollars would pay for the rent and the piano bill too. Who are these people that spend that much for performing clowns and $1000 for toy sailboats? What kinda work they do and how they live and how come we ain't in on it? Where we are is who we are, Miss Moore always pointin out. But it don't necessarily have to be that way, she always adds then waits for somebody to say that poor people have to wake up and demand their share of the pie and don't none of us know what kind of pie she talking about in the first damn place. But she ain't so smart cause I still got her four dollars from the taxi and she sure ain't gettin it. Messin up my day with this shit. Sugar nudges me in my pocket and winks.

Miss Moore lines us up in front of the mailbox where we started from, seem like years ago, and I got a headache for thinkin so hard. And we lean all over each other so we can hold up under the draggy-ass lecture she always finishes us off with at the end before we thank her for borin us to tears. But she just looks at us like she readin tea leaves. Finally she say, "Well, what did you think of F. A. O. Schwarz?"

Rosie Giraffe mumbles, "White folks crazy."

"I'd like to go there again when I get my birthday money," says Mercedes, and we shove her out the pack so she has to lean on the mailbox by herself.

"I'd like a shower. Tiring day," say Flyboy.

Then Sugar surprises me by sayin, "You know, Miss Moore, I don't think all of us here put together eat in a year what that sailboat costs." And Miss Moore lights up like somebody goosed her. "And?" she say, urging Sugar on. Only I'm standin on her foot so she don't continue.

"Imagine for a minute what kind of society it is in which some people can spend on a toy what it would cost to feed a family of six or seven. What do you think?"

"I think," say Sugar pushing me off her feet like she never done before, cause I whip her ass in a minute, "that this is not much of a democracy if you ask me. Equal chance to pursue happiness means an equal crack at the dough, don't it?" Miss Moore is beside herself and I am disgusted with Sugar's treachery. So I stand on her foot one more time to see if she'll shove me. She shuts up, and Miss Moore looks at me, sorrowfully I'm thinkin. And somethin weird is goin on, I can feel it in my chest.

"Anybody else learn anything today?" lookin dead at me. I walk away and Sugar has to run to catch up and don't even seem to notice when I shrug her arm off my shoulder.

"Well, we got four dollars anyway," she says.

"Uh hunh."

"We could go to Hascombs and get half a chocolate layer and then go to the Sunset and still have plenty money for potato chips and ice cream sodas."

"Un hunh."

"Race you to Hascombs," she say.

We start down the block and she gets ahead which is O.K. by me cause I'm going to the West End and then over to the Drive to think this day through. She can run if she want to and even run faster. But ain't nobody gonna beat me at nuthin.

[1972]

Journal Entry

According to Miss Moore, "Where we are is who we are." To what extent do you agree? Do you consider yourself the product of your social class? What other factors have contributed to your identity?

Textual Considerations

1. What does Miss Moore hope to accomplish during the class outing? What lesson does she want to teach? Does it need teaching? Why? To what extent does Miss Moore's method of teaching succeed?
2. Although the reader knows that Sylvia is angry, she will not admit her feelings to Miss Moore. Why not? Does Sylvia know what has made her angry? Explain.
3. With which character in the story do you most empathize? Why?
4. How does your attitude toward the expensive toys compare to that of the children? How do you account for similarities and/or differences in your responses?
5. How does Bambara use humor to enhance meaning in "The Lesson"? Cite examples.

Cultural Contexts

1. "White folks crazy" appears twice in "The Lesson." What situations give rise to this conclusion? What emotions are the children expressing through these words? What is the significance of Sylvia's resolve: "ain't nobody gonna beat me at nuthin"?
2. Working with your group, react to Miss Moore's assessment: "Imagine for a minute what kind of society it is in which some people can spend on a toy what it would cost to feed a family of six or seven." What does your group think?

Tillie Olsen

I Stand Here Ironing

I stand here ironing, and what you asked me moves tormented back and forth with the iron.

"I wish you would manage the time to come in and talk with me about your daughter. I'm sure you can help me understand her. She's a youngster who needs help and whom I'm deeply interested in helping."

"Who needs help." Even if I came, what good would it do? You think because I am her mother I have a key, or that in some way you could use me as a key? She has lived for nineteen years. There is all that life that has happened outside of me, beyond me.

And when is there time to remember, to sift, to weigh, to estimate, to total? I will start and there will be an interruption and I will have to gather it all together again. Or I will become engulfed with all I did or did not do, with what should have been and what cannot be helped.

She was a beautiful baby. The first and only one of our five that was beautiful at birth. You do not guess how new and uneasy her tenancy in her now-loveliness. You did not know her all those years she was thought homely, or see her poring over her baby pictures, making me tell her over and over how beautiful she had been—and would be, I would tell her—and was now, to the seeing eye. But the seeing eyes were few or non-existent. Including mine.

I nursed her. They feel that's important nowadays. I nursed all the children, but with her, with all the fierce rigidity of first motherhood, I did like the books then said. Though her cries battered me to trembling and my breasts ached with swollenness, I waited till the clock decreed.

Why do I put that first? I do not even know if it matters, or if it explains anything.

She was a beautiful baby. She blew shining bubbles of sound. She loved motion, loved light, loved colour and music and textures. She would lie on the floor in her blue overalls patting the surface so hard in ecstasy her hands and feet would blur. She was a miracle to me, but when she was eight months old I had to leave her daytimes with the woman downstairs to whom she was no miracle at all, for I worked or looked for work and for Emily's father, who "could no longer endure" (he wrote in his good-bye note) "sharing want with us."

I was nineteen. It was the pre-relief, pre-WPA world of the depression. I would start running as soon as I got off the street-car, running up the stairs, the place smelling sour, and awake or asleep to startle awake, when she saw me she would break into a clogged weeping that could not be comforted, a weeping I can yet hear.

After a while I found a job hashing at night so I could be with her days, and it was better. But it came to where I had to bring her to his family and leave her.

It took a long time to raise the money for her fare back. Then she got chicken pox and I had to wait longer. When she finally came, I hardly knew her, walking quick and nervous like her father, looking like her father, thin, and dressed in a shoddy red that yellowed her skin and glared at the pock marks. All the baby loveliness gone.

She was two. Old enough for nursery school they said, and I did not know then what I know now—the fatigue of the long day, and the lacerations of group life in nurseries that are only parking places for children.

Except that it would have made no difference if I had known. It was the only place there was. It was the only way we could be together, the only way I could hold a job.

And even without knowing, I knew. I knew the teacher that was evil because all these years it has curdled into my memory, the little boy hunched in the corner, her rasp, "why aren't you outside, because Alvin hits you? that's no reason, go out, scaredy." I knew Emily hated it even if she did not clutch and implore "don't go Mommy" like the other children, mornings.

She always had a reason why we should stay home. Momma, you look sick, Momma. I feel sick. Momma, the teachers aren't there today, they're sick. Momma, we can't go, there was a fire there last night. Momma, it's a holiday today, no school, they told me.

But never a direct protest, never rebellion. I think of our others in their three-, four-year-oldness—the explosions, the tempers, the denunciations, the demands— and I feel suddenly ill. I put the iron down. What in me demanded that goodness in her? And what was the cost, the cost to her of such goodness?

The old man living in the back once said in his gentle way: "You should smile at Emily more when you look at her." What *was* in my face when I looked at her? I loved her. There were all the acts of love.

It was only with the others I remembered what he said, and it was the face of joy, and not of care or tightness or worry I turned to them—too late for Emily. She does not smile easily, let alone almost always as her brothers and sisters do. Her face is closed and sombre, but when she wants, how fluid. You must have seen it in her pantomimes, you spoke of her rare gift for comedy on the stage that rouses a laughter out of the audience so dear they applaud and applaud and do not want to let her go.

Where does it come from, that comedy? There was none of it in her when she came back to me that second time, after I had had to send her away again. She had a new daddy now to learn to love, and I think perhaps it was a better time. Except when we left her alone nights, telling ourselves she was old enough.

"Can't you go some other time, Mommy, like tomorrow?" she would ask. "Will it be just a little while you'll be gone? Do you promise?"

The time we came back, the front door open, the clock on the floor in the hall. She rigid awake. "It wasn't just a little while. I didn't cry. Three times I called you, just three times, and then I ran downstairs to open the door so you could come faster. The clock talked loud. I threw it away, it scared me what it talked."

She said the clock talked loud again that night I went to the hospital to have Susan. She was delirious with the fever that comes before red measles, but she was fully conscious all the week I was gone and the week after we were home when she could not come near the new baby or me.

She did not get well. She stayed skeleton thin, not wanting to eat, and night after night she had nightmares. She would call for me, and I would rouse from exhaustion to sleepily call back: "You're all right, darling, go to sleep, it's just a dream," and if she still called, in a sterner voice, "now go to sleep, Emily, there's nothing to hurt you." Twice, only twice, when I had to get up for Susan anyhow, I went in to sit with her.

Now when it is too late (as if she would let me hold and comfort her like I do the others) I get up and go to her at once at her moan or restless stirring. "Are you awake, Emily? Can I get you something, dear?" And the answer is always the same: "No, I'm all right, go back to sleep, Mother."

They persuaded me at the clinic to send her away to a convalescent home in the country where "she can have the kind of food and care you can't manage for her, and you'll be free to concentrate on the new baby." They still send children to that place. I see pictures on the society page of sleek young women planning affairs to raise money for it, or dancing at the affairs, or decorating Easter eggs or filling Christmas stockings for the children.

They never have a picture of the children so I do not know if the girls still wear those gigantic red bows and the ravaged looks on the every other Sunday when parents can come to visit "unless otherwise notified"—as we were notified the first six weeks.

Oh it is a handsome place, green lawns and tall trees and fluted flower beds. High up on the balconies of each cottage the children stand, the girls in their red bows and white dresses, the boys in white suits and giant red ties. The parents stand below shrieking up to be heard and the children shriek down to be heard, and between them the invisible wall "Not To Be Contaminated by Parental Germs or Physical Affection."

There was a tiny girl who always stood hand in hand with Emily. Her parents never came. One visit she was gone. "They moved her to Rose Cottage," Emily shouted in explanation. "They don't like you to love anybody here."

She wrote once a week, the laboured writing of a seven-year-old. "I am fine. How is the baby. If I write my letter nicely I will have a star. Love." There never was a star. We wrote every other day, letters she could never hold or keep but only hear read—once. "We simply do not have room for children to keep any personal possessions," they patiently explained when we pieced one Sunday's shrieking together to plead how much it would mean to Emily, who loved so to keep things, to be allowed to keep her letters and cards.

Each visit she looked frailer. "She isn't eating," they told us.

(They had runny eggs for breakfast or mush with lumps, Emily said later, I'd hold it in my mouth and not swallow. Nothing ever tasted good, just when they had chicken.)

It took us eight months to get her released home, and only the fact that she gained back so little of her seven lost pounds convinced the social worker.

I used to try to hold and love her after she came back, but her body would stay stiff, and after a while she'd push away. She ate little. Food sickened her, and I think much of life too. Oh she had physical lightness and brightness, twinkling by on skates, bouncing like a ball up and down up and down over the jump rope, skimming over the hill; but these were momentary.

She fretted about her appearance, thin and dark and foreign-looking at a time when every little girl was supposed to look or thought she should look like a chubby blonde replica of Shirley Temple. The door-bell sometimes rang for her, but no one seemed to come and play in the house or be a best friend. Maybe because we moved so much.

There was a boy she loved painfully through two school semesters. Months later she told me how she had taken pennies from my purse to buy him candy.

"Liquorice was his favourite and I brought him some every day, but he still liked Jennifer better'n me. Why, Mommy?" The kind of question for which there is no answer.

School was a worry to her. She was not glib or quick in a world where glibness and quickness were easily confused with ability to learn. To her overworked and exasperated teachers she was an overconscientious "slow learner" who kept trying to catch up and was absent entirely too often.

I let her be absent, though sometimes the illness was imaginary. How different from my now-strictness about attendance with the others. I wasn't working. We had a new baby, I was home anyhow. Sometimes, after Susan grew old enough, I would keep her home from school, too, to have them all together.

Mostly Emily had asthma, and her breathing, harsh and laboured, would fill the house with a curiously tranquil sound. I would bring the two old dresser mirrors and her boxes of collections to her bed. She would select beads and single earrings, bottle tops and shells, dried flowers and pebbles, old postcards and scraps, all sorts of oddments; then she and Susan would play Kingdom, setting up landscapes and furniture, peopling them with action.

Those were the only times of peaceful companionship between her and Susan. I have edged away from it, that poisonous feeling between them, that terrible balancing of hurts and needs I had to do between the two, and did so badly, those earlier years.

Oh there are conflicts between the others too, each one human, needing, demanding, hurting, taking—but only between Emily and Susan, no, Emily toward Susan that corroding resentment. It seems so obvious on the surface, yet it is not obvious. Susan, the second child, Susan, golden- and curly-haired and chubby, quick and articulate and assured, everything in appearance and manner Emily was not; Susan, not able to resist Emily's precious things, losing or sometimes clumsily breaking them; Susan telling jokes and riddles to company for applause while Emily sat silent (to say to me later: that was *my* riddle, Mother, I told it to Susan); Susan, who for all the five years' difference in age was just a year behind Emily in developing physically.

I am glad for that slow physical development that widened the difference between her and her contemporaries, though she suffered over it. She was too vulnerable for that terrible world of youthful competition, of preening and parading, of constant measuring of yourself against every other, of envy, "If I had that copper hair," or "If I had that skin. . . ." She tormented herself enough about not looking like the others, there was enough of the unsureness, the having to be conscious of words before you speak, the constant caring—what are they thinking of me? What kind of an impression am I making?—there was enough without having it all magnified by the merciless physical drives.

Ronnie is calling. He is wet and I change him. It is rare there is such a cry now. That time of motherhood is almost behind me when the ear is not one's own but must always be racked and listening for the child cry, the child call. We sit for a while and I hold him, looking out over the city spread in charcoal with its soft aisles of light. "*Shoogily*," he breathes and curls closer. I carry him back to bed, asleep. *Shoogily*. A funny word, a family word, inherited from Emily, invented by her to say: *comfort*.

In this and other ways she leaves her seal, I say aloud. And startle at my saying it. What do I mean? What did I start to gather together, to try and make coherent? I was at the terrible, growing years. War years. I do not remember them well. I was working, there were four smaller ones now, there was not time for her. She had to help be a mother, and housekeeper, and shopper. She had to set her seal. Mornings of crisis and near hysteria trying to get lunches packed, hair combed, coats and shoes found, everyone to school or Child Care on time, the baby ready for transportation. And always the paper scribbled on by a smaller one, the book looked at by Susan then mislaid, the homework not done. Running out to that huge school where she was one, she was lost, she was a drop; suffering over the unpreparedness, stammering and unsure in her classes.

There was so little time left at night after the kids were bedded down. She would struggle over books, always eating (it was in those years she developed her enormous appetite that is legendary in our family) and I would be ironing, or preparing food for the next day, or writing V-mail to Bill, or tending the baby. Sometimes, to make me laugh, or out of her despair, she would imitate happenings or types at school.

I think I said once: "Why don't you do something like this in the school amateur show?" One morning she phoned me at work, hardly understandable through the weeping: "Mother, I did it. I won, I won; they gave me first prize; they clapped and clapped and wouldn't let me go."

Now suddenly she was Somebody, and as imprisoned in her difference as she had been in anonymity.

She began to be asked to perform at other high schools, even in colleges, then at city and state-wide affairs. The first one we went to, I only recognized her that first moment when thin, shy, she almost drowned herself into the curtains. Then: Was this Emily? The control, the command, the convulsing and deadly clowning, the spell, then the roaring, stamping audience, unwilling to let this rare and precious laughter out of their lives.

Afterwards: You ought to do something about her with a gift like that—but without money or knowing how, what does one do? We have left it all to her, and the gift has as often eddied inside, clogged and clotted, as been used and growing.

She is coming. She runs up the stairs two at a time with her light graceful step, and I know she is happy tonight. Whatever it was that occasioned your call did not happen today.

"Aren't you ever going to finish the ironing, Mother? Whistler painted his mother in a rocker. I'd have to paint mine standing over an ironing-board." This is one of her communicative nights and she tells me everything and nothing as she fixes herself a plate of food out of the icebox.

She is so lovely. Why did you want me to come in at all? Why were you concerned? She will find her way.

She starts up the stairs to bed. "Don't get me up with the rest in the morning." "But I thought you were having midterms." "Oh, those," she comes back in, kisses me, and says quite lightly, "in a couple of years when we'll all be atom-dead they won't matter a bit."

She has said it before. She *believes* it. But because I have been dredging the past, and all that compounds a human being is so heavy and meaningful in me, I cannot endure it tonight.

I will never total it all. I will never come in to say: She was a child seldom smiled at. Her father left me before she was a year old. I had to work her first six years when there was work, or I sent her home and to his relatives. There were years she had care she hated. She was dark and thin and foreign-looking in a world where the prestige went to blondness and curly hair and dimples, she was slow where glibness was prized. She was a child of anxious, not proud, love. We were poor and could not afford for her the soil of easy growth. I was a young mother, I was a distracted mother. There were the other children pushing up, demanding. Her younger sister seemed all that she was not. There were years she did not want me to touch her. She kept too much in herself, her life was such she had to keep too much in herself. My wisdom came too late. She has much to her and probably nothing will come of it. She is a child of her age, of depression, of war, of fear.

Let her be. So all that is in her will not bloom—but in how many does it? There is still enough left to live by. Only help her to know—help make it so there is cause for her to know that she is more than this dress on the ironing-board, helpless before the iron.

[1956]

Journal Entry

Write a journal entry describing how your relationship with your parents defined your process of coming of age. What feelings, emotions, and conflicts do you remember most?

Textual Considerations

1. Relate the title of the story to the events that occur. To what extent is the iron the dominant symbol of the story? What does it symbolize? What other symbols can you identify?
2. Examine the bonds that tie mother and daughter in Olsen's text. How well does the mother succeed in building a good relationship with her daughter? What kind of resentment might Emily feel toward her mother?
3. How does point of view function in the story? To what extent might the narrative be considered an interior monologue? What does the narrator reveal about herself? About her understanding of Emily?
4. What does the mother's statement "My wisdom came too late" mean? What kind of "wisdom" does she refer to? Explain.
5. What does the daughter's comment "Whistler painted his mother in a rocker. I'd have to paint mine standing over an ironing-board" reveal about the daughter's cultural background?

Cultural Contexts

1. Emily's mother represents the plight of single parents in the 1930s. What can be done to help young, distracted mothers of the twenty-first century who are trying to raise children by themselves? Consider, also, what these mothers might do to help themselves.
2. Olsen's story is set partly during the Depression, when the child star Shirley Temple dominated American movies. Share with your group what you feel about the narrator's criticism of that time in expressions such as "She was dark and thin and foreign-looking in a world where the prestige went to blondness and curly hair and dimples" and "She is a child of her age, of depression, of war, of fear." To what extent do you consider Emily a victim of socioeconomic circumstances?

Bharati Mukherjee

Jasmine

Jasmine came to Detroit from Port-of-Spain, Trinidad, by way of Canada. She crossed the border at Windsor in the back of a gray van loaded with mattresses and box springs. The plan was for her to hide in an empty mattress box if she heard the driver say, "All bad weather seems to come down from Canada, doesn't it?" to the customs man. But she didn't have to crawl into a box and hold her breath. The customs man didn't ask to look in.

The driver let her off at a scary intersection on Woodward Avenue and gave her instructions on how to get to the Plantations Motel in Southfield. The trick was to keep changing vehicles, he said. That threw off the immigration guys real quick.

Jasmine took money for cab fare out of the pocket of the great big raincoat that the van driver had given her. The raincoat looked like something that nuns in Port-of-Spain sold in church bazaars. Jasmine was glad to have a coat with wool lining, though; and anyway, who would know in Detroit that she was Dr. Vassanji's daughter?

All the bills in her hand looked the same. She would have to be careful when she paid the cabdriver. Money in Detroit wasn't pretty the way it was back home, or even in Canada, but she liked this money better. Why should money be pretty, like a picture? Pretty money is only good for putting on your walls maybe. The dollar bills felt businesslike, serious. Back home at work, she used to count out thousands of Trinidad dollars every day and not even think of them as real. Real money was worn and green, American dollars. Holding the bills in her fist on a street corner meant she had made it in okay. She'd outsmarted the guys at the border. Now it was up to her to use her wits to do something with her life. As her Daddy kept saying, "Girl, is opportunity come only once." The girls she'd worked with at the bank in Port-of-Spain had gone green as bananas when she'd walked in with her ticket on Air Canada. Trinidad was too tiny. That was the trouble. Trinidad was an island stuck in the middle of nowhere. What kind of place was that for a girl with ambition?

The Plantations Motel was run by a family of Trinidad Indians who had come from the tuppenny-ha'penny country town, Chaguanas. The Daboos were nobodies back home. They were lucky, that's all. They'd gotten here before the rush and bought up a motel and an ice cream parlor. Jasmine felt very superior when she saw Mr. Daboo in the motel's reception area. He was a pumpkin-shaped man with very black skin and Elvis Presley sideburns turning white. They looked like earmuffs. Mrs. Daboo was a bumpkin, too; short, fat, flapping around in house slippers. The Daboo daughters seemed very American, though. They didn't seem to know that they were nobodies, and kept looking at her and giggling.

She knew she would be short of cash for a great long while. Besides, she wasn't sure she wanted to wear bright leather boots and leotards like Viola and Loretta. The smartest move she could make would be to put a down payment on a husband. Her Daddy had told her to talk to the Daboos first chance. The Daboos ran a service fixing up illegals with islanders who had made it in legally. Daddy had paid three thousand back in Trinidad, with the Daboos and the mattress man getting part of it. They should throw in a good-earning husband for that kind of money.

The Daboos asked her to keep books for them and to clean the rooms in the new wing, and she could stay in 16B as long as she liked. They showed her 16B. They said she could cook her own roti; Mr. Daboo would bring in a stove, two gas rings that you could fold up in a metal box. The room was quite grand, Jasmine thought. It had a double bed, a TV, a pink sink and matching bathtub. Mrs. Daboo said Jasmine wasn't the big-city Port-of-Spain type she'd expected. Mr. Daboo said that he wanted her to stay because it was nice to have a neat, cheerful person around. It wasn't a bad deal, better than stories she'd heard about Trinidad girls in the States.

All day every day except Sundays Jasmine worked. There wasn't just the bookkeeping and the cleaning up. Mr. Daboo had her working on the match-up marriage service. Jasmine's job was to check up on social security cards, call clients' bosses for references, and make sure credit information wasn't false. Dermatologists and engineers living in Bloomfield Hills, store owners on Canfield and Woodward: she treated them all as potential liars. One of the first things she learned was that Ann Arbor was a magic word. A boy goes to Ann Arbor and gets an education, and all the barriers come crashing down. So Ann Arbor was the place to be.

She didn't mind the work. She was learning about Detroit, every side of it. Sunday mornings she helped unload packing crates of Caribbean spices in a shop on the next block. For the first time in her life, she was working for a black man, an African. So what if the boss was black? This was a new life, and she wanted to learn everything. Her Sunday boss, Mr. Anthony, was a courtly, Christian, church-going man, and paid her the only wages she had in her pocket. Viola and Loretta, for all their fancy American ways, wouldn't go out with blacks.

One Friday afternoon she was writing up the credit info on a Guyanese Muslim who worked in an assembly plant when Loretta said that enough was enough and there was no need for Jasmine to be her father's drudge.

"Is time to have fun," Viola said. "We're going to Ann Arbor."

Jasmine filed the sheet on the Guyanese man who probably now would never get a wife and got her raincoat. Loretta's boyfriend had a Cadillac parked out front.

It was the longest car Jasmine had ever been in and louder than a country bus. Viola's boyfriend got out of the front seat. "Oh, oh, sweet things," he said to Jasmine. "Get in front." He was a talker. She'd learned that much from working on the matrimonial match-ups. She didn't believe him for a second when he said that there were dudes out there dying to ask her out.

Loretta's boyfriend said, "You have eyes I could leap into, girl."

Jasmine knew he was just talking. They sounded like Port-of-Spain boys of three years ago. It didn't surprise her that these Trinidad country boys in Detroit were still behind the times, even of Port-of-Spain. She sat very stiff between the two men, hands on her purse. The Daboo girls laughed in the back seat.

On the highway the girls told her about the reggae night in Ann Arbor. Kevin and the Krazee Islanders. Malcolm's Lovers. All the big reggae groups in the Midwest were converging for the West Indian Students Association fall bash. The ticket didn't come cheap but Jasmine wouldn't let the fellows pay. She wasn't that kind of girl.

The reggae and steel drums brought out the old Jasmine. The rum punch, the dancing, the dreadlocks, the whole combination. She hadn't heard real music since she got to Detroit, where music was supposed to be so famous. The Daboo girls kept turning on rock stuff in the motel lobby whenever their father left the area. She hadn't danced, really *danced*, since she'd left home. It felt so good to dance. She felt hot and sweaty and sexy. The boys at the dance were more than sweet talkers; they moved with assurance and spoke of their futures in America. The bartender gave her two free drinks and said, "Is ready when you are, girl." She ignored him but she felt all hot and good deep inside. She knew Ann Arbor was a special place.

When it was time to pile back into Loretta's boyfriend's Cadillac, she just couldn't face going back to the Plantations Motel and to the Daboos with their accounting books and messy files.

"I don't know what happen, girl," she said to Loretta. "I feel all crazy inside. Maybe is time for me to pursue higher studies in this town."

"This Ann Arbor, girl, they don't just take you off the street. It *cost* like hell."

She spent the night on a bashed-up sofa in the Student Union. She was a well-dressed, respectable girl, and she didn't expect anyone to question her right to sleep on the furniture. Many others were doing the same thing. In the morning, a boy in an army parka showed her the way to the Placement Office. He was a big, blond, clumsy boy, not bad-looking except for the blond eyelashes. He didn't scare her, as did most Americans. She let him buy her a Coke and a hotdog. That evening she had a job with the Moffitts.

Bill Moffitt taught molecular biology and Lara Hatch-Moffitt, his wife, was a performance artist. A performance artist, said Lara, was very different from being an actress, though Jasmine still didn't understand what the difference might be. The Moffitts had a little girl, Muffin, whom Jasmine was to look after, though for the first few months she might have to help out with the housework and the cooking because Lara said she was deep into performance rehearsals. That was all right with her, Jasmine said, maybe a little too quickly. She explained she came from a big family and was used to heavy-duty cooking and cleaning. This wasn't the time to say anything about Ram, the family servant. Americans like the Moffitts wouldn't understand about keeping servants. Ram and she weren't in similar situations. Here mother's helpers, which is what Lara had called her—Americans were good with words to cover their shame—seemed to be as good as anyone.

Ann Arbor was a huge small town. She couldn't imagine any kind of school the size of the University of Michigan. She meant to sign up for courses in the spring. Bill brought home a catalogue bigger than the phonebook for all of Trinidad. The university had courses in everything. It would be hard to choose; she'd have to get help from Bill. He wasn't like a professor, not the ones back home where even high school teachers called themselves professors and acted like little potentates. He wore blue jeans and thick sweaters with holes in the elbows and used phrases like "in vitro" as he watched her curry up fish. Dr. Parveen back home—he called himself "doctor" when everybody knew he didn't have even a Master's degree—was never seen without his cotton jacket which had gotten really ratty at the cuffs and lapel edges. She hadn't learned anything in the two years she'd put into college. She'd learned more from working in the bank for two months than she had at college. It was the assistant manager, Personal Loans Department, Mr. Singh, who had turned her on to the Daboos and to smooth, bargain-priced emigration.

Jasmine liked Lara. Lara was easygoing. She didn't spend the time she had between rehearsals telling Jasmine how to cook and clean American-style. Mrs. Daboo did that in 16B. Mrs. Daboo would barge in with a plate of stale samosas and snoop around giving free advice on how mainstream Americans did things. As if she were dumb or something! As if she couldn't keep her own eyes open and make her mind up for herself. Sunday mornings she had to share the butcher-block workspace in the kitchen with Bill. He made the Sunday brunch from new recipes in *Gourmet* and *Cuisine*. Jasmine hadn't seen a man cook who didn't have to or wasn't getting paid to do it. Things were topsy-turvy in the Moffitt house. Lara went on two- and three-day road trips and Bill stayed home. But even her Daddy, who'd never poured himself a cup of tea, wouldn't put Bill down as a woman. The mornings Bill tried out something complicated, a Cajun shrimp, sausage, and beans dish, for instance, Jasmine skipped church services. The Moffitts didn't go to church, though they seemed to be good Christians. They just didn't talk church talk, which suited her fine.

Lara showed her the room she would have all to herself in the finished basement. There was a big, old TV, not in color like the motel's and a portable typewriter on a desk which Lara said she would find handy when it came time to turn in her term papers. Jasmine didn't say anything about not being a student. She was a student of life, wasn't she? There was a scary moment after they'd discussed what she could expect as salary, which was three times more than anything Mr. Daboo was supposed to pay her but hadn't. She thought Bill Moffitt was going to ask her about her visa or her green card[1] number and social security. But all Bill did was smile and smile at her—he had a wide, pink, baby face—and play with a button on his corduroy jacket. The button would need sewing back on, firmly.

---

[1] Work permit issued only to immigrants who have permanent resident status in the U.S.

Lara said, "I think I'm going to like you, Jasmine. You have a something about you. A something real special. I'll just bet you've acted, haven't you?" The idea amused her, but she merely smiled and accepted Lara's hug. The interview was over.

Then Bill opened a bottle of Soave and told stories about camping in northern Michigan. He'd been raised there. Jasmine didn't see the point in sleeping in tents; the woods sounded cold and wild and creepy. But she said, "Is exactly what I want to try out come summer, man. Campin and huntin."

Lara asked about Port-of-Spain. There was nothing to tell about her hometown that wouldn't shame her in front of nice white American folk like the Moffitts. The place was shabby, the people were grasping and cheating and lying and life was full of despair and drink and wanting. But by the time she finished, the island sounded romantic. Lara said, "It wouldn't surprise me one bit if you were a writer, Jasmine."

Two months passed. Jasmine knew she was lucky to have found a small, clean, friendly family like the Moffitts to build her new life around. "Man!" she'd exclaim as she vacuumed the wide-plank wood floors or ironed (Lara wore pure silk or pure cotton). "In this country Jesus givin out good luck only!" By this time they knew she wasn't a student, but they didn't care and said they wouldn't report her. They never asked if she was illegal on top of it.

To savor her new sense of being a happy, lucky person, she would put herself through a series of "what ifs": what if Mr. Singh in Port-of-Spain hadn't turned her on to the Daboos and loaned her two thousand! What if she'd been ugly like the Mintoo girl and the manager hadn't even offered! What if the customs man had unlocked the door of the van! Her Daddy liked to say, "You is a helluva girl, Jasmine."

"Thank you, Jesus," Jasmine said, as she carried on.

Christmas Day the Moffitts treated her just like family. They gave her a red cashmere sweater with a V neck so deep it made her blush. If Lara had worn it, her bosom wouldn't hang out like melons. For the holiday weekend Bill drove her to the Daboos in Detroit. "You work too hard," Bill said to her. "Learn to be more selfish. Come on, throw your weight around." She'd rather not have spent time with the Daboos, but that first afternoon of the interview she'd told Bill and Lara that Mr. Daboo was her mother's first cousin. She had thought it shameful in those days to have no papers, no family, no roots. Now Loretta and Viola in tight, bright pants seemed trashy like girls at Two-Johnny Bissoondath's Bar back home. She was stuck with the story of the Daboos being family. Village bumpkins, ha! She would break out. Soon.

Jasmine had Bill drop her off at the RenCen. The Plantations Motel, in fact, the whole Riverfront area, was too seamy. She'd managed to cut herself off mentally from anything too islandy. She loved her Daddy and Mummy, but she didn't think of them that often anymore. Mummy had expected her to be homesick and come flying right back home. "Is blowin sweat-of-brow money is what you doin, Pa," Mummy had scolded. She loved them, but she'd become her own person. That was something that Lara said: "I am my own person."

The Daboos acted thrilled to see her back. "What you drinkin, Jasmine girl?" Mr. Daboo kept asking. "You drinkin sherry or what?" Pouring her little glasses of sherry instead of rum was a sure sign he thought she had become whitefolk-fancy. The Daboo sisters were very friendly, but Jasmine considered them too wild. Both Loretta and Viola had changed boyfriends. Both were seeing black men they'd danced with in Ann Arbor. Each night at bedtime, Mr. Daboo cried. "In Trinidad we stayin we side, they stayin they side. Here, everything mixed up. Is helluva confusion, no?"

On New Year's Eve the Daboo girls and their black friends went to a dance. Mr. and Mrs. Daboo and Jasmine watched TV for a while. Then Mr. Daboo got out a brooch from his pocket and pinned it on Jasmine's red sweater. It was a Christmasy brooch, a miniature sleigh loaded down with snowed-on mistletoe. Before she could pull away, he kissed her on the lips. "Good luck for the New Year!" he said. She lifted her head and saw tears. "Is year for dreams comin true."

Jasmine started to cry, too. There was nothing wrong, but Mr. Daboo, Mrs. Daboo, she, everybody was crying.

What for? This is where she wanted to be. She'd spent some damned uncomfortable times with the assistant manager to get approval for her loan. She thought of Daddy. He would be playing poker and fanning himself with a magazine. Her married sisters would be rolling out the dough for stacks and stacks of roti, and Mummy would be steamed purple from stirring the big pot of goat curry on the stove. She missed them. But. It felt strange to think of anyone celebrating New Year's Eve in summery clothes.

In March Lara and her performing group went on the road. Jasmine knew that the group didn't work from scripts. The group didn't use a stage, either; instead, it took over supermarkets, senior citizens' centers, and school halls, without notice. Jasmine didn't understand the performance world. But she was glad that Lara said, "I'm not going to lay a guilt trip on myself. Muffie's in super hands," before she left.

Muffie didn't need much looking after. She played Trivial Pursuit all day, usually pretending to be two persons, sometimes Jasmine, whose accent she could imitate. Since Jasmine didn't know any of the answers, she couldn't help. Muffie was a quiet, precocious child with see-through blue eyes like her dad's, and red braids. In the early evenings Jasmine cooked supper, something special she hadn't forgotten from her island days. After supper she and Muffie watched some TV, and Bill read. When Muffie went to bed, Bill and she sat together for a bit with their glasses of Soave. Bill, Muffie, and she were a family, almost.

Down in her basement room that late, dark winter, she had trouble sleeping. She wanted to stay awake and think of Bill. Even when she fell asleep it didn't feel like sleep because Bill came barging into her dreams in his funny, loose-jointed, clumsy way. It was mad to think of him all the time, and stupid and sinful; but she couldn't help it. Whenever she put back a book he'd taken off the shelf to read or whenever she put his clothes through the washer and dryer, she felt sick in a giddy, wonderful way. When Lara came back things would get back to normal. Meantime she wanted the performance group miles away.

Lara called in at least twice a week. She said things like, "We've finally obliterated the margin between realspace and performancespace." Jasmine filled her in on Muffie's doings and the mail. Bill always closed with, "I love you. We miss you, hon."

One night after Lara had called—she was in Lincoln, Nebraska—Bill said to Jasmine, "Let's dance."

She hadn't danced since the reggae night she'd had too many rum punches. Her toes began to throb and clench. She untied her apron and the fraying, knotted-up laces of her running shoes.

Bill went around the downstairs rooms turning down lights. "We need atmosphere," he said. He got a small, tidy fire going in the living room grate and pulled the Turkish scatter rug closer to it. Lara didn't like anybody walking on the Turkish rug, but Bill meant to have his way. The hissing logs, the plants in the dimmed light, the thick patterned rug: everything was changed. This wasn't the room she cleaned every day.

He stood close to her. She smoothed her skirt down with both hands.

"I want you to choose the record," he said.

"I don't know your music."

She brought her hand high to his face. His skin was baby smooth.

"I want *you* to pick," he said. "You are your own person now."

"You got island music?"

He laughed, "What do you think?" The stereo was in a cabinet with albums packed tight alphabetically into the bottom three shelves. "Calypso has not been a force in my life."

She couldn't help laughing. "Calypso? Oh, man." She pulled dust jackets out at random. Lara's records. The Flying Lizards. The Violent Femmes. There was so much still to pick up on!

"This one," she said, finally.

He took the record out of her hand. "God!" he laughed. "Lara must have found this in a garage sale!" He laid the old record on the turntable. It was "Music for Lovers," something the nuns had taught her to foxtrot to way back in Port-of-Spain.

They danced so close that she could feel his heart heaving and crashing against her head. She liked it, she liked it very much. She didn't care what happened.

"Come on," Bill whispered. "If it feels right, do it." He began to take her clothes off.

"Don't Bill," she pleaded.

"Come on, baby," he whispered again. "You're a blossom, a flower."

He took off his fisherman's knit pullover, the corduroy pants, the blue shorts. She kept pace. She'd never had such an effect on a man: He nearly flung his socks and Adidas into the fire. "You feel so good," he said. "You smell so good. You're really something, flower of Trinidad."

"Flower of Ann Arbor," she said, "not Trinidad."

She felt so good she was dizzy. She'd never felt this good on the island where men did this all the time, and girls went along with it always for favors. You couldn't feel really good in a nothing place. She was thinking this as they made love on the Turkish carpet in front of the fire: she was a bright, pretty girl with no visa, no papers, and no birth certificate. No nothing other than what she wanted to invent and tell. She was a girl rushing wildly into the future.

His hand moved up her throat and forced her lips apart and it felt so good, so right, that she forgot all the dreariness of her new life and gave herself up to it.

[1988]

Journal Entry

How do you feel about the entry of illegal immigrants into the United States? Compare how Americans and Europeans react toward this crucial issue. What kinds of policies has the United States recently adopted toward illegal immigration?

Textual Considerations

1. How does Jasmine react to racism, class distinctions, sexuality, and gender issues? How does she view herself in relation to the Daboos and the young men from Trinidad? How does she express her sexuality?
2. Jasmine is described as "a girl with ambition." What is she ambitious for? Does she accomplish her ambition? How? What are her other outstanding characteristics? Compare her experiences in Michigan with those in Trinidad.
3. Jasmine thinks that what she learned about "bargain-priced emigration" from the assistant bank manager in Trinidad was more important than anything she learned in two years of college. What does this tell us about Jasmine? What is the tone of the phrase "bargain-priced emigration"? How do you interpret the sentence "She'd spent some damned uncomfortable times with the assistant manager to get approval for her loan"?
4. Trace the development of Jasmine's change from the moment she arrives in the United States to the moment she forms a new identity. Compare her description of herself as "Flower of Ann Arbor" with Bill's description of her as "Flower of Trinidad." What do they tell us about Jasmine's sense of self?
5. Stories develop mainly from conflict: between two or more characters, within a character as the result of some psychological force (guilt, jealousy), or between a character and some impersonal force such as poverty or disease. What is the main conflict in this story? Between what or whom? Is the struggle resolved?

Cultural Contexts

1. "In this country Jesus givin out good luck only!" Why did Jasmine think Ann Arbor was "the place to be"? To what extent was she captured by the promise of the American Dream? Was she lucky to work for the Moffitts? Why or why not?
2. Examine with your group the portrait of the American family as exemplified by the Moffits. To what extent does your group share their values?

Kate Chopin

Désirée's Baby

As the day was pleasant, Madame Valmondé drove over to L'Abri to see Désirée and the baby.

It made her laugh to think of Désirée with a baby. Why, it seemed but yesterday that Désirée was little more than a baby herself; when Monsieur in riding through the gateway of Valmondé had found her lying asleep in the shadow of the big stone pillar.

The little one awoke in his arms and began to cry for "Dada." That was as much as she could do or say. Some people thought she might have strayed there of her own accord, for she was of the toddling age. The prevailing belief was that she had been purposely left by a party of Texans, whose canvas-covered wagon, late in the day, had crossed the ferry that Coton Maïs kept, just below the plantation. In time Madame Valmondé abandoned every speculation but the one that Désirée had been sent to her by a beneficent Providence to be the child of her affection, seeing that she was without child of the flesh. For the girl grew to be beautiful and gentle, affectionate and sincere—the idol of Valmondé.

It was no wonder, when she stood one day against the stone pillar in whose shadow she had lain asleep, eighteen years before, that Armand Aubigny riding by and seeing her there, had fallen in love with her. That was the way all the Aubignys fell in love, as if struck by a pistol shot. The wonder was that he had not loved her before; for he had known her since his father brought him home from Paris, a boy of eight, after his mother died there. The passion that awoke in him that day, when he saw her at the gate, swept along like an avalanche, or like a prairie fire, or like anything that drives headlong over all obstacles.

Monsieur Valmondé grew practical and wanted things well considered; that is, the girl's obscure origin. Armand looked into her eyes and did not care. He was reminded that she was nameless. What did it matter about a name when he could give her one of the oldest and proudest in Louisiana? He ordered the *corbeille*[1] from Paris, and contained himself with what patience he could until it arrived; then they were married.

Madame Valmondé had not seen Désirée and the baby for four weeks. When she reached L'Abri she shuddered at the first sight of it, as she always did. It was a sad looking place, which for many years had not known the gentle presence of a mistress, old Monsieur Aubigny having married and buried his wife in France, and she having loved her own land too well ever to leave it. The roof came down steep and black like a cowl, reaching out beyond the wide galleries that encircled the yellow stuccoed house. Big, solemn oaks grew close to it, and their thick-leaved, far-reaching branches shadowed it like a pall. Young Aubigny's rule was a strict one,

---

[1] Wedding presents given by the groom.

too, and under it his negroes had forgotten how to be gay, as they had been during the old master's easy-going and indulgent lifetime.

The young mother was recovering slowly, and lay full length, in her soft white muslins and laces, upon a couch. The baby was beside her, upon her arm, where he had fallen asleep, at her breast. The yellow nurse woman sat beside a window fanning herself.

Madame Valmondé bent her portly figure over Désirée and kissed her, holding her an instant tenderly in her arms. Then she turned to the child.

"This is not the baby!" she exclaimed, in startled tones. French was the language spoken at Valmondé in those days.

"I knew you would be astonished," laughed Désirée, "at the way he has grown. The little *cochon de lait!*[2] Look at his legs, mamma, and his hands and finger-nails,— real finger-nails. Zandrine had to cut them this morning. Isn't it true, Zandrine?"

The woman bowed her turbaned head majestically, "Mais si, Madame."

"And the way he cries," went on Désirée, "is deafening. Armand heard him the other day as far away as La Blanche's cabin."

Madame Valmondé had never removed her eyes from the child. She lifted it and walked with it over to the window that was lightest. She scanned the baby narrowly, then looked as searchingly at Zandrine, whose face was turned to gaze across the fields.

"Yes, the child has grown, has changed," said Madame Valmondé, slowly, as she replaced it beside its mother. "What does Armand say?"

Désirée's face became suffused with a glow that was happiness itself.

"Oh, Armand is the proudest father in the parish, I believe, chiefly because it is a boy, to bear his name; though he says not,—that he would have loved a girl as well. But I know it isn't true. I know he says that to please me. And mamma," she added, drawing Madame Valmondé's head down to her, and speaking in a whisper, "he hasn't punished one of them—not one of them—since baby is born. Even Négrillon, who pretended to have burnt his leg that he might rest from work—he only laughed, and said Négrillon was a great scamp. Oh, mamma, I'm so happy; it frightens me."

What Désirée said was true. Marriage, and later the birth of his son, had softened Armand Aubigny's imperious and exacting nature greatly. This was what made the gentle Désirée so happy, for she loved him desperately. When he frowned she trembled, but loved him. When he smiled, she asked no greater blessing of God. But Armand's dark, handsome face had not often been disfigured by frowns since the day he fell in love with her.

When the baby was about three months old, Désirée awoke one day to the conviction that there was something in the air menacing her peace. It was at first too subtle to grasp. It had only been a disquieting suggestion; an air of mystery among the blacks; unexpected visits from far-off neighbors who could hardly account for their coming. Then a strange, an awful change in her husband's manner, which she dared not ask him to explain. When he spoke to her, it was with averted eyes, from which the old love-light seemed to have gone out. He absented himself from home;

[2] Suckling pig.

and when there, avoided her presence and that of her child, without excuse. And the very spirit of Satan seemed suddenly to take hold of him in his dealings with the slaves. Désirée was miserable enough to die.

She sat in her room, one hot afternoon, in her *peignoir*,[3] listlessly drawing through her fingers the strands of her long, silky brown hair that hung about her shoulders. The baby, half naked, lay asleep upon her own great mahogany bed, that was like a sumptuous throne, with its satin-lined half-canopy. One of La Blanche's little quadroon boys—half naked too—stood fanning the child slowly with a fan of peacock feathers. Désirée's eyes had been fixed absently and sadly upon the baby, while she was striving to penetrate the threatening mist that she felt closing about her. She looked from her child to the boy who stood beside him, and back again; over and over. "Ah!" It was a cry that she could not help; which she was not conscious of having uttered. The blood turned like ice in her veins, and a clammy moisture gathered upon her face.

She tried to speak to the little quadroon boy; but no sound would come, at first. When he heard his name uttered, he looked up, and his mistress was pointing to the door. He laid aside the great, soft fan, and obediently stole away, over the polished floor, on his bare tiptoes.

She stayed motionless, with gaze riveted upon her child, and her face the picture of fright.

Presently her husband entered the room, and without noticing her, went to a table and began to search among some papers which covered it.

"Armand," she called to him, in a voice which must have stabbed him, if he was human. But he did not notice. "Armand," she said again. Then she rose and tottered towards him. "Armand," she panted once more, clutching his arm, "look at our child. What does it mean? Tell me."

He coldly but gently loosened her fingers from about his arm and thrust the hand away from him. "Tell me what it means!" she cried despairingly.

"It means," he answered lightly, "that the child is not white; it means that you are not white."

A quick conception of all that this accusation meant for her nerved her with unwonted courage to deny it, "It is a lie; it is not true, I am white! Look at my hair, it is brown; and my eyes are gray, Armand, you know they are gray. And my skin is fair," seizing his wrist. "Look at my hand; whiter than yours, Armand," she laughed hysterically.

"As white as La Blanche's," he returned cruelly; and went away leaving her alone with their child.

When she could hold a pen in her hand, she sent a despairing letter to Madame Valmondé.

"My mother, they tell me I am not white. Armand has told me I am not white. For God's sake tell them it is not true. You must know it is not true. I shall die. I must die. I cannot be so unhappy, and live."

The answer that came was as brief:

---

[3] Dressing gown.

"My own Désirée: Come home to Valmondé; back to your mother who loves you. Come with your child."

When the letter reached Désirée she went with it to her husband's study, and laid it open upon the desk before which he sat. She was like a stone image: silent, white, motionless after she placed it there.

In silence he ran his cold eyes over the written words. He said nothing. "Shall I go, Armand?" she asked in tones sharp with agonized suspense.

"Yes, go."

"Do you want me to go?"

He thought Almighty God had dealt cruelly and unjustly with him; and felt, somehow, that he was paying Him back in kind when he stabbed thus into his wife's soul. Moreover, he no longer loved her, because of the unconscious injury she had brought upon his home and his name.

She turned away like one stunned by a blow, and walked slowly towards the door, hoping he could call her back.

"Good-by, Armand," she moaned.

He did not answer her. That was his last blow at fate.

Désirée went in search of her child. Zandrine was pacing the sombre gallery with it. She took the little one from the nurse's arms with no word of explanation, and descending the steps, walked away, under the live-oak branches.

It was an October afternoon; the sun was just sinking. Out in the still fields the negroes were picking cotton.

Désirée had not changed the thin white garment nor the slippers she wore. Her hair was uncovered and the sun's rays brought a golden gleam from its brown meshes. She did not take the broad, beaten road which led to the far-off plantation of Valmondé. She walked across a deserted field, where the stubble bruised her tender feet, so delicately shod, and tore her thin gown to shreds.

She disappeared among the reeds and willows that grew thick along the banks of the deep, sluggish bayou; and she did not come back again.

Some weeks later there was a curious scene at L'Abri. In the centre of the smoothly swept back yard was a great bonfire. Armand Aubigny sat in the wide hallway that commanded a view of the spectacle; and it was he who dealt out to a half dozen negroes the material which kept this fire ablaze.

A graceful cradle of willow, with all its dainty furbishings, was laid upon the pyre, which had already been fed with the richness of a priceless *layette*.[4] Then there were silk gowns, and velvet and satin ones added to these; laces, too, and embroideries; bonnets and gloves; for the *corbeille* had been of rare quality.

The last thing to go was a tiny bundle of letters; innocent little scribblings that Désirée had sent to him during the days of their espousal. There was the remnant of one back in the drawer from which he took them. But it was not Désirée's; it was part of an old letter from his mother to his father. He read it. She was thanking God for the blessing of her husband's love:—

---

[4] A complete outfit of clothing and equipment for a newborn infant.

"But, above all," she wrote, "night and day, I thank God for having so arranged our lives that our dear Armand will never know that his mother, who adores him, belongs to the race that is cursed with the brand of slavery."

[1893]

Journal Entry

What knowledge and experience of interracial marriages do you bring to the reading of this text? Do you believe that interracial marriages have the same chance of succeeding as marriages of people with the same ethnic origins?

Textual Considerations

1. Characterize Désirée and Armand. What specific images and descriptions does Chopin use to portray them? How similar or different are they?
2. Ancestry and heritage play an important role in Chopin's story. How do these issues apply to Armand and Désirée? Is it important to the development of the story that Désirée was a foundling, adopted by the Valmondés? How does this issue connect with the theme of racism in the story?
3. Describe the setting of L'Abri. What does its dilapidated condition and "solemn oaks" indicate about the Aubigny property? What other symbols can you cite in the story? How do you interpret them?
4. What do the background characters, including Négrillon, and the quadroon's boys add to the reader's understanding of the story?
5. How do you view the "letter device" Chopin uses in "Désirée's Baby"? Do you consider it effective from the narrative point of view? Can you think of any other narrative tool Chopin could have used to reveal to Armand the truth about his own black ancestry?

Cultural Contexts

1. Examine the extent to which the presence of the French, American, and African elements in L'Abri contribute to its ethnic and cultural diversity. How integrated are they?
2. How does Chopin explore the issue of racial prejudice in her story? Discuss with your group whether Armand Aubigny's values—placing racial prejudices above marriage, love, and family ties—in the late nineteenth-century still exist today. How does your group react toward interracial marriage?

ESSAYS

Judith Ortiz Cofer

Silent Dancing

We have a home movie of this party. Several times my mother and I have watched it together, and I have asked questions about the silent revelers coming in and out of focus. It is grainy and of short duration, but it's a great visual aid to my memory of life at that time. And it is in color—the only complete scene in color I can recall from those years.

We lived in Puerto Rico until my brother was born in 1954. Soon after, because of economic pressures on our growing family, my father joined the United States Navy. He was assigned to duty on a ship in Brooklyn Yard—a place of cement and steel that was to be his home base in the States until his retirement more than twenty years later. He left the Island first, alone, going to New York City and tracking down his uncle who lived with his family across the Hudson River in Paterson, New Jersey. There my father found a tiny apartment in a huge tenement that had once housed Jewish families but was just being taken over and transformed by Puerto Ricans, overflowing from New York City. In 1953 he sent for us. My mother was only twenty years old, I was not quite three, and my brother was a toddler when we arrived at El Building, as the place had been christened by its newest residents.

My memories of life in Paterson during those first few years are all in shades of gray. Maybe I was too young to absorb vivid colors and details, or to discriminate between the slate blue of the winter sky and the darker hues of the snow-bearing clouds, but that single color washes over the whole period. The building we lived in was gray, as were the streets, filled with slush the first few months of my life there. The coat my father had bought for me was similar in color and too big; it sat heavily on my thin frame.

I do remember the way the heater pipes banged and rattled, startling all of us out of sleep until we got so used to the sound that we automatically shut it out or raised our voices above the racket. The hiss from the valve punctuated my sleep (which has always been fitful) like a nonhuman presence in the room—a dragon sleeping at the entrance of my childhood. But the pipes were also a connection to all the other lives being lived around us. Having come from a house designed for a single family back in Puerto Rico—my mother's extended-family home—it was curious to know that strangers lived under our floor and above our heads, and that the heater pipe went through everyone's apartment. (My first spanking in Paterson came as a result of playing tunes on the pipes in my room to see if there would be an answer.) My mother was as new to this concept of beehive life as I was, but she had been given strict orders by my father to keep the doors locked, the noise down, ourselves to ourselves.

It seems that Father had learned some painful lessons about prejudice while searching for an apartment in Paterson. Not until years later did I hear how much resistance he had encountered with landlords who were panicking at the influx of Latinos into a neighborhood that had been Jewish for a couple of generations. It made no difference that it was the American phenomenon of ethnic turnover which was changing the urban core of Paterson, and that the human flood could not be held back with an accusing finger.

"You Cuban?" one man had asked my father, pointing at his name tag on the navy uniform—even though my father had the fair skin and light brown hair of his northern Spanish background, and the name Ortiz is as common in Puerto Rico as Johnson is in the United States.

"No," my father had answered, looking past the finger into his adversary's angry eyes. "I'm Puerto Rican."

"Same shit." And the door closed.

My father could have passed as European, but we couldn't. My brother and I both have our mother's black hair and olive skin, and so we lived in El Building and visited our great-uncle and his fair children on the next block. It was their private joke that they were the German branch of the family. Not many years later that area too would be mainly Puerto Rican. It was as if the heart of the city map were being gradually colored brown—*café con leche* brown. Our color.

The movie opens with a sweep of the living room. It is a "typical" immigrant Puerto Rican decor for the time: the sofa and chairs are square and hard-looking, upholstered in bright colors (blue and yellow in this instance) and covered with the transparent plastic that furniture salesmen then were so adept at convincing women to buy. The linoleum on the floor is light blue; where it had been subjected to spike heels, as it was in most places, there were dime-size indentations all over it that cannot be seen in this movie. The room is full of people dressed up: dark suits for the men, red dresses for the women. When I have asked my mother why most of the women are in red that night, she has shrugged and said, "I don't remember. Just a coincidence." She doesn't have my obsession for assigning symbolism to everything.

The three women in red sitting on the couch are my mother, my eighteen-year-old cousin, and her brother's girlfriend. The novia *is just up from the Island, which is apparent in her body language. She sits up formally, her dress pulled over her knees. She is a pretty girl, but her posture makes her look insecure, lost in her full-skirted dress, which she has carefully tucked around her to make room for my gorgeous cousin, her future sister-in-law. My cousin has grown up in Paterson and is in her last year of high school. She doesn't have a trace of what Puerto Ricans call* la mancha *(literally, the stain: the mark of the new immigrant—something about the posture, the voice, or the humble demeanor that makes it obvious to everyone the person has just arrived on the mainland). My cousin is wearing a tight, sequined, cocktail dress. Her brown hair has been lightened with peroxide around the bangs, and she is holding a cigarette expertly between her fingers, bringing it up to her mouth in a sensuous arc of her arm as she talks animatedly. My mother, who has come up to sit between the two women, both only a few years younger than herself, is somewhere between the poles they represent in our culture.*

• • •

It became my father's obsession to get out of the barrio, and thus we were never permitted to form bonds with the place or with the people who lived there. Yet El Building was a comfort to my mother, who never got over yearning for *la isla*. She felt surrounded by her language: the walls were thin, and voices speaking and arguing in Spanish could be heard all day. *Salsas* blasted out of radios, turned on early in the morning and left on for company. Women seemed to cook rice and beans perpetually—the strong aroma of boiling red kidney beans permeated the hallways.

Though Father preferred that we do our grocery shopping at the supermarket when he came home on weekend leaves, my mother insisted that she could cook only with products whose labels she could read. Consequently, during the week I accompanied her and my little brother to La Bodega—a hole-in-the-wall grocery store across the street from El Building. There we squeezed down three narrow aisles jammed with various products. Goya and Libby's—those were the trademarks that were trusted by her *mamá*, so my mother bought many cans of Goya beans, soups, and condiments, as well as little cans of Libby's fruit juices for us. And she also bought Colgate toothpaste and Palmolive soap. (The final *e* is pronounced in both these products in Spanish, so for many years I believed that they were manufactured on the Island. I remember my surprise at first hearing a commercial on television in which "Colgate" rhymed with "ate.") We always lingered at La Bodega, for it was there that Mother breathed best, taking in the familiar aromas of the foods she knew from Mamá's kitchen. It was also there that she got to speak to the other women of El Building without violating outright Father's dictates against fraternizing with our neighbors.

Yet Father did his best to make our "assimilation" painless. I can still see him carrying a real Christmas tree up several flights of stairs to our apartment, leaving a trail of aromatic pine. He carried it formally, as if it were a flag in a parade. We were the only ones in El Building that I knew of who got presents on both Christmas and *día de Reyes*, the day when the Three Kings brought gifts to Christ and Hispanic children.

Our supreme luxury in El Building was having our own television set. It must have been a result of Father's guilt feelings over the isolation he had imposed on us, but we were among the first in the barrio to have one. My brother quickly became an avid watcher of Captain Kangaroo and Jungle Jim, while I loved all the series showing families. By the time I started first grade, I could have drawn a map of Middle America as exemplified by the lives of characters in *Father Knows Best, The Donna Reed Show, Leave It to Beaver, My Three Sons*, and (my favorite) *Bachelor Father*, where John Forsythe treated his adopted teenage daughter like a princess because he was rich and had a Chinese houseboy to do everything for him. In truth, compared to our neighbors in El Building *we* were rich. My father's navy check provided us with financial security and a standard of living that the factory workers envied. The only thing his money could not buy us was a place to live away from the barrio—his greatest wish, Mother's greatest fear.

In the home movie the men are shown next, sitting around a card table set up in one corner of the living room, playing dominoes. The clack of the ivory pieces was a familiar sound. I heard it in many houses on the Island and in many apartments in Paterson. In Leave It to Beaver, *the Cleavers played bridge in every other episode; in my childhood, the men started every social occasion with a hotly debated round of dominoes. The women would sit around and watch, but they never participated in the games.*

Here and there you can see a small child. Children were always brought to parties and, whenever they got sleepy, were put to bed in the host's bedroom. Babysitting was a concept unrecognized by the Puerto Rican women I knew: a responsible mother did not leave her children with any stranger. And in a culture where children are not considered intrusive, there was no need to leave the children at home. We went where our mother went.

Of my preschool years I have only impressions: the sharp bite of the wind in December as we walked with our parents toward the brightly lit stores downtown; how I felt like a stuffed doll in my heavy coat, boots, and mittens; how good it was to walk into the five-and-dime and to sit at the counter drinking hot chocolate. On Saturdays our whole family would walk downtown to shop at the big department stores on Broadway. Mother bought all our clothes at Penney's and Sears, and she liked to buy her dresses at the women's specialty shops like Lerner's and Diana's. At some point we'd go into Woolworth's and sit at the soda fountain to eat.

We never ran into other Latinos at these stores or when eating out, and it became clear to me only years later that the women from El Building shopped mainly in other places—stores owned by other Puerto Ricans or by Jewish merchants who had philosophically accepted our presence in the city and decided to make us their good customers, if not real neighbors and friends. These establishments were located not downtown but in the blocks around our street, and they were referred to generically as La Tienda, El Bazar, La Bodega, La Botánica. Everyone knew what was meant. These were the stores where your face did not turn a clerk to stone, where your money was as green as anyone else's.

One New Year's Eve we were dressed up like child models in the Sears catalogue: my brother in a miniature man's suit and bow tie, and I in black patent-leather shoes and a frilly dress with several layers of crinoline underneath. My mother wore a bright red dress that night, I remember, and spike heels; her long black hair hung to her waist. Father, who usually wore his navy uniform during his short visits home, had put on a dark civilian suit for the occasion: we had been invited to his uncle's house for a big celebration. Everyone was excited because my mother's brother Hernan—a bachelor who could indulge himself with luxuries—had bought a home movie camera, which he would be trying out that night.

Even the home movie cannot fill in the sensory details such a gathering left imprinted in a child's brain. The thick sweetness of women's perfumes mixing with the ever-present smells of food cooking in the kitchen: meat and plantain *pasteles*, as well as the ubiquitous rice dish made special with pigeon peas—*gandules*—and seasoned with precious *sofrito* sent up from the Island by somebody's mother or smuggled in by a recent traveler. *Sofrito* was one of the items that women hoarded, since it was hardly ever in stock at La Bodega. It was the flavor of Puerto Rico.

The men drank Palo Viejo rum, and some of the younger ones got weepy. The first time I saw a grown man cry was at a New Year's Eve party: he had been reminded of his mother by the smells in the kitchen. But what I remember most were the boiled *pasteles*, plantain or yucca rectangles stuffed with corned beef or other meats, olives, and many other savory ingredients, all wrapped in banana leaves. Everybody had to fish one out with a fork. There was always a "trick" *pastel*—one without stuffing—and whoever got that one was the "New Year's Fool."

There was also the music. Long-playing albums were treated like precious china in these homes. Mexican recordings were popular, but the songs that brought tears to my mother's eyes were sung by the melancholy Daniel Santos, whose life as a drug addict was the stuff of legend. Felipe Rodriguez was a particular favorite of couples, since he sang about faithless women and brokenhearted men. There is a snatch of one lyric that has stuck in my mind like a needle on a worn groove: *De piedra ha de ser mi cama, de piedra la cabezera . . . la mujer que a mi me quiera . . . ha de quererme de veras. Ay, Ay, Ay, corazón, porque no amas . . .* I must have heard it a thousand times since the idea of a bed made of stone, and its connection to love, first troubled me with its disturbing images.

The five-minute home movie ends with people dancing in a circle—the creative filmmaker must have set it up, so that all of them could file past him. It is both comical and sad to watch silent dancing. Since there is no justification for the absurd movements that music provides for some of us, people appear frantic, their faces embarrassingly intense. It's as if you were watching sex. Yet for years, I've had dreams in the form of this home movie. In a recurring scene, familiar faces push themselves forward into my mind's eye, plastering their features into distorted close-ups. And I'm asking them: "Who is *she*? Who is the old woman I don't recognize? Is she an aunt? Somebody's wife? Tell me who she is."

"See the beauty mark on her cheek as big as a hill on the lunar landscape of her face—well, that runs in the family. The women on your father's side of the family wrinkle early; it's the price they pay for that fair skin. The young girl with the green stain on her wedding dress is *la novia*—just up from the Island. See, she lowers her eyes when she approaches the camera, as she's supposed to. Decent girls never look at you directly in the face. *Humilde*, humble, a girl should express humility in all her actions. She will make a good wife for your cousin. He should consider himself lucky to have met her only weeks after she arrived here. If he marries her quickly, she will make him a good Puerto Rican–style wife; but if he waits too long, she will be corrupted by the city, just like your cousin there."

"She means me, I do what I want. This is not some primitive island I live on. Do they expect me to wear a black mantilla on my head and go to mass every day? Not me. I'm an American woman, and I will do as I please. I can type faster than anyone in my senior class at Central High, and I'm going to be a secretary to a lawyer when I graduate. I can pass for an American girl anywhere—I've tried it. At least for Italian, anyway—I never speak Spanish in public. I hate these parties, but I wanted the dress. I look better than any of these *humildes* here. *My* life is going to be different. I have an American boyfriend. He is older and has a car. My parents don't know it, but I sneak out of the house late at night sometimes to be with him. If I marry him, even my name will be American. I hate rice and beans—that's what makes these women fat."

"Your *prima* is pregnant by that man she's been sneaking around with. Would I lie to you? I'm your *tía política*, your great-uncle's common-law wife—the one he abandoned on the Island to go marry your cousin's mother. *I* was not invited to this party, of course, but I came anyway. I came to tell you that story about your cousin that you've always wanted to hear. Do you remember the comment your mother made to a neighbor that has always haunted you? The only thing you heard was your cousin's name, and then you saw your mother pick up your doll from the couch and say: 'It was as big as this doll when they flushed it down the toilet.' This image has bothered you for years, hasn't it? You had nightmares about babies being flushed down the toilet, and you wondered why anyone would do such a horrible thing. You didn't dare ask your mother about it. She would only tell you that you had not heard her right, and yell at you for listening to adult conversations. But later, when you were old enough to know about abortions, you suspected."

"I am here to tell you that you were right. Your cousin was growing an *americanito* in her belly when this movie was made. Soon after, she put something long and pointy into her pretty self, thinking maybe she could get rid of the problem before breakfast and still make it to her first class at the high school. Well, *niña*, her screams could be heard downtown. Your aunt, her *mamá*, who had been a midwife on the Island, managed to pull the little thing out. Yes, they probably flushed it down the toilet. What else could they do with it—give it a Christian burial in a little white casket with blue bows and ribbons? Nobody wanted that baby—least of all the father, a teacher at her school with a house in West Paterson that he was filling with real children, and a wife who was a natural blonde."

"Girl, the scandal sent your uncle back to the bottle. And guess where your cousin ended up? Irony of ironies. She was sent to a village in Puerto Rico to live with a relative on her mother's side: a place so far away from civilization that you have to ride a mule to reach it. A real change in scenery. She found a man there—women like that cannot live without male company—but believe me, the men in Puerto Rico know how to put a saddle on a woman like her. *La gringa*, they call her. Ha, ha, ha. *La gringa* is what she always wanted to be . . ."

The old woman's mouth becomes a cavernous black hole I fall into. And as I fall, I can feel the reverberations of her laughter. I hear the echoes of her last mocking words: *la gringa, la gringa!* And the conga line keeps moving silently past me. There is no music in my dream for the dancers.

When Odysseus visits Hades to see the spirit of his mother, he makes an offering of sacrificial blood, but since all the souls crave an audience with the living, he has to listen to many of them before he can ask questions. I, too, have to hear the dead and the forgotten speak in my dream. Those who are still part of my life remain silent, going around and around in their dance. The others keep pressing their faces forward to say things about the past.

My father's uncle is last in line. He is dying of alcoholism, shrunken and shriveled like a monkey, his face a mass of wrinkles and broken arteries. As he comes closer I realize that in his features I can see my whole family. If you were to stretch that rubbery flesh, you could find my father's face, and deep within *that* face—my own. I don't want to look into those eyes ringed in purple. In a few years he will retreat into silence, and take a long, long time to die. *Move back. Tío,* I tell him. *I don't want to hear what you have to say. Give the dancers room to move. Soon it will be midnight. Who is the New Year's Fool this time?*

[1990]

Journal Entry

Brainstorm on your associations with "whiteness." Are your responses in part attributable to your ethnicity? Explain.

Textual Considerations

1. How did Cofer's father's policy of isolating his family affect the family, and Cofer specifically? Was assimilation the goal of this policy of isolation? If so, how would you have expected Cofer's father to regard the cousin—as, for example, a model for his family?
2. Can you find evidence to show Cofer's own attitude toward this policy of isolation?
3. How do you interpret the statement "*La Gringa* is what she always wanted to be"? What point about assimilation does the cousin's life make?
4. Why do you think Cofer sees her whole family in her alcoholic uncle's face?
5. What would you say are Cofer's feelings about the dead and the forgotten relations that make her think of Odysseus in Hades? If she identifies or sympathizes with them, why does she say, "I don't want to hear what you have to say"?

Cultural Contexts

1. Cofer's father rejected his Puerto Rican culture while her mother embraced it. How well does Cofer understand both parents? How have their attitudes toward assimilation affected hers? With whose view on assimilation do you agree? Why?
2. Cofer describes the family home movie as a powerful visual aid to her childhood memories. Working with your group, examine how her visual recollections affect the meaning of her essay. Where in her descriptions do you also find Cofer appealing to taste and smell? How do these relate to her cultural heritage?

Frederick Douglass
How I Learned to Read and Write

I lived in Master Hugh's family about seven years. During this time, I succeeded in learning to read and write. In accomplishing this, I was compelled to resort to various stratagems. I had no regular teacher. My mistress, who had kindly commenced to instruct me, had, in compliance with the advice and direction of her husband, not only ceased to instruct, but had set her face against my being instructed by any one else. It is due, however, to my mistress to say of her, that she did not adopt this course of treatment immediately. She at first lacked the depravity indispensable to shutting me up in mental darkness. It was at least necessary for her to have some training in the exercise of irresponsible power, to make her equal to the task of treating me as though I were a brute.

My mistress was, as I have said, a kind and tender-hearted woman; and in the simplicity of her soul she commenced, when I first went to live with her, to treat me as she supposed one human being ought to treat another. In entering upon the duties of a slaveholder, she did not seem to perceive that I sustained to her the relation of a mere chattel, and that for her to treat me as a human being was not only wrong, but dangerously so. Slavery proved as injurious to her as it did to me. When I went there, she was a pious, warm, and tenderhearted woman. There was no sorrow or suffering for which she had not a tear. She had bread for the hungry, clothes for the naked, and comfort for every mourner that came within her reach. Slavery soon proved its ability to divest her of these heavenly qualities. Under its influence, the tender heart became stone, and the lamblike disposition gave way to one of tiger-like fierceness. The first step in her downward course was in her ceasing to instruct me. She now commenced to practise her husband's precepts. She finally became even more violent in her opposition than her husband himself. She was not satisfied with simply doing as well as he had commanded; she seemed anxious to do better. Nothing seemed to make her more angry than to see me with a newspaper. She seemed to think that here lay the danger. I have had her rush at me with a face made all up of fury, and snatch from me a newspaper, in a manner that fully revealed her apprehension. She was an apt woman; and a little experience soon demonstrated, to her satisfaction, that education and slavery were incompatible with each other.

From this time I was most narrowly watched. If I was in a separate room any considerable length of time, I was sure to be suspected of having a book, and was at once called to give an account of myself. All this, however, was too late. The first step had been taken. Mistress, in teaching me the alphabet, had given me the *inch*, and no precaution could prevent me from taking the *ell*.

The plan which I adopted, and the one by which I was most successful, was that of making friends of all the little white boys whom I met in the street. As many of these as I could, I converted into teachers. With their kindly aid, obtained at different times and in different places, I finally succeeded in learning to read. When I was sent on errands, I always took my book with me, and by doing one part of my errand quickly, I found time to get a lesson before my return. I used also to carry bread with me, enough of which was always in the house, and to which I was always welcome; for I was much better off in this regard than many of the poor white children in our neighborhood. This bread I used to bestow upon the hungry little urchins, who, in return, would give me that more valuable bread of knowledge. I am strongly tempted to give the names of two or three of those little boys, as a testimonial of the gratitude and affection I bear them; but prudence forbids;—not that it would injure me, but it might embarrass them; for it is almost an unpardonable offence to teach slaves to read in this Christian country. It is enough to say of the dear little fellows, that they lived on Philpot Street, very near Durgin and Bailey's shipyard. I used to talk this matter of slavery over with them. I would sometimes say to them, I wished I could be as free as they would be when they got to be men. "You will be free as soon as you are twenty-one, *but I am a slave for life!* Have not I as good a right to be free as you have?" These words used to trouble them; they would express for me the liveliest sympathy, and console me with the hope that something would occur by which I might be free.

I was now about twelve years old, and the thought of being *a slave for life* began to bear heavily upon my heart. Just about this time, I got hold of a book entitled "The Columbian Orator." Every opportunity I got, I used to read this book. Among much of other interesting matter, I found in it a dialogue between a master and his slave. The slave was represented as having run away from his master three times. The dialogue represented the conversation which took place between them, when the slave was retaken the third time. In this dialogue, the whole argument in behalf of slavery was brought forward by the master, all of which was disposed of by the slave. The slave was made to say some very smart as well as impressive things in reply to his master—things which had the desired though unexpected effect; for the conversation resulted in the voluntary emancipation of the slave on the part of the master.

In the same book, I met with one of Sheridan's mighty speeches on and in behalf of Catholic emancipation. These were choice documents to me. I read them over and over again with unabated interest. They gave tongue to interesting thoughts of my own soul, which had frequently flashed through my mind, and died away for want of utterance. The moral which I gained from the dialogue was the power of truth over the conscience of even a slaveholder. What I got from Sheridan was a bold denunciation of slavery, and a powerful vindication of human rights. The reading of these documents enabled me to utter my thoughts, and to meet the arguments brought forward to sustain slavery; but while they relieved me of one difficulty, they brought on another even more painful than the one of which I was relieved. The more I read, the more I was led to abhor and detest my enslavers. I could regard them in no other light than a band of successful robbers, who had left their homes, and gone to Africa, and stolen us from our homes, and in a strange land reduced us to slavery. I loathed them as being the meanest as well as the most wicked of men. As I read and contemplated the subject, behold! that very discontentment which Master Hugh had predicted would follow my learning to read had already come, to torment and sting my soul to unutterable anguish. As I writhed under it, I would at times feel that learning to read had been a curse rather than a blessing. It had given me a view of my wretched condition, without the remedy. It opened my eyes to the horrible pit, but to no ladder upon which to get out. In moments of agony, I envied my fellow-slaves for their stupidity. I have often wished myself a beast. I preferred the condition of the meanest reptile to my own. Any thing, no matter what, to get rid of thinking! It was this everlasting thinking of my condition that tormented me. There was no getting rid of it. It was pressed upon me by every object within sight or hearing, animate or inanimate. The silver trump of freedom had roused my soul to eternal wakefulness. Freedom now appeared, to disappear no more forever. It was heard in every sound, and seen in every thing. It was ever present to torment me with a sense of my wretched condition. I saw nothing without seeing it, I heard nothing without hearing it, and felt nothing without feeling it. It looked from every star, it smiled in every calm, breathed in every wind, and moved in every storm.

I often found myself regretting my own existence, and wishing myself dead; and but for the hope of being free, I have no doubt but that I should have killed myself, or done something for which I should have been killed. While in this state of mind, I was eager to hear any one speak of slavery. I was a ready listener. Every little while, I could hear something about the abolitionists. It was some time before I found what the word meant. It was always used in such connections as to make it an interesting word to me. If a slave ran away and succeeded in getting clear, or if a slave killed his master, set fire to a barn, or did any thing very wrong in the mind of a slaveholder, it was spoken of as the fruit of *abolition*. Hearing the word in this connection very often, I set about learning what it meant. The dictionary afforded me little or no help. I found it was "the act of abolishing"; but then I did not know what was to be abolished. Here I was perplexed. I did not dare to ask any one about its meaning, for I was satisfied that it was something they wanted me to know very little about. After a patient waiting, I got one of our city papers, containing an account of the number of petitions from the north, praying for the abolition of slavery in the District of Columbia, and of the slave trade between the States. From this time I understood the words *abolition* and *abolitionist*, and always drew near when that word was spoken, expecting to hear something of importance to myself and fellow-slaves. The light broke in upon me by degrees. I went one day down to the wharf of Mr. Waters; and seeing two Irishmen unloading a scow of stone, I went, unasked, and helped them. When we had finished, one of them came to me and asked me if I were a slave. I told him I was. He asked, "Are ye a slave for life?" I told him that I was. The good Irishman seemed to be deeply affected by the statement. He said to the other that it was a pity so fine a little fellow as myself should be a slave for life. He said it was a shame to hold me. They both advised me to run away to the north; that I should find friends there, and that I should be free. I pretended not to be interested in what they said, and treated them as if I did not understand them; for I feared they might be treacherous. White men have been known to encourage slaves to escape, and then, to get the reward, catch them and return them to their masters. I was afraid that these seemingly good men might use me so; but I nevertheless remembered their advice, and from that time I resolved to run away. I looked forward to a time at which it would be safe for me to escape. I was too young to think of doing so immediately; besides, I wished to learn how to write, as I might have occasion to write my own pass. I consoled myself with the hope that I should one day find a good chance. Meanwhile, I would learn to write.

The idea as to how I might learn to write was suggested to me by being in Durgin and Bailey's ship-yard, and frequently seeing the ship carpenters, after hewing, and getting a piece of timber ready for use, write on the timber the name of that part of the ship for which it was intended. When a piece of timber was intended for the larboard side, it would be marked thus—"L." When a piece was for the starboard side, it would be marked thus—"S." A piece for the larboard side forward, would be marked thus—"L. F." When a piece was for starboard side forward, it would be marked thus—"S. F." For larboard aft, it would be marked thus—"L. A." For starboard aft, it would be marked thus— "S. A." I soon learned the names of these letters, and for what they were intended when placed upon a piece of timber in the ship-yard. I immediately commenced copying them, and in a short time was able to make the four letters named. After that, when I met with any boy who I knew could write, I would tell him I could write as well as he. The next word would be, "I don't believe you. Let me see you try it." I would then make the letters which I had been so fortunate as to learn, and ask him to beat that. In this way I got a good many lessons in writing, which it is quite possible I should never have gotten in any other way. During this time, my copy-book was the board fence, brick wall, and pavement; my pen and ink was a lump of chalk. With these, I learned mainly how to write. I then commenced and continued copying the Italics in Webster's Spelling Book, until I could make them all without looking on the book. By this time, my little Master Thomas had gone to school, and learned how to write, and had written over a number of copy-books. These had been brought home, and shown to some of our near neighbors, and then laid aside. My mistress used to go to class meeting at the Wilk Street meetinghouse every Monday afternoon, and leave me to take care of the house. When left thus, I used to spend the time in writing in the spaces left in Master Thomas's copy-book, copying what he had written. I continued to do this until I could write a hand very similar to that of Master Thomas. Thus, after a long, tedious effort for years, I finally succeeded in learning how to write.

[1845]

Journal Entry

What is your first reading or writing memory, either at home or at school? When was the first time you realized that something you wrote had an effect on someone?

Textual Considerations

1. What portrait of Douglass's mistress emerges from paragraphs 1 and 2?
2. Why would slaveholders wish slaves to remain illiterate?
3. What does Douglass learn from reading "The Columbian Orator"?
4. Select two or three paragraphs from Douglass's essay and show how his examples support his thesis in each case.

5. How does Douglass use the statement in paragraph 1, "I was compelled to resort to various stratagems," to organize his account of learning to read and write?
6. How many examples of such stratagems can you find? Why do you think Douglass chose this particular word?
7. Douglass uses irony and **figurative language** to enhance his narrative. Cite examples.

Cultural Contexts

1. Douglass's determination to educate himself involves acts of rebellion and self-reliance. To what extent does he succeed in challenging and refuting racial stereotypes about African American slaves? Can you imagine sacrificing as he does to acquire an education?
2. How did language acquisition change Douglass's concept of himself? Do you think of language as empowerment? Were there obstacles you had to overcome? Discuss these issues with your group and compare your responses.

Paul Monette

Borrowed Time: An AIDS Memoir

I don't know if I will live to finish this. Doubtless there's a streak of self-importance in such an assertion, but who's counting? Maybe it's just that I've watched too many sicken in a month and die by Christmas, so that a fatal sort of realism comforts me more than magic. All I know is this: The virus ticks in me. And it doesn't care a whit about our categories—when is full-blown, what's AIDS-related, what is just sick and tired? No one has solved the puzzle of its timing. I take my drug from Tijuana twice a day. The very friends who tell me how vigorous I look, how well I seem, are the first to assure me of the imminent medical break-through. What they don't seem to understand is, I used up all my optimism keeping my friend alive. Now that he's gone, the cup of my own health is neither half full nor half empty. Just half.

Equally difficult, of course, is knowing where to start. The world around me is defined now by its endings and its closures—the date on the grave that follows the hyphen. Roger Horwitz, my beloved friend, died of complications of AIDS on October 22, 1986, nineteen months and ten days after his diagnosis. That is the only real date anymore, casting its icy shadow over all the secular holidays lovers mark their calendars by. Until that long night in October, it didn't seem possible that any day could supplant the brute equinox of March 12—the day of Roger's diagnosis in 1985, the day we began to live on the moon.

The fact is, no one knows where to start with AIDS. Now, in the seventh year of the calamity, my friends in L.A. can hardly recall what it felt like any longer, the time before the sickness. Yet we all watched the toll mount in New York, then in San Francisco, for years before it ever touched us here. It comes like a slowly dawning horror. At first you are equipped with a hundred different amulets to keep it far

away. Then someone you know goes into the hospital, and suddenly you are at high
noon in full battle gear. They have neglected to tell you that you will be issued no
weapons of any sort. So you cobble together a weapon out of anything that lies at
hand, like a prisoner honing a spoon handle into a stiletto. You fight tough, you
fight dirty, but you cannot fight dirtier than it.

I remember a Saturday in February 1982, driving Route 10 to Palm Springs
with Roger to visit his parents for the weekend. While Roger drove, I read aloud an
article from *The Advocate*: "Is Sex Making Us Sick?" There was the slightest edge of
irony in the query, an urban cool that seems almost bucolic now in its innocence.
But the article didn't mince words. It was the first in-depth reporting I'd read that
laid out the shadowy nonfacts of what till then had been the most fragmented of
rumors. The first cases were reported to the Centers for Disease Control (CDC)
only six months before, but they weren't in the newspapers, not in L.A. I note in my
diary in December 1981 ambiguous reports of a "gay cancer," but I know I didn't
have the slightest picture of the thing. Cancer of the *what*? I would have asked, if
anyone had known anything.

I remember exactly what was going through my mind while I was reading,
though I can't now recall the details of the piece. I was thinking: How is this not
me? Trying to find a pattern I was exempt from. It was a brand of denial I would
watch grow exponentially during the next few years, but at the time I was simply
relieved. Because the article appeared to be saying that there was a grim progression
toward this undefined catastrophe, a set of preconditions—chronic hepatitis,
repeated bouts of syphilis, exotic parasites. No wonder my first baseline response
was to feel safe. It was *them*—by which I meant the fast-lane Fire Island crowd, the
Sutro Baths, the world of High Eros.

Not us.

I grabbed for that relief because we'd been through a rough patch the previous
autumn. Till then Roger had always enjoyed a sort of no-nonsense good health: not
an abuser of anything, with a constitutional aversion to hypochondria, and not wed
to his mirror save for a minor alarm as to the growing dimensions of his bald spot.
In the seven years we'd been together I scarcely remember him having a cold or taking an aspirin. Yet in October 1981 he had struggled with a peculiar bout of intestinal flu. Nothing special showed up in any of the blood tests, but over a period of
weeks he experienced persistent symptoms that didn't neatly connect: pains in his
legs, diarrhea, general malaise. I hadn't been feeling notably bad myself, but on the
other hand I was a textbook hypochondriac, and I figured if Rog was harboring
some kind of bug, so was I.

The two of us finally went to a gay doctor in the Valley for a further set of blood
tests. It's a curious phenomenon among gay middle-class men that anything faintly
venereal had better be taken to a doctor who's "on the bus." Is it a sense of fellow
feeling perhaps, or a way of avoiding embarrassment? Do we really believe that only
a doctor who's *our* kind can heal us of the afflictions that attach somehow to our
secret hearts? There is so much magic to medicine. Of course we didn't know then
that those few physicians with a large gay clientele were about to be swamped
beyond all capacity to cope.

The tests came back positive for amoebiasis. Roger and I began the highly toxic treatment to kill the amoeba, involving two separate drugs and what seems in memory thirty pills a day for six weeks, till the middle of January. It was the first time I'd experienced the phenomenon of the cure making you sicker. By the end of treatment we were both weak and had lost weight, and for a couple of months afterward were susceptible to colds and minor infections.

It was only after the treatment was over that a friend of ours, diagnosed with amoebas by the same doctor, took his slide to the lab at UCLA for a second opinion. And that was my first encounter with lab error. The doctor at UCLA explained that the slide had been misread; the squiggles that looked like amoebas were in fact benign. The doctor shook his head and grumbled about "these guys who do their own lab work." Roger then retrieved his slide, took it over to UCLA and was told the same: no amoebas. We had just spent six weeks methodically ingesting poison for no reason at all.

So it wasn't the *Advocate* story that sent up the red flag for us. We'd been shaken by the amoeba business, and from that point on we operated at a new level of sexual caution. What is now called safe sex did not used to be so clearly defined. The concept didn't exist. But it was quickly becoming apparent, even then, that we couldn't wait for somebody else to define the parameters. Thus every gay man I know has had to come to a point of personal definition by way of avoiding the chaos of sexually transmitted diseases, or STD as we call them in the trade. There was obviously no one moment of conscious decision, a bolt of clarity on the shimmering freeway west of San Bernadino, but I think of that day when I think of the sea change. The party was going to have to stop. The evidence was too ominous: *We were making ourselves sick*.

Not that Roger and I were the life of the party. Roger especially didn't march to the different drum of *so many men, so little time*, the motto and anthem of the sun-struck summers of the mid-to-late seventies. He'd managed not to carry away from his adolescence the mark of too much repression, or indeed the yearning to make up for lost time. In ten years he had perhaps half a dozen contacts outside the main frame of our relationship, mostly when he was out of town on business. He was comfortable with relative monogamy, even at a time when certain quarters of the gay world found the whole idea trivial and bourgeois. I realized that in the world of the heterosexual there is a generalized lip service paid to exclusive monogamy, a notion most vividly honored in the breach. I leave the matter of morality to those with the gift of tongues; it was difficult enough for us to fashion a sexual ethics just for us. In any case, I was the one in the relationship who suffered from lost time. I was the one who would go after a sexual encounter as if it were an ice cream cone—casual, quick, good-by.

But as I say, who's counting? I only want to make it plain to start with that we got very alert and very careful as far back as the winter of 1982. That gut need for safety took hold and lingered, even as we got better again and strong. Thus I'm not entirely sure what I thought on another afternoon a year and a half later, when a friend of ours back from New York reported a conversation he'd had with a research man from Sloan-Kettering.

"He thinks all it takes is one exposure," Charlie said, this after months of articles about the significance of repeated exposure. More tenaciously than ever, we all wanted to believe the whole deepening tragedy was centered on those at the sexual frontlines who were fucking their brains out. The rest of us were fashioning our own little Puritan forts, as we struggled to convince ourselves that a clean slate would hold the nightmare at bay.

Yet with caution as our watchword starting in February of 1982, Roger was diagnosed with AIDS three years later. So the turning over of new leaves was not to be on everybody's side. A lot of us were already ticking and didn't even know. The magic circle my generation is trying to stay within the borders of is only as real as the random past. Perhaps the young can live in the magic circle, but only if those of us who are ticking will tell our story. Otherwise it goes on being *us* and *them* forever, built like a wall higher and higher, till you no longer think to wonder if you are walling it out or in.

For us the knowing began in earnest on the first of September, 1983. I'd had a call a couple of days before from my closest friend, Cesar Albini, who'd just returned to San Francisco after a summer touring Europe with a group of students. He said he'd been having trouble walking because of a swollen gland in his groin, and he was going to the hospital to have it biopsied. He reassured me he was feeling fine and wasn't expecting anything ominous, but figured he'd check it out before school started again. AIDS didn't even cross my mind, though cancer did. Half joking, Cesar wondered aloud if he dared disturb our happy friendship with bad news.

"If it's bad," I said, "we'll handle it, okay?"

But I really didn't clutch with fear, or it was only a brief stab of the hypochondriacal sort. Roger and I were just getting ready for a four-day trip to Big Sur, something we'd done almost yearly since moving to California in 1977. We were putting the blizzard of daily life on hold, looking forward to a dose of raw sublime that coincided with our anniversary—September 3, the day we met.

Cesar was forty-three, only ten months older than Roger. Born in Uruguay, possessed of a great heart and inexhaustible energy, he had studied in Europe and traveled all over, once spending four months going overland from Paris to China at a total cost of five hundred dollars. He was the first Uruguayan ever to enter Afghanistan through the mountains—on a camel, if I remember right. He spoke French, Italian, Spanish and English with equal fluency, and he tended to be the whole language department of a school. We'd both been teaching at secondary schools in Massachusetts when we met, and goaded one another to make the move west that had always been our shared dream. Thus Cesar had relocated to San Francisco in July of 1976, and Roger and I landed in L.A. four days after Thanksgiving the following year.

Cesar wasn't lucky in matters of the heart. He was still in the closet during his years back East, and the move to San Francisco was an extraordinary rite of passage for him. He always wanted a great love, but the couple of relationships he'd been involved in scarcely left the station. Still, he was very proud and indulged in no self-pity. He learned to accept the limited terms of the once-a-week relations he found in San Francisco, and broke through to the freedom of his own manhood without the mythic partner. The open sexual exultation that marked San Francisco in those days was something he rejoiced in.

Yet even though he went to the baths a couple of times a week, Cesar wasn't into anything *weird*—or that's how I might have put it at that stage of my own denial. No hepatitis, no history of VD, built tall and fierce—of course he was safe. The profile of AIDS continued to be mostly a matter of shadows. The L.A. *Times* wasn't covering it, though by then I had come to learn how embattled things had grown in New York. The Gay Men's Health Crisis was up to its ears in clients; Larry Kramer was screaming at the mayor; and the body count was appearing weekly in the *Native*. A writer I knew slightly was walking around with Kaposi's sarcoma. A young composer kept getting sicker and sicker, though he stubbornly didn't fit the CDC's hopelessly narrow categories, so the case was still officially a toss-up. And again, we're talking New York.

I came home at six on the evening of the first, and Roger met me gravely at the door. "There's a message from Cesar," he said. "It's not good."

Numbly I played back the answering machine, where so much appalling misery would be left on tape over the years to come, as if a record were crying out to be kept. "I have a little bit of bad news." Cesar's voice sounded strained, almost embarrassed. He left no details. I called and called him throughout the evening, convinced I was about to hear cancer news. The lymph nodes, of course—a hypochondriac knows all there is to know about the sites of malignancy. Already I was figuring what the treatments might be; no question in my mind but that it was treatable. I had Cesar practically cured by the time I reached Tom, a friend and former student of his. But as usual with me in crisis, I was jabbering and wouldn't let Tom get a word in. Finally he broke through: "He's got it."

"Got what?"

It's not till you first hear it attached to someone you love that you realize how little you know about it. My mind went utterly blank. The carefully constructed wall collapsed as if a 7.5 quake had rumbled under it. At that point I didn't even know the difference between KS and the opportunistic infections. I kept picturing that swollen gland in his groin, thinking: What's *that* got to do with AIDS? And a parallel track in my mind began careening with another thought: the swollen glands in my own groin, always dismissed by my straight doctor as herpes-related and "not a significant sign."

"We're not going to die young," Cesar used to say with a wag of his finger, his black Latin eyes dancing. "We won't get out of it *that* easily!" Then he would laugh and clap his hands, downing the coffee he always took with cream and four sugars. It looked like pudding.

I reached him very late that night and mouthed again the same words I'd said so bravely two days before: We'll deal with it. There is no end to the litany of reassurance that springs to your lips to ward away the specter. They've caught it early; you're fine; there's got to be some kind of treatment. That old chestnut, the imminent breakthrough. You fling these phrases instinctively, like pennies down a well.

Cesar and I bent backward to calm each other. It was just a couple of lesions in the groin; you could hardly see them. And the reason everything was going to be all right was really very simple: We would fight this thing like demons.

But the hollowness and disbelief pursued Roger and me all the way up the gold coast. Big Sur was towering and bracing as ever—exalted as Homer's Ithaca, as Robinson Jeffers described it. We were staying at Ventana, the lavish inn high in the hills above the canyon of the Big Sur River. We used the inn as a base camp for our day-long hikes, returning in the evening to posh amenities worthy of an Edwardian big-game hunt. On the second morning we walked out to Andrew Molera Beach, where the Big Sur empties into the Pacific. Molera stretches unblemished for five miles down the coast, curving like a crescent moon, with weathered headlands clean as Scotland. It was a kind of holy place for Roger and me, like the yearly end of a quest.

"What if we got it?" I said, staring out at the otters belly up in the kelp beds, taking the sun.

I don't remember how we answered that, because of course there wasn't any answer. Merely to pose the question was by way of another shot at magic. Mention the unmentionable and it will go away, like shining a light around a child's bedroom to shoo the monster. The great ache we were feeling at that moment was for our stricken friend, and we were too ignorant still to envision the medieval tortures that might await him.

But I know that the roll of pictures I took that day was my first conscious memorializing of Roger and me, as if I could hold the present as security on the future. There's one of me on the beach, then a mirror image of him as we traded off the camera, both of us squinting in the clear autumn light with the river mouth behind. Back at the inn, I took a picture of Rog in a rope hammock, his blue eyes resting on me as if the camera weren't even there, in total equilibrium, nine years to the day since our paths crossed on Revere Street. His lips are barely curved in a quarter-smile, his hands at rest in his lap as the last wave of the westering sun washes his left side through the diamond weave of the rope.

[1988]

Journal Entry

Imagine yourself as a young gay man or as a young lesbian, and write a letter to your parents explaining your sexual preference.

Textual Considerations

1. Characterize Paul and Roger's relationship.
2. Review paragraphs 3–6. Why does the author view the AIDS epidemic in terms of "us" and "them"?
3. How did the false diagnosis of amoebiasis affect their sexual relationship?
4. Why does Monette include Cesar in his memoir? What does the author's response to Cesar's diagnosis reveal about him?
5. Monette uses many metaphors to enhance his narrative. Cite examples.

Cultural Contexts

1. Examine the implication of AIDS for your generation, including its effects on gender relationships and on individual and family lives.
2. Write a paragraph summarizing your attitude toward AIDS *before* reading Monette's memoir. Then write a second paragraph recording your responses to Monette's autobiographical account of coming to terms with the epidemic. Share both paragraphs with members of your group. How similar are your reactions? To what factors do you attribute differences in responses? Write a third paragraph summarizing your group's attitudes.

Eric Liu

A Chinaman's Chance: Reflections on the American Dream

A lot of people my age seem to think that the American Dream is dead. I think they're dead wrong.

Or at least only partly right. It is true that for those of us in our twenties and early thirties, job opportunities are scarce. There looms a real threat that we will be the first American generation to have a lower standard of living than our parents.

But what is it that we mean when we invoke the American Dream?

In the past, the American Dream was something that held people of all races, religions, and identities together. As James Comer has written, it represented a shared aspiration among all Americans—black, white, or any other color—"to provide well for themselves and their families as valued members of a democratic society." Now, all too often, it seems the American Dream means merely some guarantee of affluence, a birthright of wealth.

At a basic level, of course, the American Dream is about prosperity and the pursuit of material happiness. But to me, its meaning extends beyond such concerns. To me, the dream is not just about buying a bigger house than the one I grew up in or having shinier stuff now than I had as a kid. It also represents a sense of opportunity that binds generations together in commitment, so that the young inherit not only property but also perseverance, not only money but also a mission to make good on the strivings of their parents and grandparents.

The poet Robert Browning once wrote that "a man's reach must exceed his grasp—else what's a heaven for?" So it is in America. Every generation will strive, and often fail. Every generation will reach for success, and often miss the mark. But Americans rely as much on the next generation as on the next life to prove that such struggles and frustrations are not in vain. There may be temporary setbacks, cutbacks, recessions, depressions. But this is a nation of second chances. So long as there are young Americans who do not take what they have—or what they can do—for granted, progress is always possible.

My conception of the American Dream does not take progress for granted. But it does demand the *opportunity* to achieve progress—and values the opportunity as much as the achievement. I come at this question as the son of immigrants. I see just as clearly as anyone else the cracks in the idealist vision of fulfillment for all. But because my parents came here with virtually nothing, because they did build something, I see the enormous potential inherent in the ideal.

I happen still to believe in our national creed: freedom and opportunity, and our common responsibility to uphold them. This creed is what makes America unique. More than any demographic statistic or economic indicator, it animates the American Dream. It infuses our mundane struggles—to plan a career, do good work, get ahead—with purpose and possibility. It makes America the only country that could produce heroes like Colin Powell—heroes who rise from nothing, who overcome the odds.

I think of the sacrifices made by my own parents. I appreciate the hardship of the long road traveled by my father—one of whose first jobs in America was painting the yellow line down a South Dakota interstate—and by my mother—whose first job here was filing pay stubs for a New York restaurant. From such beginnings, they were able to build a comfortable life and provide me with a breadth of resources—through arts, travel, and an Ivy League education. It was an unspoken obligation for them to do so.

I think of my boss in my first job after college, on Capitol Hill. George is a smart, feisty, cigar-chomping, take-no-shit Greek-American. He is about fifteen years older than I, has different interests, a very different personality. But like me, he is the son of immigrants, and he would joke with me that the Greek-Chinese mafia was going to take over one day. He was only half joking. We'd worked harder, our parents doubly harder, than almost anyone else we knew. To people like George, talk of the withering of the American Dream seems foreign.

It's undeniable that principles like freedom and opportunity, no matter how dearly held, are not enough. They can inspire a multiracial March on Washington, but they can not bring black salaries in alignment with white salaries. They can draw wave after wave of immigrants here, but they can not provide them the means to get out of our ghettos and barrios and Chinatowns. They are not sufficient for fulfillment of the American Dream.

But they are necessary. They are vital. And not just to the children of immigrants. These ideals form the durable thread that weaves us all in union. Put another way, they are one of the few things that keep America from disintegrating into a loose confederation of zip codes and walled-in communities.

What alarms me is how many people my age look at our nation's ideals with a rising sense of irony. What good is such a creed if you are working for hourly wages in a deadend job? What value do such platitudes have if you live in an urban war zone? When the only apparent link between homeboys and housepainters and bike messengers and investment bankers is pop culture—MTV, the NBA, movies, dance music—then the social fabric is flimsy indeed.

My generation has come of age at a time when the country is fighting off bouts of defeatism and self-doubt, at a time when racism and social inequities seem not only persistent but intractable. At a time like this, the retreat to one's own kind is seen by more and more of my peers as an advance. And that retreat has given rise again to the notion that there are essential and irreconcilable differences among the races—a notion that was supposed to have disappeared from American discourse by the time my peers and I were born in the sixties.

Not long ago, for instance, my sister called me a "banana."

I was needling her about her passion for rap and hip-hop music. Every time I saw her, it seemed, she was jumping and twisting to Arrested Development or Chubb Rock or some other funky group. She joked that despite being the daughter of Chinese immigrants, she was indeed "black at heart." And then she added, light-heartedly, "You, on the other hand—well, you're basically a banana." Yellow on the outside, but white inside.

I protested, denied her charge vehemently. But it was too late. She was back to dancing. And I stood accused.

Ever since then, I have wondered what it means to be black, or white, or Asian "at heart"—particularly for my generation. Growing up, when other kids would ask whether I was Chinese or Korean or Japanese, I would reply, a little petulantly, "American." Assimilation can still be a sensitive subject. I recall reading about a Korean-born Congressman who had gone out of his way to say that Asian-Americans should expect nothing special from him. He added that he was taking speech lessons "to get rid of this accent." I winced at his palpable self-hate. But then it hit me: Is this how my sister sees me?

There is no doubt that minorities like me can draw strength from our communities. But in today's environment, anything other than ostentatious tribal fealty is taken in some communities as a sign of moral weakness, a disappointing dilution of character. In times that demand ever-clearer thinking, it has become too easy for people to shut off their brains: "It's a black/Asian/Latino/white thing," says the variable T-shirt. "You wouldn't understand." Increasingly, we don't.

The civil-rights triumphs of the sixties and the cultural revolutions that followed made it possible for minorities to celebrate our diverse heritages. I can appreciate that. But I know, too, that the sixties—or at least, my generation's grainy, hazy vision of the decade—also bequeathed to young Americans a legacy of near-pathological race consciousness.

Today's culture of entitlement—and of race entitlement in particular—tells us plenty about what we get if we are black or white or female or male or old or young.

It is silent, though, on some other important issues. For instance: What do we "get" for being American? And just as importantly, What do we owe? These are questions around which young people like myself must tread carefully, since talk of common interests, civic culture, responsibility, and integration sounds a little too "white" for some people. To the new segregationists, the "American Dream" is like the old myth of the "Melting Pot": an oppressive fiction, an opiate for the unhappy colored masses.

How have we allowed our thinking about race to become so twisted? The formal obstacles and the hateful opposition to civil rights have long faded into memory. By most external measures, life for minorities is better than it was a quarter century ago. It would seem that the opportunities for tolerance and cooperation are commonplace. Why, then, are so many of my peers so cynical about our ability to get along with one another?

The reasons are frustratingly ambiguous. I got a glimpse of this when I was in college. It was late in my junior year, and as the editor of a campus magazine, I was sitting on a panel to discuss "The White Press at Yale: What Is to Be Done?" The assembly hall was packed, a diverse and noisy crowd. The air was heavy, nervously electric.

Why weren't there more stories about "minority issues" in the Yale *Daily News*? Why weren't there more stories on Africa in my magazine, the foreign affairs journal? How many "editors of color" served on the boards of each of the major publications? The questions were volleyed like artillery, one round after another, punctuated only by the applause of an audience spoiling for a fight. The questions were not at all unfair. But it seemed that no one—not even those of us on the panel who *were* people of color—could provide, in this context, satisfactory answers.

Toward the end of the discussion, I made a brief appeal for reason and moderation. And afterward, as students milled around restlessly, I was attacked: for my narrow-mindedness—How dare you suggest that Yale is not a fundamentally prejudiced place!—for my simplemindedness—Have you, too, been co-opted?

And for my betrayal—Are you just white inside?

My eyes were opened that uncomfortably warm early summer evening. Not only to the cynical posturing and the combustible opportunism of campus racial politics. But more importantly, to the larger question of identity—my identity—in America. Never mind that the aim of many of the loudest critics was to generate headlines in the very publications they denounced. In spite of themselves—against, it would seem, their true intentions—they got me to think about who I am.

In our society today, and especially among people of my generation, we are congealing into clots of narrow commonality. We stick with racial and religious comrades. This tribal consciousness-raising can be empowering for some. But while America was conceived in liberty—the liberty, for instance, to associate with whomever we like—it was never designed to be a mere collection of subcultures. We forget that there is in fact such a thing as a unique American identity that transcends our sundry tribes, sets, gangs, and cliques.

I have grappled, wittingly or not, with these questions of identity and allegiance all my life. When I was in my early teens, I would invite my buddies overnight to watch movies, play video games, and beat one another up. Before too long, my dad would come downstairs and start hamming it up—telling stories, asking gently nosy questions, making corny jokes, all with his distinct Chinese accent. I would stand back, quietly gauging everyone's reaction. Of course, the guys loved it. But I would feel uneasy.

What was then cause for discomfort is now a source of strength. Looking back on such episodes, I take pride in my father's accented English; I feel awe at his courage to laugh loudly in a language not really his own.

It was around the same time that I decided that continued attendance at the community Chinese school on Sundays was uncool. There was no fanfare; I simply stopped going. As a child, I'd been too blissfully unaware to think of Chinese school as anything more than a weekly chore, with an annual festival (dumplings and spring rolls, games and prizes). But by the time I was a peer-pressured adolescent, Chinese school seemed like a badge of the woefully unassimilated. I turned my back on it.

Even as I write these words now, it feels as though I am revealing a long-held secret. I am proud that my ancestors—scholars, soldiers, farmers—came from one of the world's great civilizations. I am proud that my grandfather served in the Chinese Air Force. I am proud to speak even my clumsy brand of Mandarin, and I feel blessed to be able to think idiomatically in Chinese, a language so much richer in nuance and subtle poetry than English.

Belatedly, I appreciate the good fortune I've had to be the son of immigrants. As a kid, I could play Thomas Jefferson in the bicentennial school play one week and the next week play the poet Li Bai at the Chinese school festival. I could come home from an afternoon of teen slang at the mall and sit down to dinner for a rollicking conversation in our family's hybrid of Chinese and English. I understood, when I went over to visit friends, that my life was different. At the time, I just never fully appreciated how rich it was.

Yet I know that this pride in my heritage does not cross into prejudice against others. What it reflects is pride in what my country represents. That became clear to me when I went through Marine Corps Officer Candidates' School. During the summers after my sophomore and junior years of college, I volunteered for OCS, a grueling boot camp for potential officers in the swamps and foothills of Quantico, Virginia.

And once I arrived—standing 5'4", 135 pounds, bespectacled, a Chinese Ivy League Democrat—I was a target straight out of central casting. The wiry, raspy-voiced drill sergeant, though he was perhaps only an inch or two taller than I, called me "Little One" with as much venom as can be squeezed into such a moniker. He heaped verbal abuse on me, he laughed when I stumbled, he screamed when I hesitated. But he also never failed to remind me that just because I was a little shit didn't mean I shouldn't run farther, climb higher, think faster, hit harder than anyone else.

That was the funny thing about the Marine Corps. It is, ostensibly, one of the most conservative institutions in the United States. And yet, for those twelve weeks, it represented the kind of color-blind equality of opportunity that the rest of society struggles to match. I did not feel uncomfortable at OCS to be of Chinese descent. Indeed, I drew strength from it. My platoon was a veritable cross section of America: forty young men of all backgrounds, all regions, all races, all levels of intelligence and ability, displaced from our lives (if only for a few weeks) with nowhere else to go.

Going down the list of names—Courtemanche, Dougherty, Grella, Hunt, Liu, Reeves, Schwarzman, and so on— brought to mind a line from a World War II documentary I once saw, which went something like this: The reason why it seemed during the war that America was as good as the rest of the world put together was that America *was* the rest of the world put together.

Ultimately, I decided that the Marines was not what I wanted to do for four years and I did not accept the second lieutenant's commission. But I will never forget the day of the graduation parade: bright sunshine, brisk winds, the band playing Sousa as my company passed in review. As my mom and dad watched and photographed the parade from the rafters, I thought to myself: this is the American Dream in all its cheesy earnestness. I felt the thrill of truly being part of something larger and greater than myself.

I do know that American life is not all Sousa marches and flag-waving. I know that those with reactionary agendas often find it convenient to cloak their motives in the language of Americanism. The "American Party" was the name of a major nativist organization in the nineteenth century. "America First" is the siren song of the isolationists who would withdraw this country from the world and expel the world from this country. I know that our national immigration laws were once designed explicitly to cut off the influx from Asia.

I also know that discrimination is real. I am reminded of a gentle old man who, after Pearl Harbor, was stripped of his possessions without warning, taken from his home, and thrown into a Japanese internment camp. He survived, and by many measures has thrived, serving as a community leader and political activist. But I am reluctant to share with him my wide-eyed patriotism.

I know the bittersweet irony that my own father—a strong and optimistic man—would sometimes feel when he was alive. When he came across a comically lost cause—if the Yankees were behind 14–0 in the ninth, or if Dukakis was down ten points in the polls with a week left—he would often joke that the doomed party had "a Chinaman's chance" of success. It was one of those insensitive idioms of a generation ago, and it must have lodged in his impressionable young mind when he first came to America. It spoke of a perceived stacked deck.

I know, too, that for many other immigrants, the dream simply does not work out. Fae Myenne Ng, the author of *Bone*, writes about how her father ventured here from China under a false identity and arrived at Angel Island, the detention center outside the "Gold Mountain" of San Francisco. He got out, he labored, he struggled, and he suffered "a bitter no-luck life" in America. There was no glory. For him, Ng suggests, the journey was not worth it.

But it is precisely because I know these things that I want to prove that in the long run, over generations and across ethnicities, it *is* worth it. For the second-generation American, opportunity is obligation. I have seen and faced racism. I understand the dull pain of dreams deferred or unmet. But I believe still that there is so little stopping me from building the life that I want. I was given, through my parents' labors, the chance to bridge that gap between ideals and reality. Who am I to throw away that chance?

Plainly, I am subject to the criticism that I speak too much from my own experience. Not everyone can relate to the second-generation American story. When I have spoken like this with some friends, the issue has been my perspective. *What you say is fine for you. But unless you grew up where I did, unless you've had people avoid you because of the color of your skin, don't talk to me about common dreams.*

But are we then to be paralyzed? Is respect for different experiences supposed to obviate the possibility of shared aspirations? Does the diversity of life in America doom us to a fractured understanding of one another? The question is basic: Should the failure of this nation thus far to fulfill its stated ideals incapacitate its young people, or motivate us?

Our country was built on, and remains glued by, the idea that everybody deserves a fair shot and that we must work together to guarantee that opportunity—the original American Dream. It was this idea, in some inchoate form, that drew every immigrant here. It was this idea, however sullied by slavery and racism, that motivated the civil-rights movement. To write this idea off—even when its execution is spotty—to let American life descend into squabbles among separatist tribes would not just be sad. It would be a total mishandling of a legacy, the squandering of a great historical inheritance.

Mine must not be the first generation of Americans to lose America. Just as so many of our parents journeyed here to find their version of the American Dream, so must young Americans today journey across boundaries of race and class to rediscover one another. We are the first American generation to be born into an integrated society, and we are accustomed to more race mixing than any generation before us. We started open-minded, and it's not too late for us to stay that way.

Time is of the essence. For in our national political culture today, the watchwords seem to be *decline* and *end*. Apocalyptic visions and dark millennial predictions abound. The end of history. The end of progress. The end of equality. Even something as ostensibly positive as the end of the Cold War has a bittersweet tinge, because for the life of us, no one in America can get a handle on the big question, "What Next?"

For my generation, this fixation on endings is particularly enervating. One's twenties are supposed to be a time of widening horizons, of bright possibilities. Instead, America seems to have entered an era of limits. Whether it is the difficulty of finding jobs from some place other than a temp agency, or the mountains of debt that darken our future, the message to my peers is often that this nation's time has come and gone; let's bow out with grace and dignity.

A friend once observed that while the Chinese seek to adapt to nature and yield to circumstance, Americans seek to conquer both. She meant that as a criticism of America. But I interpreted her remark differently. I *do* believe that America is exceptional. And I believe it is up to my generation to revive that spirit, that sense that we do in fact have control over our own destiny—as individuals and as a nation.

If we are to reclaim a common destiny, we must also reach out to other generations for help. It was Franklin Roosevelt who said that while America can't always build the future for its youth, it can—and must—build its youth for the future. That commitment across generations is as central to the American Dream as any I have enunciated. We are linked, black and white, old and young, one and inseparable.

I know how my words sound. I am old enough to perceive my own naïveté but young enough still to cherish it. I realize that I am coming of age just as the American Dream is showing its age. Yet I still have faith in this country's unique destiny—to create generation after generation of hyphenates like me, to channel this new blood, this resilience and energy into an ever more vibrant future for *all* Americans.

And I want to prove—for my sake, for my father's sake, and for my country's sake—that a Chinaman's chance is as good as anyone else's.

[1994]

Journal Entry

What concepts, experiences, associations, or images of the American dream can you bring to your reading of Liu's text?

Textual Considerations

1. Why does Liu include so many details about his parents' experience? How does this affect his argument?
2. "What alarms me is how many people my age look at our nation's ideals with a rising sense of irony" (paragraph 13). What evidence does Liu offer to support his thesis? To what extent do you agree with him?
3. Liu is an assimilationist, yet he is proud of his Chinese American heritage. How does he reconcile these different aspects of his philosophy?
4. Liu's essay was originally published in 1994 in a collection of essays titled *Next: Young American Writers on the New Generation*, which he edited. Who was his intended audience?
5. Characterize your response to Liu's essay. Was his purpose in his essay to inform or persuade? Explain.

Cultural Contexts

1. Liu is disturbed by the fact that in recent times, "America seems to have entered an era of limits." What challenges does he issue to his own generation? How do you respond to his call to action? Does his summons transcend generational limitations? How?
2. If you were forced to emigrate from your country and found yourself raising a family in another culture, what aspects of your native culture would you attempt to preserve and share with your children? Discuss this issue with members of your group.

POETRY

Walt Whitman

I Hear America Singing

I hear America singing, the varied carols I hear,
Those of mechanics, each one singing his as it should be blithe and strong,
The carpenter singing his as he measures his plank or beam,
The mason singing his as he makes ready for work, or leaves off work,
The boatman singing what belongs to him on his boat, the deck-hand
    singing on the steamboat deck,   5
The shoemaker singing as he sits on his bench, the hatter singing as he
    stands,
The wood-cutter's song, the ploughboy's on his way in the morning, or
    at noon intermission or at sundown,
The delicious singing of the mother, or of the young wife at work, or of
    the girl sewing or washing,
Each singing what belongs to him or her and to none else,
The day what belongs to the day—at night the party of young fellows,
    robust, friendly,   10
Singing with open mouths their strong melodious songs.

[1865]

Denise Levertov

Poet Power

Riding by taxi, Brooklyn to Queens,
a grey spring day. The Hispanic driver,
when I ask, 'Es usted Mexicano?' tells me
No, he's an exile from Uruguay. And I say,
'The only other Uraguayan I've met   5

was a writer—maybe
you know his name?—
                              Mario Benedetti?
    And he takes both hands
off the wheel and swings round,   10
glittering with joy: '*Benedetti!*
Mario Benedetti!!'
                         There are
hallelujahs in his voice—
we execute a perfect   15
figure 8 on the shining highway,
and rise aloft, high above traffic, flying
all the rest of the way in the blue sky, azul, azul!

                                                         [1987]

Journal Entry

Whitman and Levertov celebrate the diversity of the United States. What experiences or knowledge of ethnic or cultural diversity can you bring to your reading of these texts?

Textual Considerations

1. What is the thematic significance of the titles of the two poems?
2. Discuss the effectiveness of the metaphor of song to reinforce meaning in Whitman's text. Which "songs" did you find most appealing?
3. What images in Levertov's text best express the joy of the taxi driver?
4. What emotions is Levertov trying to capture in this poem? Explain.
5. Discuss the parallel structure of Whitman's poem. How does it contribute to rhythm, imagery, and idea? How does it compare to the stanzaic structure of Levertov's poem?

Cultural Considerations

1. Whitman was the first American poet who tried to express and celebrate democracy and cultural diversity in the language of the people. Is his concept of social equality applicable to the twenty-first century? Explain.
2. According to fiction writer Grace Paley, "If you say what's on your mind in the language that comes to you from your parents and your street and your friends, you'll probably say something beautiful." Test Paley's thesis with your group members and write a short poem in your own language.

ERDRICH AND GILLAN

Louise Erdrich

Indian Boarding School: The Runaways

Home's the place we head for in our sleep.
Boxcars stumbling north in dreams
don't wait for us. We catch them on the run.
The rails, old lacerations that we love,
shoot parallel across the face and break   5
just under Turtle Mountains. Riding scars
you can't get lost. Home is the place they cross.

The lame guard strikes a match and makes the dark
less tolerant. We watch through cracks in boards
as the land starts rolling, rolling till it hurts   10
to be here, cold in regulation clothes.
We know the sheriff's waiting at midrun
to take us back. His car is dumb and warm.
The highway doesn't rock, it only hums
like a wing of long insults. The worn-down welts   15
of ancient punishments lead back and forth.

All runaways wear dresses, long green ones,
the color you would think shame was. We scrub
the sidewalks down because it's shameful work.
Our brushes cut the stone in watered arcs   20
and in the soak frail outlines shiver clear
a moment, things us kids pressed on the dark
face before it hardened, place, remembering
delicate old injuries, the spines of names and leaves.

[1984]

Maria Mazziotti Gillan

Public School No. 18: Paterson, New Jersey

Miss Wilson's eyes, opaque
as blue glass, fix on me:
"We must speak English.
We're in America now."
I want to say, "I am American,"   5
but the evidence is stacked against me.

My mother scrubs my scalp raw, wraps
my shining hair in white rags
to make it curl; Miss Wilson
drags me to the window, checks my hair   10
for lice. My face wants to hide.

At home, my words smooth in my mouth,
I chatter and am proud. In school,
I am silent; I grope for the right English
words, fear the Italian word will sprout   15
from my mouth like a rose.

I fear the progression of teachers
in their sprigged dresses,
their Anglo-Saxon faces.

Without words, they tell me   20
to be ashamed.
I am.
I deny that booted country
even from myself,
want to be still   25
and untouchable
as these women
who teach me to hate myself.

Years later, in a white
Kansas City house,   30
the psychology professor tells me
I remind him of the Mafia leader
on the cover of *Time* magazine.
My anger spits
venomous from my mouth: 35

I am proud of my mother,
dressed all in black,
proud of my father
with his broken tongue,
proud of the laughter   40
and noise of our house.

Remember me, ladies,
the silent one?
I have found my voice
and my rage will blow   45
your house down.

[1984]

Journal Entry

What experiences, memories, or emotions of being an ethnic outsider in a classroom can you bring to your reading of these texts?

Textual Considerations

1. Describe the situation in Erdrich's text. Is it imagined or real? Explain.
2. What images of home in the first stanza of "Indian Boarding School: The Runaways" do you find most effective? Identify them and explain how they relate to the full meaning of the poem. What kinds of experiences do they evoke?
3. Why do the children in Erdrich's poem run away if they know they will be caught?
4. How do the railroad tracks, work uniform, and highways function literally and symbolically in "Indian Boarding School: The Runaways"?
5. Why does the speaker in Gillan's poem feel like an outsider?
6. How do the teachers in Gillan's poem contribute to her humiliation and exclusion?
7. Characterize the tone of Gillan's poem. Is it consistent throughout? How does it compare with the tone of Erdrich's poem?

Cultural Contexts

1. Erdrich is a Native American of German and Chippewa heritage. What preconceptions about Native Americans and reservations did you bring to this text? Did you modify them in any way after this experience? How?
2. Should a schoolteacher serve as a role model for students? How important is it that he or she be a member of the students' ethnic group? Do teachers have too much or too little influence on their students? Discuss these issues with your group and record your responses.

Langston Hughes

The Weary Blues

Droning a drowsy syncopated tune,
Rocking back and forth to a mellow croon,
   I heard a Negro play.
Down on Lenox Avenue° the other night
By the pale dull pallor of an old gas light   5
   He did a lazy sway . . .
   He did a lazy sway . . .
To the tune o' those Weary Blues.
With his ebony hands on each ivory key
He made that poor piano moan with melody.   10
   O Blues!
Swaying to and fro on his rickety stool
He played that sad raggy tune like a musical fool.
   Sweet Blues!
Coming from a black man's soul.   15
   O Blues!

In a deep song voice with a melancholy tone
I heard that Negro sing, that old piano moan—
   "Ain't got nobody in all this world,
   Ain't got nobody but ma self.   20
   I's gwine° to quit ma frownin'
   And put ma troubles on the shelf."
Thump, thump, thump, went his foot on the floor.
He played a few chords then he sang some more—
   "I got the Weary Blues   25
   And I can't be satisfied.
   Got the Weary Blues
   And can't be satisfied—
   I ain't happy no mo'
   And I wish that I had died."   30
And far into the night he crooned that tune.
The stars went out and so did the moon.
The singer stopped playing and went to bed
While the Weary Blues echoed through his head.
He slept like a rock or a man that's dead.   35

[1923]

4 **Lenox Avenue:** was a main street in Harlem.   21 **"gwine":** "going."

Langston Hughes

Dream Variations

To fling my arms wide
In some place of the sun,
To whirl and to dance
Till the white day is done.
Then rest at cool evening   5
Beneath a tall tree
While night comes on gently,
　　Dark like me—
That is my dream!

To fling my arms wide   10
In the face of the sun,
Dance! Whirl! Whirl!
Till the quick day is done.
Rest at pale evening . . .
A tall, slim tree . . .   15
Night coming tenderly
　　Black like me.

　　　　　　　　　　　　　　　　　　[1926]

Langston Hughes

Harlem (A Dream Deferred)

What happens to a dream deferred?

　　Does it dry up
　　like a raisin in the sun?
　　Or fester like a sore—
　　And then run?   5
　　Does it stink like rotten meat?
　　Or crust and sugar over—
　　like a syrupy sweet?

　　Maybe it just sags
　　like a heavy load.   10

　　Or does it explode?

　　　　　　　　　　　　　　　　　　[1951]

Journal Entry

What knowledge of jazz, blues, or Harlem can you bring to your reading of these poems?

Textual Considerations

1. How does the speaker use color imagery to enhance theme in "Dream Variations"?
2. What does the second stanza of "The Weary Blues" add to the first? To what extent does the poem's structure underline meaning?
3. What strategies does the speaker of "The Weary Blues" use to reinforce the influence of blues and jazz in his poetry?
4. To what extent does the speaker of "The Weary Blues" find refuge in the blues?
5. How does setting function in "Dream Variations"?
6. Evaluate the effectiveness of the speakers' voices in "The Weary Blues," "Dream Variations," and "Harlem." Consider tone, direct speech, punctuation, and the use of questions and answers.

Cultural Contexts

1. Hughes published "Harlem" in 1951 in response to his having witnessed the gradual erosion of the dreams of his people in the previous two decades. To what extent was his prophecy of violence fulfilled? Does the poem have any relevance to the dreams of your generation? Explain.
2. In the 1920s, during the Harlem Renaissance, many critics, both black and white, criticized Hughes's poetry because it reflected the seedy side of Harlem with its portrayals of musicians in bars and bordellos, suggestive of the lowdown aspects of the jazz life. How do your group members respond to that criticism? Are musicians particularly vulnerable to societal critiques? How did you respond to Hughes's poetry?

SOYINKA AND OLDS

Wole Soyinka

Telephone Conversation

The price seemed reasonable, location
Indifferent. The landlady swore she lived
Off premises. Nothing remained
But self-confession. "Madam," I warned,
"I hate a wasted journey—I am African."   5
Silence. Silenced transmission of
Pressurized good-breeding. Voice, when it came,
Lipstick coated, long gold-rolled
Cigarette-holder pipped. Caught I was, foully.
"HOW DARK?". . . I had not misheard. . . "ARE YOU LIGHT   10
OR VERY DARK?" Button B. Button A. Stench
Of rancid breath of public hide-and-speak.
Red booth. Red pillar-box. Red double-tiered
Omnibus squelching tar. It *was* real! Shamed
By ill-mannered silence, surrender   15
Pushed dumbfoundment to beg simplification.
Considerate she was, varying the emphasis—
"ARE YOU DARK? OR VERY LIGHT?" Revelation came.
"You mean—like plain or milk chocolate?"
Her assent was clinical, crushing in its light   20
Impersonality. Rapidly, wave-length adjusted,
I chose. "West African sepia"—and as afterthought,
"Down in my passport." Silence for spectroscopic
Flight of fancy, till truthfulness clanged her accent
Hard on the mouthpiece. "WHAT'S THAT?" conceding   25
"DON'T KNOW WHAT THAT IS." "Like brunette."
"THAT'S DARK, ISN'T IT?" "Not altogether.
Facially, I am brunette, but madam, you should see
The rest of me. Palm of my hand, soles of my feet
Are a peroxide blonde. Friction, caused—   30
Foolishly madam—by sitting down, has turned
My bottom raven black—One moment madam!"—sensing
Her receiver rearing on the thunderclap
About my ears—"Madam," I pleaded, "wouldn't you rather
See for yourself?"   35

[1960]

Sharon Olds

On the Subway

The boy and I face each other.
His feet are huge, in black sneakers
laced with white in a complex pattern like a
set of intentional scars. We are stuck on
opposite sides of the car, a couple of   5
molecules stuck in a rod of light
rapidly moving through darkness. He has the
casual cold look of a mugger,
alert under hooded lids. He is wearing
red, like the inside of the body   10
exposed. I am wearing dark fur, the
whole skin of an animal taken and
used. I look at his raw face,
he looks at my fur coat, and I don't
know if I am in his power—   15
he could take my coat so easily, my
briefcase, my life—
or if he is in my power, the way I am
living off his life, eating the steak
he does not eat, as if I am taking   20
the food from his mouth. And he is black
and I am white, and without meaning or
trying to I must profit from his darkness,
the way he absorbs the murderous beams of the
nation's heart, as black cotton   25
absorbs the heat of the sun and holds it. There is
no way to know how easy this
white skin makes my life, this
life he could take so easily and
break across his knee like a stick the way his   30
own back is being broken, the
rod of his soul that at birth was dark and
fluid and rich as the heart of a seedling
ready to thrust up into any available light.

[1987]

Journal Entry

Define racism and stereotyping. How do they differ in meaning and connotation?

Textual Considerations

1. Create a profile of the landlady in "Telephone Conversation." How does the speaker use visual and sensory imagery to communicate her attitude toward skin color? Cite examples.
2. What profile of the speaker emerges in Soyinka's poem? How do the poet's stylistic techniques, such as short sentences and unusual syntax, enhance theme? How do you interpret the last four lines?
3. How does Olds use color to heighten differences in race and social class in "On the Subway"?
4. Explain lines 20–25 of "On the Subway." To what extent do you agree with the speaker that exploitation on the basis of race continues today as it did in the days of slavery?
5. Compare and contrast the conflict in each poem. Is it between the speaker and an antagonist? or within the speaker himself/herself? Explain.

Cultural Contexts

1. In addition to race, both poems address class, social injustice, power, and powerlessness. Who wins or loses in each text?
2. Is the community in which you are currently living integrated, or are there ethnic groups that would make you feel unwelcome? If so, how would your group explain or change the situation?

CHOCK AND LAVIERA

Eric Chock

Chinese Fireworks Banned in Hawaii
for Uncle Wongie, 1987

Almost midnight, and the aunties
are wiping the dinner dishes
back to their shelves,
cousins eat jook° from the huge vat
in the kitchen, and small fingers   5
help to mix the clicking ocean
of mah jong tiles, so the uncles can play
through another round of seasons.
And you put down your whiskey
and go outside to find your long bamboo pole   10
so Uncle Al can help you tie on
a ten foot string of good luck,
red as the raw fish we want
on our plates every New Year's.
As you hang this fish over the railing   15
Uncle Al walks down the steps
and with his cigarette lighter
ignites it and jumps out of the way.
You lean back and jam the pole
into the bottom of your guts,   20
waving it across the sky,
whipping sparks of light from its tail,
your face in a laughing Buddha smile
as you trace your name in the stars
the way we teach our kids to do   25
with their sparklers.
This is the family picture
that never gets taken, everyone
drawn from dishes and food and games
and frozen at the sound   30
of 10,000 wishes filling our bodies
and sparkling our eyes.
You play the fish till its head explodes
into a silence that echoes,
scattering red scales to remind us of spirits   35

that live with us in Hawaii.
Then, as we clap and cheer,
the collected smoke of our consciousness
floats over Honolulu, as it has
each year for the last century.   40
But tonight, as we leave,
Ghislaine stuffs her styrofoam tea cup
full of red paper from the ground.
This is going to be history, she says.
Let's take some home.   45

[1989]

4 jook: Asian rice dish

Tato Laviera

Latero° Story

i am a twentieth-century welfare recipient
moonlighting in the sun as a latero
a job invented by national state laws
designed to re-cycle aluminum cans
returned to consumer's acid laden   5
gastric inflammation pituitary glands
coca diet rites low cal godsons
of artificially flavored malignant
indigestions somewhere down the line
of a cancerous cell   10

i collect garbage cans in outdoor facilities
congested with putrid residues
my hands shelving themselves
opening plastic bags never knowing
what they'll encounter   15

several times a day i touch evil rituals
cut throats of chickens
tongues of poisoned rats
salivating my index finger
smells of month old rotten foods   20

next to pamper's diarrhea
    dry blood infectious diseases
hypodermic needles tissued with
heroin water drops pilfered in
slimy greases hazardous waste materials
but i cannot use rubber gloves
they undermine my daily profits

i am a twentieth-century welfare recipient
moonlighting in the day as a latero
that is the only opportunity i have
to make it big in america
some day i might become experienced enough
to offer technical assistance
to other lateros
i am thinking of publishing
my own guide to latero's collection
and a latero's union offering
medical dental benefits

i am a twentieth-century welfare recipient
moonlighting in the night as a latero
i am considered some kind of expert
at collecting cans during fifth avenue parades
i can now hire workers at twenty
five cents an hour guaranteed salary
and fifty per cent two and one half cents
profit on each can collected

i am a twentieth-century welfare recipient
moonlighting in midnight as a latero
i am becoming an entrepreneur
an american success story
i have hired bag ladies to keep peddlers
from my territories
i have read in some guide to success
that in order to get rich
to make it big
i have to sacrifice myself
moonlighting until dawn by digging
deeper into the extra can
margin of profit
i am on my way up the opportunistic
ladder of success
in ten years i will quit welfare
to become a legitimate businessman

i'll soon become a latero executive
with corporate conglomerate intents
god bless america

65

[1988]

Latero: From Spanish *lata*: can. A man who picks up cans from garbage containers and the streets.

Journal Entry

What associations, images, experiences, or memories of alienation or displacement can you bring to your reading of these texts?

Textual Considerations

1. Who is the speaker addressing in Chock's poem, and on what occasion?
2. Speculate on the significance and identity of the spirits in Chock's poem.
3. How do you interpret the next-to-last line of "Chinese Fireworks Banned in Hawaii"?
4. Laviera uses irony and repetition to satirize the values of corporate America in "Latero Story." Cite lines you find most effective. What is your response to his point of view?
5. Much of Laviera's poetry belongs to oral tradition. What does that suggest about his purpose and audience? How does it compare to the purpose and audience in Chock's poem?

Cultural Contexts

1. Chock and Laviera use poetry to transmit individual and cultural experiences. Experiment with writing a short poem about an experience, image, or emotion that has cultural implications for you.
2. Chock is an Asian of Hawaiian descent, while Laviera is an immigrant from Puerto Rico. Why might the preservation of their ethnic and cultural heritage inform their poetry? What does it mean to break traditions? How important is it to transmit and preserve communal rituals? Did your group reach a consensus?

May Sarton

AIDS

We are stretched to meet a new dimension
Of love, a more demanding range
Where despair and hope must intertwine.
How grow to meet it? Intention
Here can neither move nor change   5
The raw truth. Death is on the line.
It comes to separate and estrange
Lover from lover in some reckless design.
Where do we go from here?

Fear.   Fear.   Fear.   Fear.   10

Our world has never been more stark
Or more in peril.

It is very lonely now in the dark.
Lonely and sterile.

And yet in the simple turn of a head   15
Mercy lives. I heard it when someone said
"I must go now to a dying friend.
Every night at nine I tuck him into bed,
And give him a shot of morphine,"
And added, "I go where I have never been."   20
I saw he meant into a new discipline
He had not imagined before, and a new grace.

Every day now we meet face to face.
Every day now devotion is the test.
Through the long hours, the hard, caring nights   25
We are forging a new union. We are blest.
As closed hands open to each other
Closed lives open to strange tenderness.
We are learning the hard way how to mother.
Who says it is easy? But we have the power.   30
I watch the faces deepen all around me.
It is the time of change, the saving hour.
The word is not fear, the word we live,

But an old word suddenly made new,
As we learn it again, as we bring it alive: 35

Love.   Love.   Love.   Love.

[1988]

Michael Lassell

How to Watch Your Brother Die

When the call comes, be calm
Say to your wife, "My brother is dying. I have
to fly to California."
Try not to be shocked that he already looks like a cadaver.
Say to the young man sitting by your brother's side,   5
"I'm his brother."
Try not to be shocked when the young man says,
"I'm his lover. Thanks for coming."

Listen to the doctor with a steel face on.
Sign the necessary forms.   10
Tell the doctor you will take care of everything.
Wonder why doctors are so remote.

Watch the lover's eyes as they stare into
your brother's eyes as they stare into
space.   15
Wonder what they see there.
Remember the time he was jealous and
opened your eyebrows with a sharp stick.
Forgive him out loud
even if he can't understand you.   20
Realize the scar will be
all that's left of him.

Over coffee in the hospital cafeteria
say to the lover, "You're an extremely good-looking
young man."   25
Hear him say,
"I never thought I was good enough looking to
deserve your brother."
Watch the tears well up in his eyes. Say,
"I'm sorry. I don't know what it means to be   30
the lover of another man."

Hear him say,
"It's just like a wife, only the commitment is
deeper because the odds against you are so much
greater."   35
Say nothing, but
take his hand like a brother's.

Drive to Mexico for unproven drugs that might
help him live longer.
Explain what they are to the border guard.   40
Fill with rage when he informs you,
"You can't bring those across."
Begin to grow loud.
Feel the lover's hand on your arm,
restraining you. See in the guard's eye   45
how much a man can hate another man.
Say to the lover, "How can you stand it?"
Hear him say, "You get used to it."
Think of one of your children getting used to
another man's hatred.   50

Call your wife on the telephone. Tell her
"He hasn't much time.
I'll be home soon." Before you hang up, say,
"How could anyone's commitment be deeper than
a husband and wife?" Hear her say,   55
"Please, I don't want to know all the details."

When he slips into an irrevocable coma
hold his lover in your arms while he sobs,
no longer strong. Wonder how much longer
you will be able to be strong.   60
Feel how it feels to hold a man in your arms
whose arms are used to holding men.
Offer God anything to bring your brother back.
Know you have nothing God could possibly want.
Curse God, but do not   65
abandon Him.

Stare at the face of the funeral director
when he tells you he will not
embalm the body for fear of
contamination. Let him see in your eyes   70
how much a man can hate a man.

Stand beside a casket covered in flowers,
white flowers. Say,

"Thank you for coming" to each of several hundred men
who file past in tears, some of them   75
holding hands. Know that your brother's life
was not what you imagined. Overhear two mourners say,
"I wonder who'll be next."

Arrange to take an early flight home.
His lover will drive you to the airport.   80
When your flight is announced say,
awkwardly, "If I can do anything, please
let me know." Do not flinch when he says,
"Forgive yourself for not wanting to know him
after he told you. He did."   85
Stop and let it soak in. Say,
"He forgave me, or he knew himself?"
"Both," the lover will say, not knowing what else
to do. Hold him like a brother while he
kisses you on the cheek. Think that   90
you haven't been kissed by a man since
your father died. Think,
"This is no moment not to be strong." Fly
first class and drink scotch. Stroke
your split eyebrow with a finger   95
and think of your brother alive. Smile
at the memory and think
how your children will feel in your arms,
warm and friendly and without challenge.

                                                                [1985]

Journal Entry

What attitudes, opinions, or knowledge of AIDS do you bring to your reading of these texts?

Textual Considerations

1. To what extent do you agree with the speaker in "AIDS" that "Our world has never been more stark / Or more in peril"?
2. How do you respond to the idea that words like *fear, mercy,* and *love* evoke new meanings in the context of AIDS?
3. Lassell uses contrasting images of love and hate in "How to Watch Your Brother Die." Cite examples of each.
4. Analyze the function of dialogue in Lassell's poem. Consider, for example, what the speaker's "conversations" reveal about himself, his wife, and his relationship to his brother and to his brother's lover.
5. Explain the last two words of Lassell's poem. How does it compare with the last line of Sarton's poem?

Cultural Contexts

1. Are homosexuals an oppressed group in the United States? Make a list of the arguments and evidence you would offer to support or refute this thesis.
2. Review with your group your responses to question 4. What do the various conversations suggest about the relationship of the gay community to the larger society? Make a list of the images that you associate with gays and lesbians. To what extent do you agree that people should be free to express their sexual preferences?

Martín Espada

Cross Plains, Wisconsin

Blue bandanna
across the forehead,
beard bristling
like a straw broom,
sleeveless T-shirt   5
of the Puerto Rican flag
with Puerto Rico stamped
across the chest,
a foreign name on the license,
evidence enough   10
for the cop to announce
that the choice is cash or jail,
that today
the fine for speeding
is exactly   15
sixty-seven dollars,
and his car
will follow my car
out of town

[1990]

Martín Espada

Federico's Ghost

The story is
that whole families of fruitpickers
still crept between the furrows
of the field at dusk,
when for reasons of whiskey or whatever   5
the cropduster plane sprayed anyway,
floating a pesticide drizzle
over the pickers

who thrashed like dark birds
in a glistening white net,   10
except for Federico,
a skinny boy who stood apart
in his own green row,
and, knowing the pilot
would not understand in Spanish   15
that he was the son of a whore,
instead jerked his arm
and thrust an obscene finger.

The pilot understood.
He circled the plane and sprayed again,   20
watching a fine gauze of poison
drift over the brown bodies
that cowered and scurried on the ground,
and aiming for Federico,
leaving the skin beneath his shirt   25
wet and blistered,
but still pumping his finger at the sky.

After Federico died,
rumors at the labor camp
told of tomatoes picked and smashed at night,   30
growers muttering of vandal children
or communists in camp,
first threatening to call Immigration,
then promising every Sunday off
if only the smashing of tomatoes would stop.   35

Still tomatoes were picked and squashed
in the dark,
and the old women in camp
said it was Federico,
laboring after sundown   40
to cool the burns on his arms,
flinging tomatoes
at the cropduster
that hummed like a mosquito
lost in his ear,   45
and kept his soul awake.

[1990]

Martín Espada

Tony Went to the Bodega° but He Didn't Buy Anything

para° Angel Guadalupe

Tony's father left the family
and the Long Island city projects,
leaving a mongrel-skinny puertorriqueño boy
nine years old
who had to find work.   5

Makengo the Cuban
let him work at the bodega.
In grocery aisles
he learned the steps of the dry-mop mambo,
banging the cash register   10
like piano percussion
in the spotlight of Machito's orchestra,
polite with the abuelas° who bought on credit,
practicing the grin on customers
he'd seen Makengo grin   15
with his bad yellow teeth.

Tony left the projects too,
with a scholarship for law school.
But he cursed the cold primavera°
in Boston;   20
the cooking of his neighbors
left no smell in the hallway,
and no one spoke Spanish
(not even the radio).

So Tony walked without a map   25
through the city,
a landscape of hostile condominiums
and the darkness of white faces,
sidewalk-searcher lost
till he discovered the projects.   30

Tony went to the bodega
but he didn't buy anything:
he sat by the doorway satisfied
to watch la gente° (people
island-brown as him)   35

crowd in and out,
hablando español,°
thought: this is beautiful,
and grinned
his bodega grin.   40

This is a rice and beans
success story:
Today Tony lives on Tremont Street,
above the bodega.

[1987]

Bodega: Grocery and liquor store. **para:** in the dedication, after the title, means "for."   **13 abuelas:** Grandmothers.   **19 primavera:** Spring season.   **34 la gente:** The people.   **37 hablando español:** Speaking Spanish.

Journal Entry

How does Espada's philosophy that "any oppressive social condition, before it can be changed, must be named and condemned in words that pervade by stirring the emotions, awakening the senses" apply to his poetry?

Textual Considerations

1. Analyze the effects of withholding the use of the personal pronouns until the end of "Cross Plains, Wisconsin." Describe the meaning of the dramatic contrasts imposed by the use of the pronouns.
2. What factors contributed to the fine imposed by the policeman in "Cross Plains, Wisconsin"? Identify them and interpret the meaning they acquire in the context of the poem.
3. Characterize the speaker's tone in "Cross Plains, Wisconsin." How does the cop react to him and the collection of physical traits that identify his ethnic origin? Does the fact the incident takes place in Cross Plains, Wisconsin, affect the cop's decision? Why or why not?
4. Why does Federico act as he does in "Federico's Ghost"? What is your response to his actions? Explain.
5. How do the growers modify their first reactions to the migrant workers in "Federico's Ghost"? Why?
6. Explain the significance of the final simile in "Federico's Ghost."
7. Characterize Tony. Why does he return to his roots? How do you respond to that decision?
8. Why does Espada mention Tony's father in the first part of the poem?

Cultural Contexts

1. Espada's poems—poems of political imagination—document racism, dehumanizing labor, and personal and political resistance. To what extent do you agree or disagree that the poet should protest social injustices?
2. Debate with your group the idea that Espada's poems present life well by transforming everyday reality into art but that their lack of commitment to a clearly imposed poetic form make them inferior to poems that excel in both—a fusion of form, elegance, and artistic structure with the imaginative transformation of reality into art. Record your findings.

DRAMA

William Shakespeare

Othello, the Moor of Venice

CHARACTERS

OTHELLO, *the Moor*
BRABANTIO, *a senator, father to* DESDEMONA
CASSIO, *an honourable lieutenant to* OTHELLO
IAGO, OTHELLO'S *ancient, a villain.*
RODERIGO, *a gulled gentleman.*
DUKE OF VENICE
SENATORS *of Venice.*
MONTANO, *governor of Cyprus.*
LODOVICO *and* GRATIANO, *kinsmen to* BRABANTIO, *two noble Venetians*
Sailors
Clown
DESDEMONA, *daughter to* BRABANTIO *and wife to* OTHELLO
EMILIA, *wife to* IAGO
BIANCA, *a courtesan and mistress to* CASSIO
Messenger, Herald, Officers, Gentlemen, Musicians, and Attendants

(SCENE: *Venice: a sea-port in Cyprus*)

ACT I

SCENE I.

Venice. A street.

(*Enter* RODERIGO *and* IAGO.)

ROD: Tush! never tell me; I take it much unkindly
  That thou, Iago, who hast had my purse
  As if the strings were thine, shouldst know of this.
IAGO: 'Sblood,° but you'll not hear me:
  If ever I did dream of such a matter,
  Abhor me.   5
ROD: Thou told'st me thou didst hold him in thy hate.
IAGO: Despise me, if I do not. Three great ones of the city,°

I.i. 4. 'Sblood: an oath, "by God's blood."   **8. great ones of the city:** Iago means to indicate his importance in the community; this is suggested also by his use of the word *worth* in line 11.

In personal suit to make me his lieutenant,
Off-capp'd to him°: and, by the faith of man, 10
I know my price, I am worth no worse a place:
But he, as loving his own pride and purposes,
Evades them, with a bombast circumstance
Horribly stuff'd with epithets of war;
And, in conclusion, 15
Nonsuits° my mediators; for, "Certes," says he,
"I have already chose my officer."
And what was he?
Forsooth, a great arithmetician,°
One Michael Cassio, a Florentine, 20
A fellow almost damn'd in a fair wife°;
That never set a squadron in the field,
Nor the division° of a battle knows
More than a spinster; unless the bookish theoric,°
Wherein the toged° consuls can propose° 25
As masterly as he: mere prattle, without practice,
Is all his soldiership. But he, sir, had th' election:
And I, of whom his eyes had seen the proof
At Rhodes, at Cyprus° and on other grounds
Christian and heathen, must be be-lee'd and calm'd 30
By debitor and creditor: this counter-caster,°
He, in good time,° must his lieutenant be,
And I—God bless the mark!°—his Moorship's ancient.°
ROD: By heaven, I rather would have been his hangman.
IAGO: Why, there's no remedy; 'tis the curse of service, 35
Preferment goes by letter and affection,
And not by old gradation,° where each second
Stood heir to th' first. Now, sir, be judge yourself,
Whether I in any just term am affin'd°
To love the Moor.
ROD: I would not follow then. 40
IAGO: O, sir, content you;
I follow him to serve my turn upon him:
We cannot all be masters, nor all masters

10. him: Othello.   **16. Nonsuits:** rejects.   **19. arithmetician:** a man whose military knowledge was merely theoretical, based on books of tactics.   **21. A . . . wife:** Cassio does not seem to be married, but his counterpart in Shakespeare's source did have a wife.   **23. division:** disposition of a battle line. **24. theoric:** theory.   **25. toged:** wearing the toga.   **25. propose:** discuss.   **29. Rhodes, Cyprus:** islands in the Mediterranean south of Asia Minor, long subject to contention between the Venetians and the Turks.   **31. counter-caster:** a sort of bookkeeper; contemptuous term.   **32. in good time:** forsooth.   **33. God bless the mark:** anciently, a pious interjection to avert evil omens.   **33. ancient:** standardbearer, ensign.   **37. old gradation:** seniority; Iago here expresses a characteristic prejudice of professional soldiers.   **39. affin'd:** bound.

Cannot be truly follow'd. You shall mark
Many a duteous and knee-crooking knave,   45
That, doting on his own obsequious bondage,
Wears out his time, much like his master's ass,
For nought but provender, and when he's old, cashier'd:
Whip me such honest knaves. Others there are
Who, trimm'd in forms and visages of duty,   50
Keep yet their hearts attending on themselves,
And, throwing but shows of service on their lords,
Do well thrive by them and when they have lin'd their coats
Do themselves homage: these fellows have some soul;
And such a one do I profess myself. For, sir,   55
It is as sure as you are Roderigo,
Were I the Moor, I would not be Iago°:
In following him, I follow but myself;
Heaven is my judge, nor I for love and duty,
But seeming so, for my peculiar end: 60
For when my outward action doth demonstrate
The native act and figure of my heart
In compliment extern,° 'tis not long after
But I will wear my heart upon my sleeve
For daws to peck at: I am not what I am.   65
ROD: What a full fortune does the thick-lips° owe,
    If he can carry 't thus!
IAGO: Call up her father,
    Rouse him: make after him, poison his delight,
    Proclaim him in the streets; incense her kinsmen,
    And, though he in a fertile climate dwell,   70
    Plague him with flies: though that his joy be joy,
    Yet throw such changes of vexation on 't,
    As it may lose some colour.
ROD: Here is her father's house; I'll call aloud.
IAGO: Do, with like timorous° accent and dire yell   75
    As when, by night and negligence, the fire
    Is spied in populous cities.
ROD: What, ho, Brabantio! Signior Brabantio, ho!
IAGO: Awake! what, ho, Brabantio! thieves! thieves! thieves!
    Look to your house, your daughter and your bags!   80
    Thieves! thieves!

    (BRABANTIO *appears above at a window.*)

---

57. Were . . . Iago: Were I in the position of the Moor, I should not feel as Iago feels.   **63. compliment extern:** outward civility.   **66. thick-lips:** Elizabethans often applied the term *Moor* to Africans.
75. timorous: frightening.

BRA: What is the reason of this terrible summons?
    What is the matter there?

ROD: Signior, is all your family within?

IAGO: Are your doors lock'd?

BRA: Why, wherefore ask you this?   85

IAGO: 'Zounds, sir, y' are robb'd; for shame, put on your gown;
    Your heart is burst, you have lost half your soul;
    Even now, now, very now, an old black ram
    Is tupping your white ewe. Arise, arise:
    Awake the snorting° citizens with the bell,   90
    Or else the devil will make a grandsire of you:
    Arise, I say.

BRA: What, have you lost your wits?

ROD: Most reverend signior, do you know my voice?

BRA: Not I: what are you?

ROD: My name is Roderigo.

BRA: The worser welcome: 95
    I have charg'd thee not to haunt about my doors:
    In honest plainness thou has heard me say
    My daughter is not for thee; and now, in madness,
    Being full of supper and distemp'ring draughts,
    Upon malicious bravery,° doest thou come   100
    To start° my quiet.

ROD: Sir, sir, sir,—

BRA: But thou must needs be sure
    My spirit and my place have in them power
    To make this bitter to thee.

ROD: Patience, good sir.

BRA: What tell'st thou me of robbing? this is Venice;   105
    My house is not a grange.°

ROD: Most grave Brabantio,
    In simple and pure soul I come to you.

IAGO: 'Zounds, sir, you are one of those that will not serve God, if the devil bid
    you. Because we come to do you service and you think we are ruffians, you'll have
    your daughter covered with a Barbary horse, you'll have your nephews° neigh to   110
    you; you'll have coursers for cousins and gennets° for germans.°

BRA: What profane wretch art thou?

IAGO: I am one, sir, that comes to tell you your daughter and the Moor are now
    making the beast with two backs.

BRA: Thou art a villain.

IAGO: You are—a senator.   115

---

90. snorting: snoring.   **100. bravery:** defiance, bravado.   **101. start:** disrupt.   **106. grange:** isolated
farmhouse.   **110. nephews:** grandsons.   **111. gennets:** small Spanish horses.   **111. germans:** near
relatives.

BRA: This thou shalt answer; I know thee, Roderigo.
ROD: Sir, I will answer any thing. But, I beseech you,
   If 't be your pleasure and most wise consent,
   As partly I find it is, that your fair daughter,
   At this odd-even° and dull watch o' th' night,   120
   Transported, with no worse nor better guard
   But with a knave of common hire, a gondolier,
   To the gross clasps of a lascivious Moor,—
   If this be known to you and your allowance,°
   We then have done you bold and saucy wrongs;   125
   But if you know not this, my manners tell me
   We have your wrong rebuke. Do not believe
   That, from° the sense of all civility,
   I thus would play and trifle with your reverence:
   Your daughter, if you have not given her leave,   130
   I say again, hath made a gross revolt;
   Tying her duty, beauty, wit and fortunes
   In an extravagant° and wheeling° stranger
   Of here and every where. Straight satisfy yourself:
   If she be in her chamber or your house,   135
   Let loose on me the justice of the state
   For thus deluding you.
BRA: Strike on the tinder,° ho!
   Give me a taper! call up my people!
   This accident° is not unlike my dream:
   Belief of it oppresses me already.   140
   Light, I say! light?   *(Exit above.)*
IAGO: Farewell; for I must leave you:
   It seems not meet, nor wholesome to my place,
   To be produc'd—as, if I stay, I shall—
   Against the Moor: for I do know the state,
   However this may gall him with some check,°   145
   Cannot with safety cast° him, for he's embark'd
   With such loud reason to the Cyprus wars,
   Which even now stand in act,° that, for their souls,
   Another of his fathom° they have none,
   To lead their business: in which regard,   150
   Though I do hate him as I do hell-pains,
   Yet, for necessity of present life,
   I must show out a flag and sign of love,

---

120. odd-even: between night and morning.   **124. allowance:** permission.   **128. from:** contrary to.
133. extravagant: wandering.   **133. wheeling:** vagabond.   **137. tinder:** charred linen kept in a metal box, and ignited by a spark from flint and steel.   **139. accident:** occurrence, event.   **145. check:** rebuke.   **146. cast:** dismiss.   **148. stand in act:** are going on.   **149. fathom:** ability.

Which is indeed but sign. That you shall surely find him,
Lead to the Sagittary° the raised search: 155
And there will I be with him. So, farewell.   (*Exit.*)

(*Enter below* Brabantio *with* Servants *and torches.*)

BRA: It is too true an evil; gone she is;
    And what's to come of my despised time
    Is nought but bitterness. Now, Roderigo,
    Where didst thou see her? O unhappy girl!   160
    With the Moor, say'st thou? Who would be a father!
    How didst thou know 'twas she? O, she deceives me
    Past thought! What said she to you? Get moe° tapers:
    Raise all my kindred. Are they married, think you?
ROD: Truly, I think they are.   165
BRA: O heaven! How got she out? O treason of the blood!
    Fathers, from hence trust not your daughters' minds
    By what you see them act. Is° there not charms
    By which the property° of youth and maidhood
    May be abus'd? Have you not read, Roderigo,   170
    Of some such thing?
ROD: Yes, sir, I have indeed.
BRA: Call up my brother. O, would you° had had her!
    Some one way, some another. Do you know
    Where we may apprehend her and the Moor?
ROD: I think I can discover him, if you please   175
    To get good guard and go along with me.
BRA: Pray you, lead on. At every house I'll call;
    I may command at most. Get weapons, ho!
    And raise some special officers of night.°
    On, good Roderigo: I will deserve your pains.   (*Exeunt.*) 180

SCENE II.

Another street.

(*Enter* Othello, Iago, Attendants *with torches.*)

IAGO: Though in the trade of war I have slain men,
    Yet do I hold it very stuff o' th' conscience
    To do no contriv'd murder: I lack iniquity
    Sometime to do me service: nine or ten times
    I had thought t' have yerk'd° him here under the ribs.   5
OTH: 'Tis better as it is.
IAGO: Nay, but he prated,

---

155. Sagittary: probably an inn.   **163. moe:** more.   **168. Is:** are.   **169. property:** special quality.
172. you: Roderigo.   **179. officers of night:** police.   **I.ii. 5. yerk'd:** stabbed.

And spoke such scurvy and provoking terms
Against your honour
That, with the little godliness I have,
I did full hard forbear him. But, I pray you, sir,   10
Are you fast married? Be assur'd of this,
That the magnifico° is much belov'd,
And hath in his effect° a voice potential°
As double° as the duke's: he will divorce you;
Or put upon you what restraint and grievance   15
The law, with all his might to enforce it on,
Will give him cable.

OTH: Let him do his spite;
My services, which I have done the signiory°
Shall out-tongue his complaints. 'Tis yet to know—
Which, when I know that boasting is an honour,   20
I shall promulgate—I fetch my life and being
From men of royal siege,° and my demerits°
May speak unbonneted° to as proud a fortune
As this that I have reach'd: for know, Iago,
But that I love the gentle Desdemona,   25
I would not my unhoused free condition
Put into circumscription and confine
For the sea's worth. But, look! what lights come yond?

IAGO: Those are the raised father and his friends:
You were best go in.

OTH: Not I; I must be found: 30
My parts, my title and my perfect soul°
Shall manifest me rightly. Is it they?

IAGO: By Janus, I think no.

(*Enter* CASSIO *and certain* OFFICERS *with torches.*)

OTH: The servants of the duke, and my lieutenant.
The goodness of the night upon you, friends!   35
What is the news?

CAS: The duke does greet you, general,
And he requires your haste-post-haste appearance,
Even on the instant.

OTH: What is the matter, think you?

CAS: Something from Cyprus, as I may divine:
It is a business of some heat: the galleys   40
Have sent a dozen sequent° messengers

---

12. magnifico: Venetian grandee (i.e., Brabantio).   **13. effect:** influence.   **13. potential:** powerful.
14. double: twice as influential as most men's.   **18. signiory:** Venetian government.   **22. siege:** rank.
22. demerits: deserts.   **23. unbonneted:** on equal terms.   **31. perfect soul:** unflawed conscience.
41. sequent: successive.

This very night at one another's heels,
And many of the consuls,° rais'd and met,
Are at the duke's already: you have been hotly call'd for;
When, being not at your lodging to be found,   45
The senate hath sent about three several° quests
To search you out.
OTH: 'Tis well I am found by you.
I will but spend a word here in the house.
And go with you.   (*Exit.*)
CAS: Ancient, what makes he here?
IAGO: 'Faith, he to-night hath boarded a land carack°:   50
If it prove lawful prize, he's made for ever.
CAS: I do not understand.
IAGO: He's married.
CAS: To who?

            (*Enter* OTHELLO.)

IAGO: Marry, to—Come, captain, will you go?
OTH: Have with you.
CAS: Here comes another troop to seek for you.

        (*Enter* BRABANTIO, RODERIGO, *with* OFFICERS *and torches.*)

IAGO: It is Brabantio. General, be advis'd;   55
He comes to bad intent.
OTH: Holla! stand there!
ROD: Signior, it is the Moor.
BRA: Down with him, thief!   (*They draw on both sides.*)
IAGO: You, Roderigo! come, sir, I am for you.
OTH: Keep up your bright swords, for the dew will rust them.
Good Signior, you shall more command with years   60
Than with your weapons.
BRA: O thou foul thief, where hast thou stow'd my daughter?
Damn'd as thou art, thou has enchanted her;
For I'll refer me to all things of sense,°
If she in chains of magic were not bound,   65
Whether a maid so tender, fair and happy,
So opposite to marriage that she shunn'd
The wealthy curled darlings of our nation,
Would ever have, t' incur a general mock
Run from her guardage° to the sooty bosom   70
Of such a thing as thou, to fear, not to delight
Judge me the world, if 'tis not gross in sense°

---

43. consuls: senators.   **46. several:** separate.   **50. carack:** large merchant ship.   **64. things of sense:**
commonsense understandings of the natural order.   **70. guardage:** guardianship.   **72. gross in sense:**
easily discernible in apprehension or perception.

That thou has practis'd on her with foul charms,
Abus'd her delicate youth with drugs or minerals°
That weaken motion°: I'll have't disputed on°;   75
'Tis probable and palpable to thinking.
I therefore apprehend and do attach thee
For an abuser of the world,° a practiser
Of arts inhibited° and out of warrant.
Lay hold upon him: if he do resist,   80
Subdue him at his peril.

OTH: Hold your hands,
Both you of my inclining,° and the rest:
Were it my cue to fight, I should have known it
Without a prompter. Whither will you that I go
To answer this charge?

BRA: To prison, till fit time   85
Of law and course of direct session°
Call thee to answer.

OTH: What if I do obey?
How may the duke be therewith satisfied,
Whose messengers are here about my side,
Upon some present business of the state   90
To bring me to him?

FIRST OFF: 'Tis true, most worthy signior;
The duke's in council, and your noble self,
I am sure, is sent for.

BRA: How! the duke in council!
In this time of night! Bring him away:
Mine's not an idle cause: the duke himself,   95
Or any of my brothers of the state
Cannot but feel this wrong as 'twere their own;
For if such actions may have passage free,
Bond-slaves and pagans° shall our statesmen be.   [*Exeunt.*]

SCENE III.

A council-chamber.

(*Enter* DUKE, SENATORS *and* OFFICERS *set at a table, with lights and* ATTENDANTS.)

DUKE: There is no composition in these news
That gives them credit.

FIRST SEN: Indeed, they are disproportion'd°;

---

74. minerals: medicine, poison.   **75. motion:** thought, reason.   **75. disputed on:** argued in court by professional counsel.   **78. abuser of the world:** corrupter of society.   **79. inhibited:** prohibited.   **82. inclining:** following, party.   **86. course of direct session:** regular legal proceedings.   **99. Bond-slaves and pagans:** contemptuous reference to Othello's past history.   **I. iii. 2. disproportion'd:** inconsistent.

    My letters say a hundred and seven galleys.
DUKE: And mine, a hundred forty.
SEC. SEN: And mine, two hundred:
    But though they jump° not on a just account,—   5
    As in these cases, where the aim° reports,
    'Tis oft with difference—yet do they all confirm
    A Turkish fleet, and bearing up to Cyprus.
DUKE: Nay, it is possible enough to judgment:
    I do not so secure me° in the error,   10
    But the main article° I do approve
    In fearful sense.
SAILOR (*Within*):   What, ho! what, ho! what, ho!
FIRST OFF: A messenger from the galleys.

          (*Enter* SAILOR.)

DUKE: Now, what's the business?
SAIL: The Turkish preparation makes for Rhodes;
    So was I bid report here to the state   15
    By Signior Angelo.
DUKE: How say you by this change?
FIRST SEN: This cannot be,
    By no assay° of reason: 'tis a pageant,
    To keep us in false gaze. When we consider
    Th' importancy of Cyprus to the Turk,   20
    And let ourselves again but understand,
    That as it more concerns the Turk than Rhodes,
    So may he with more facile question° bear it,
    For that it stands not in such warlike brace,°
    But altogether lacks th' abilities   25
    That Rhodes is dress'd in: if we make thought of this,
    We must not think the Turk is so unskilful
    To leave that latest which concerns him first,
    Neglecting an attempt of ease and gain,
    To wake and wage a danger profitless.   30
DUKE: Nay, in all confidence, he's not for Rhodes.
FIRST OFF: Here is more news.

          (*Enter a* MESSENGER.)

MESS: The Ottomites, reverend and gracious,
    Steering with due course toward the isle of Rhodes,
    Have there injointed them with an after fleet.   35

---

5. **jump:** agree.   6. **aim:** conjecture.   10. **secure me:** feel myself secure.   11. **main article:** i.e., that the Turkish fleet is threatening.   18. **assay:** test.   23. **more facile question:** greater facility of effort. 24. **brace:** state of defense.

FIRST SEN: Ay, so I thought. How many, as you guess?
MESS: Of thirty sail: and now they do re-stem°
  Their backward course, bearing with frank appearance
  Their purposes toward Cyprus. Signior Montano,
  Your trusty and most valiant servitor,   40
  With his free duty recommends you thus,
  And prays you to believe him.
DUKE: 'Tis certain, then, for Cyprus.
  Marcus Luccicos, is not he in town?
FIRST SEN: He's now in Florence.   45
DUKE: Write from us to him; post-posthaste dispatch.
FIRST SEN: Here comes Brabantio and the valiant Moor.

(*Enter* BRABANTIO, OTHELLO, CASSIO, IAGO, RODERIGO, *and* OFFICERS.)

DUKE: Valiant Othello, we must straight employ you
  Against the general enemy Ottoman.
  (*To* BRABANTIO) I did not see you; welcome, gentle signior;   50
  We lack'd your counsel and your help to-night.
BRA: So did I yours. Good your grace, pardon me;
  Neither my place nor aught I heard of business
  Hath rais'd me from my bed, nor does the general care
  Take hold on me, for my particular grief
  Is of so flood-gate and o'erbearing nature   55
  That it engluts° and swallows other sorrows
  And it is still itself.
DUKE: Why, what's the matter?
BRA: My daughter! O, my daughter!
DUKE *and* SEN: Dead?
BRA: Ay, to me;
  She is abus'd, stol'n from me, and corrupted   60
  By spells and medicines bought of mountebanks;
  For nature so preposterously to err,
  Being not deficient, blind, or lame of sense,
  Sans witchcraft could not.
DUKE: Whoe'er he be that in this foul proceeding   65
  Hath thus beguil'd your daughter of herself
  And you of her, the bloody book of law
  You shall yourself read in the bitter letter
  After your own sense, yea, though our proper son
  Stood in your action.°
BRA: Humbly I thank your grace.   70
  Here is the man, this Moor, whom now, it seems,

---

37. re-stem: steer again.   **57. engluts:** engulfs.   **70. Stood . . . action:** was under your accusation.

Your special mandate for the state-affairs
Hath hither brought.
DUKE *and* SEN: We are very sorry for 't.
DUKE (*To* OTHELLO):   What, in your own part, can you say to this?
BRA: Nothing, but this is so.   75
OTH: Most potent, grave, and reverend signiors,
My very noble and approv'd good masters,
That I have ta'en away this old man's daughter,
It is most true; true, I have married her:
The very head and front of my offending   80
Hath this extent, no more. Rude am I in my speech,
And little bless'd with the soft phrase of peace;
For since these arms of mine had seven years' pith,°
Till now some nine moons wasted, they have us'd
Their dearest action in the tented field,   85
And little of this great world can I speak,
More than pertains to feats of broil and battle,
And therefore little shall I grace my cause
In speaking for myself. Yet, by your gracious patience,°
I will a round unvarnish'd tale deliver   90
Of my whole course of love; what drugs, what charms,
What conjuration and what mighty magic,
For such proceeding I am charg'd withal,
I won his daughter.
BRA: A maiden never bold;   95
Of spirit so still and quiet, that her motion
Blush'd at herself°; and she, in spite of nature,
Of years, of country, credit, every thing,
To fall in love with what she fear'd to look on!
It is a judgement maim'd and most imperfect   100
That will confess perfection so could err
Against all rules of nature, and must be driven
To find our practices of cunning hell,
Why this should be. I therefore vouch° again
That with some mixtures pow'rful o'er the blood,   105
Or with some dram conjur'd to this effect,
He wrought upon her.
DUKE: To vouch this, is no proof,
Without more wider and more overt test
Than these thin habits and poor likelihoods
Of modern seeming do prefer against him.
FIRST SEN: But, Othello, speak: 110

---

83. pith: strength, vigor.   **89. patience:** suffering, permission.   **96. motion . . . herself:** inward
impulses blushed at themselves.   **103. vouch:** assert.

Did you by indirect and forced courses
Subdue and poison this young maid's affections?
Or came it by request and such fair question
As soul to soul affordeth?

OTH: I do beseech you,
Send for the lady to the Sagittary,   115
And let her speak of me before her father:
If you do find me foul in her report,
The trust, the office I do hold of you,
Not only take away, but let your sentence
Even fall upon my life.

DUKE: Fetch Desdemona hither.   120
OTH: Ancient, conduct them; you best know the place.

                                    (*Exeunt* IAGO *and* ATTENDANTS.)

And, till she come, as truly as to heaven
I do confess the vices of my blood,
So justly to your grave ear I'll present
How I did thrive in this fair lady's love,   125
And she in mine.

DUKE: Say it, Othello.
OTH: Her father lov'd me; oft invited me;
Still question'd me the story of my life,
From year to year, the battles, sieges, fortunes,   130
That I have pass'd.
I ran it through, even from my boyish days,
To th' very moment that he bade me tell it;
Wherein I spake of most disastrous chances,
Of moving accidents by flood and field,   135
Of hair-breadth scapes i' th' imminent° deadly breach,
Of being taken by the insolent foe
And sold to slavery, of my redemption thence
And portance° in my travels' history:
Wherein of antres° vast and deserts idle,°   140
Rough quarries, rocks and hills whose heads touch heaven,
It was my hint° to speak,—such was the process;
And of the Cannibals that each other eat,°
The Anthropophagi° and men whose heads
Do grow beneath their shoulders. This to hear   145
Would Desdemona seriously incline:
But still the house-affairs would draw her thence:
Which ever as she could with haste dispatch,

---

136. imminent: i.e., impending parts when a gap has been made in a fortification.   **139. portance:**
conduct.   **140. antres:** caverns.   **140. idle:** barren, unprofitable.   **142. hint:** occasion.   **143. eat:**
ate.   **144. Anthropophagi:** man-eaters.

She 'ld come again, and with a greedy ear
Devour up my discourse: which I observing,   150
Took once a pliant hour, and found good means
To draw from her a prayer of earnest heart
That I would all my pilgrimage dilate,°
Whereof by parcels she had something heard,
But not intentively°; I did consent,   155
And often did beguile her of her tears,
When I did speak some distressful stroke
That my youth suffer'd. My story being done,
She gave me for my pains a world of sighs:
She swore, in faith, 'twas strange, 'twas passing strange,   160
'Twas pitiful, 'twas wondrous pitiful:
She wish'd she had not heard it, yet she wish'd
That heaven had made her such a man: she thank'd me,
And bade me, if I had a friend that lov'd her,
I should but teach him how to tell my story,   165
And that would woo her. Upon this hint I spake:
She lov'd me for the dangers I had pass'd,
And I lov'd her that she did pity them.
This only is the witchcraft I have us'd:
Here comes the lady; let her witness it.   170

(*Enter* DESDEMONA, IAGO *and* ATTENDANTS.)

DUKE: I think this tale would win my daughter too.
    Good Brabantio,
    Take up this mangled matter at the best:
    Men do their broken weapons rather use
    Than their bare hands.
BRA: I pray you, hear her speak: 175
    If she confess that she was half the wooer,
    Destruction on my head, if my bad blame
    Light on the man! Come hither, gentle mistress:
    Do you perceive in all this noble company
    Where most you owe obedience?
DES: My noble father,   180
    I do perceive here a divided duty°:
    To you I am bound for life and education;
    My life and education both do learn me
    How to respect you; you are the lord of duty;
    I am hitherto your daughter: but here's my husband,   185
    And so much duty as my mother show'd

---

153. dilate: relate in detail.   **155. intentively:** with full attention.   **181. divided duty:** Desdemona recognizes that she still owes a duty to her father even after marriage.

To you, preferring you before her father,
So much I challenge that I may profess
Due to the Moor my lord.

BRA: God be with you! I have done.
  Please it your grace, on to° the state-affairs: 190
  I had rather to adopt a child than get° it.
  Come hither, Moor:
  I here do give thee that with all my heart
  Which, but thou hast already, with all my heart
  I would keep from thee. For your sake,° jewel,   195
  I am glad at soul I have no other child;
  For thy escape would teach me tyranny,
  To hang clogs on them. I have done, my lord.

DUKE: Let me speak like yourself,° and lay a sentence,°
  Which, as a grise° or step, may help these lovers   200
  Into your favour.
  When remedies are past, the griefs are ended
  By seeing the worst, which late on hopes depended.
  To mourn a mischief that is past and gone
  Is the next° way to draw new mischief on.   205
  Which cannot be preserv'd when fortune takes,
  Patience her injury a mock'ry makes.
  The robb'd that smiles steals something from the thief;
  He robs himself that spends a bootless grief.

BRA: So let the Turk of Cyprus us beguile;   210
  We lost it now, so long as we can smile.
  He bears the sentence well that nothing bears
  But the free comfort° which from thence he hears,
  But he bears both the sentence and the sorrow
  That, to pay grief, must of poor patience borrow.   215
  These sentences, to sugar, or to gall,
  Being strong on both sides, are equivocal:
  But words are words; I never yet did hear
  That the bruis'd heart was pierced through the ear.
  I humbly beseech you, proceed to th' affairs of state.   220

DUKE: The Turk with a most mighty preparation makes for Cyprus. Othello, the
fortitude° of the place is best known to you; and though we have there a substitute of most allowed° sufficiency, yet opinion, a sovereign mistress of effects,
throws a more safer voice on you°: you must therefore be content to slubber° the
gloss of your new fortunes with this more stubborn and boist'rous expedition.   225

190. on to: i.e., proceed with.   **191. get:** beget.   **195. For your sake:** on your account.   **199. like
yourself:** i.e., as you would, in your proper temper.   **199. sentence:** maxim.   **200. grise:** step.
205. next: nearest.   **213. comfort:** i.e., the consolation that it may be borne with patience.   **222. fortitude:** strength.   **223. allowed:** acknowledged.   **223–224. opinion . . . on you:** public opinion, an
important determiner of affairs, chooses you as the best man.   **224. slubber:** soil, sully.

OTH: The tyrant custom, most grave senators,
    Hath made the flinty and steel couch of war
    My thrice-driven° bed of down: I do agnize°
    A natural and prompt alacrity
    I find in hardness° and do undertake   230
    These present wars against the Ottomites.
    Most humbly therefore bending to your state,
    I crave fit disposition for my wife,
    Due reference of place and exhibition,°
    With such accommodation and besort°   235
    As levels with her breeding.
DUKE: If you please,
    Be 't at her father's.
BRA: I'll not have it so.
OTH: Nor I.
DES: Nor I; I would not there reside,
    To put my father in impatient thoughts
    By being in his eye. Most gracious duke,   240
    To my unfolding lend your prosperous° ear
    And let me find a charter° in your voice,
    T' assist my simpleness.°
DUKE: What would you, Desdemona?
DES: That I did love the Moor to live with him,   245
    My downright violence and storm of fortunes
    May trumpet to the world: my heart's subdu'd
    Even to the very quality of my lord:
    I saw Othello's visage in his mind,
    And to his honours and his valiant parts   250
    Did I my soul and fortunes consecrate.
    So that, dear lords, if I be left behind,
    A moth of peace, and he go to the war,
    The rites for why I love him are bereft me,
    And I a heavy interim shall support   255
    By his dear absence. Let me go with him.
OTH: Let her have your voices.
    Vouch with me, heaven, I therefore beg it not,
    To please the palate of my appetite,
    Nor to comply with heat—the young affects°   260
    In me defunct—and proper satisfaction,
    But to be free and bounteous to her mind:
    And heaven defend your good souls, that you think

---

228. thrice-driven: thrice sifted.   **228. agnize:** know in myself.   **230. hardness:** hardship.
234. exhibition: allowance.   **235. besort:** suitable company.   **241. prosperous:** propitious.
242. charter: privilege.   **243. simpleness:** simplicity.   **260. affects:** inclinations, desires.

I will your serious and great business scant
When she is with me: no, when light-wing'd toys 265
Of feather'd Cupid seel° with wanton dullness
My speculative and offic'd instruments,°
That° my disports° corrupt and taint° my business,
Let housewives make a skillet of my helm,
And all indign° and base adversities 270
Make head against my estimation!°

DUKE: Be it as you shall privately determine,
Either for her stay or going: th' affair cries haste,
And speed must answer for it.

FIRST SEN: You must away to-night.

OTH: With all my heart. 275

DUKE: At nine i' th' morning here we'll meet again.
Othello, leave some officer behind,
And he shall our commission bring to you;
With such things else of quality and respect
As doth import° you.

OTH: So please your grace, my ancient; 280
A man he is of honesty and trust:
To his conveyance I assign my wife,
With what else needful your good grace shall think
To be sent after me.

DUKE: Let it be so.
Good night to every one. (*To* BRA.) And, noble signior, 285
If virtue no delighted° beauty lack,
Your son-in-law is far more fair than black.

FIRST SEN: Adieu, brave Moor; use Desdemona well.

BRA: Look to her, Moor, if thou hast eyes to see;
She has deceiv'd her father, and may thee. 290

                                    (*Exeunt* DUKE, SENATORS, OFFICERS, &c.)

OTH: My life upon her faith! Honest Iago,°
My Desdemona must I leave to thee:
I prithee, let thy wife attend on her;
And bring them after in the best advantage.
Come, Desdemona; I have but an hour 295
Of love, of worldly matters and direction,
To spend with thee: we must obey the time.   (*Exit with* DESDEMONA.)

ROD: Iago—

---

266. seel: in falconry, to make blind by sewing up the eyes of the hawk in training.   **267. specula-tive . . . instruments:** ability to see and reason clearly.   **268. That:** so that.   **268. disports:** pastimes.   **268. taint:** impair.   **270. indign:** unworthy, shameful.   **271. estimation:** reputation.   **280. import:** concern.   **286. delighted:** delightful.   **291. Honest Iago:** an evidence of Iago's carefully built reputation.

IAGO: What say'st thou, noble heart?

ROD: What will I do, thinkest thou?   300

IAGO: Why, go to bed, and sleep.

ROD: I will incontinently° drown myself.

IAGO: If thou dost, I shall never love thee after. Why, thou silly gentleman!

ROD: It is silliness to live when to live is torment; and then have we a prescription
to die when death is our physician.   305

IAGO: O villainous! I have looked upon the world for four times seven years; and
since I could distinguish betwixt a benefit and an injury, I never found man that
knew how to love himself. Ere I would say, I would drown myself for the love of a
guinea-hen, I would change my humanity with a baboon.

ROD: What should I do? I confess it is my shame to be so fond; but it is not in my   310
virtue° to amend it.

IAGO: Virtue! a fig! 'tis in ourselves that we are thus or thus. Our bodies are our
gardens, to the which our wills are gardeners; so that if we will plant nettles,
or sow lettuce, set hyssop° and weed up thyme, supply it with one gender°
of herbs, or distract it with many, either to have it sterile with idleness,° or   315
manured with industry, why, the power and corrigible authority° of this lies in
our wills. If the balance of our lives had not one scale of reason to poise another
of sensuality, the blood and baseness of our natures would conduct us to most
preposterous conclusions°: but we have reason to cool our raging motions,° our
carnal stings, our unbitted° lusts, whereof I take this that you call love to be a   320
sect° or scion.

ROD: It cannot be.

IAGO: It is merely a lust of the blood and a permission of the will. Come, be a
man. Drown thyself! drown cats and blind puppies. I have professed me thy
friend and I confess me knit to thy deserving with cables of perdurable°   325
toughness; I could never better stead thee than now. Put money in thy purse;
follow thou the wars; defeat thy favour° with an usurped beard; I say, put
money in thy purse. It cannot be that Desdemona should long continue her
love to the Moor,—put money in thy purse,—nor he his to her: it was a violent
commencement in her, and thou shalt see an answerable sequestration°:—put   330
but money in thy purse. These Moors are changeable in their wills:—fill thy
purse with money:—the food that to him now is as luscious as locusts,° shall be
to him shortly as bitter as coloquintida.° She must change for youth: when
she is sated with his body, she will find the error of her choice: she must have
change, she must: therefore put money in thy purse. If thou wilt needs damn   335

---

302. incontinently: immediately.   **311. virtue:** strength.   **314. hyssop:** an herb of the mint family.
314. gender: kind.   **315. idleness:** want of cultivation.   **316. corrigible authority:** the power to correct.   **317–319. reason . . . conclusions:** Iago understands the warfare between reason and sensuality,
but his ethics are totally inverted; reason works in him not good, as it should according to natural law,
but evil, which he has chosen for his good.   **319. motions:** appetites.   **320. unbitted:** uncontrolled.
321. sect: cutting.   **325. perdurable:** very durable.   **327. defeat thy favour:** disguise and disfigure
thy face.   **330. answerable sequestration:** a separation corresponding.   **332. locusts:** of doubtful
meaning; defined as fruit of the carob tree, as honeysuckle, and as lollipops or sugar sticks.
333. coloquintida: colocynth, or bitter apple, a purgative.

thyself, do it a more delicate way than drowning. Make all the money thou canst: if sanctimony and a frail vow betwixt an erring° barbarian and a super-subtle Venetian be not too hard for my wits and all the tribe of hell, thou shalt enjoy her; therefore make money. A pox of drowning thyself! it is clean out of the way: seek thou rather to be hanged in compassing thy joy than to be drowned and go with- 340 out her.

ROD: Wilt thou be fast to my hopes, if I depend on the issue?

IAGO: Thou art sure of me:—go, make money:—I have told thee often, and I re- tell thee again and again, I hate the Moor: my cause is hearted°; thine hath no less reason. Let us be conjunctive° in our revenge against him; if thou canst cuckold 345 him, thou dost thyself a pleasure, me a sport. There are many events in the womb of time which will be delivered. Traverse!° go, provide thy money. We shall have more of this to-morrow. Adieu.

ROD: Where shall we meet i' the morning?

IAGO: At my lodging. 350

ROD: I'll be with thee betimes.

IAGO: Go to; farewell. Do you hear, Roderigo?

ROD: What say you?

IAGO: No more of drowning, do you hear?

ROD: I am changed: I'll go sell all my land.   *(Exit.)* 355

IAGO: Thus do I ever make my fool my purse;
For I mine own gain'd knowledge should profane,
If I would time expend with such a snipe,°
But for my sport and profit. I hate the Moor;
And it is thought abroad, that 'twixt my sheets 360
H' as done my office: I know not if 't be true;
But I, for mere suspicion in that kind,
Will do as if for surety. He holds me well;
The better shall my purpose work on him.
Cassio's a proper man: let me see now: 365
To get his place and to plume up° my will
In double knavery—How, how?—Let's see:—
After some time, to abuse Othello's ears
That he° is too familiar with his wife.
He hath a person and a smooth dispose° 370
To be suspected, fram'd to make women false.
The Moor is of a free° and open nature,
That thinks men honest that but seem to be so,
And will as tenderly be led by th' nose
As asses are. 375
I have 't. It is engend'red. Hell and night
Must bring this monstrous birth to the world's light.   *(Exit.)*

---

337. erring: wandering.   **344. hearted:** fixed in the heart.   **345. conjunctive:** united.   **347. Tra- verse:** go (military term).   **358. snipe:** gull, fool.   **366. plume up:** glorify, gratify.   **369. he:** i.e., Cas- sio   **370. dispose:** external manner.   **372. free:** frank.

ACT II

SCENE I.

A Sea-port in Cyprus. An open place near the quay.

(*Enter* MONTANO *and two* GENTLEMEN.)

MON: What from the cape can you discern at sea?

FIRST GENT: Nothing at all: it is a high-wrought flood;
  I cannot, 'twixt the heaven and the main,
  Descry a sail.

MON: Methinks the wind hath spoke aloud at land;   5
  A fuller blast ne'er shook our battlements:
  If it hath ruffian'd° so upon the sea,
  What ribs of oak, what mountains melt on them,
  Can hold the mortise?° What shall we hear of this?

SEC. GENT: A segregation° of the Turkish fleet: 10
  For do but stand upon the foaming shore,
  The chidden billow seems to pelt the clouds:
  The wind-shak'd surge, with high and monstrous mane,
  Seems to cast water on the burning bear,°
  And quench the guards° of th' ever-fixed pole: 15
  I never did like molestation view
  On the enchafed° flood.

MON: If that the Turkish fleet
  Be not enshelter'd and embay'd, they are drown'd;
  It is impossible they bear it out.

(*Enter a third* GENTLEMAN.)

THIRD GENT: News, lads! our wars are done   20
  The desperate tempest hath so bang'd the Turks,
  That their designment° halts: a noble ship of Venice
  Hath seen a grievous wrack and sufferance°
  On most part of their fleet.

MON: How! is this true?

THIRD GENT: The ship is here put in,   25
  A Veronesa; Michael Cassio,
  Lieutenant to the warlike Moor Othello,
  Is come on shore: the Moor himself at sea,
  And is in full commission here for Cyprus.

MON: I am glad on 't; 'tis a worthy governor.   30

II.i. 7. ruffian'd: raged.   **9. mortise:** the socket hollowed out in fitting timbers.   **10. segregation:** dispersion.   **14. bear:** a constellation.   **15. quench the guards:** overwhelm the stars near the polestar. **17. enchafed:** angry.   **22. designment:** enterprise.   **23. sufferance:** disaster.

THIRD GENT: But this same Cassio, though he speak of comfort
   Touching the Turkish loss, yet he looks sadly,
   And prays the Moor be safe; for they were parted
   With foul and violent tempest.
MON: Pray heavens he be;
   For I have serv'd him, and the man commands   35
   Like a full° soldier. Let's to the seaside, ho!
   As well to see the vessel that's come in
   As to throw out our eyes for brave Othello,
   Even till we make the main and th' aerial blue
   And indistinct regard.°
THIRD GENT: Come, let's do so;   40
   For every minute is expectancy
   Of more arrivance.°

      (Enter CASSIO.*)*

CAS: Thanks, you the valiant of this warlike isle,
   That so approve the Moor! O, let the heavens
   Give him defence against the elements,   45
   For I have lost him on a dangerous sea.
MON: Is he well shipp'd?
CAS: His bark is stoutly timber'd, and his pilot
   Of very expert and approv'd allowance°;
   Therefore my hopes, not surfeited to death,   50
   Stand in bold cure. *(A cry within.)* "A sail, a sail, a sail!"

      (Enter a fourth GENTLEMAN.*)*

CAS: What noise?
FOURTH GENT: The town is empty; on the brow o' th' sea
   Stand ranks of people, and they cry "A sail!"
CAS: My hopes do shape him for the governor.   *(Guns heard.)* 55
SEC. GENT: They do discharge their shot of courtesy:
   Our friends at least.
CAS: I pray you, sir, go forth,
   And give us truth who 'tis that is arriv'd.
SEC. GENT: I shall.   *(Exit.)*
MON: But, good lieutenant, is your general wiv'd?   60
CAS: Most fortunately: he hath achiev'd a maid
   That paragons° description and wild fame;
   One that excels the quirks° of blazoning° pens,

---

36. full: perfect.   **39–40. make . . . regard:** cause the blue of the sea and the air to grow indistinguishable in our view.   **42. arrivance:** arrival.   **49. allowance:** reputation.   **62. paragons:** surpasses.
63. quirks: witty conceits.   **63. blazoning:** setting forth honorably in words.

And in th' essential vesture of creation°
Does tire the ingener.°

(*Enter second* GENTLEMAN.)

              How now! who has put in?   65
SEC. GENT: 'Tis one Iago, ancient to the general.
CAS: Has had most favourable and happy speed:
    Tempests themselves, high seas and howling winds,
    The gutter'd° rocks and congregated sands,—
    Traitors ensteep'd° to clog the guiltless keel,—   70
    As having sense of beauty, do omit
    Their mortal° natures, letting go safely by
    The divine Desdemona.
MON: What is she?
CAS: She that I spake of, our great captain's captain,
    Left in the conduct of the bold Iago,   75
    Whose footing here anticipates our thoughts
    A se'nnight's° speed. Great Jove, Othello guard,
    And swell his sail with thine own powr'ful breath,
    That he may bless this bay with his tall ship,
    Make love's quick pants in Desdemona's arms,   80
    Give renew'd fire to our extinced spirits,
    And bring all Cyprus comfort!

(*Enter* DESDEMONA, IAGO, RODERIGO, *and* EMILIA *with* ATTENDANTS.)

              O, behold!
    The riches of the ship is come on shore!
    You men of Cyprus, let her have your knees.
    Hail to thee, lady! and the grace of heaven,   85
    Before, behind thee and on every hand,
    Enwheel thou round!
DES: I thank you, valiant Cassio.
    What tidings can you tell me of my lord?
CAS: He is not yet arriv'd: nor know I aught
    But that he's well and will be shortly here.   90
DES: O, but I fear—How lost you company?
CAS: The great contention of the sea and skies
    Parted our fellowship—But, hark! a sail.
    (*Within*) "A sail, a sail!" (*Guns heard.*)
SEC. GENT: They give their greeting to the citadel: 95
    This likewise is a friend.

---

64. vesture of creation: the real qualities with which creation has invested her.   **65. ingener:** inventor,
praiser.   **69. gutter'd:** jagged, trenched.   **70. ensteep'd:** lying under water.   **72. mortal:** deadly.
77. se'nnight's: week's.

CAS: See for the news.   (*Exit* GENTLEMAN.)
   Good ancient, you are welcome. (*To* EMILIA) Welcome, mistress:
   Let it not gall your patience, good Iago,
   That I extend my manners; 'tis my breeding
   That gives me this bold show of courtesy. (*Kissing her.*)   100
IAGO: Sir, would she give you so much of her lips
   As of her tongue she oft bestows on me,
   You would have enough.
DES: Alas, she has no speech.
IAGO: In faith, too much;
   I find it still, when I have list to sleep: 105
   Marry, before your ladyship, I grant,
   She puts her tongue a little in her heart,
   And chides with thinking.
EMIL: You have little cause to say so.
IAGO: Come on, come on; you are pictures out of doors,   110
   Bells in your parlours, wild-cats in your kitchens,
   Saints in your injuries, devils being offended,
   Players in your housewifery, and housewives° in your beds.
DES: O, fie upon thee, slanderer!
IAGO: Nay, it is true, or else I am a Turk: 115
   You rise to play and go to bed to work.
EMIL: You shall not write my praise.
IAGO: No, let me not.
DES: What wouldst thou write of me, if thou shouldst praise me?
IAGO: O gentle lady, do not put me to 't;
   For I am nothing, if not critical.°   120
DES: Come on, assay. There's one gone to the harbour?
IAGO: Ay, madam.
DES: I am not merry; but I do beguile
   The thing I am, by seeming otherwise.
   Come, how wouldst thou praise me?   125
IAGO: I am about it; but indeed my invention
   Comes from my pate as birdlime° does from frieze°;
   It plucks out brains and all: but my Muse labours,
   And thus she is deliver'd.
   If she be fair and wise, fairness and wit,   130
   The one's for use, the other useth it.
DES: Well praised! How if she be black and witty?
IAGO: If she be black, and thereto have a wit,
   She'll find a white° that shall her blackness fit.

---

113. housewives: hussies.   **120. critical:** censorious.   **127. birdlime:** sticky substance smeared on twigs to catch small birds.   **127. frieze:** coarse woolen cloth.   **134. white:** a fair person, with a word-play on *wight*.

DES: Worse and worse.   135

EMIL: How if fair and foolish?

IAGO: She never yet was foolish that was fair;
  For even her folly help'd her to an heir.

DES: These are old fond° paradoxes to make fools laugh i' the alehouse.
  What miserable praise hast thou for her that's foul and foolish?   140

IAGO: There's none so foul and foolish thereunto,
  But does foul pranks which fair and wise ones do.

DES: O heavy ignorance! thou praisest the worst best. But what praise couldst
  thou bestow on a deserving woman indeed, one that, in the authority of her
  merit, did justly put on the vouch° of her malice itself?   145

IAGO: She that was ever fair and never proud,
  Had tongue at will and yet was never loud,
  Never lack'd gold and yet went never gay,
  Fled from her wish and yet said "Now I may,"
  She that being ang'rd, her revenge being nigh,   150
  Bade her wrong stay and her displeasure fly,
  She that in wisdom never was so frail
  To change the cod's head for the salmon's tail,°
  She that could think and ne'er disclose her mind,
  See suitors following and not look behind,   155
  She was a wight, if ever such wight were,—

DES: To do what?

IAGO: To suckle fools and chronicle small beer.°

DES: O most lame and impotent conclusion! Do not learn of him, Emilia, though
  he be thy husband. How say you, Cassio? is he not a most profane and liberal° 160
  counsellor?

CAS: He speaks home,° madam: you may relish him more in the soldier than in the
  scholar.

IAGO (*Aside*):   He takes her by the palm: ay, well said, whisper: with as little a web as
  this will I ensnare as great a fly as Cassio. Ay, smile upon her, do; I will gyve° thee 165
  in thine own courtship.° You say true; 'tis so, indeed: if such tricks as these strip
  you out of your lieutenantry, it had been better you had not kissed your three fin-
  gers° so oft, which now again you are most apt to play the sir° in. Very good; well
  kissed! an excellent courtesy! 'tis so, indeed. Yet again your fingers to your lips?
  would they were clyster-pipes° for your sake. (*Trumpet within.*) The Moor! I 170
  know his trumpet.

CAS: 'Tis truly so.

DES: Let's meet him and receive him.

CAS: Lo, where he comes!

---

139. fond: foolish.   **145. put on the vouch:** compel the approval.   **153. To change . . . tail:** to
exchange a delicacy for mere refuse.   **158. chronicle small beer:** keep petty household accounts.
160. liberal: licentious.   **162. speaks home:** i.e., without reserve.   **165. gyve:** fetter, shackle.
166. courtship: courtesy.   **167–168. kissed your three fingers:** he kisses his own hand as a token of
reverence.   **168. the sir:** i.e., the fine gentleman.   **170. clyster-pipes:** tubes used for enemas.

(*Enter* OTHELLO *and* ATTENDANTS.)

OTH: O my fair warrior!
DES: My dear Othello!   175
OTH: It gives me wonder great as my content
  To see you here before me. O my soul's joy!
  If after every tempest come such calms,
  May the winds blow till they have waken'd death!
  And let the labouring bark climb hills of seas   180
  Olympus-high and duck again as low
  As hell 's from heaven! If it were now to die,
  'Twere now to be most happy; for, I fear,
  My soul hath her content so absolute
  That not another comfort like to this   185
  Succeeds in unknown fate.
DES: The heavens forbid
  But that our loves and comforts should increase,
  Even as our days grow!
OTH: Amen to that, sweet powers!
  I cannot speak enough of this content;
  It stops me here; it is too much of joy;   190
  And this, and this, the greatest discords be (*Kissing her*)
  That e'er our hearts shall make!
IAGO (*Aside*):   O, you are well tun'd now!
  But I'll set down the pegs° that make this music,
  As honest as I am.
OTH: Come, let us to the castle.
  News, friends, our wars are done, the Turks are drowned.   195
  How does my old acquaintance of this isle?
  Honey, you shall be well desir'd in Cyprus;
  I have found greatest love amongst them. O my sweet,
  I prattle out of fashion, and I dote
  In mine own comforts. I prithee, good Iago,   200
  Go to the bay and disembark my coffers:
  Bring thou the master to the citadel;
  He is a good one, and his worthiness
  Does challenge much respect. Come, Desdemona,
  Once more, well met at Cyprus.   205
                (*Exeunt* OTHELLO *and* DESDEMONA *and all but* IAGO *and* RODERIGO.)
IAGO (*to an* ATTENDANT): Do thou meet me presently at the harbour. (*To* ROD.)
  Come hither. If thou be'st valiant,—as, they say, base men being in love have then
  a nobility in their natures more than is native to them,—list me. The lieutenant
  tonight watches on the court of guard.°—First, I must tell thee this—Desdemona
  is directly in love with him.   210

---

193. set down the pegs: lower the pitch of the strings, i.e., disturb the harmony. **209. court of guard:** guardhouse.

ROD: With him! why 'tis not possible.

IAGO: Lay thy finger thus, and let thy soul be instructed. Mark me with what violence she first loved the Moor, but for bragging and telling her fantastical lies: and will she love him still for prating? let not thy discreet heart think it. Her eye must be fed; and what delight shall she have to look on the devil? When the blood   215 is made dull with the act of sport, there should be, again to inflame it and to give satiety a fresh appetite, loveliness in favour, sympathy in years, manners and beauties; all which the Moor is defective in: now, for want of these required conveniences, her delicate tenderness will find itself abused, begin to heave the gorge, disrelish and abhor the Moor; very nature will instruct her in it and compel   220 her to some second choice. Now, sir, this granted,—as it is a most pregnant and unforced position—who stands so eminent in the degree of this fortune as Cassio does? a knave very voluble; no further conscionable° than in putting on the mere form of civil and humane seeming, for the better compassing of his salt° and most hidden loose affection? why, none; why, none: a slipper° and subtle   225 knave, a finder of occasions, that has an eye can stamp and counterfeit advantages, though true advantage never present itself; a devilish knave. Besides, the knave is handsome, young, and hath all those requisites in him that folly and green minds look after: a pestilent complete knave; and the woman hath found him already.   230

ROD: I cannot believe that in her; she's full of most blessed condition.

IAGO: Blessed fig's-end! the wine she drinks is made of grapes: if she had been blessed, she would never have loved the Moor. Blessed pudding! Didst thou not see her paddle with the palm of his hand? didst not mark that?

ROD: Yes, that I did; but that was but courtesy.   235

IAGO: Lechery, by this hand; an index and obscure prologue to the history of lust and foul thoughts. They met so near with their lips that their breaths embraced together. Villainous thoughts, Roderigo! when these mutualities so marshall the way, hard at hand comes the master and main exercise, the incorporate conclusion. Pish! But, sir, be you ruled by me: I have brought you from Venice. Watch   240 you to-night; for the command, I'll lay't upon you. Cassio knows you not. I'll not be far from you: do you find some occasion to anger Cassio, either by speaking too loud, or tainting° his discipline; or from what other course you please, which the time shall more favourably minister.

ROD: Well.   245

IAGO: Sir, he is rash and very sudden in choler, and haply may strike at you: provoke him, that he may; for even out of that will I cause these of Cyprus to mutiny; whose qualification° shall come into no true taste again but by the displanting of Cassio. So shall you have a shorter journey to your desires by the means I shall then have to prefer them; and the impediment most profitably removed, without   250 the which there were no expectation of our prosperity.

---

223. conscionable: conscientious.   **224. salt:** licentious.   **225. slipper:** slippery.   **243. tainting:** disparaging.   **248. qualification:** appeasement.

Rod: I will do this if I can bring it to any opportunity.

Iago: I warrant thee. Meet me by and by° at the citadel: I must fetch his necessaries ashore. Farewell.

Rod: Adieu. (*Exit.*) 255

Iago: That Cassio loves her, I do well believe 't;
That she loves him, 'tis apt° and of great credit°:
The Moor, howbeit that I endure him not,
Is of a constant, loving, noble nature,
And I dare think he'll prove to Desdemona 260
A most dear husband. Now I do love her too;
Not out of absolute lust, though peradventure
I stand accountant for as great a sin,
But partly led to diet my revenge,
For that I do suspect the lusty Moor 265
Hath leap'd into my seat; the thought whereof
Doth, like a poisonous mineral, gnaw my inwards;
And nothing can or shall content my soul
Till I am even'd with him, wife for wife,
Or failing so, yet that I put the Moor 270
At least into a jealousy so strong
That judgement cannot cure. Which thing to do,
If this poor trash° of Venice, whom I trash°
For his quick hunting, stand the putting on,°
I'll have Michael Cassio on the hip,° 275
Abuse him to the Moor in the rank garb—
For I fear Cassio with my night-cap too—
Make the Moor thank me, love me and reward me,
For making him egregiously an ass
And practicing upon his peace and quiet 280
Even to madness. 'Tis here, but yet confus'd:
Knavery's plain face is never seen till us'd. (*Exit.*)

Scene II.

A street.

(*Enter Othello's* Herald *with a proclamation.*)

Her: It is Othello's pleasure, our noble and valiant general, that, upon certain tidings now arrived, importing the mere perdition° of the Turkish fleet, every man
put himself into triumph; some to dance, some to make bonfires, each man to
what sport and revels his addiction leads him: for, besides these beneficial news, it

---

253. by and by: immediately. **257. apt:** probable. **257. credit:** credibility. **273. trash:** worthless
thing (Roderigo). **273. trash:** hold in check. **274. putting on:** incitement to quarrel. **275. on the
hip:** at my mercy (wrestling term). **II.ii. 2. mere perdition:** complete destruction.

is the celebration of his nuptial. So much was his pleasure should be proclaimed.　5
All offices° are open, and there is full liberty of feasting from this present hour of
five till the bell have told eleven. Heaven bless the isle of Cyprus and our general
Othello!　　　　　　　　　　　　　　　　　　　　　　　　　　　　　(*Exit.*)

SCENE III.

A hall in the castle.

(*Enter* OTHELLO, DESDEMONA, CASSIO, *and* ATTENDANTS.)

OTH:　Good Michael, look you to the guard to-night:
Let's teach ourselves that honourable stop,°
Not to outsport discretion.

CAS:　Iago hath direction what to do;
But, notwithstanding, with my personal eye　　　　　　　　　　　　　　5
Will I look to 't.

OTH:　　　　　　　　Iago is most honest.
Michael, goodnight: to-morrow with your earliest
Let me have speech with you. (*To* DESDEMONA) Come, my dear love,
The purchase made, the fruits to ensue;
That profit's yet to come 'tween me and you.　　　　　　　　　　　　10
Good night.　　　　　　　(*Exit* OTHELLO, *with* DESDEMONA *and* ATTENDANTS.]

(*Enter* IAGO.)

CAS:　Welcome, Iago; we must to the watch.

IAGO:　Not this hour, lieutenant; 'tis not yet ten o' the clock. Our general cast° us
thus early for the love of his Desdemona; who let us not therefore blame: he hath
not yet made wanton the night with her; and she is sport for Jove.　　　　15

CAS:　She's a most exquisite lady.

IAGO:　And, I'll warrant her, full of game.

CAS:　Indeed, she's a most fresh and delicate creature.

IAGO:　What an eye she has! methinks it sounds a parley of provocation.

CAS:　An inviting eye; and yet methinks right modest.　　　　　　　　20

IAGO:　And when she speaks, is it not an alarum to love?

CAS:　She is indeed perfection.

IAGO:　Well, happiness to their sheets! Come, lieutenant, I have a stoup° of wine;
and here without are a brace of Cyprus gallants that would fain have a measure to
the health of black Othello.　　　　　　　　　　　　　　　　　　　25

CAS:　Not to-night, good Iago: I have very poor and unhappy brains for drinking: I
could well wish courtesy would invent some other custom of entertainment.

IAGO:　O, they are our friends; but one cup: I'll drink for you.

6. offices: rooms where food and drink were kept.　**II.iii. 2. stop:** restraint.　**13. cast:** dismissed.
23. stoup: measure of liquor, two quarts.

CAS: I have drunk but one cup to-night, and that was craftily qualified° too, and,
behold, what innovation° it makes here°: I am unfortunate in the infirmity, and 30
dare not task my weakness with any more.

IAGO: What, man! 'tis a night of revels: the gallants desire it.

CAS: Where are they?

IAGO: Here at the door; I pray you, call them in.

CAS: I'll do 't; but it dislikes me. (*Exit.*) 35

IAGO: If I can fasten but one cup upon him,
With that which he hath drunk to-night already,
He'll be as full of quarrel and offence
As my young mistress' dog. Now, my sick fool Roderigo,
Whom love hath turn'd almost the wrong side out, 40
To Desdemona hath to-night carous'd
Potations pottle-deep°; and he's to watch:
Three lads of Cyprus, noble swelling spirits,
That hold their honours in a wary distance,°
The very elements° of this warlike isle, 45
Have I to-night fluster'd with flowing cups,
And they watch° too. Now, 'mongst this flock of drunkards,
Am I to put our Cassio in some action
That may offend the isle.—But here they come:

(*Enter* CASSIO, MONTANO, *and* GENTLEMEN; SERVANTS *following with wine.*)

If consequence do but approve° my dream, 50
My boat sails freely, both with wind and stream.

CAS: 'Fore God, they have given me a rouse° already.

MON: Good faith, a little one; not past a pint, as I am a soldier.

IAGO: Some wine, ho!
(*Sings*) And let me the canakin° clink, clink; 55
And let me the canakin clink:
A soldier's a man;
A life's but a span;
Why, then, let a soldier drink.
Some wine, boys! 60

CAS: 'Fore God, an excellent song.

IAGO: I learned it in England, where, indeed, they are most potent in potting: your
Dane, your German, and your swag-bellied Hollander—Drink, ho!—are nothing to your English.

CAS: Is your Englishman so expert in his drinking? 65

---

29. qualified: diluted. **30. innovation:** disturbance. **30. here:** i.e., in Cassio's head. **42. pottle-
deep:** to the bottom of the tankard. **44. hold . . . distance:** i.e., are extremely sensitive of their honor.
45. very elements: true representatives. **47. watch:** are members of the guard. **50. approve:** confirm. **52. rouse:** full draft of liquor. **55. canakin:** small drinking vessel.

IAGO: Why, he drinks you, with facility, your Dane dead drunk; he sweats not to overthrow your Almain°; he gives your Hollander a vomit, ere the next pottle can be filled.

CAS: To the health of our general!

MON: I am for it, lieutenant; and I'll do you justice.°   70

IAGO: O sweet England! (*Sings.*)
　　King Stephen was a worthy peer,
　　　　His breeches cost him but a crown;
　　He held them sixpence all too dear,
　　　　With that he call'd the tailor lown.°   75
　　He was a wight of high renown,
　　　　And thou art but of low degree:
　　'Tis pride that pulls the country down;
　　　　Then take thine auld cloak about thee.
　　Some wine, ho!   80

CAS: Why, this is a more exquisite song than the other.

IAGO: Will you hear't again?

CAS: No; for I hold him to be unworthy of his place that does those things. Well, God's above all; and there be souls must be saved, and there be souls must not be saved.   85

IAGO: It's true, good lieutenant.

CAS: For mine own part,—no offence to the general, nor any man of quality,—I hope to be saved.

IAGO: And so do I too, lieutenant.

CAS: Ay, but, by your leave, not before me; the lieutenant is to be saved before the   90
ancient. Let's have no more of this; let 's to our affairs.—God forgive us our sins!—Gentlemen, let's look to our business. Do not think, gentlemen, I am drunk: this is my ancient; this is my right hand, and this is my left: I am not drunk now; I can stand well enough, and speak well enough.

ALL: Excellent well.   95

CAS: Why, very well then; you must not think then that I am drunk.   (*Exit.*)

MON: To th' platform, masters; come, let's set the watch.

IAGO: You see this fellow that is gone before;
　　He's soldier fit to stand by Caesar
　　And give direction: and do but see his vice;   100
　　'Tis to his virtue a just equinox,°
　　The one as long as th' other: 'tis pity of him.
　　I fear the trust Othello puts him in,
　　On some odd time of his infirmity,
　　Will shake this island.

MON: But is he often thus?   105

IAGO: 'Tis evermore the prologue to his sleep:

---

67. Almain: German.   **70. I'll . . . justice:** i.e., drink as much as you.   **75. lown:** lout, loon.
101. equinox: equal length of days and nights; used figuratively to mean "counterpart."

He'll watch the horologe° a double set,°
If drink rock not his cradle.
MON: It were well
The general were put in mind of it.
Perhaps he sees it not; or his good nature   110
Prizes the virtue that appears in Cassio,
And looks not on his evils: is not this true?

        (*Enter* RODERIGO.)

IAGO (*Aside to him*):   How now, Roderigo!
I pray you, after the lieutenant; go.   (*Exit* RODERIGO.)
MON: And 'tis great pity that the noble Moor   115
Should hazard such a place as his own second
With one of an ingraft° infirmity:
It were an honest action to say
So to the Moor.
IAGO: Not I, for this fair island:
I do love Cassio well; and would do much   120
To cure him of this evil—But, hark! what noise? (*Cry within:* "Help! help!")

        (*Enter* CASSIO, *pursuing* RODERIGO.)

CAS: 'Zounds, you rogue! you rascal!
MON: What's the matter, lieutenant?
CAS: A knave teach me my duty!
I'll beat the knave into a twiggen° bottle.
ROD: Beat me!
CAS: Dost thou prate, rogue? (*Striking* RODERIGO.)
MON: Nay, good lieutenant; (*Staying him.*)   125
I pray you, sir, hold your hand.
CAS: Let me go, sir,
Or I'll knock you o'er the mazzard.°
MON: Come, come, you're drunk.
CAS: Drunk! (*They fight.*)
IAGO (*aside to* RODERIGO):   Away, I say; go out, and cry a mutiny.

                    (*Exit* RODERIGO.)

Nay, good lieutenant,—God's will, gentlemen;—   130
Help, ho!—Lieutenant,—sir,—Montano,—sir,—
Help, masters!—Here's a goodly watch indeed! (*Bell rings.*)
Who's that which rings the bell?—Diablo,° ho!
The town will rise°: God's will, lieutenant, hold!
You'll be asham'd for ever.

---

107. horologe: clock. **107. double set:** twice around. **117. ingraft:** ingrafted, inveterate. **124. twiggen:** covered with woven twigs. **127. mazzard:** head. **133. Diablo:** the devil. **134. rise:** grow riotous.

(*Enter* OTHELLO *and* ATTENDANTS.)

OTH: What is the matter here?   135
MON: 'Zounds, I bleed still; I am hurt to th' death.
  He dies! (*Thrusts at* CASSIO.)
OTH: Hold, for your lives!
IAGO: Hold, ho! Lieutenant,—sir,—Montano,—gentlemen,—
  Have your forgot all sense of place and duty?   140
  Hold! the general speaks to you; hold, for shame!
OTH: Why, how now, ho! from whence ariseth this?
  Are we turn'd Turks° and to ourselves do that
  Which heaven hath forbid the Ottomites?
  For Christian shame, put by this barbarous brawl: 145
  He that stirs next to carve for° his own rage
  Holds his soul light; he dies upon his motion.
  Silence that dreadful bell: it frights the isle
  From her propriety.° What is the matter, masters?
  Honest Iago, that looks dead with grieving,   150
  Speak, who began this? on thy love, I charge thee.
IAGO: I do not know: friends all but now, even now,
  In quarter,° and in terms like bride and groom
  Devesting them for bed; and then, but now—
  As if some planet had unwitted men—   155
  Swords out, and tilting one at other's breast,
  In opposition bloody. I cannot speak
  Any beginning to this peevish odds°;
  And would in action glorious I had lost
  Those legs that brought me to a part of it!   160
OTH: How comes it, Michael, you are thus forgot?
CAS: I pray you, pardon me; I cannot speak.
OTH: Worthy Montano, you were wont to be civil;
  The gravity and stillness of your youth
  The world hath noted, and your name is great   165
  In mouths of wisest censure°: what's the matter,
  That you unlace° your reputation thus
  And spend your rich opinion for the name
  Of a night-brawler? give me answer to it.
MON: Worthy Othello, I am hurt to danger: 170
  Your officer, Iago, can inform you,—
  While I spare speech, which something now offends me,—
  Of all that I do know: nor know I aught

---

143. **turn'd Turks:** changed completely for the worse; proverbial.   146. **carve for:** indulge.
149. **propriety:** proper state or condition.   153. **In quarter:** on terms.   158. **peevish odds:** childish
quarrel.   166. **censure:** judgment.   167. **unlace:** degrade.

By me that's said or done amiss this night;
Unless self-charity be sometimes a vice,   175
And to defend ourselves it be a sin
When violence assails us.
OTH: Now, by heaven,
My blood begins my safer guides to rule;
And passion, having my best judgement collied,°
Assays to lead the way: if I once stir,   180
Or do but lift this arm, the best of you
Shall sink in my rebuke. Give me to know
How this foul rout began, who set it on;
And he that is approv'd in° this offence,
Though he had twinn'd with me, both at birth,   185
Shall lose me. What! in a town of war,
Yet wild, the people's hearts brimful of fear,
To manage private and domestic quarrel,
In night, and on the court and guard° of safety!
'Tis monstrous. Iago, who began 't?   190
MON: If partially affin'd,° or leagu'd in office,
Thou dost deliver more or less than truth,
Thou art no soldier.
IAGO: Touch me not so near:
I had rather have this tongue cut from my mouth
Than it should do offence to Michael Cassio;   195
Yet, I persuade myself, to speak the truth,
Shall nothing wrong him. Thus it is, general.
Montano and myself being in speech,
There comes a fellow crying out for help;
And Cassio following him with determin'd sword,
To execute° upon him. Sir, this gentleman   200
Steps in to Cassio, and entreats his pause:
Myself the crying fellow did pursue,
Lest by his clamour—as it so fell out—
The town might fall in fright: he, swift of foot,   205
Outran my purpose; and I return'd the rather
For that I heard the clink and fall of swords,
And Cassio high in oath; which till to-night
I ne'er might say before. When I came back—
For this was brief—I found them close together,   210
At blow and thrust; even as again they were
When you yourself did part them.
More of this matter cannot I report:

---

179. **collied:** darkened.   184. **approv'd in:** found guilty of.   189. **court and guard:** spot and guarding place, i.e., the main guardhouse.   191. **affin'd:** bound by a tie.   201. **execute:** give effect to (his anger).

But men are men; the best sometimes forget:
Though Cassio did some little wrong to him, 215
As men in rage strike those that wish them best,
Yet surely, Cassio, I believe, receive'd
From him that fled some strange indignity,
Which patience could not pass.

OTH: I know, Iago,
Thy honesty and love doth mince this matter, 220
Making it light to Cassio. Cassio, I love thee;
But never more be officer of mine.

             (*Enter* DESDEMONA, *attended.*)

Look, if my gentle love be not rais'd up!
I'll make thee an example.

DES: What's the matter?

OTH: All's well now, sweeting; come away to bed. 225
Sir, for your hurts, myself will be your surgeon:
Lead him off. (*To* MONTANO, *who is led off.*]
Iago, look with care about the town,
And silence those whom this vile brawl distracted.
Come, Desdemona: 'tis the soldier's life 230
To have their balmy slumbers wak'd with strife.

         (*Exit with all but* IAGO *and* CASSIO.)

IAGO: What, are you hurt, lieutenant?

CAS: Ay, past all surgery.

IAGO: Marry, God forbid!

CAS: Reputation, reputation, reputation! O, I have lost my reputation! I have lost 235
the immortal part of myself, and what remains is bestial. My reputation, Iago, my
reputation!

IAGO: As I am an honest man, I thought you had received some bodily wound;
there is more sense in that than in reputation. Reputation is an idle and most false
imposition; oft got without merit, and lost without deserving: you have lost no 240
reputation at all, unless you repute yourself such a loser. What, man! there are
ways to recover the general again: you are but now cast in his mood, a punishment more in policy than in malice; even so as one would beat his offenceless dog
to affright an imperious lion: sue to him again, and he 's yours.

CAS: I will rather sue to be despised than to deceive so good a commander with so 245
slight, so drunken, and so indiscreet an officer. Drunk? and speak parrot?° and
squabble? swagger? swear? and discourse fustian° with one's own shadow? O
thou invisible spirit of wine, if thou has no name to be known by, let us call thee
devil!

IAGO: What was he that you followed with your sword? What had he done to you? 250

CAS: I know not.

---

246. speak parrot: talk nonsense.   **247. discourse fustian:** talk nonsense.

IAGO: Is't possible?

CAS: I remember a mass of things, but nothing distinctly; a quarrel, but nothing
wherefore. O God, that men should put an enemy in their mouths to steal away
their brains! that we should, with joy, pleasance, revel and applause, transform   255
ourselves into beasts!

IAGO: Why, but you are now well enough: how came you thus recovered?

CAS: It hath pleased the devil drunkenness to give place to the devil wrath: one
unperfectness° shows me another, to make me frankly despise myself.

IAGO: Come, you are too severe a moraler: as the time, the place, and the condi-   260
tion of this country stands, I could heartily wish this had not befallen; but, since it
is as it is, mend it for your own good.

CAS: I will ask him for my place again; he shall tell me I am a drunkard! Had I
as many mouths as Hydra,° such an answer would stop them all. To be now a sensible man, by and by a fool, and presently a beast! O strange! Every inordinate   265
cup is unblessed and the ingredient is a devil.

IAGO: Come, come, good wine is a good familiar creature, if it be well used:
exclaim no more against it. And, good lieutenant, I think you think I love you.

CAS: I have well approved° it, sir. I drunk!

IAGO: You or any man living may be a drunk at a time, man. I'll tell you what you   270
shall do. Our general's wife is now the general: I may say so in this respect, for
that he hath devoted and given up himself to the contemplation, mark, and
denotement° of her parts and graces: confess yourself freely to her; importune
her help to put you in your place again: she is of so free, so kind, so apt, so blessed
a dispositon, she holds it a vice in her goodness not to do more than she is   275
requested: this broken joint between you and her husband entreat her to
splinter°; and, my fortunes against any lay° worth naming, this crack of your love
shall grow stronger than it was before.

CAS: You advise me well.

IAGO: I protest, in the sincerity of love and honest kindness.   280

CAS: I think it freely; and betimes in the morning I will beseech the virtuous Desdemona to undertake for me: I am desperate of my fortunes if they check° me
here.

IAGO: You are in the right. Good night, lieutenant; I must to the watch.

CAS: Good night, honest Iago.   (*Exit* CASSIO.)   285

IAGO: And what's he then that says I play the villain?
When this advice is free I give and honest,
Probal° to thinking and indeed the course
To win the Moor again? For 'tis most easy
Th' inclining° Desdemona to subdue°   290
In any honest suit: she's fram'd as fruitful

---

259. unperfectness: imperfection.   **264. Hydra:** a monster with many heads, slain by Hercules as
the second of his twelve labors.   **269. approved:** proved.   **273. denotement:** observation.
277. splinter: bind with splints.   **277. lay:** stake, wager.   **282. check:** repulse.   **288. Probal:** probable.   **290. inclining:** favorably disposed.   **290. subdue:** persuade.

As the free elements. And then for her
To win the Moor—were 't to renounce his baptism,
All seals and symbols of redeemed sin,
His soul is so enfetter'd to her love,   295
That she may make, unmake, do what she list,
Even as her appetite shall play the god
With his weak function. How am I then a villain
To counsel Cassio to this parallel° course,
Directly to his good? Divinity of hell!   300
When devils will the blackest sins put on,°
They do suggest° at first with heavenly shows,
As I do now; for whiles this honest fool
Plies Desdemona to repair his fortunes
And she for him pleads strongly to the Moor,   305
I'll pour this pestilence into his ear,
That she repeals him° for her body's lust;
And by how much she strives to do him good,
She shall under her credit with the Moor,
So will I turn her virtue into pitch,   310
And out of her own goodness make the net
That shall enmesh them all.

         (*Enter* RODERIGO.)

                        How now, Roderigo!

ROD: I do not follow here in the chase, not like a hound that hunts, but one that
fills up the cry.° My money is almost spent; I have been tonight exceedingly
well cudgelléd; and I think the issue will be, I shall have so much experience   315
for my pains, and so, with no money at all and a little more wit, return again to
Venice.

IAGO: How poor are they that have not patience!
What wound did ever heal but by degrees?
Thou know'st we work by wit, and not by witchcraft;   320
And wit depends on dilatory time.
Does 't not go well? Cassio hath beaten thee,
And thou, by that small hurt, hast cashier'd° Cassio:
Though other things grow fair against the sun,
Yet fruits that blossom first will first be ripe: 325
Content thyself awhile. By th' mass, 'tis morning;
Pleasure and action make the hours seem short.
Retire thee; go where thou art billeted:
Away, I say; thou shalt know more hereafter:
Nay, get thee gone.   (*Exit* RODERIGO.)

---

299. parallel: probably, corresponding to his best interest. **301. put on:** further. **302. suggest:**
tempt. **307. repeals him:** i.e., attempts to get him restored. **314. cry:** pack. **323. cashier'd:** dismissed from service.

Two things are to be done: 330
My wife must move for Cassio to her mistress;
I'll set her on;
Myself the while to draw the Moor apart,
And bring him jump° when he may Cassio find
Soliciting his wife: ay, that's the way: 335
Dull not device by coldness and delay. (*Exit.*)

ACT III

SCENE I.

Before the castle.

(*Enter* CASSIO *and* MUSICIANS.)

CAS: Masters, play here; I will content° your pains;
Something that's brief; and bid "Good morrow, general." (*They play.*)

(*Enter* CLOWN.)

CLO: Why, masters, have your instruments been in Naples, that they speak i' the
nose° thus?
FIRST MUS: How, sir, how! 5
CLO: Are these, I pray you, wind-instruments?
FIRST MUS: Ay, marry, are they, sir.
CLO: O, thereby hangs a tail.
FIRST MUS: Whereby hangs a tale,° sir?
CLO: Marry, sir, by many a wind-instrument that I know. But, masters, here 's 10
money for you: and the general so likes your music, that he desires you, for love's
sake, to make no more noise with it.
FIRST MUS: Well, sir, we will not.
CLO: If you have any music that may not be heard, to 't again: but, as they say, to
hear music the general does not greatly care. 15
FIRST MUS: We have none such, sir.
CLO: Then put up your pipes in your bag, for I'll away: go; vanish into air;
away! (*Exeunt* MUSICIANS.)
CAS: Dost thou hear, my honest friend?
CLO: No, I hear not your honest friend; I hear you. 20
CAS: Prithee, keep up thy quillets. There's a poor piece of gold for thee: if the
gentlewoman that attends the general's wife be stirring, tell her there 's one Cas-
sio entreats her a little favour of speech: wilt thou do this?
CLO: She is stirring, sir: if she will stir hither, I shall seem to notify unto her.
CAS: Do, good my friend. (*Exit* CLOWN.)

334. jump: precisely.   **III.i. 1. content:** reward.   **3–4. speak i' the nose:** i.e., like Neapolitans, who
spoke a nasal dialect (with a joke on syphilis, which attacks the nose).   **9. tale:** pun on *tail*, a wind instrument of sorts.

(*Enter* IAGO.)

In happy time, Iago.   25

IAGO: You have not been a-bed, then?

CAS: Why, no; the day had broke
Before we parted. I have made bold, Iago,
To send in to your wife: my suit to her
Is, that she will to virtuous Desdemona   30
Procure me some access.

IAGO: I'll send her to you presently;
And I'll devise a means to draw the Moor
Out of the way, that your converse and business
May be more free.

CAS: I humbly thank you for 't.   (*Exit* IAGO.)

I never knew   35
A Florentine more kind and honest.

(*Enter* EMILIA.)

EMIL: Good morrow, good lieutenant: I am sorry
For your displeasure; but all will sure be well.
The general and his wife are talking of it;
And she speaks for you stoutly: the Moor replies,   40
That he you hurt is of great fame in Cyprus
And great affinity° and that in wholesome wisdom
He might not but refuse you, but he protests he loves you
And needs no other suitor but his likings
To take the safest occasion by the front°   45
To bring you in again.

CAS: Yet, I beseech you,
If you think fit, or that it may be done,
Give me advantage of some brief discourse
With Desdemona alone.

EMIL: Pray you, come in:
I will bestow you where you shall have time   50
To speak your bosom freely.

CAS: I am much bound to you.   (*Exeunt.*)

SCENE II.

A room in the castle.

(*Enter* OTHELLO, IAGO, *and* GENTLEMEN.)

OTH: These letters give, Iago, to the pilot;
And by him do my duties to the senate:

---

42. affinity: kindred, family connection.   **45. by the front:** i.e., by the forelock.

That done, I will be walking on the works°:
Repair there to me.
IAGO: Well, my good lord, I'll do 't.
OTH: This fortification, gentlemen, shall we see 't?   5
GENT: We'll wait upon your lordship.   (*Exeunt.*)

SCENE III.

The garden of the castle.

(*Enter* DESDEMONA, CASSIO, *and* EMILIA.)

DES: Be thou assur'd, good Cassio, I will do
All my abilities in thy behalf.
EMIL: Good madam, do: I warrant it grieves my husband,
As if the case were his.
DES: O, that 's an honest fellow. Do not doubt, Cassio,   5
But I will have my lord and you again
As friendly as you were.
CAS: Bounteous madam,
Whatever shall become of Michael Cassio,
He's never any thing but your true servant.
DES: I know 't; I thank you. You do love my lord: 10
You have known him long; and be you well assur'd
He shall in strangeness° stand no farther off
Than in a politic distance.
CAS: Ay, but lady,
That policy may either last so long
Or feed upon such nice and waterish diet,   15
Or breed itself so out of circumstance,°
That, I being absent and my place supplied,
My general will forget my love and service.
DES: Do not doubt° that; before Emilia here
I give thee warrant of thy place: assure thee,   20
If I do vow a friendship, I'll perform it
To the last article: my lord shall never rest;
I'll watch him tame° and talk him out of patience;
His bed shall seem a school, his board a shrift°;
I'll intermingle every thing he does   25
With Cassio's suit: therefore be merry, Cassio;
For thy solicitor shall rather die
Than give thy cause away.°

III.ii. 3. works: earthworks, fortifications. **III.iii. 12. strangeness:** distant behavior. **16. breed . . . circumstance:** increase itself so on account of accidents. **19. doubt:** fear. **23. watch him tame:** tame
him by keeping him from sleeping (a term from falconry). **24. shrift:** confessional. **28. away:** up.

(*Enter* OTHELLO *and* IAGO *at a distance.*)

EMIL: Madam, here comes my lord.

CAS: Madam, I'll take my leave.   30

DES: Why, stay, and hear me speak.

CAS: Madam, not now: I am very ill at ease,
Unfit for mine own purposes.

DES: Well, do your discretion.   (*Exit* CASSIO.)

IAGO: Ha! I like not that.

OTH: What dost thou say?   35

IAGO: Nothing, my lord: or if—I know not what.

OTH: Was not that Cassio parted from my wife?

IAGO: Cassio, my lord! No, sure, I cannot think it,
That he would steal away so guilty-like,
Seeing you coming.

OTH: I do believe 'twas he.   40

DES: How now, my lord!
I have been talking with a suitor here,
A man that languishes in your displeasure.

OTH: Who is 't you mean?

DES: Why, your lieutenant, Cassio. Good my lord,   45
If I have any grace or power to move you,
His present reconciliation take;
For if he be not one that truly loves you,
That errs in ignorance and not in cunning,
I have no judgement in an honest face: 50
I prithee, call him back.

OTH: Went he hence now?

DES: Ay, sooth; so humbled
That he hath left part of his grief with me,
To suffer with him. Good love, call him back.

OTH: Not now, sweet Desdemona; some other time.   55

DES: But shall 't be shortly?

OTH: The sooner, sweet, for you.

DES: Shall 't be to-night at supper?

OTH: No, not to-night.

DES: To-morrow dinner, then?

OTH: I shall not dine at home;
I meet the captains at the citadel.

DES: Why, then, to-morrow night; or Tuesday morn;   60
On Tuesday noon, or night; on Wednesday morn:
I prithee, name the time, but let it not
Exceed three days: in faith, he's penitent;
And yet his trespass, in our common reason°—

64. common reason: everyday judgments.

Save that, they say, the wars must make examples 65
Out of their best—is not almost a fault
T' incur a private check. When shall he come?
Tell me, Othello: I wonder in my soul,
What you would ask me, that I should deny,
Or stand so mamm'ring on.° What! Michael Cassio, 70
That came a-wooing with you, and so many a time,
When I have spoke of you dispraisingly,
Hath ta'en your part; to have so much to do
To bring him in! Trust me, I could do much,—
OTH: Prithee, no more: let him come when he will; 75
I will deny thee nothing.
DES: Why, this is not a boon;
'Tis as I should entreat you wear your gloves,
Or feed on nourishing dishes, or keep you warm,
Or sue to you to do a peculiar profit
To your own person: nay, when I have a suit 80
Wherein I mean to touch your love indeed,
It shall be full of poise° and difficult weight
And fearful to be granted.
OTH: I will deny thee nothing:
Whereon, I do beseech thee, grant me this,
To leave me but a little to myself. 85
DES: Shall I deny you? no: farewell, my lord.
OTH: Farewell, my Desdemona: I'll come to thee straight.
DES: Emilia, come. Be as your fancies teach you;
Whate'er you be, I am obedient.   (*Exit with* EMILIA.)
OTH: Excellent wretch!° Perdition catch my soul, 90
But I do love thee! and when I love thee not,
Chaos is come again.
IAGO: My noble lord,—
OTH: What dost thou say, Iago?
IAGO: Did Michael Cassio, when you woo'd my lady,
Know of your love? 95
OTH: He did, from first to last: why dost thou ask?
IAGO: But for a satisfaction of my thought;
No further harm.
OTH: Why of thy thought, Iago?
IAGO: I did not think he had been acquainted with her.
OTH: O, yes; and went between us very oft. 100
IAGO: Indeed!
OTH: Indeed! ay, indeed: discern'st thou aught in that?
Is he not honest?

---

70. mamm'ring on: wavering. **82. poise:** weight, heaviness. **90. wretch:** term of affectionate endearment with a connotation of pity.

IAGO:	Honest, my lord!
OTH:	Honest! ay, honest.
IAGO:	My lord, for aught I know.
OTH:	What dost thou think?
IAGO:	Think, my lord!
OTH:	Think, my lord!

105

By heaven, he echoes me,
As if there were some monster in his thought
Too hideous to be shown. Thou dost mean something:
I heard thee say even now, thou lik'st not that,
When Cassio left my wife: what didst not like? 110
And when I told thee he was of my counsel
In my whole course of wooing, thou criedst "Indeed!"
And didst contract and purse thy brow together,
As if thou then hadst shut up in thy brain
Some horrible conceit: if thou dost love me, 115
Show me thy thought.

IAGO: My lord, you know I love you.

OTH: I think thou dost;
And, for I know thou 'rt full of love and honesty,
And weigh'st thy words before thou giv'st them breath,
Therefore these stops of thine fright me more: 120
For such things in a false disloyal knave
Are tricks of custom, but in a man that's just
They 're close delations,° working from the heart
That passion cannot rule.

IAGO: For Michael Cassio,
I dare be sworn I think that he is honest. 125

OTH: I think so too.

IAGO: Men should be what they seem;
Or those that be not, would they might seem none!

OTH: Certain, men should be what they seem.

IAGO: Why, then, I think Cassio 's an honest man.

OTH: Nay, yet there 's more in this: 130
I prithee, speak to me as to thy thinkings,
As thou dost ruminate, and give thy worst of thoughts
The worst of words.

IAGO: Good my lord, pardon me:
Though I am bound to every act of duty,
I am not bound to that all slaves are free to. 135
Utter my thoughts? Why, say they are vile and false:
As where 's that palace whereinto foul things
Sometimes intrude not? who has a breast so pure,

---

123. close delations: secret or involuntary accusations.

But some uncleanly apprehensions
Keep leets° and law-days° and in sessions sit   140
With meditations lawful?
OTH: Thou dost conspire against thy friend, Iago,
If thou but think'st him wrong'd and mak'st his ear
A stranger to thy thoughts.
IAGO: I do beseech you—
Though I perchance am vicious° in my guess,   145
As, I confess, it is my nature's plague
To spy into abuses, and oft my jealousy°
Shapes faults that are not—that your wisdom yet,
From one that so imperfectly conceits,°
Would take no notice, nor build yourself a trouble   150
Out of his scattering and unsure observance.
It were not for your quiet nor your good,
Nor for my manhood, honesty, or wisdom,
To let you know my thoughts.
OTH: What dost thou mean?
IAGO: Good name in man and woman, dear my lord,   155
Is the immediate jewel of their souls:
Who steals my purse steals trash: 'tis something, nothing;
'Twas mine, 'tis his, and has been slave to thousands;
But he that filches from me my good name
Robs me of that which not enriches him   160
And makes me poor indeed.
OTH: By heaven, I'll know thy thoughts.
IAGO: You cannot, if my heart were in your hand;
Nor shall not, whilst 'tis in my custody.
OTH: Ha!
IAGO: Oh, beware, my lord, of jealousy;   165
It is the green-ey'd monster which doth mock
The meat it feeds on: that cuckold lives in bliss
Who certain of his fate, loves not his wronger;
But, O, what damned minutes tells her o'er
Who dotes, yet doubts, suspects, yet strongly loves!   170
OTH: O misery!
IAGO: Poor and content is rich and rich enough,
But riches fineless° is as poor as winter
To him that ever fears he shall be poor.
Good God, the souls of all my tribe defend   175
From jealousy!
OTH: Why, why is this?

---

140. Keep leets: hold courts.   **140. law-days:** court days.   **145. vicious:** wrong.   **147. jealousy:** suspicion of evil.   **149. conceits:** judges.   **173. fineless:** boundless.

Think'st thou I'd make a life of jealousy,
To follow still the changes of the moon
With fresh suspicions? No; to be once in doubt
Is once to be resolv'd: exchange me for a goat,   180
When I shall turn the business of my soul
To such exsufflicate and blown° surmises,
Matching thy inference. 'Tis not to make me jealous
To say my wife is fair, feeds well, loves company,
Is free of speech, sings, plays and dances well;   185
Where virtue is, these are more virtuous;
Nor from mine own weak merits will I draw
The smallest fear or doubt of her revolt:
For she had eyes, and chose me. No, Iago;
I'll see before I doubt; when I doubt, prove;   190
And on the proof, there is no more but this,—
Away at once with love or jealousy!

IAGO: I am glad of this; for now I shall have reason
To show the love and duty that I bear you
With franker spirit: therefore, as I am bound,   195
Receive it from me. I speak not yet of proof.
Look to your wife; observe her well with Cassio;
Wear your eye thus, not jealous nor secure.°
I would not have your free and noble nature,
Out of self-bounty,° be abus'd; look to 't: 200
I know our country disposition well;
In Venice they do let heaven see the pranks
They dare not show their husbands; their best conscience
Is not to leave 't undone, but keep 't unknown.

OTH: Dost thou say so?   205

IAGO: She did deceive her father, marrying you;
And when she seem'd to shake and fear your looks,
She lov'd them most.

OTH: And so she did.

IAGO: Why, go to then;
She that, so young, could give out such a seeming,°
To seel° her father's eyes up close as oak—   210
He thought 'twas witchcraft—but I am much to blame;
I humbly do beseech you of your pardon
For too much loving you.

OTH: I am bound to thee for ever.

IAGO: I see this hath a little dash'd your spirits.

---

182. exsufflicate and blown: unsubstantial and inflated, flyblown.   **198. secure:** free from uneasiness.
200. self-bounty: inherent or natural goodness.   **209. seeming:** false appearance.   **210. seel:** blind (a
term from falconry).

OTH: Not a jot, not a jot.

IAGO: I' faith, I fear it has.   215
  I hope you will consider what is spoke
  Comes from my love. But I do see y' are mov'd:
  I am to pray you not to strain my speech
  To grosser issues nor to larger reach°
  Than to suspicion.   220

OTH: I will not.

IAGO: Should you do so, my lord,
  My speech would fall into such vile success
  As my thoughts aim not at. Cassio 's my worthy friend—
  My lord, I see y' are mov'd.

OTH: No, not much mov'd:
  I do not think but Desdemona's honest.   225

IAGO: Long live she so! and long live you to think so!

OTH: And yet, how nature erring from itself,—

IAGO: Ay, there's the point: as—to be bold with you—
  Not to affect many proposed matches
  Of her own clime, complexion, and degree,   230
  Whereto we see in all things nature tends—
  Foh! one may smell in such a will° most rank,
  Foul disproportion,° thoughts unnatural.
  But pardon me; I do not in position°
  Distinctly speak of her; though I may fear   235
  Her will, recoiling to° her better judgment,
  May fall to match you with her country forms°
  And happily repent.°

OTH: Farewell, farewell:
  If more thou dost perceive, let me know more;
  Set on thy wife to observe: leave me, Iago.   240

IAGO (*going*):   My lord I take my leave.

OTH: Why did I marry? This honest creature doubtless
  Sees and knows more, much more, than he unfolds.

IAGO (*returning*):   My lord, I would I might entreat your honour
  To scan this thing no farther; leave it to time: 245
  Although 'tis fit that Cassio have his place,
  For, sure, he fills it up with great ability,
  Yet, if you please to hold him off awhile,
  You shall by that perceive him and his means:
  Note, if your lady strain his entertainment°   250

---

219. reach: meaning.   **232. will:** sensuality.   **233. disproportion:** abnormality.   **234. position:** general argument.   **236. recoiling to:** falling back upon, or recoiling against.   **237. fall . . . forms:** happen to compare you with Venetian norms of handsomeness.   **238. repent:** i.e., of her marriage. **250. strain his entertainment:** urge his reinstatement.

With any strong or vehement importunity;
Much will be seen in that. In the mean time,
Let me be thought too busy in my fears—
As worthy cause I have to fear I am—
And hold her free,° I do beseech your honour.   255

OTH: Fear not my government.°

IAGO: I once more take my leave.   (*Exit.*)

OTH: This fellow 's of exceeding honesty,
And knows all qualities, with a learned spirit,
Of human dealings. If I do prove her haggard,°   260
Though that her jesses° were my dear heartstrings,
I 'ld whistle her off and let her down the wind,
To prey at fortune.° Haply, for I am black
And have not those soft parts of conversation
That chamberers° have, or for I am declin'd   265
Into the vale of years,—yet that 's not much—
She 's gone. I am abus'd: and my relief
Must be to loathe her. O curse of marriage,
That we can call these delicate creatures ours,
And not their appetites! I had rather be a toad,   270
And live upon the vapour of a dungeon,
Than keep a corner in the thing I love
For others' uses. Yet, 'tis the plague of great ones;
Prerogativ'd° are they less than the base;
'Tis destiny unshunnable, like death: 275
Even then this forked° plague is fated to us
When we do quicken.° Look where she comes:

(*Enter* DESDEMONA *and* EMILIA.)

If she be false, O, then heaven mocks itself!
I'll not believe 't.

DES: How now, my dear Othello!
Your dinner, and the generous° islanders   280
By you invited, do attend your presence.

OTH: I am to blame.

DES: Why do you speak so faintly?
Are you not well?

OTH: I have a pain upon my forehead here.

DES: 'Faith, that 's with watching°; 'twill away again: 285

---

255. hold her free: regard her as innocent. **256. government:** self-control. **260. haggard:** a wild female duck. **261. jesses:** straps fastened around the legs of a trained hawk. **263. at fortune:** at random. **265. chamberers:** gallants. **274. Prerogativ'd:** privileged. **276. forked:** an allusion to the horns of the cuckold. **277. quicken:** receive life. **280. generous:** noble. **285. watching:** working late.

Let me but bind it hard, within this hour
It will be well.

OTH: Your napkin is too little: (*He puts the handkerchief from him; and*
 it drops.)
Let it alone. Come, I'll go in with you.

DES: I am very sorry that you are not well.   (*Exit with* OTHELLO.)

EMIL: I am glad I have found this napkin: 290
This was her first remembrance from the Moor:
My wayward husband hath a hundred times
Woo'd me to steal it; but she so loves the token,
For he conjur'd her she should ever keep it,
That she reserves it evermore about her   295
To kiss and talk to. I'll have the work ta'en out,°
And give 't Iago: what he will do with it
Heaven knows, not I;
I nothing but to please his fantasy.

   (*Enter* IAGO.)

IAGO: How now! what do you here alone?   300
EMIL: Do not you chide; I have a thing for you.
IAGO: A thing for me? it is a common thing°—
EMIL: Ha!
IAGO: To have a foolish wife.
EMIL: O, is that all? What will you give me now   305
For that same handkerchief?
IAGO: What handkerchief?
EMIL: What handkerchief!
 Why, that the Moor first gave Desdemona;
 That which so often you did bid me steal.
IAGO: Hast stol'n it from her?   310
EMIL: No, 'faith; she let it drop by negligence,
 And, to th' advantage, I, being here, took 't up.
 Look, here it is.
IAGO: A good wench; give it to me.
EMIL: What will you do with 't, that you have been so earnest
 To have me filch it?
IAGO: (*Snatching it*) Why, what is that to you?   315
EMIL: If it be not for some purpose of import,
 Give 't me again: poor lady, she'll run mad
 When she shall lack it.
IAGO: Be not acknown on 't°; I have use for it.
 Go, leave me.   (*Exit* EMILIA.) 320

---

296. work ta'en out: design copied. **302. common thing:** *common* suggests coarseness and availability
to all, and *thing* is slang for female sexual organs. **319. Be . . . on 't:** do not confess knowledge of it.

I will in Cassio's lodging lose this napkin,
And let him find it. Trifles light as air
Are to the jealous confirmations strong
As proofs of holy writ: this may do something.
The Moor already changes with my poison: 325
Dangerous conceits are, in their natures, poisons,
Which at the first are scarce found to distaste,
But with a little act° upon the blood,
Burn like the mines of sulphur. I did say so:

    (*Enter* OTHELLO.)

Look, where he comes! Not poppy, nor mandragora,   330
Nor all the drowsy syrups of the world,
Shall ever medicine thee to that sweet sleep
Which thou owedst yesterday.
OTH: Ha! ha! false to me?
IAGO: Why, how now, general! no more of that.
OTH: Avaunt! be gone! thou has set me on the rack;   335
  I swear 'tis better to be much abus'd
  Than but to know 't a little.
IAGO: How now, my lord!
OTH: What sense had I of her stol'n hours of lust?
  I saw 't not, thought it not, it harm'd not me:
  I slept the next night well, fed well, was free and merry; 340
  I found not Cassio's kisses on her lips:
  He that is robb'd, not wanting what is stol'n,
  Let him not know 't, and he 's not robb'd at all.
IAGO: I am sorry to hear this.
OTH: I had been happy, if the general camp,   345
  Pioners° and all, had tasted her sweet body,
  So I had nothing known. O, now, for ever
  Farewell the tranquil mind! farewell content!
  Farewell the plumed troop, and the big wars,
  That make ambition virtue! O, farewell!   350
  Farewell the neighing steed, and the shrill trump,
  The spirit-stirring drum, th' ear-piercing fife,
  The royal banner, and all quality,
  Pride, pomp and circumstance° of glorious war!
  And, O you mortal engines,° whose rude throats   355
  Th' immortal Jove's dread clamours counterfeit,
  Farewell! Othello's occupation 's gone!
IAGO: Is 't possible, my lord?

---

328. act: action, working. **346. Pioners:** sappers, a low grade of soldiers. **354. circumstance:** attendant fact; here, formal display. **355. mortal engines:** i.e., cannon.

OTH: Villain, be sure thou prove my love a whore,
    Be sure of it; give me the ocular proof;   360
    Or, by the worth of mine eternal soul,
    Thou hadst been better have been born a dog
    Than answer my wak'd wrath!
IAGO: Is 't come to this?
OTH: Make me to see 't; or, at the least, so prove it,
    That the probation bear no hinge nor loop   365
    To hang a doubt on; or woe upon thy life!
IAGO: My noble lord,—
OTH: If thou dost slander her and torture me,
    Never pray more; abandon all remorse;
    On horror's head horrors° accumulate;   370
    Do deeds to make heaven weep, all earth amaz'd;
    For nothing canst thou to damnation add
    Greater than that.
IAGO: O grace! O heaven forgive me!
    Are you a man? have you a soul or sense?
    God be wi' you; take mine office. O wretched fool,   375
    That liv'st to make thine honesty a vice!
    O monstrous world! Take note, take note, O world,
    To be direct and honest is not safe.
    I thank you for this profit; and from hence
    I'll love no friend, sith love breeds such offence.   380
OTH: Nay, stay: thou shouldst be honest.
IAGO: I should be wise, for honesty 's a fool
    and loses that it works for.
OTH: By the world,
    I think my wife be honest and think she is not;
    I think thou are just and think thou are not.   385
    I'll have some proof. Her name, that was as fresh
    As Dian's visage, is now begrim'd and black
    As mine own face. If there be cords, or knives,
    Poison, or fire, or suffocating streams,
    I'll not endure it. Would I were satisfied!   390
IAGO: I see, sir, you are eaten up with passion:
    I do repent me that I put it to you.
    You would be satisfied!
OTH: Would! nay, I will.
IAGO: And may: but, how? how satisfied, my lord?
    Would you, the supervisor, grossly gape on—   395
    Behold her topp'd?
OTH: Death and damnation! O!

370. horrors: object of *accumulate*.

IAGO: It were a tedious difficulty, I think,
   To bring them to that prospect: damn them then,
   If ever mortal eyes do see them bolster°
   More than their own! What then? how then?   400
   What shall I say? Where 's satisfaction?
   It is impossible you should see this,
   Were they as prime as goats, as hot as monkeys,
   As salt° as wolves in pride, and fools as gross
   As ignorance made drunk. But yet, I say,   405
   If imputation° and strong circumstances,
   Which lead directly to the door of truth,
   Will give you satisfaction, you may have 't.
OTH: Give me a living reason she 's disloyal.
IAGO: I do not like the office: 410
   But, sith I am ent'red in this cause so far,
   Prick'd to 't by foolish honesty and love,
   I will go on. I lay with Cassio lately;
   And, being troubled with a raging tooth,
   I could not sleep.   415
   There are a kind of men so loose of soul,
   That in their sleeps will mutter their affairs:
   One of this kind is Cassio:
   In sleep I heard him say "Sweet Desdemona,
   Let us be wary, let us hide our loves";   420
   And then, sir, would he grip and wring my hand,
   Cry, "O sweet creature!" and then kiss me hard,
   As if he pluck'd up kisses by the roots
   That grew upon my lips: then laid his leg
   Over my thigh, and sigh'd, and kiss'd; and then   425
   Cried "Cursed fate that gave thee to the Moor!"
OTH: O monstrous! monstrous!
IAGO: Nay, this was but his dream.
OTH: But this denoted a foregone conclusion°:
   'Tis a shrewd doubt, though it be but a dream.
IAGO: And this may help to thicken other proofs   430
   That do demonstrate thinly.
OTH: I'll tear her all to pieces.
IAGO: Nay, but be wise; yet we see nothing done;
   She may be honest yet. Tell me but this,
   Have you not sometimes seen a handkerchief
   Spotted with strawberries in your wife's hand?   435

---

399. bolster: lie together.   **404. salt:** wanton, sexual.   **406. imputation:** i.e., opinion founded on strong circumstantial evidence.   **428. foregone conclusion:** previous trial or experience (not used in our sense).

OTH: I gave her such a one; 'twas my first gift.
IAGO: I know not that: but such a handkerchief—
        I am sure it was your wife's—did I to-day
        See Cassio wipe his beard with.
OTH: If it be that,—
IAGO: If it be that, or any that was hers,   440
        It speaks against her with the other proofs.
OTH: O, that the slave had forty thousand lives!
        One is too poor, too weak for my revenge.
        Now do I see 'tis true. Look here, Iago;
        All my fond love thus do I blow to heaven.   445
        'Tis gone.
        Arise, black vengeance, from the hollow hell!
        Yield up, O love, thy crown and hearted° throne
        To tyrannous hate! Swell, bosom, with thy fraught,°
        For 'tis of aspics'° tongues!
IAGO: Yet be content.   450
OTH: O, blood, blood, blood!
IAGO: Patience, I say; your mind perhaps may change.
OTH: Never, Iago. Like to the Pontic sea,
        Whose icy current and compulsive course
        Ne'er feels retiring ebb, but keeps due on   455
        To the Propontic and the Hellespont,
        Even so my bloody thoughts, with violent pace,
        Shall ne'er look back, ne'er ebb to humble love,
        Till that a capable and wide revenge
        Swallow them up. Now, by yond marble° heaven,   460
        (*Kneels*) In the due reverence of a sacred vow
        I here engage my words.
IAGO: Do not rise yet.
        (*Kneels*) Witness, you ever-burning lights above,
        You elements that clip us round about,
        Witness that here Iago doth give up   465
        The execution° of his wit, hands, heart,
        To wrong'd Othello's service! Let him command,
        And to obey shall be in me remorse,°
        What bloody business ever. (*They rise.*)
OTH: I greet thy love,
        Not with vain thanks, but with acceptance bounteous,   470
        And will upon the instant put thee to 't:
        Within these three days let me hear thee say

---

448. hearted: fixed in the heart.   **449. fraught:** freight, burden.   **450. aspics':** venomous serpents'.
460. marble: i.e., gleaming like marble.   **466. execution:** exercise.   **468. remorse:** pity for Othello's
wrongs.

That Cassio 's not alive.

IAGO: My friend is dead; 'tis done at your request:
But let her live.   475

OTH: Damn her, lewd minx! O, damn her! damn her!
Come, go with me apart; I will withdraw,
To furnish me with some swift means of death
For the fair devil. Now art thou my lieutenant.

IAGO: I am your own for ever.   *(Exeunt.)* 480

SCENE IV.

Before the castle.

(Enter DESDEMONA, EMILIA, *and* CLOWN.)

DES: Do you know, sirrah, where Lieutenant Cassio lies?

CLO: I dare not say he lies any where.

DES: Why, man?

CLO: He's a soldier, and for one to say a soldier lies, is stabbing.

DES: Go to; where lodges he?   5

CLO: To tell you where he lodges, is to tell you where I lie.

DES: Can any thing be made of this?

CLO: I know not where he lodges, and for me to devise a lodging and say he lies
here or he lies there, were to lie in mine own throat.

DES: Can you inquire him out, and be edified by report?   10

CLO: I will catechize the world for him, that is, make questions, and by them
answer.

DES: Seek him, bid him come hither: tell him I have moved my lord on his behalf,
and hope all will be well.

CLO: To do this is within the compass of man's wit; and therefore I will attempt   15
the doing it.   *(Exit* CLOWN.)

DES: Where should I lose that handkerchief, Emilia?

EMIL: I know not, madam.

DES: Believe me, I had rather lost my purse
Full of crusadoes°: and, but my noble Moor   20
Is true of mind and made of no such baseness
As jealous creatures are, it were enough
To put him to ill thinking.

EMIL: Is he not jealous?

DES: Who, he? I think the sun where he was born
Drew all such humours from him.

EMIL: Look, where he comes.   25

(Enter OTHELLO.)

DES: I will not leave him now till Cassio
Be call'd to him.—How is 't with you, my lord?

II.iv. 20. crusadoes: Portuguese gold coins.

OTH: Well, my good lady. (*Aside*) O, hardness, to dissemble!—
  How do you do, Desdemona?
DES: Well, my good lord.
OTH: Give me your hand: this hand is moist, my lady.   30
DES: It yet hath felt no age nor known no sorrow.
OTH: This argues fruitfulness and liberal heart:
  Hot, hot, and moist: this hand of yours requires
  A sequester° from liberty, fasting and prayer,
  Much castigation, exercise devout;   35
  For here 's a young and sweating devil here,
  That commonly rebels. 'Tis a good hand,
  A frank one.
DES: You may, indeed, say so:
  For 'twas that hand that gave away my heart.
OTH: A liberal hand: the hearts of old gave hands;   40
  But our new heraldry is hands, not hearts.°
DES: I cannot speak of this. Come now, your promise.
OTH: What promise, chuck?
DES: I have sent to bid Cassio come speak with you.
OTH: I have a salt and sorry rheum° offends me;   45
  Lend me thy handkerchief.
DES: Here, my lord.
OTH: That which I gave you.
DES: I have it not about me.
OTH: Not?
DES: No, indeed, my lord.
OTH: That 's a fault.
  That handkerchief
  Did an Egyptian° to my mother give;   50
  She was a charmer, and could almost read
  The thoughts of people: she told her, while she kept it,
  'Twould make her amiable and subdue my father
  Entirely to her love, but if she lost it
  Or made a gift of it, my father's eye   55
  Should hold her loathed and his spirits should hunt
  After new fancies: she, dying, gave it me;
  And bid me, when my fate would have me wive,
  To give it her. I did so: and take heed on 't;
  Make it a darling like your precious eye;   60
  To lose 't or give 't away were such perdition
  As nothing else could match.
DES: Is 't possible?

---

34. sequester: separation, sequestration.   **41. new . . . hearts:** a current expression referring to marriages in which there is a joining of hands without the giving of hearts.   **45. sorry rheum:** distressful head cold.   **50. Egyptian:** gypsy.

OTH: 'Tis true: there 's magic in the web of it:
  A sibyl, that had numb'red in the world
  The sun to course two hundred compasses, 65
  In her prophetic fury sew'd the work;
  The worms were hallow'd that did breed the silk;
  And it was dy'd in mummy° which the skilful
  Conserv'd of° maidens' hearts.

DES: Indeed! is 't true?

OTH: Most veritable; therefore look 't well. 70

DES: Then would to God that I had never seen 't!

OTH: Ha! wherefore?

DES: Why do you speak so startingly and rash?

OTH: Is 't lost? is 't gone? speak, is it out o' the way?

DES: Heaven bless us! 75

OTH: Say you?

DES: It is not lost; but what if it were?

OTH: How!

DES: I say, it is not lost.

OTH: Fetch 't, let me see 't.

DES: Why, so I can sir, but I will not now. 80
  This is a trick to put me from my suit:
  Pray you, let Cassio be receiv'd again.

OTH: Fetch me the handkerchief: my mind misgives.

DES: Come, come:
  You'll never meet a more sufficient man. 85

OTH: The handkerchief!

DES: I pray, talk me of Cassio.

OTH: The handkerchief!

DES: A man that all his time
  Hath founded his good fortunes on your love,
  Shar'd dangers with you,—

OTH: The handkerchief! 90

DES: In sooth, you are to blame.

OTH: Away!   (*Exit* OTHELLO.)

EMIL: Is not this man jealous?

DES: I ne'er saw this before.
  Sure, there 's some wonder in this handkerchief: 95
  I am most unhappy in the loss of it.

EMIL: 'Tis not a year or two shows us a man:
  They are all but stomachs, and we all but food;
  They eat us hungerly, and when they are full,
  They belch us.

---

68. mummy: medicinal or magical preparation drained from the flesh of mummified bodies.   **69. Conserv'd of:** preserved out of.

(*Enter* IAGO *and* CASSIO.)

Look you, Cassio and my husband!   100
IAGO: There is no other way; 'tis she must do 't:
   And, lo, the happiness! go, and importune her.
DES: How now, good Cassio! what 's the news with you?
CAS: Madam, my former suit: I do beseech you
   That by your virtuous means I may again   105
   Exist, and be a member of his love
   Whom I with all the office of my heart
   Entirely honour: I would not be delay'd.
   If my offence be of such mortal kind
   That nor my service past, nor present sorrows,   110
   Nor purpos'd merit in futurity,
   Can ransom me into his love again,
   But to know so much be my benefit°;
   So shall I clothe me in a forc'd content,
   And shut myself up in some other course,   115
   To fortune's alms.
DES: Alas, thrice-gentle Cassio!
   My advocation° is not now in tune;
   My lord is not my lord; nor should I know him,
   Were he in favour as in humour alter'd.
   So help me every spirit sanctified   120
   As I have spoken for you all my best
   And stood within the blank° of his displeasure
   For my free speech! You must awhile be patient:
   What I can do I will; and more I will
   Than for myself I dare: let that suffice you.   125
IAGO: Is my lord angry?
EMIL: He went hence but now,
   And certainly in strange unquietness.
IAGO: Can he be angry? I have seen the cannon,
   When it hath blown his ranks into the air,
   And, like the devil, from his very arm   130
   Puff'd his own brother:—and can he be angry?
   Something of moment then: I will go meet him:
   There 's matter in 't indeed, if he be angry.
DES: I prithee, do so.   (*Exit* IAGO.)
                        Something, sure, of state,
   Either from Venice, or some unhatch'd practice   135
   Made demonstrable here in Cyprus to him,

---

113. to know . . . benefit: to know that my case is hopeless will end my vain endeavor.   **117. advocation:** advocacy.   **122. blank:** white spot in the center of a target; here, range.

Hath puddled° his clear spirit; and in such cases
Men's natures wrangle with inferior things,
Though great ones are their object. 'Tis even so;
For let our finger ache, and it indues°   140
Our other healthful members even to a sense
Of pain: nay, we must think men are not gods,
Nor of them look for such observancy
As fits the bridal. Beshrew me much, Emilia,
I was, unhandsome° warrior as I am,   145
Arraigning his unkindness with my soul;
But now I find I had suborn'd the witness,
And he 's indicted falsely.
EMIL: Pray heaven it be state-matters, as you think,
And no conception° nor no jealous toy   150
Concerning you.
DES: Alas the day! I never gave him cause.
EMIL: But jealous souls will not be answer'd so;
They are not ever jealous for the cause,
But jealous for they are jealous: 'tis a monster   155
Begot upon itself, born on itself.
DES: Heaven keep that monster from Othello's mind!
EMIL: Lady, amen.
DES: I will go seek him. Cassio, walk here about:
If I do find him fit, I'll move your suit   160
And seek to effect it to my uttermost.
CAS: I humbly thank your ladyship.   (*Exit* DESDEMONA *with* EMILIA.)

    (*Enter* BIANCA.)

BIAN: Save you, friend Cassio!
CAS: What make you from home?
How is 't with you, my most fair Bianca?
I' faith, sweet love, I was coming to your house.   165
BIAN: And I was going to your lodging, Cassio.
What, keep a week away? seven days and nights?
Eight score eight hours? and lovers' absent hours,
More tedious than the dial eight score times?
O weary reck'ning!
CAS: Pardon me, Bianca.   170
I have this while with leaden thoughts been press'd;
But I shall, in a more continuate° time,
Strike off this score of absence. Sweet Bianca, (*Giving her* DESDEMONA'*s
    handkerchief.*)

---

137. puddled: sullied the purity of.   **140. indues:** brings to the same condition.   **145. unhandsome:**
unfair.   **150. conception:** mere fancy.   **172. continuate:** uninterrupted.

Take me this work out.°
BIAN: O Cassio, whence came this?
This is some token from a newer friend: 175
To the felt absence now I feel a cause:
Is 't come to this? Well, well.
CAS: Go to, woman!
Throw your vile guesses in the devil's teeth,
From whence you have them. You are jealous now
That this is from some mistress, some remembrance: 180
No, in good troth, Bianca.
BIAN: Why, whose is it?
CAS: I know not, sweet: I found it in my chamber.
I like the work well: ere it be demanded—
As like enough it will—I would have it copied:
Take it, and do 't; and leave me for this time.   185
BIAN: Leave you! wherefore?
CAS: I do attend here on the general;
And think it no addition, nor my wish,
To have him see me woman'd.
BIAN: Why, I pray you?
CAS: Not that I love you not.
BIAN: But that you do not love me.   190
I pray you, bring me on the way a little,
And say if I shall see you soon at night.
CAS: 'Tis but a little way that I can bring you;
For I attend here: but I'll see you soon.
BIAN: 'Tis very good; I must be circumstance'd.°   *(Exeunt omnes.)* 195

ACT IV

SCENE I.

Cyprus. Before the castle.

(Enter OTHELLO *and* IAGO.*)*

IAGO: Will you think so?
OTH: Think so, Iago!
IAGO: What,
To kiss in private?
OTH: An unauthoriz'd kiss.
IAGO: Or to be naked with her friend in bed
An hour or more, not meaning any harm?
OTH: Naked in bed, Iago, and not mean harm!   5

---

174. Take . . . out: i.e., copy this embroidery for me.   **195. circumstance'd:** governed by circumstances.

It is hypocrisy against the devil:
They that mean virtuously, and yet do so,
The devil their virtue tempts, and they tempt heaven.

IAGO: So° they do nothing, 'tis a venial slip:
But if I give my wife a handkerchief,—   10

OTH: What then?

IAGO: Why, then, 'tis hers, my lord: and, being hers,
She may, I think, bestow 't on any man.

OTH: She is protectress of her honour too:
May she give that?   15

IAGO: Her honour is an essence that 's not seen;
They have it very oft that have it not:
But, for the handkerchief,—

OTH: By heaven, I would most gladly have forgot it.
Thou said'st—O, it comes o'er my memory,   20
As doth the raven o'er the infected house,°
Boding to all—he had my handkerchief.

IAGO: Ay, what of that?

OTH: That's not so good now.

IAGO: What,
If I had said I had seen him do you wrong?
Or hear him say,—as knaves be such abroad,   25
Who having, by their own importunate suit,
Or voluntary dotage of some mistress,
Convinced or supplied° them, cannot choose
But they must blab—

OTH: Hath he said anything?

IAGO: He hath, my lord; but be you well assur'd,   30
No more than he'll unswear.

OTH: What hath he said?

IAGO: 'Faith, that he did—I know not what he did.

OTH: What? What?

IAGO: Lie—

OTH: With her?

IAGO: With her, on her; what you will.

OTH: Lie with her! lie on her! We say lie on her, when they belie her. Lie with her!   35
that's fulsome.—Handkerchief—confessions—handkerchief!—To confess, and
be hanged for his labour;—first, to be hanged, and then to confess.— I tremble at
it. Nature would not invest herself in such shadowing passion without some
instruction.° It is not words that shake me thus. Pish! Noses, ears, and lips.—Is 't
possible?—Confess—handkerchief—O devil! (*Falls in a trance.*)   40

IV.i. 9. So: as long as.   21. raven . . . house: allusion to the belief that the raven hovered over a house
of sickness or infection.   28. Convinced or supplied: i.e., mistresses gained by importunity and those
who doted voluntarily.   38–39. Nature . . . instruction: i.e., my jealousy cannot be merely the result of
natural imagination, but must have some foundation in fact.

IAGO: Work on,
  My medicine, work! Thus credulous fools are caught;
  And many worthy and chaste dames even thus,
  All guiltless, meet reproach. What, ho! my lord!
  My lord, I say! Othello!

  (*Enter* CASSIO.)

                        How now, Cassio!   45
CAS: What 's the matter?
IAGO: My lord is fall'n into an epilepsy:
  This is his second fit; he had one yesterday.
CAS: Rub him about the temples.
IAGO: No, forbear;
  The lethargy° must have his quiet course: 50
  If not, he foams at mouth and by and by
  Breaks out to savage madness. Look, he stirs:
  Do you withdraw yourself a little while,
  He will recover straight: when he is gone,
  I would on great occasion speak with you.   (Exit CASSIO.) 55
  How is it, general? have you not hurt your head?
OTH: Dost thou mock me?
IAGO: I mock you! no, by heaven.
  Would you would bear your fortune like a man!
OTH: A horned man 's a monster and a beast.
IAGO: There 's many a beast then in a populous city,   60
  And many a civil° monster.
OTH: Did he confess it?
IAGO: Good sir, be a man;
  Think every bearded fellow that 's but yok'd
  May draw with you°: there 's millions now alive
  That nightly lie in those unproper° beds   65
  Which they dare swear peculiar°: your case is better.
  O, 'tis the spite of hell, the fiend's arch-mock,
  To lip a wanton in a secure couch,
  And to suppose her chaste! No, let me know;
  And knowing what I am, I know what she shall be.   70
OTH: O, thou art wise; 'tis certain.
IAGO: Stand you awhile apart;
  Confine yourself but in a patient list.°
  Whilst you were here o'erwhelmed with your grief—
  A passion most unsuiting such a man—
  Cassio came hither: I shifted him away,   75

---

50. lethargy: unconscious condition.   **61. civil:** i.e., in civilized society.   **64. draw with you:** i.e., share your fate as cuckold.   **65. unproper:** not belonging exclusively to an individual.   **66. peculiar:** private, one's own.   **72. patient list:** within the bounds of patience.

And laid good 'scuse upon your ecstasy,
Bade him anon return and here speak with me;
The which he promis'd. Do but encave° yourself,
And mark the fleers,° the gibes, and notable scorns,
That dwell in every region of his face;   80
For I will make him tell the tale anew,
Where, how, how oft, how long ago, and when
He hath, and is again to cope your wife:
I say, but mark his gesture. Marry, patience;
Or I shall say y' are all in all in spleen,   85
And nothing of a man.
OTH: Dost thou hear, Iago?
I will be found most cunning in my patience;
But—dost thou hear?—most bloody.
IAGO: That 's not amiss;
But yet keep time° in all. Will you withdraw? (OTHELLO *retires.*)
Now will I question Cassio of Bianca,   90
A housewife that by selling her desires
Buys herself bread and clothes: it is a creature
That dotes on Cassio; as 'tis the strumpet's plague
To beguile many and be beguil'd by one:
He, when he hears of her, cannot refrain   95
From the excess of laughter. Here he comes:

     (*Enter* CASSIO.)

As he shall smile, Othello shall go mad;
And his unbookish° jealousy must conster°
Poor Cassio's smiles, gestures and light behaviour,
Quite in the wrong. How do you now, lieutenant?   100
CAS: The worser that you give me the addition°
Whose want even kills me.
IAGO: Ply Desdemona well, and you are sure on 't.
(*Speaking lower*) Now, if this suit lay in Bianca's power,
How quickly should you speed!
CAS: Alas, poor caitiff!   105
OTH: Look, how he laughs already!
IAGO: I never knew woman love man so.
CAS: Alas, poor rogue! I think, i' faith, she loves me.
OTH: Now he denies it faintly, and laughs it out.
IAGO: Do you hear, Cassio?
OTH: Now he importunes him   110
To tell o'er: go to; well said, well said.

---

78. encave: conceal.   **79. fleers:** sneers.   **89. keep time:** use judgment and order.   **98. unbookish:**
uninstructed.   **98. conster:** construe.   **101. addition:** title.

IAGO: She gives it out that you shall marry her:
  Do you intend it?

CAS: Ha, ha, ha!

OTH: Do you triumph, Roman?° do you triumph?   115

CAS: I marry her! what? a customer!° Prithee, bear some charity to my wit; do not
  think it so unwholesome. Ha, ha, ha!

OTH: So, so, so, so: they laugh that win.

IAGO: 'Faith, the cry goes that you shall marry her.

CAS: Prithee, say true.   120

IAGO: I am a very villain else.

OTH: Have you scored me?° Well.

CAS: This is the monkey's own giving out: she is persuaded I will marry her, out of
  her own love and flattery, not out of my promise.

OTH: Iago beckons me; now he begins the story.   125

CAS: She was here even now; she haunts me in every place. I was the other day
  talking on the seabank with certain Venetians; and thither comes the bauble,°
  and, by this hand, she falls me thus about my neck—

OTH: Crying, 'O dear Cassio!' as it were: his gesture imports it.

CAS: So hangs, and lolls, and weeps upon me; so shakes, and pulls me: ha, ha, ha! 130

OTH: Now he tells how she plucked him to my chamber. O, I see that nose of
  yours, but not that dog I shall throw it to.

CAS: Well, I must leave her company.

IAGO: Before me!° look, where she comes.

  (*Enter* BIANCA.)

CAS: 'Tis such another fitchew!° marry, a perfumed one.—What do you mean by   135
  this haunting of me?

BIAN: Let the devil and his dam haunt you! What did you mean by that same
  handkerchief you gave me even now? I was a fine fool to take it. I must take out
  the work?—A likely piece of work, that you should find it in your chamber, and
  not know who left it there! This is some minx's token, and I must take out the   140
  work? There; give it your hobby-horse°: wheresoever you had it, I'll take out no
  work on 't.

CAS: How now, my sweet Bianca! how now! how now!

OTH: By heaven, that should be my handkerchief!

BIAN: An you'll come to supper to-night, you may; an' you will not, come when   145
  you are next prepared for.   (*Exit.*)

IAGO: After her, after her.

CAS: 'Faith, I must; she'll rail in the street else.

IAGO: Will you sup there?

---

115. Roman: epithet arising from the association of the Romans with the idea of triumph.   **116. customer:** prostitute.   **122. scored me:** made up my reckoning, or branded me.   **127. bauble:** plaything.
134. Before me!: On my soul!   **135. fitchew:** polecat (because of her strong perfume; also, slang word
for a prostitute).   **141. hobby-horse:** harlot.

CAS: Yes, I intend so. 150
IAGO: Well, I may chance to see you; for I would very fain speak with you.
CAS: Prithee, come; will you?
IAGO: Go to; say no more. (*Exit* CASSIO.)
OTH (*advancing*): How shall I murder him, Iago?
IAGO: Did you perceive how he laughed at his vice? 155
OTH: O Iago!
IAGO: And did you see the handkerchief?
OTH: Was that mine?
IAGO: Yours, by this hand: and to see how he prizes the foolish woman your wife!
She gave it him, and he hath given it his whore. 160
OTH: I would have him nine years a-killing. A fine woman! a fair woman! a sweet
woman!
IAGO: Nay, you must forget that.
OTH: Ay, let her rot, and perish, and be damned to-night; for she shall not live: no,
my heart is turned to stone; I strike it, and it hurts my hand. O, the world hath 165
not a sweeter creature: she might lie by an emperor's side and command him
tasks.
IAGO: Nay, that's not your way.°
OTH: Hang her! I do but say what she is: so delicate with her needle: an admirable
musician: O! she will sing the savageness out of a bear: of so high and plenteous 170
wit and invention:—
IAGO: She's the worse for all this.
OTH: O, a thousand thousand times: and then, of so gentle a condition!
IAGO: Ay, too gentle.
OTH: Nay, that's certain: but yet the pity of it, Iago! O Iago, the pity of it, Iago! 175
IAGO: If you are so fond over her iniquity, give her patent° to offend; for, if it touch
not you, it comes near nobody.
OTH: I will chop her into messes°; cuckold me!
IAGO: O, 'tis foul in her.
OTH: With mine officer! 180
IAGO: That's fouler.
OTH: Get me some poison, Iago; this night: I'll not expostulate with her, lest her
body and beauty unprovide° my mind again: this night, Iago.
IAGO: Do it not with poison, strangle her in her bed, even the bed she hath
contaminated. 185
OTH: Good, good: the justice of it pleases: very good.
IAGO: And for Cassio, let me be his undertaker°: you shall hear more by midnight.
OTH: Excellent good. (*A trumpet within.*) What trumpet is that same?
IAGO: I warrant something from Venice.

(*Enter* LODOVICO, DESDEMONA, *and* ATTENDANTS.)

---

168. your way: i.e., the way you should think of her. **176. patent:** license. **178. messes:** dishes of
food. **183. unprovide:** weaken, unfit. **187. let . . . undertaker:** i.e., let me settle with him.

'Tis Lodovico.
This comes from the duke: and, see, your wife's with him.   190
Lod: God save you, worthy general!
Oth: With all my heart, sir.
Lod: The duke and the senators of Venice greet you. (*Gives him a letter.*)
Oth: I kiss the instrument of their pleasures. (*Opens the letter, and reads.*)
Des: And what's the news, good cousin Lodovico?
Iago: I am very glad to see you, signior;   195
Welcome to Cyprus.
Lod: I thank you. How does Lieutenant Cassio?
Iago: Lives, sir.
Des: Cousin, there's fall'n between him and my lord
An unkind breach: but you shall make all well.   200
Oth: Are you sure of that?
Des: My lord?
Oth (*reads*):   "This fail you not to do, as you will—"
Lod: He did not call; he's busy in the paper.
Is there division 'twixt my lord and Cassio?   205
Des: A most unhappy one: I would do much
T' atone them, for the love I bear to Cassio.
Oth: Fire and brimstone!
Des: My lord?
Oth: Are you wise?
Des: What, is he angry?
Lod: May be the letter mov'd him:
For, as I think, they do command him home,   210
Deputing Cassio in his government.°
Des: Trust me, I am glad on 't.
Oth: Indeed!
Des: My lord?
Oth: I am glad to see you mad.
Des: Why, sweet Othello,—
Oth (*striking her*):   Devil!
Des: I have not deserv'd this.   215
Lod: My lord, this would not be believ'd in Venice,
Though I should swear I saw 't; 'tis very much:
Make her amends; she weeps.
Oth: O devil, devil!
If that the earth could teem with woman's tears,
Each drop she falls would prove a crocodile.°   220
Out of my sight!
Des: I will not stay to offend you. (*Going.*)

---

211. **government:** office.   220. **prove a crocodile:** i.e., by weeping crocodile tears; it was believed the crocodile shed tears over the body of the person it was eating.

LOD: Truly, an obedient lady:
  I do beseech your lordship, call her back.
OTH: Mistress!
DES: My lord?
OTH: What would you with her, sir?
LOD: Who, I, my lord?   225
OTH: Ay; you did wish that I would make her turn:
  Sir, she can turn, and turn, and yet go on,
  And turn again; and she can weep, sir, weep;
  And she 's obedient, as you say, obedient,
  Very obedient. Proceed you in your tears.   230
  Concerning this, sir,—O well-painted passion,°—
  I am commanded home. Get you away;
  I'll send for you anon. Sir, I obey the mandate,
  And will return to Venice. Hence, avaunt!   (*Exit* DESDEMONA.)
  Cassio shall have my place. And, sir, to-night,   235
  I do entreat that we may sup together:
  You are welcome, sir, to Cyprus.—Goats and monkeys!   (*Exit.*)
LOD: Is this the noble Moor whom our full senate
  Call all in all sufficient? Is this the nature
  Whom passion could not shake? whose solid virtue   240
  The shot of accident, nor dart of chance,
  Could neither graze nor pierce?
IAGO: He is much chang'd.
LOD: Are his wits safe? is he not light of brain?
IAGO: He 's that he is: I may not breathe my censure
  What he might be: if what he might he is not,   245
  I would to heaven he were!
LOD: What, strike his wife!
IAGO: 'Faith, that was not so well; yet would I knew
  That stroke would prove the worst!
LOD: Is it his use?
  Or did the letters work upon his blood,
  And new-create this fault?   250
IAGO: Alas, alas!
  It is not honesty in me to speak
  What I have seen and known. You shall observe him,
  And his own courses will denote him so
  That I may save my speech: do but go after,
  And mark how he continues.   255
LOD: I am sorry that I am deceiv'd in him.   (*Exeunt.*)

231. well-painted passion: well-simulated emotion.

SCENE II.

A room in the castle.

(*Enter* OTHELLO *and* EMILIA.)

OTH:	You have seen nothing then?	
EMIL:	Nor ever heard, nor ever did suspect.	
OTH:	Yes, you have seen Cassio and she together.	
EMIL:	But then I saw no harm, and then I heard	

Each syllable that breath made up between them.   5

OTH:	What, did they never whisper?	
EMIL:		Never, my lord.
OTH:	Nor send you out 'o th' way?	
EMIL:	Never.	
OTH:	To fetch her fan, her gloves, her mask, nor nothing?	
EMIL:	Never, my lord. 10	
OTH:	That 's strange.	
EMIL:	I durst, my lord, to wager she is honest,	

Lay down my soul at stake: if you think other,
Remove your thought: it doth abuse your bosom.
If any wretch have put this in your head,   15
Let heaven requite it with the serpent's curse!
For, if she be not honest, chaste, and true,
There 's no man happy; the purest of their wives
Is foul as slander.

OTH: Bid her come hither: go.   (*Exit* EMILIA.)
She says enough; yet she 's a simple bawd   20
That cannot say as much. This is a subtle whore,
A closet lock and key° of villainous secrets:
And yet she'll kneel and pray; I have seen her do 't.

(*Enter* DESDEMONA *and* EMILIA.)

DES:	My lord, what is your will?	
OTH:		Pray, chuck, come hither.
DES:	What is your pleasure?	
OTH:		Let me see your eyes; 25

Look in my face.

DES: What horrible fancy 's this?

OTH (*to* EMILIA):   Some of your function,° mistress;
Leave procreants° alone and shut the door;
Cough, or cry "hem," if any body come:
Your mystery, your mystery°: nay, dispatch.   (*Exit* EMILIA.)   30

IV.ii. 22. closet lock and key: complete storeroom.   **27. Some . . . function:** i.e., set to work in your chosen profession, that of bawd.   **28. procreants:** mating couples.   **30. mystery:** trade, occupation.

DES: Upon my knees, what doth your speech import?
    I understand a fury in your words,
    But not the words.
OTH: Why, what art thou?
DES: Your wife, my lord; your true
    And loyal wife.
OTH: Come, swear it, damn thyself;   35
    Lest, being like one of heaven, the devils themselves
    Should fear to seize thee: therefore be double damn'd:
    Swear thou are honest.
DES: Heaven doth truly know it.
OTH: Heaven truly knows that thou art false as hell.
DES: To whom, my lord? with whom? how am I false?   40
OTH: O Desdemona! away! away! away!
DES: Alas the heavy day! Why do you weep?
    Am I the motive of these tears, my lord?
    If haply you my father do suspect
    An instrument of this your calling back,   45
    Lay not your blame on me: if you have lost him,
    Why, I have lost him too.
OTH: Had it pleas'd heaven
    To try me with affliction; had they° rain'd
    All kinds of sores and shames on my bare head,
    Steep'd me in poverty to the very lips,   50
    Given to captivity me and my utmost hopes,
    I should have found in some place of my soul
    A drop of patience: but, alas, to make me
    A fixed figure for the time of scorn
    To point his slow unmoving finger at!°   55
    Yet could I bear that too; well, very well:
    But there, where I have garner'd up my heart,
    Where either I must live, or bear no life;
    The fountain from the which my current runs,
    Or else dries up; to be discarded thence!   60
    Or keep it as a cistern for foul toads
    To knot and gender° in! Turn thy complexion° there,
    Patience, thou young and rose-lipp'd cherubin,—
    Ay, there, look grim as hell!
DES: I hope my noble lord esteems me honest.   65

---

48. they: heavenly powers.   **54–55. A . . . at:** Othello possibly thinks of himself as a man set in a pillory
at whom the scornful world points in mockery. There seems to be a comparison with the sundial, whose
gnomon, or indicator, becomes the finger of scornful time.   **62. gender:** engender.   **62. Turn thy
complexion:** grow pale.

OTH: O, ay; as summer flies are in the shambles,°
  That quicken° even with blowing. O thou weed,
  Who are so lovely fair and smell'st so sweet
  That the sense aches at thee, would thou hads't ne'er been born!
DES: Alas, what ignorant sin have I committed?   70
OTH: Was this fair paper, this most goodly book,
  Made to write "whore" upon? What committed!
  Committed! O thou public commoner!°
  I should make very forges of my cheeks,
  That would to cinders burn up modesty,   75
  Did I but speak thy deeds. What committed!
  Heaven stops the nose at it and the moon winks,
  The bawdy wind that kisses all it meets
  Is hush'd within the hollow mine of earth,
  And will not hear it. What committed!   80
  Impudent strumpet!
DES: By heaven, you do me wrong.
OTH: Are not you a strumpet?
DES: No, as I am a Christian:
  If to preserve this vessel° for my lord
  From any other foul unlawful touch
  Be not to be a strumpet, I am none.   85
OTH: What, not a whore?
DES: No, as I shall be sav'd.
OTH: Is 't possible?
DES: O, heaven forgive us!
OTH: I cry you mercy, then:
  I took you for the cunning whore of Venice
  That married with Othello. (*Raising his voice.*) You, mistress,   90
  That have the office opposite to Saint Peter,
  And keep the gate of hell!

       (*Enter* EMILIA.)

               You, you, ay, you!
We have done our course; there's money for your pains:
  I pray you, turn the key and keep our counsel.   (*Exit.*)
EMIL: Alas, what does this gentleman conceive?   95
  How do you, madam? how do you, my good lady?
DES: 'Faith, half asleep.
EMIL: Good madam, what's the matter with my lord?
DES: With who?

---

66. shambles: slaughterhouse.   **67. quicken:** come to life.   **73. commoner:** prostitute.   **83. vessel:** body.

EMIL: Why, with my lord, madam.   100
DES: Who is thy lord?
EMIL: He that is yours, sweet lady.
DES: I have none: do not talk to me, Emilia;
   I cannot weep; nor answers have I none,
   But what should go by water.° Prithee, tonight
   Lay on my bed my wedding sheets: remember;   105
   And call thy husband hither.
EMIL: Here 's a change indeed!   *(Exit.)*
DES: 'Tis meet I should be us'd so, very meet.
   How have I been behav'd, that he might stick
   The small'st opinion on my least misuse?°

(*Enter* IAGO *and* EMILIA.)

IAGO: What is your pleasure, madam? How is 't with you?   110
DES: I cannot tell. Those that do teach young babes
   Do it with gentle means and easy tasks:
   He might have chid me so; for, in good faith,
   I am a child to chiding.
IAGO: What is the matter, lady?
EMIL: Alas, Iago, my lord hath so bewhor'd her,   115
   Thrown such despite° and heavy terms upon her,
   As true hearts cannot bear.
DES: Am I that name, Iago?
IAGO: What name, fair lady?
DES: Such as she said my lord did say I was.
EMIL: He call'd her whore: a beggar in his drink   120
   Could not have laid such terms upon his callet.°
IAGO: Why did he so?
DES: I do not know; I am sure I am none such.
IAGO: Do not weep, do not weep. Alas the day!
EMIL: Hath she forsook so many noble matches,   125
   Her father and her country and her friends,
   To be call'd whore? would it not make one weep?
DES: It is my wretched fortune.
IAGO: Beshrew him for 't!
   How comes this trick upon him?
DES: Nay, heaven doth know.
EMIL: I will be hang'd, if some eternal villain,   130
   Some busy and insinuating rogue,
   Some cogging,° cozening slave, to get some office,
   Have not devis'd this slander; I will be hang'd else.

---

104. go by water: be expressed by tears.   **109. misuse:** evil conduct.   **116. despite:** contempt, scorn.
121. callet: lewd woman.   **132. cogging:** cheating.

IAGO: Fie, there is no such man; it is impossible.
DES: If any such there be, heaven pardon him!   135
EMIL: A halter pardon him! and hell gnaw his bones!
 Why should he call her whore? who keeps her company?
 What place? what time? what form? what likelihood?
 The Moor's abus'd by some most villainous knave,
 Some base notorious knave, some scurvy fellow.   140
 O heaven, that such companions thou 'ldst unfold,
 And put in every honest hand a whip
 To lash the rascals naked through the world
 Even from the east to th' west!
IAGO: Speak within door.°
EMIL: O, fie upon them! Some such squire he was   145
 That turn'd your wit the seamy side without,
 And made you to suspect me with the Moor.
IAGO: You are a fool; go to.
DES: Alas, Iago.
 What shall I do to win my lord again?
 Good friend, go to him; for, by this light of heaven,   150
 I know not how I lost him. Here I kneel:
 If e'er by will did trespass 'gainst his love,
 Either in discourse of thought or actual deed,
 Or that mine eyes, mine ears, or any sense,
 Delighted them in any other form;   155
 Or that I do not yet, and ever did,
 And ever will—though he do shake me off
 To beggarly divorcement—love him dearly,
 Comfort forswear me! Unkindness may do much;
 And his unkindness may defeat my life,   160
 But never taint my love. I cannot say "whore":
 It doth abhor me now I speak the word;
 To do the act that might the addition° earn
 Not the world's mass of vanity could make me.
IAGO: I pray you, be content; 'tis but his humour: 165
 The business of the state does him offence,
 And he does chide with you.
DES: If 'twere no other,—
IAGO: 'Tis but so, I warrant. (*Trumpets within.*)
 Hark, how these instruments summon to supper!
 The messengers of Venice stay the meat°;   170
 Go in, and weep not; all things shall be well.   (*Exeunt* DESDEMONA *and* EMILIA.)

---

144. Speak . . . door: i.e., not so loud.   **163. addition:** title.   **170. stay the meat:** are waiting for
supper.

(*Enter* RODERIGO.)

How now, Roderigo!

ROD: I do not find that thou dealest justly with me.

IAGO: What in the contrary?

ROD: Everyday thou daffest me° with some device, Iago; and rather, as it seems to   175
me now, keepest from me all conveniency° than suppliest me with the least
advantage of hope. I will indeed no longer endure it, nor am I yet persuaded to
put up° in peace what already I have foolishly suffered.

IAGO: Will you hear me, Roderigo?

ROD: 'Faith, I have heard too much, for your words and performances are no kin   180
together.

IAGO: You charge me most unjustly.

ROD: With nought but truth. I have wasted myself out of my means. The jewels
you have had from me to deliver to Desdemona would half have corrupted a
votarist°: you have told me she hath received them and returned me expectations   185
and comforts of sudden respect and acquaintance, but I find none.

IAGO: Well; go to; very well.

ROD: Very well! go to! I cannot go to, man; nor 'tis not very well: nay, I think it is
scurvy, and begin to find myself fopped° in it.

IAGO: Very well.   190

ROD: I tell you 'tis not very well. I will make myself known to Desdemona: if she
will return me my jewels, I will give over my suit and repent my unlawful solicita-
tion; if not, assure yourself I will seek satisfaction of you.

IAGO: You have said now.°

ROD: Ay, and said nothing but what I protest intendment° of doing.   195

IAGO: Why, now I see there 's mettle in thee, and even from this instant do build
on thee a better opinion than ever before. Give me thy hand, Roderigo: thou hast
taken against me a most just exception; but yet, I protest, I have dealt most
directly in thy affair.

ROD: It hath not appeared.   200

IAGO: I grant indeed it had not appeared, and your suspicion is not without wit and
judgement. But, Roderigo, if thou hast that in thee indeed, which I have greater
reason to believe now than ever, I mean purpose, courage and valour, this night
show it: if thou the next night following enjoy not Desdemona, take me from this
world with treachery and devise engines for° my life.   205

ROD: Well, what is it? is it within reason and compass?

IAGO: Sir, there is especial commission come from Venice to depute Cassio in
Othello's place.

ROD: Is that true? why, then Othello and Desdemona return again to Venice.

---

175. daffest me: puts me off with an excuse.   **176. conveniency:** advantage, opportunity.   **178. put
up:** submit to.   **185. votarist:** nun.   **189. fopped:** fooled.   **194. You . . . now:** well said, quite right.
195. intendment: purpose, intention.   **205. engines for:** plots against.

IAGO: O, no; he goes into Mauritania° and takes away with him the fair Desde-   210
mona, unless his abode be lingered here by some accident: wherein none can be
so determinate° as the removing of Cassio.

ROD: How do you mean, removing of him?

IAGO: Why, by making him uncapable of Othello's place; knocking out his brains.

ROD: And that you would have me to do?   215

IAGO: Ay, if you dare do yourself a profit and a right. He sups to-night with a harlotry,° and thither will I go to him: he knows not yet of his honourable fortune. If
you will watch his going thence, which I will fashion to fall out between twelve
and one, you may take him at your pleasure: I will be near to second your
attempt, and he shall fall between us. Come, stand not amazed at it, but go along   220
with me; I will show you such a necessity in his death that you shall think yourself
bound to put it to him. It is now high° supper-time, and the night grows to waste:
about it.

ROD: I will hear further reason for this.

IAGO: And you shall be satisfied.   *(Exeunt.)*   225

SCENE III.

Another room in the castle.

(*Enter* OTHELLO, LODOVICO, DESDEMONA, EMILIA, *and* ATTENDANTS.)

LOD: I do beseech you, sir, trouble yourself no further.

OTH: O, pardon me; 'twill do me good to walk.

LOD: Madam, good night; I humbly thank your ladyship.

DES: Your honour is most welcome.

OTH: Will you walk, sir?

O,—Desdemona,—   5

DES: My lord?

OTH: Get you to bed on th' instant; I will be returned forthwith: dismiss your
attendant there: look 't be done.

DES: I will, my lord.   (*Exit* OTHELLLO, *with* LODOVICO *and* ATTENDANTS.)

EMIL: How goes it now? he looks gentler than he did.   10

DES: He says he will return incontinent°:
He hath commanded me to go to bed,
And bade me to dismiss you.

EMIL: Dismiss me!

DES: It was his bidding; therefore, good Emilia,
Give me my nightly wearing, and adieu: 15
We must not now displease him.

EMIL: I would you had never seen him!

DES: So would not I: my love doth so approve him,

---

210. Mauritania: Roman name of northwest Africa, supposed land of the Moors.   **212. determinate:**
decisive.   **216–217. harlotry:** courtesan.   **222. high:** quite.   **IV.iii. 11. incontinent:** immediately.

That even his stubbornness,° his checks,° his frowns,—
Prithee, unpin me,—have grace and favour in them.   20
EMIL: I have laid those sheets you bade me on the bed.
DES: All 's one. Good faith, how foolish are our minds!
    If I do die before thee, prithee, shroud me
    In one of those same sheets.
EMIL: Come, come, you talk.
DES: My mother had a maid call'd Barbary: 25
    She was in love, and he she lov'd prov'd mad
    And did forsake her: she had a song of 'willow';
    An old thing 'twas, but it express'd her fortune,
    And she died singing it: that song to-night
    Will not go from my mind; I have much to do,   30
    But to° go hang my head all at one side,
    And sing it like poor Barbary. Prithee, dispatch.
EMIL: Shall I go fetch your night-gown?°
DES: No, unpin me here.
    This Lodovico is a proper man.
EMIL: A very handsome man.   35
DES: He speaks well.
EMIL: I know a lady in Venice would have walked barefoot to Palestine for a
    touch of his nether lip.
DES (*Singing*):   The poor soul sat sighing by a sycamore tree,
        Sing all a green willow;   40
    Her hand on her bosom, her head on her knee,
        Sing willow, willow, willow:
    The fresh streams ran by her, and murmur'd her moans;
        Sing willow, willow, willow;
    Her salt tears fell from her, and soft'ned the stones;—   45
    Lay by these:—
    (*Singing*) Sing willow, willow, willow;
    Prithee, hie thee; he'll come anon:—
    (*Singing*) Sing all a green willow must be my garland.
        Let nobody blame him; his scorn I approve,—   50
    Nay, that 's not next.—Hark! who is 't that knocks?
EMIL: It 's the wind.
DES (*Singing*): I call'd my love false love; but what said he then?
        Sing willow, willow, willow:
        If I court moe women, you'll couch with moe men.—   55
    So, get thee gone; good night. Mine eyes do itch;
    Doth that bode weeping?
EMIL: 'Tis neither here nor there.

---

19. stubbornness: harshness.   **19. checks:** rebukes.   **31. But to:** not to.   **33. night-gown:** dressing
gown.

DES: I have heard it said so. O, these men, these men!
  Dost thou in conscience think,—tell me, Emilia,—
  That there be women do abuse their husbands   60
  In such gross kind?
EMIL: There be some such, no question.
DES: Wouldst thou do such a deed for all the world?
EMIL: Why, would not you?
DES: No, by this heavenly light!
EMIL: Nor I neither by this heavenly light; I might do't as well i' the dark.
DES: Wouldst thou do such a deed for all the world?   65
EMIL: The world 's a huge thing: it is a great price
  For a small vice.
DES: In troth, I think thou wouldst not.
EMIL: In troth, I think I should; and undo 't when I had done. Marry, I would not
  do such a thing for a joint-ring,° nor for measures of lawn, nor for gowns, petti-   70
  coats, nor caps, nor any petty exhibition°; but, for all the whole world,—why,
  who would not make her husband a cuckold to make him a monarch? I should
  venture purgatory for 't.
DES: Beshrew me, if I would do such a wrong
  For the whole world.
EMIL: Why, the wrong is but a wrong i' the world; and having the world for your   75
  labour, 'tis a wrong in your own world, and you might quickly make it right.
DES: I do not think there is any such woman.
EMIL: Yes, a dozen; and as many to the vantage° as would store the world they
    played for.   80
  But I do think it is their husband's faults
  If wives do fall: say that they slack their duties,
  And pour our treasures into foreign laps,°
  Or else break out in peevish jealousies,
  Throwing restraint upon us; or say they strike us,   85
  Or scant our former having in despite°;
  Why, we have galls,° and though we have some grace,
  Yet have we some revenge. Let husbands know
  Their wives have sense like them: they see and smell
  And have their palates both for sweet and sour,   90
  As husbands have. What is it that they do
  When they change us for others? Is it sport?
  I think it is: and doth affection breed it?
  I think it doth: is 't frailty that thus errs?
  It is so too: and have not we affections,   95
  Desires for sport, and frailty, as men have?

---

70. joint-ring: a ring made in separable halves as a lover's token.   **71. exhibition:** gift, present.   **79. to the vantage:** in addition.   **83. pour . . . laps:** i.e., are unfaithful.   **86. scant . . . despite:** reduce our allowance to spite us.   **87. have galls:** are capable of resenting injury and insult.

Then let them use us well: else let them know,
The ills we do, their ills instruct us so.

DES: Good night, good night: heaven me such uses send,
Not to pick bad from bad, but by bad mend!   (*Exeunt.*)   100

ACT V

SCENE I.

Cyprus. A street.

(*Enter* IAGO *and* RODERIGO.)

IAGO: Here stand behind this bulk°; straight will he come:
Wear thy good rapier bare, and put it home:
Quick, quick; fear nothing; I'll be at they elbow:
It makes us, or it mars us; think on that,
And fix most firm thy resolution.   5

ROD: Be near at hand; I may miscarry in 't.

IAGO: Here, at thy hand: be bold, and take thy stand. (*Retires.*)

ROD: I have no great devotion to the deed;
And yet he hath given me satisfying reasons:
'Tis but a man gone. Forth, my sword: he dies.   10

IAGO: I have rubb'd this young quat° almost to the sense,°
And he grows angry. Now, whether he kill Cassio,
Or Cassio him, or each do kill the other,
Every way makes my gain: live Roderigo,
He calls me to a restitution large   15
Of gold and jewels that I bobb'd° from him,
As gifts to Desdemona;
It must not be: if Cassio do remain,
He hath a daily beauty in his life
That makes me ugly; and, besides, the Moor   20
May unfold me to him; there stand I in much peril:
No, he must die. But so: I hear him coming.

(*Enter* CASSIO.)

ROD: I know his gait, 'tis he.—Villain, thou diest! (*Makes a pass at* CASSIO.)

CAS: That thrust had been mine enemy indeed,
But that my coat° is better than thou know'st: 25
I will make proof of thine. (*Draws, and wounds* RODERIGO.)

ROD: O, I am slain!

(IAGO *from behind wounds* CASSIO *in the leg, and exits.*)

CAS: I am maim'd for ever. Help, ho! murder! murder! (*Falls.*)

V.i. 1. bulk: framework projecting from the front of a shop.   **11. quat:** pimple, pustule; used contemptuously.   **11. to the sense:** to the quick.   **16. bobb'd:** filched cunningly.   **25. coat:** coat of mail.

(*Enter* OTHELLO.)

OTH:	The voice of Cassio: Iago keeps his word.
ROD:	O, villain that I am!
OTH:	It is even so.
CAS:	O, help, ho! light! a surgeon!
OTH:	'Tis he:—O brave Iago, honest and just,

That hast such noble sense of thy friend's wrong!
Thou teachest me. Minion, your dear lies dead,
And your unblest fate hies: strumpet, I come.
Forth of my heart those charms, thine eyes, are blotted;
Thy bed, lust-stain'd, shall with lust's blood be spotted.   (*Exit* OTHELLO.)

(*Enter* LODOVICO *and* GRATIANO.)

CAS:	What, ho! no watch? no passage?° murder! murder!
GRA:	'Tis some mischance; the cry is very direful.
CAS:	O, help!
LOD:	Hark!
ROD:	O wretched villain!
LOD:	Two or three groan: it is a heavy° night;

These may be counterfeits: let 's think 't unsafe
To come in to the cry without more help.

ROD:	Nobody come? then shall I bleed to death.
LOD:	Hark!

(*Enter* IAGO *with a light.*)

GRA:	Here 's one comes in his shirt, with light and weapons.
IAGO:	Who 's there? whose noise is this that cries on° murder?
LOD:	We do not know.
IAGO:	Did not you hear a cry?
CAS:	Here, here! for heaven's sake, help me!
IAGO:	What's the matter?
GRA:	This is Othello's ancient, as I take it.
LOD:	The same indeed; a very valiant fellow.
IAGO:	What are you here that cry so grievously?
CAS:	Iago? O, I am spoil'd, undone by villains!

Give me some help.

IAGO:	O me, lieutenant! what villains have done this?
CAS:	I think that one of them is hereabout,

And cannot make away.

IAGO:	O treacherous villains!

What are you there? come in, and give some help. (*To* LODOVICO *and* GRATIANO.)

ROD:	O, help me here!
CAS:	That 's one of them.

37. passage: people passing.   **42. heavy:** thick, cloudy.   **48. cries on:** cries out.

IAGO: O murd'rous slave! O villain! (*Stabs* RODERIGO.)
ROD: O damn'd Iago! O inhuman dog!
IAGO: Kill men i' th' dark!—Where be these bloody thieves?—
    How silent is this town!—Ho! murder! murder!—
    What° may you be? are you of good or evil?   65
LOD: As you shall prove us, praise us.
IAGO: Signior Lodovico?
LOD: He, sir.
IAGO: I cry you mercy. Here 's Cassio hurt by villains.
GRA: Cassio!   70
IAGO: How is 't, brother!
CAS: My leg is cut in two.
IAGO: Marry, heaven forbid!
    Light, gentlemen: I'll bind it with my shirt.

       (*Enter* BIANCA.)

BIAN: What is the matter, ho? who is 't that cried?
IAGO: Who is 't that cried?   75
BIAN: O my dear Cassio! my sweet Cassio!
    O Cassio, Cassio, Cassio!
IAGO: O notable strumpet! Cassio, may you suspect
    Who they should be that have thus mangled you?
CAS: No.   80
GRA: I am sorry to find you thus: I have been to seek you.
IAGO: Lend me a garter. So. O, for a chair,°
    To bear him easily hence!
BIAN: Alas, he faints! O Cassio, Cassio, Cassio!
IAGO: Gentlemen all, I do suspect this trash°   85
    To be a party in this injury.
    Patience awhile, good Cassio. Come, come;
    Lend me a light. Know we this face or no?
    Alas, my friend and my dear countryman
    Roderigo! no:—yes, sure:—O heaven! Roderigo.   90
GRA: What, of Venice?
IAGO: Even he, sir: did you know him?
GRA: Know him! ay.
IAGO: Signior Gratiano? I cry your gentle pardon;
    These bloody accidents must excuse my manners,
    That so neglected you.
GRA: I am so glad to see you.   95
IAGO: How do you, Cassio? O, a chair, a chair!
GRA: Roderigo!
IAGO: He, he, 'tis he. (*A chair brought in.*) O, that's well said; the chair.
    Some good man bear him carefully from hence;

65. What: who.   **82. chair:** sedan chair.   **85. trash:** worthless thing, i.e., Bianca.

I'll fetch the general's surgeon. (*To* Bianca) For you, mistress, 100
Save you your labour. He that lies slain here, Cassio,
Was my dear friend: what malice was between you?
Cas: None in the world; nor do I know the man.
Iago (*To* Bian.):   What, look you pale? O, bear him out o' th' air.

(Cassio *and* Roderigo *are borne off.*)

Stay you, good gentlemen. Look you pale, mistress? 105
Do you perceive the gastness° of her eye?
Nay, if you stare, we shall hear more anon.
Behold her well; I pray you, look upon her:
Do you see, gentlemen? nay, guiltiness will speak,
Though tongues were out of use. 110

(*Enter* Emilia.)

Emil: 'Las, what's the matter? what's the matter, husband?
Iago: Cassio hath here been set on in the dark
By Roderigo and fellows that are scap'd:
He's almost slain, and Roderigo dead.
Emil: Alas, good gentlemen! alas, good Cassio! 115
Iago: This is the fruit of whoring. Prithee, Emilia.
Go know of Cassio where he supp'd to-night.
(*To* Bianca) What, do you shake at that?
Bian: He supp'd at my house; but I therefore shake not.
Iago: O, did he so? I charge you, go with me. 120
Emil: Fie, fie upon thee, strumpet!
Bian: I am no strumpet; but of life as honest
As you that thus abuse me.
Emil: As I! foh! fie upon thee!
Iago: Kind gentlemen, let's go see poor Cassio dress'd.
Come, mistress, you must tell's another tale. 125
Emilia, run you to the citadel,
And tell my lord and lady what hath happ'd.
Will you go on afore? (*Aside*) This is the night
That either makes me or fordoes° me quite.   (*Exeunt.*)

SCENE II.

A bedchamber in the castle.

(*Enter* Othello *with a light;* Desdemona *in her bed.*)

Oth: It is the cause, it is the cause,° my soul,—
Let me not name it to you, you chaste stars!—

---

106. gastness: terror, ghastliness.   **129. fordoes:** undoes, ruins.   **V.ii. 1. It is the cause:** i.e., the cause of justice on which Othello must act, Desdemona's deed, which is too unmentionable to be named to the chaste stars.

It is the cause. Yet I'll not shed her blood;
Nor scar that whiter skin of hers than snow,
And smooth as monumental alabaster.   5
Yet she must die, else she'll betray more men.
Put out the light, and then put out the light:
If I quench thee, thou flaming minister,
I can again thy former light restore,
Should I repent me: but once put out thy light,   10
Thou cunning'st pattern of excelling nature,
I know not where is that Promethean heat°
That can thy light relume.° When I have pluck'd the rose,
I cannot give it vital growth again,
It needs must wither: I'll smell thee on the tree. (*Kissing her.*)   15
O balmy breath, that dost almost persuade
Justice to break her sword! One more, one more.
Be thus when thou art dead, and I will kill thee,
And love thee after. One more, and that's the last:
So sweet was ne'er so fatal. I must weep,   20
But they are cruel tears: this sorrow's heavenly°;
It strikes where it doth love. She wakes.

DES: Who's there? Othello?
OTH: Ay, Desdemona.
DES: Will you come to bed, my lord?
OTH: Have you pray'd to-night, Desdemona?
DES: Ay, my lord.   25
OTH: If you bethink yourself of any crime
        Unreconcil'd as yet to heaven and grace,
        Solicit for it straight.
DES: Alack, my lord, what may you mean by that?
OTH: Well, do it, and be brief; I will walk by: 30
        I would not kill thy unprepared spirit;
        No; heaven forfend! I would not kill thy soul.
DES: Talk you of killing?
OTH: Ay, I do.
DES: Then heaven
        Have mercy on me!
OTH: Amen, with all my heart!
DES: If you say so, I hope you will not kill me.   35
OTH: Hum!
DES: And yet I fear you; for you're fatal then
        When your eyes roll so: why I should fear I know not,

---

12. Promethean heat: divine fire; allusion to the theft of fire from heaven by Prometheus. **13. relume:** rekindle. **21. this . . . heavenly:** this tenderness, with which I lament the punishment which justice compels me to inflict, is a holy passion.

Since guiltiness I know not; but yet I feel I fear.

OTH: Think on thy sins.

DES: They are loves I bear to you.   40

OTH: Ay, and for that thou diest.

DES: That death 's unnatural that kills for loving.
Alas, why gnaw you so your nether lip?
Some bloody passion shakes your very frame:
These are portents; but yet I hope, I hope,   45
They do not point on me.

OTH: Peace, and be still!

DES: I will so. What 's the matter?

OTH: That handkerchief which I so lov'd and gave thee
Thou gav'st to Cassio.

DES: No, by my life and soul!
Send for the man, and ask him.

OTH: Sweet soul, take heed,   50
Take heed of perjury; thou are on thy deathbed.

DES: Ay, but not yet to die.

OTH: Yes, presently:
Therefore confess thee freely of thy sin;
For to deny each article with oath
Cannot remove nor choke the strong conception°   55
That I do groan withal. Thou art to die.

DES: Then Lord have mercy on me!

OTH: I say, amen.

DES: And have you mercy too! I never did
Offend you in my life; never lov'd Cassio
But with such general warranty of heaven
As I might love; I never gave him token.   60

OTH: By heaven, I saw my handkerchief in 's hand.
O perjur'd woman! thou dost stone° my heart,
And makest me call what I intend to do
A murder, which I thought a sacrifice: 65
I saw the handkerchief.

DES: He found it then;
I never gave it him: send for him hither;
Let him confess a truth.

OTH: He hath confess'd.

DES: What, my Lord?

OTH: That he hath us'd thee.

DES: How? unlawfully?

OTH: Ay.   70

---

55. conception: plan, intention.   **63. stone:** turn to stone, harden; Othello means that he will be tempted to kill her in sheer anger because of her perjury.

DES: He will not say so.

OTH: No, his mouth is stopp'd;
 Honest Iago hath ta'en order° for 't.

DES: O! my fear interprets: what, is he dead?

OTH: Had all his hairs been lives, my great revenge
 Had stomach for them all.   75

DES: Alas! he is betray'd and I undone.

OTH: Out, strumpet! weep'st thou for him to my face?

DES: O, banish me, my lord, but kill me not!

OTH: Down, strumpet!

DES: Kill me to-morrow: let me live to-night!   80

OTH: Nay, if you strive,—

DES: But half an hour!

OTH: Being done, there is no pause.°

DES: But while I say one prayer!

OTH: It is too late. (*Smothers her.*)

EMIL (*at the door*):   My lord, my lord! what, ho! my lord, my lord!

OTH: What noise is this? Not dead? not yet quite dead?   85
 I that am cruel am yet merciful;
 I would not have thee linger in thy pain:
 So, so.

EMIL (*within*):   What, ho! my lord, my lord!

OTH: Who's there?

EMIL (*within*):   O, good my lord, I would speak a word with you!   90

OTH: Yes: 'tis Emilia. By and by. She 's dead.
 'Tis like she comes to speak of Cassio's death.—
 The noise was here. Ha! no more moving?
 Still as the grave. Shall she come in? were 't good?—
 I think she stirs again:—no. What 's best to do?   95
 If she come in, she'll sure speak to my wife:
 My wife! my wife! what wife? I have no wife.
 O, insupportable! O heavy hour!
 Methinks it should be now a huge eclipse
 Of sun and moon, and that th' affrighted globe   100
 Should yawn° at alteration.°

EMIL: (*Within*) I do beseech you
 That I may speak with you, O, good my lord!

OTH: I had forgot thee: O, come in, Emilia:
 Soft; by and by. Let me the curtains draw.
 Where art thou? (*Closes bed-curtains and opens door.*)

---

72. ta'en order: taken measures.   **82. Being . . . pause:** i.e., when the execution of the deed has once begun, there is no stopping.   **101. yawn:** gape in amazement.   **101. at alteration:** at the change.

(*Enter* EMILIA.)

	What 's the matter with thee now?	105

EMIL: O, my good lord, yonder's foul murders done!

OTH: What, now?

EMIL: But now, my lord.

OTH: It is the very error° of the moon;
She comes more nearer earth than she was wont, 110
And makes men mad.

EMIL: Cassio, my lord, hath kill'd a young Venetian
Call'd Roderigo.

OTH: Roderigo kill'd!
And Cassio kill'd!

EMIL: No, Cassio is not kill'd.

OTH: Not Cassio kill'd! then murder 's out of tune, 115
And sweet revenge grows harsh.

DES: O, falsely, falsely murder'd!

EMIL: Alas, what cry is that?

OTH: That! what!

EMIL: Out, and alas! that was my lady's voice.
Help, help, ho! help. O lady, speak again! 120
Sweet Desdemona! O sweet mistress, speak!

DES: A guiltless death I die.

EMIL: O, who hath done this deed?

DES: Nobody; I myself. Farewell:
Commend me to my kind lord: O, farewell! (*Dies.*) 125

OTH: Why, how should she be murd'red?

EMIL: Alas, who knows?

OTH: You heard her say herself, it was not I.

EMIL: She said so: I must needs report the truth.

OTH: She's, like a liar, gone to burning hell:
'Twas I that kill'd her.

EMIL: O, the more angel she, 130
And you the blacker devil!

OTH: She turn'd to folly,° and she was a whore.

EMIL: Thou dost belie her, and thou art a devil.

OTH: She was false as water.

EMIL: Thou art rash as fire, to say
That she was false: O, she was heavenly true! 135

OTH: Cassio did top her; ask thy husband else.
O, I were damned beneath all depth in hell,
But that I did proceed upon just grounds

---

109. error: irregularity.   **132. folly:** unchastity.

To this extremity. Thy husband knew it all.

EMIL: My husband!   140

OTH: Thy husband.

EMIL: That she was false to wedlock?

OTH: Ay, with Cassio. Nay, had she been true,
If heaven would make me such another world
Of one entire and perfect chrysolite,°   145
I'ld not have sold her for it.

EMIL: My husband!

OTH: Ay, 'twas he that told me first:
An honest man he is, and hates the slime
That sticks on filthy deeds.

EMIL: My husband!

OTH: What needs this iterance,° woman? I say thy husband.   150

EMIL: O mistress, villainy hath made mocks with° love!
My husband say that she was false!

OTH: He, woman;
I say thy husband: dost understand the word?
My friend, thy husband, honest, honest Iago.

EMIL: If he say so, may his pernicious soul   155
Rot half a grain a day! he lies to th' heart:
She was too fond of her most filthy bargain.

OTH: Ha!

EMIL: Do thy worst:
This deed of thine is no more worthy heaven   160
Than thou wast worthy her.

OTH: Peace, you were best.

EMIL: Thou hast not half that power to do me harm
As I have to be hurt.° O gull! O dolt!
As ignorant as dirt! thou hast done a deed—
I care not for thy sword; I'll make thee known,   165
Though I lost twenty lives.—Help! help, ho! help!
The Moor hath kill'd my mistress! Murder! murder!

(Enter MONTANO, GRATIANO, *and* IAGO *with others.)*

MON: What is the matter! How now, general!

EMIL: O, are you come, Iago? you have done well,
That men must lay their murders on your neck.   170

GRA: What is the matter?

EMIL: Disprove this villain, if thou be'st a man:
He says thou told'st him that his wife was false:

---

145. chrysolite: the golden stone; a name given to various precious stones of green color.   **150. iterance:** iteration, repetition.   **151. made mocks with:** derided, made sport of.   **163. to be hurt:** i.e., to endure hurting.

I know thou didst not, thou 'rt not such a villain:
  Speak, for my heart is full.   175
IAGO: I told him what I thought, and told no more
  Than what he found himself was apt° and true.
EMIL: But did you ever tell him she was false?
IAGO: I did.
EMIL: You told a lie; an odious, damned lie;   180
  Upon my soul, a lie, a wicked lie.
  She false with Cassio!—did you say with Cassio?
IAGO: With Cassio, mistress. Go to, charm° your tongue.
EMIL: I will not charm my tongue; I am bound to speak:
  My mistress here lies murdered in her bed,—   185
ALL: O heavens forfend!
EMIL: And your reports have set the murder on.
OTH: Nay, stare not, masters: it is true, indeed.
GRA: 'Tis a strange truth.
MON: O monstrous act!
EMIL: Villainy, villainy, villainy!   190
  I think upon 't, I think: I smell 't: O villainy—
  I thought so then°: I'll kill myself for grief:—
  O villainy, villainy!
IAGO: What, are you mad? I charge you, get you home.
EMIL: Good gentlemen, let me have leave to speak: 195
  'Tis proper I obey him, but not now.
  Perchance, Iago, I will ne'er go home.
OTH: O! O! O! (*He falls on the bed.*)
EMIL: Nay, lay thee down and roar;
  For thou hast kill'd the sweetest innocent
  That e'er did lift up eye.
OTH: (*Rising*) O, she was foul!   200
  I scarce did know you, uncle: there lies your niece,
  Whose breath, indeed, these hands have newly stopp'd:
  I know this act shows horrible and grim.
GRA: Poor Desdemona! I am glad thy father's dead:
  Thy match was mortal to him, and pure grief   205
  Shore° his old thread in twain: did he live now,
  This sight would make him do a desperate turn,
  Yea, curse his better angel from his side,
  And fall to reprobation.°
OTH: 'Tis pitiful; but yet Iago knows   210
  That she with Cassio hath the act of shame

---

177. apt: natural, likely.   **183. charm:** keep silent.   **192. then:** i.e., at some earlier time, probably IV,
ii, when she suspected the machinations of *some eternal villain*; she did not, however, know that villain to
be Iago until this moment.   **206. Shore:** cut   **209. reprobation:** damnation, rejection by God.

A thousand times committed; Cassio confess'd it:
And she did gratify his amorous works
With that recognizance° and pledge of love
Which I first gave her; I saw it in his hand: 215
It was a handkerchief, an antique token
My father gave my mother.

EMIL: O heaven! O heavenly pow'rs!

IAGO: Come, hold your peace.

EMIL: 'Twill out, 'twill out: I peace!
No, I will speak as liberal as the north°:   220
Let heaven and men and devils, let them all,
All, all, cry shame against me, yet I'll speak.

IAGO: Be wise, and get you home.

EMIL: I will not! (IAGO *offers to stab* EMILIA.)

GRA: Fie!
Your sword upon a woman?

EMIL: O thou dull Moor! that handkerchief thou speak'st of   225
I found by fortune° and did give my husband;
For often, with solemn earnestness,
More than indeed belong'd to such a trifle,
He begg'd me to steal it.

IAGO: Villainous whore!

EMIL: She give it Cassio! no, alas! I found it,   230
And I did give 't my husband.

IAGO: Filth, thou liest!

EMIL: By heaven, I do not, I do not, gentlemen.
O murd'rous coxcomb!° what should such a fool
Do with so good a wife!

OTH: Are there no stones in heaven°
But what serves for the thunder?—Precious villain!   235

              (*He runs at* IAGO: IAGO, *from behind, stabs* EMILIA, *and exits.*)

GRA: The woman falls; sure, he hath kill'd his wife.

EMIL: Ay, ay: O, lay me by my mistress' side.

GRA: He 's gone, but his wife 's kill'd.

MON: 'Tis a notorious villain. Take you this weapon,
Which I have here recover'd from the Moor: 240
Come, guard the door without; let him not pass,
But kill him rather. I'll after that same villain,
For 'tis a damned slave.   (*Exit with all but* OTHELLO *and* EMILIA.)

OTH: I am not valiant neither,
But every puny whipster° gets my sword:

---

214. recognizance: token.   **220. liberal as the north:** freely as the north wind.   **226. fortune:** chance.   **233. coxcomb:** fool; addressed to Othello.   **234. stones in heaven:** thunderbolts. It was supposed that real stones fell with the thunder and caused the damage.   **244. whipster:** contemptible fellow.

But why should honour outlive honesty?°   245
  Let it go all.
EMIL: What did thy song bode, lady?
  Hark, canst thou hear me? I will play the swan,
  And die in music. (*Singing*) Willow, willow, willow.—
  Moor, she was chaste; she lov'd thee, cruel Moor;
  So come my soul to bliss, as I speak true;   250
  So speaking as I think, I die, I die. (*Dies.*)
OTH: I have another weapon in this chamber;
  It is a sword of Spain, the ice-brook's temper°:—
  O, here it is. Uncle, I must come forth.
GRA (*within*): If thou attempt it, it will cost thee dear: 255
  Thou hast no weapon, and perforce must suffer.
OTH: Look in upon me then and speak with me,
  Or, naked° as I am, I will assault thee.

      (*Enter* GRATIANO.)

GRA: What is the matter?
OTH: Behold, I have a weapon;
  A better never did itself sustain   260
  Upon a soldier's thigh: I have seen the day,
  That, with this little arm and this good sword,
  I have made my way through more impediments
  Than twenty times your stop°: but, O vain boast!
  Who can control his fate? 'tis not so now.   265
  Be not afraid, though you do see me weapon'd;
  Here is my journey's end, here is my butt,°
  And very sea-mark° of my utmost sail.
  Do you go back dismay'd? 'tis a lost fear;
  Man° but a rush° against Othello's breast,   270
  And he retires. Where should Othello go?
  Now, how dost thou look now? O ill-starr'd wench!
  Pale as thy smock! when we shall meet at compt,°
  This look of thine will hurl my soul from heaven,
  And fiends will snatch at it. Cold, cold, my girl!   275
  Even like thy chastity. O cursed, cursed slave!
  Whip me, ye devils,
  From the possession of this heavenly sight!
  Blow me about in winds! roast me in sulphur!
  Wash me in steep-down gulfs of liquid fire!   280

---

245. honour outlive honesty: Othello realizes that he has done a shameful deed; he asks why his reputation for valor should endure.   **253. ice-brook's temper:** usually defined as "tempered in ice-cold water."   **258. naked:** unarmed.   **264. stop:** power.   **267. butt:** mark for archery, goal, limit.   **268. sea-mark:** beacon (marking his destination or limit).   **270. Man:** provide, as in manning a gun.   **270. rush:** reed.   **273. compt:** account, judgment day.

O Desdemona! Dead Desdemona! dead!
Oh! Oh!

> (*Enter* LODOVICO, CASSIO, *carried in a chair*, MONTANO, *and* IAGO, *prisoner*,
> *with* OFFICERS.)

LOD: Where is this rash and most unfortunate man?
OTH: That 's he that was Othello: here I am.
LOD: Where is that viper? bring the villain forth.   285
OTH: I look down towards his feet°; but that 's a fable.
   If that thou be'st a devil, I cannot kill thee. (*Wounds* IAGO.]
LOD: Wrench his sword from him.
IAGO: I bleed sir; but not kill'd.
OTH: I am not sorry neither: I 'ld have thee live;
   For, in my sense, 'tis happiness to die.   290
LOD: O thou Othello, that wert once so good,
   Fall'n in the practice of a damned slave,
   What shall be said to thee?
OTH: Why, any thing:
   An honourable murder, if you will;
   For nought I did in hate, but all in honour.   295
LOD: This wretch hath part confess'd his villainy:
   Did you and he consent in Cassio's death?
OTH: Ay.
CAS: Dear general, I never gave you cause.
OTH: I do believe it, and I ask your pardon.   300
   Will you, I pray, demand that demi-devil
   Why he hath thus ensnar'd my soul and body?
IAGO: Demand me nothing: what you know, you know:
   From this time forth I never will speak word.
LOD: What, not to pray?
GRA: Torments will ope your lips.   305
OTH: Well, thou dost best.
LOD: Sir, you shall understand what hath befall'n,
   Which, as I think, you know not. Here is a letter
   Found in the pocket of the slain Roderigo;
   And here another: the one of them imports   310
   The death of Cassio to be undertook
   By Roderigo.
OTH: O villain!
CAS: Most heathenish and most gross!
LOD: Now here 's another discontented° paper,
   Found in his pocket too; and this, it seems,   315
   Roderigo meant t' have sent this damned villain;

---

286. towards his feet: i.e., to see if they were cloven like a devil's.   **314. discontented:** expressing dissatisfaction.

But that belike Iago in the interim
Came in and satisfied him.

OTH: O thou pernicious caitiff!°—
How came you, Cassio, by that handkerchief
That was my wife's?

CAS: I found it in my chamber: 320
And he himself confess'd but even now
That there he dropp'd it for a special purpose
Which wrought to his desire.

OTH: O fool! O fool! fool!

CAS: There is besides in Roderigo's letter,
How he upbraids Iago, that he made him   325
Brave° me upon the watch; whereon it came
That I was cast°: and even but now he spake,
After long seeming dead, Iago hurt him,
Iago set him on.

LOD: You must forsake this room, and go with us: 330
Your power and your command is taken off,°
And Cassio rules in Cyprus. For this slave,
If there be any cunning cruelty
That can torment him much and hold him long,
It shall be his. You shall close prisoner rest,   335
Till that the nature of your fault be known
To the Venetian state. Come, bring him away.

OTH: Soft you; a word or two before you go.
I have done the state some service, and they know 't.
No more of that. I pray you, in your letters,   340
When you shall these unlucky deeds relate,
Speak of me as I am; nothing extenuate,°
Nor set down aught in malice: then must you speak
Of one that lov'd not wisely but too well;
Of one not easily jealous, but being wrought,   345
Perplex'd° in the extreme; of one whose hand,
Like the base Judean,° threw a pearl away
Richer than all his tribe; of one whose subdu'd eyes,
Albeit unused to the melting mood,
Drop tears as fast as the Arabian trees   350
Their medicinal gum. Set you down this;
And say besides, that in Aleppo° once,
Where a malignant and a turban'd Turk

---

318. caitiff: wretch.   **326. Brave:** defy.   **327. cast:** dismissed.   **331. taken off:** taken away.
342. extenuate: diminish, depreciate; the idea is contrasted with the thought of *malice* in the following
line.   **346. Perplex'd:** confounded, distracted.   **347. Judean:** infidel or disbeliever.   **352. Aleppo:** a
Turkish city where the Venetians had special trading privileges. It is stated that it was immediate death
for a Christian to strike a Turk in Aleppo; Othello risked his life for the honor of Venice.

Beat a Venetian and traduc'd the state,
I took by th' throat the circumcised dog,   355
And smote him, thus. (*Stabs himself.*)

LOD: O bloody period!°
GRA: All that is spoke is marr'd.
OTH: I kiss'd thee ere I kill'd thee: no way but this;
Killing myself, to die upon a kiss.

(*Falls on the bed, and dies.*)

CAS: This did I fear, but thought he had no weapon;   360
For he was great of heart.
LOD: (*To* IAGO) O Spartan dog,°
More fell than anguish, hunger, or the sea!
Look on the tragic loading of this bed;
This is thy work: the object poisons sight;
Let it be hid, Gratiano, keep the house,   365
And seize upon the fortunes of the Moor,
For they succeed on you. To you, lord governor,
Remains the censure of this hellish villain;
The time, the place, the torture: O, enforce it!
Myself will straight abroad; and to the state   370
This heavy act with heavy heart relate.   (*Exeunt.*)

[1604]

357. period: termination, conclusion.   **361. Spartan dog:** Spartan dogs were noted for their savagery.

Journal Entry

How effective is Shakespeare's play in portraying the presence of a black moor in a white society? Consider Brabantio's, the Duke's, Iago's, and Othello's various attitudes toward the issue of race relations.

Textual Considerations

1. To analyze the structural development of *Othello*, consider Othello's autobiographical speeches in act 1, scene 3. Explain how Othello's portrait of himself and his cultural background might have contributed to his manipulation by Iago.
2. Analyze the images of women in *Othello* from the viewpoint of gender and class. What role do the women fulfill in the patriarchal system? What position do they occupy in Venetian society?. Don't overlook Cassio's treatment of Desdemona and Bianca as well as the various images of women with which Iago entertains his audience in act 2, scene 1.
3. Consider the extent to which the settings of the play suggest a symbolic contrast between the social and political orders of Venice and Cyprus. To what extent do these symbolic settings reflect psychological changes in Othello?
4. What kinds of responses do Iago's soliloquies and asides elicit from the audience? Consider the audience's feelings of comfort, discomfort, fear, sympathy, repulsion, expectation, and suspense.

5. Analyze the images of women that Desdemona uses in act 1, scene 3, lines 185–88, and in act 4, scene 3, lines 25–32. To what extent do these images help Desdemona justify her actions and communicate her feelings and emotions? How effective is Desdemona's use of language in both passages?

Cultural Contexts

1. The explanations behind Iago's motives for destroying Othello have ranged from Iago's dissatisfaction with Othello's poor distribution of power within the ranks of his army, to Iago's pleasure and excitement in manipulating people, to Iago's "motiveless malignity." What other motives can you and your classmates attribute to Iago? How effective are these motives in view of the closure Iago imposes on this issue at the end of the play: "what you know, you know: From this time forth I never will speak a word" (act 5, scene 2, lines 303–304)?
2. Some of the lines in *Othello*, such as "Were I the Moor, I would not be Iago" (act 1, scene 1, line 57), suggest Iago's dissatisfaction with his sense of self. Identify other lines and speeches that support the viewpoint that Iago is continuously fashioning a new identity for himself.

Performance Exercises

PERFORMANCE EXPRESS (45 MINUTES)

Propose a cast for all the roles in *Othello*, using your classmates as actors. To identify themselves to their audience, ask actors to stick paper tags with their names to their garments. After a brief (ten-minute) rehearsal, bring them in front of the classroom audience to talk about their characters and discuss their roles in the play. Encourage the actors to explore voice, physical action, and the emotional possibilities of their roles. To create a good dynamic *ensemble*, invite the class to interact with the actors.

PERFORMANCE PROJECTS

1. One of the most reputable Shakespearean critics, A.C. Bradley (1851–1935), defined Othello as "by far the most romantic figure among Shakespeare's heroes." Working with your group, search for character traits that emphasize Othello's romantic background in his famous speech, "Her father lov'd me" (1.3.128–170). Break the script into its smallest parts and devise the character's intention for each part or beat. Discuss and encourage the actors cast in the role of Othello to present a variety of vocal, physical, and emotion choices. The group should also decide on scenic design, music, and costume to support this romantic staging of Othello's speech.
2. Iago was cast as a gloomy malcontent and self-centered individualist in the film adaptations of *Othello* by Orson Welles (1952) and Oliver Parker (1995). Working with your group, stage a production of Iago's soliloquies to show your own dramatic interpretation of Iago. Consider the importance of voice, movement, constumes, and emotional focus, as well as the context or situation in which Iago finds himself for his solo performance of each soliloquy.

Manuel Puig

Kiss of the Spider Woman°

Translated by Allan J. Baker

ACT I

SCENE I.

(SCENE: *A small cell in the Villa Devoto prison in Buenos Aires. The stage is in total darkness. Suddenly two overhead white spots light up the heads of the two men. They are sitting down, looking in opposite directions.*)

MOLINA: You can see there's something special about her, that she's not any ordinary woman. Quite young . . . and her face more round than oval, with a little pointy chin like a cat's.

VALENTIN: And her eyes?

MOLINA: Most probably green. She looks up at the model, the black panther lying down in its cage in the zoo. But she scratches her pencil against the sketch pad and the panther sees her.

VALENTIN: How come it didn't smell her before?

MOLINA (*deliberately not answering*): But, who's that behind her? Someone trying to light a cigarette, but the wind blows out the match.

VALENTIN: Who is it?

MOLINA: Hold on. She flusters. He's no matinée idol but he's nice-looking, in a hat with a low brim. He touches the brim like he's saluting and says the drawing is terrific. She fiddles with the curls of her fringe.

VALENTIN: Go on.

MOLINA: He can tell she's a foreigner by her accent. She tells him that she came to New York when the war broke out. He asks her if she's homesick. And then it's like a cloud passes across her eyes and she tells him she comes from the mountains, someplace not far from Transylvania.

VALENTIN: Where Dracula comes from.

MOLINA: The next day he's in his office with some colleagues—he's an architect— and this girl, another architect he works with—and when the clock strikes three he just wants to drop everything and go to the zoo. It's right across the street. And the architect girl asks him why he's so happy. Deep down, she's really in love with him, no use her pretending otherwise.

VALENTIN: Is she a dog?

MOLINA: No, nothing out of this world: chestnut hair, but pleasant enough. But the other one, the one at the zoo, Irene—no, Irina—has disappeared. As time

Kiss of the Spider Woman: A play based on his novel of the same title.

goes by he just can't get her out of his mind until one day he's walking down this fashionable avenue and he notices something in the window of an art gallery. They're pictures by an artist who only paints. . . panthers. The guy goes in and there's Irina being congratulated by all the guests. And I don't remember what comes next.

VALENTIN: Try to remember . . .

MOLINA: Hold on a sec . . . Okay, . . . then the architect goes up and congratulates her too. She drops the critics and walks off with him. He tells her that he just happened to be passing by, really he was on his way to buy a present.

VALENTIN: For the girl architect.

MOLINA: Now he's wondering if he's got enough money with him to buy two presents. And he stops outside a shop and she gets a funny feeling when she sees what kind of shop it is. There are all different kinds of birds in little cages sipping fresh water from their bowls.

VALENTIN: Excuse me . . . is there any water in the bottle?

MOLINA: Yes, I filled it up when they let us out to the toilet.

> (*The white light which up till now has lit just their heads widens to fully light both actors: we see the cell for the first time.*)

VALENTIN: That's okay then.

MOLINA: Do you want some? It's nice and cool.

VALENTIN: No or we won't have enough for tea in the morning. Go on.

MOLINA: Don't exaggerate. We've got enough to last all day.

VALENTIN: Don't spoil me. I forgot to fetch some when they let us out to shower. If it wasn't for you we wouldn't have any.

MOLINA: Look, there's plenty . . . Anyway, when they go inside that shop it's like— I don't know what—it's like the devil just came in. The birds, blind with fear, fly into the wire mesh and hurt their wings. She grabs his hand and drags him outside. Straight away the birds calm down. She asks him to let her go home. When he comes back into the shop the birds are chirruping and singing just like normal and he buys one for the other girl's birthday. And then . . . it's no good, I can't remember what happens next, I'm pooped.

VALENTIN: Just a little more.

MOLINA: When I'm sleepy my memory goes. I'll carry on with the morning tea.

VALENTIN: No, it's better at night. During the day I don't want to bother with this trivia. There are more important things . . . (MOLINA *shrugs.*) If I'm not reading and I'm keeping quiet it's because I'm thinking. But don't take it wrong.

MOLINA (*upset by* VALENTIN'S *remark. With almost concealed irony*):   I shan't bother you. You can count on that!

VALENTIN: I see you understand. See you in the morning. (*He settles down to sleep.*)

MOLINA: Till tomorrow. Pleasant dreams of Irina. (MOLINA *settles down too, but he is troubled by something.*)

VALENTIN: I prefer the architect girl.

MOLINA: I'd already guessed that.

SCENE II.

(SCENE: MOLINA *and* VALENTIN *are sitting in different positions. They do not look at one another. Only their heads are lit: seconds later the night light comes on.*)

MOLINA: So they go on seeing each other and they fall in love. She pampers him, cuddles up in his arms, but when he wants to hold her tight and kiss her she slips away from him. She asks him not to kiss her but to let her kiss him with her full lips, but she keeps her mouth shut tight. (VALENTIN *is about to interrupt but* MOLINA *forges ahead.*) So, on their next date they go to this quaint restaurant. He tells her she's prettier than ever in her shimmering black blouse. But she's lost her appetite, she can't manage a thing, and they leave. It's snowing gently. The noise of the city is muffled but far away you can just hear the growling of wild animals. The zoo's close, that's why. Barely in a whisper she says she's afraid to return to her house and spend the night alone. He hails a taxi and they go to his house. It's a huge place, all *fin de siècle;* it used to be his mother's.

VALENTIN: And what does he do?

MOLINA: Nothing. He lights up his pipe and looks over at her. You always guessed he had a kind heart.

VALENTIN: I'd like to ask you something: how do you picture his mother?

MOLINA: So you can make fun of her?

VALENTIN: I swear I won't.

MOLINA: I don't know . . . someone really charming. She made her husband happy and her children too. She's always well groomed.

VALENTIN: And do you picture her scrubbing floors?

MOLINA: No, she's always impeccable. The high-necked dress hides the wrinkles round her throat.

VALENTIN: Always impeccable. With servants. People with no other choice than to fetch and carry for her. And, of course, she was happy with her husband who also exploited her in his turn, kept her locked up in the house like a slave, waiting for him . . .

MOLINA: . . . Listen . . .

VALENTIN: . . . waiting for him to come home every night from his chambers or his surgery. And she condoned the system, fed all this crap to her son and now he trips over the panther woman. Serves him right.

MOLINA (*irritated*): Why did you have to bring up all that? . . . I'd forgotten all about this dump while I was telling you the movie.

VALENTIN: I'd forgotten about it too.

MOLINA: Well, then . . . Why d'you have to go and break the spell?

VALENTIN: Let me explain . . . .

MOLINA: Fine, but not now, tomorrow. . . . Why did I get lumbered with you and not the panther woman's boyfriend?

VALENTIN: That's another story and one that doesn't interest me.

MOLINA: Are you frightened to talk about it?

VALENTIN: It bores me. I know all about it—even though you've never said a word.

MOLINA: Fine. I told you I got done for corruption of minors. There's nothing else to add. So don't come the psychologist with me.

VALENTIN (*shielding himself behind humor*): Admit that you like him because he smokes a pipe.

MOLINA: No, it's not that. It's because he's gentle and understanding.

VALENTIN: His mother castrated him, that's all.

MOLINA: I like him and that's that. And you like the architect girl—what's so Bolshy about her?

VALENTIN: I prefer her to the panther woman, that's for sure. But the guy with the pipe won't suit you.

MOLINA: Why not?

VALENTIN: Your intentions aren't exactly chaste, are they?

MOLINA: Of course not.

VALENTIN: Exactly. He likes Irina because she's frigid and he doesn't have to pounce on her and that's why he takes her to the house where his mother is still present even if she is dead.

MOLINA (*getting angrier and angrier*): Continue.

VALENTIN: If he's still kept all his mother's things it's because he wants to remain a child. He doesn't bring home a woman but a child to play with.

MOLINA: That's all in your head. I don't even know if the place is his mother's—I said that because I liked the place and since I saw antiques there I told you it belonged to his mother. For all I know he rents it furnished.

VALENTIN: So you're making up half the movie?

MOLINA: I'm not, I swear. But—you know—there are some things I add to fill it out for you. The house, for example. And, in any case, don't forget I'm a window dresser and that's almost like being an interior designer. . . . Well, she begins to tell him her story but I don't remember all the details. . . . I remember that in her village, a long time ago, there used to be panther-women. And these tales frightened her a lot when she was a little girl.

VALENTIN: And the birds? . . . Why were they afraid of her?

MOLINA: That's what the architect asks her. And what does she say? She doesn't say anything! And the scene ends with him in pyjamas and a dressing gown, good quality, no pattern, something serviceable—and he looks at her sleeping on the sofa from his bedroom door and he lights up his pipe and stands there . . . thoughtful.

VALENTIN: Do you know what I like about it? That it's like an allegory of women's fear of submitting to the male, because when it comes to sex, the animal part takes over. You see?

MOLINA (*he doesn't approve of* VALENTIN's *comments*): Irina wakes up, it's morning already.

VALENTIN: She wakes up because of the cold, like us.

MOLINA (*irritated*): I knew you were going to say that. . . . She's woken up by the canary, singing in its cage. At first she's afraid to go near it, but the little bird is chirpy so she dares to move a little closer. She heaves a big sigh of relief because the bird isn't frightened of her. And then she makes breakfast . . . toast and cereals and pancakes . . .

VALENTIN: Don't mention food.

MOLINA: . . . and pancakes . . .

VALENTIN: I'm serious. Neither food nor women.

MOLINA: She wakes him up and he's all happy to see her settling in and so he asks her to stay there forever and marry him. And she says, yes, from the bottom of her heart and she looks around and the curtains look so beautiful to her, they're made of thick dark velvet.

(*Aggressively.*) And now you can fully appreciate the *fin de siècle* decor. Then Irina asks him if he truly wants her to be his wife to give her just a little more time, just long enough for her to get over her fears.

VALENTIN: You can see what's going on with her, can't you?

MOLINA: Hold on. He agrees and they get married. And on their wedding night she sleeps in the bed and he sleeps on the couch.

VALENTIN: Looking at his mother's ornaments. Admit it, it's your ideal home, isn't it?

MOLINA: Of course it is! Now I've got to put up with you telling me the same thing they all say.

VALENTIN: What d'you mean? What do they all say?

MOLINA: They're all the same, they all tell me the same thing.

VALENTIN: What?

MOLINA: That I was fussed over as a kid and that's why I'm like I am now, that I was clinging to my mother's skirts, but it's never too late to straighten out and all I need is a good woman because there's nothing better than a good woman.

VALENTIN: And that's what they all tell you?

MOLINA: And this is what I tell them. . . . You're dead right! . . . and since there's nothing better than a woman . . . I want to be one! So spare me the advice please, because I know what I feel like and it's all as clear as day to me.

VALENTIN: I don't see it as clear—at least, not the way you've just put it.

MOLINA: I don't need you telling me what's what—if you want I'll go on with the picture, if not, ciao. . . . I'll just whisper it to myself, and *arrivederci*, Sparafucile!

VALENTIN: Who's Sparafucile?

MOLINA: You don't have a clue about opera. He's the hatchet man in *Rigoletto*. . . . Where were we?

VALENTIN: The wedding night. He hasn't laid a finger on her.

MOLINA: And I forgot to tell you that they'd agreed she'd go and see a psychoanalyst.

VALENTIN: Excuse me again . . . don't get upset.

MOLINA: What is it?

VALENTIN (*less communicative than ever, somber*):   I can't keep my mind on the story.

MOLINA: Is it boring you?

VALENTIN: No, it's not that. It's . . . My head is in a state. (*He talks more to himself than to* MOLINA.) I just want to be quiet for a while. I don't know if this has ever happened to you, that you're just about to understand something, you've got the end of the thread and if you don't yank it now . . . you'll lose it.

MOLINA: Why do you like the architect girl?

VALENTIN: It has to come out some way or other. . . . (*Self-contemptuous.*) Weakness, I mean . . .

MOLINA: Ttt . . . it's not weakness.

VALENTIN (*bitter, impersonally*):   Funny how you just can't avoid getting attached to something. It's . . . it's as if the mind just oozed sentiment constantly.

MOLINA: Is that what you believe?

VALENTIN: Like a leaky tap. Drips falling over anything.

MOLINA: Anything?

VALENTIN: You can't stop the drips.

MOLINA: And you don't want to be reminded of your girlfriend, is that it?

VALENTIN (*mistrustful*):   How do you know whether I have a girlfriend?

MOLINA: It's only natural.

VALENTIN: I can't help it. . . . I get attached to anything that reminds me of her. Anyway, I'd do better to get my mind on what I ought to, right?

MOLINA: Yank the thread.

VALENTIN: Exactly.

MOLINA: And if you get it all in a tangle, Missy Valentina, you'll flunk needlework.

VALENTIN: Don't worry on my account.

MOLINA: Okay, I won't say another word.

VALENTIN: And don't call me Valentina. I'm not a woman.

MOLINA: How should I know?

VALENTIN: I'm sorry, Molina, but I don't give demonstrations.

MOLINA: I wasn't asking for one.

SCENE III.

(SCENE: *Night. The prison light is on.* MOLINA *and* VALENTIN *are sitting on the floor, eating.*)

VALENTIN (*speaking as soon as he finishes his last mouthful*):   You're a good cook.

MOLINA: Thank you, Valentin.

VALENTIN: It could cause problems later on. I'm getting spoiled.

MOLINA: You're crazy. Live for today!

VALENTIN: I don't believe in that live for today crap. We haven't earned that paradise yet.

MOLINA: Do you believe in Heaven and Hell?

VALENTIN: Hold on a minute. If we're going to have a discussion then we need a framework. Otherwise you'll just ramble on.

MOLINA: I'm not going to ramble.

VALENTIN: Okay. I'll state an opening proposition. Let me put it to you like this.

MOLINA: Put it any way you like.

VALENTIN: I can't live just for today. All I do is determined by the ongoing political struggle. D'you get me? Everything that I endure here, which is bad enough . . . is nothing if you compare it to torture . . . but you don't know what that's like.

MOLINA: I can imagine.

VALENTIN: No, Molina, you can't imagine what it's like. . . . Well, anyway, I can put up with all this because there's a blueprint. The essential thing is the social revolution and the pleasures of the senses come second. The greatest pleasure, well, it's knowing that I'm part of the most noble cause . . . my ideas, for instance . . . (*The prison lights go out. The BLUE nighttime light stays on.*) It's eight . . .

MOLINA: What do you mean "your ideas"?

VALENTIN: My ideals. Marxism. And that good feeling is one I can experience anywhere, even here in this cell, and even in torture. And that's my strength.

MOLINA: And what about your girlfriend?

VALENTIN: That has to be second too. And I'm second for her. Because she also knows what's most important. (MOLINA *remains silent.*) You don't look convinced.

MOLINA: Don't mind me. I'm going to turn in soon.

VALENTIN: You're mad! What about the panther-woman?

MOLINA: Tomorrow.

VALENTIN: What's up?

MOLINA: Look, Valentin, that's me. I get hurt easy. I cooked that food for you, with my supplies, and worse still I give you half my avocado—which is my favorite and could have eaten tomorrow . . . Result? You throw it in my face that I'm spoiling you. . . .

VALENTIN: Don't be so soft! It's just like a . . .

MOLINA: Say it!

VALENTIN: Say what?

MOLINA: I know what you were going to say, Valentin.

VALENTIN: Cut it out.

MOLINA: "It's just like a woman." That's what you were going to say.

VALENTIN: Yes.

MOLINA: And what's wrong with being soft like a woman? Why can't a man—or whatever—a dog, or a fairy—why can't he be sensitive if he feels like it?

VALENTIN: In excess, it can get in a man's way.

MOLINA: In the way of what? Of torturing someone?

VALENTIN: No, of getting rid of the torturers.

MOLINA: But if all men were like women then there'd be no torturers.

VALENTIN: And what would you do without men?

MOLINA: You're right. They're brutes, but I need them.

VALENTIN: Molina . . . you just said that if all men were like women there'd be no torturers. You've got a point there; kind of weird, but a point at least.

MOLINA: The way you say things. (*Imitating* VALENTIN.) "A point at least."

VALENTIN: I'm sorry I upset you.

MOLINA: I'm not upset.

VALENTIN: Well, cheer up, don't reproach me.

MOLINA: Do you want me to go on with the picture?

VALENTIN: Yeah, man, of course.

MOLINA: Man? What man? Tell me so he won't get away.

VALENTIN (*trying to hide that he finds this funny*): Start.

MOLINA: Irina goes along to the psychoanalyst who's a ladykiller, real handsome.

VALENTIN: Tell me what you mean by real handsome. I'd like to know.

MOLINA: Well, let's get this straight, he isn't my type at all.

VALENTIN: Who's the actor?

MOLINA: I don't remember. Too skinny for my taste. With a pencil moustache. But there's something about him, so full of himself, he just puts you off. And he puts off Irina. She skips the next appointment, she lies to her husband and instead of going to the doctor's she puts on that black fleecy coat and goes to the zoo, to look at the panther. The keeper comes along, opens the cage, throws in the meat and closes the door again. But he's absent-minded and leaves the key in the lock. Irina sneaks up to the door and puts her hand on the key. And she just stands there, musing, rapt in her thoughts.

VALENTIN: What does she do then?

MOLINA: That's all for tonight. I'll continue tomorrow.

VALENTIN: At least, let me ask you something.

MOLINA: What?

VALENTIN: Who do you identify with? Irina or the architect girl?

MOLINA: With Irina—who do you think? *Moi*—always with the leading lady.

VALENTIN: Continue.

MOLINA: What about you? I guess you're stuck because the guy is such a wimp.

VALENTIN: Don't laugh—with the psychoanalyst. But I didn't say anything about your choice, so don't mock mine. . . . You know something? I'm finding it hard to keep my mind on it.

MOLINA: What's the problem?

VALENTIN: Nothing.

MOLINA: Come on, open up a little.

VALENTIN: When you said the girl was there in front of the cage, I imagined it was my girl who was in danger.

MOLINA: I understand.

VALENTIN: I shouldn't be telling you this, Molina. But I guess you've figured it all out for yourself anyhow. My girl is in the organization too.

MOLINA: So what.

VALENTIN: It's only that I don't want to burden you with information it's better you don't know.

MOLINA: With me, it's not a woman, a girlfriend I mean. It's my mother. She's got blood pressure and a weak heart.

VALENTIN: People can live for years with that.

MOLINA: Sure, but they don't need more aggravation, Valentin. Imagine the shame of having a son inside—and why.

VALENTIN: Look, the worst has already happened, hasn't it?

MOLINA: Yes, but the risk is ever-present inside her. It's that dodgy heart.

VALENTIN: She's waiting for you. Eight years'll fly by, what with remission and all that. . . .

MOLINA (*a little contrived*):   Tell me about your girlfriend if you like. . . .

VALENTIN: I'd give anything to hold her in my arms right now.

MOLINA: It won't be long. You're not in for life.

VALENTIN: Something might happen to her.

MOLINA: Write to her, tell her not to take chances, that you need her.

VALENTIN: Never. Impossible. If you think like that you'll never change anything in the world.

MOLINA (*not realizing he's mocking* VALENTIN):   And you think you're going to change the world?

VALENTIN: Yes, and I don't care that you laugh. It makes people laugh to hear this, but what I have to do before anything is to change the world.

MOLINA: Sure, but you can't do it just like that, *and* on your own.

VALENTIN: But I'm not on my own—that's it! I'm with her and all those other people who think like we do. That's the end of the thread that slips through my fingers . . . I'm not apart from my comrades—I'm with them, right now! . . . It doesn't matter whether I can see them or not.

MOLINA (*with a slight drawl, skeptically*):   If that makes you feel good, terrific!

VALENTIN: Christ, what a moron!

MOLINA: Sticks and stones . . .

VALENTIN: Don't provoke me then. I'm not some loudmouth who just spouts off about politics in a bar. The proof is that I'm in here.

MOLINA: I'm sorry.

VALENTIN: It's okay . . .

MOLINA (*pretending not to pry*):   You were going to tell me something . . . about your girlfriend.

VALENTIN: We'd better drop that.

MOLINA: As you like . . .

VALENTIN: Why it gets me so upset, I can't fathom.

MOLINA: Better not, then, if it upsets you . . .

VALENTIN: The one thing I shouldn't tell you is her name.

MOLINA: What sort of girl is she?

VALENTIN: She's twenty-four, two years younger than me.

MOLINA: Thirteen years younger than me. . . . No, I tell a lie, sixteen.

VALENTIN: She was always politically conscious. First it was . . . well, I needn't be shy with you, at first it was because of the sexual revolution.

MOLINA (*bracing himself for some saucy tidbit*):   That I wouldn't miss.

VALENTIN: She comes from a bourgeois family, not really wealthy, but comfortably off. But as a kid and all through her adolescence she had to watch her parents destroy each other. Her father was cheating her mother, you know what I mean?

MOLINA: No, I don't.

VALENTIN: Cheating her by not telling her he needed other relationships. I don't hold with monogamy.

MOLINA: But it's beautiful when a couple love each other for ever and ever.

VALENTIN: Is that what you'd like?

MOLINA: It's my dream.

VALENTIN: Why do you like men then?

MOLINA: What's that got to do with it? I want to marry a man—to love and to cherish, for ever and ever.

VALENTIN: So, basically, you're just a bourgeois man?

MOLINA: A bourgeois lady, please.

VALENTIN: If you were a woman you'd think otherwise.

MOLINA: The only thing I want is to live forever with a wonderful man.

VALENTIN: And that's impossible because . . . well, if he's a man, he wants a woman . . . you'll always be living in a fool's paradise.

MOLINA: Go on about your girlfriend. I don't want to talk about me.

VALENTIN: She was brought up to be the lady of the house. Piano lessons, French, drawing. . . . I'll tell you the rest tomorrow, Molina . . . I want to think about something I was studying today.

MOLINA: Now you're getting your own back.

VALENTIN: No, silly. I'm tired, too.

MOLINA: I'm not sleepy at all.

SCENE IV.

(SCENE: *Night. The prison lights are on.* VALENTIN *is engrossed in a book.* MOLINA, *restless, is flicking through a magazine he already knows backwards.*)

VALENTIN (*lifting his head from the book*):   Why are they late with dinner? Next door had it ages ago.

MOLINA (*ironic*):   Is *that* all you're studying tonight? I'm not hungry, thank goodness.

VALENTIN: That's unusual. Don't you feel well?

MOLINA: No, just nerves.

VALENTIN: Listen . . . I think they're coming.

MOLINA: Hide the magazines or they'll pinch them.

VALENTIN: I'm famished.

MOLINA: Please Valentin, don't make a scene with the guards.

VALENTIN: No.

(*Through the grille in the door come two plates of porridge—one visibly more loaded than the other.* MOLINA *looks at* VALENTIN.)

VALENTIN: Porridge.

MOLINA: Yes. (MOLINA *looks at the two plates which* VALENTIN *has collected from the hatch. Exchanging an enigmatic glance with the invisible guard*). Thank you.

VALENTIN (*to guard*):   What about this one? Why's it got less? (*To* MOLINA.) I didn't say anything for your sake. Otherwise I'd have thrown it in his face, this bloody glue.

MOLINA: What's the use of complaining?

VALENTIN: One plate's only got half as much as the other. That bastard guard, he's out of his fucking mind.

MOLINA: It's okay, Valentin, I'll take the small portion.

VALENTIN (*serving* MOLINA *the large one*):   No, you like porridge, you always lap it up.

MOLINA: Skip the chivalry. You have it.

VALENTIN: I told you no.

MOLINA: Why should I have the big one?

VALENTIN: Because I know you like porridge.

MOLINA: But I'm not hungry.

VALENTIN: Eat it, it'll do you good. (VALENTIN *starts eating from the small plate.*)

MOLINA: No.

VALENTIN: It's not too bad today.

MOLINA: I don't want it.

VALENTIN: Afraid of putting on weight?

MOLINA: No.

VALENTIN: Get stuck in then. This porridge à la glue isn't so bad today. This small plate is plenty for me.

MOLINA (*starts eating, overcoming his resistance; his voice nostalgic now*):   Thursday. Ladies day. The cinema in my neighborhood used to show a romantic triple feature on Thursdays. Years ago now.

VALENTIN: Is that where you saw the panther-woman?

MOLINA: No, that was in a smart little cinema in that German neighborhood where all those posh houses with gardens are. My house was near there, but in the rundown part. Every Monday they'd show a German-language feature. Even during the war. They still do.

VALENTIN: Nazi propaganda films.

MOLINA: But the musical numbers were fabulous!

VALENTIN: You're touched. (*He finishes his dinner.*) They'll be turning off the lights soon, that's it for studying today. (*Unconsciously authoritarian.*) You can go on with the film now—Irina's hand was on the key in the lock.

MOLINA (*picking at his porridge*):   She takes the key out of the lock and gives it back to the keeper. The old fellow thanks her and she goes back home to wait for her husband. She's all out to kiss him, on the mouth this time.

VALENTIN (*absorbed*):   Mmmm . . .

MOLINA: Irina calls him up at his office, it's getting late, and the girl architect answers. Irina hangs up. She's eaten up with jealousy. She paces up and down the apartment like a caged beast, and when she walks by the bird cage she notices that the bird's wings are flapping frenetically. She can't control herself and she opens the little door and puts her hand right inside the cage. The little bird drops stone dead before she even touches it. Irina panics and flees from the house looking for her husband, but, of course, she has to go past the bar on the corner and she sees them both inside. And she just wants to tear the other woman to shreds. Irina only wears black clothes but she's never again worn that blouse he liked so much, the one in the restaurant scene, with all the rhinestones.

VALENTIN: What are they?

MOLINA (*shocked*): Rhinestones! I don't believe this! You don't know . . . ?

VALENTIN: I haven't the faintest.

MOLINA: They're like diamonds only worthless; little pieces of glass that shine.

> (*At this moment the cell light goes out.*)

VALENTIN: I'm going to turn in early tonight. I've had enough of all this drivel.

MOLINA (*overreacting, but deeply hurt*): Thank goodness there's no light so I don't have to see your face. Don't ever speak another word to me!

> (*Note: The production must establish that when the blue light is on—meaning nighttime—THEY CANNOT SEE EACH OTHER, and so are free to express themselves as they like in gestures and body language.*)

VALENTIN: I'm sorry . . . (MOLINA *stays silent.*) Really, I'm sorry, I didn't think you'd get so upset.

MOLINA: You upset me because it's one of my favorite movies, you can't know . . . (*He starts to cry.*) . . . you didn't see it.

VALENTIN: Are you crazy? It's nothing to cry about.

MOLINA: I'll . . . I'll cry if I feel like it.

VALENTIN: Suit yourself. . . . I'm very sorry.

MOLINA: And don't get the idea you've made me cry. It's because today's my mother's birthday and I'm dying to be with her. . . . And not with you. (*Pause.*) Ay! . . . Ay! . . . I don't feel well.

VALENTIN: What's wrong?

MOLINA: Ay! . . . Ay!

VALENTIN: What is it? What's the matter?

MOLINA: The girl's fucked!

VALENTIN: Which girl?

MOLINA: Me, dummy. It's my stomach.

VALENTIN: Do you want to throw up?

MOLINA: The pain's lower down. It's in my guts.

VALENTIN: I'll call the guard, okay?

MOLINA: No, it'll pass, Valentin.

VALENTIN: The food didn't do anything to me.

MOLINA: I bet it's my nerves. I've been on edge all day. I think it's letting up now.

VALENTIN: Try to relax. Relax your arms and legs, let them go loose.

MOLINA: Yes, that's better. I think it's going.

VALENTIN: Do you want to go to sleep?

MOLINA: I don't know . . . Ugh! it's awful . . .

VALENTIN: Maybe it'd be better if you talk, it'll take your mind off the pain.

MOLINA: You mean the movie?

VALENTIN: Where had we got to?

MOLINA: Afraid I'm going to croak before we get to the end?

VALENTIN: This is for your benefit. We broke off when they were in the bar on the corner.

MOLINA: Okay . . . the two of them get up together to leave and Irina takes cover behind a tree. The architect girl decides to take the shortcut home through the park. He told her everything while they were in the bar, that Irina doesn't make love to him, that she has nightmares about panther-women and all. The other girl, who'd just got used to the idea that she'd lost him, now begins to think maybe she has a chance again. So she's walking along and then you hear heels clicking behind her. She turns round and sees the silhouette of a woman. And then the clicking gets faster and now, right, the girl begins to get frightened, because you know what it's like when you've been talking about scary things. . . . But she's right in the middle of the park and if she starts to run she'll be in even worse trouble . . . and, then, suddenly, you can't hear the human footsteps anymore. . . . Ay! . . . Ay! . . . it's still hurting me.

SCENE V.

(SCENE: *Day.* VALENTIN *is lying down, doubled up with stomach pains.* MOLINA *stands looking on at him.*)

VALENTIN: You can't imagine how much it hurts. Like a stabbing pain.

MOLINA: Just what I had two days ago.

VALENTIN: And each time it gets worse, Molina.

MOLINA: You should go to the clinic.

VALENTIN: Don't be thick, I already told you I don't want to go.

MOLINA: They'll only give you a little Seconal. It can't harm you.

VALENTIN: Of course it can; you can get hooked on it. You don't have a clue.

MOLINA: About what?

VALENTIN: Nothing.

MOLINA: Go on, tell me. Don't be like that.

VALENTIN: It happened to one of my comrades once. They got him hooked, his will power just went. A political prisoner can't afford to end up in a prison hospital. You follow me? Never. Once you're in there they come along and interrogate you and you have no resistance. . . . Ay! . . . Ay! . . . It feels like my guts are splitting open. Aaargh!

MOLINA: I told you not to gobble down your food like that.

VALENTIN (*raising himself with difficulty*):   You were right. I'm ready to burst.

MOLINA: Stretch out a little.

VALENTIN: No, I don't want to sleep, I had nightmares all last night and this morning.

MOLINA (*relenting, like a middle-class housewife*):   I swore I wouldn't tell you another film. I'll probably go to hell for breaking my word.

VALENTIN: Ay! . . . Oh, fucking hell . . . (MOLINA *hesitates.*) You carry on. Pay no attention if I groan.

MOLINA: I'll tell you another movie, one for tummy ache. Now, you seemed keen on those German movies, am I right?

VALENTIN: In their propaganda machine . . . but, listen, go on with the panther-woman. We left off where the architect girl stopped hearing the human footsteps behind her in the park.

MOLINA: Well . . . she's shaking with fear, she won't dare turn around in case she sees the panther. She stops for a second to see if she still can't hear the woman's footsteps, but there's nothing, absolute silence, and then suddenly she begins to notice this rustling noise coming from the bushes being stirred by the wind . . . or maybe by something else. . . . (*Molina imitates the actions he describes.*) And she turns round with a start.

VALENTIN: I think I want to go to the toilet again.

MOLINA: Shall I call them to open up?

VALENTIN: They'll catch on that I'm ill.

MOLINA: They're not going to whip you into hospital for a dose of the runs.

VALENTIN: It'll go away, carry on with the story.

MOLINA: Okay . . . (*Repeating the same actions.*) . . . she turns around with a start . . .

VALENTIN: Ay! . . . ay! the pain . . .

MOLINA (*suddenly*): Tell me something: you never told me why your mother doesn't bring you any food.

VALENTIN: She's a . . . a difficult woman. That's why I don't talk about her. She could never stand my ideas—she believes she's entitled to everything she's got, her family's got a certain position to keep up.

MOLINA: The family name.

VALENTIN: Only second league, but a name all the same.

MOLINA: Let her know that she can bring you a week's supplies at a time. You're only spiting yourself.

VALENTIN: If I'm in here it's because I brought it on myself, it's got nothing to do with her.

MOLINA: My mother didn't visit lately 'cos she's ill, did I tell you?

VALENTIN: You never mentioned it.

MOLINA: She thinks she's going to recover from one minute to the next. She won't let anyone but her bring me food, so I'm in a pickle.

VALENTIN: If you could get out of this hole she'd improve, right?

MOLINA: You're a mind reader. . . . Okay, let's get on with it. (*Repeating the same action as before.*) She turns round with a start.

VALENTIN: Ay! . . . Ay! . . . What have I gone and done? I'm sorry.

MOLINA: No, no. . . hold still, don't clean yourself with the sheet, wait a second.

VALENTIN: No, not your shirt . . .

MOLINA: Here, take it, wipe yourself with it. You'll need the sheet to keep warm.

VALENTIN: No, you haven't got a change of shirt.

MOLINA: Wait . . . get up, that way it won't go through . . . like this . . . mind it doesn't soil the sheet.

VALENTIN: Did it go through?

MOLINA: Your underpants held it in. Here, take them off . . .

VALENTIN: I'm embarrassed . . .

MOLINA: Didn't you say you have to be a man . . . ? So what's all this about being embarrassed?

VALENTIN: Wrap my underpants up well, Molina, so they don't smell.

MOLINA: I know how to handle this. You see . . . all wrapped up in the shirt. It'll be easier to wash than the sheet. Take the toilet paper.

VALENTIN: No, not yours. You'll have none left.

MOLINA: You never had any. So cut it out.

VALENTIN: Thank you. (*He takes the tissue and wipes himself and hands the roll back to* MOLINA.)

MOLINA: You're welcome. Relax a little, you're shaking.

VALENTIN: It's with rage. I could cry . . . I'm furious for letting myself get caught.

MOLINA: Calm down. Pull yourself together. (VALENTIN *watches* MOLINA *wrap the shirt and soiled tissue in a newspaper.*)

VALENTIN: Good idea . . . so it won't smell, eh?

MOLINA: Clever, isn't it?

VALENTIN: I'm freezing.

MOLINA (*Meanwhile lighting the stove and putting water on to boil*):   I'm just making some tea. We're down to the last little bag. It's camomile, good for the nerves.

VALENTIN: No, leave it, it'll go away now.

MOLINA: Don't be silly.

VALENTIN: You're crazy—you're using up all your supplies.

MOLINA: I'll be getting more soon.

VALENTIN: But your mother's sick and can't come.

MOLINA: I'll continue. (*With irony. Repeating the same gestures as before but without the same élan.*) She turns round with a start. The rustling noise gets nearer and she lets rip with a desperate scream, when . . . whack! the door of the bus opens in front of her. The driver saw her standing there and stopped for her. . . . The tea's almost ready. (MOLINA *pours the hot water.*)

VALENTIN: Thanks. I mean that sincerely. And I want to apologize. . . . sometimes I get too rough and hurt people without thinking.

MOLINA: Don't talk nonsense.

VALENTIN: Instead of a film, I want to tell you something real. About me. I lied when I told you about my girlfriend. I was talking about another one, someone I loved very much. I didn't tell you the truth about my real girlfriend, you'd like her a lot, she's just a sweet and simple kid, but really courageous.

MOLINA: Please don't tell me anything about her. I don't want to know anything about your political business.

VALENTIN: Don't be dumb. Who's going to question you about me?

MOLINA: They might interrogate me.

VALENTIN (*finishing his tea; much improved*):   You trust me, don't you?

MOLINA: Yes . . .

VALENTIN: Well, then . . . Inside here it's got to be share and share alike.

MOLINA: It's not that . . .

VALENTIN (*he lies down on the pillow, relaxing*):   There's nothing worse than feeling bad about having hurt someone. And I hurt her, I forced her to join the organization when she wasn't ready for it, she's very . . . unsophisticated.

MOLINA: But don't tell me anymore now. I'm doing the telling for the moment. Where were we? Where did we stop? . . . (*Hearing no response, Molina looks at Valentin who has fallen asleep.*) How did it continue? What comes next? (*Molina feels proud of having helped his fellow cellmate.*)

SCENE VI.

(SCENE: *Daylight. Both* MOLINA *and* VALENTIN *are stretched out on their beds, lost in a private sorrow. In the distance we hear a bolero tune.*)

MOLINA (*singing softly*):   "My love, I write to you again
   The night brings an urge to inquire
   If you, too, dear, recall the tender pain
   And the sad dreams our love would inspire."

VALENTIN: What's that you're singing?

MOLINA: A bolero. "My letter."

VALENTIN: Only you would go for that stuff.

MOLINA: What's wrong with it?

VALENTIN: It's romantic eyewash, that's what. You're daft.

MOLINA: I'm sorry. I think I've put my foot in it.

VALENTIN: In what?

MOLINA: Well, after you got that letter you were really down in the dumps and here I am singing about sad love letters.

VALENTIN: It was some bad news. You can read it if you like.

MOLINA: Better not.

VALENTIN: Don't start all that again; no one's going to ask you anything. Besides, they read it through before I did. (*He unfolds the letter and reads it as he talks.*)

MOLINA: The handwriting's like hen's tracks.

VALENTIN: She didn't have much education. . . . One of the comrades was killed, and now she's leader of the group. It's all written in CODE.

MOLINA: Ah . . .

VALENTIN: And she writes that she's having relations with another of the lads, just like I told her.

MOLINA: What relations?

VALENTIN: She was missing me too much. In the organization we take an oath not to get too involved with someone because it can paralyze you when you go into action.

MOLINA: Into action?

VALENTIN: Direct action. Risking your life. . . . We can't afford to worry about someone who wants us to go on living because it makes you scared of dying.

Well, maybe not scared exactly, but you hate the suffering it'll cause others. And that's why she's having a relationship with another comrade.

MOLINA: You said that your girlfriend wasn't really the one you told me about.

VALENTIN: Damn, staring at this letter has made me dizzy again.

MOLINA: You're still weak.

VALENTIN: I'm shivering and I feel queasy. (*He covers himself with the sheet.*)

MOLINA: I told you not to start taking food again.

VALENTIN: But I was famished. (MOLINA *helps* VALENTIN *wrap up well.*)

MOLINA: You were getting better yesterday and then you went and ate and got sick again. And today it's the same story. Promise me you won't touch a thing tomorrow.

VALENTIN: The girl I told you about, the bourgeois one, she joined the organization with me but she dropped out and tried to persuade me to split with her.

MOLINA: Why?

VALENTIN: She loved life too much and she was happy just to be with me, that's all she wanted. So we had to break up.

MOLINA: Because you loved each other too much.

VALENTIN: You make it sound like one of your boleros.

MOLINA: The truth is you mock those songs because they're too close to home. You laugh to keep from crying. As a tango says.

VALENTIN: I was lying low for a while in that guy's flat, the one they killed. With his wife and kid. I even used to change the kid's nappies. . . . And do you want to know what the worst of it is? I can't write to a single one of them without blowing them to the police.

MOLINA: Not even to your girlfriend?

VALENTIN (*struggling to hold back his tears*):   Oh, God! . . . what a mess! . . . it's all so sad!

MOLINA: There's nothing you can do.

VALENTIN: Help me get my arm from under . . . the blanket.

MOLINA: What for?

VALENTIN: Give me your hand, Molina. Squeeze hard . . .

MOLINA: Hold it tight.

VALENTIN: There's something else. It's wrecking me. It's shameful, awful . . .

MOLINA: Tell me, get it off your chest.

VALENTIN: It's . . . the girl I want to hear from, the one I want to have next to me right now and hug and kiss . . . it's not the one in the movement, but the other one . . . Marta, that's her name . . .

MOLINA: If that's what you feel deep down . . . Oh, I forgot, if your stomach feels real empty, there's a few digestives I'd forgotten all about. (*Without taking his hand from* VALENTIN's *he reaches for the packet of digestives.*)

VALENTIN: For all I shoot my mouth off about progress . . . when it comes to women, what I really like is a woman with class and I'm just like all the reactionary sons-of-bitches that killed my comrade. . . . The same, exactly the same . . .

MOLINA: That's not true . . .

VALENTIN: And sometimes I think maybe I don't even love Marta because of who she is but because she's got . . . class . . . I'm just like all the other class-conscious sons-of-bitches . . . in the world.

GUARD'S VOICE: Luis Alberto Molina! To the visiting room!

(VALENTIN *and* MOLINA *let go of each other's hand as if caught in a shameful act. The cell door opens and* MOLINA *exits, but not before he's managed to slip the biscuits under* VALENTIN's *blanket. Hereafter, the dialogue is on prerecorded tape. Meanwhile,* VALENTIN *remains on stage and takes the biscuits from under his covers, manages to find just three at the bottom of the large packet and begins to eat them, one at a time, savoring each one.*)

WARDEN'S VOICE: Stop shaking, man, no one's going to do anything to you.

MOLINA'S VOICE: I had a bad stomach ache before, sir, but I'm fine now.

WARDEN'S VOICE: You've got nothing to be afraid of. We've made it look like you've had a visitor. The other one won't suspect a thing.

MOLINA'S VOICE: No, he won't suspect anything.

WARDEN'S VOICE: At home last night I had dinner with your protector and he had some good news for you. Your mother is on the road to recovery . . . it seems the chance of your pardon is doing her good . . .

MOLINA'S VOICE: Are you sure?

WARDEN'S VOICE: What's the matter with you? Why are you trembling? . . . You should be jubilant. . . . Well, have you got any news for me yet? Has he told you anything? Is he opening up to you?

MOLINA'S VOICE: No, sir, not so far. You have to take these things a step at a time.

WARDEN'S VOICE: Didn't it help at all when we weakened him physically?

MOLINA'S VOICE: I had to eat the first plate of fixed food myself.

WARDEN'S VOICE: You shouldn't have done that.

MOLINA'S VOICE: The truth is he doesn't like porridge and since one portion was bigger than the other . . . he insisted I eat it. If I'd refused he might have got suspicious. You told me, sir, that the doctored food would be on the newest plate but they made a mistake piling it high like that.

WARDEN'S VOICE: Ah, well, in that case, I'm obliged to you, Molina. I'm sorry about the mistake.

MOLINA'S VOICE: Now you should let him get some of his strength back.

WARDEN'S VOICE (*irritated*): That's for us to decide. We know what we're doing. And when you get back to your cell say you had a visit from your mother. That'll explain why you're so excited.

MOLINA'S VOICE: No, I couldn't say that, she always brings me a food parcel.

WARDEN'S VOICE: Okay, we'll send out for some groceries. Think of it as a reward for the trouble with the porridge. Poor Molina!

MOLINA'S VOICE: Thank you, Warden.

WARDEN'S VOICE: Reel off a list of what she usually brings. (*Pause.*) Now!

MOLINA'S VOICE: To you?

WARDEN'S VOICE: Yes, and be quick about it, I've got work to catch up with.

MOLINA'S VOICE (*as the curtain falls*):   A tin of treacle, a can of peaches . . . two roast chickens . . . a big bag of sugar . . . two packs of tea, one breakfast, one camomile . . . powdered milk, a bar of soap, bathsize . . . oh, let me think a second, my mind's a complete blank . . .

ACT II

SCENE VII.

(SCENE: *Lighting as in previous scene. The cell door opens and* MOLINA *enters with a shopping bag.*)

MOLINA: Look what I've got!!!

VALENTIN: No! Your mother?

MOLINA: Yes!!

VALENTIN: So she's better now?

MOLINA: A little better. . . . And look what she brought me. Ooops! Sorry, brought us!

VALENTIN (*secretly flattered*):   No, it's for you. Cut the nonsense.

MOLINA: Shut it, you're the invalid. The chickens are for you, they'll get you back on your feet.

VALENTIN: No, I won't let you do this.

MOLINA: It's no sacrifice. I can go without the chicken if it means I don't have to put up with your pong . . . No, listen, I'm being serious now, you've got to stop eating this pig swill they serve in here. At least for a day or two.

VALENTIN: You think so?

MOLINA: And then when you're better . . . Close your eyes. (VALENTIN *closes his eyes and* MOLINA *places a large tin in one of his hands.*) Three guesses . . .

VALENTIN: Ahem . . . er . . . er . . . (*Enjoying the game.* MOLINA *places an identical one in* VALENTIN'*s other hand.*)

MOLINA: The weight ought to help you . . .

VALENTIN: Heavy all right . . . I give up.

MOLINA: Open your eyes.

VALENTIN: Treacle!

MOLINA: But you can't have it yet, not until you're better. And this is for both of us.

VALENTIN: Marvellous.

MOLINA: First . . . we'll have a cup of camomile tea because my nerves are shot and you can have a drumstick, no, better not, it's only five. . . . Anyway, we can have tea and some biscuits, they're even lighter than those digestives.

VALENTIN: Please, can't I have one right away?

MOLINA: Why not! But no treacle on it—just marmalade! . . . Luckily, everything she brought is easy to get down so it won't give you any trouble. Except the treacle for the time being.

VALENTIN: Oh, Molina, I'm wilting with hunger. Why won't you let me have that chicken leg now?

MOLINA (*he hesitates a moment*):   Here . . .

VALENTIN (*wolfing down the chicken*):   Honest, I really was beginning to feel bad. . . . (*He devours the chicken.*) Thanks . . .

MOLINA: You're welcome.

VALENTIN (*his mouth full*):   But there's just one thing missing to round off the picnic.

MOLINA: Tut, and I thought I was supposed to be the pervert here.

VALENTIN: Stop fooling around! What we need is a movie . . .

MOLINA: Ah! . . . Well, now there's a scene where Irina has a completely new hair-style.

VALENTIN: Oh, I'm sorry, I don't feel too good, it's that dizziness again.

MOLINA: Are you positive?

VALENTIN: Yes, it's been threatening all night.

MOLINA: But it can't be the chicken. Maybe you're imagining it.

VALENTIN: I felt full up all of a sudden.

MOLINA: That's because you wolfed it down without even chewing.

VALENTIN: And this itching is driving me wild. I don't know when I last had a bath.

MOLINA: Don't even think about that. That freezing water in your present state! (*Pause.*) Anyway, she looks stunning here, you can see her reflection in a windowpane, it's drizzling and all the drops are running down the glass. She's got raven black hair and it's all scooped up in a bun. Let me describe it to you. . . .

VALENTIN: It's all scooped up, okay, never mind the silly details. . . .

MOLINA: Silly, my foot! And she's got a rhinestone flower in her hair.

VALENTIN (*very agitated now because of his itch*):   I know what rhinestones are so you can save your breath!

MOLINA: My, you are touchy today!

VALENTIN: Do you mind if I say something?

MOLINA: Go ahead.

VALENTIN: I feel all screwed up—and confused. If it's not too much trouble I'd like to dictate a letter to her. Would you mind taking it down? . . . I get dizzy if I try to focus my eyes too hard.

MOLINA: Let me get a pencil.

VALENTIN: You're very kind to me.

MOLINA: We'll do a rough draft first on a bit of paper.

VALENTIN: Here, take my pen-case.

MOLINA: Wait till I sharpen this pencil.

VALENTIN (*short-tempered*):   I told you! Use one of mine!

MOLINA: Okay, don't blow your top!

VALENTIN: I'm sorry, it's just that everything is going black.

MOLINA: Okay, ready, shoot . . .

VALENTIN (*very sad*):   Dear Marta . . . you don't expect this letter. . . . In your case, it won't endanger you. . . . I'm feeling . . . lonely, I need you, I want to be . . . near you . . . I want you to give me . . . a word of encouragement.

MOLINA: . . . "of encouragement" . . .

VALENTIN: . . . in this moment I couldn't face my comrades, I'd be ashamed of being so weak. . . . I have sores all over inside, I need somebody to pour some honey . . . over my wounds. . . . And only you could understand . . . because you too were brought up in a nice clean house to enjoy life to the full, . . . I can't accept becoming a martyr, it makes me angry to be one . . . or, it isn't that, I see it clearer now . . . I'm afraid because I'm sick, horribly afraid of dying . . . that it may just end here, that my life has amounted to nothing more than this, I never exploited anyone . . . and ever since I had any sense I've been struggling against the exploitation of my fellow man . . .

MOLINA: Go on.

VALENTIN: Where was I?

MOLINA: "My fellow man" . . .

VALENTIN: . . . because I want to go out into the street one day and not die. And sometimes I get this idea that never ever again will I be able to touch a woman, and I can't accept it, and when I think of women I only see you, and what a relief it would be to believe that right until I finish writing this letter you'll be thinking of me . . . and that you'll be running your hands over your body I so well remember . . .

MOLINA: Hold on, don't go so fast.

VALENTIN: over your body I so well remember, and you'll be thinking that it's my hand . . . it would be as if I were touching you, darling . . . because there's still something of me inside you, isn't that so? Just as your own scent has stayed in my nose . . . beneath my fingertips lies a sort of memory of your skin, do you understand me? Although it's not a matter of understanding . . . it's a matter of believing, and sometimes I'm convinced that I took something of you with me . . . and that I haven't lost it, and then sometimes not, I feel there's just me all alone in this cell . . . (*Pause.*)

MOLINA: Yes, "all alone in this cell" . . . Go on.

VALENTIN: . . . because nothing leaves any trace, and my luck in having had such happiness with you, of spending those nights and afternoons and mornings of sheer enjoyment, none of this is any use now, just the opposite, it all turns against me, because I miss you madly, and all I can feel is the torture of my loneliness, and in my nose there is only the stench of this cell, and of myself . . . and I can't have a wash because I'm ill, really weak, and the cold water would give me pneumonia and beneath my fingertips what I feel is the chill of my fear of death, I can feel it in my joints . . . what a terrible thing to lose hope and that's what's happened to me . . .

MOLINA: I'm sorry for butting in . . .

VALENTIN: What is it?

MOLINA: When you finish dictating the letter there's something I want to say.

VALENTIN (*wound up*):   What?

MOLINA: Because if you take one of those freezing showers it'll kill you.

VALENTIN (*almost hysterical*):   And? . . . So what? Tell me, for Christ's sake.

MOLINA: I could help you to get cleaned up. You see, we've got the hot water we were going to use to boil the potatoes and we've got two towels, so we lather one of them and you do your front and I'll do the back and then you can dry yourself with the other towel.

VALENTIN: And then I'd stop itching?

MOLINA: Sure. And we'd clean a bit at a time so you won't catch cold.

VALENTIN: And you'll help me?

MOLINA: Of course I will.

VALENTIN: When?

MOLINA: Now, if you like. The water's boiling, we can mix it with a little cold water. (MOLINA *starts to do this.*)

VALENTIN (*who can't believe in such happiness*):   And I'd be able to get to sleep without scratching?

MOLINA: Take your shirt off. I'll put some more water on. (*He mixes the hot and cold water.*)

VALENTIN: Give me the letter, Molina.

MOLINA: What for?

VALENTIN: Just hand it over.

MOLINA: Here. (VALENTIN *tears it up.*) What are you doing???

VALENTIN: This. (*He tears it into quarters.*) Let's not mention it again.

MOLINA: As you like . . .

VALENTIN: It's wrong to get carried away like that by despair.

MOLINA: But it's good to get it into the open. You said so yourself.

VALENTIN: But it's bad for me. I have to learn to restrain myself. (*Pause.*) Listen, I mean it, one day I'll thank you properly for all this. (MOLINA *puts more water on the stove.*) Are you going to waste all that water?

MOLINA: Yes . . . and don't be daft, there's no need to thank me. (MOLINA *signals to* VALENTIN *to turn around.*)

VALENTIN: Tell me, how does the movie end, just the last scene.

MOLINA (*scrubbing* VALENTIN's *back*):   It's either all or nothing.

VALENTIN: Why?

MOLINA: Because of the details. Her hairdo is important, it's the style that women wear, or used to wear, when they wanted to show that this was a crucial moment in their lives, because the hair all scooped up in a bun which left the neck bare, gave the woman's face a certain nobility. (VALENTIN, *despite the tensions and turmoil of the difficult day, changes his expression and smiles.*) Why have you got that mocking little grin on your face? I don't see anything to laugh at.

VALENTIN: Because my back doesn't itch anymore!

SCENE VIII.

(SCENE: *Day.* MOLINA *is tidying up his belongings with extreme care so as not to wake* VALENTIN. VALENTIN, *nevertheless, wakes up. Both of them are charged with renewed energy and the dialogue begins at its normal pace but accelerates rapidly into tenseness.*)

VALENTIN: Good morning.

MOLINA: Good morning.

VALENTIN: What's the time?

MOLINA: Ten past ten. I call my mother "ten past ten," the poor dear, because of the way her feet stick out when she walks.

VALENTIN: It's late.

MOLINA: When they brought the tea round you just turned over and carried on sleeping.

VALENTIN: What were you saying about your old lady?

MOLINA: Look who's still sleeping. Nothing. Sleep well?

VALENTIN: I feel a lot better.

MOLINA: You don't feel dizzy?

VALENTIN: Lying in bed, no.

MOLINA: Great—why don't you try to walk a little?

VALENTIN: No—you'll laugh.

MOLINA: At what?

VALENTIN: Something that happens to a normal healthy man when he wakes up in the morning with too much energy.

MOLINA: You've got a hard-on? Well, God bless . . .

VALENTIN: But look away, please. I get embarrassed. (*He gets up to wash his face with water from the jug.*)

MOLINA (*he puts his hand over his eyes and looks away*):   My eyes are shut tight.

VALENTIN: It's all thanks to your food. My legs are a bit shaky still, but I don't feel queasy. You can look now. (*He gets back into bed.*) I'll lie down a bit more.

MOLINA (*overprotective and smothering*):   I'll put the water on for tea.

VALENTIN: No, just reheat the crap they brought us this morning.

MOLINA: I threw it out when I went to the loo. You must look after yourself properly if you want to get better.

VALENTIN: It embarrasses me to use up your things. I'm better now.

MOLINA: Button it.

VALENTIN: No, listen . . .

MOLINA: Listen nothing. My mother's bringing stuff again.

VALENTIN: Okay, thanks, but just for today. (*He collects his books together.*)

MOLINA: And no reading. Rest! . . . I'll start another film while I'm making the tea.

VALENTIN: I'd better try and study, if I can, now that I'm on form. (*He starts to read.*)

MOLINA: Won't it be too tiring?

VALENTIN: I'll give it a go.

MOLINA: You're a real fanatic.

VALENTIN (*throwing the book to the ground as his tenseness increases*):   I can't . . . the words are jumping around.

MOLINA: I told you so. Are you feeling dizzy?

VALENTIN: Only when I try to read.

MOLINA: You know what it is? It's probably just a temporary weakness—if you have a ham sandwich you'll be right as rain.

VALENTIN: Do you think so?

MOLINA: Sure, and then later, after you've had lunch and another little snooze you'll feel up to studying again.

VALENTIN: I feel lazy as hell. I'll just lie down.

MOLINA (*schoolmistressy*):   No, lying in bed only weakens the constitution, you'd be better standing or at least sitting up. (MOLINA *hands him the tea.*)

VALENTIN: This is the last day I'm taking any more of this.

MOLINA (*mistress of the situation*):   Ha! Ha! I already told the guard not to bring you any more tea in the morning.

VALENTIN: Listen, you decide what you want for yourself, but I want them to bring me the tea even if it is horse's piss.

MOLINA: You don't know the first thing about a healthy diet.

VALENTIN (*trying to control himself*):   I'm not joking Molina, I don't like other people controlling my life.

MOLINA (*counting on his fingers*):   Today is Wednesday . . . everything will hang on what happens on Monday. That's what my lawyer says. I don't believe in appeals and all that but if there's someone who can pull a few strings, maybe there's a chance.

VALENTIN: I hope so.

MOLINA (*with concealed cunning, as he makes more tea*):   If they let me out . . . who knows who you'll get as a cellmate.

VALENTIN: Haven't you had breakfast yet?

MOLINA: I didn't want to disturb you. You were sleeping. (*He takes* VALENTIN's *cup to refill it.*) Will you join me in another cup?

VALENTIN: No, thanks.

MOLINA (*opening a new packet, not letting* VALENTIN *see*):   Tell me, what are you going to study later on?

VALENTIN: What are you doing?

MOLINA: A surprise. Tell me what you're reading.

VALENTIN: Nothing . . .

MOLINA: Cat got your tongue? . . . And now . . . we untie the mystery parcel . . . which I had hidden about my person . . . and, what have we got here? . . . Something that goes a treat with tea . . . a cherry madeira!

VALENTIN: No, thanks.

MOLINA: What d'you mean "no"? . . . the kettle's on . . . Oh, I know why not—you want to go to the loo. Ask them to open up and then fly back here.

VALENTIN: For Christ's sake, don't tell me what to do!

MOLINA (*he squeezes* VALENTIN's *chin*):   Oh, come on, let me pamper you a little.

VALENTIN: That's enough . . . you prick!

MOLINA: Are you crazy? . . . What's the matter with you?

VALENTIN (*he hurls the teacup and the cake against the wall*):   Shut your fucking trap!

MOLINA: The cake . . . (VALENTIN *is silent.*) Look what you've done. . . if the stove's broke, we're done for. . . . (*Pause.*) . . . and the saucer . . . (*Pause.*) . . . and the tea . . .

VALENTIN: I'm sorry . . . (MOLINA *is silent now.*) I lost control . . . I'm really sorry. (MOLINA *remains silent.*) The stove is okay; but the paraffin spilled. (MOLINA *still doesn't answer.*) . . . I'm sorry I got carried away, forgive me. . . .

MOLINA (*deeply wounded*):   There's nothing to forgive.

VALENTIN: There is. A lot.

MOLINA: Forget it. Nothing happened.

VALENTIN: It did, I'm dying with shame. (MOLINA *says nothing.*) . . . I behaved like an animal. . . . Look, I'll call the guard and fill up the bottle while I'm at it. We're almost out of water. . . . Molina, please, look at me. Raise your head. (MOLINA *remains silent.*)

GUARD'S VOICE: Luis Alberto Molina. To the visiting room!

(The door opens and MOLINA *exits. The recorded dialogue begins as soon as* MOLINA *moves toward the door.* MOLINA *returns with the provisions to find* VALENTIN *picking up the things he has just thrown on the floor.* MOLINA *starts to unpack the shopping bag. The recorded dialogue is heard while the action takes place on stage.)*

WARDEN'S VOICE: Today's Monday, Molina, what have you got for me?

MOLINA'S VOICE: Nothing, I'm afraid, sir.

WARDEN'S VOICE: Indeed.

MOLINA'S VOICE: But he's taking me more into his confidence.

WARDEN'S VOICE: The problem is they're putting pressure on me, Molina. From the top: from the President's private office. You understand what I'm saying to you, Molina? They want to try interrogation again. Less carrot, more stick.

MOLINA'S VOICE: Not that sir. It'd be even worse if you lost him in interrogation.

WARDEN'S VOICE: That's what I tell them, but they won't listen.

MOLINA'S VOICE: Just one more week, sir. Please. I have an idea . . .

WARDEN'S VOICE: What?

MOLINA'S VOICE: He's a hard nut but he has an emotional side.

WARDEN'S VOICE: So?

MOLINA'S VOICE: Well, if the guard were to come and say they're moving me to another block in a week's time because of the appeal, that might really soften him up.

WARDEN'S VOICE: What are you driving at?

MOLINA'S VOICE: Nothing, I swear. It's just a hunch. If he thinks I'm leaving soon he'll feel like opening up even more with me. Prisoners are like that, sir . . . when one of their pals is leaving they feel more defenseless than ever.

(At this moment MOLINA *is back in the cell and he takes out the food as the* WARDEN'S VOICE *mentions each item.* VALENTIN *looks at* MOLINA.)

WARDEN'S VOICE: Guard, take this down: two roast chickens, four baked apples, one carton of coleslaw, one pound of bacon, one pound of cooked ham, four French loaves, four pieces of crystallized fruit *(the recorded voice begins to fade out)* . . . a carton of orange juice, two cherry madeiras . . .

MOLINA *(very calm and very sad; still upset by* VALENTIN's *remarks)*: This is the bacon and this one's the ham. I'm going to make a sandwich while the bread's fresh. You fix yourself whatever you want.

VALENTIN *(deeply ashamed)*: Thank you.

MOLINA *(reserved, calm)*: I'm going to cut this roll in half and spread it with butter and have a ham sandwich. And a baked apple.

VALENTIN: Sounds delicious.

MOLINA: If you'd like some of the chicken while it's still warm, go ahead. Feel free.

VALENTIN: Thank you, Molina.

MOLINA: We'll each fend for ourselves. Then I won't get on your nerves.

VALENTIN: If that's what you prefer.

MOLINA: There's some crystallized fruit, too. All I ask is you leave me the pumpkin. Otherwise, take what you want.

VALENTIN (*finding it hard to apologize*):   I'm still embarrassed . . . because of that tantrum.

MOLINA: Don't be silly.

VALENTIN: If I got annoyed with you . . . it was because you were kind to me . . . and I didn't want . . . to treat you the same way.

MOLINA: Look, I've been thinking too and I remembered something you once said, right? . . . that when you're involved in a struggle like that, well, it's not too convenient to get fond of someone. Well, fond is maybe going too far. . . . Or, why not? Fond as a friend.

VALENTIN: That's a very noble way of looking at it.

MOLINA: You see, sometimes I do understand what you tell me.

VALENTIN: But are we so fettered by the world outside that we can't act like human beings just for a minute . . . ? Is the enemy out there that powerful?

MOLINA: I don't follow.

VALENTIN: Our persecutors are on the outside, not inside this cell. . . . The problem is I'm so brainwashed that it freaks me out when someone is nice to me without asking anything in return.

MOLINA: I don't know about that . . .

VALENTIN: About what?

MOLINA: Don't get me wrong, but if I'm nice to you, well, it's because I want you to be my friend . . . and why not admit it? . . . I want your affection. Just like I treat my mother well because she's a good person and I want her to love me. And you're a good person too, and unselfish because you're risking your life for an ideal . . . that I don't understand but, all the same, it's not just for yourself. . . . Don't look away like that, are you embarrassed?

VALENTIN: A bit. (*He looks* MOLINA *in the face.*)

MOLINA: And that's why I respect you and have warm feelings toward you . . . and why I want you to like me . . . because, you see, my mother's love is the only good thing I've felt in my life, because she likes me . . . just the way I am.

VALENTIN (*pointing to the loaf* MOLINA *put aside*):   Can I cut the loaf for you?

MOLINA: Of course . . .

VALENTIN (*cutting the loaf*):   And did you never have good friends that meant a lot to you?

MOLINA: My friends were all . . . screaming queens, like me, we never really count on each other because . . . how can I express it?—because we know we're so easily frightened off. We're always looking, you know, for friendship, or whatever, with somebody more serious, with a man, you see? And that just doesn't happen, right? Because what a man wants is a woman.

VALENTIN (*taking a slice of ham for* MOLINA's *sandwich*):   And are all homosexuals like that?

MOLINA: Oh no, there are some who fall in love with each other. But me and my friends we're women. One hundred percent. We don't go in for those little games. We're normal women; *we* only go to bed with men.

VALENTIN (*too absorbed to see the funny side of this*): Butter?

MOLINA: Yes, thanks. There's something I have to tell you.

VALENTIN: Of course, the movie . . .

MOLINA (*with cunning, but nervous all the same*): My lawyer said things were looking up.

VALENTIN: What a creep I am! I didn't ask you.

MOLINA: And when there's an appeal pending, the prisoner gets moved to another block in the prison. They'll probably shift me within a week or so.

VALENTIN (*upset by this but dissimulating*): That's terrific . . . you ought to be pleased.

MOLINA: I don't want to dwell on it too much, build my hopes. . . . Have some coleslaw.

VALENTIN: Should I?

MOLINA: It's very good.

VALENTIN: Your news made me lose my appetite. (*He gets up.*)

MOLINA: Pretend I didn't say anything, nothing's settled yet.

VALENTIN: No, it all looks good for you, we should be happy.

MOLINA: Have some salad.

VALENTIN: I don't know what's wrong, but all of a sudden I don't feel too good.

MOLINA: Is your stomach hurting?

VALENTIN: No . . . it's my head. I'm all confused.

MOLINA: About what?

VALENTIN: Let me rest for a while.

> (VALENTIN *sits down again, resting his head in his palms. The light changes to indicate a shift to a different time—the two characters stay where they are: there is a special tension, a hypersensitivity in the air.*)

MOLINA: The guy is all muddled up, he doesn't know how to handle this freaky wife of his. She comes in, sees that he's dead serious and goes to the bathroom to put away her shoes, all dirty with mud. He says he went to the doctor's to look for her and found out that she didn't go anymore. Then she breaks into tears and tells him that she's just what she always feared, a mad woman with hallucinations or even worse, a panther-woman. Then he gives in and takes her in his arms and you were right, she's really just a little girl for him, because when he sees her so defenseless and lost, he feels again he loves her with all his heart and tells her that everything will sort itself out. . . . (MOLINA *sighs deeply.*) Ahhh . . . !

VALENTIN: What a sigh!

MOLINA: Life is so difficult. . . .

VALENTIN: What's the matter?

MOLINA: I don't know, I'm afraid of building up my hopes of getting out of here . . . and that I'll get put in some other cell and spend my life there with God knows what sort of creep.

VALENTIN: Don't lose sight of this. Your mother's health is the most precious thing to you, right?

MOLINA: Yes . . .

VALENTIN: Think about her recovery. Period!

MOLINA (*he laughs involuntarily in his distress*): I don't want to think about it.

VALENTIN: What's wrong?

MOLINA: Nothing!

VALENTIN: Don't bury your head in the pillow. . . . Are you keeping something from me?

MOLINA: It's . . .

VALENTIN: It's what? . . . Look, when you get out of here you're going to be a free man. You can join a political organization if you like.

MOLINA: You're crazy! They won't trust a fag.

VALENTIN: But I can tell you who to speak to. . . .

MOLINA (*suddenly forceful, raising his head from the pillow*): Promise me on whatever you hold most dear, never, never, you understand, never tell me anything about your comrades.

VALENTIN: But who would ever think you're seeing them?

MOLINA: They could interrogate me, whatever, but if I know nothing, I say nothing.

VALENTIN: In any case, there are all kinds of groups, of political action; there are even some who just sit and talk. When you get out things'll be different.

MOLINA: Things *won't* be different. That's the worst of it.

VALENTIN: How many times have I seen you cry? Come on, you annoy me with your sniveling.

MOLINA: It's just that I can't take any more. . . . I've had nothing but bad luck . . . always. (*The prison light goes out.*)

VALENTIN: Lights out already? . . . In the first place you must join a group, avoid being alone.

MOLINA: I don't understand any of that . . . (*Suddenly grave.*) . . . and I don't believe in it much either.

VALENTIN (*tough*): Then like it or lump it.

MOLINA (*still crying a little*): Let's . . . skip it.

VALENTIN (*conciliatory*): Come on, don't be like that. . . . (*He pats* MOLINA *on the back affectionately.*)

MOLINA: I'm asking you . . . please don't touch me.

VALENTIN: Can't a friend pat you on the back?

MOLINA: It makes it worse. . . .

VALENTIN: Why? . . . Tell me what's troubling you. . . .

MOLINA (*with deep, deep feeling*): I'm so tired, Valentin. . . . I'm tired of suffering. I hurt all over inside.

VALENTIN: Where does it hurt you?

MOLINA: Inside my chest and my throat. . . . Why does sadness always get you there? It's choking me, like a knot. . . .

VALENTIN: It's true, that's where people always feel it. (MOLINA *is quiet.*) Is it hurting you a lot, this knot?

MOLINA: Yes.

VALENTIN: Is it here?

MOLINA: Yes.

VALENTIN: Want me to stroke it . . . here?

MOLINA: Yes.

VALENTIN (*after a short pause*):   This is relaxing. . . .

MOLINA: Why relaxing, Valentin?

VALENTIN: Not to think about myself for a while. Thinking about you, that you need me, and I can be of some use to you.

MOLINA: You're always looking for explanations. . . . You're crazy.

VALENTIN: I don't want events to get the better of me. I want to know why they happen.

MOLINA: Can I touch you?

VALENTIN: Yes . . .

MOLINA: I want to touch that mole—the little round one over your eye. (*Pause.* MOLINA *touches the mole.*) You're very kind.

VALENTIN: No, you're the one who's kind.

MOLINA: If you like you can do what you want with me . . . because I want it too. . . . If it won't disgust you . . .

VALENTIN: Don't say that—let's not say anything. (VALENTIN *goes under* MOLINA's *top sheet.*) Shift a bit closer to the wall. . . . (*Pause.*) You can't see a thing it's so dark.

MOLINA: Gently . . . (*Pause.*) No, it hurts too much like that. (*Pause.*) Slowly please . . . (*Pause.*) That's it . . . (*Pause.*) . . . thanks . . .

VALENTIN: Thank you, too. Are you feeling better?

MOLINA: Yes. And what about you, Valentin?

VALENTIN: Don't ask me. . . . I don't know anything anymore. . . .

MOLINA: Oh, . . . it's beautiful . . .

VALENTIN: Don't say anything . . . not for now . . .

MOLINA: It's just that I feel . . . such strange things. . . . Without thinking, I just lifted my hand to my eye, looking for that mole.

VALENTIN: What mole? . . . *I'm* the one with the mole, not you.

MOLINA: I know, but I just lifted up my hand . . . to touch the mole . . . I don't have.

VALENTIN: Ssh, try and keep quiet for a while. . . .

MOLINA: And do you know what else I felt, but only for a minute, no longer . . .

VALENTIN: Tell me, but keep still, like that. . . .

MOLINA: For just a minute, it felt like I wasn't here . . . not in here, nor anywhere else . . . (*Pause.*) It felt like I wasn't here, there was just you. . . . Or that I wasn't me anymore. As if I was . . . you.

SCENE IX.

(SCENE: *Day.* MOLINA *and* VALENTIN *are in their beds.*)

VALENTIN: Good morning. (*He is reinvigorated, happy.*)

MOLINA (*also highly charged*):   Good morning, Valentin.

VALENTIN: Did you sleep well?

MOLINA: Yes. (*Calmly, not insisting.*) Would you like tea or coffee?

VALENTIN: Coffee. To wake me up well—and study. Try to get back into the swing of things. . . . What about you? Is the gloom over? Or not?

MOLINA: Yes it is, but I feel groggy. I can't think . . . my mind's a blank.

VALENTIN: I don't want to think about anything either, so I'm going to read. That'll keep my mind off things.

MOLINA: Off what? Feeling guilty about what happened?

VALENTIN: I'm more and more convinced that sex is innocence itself.

MOLINA: Can I ask you a favor? . . . Let's not discuss anything, just for today.

VALENTIN: Whatever you like.

MOLINA: I feel . . . fine and I don't want anything to rob me of that feeling. I haven't felt so good since I was a kid. Since my mother bought me some toy.

VALENTIN: Do you remember what toy you liked most?

MOLINA: A doll.

VALENTIN: Ay!! (*He starts to laugh.*)

MOLINA: What's funny about that?

VALENTIN: As a psychologist I would starve.

MOLINA: Why?

VALENTIN: Nothing . . . I was just wondering if there was any link between your favorite toy and . . . me.

MOLINA (*playing along*):   It was your own fault for asking.

VALENTIN: Are you sure it wasn't a boy doll?

MOLINA: Absolutely. She had blond braids and a little Tyrolese folk dress. (*They laugh together, unself-consciously.*)

VALENTIN: One question. . . . Physically, you're as much a man as I am.

MOLINA: Ummm . . .

VALENTIN: Why then don't you behave like a man. . . . I don't mean with women if you're not attracted to them, but with another man?

MOLINA: It's not me. I only enjoy myself like that.

VALENTIN: Well, if you like being a woman. . . you shouldn't feel diminished because of that. (MOLINA *doesn't answer.*) I mean you shouldn't feel you owe anyone, or feel obliged to them because that's what you happen to like. . . . You shouldn't yield . . .

MOLINA: But if a man is . . . my husband, he has to be boss to feel good. That's only natural.

VALENTIN: No, the man and the woman should be equal partners inside the home. Otherwise, it's exploitation. Don't you see?

MOLINA: But there's no thrill in that.

VALENTIN: What?

MOLINA: Since you want to know about it. . . . The thrill is that when a man embraces you, you're a bit afraid.

VALENTIN: Who put that idea into your head? That's all crap.

MOLINA: But it's what I feel.

VALENTIN: It's not what you feel—it's what you were taught to feel. Being a woman doesn't make you . . . how should I say? . . . a martyr. And if I didn't think it would hurt like hell I'd ask you to do it to me, to show you that all this business about being macho doesn't give anyone rights over another person.

MOLINA (*now disturbed*):   This is getting us nowhere.

VALENTIN: On the contrary, I want to talk about it.

MOLINA: Well, I don't, so that's it. I'm begging you, no more please.

GUARD'S VOICE: Prisoner Luis Alberto Molina! To the visiting room!

> (*The door opens and* MOLINA *exits.* VALENTIN, *contented, sorts through his books, lays out his pencil and paper and begins to read. Meanwhile, we hear the* WARDEN'S VOICE.)

WARDEN'S VOICE: Put me through to your boss, please. . . . How's it going? Nothing this end. Yes, that's why I called. He's on his way here now. . . . Yes, they need the information, I'm aware of that. . . . And if Molina still hasn't found out anything, what should I do with him? . . . Are you sure? . . . Let him out today? . . . But why today? . . . Yes, of course, there's no time to lose. Quite, and if the other one gives him a message Molina will lead us straight to the group. . . . I've got it, yes, we'll give him just enough time for the other to pass on the message. . . . The tricky thing will be if Molina catches on that he's under surveillance. . . . It's hard to anticipate the reactions of someone like Molina: a pervert after all.

> (*The cell door opens and* MOLINA *comes back in, totally deflated.*)

MOLINA: Poor Valentin, you're looking at my hands.

VALENTIN: I didn't mean to.

MOLINA: Your eyes give you away, poor love. . . .

VALENTIN: Such language. . .

MOLINA: I didn't get a parcel. You'll have to forgive me. . . . Ay! Valentin . . .

VALENTIN: What's wrong?

MOLINA: Ay, you can't imagine . . .

VALENTIN: What's up? Tell me!

MOLINA: I'm going.

VALENTIN: To another cell. . . . What a nuisance!

MOLINA: No, they're releasing me.

VALENTIN: No.

MOLINA: I'm out on parole.

VALENTIN (*exploding with unexpected happiness*):   But that's incredible!

MOLINA (*confused by the way* VALENTIN'*s taking this*):   You're very kind to be so pleased for me.

VALENTIN: I'm happy for you too, of course . . . but, it's terrific! And I guarantee there's not the slightest risk.

MOLINA: What are you saying?

VALENTIN: Listen, . . . I had to get urgent information out to my people and I was dying with frustration because I couldn't do anything about it. I was racking my brains trying to find a way. . . . And you come and serve it to me on a plate.

MOLINA (*as if he'd just had an electric shock*):   I can't do that, you're out of your head.

VALENTIN: You'll memorize it in a minute. That's how easy it is. All you have to do is tell them that Number Three Command has been knocked out and they have to go to Corrientes for new orders.

MOLINA: No, I'm on parole, they can lock me up again for anything.

VALENTIN: I give you my word there's no risk.

MOLINA: I'm pleading with you. I don't want to hear another word. Not who they are or where they are. Nothing.

VALENTIN: Don't you want me to get out one day too?

MOLINA: Of here?

VALENTIN: Yes, to be free.

MOLINA: There's nothing I want more. But listen to me, I'm telling you for your own good. . . . I'm not good at this sort of thing, if they catch me, I'll spill everything.

VALENTIN: I'll answer for my comrades. You just have to wait a few days and then call from a public telephone, and make an appointment with someone in some bogus place.

MOLINA: What do you mean "a bogus place"?

VALENTIN: You just give them a name in code, let's say the Ritz cinema, and that means a certain bench in a particular square.

MOLINA: I'm frightened.

VALENTIN: You won't be when I explain the procedure to you.

MOLINA: But if the phone's tapped I'll get in trouble.

VALENTIN: Not from a public callbox and if you disguise your voice. It's the easiest thing in the world, I'll show you how to do it. There are millions of ways—a sweet in your mouth, or a toothpick under your tongue . . .

MOLINA: No.

VALENTIN: We'll discuss it later.

MOLINA: No!!!

VALENTIN: Whatever you say. (MOLINA *flops on the bed, all done in, and buries his face in the pillow.*) Look at me please.

MOLINA (*not looking at* VALENTIN):   I made a promise, I don't know who to, maybe God, even though I don't much believe in that.

VALENTIN: Yes . . .

MOLINA: I swore that I'd sacrifice anything if I could only get out of here and look after my mother. And my wish has come true.

VALENTIN: It was very generous of you to put someone else first.

MOLINA: But where's the justice in it? I always get left with nothing . . .

VALENTIN: You have your mother and she needs you. You have to assume that responsibility.

MOLINA: Listen, my mother's already had her life, she's lived, been married, had a child . . . she's old now, and her life is almost finished. . . .

VALENTIN: But she's still alive. . . .

MOLINA: And so am I . . . But when is my life going to begin? . . . When is it my turn for something good to happen? To have something for myself?

VALENTIN: You can start a new life outside. . . .

MOLINA: All I want is to stay with you. . . . (VALENTIN *doesn't say anything.*) Does that embarrass you?

VALENTIN: No, . . . er, well, yes . . .

MOLINA: Yes what?

VALENTIN: That . . . it makes me a little embarrassed.

MOLINA: If I can relay the information will you get out sooner?

VALENTIN: It's a way of helping the cause.

MOLINA: But you won't get out quickly? You just think it'll bring the revolution a bit closer.

VALENTIN: Yes, Molinita. . . . Don't dwell on it, we'll discuss it later.

MOLINA: There's no time left to discuss.

VALENTIN: Besides, we have to finish the panther movie.

MOLINA: It's a sad ending.

VALENTIN: How?

MOLINA: She's a flawed woman. (*With his usual irony.*) All of us flawed women come to a sad ending.

VALENTIN (*laughing*):   And the psychoanalyst? Does he get her in the end?

MOLINA: She gets him! And good! No, it's not so terrible, she just tears him to pieces.

VALENTIN: Does she kill him?

MOLINA: In the movie, yes. In real life, no.

VALENTIN: Tell me.

MOLINA: Let's see. Irina goes from bad to worse, she's insanely jealous of the other girl and tries to kill her. But the other one's lucky like hell and she gets away. Then one day the husband, who's at his wits' end now, arranges to meet the psychoanalyst at their house while she's out. But things get all muddled up and when the psychoanalyst arrives she's there on her own. He tries to take advantage of the situation and throws himself at her and kisses her. And right there she turns into a panther. By the time the husband gets home the guy's bled to death. Meanwhile, Irina has made it to the zoo and she sidles up to the panther's cage. She's all alone, in the night. That afternoon she got the key when the keeper left it in the lock. It's like Irina's in another world. The husband is on his way with the cops at top speed. Irina opens the panther's cage and it pounces on her and mortally wounds her with the first blow. The animal is scared away by the police siren, it dashes out into the street, a car runs over it and kills it.

VALENTIN: I'm going to miss you, Molinita.

MOLINA: The movies, at least.

VALENTIN: At least.

MOLINA: I want to ask you for a going away present. Something that we never did, although we got up to worse.

VALENTIN: What?

MOLINA: A kiss.

VALENTIN: It's true. We never did.

MOLINA: But right at the end, just as I'm leaving.

VALENTIN: Okay.

MOLINA: I'm curious. . . . Did the idea of kissing me disgust you?

VALENTIN: Ummm . . . Maybe I was afraid you'd turn into a panther.

MOLINA: I'm not the panther-woman.

VALENTIN: I know.

MOLINA: It's not fun to be a panther-woman, no one can kiss you. Or anything else.

VALENTIN: You're the spider-woman who traps men in her web.

MOLINA (*flattered*):   How sweet! I like that!

VALENTIN: And now it's your turn to promise me something: that you'll make
people respect you, that you won't let anybody take advantage of you. . . .
Promise me you won't let anybody degrade you.

GUARD'S VOICE: Prisoner Luis Alberto Molina, be ready with your belongings!

MOLINA: Valentin . . .

VALENTIN: What?

MOLINA: Nothing, it doesn't matter. . . . (*Pause.*) Valentin . . .

VALENTIN: What is it?

MOLINA: Rubbish, skip it.

VALENTIN: Do you want . . . ?

MOLINA: What?

VALENTIN: The kiss.

MOLINA: No, it was something else.

VALENTIN: Don't you want your kiss now?

MOLINA: Yes, if it won't disgust you.

VALENTIN: Don't get me mad. (*He walks over to* MOLINA *and timidly gives him a kiss
on the mouth.*)

MOLINA: Thank you.

VALENTIN: Thank you.

MOLINA (*after a long pause*):   And now give me the number of your comrades.

VALENTIN: If you want.

MOLINA: I'll get the message to them.

VALENTIN: Okay . . . Is that what you wanted to ask?

MOLINA: Yes.

VALENTIN (*he kisses* MOLINA *one more time*):   You don't know how happy you've made
me. It's 323–1025.

> (*Bolero music starts playing: it chokes* VALENTIN's *voice as he gives his instruc-
> tions.* MOLINA *and* VALENTIN *separate slowly.* MOLINA *puts all his belongings
> into a duffel bag. They are now openly brokenhearted;* MOLINA *can hardly
> keep his mind on what he's doing.* VALENTIN *looks at him in total helplessness.
> Their taped voices are heard as all this action takes place on stage.*)

MOLINA'S VOICE: What happened to me, Valentin, when I got out of here?

VALENTIN'S VOICE: The police kept you under constant surveillance, listened in on
your phone, everything. The first call you got was from an uncle, your godfather: he told you not to dally with minors again. You told him what he

deserved, that he should go to hell, because in jail you'd learned what dignity was. Your friends telephoned and you called each other Greta and Marlene and Marilyn and the police thought maybe it was a secret code. You got a job as a window dresser and then finally one day you called my comrades. You took your mother to the movies and bought her some fashion magazines. And one day you went to meet my friends but the police were shadowing you and they arrested you. My friends opened fire and killed you from their getaway car as you'd asked them to if the police caught you. And that was all. . . . And what about me, Molina, what happened to me?

MOLINA'S VOICE: They tortured you a lot . . . and then your wounds turned septic. A nurse took pity on you and secretly he gave you some morphine and you had a dream.

VALENTIN'S VOICE: About what?

MOLINA'S VOICE: You dreamed that inside you, in your chest, you were carrying Marta and that you'd never ever be apart from one another. And she asked you if you regretted what had happened to me, my death, which she said was your fault.

VALENTIN'S VOICE: And what did I answer her?

MOLINA'S VOICE: You replied that I had died for a noble and selfless ideal. And she said that wasn't true, she said that I had sacrificed myself just so I could die like the heroine in a movie. And you said that only I knew the answer. And you dreamed you were very hungry when you escaped from prison and that you ended up on a savage island and in the middle of the jungle you met a spider woman who gave you food to eat. And she was so lonely there in the jungle but you had to carry on with your struggle and go back to join your comrades, and your strength was restored by the food the spider woman gave you.

VALENTIN'S VOICE: And, at the end, did I get away from the police or did they catch up with me?

MOLINA'S VOICE: No, at the end you left the island, you were glad to be reunited with your comrades in the struggle, because it was a short dream, but a pleasant one. . . .

> (*The door opens.* MOLINA *and* VALENTIN *embrace one another with infinite sadness.* MOLINA *exits. The door closes behind him. Curtain.*)

[1981]

Journal Entry

Among many others issues, *Kiss of the Spider Woman* explores the appeal of film as pop culture. How is film represented in Puig's text? What is its relation to politics, ideology, and art?

Textual Considerations

1. Characterize Molina. What has his life been like? Why does he feel so deeply about the film he narrates? How and why does Valentin affect him?

2. Characterize Valentin. What has his life been like? What are his values? What political changes does he want to effect? How does he respond to the story of the panther woman? How and why does Molina affect him?
3. How does Puig use setting to enhance the theme of physical and symbolic imprisonment? How do the characters respond to the restrictions to which they are subjected? Consider, too, their emotional and psychological entrapments.
4. Although Molina is gay and Valentin is heterosexual, to what extent are their views about male–female relations stereotypical? Explain.
5. In what ways have Molina and Valentin changed by the end of the play? How has your attitude toward them changed? Explain.

Cultural Contexts

1. The play dramatizes the brutality of contemporary Latin American military regimes and their imprisonment of homosexuals and political dissidents, as well as the effects of surveillance and torture on political and sexual identity. What kind of political change does Puig advocate through the friendship between Molina and Valentin? Is Puig's drama mostly concerned with homosexuality? Why or why not?
2. Respond to the link that Puig establishes between the discourse of imprisonment and Theodore Roszak's idea that the "kind of woman who is most in need of liberation, and desperately so, is the woman every man keeps locked in the dungeons of his psyche" (Ronald Christ, "Last Interview With Manuel Puig").

Performance Exercises

PERFORMANCE EXPRESS (45 MINUTES)

For your semester performance of *Kiss of the Spider Woman*, ask your classmates to audition for the roles of Molina and Valentin. Group students in pairs (women included), and ask them to select a dialogue, rehearse for about ten minutes, and render a spontaneous, improvised version of their scene to the whole class. The students who are not auditioning for the main roles should critique their classmates' performance constructively, considering their voice (is it audible, strong, colorful?), physical presence (Are their gestures controlled? Do they serve a purpose?), and emotions (Do they vary?), and finally should select the best actors for the semester's performance project.

PERFORMANCE PROJECTS

1. Expand the roles of Molina's mother, Valentin's girlfriend, and the prison's warden by recreating them as a Greek chorus. Make them speak in unison or alternate their voices as they comment on and make general observations on the dramatic action that unfolds before their eyes. Like the Greek chorus, their comments should lead the audience to realize the greater significance of the actions unfolding before their eyes.
2. Following the lead of the Broadway musical, choreograph a tango performance for *Kiss of the Spider Woman* in which your classmates, as Molina and Valentin, take turns dancing with the spider woman. Decide on the music, costumes, and makeup for a performance that should attempt to capture, through music and dancing, some of the major themes of Puig's text, including the original spider woman legend, in which, after coupling, she devours her partner.

TOPICS FOR DISCUSSION
AND WRITING

Writing Topics

1. Identify and analyze the sources of racial hostility in "Cross Plains, Wisconsin," "Telephone Conversation," and "On the Subway." To what extent do the poems reinforce or negate the concept that people can modify ingrained assumptions about race?
2. Poverty, economic inequity, immigration, exile, and displacement are subtexts in the poems by Espada and Laviera. Compare and contrast their speakers' responses to their situations. What knowledge do they bring to this topic?
3. Compare and contrast the portrayals of the American dream in the texts by Hughes, Liu, Olsen, and Mukherjee. What factors might account for differences in their point of view? Limit your discussion to three texts.
4. Compare and contrast the themes of ethnic identification and cultural assimilation in the texts by Liu, Douglass, Hughes, Mukherjee, and Cofer. What functions might account for differences in their point of view? Focus on three texts.
5. Compare and contrast images of whiteness in the poems by Soyinka, Olds, and Hughes and the short stories by Bambara, Chopin, and Gordimer. Limit yourself to three texts.
6. Several texts use stereotypes to show how one racial group envisions the other. Write an essay in which you test these stereotypes against reality by comparing them to facts or to your own observations about stereotypes.
7. Using texts by Mukherjee and Espada, write an analysis of the cost of being an immigrant, migrant worker, or illegal alien in the United States.
8. Choose two or three texts that support or refute African American critic Shelby Steele's thesis that "black anger always in a way flatters white power."
9. Several texts focus on the relation between exclusion and social class. Discuss their portrayal in "I Stand Here Ironing," "Latero Story," and "On the Subway."
10. A lack of awareness of cultural differences or the assumption by one cultural group that another is inferior often results in painful personal and social encounters. Apply this thesis to any three texts.
11. Personal and cultural alienation is a motif in the poetry of Gillan, Erdrich, and Espada. Analyze the causes and effects of the various speakers' sense of exclusion. To what extent are anger and rebellion part of their responses, to what effect?
12. Write an essay on the issue of race in *Othello*. Identify the racists in the play, and discuss their effect on Othello. Pay particular attention to Iago's determination to undermine Othello's self-confidence by focusing on his being not only black but also an outsider in Venetian society.
13. Discuss the issue of gender relations in *Othello*. Consider, for example, how social class and the patriarchal tradition have shaped the personal identities of Iago, Emilia, and Desdemona.

14. In *Kiss of the Spider Woman*, setting functions as the third character. Analyze the effects of the play's setting on the relationship of Molina and Valentin, as well as on the dual themes of sexual preference and political oppression.

15. Write an essay analyzing the discourse of entrapment in *Othello* and *Kiss of the Spider Woman*. Focus on the characters' emotional, psychological, and sexual restrictions. Include Iago in your discussion of *Othello* and explain how Puig relates this theme to ideas about gender, race, violence, and sexuality.

Research Topics

1. Many Asian Americans have made important contributions to the arts, movies, television, and business. Research biographical material on one of the following prominent Asian Americans and write a profile of that individual that highlights the nature of his or her contribution: Yo Yo Ma, Maya Lin, Maxine Hong Kingston, David Henry Hwang, Amy Tan, Connie Chung, Chang-Rae Lee, and Garrett Hongo.

2. Focus on the contributions African Americans have made to arts, movies, literature, television, business, sports, government, and the armed forces. Research biographical material on one prominent African American of your choice, and write a profile of that individual that highlights the nature of his or her contribution: Toni Morrison, Wynton Marsalis, Tiger Woods, Oprah Winfrey, the Williams sisters (Venus and Serena), Alice Walker, or Colin Powell are just some of the people you could consider.

3. When interviewed by Ronald Christ in 1991, Manuel Puig stated: "For me, the only natural sexuality is bisexuality: that is total sexuality. It's all a matter of sexuality, not homosexuality, not heterosexuality. . . . In a free society though, where women and men would stop acting within the limitations of roles, their children would be free too. But certainly, not people of our generation" (Christ, "A Last Interview" 578).

   Consult Ronald Christ's "A Last Interview with Manuel Puig" as well as the other articles on Puig in *World Literature Today: A Literary Quarterly of the University of Oklahoma* (Autumn 1991) to fully understand what Puig describes as "total sexuality." Examine the extent to which Puig succeeds in combining his theory of "total sexuality" to ideas related to politics, ideology, and film in *Kiss of the Spider Woman*.

Group Research Topic

. The literature of AIDS has flourished in the last decade, providing readers with new voices and perspectives from which to view the epidemic and its inherent sense of loss. Working with your group, examine at least three works—poems, short stories, or plays—that explore the AIDS issue. Investigate the premises these texts advance in relation to the epidemic, the discourse of AIDS, and the emotional outlets that help people deal with the presence and absence of AIDS victims.

Sources you might consult include the following:

Doty, Mark. *Heaven's Coast: A Memoir*. New York: HarperCollins, 1997.

Gross, Gregory D. "Coming Up for Air: Three AIDS Plays." *Journal of American Culture 15* (Summer 1992): 63–67.

Klein, Michael, ed. *Poets for Life: Seventy-six Poets Respond to AIDS*. New York: Crown, 1989.

Lily, Mark, ed. *Lesbian and Gay Writing*. Philadelphia: Temple UP, 1990.

Mars-Jones, Adam. "Remission." In *The Darker Proof: Stories from a Crisis*. Eds. Edmund White and Adam Mars-Jones. New York: New American Library, 1988.

Morse, Carl, and Joan Larkin, eds. *Gay and Lesbian Poetry in Our Time: An Anthology*. New York: St. Martin's Press, 1988.

Osborn, M. Elizabeth, ed. *The Way We Live Now: American Plays and the AIDS Crisis*. New York: Theater Communications Group, 1990.

Preston, John, ed. *Personal Dispatches: Writers Confront AIDS*. New York: St. Martin's Press, 1991.

FILM ANGLES

RACE AND DIFFERENCE: THE FILM ANGLE

As the literary selections of this part affirm, both race and difference concern the existence of the "other"—an individual or group considered to be outside the "norms" of and often denied the same rights as the majority. The other is often perceived as a threat to the beliefs, values, and institutions that sustain society.

History is strewn with ugly illustrations of how societies have dealt with such phenomena as racial and religious difference. Examples include the history of slavery and segregation in America, the Holocaust in Nazi Germany, and the colonial occupations of Africa and Asia by various European nations. Although mainstream filmmakers have addressed these subjects, they tend to sanitize or understate their more horrific aspects in order to appeal to a mass audience. For example, neither Steven Spielberg's *Amistad* (1997) nor his *The Color Purple* (1985), both dealing with slavery, avoids typical Hollywood production values and cliches. The black protagonist of the former, for example, is saved by a white Anglo-Saxon hero. The same is true of Spielberg's *Schindler's List* (1993), which is less about the fate of the millions of Jews who died in the Holocaust than about the rescue of the fortunate few by a "good Nazi."

By avoiding the more troubling aspects of these subjects, popular movies have often perpetuated ignorance and prejudice. For the greater part of its history, Hollywood characterized people of color, Jews, Italians, Hispanics, Arabs, Asians, lesbians, and homosexuals as negative or comic stereotypes, rather than as full-bodied, three-dimensional individuals. As social attitudes have replaced ignorance and prejudice with knowledge and tolerance, movies have projected more enlightened views. Although foreign films often treat racial and sexual differences more openly, they, too, have been affected by the climate of the times. A recent film, *Nowhere in Africa* (d. Caroline Link, Germany), which won the Academy Award for Best Foreign Film of 2002, poses the question of the other in an intriguing cross-cultural context.

Based on an autobiographical novel by Stefanie Zweig, the story concerns a German-Jewish couple who flee to Africa with their young daughter in 1938—just before German Jews were sent to concentration camps. Although the couple's marriage and lifestyle suffer from the uprooting, the daughter learns the tribal languages of various people in Kenya and assimilates cultural values completely foreign to her European-Judaic roots. Although her mother treats the Africans as outsiders, it is she and her family, as Europeans, who are the real "others."

Question to Consider

1. Examine several scenes in *Nowhere in Africa* that illustrate the different attitudes of members of the family. Do these attitudes change in the course of the film? What lessons do the daughter, her mother, and her father learn about living with the "other"? What do they learn about themselves?

RACE AND ETHNIC DIFFERENCE: HISTORY AND GENRE

Representations of Blacks in Movies

No better film example of the racial conflict that has stained American history and continues to divide society can be found than D. W. Griffith's controversial Civil War epic, *The Birth of a Nation* (1915). The film made instant cultural history: It advanced the art of narrative filmmaking exponentially with its complex interweaving of characters against an historical backdrop, yet it also espoused a racist ideology with its regressive depiction of blacks and heroic images of the Ku Klux Klan as preservers of racial purity. Upon its release, it aroused vociferous protests across America, signaling the astounding impact movies would have on society. Although film historians do not deny the film's artistic achievement, neither can they deny its undisguised racism. Many object to public screenings of the film, while others argue that suppressing it is equivalent to denying the disturbing circumstances and sentiments it reflects. If we want to learn from the past, scholars and historians assert, we cannot ignore the records and artworks that document it—however unpleasant they may be.

For decades, popular movies reflected an ingrained prejudice toward African Americans by perpetuating stereotypical images. Until the 1950s, it was the rare film that did not restrict them to menial character roles (e.g., maids, butlers, bellhops) or treat them as objects of humor. The only black actor to win an Academy Award between 1929 and 1963 was Hattie McDaniel as Scarlett O'Hara's Mammy in *Gone With the Wind* (d. Victor Fleming, 1939).

This tendency began to change after World War II, with films such as *Pinky* (d. Elia Kazan), *Home of the Brave* (d. Mark Robson), *Intruder in the Dust* (d. Clarence Brown), and *Lost Boundaries* (d. Alfred L. Werker), all released in 1949—all with more fully developed black characters. Independent films in the 1960s, such as *Nothing But a Man* (d. Michael Roemer) and *One Potato, Two Potato* (d. Larry Peerce), both 1964, dealt more openly with the effect of prejudice on the everyday worker and with interracial marriage, a theme tackled by Hollywood three years later in the popular *Guess Who's Coming to Dinner* (d. Stanley Kramer, 1967).

Today African Americans are actively engaged in filmmaking. Spike Lee's films range from depictions of racial conflict in New York neighborhoods (*Do the Right Thing*, 1989; *Clockers*, 1995), to biographical drama (*Malcolm X*, 1992) and satire (*Bamboozled*, 2002). Comedies and melodramas with all-black casts are commonplace, and documentaries like *Love and Diane* (d. Jennifer Dworkin, 2003) deal with ongoing social problems that beset the African American community.

Representations of Other Ethnic Groups in Films

From the treatment of the Native American in countless westerns to stereotypes of Jews, Italians, Asians, Irish, and others, Hollywood movies are rife with examples of how ethnicity is represented in films. Many groups protest what they believe are negative images. Some Italian Americans object to films like *The Godfather* (d. Francis Ford Coppola, 1972) and *Goodfellas* (d. Martin Scorsese, 1990), and the TV series *The Sopranos* because they allegedly reinforce the belief that all Italians are associated with crime and the Mafia.

Genres often perpetuate **character types** and formulaic images of ethnic groups (e.g., the Italian mobster, the Irish cop, the Jewish businessman). Perhaps the best illustration of how genre has shaped popular conception of an ethnic group is the western. Westerns proliferated from the 1910s through the 1950s, moved to television in the 1950s and 1960s, and made a sporadic return with *Dances With Wolves* (d. Kevin Costner, 1990) and *Unforgiven* (d. Clint Eastwood, 1992). Many exploited the image of the Native American as a threat to civilized life who had to be eradicated to make way for progress. It was through the western that generations of children learned to play "cowboys and Indians," a game that not so innocently reenacted the history of territorial expansion and communal settlement across America—both at the expense of the cultures and peoples of Indian nations. As in the history and the films, so with the games: The Indians never won.

John Ford, the most revered director in Hollywood's history, did as much as anyone to propagate this myth, symbolized in his westerns as the clash between the "garden" (civilization) and the "wilderness" (untamed nature). Yet he also made *The Searchers* (1956)—judged by film scholars to be among the ten greatest movies ever made—whose hero's pathological hatred of the Indian is scrutinized in the film.

Pathological hatred also underlies anti-Semitic sentiments in America, Europe, and other parts of the world. The Holocaust has been the subject of documentaries (e.g., Claude Lanzmann's *Shoah*, 1985) and narrative films (e.g., Sidney Lumet's *The Pawnbroker*, 1965; *Schindler's List*; and Roman Polanski's *The Pianist*, 2002). Unfortunately, anti-Semitism did not end with the horrors of the Holocaust. It was treated in such Hollywood films as *Gentleman's Agreement* (d. Elia Kazan, 1947) and *Crossfire* (d. Edward Dmytryk, 1947) and continues to be an important subject.

Questions to Consider

1. Stereotypes use features familiar to viewers from various aspects of a culture. Can you think of a film that uses stereotypes in this way? What are the familiar features it relies on?
2. Think of a recent film in which an individual or a group is treated unjustly because of their racial or ethnic difference. How are these people characterized in the film? Does the film resort to stereotyping? Is the difference treated as a "problem" that the community must deal with?
3. Think of a recent film, TV movie, or series that might invite the kind of controversy that surrounds *The Birth of a Nation*. Should a film be denied public exhibition because it may offend certain members of the audience? Is this a result of "political correctness"? If so, how does it differ from censorship? Doesn't freedom of speech and of the press preclude censorship?
4. What is the difference between a character type and a three-dimensional character? Can you think of a recent movie that illustrates the difference? What is the effect of each of these on your impressions of a character of a particular race or ethnic group?

CASE STUDIES

To Kill a Mockingbird and *The Searchers*

Films about outsiders raise questions about viewer identification discussed in earlier units. It is generally assumed that viewers will identify with the most admirable character, either because we approve how that character acts in a given situation or because the character's principles and ideas provide the most lucid and morally acceptable guide through whatever controversies the film presents. In *To Kill a Mockingbird* (d. Robert

Mulligan, 1962), the film version of Harper Lee's novel, this character is the courageous lawyer who defends a black man on trial for rape.

Imagine a black member of the audience in the South, however—someone who had been directly or indirectly affected by events like the one in the film. Would this person identify with the film's "hero"—the white lawyer—or with the accused black man? Assuming the latter would be a form of stereotyping, since it would presume that a black member of the audience would naturally identify with the underdog. Suppose, however, that this same viewer had aspirations to improve society—perhaps to become a lawyer or to help his or her son or grandson become a lawyer and fight the hatred, prejudice, and stereotyping that led to many such situations. Might not such a person also identify with the white lawyer?

Having to split one's identification is not an uncommon effect of movies. Ethan Edwards, the ostensible hero in *The Searchers*, is both the courageous, experienced, and knowledgeable character determined to track down the Indians who murdered his family and abducted his nieces *and* a person consumed by his blinding hatred of Indians. While we respect his positive features, we may be repelled by his irrational ones. The film provides us with a younger, less experienced character, no less determined and courageous, who accompanies Ethan on the search and, like the viewer, aligns himself with Ethan's good features while repudiating the bad.

Questions to Consider

1. Both *To Kill a Mockingbird* and *The Searchers* confirm that the more complex a character's makeup and situation are, the more complex the viewer's reaction and ability to identify will be. Why might this be an especially appropriate position for the viewer in a film dealing with race and difference?
2. Consider the film *Training Day* (d. Antoine Fuqua, 2001) from the perspective of identification. How is the Denzel Washington character initially presented? Do your first impressions change as the film progresses? Why? Does the Ethan Hawke character act as the surrogate for the viewer's ambivalence?

OTHELLO

As a play, *Othello* has a more direct, visceral appeal than *Hamlet*—its plot and passions less ambiguous. As a character, Othello can be discussed in terms of race and difference, since, despite his preeminent position as the commander of the Venetian fleet, he is a stranger to the culture, racially and otherwise, which makes him doubly vulnerable to Iago's attacks on his peace of mind. Othello is both a man of status and the ultimate outsider, so ignorant of the ways of the court that he cannot contradict Iago's shrewd, licentious characterizations of Venetian women, including his wife. These qualities of innocence and naïveté, coupled with Othello's military reputation and presumed sexual prowess, no doubt feed Iago's jealously and hatred, well beyond the motives Shakespeare provides for his evil machinations.

Yet Iago's plan of destruction extends to Desdemona and Cassio, and to his own wife Emilia as well. As his soliloquies reveal, his is a philosophically grounded hatred of virtue in people, and the presence of such virtue makes his life and person meaner by contrast. In this sense, the play explores the psychological underpinnings of hatred of the other, whose difference acts as a foil, exposing the inadequacies and inferiority of the one who hates. To different degrees, each film version of *Othello* explores these facets of the characters.

The Range of Film Treatments

Like *Hamlet*, *Othello* was filmed in abridged and wordless form in silent movies. Understandably, its most notable film treatments are those of Shakespearean actor-directors Laurence Olivier and Orson Welles. Opera and film director Franco Zeffirelli also made a film in 1986 of Verdi's opera *Otello*, with Placido Domingo as the Moor. The opera is a consummate fusion of music and drama thanks to the play's tight construction and generous supply of dramatic high points. The film, however, illustrates how filmmakers, in order to make a play more cinematic, often mislead the viewer. In the scene when Iago is trying to convince Othello that Desdemona and Cassio are lovers, Zeffirelli shows us Iago sleeping next to Cassio as the latter tosses and turns, presumably "dreaming" of Desdemona. This is not only gratuitous, but it tends to validate as fact what the play presents as fabrication.

In Oliver Parker's film (1995), Laurence Fishburne is a physically imposing Othello, and Shakespearean actor Kenneth Branagh a convincingly menacing Iago, yet neither seems to have grasped the complexities of the characters. Fishburne's forcefulness, for example, is unrelenting, even when he should be conveying Othello's susceptibility to Iago's schemes. Huge close-ups of Branagh in his soliloquies misfire, giving undue stress to Iago's motives and reducing this most ambiguous of Shakespeare's villains to simplistic sentiments.

Othello has also been modernized in various ways. In a production made for British television in 2001 (d. Geoffrey Saxe), the protagonist is a police lieutenant elevated to captain because he has the clout, and is of the complexion, to calm protests in black communities. His nemesis is jealous that he has been overlooked and, as in the play, believes the captain has seduced his wife. In *O* (d. Tim Blake Nelson, 2001), the protagonist is Odin, a star basketball player at a private school, loved by everyone, including his coach, whose son Hugo (Iago) becomes jealous. Although it stretches credibility, the film, in making the villain the coach's son, infuses his motives with a convincing sense of fraternal rivalry.

Both Orson Welles and Laurence Olivier were experienced Shakespearean artists whose knowledge of film and theater made them especially suited to transpose Shakespeare to the screen. Welles directed the Negro Theater's production of *Macbeth* in Harlem in 1936—a landmark work in the history of the American theater. Like his other film treatments of Shakespeare (*Macbeth* in 1948, *Falstaff* [aka *Chimes at Midnight*] in 1966), his *Othello* is more than a simple rendering of the play. He explores the tensions between language (the strength of the theater) and the visual (the strength of the cinema). His *Othello*, therefore, is as much a rich cinematic experience as it is a powerful interpretation of the play. This is immediately evident in the brief, wordless prologue—a flash-forward scene of Welles's invention—in which the bodies of Othello and Desdemona are carried aloft to their burial, the funeral procession etched in stark black and white images against the sky. He condenses the play—one of Shakespeare's most dramatically focused—to a fast-moving ninety-two minutes, eliminating many lines, including most of Iago's soliloquies, and transposing others to different scenes. Through ingenious editing and overlapping dialogue, much of the action is collapsed into brief passages. Although purists might object to these changes, key speeches and dramatic exchanges retain their privileged places, and the performances are strong, especially those by Welles—a larger-than-life Othello with a grave, sonorous voice—and Michael MacLiammoir, whose less than physically imposing Iago is nonetheless malevolent.

Olivier's film, running close to three hours, follows the play's action more faithfully and offers the most controversial portrait of the Moor. Neither noble nor admirable, Olivier's Othello is a pompous, self-centered figure whose blackness is flamboyantly, even crudely emphasized. Though no doubt politically incorrect, this version stresses Othello's otherness more bluntly and disturbingly than any other. Indeed, in putting Othello's race front and center, Olivier seems to answer scholar E. A. J. Honigmann's remark: "Who would dare to say, in the more liberal 1990s, that we have changed so completely that Othello's 'otherness' no longer affects us in the theatre?" (Introduction to the Arden edition of the play, 1997). The boldness of Olivier's portrayal, raising issues of the visibility or invisibility of blackness, is reason enough for classroom viewing and discussion.

Comparing Interpretive and Cinematic Features

Like many filmed versions of plays, Olivier's *Othello* is more concerned with preserving on film the interpretation and performance of a famous actor. It is more an archival treasure than a work of cinematic imagination. Such records are important, because the texts of Shakespeare's plays lack directions as to how lines should be delivered, or who might be listening, and concerning various aspects of stage design that affect the audience's understanding of the action.

For a more cinematically-minded director, a convention such as the soliloquy poses a problem. Welles gets around it by virtually eliminating Iago's soliloquies—in which he tells us his true intentions and lays out his evil plans—by incorporating sections of them into his interactions with Roderigo. Othello's first soliloquy, declaring that he could stand almost anything but Desdemona's betrayal, is spoken as part of a scene with Desdemona; and his final one is spoken as a voice-over/interior monologue, since he is in shadows and we never see his mouth moving. Thus, Welles converts the stage convention into the more realistic terms of film language.

Such cinematographic elements as camera angles, camera movements, and lighting enhance aspects of the text and create specific moods that either intensify or counteract what characters are doing and saying. Welles makes frequent use of these features to make the space in which the play occurs a dynamic character, subject to the shifts and turns of the action. Examples of this are when the camera revolves from ground level to perusing the sky to express Othello's collapse into an epileptic fit as if from his point of view, and the way it spins dizzily at the end to mimic Othello's reeling condition in his final moments.

Equally expressive is Welles's way of filming and lighting the architecture and set, making them eloquent participants in the action rather than static backdrops. At the height of his rage over the thought of his wife's infidelity, Othello moves quickly with Iago through the castle's spaces and outdoors, in each shot framed and caught in a web of crisscrossing beams and shadows that increasingly express not only the distortions of his mind but his inability to free himself from what Iago calls the "net that shall enmesh them all." In such ways, Welles, as great a filmmaker as he was a Shakespearean, creates cinematic imagery to match the play's verse. To fully appreciate what a filmmaker can add to a work of literature requires close scrutiny of the film's parallel visual text, rich in connotative meanings and metaphorical implications.

Questions to Consider

1. What problems are there in trying to adapt a Shakespeare play to a contemporary setting—as in *O* and the British television film *Othello*? Do you think these problems have been solved in either film? Are there advantages to being introduced to the play in such forms?

2. What effect do you think the emphasis on Othello's blackness—as in Olivier's film— would have on today's viewers? Would it distract from other aspects of the play? Would it distort the play's meaning in any way? Do you think black viewers and white viewers would form different impressions of the characters or the play?

3. In Welles's film, in the scene when Iago makes Othello doubt why Desdemona married him, Othello looks into a mirror in three different shots. What is the significance of this gesture in this context? What idea does the mirror visualize? Is it related to Othello's awareness of his blackness?

Research Topics

1. In his critical study *Shakespeare: The Invention of the Human*, Harold Bloom argues that a major reason for Othello's vulnerability to Iago's lies is that he has not consummated his marriage to Desdemona. If, Bloom suggests, in addition to Othello's lack of experience of Venetian women, he has no physical verification of his wife's virginity, then he cannot know for certain that she has been faithful. Since no scene in the play absolutely confirms the issue one way or the other, use Bloom's thesis as a guide and look for evidence in several of the films that would indicate where each filmmaker stands on the issue.

2. Compare any two performances of actors or actresses in film versions of *Othello*. What are the strong or weak points in each? Which seem to lend themselves better to the film medium as opposed to the stage?

SEXUAL DIFFERENCE: HISTORY AND GENRE

Among the other groups whose identity has been the object of "the politics of exclusion" are homosexuals and lesbians. For decades, homosexuality was a taboo subject in Hollywood movies. When Lillian Hellman's play *The Children's Hour* was filmed in 1936 as *These Three*, all references to lesbianism were eliminated. Instead, the scandal involved an alleged love affair between a female teacher and her boyfriend. William Wyler, the director of that film, remade it in 1962, restoring the original theme.

Similarly, in other films of the period—such as *Tea and Sympathy* (d. Vincente Minnelli, 1956) and *Advise and Consent* (d. Otto Preminger, 1962)—the male homosexuality of the literary source is either awkwardly skirted or treated as a dirty secret. We should not so much criticize the narrow-mindedness of such films, however, as realize that they were accurate reflections of prevailing attitudes toward the subject at the time.

In *The Celluloid Closet*, a study of homosexuality in the movies, author Vito Russo notes that for decades in Hollywood movies, the taboos against male intimacy and homosexuality as a viable option were so strong that dozens of scripts were altered and sanitized to avoid any such implications in the establishment of male camaraderie. Nevertheless, emotional bonding between men can be seen in many genres—especially westerns, war films, and action, crime, and gangster films—often overshadowing heterosexual relationships in the same films. The term "buddy movie" is used to describe films in which the relationship between two male characters is the dominant one. This phenomenon can be traced back to the silent era—for example, the first version of *Ben-Hur* (d. Fred Niblo, 1926)—and was prominent in such popular movies as the 1959 *Ben-Hur* (d. William Wyler), *Butch Cassidy and the Sundance Kid* (d. George Roy Hill, 1969), *Midnight Cowboy* (d. John Schlesinger, 1969), and the *Lethal Weapon* series. Many of the actors in these films have said that they deliberately played scenes with an intensity that indicated they understood the homosexual subtext but realized it could not be acknowledged.

The treatment was equally delicate in films from other cultures, where the homosexual was often a marginal figure—as in *The Rules of the Game* (d. Jean Renoir, France, 1939) and *Ossessione* (d. Luchino Visconti, Italy, 1942)—and where homosexual desire was presented as a forbidden theme—as in Visconti's *Rocco and His Brothers* (Italy, 1960). Both *Victim* (d. Basil Dearden, 1961) and *Sunday Bloody Sunday* (d. John Schlesinger, 1971) were breakthrough British films—the former about a lawyer who risks his reputation confronting the gang that caused his ex-lover's death, and the latter about a married couple who are both in love with the same man. It is only recently that Chinese cinema has dealt with homosexuality, in such films as *Happy Together* (d. Wong Kar-wai, 1997).

Although the subject has been treated more openly in recent decades, it is still rare to find a mainstream film with a nonstereotypical homosexual main character—such as the bank robber played by Al Pacino in *Dog Day Afternoon* (d. Sidney Lumet, 1975), the Olympic athlete played by Mariel Hemingway in *Personal Best* (d. Robert Towne, 1982), or the lawyer afflicted with AIDS played by Tom Hanks in *Philadelphia* (d. Jonathan Demme, 1993). It is still more common to see homosexuals as flamboyant, wise-cracking objects of humor—as in *La Cage Aux Folles* (d. Eduardo Molinaro, Italy/France, 1978) and its Hollywood remake, *The Birdcage* (d. Mike Nichols, 1996).

Foreign and independent filmmakers continue to be venturesome, however, with such films as *My Beautiful Laundrette* (d. Stephen Frears, Great Britain, 1985), *My Own Private Idaho* (d. Gus Van Sant, 1991), *The Crying Game* (d. Neil Jordan, Great Britain, 1992), *Adventures of Priscilla, Queen of the Desert* (d. Stephan Elliott, Australia, 1994), *Beautiful Thing* (d. Hettie MacDonald, Great Britain, 1996), *Gods and Monsters* (d. Bill Condon, 1998), and *Boys Don't Cry* (d. Kimberley Pierce, 1999). Ironically, homosexuals have become more visible on television, both in the "safer" comic contexts of regular network shows such as *Will and Grace*, and in a more serious and explicit vein in cable shows such as *Six Feet Under* and *Queer as Folk*.

Question to Consider

1. In mainstream Hollywood films of the past, a homosexual character was often a guilt-ridden, tragic figure who had to suffer exclusion and guilt and be purged from "normal" social life—as in the 1962 version of *The Children's Hour*, in which the lesbian commits suicide. Is such treatment tenable in today's society? What social changes affect the way homosexuals and lesbians are portrayed in movies? Do you think there are other movie stereotypes of gay people?

CASE STUDY

Far from Heaven

Todd Haynes' *Far from Heaven* (2002), a melodrama set in the 1950s, is, among other things, an homage to and a partial remake of Douglas Sirk's *All That Heaven Allows*

(1955)—a classic of the genre that dealt with class difference, gender expectations, and social alienation. *Far from Heaven* deliberately imitates the look and style of Sirk's film, and even much of its plot. Here, a young couple's picture-perfect life in a New England (Connecticut) community is shattered when the wife discovers that her husband, a successful sales executive, is living a secret life as a homosexual. She finds solace temporarily with her black gardener, a relationship that deepens into a possible romance, only to realize in the end that a future together would be impossible. The film touches more explicitly on many aspects of difference—class, racial, and sexual—that could not have been presented as directly in a Hollywood film of the 1950s.

This film is a good example of how an important film genre adjusts to the changing views of a contemporary audience without violating genre "rules" or renouncing the visual stylistics of the original. By evoking Sirk's film in its use of rich New England autumn colors and interior shadows, Haynes's film sustains a dialogue not only with the Sirk film but with the genre of the melodrama and film history. The added tension provided by the racial and sexual themes makes us aware of how difficult it was for a Hollywood film to face these issues honestly in the 1950s, an indication of how ill-prepared society itself was to do so as well. Of course, *Far from Heaven* reflects contemporary attitudes and is looking at the 1950s with hindsight.

Questions to Consider

1. How is the subject of race handled in *Far from Heaven*? Given their social roles, do you think the wife and the gardener behave in credible ways? If the film were set in the present, how different would their behavior be? What prevents their having a future together?
2. How is the homosexual issue treated in the film? Which elements in the film—acting, dialogue, mise-en-scène—seem most effective in presenting this theme? Do we sympathize with the husband's dilemma as much as the wife's? Why or why not?
3. On the surface, the domestic situation presented in the film seems to perfectly embody the ideal American dream—until race and forbidden sexuality enter the picture. What message does the film convey about such concepts as the American dream? What point do you think the director wants to make about what lies under the surface of middle class life?

Research Topics

1. Watch both *All That Heaven Allows* and *Far from Heaven* and compare the way each film uses the genre of the melodrama. (See a description of the melodrama in the film unit of Part Two.) How are the characters presented in each film? Are they driven by a single emotion, as is often the case in melodramas, or do they seem more complex? If the latter, how important is the acting and dialogue in conveying this complexity? What cinematic means, other than acting and dialogue, helps to convey it? How are love and sexuality handled in each film?
2. Compare any two films that deal with the subject of female homosexuality (*The Children's Hour, High Art, Personal Best*) or male homosexuality (*Beautiful Thing, My Beautiful Laundrette, My Own Private Idaho, Torch Song Trilogy, Philadelphia*) in terms of how each presents the subject. Are the characters stereotypical or three-dimensional? Does the film have a moral attitude toward homosexuality?

INDIVIDUALISM AND COMMUNITY

813

"**P**ostmodern life will place a premium on relationships, not individualism," predicted a contemporary psychologist as he looked ahead to the new century. Yet at the beginning of the twenty-first century, many sociological studies show marked variations in Americans' attitudes toward their roles in traditional communities such as the family, neighborhood, workplace, and religious institution. According to Robert Bellah, a contemporary American sociologist, ours "is a society in which the individual can rarely and with difficulty understand himself and his activities as interrelated in morally meaningful ways with those of other, different Americans."

Novelist Toni Morrison views the issue of individualism from a different perspective in her speech to the 2001 graduates of Smith College in which she urges them to resist conformity and focus on their individuality:

> You need not settle for any defining category: taxpayers, consumers, minority, majority. Of course, you are general. But you're also specific. Of course, you're more citizen than consumer. But you are also a person like no other on the planet. Nobody has your exact memory but you. You are your own stories and therefore, free to imagine, to discover, and to implement what it is to be human without wealth. What it feels like to be human without dominion over others, without reckless arrogance, without fear and without plundering others unlike you. Without rotating, rehearsing, and reinventing the hatreds learned in the sandbox. And although you don't have complete control of the narrative—no author does—you can, nevertheless, create it.

How do we resolve the issues of individualism and community in the complex and diverse society of the twenty-first century? What questions about the relation between our private and communal selves do we need to answer? How can we reconcile our individual quests for identity with the sometimes conflicting demands of social responsibility? To what extent should we rebel against social conformity? What kinds of threats, if any, do individuals pose to the community? Are individual rights and social responsibility irreconcilable? What are the necessary preconditions for individual participation in any society?

According to anthropologist Bronislaw Malinowski, culture is the "artificial, secondary environment" that human beings superimpose on nature. We human beings, then, are in both nature and culture, and both influence our choices. A diversity of cultures, which the following selections illustrate, creates many opportunities for choices and sometimes leads to great difficulty in actually choosing. While nature is passively selecting the fittest organisms for survival, we humans are actively, sometimes painfully, making a variety of choices—personal, ethical, political, economic—for a number of reasons, both rational and emotional. Many of these choices concern other people and our relations to them; others involve coming to terms with our cultural or institutional pasts. Are cultural and historical factors limitations on freedom of choice, or do they allow more opportunity for individual action and imagination? Do we increase our individual choices to the degree that we free ourselves from history and culture?

Several stories in Part Five will also engage you in various debates raised by the voices of the individual and the community in different historical and cross-cultural contexts. To what extent are the choices of the protagonists in "Eveline" and "The Boarding House"—set in Dublin at the turn of the twentieth century—shaped by religious, economic, familial, and societal forces? What kinds of pressure does the town of Jefferson suffer from Miss Emily Grierson when she becomes "a tradition, a duty, and a care; a sort of hereditary obligation upon the town" in William Faulkner's short story "A Rose for Emily"?

The way in which communities deal with threats against their authority is the subject of "The Guest," which takes place in Algeria in the 1950s and explores the choice of the protagonist to treat a murderer as a guest and allow him to make his own decision about handing himself over to the authorities. And in "Dead Men's Path," set in Africa in the 1970s, you will witness the consequences of cultural clashes between the old and the new.

The poems by William Blake and William Wordsworth portray their concern with social problems in nineteenth-century London, including child labor, and the degree to which religious and political institutions failed to respond to these problems, whereas the texts by Dickinson, Stevens, and Cummings focus on the cost to individuals who conform to rigidly assigned societal roles. "People," "Street Kid," and "Danse Russe" extend the discussion of individualism and community through their celebration of the uniqueness of human beings, while other texts, such as "Constantly Risking Absurdity" and "The Writer," explore the dual, paradoxical role of the artist who needs solitude to create and society to respond to his or her creations.

The dramas in Part Five explore issues related to civil disobedience and religious hypocrisy. Although Sophocles' *Antigone* presents conflicts such as those between male and female, youth and age, and religious and secular beliefs, the main issue is the decision of Antigone to insist on obeying her conscience, even if it means violating the laws of the state. Molière's *Tartuffe*, banned from the French stage in 1664 and 1667, presents the debate between reason and religious affectation.

As you read these and other texts in this part, you, too, will be asked to make judgments about issues such as personal freedom and social responsibility, rebellion and conformity, the right of an individual to participate in acts of civil disobedience, the conflicting demands of individual preference and familial obligation, and the extent to which personal identity is shaped by external social forces.

FICTION

Shirley Jackson

The Lottery

The morning of June 27th was clear and sunny, with the fresh warmth of a full-summer day; the flowers were blossoming profusely and the grass was richly green. The people of the village began to gather in the square, between the post office and the bank, around ten o'clock; in some towns there were so many people that the lottery took two days and had to be started on June 26th, but in this village, where there were only about three hundred people, the whole lottery took less than two hours, so it could begin at ten o'clock in the morning and still be through in time to allow the villagers to get home for noon dinner.

The children assembled first, of course. School was recently over for the summer, and the feeling of liberty sat uneasily on most of them; they tended to gather together quietly for a while before they broke into boisterous play, and their talk was still of the classroom and the teacher, of books and reprimands. Bobby Martin had already stuffed his pockets full of stones, and the other boys soon followed his example, selecting the smoothest and roundest stones; Bobby and Harry Jones and Dickie Delacroix—the villagers pronounced this name "Dellacroy"—eventually made a great pile of stones in one corner of the square and guarded it against the raids of the other boys. The girls stood aside, talking among themselves, looking over their shoulders at the boys, and the very small children rolled in the dust or clung to the hands of their older brothers or sisters.

Soon the men began to gather, surveying their own children, speaking of planting and rain, tractors and taxes. They stood together, away from the pile of stones in the corner, and their jokes were quiet and they smiled rather than laughed. The women, wearing faded house dresses and sweaters, came shortly after their menfolk. They greeted one another and exchanged bits of gossip as they went to join their husbands. Soon the women, standing by their husbands, began to call to their children, and the children came reluctantly, having to be called four or five times. Bobby Martin ducked under his mother's grasping hand and ran, laughing, back to the pile of stones. His father spoke up sharply, and Bobby came quickly and took his place between his father and his oldest brother.

The lottery was conducted—as were the square dances, the teenage club, the Halloween program—by Mr. Summers, who had time and energy to devote to civic activities. He was a round-faced, jovial man and he ran the coal business, and people were sorry for him, because he had no children and his wife was a scold. When he arrived in the square, carrying the black wooden box, there was a murmur of conversation among the villagers, and he waved and called, "Little late today, folks."

817

The postmaster, Mr. Graves, followed him, carrying a three-legged stool, and the stool was put in the center of the square and Mr. Summers set the black box down on it. The villagers kept their distance, leaving a space between themselves and the stool, and when Mr. Summers said, "Some of you fellows want to give me a hand?" there was a hesitation before two men, Mr. Martin and his oldest son, Baxter, came forward to hold the box steady on the stool while Mr. Summers stirred up the papers inside it.

The original paraphernalia for the lottery had been lost long ago, and the black box now resting on the stool had been put into use even before Old Man Warner, the oldest man in town, was born. Mr. Summers spoke frequently to the villagers about making a new box, but no one liked to upset even as much tradition as was represented by the black box. There was a story that the present box had been made with some pieces of the box that had preceded it, the one that had been constructed when the first people settled down to make a village here. Every year, after the lottery, Mr. Summers began talking again about a new box, but every year the subject was allowed to fade off without anything's being done. The black box grew shabbier each year; by now it was no longer completely black but splintered badly along one side to show the original wood color, and in some places faded or stained.

Mr. Martin and his oldest son, Baxter, held the black box securely on the stool until Mr. Summers had stirred the papers thoroughly with his hand. Because so much of the ritual had been forgotten or discarded, Mr. Summers had been successful in having slips of paper substituted for the chips of wood that had been used for generations. Chips of wood, Mr. Summers had argued, had been all very well when the village was tiny, but now that the population was more than three hundred and likely to keep on growing, it was necessary to use something that would fit more easily into the black box. The night before the lottery, Mr. Summers and Mr. Graves made up the slips of paper and put them in the box, and it was then taken to the safe of Mr. Summers's coal company and locked up until Mr. Summers was ready to take it to the square next morning. The rest of the year, the box was put away, sometimes one place, sometimes another; it had spent one year in Mr. Graves's barn and another year underfoot in the post office, and sometimes it was set on a shelf in the Martin grocery and left there.

There was a great deal of fussing to be done before Mr. Summers declared the lottery open. There were the lists to make up—of heads of families, heads of households in each family, members of each household in each family. There was the proper swearing-in of Mr. Summers by the postmaster, as the official of the lottery; at one time, some people remembered, there had been a recital of some sort, performed by the official of the lottery, a perfunctory, tuneless chant that had been rattled off duly each year; some people believed that the official of the lottery used to stand just so when he said or sang it, others believed that he was supposed to walk among the people, but years and years ago this part of the ritual had been allowed to lapse. There had been, also, a ritual salute, which the official of the lottery had had to use in addressing each person who came up to draw from the box, but this also had changed with time, until now it was felt necessary only for the official to speak to each person approaching. Mr. Summers was very good at all this; in his clean white shirt and blue jeans, with one hand resting carelessly on the black box, he seemed very proper and important as he talked interminably to Mr. Graves and the Martins.

Just as Mr. Summers finally left off talking and turned to the assembled villagers, Mrs. Hutchinson came hurriedly along the path to the square, her sweater thrown over her shoulders, and slid into place in the back of the crowd. "Clean forgot what day it was," she said to Mrs. Delacroix, who stood next to her, and they both laughed softly. "Thought my old man was out back stacking wood," Mrs. Hutchinson went on, "and then I looked out the window and the kids was gone, and then I remembered it was the twenty-seventh and came a-running." She dried her hands on her apron, and Mrs. Delacroix said, "You're in time, though. They're still talking away up there."

Mrs. Hutchinson craned her neck to see through the crowd and found her husband and children standing near the front. She tapped Mrs. Delacroix on the arm as a farewell and began to make her way through the crowd. The people separated good-humoredly to let her through; two or three people said, in voices just loud enough to be heard across the crowd, "Here comes your Missus, Hutchinson," and "Bill, she made it after all." Mrs. Hutchinson reached her husband, and Mr. Summers, who had been waiting, said cheerfully. "Thought we were going to have to get on without you, Tessie." Mrs. Hutchinson said, grinning, "Wouldn't have me leave m'dishes in the sink, now, would you, Joe?" and soft laughter ran through the crowd as the people stirred back into position after Mrs. Hutchinson's arrival.

"Well, now," Mr. Summers said soberly, "guess we better get started, get this over with, so's we can go back to work. Anybody ain't here?"

"Dunbar," several people said. "Dunbar, Dunbar."

Mr. Summers consulted his list. "Clyde Dunbar," he said. "That's right. He's broke his leg, hasn't he? Who's drawing for him?"

"Me, I guess," a woman said, and Mr. Summers turned to look at her. "Wife draws for her husband," Mr. Summers said. "Don't you have a grown boy to do it for you, Janey?" Although Mr. Summers and everyone else in the village knew the answer perfectly well, it was the business of the official of the lottery to ask such questions formally. Mr. Summers waited with an expression of polite interest while Mrs. Dunbar answered.

"Horace's not but sixteen yet," Mrs. Dunbar said regretfully. "Guess I gotta fill in for the old man this year."

"Right," Mr. Summers said. He made a note on the list he was holding. Then he asked, "Watson boy drawing this year?"

A tall boy in the crowd raised his hand. "Here," he said. "I'm drawing for m'mother and me." He blinked his eyes nervously and ducked his head as several voices in the crowd said things like "Good fellow, Jack," and "Glad to see your mother's got a man to do it."

"Well," Mr. Summers said, "guess that's everyone. Old Man Warner make it?"

"Here," a voice said, and Mr. Summers nodded.

A sudden hush fell on the crowd as Mr. Summers cleared his throat and looked at the list. "All ready?" he called. "Now, I'll read the names—heads of families first—and the men come up and take a paper out of the box. Keep the paper folded in your hand without looking at it until everyone has had a turn. Everything clear?"

The people had done it so many times that they only half listened to the directions; most of them were quiet, wetting their lips, not looking around. Then Mr. Summers raised one hand high and said, "Adams." A man disengaged himself from the crowd and came forward. "Hi, Steve," Mr. Summers said, and Mr. Adams said, "Hi, Joe." They grinned at one another humorlessly and nervously. Then Mr. Adams reached into the black box and took out a folded paper. He held it firmly by one corner as he turned and went hastily back to his place in the crowd, where he stood a little apart from his family, not looking down at his hand.

"Allen," Mr. Summers said, "Anderson . . . Bentham."

"Seems like there's no time at all between lotteries any more," Mrs. Delacroix said to Mrs. Graves in the back row. "Seems like we got through with the last one only last week."

"Time sure goes fast," Mrs. Graves said.

"Clark . . . Delacroix."

"There goes my old man," Mrs. Delacroix said. She held her breath while her husband went forward.

"Dunbar," Mr. Summers said, and Mrs. Dunbar went steadily to the box while one of the women said, "Go on, Janey," and another said, "There she goes."

"We're next," Mrs. Graves said. She watched while Mr. Graves came around from the side of the box, greeted Mr. Summers gravely, and selected a slip of paper from the box. By now, all through the crowd there were men holding the small folded papers in their large hands, turning them over and over nervously. Mrs. Dunbar and her two sons stood together, Mrs. Dunbar holding the slip of paper.

"Harburt . . . Hutchinson."

"Get up there, Bill," Mrs. Hutchinson said, and the people near her laughed.

"Jones."

"They do say," Mr. Adams said to Old Man Warner, who stood next to him, "that over in the north village they're talking of giving up the lottery."

Old Man Warner snorted. "Pack of crazy fools," he said. "Listening to the young folks, nothing's good enough for *them.* Next thing you know, they'll be wanting to go back to living in caves, nobody work any more, live *that* way for a while. Used to be a saying about 'Lottery in June, corn be heavy soon.' First thing you know, we'd all be eating stewed chickweed and acorns. There's *always* been a lottery," he added petulantly. "Bad enough to see young Joe Summers up there joking with everybody."

"Some places have already quit lotteries," Mrs. Adams said.

"Nothing but trouble in *that,*" Old Man Warner said stoutly. "Pack of young fools."

"Martin." And Bobby Martin watched his father go forward. "Overdyke . . . Percy."

"I wish they'd hurry," Mrs. Dunbar said to her oldest son. "I wish they'd hurry."

"They're almost through," her son said.

"You get ready to run tell Dad," Mrs. Dunbar said.

Mr. Summers called his own name and then stepped forward precisely and selected a slip from the box. Then he called, "Warner."

"Seventy-seventh year I been in the lottery," Old Man Warner said as he went through the crowd. "Seventy-seventh time."

"Watson." The tall boy came awkwardly through the crowd. Someone said, "Don't be nervous, Jack," and Mr. Summers said, "Take your time, son."

"Zanini."

After that, there was a long pause, a breathless pause, until Mr. Summers, holding his slip of paper in the air, said, "All right, fellows." For a minute, no one moved, and then all the slips of paper were opened. Suddenly, all the women began to speak at once, saying, "Who is it?" "Who's got it?" "Is it the Dunbars?" "Is it the Watsons?" Then the voices began to say, "It's Hutchinson. It's Bill." "Bill Hutchinson's got it."

"Go tell your father," Mrs. Dunbar said to her older son.

People began to look around to see the Hutchinsons. Bill Hutchinson was standing quiet, staring down at the paper in his hand. Suddenly, Tessie Hutchinson shouted to Mr. Summers, "You didn't give him time enough to take any paper he wanted. I saw you. It wasn't fair!"

"Be a good sport, Tessie," Mrs. Delacroix called, and Mrs. Graves said, "All of us took the same chance."

"Shut up, Tessie," Bill Hutchinson said.

"Well, everyone," Mr. Summers said, "that was done pretty fast, and now we've got to be hurrying a little more to get done in time." He consulted his next list. "Bill," he said, "you draw for the Hutchinson family. You got any other households in the Hutchinsons?"

"There's Don and Eva," Mrs. Hutchinson yelled. "Make *them* take their chance!"

"Daughters drew with their husbands' families, Tessie," Mr. Summers said gently. "You know that as well as anyone else."

"It wasn't *fair*," Tessie said.

"I guess not, Joe," Bill Hutchinson said regretfully. "My daughter draws with her husband's family, that's only fair, And I've got no other family except the kids."

"Then, as far as drawing for families is concerned, it's you," Mr. Summers said in explanation, "and as far as drawing for households is concerned, that's you, too. Right?"

"Right," Bill Hutchinson said.

"How many kids, Bill?" Mr. Summers asked formally.

"Three," Bill Hutchinson said. "There's Bill, Jr., and Nancy, and little Dave. And Tessie and me."

"All right, then," Mr. Summers said. "Harry, you got their tickets back?"

Mr. Graves nodded and held up the slips of paper. "Put them in the box, then," Mr. Summers directed. "Take Bill's and put it in."

"I think we ought to start over," Mrs. Hutchinson said, as quietly as she could. "I tell you it wasn't *fair*. You didn't give him time enough to choose. *Every*body saw that."

Mr. Graves had selected the five slips and put them in the box, and he dropped all the papers but those onto the ground, where the breeze caught them and lifted them off.

"Listen, everybody," Mrs. Hutchinson was saying to the people around her.

"Ready, Bill?" Mr. Summers asked, and Bill Hutchinson, with one quick glance around at his wife and children, nodded.

"Remember," Mr. Summers said, "take the slips and keep them folded until each person has taken one. Harry, you help little Dave." Mr. Graves took the hand of the little boy, who came willingly with him up to the box. "Take a paper out of the box, Davy," Mr. Summers said. Davy put his hand into the box and laughed. "Take just *one* paper," Mr. Summers said. "Harry, you hold it for him." Mr. Graves took the child's hand and removed the folded paper from the tight fist and held it while little Dave stood next to him and looked up at him wonderingly.

"Nancy next," Mr. Summers said. Nancy was twelve, and her school friends breathed heavily as she went forward, switching her skirt, and took a slip daintily from the box. "Bill, Jr.," Mr. Summers said, and Billy, his face red and his feet over-large, nearly knocked the box over as he got a paper out. "Tessie," Mr. Summers said. She hesitated for a minute, looking around defiantly, and then set her lips and went up to the box. She snatched a paper out and held it behind her.

"Bill," Mr. Summers said, and Bill Hutchinson reached into the box and felt around, bringing his hand out at last with the slip of paper in it.

The crowd was quiet. A girl whispered, "I hope it's not Nancy," and the sound of the whisper reached the edges of the crowd.

"It's not the way it used to be," Old Man Warner said clearly. "People ain't the way they used to be."

"All right," Mr. Summers said. "Open the papers. Harry, you open little Dave's."

Mr. Graves opened the slip of paper and there was a general sigh through the crowd as he held it up and everyone could see that it was blank. Nancy and Bill, Jr., opened theirs at the same time, and both beamed and laughed, turning around to the crowd and holding their slips of paper above their heads.

"Tessie," Mr. Summers said. There was a pause, and then Mr. Summers looked at Bill Hutchinson, and Bill unfolded his paper and showed it. It was blank.

"It's Tessie," Mr. Summers said, and his voice was hushed. "Show us her paper, Bill."

Bill Hutchinson went over to his wife and forced the slip of paper out of her hand. It had a black spot on it, the black spot Mr. Summers had made the night before with the heavy pencil in the coal-company office. Bill Hutchinson held it up and there was a stir in the crowd.

"All right, folks," Mr. Summers said. "Let's finish quickly."

Although the villagers had forgotten the ritual and lost the original black box, they still remembered to use stones. The pile of stones the boys had made earlier was ready; there were stones on the ground with the blowing scraps of paper that had come out of the box. Mrs. Delacroix selected a stone so large she had to pick it up with both hands and turned to Mrs. Dunbar, "Come on," she said. "Hurry up."

Mrs. Dunbar had small stones in both hands, and she said, gasping for breath, "I can't run at all. You'll have to go ahead and I'll catch up with you."

The children had stones already, and someone gave little Davy Hutchinson a few pebbles.

Tessie Hutchinson was in the center of a cleared space by now, and she held her hands out desperately as the villagers moved in on her. "It isn't fair," she said. A stone hit her on the side of the head.

Old Man Warner was saying, "Come on, come on, everyone." Steve Adams was in the front of the crowd of villagers, with Mrs. Graves beside him.

"It isn't fair, it isn't right," Mrs. Hutchinson screamed and then they were upon her.

[1948]

Journal Entry

What are your associations with a lottery? What images and situations does the word evoke?

Textual Considerations

1. What do the villagers mean by "fairness"? What is implied by the fact that the only villager to complain about the lottery's consequences is Tessie Hutchinson?
2. Why does Jackson use a flat, reportorial style to describe an event that would normally be headline news?
3. Consider the role of irony in the story.
4. How important is it that the story is set in New England in the mid 1950s? How for example, would its influence differ if it were set in Aztec Mexico, a culture that routinely practiced human sacrifice?
5. What indications are there that the villagers have lost interest in the process that leads up to the choosing of the slip?

Cultural Contexts

1. When Jackson's story was first published in *The New Yorker* in 1948, she received hundreds of letters from people "who wanted to know where the lotteries were held, and whether they could go there and watch." Examine what these responses reveal about human nature. What is your own response to the story?
2. By showing the process involved in the lottery, what is Jackson implying about traditions, mass psychology, and social pressure? How did your group's response to this question compare with that of other groups in your class?

Franz Kafka

The Metamorphosis

Translated by Will and Edwin Muir

I

As Gregor Samsa awoke one morning from uneasy dreams he found himself transformed in his bed into a gigantic insect. He was lying on his hard, as it were armor-plated, back and when he lifted his head a little he could see his dome-like brown belly divided into stiff arched segments on top of which the bed quilt could hardly keep in position and was about to slide off completely. His numerous legs, which were pitifully thin compared to the rest of his bulk, waved helplessly before his eyes.

What has happened to me? he thought. It was no dream. His room, a regular human bedroom, only rather too small, lay quiet between the four familiar walls. Above the table on which a collection of cloth samples was unpacked and spread out—Samsa was a commercial traveler—hung the picture which he had recently cut out of an illustrated magazine and put into a pretty gilt frame. It showed a lady, with a fur cap on and a fur stole, sitting upright and holding out to the spectator a huge fur muff into which the whole of her forearm had vanished!

Gregor's eyes turned next to the window, and the overcast sky—one could hear rain drops beating on the window gutter—made him quite melancholy. What about sleeping a little longer and forgetting all this nonsense, he thought, but it could not be done, for he was accustomed to sleep on his right side and in his present condition he could not turn himself over. However violently he forced himself towards his right side he always rolled on to his back again. He tried it at least a hundred times, shutting his eyes to keep from seeing his struggling legs, and only desisted when he began to feel in his side a faint dull ache he had never experienced before.

Oh God, he thought, what an exhausting job I've picked on! Traveling about day in, day out. It's much more irritating work than doing the actual business in the office, and on top of that there's the trouble of constant traveling, of worrying about train connections, the bed and irregular meals, casual acquaintances that are always new and never become intimate friends. The devil take it all! He felt a slight itching up on his belly; slowly pushed himself on his back nearer to the top of the bed so that he could lift his head more easily; identified the itching place which was surrounded by many small white spots the nature of which he could not understand and made to touch it with a leg, but drew the leg back immediately, for the contact made a cold shiver run through him.

He slid down again into his former position. This getting up early, he thought, makes one quite stupid. A man needs his sleep. Other commercials live like harem women. For instance, when I come back to the hotel of a morning to write up the orders I've got, these others are only sitting down to breakfast. Let me just try that with my chief; I'd be sacked on the spot. Anyhow, that might be quite a good thing for me, who can tell? If I didn't have to hold my hand because of my parents I'd have given notice long ago. I'd have gone to the chief and told him exactly what I think of him. That would knock him endways from his desk! It's a queer way of doing, too, this sitting on high at a desk and talking down to employees, especially when they have to come quite near because the chief is hard of hearing. Well, there's still hope; once I've saved enough money to pay back my parents' debts to him—that should take another five or six years—I'll do it without fail. I'll cut myself completely loose then. For the moment, though, I'd better get up, since my train goes at five.

He looked at the alarm clock ticking on the chest. Heavenly Father! he thought. It was half-past six o'clock and the hands were quietly moving on, it was even past the half-hour, it was getting on toward a quarter to seven. Had the alarm clock not gone off? From the bed one could see that it had been properly set for four o'clock; of course it must have gone off. Yes, but was it possible to sleep quietly through that ear-splitting noise? Well, he had not slept quietly, yet apparently all the more soundly for that. But what was he to do now? The next train went at seven o'clock; to catch that he would need to hurry like mad and his samples weren't even packed up, and he himself wasn't feeling particularly fresh and active. And even if he did catch the train he wouldn't avoid a row with the chief, since the firm's porter would have been waiting for the five o'clock train and would long since have reported his failure to turn up. The porter was a creature of the chief's, spineless and stupid. Well, supposing he were to say he was sick? But that would be most unpleasant and would look suspicious, since during his five years' employment he had not been ill once. The chief himself would be sure to come with the sick-insurance doctor, would reproach his parents with their son's laziness and would cut all excuses short by referring to the insurance doctor, who of course regarded all mankind as perfectly healthy malingerers. And would he be so far wrong on this occasion? Gregor really felt quite well, apart from a drowsiness that was utterly superfluous after such a long sleep, and he was even unusually hungry.

As all this was running through his mind at top speed without his being able to decide to leave his bed—the alarm clock had just struck a quarter to seven—there came a cautious tap at the door behind the head of his bed. "Gregor," said a voice—it was his mother's—"it's a quarter to seven. Hadn't you a train to catch?" That gentle voice! Gregor had a shock as he heard his own voice answering hers, unmistakably his own voice, it was true, but with a persistent horrible twittering squeak behind it like an undertone, that left the words in their clear shape only for the first moment and then rose up reverberating round them to destroy their sense, so that one could not be sure one had heard them rightly. Gregor wanted to answer at length and explain everything, but in the circumstances he confined himself to saying: "Yes, yes, thank you, Mother, I'm getting up now." The wooden door between them must have kept the change in his voice from being noticeable outside, for his mother contented herself with this statement and shuffled away. Yet this brief exchange of words had made the other members of the family aware that Gregor was still in the house, as they had not expected, and at one of the side doors his father was already knocking, gently, yet with his fist. "Gregor, Gregor," he called, "what's the matter with you?" And after a little while he called again in a deeper voice: "Gregor! Gregor!" At the other side door his sister was saying in a low, plaintive tone: "Gregor? Aren't you well? Are you needing anything?" He answered them both at once: "I'm just ready," and did his best to make his voice sound as normal as possible by enunciating the words very clearly and leaving long pauses between them. So his father went back to his breakfast, but his sister whispered: "Gregor, open the door, do." However, he was not thinking of opening the door, and felt thankful for the prudent habit he had acquired in traveling of locking all doors during the night, even at home.

His immediate attention was to get up quietly without being disturbed, to put on his clothes and above all eat his breakfast, and only then to consider what else was to be done, since in bed, he was well aware, his meditations would come to no sensible conclusion. He remembered that often enough in bed he had felt small aches and pains, probably caused by awkward postures, which had proved purely imaginary once he got up, and he looked forward eagerly to seeing this morning's delusions gradually fall away. That the change in his voice was nothing but the precursor of a severe chill, a standing ailment of commercial travelers, he had not the least possible doubt.

To get rid of the quilt was quite easy; he had only to inflate himself a little and it fell off by itself. But the next move was difficult, especially because he was so uncommonly broad. He would have needed arms and hands to hoist himself up; instead he had only the numerous little legs which never stopped waving in all directions and which he could not control in the least. When he tried to bend one of them it was the first to stretch itself straight; and did he succeed at last in making it do what he wanted, all the other legs meanwhile waved the more wildly in a high degree of unpleasant agitation. "But what's the use of lying idle in bed," said Gregor to himself.

He thought that he might get out of bed with the lower part of his body first, but this lower part, which he had not yet seen and of which he could form no clear conception, proved too difficult to move; it shifted so slowly, and when finally, almost wild with annoyance, he gathered his forces together and thrust out recklessly, he had miscalculated the direction and bumped heavily against the lower end of the bed, and the stinging pain he felt informed him that precisely this lower part of his body was at the moment probably the most sensitive.

So he tried to get the top part of himself out first, and cautiously moved his head towards the edge of the bed. That proved easy enough, and despite its breadth and mass the bulk of his body at last slowly followed the movement of his head. Still, when he finally got his head free over the edge of the bed he felt too scared to go on advancing, for after all if he let himself fall in this way it would take a miracle to keep his head from being injured. And at all costs he must not lose consciousness now, precisely now; he would rather stay in bed.

But when after a repetition of the same efforts he lay in his former position again, sighing, and watched his little legs struggling against each other more wildly than ever, if that were possible, and saw no way of bringing any order into this arbitrary confusion, he told himself again that it was impossible to stay in bed and that the most sensible course was to risk everything for the smallest hope of getting away from it. At the same time he did not forget meanwhile to remind himself that cool reflection, the coolest possible, was much better than desperate resolves. In such

moments he focused his eyes as sharply as possible on the window, but, unfortunately, the prospect of the morning fog, which muffled even the other side of the
narrow street, brought him little encouragement and comfort. "Seven o'clock already," he said to himself when the alarm clock chimed again, "seven o'clock
already and still such a thick fog." And for a little while he lay quiet, breathing
lightly, as if perhaps expecting such complete repose to restore all things to their
real and normal condition.

But then he said to himself: "Before it strikes a quarter past seven I must be
quite out of this bed, without fail. Anyhow, by that time someone will have come
from the office to ask for me, since it opens before seven." And he set himself to
rocking his whole body at once in a regular rhythm, with the idea of swinging it out
of the bed. If he tipped himself out in that way he could keep his head from injury
by lifting it at an acute angle when he fell. His back seemed to be hard and was not
likely to suffer from a fall on the carpet. His biggest worry was the loud crash he
would not be able to help making, which would probably cause anxiety, if not terror,
behind all the doors. Still, he must take the risk.

When he was already half out of the bed—the new method was more a game
than an effort, for he needed only to hitch himself across by rocking to and fro—it
struck him how simple it would be if he could get help. Two strong people—he
thought of his father and the servant girl—would be amply sufficient; they would
only have to thrust their arms under his convex back, lever him out of the bed, bend
down with their burden and then be patient enough to let him turn himself right
over on to the floor, where it was to be hoped his legs would then find their proper
function. Well, ignoring the fact that the doors were all locked, ought he really to
call for help? In spite of his misery he could not suppress a smile at the very idea of it.

He had got so far that he could barely keep his equilibrium when he rocked
himself strongly, and he would have to nerve himself very soon for the final decision
since in five minutes' time it would be a quarter past seven—when the front door
bell rang. "That's someone from the office," he said to himself, and grew almost
rigid, while his little legs jigged about all the faster. For a moment everything stayed
quiet. "They're not going to open the door," said Gregor to himself, catching at
some kind of irrational hope. But then of course the servant girl went as usual to the
door with her heavy tread and opened it. Gregor needed only to hear the first good
morning of the visitor to know immediately who it was—the chief clerk himself.
What a fate, to be condemned to work for a firm where the smallest omission at
once gave rise to the gravest suspicion! Were all employees in a body nothing but
scoundrels, was there not among them one single loyal devoted man who, had he
wasted only an hour or so of the firm's time in a morning, was so tormented by conscience as to be driven out of his mind and actually incapable of leaving his bed?
Wouldn't it really have been sufficient to send an apprentice to inquire—if any
inquiry were necessary at all—did the chief clerk himself have to come and thus
indicate to the entire family, an innocent family, that this suspicious circumstance
could be investigated by no one less versed in affairs than himself? And more
through the agitation caused by these reflections than through any act of will Gregor swung himself out of bed with all his strength. There was a loud thump, but it

was not really a crash. His fall was broken to some extent by the carpet, his back, too, was less stiff than he thought, and so there was merely a dull thud, not so very startling. Only he had not lifted his head carefully enough and had hit it; he turned it and rubbed it on the carpet in pain and irritation.

"That was something falling down in there," said the chief clerk in the next room to the left. Gregor tried to suppose to himself that something like what had happened to him today might some day happen to the chief clerk; one really could not deny that it was possible. But as if in brusque reply to this supposition the chief clerk took a couple of firm steps in the next-door room and his patent leather boots creaked. From the right-hand room his sister was whispering to inform him of the situation: "Gregor, the chief clerk's here." "I know," muttered Gregor to himself; but he didn't dare to make his voice loud enough for his sister to hear it.

"Gregor," said his father now from the left-hand room, "the chief clerk has come and wants to know why you didn't catch the early train. We don't know what to say to him. Besides, he wants to talk to you in person. So open the door, please. He will be good enough to excuse the untidiness of your room." "Good morning, Mr. Samsa," the chief clerk was calling amiably meanwhile. "He's not well," said his mother to the visitor, while his father was still speaking through the door, "he's not well, sir, believe me. What else would make him miss a train! The boy thinks about nothing but his work. It makes me almost cross the way he never goes out in the evenings; he's been here the last eight days and has stayed at home every single evening. He just sits there quietly at the table reading a newspaper or looking through railway timetables. The only amusement he gets is doing fretwork. For instance, he spent two or three evenings cutting out a little picture frame; you would be surprised to see how pretty it is; it's hanging in his room; you'll see it in a minute when Gregor opens the door. I must say I'm glad you've come, sir; we should never have got him to unlock the door by ourselves; he's so obstinate; and I'm sure he's unwell, though he wouldn't have it to be so this morning." "I'm just coming," said Gregor slowly and carefully, not moving an inch for fear of losing one word of the conversation. "I can't think of any other explanation, madam," said the chief clerk, "I hope it's nothing serious. Although on the other hand I must say that we men of business—fortunately or unfortunately—very often simply have to ignore any slight indisposition, since business must be attended to." "Well, can the chief clerk come in now?" asked Gregor's father impatiently, again knocking on the door. "No," said Gregor. In the left-hand room a painful silence followed this refusal, in the right-hand room his sister began to sob.

Why didn't his sister join the others? She was probably newly out of bed and hadn't even begun to put on her clothes yet. Well, why was she crying? Because he wouldn't get up and let the chief clerk come in, because he was in danger of losing his job, and because the chief would begin dunning his parents again for the old debts? Surely these were things one didn't need to worry about for the present. Gregor was still at home and not in the least thinking of deserting the family. At the moment, true, he was lying on the carpet and no one who knew the condition he was in could seriously expect him to admit the chief clerk. But for such a small dis-courtesy, which could plausibly be explained away somehow later on, Gregor could hardly be dismissed on the spot. And it seemed to Gregor that it would be much more sensible to leave him in peace for the present than to trouble him with tears and entreaties. Still, of course, their uncertainty bewildered them all and excused their behavior.

"Mr. Samsa," the chief clerk called now in a louder voice, "what's the matter with you? Here you are, barricading yourself in your room, giving only 'yes' and 'no' for answers, causing your parents a lot of unnecessary trouble and neglecting— I mention this only in passing—neglecting your business duties in an incredible fashion. I am speaking here in the name of your parents and of your chief, and I beg you quite seriously to give me an immediate and precise explanation. You amaze me, you amaze me. I thought you were a quiet, dependable person, and now all at once you seem bent on making a disgraceful exhibition of yourself. The chief did hint to me early this morning a possible explanation for your disappearance—with reference to the cash payments that were entrusted to you recently—but I almost pledged my solemn word of honor that this could not be so. But now that I see how incredibly obstinate you are, I no longer have the slightest desire to take your part at all. And your position in the firm is not so unassailable. I came with the intention of telling you all this in private, but since you are wasting my time so needlessly I don't see why your parents shouldn't hear it too. For some time past your work has been most unsatisfactory; this is not the season of the year for a business boom, of course, we admit that, but a season of the year for doing no business at all, that does not exist, Mr. Samsa, must not exist."

"But sir," cried Gregor, beside himself and in his agitation forgetting everything else, "I'm just going to open the door this very minute. A slight illness, an attack of giddiness, has kept me from getting up. I'm still lying in bed. But I feel all right again. I'm getting out of bed now. Just give me a moment or two longer! I'm not quite so well as I thought. But I'm all right, really. How a thing like that can suddenly strike one down! Only last night I was quite well, my parents can tell you, or rather I did have a slight presentiment. I must have showed some sign of it. Why didn't I report it at the office! But one always thinks that an indisposition can be got over without staying in the house. Oh sir, do spare my parents! All that you're reproaching me with now has no foundation; no one has ever said a word to me about it. Perhaps you haven't looked at the last orders I sent in. Anyhow, I can still catch the eight o'clock train, I'm much the better for my few hours' rest. Don't let me detain you here, sir; I'll be attending to business very soon, and do be good enough to tell the chief so and to make my excuses to him!"

And while all this was tumbling out pell-mell and Gregor hardly knew what he was saying, he had reached the chest quite easily, perhaps because of the practice he had had in bed, and was now trying to lever himself upright by means of it. He meant actually to open the door, actually to show himself and speak to the chief clerk; he was eager to find out what the others, after all their insistence, would say at the sight of him. If they were horrified then the responsibility was no longer his and he could stay quiet. But if they took it calmly, then he had no reason either to be upset, and could really get to the station for the eight o'clock train if he hurried. At first he slipped down a few times from the polished surface of the chest, but at length with a last heave he stood upright; he paid no more attention to the pains in the lower part of his body, however they smarted. Then he let himself fall against the back of a near-by chair, and clung with his little legs to the edges of it. That brought him into control of himself again and he stopped speaking, for now he could listen to what the chief clerk was saying.

"Did you understand a word of it?" the chief clerk was asking; "surely he can't be trying to make fools of us?" "Oh dear," cried his mother, in tears, "perhaps he's terribly ill and we're tormenting him. Grete! Grete!" she called out then. "Yes Mother?" called his sister from the other side. They were calling to each other across Gregor's room. "You must go this minute for the doctor. Gregor is ill. Go for the doctor, quick. Did you hear how he was speaking?" "That was no human voice," said the chief clerk in a voice noticeably low beside the shrillness of the mother's. "Anna! Anna!" his father was calling through the hall to the kitchen, clapping his hands, "get a locksmith at once!" And the two girls were already running through the hall with a swish of skirts—how could his sister have got dressed so quickly?—and were tearing the front door open. There was no sound of its closing again; they had evidently left it open, as one does in houses where some great misfortune has happened.

But Gregor was now much calmer. The words he uttered were no longer understandable, apparently, although they seemed clear enough to him, even clearer than before, perhaps because his ear had grown accustomed to the sound of them. Yet at any rate people now believed that something was wrong with him, and were ready to help him. The positive certainty with which these first measures had been taken comforted him. He felt himself drawn once more into the human circle and hoped for great and remarkable results from both the doctor and the locksmith, without really distinguishing precisely between them. To make his voice as clear as possible for the decisive conversation that was now imminent he coughed a little, as quietly as he could, of course, since this noise too might not sound like a human cough for all he was able to judge. In the next room meanwhile there was complete silence. Perhaps his parents were sitting at the table with the chief clerk, whispering, perhaps they were all leaning against the door and listening.

Slowly Gregor pushed the chair towards the door, then let go of it, caught hold of the door for support—the soles at the end of his little legs were somewhat sticky—and rested against it for a moment after his efforts. Then he set himself to turning the key in the lock with his mouth. It seemed, unhappily, that he hadn't really any teeth—what could he grip the key with?—but on the other hand his jaws were certainly very strong; with their help he did manage to set the key in motion, heedless of the fact that he was undoubtedly damaging them somewhere, since a brown fluid issued from his mouth, flowed over the key and dripped on the floor. "Just listen to that," said the chief clerk next door; "he's turning the key." That was a great encouragement to Gregor; but they should all have shouted encouragement to him, his father and mother too: "Go on, Gregor," they should have called out, "keep going, hold on to that key!" And in the belief that they were all following his efforts intensely, he clenched his jaws recklessly on the key with all the force at his command. As the turning of the key progressed he circled round the lock, holding on now only with his mouth, pushing on the key, as required, or pulling it down again with all the weight of his body. The louder click of the finally yielding lock literally quickened Gregor. With a deep breath of relief he said to himself: "So I didn't need the locksmith," and laid his head on the handle to open the door wide.

Since he had to pull the door towards him, he was still invisible when it was really wide open. He had to edge himself slowly round the near half of the double door, and to do it very carefully if he was not to fall plump upon his back just on the threshold. He was still carrying out this difficult manoeuvre, with no time to observe anything else, when he heard the chief clerk utter a loud "Oh!"—it sounded like a gust of wind—and now he could see the man, standing as he was nearest to the door, clapping one hand before his open mouth and slowly backing away as if driven by some invisible steady pressure. His mother—in spite of the chief clerk's being there her hair was still undone and sticking up in all directions—first clasped her hands and looked at his father, then took two steps towards Gregor and fell on the floor among her outspread skirts, her face quite hidden on her breast. His father knotted his fist with a fierce expression on his face as if he meant to knock Gregor back into his room, then looked uncertainly round the living room, covered his eyes with his hands and wept till his great chest heaved.

Gregor did not go now into the living room, but leaned against the inside of the firmly shut wing of the door, so that only half his body was visible and his head above it bending sideways to look at the others. The light had meanwhile strengthened; on the other side of the street one could see clearly a section of the endlessly long, dark gray building opposite—it was a hospital—abruptly punctuated by its row of regular windows; the rain was still falling, but only in large singly discernible and literally singly splashing drops. The breakfast dishes were set out on the table lavishly, for breakfast was the most important meal of the day to Gregor's father, who lingered it out for hours over various newspapers. Right opposite Gregor on the wall hung a photograph of himself on military service, as a lieutenant, hand on sword, a carefree smile on his face, inviting one to respect his uniform and military bearing. The door leading to the hall was open, and one could see that the front door stood open too, showing the landing beyond and the beginning of the stairs going down.

"Well," said Gregor, knowing perfectly that he was the only one who had retained any composure, "I'll put my clothes on at once, pack up my samples and start off. Will you only let me go? You see, sir, I'm not obstinate, and I'm willing to work; traveling is a hard life, but I couldn't live without it. Where are you going, sir? To the office? Yes? Will you give a true account of all this? One can be temporarily incapacitated, but that's just the moment for remembering former services and bearing in mind that later on, when the incapacity has been got over, one will certainly work with all the more industry and concentration. I'm loyally bound to serve the chief, you know that very well. Besides, I have to provide for my parents and my sister. I'm in great difficulties, but I'll get out of them again. Don't make things any worse for me than they are. Stand up for me in the firm. Travelers are not popular there, I know. People think they earn sacks of money and just have a good time. A prejudice there's no particular reason for revising. But you, sir, have a more comprehensive view of affairs than the rest of the staff, yes, let me tell you in confidence, a more comprehensive view than the chief himself, who, being the owner, lets his judgment easily be swayed against one of his employees. And you know very well that the traveler, who is never seen in the office almost the whole year round, can so easily fall a victim to gossip and ill luck and unfounded complaints, which he mostly knows nothing about, except when he comes back exhausted from his rounds, and only then suffers in person from their evil consequences, which he can no longer trace back to the original causes. Sir, sir, don't go away without a word to me to show that you think me in the right at least to some extent!"

But at Gregor's very first words the chief clerk had already backed away and only stared at him with parted lips over one twitching shoulder. And while Gregor was speaking he did not stand still one moment but stole away towards the door, without taking his eyes off Gregor, yet only an inch at a time, as if obeying some secret injunction to leave the room. He was already at the hall, and the suddenness with which he took his last step out of the living room would have made one believe he had burned the sole of his foot. Once in the hall he stretched his right arm before him towards the staircase, as if some supernatural power were waiting there to deliver him.

Gregor perceived that the chief clerk must on no account be allowed to go away in this frame of mind if his position in the firm were not to be endangered to the utmost. His parents did not understand this so well; they had convinced themselves in the course of years that Gregor was settled for life in this firm, and besides they were so occupied with their immediate troubles that all foresight had forsaken them. Yet Gregor had this foresight. The chief clerk must be detained, soothed, persuaded and finally won over; the whole future of Gregor and his family depended on it! If only his sister had been there! She was intelligent; she had begun to cry while Gregor was still lying on his back. And no doubt the chief clerk, so partial to ladies, would have been guided by her; she would have shut the door of the flat and in the hall talked him out of his horror. But she was not there, and Gregor would have to handle the situation himself. And without remembering that he was still unaware what powers of movement he possessed, without even remembering that his words in all possibility, indeed in all likelihood, would again be unintelligible, he let go of the wing of the door, pushed himself through the opening, started to walk towards the chief clerk, who was already ridiculously clinging with both hands to the railing on the landing; but immediately, as he was feeling for a support, he fell down with a little cry upon all his numerous legs. Hardly was he down when he experienced for the first time a sense of physical comfort; his legs had firm ground under them; they were completely obedient, as he noted with joy; they even strove to carry him forward in whatever direction he chose; and he was inclined to believe that a final relief from all his sufferings was at hand. But in the same moment as he found himself on the floor, rocking with suppressed eagerness to move, not far from his mother, indeed just in front of her, she, who had seemed so completely crushed, sprang all at once to her feet, her arms and fingers outspread, cried: "Help, for God's sake, help!" bent her head down as if to see Gregor better, yet on the contrary kept backing senselessly away; had quite forgotten that the laden table stood behind her; sat upon it hastily, as if in absence of mind, when she bumped into it; and seemed altogether unaware that the big coffee pot beside her was upset and pouring coffee in a flood over the carpet.

"Mother, Mother," said Gregor in a low voice, and looked up at her. The chief clerk, for the moment, had quite slipped from his mind; instead, he could not resist snapping his jaws together at the sight of the streaming coffee. That made his mother scream again, she fled from the table and fell into the arms of his father, who hastened to catch her. But Gregor had now no time to spare for his parents; the chief clerk was already on the stairs; with his chin on the banisters he was taking one last backward look. Gregor made a spring, to be as sure as possible of overtaking him; the chief clerk must have divined his intention, for he leaped down several steps and vanished; he was still yelling "Ugh!" and it echoed through the whole staircase.

Unfortunately, the flight of the chief clerk seemed completely to upset Gregor's father, who had remained relatively calm until now, for instead of running after the man himself, or at least not hindering Gregor in his pursuit, he seized in his right hand the walking stick which the chief clerk had left behind on a chair, together with a hat and greatcoat, snatched in his left hand a large newspaper from the table and began stamping his feet and flourishing the stick and the newspaper to drive Gregor back into his room. No entreaty of Gregor's availed, indeed no entreaty was even understood, however humbly he bent his head his father only stamped on the floor the more loudly. Behind his father his mother had torn open a window, despite the cold weather, and was leaning far out of it with her face in her hands. A strong draught set in from the street to the staircase, the window curtains blew in, the newspapers on the table fluttered, stray pages whisked over the floor. Pitilessly Gregor's father drove him back, hissing and crying "Shoo!" like a savage. But Gregor was quite unpracticed in walking backwards, it really was a slow business. If he only had a chance to turn round he could get back to his room at once, but he was afraid of exasperating his father by the slowness of such a rotation and at any moment the stick in his father's hand might hit him a fatal blow on the back or on the head. In the end, however, nothing else was left for him to do since to his horror he observed that in moving backwards he could not even control the direction he took; and so, keeping an anxious eye on his father all the time over his shoulder, he began to turn round as quickly as he could, which was in reality very slowly. Perhaps his father noted his good intentions, for he did not interfere except every now and then to help him in the manoeuvre from a distance with the point of the stick. If only he would have stopped making that unbearable hissing noise! It made Gregor quite lose his head. He had turned almost completely round when the hissing noise so distracted him that he even turned a little the wrong way again. But when at last his head was fortunately right in front of the doorway, it appeared that his body was too broad simply to get through the opening. His father, of course, in his present mood was far from thinking of such a thing as opening the other half of the door, to let Gregor have enough space. He had merely the fixed idea of driving Gregor back into his room as quickly as possible. He would never have suffered Gregor to make the circumstantial preparations for standing up on end and perhaps slipping his way through the door. Maybe he was now making more noise than ever to urge Gregor forward, as if no obstacle impeded him; to Gregor, anyhow, the noise in his rear sounded no longer like the voice of one single father; this was really no joke, and Gregor thrust himself—come what might—into the doorway. One side of his body rose up, he was tilted at an angle in the doorway, his flank was quite bruised, horrid blotches stained the white door, soon he was stuck fast and, left to himself, could not have moved at all, his legs on one side fluttered trembling in the air, those on the other were crushed painfully to the floor—when from behind his father gave him a strong push which was literally a deliverance and he flew far into the room, bleeding freely. The door was slammed behind him with the stick, and then at last there was silence.

II

Not until it was twilight did Gregor awake out of a deep sleep, more like a swoon than a sleep. He would certainly have waked up of his own accord not much later, for he felt himself sufficiently rested and well-slept, but it seemed to him as if a fleeting step and a cautious shutting of the door leading into the hall had aroused him. The electric lights in the street cast a pale sheen here and there on the ceiling and the upper surfaces of the furniture, but down below, where he lay, it was dark. Slowly, awkwardly trying out his feelers, which he now first learned to appreciate, he pushed his way to the door to see what had been happening there. His left side felt like one single long, unpleasantly tense scar, and he had actually to limp on his two rows of legs. One little leg, moreover, had been severely damaged in the course of that morning's events—it was almost a miracle that only one had been damaged—and trailed uselessly behind him.

He had reached the door before he discovered what had really drawn him to it: the smell of food. For there stood a basin filled with fresh milk in which floated little sops of white bread. He could almost have laughed with joy, since he was now still hungrier than in the morning, and he dipped his head almost over the eyes straight into the milk. But soon in disappointment he withdrew it again; not only did he find it difficult to feed because of his tender left side—and he could only feed with the palpitating collaboration of his whole body—he did not like the milk either, although milk had been his favorite drink and that was certainly why his sister had set it there for him, indeed it was almost with repulsion that he turned away from the basin and crawled back to the middle of the room.

He could see through the crack of the door that the gas was turned on in the living room, but while usually at this time his father made a habit of reading the afternoon newspaper in a loud voice to his mother and occasionally to his sister as well, not a sound was now to be heard. Well, perhaps his father had recently given up this habit of reading aloud, which his sister had mentioned so often in conversation and in her letters. But there was the same silence all around, although the flat was certainly not empty of occupants. "What a quiet life our family has been leading," said Gregor to himself, and as he sat there motionless staring into the darkness he felt great pride in the fact that he had been able to provide such a life for his parents and sister in such a fine flat. But what if all the quiet, the comfort, the contentment were now to end in horror? To keep himself from being lost in such thoughts Gregor took refuge in movement and crawled up and down the room.

Once during the long evening one of the side doors was opened a little and quickly shut again, later the other side door too; someone had apparently wanted to come in and then thought better of it. Gregor now stationed himself immediately before the living room door, determined to persuade any hesitating visitor to come in or at least to discover who it might be; but the door was not opened again and he waited in vain. In the early morning, when the doors were locked, they had all wanted to come in, now that he had opened one door and the other had apparently been opened during the day, no one came in and even the keys were on the other side of the doors.

It was late at night before the gas went out in the living room, and Gregor could easily tell that his parents and his sister had all stayed awake until then, for he could clearly hear the three of them stealing away on tiptoe. No one was likely to visit him, not until the morning, that was certain; so he had plenty of time to meditate at his leisure on how he was to arrange his life afresh. But the lofty, empty room in which he had to lie flat on the floor filled him with an apprehension he could not account for, since it had been his very own room for the past five years—and with a half-unconscious action, not without a slight feeling of shame, he scuttled under the sofa, where he felt comfortable at once, although his back was a little cramped and he could not lift his head up, and his only regret was that his body was too broad to get the whole of it under the sofa.

He stayed there all night, spending his time partly in a light slumber, from which his hunger kept waking him up with a start, and partly in worrying and sketching vague hopes, which all led to the same conclusion, that he must lie low for the present and, by exercising patience and the utmost consideration, help the family to bear the inconvenience he was bound to cause them in his present condition.

Very early in the morning, it was still almost night, Gregor had the chance to test the strength of his new resolutions, for his sister, nearly fully dressed, opened the door from the hall and peered in. She did not see him at once, yet when she caught sight of him under the sofa—well, he had to be somewhere, he couldn't have flown away, could he?—she was so startled that without being able to help it she slammed the door shut again. But as if regretting her behavior she opened the door again immediately and came in on tiptoe, as if she were visiting an invalid or even a stranger. Gregor had pushed his head forward to the very edge of the sofa and watched her. Would she notice that he had left the milk standing, and not for lack of hunger, and would she bring in some other kind of food more to his taste? If she did not do it of her own accord, he would rather starve than draw her attention to the fact, although he felt a wild impulse to dart out from under the sofa, throw himself at her feet and beg her for something to eat. But his sister at once noticed, with surprise, that the basin was still full, except for a little milk that had been spilt all around it, she lifted it immediately, not with her bare hands, true, but with a cloth and carried it away. Gregor was wildly curious to know what she would bring instead, and made various speculations about it. Yet what she actually did next, in the goodness of her heart, he could never have guessed at. To find out what he liked she brought him a whole selection of food, all set out on an old newspaper. There were old, half-decayed vegetables, bones from last night's supper covered with a white sauce that had thickened; some raisins and almonds; a piece of cheese that Gregor would have called uneatable two days ago; a dry roll of bread, a buttered roll, and a roll both buttered and salted. Besides all that, she set down again the same basin, into which she had poured some water, and which was apparently to be reserved for his exclusive use. And with fine tact, knowing that Gregor would not eat in her presence, she withdrew quickly and even turned the key, to let him understand that he could take his ease as much as he liked. Gregor's legs all whizzed towards the food. His wounds must have healed completely, moreover, for he felt no disability, which amazed him and made him reflect how more than a month ago he had cut one finger a little with a knife and had still suffered pain from the wound only the day before yesterday. Am I less sensitive now? he thought, and sucked greedily at the cheese, which above all the other edibles attracted him at once and strongly. One after another and with tears of satisfaction in his eyes he quickly devoured the cheese, the vegetables and the sauce; the fresh food, on the other hand, had no charms for him, he could not even stand the smell of it and actually dragged away to some little distance the things he could eat. He had long finished his meal and was only lying lazily on the same spot when his sister turned the key slowly as a sign for him to retreat. That roused him at once, although he was nearly asleep, and he hurried under the sofa again. But it took considerable self-control for him to stay under the sofa, even for the short time his sister was in the room, since the large meal had swollen his body somewhat and he was so cramped he could hardly breathe. Slight attacks of breathlessness afflicted him and his eyes were starting a little out of his head as he watched his unsuspecting sister sweeping together with a broom not only the remains of what he had eaten but even the things he had not touched, as if these were now of no use to anyone, and hastily shoveling it all into a bucket, which she covered with a wooden lid and carried away. Hardly had she turned her back when Gregor came from under the sofa and stretched and puffed himself out.

In this manner Gregor was fed, once in the early morning while his parents and the servant girl were still asleep, and a second time after they had all had their mid-day dinner, for then his parents took a short nap and the servant girl could be sent out on some errand or other by his sister. Not that they would have wanted him to starve, of course, but perhaps they could not have borne to know more about his feeding than from hearsay, perhaps too his sister wanted to spare them such little anxieties wherever possible, since they had quite enough to bear as it was.

Under what pretext the doctor and the locksmith had been got rid of on that first morning Gregor could not discover, for since what he said was not understood by the others it never struck any of them, not even his sister, that he could under-stand what they said, and so whenever his sister came into his room he had to con-tent himself with hearing her utter only a sigh now and then and an occasional appeal to the saints. Later on, when she had got a little used to the situation—of course she could never get completely used to it—she sometimes threw out a remark which was kindly meant or could be so interpreted. "Well, he liked his din-ner today," she would say when Gregor had made a good clearance of his food; and when he had not eaten, which gradually happened more and more often, she would say almost sadly: "Everything's been left standing again."

But although Gregor could get no news directly, he overheard a lot from the neighboring rooms, and as soon as voices were audible, he would run to the door of the room concerned and press his whole body against it. In the first few days especially there was no conversation that did not refer to him somehow, even if only indirectly. For two whole days there were family consultations at every mealtime about what should be done; but also between meals the same subject was discussed, for there were always at least two members of the family at home, since no one wanted to be alone in the flat and to leave it quite empty was unthinkable. And on the very first of these days the household cook—it was not quite clear what and how much she knew of the situation—went down on her knees to his mother and begged leave to go, and when she departed, a quarter of an hour later, gave thanks for her dismissal with tears in her eyes as if for the greatest benefit that could have been conferred on her, and without any prompting swore a solemn oath that she would never say a single word to anyone about what had happened.

Now Gregor's sister had to cook too, helping her mother; true, the cooking did not amount to much, for they ate scarcely anything. Gregor was always hearing one of the family vainly urging another to eat and getting no answer but: "Thanks, I've had all I want," or something similar. Perhaps they drank nothing either. Time and again his sister kept asking his father if he wouldn't like some beer and offered kindly to go and fetch it herself, and when he made no answer suggested that she could ask the concierge to fetch it, so that he need feel no sense of obligation, but then a round "No" came from his father and no more was said about it.

In the course of that very first day Gregor's father explained the family's financial position and prospects to both his mother and his sister. Now and then he rose from the table to get some voucher or memorandum out of the small safe he had rescued from the collapse of his business five years earlier. One could hear him opening the complicated lock and rustling papers out and shutting it again. This statement made by his father was the first cheerful information Gregor had heard since his imprisonment. He had been of the opinion that nothing at all was left over from his father's business, at least his father had never said anything to the contrary, and of course he had not asked him directly. At that time Gregor's sole desire was to do his utmost to help the family to forget as soon as possible the catastrophe which had overwhelmed the business and thrown them all into a state of complete despair. And so he had set to work with unusual ardor and almost overnight had become a commercial traveler instead of a little clerk, with of course much greater chances of earning money, and his success was immediately translated into good round coin which he could lay on the table for his amazed and happy family. These had been fine times, and they had never recurred, at least not with the same sense of glory, although later on Gregor had earned so much money that he was able to meet the expenses of the whole household and did so. They had simply got used to it, both the family and Gregor; the money was gratefully accepted and gladly given, but there was no special uprush of warm feeling. With his sister alone had he remained intimate, and it was a secret plan of his that she, who loved music, unlike himself, and could play movingly on the violin, should be sent next year to study at the Conservatorium, despite the great expense that would entail, which must be made up in some other way. During his brief visits home the Conservatorium was often mentioned in the talks he had with his sister, but always merely as a beautiful dream which could never come true, and his parents discouraged even those innocent references to it; yet Gregor had made up his mind firmly about it and meant to announce the fact with due solemnity on Christmas Day.

Such were the thoughts, completely futile in his present condition, that went through his head as he stood clinging upright to the door and listening. Sometimes out of sheer weariness he had to give up listening and let his head fall negligently against the door, but he always had to pull himself together again at once, for even the slight sound his head made was audible next door and brought all conversation to a stop. "What can he be doing now?" his father would say after a while, obviously turning towards the door, and only then would the interrupted conversation gradually be set going again.

Gregor was now informed as amply as he could wish—for his father tended to repeat himself in his explanations, partly because it was a long time since he had handled such matters and partly because his mother could not always grasp things at once—that a certain amount of investments, a very small amount it was true, had survived the wreck of their fortunes and had even increased a little because the dividends had not been touched meanwhile. And besides that, the money Gregor brought home every month—he had kept only a few dollars for himself—had never been quite used up and now amounted to a small capital sum. Behind the door Gregor nodded his head eagerly, rejoiced at this evidence of unexpected thrift and foresight. True, he could really have paid off some more of his father's debts to the chief with his extra money, and so brought much nearer the day on which he could quit his job, but doubtless it was better the way his father had arranged it.

Yet this capital was by no means sufficient to let the family live on the interest of it; for one year, perhaps, or at the most two, they could live on the principal, that was all. It was simply a sum that ought not to be touched and should be kept for a rainy day; money for living expenses would have to be earned. Now his father was still hale enough but an old man, and he had done no work for the past five years and could not be expected to do much; during these five years, the first years of leisure in his laborious though unsuccessful life, he had grown rather fat and become sluggish. And Gregor's old mother, how was she to earn a living with her asthma, which troubled her even when she walked through the flat and kept her lying on a sofa every other day panting for breath beside an open window? And was his sister to earn her bread, she who was still a child of seventeen and whose life hitherto had been so pleasant, consisting as it did in dressing herself nicely, sleeping long, helping in the housekeeping, going out to a few modest entertainments and above all playing the violin? At first whenever the need for earning money was mentioned Gregor let go his hold on the door and threw himself down on the cool leather sofa beside it, he felt so hot with shame and grief.

Often he just lay there the long nights through without sleeping at all, scrabbling for long hours on the leather. Or he nerved himself to the great effort of pushing an armchair to the window, then crawled up over the window sill and, braced against the chair, leaned against the window panes, obviously in some recollection of the sense of freedom that looking out of a window always used to give him. For in reality day by day things that were even a little way off were growing dimmer to his sight; the hospital across the street, which he used to execrate for being all too often before his eyes, was now quite beyond his range of vision, and if he had not known that he lived in Charlotte Street, a quiet street but still a city street, he might have believed that his window gave on a desert waste where gray sky and gray land blended indistinguishably into each other. His quick-witted sister only needed to observe twice that the armchair stood by the window; after that whenever she had tidied the room she always pushed the chair back to the same place at the window and even left the inner casements open.

If he could have spoken to her and thanked her for all she had to do for him, he could have borne her ministrations better; as it was, they oppressed him. She certainly tried to make as light as possible of whatever was disagreeable in her task, and as time went on she succeeded, of course, more and more, but time brought more enlightenment to Gregor too. The very way she came in distressed him. Hardly was she in the room when she rushed to the window, without even taking time to shut the door, careful as she was usually to shield the sight of Gregor's room from the others, and as if she were almost suffocating tore the casements open with hasty fingers, standing then in the open draught for a while even in the bitterest cold and drawing deep breaths. This noisy scurry of hers upset Gregor twice a day; he would crouch trembling under the sofa all the time, knowing quite well that she would certainly have spared him such a disturbance had she found it at all possible to stay in his presence without opening the window.

On one occasion, about a month after Gregor's metamorphosis, when there was surely no reason for her to be still startled at his appearance, she came a little earlier than usual and found him gazing out the window, quite motionless, and thus well placed to look like a bogey. Gregor would not have been surprised had she not come in at all, for she could not immediately open the window while he was there, but not only did she retreat, she jumped back as if in alarm and banged the door shut; a stranger might well have thought that he had been lying in wait for her there meaning to bite her. Of course he hid himself under the sofa at once, but he had to wait until midday before she came again, and seemed more ill at ease than usual. This made him realize how repulsive the sight of him still was to her, and that it was bound to go on being repulsive, and what an effort it must cost her not to run away even from the sight of the small portion of his body that stuck out from under the sofa. In order to spare her that, therefore, one day he carried a sheet on his back to the sofa—it cost him four hours' labor—and arranged it there in such a way as to hide him completely, so that even if she were to bend down she could not see him. Had she considered the sheet unnecessary, she would certainly have stripped it off the sofa again, for it was clear enough that this curtaining and confining of himself was not likely to conduce Gregor's comfort, but she left it where it was, and Gregor even fancied that he caught a thankful glance from her eye when he lifted the sheet carefully a very little with his head to see how she was taking the new arrangement.

For the first fortnight his parents could not bring themselves to the point of entering his room, and he often heard them expressing their appreciation of his sister's activities, whereas formerly they had frequently scolded her for being as they thought a somewhat useless daughter. But now, both of them often waited outside the door, his father and his mother, while his sister tidied his room, and as soon as she came out she had to tell them exactly how things were in the room, what Gregor had eaten, how he had conducted himself this time and whether there was not perhaps some slight improvement in his condition. His mother, moreover, began relatively soon to want to visit him, but his father and sister dissuaded her at first with arguments which Gregor listened to very attentively and altogether approved. Later, however, she had to be held back by main force, and when she cried out: "Do let me in to Gregor, he is my unfortunate son! Can't you understand that I must go in to him?" Gregor thought that it might be well to have her come in, not every day, of course, but perhaps once a week; she understood things, after all, much better than his sister, who was only a child despite the efforts she was making and had perhaps taken on so difficult a task merely out of childish thoughtlessness.

Gregor's desire to see his mother was soon fulfilled. During the daytime he did not want to show himself at the window, out of consideration for his parents, but he could not crawl very far around the few square yards of floor space he had, nor could he bear lying quietly at rest all during the night, while he was fast losing any interest he had ever taken in food, so that for mere recreation he had formed the habit of crawling crisscross over the walls and ceiling. He especially enjoyed hanging suspended from the ceiling; it was much better than lying on the floor; one could breathe more freely; one's body swung and rocked lightly; and in the almost blissful absorption induced by this suspension it could happen to his own surprise that he let go and fell plump on the floor. Yet he now had his body much better under control than formerly, and even such a big fall did him no harm. His sister at once remarked the new distraction Gregor had found for himself—he left traces behind him of the sticky stuff on his soles wherever he crawled—and she got the idea in her head of giving him as wide a field as possible to crawl in and of removing the pieces of furniture that hindered him, above all the chest of drawers and the writing desk. But that was more than she could manage all by herself; she did not dare ask her father to help her; and as for the servant girl, a young creature of sixteen who had had the courage to stay on after the cook's departure, she could not be asked to help, for she had begged as an especial favor that she might keep the kitchen door locked and open it only on a definite summons; so there was nothing left but to apply to her mother at an hour when her father was out. And the old lady did come, with exclamations of joyful eagerness, which, however, died away at the door of Gregor's room. Gregor's sister, of course, went in first, to see that everything was in order before letting his mother enter. In great haste Gregor pulled the sheet lower and rucked it more in folds so that it really looked as if it had been thrown accidentally over the sofa. And this time he did not peer out from under it; he renounced the pleasure of seeing his mother on this occasion and was only glad that she had come at all. "Come in, he's out of sight," said his sister, obviously leading her mother in by the hand. Gregor could now hear the two women struggling to shift the heavy old chest from its place, and his sister claiming the greater part of the labor for herself, without listening to the admonitions of her mother who feared she might overstrain herself. It took a long time. After at least a quarter of an hour's tugging his mother objected that the chest had better be left where it was, for in the first place it was too heavy and could never be got out before his father came home, and standing in the middle of the room like that it would only hamper Gregor's movements, while in the second place it was not at all certain that removing the furniture would be doing a service to Gregor. She was inclined to think to the contrary; the sight of the naked walls made her own heart heavy, and why shouldn't Gregor have the same feeling, considering that he had been used to his furniture for so long and might feel forlorn without it. "And doesn't it look," she concluded in a low voice—in fact she had been almost whispering all the time as if to avoid letting Gregor, whose exact whereabouts she did not know, hear even the tones of her voice, for she was convinced that he could not understand her words—"doesn't it look as if we were showing him, by taking away his furniture, that we have given up hope of his ever getting better and are just leaving him coldly to himself? I think it would be best to keep his room exactly as it has always been, so that when he comes back to us he will find everything unchanged and be able all the more easily to forget what has happened in between."

On hearing these words from his mother Gregor realized that the lack of all direct human speech for the past two months together with the monotony of family life must have confused his mind, otherwise he could not account for the fact that he had quite earnestly looked forward to having his room emptied of furnishing. Did he really want his warm room, so comfortably fitted with old family furniture, to be turned into a naked den in which he would certainly be able to crawl unhampered in all directions but at the price of shedding simultaneously all recollection of his human background? He had indeed been so near the brink of forgetfulness that only the voice of his mother, which he had not heard for so long, had drawn him back from it. Nothing should be taken out of his room; everything must stay as it was; he could not dispense with the good influence of the furniture on his state of mind; and even if the furniture did hamper him in his senseless crawling round and round, that was no drawback but a great advantage.

Unfortunately his sister was of the contrary opinion; she had grown accustomed, and not without reason, to consider herself an expert in Gregor's affairs as against her parents, and so her mother's advice was now enough to make her determined on the removal not only of the chest and the writing desk, which had been her first intention, but of all the furniture except the indispensable sofa. This determination was not, of course, merely the outcome of childish recalcitrance and of the self-confidence she had recently developed so unexpectedly and at such cost; she had in fact perceived that Gregor needed a lot of space to crawl about in, while on the other hand he never used the furniture at all, so far as could be seen. Another factor might have been also the enthusiastic temperament of an adolescent girl, which seeks to indulge itself on every opportunity and which now tempted Grete to exaggerate the horror of her brother's circumstances in order that she might do all the more for him. In a room where Gregor lorded it all alone over empty walls no one save herself was likely ever to set foot.

And so she was not to be moved from her resolve by her mother who seemed moreover to be ill at ease in Gregor's room and therefore unsure of herself, was soon reduced to silence and helped her daughter as best she could to push the chest outside. Now, Gregor could do without the chest, if need be, but the writing desk he must retain. As soon as the two women had got the chest out of his room, groaning as they pushed it, Gregor stuck his head out from under the sofa to see how he might intervene as kindly and cautiously as possible. But as bad luck would have it, his mother was the first to return, leaving Grete clasping the chest in the room next door where she was trying to shift it all by herself, without of course moving it from the spot. His mother however was not accustomed to the sight of him, it might sicken her and so in alarm Gregor backed quickly to the other end of the sofa, yet could not prevent the sheet from swaying a little in front. That was enough to put her on the alert. She paused, stood still for a moment and then went back to Grete.

Although Gregor kept reassuring himself that nothing out of the way was happening, but only a few bits of furniture were being changed around, he soon had to admit that all this trotting to and fro of the two women, their little ejaculations and the scraping of furniture along the floor affected him like a vast disturbance coming from all sides at once, and however much he tucked in his head and legs and cowered to the very floor he was bound to confess that he would not be able to stand it for long. They were clearing his room out; taking away everything he loved; the chest in which he kept his fret saw and other tools was already dragged off; they were now loosening the writing desk which had almost sunk into the floor, the desk at which he had done all his homework when he was at the commercial academy, at the grammar school before that, and, yes, even at the primary school—he had no more time to waste in weighing the good intentions of the two women, whose existence he had by now forgotten, for they were so exhausted that they were laboring in silence and nothing could be heard but the heavy scuffling of their feet.

And so he rushed out—the women were just leaning against the writing desk in the next room to give themselves a breather—and four times changed his direction, since he really did not know what to rescue first, then on the wall opposite, which was already otherwise cleared, he was struck by the picture of the lady muffled in so much fur and quickly crawled up to it and pressed himself to the glass, which was a good surface to hold on to and comforted his hot belly. This picture at least, which was entirely hidden beneath him, was going to be removed by nobody. He turned his head towards the door of the living room so as to observe the women when they came back.

They had not allowed themselves much of a rest and were already coming; Grete had twined her arm round her mother and was almost supporting her. "Well, what shall we take now?" said Grete, looking round. Her eyes met Gregor's from the wall. She kept her composure, presumably because of her mother, bent her head down to her mother, to keep her from looking up, and said, although in a fluttering, unpremeditated voice: "Come, hadn't we better go back to the living room for a moment?" Her intentions were clear enough to Gregor, she wanted to bestow her mother in safety and then chase him down from the wall. Well, just let her try it! He clung to his picture and would not give it up. He would rather fly in Grete's face.

But Grete's words had succeeded in disquieting her mother, who took a step to one side, caught sight of the huge brown mass on the flowered wallpaper, and before she was really conscious that what she saw was Gregor screamed in a loud, hoarse voice: "Oh God, oh God!" fell with outspread arms over the sofa as if giving up and did not move. "Gregor!" cried his sister, shaking her fist and glaring at him. This was the first time she had directly addressed him since his metamorphosis. She ran into the next room for some aromatic essence with which to rouse her mother from her fainting fit. Gregor wanted to help too—there was still time to rescue the picture— but he was stuck fast to the glass and had to tear himself loose; he then ran after his sister into the next room as if he could advise her, as he used to do; but then had to stand helplessly behind her; she meanwhile searched among various small bottles and when she turned round started in alarm at the sight of him; one bottle fell on the floor and broke; a splinter of glass cut Gregor's face and some kind of corrosive med- icine splashed him; without pausing a moment longer Grete gathered up all the bottles she could carry and ran to her mother with them; she banged the door shut with her foot. Gregor was now cut off from his mother, who was perhaps nearly dying because of him; he dared not open the door for fear of frightening away his sis- ter, who had to stay with her mother; there was nothing he could do but wait; and harassed by self-reproach and worry he began now to crawl to and fro, over every- thing, walls, furniture, and ceiling, and finally in his despair, when the noble room seemed to be reeling round him, fell down on to the middle of the big table.

A little while elapsed. Gregor was still lying there feebly and all around was quiet, perhaps that was a good omen. Then the doorbell rang. The servant girl was of course locked in her kitchen, and Grete would have to open the door. It was his father. "What's been happening?" were his first words; Grete's face must have told him everything. Grete answered in a muffled voice, apparently hiding her head on his breast: "Mother has been fainting, but she's better now. Gregor's broken loose." "Just what I expected," said his father, "just what I've been telling you, but you women would never listen." It was clear to Gregor that his father had taken the worst interpretation of Grete's all too brief statement and was assuming that Gre- gor had been guilty of some violent act. Therefore Gregor must now try to propiti- ate his father, since he had neither time nor means for an explanation. And so he fled to the door of his own room and crouched against it, to let his father see as soon as he came in from the hall that his son had the good intention of getting back into his room immediately and that it was not necessary to drive him there, but that if only the door were opened he would disappear at once.

Yet his father was not in the mood to perceive such fine distinctions. "Ah!" he cried as soon as he appeared, in a tone which sounded at once angry and exultant. Gregor drew his head back from the door and lifted it to look at his father. Truly, this was not the father he had imagined to himself; admittedly he had been too absorbed of late in his new recreation of crawling over the ceiling to take the same interest as before in what was happening elsewhere in the flat, and he ought really to be pre- pared for some changes. And yet, and yet, could that be his father? The man who used to lie wearily sunk in bed whenever Gregor set out on a business journey; who welcomed him back of an evening lying in a long chair in a dressing gown; who could not really rise to his feet but only lifted his arms in greeting, and on the rare occa- sions when he did go out with his family, on one or two Sundays a year and on high holidays, walked between Gregor and his mother, who were slow walkers anyhow, even more slowly than they did, muffled in his old greatcoat, shuffling laboriously forward with the help of his crook-handled stick which he set down most cautiously at every step and, whenever he wanted to say anything, nearly always came to a full stop and gathered his escort around him? Now he was standing there in fine shape; dressed in a smart blue uniform with gold buttons, such as bank messengers wear; his strong double chin bulged over the stiff high collar of his jacket; from under his bushy eyebrows his black eyes darted fresh and penetrating glances; his onetime tangled white hair had been combed flat on either side of a shining and carefully exact parting. He pitched his cap, which bore a gold monogram, probably the badge of some bank, in a wide sweep across the whole room on to a sofa and with the tail-ends of his jacket thrown back, his hands in his trouser pockets, advanced with a grim visage towards Gregor. Likely enough he did not himself know what he meant to do; at any rate he lifted his feet uncommonly high, and Gregor was dumb-founded at the enormous size of his shoe soles. But Gregor could not risk standing up to him, aware as he had been from the very first day of his new life that his father believed only the severest measures suitable for dealing with him. And so he ran before his father, stopping when he stopped and scuttling forward again when his father made any kind of move. In this way they circled the room several times without anything decisive happening; indeed the whole operation did not even look like a pursuit because it was carried out so slowly. And so Gregor did not leave the floor, for he feared that his father might take as a piece of peculiar wickedness any excursion of his over the walls or the ceiling. All the same, he could not stay this course much longer, for while his father took one step he had to carry out a whole series of movements. He was already beginning to feel breathless, just as in his former life his lungs had not been very dependable. As he was staggering along, trying to concentrate his energy on running, hardly keeping his eyes open; in his dazed state never even thinking of any other escape than simply going forward; and having almost forgotten that the walls were free to him, which in this room were well provided with finely carved pieces of furniture full of knobs and crevices—suddenly something lightly flung landed close behind him and rolled before him. It was an apple; a second apple followed immediately; Gregor came to a stop in alarm; there was no point in running on, for his father was determined to bombard him. He had filled his pockets with fruit from the dish on the sideboard and was now shying apple after apple, without taking particularly good aim for the moment. The small red apples rolled about the floor as if magnetized and cannoned into each other. An apple thrown without much force grazed Gregor's back and glanced off harmlessly. But another following immediately landed right on his back and sank in; Gregor wanted to drag himself forward, as if this startling, incredible pain could be left behind him; but he felt as if nailed to the spot and flattened himself out in a complete derangement of all his senses. With his last conscious look he saw the door of his room being torn open and his mother rushing out ahead of his screaming sister, in her underbodice, for her daughter had loosened her clothing to let her breathe more freely and recover from her swoon, he saw his mother rushing toward his father, leaving one after another behind her on the floor her loosened petticoats, stumbling over her petticoats straight to his father and embracing him, in complete union with him—but here Gregor's sight began to fail—with her hands clasped round his father's neck as she begged for her son's life.

III

The serious injury done to Gregor, which disabled him for more than a month—the apple went on sticking in his body as a visible reminder, since no one bothered to remove it—seemed to have made even his father recollect that Gregor was a member of the family, despite his present unfortunate and repulsive shape, and ought not to be treated as an enemy, that, on the contrary, family duty required the suppression of disgust and the exercise of patience, nothing but patience.

And although his injury had impaired, probably for ever, his power of movement, and for the time being it took him long, long minutes to creep across his room like an old invalid—there was no question now of crawling up the wall—yet in his own opinion he was sufficiently compensated for this worsening of his condition by the fact that towards evening the living-room door, which he used to watch intently for an hour or two beforehand, was always thrown open, so that lying in the darkness of his room, invisible to the family, he could see them all at the lamp-lit table and listen to their talk, by general consent as it were, very different from his earlier eavesdropping.

True, their intercourse lacked the lively character of former times, which he had always called to mind with a certain wistfulness in the small hotel bedrooms where he had been wont to throw himself down, tired out, on damp bedding. They were now mostly very silent. Soon after supper his father would fall asleep in his armchair; his mother and sister would admonish each other to be silent; his mother, bending low over the lamp, stitched at fine sewing for an underwear firm; his sister, who had taken a job as a salesgirl, was learning shorthand and French in the evenings on the chance of bettering herself. Sometimes his father woke up, and as if quite unaware that he had been sleeping said to his mother: "What a lot of sewing you're doing today!" and at once fell asleep again, while the two women exchanged a tired smile.

With a kind of mulishness his father persisted in keeping his uniform on even in the house; his dressing gown hung uselessly on its peg and he slept fully dressed where he sat, as if he were ready for service at any moment and even here only at the beck and call of his superior. As a result, his uniform, which was not brand-new to start with, began to look dirty, despite all the loving care of the mother and sister to keep it clean, and Gregor often spent whole evenings gazing at the many greasy spots on the garment, gleaming with gold buttons always in a high state of polish, in which the old man sat sleeping in extreme discomfort and yet quite peacefully.

As soon as the clock struck ten his mother tried to rouse his father with gentle words and to persuade him after that to get into bed, for sitting there he could not have a proper sleep and that was what he needed most, since he had to go to duty at six. But with the mulishness that had obsessed him since he became a bank messenger he always insisted on staying longer at the table, although he regularly fell asleep again and in the end only with the greatest trouble could be got out of his armchair and into his bed. However insistently Gregor's mother and sister kept urging him with gentle reminders, he would go on slowly shaking his head for a quarter of an hour, keeping his eyes shut, and refuse to get to his feet. The mother plucked at his sleeve, whispering endearments in his ear, the sister left her lessons to come to her mother's help, but Gregor's father was not to be caught. He would only sink down deeper in his chair. Not until the two women hoisted him up by the armpits did he open his eyes and look at them both, one after the other, usually with the remark: "This is a life. This is the peace and quiet of my old age." And leaning on the two of them he would heave himself up, with difficulty, as if he were a great burden to himself, suffer them to lead him as far as the door and then wave them off and go on alone, while the mother abandoned her needlework and the sister her pen in order to run after him and help him farther.

Who could find time, in this overworked and tired-out family, to bother about Gregor more than was absolutely needful? The household was reduced more and more; the servant girl was turned off; a gigantic bony charwoman with white hair flying round her head came in morning and evening to do the rough work; everything else was done by Gregor's mother, as well as great piles of sewing. Even various family ornaments, which his mother and sister used to wear with pride at parties and celebrations, had to be sold, as Gregor discovered of an evening from hearing them all discuss the prices obtained. But what they lamented most was the fact that they could not leave the flat which was much too big for their present circumstances, because they could not think of any way to shift Gregor. Yet Gregor saw well enough that consideration for him was not the main difficulty preventing the removal, for they could have easily shifted him in some suitable box with a few air holes in it; what really kept them from moving into another flat was rather their own complete hopelessness and the belief that they had been singled out for a misfortune such as had never happened to any of their relations or acquaintances. They fulfilled to the uttermost all that the world demands of poor people, the father fetched breakfast for the small clerks in the bank, the mother devoted her energy to making underwear for strangers, the sister trotted to and fro behind the counter at the behest of customers, but more than this they had not the strength to do. And the wound in Gregor's back began to nag at him afresh when his mother and sister, after getting his father into bed, came back again, left their work lying, drew close to each other and sat cheek by cheek; when his mother, pointing towards his room, said: "Shut that door now, Grete," and he was left again in darkness, while next door the women mingled their tears or perhaps sat dry-eyed staring at the table.

Gregor hardly slept at all by night or by day. He was often haunted by the idea that next time the door opened he would take the family's affairs in hand again just as he used to do; once more, after this long interval, there appeared in his thoughts the figures of the chief and the chief clerk, the commercial travelers and the apprentices, the porter who was so dull-witted, two or three friends in other firms, a chambermaid in one of the rural hotels, a sweet and fleeting memory, a cashier in a milliner's shop, whom he had wooed earnestly but too slowly—they all appeared, together with strangers or people he had quite forgotten, but instead of helping him and his family they were one and all unapproachable and he was glad when they vanished. At other times he would not be in the mood to bother about his family, he was only filled with rage at the way they were neglecting him, and although he had no clear idea of what he might care to eat he would make plans for getting into the larder to take the food that was after all his due, even if he were not hungry. His sister no longer took thought to bring him what might especially please him, but in the morning and at noon before she went to business hurriedly pushed into his room with her foot any food that was available, and in the evening cleared it out again with one sweep of the broom, heedless of whether it had been merely tasted, or—as most frequently happened—left untouched. The cleaning of his room, which she now always did in the evenings, could not have been more hastily done. Streaks of dirt stretched along the walls, here and there lay balls of dust and filth. At first Gregor used to station himself in some particularly filthy corner when his sister arrived, in order to reproach her with it, so to speak. But he could have sat there for weeks without getting her to make any improvements; she could see the dirt as well as he did, but she had simply made up her mind to leave it alone. And yet, with a touchiness that was new to her, which seemed anyhow to have infected the whole family, she jealously guarded her claim to be the sole caretaker of Gregor's room. His mother once subjected his room to a thorough cleaning, which was achieved only by means of several buckets of water—all this dampness of course upset Gregor too and he lay widespread, sulky and motionless on the sofa—but she was well punished for it. Hardly had his sister noticed the changed aspect of his room that evening than she rushed in high dudgeon into the living room and, despite the imploringly raised hands of her mother, burst into a storm of weeping, while her parents—her father had of course been startled out of his chair—looked on at first in helpless amazement; then they too began to go into action; the father reproached the mother on his right for not having left the cleaning of Gregor's room to his sister; shrieked at the sister on his left that never again was she allowed to clean Gregor's room; while the mother tried to pull the father into his bedroom, since he was beyond himself with agitation; the sister, shaken with sobs, then beat upon the table with her small fists; and Gregor hissed loudly with rage because not one of them thought of shutting the door to spare him such a spectacle and so much noise.

Still, even if the sister, exhausted by her daily work, had grown tired of looking after Gregor as she did formerly, there was no need for his mother's intervention or for Gregor's being neglected at all. The charwoman was there. This old widow, whose strong bony frame had enabled her to survive the worst a long life could offer, by no means recoiled from Gregor. Without being in the least curious she had once by chance opened the door of his room and at the sight of Gregor, who, taken by surprise, began to rush to and fro although no one was chasing him, merely stood there with her arms folded. From that time she never failed to open his door a little for a moment, morning and evening, to have a look at him. At first she even used to call him to her, with words which apparently she took to be friendly, such as: "Come along, then, you old dung beetle!" or "Look at the old dung beetle, then!" To such allocutions Gregor made no answer, but stayed motionless where he was, as if the door had never been opened. Instead of being allowed to disturb him so senselessly whenever the whim took her, she should rather have been ordered to clean out his room daily, that charwoman! Once, early in the morning—heavy rain was lashing on the windowpanes, perhaps a sign that spring was on the way—Gregor was so exasperated when she began addressing him again that he ran at her, as if to attack her, although slowly and feebly enough. But the charwoman instead of showing fright merely lifted high a chair that happened to be beside the door, and as she stood there with her mouth wide open it was clear that she meant to shut it only when she brought the chair down on Gregor's back. "So you're not coming any nearer?" she asked, as Gregor turned away again, and quietly put the chair back into the corner.

Gregor was now eating hardly anything. Only when he happened to pass the food laid out for him did he take a bit of something in his mouth as a pastime, kept it there for an hour at a time and usually spat it out again. At first he thought it was chagrin over the state of his room that prevented him from eating, yet he soon got used to the various changes in his room. It had become a habit in the family to push into his room things there was no room for elsewhere, and there were plenty of these now, since one of the rooms had been let to three lodgers. Three serious gentlemen—all three of them with full beards, as Gregor once observed through a crack in the door—had a passion for order, not only in their own room but, since they were now members of the household, in all its arrangements, especially in the kitchen. Superfluous, not to say dirty, objects they could not bear. Besides, they had brought with them most of the furnishings they needed. For this reason many things could be dispensed with that it was no use trying to sell but that should not be thrown away either. All of them found their way into Gregor's room. The ash can likewise and the kitchen garbage can. Anything that was not needed for the moment was simply flung into Gregor's room by the charwoman, who did everything in a hurry; fortunately Gregor usually saw only the object, whatever it was, and the hand that held it. Perhaps she intended to take the things away again as time and opportunity offered, or to collect them until she could throw them all out in a heap, but in fact they just lay wherever she happened to throw them, except when Gregor pushed his way through the junk heap and shifted it somewhat, at first out of necessity, because he had not room enough to crawl, but later with increasing enjoyment, although after such excursions, being sad and weary to death, he would lie motionless for hours. And since the lodgers often ate their supper at home in the common living room, the living-room door stayed shut many an evening, yet Gregor reconciled himself quite easily to the shutting of the door, for often enough on evenings when it was opened he had disregarded it entirely and lain in the darkest corner of his room, quite unnoticed by the family. But on one occasion the charwoman left the door open a little and it stayed ajar even when the lodgers came in for supper and the lamp was lit. They set themselves at the top end of the table where formerly Gregor and his father and mother had eaten their meals, unfolded their napkins and took knife and fork in hand. At once his mother appeared in the other doorway with a dish of meat and close behind her his sister with a dish of potatoes piled high. The food steamed with a thick vapor. The lodgers bent over the food set before them as if to scrutinize it before eating, in fact the man in the middle, who seemed to pass for an authority with the other two, cut a piece of meat as it lay on the dish, obviously to discover if it were tender or should be sent back to the kitchen. He showed satisfaction, and Gregor's mother and sister, who had been watching anxiously, breathed freely and began to smile.

The family itself took its meals in the kitchen. None the less, Gregor's father came into the living room before going into the kitchen and with one prolonged bow, cap in hand, made a round of the table. The lodgers all stood up and murmured something in their beards. When they were alone again they ate their food in almost complete silence. It seemed remarkable to Gregor that among the various noises coming from the table he could always distinguish the sound of their masticating teeth, as if this were a sign to Gregor that one needed teeth in order to eat, and that with toothless jaws even of the finest make one could do nothing. "I'm hungry enough," said Gregor sadly to himself, "but not for that kind of food. How these lodgers are stuffing themselves, and here am I dying of starvation!"

On that very evening—during the whole of his time there Gregor could not remember ever having heard the violin—the sound of violin-playing came from the kitchen. The lodgers had already finished their supper, the one in the middle had brought out a newspaper and given the other two a page apiece, and now they were leaning back at ease reading and smoking. When the violin began to play they pricked up their ears, got to their feet, and went on tiptoe to the hall door where they stood huddled together. Their movements must have been heard in the kitchen, for Gregor's father called out: "Is the violin-playing disturbing you, gentlemen? It can be stopped at once." "On the contrary," said the middle lodger, "could not Fräulein Samsa come and play in this room, beside us, where it is much more convenient and comfortable?" "Oh certainly," cried Gregor's father, as if he were the violin-player. The lodgers came back into the living room and waited. Presently Gregor's father arrived with the music stand, his mother carrying the music and his sister with the violin. His sister quietly made everything ready to start playing; his parents, who had never let rooms before and so had an exaggerated idea of the courtesy due to lodgers, did not venture to sit down on their own chairs; his father leaned against the door, the right hand thrust between two buttons of his livery coat, which was formally buttoned up; but his mother was offered a chair by one of the lodgers and, since she left the chair just where he had happened to put it, sat down in a corner to one side.

Gregor's sister began to play; the father and mother, from either side, intently watched the movements of her hands. Gregor, attracted by the playing, ventured to move forward a little until his head was actually inside the living room. He felt hardly any surprise at his growing lack of consideration for the others; there had been a time when he prided himself on being considerate. And yet just on this occasion he had more reason than ever to hide himself, since owing to the amount of dust which lay thick in his room and rose into the air at the slightest movement, he too was covered with dust; fluff and hair and remnants of food trailed with him, caught on his back and along his sides; his indifference to everything was much too great for him to turn on his back and scrape himself clean on the carpet, as once he had several times a day. And in spite of his condition, no shame deterred him from advancing a little over the spotless floor of the living room.

To be sure, no one was aware of him. The family was entirely absorbed in the violin-playing; the lodgers, however, who first of all had stationed themselves, hands in pockets, much too close behind the music stand so that they could all have read the music, which must have bothered his sister, had soon retreated to the window, half-whispering with downbent heads, and stayed there while his father turned an anxious eye on them. Indeed, they were making it more than obvious that they had been disappointed in their expectation of hearing good or enjoyable violin-playing, that they had had more than enough of the performance and only out of courtesy suffered a continued disturbance of their peace. From the way they all kept blowing the smoke of their cigars high in the air through nose and mouth one could divine their irritation. And yet Gregor's sister was playing so beautifully. Her face leaned sideways, intently and sadly her eyes followed the notes of music. Gregor crawled a little farther forward and lowered his head to the ground so that it might be possible for his eyes to meet hers. Was he an animal, that music had such an effect upon him? He felt as if the way were opening before him to the unknown nourishment he craved. He was determined to push forward till he reached his sister, to pull at her skirt and so let her know that she was to come into his room with her violin, for no one here appreciated her playing as he would appreciate it. He would never let her out of his room, at least, not so long as he lived; his frightful appearance would become, for the first time, useful to him; he would watch all the doors of his room at night and spit at intruders; but his sister should need no constraint, she should stay with him of her own free will; she should sit beside him on the sofa, bend down her ear to him and hear him confide that he had had the firm intention of sending her to the Conservatorium, and that, but for his mishap, last Christmas—surely Christmas was long past?—he would have announced it to everybody without allowing a single objection. After this confession his sister would be so touched that she would burst into tears, and Gregor would then raise himself to her shoulder and kiss her on the neck, which, now that she went to business, she kept free of any ribbon or collar.

"Mr. Samsa!" cried the middle lodger, to Gregor's father, and pointed, without wasting any more words, at Gregor, now working himself slowly forwards. The violin fell silent, the middle lodger first smiled to his friends with a shake of the head and then looked at Gregor again. Instead of driving Gregor out, his father seemed to think it more needful to begin by soothing the lodgers, although they were not at all agitated and apparently found Gregor more entertaining than the violin-playing. He hurried towards them and, spreading out his arms, tried to urge them back into their own room and at the same time to block their view of Gregor. They now began to be really a little angry, one could not tell whether because of the old man's behavior or because it had just dawned on them that all unwittingly they had such a neighbor as Gregor next door. They demanded explanations of his father, they waved their arms like him, tugged uneasily at their beards, and only with reluctance backed towards their room. Meanwhile Gregor's sister, who stood there as if lost when her playing was so abruptly broken off, came to life again, pulled herself together all at once after standing for a while holding violin and bow in nervelessly hanging hands and staring at her music, pushed her violin into the lap of her mother, who was still sitting in her chair fighting asthmatically for breath, and ran into the lodgers' room to which they were now being shepherded by her father more quickly than before. One could see the pillows and blankets on the beds flying under her accustomed fingers and being laid in order. Before the lodgers had actually reached their room she had finished making the beds and slipped out.

The old man seemed once more to be so possessed by his mulish self-assertiveness that he was forgetting all the respect he should show to his lodgers. He kept driving them on and driving them on until in the very door of the bedroom the middle lodger stamped his foot loudly on the floor and so brought him to a halt. "I beg to announce," said the lodger, lifting one hand and looking also at Gregor's mother and sister, "that because of the disgusting conditions prevailing in this household and family"—here he spat on the floor with emphatic brevity—"I give you notice on the spot. Naturally I won't pay you a penny for the days I have lived here, on the contrary I shall consider bringing an action for damages against you, based on claims—believe me—that will be easily susceptible of proof." He ceased and stared straight in front of him, as if he expected something. In fact his two friends at once rushed into the breach with these words: "And we too give notice on the spot." On that he seized the door-handle and shut the door with a slam.

Gregor's father, groping with his hands, staggered forward and fell from his chair; it looked as if he were stretching himself there for his ordinary evening nap, but the marked jerkings of his head, which was as if uncontrollable, showed that he was far from asleep. Gregor had simply stayed quietly all the time on the spot where the lodgers had espied him. Disappointment at the failure of his plan, perhaps also the weakness arising from extreme hunger, made it impossible for him to move. He feared, with a fair degree of certainty, that at any moment the general tension would discharge itself in a combined attack upon him, and he lay waiting. He did not react even to the noise made by the violin as it fell off his mother's lap from under her trembling fingers and gave out a resonant note.

"My dear parents," said his sister, slapping her hand on the table by way of introduction, "things can't go on like this. Perhaps you don't realize that, but I do. I won't utter my brother's name in the presence of this creature, and so all I say is: we must try to get rid of it. We've tried to look after it and to put up with it as far as is humanly possible, and I don't think anyone could reproach us in the slightest."

"She is more than right," said Gregor's father to himself. His mother, who was still choking for lack of breath, began to cough hollowly into her hand with a wild look in her eyes.

His sister rushed over to her and held her forehead. His father's thoughts seemed to have lost their vagueness at Grete's words, he sat more upright, fingering his service cap that lay among the plates still lying on the table from the lodgers' supper, and from time to time looked at the still form of Gregor.

"We must try to get rid of it," his sister now said explicitly to her father, since her mother was coughing too much to hear a word, "it will be the death of both of you, I can see that coming. When one has to work as hard as we do, all of us, one can't stand this continual torment at home on top of it. At least I can't stand it any longer." And she burst into such a passion of sobbing that her tears dropped on her mother's face, where she wiped them off mechanically.

"My dear," said the old man sympathetically, and with evident understanding, "but what can we do?"

Gregor's sister merely shrugged her shoulders to indicate the feeling of helplessness that had now overmastered her during her weeping fit, in contrast to her former confidence.

"If he could understand us," said her father, half questioningly; Grete, still sobbing, vehemently waved a hand to show how unthinkable that was.

"If he could understand us," repeated the old man, shutting his eyes to consider his daughter's conviction that understanding was impossible, "then perhaps we might come to some agreement with him. But as it is—"

"He must go," cried Gregor's sister, "that's the only solution, Father. You must just try to get rid of the idea that this is Gregor. The fact that we've believed it for so long is the root of all our trouble. But how can it be Gregor? If this were Gregor, he would have realized long ago that human beings can't live with such a creature, and he'd have gone away on his own accord. Then we wouldn't have any brother, but we'd be able to go on living and keep his memory in honor. As it is, this creature persecutes us, drives away our lodgers, obviously wants the whole apartment to himself and would have us all sleep in the gutter. Just look, Father," she shrieked all at once, "he's at it again!" And in an access of panic that was quite incomprehensible to Gregor she even quitted her mother, literally thrusting the chair from her as if she would rather sacrifice her mother than stay so near to Gregor, and rushed behind her father, who also rose up, being simply upset by her agitation, and half-spread his arms out as if to protect her.

Yet Gregor had not the slightest intention of frightening anyone, far less his sister. He had only begun to turn round in order to crawl back to his room, but it was certainly a startling operation to watch, since because of his disabled condition he could not execute the difficult turning movements except by lifting his head and then bracing it against the floor over and over again. He paused and looked round. His good intentions seemed to have been recognized; the alarm had been only momentary. Now they were all watching him in melancholy silence. His mother lay in her chair, her legs stiffly outstretched and pressed together, her eyes almost closing for sheer weariness; his father and his sister were sitting beside each other, his sister's arm around the old man's neck.

Perhaps I can go on turning round now, thought Gregor, and began his labors again. He could not stop himself from panting with the effort, and had to pause now and then to take breath. Nor did anyone harass him, he was left entirely to himself. When he had completed the turn-round he began at once to crawl straight back. He was amazed at the distance separating him from his room and could not understand how in his weak state he had managed to accomplish the same journey so recently, almost without remarking it. Intent on crawling as fast as possible, he barely noticed that not a single word, not an ejaculation from his family, interfered with his progress. Only when he was already in the doorway did he turn his head round, not completely, for his neck muscles were getting stiff, but enough to see that nothing had changed behind him except that his sister had risen to her feet. His last glance fell on his mother, who was now quite overcome by sleep.

Hardly was he well inside his room when the door was hastily pushed shut, bolted and locked. The sudden noise in his rear startled him so much that his little legs gave beneath him. It was his sister who had shown such haste. She had been standing ready waiting and had made a light spring forward, Gregor had not even heard her coming, and she cried "At last!" to her parents as she turned the key in the lock.

"And what now?" said Gregor to himself, looking round in the darkness. Soon he made the discovery that he was unable to stir a limb. This did not surprise him, rather it seemed unnatural that he should ever actually have been able to move on these feeble little legs. Otherwise he felt relatively comfortable. True, his whole body was aching, but it seemed that the pain was gradually growing less and would finally pass away. The rotting apple in his back and the inflamed area around it, all covered with soft dust, already hardly troubled him. He thought of his family with tenderness and love. The decision that he must disappear was one that he held to even more strongly than his sister, if that were possible. In this state of vacant and peaceful meditation he remained until the tower clock struck three in the morning. The first broadening of light in the world outside the window entered his consciousness once more. Then his head sank to the floor of its own accord and from his nostrils came the last faint flicker of his breath.

When the charwoman arrived early in the morning—what between her strength and her impatience she slammed all the doors so loudly, never mind how often she had been begged not to do so, that no one in the whole apartment could enjoy any quiet sleep after her arrival—she noticed nothing unusual as she took her customary peep into Gregor's room. She thought he was lying motionless on purpose, pretending to be in the sulks; she credited him with every kind of intelligence. Since she happened to have the long-handled broom in her hand she tried to tickle him up with it from the doorway. When that too produced no reaction she felt provoked and poked at him a little harder, and only when she had pushed him along the floor without meeting any resistance was her attention aroused. It did not take her long to establish the truth of the matter, and her eyes widened, she let out a whistle, yet did not waste much time over it but tore open the door of the Samsas' bedroom and yelled into the darkness at the top of her voice: "Just look at this, it's dead; it's lying here dead and done for!"

Mr. and Mrs. Samsa started up in their double bed and before they realized the nature of the charwoman's announcement had some difficulty in overcoming the shock of it. But then they got out of bed quickly, one on either side, Mr. Samsa throwing a blanket over his shoulders, Mrs. Samsa in nothing but her nightgown; in this array they entered Gregor's room. Meanwhile the door of the living room opened, too, where Grete had been sleeping since the advent of the lodgers; she was completely dressed as if she had not been to bed, which seemed to be confirmed also by the paleness of her face. "Dead?" said Mrs. Samsa, looking questioningly at the charwoman, although she could have investigated for herself, and the fact was obvious enough without investigation. "I should say so," said the charwoman, proving her words by pushing Gregor's corpse a long way to one side with her broomstick. Mrs. Samsa made a movement as if to stop her, but checked it. "Well," said Mr. Samsa, "now thanks be to God." He crossed himself, and the three women followed his example.

Grete, whose eyes never left the corpse, said: "Just see how thin he was. It's such a long time since he's eaten anything. The food came out again just as it went in." Indeed, Gregor's body was completely flat and dry, as could only now be seen when it was no longer supported by the legs and nothing prevented one from looking closely at it.

"Come in beside us, Grete, for a little while," said Mrs. Samsa with a tremulous smile, and Grete, not without looking back at the corpse, followed her parents into their bedroom. The charwoman shut the door and opened the window wide. Although it was so early in the morning a certain softness was perceptible in the fresh air. After all, it was already the end of March.

The three lodgers emerged from their room and were surprised to see no breakfast; they had been forgotten. "Where's our breakfast?" said the middle lodger peevishly to the charwoman. But she put her finger to her lips and hastily, without a word, indicated by gestures that they should go into Gregor's room. They did so and stood, their hands in the pockets of their somewhat shabby coats, around Gregor's corpse in the room where it was now fully light.

At that the door of the Samsas' bedroom opened and Mr. Samsa appeared in his uniform, his wife on one arm, his daughter on the other. They all looked a little as if they had been crying; from time to time Grete hid her face on her father's arm.

"Leave my house at once!" said Mr. Samsa, and pointed to the door without disengaging himself from the women. "What do you mean by that?" said the middle lodger, taken somewhat aback, with a feeble smile. The two others put their hands behind them and kept rubbing them together, as if in gleeful expectation of a fine set-to in which they were bound to come off the winners. "I mean just what I say," answered Mr. Samsa, and advanced in a straight line with his two companions towards the lodger. He stood his ground at first quietly, looking at the floor as if his thoughts were taking a new pattern in his head. "Then let us go, by all means," he said, and looked up at Mr. Samsa as if in a sudden access of humility he were expecting some renewed sanction for this decision. Mr. Samsa merely nodded briefly once or twice with meaning eyes. Upon that the lodger really did go with long strides into the hall, his two friends had been listening and had quite stopped rubbing their hands for some moments and now went scuttling after him as if afraid that Mr. Samsa might get into the hall before them and cut them off from their leader. In the hall they all three took their hats from the rack, their sticks from the umbrella stand, bowed in silence and quitted the apartment. With a suspiciousness which proved quite unfounded Mr. Samsa and the two women followed them out to the landing; leaning over the banister they watched the three figures slowly but surely going down the long stairs, vanishing from sight at a certain turn of the staircase on every floor and coming into view again after a moment or so; the more they dwindled, the more the Samsa family's interest in them dwindled, and when a butcher's boy met them and passed them on the stairs coming up proudly with a tray on his head, Mr. Samsa and the two women soon left the landing and as if a burden had been lifted from them went back into their apartment.

They decided to spend this day in resting and going for a stroll; they had not only deserved such a respite from work, but absolutely needed it. And so they sat down at the table and wrote three notes of excuse, Mr. Samsa to his board of management, Mrs. Samsa to her employer and Grete to the head of her firm. While they were writing, the charwoman came in to say that she was going now, since her morning's work was finished. At first they only nodded without looking up, but as she kept hovering there they eyed her irritably. "Well?" said Mr. Samsa. The charwoman stood grinning in the doorway as if she had good news to impart to the family but meant not to say a word unless properly questioned. The small ostrich feather standing upright on her hat, which had annoyed Mr. Samsa ever since she was engaged, was waving gaily in all directions. "Well, what is it, then?" asked Mrs. Samsa, who obtained more respect from the charwoman than the others. "Oh," said the charwoman, giggling so amiably that she could not at once continue, "just this, you don't need to bother about how to get rid of the thing next door. It's been seen to already." Mrs. Samsa and Grete bent over their letters again, as if preoccupied; Mr. Samsa, who perceived that she was eager to begin describing it all in detail, stopped her with a decisive hand. But since she was not allowed to tell her story, she remembered the great hurry she was in, being obviously deeply huffed: "Bye, everybody," she said, whirling off violently, and departed with a frightful slamming of doors.

"She'll be given notice tonight," said Mr. Samsa, but neither from his wife nor his daughter did he get any answer, for the charwoman seemed to have shattered again the composure they had barely achieved. They rose, went to the window and stayed there, clasping each other tight. Mr. Samsa turned in his chair to look at them and quietly observed them for a little. Then he called out: "Come along, now, do. Let bygones be bygones. And you might have some consideration for me." The two of them complied at once, hastened to him, caressed him and quickly finished their letters.

Then they all three left the apartment together, which was more than they had done for months, and went by tram into the open country outside the town. The tram, in which they were the only passengers, was filled with warm sunshine. Leaning comfortably back in their seats they canvassed their prospects for the future, and it appeared on closer inspection that these were not at all bad, for the jobs they had got, which so far they had never really discussed with each other, were all three admirable and likely to lead to better things later on. The greatest immediate improvement in their condition would of course arise from moving to another house; they wanted to take a smaller and cheaper but also better situated and more easily run apartment than the one they had, which Gregor had selected. While they were thus conversing, it struck both Mr. and Mrs. Samsa, almost at the same moment, as they became aware of their daughter's increasing vivacity, that in spite of all the sorrow of recent times, which had made her cheeks pale, she had bloomed into a pretty girl with a good figure. They grew quieter and half unconsciously exchanged glances of complete agreement, having come to the conclusion that it would soon be time to find a good husband for her. And it was like a confirmation of their new dreams and excellent intentions that at the end of their journey their daughter sprang to her feet first and stretched her young body.

[1915]

Journal Entry

How do you respond to the first sentence of "The Metamorphosis"? Characterize the narrator's tone.

Textual Considerations

1. Characterize the narrator's attitude toward Gregor. What does he reveal about Gregor, his job, and his relationship with his boss?
2. Analyze Gregor's relationship with his sister. Explain how her treatment of Gregor changes as the story continues. To what extent is her final betrayal inevitable?
3. Food plays an important role in the story. How does it affect the main ideas Kafka explores in the story? Explain.
4. Characterize Gregor's father. To what extent has he exploited Gregor? Why is it ironic that as Gregor's situation deteriorates that of his family improves?
5. Consider the roles of the three lodgers and the charwoman. How are their attitudes toward Gregor similar to or different from those of his family?
6. Compare and contrast Kafka's treatment of time in parts I and II. How is it reflective of Gregor's psychological state?
7. How many "metamorphoses" occur in the story? Consider, for example, the final scene. How does it differ stylistically from the rest of the story?

Cultural Contexts

1. Analyze the extent to which Gregor is responsible for his sense of alienation. Does he deserve his fate? Of what is he guilty? Is he a victim of the selfishness or manipulation of others? What might Kafka be implying about one's relationship to oneself versus responsibility to family and community?
2. Many critics attribute Kafka's thematic preoccupation with exile and alienation to his biographical circumstances. Kafka was a Jew raised in a Gentile world, suffered from tuberculosis, was terrified of his domineering and judgmental father, and was a sensitive artist in a typical middle-class society. Debate with your group the degree to which Gregor's sense of isolation may be explained solely by these circumstances.

James Joyce

Eveline

She sat at the window watching the evening invade the avenue. Her head was leaned against the window curtains and in her nostrils was the odor of dusty cretonne. She was tired.

Few people passed. The man out of the last house passed on his way home; she heard his footsteps clicking along the concrete pavement and afterwards crunching on the cinder path before the new red houses. One time there used to be a field there in which they used to play every evening with other people's children. Then a man from Belfast bought the field and built houses in it—not like their little brown houses but bright brick houses with shining roofs. The children of the avenue used to play together in that field—the Devines, the Waters, the Dunns, little Keogh the cripple, she and her brothers and sisters. Ernest, however, never played: he was too grown up. Her father used often to hunt them in out of the field with his blackthorn stick; but usually little Keogh used to keep *nix* and call out when he saw her father coming. Still they seemed to have been rather happy then. Her father was not so bad then; and besides, her mother was alive. That was a long time ago; she and her brothers and sisters were all grown up; her mother was dead. Tizzie Dunn was dead, too, and the Waters had gone back to England. Everything changes. Now she was going to go away like the others, to leave her home.

Home! She looked round the room, reviewing all its familiar objects which she had dusted once a week for so many years, wondering where on earth all the dust came from. Perhaps she would never see again those familiar objects from which she had never dreamed of being divided. And yet during all those years she had never found out the name of the priest whose yellowing photograph hung on the wall above the broken harmonium beside the colored print of the promises made to Blessed Margaret Mary Alacoque. He had been a school friend of her father. Whenever he showed the photograph to a visitor her father used to pass it with a casual word:

—He is in Melbourne now.

She had consented to go away, to leave her home. Was that wise? She tried to weigh each side of the question. In her home anyway she had shelter and food; she had those whom she had known all her life about her. Of course she had to work hard both in the house and at business. What would they say of her in the Stores when they found out that she had run away with a fellow? Say she was a fool, perhaps; and her place would be filled up by advertisement. Miss Gavan would be glad. She had always had an edge on her, especially whenever there were people listening.

—Miss Hill, don't you see these ladies are waiting?

—Look lively, Miss Hill, please.

She would not cry many tears at leaving the Stores.

But in her new home, in a distant unknown country, it would not be like that. Then she would be married—she, Eveline. People would treat her with respect then. She would not be treated as her mother had been. Even now, though she was over nineteen, she sometimes felt herself in danger of her father's violence. She knew it was that that had given her the palpitations. When they were growing up he had never gone for her, like he used to go for Harry and Ernest, because she was a girl; but latterly he had begun to threaten her and say what he would do to her only for her dead mother's sake. And now she had nobody to protect her. Ernest was dead and Harry, who was in the church decorating business, was nearly always down somewhere in the country. Besides, the invariable squabble for money on Saturday nights had begun to weary her unspeakably. She always gave her entire wages—seven shillings—and Harry always sent up what he could but the trouble was to get any money from her father. He said she used to squander the money, that she had no head, that he wasn't going to give her his hard-earned money to throw about the streets, and much more, for he was usually fairly bad of a Saturday night. In the end he would give her the money and ask her had she any intention of buying Sunday's dinner. Then she had to rush out as quickly as she could and do her marketing, holding her black leather purse tightly in her hand as she elbowed her way through the crowds and returning home late under her load of provisions. She had hard work to keep the house together and to see that the two young children who had been left to her charge went to school regularly and got their meals regularly. It was hard work—a hard life—but now that she was about to leave it she did not find it a wholly undesirable life.

She was about to explore another life with Frank. Frank was very kind, manly, open-hearted. She was to go away with him by the night-boat to be his wife and to live with him in Buenos Ayres where he had a home waiting for her. How well she remembered the first time she had seen him; he was lodging in a house on the main road where she used to visit. It seemed a few weeks ago. He was standing at the gate, his peaked cap pushed back on his head and his hair tumbled forward over a face of bronze. Then they had come to know each other. He used to meet her outside the Stores every evening and see her home. He took her to see *The Bohemian Girl* and she felt elated as she sat in an unaccustomed part of the theatre with him. He was awfully fond of music and sang a little. People knew that they were courting and, when he sang about the lass that loves a sailor, she always felt pleasantly confused. He used to call her Poppens out of fun. First of all it had been an excitement for her to have a fellow and then she had begun to like him. He had tales of distant countries. He had started as a deck boy at a pound a month on a ship of the Allan Line going out to Canada. He told her the names of the ships he had been on and the names of the different services. He had sailed through the Straits of Magellan and he told her stories of the terrible Patagonians. He had fallen on his feet in Buenos Ayres, he said, and had come over to the old country just for a holiday. Of course, her father had found out the affair and had forbidden her to have anything to say to him.

—I know these sailor chaps, he said.

One day he had quarrelled with Frank and after that she had to meet her lover secretly.

The evening deepened in the avenue. The white of two letters in her lap grew indistinct. One was to Harry; the other was to her father. Ernest had been her favorite but she liked Harry too. Her father was becoming old lately, she noticed; he would miss her. Sometimes he could be very nice. Not long before, when she had been laid up for a day, he had read her out a ghost story and made toast for her at the fire. Another day, when their mother was alive, they had all gone for a picnic to the Hill of Howth. She remembered her father putting on her mother's bonnet to make the children laugh.

Her time was running out but she continued to sit by the window, leaning her head against the window curtain, inhaling the odor of dusty cretonne. Down far in the avenue she could hear a street organ playing. She knew the air. Strange that it should come that very night to remind her of the promise to her mother, her promise to keep the home together as long as she could. She remembered the last night of her mother's illness; she was again in the close dark room at the other side of the hall and outside she heard a melancholy air of Italy. The organ-player had been ordered to go away and given sixpence. She remembered her father strutting back into the sickroom saying:

—Damned Italians! coming over here!

As she mused, the pitiful vision of her mother's life laid its spell on the very quick of her being—that life of commonplace sacrifices closing in final craziness. She trembled as she heard again her mother's voice saying constantly with foolish insistence:

—Derevaun Seraun! Derevaun Seraun!

She stood up in a sudden impulse of terror. Escape! She must escape! Frank would save her. He would give her life, perhaps love, too. But she wanted to live. Why should she be unhappy? She had a right to happiness. Frank would take her in his arms, fold her in his arms. He would save her.

She stood among the swaying crowd in the station at the North Wall. He held her hand and she knew that he was speaking to her, saying something about the passage over and over again. The station was full of soldiers with brown baggages. Through the wide doors of the sheds she caught a glimpse of the black mass of the boat, lying in beside the quay wall, with illumined portholes. She answered nothing. She felt her cheek pale and cold and, out of a maze of distress, she prayed to God to direct her, to show her what was her duty. The boat blew a long mournful whistle into the mist. If she went, tomorrow she would be on the sea with Frank, steaming towards Buenos Ayres. Their passage had been booked. Could she still draw back after all he had done for her? Her distress awoke a nausea in her body and she kept moving her lips in silent fervent prayer.

A bell clanged upon her heart. She felt him seize her hand:

—Come!

All the seas of the world tumbled about her heart. He was drawing her into them: he would drown her. She gripped with both hands at the iron railing.

—Come!

No! No! No! It was impossible. Her hands clutched the iron in frenzy. Amid the seas she sent a cry of anguish!

—Eveline! Evvy!

He rushed beyond the barrier and called to her to follow. He was shouted at to go on but he still called to her. She set her white face to him, passive, like a helpless animal. Her eyes gave him no sign of love or farewell or recognition.

[1916]

Journal Entry

Imagine yourself in Eveline's position and defend the choice you have made. How might your choice be similar or different from hers? Explain.

Textual Considerations

1. How does Eveline define "home" in paragraphs 3–5 of Joyce's story? To what extent does her definition of home differ from or contrast with her definition of "new home"?
2. What do the first paragraphs of the story reveal about Eveline? How emotionally connected is she to her physical surroundings?

3. Characterize Frank. To what extent is he a romantic figure? Identify the romantic elements he uses to court Eveline. How does Eveline's father react to Frank? Why is Frank unable to persuade Eveline to overcome her "fixed gender identity?"
4. Discuss the appropriateness of dust as the dominant symbol in "Eveline." Can you find other symbols in that story?
5. To what extent is Eveline's inability to choose her own happiness attributable to her role as daughter and as a single woman in an Irish Catholic environment at the turn of the century? What other factors might have contributed to her sense of paralysis?

Cultural Contexts

1. Compare and contrast Frank's philosophy of life with the view Eveline's mother expresses through her insistent statement that "the end of pleasure is pain" ("Deveraun Seraun").
2. Initiate a group discussion of "Eveline" by locating the conflict between the forces of tradition and change in Joyce's story.

James Joyce

The Boarding House

Mrs. Mooney was a butcher's daughter. She was a woman who was quite able to keep things to herself: a determined woman. She had married her father's foreman and opened a butcher's shop near Spring Gardens. But as soon as his father-in-law was dead Mr. Mooney began to go to the devil. He drank, plundered the till, ran headlong into debt. It was no use making him take the pledge: he was sure to break out again a few days after. By fighting his wife in the presence of customers and by buying bad meat he ruined his business. One night he went for his wife with the cleaver and she had to sleep in a neighbour's house.

After that they lived apart. She went to the priest and got a separation from him with care of the children. She would give him neither money nor food nor house-room; and so he was obliged to enlist himself as a sheriff's man. He was a shabby stooped little drunkard with a white face and a white moustache and white eyebrows, pencilled above his little eyes, which were pink-veined and raw; and all day long he sat in the bailiff's room, waiting to be put on a job. Mrs. Mooney, who had taken what remained of her money out of the butcher business and set up a boarding house in Hardwicke Street, was a big imposing woman. Her house had a floating population made up of tourists from Liverpool and the Isle of Man and, occasionally, *artistes* from the music halls. Its resident population was made up of clerks from the city. She governed the house cunningly and firmly, knew when to give credit, when to be stern and when to let things pass. All the resident young men spoke of her as *The Madam*.

Mrs. Mooney's young men paid fifteen shillings a week for board and lodgings (beer or stout at dinner excluded). They shared in common tastes and occupations and for this reason they were very chummy with one another. They discussed with one another the chances of favourites and outsiders. Jack Mooney, the Madam's son, who was clerk to a commission agent in Fleet Street, had the reputation of being a hard case. He was fond of using soldiers' obscenities: usually he came home in the small hours. When he met his friends he had always a good one to tell them and he was always sure to be on to a good thing—that is to say, a likely horse or a likely *artiste*. He was also handy with the mits and sang comic songs. On Sunday nights there would often be a reunion in Mrs. Mooney's front drawing-room. The music-hall *artistes* would oblige; and Sheridan played waltzes and polkas and vamped accompaniments. Polly Mooney, the Madam's daughter, would also sing. She sang:

> "*I'm a . . . naughty girl*
> *You needn't sham:*
> *You know I am.*"

Polly was a slim girl of nineteen; she had light soft hair and a small full mouth. Her eyes, which were grey with a shade of green through them, had a habit of glancing upwards when she spoke with anyone, which made her look like a little perverse madonna. Mrs. Mooney had first sent her daughter to be a typist in a corn-factor's office but, as a disreputable sheriff's man used to come every other day to the office, asking to be allowed to say a word to his daughter, she had taken her daughter home again and set her to do housework. As Polly was very lively the intention was to give her the run of the young men. Besides, young men like to feel that there is a young woman not very far away. Polly, of course, flirted with the young men but Mrs. Mooney, who was a shrewd judge, knew that the young men were only passing the time away: none of them meant business. Things went on so for a long time and Mrs. Mooney began to think of sending Polly back to typewriting when she noticed that something was going on between Polly and one of the young men. She watched the pair and kept her own counsel.

Polly knew that she was being watched, but still her mother's persistent silence could not be misunderstood. There had been no open complicity between mother and daughter, no open understanding but, though people in the house began to talk of the affair, still Mrs. Mooney did not intervene. Polly began to grow a little strange in her manner and the young man was evidently perturbed. At last, when she judged it to be the right moment, Mrs. Mooney intervened. She dealt with moral problems as a cleaver deals with meat: and in this case she had made up her mind.

It was a bright Sunday morning of early summer, promising heat, but with a fresh breeze blowing. All the windows of the boarding house were open and the lace curtains ballooned gently towards the street beneath the raised sashes. The belfry of George's Church sent out constant peals and worshippers, singly or in groups, traversed the little circus before the church, revealing their purpose by their self-contained demeanour no less than by the little volumes in their gloved hands. Breakfast was over in the boarding house and the table of the breakfast-room was covered with plates on which lay yellow streaks of eggs with morsels of bacon-fat and bacon-rind. Mrs. Mooney sat in the straw arm-chair and watched the servant Mary remove the breakfast things. She made Mary collect the crusts and pieces of broken bread to help to make Tuesday's bread-pudding. When the table was cleared, the broken bread collected, the sugar and butter safe under lock and key, she began to reconstruct the interview which she had had the night before with Polly. Things were as she had suspected: she had been frank in her questions and Polly had been frank in her answers. Both had been somewhat awkward, of course. She had been made awkward by her not wishing to receive the news in too cavalier a fashion or to seem to have connived and Polly had been made awkward not merely because allusions of that kind always made her awkward but also because she did not wish it to be thought that in her wise innocence she had divined the intention behind her mother's tolerance.

Mrs. Mooney glanced instinctively at the little gilt clock on the mantelpiece as soon as she had become aware through her revery that the bells of George's Church had stopped ringing. It was seventeen minutes past eleven: she would have lots of time to have the matter out with Mr. Doran and then catch short twelve at Marlborough Street. She was sure she would win. To begin with she had all the weight of social opinion on her side: she was an outraged mother. She had allowed him to live beneath her roof, assuming that he was a man of honour, and he had simply abused her hospitality. He was thirty-four or thirty-five years of age, so that youth could not be pleaded as his excuse; nor could ignorance be his excuse since he was a man who had seen something of the world. He had simply taken advantage of Polly's youth and inexperience: that was evident. The question was: What reparation would he make?

There must be reparation made in such cases. It is all very well for the man: he can go his ways as if nothing had happened, having had his moment of pleasure, but the girl has to bear the brunt. Some mothers would be content to patch up such an affair for a sum of money; she had known cases of it. But she would not do so. For her only one reparation could make up for the loss of her daughter's honour: marriage.

She counted all her cards again before sending Mary up to Mr. Doran's room to say that she wished to speak with him. She felt sure she would win. He was a serious young man, not rakish or loud-voiced like the others. If it had been Mr. Sheridan or Mr. Meade or Bantam Lyons her task would have been much harder. She did not think he would face publicity. All the lodgers in the house knew something of the affair; details had been invented by some. Besides, he had been employed for thirteen years in a great Catholic wine-merchant's office and publicity would mean for him, perhaps, the loss of his job. Whereas if he agreed all might be well. She knew he had a good screw for one thing and she suspected he had a bit of stuff put by.

Nearly the half-hour! She stood up and surveyed herself in the pierglass. The decisive expression of her great florid face satisfied her and she thought of some mothers she knew who could not get their daughters off their hands.

Mr. Doran was very anxious indeed this Sunday morning. He had made two attempts to shave but his hand had been so unsteady that he had been obliged to desist. Three days' reddish beard fringed his jaws and every two or three minutes a mist gathered on his glasses so that he had to take them off and polish them with his pocket-handkerchief. The recollection of his confession of the night before was a cause of acute pain to him; the priest had drawn out every ridiculous detail of the affair and in the end had so magnified his sin that he was almost thankful at being afforded a loophole of reparation. The harm was done. What could he do now but marry her or run away? He could not brazen it out. The affair would be sure to be talked of and his employer would be certain to hear of it. Dublin is such a small city:

everyone knows everyone else's business. He felt his heart leap warmly in his throat as he heard in his excited imagination old Mr. Leonard calling out in his rasping voice: "Send Mr. Doran here, please."

All his long years of service gone for nothing! All his industry and diligence thrown away! As a young man he had sown his wild oats, of course; he had boasted of his free-thinking and denied the existence of God to his companions in public-houses. But that was all passed and done with . . . nearly. He still bought a copy of *Reynold's Newspaper* every week but he attended to his religious duties and for nine-tenths of the year lived a regular life. He had money enough to settle down on; it was not that. But the family would look down on her. First of all there was her dis-reputable father and then her mother's boarding house was beginning to get a cer-tain fame. He had a notion that he was being had. He could imagine his friends talking of the affair and laughing. She *was* a little vulgar; sometimes she said "I seen" and "If I had've known." But what would grammar matter if he really loved her? He could not make up his mind whether to like her or despise her for what she had done. Of course he had done it too. His instinct urged him to remain free, not to marry. Once you are married you are done for, it said.

While he was sitting helplessly on the side of the bed in shirt and trousers she tapped lightly at his door and entered. She told him all, that she had made a clean breast of it to her mother and that her mother would speak with him that morning. She cried and threw her arms round his neck, saying:

"O Bob! Bob! What am I to do? What am I to do at all?"

She would put an end to herself, she said.

He comforted her feebly, telling her not to cry, that it would be all right, never fear. He felt against his shirt the agitation of her bosom.

It was not altogether his fault that it had happened. He remembered well, with the curious patient memory of the celibate, the first casual caresses her dress, her breath, her fingers had given him. Then late one night as he was undressing for bed she had tapped at his door, timidly. She wanted to relight her candle at his for hers had been blown out by a gust. It was her bath night. She wore a loose open combing-jacket of printed flannel. Her white instep shone in the opening of her furry slippers and the blood glowed warmly behind her perfumed skin. From her hands and wrists too as she lit and steadied her candle a faint perfume arose.

On nights when he came in very late it was she who warmed up his dinner. He scarcely knew what he was eating feeling her beside him alone, at night, in the sleeping house. And her thoughtfulness! If the night was anyway cold or wet or windy there was sure to be a little tumbler of punch ready for him. Perhaps they could be happy together. . . .

They used to go upstairs together on tiptoe, each with a candle, and on the third landing exchange reluctant good-nights. They used to kiss. He remembered well her eyes, the touch of her hand and his delirium. . . .

But delirium passes. He echoed her phrase, applying it to himself: *"What am I to do?"* The instinct of the celibate warned him to hold back. But the sin was there; even his sense of honour told him that reparation must be made for such a sin.

While he was sitting with her on the side of the bed Mary came to the door and said that the missus wanted to see him in the parlour. He stood up to put on his coat and waistcoat, more helpless than ever. When he was dressed he went over to her to comfort her. It would be all right, never fear. He left her crying on the bed and moaning softly: *"O my God!"*

Going down the stairs his glasses became so dimmed with moisture that he had to take them off and polish them. He longed to ascend through the roof and fly away to another country where he would never hear again of his trouble, and yet a force pushed him downstairs step by step. The implacable faces of his employer and of the Madam stared upon his discomfiture. On the last flight of stairs he passed Jack Mooney who was coming up from the pantry nursing two bottles of *Bass*. They saluted coldly; and the lover's eyes rested for a second or two on a thick bulldog face and a pair of thick short arms. When he reached the foot of the staircase he glanced up and saw Jack regarding him from the door of the return-room.

Suddenly he remembered the night when one of the music-hall *artistes*, a little blond Londoner, had made a rather free allusion to Polly. The reunion had been almost broken up on account of Jack's violence. Everyone tried to quiet him. The music-hall *artiste*, a little paler than usual, kept smiling and saying that there was no harm meant: but Jack kept shouting at him that if any fellow tried that sort of a game on with his sister he'd bloody well put his teeth down his throat, so he would.

Polly sat for a little time on the side of the bed, crying. Then she dried her eyes and went over to the looking-glass. She dipped the end of the towel in the water-jug and refreshed her eyes with the cool water. She looked at herself in profile and read-justed a hairpin above her ear. Then she went back to the bed again and sat at the foot. She regarded the pillows for a long time and the sight of them awakened in her mind secret, amiable memories. She rested the nape of her neck against the cool iron bed-rail and fell into a revery. There was no longer any perturbation visible on her face.

She waited on patiently, almost cheerfully, without alarm, her memories gradu-ally giving place to hopes and visions of the future. Her hopes and visions were so intricate that she no longer saw the white pillows on which her gaze was fixed or remembered that she was waiting for anything.

At last she heard her mother calling. She started to her feet and ran to the banisters.

"Polly! Polly!"

"Yes, mamma?"

"Come down, dear. Mr. Doran wants to speak to you."

Then she remembered what she had been waiting for.

[1916]

Journal Entry

How does Mr. Doran feel about becoming a member of the Mooney family?

Textual Considerations

1. Characterize Mr. Doran. How emotionally connected is he with the boarding house? What idea of home is reflected in Mrs. Mooney's boarding house?
2. Consider the role of religion and honor in "The Boarding House." How do they contribute to Mr. Doran's paralysis? What other factors might also be cited?
3. Would you characterize Mr. Doran's and Polly's affair as romantic? Are they in love with each other? Make a character sketch of Polly. Why has she chosen Mr. Doran over the other young men in the boarding house?
4. Discuss Mrs. Mooney's attitude toward marriage. Consider her own marriage and how it influenced the way she raised Polly and built up her expectations about Polly's future.
5. What role does the concept of "honor" play in the story? What does it say about gender relations in Joyce's story?

Cultural Contexts

1. Initiate a group discussion of "The Boarding House" by locating the forces of tradition and change that shape Joyce's story.
2. Discuss Joyce's story as a social document that reflects or criticizes the values of the Irish community.

William Faulkner

A Rose for Emily

I

When Miss Emily Grierson died, our whole town went to her funeral: the men through a sort of respectful affection for a fallen monument, the women mostly out of curiosity to see the inside of her house, which no one save an old manservant—a combined gardener and cook—had seen in at least ten years.

It was a big, squarish frame house that had once been white, decorated with cupolas and spires and scrolled balconies in the heavily lightsome style of the seventies, set on what had once been our most select street. But garages and cotton gins had encroached and obliterated even the august names of that neighborhood; only Miss Emily's house was left, lifting its stubborn and coquettish decay above the cotton wagons and the gasoline pumps—an eyesore among eyesores. And now Miss Emily had gone to join the representatives of those august names where they lay in the cedar-bemused cemetery among the ranked and anonymous graves of Union and Confederate soldiers who fell at the battle of Jefferson.

Alive, Miss Emily had been a tradition, a duty, and a care; a sort of hereditary obligation upon the town, dating from that day in 1894 when Colonel Sartoris,[1] the mayor—he who fathered the edict that no Negro woman should appear on the streets without an apron—remitted her taxes, the dispensation dating from the death

---

[1] A major figure among Faulkner's fictional inhabitants of Yoknapatawpha County.

of her father on into perpetuity. Not that Miss Emily would have accepted charity. Colonel Sartoris invented an involved tale to the effect that Miss Emily's father had loaned money to the town, which the town, as a matter of business, preferred this way of repaying. Only a man of Colonel Sartoris' generation and thought could have invented it, and only a woman could have believed it.

When the next generation, with its more modern ideas, became mayors and aldermen, this arrangement created some little dissatisfaction. On the first of the year they mailed her a tax notice. February came, and there was no reply. They wrote her a formal letter, asking her to call at the sheriff's office at her convenience. A week later the mayor wrote her himself, offering to call or to send his car for her, and received in reply a note on paper of an archaic shape, in a thin, flowing calligraphy in faded ink, to the effect that she no longer went out at all. The tax notice was also enclosed, without comment.

They called a special meeting of the Board of Aldermen. A deputation waited upon her, knocked at the door through which no visitor had passed since she ceased giving china-painting lessons eight or ten years earlier. They were admitted by the old Negro into a dim hall from which a stairway mounted into still more shadow. It smelled of dust and disuse—a close, dank smell. The Negro led them into the parlor. It was furnished in heavy, leather-covered furniture. When the Negro opened the blinds of one window, a faint dust rose sluggishly about their thighs, spinning with slow motes in the single sun-ray. On a tarnished gilt easel before the fireplace stood a crayon portrait of Miss Emily's father.

They rose when she entered—a small, fat woman in black, with a thin gold chain descending to her waist and vanishing into her belt, leaning on an ebony cane with a tarnished gold head. Her skeleton was small and spare; perhaps that was why what would have been merely plumpness in another, was obesity in her. She looked bloated, like a body long submerged in motionless water, and of that pallid hue. Her eyes, lost in the fatty ridges of her face, looked like two small pieces of coal pressed into a lump of dough as they moved from one face to another while the visitors stated their errand.

She did not ask them to sit. She just stood in the door and listened quietly until the spokesman came to a stumbling halt. Then they could hear the invisible watch ticking at the end of the gold chain. Her voice was dry and cold. "I have no taxes in Jefferson. Colonel Sartoris explained it to me. Perhaps one of you can gain access to the city records and satisfy yourselves."

"But we have. We are the city authorities, Miss Emily. Didn't you get a notice from the sheriff, signed by him?"

"I received a paper, yes," Miss Emily said. "Perhaps he considers himself the sheriff. . . . I have no taxes in Jefferson."

"But there is nothing on the books to show that, you see. We must go by the—"

"See Colonel Sartoris. I have no taxes in Jefferson."

"But, Miss Emily—"

"See Colonel Sartoris." (Colonel Sartoris had been dead almost ten years.) "I have no taxes in Jefferson. Tobe!" The Negro appeared. "Show these gentlemen out."

II

So she vanquished them, horse and foot, just as she had vanquished their fathers thirty years before about the smell. That was two years after her father's death and a short time after her sweetheart—the one we believed would marry her—had deserted her. After her father's death she went out very little; after her sweetheart went away, people hardly saw her at all. A few of the ladies had the temerity to call, but were not received, and the only sign of life about the place was the Negro man—a young man then—going in and out with a market basket.

"Just as if a man—any man—could keep a kitchen properly," the ladies said; so they were not surprised when the smell developed. It was another link between the gross, teeming world and the high and mighty Griersons.

A neighbor, a woman, complained to the mayor, Judge Stevens, eighty years old.

"But what will you have me do about it, madam?" he said.

"Why, send her word to stop it," the woman said. "Isn't there a law?"

"I'm sure that won't be necessary," Judge Stevens said. "It's probably just a snake or a rat that nigger of hers killed in the yard. I'll speak to him about it."

The next day he received two more complaints, one from a man who came in diffident deprecation. "We really must do something about it, Judge. I'd be the last one in the world to bother Miss Emily, but we've got to do something." That night the Board of Aldermen met—three gray-beards and one younger man, a member of the rising generation.

"It's simple enough," he said. "Send her word to have her place cleaned up. Give her a certain time to do it in, and if she don't . . ."

"Dammit, sir," Judge Stevens said, "will you accuse a lady to her face of smelling bad?"

So the next night, after midnight, four men crossed Miss Emily's lawn and slunk about the house like burglars, sniffing along the base of the brickwork and at the cellar openings while one of them performed a regular sowing motion with his hand out of a sack slung from his shoulder. They broke open the cellar door and sprinkled lime there, and in all the outbuildings. As they recrossed the lawn, a window that had been dark was lighted and Miss Emily sat in it, the light behind her, and her upright torso motionless as that of an idol. They crept quietly across the lawn and into the shadow of the locusts that lined the street. After a week or two the smell went away.

That was when people had begun to feel really sorry for her. People in our town, remembering how old lady Wyatt, her great-aunt, had gone completely crazy at last, believed that the Griersons held themselves a little too high for what they really were. None of the young men were quite good enough for Miss Emily and such. We had long thought of them as a tableau; Miss Emily a slender figure in white in the background, her father a spraddled silhouette in the foreground, his back to her and clutching a horsewhip,[2] the two of them framed by the back-flung front door. So when she got to be thirty and was still single, we were not pleased

[2] The horsewhip was the legendary weapon used by American fathers to protect their daughters from unwelcome suitors.

exactly, but vindicated; even with insanity in the family she wouldn't have turned down all of her chances if they had really materialized.

When her father died, it got about that the house was all that was left to her; and in a way, people were glad. At last they could pity Miss Emily. Being left alone, and a pauper, she had become humanized. Now she too would know the old thrill and the old despair of a penny more or less.

The day after his death all the ladies prepared to call at the house and offer condolence and aid, as is our custom. Miss Emily met them at the door, dressed as usual and with no trace of grief on her face. She told them that her father was not dead. She did that for three days, with the ministers calling on her, and the doctors, trying to persuade her to let them dispose of the body. Just as they were about to resort to law and force, she broke down, and they buried her father quickly.

We did not say she was crazy then. We believed she had to do that. We remembered all the young men her father had driven away, and we knew that with nothing left, she would have to cling to that which had robbed her, as people will.

III

She was sick for a long time. When we saw her again, her hair was cut short, making her look like a girl, with a vague resemblance to those angels in colored church windows—sort of tragic and serene.

The town had just let the contracts for paving the sidewalks, and in the summer after her father's death they began to work. The construction company came with niggers and mules and machinery, and a foreman named Homer Barron, a Yankee—a big, dark, ready man, with a big voice and eyes lighter than his face. The little boys would follow in groups to hear him cuss the niggers, and the niggers singing in time to the rise and fall of picks. Pretty soon he knew everybody in town. Whenever you heard a lot of laughing anywhere about the square, Homer Barron would be in the center of the group. Presently we began to see him and Miss Emily on Sunday afternoons driving in the yellow-wheeled buggy and the matched team of bays from the livery stable.

At first we were glad that Miss Emily would have an interest, because the ladies all said, "Of course a Grierson would not think seriously of a Northerner, a day laborer." But there were still others, older people, who said that even grief could not cause a real lady to forget *noblesse oblige*[3]—without calling it *noblesse oblige*. They just said, "Poor Emily. Her kinsfolk should come to her." She had some kin in Alabama; but years ago her father had fallen out with them over the estate of old lady Wyatt, the crazy woman, and there was no communication between the two families. They had not even been represented at the funeral.

And as soon as the old people said, "Poor Emily," the whispering began. "Do you suppose it's really so?" they said to one another. "Of course it is. What else could . . ." This behind their hands; rustling of craned silk and satin behind jalousies closed upon the sun of Sunday afternoon as the thin, swift clop-clop-clop of the matched team passed: "Poor Emily."

---

[3] The obligations of the upper class.

She carried her head high enough—even when we believed that she was fallen. It was as if she demanded more than ever the recognition of her dignity as the last Grierson; as if it had wanted that touch of earthiness to reaffirm her imperviousness. Like when she bought the rat poison, the arsenic. That was over a year after they had begun to say "Poor Emily," and while the two female cousins were visiting her.

"I want some poison," she said to the druggist. She was over thirty then, still a slight woman, though thinner than usual, with cold, haughty black eyes in a face the flesh of which was strained across the temples and about the eyesockets as you imagine a lighthouse-keeper's face ought to look. "I want some poison," she said.

"Yes, Miss Emily. What kind? For rats and such? I'd recom—"

"I want the best you have. I don't care what kind."

The druggist named several. "They'll kill anything up to an elephant. But what you want is—"

"Arsenic," Miss Emily said. "Is that a good one?"

"Is . . . arsenic? Yes ma'am. But what you want—"

"I want arsenic."

The druggist looked down at her. She looked back at him, erect, her face like a strained flag. "Why, of course," the druggist said. "If that's what you want. But the law requires you to tell what you are going to use it for."

Miss Emily just stared at him, her head tilted back in order to look him eye for eye, until he looked away and went and got the arsenic and wrapped it up. The Negro delivery boy brought her the package; the druggist didn't come back. When she opened the package at home there was written on the box, under the skull and bones: "For rats."

IV

So the next day we all said, "She will kill herself"; and we said it would be the best thing. When she had first begun to be seen with Homer Barron, we had said, "She will marry him." Then we said, "She will persuade him yet," because Homer himself had remarked—he liked men, and it was known that he drank with the younger men in the Elk's Club—that he was not a marrying man. Later we said, "Poor Emily," behind the jalousies as they passed on Sunday afternoon in the glittering buggy, Miss Emily with her head high and Homer Barron with his hat cocked and a cigar in his teeth, reins and whip in a yellow glove.

Then some of the ladies began to say that it was a disgrace to the town and a bad example to the young people. The men did not want to interfere, but at last the ladies forced the Baptist minister—Miss Emily's people were Episcopal—to call upon her. He would never divulge what happened during that interview, but he refused to go back again. The next Sunday they again drove about the streets, and the following day the minister's wife wrote to Miss Emily's relations in Alabama.

So she had blood-kin under her roof again and we sat back to watch developments. At first nothing happened. Then we were sure that they were to be married. We learned that Miss Emily had been to the jeweler's and ordered a man's toilet set in silver, with the letters H. B. on each piece. Two days later we learned that she had bought a complete outfit of men's clothing, including a nightshirt, and we said,

"They are married." We were really glad. We were glad because the two female cousins were even more Grierson than Miss Emily had ever been.

So we were not surprised when Homer Barron—the streets had been finished some time since—was gone. We were a little disappointed that there was not a public blowing-off, but we believed that he had gone on to prepare for Miss Emily's coming, or to give her a chance to get rid of the cousins. (By that time it was a cabal, and we were all Miss Emily's allies to help circumvent the cousins.) Sure enough, after another week they departed. And, as we had expected all along, within three days Homer Barron was back in town. A neighbor saw the Negro man admit him at the kitchen door at dusk one evening.

And that was the last we saw of Homer Barron. And of Miss Emily for some time. The Negro man went in and out with the market basket, but the front door remained closed. Now and then we would see her at a window for a moment, as the men did that night when they sprinkled the lime, but for almost six months she did not appear on the streets. Then we knew that this was to be expected too; as if that quality of her father which had thwarted her woman's life so many times had been too virulent and too furious to die.

When we next saw Miss Emily, she had grown fat and her hair was turning gray. During the next few years it grew grayer and grayer until it attained an even pepper-and-salt iron-gray, when it ceased turning. Up to the day of her death at seventy-four it was still that vigorous iron-gray, like the hair of an active man.

From that time on her front door remained closed, save for a period of six or seven years, when she was about forty, during which she gave lessons in china-painting. She fitted up a studio in one of the downstairs rooms, where the daughters and granddaughters of Colonel Sartoris' contemporaries were sent to her with the same regularity and in the same spirit that they were sent on Sundays with a twenty-five cent piece for the collection plate. Meanwhile her taxes had been remitted.

Then the newer generation became the backbone and the spirit of the town, and the painting pupils grew up and fell away and did not send their children to her with boxes of color and tedious brushes and pictures cut from the ladies' magazines. The front door closed upon the last one and remained closed for good. When the town got free postal delivery Miss Emily alone refused to let them fasten the metal numbers above her door and attach a mailbox to it. She would not listen to them.

Daily, monthly, yearly we watched the Negro grow grayer and more stooped, going in and out with the market basket. Each December we sent her a tax notice, which would be returned by the post office a week later, unclaimed. Now and then we would see her in one of the downstairs windows—she had evidently shut up the top floor of the house—like the carven torso of an idol in a niche, looking or not looking at us, we could never tell which. Thus she passed from generation to generation—dear, inescapable, impervious, tranquil, and perverse.

And so she died. Fell ill in the house filled with dust and shadows, with only a doddering Negro man to wait on her. We did not even know she was sick; we had long since given up trying to get any information from the Negro. He talked to no one, probably not even to her, for his voice had grown harsh and rusty, as if from disuse.

She died in one of the downstairs rooms, in a heavy walnut bed with a curtain, her gray head propped on a pillow yellow and moldy with age and lack of sunlight.

V

The Negro met the first of the ladies at the front door and let them in, with their hushed, sibilant voices and their quick, curious glances, and then he disappeared. He walked right through the house and out the back and was not seen again.

The two female cousins came at once. They held the funeral on the second day, with the town coming to look at Miss Emily beneath a mass of bought flowers, with the crayon face of her father musing profoundly above the bier and the ladies sibilant and macabre; and the very old men—some in their brushed Confederate uniforms—on the porch and the lawn, talking of Miss Emily as if she had been a contemporary of theirs, believing that they had danced with her and courted her perhaps, confusing time with its mathematical progression, as the old do, to whom all the past is not a diminishing road, but, instead, a huge meadow which no winter ever quite touches, divided from them now by the narrow bottleneck, of the most recent decade of years.

Already we knew that there was one room in that region above stairs which no one had seen in forty years, and which would have to be forced. They waited until Miss Emily was decently in the ground before they opened it.

The violence of breaking down the door seemed to fill this room with pervading dust. A thin, acrid pall as of the tomb seemed to lie everywhere upon this room decked and furnished as for a bridal: upon the valance curtains of faded rose color, upon the rose-shaded lights, upon the dressing table, upon the delicate array of crystal and the man's toilet things backed with tarnished silver, silver so tarnished that the monogram was obscured. Among them lay a collar and tie, as if they had just been removed, which, lifted, left upon the surface a pale crescent in the dust. Upon a chair hung the suit, carefully folded; beneath it the two mute shoes and the discarded socks.

The man himself lay in the bed.

For a long while we just stood there, looking down at the profound and fleshless grin. The body had apparently once lain in the attitude of an embrace, but now the long sleep that outlasts love, that conquers even the grimace of love, had cuckolded him. What was left of him, rotted beneath what was left of the nightshirt, had become inextricable from the bed in which he lay; and upon him and upon the pillow beside him lay that even coating of the patient and biding dust.

Then we noticed that in the second pillow was the indentation of a head. One of us lifted something from it, and leaning forward, that faint and invisible dust dry and acrid in the nostrils, we saw a long strand of iron-gray hair.

[1930]

Journal Entry

Did Emily kill Homer because of loneliness or jealousy? Is it possible to love someone too much?

Textual Considerations

1. Several characters influence Miss Emily's actions. Analyze her father's influence on her life. What kind of person is Homer? What is his role in the story? Why does Miss Emily's servant stay with her so faithfully during her life and leave so abruptly after her death?
2. Symbols of decay abound in the story. Identify at least three. How far has Emily Grierson, the "fallen monument," actually fallen? What does the last line of the story mean?
3. This story presents a series of character glimpses that when put together create a montage of the life of Emily Grierson. How does the author move from one scene to another? What effect is achieved by his disjointed chronology? What, for instance, would have happened had he started at the beginning and moved in chronological sequence to the end? Recreate the actual sequence of events.
4. What is the role of the narrator in the story? Why does Faulkner tell the story through the eyes of an anonymous townsperson?
5. How important is the setting of the story? Miss Emily's position in the town? The passage of time?

Cultural Contexts

1. Characterize the narrator and the townspeople. How do they regard the Grierson family? What is Miss Emily's attitude toward them?
2. Discuss with your group Faulkner's purpose in writing this story. What philosophical, social, and moral ideas does he explore in "A Rose for Emily"? What does Faulkner's story reveal about the disintegration of Southern culture?

Albert Camus

The Guest

Translated by Justin O'Brien

The schoolmaster was watching the two men climb toward him. One was on horseback, the other on foot. They had not yet tackled the abrupt rise leading to the schoolhouse built on the hillside. They were toiling onward, making slow progress in the snow, among the stones, on the vast expanse of the high, deserted plateau. From time to time the horse stumbled. Without hearing anything yet, he could see the breath issuing from the horse's nostrils. One of the men, at least, knew the region. They were following the trail although it had disappeared days ago under a layer of dirty white snow. The schoolmaster calculated that it would take them half an hour to get onto the hill. It was cold; he went back into the school to get a sweater.

He crossed the empty, frigid classroom. On the blackboard the four rivers of France, drawn with four different colored chalks, had been flowing toward their estuaries for the past three days. Snow had suddenly fallen in mid-October after eight months of drought without the transition of rain, and the twenty pupils, more or less, who lived in the villages scattered over the plateau had stopped coming. With fair weather they would return. Daru now heated only the single room that was his lodging, adjoining the classroom and giving also onto the plateau to the east. Like the class windows, his window looked to the south too. On that side the school was a few kilometers from the point where the plateau began to slope toward the south. In clear weather could be seen the purple mass of the mountain range where the gap opened onto the desert.

Somewhat warmed, Daru returned to the window from which he had first seen the two men. They were no longer visible. Hence they must have tackled the rise. The sky was not so dark, for the snow had stopped falling during the night. The morning had opened with a dirty light which had scarcely become brighter as the ceiling of clouds lifted. At two in the afternoon it seemed as if the day were merely beginning. But still this was better than those three days when the thick snow was falling amidst unbroken darkness with little gusts of wind that rattled the double door of the classroom. Then Daru had spent long hours in his room, leaving it only to go to the shed and feed the chickens or get some coal. Fortunately the delivery truck from Tadjid, the nearest village to the north, had brought his supplies two days before the blizzard. It would return in forty-eight hours.

Besides, he had enough to resist a siege, for the little room was cluttered with bags of wheat that the administration left as a stock to distribute to those of his pupils whose families had suffered from the drought. Actually they had all been victims because they were all poor. Every day Daru would distribute a ration to the children. They had missed it, he knew, during these bad days. Possibly one of the fathers or big brothers would come this afternoon and he could supply them with grain. It was just a matter of carrying them over to the next harvest. Now shiploads of wheat were arriving from France and the worst was over. But it would be hard to forget that poverty, that army of ragged ghosts wandering in the sunlight, the plateaus burned to a cinder month after month, the earth shriveled up little by little, literally scorched, every stone bursting into dust under one's foot. The sheep had died then by thousands and even a few men, here and there, sometimes without anyone's knowing.

In contrast with such poverty, he who lived almost like a monk in his remote schoolhouse, nonetheless satisfied with the little he had and with the rough life, had felt like a lord with his white-washed walls, his narrow couch, his unpainted shelves, his well, and his provision of water and food. And suddenly this snow, without warning, without the foretaste of rain. This is the way the region was, cruel to live in, even without men—who didn't help matters either. But Daru had been born here. Everywhere else, he felt exiled.

He stepped out onto the terrace in front of the schoolhouse. The two men were now halfway up the slope. He recognized the horseman as Balducci, the old gendarme he had known for a long time. Balducci was holding on the end of a rope an Arab who was walking behind him with hands bound and head lowered. The gendarme waved a greeting to which Daru did not reply, lost as he was in contemplation of the Arab dressed in a faded blue jellaba, his feet in sandals but covered with socks of heavy raw wool, his head surmounted by a narrow, short *chèche*. They were approaching. Balducci was holding back his horse in order not to hurt the Arab and the group was advancing slowly.

Within earshot, Balducci shouted: "One hour to do the three kilometers from El Ameur!" Daru did not answer. Short and square in his thick sweater, he watched them climb. Not once had the Arab raised his head. "Hello," said Daru when they got up onto the terrace. "Come in and warm up." Balducci painfully got down from his horse without letting go the rope. From under his bristling mustache he smiled at the schoolmaster. His little dark eyes, deep-set under a tanned forehead, and his mouth surrounded with wrinkles made him look attentive and studious. Daru took the bridle, led the horse to the shed, and came back to the two men, who were now waiting for him in the school. He led them into his room. "I am going to heat up the classroom," he said. "We'll be more comfortable there." When he entered the room again, Balducci was on the couch. He had undone the rope tying him to the Arab, who had squatted near the stove. His hands still bound, the *chèche* pushed back on his head, he was looking toward the window. At first Daru noticed only his huge lips, fat, smooth, almost Negroid; yet his nose was straight, his eyes were dark and full of fever. The *chèche* revealed an obstinate forehead and, under the weathered skin now rather discolored by the cold, the whole face had a restless and rebellious look that struck Daru when the Arab, turning his face toward him, looked him straight in the eyes. "Go into the other room," said the schoolmaster, "and I'll make you some mint tea." "Thanks," Balducci said. "What a chore! How I long for retirement." And addressing his prisoner in Arabic: "Come on, you." The Arab got up and, slowly, holding his bound wrists in front of him, went into the classroom.

With the tea, Daru brought a chair. But Balducci was already enthroned on the nearest pupil's desk and the Arab had squatted against the teacher's platform facing the stove, which stood between the desk and the window. When he held out the glass of tea to the prisoner, Daru hesitated at the sight of his bound hands. "He might perhaps be untied." "Sure," said Balducci. "That was for the trip." He started to get to his feet. But Daru, setting the glass on the floor, had knelt beside the Arab. Without saying anything, the Arab watched him with his feverish eyes. Once his hands were free, he rubbed his swollen wrists against each other, took the glass of tea, and sucked up the burning liquid in swift little sips.

"Good," said Daru. "And where are you headed?"

Balducci withdrew his mustache from the tea. "Here, son."

"Odd pupils! And you're spending the night?"

"No. I'm going back to El Ameur. And you will deliver this fellow to Tinguit. He is expected at police headquarters."

Balducci was looking at Daru with a friendly little smile.

"What's this story?" asked the schoolmaster. "Are you pulling my leg?"

"No, son. Those are the orders."

"The orders? I'm not . . ." Daru hesitated, not wanting to hurt the old Corsican. "I mean, that's not my job."

"What! What's the meaning of that? In wartime people do all kinds of jobs."

"Then I'll wait for the declaration of war!"

Balducci nodded.

"O.K. But the orders exist and they concern you too. Things are brewing, it appears. There is talk of a forthcoming revolt. We are mobilized, in a way."

Daru still had his obstinate look.

"Listen, son," Balducci said. "I like you and you must understand. There's only a dozen of us at El Ameur to patrol throughout the whole territory of a small department and I must get back in a hurry. I was told to hand this guy over to you and return without delay. He couldn't be kept there. His village was beginning to stir; they wanted to take him back. You must take him to Tinguit tomorrow before the day is over. Twenty kilometers shouldn't faze a husky fellow like you. After that, all will be over. You'll come back to your pupils and your comfortable life."

Behind the wall the horse could be heard snorting and pawing the earth. Daru was looking out the window. Decidedly, the weather was clearing and the light was increasing over the snowy plateau. When all the snow was melted, the sun would take over again and once more would burn the fields of stone. For days, still, the unchanging sky would shed its dry light on the solitary expanse where nothing had any connection with man.

"After all," he said, turning around toward Balducci, "what did he do?" And, before the gendarme had opened his mouth, he asked: "Does he speak French?"

"No, not a word. We had been looking for him for a month, but they were hiding him. He killed his cousin."

"Is he against us?"

"I don't think so. But you can never be sure."

"Why did he kill?"

"A family squabble, I think. One owed the other grain, it seems. It's not at all clear. In short, he killed his cousin with a billhook. You know, like a sheep, *kreezk!*"

Balducci made the gesture of drawing a blade across his throat and the Arab, his attention attracted, watched him with a sort of anxiety. Daru felt a sudden wrath against the man, against all men with their rotten spite, their tireless hates, their blood lust.

But the kettle was singing on the stove. He served Balducci more tea, hesitated, then served the Arab again, who, a second time, drank avidly. His raised arms made the jellaba fall open and the schoolmaster saw his thin, muscular chest.

"Thanks, kid," Balducci said. "And now, I'm off."

He got up and went toward the Arab, taking a small rope from his pocket.

"What are you doing?" Daru asked dryly.

Balducci, disconcerted, showed him the rope.

"Don't bother."

The old gendarme hesitated. "It's up to you. Of course, you are armed?"

"I have my shotgun."

"Where?"

"In the trunk."

"You ought to have it near your bed."

"Why? I have nothing to fear."

"You're crazy, son. If there's an uprising, no one is safe, we're all in the same boat."

"I'll defend myself. I'll have time to see them coming."

Balducci began to laugh, then suddenly the mustache covered the white teeth.

"You'll have time? O.K. That's just what I was saying. You have always been a little cracked. That's why I like you, my son was like that."

At the same time he took out his revolver and put it on the desk.

"Keep it; I don't need two weapons from here to El Ameur."

The revolver shone against the black paint of the table. When the gendarme turned toward him, the schoolmaster caught the smell of leather and horseflesh.

"Listen, Balducci," Daru said suddenly, "every bit of this disgusts me, and first of all your fellow here. But I won't hand him over. Fight, yes, if I have to. But not that."

The old gendarme stood in front of him and looked at him severely.

"You're being a fool," he said slowly. "I don't like it either. You don't get used to putting a rope on a man even after years of it, and you're even ashamed—yes, ashamed. But you can't let them have their way."

"I won't hand him over," Daru said again.

"It's an order, son, and I repeat it."

"That's right. Repeat to them what I've said to you: I won't hand him over."

Balducci made a visible effort to reflect. He looked at the Arab and at Daru. At last he decided.

"No, I won't tell them anything. If you want to drop us, go ahead; I'll not denounce you. I have an order to deliver the prisoner and I'm doing so. And now you'll just sign this paper for me."

"There's no need. I'll not deny that you left him with me."

"Don't be mean with me. I know you'll tell the truth. You're from hereabouts and you are a man. But you must sign, that's the rule."

Daru opened his drawer, took out a little square bottle of purple ink, the red wooden penholder with the "sergeant-major" pen he used for making models of penmanship, and signed. The gendarme carefully folded the paper and put it into his wallet. Then he moved toward the door.

"I'll see you off," Daru said.

"No," said Balducci. "There's no use being polite. You insulted me."

He looked at the Arab, motionless in the same spot, sniffed peevishly, and turned away toward the door. "Good-by, son," he said. The door shut behind him. Balducci appeared suddenly outside the window and then disappeared. His footsteps were muffled by the snow. The house stirred on the other side of the wall and several chickens fluttered in fright. A moment later Balducci reappeared outside the window leading the horse by the bridle. He walked toward the little rise without turning around and disappeared from sight with the horse following him. A big stone could be heard bouncing down. Daru walked back toward the prisoner, who, without stirring, never took his eyes off him. "Wait," the schoolmaster said in Arabic and went toward the bedroom. As he was going through the door, he had a second thought, went to the desk, took the revolver, and stuck it in his pocket. Then, without looking back, he went into his room.

For some time he lay on his couch watching the sky gradually close over, listening to the silence. It was this silence that had seemed painful to him during the first days here, after the war. He had requested a post in the little town at the base of the foothills separating the upper plateaus from the desert. There, rocky walls, green and black to the north, pink and lavender to the south, marked the frontier of eternal summer. He had been named to a post farther north, on the plateau itself. In the beginning, the solitude and the silence had been hard for him on those wastelands peopled only by stones. Occasionally, furrows suggested cultivation, but they had been dug to uncover a certain kind of stone good for building. The only plowing here was to harvest rocks. Elsewhere a thin layer of soil accumulated in the hollows would be scraped out to enrich paltry village gardens. This is the way it was: bare rock covered three quarters of the region. Towns sprang up, flourished, then disappeared; men came by, loved one another or fought bitterly, then died. No one in this desert, neither he nor his guest, mattered. And yet, outside this desert neither of them, Daru knew, could have really lived.

When he got up, no noise came from the classroom. He was amazed at the unmixed joy he derived from the mere thought that the Arab might have fled and that he would be alone with no decision to make. But the prisoner was there. He had merely stretched out between the stove and the desk. With eyes open, he was staring at the ceiling. In that position, his thick lips were particularly noticeable, giving him a pouting look. "Come," said Daru. The Arab got up and followed him. In the bedroom, the schoolmaster pointed to a chair near the table under the window. The Arab sat down without taking his eyes off Daru.

"Are you hungry?"

"Yes," the prisoner said.

Daru set the table for two. He took flour and oil, shaped a cake in a frying-pan, and lighted the little stove that functioned on bottled gas. While the cake was cooking, he went out to the shed to get cheese, eggs, dates, and condensed milk. When the cake was done he set it on the window sill to cool, heated some condensed milk diluted with water, and beat up the eggs into an omelette. In one of his motions he knocked against the revolver stuck in his right pocket. He set the bowl down, went into the classroom, and put the revolver in his desk drawer. When he came back to the room, night was falling. He put on the light and served the Arab. "Eat," he said. The Arab took a piece of the cake, lifted it eagerly to his mouth, and stopped short.

"And you?" he asked.

"After you. I'll eat too."

The thick lips opened slightly. The Arab hesitated, then bit into the cake determinedly.

The meal over, the Arab looked at the schoolmaster. "Are you the judge?"

"No, I'm simply keeping you until tomorrow."

"Why do you eat with me?"

"I'm hungry."

The Arab fell silent. Daru got up and went out. He brought back a folding bed from the shed, set it up between the table and the stove, perpendicular to his own bed. From a large suitcase which, upright in a corner, served as a shelf for papers, he took two blankets and arranged them on the camp bed. Then he stopped, felt useless, and sat down on his bed. There was nothing more to do or to get ready. He had to look at this man. He looked at him, therefore, trying to imagine his face bursting with rage. He couldn't do so. He could see nothing but the dark yet shining eyes and the animal mouth.

"Why did you kill him?" he asked in a voice whose hostile tone surprised him.

The Arab looked away.

"He ran away. I ran after him."

He raised his eyes to Daru again and they were full of a sort of woeful interrogation. "Now what will they do to me?"

"Are you afraid?"

He stiffened, turning his eyes away.

"Are you sorry?"

The Arab stared at him openmouthed. Obviously he did not understand. Daru's annoyance was growing. At the same time he felt awkward and self-conscious with his big body wedged between the two beds.

"Lie down there," he said impatiently. "That's your bed."

The Arab didn't move. He called to Daru:

"Tell me!"

The schoolmaster looked at him.

"Is the gendarme coming back tomorrow?"

"I don't know."

"Are you coming with us?"

"I don't know. Why?"

The prisoner got up and stretched out on top of the blankets, his feet toward the window. The light from the electric bulb shone straight into his eyes and he closed them at once.

"Why?" Daru repeated, standing beside the bed.

The Arab opened his eyes under the blinding light and looked at him, trying not to blink.

"Come with us," he said.

In the middle of the night, Daru was still not asleep. He had gone to bed after undressing completely; he generally slept naked. But when he suddenly realized that he had nothing on, he hesitated. He felt vulnerable and the temptation came to him to put his clothes back on. Then he shrugged his shoulders; after all, he wasn't a child and, if need be, he could break his adversary in two. From his bed he could observe him, lying on his back, still motionless with his eyes closed under the harsh light. When Daru turned out the light, the darkness seemed to coagulate all of a sudden. Little by little, the night came back to life in the window where the starless sky was stirring gently. The schoolmaster soon made out the body lying at his feet. The Arab still did not move, but his eyes seemed open. A faint wind was prowling around the schoolhouse. Perhaps it would drive away the clouds and the sun would reappear.

During the night the wind increased. The hens fluttered a little and then were silent. The Arab turned over on his side with his back to Daru, who thought he heard him moan. Then he listened for his guest's breathing; it became heavier and more regular. He listened to that breath so close to him and mused without being able to go to sleep. In this room where he had been sleeping alone for a year, this presence bothered him. But it bothered him also by imposing on him a sort of brotherhood he knew well but refused to accept in the present circumstances. Men who share the same rooms, soldiers or prisoners, develop a strange alliance as if, having cast off their armor with their clothing, they fraternized every evening, over and above their differences, in the ancient community of dream and fatigue. But Daru shook himself; he didn't like such musings, and it was essential to sleep.

A little later, however, when the Arab stirred slightly, the schoolmaster was still not asleep. When the prisoner made a second move, he stiffened, on the alert. The Arab was lifting himself slowly on his arms with almost the motion of a sleepwalker. Seated upright in bed, he waited motionless without turning his head toward Daru, as if he were listening attentively. Daru did not stir; it had just occurred to him that the revolver was still in the drawer of his desk. It was better to act at once. Yet he continued to observe the prisoner, who, with the same slithery motion, put his feet on the ground, waited again, then began to stand up slowly. Daru was about to call out to him when the Arab began to walk, in a quite natural but extraordinarily silent way. He was heading toward the door at the end of the room that opened into the shed. He lifted the latch with precaution and went out, pushing the door behind him but without shutting it. Daru had not stirred. "He is running away," he merely thought. "Good riddance!" Yet he listened attentively. The hens were not fluttering; the guest must be on the plateau. A faint sound of water reached him, and he didn't know what it was until the Arab again stood framed in the doorway, closed the door carefully, and came back to bed without a sound. Then Daru turned his back on him and fell asleep. Still later he seemed, from the depths of his sleep, to hear furtive steps around the schoolhouse. "I'm dreaming! I'm dreaming!" he repeated to himself. And he went on sleeping. When he awoke, the sky was clear; the loose window let in a cold, pure air. The Arab was asleep, hunched up under the blankets now, his mouth open, utterly relaxed. But when Daru shook him, he started dreadfully, staring at Daru with wild eyes as if he had never seen him and such a frightened expression that the schoolmaster stepped back. "Don't be afraid. It's me. You must eat." The Arab nodded his head and said yes. Calm had returned to his face, but his expression was vacant and listless.

The coffee was ready. They drank it together on the folding bed as they munched their pieces of the cake. Then Daru led the Arab under the shed and showed him the faucet where he washed. He went back into the room, folded the blankets and the bed, made his own bed and put the room in order. Then he went through the classroom and out onto the terrace. The sun was already rising in the blue sky; a soft, bright light was bathing the deserted plateau. On the ridge the snow was melting in spots. The stones were about to reappear. Crouched on the edge of the plateau, the schoolmaster looked at the deserted expanse. He thought of Balducci. He had hurt him, for he had sent him off in a way as if he didn't want to be associated with him. He could still hear the gendarme's farewell and, without knowing why, he felt strangely empty and vulnerable. At that moment, from the other side of the schoolhouse, the prisoner coughed. Daru listened to him almost despite himself and then, furious, threw a pebble that whistled through the air before sinking in the snow. That man's stupid crime revolted him, but to hand him over was contrary to honor. Merely thinking of it made him smart with humiliation. And he cursed at one and the same time his own people who had sent him this Arab and the Arab too who had dared to kill and not managed to get away. Daru got up, walked in a circle on the terrace, waited motionless, and then went back into the schoolhouse.

The Arab, leaning over the cement floor of the shed, was washing his teeth with two fingers. Daru looked at him and said: "Come." He went back into the room ahead of the prisoner. He slipped a hunting-jacket on over his sweater and put on walking-shoes. Standing, he waited until the Arab had put on his *chèche* and sandals. They went into the classroom and the schoolmaster pointed to the exit, saying: "Go head." The fellow didn't budge. "I'm coming," said Daru. The Arab went out. Daru went back into the room and made a package of pieces of rusk, dates, and sugar. In the classroom, before going out, he hesitated a second in front of his desk, then crossed the threshold and locked the door. "That's the way," he said. He started toward the east, followed by the prisoner. But, a short distance from the school-house, he thought he heard a slight sound behind them. He retraced his steps and examined the surroundings of the house; there was no one there. The Arab watched him without seeming to understand. "Come on," said Daru.

They walked for an hour and rested beside a sharp peak of limestone. The snow was melting faster and faster and the sun was drinking up the puddles at once, rapidly cleaning the plateau, which gradually dried and vibrated like the air itself. When they resumed walking, the ground rang under their feet. From time to time a bird rent the space in front of them with a joyful cry. Daru breathed in deeply the fresh morning light. He felt a sort of rapture before the vast familiar expanse, now almost entirely yellow under its dome of blue sky. They walked an hour more, descending toward the south. They reached a level height made up of crumbly rocks. From there on, the plateau sloped down, eastward, toward a low plain where there were a few spindly trees and, to the south, toward outcroppings of rock that gave the landscape a chaotic look.

Daru surveyed the two directions. There was nothing but the sky on the horizon. Not a man could be seen. He turned toward the Arab, who was looking at him blankly. Daru held out the package to him. "Take it," he said. "There are dates, bread, and sugar. You can hold out for two days. Here are a thousand francs too." The Arab took the package and the money but kept his full hands at chest level as if he didn't know what to do with what was being given him. "Now look," the school-master said as he pointed in the direction of the east, "there's the way to Tinguit. You have a two-hour walk. At Tinguit you'll find the administration and the police. They are expecting you." The Arab looked toward the east, still holding the pack-age and the money against his chest. Daru took his elbow and turned him rather roughly toward the south. At the foot of the height on which they stood could be seen a faint path. "That's the trail across the plateau. In a day's walk from here you'll find pasturelands and the first nomads. They'll take you in and shelter you accord-ing to their law." The Arab had now turned toward Daru and a sort of panic was vis-ible in his expression. "Listen," he said. Daru shook his head: "No, be quiet. Now I'm leaving you." He turned his back on him, took two long steps in the direction of the school, looked hesitantly at the motionless Arab, and started off again. For a few minutes he heard nothing but his own step resounding on the cold ground and did not turn his head. A moment later, however, he turned around. The Arab was still there on the edge of the hill, his arms hanging now, and he was looking at the schoolmaster. Daru felt something rise in his throat. But he swore with impatience, waved vaguely, and started off again. He had already gone some distance when he again stopped and looked. There was no longer anyone on the hill.

Daru hesitated. The sun was now rather high in the sky and was beginning to beat down on his head. The schoolmaster retraced his steps, at first somewhat uncertainly, then with decision. When he reached the little hill, he was bathed in sweat. He climbed it as fast as he could and stopped, out of breath, at the top. The rock-fields to the south stood out sharply against the blue sky, but on the plain to the east a steamy heat was already rising. And in that slight haze, Daru, with heavy heart, made out the Arab walking slowly on the road to prison.

A little later, standing before the window of the classroom, the schoolmaster was watching the clear light bathing the whole surface of the plateau, but he hardly saw it. Behind him on the blackboard, among the winding French rivers, sprawled the clumsily chalked-up words he had just read: "You handed over our brother. You will pay for this." Daru looked at the sky, the plateau, and, beyond, the invisible lands stretching all the way to the sea. In this vast landscape he had loved so much, he was alone.

[1957]

Journal Entry

Assume the persona of the Arab and record your impressions of Daru.

Textual Considerations

1. The narrator describes this part of Algeria as "cruel to live in." What details reinforce this description? Why doesn't Daru leave? Where in the story does he indicate his attitude toward the land?
2. What does Daru think of humanity? What connection is there between his attitude toward people and his profession?
3. Describe the relationship between Balducci and Daru. To what extent are they foils for each other?
4. Daru, the French Algerian, must play host to an Arab. How does he behave toward his guest? How does the guest respond to his host?
5. To what extent do we see the action through Daru's eyes? Do we enter the mind of any character other than Daru? Could the story have been written in the first person? What different effects would a first-person narration create?

Cultural Contexts

1. "That stupid man's crime revolted him, but to hand him over was contrary to honor." Why does Daru's philosophy make it dishonorable to turn in a murderer? What is your response to such a philosophy?
2. Why does Daru give the Arab a choice, rather than setting him on the path to freedom? Why does Daru observe the Arab's choice with "heavy heart"? What is your group's response? What irony is implicit in the last paragraph?

Chinua Achebe

Dead Men's Path

Michael Obi's hopes were fulfilled much earlier than he had expected. He was appointed headmaster of Ndume Central School in January 1949. It had always been an unprogressive school, so the Mission authorities decided to send a young and energetic man to run it. Obi accepted this responsibility with enthusiasm. He had many wonderful ideas and this was an opportunity to put them into practice. He had had sound secondary school education which designated him a "pivotal teacher" in the official records and set him apart from the other headmasters in the mission field. He was outspoken in his condemnation of the narrow views of these older and often less-educated ones.

"We shall make a good job of it, shan't we?" he asked his young wife when they first heard the joyful news of his promotion.

"We shall do our best," she replied. "We shall have such beautiful gardens and everything will be just *modern* and delightful . . ." In their two years of married life she had become completely infected by his passion for "modern methods" and his denigration of "these old and superannuated people in the teaching field who would be better employed as traders in the Onitsha market." She began to see herself already as the admired wife of the young headmaster, the queen of the school.

The wives of the other teachers would envy her position. She would set the fashion in everything . . . Then, suddenly, it occurred to her that there might not be other wives. Wavering between hope and fear, she asked her husband, looking anxiously at him.

"All our colleagues are young and unmarried," he said with enthusiasm which for once she did not share. "Which is a good thing," he continued.

"Why?"

"Why? They will give all their time and energy to the school."

Nancy was downcast. For a few minutes she became skeptical about the new school; but it was only for a few minutes. Her little personal misfortune could not blind her to her husband's happy prospects. She looked at him as he sat folded up in a chair. He was stoop-shouldered and looked frail. But he sometimes surprised people with sudden bursts of physical energy. In his present posture, however, all his bodily strength seemed to have retired behind his deep-set eyes, giving them an extraordinary power of penetration. He was only twenty-six, but looked thirty or more. On the whole, he was not unhandsome.

"A penny for your thoughts, Mike," said Nancy after a while, imitating the woman's magazine she read.

"I was thinking what a grand opportunity we've got at last to show these people how a school should be run."

Ndume School was backward in every sense of the word. Mr. Obi put his whole life into the work, and his wife hers too. He had two aims. A high standard of teaching was insisted upon, and the school compound was to be turned into a place of beauty. Nancy's dream-gardens came to life with the coming of the rains, and blossomed. Beautiful hibiscus and allamanda hedges in brilliant red and yellow marked out the carefully tended school compound from the rank neighbourhood bushes.

One evening as Obi was admiring his work he was scandalized to see an old woman from the village hobble right across the compound, through a marigold flower-bed and the hedges. On going up there he found faint signs of an almost disused path from the village across the school compound to the bush on the other side.

"It amazes me," said Obi to one of his teachers who had been three years in the school, "that you people allowed the villagers to make use of this footpath. It is simply incredible." He shook his head.

"The path," said the teacher apologetically, "appears to be very important to them. Although it is hardly used, it connects the village shrine with their place of burial."

"And what has that got to do with the school?" asked the headmaster.

"Well, I don't know," replied the other with a shrug of the shoulders. "But I remember there was a big row some time ago when we attempted to close it."

"That was some time ago. But it will not be used now," said Obi as he walked away. "What will the Government Education Officer think of this when he comes to inspect the school next week? The villagers might, for all I know, decide to use the schoolroom for a pagan ritual during the inspection."

Heavy sticks were planted closely across the path at the two places where it entered and left the school premises. These were further strengthened with barbed wire.

Three days later the village priest of *Ani* called on the headmaster. He was an old man and walked with a slight stoop. He carried a stout walking-stick which he usually tapped on the floor, by way of emphasis, each time he made a new point in his argument.

"I have heard," he said after the usual exchange of cordialities, "that our ancestral footpath has recently been closed . . ."

"Yes," replied Mr. Obi. "We cannot allow people to make a highway of our school compound."

"Look here, my son," said the priest bringing down his walking-stick, "this path was here before you were born and before your father was born. The whole life of this village depends on it. Our dead relatives depart by it and our ancestors visit us by it. But most important, it is the path of children coming in to be born . . ."

Mr. Obi listened with a satisfied smile on his face.

"The whole purpose of our school," he said finally, "is to eradicate just such beliefs as that. Dead men do not require footpaths. The whole idea is just fantastic. Our duty is to teach your children to laugh at such ideas."

"What you say may be true," replied the priest, "but we follow the practices of our fathers. If you re-open the path we shall have nothing to quarrel about. What I always say is: let the hawk perch and let the eagle perch." He rose to go.

"I am sorry," said the young headmaster. "But the school compound cannot be a thoroughfare. It is against our regulations. I would suggest your constructing another path, skirting our premises. We can even get our boys to help in building it. I don't suppose the ancestors will find the little detour too burdensome."

"I have no more words to say," said the old priest, already outside.

Two days later a young woman in the village died in childbed. A diviner was immediately consulted and he prescribed heavy sacrifices to propitiate ancestors insulted by the fence.

Obi woke up next morning among the ruins of his work. The beautiful hedges were torn up not just near the path but right round the school, the flowers trampled to death and one of the school buildings pulled down . . . That day, the white Supervisor came to inspect the school and wrote a nasty report on the state of the premises but more seriously about the "tribal-war situation developing between the school and the village, arising in part from the misguided zeal of the new headmaster."

[1972]

Journal Entry

With which characters in Chinua Achebe's story do you identify most? Explain.

Textual Considerations

1. Characterize Obi's attitude toward the teachers and the people in the community.
2. Speculate on the implications of the story's title. To what extent do you agree with Obi's reasons for closing the path?
3. Explain what the supervisor means by "misguided zeal." What is ironic about this statement? Does Obi deserve his censure? Why or why not?
4. Draw a character sketch of Nancy, including an analysis of her personality traits and her attitude toward life.
5. How does the story explore the cultural clash between two different kinds of knowledge, experience, and attitudes toward life? Identify them and explain why they oppose each other.

Cultural Contexts

1. The conflict between individual aspirations and communal rites is central to this story. With whom do you empathize—Obi, who insisted on "civilizing the pagans," or the villagers, who used the path that "connects the village shrine with their place of burial"?
2. Consider with your group why Obi and the village priest are unable to negotiate a compromise. Explain the implications of the priest's plea to "let the hawk perch and let the eagle perch."

ESSAYS

May Sarton

The Rewards of Living a Solitary Life

The other day an acquaintance of mine, a gregarious and charming man, told me he had found himself unexpectedly alone in New York for an hour or two between appointments. He went to the Whitney and spent the "empty" time looking at things in solitary bliss. For him it proved to be a shock nearly as great as falling in love to discover that he could enjoy himself so much alone.

What had he been afraid of, I asked myself? That, suddenly alone, he would discover that he bored himself, or that there was, quite simply, no self there to meet? But having taken the plunge, he is now on the brink of adventure; he is about to be launched into his own inner space, space as immense, unexplored, and sometimes frightening as outer space to the astronaut. His every perception will come to him with a new freshness and, for a time, seem startlingly original. For anyone who can see things for himself with a naked eye becomes, for a moment or two, something of a genius. With another human being present vision becomes double vision, inevitably. We are busy wondering, what does my companion see or think of this, and what do I think of it? The original impact gets lost, or diffused.

"Music I heard with you was more than music."[1] Exactly. And therefore music *itself* can only be heard alone. Solitude is the salt of personhood. It brings out the authentic flavor of every experience.

"Alone one is never lonely: the spirit adventures, walking/In a quiet garden, in a cool house, abiding single there."

Loneliness is most acutely felt with other people, for with others, even with a lover sometimes, we suffer from our differences of taste, temperament, mood. Human intercourse often demands that we soften the edge of perception, or withdraw at the very instant of personal truth for fear of hurting, or of being inappropriately present, which is to say naked, in a social situation. Alone we can afford to be wholly whatever we are, and to feel whatever we feel absolutely. That is a great luxury!

For me the most interesting thing about a solitary life, and mine has been that for the last twenty years, is that it becomes increasingly rewarding. When I can wake up and watch the sun rise over the ocean, as I do most days, and know that I have an entire day ahead, uninterrupted, in which to write a few pages, take a walk with my dog, lie down in the afternoon for a long think (why does one think better in a horizontal position?), read and listen to music, I am flooded with happiness.

I am lonely only when I am overtired, when I have worked too long without a break, when for the time being I feel empty and need filling up. And I am lonely

---

[1] A line from Conrad Aiken's *Bread and Music* (1914).

sometimes when I come back home after a lecture trip, when I have seen a lot of people and talked a lot, and am full to the brim with experience that needs to be sorted out.

Then for a little while the house feels huge and empty, and I wonder where my self is hiding. It has to be recaptured slowly by watering the plants, perhaps, and looking again at each one as though it were a person, by feeding the two cats, by cooking a meal.

It takes a while, as I watch the surf blowing up in fountains at the end of the field, but the moment comes when the world falls away, and the self emerges again from the deep unconscious; bringing back all I have recently experienced to be explored and slowly understood, when I can converse again with my hidden powers, and so grow, and so be renewed, till death do us part.

[1990]

Journal Entry

To what extent do you agree with the author's statement: "Loneliness is most acutely felt with other people"?

Textual Considerations

1. Explain the statement that "anyone who can see things for himself with a naked eye becomes, for a moment or two, something of a genius."
2. What evidence is there to support Sarton's thesis that solitude is rewarding?
3. How does Sarton's conclusion connect with her introduction?
4. Is Sarton seeking to inform or persuade her audience? To what extent does she persuade you?
5. How does Sarton describe loneliness in paragraph seven?

Cultural Contexts

1. Explain the differences between being *alone* and being *lonely*. Is it possible to feel alone in a room full of people? Why or why not?
2. Can your group reach a consensus about what would happen to "relatedness" and community values if everybody established "loneliness" as an ideal?

Thomas Jefferson
The Declaration of Independence

When in the course of human events, it becomes necessary for one people to dissolve the political bands which have connected them with another, and to assume among the Powers of the earth, the separate and equal station to which the Laws of Nature and of Nature's God entitle them, a decent respect to the opinions of mankind requires that they should declare the causes which impel them to the separation.

We hold these truths to be self-evident, that all men are created equal, that they are endowed by their Creator with certain unalienable Rights, that among these are Life, Liberty and the pursuit of Happiness. That to secure these rights, Governments are instituted among Men deriving their just powers from the consent of the governed. That whenever any Form of Government becomes destructive of these ends, it is the Right of the People to alter or to abolish it, and to institute new Government, laying its foundation on such principles and organizing its powers in such form, as to them shall seem most likely to effect their Safety and Happiness. Prudence, indeed, will dictate that Governments long established should not be changed for light and transient causes; and accordingly all experience hath shown, that mankind are more disposed to suffer, while evils are sufferable, than to right themselves by abolishing the forms to which they are accustomed. But when a long train of abuses and usurpations pursuing invariably the same Object evinces a design to reduce them under absolute Despotism, it is their right, it is their duty, to throw off such government, and to provide new Guards for their future security. Such has been the patient sufferance of these Colonies; and such is now the necessity which constrains them to alter their former Systems of Government. The history of the present King of Great Britain is a history of repeated injuries and usurpations, all having in direct object the establishment of an absolute Tyranny over these States. To prove this, let Facts be submitted to a candid world.

He has refused his Assent to laws, the most wholesome and necessary for the public good.

He has forbidden his Governors to pass Laws of immediate and pressing importance, unless suspended in their operation till his Assent should be obtained; and when so suspended, he has utterly neglected to attend to them.

He has refused to pass other Laws for the accommodation of large districts of people, unless those people would relinquish the right of Representation in the Legislature, a right inestimable to them and formidable to tyrants only.

He has called together legislative bodies at places unusual, uncomfortable, and distant from the depository of their Public Records, for the sole purpose of fatiguing them into compliance with his measures.

He has dissolved Representative Houses repeatedly, for opposing with manly firmness his invasions on the rights of the people.

He has refused for a long time, after such dissolutions, to cause others to be elected; whereby the Legislative Powers, incapable of Annihilation, have returned to the People at large for their exercise; the State remaining in the mean time exposed to all the dangers of invasion from without, and convulsions within.

He has endeavoured to prevent the population of these States; for that purpose obstructing the Laws of Naturalization of Foreigners; refusing to pass others to encourage their migration hither, and raising the conditions of new Appropriations of Lands.

He has obstructed the Administration of Justice, by refusing his Assent to Laws for establishing Judiciary Powers.

He has made Judges dependent on his Will alone, for the tenure of their offices, and the amount and payment of their salaries.

He has erected a multitude of New Offices, and sent hither swarms of Officers to harass our People, and eat out their substance.

He has kept among us, in time of peace. Standing Armies without the Consent of our Legislature.

He has affected to render the Military independent of and superior to the Civil Power.

He has combined with others to subject us to jurisdictions foreign to our constitution, and unacknowledged by our laws: giving his Assent to their acts of pretended Legislation:

For quartering large bodies of armed troops among us:

For protecting them, by a mock Trial, from Punishment for any Murders which they should commit on the Inhabitants of these States:

For cutting off our Trade with all parts of the world:

For imposing Taxes on us without our Consent:

For depriving us in many cases, of the benefits of Trial by Jury:

For transporting us beyond Seas to be tried for pretended offenses:

For abolishing the free System of English Laws in a Neighbouring Province, establishing therein an Arbitrary government, and enlarging its boundaries so as to render it at once an example and fit instrument for introducing the same absolute rule into these Colonies:

For taking away our Charters, abolishing our most valuable Laws, and altering fundamentally the Forms of our Governments:

For suspending our own Legislatures, and declaring themselves invested with Power to legislate for us in all cases whatsoever.

He has abdicated Government here, by declaring us out of his Protection and waging War against us.

He has plundered our seas, ravaged our Coasts, burnt our towns and destroyed the Lives of our people.

He is at this time transporting large Armies of foreign Mercenaries to compleat works of death, desolation and tyranny, already begun with circumstances of Cruelty & perfidy scarcely paralleled in the most barbarous ages, and totally unworthy the Head of a civilized nation.

He has constrained our fellow Citizens taken Captive on the high Seas to bear Arms against their Country, to become the executioners of their friends and Brethren, or to fall themselves by their Hands.

He has excited domestic insurrections amongst us, and has endeavoured to bring on the inhabitants of our frontiers, the merciless Indian Savages, whose known rule of warfare, is an undistinguished destruction of all ages, sexes and conditions.

In every stage of these Oppressions We have Petitioned for Redress in the most humble terms: Our repeated Petitions have been answered only by repeated injury. A Prince, whose character is thus marked by every act which may define a Tyrant, is unfit to be the ruler of a free People.

Nor have We been wanting in attention to our British brethren. We have warned them from time to time of attempts by their legislature to extend an unwarrantable jurisdiction over us. We have reminded them of the circumstances of our emigration and settlement here. We have appealed to their native justice and magnanimity, and we have conjured them by the ties of our common kindred to disavow these usurpations, which would inevitably interrupt our connections and correspondence. They too have been deaf to the voice of justice and of consanguinity. We must, therefore, acquiesce in the necessity, which denounces our Separation, and hold them, as we hold the rest of mankind, Enemies in War, in Peace Friends.

We, therefore, the Representatives of the united States of America, in General Congress, Assembled, appealing to the Supreme Judge of the world for the rectitude of our intentions, do, in the Name, and by Authority of the good People of these Colonies, solemnly publish and declare, That these United Colonies are, and of Right ought to be Free and Independent States; that they are Absolved from all Allegiance to the British Crown, and that all political connection between them and the State of Great Britain, is and ought to be totally dissolved; and that as Free and Independent States, they have full Power to levy War, conclude Peace, contract Alliances, establish Commerce, and to do all other Acts and Things which Independent States may of right do. And for the support of this Declaration, with a firm reliance on the Protection of Divine Providence, we mutually pledge to each other our Lives, our Fortunes and our sacred Honor.

[1776]

Journal Entry

Freewrite on your associations with democracy. What images, emotions, and ideas does the word evoke?

Textual Considerations

1. According to the Declaration, what is the purpose of government? How is this point important in the Declaration?
2. What is Jefferson's purpose in drafting the Declaration of Independence?
3. Does the Declaration of Independence appeal primarily to the reader's intellect, emotions, or both? Explain.
4. According to the Declaration, what are people more likely to do—rebel or put up with injustice?
5. What does the last paragraph of the Declaration proclaim? How is it related to the rest of the document?

Cultural Contexts

1. We have all heard the phrase "all men are created equal" so often that we don't really hear it anymore. What does it mean in this context? Is it true outside this context? In what sense is it true or not true?
2. Collaborate with your group in writing your own Declaration of Independence for the twenty-first century. What focus would you include that is not present in the original document?

Martin Luther King Jr.

I Have a Dream

I am happy to join with you today in what will go down in history as the greatest demonstration for freedom in the history of our nation.

Five score years ago, a great American in whose symbolic shadow we stand today, signed the Emancipation Proclamation. This momentous decree came as a great beacon light of hope to millions of Negro slaves who had been seared in the flames of withering injustice. It came as a joyous daybreak to end the long night of their captivity. But one hundred years later, the Negro still is not free. One hundred years later, the life of the Negro is still sadly crippled by the manacles of segregation and the chains of discrimination. One hundred years later, the Negro lives on a lonely island of poverty in the midst of a vast ocean of material prosperity. One hundred years later, the Negro is still anguished in the corners of American society and finds himself in exile in his own land. And so we have come here today to dramatize a shameful condition.

In a sense we have come to our nation's capital to cash a check. When the architects of our republic wrote the magnificent words of the Constitution and the Declaration of Independence, they were signing a promissory note to which every American was to fall heir. This note was the promise that all men—yes, Black men as well as white men—would be guaranteed the inalienable rights of life, liberty, and the pursuit of happiness.

It is obvious today that America has defaulted on this promissory note insofar as her citizens of color are concerned. Instead of honoring this sacred obligation, America has given the Negro people a bad check, a check which has come back marked "insufficient funds." But we refuse to believe that the bank of justice is bankrupt. We refuse to believe that there are insufficient funds in the great vaults of opportunity of this nation; and so we have come to cash this check, a check that will give us upon demand the riches of freedom and the security of justice.

We have also come to this hallowed spot to remind America of the fierce urgency of *now*. This is no time to engage in the luxury of cooling off or to take the tranquilizing drug of gradualism. *Now* is the time to make real the promises of democracy. *Now* is the time to rise from the dark and desolate valley of segregation to the sunlit path of racial justice. *Now* is the time to lift our nation from the quicksands of racial injustice to the solid rock of brotherhood. Now is the time to make justice a reality for all of God's children.

It would be fatal for the nation to overlook the urgency of the moment. This sweltering summer of the Negro's legitimate discontent will not pass until there is an invigorating autumn of freedom and equality. Nineteen Sixty-three is not an end, but a beginning. And those who hope that the Negro needed to blow off steam and will now be content will have a rude awakening if the nation returns to business as usual. There will be neither rest nor tranquility in America until the Negro is granted his citizenship rights. The whirlwinds of revolt will continue to shake the foundations of our nation until the bright day of justice emerges.

But there is something that I must say to my people who stand on the warm threshold which leads into the palace of justice. In the process of gaining our rightful place, we must not be guilty of wrongful deeds. Let us not seek to satisfy our thirst for freedom by drinking from the cup of bitterness and hatred. We must forever conduct our struggle on the high plane of dignity and discipline. We must not allow our creative protest to degenerate into physical violence. Again and again we must rise to the majestic heights of meeting physical force with soul force. And the marvelous new militancy which has engulfed the Negro community must not lead us to a distrust of all white people; for many of our white brothers, as evidenced by their presence here today, have come to realize that their destiny is tied up with our destiny, and they have come to realize that their freedom is inextricably bound to our freedom.

We cannot walk alone. And as we walk we must make the pledge that we shall always march ahead. We cannot turn back. There are those who are asking the devotees of civil rights, "When will you be satisfied?" We can never be satisfied as long as the Negro is the victim of the unspeakable horrors of police brutality. We can never be satisfied as long as our bodies, heavy with the fatigue of travel, cannot gain lodging in the motels of the highways and the hotels of the cities. We cannot be satisfied as long as the Negro's basic mobility is from a smaller ghetto to a larger one. We can never be satisfied as long as our children are stripped of their selfhood and robbed of their dignity by signs stating "For Whites Only." We cannot be satisfied as long as the Negro in Mississippi cannot vote and a Negro in New York believes he has nothing for which to vote. No, no, we are not satisfied, and we will not be satisfied until justice rolls down like waters and righteousness like a mighty stream.

I am not unmindful that some of you have come here out of great trials and tribulations. Some of you have come fresh from narrow jail cells. Some of you have come from areas where your quest for freedom left you battered by the storms of persecution and staggered by the winds of police brutality. You have been the veterans of creative suffering. Continue to work with the faith that unearned suffering is redemptive.

Go back to Mississippi, and go back to Alabama. Go back to South Carolina. Go back to Georgia. Go back to Louisiana. Go back to the slums and ghettos of our Northern cities, knowing that somehow this situation can and will be changed. Let us not wallow in the valley of despair.

I say to you today, my friends, even though we face the difficulties of today and tomorrow, I still have a dream. It is a dream deeply rooted in the American dream. I have a dream that one day this nation will rise up and live out the true meaning of its creed: "We hold these truths to be self-evident, that all men are created equal." I have a dream that one day, on the red hills of Georgia, sons of former slaves and the sons of former slave owners will be able to sit down together at the table of brotherhood. I have a dream that one day even the state of Mississippi, a state sweltering with the heat of injustice, sweltering with the heat of oppression, will be transformed into an oasis of freedom and justice. I have a dream that my four children will one day live in a nation where they will not be judged by the color of their skin, but by the content of their character.

I have a dream today. I have a dream that one day down in Alabama—with its vicious racists, with its governor's lips dripping with the words of interposition and nullification—one day right there in Alabama, little Black boys and Black girls will be able to join hands with little white boys and white girls as sisters and brothers.

I have a dream today. I have a dream that one day every valley shall be exalted and every hill and mountain shall be made low, the rough places will be made plain and the crooked places will be made straight, and the glory of the Lord shall be revealed, and all flesh shall see it together.

This is our hope. This is the faith that I go back to the South with. And with this faith we will be able to hew out of the mountain of despair a stone of hope. With this faith we will be able to transform the jangling discords of our nation into a beautiful symphony of brotherhood. With this faith we will be able to work together, to play together, to struggle together, to go to jail together, to stand up for freedom together, knowing that we will be free one day.

And this will be the day—this will be the day when all God's children will be able to sing with new meaning:

> My country, 'tis of thee,
>> Sweet land of liberty;
>>> Of thee I sing;
>> Land where my fathers died,
>> Land of the Pilgrims' pride,
>> From every Mountainside
>>> Let freedom ring.

And if America is to be a great nation, this must become true.

And so let freedom ring from the prodigious hilltops of New Hampshire. Let freedom ring from the mighty mountains of New York. Let freedom ring from the heightening Alleghenies of Pennsylvania. Let freedom ring from the snowcapped Rockies of Colorado. Let freedom ring from the curvaceous slopes of California.

But not only that. Let freedom ring from Stone Mountain of Georgia. Let freedom ring from Lookout Mountain of Tennessee. Let freedom ring from every hill and molehill of Mississippi. "From every Mountainside let freedom ring."

And when this happens—when we allow freedom to ring, when we let it ring from every village and every hamlet, from every state and every city—we will be able to speed up that day when all of God's children, Black men and white men, Jews and Gentiles, Protestants and Catholics, will be able to join hands and sing in the words of the old Negro spiritual: "Free at last! Free at last! Thank God Almighty. We are free at last!"

[1963]

Journal Entry

King uses the word *freedom* several times in his speech. What do you think he means by it? Consider the different possible meanings of freedom to the various members of his audience. What does it mean to you?

Textual Considerations

1. Why is the phrase "Five score years ago" more appropriate than "a hundred years ago" or "in 1863"? Why does King later repeat the phrase "one hundred years later" so often?
2. When King speaks of "cash [ing] a check" or "insufficient funds," is he talking about money? Explain.
3. What evidence is there that King is writing for an audience that includes whites?
4. King states: "You have been the veterans of creative suffering." Can suffering be creative? How?
5. One characteristic of persuasion is that it uses connotative diction and figurative language to appeal to the reader's emotions. What words or expressions do you find in this speech that make you react emotionally?
6. Characterize the tone of the speech. Is it objective, angry, neutral? Explain your answer.

Cultural Contexts

1. King says his dream is "rooted in the American dream." What is that? Explain King's quotation, and connect it with the Declaration of Independence. Is the American dream more than the hopes and rights expressed in that document? If so, in what way?
2. Working with your group, discuss what events in Mississippi in the early 1960s might have caused King to single out that state? Why would he specifically mention Georgia? Why Alabama?

Toni Morrison

The Nobel Lecture in Literature

Your Majesties, Your Highnesses, Ladies and Gentlemen:

Narrative has never been merely entertainment for me. It is, I believe, one of the principal ways in which we absorb knowledge. I hope you will understand, then, why I begin these remarks with the opening phrase of what must be the oldest sentence in the world, and the earliest one we remember from childhood: "Once upon a time . . ."

"Once upon a time there was an old woman. Blind but wise." Or was it an old man? A guru, perhaps. Or a *griot* soothing restless children. I have heard this story, or one exactly like it in the lore of several cultures.

"Once upon a time there was an old woman. Blind. Wise."

In the version I know the woman is the daughter of slaves, black, American, and lives alone in a small house outside of town. Her reputation for wisdom is without peer and without question.

Among her people she is both the law and its transgression. The honor she is paid and the awe in which she is held reach beyond her neighborhood to places far away, to the city where the intelligence of rural prophets is the source of much amusement.

One day the woman is visited by some young people who seem to be bent on disproving her clairvoyance and showing her up for the fraud they believe she is. Their plan is simple: they enter her house and ask the one question the answer to which rides solely on her difference from them, a difference they regard as a profound disability: her blindness. They stand before her, and one of them says,

"Old woman, I hold in my hand a bird. Tell me whether it is living or dead." She does not answer, and the question is repeated. "Is the bird I am holding living or dead?" Still she does not answer. She is blind and cannot see her visitors, let alone what is in their hands. She does not know their color, gender or homeland. She only knows their motive. The old woman's silence is so long; the young people have trouble holding their laughter.

Finally she speaks and her voice is soft but stern. "I don't know," she says. "I don't know whether the bird you are holding is dead or alive, but what I do know is that it is in your hands. It is in your hands."

Her answer can be taken to mean: if it is dead, you have either found it that way or you have killed it. If it is alive, you can still kill it. Whether it is to stay alive is your decision. Whatever the case it is your responsibility.

For parading their power and her helplessness, the young visitors are reprimanded, told they are responsible not only for the act of mockery but also for the small bundle of life sacrificed to achieve its aims. The blind woman shifts attention away from the assertions of power to the instrument through which that power is exercised.

Speculation on what (other than its own frail body) that bird in the hand might signify has always been attractive to me, but especially so now, thinking as I have been about the work I do that has brought me to this company. So I choose to read the bird as language and the woman as a practiced writer.

She is worried about how the language she dreams in, given to her at birth, is handled, put into service, even withheld from her for certain nefarious purposes. Being a writer, she thinks of language partly as a system, partly as a living thing over which one has control, but mostly as agency—as an act with consequences. So the question the children put to her, "Is it living or dead?" is not unreal, because she thinks of language as susceptible to death, erasure; certainly imperiled and salvageable only by an effort of the will. She believes that if the bird in the hands of her visitors is dead, the custodians are responsible for the corpse. For her a dead language is not only one no longer spoken or written, it is unyielding language content to admire its own paralysis. Like statist language, censored and censoring, ruthless in its policing duties, it has no desire or purpose other than to maintain the free range of its own narcotic narcissism, its own exclusivity and dominance. However moribund, it is not without effect, for it actively thwarts the intellect, stalls conscience, suppresses human potential. Unreceptive to interrogation, it cannot form or tolerate new ideas, shape other thoughts, tell another story, fill baffling silences. Official language smitheried to sanction ignorance and preserve privilege is a suit of armor, polished to shocking glitter, a husk from which the knight departed long ago. Yet there it is, dumb, predatory, sentimental: exciting reverence in schoolchildren, providing shelter for despots, summoning false memories of stability, harmony among the public.

She is convinced that when language dies, out of carelessness, disuse, indifference, and absence of esteem, or killed by fiat, not only she herself but all users and makers are accountable for its demise. In her country children have bitten their tongues off and use bullets instead to iterate the void of speechlessness, of disabled and disabling language, of language adults have abandoned altogether as a device for grappling with meaning, providing guidance, or expressing love. But she knows tongue-suicide is not only the choice of children. It is common among the infantile heads of state and power merchants whose evacuated language leaves them with no access to what is left of their human instincts, for they speak only to those who obey, or in order to force obedience.

The systematic looting of language can be recognized by the tendency of its users to forgo its nuanced, complex, mid-wifery properties, replacing them with menace and subjugation. Oppressive language does more than represent violence; it is violence; does more than represent the limits of knowledge; it limits knowledge. Whether it is obscuring state language or the faux language of mindless media; whether it is the round but calcified language of the academy or the commodity-driven language of science; whether it is the malign language of law-without-ethics, or language designed for the estrangement of minorities, hiding its racist plunder in its literary cheek—it must be rejected, altered, and exposed. It is the language that drinks blood, laps vulnerabilities, tucks its fascist boots under crinolines of respectability and patriotism as it moves relentlessly toward the bottom line and the bottomed-out mind. Sexist language, racist language, theistic language—all are typical of the policing languages of mastery, and cannot, do not, permit new knowledge or encourage the mutual exchange of ideas.

The old woman is keenly aware that no intellectual mercenary or insatiable dictator, no paid-for politician or demagogue, no counterfeit journalist would be persuaded by her thoughts. There is and will be rousing language to keep citizens armed and arming; slaughtered and slaughtering in the malls, courthouses, post offices, playgrounds, bedrooms and boulevards; stirring, memorializing language to mask the pity and waste of needless death. There will be more diplomatic language to countenance rape, torture, assassination. There is and will be more seductive, mutant language designed to throttle women, to pack their throats like pate-producing geese with their own unsayable, transgressive words; there will be more of the language of surveillance disguised as research; of politics and history calculated to render the suffering of millions mute; language glamorized to thrill the dissatisfied and bereft into assaulting their neighbors; arrogant pseudo-empirical language crafted to lock creative people into cages of inferiority and hopelessness.

Underneath the eloquence, the glamour, the scholarly associations, however stirring or seductive, the heart of such language is languishing, or perhaps not beating at all—if the bird is already dead.

She has thought about what could have been the intellectual history of any discipline if it had not insisted upon, or been forced into, the waste of time and life that rationalizations for and representation of dominance required—lethal discourses of exclusion blocking access to cognition for both the excluder and the excluded.

The conventional wisdom of the Tower of Babel story is that the collapse was a misfortune. That it was the distraction or the weight of many languages that precipitated the tower's failed architecture. That one monolithic language would have expedited the building and heaven would have been reached. Whose heaven, she wonders? And what kind? Perhaps the achievement of Paradise was premature, a little hasty if no one could take the time to understand other languages, other views, other narratives. Had they, the heaven they imagined might have been found at their feet. Complicated, demanding, yes, but a view of heaven as life; not heaven as post-life.

She would not want to leave her young visitors with the impression that language should be forced to stay alive merely to be. The vitality of language lies in its ability to limn the actual, imagined, and possible lives of its speakers, readers, writers. Although its poise is sometimes in displacing experience, it is not a substitute for it. It arcs toward the place where meaning may lie. When a President of the United States thought about the graveyard his country had become, and said, "The world will little note nor long remember what we say here. But it will never forget what they did here." His simple words were exhilarating in their life-sustaining properties because they refused to encapsulate the reality of 600,000 dead men in a cataclysmic race war. Refusing to monumentalize, disdaining the "final word," the precise "summing up," acknowledging their words signal deference to the uncapturability of the life it mourns. It is the deference that moves her, that recognition that language can never live up to life once and for all. Nor should it. Language can never "pin down" slavery, genocide, war. Nor should it yearn for the arrogance to be able to do so. Its force, its felicity, is in its reach toward the ineffable.

Be it broad or slender, burrowing, blasting, or refusing to sanctify; whether it laughs out loud or is a cry without an alphabet, the choice word or the chosen silence, unmolested language surges toward knowledge, not its destruction. But who does not know of literature banned because it is interrogative; discredited because it is critical; erased because alternate? And how many are outraged by the thought of a self-ravaged tongue?

Word-work is sublime, she thinks, because it is generative; it makes meaning that secures our difference, our human difference—the way in which we are like no other life.

We die. That may be the meaning of life. But we do language. That may be the measure of our lives.

"Once upon time . . ." Visitors ask an old woman a question. Who are they, these children? What did they make of that encounter? What did they hear in those final words: "the bird is in your hands"? A sentence that gestures toward possibility, or one that drops a latch? Perhaps what the children heard was, "It is not my problem. I am old, female, black, blind. What wisdom I have now is in knowing I cannot help you. The future of language is yours."

They stand there. Suppose nothing was in their hands. Suppose the visit was only a ruse, a trick to get to be spoken to, taken seriously, as they have not been before. A chance to interrupt, to violate the adult world, its miasma of discourse about them. Urgent questions are at stake, including the one they have asked: "Is the bird we hold living or dead?" Perhaps the question meant: "Could someone tell us what is life? What is death?" No trick at all, no silliness. A straightforward question worthy of the attention of a wise one. An old one. And if the old and wise who have lived life and faced death cannot describe either, who can?

But she does not; she keeps her secret, her good opinion of herself, gnomic pronouncements, her art without commitment. She keeps her distance, enforces it and retreats into the singularity of isolation, in sophisticate privileged space.

Nothing, no word follows her declaration of transfer. That silence is deep, deeper than the meaning available in the words she has spoken. It shivers this silence, and the children, annoyed, fill it with language invented on the spot.

"Is there no speech," they ask her, "no words you can give us that help us break through your dossier of failures?" through the education you have just given us that is no education at all because we are paying close attention to what you have done as well as to what you have said? to the barrier you have erected between generosity and wisdom?

"We have no bird in our hands, living or dead. We have only you and our important question. Is the nothing in our hands something you could not bear to contemplate, to even guess? Don't you remember being young, when language was magic without meaning? When what you could say, could not mean? When the invisible was what imagination strove to see? When questions and demands for answers burned so brightly you trembled with fury at not knowing?

"Do we have to begin consciousness with a battle heroes and heroines like you have already fought and lost, leaving us with nothing in our hands except what you have imagined is there? Your answer is artful, but its artfulness embarrasses us and ought to embarrass you. Your answer is indecent in its self-congratulation. A made-for-television script that makes no sense if there is nothing in our hands.

"Why didn't you reach out, touch us with your soft fingers, delay the sound bite, the lesson, until you knew who we were? Did you so despise our trick, our *modus operandi*, that you could not see that we were baffled about how to get your attention? We are young. Unripe. We have heard all our short lives that we have to be responsible. What could that possibly mean in the catastrophe this world has become; where, as a poet said, 'nothing needs to be exposed since it is already barefaced'? Our inheritance is an affront. You want us to have your old blank eyes and see only cruelty and mediocrity. Do you think we are stupid enough to perjure ourselves again and again with the fiction of nationhood? How dare you talk to us of duty when we stand waist deep in the toxins of your past?

"You trivialize us and trivialize the bird that is not in our hands. Is there no context for our lives? No song, no literature, no poem full of vitamins, no history connected to experience that you can pass along to help us start strong? You are an adult. The old one, the wise one. Stop thinking about saving your face. Think of our lives and tell us your particularized world. Make up a story. Narrative is radical, creating us at the very moment it is being created. We will not blame you if your reach exceeds your grasp; if love so ignites your words that they go down in flames and nothing is left but their scald. Or if, with the reticence of a surgeon's hands, your words suture only the places where blood might flow. We know you can never do it properly—once and for all. Passion is never enough; neither is skill. But try. For our sake and yours forget your name in the street; tell us what the world has been to you in the dark places and in the light. Don't tell us what to believe, what to fear. Show us belief's wide skirt and the stitch that unravels fear's caul. You, old woman, blessed with blindness, can speak the language that tells us what only language can: how to see without pictures. Language alone protects us from the scariness of things with no names. Language alone is meditation.

"Tell us what it is to be a woman so that we may know what it is to be a man. What moves at the margin. What it is to have no home in this place. To be set adrift from the one you knew. What it is to live at the edge of towns that cannot bear your company.

"Tell us about ships turned away from shorelines at Easter, placental in a field. Tell us about a wagonload of slaves, how they sang so softly their breath was indistinguishable from the falling snow. How they knew from the hunch of the nearest shoulder that the next stop would be their last. How, with hands prayered in their sex, they thought of heat, then sun. Lifting their faces as though it was there for the taking. Turning as though there for the taking. They stop at an inn. The driver and his mate go in with the lamp, leaving them humming in the dark. The horses void steams into the snow beneath its hooves and the hiss and melt are the envy of the freezing slaves.

"The inn door opens: a girl and a boy step away from its light. They club into the wagon bed. The boy will have a gun in three years, but now he carries a lamp and a jug of warm cider. They pass it from mouth to mouth. The girl offers bread, pieces of meat and something more, a glance into the eyes of the one she serves. One helping for each man, two for each woman. And a look. They look back. The next stop will be their last. But not this one. This one is warmed."

It's quiet again when the children finish speaking, until the woman breaks into the silence.

"Finally," she says. "I trust you now. I trust you with the bird that is not in your hands because you have truly caught it. Look. How lovely it is, this thing we have done—together."

I entered this hall pleasantly haunted by those who have entered it before me. That company of laureates is both daunting and welcoming, for among its lists are names of persons whose work has made whole worlds available to me. The sweep and specificity of their art have sometimes broken my heart with the courage and clarity of its vision. The astonishing brilliance with which they practiced their craft has challenged and nurtured my own. My debt to them rivals the profound one I owe to the Swedish Academy for having selected me to join that distinguished alumni.

Early in October an artist friend left a message which I kept on the answering service for weeks and played back every once in a while just to hear the trembling pleasure in her voice and the faith in her words. "My dear sister," she said, "the prize that is yours is also ours and could not have been placed in better hands." The spirit of her message with its earned optimism and sublime trust marks this day for me.

I will leave this hall, however, with a new and much more delightful haunting than the one I felt upon entering: this is the company of the laureates yet to come. Those who, even as I speak, are mining, sifting and polishing languages for illuminations none of us has dreamed of. But whether or not anyone of them secures a place in this pantheon, the gathering of these writers is unmistakable and mounting. Their voices bespeak civilizations gone and yet to be; the precipice from which their imagination's gaze will rivet us; they do not blink or turn away. It is therefore mindful to the gifts of my predecessors, the blessing of my sisters, in joyful anticipation of writers to come that I accept the honor the Swedish Academy has done me, and ask you to share what is for me a moment of grace.

[1993]

Journal Entry

What memories, images, and emotions does the phrase "Once upon a time" evoke for you?

Textual Considerations

1. What is a guru or a griot? Is it significant that the old woman is blind? Explain.
2. Why does she reprimand the young people?
3. Review paragraph 11 and identify the deadening characteristics of the statist language to which Morrison refers.
4. Who does she blame for the looting of language in paragraph 13?
5. In paragraph 18 Morrison states that language can never be a substitute for life itself. What does she mean by her statement, "Its force, its felicity, is in its reach toward the ineffable"?
6. What is the significance of the questions the young people ask?
7. What does their story about slaves in a wagon mean to the old woman?
8. What is it that they have "done together"?

Cultural Contexts

1. Explain the significance of Morrison's allusion to the Tower of Babel. What is your response to monolingualism as opposed to multilingualism?
2. In another context, Morrison has posed this challenge to your generation: "Although you don't have complete control of the narrative—no author does—you can nevertheless, create it. . . . The theme you choose may change or elude you, but being your story means you can always choose the tone, the style. It also means you can invent the language to say who you are and what you mean." Discuss this proposition with your group. What elements would you include in your narrative thus far?

POETRY

James Wright

A Blessing

Just off the highway to Rochester, Minnesota,
Twilight bounds softly forth on the grass.
And the eyes of those two Indian ponies
Darken with kindness.
They have come gladly out of the willows   5
To welcome my friend and me.
We step over the barbed wire into the pasture
Where they have been grazing all day, alone.
They ripple tensely, they can hardly contain their happiness
That we have come.   10
They bow shyly as wet swans. They love each other.
There is no loneliness like theirs.
At home once more,
They begin munching the young tufts of spring in the darkness.
I would like to hold the slenderer one in my arms,   15
For she has walked over to me
And nuzzled my left hand.
She is black and white,
Her mane falls wild on her forehead,
And the light breeze moves me to caress her long ear   20
That is delicate as the skin over a girl's wrist.
Suddenly I realize
That if I stepped out of my body I would break
Into blossom.

[1961]

William Carlos Williams

Danse Russe

If when my wife is sleeping
and the baby and Kathleen
are sleeping
and the sun is a flame-white disc
in silken mists   5
above shining trees,—
if I in my north room
dance naked, grotesquely
before my mirror
waving my shirt round my head   10
and singing softly to myself:

"I am lonely, lonely.
I was born to be lonely,
I am best so!"
If I admire my arms, my face,   15
my shoulders, flanks, buttocks
against the yellow drawn shades,—
Who shall say I am not
the happy genius of my household?

[1938]

Journal Entry

Freewrite on your associations, experiences, memories, or images of loneliness. Is it possible to be alone and not be lonely? Explain.

Textual Considerations

1. What figures of speech enhance the poet's descriptions of the ponies and the setting in Wright's text?
2. How do you interpret the juxtaposition of lines 11 and 12 in "A Blessing"?
3. What blessing is referred to in the title of Wright's poem?
4. What several connotations do the speakers in "A Blessing" and "Danse Russe" give to the words *blessing* and *lonely*, respectively?
5. What effect does the place of the sun as well as its description have on the speaker's Russian dance? What are his motivations for dancing?
6. Why does the speaker dance in front of the mirror? Is he narcissistic? Explain.

Cultural Contexts

1. Explain the connotations of the word *epiphany* in the contexts "A Blessing" and "Danse Russe." What kinds of experiences are both poets celebrating? How do you respond to the concluding lines of both texts?
2. Discuss with your group the metaphor "solitude is the salt of personhood." Did you reach a consensus?

E. E. Cummings

the Cambridge ladies
who live in furnished souls

the Cambridge ladies who live in furnished souls
are unbeautiful and have comfortable minds
(also, with the church's protestant blessings
daughters, unscented shapeless spirited)
they believe in Christ and Longfellow, both dead,   5
are invariably interested in so many things—
at the present writing one still finds
delighted fingers knitting for the is it Poles?
perhaps. While permanent faces coyly bandy
scandal of Mrs. N. and Professor D   10
. . . . the Cambridge ladies do not care, above
Cambridge if sometimes in its box of
sky lavender and cornerless, the
moon rattles like a fragment of angry candy

[1923]

Wallace Stevens

Disillusionment of Ten O'Clock

The houses are haunted
By white night-gowns.
None are green,
Or purple with green rings,
Or green with yellow rings,   5
Or yellow with blue rings.
None of them are strange,
With socks of lace
And beaded ceintures.
People are not going   10
To dream of baboons and periwinkles.

> Only, here and there, an old sailor,
> Drunk and asleep in his boots,
> Catches tigers
> In red weather.   15
>
>   [1951]

Journal Entry

How would you define yourself? Are you a curious person? Can curiosity be dangerous? Explain.

Textual Considerations

1. What does the speaker in "The Cambridge Ladies" mean by "live in furnished souls"?
2. What effect has the church had on these women in E. E. Cummings's poem?
3. Does the speaker in the Cummings poem reverse his attitude toward the women in the line "[they] are invariably interested in so many things"? Explain.
4. Explain lines 7–10 in the Cummings poem. What is their motivation for what they do and say?
5. Analyze the double meanings of the image in the first two lines of Stevens's text.
6. What attitude does the speaker convey toward dreaming of "baboons and periwinkles" in "Disillusionment of Ten O'Clock"?
7. Compare the functions that the Cambridge ladies and the old sailor have in the Cummings and Stevens poems.
8. What is the effect of listing the colored nightgowns in the Stevens poem?

Cultural Contexts

1. What kind of people wear white nightgowns and have "furnished souls"? Would you enjoy a conversation with them? Why or why not?
2. Do you consider yourself a dreamer? Do you have a "dream"? How do you and your group interpret the last four lines of the Cummings text? What connection do they have to dreaming?

WHITMAN AND SHELLEY

Walt Whitman

What Is the Grass?

A child said *What is the grass?* fetching it to me with full hands,
How could I answer the child? I do not know what it is any more
    than he.

I guess it must be the flag of my disposition, out of hopeful green stuff
    woven.

Or I guess it is the handkerchief of the Lord,
A scented gift and remembrancer designedly dropt,   5
Bearing the owner's name someway in the corners, that we may see and
    remark, and say *Whose?*

Or I guess the grass is itself a child, the produced babe of the
    vegetation.

Or I guess it is a uniform hieroglyphic,
And it means, Sprouting alike in broad zones and narrow zones,
Growing among black folks as among white,   10
Kanuck, Tuckahoe, Congressman, Cuff, I give them the same, I receive
    them the same.

And now it seems to me the beautiful uncut hair of graves.

Tenderly will I use you curling grass,
It may be you transpire from the breasts of young men,
It may be if I had known them I would have loved them,   15
It may be you are from old people, or from offspring taken soon out of
    their mothers' laps,
And here you are the mothers' laps.
This grass is very dark to be from the white heads of old mothers,
Darker than the colorless beards of old men,
Dark to come from under the faint red roofs of mouths.   20
O I perceive after all so many uttering tongues,
And I perceive they do not come from the roofs of mouths for nothing.

I wish I could translate the hints about the dead young men and
    women,
And the hints about old men and mothers, and the offspring taken soon
    out of their laps.

What do you think has become of the young and old men?   25
And what do you think has become of the women and children?

They are alive and well somewhere,
The smallest sprout shows there is really no death,
And if ever there was it led forward life, and does not wait at the end to
    arrest it,
And ceas'd the moment life appear'd.   30
All goes onward and outward, nothing collapses,
And to die is different from what any one supposed, and luckier.

[1886]

Percy Bysshe Shelley

Ozymandias°

I met a traveller from an antique land
Who said: Two vast and trunkless legs of stone
Stand in the desert . . . Near them, on the sand,
Half sunk, a shattered visage lies, whose frown,
And wrinkled lip, and sneer of cold command,   5
Tell that its sculptor well those passions read
Which yet survive, stamped on these lifeless things,
The hand that mocked them, and the heart that fed:
And on the pedestal these words appear:
"My name is Ozymandias, king of kings: 10
Look on my works, ye Mighty, and despair!"
Nothing beside remains. Round the decay
Of that colossal wreck, boundless and bare
The lone and level sands stretch far away.

[1818]

Ozymandias: Egyptian monarch of the thirteenth century B.C., said to have erected a huge statue of himself.

Journal Entry

How would you answer the question in Whitman's title?

Textual Considerations

1. The speaker in "What Is the Grass?" strikes the pose of an old man pondering the questions of youth. What evidence in the poem indicates that he is probing for answers?

2. In responding to the child's question, the speaker in Whitman's poem postulates several answers. What are they?
3. One answer seems more satisfactory to the speaker in "What Is the Grass?" than the others, because he emphasizes it in an obvious way. Which answer is it, and how does the speaker emphasize it?
4. How do the structures of "What Is the Grass" and "Ozymandias" emphasize meaning? What is the significance of the lines printed completely separate from the others in "What Is the Grass?"? What is the significance of the compact stanza of Shelley's poem?
5. How is the sculptor depicted in "Ozymandias"?
6. In what condition is this ancient statue? Why is it located alone in an empty desert?
7. What irony is implied in the inscription on the pedestal of Ozymandias?

Cultural Contexts

1. Discuss with your group Whitman's philosophy of death as he presents it in the poem. How does his point of view compare to yours? Explain.
2. Shelley was an English Romantic poet who rebelled against authority. What evidence of this do you find in the poem? To what extent does your group agree or disagree with his point of view?

BLAKE AND WORDSWORTH

William Blake

London

I wander through each chartered° street,
Near where the chartered Thames does flow
And mark in every face I meet
Marks of weakness, marks of woe.

In every cry of every man,   5
In every infant's cry of fear,
In every voice; in every ban,
The mind-forged manacles I hear:

How the chimney-sweeper's cry
Every blackening church appalls,   10
And the hapless soldier's sigh
Runs in blood down palace-walls.

But most, through midnight streets I hear
How the youthful harlot's curse
Blasts the new-born infant's tear,   15
And blights with plagues the marriage-hearse.

[1794]

1 **chartered:** Preempted by the state and leased out under royal patent.

William Wordsworth

London, 1802

Milton! thou should'st be living at this hour:
England hath need of thee: she is a fen
Of stagnant waters: altar, sword, and pen,
Fireside, the heroic wealth of hall and bower,
Have forfeited their ancient English dower   5
Of inward happiness. We are selfish men;
Oh! raise us up, return to us again;
And give us manners, virtue, freedom, power.

Thy soul was like a Star, and dwelt apart:
Thou hadst a voice whose sound was like the sea: 10
Pure as the naked heavens, majestic, free,
So didst thou travel on life's common way,
In cheerful godliness; and yet thy heart
The lowliest duties on herself did lay.

[1802]

William Wordsworth
The World Is Too Much with Us

The world is too much with us; late and soon,
Getting and spending, we lay waste our powers:
Little we see in Nature that is ours;
We have given our hearts away, a sordid boon!
This Sea that bares her bosom to the moon;   5
The winds that will be howling at all hours,
And are up-gathered now like sleeping flowers;
For this, for every thing, we are out of tune;
It moves us not.—Great God! I'd rather be
A Pagan suckled in a creed outworn;   10
So might I, standing on this pleasant lea,
Have glimpses that would make me less forlorn;
Have sight of Proteus° rising from the sea;
Or hear old Triton blow his wreathéd horn.°

[1807]

13 **Proteus:** An old man of the sea who (in the *Odyssey*) could assume a variety of shapes.
14 **Triton:** A sea deity, usually represented as blowing on a conch shell.

Journal Entry

What associations, attitudes, or ideas about institutions do you bring to your reading of these poems?

Textual Considerations

1. What pictures of London do Blake and Wordsworth present? Which aspects of the speakers' descriptions are not meant literally? How do these pictures compare with Wordsworth's picture of the world in "The World Is Too Much with Us"?
2. Why does Blake use the word *chartered* twice? Explain the meaning in each case.

3. What effect does Blake achieve through repetition of words from line to line and sometimes within the same line? How does repetition affect the mood of the poem?
4. What aspects of English life and institutions does the speaker portray as stagnant in Wordsworth's "London, 1802"?
5. What evidence does he offer in the first six lines of "London, 1802" to support this charge? Summarize the theme of the last eight lines of Wordsworth's sonnet.
6. What contrasts between "The world" and "Nature" does the speaker make in "The World Is Too Much with Us"?

Cultural Contexts

1. In both poems about London, the speakers lament the demise of institutions and their suppression of the human spirit. To what extent do their critiques apply to life in urban centers today? Are these poems anti-city? Explain.
2. Why does Wordsworth invoke Milton in "London, 1802" and Proteus and Triton in "The World Is Too Much with Us," while Blake invokes the images of "the chimney-sweeper's cry," "the hapless soldier's sigh," and "the youthful harlot's curse"? Which belief do you tend to share—that human beings can rekindle humanity's sense of awe or that they themselves are responsible for the creation of evil?

YEVTUSHENKO AND NIATUM

Yevgeny Yevtushenko

People

No people are uninteresting.
Their fate is like the chronicle of planets.

Nothing in them is not particular,
and planet is dissimilar from planet.

And if a man lived in obscurity   5
making his friends in that obscurity
obscurity is not uninteresting.

To each his world is private,
and in that world one excellent minute.

And in that world one tragic minute.   10
These are private.

In any man who dies there dies with him
his first snow and kiss and fight.
It goes with him.

They are left books and bridges   15
and painted canvas and machinery.

Whose fate is to survive.
But what has gone is also not nothing:

by the rule of the game something has gone.
Not people die but worlds die in them.   20

Whom we knew as faulty, the earth's creatures.
Of whom, essentially, what did we know?

Brother of a brother? Friend of friends?
Lover of lover?

We who knew our fathers   25
in everything, in nothing.

They perish. They cannot be brought back.
The secret worlds are not regenerated.

And every time again and again
I make my lament against destruction.   30

[1962]

Duane Niatum

Street Kid

I stand before the window that opens
to a field of sagebrush—
California country northeast of San Francisco.
Holding to the earth and its shield of silence,
The sun burns my thirteen years into the hill.   5
The white breath of twilight
Whirrs with insects crawling down the glass
Between the bars. But it is the meadowlark
Warbling at the end of the fence
That sets me apart from the rest of the boys,   10
The cool toughs playing ping pong
And cards before lock-up.
When this new home stops calling on memory,
As well as my nickname, Injun Joe,
Given to me by the brothers,   15
The Blacks, the Chicanos, the others growing
Lean as this solitude, I step
From the window into the darkness
Reach my soul building a nest against the wall.

[1978]

Journal Entry

To what extent do you agree with Yevtushenko that "no people are uninteresting"?

Textual Considerations

1. Analyze Yevtushenko's use of symbolism in "People." To what events might the "excellent minute" and the "tragic minute" refer? What other examples reinforce the poem's meanings about individual uniqueness, mortality, and our ability to know another person?
2. What is the significance of the contrast between "first snow and kiss and fight" and "books and bridges and painted canvas and machinery" in "People"?
3. Explain the line "Not people die but worlds die in them" in Yevtushenko's poem. Characterize your response to it.
4. The speaker in "Street Kid" is Native American. What role does ethnicity play in the text?
5. How do the speakers' identification with people and "the meadowlark" in "People" and "Street Kid," respectively, help us to understand them?

Cultural Contexts

1. The speaker in "Street Kid" is thirteen. For what reasons does he feel alienated from his peers? Is this kind of isolation particularly painful in adolescence? Explain.

2. Discuss with your group Yevtushenko's idea that "obscurity is not uninteresting." What does he mean by "obscurity"? Is there an ordinary person that you consider interesting? What makes a person interesting? Did your group reach a consensus?

Sharon Olds

Summer Solstice, New York City

By the end of the longest day of the year he could not stand it,
he went up the iron stairs through the roof of the building
and over the soft, tarry surface
to the edge, put one leg over the complex green tin cornice
and said if they came a step closer that was it.   5
Then the huge machinery of the earth began to work for his life,
the cops came in their suits blue-gray as the sky on a cloudy evening,
and one put on a bulletproof vest, a
black shell around his own life,
life of his children's father, in case   10
the man was armed, and one, slung with a
rope like the sign of his bounden duty,
came up out of a hole in the top of the neighboring building,
like the gold hole they say is in the top of the head,
and began to lurk toward the man who wanted to die.   15
The tallest cop approached him directly,
softly, slowly, talking to him, talking, talking,
while the man's leg hung over the lip of the next world,
and the crowd gathered in the street, silent, and the
dark hairy net with its implacable grid was   20
unfolded near the curb and spread out and
stretched as the sheet is prepared to receive at a birth.
Then they all came a little closer
where he squatted next to his death, his shirt
glowing its milky glow like something   25
growing in a dish at night in the dark in a lab, and then
everything stopped
as his body jerked and he
stepped down from the parapet and went toward them
and they closed on him, I thought they were going to   30
beat him up, as a mother whose child has been
lost will scream at the child when it's found, they
took him by the arms and held him up and
leaned him against the wall of the chimney and the
tall cop lit a cigarette   35
in his own mouth, and gave it to him, and

then they all lit cigarettes, and the
red glowing ends burned like the
tiny campfires we lit at night
back at the beginning of the world.   40

[1987]

Leo Romero

What the Gossips Saw

Everyone pitied Escolastica, her leg
had swollen like a watermelon in the summer
It had practically happened over night
She was seventeen, beautiful and soon
to be married to Guillermo who was working   5
in the mines at Terreros, eighty miles away
far up in the mountains, in the wilderness
Poor Escolastica, the old women would say
on seeing her hobble to the well with a bucket
carrying her leg as if it were the weight   10
of the devil, surely it was a curse from heaven
for some misdeed, the young women who were
jealous would murmur, yet they were grieved too
having heard that the doctor might cut
her leg, one of a pair of the most perfect legs   15
in the valley, and it was a topic of great
interest and conjecture among the villagers
whether Guillermo would still marry her
if she were crippled, a one-legged woman—
as if life weren't hard enough for a woman   20
with two legs—how could she manage

Guillermo returned and married Escolastica
even though she had but one leg, the sound
of her wooden leg pounding down the wooden aisle
stayed in everyone's memory for as long   25
as they lived, women cried at the sight
of her beauty, black hair so dark
that the night could get lost in it, a face
more alluring than a full moon

Escolastica went to the dances with her husband   30
and watched and laughed but never danced

though once she had been the best dancer
and could wear holes in a pair of shoes
in a matter of a night, and her waist had been
as light to the touch as a hummingbird's flight   35
And Escolastica bore five children, only half
what most women bore, yet they were healthy
In Escolastica's presence, no one would mention
the absence of her leg, though she walked heavily
And it was not long before the gossips   40
spread their poison, that she must be in cahoots
with the devil, had given him her leg
for the power to bewitch Guillermo's heart
and cloud his eyes so that he could not see
what was so clear to them all   45

[1981]

Journal Entry

What associations or attitudes toward suicide can you bring to your reading of Olds's text?

Textual Considerations

1. How does setting contribute to the theme of "Summer Solstice, New York City"?
2. How are the cops portrayed in Olds's poem? Cite specific lines.
3. Explain the last three lines of "Summer Solstice, New York City."
4. Consider the importance of the word *saw* in Romero's title. What other allusions to sight do you find in the poem?
5. What issue seems to be of greatest concern to the communities in Olds's and Romero's texts? Chart the course of the speakers' reactions to the suicidal man in Olds's poem and to Escolastica and Guillermo in Romero's poem.

Cultural Contexts

1. Olds and Romero address the issue of boundaries, or fences, in relationships—our often conflicting needs for solitude and solidarity, identity and community, and personal space and relatedness. What new meanings about relationships can you draw from these poems?
2. Working with your group, reconstruct the circumstances under which each of you would risk your life to save another's. Can you imagine yourself in the place of the cops in Olds's poem? How does the poem address the conflict between individual rights and the claims of communal obligation? Were the cops only doing their jobs? Explain.

FERLINGHETTI AND WILBUR

Lawrence Ferlinghetti
Constantly Risking Absurdity

Constantly risking absurdity
           and death
     whenever he performs
         above the heads
            of his audience   5
    the poet like an acrobat
         climbs on rime
           to a high wire of his own making
  and balancing on eyebeams
         above a sea of faces   10
      paces his way
         to the other side of day
    performing entrechats
         and sleight-of-foot tricks
  and other high theatrics   15
         and all without mistaking
     any thing
       for what it may not be
  For he's the super realist
         who must perforce perceive   20
     taut truth
        before the taking of each stance or step
  in his supposed advance
       toward that still higher perch
where Beauty stands and waits   25
       with gravity
          to start her death-defying leap
  And he
    a little charleychaplin man
        who may or may not catch   30
    her fair eternal form
       spreadeagled in the empty air
    of existence

                             [1958]

Richard Wilbur

The Writer

In her room at the prow of the house
Where light breaks, and the windows are tossed with linden,
My daughter is writing a story.

I pause in the stairwell, hearing
From her shut door a commotion of typewriter-keys   5
Like a chain hauled over a gunwale.

Young as she is, the stuff
Of her life is a great cargo, and some of it heavy:
I wish her a lucky passage.

But now it is she who pauses,   10
As if to reject my thought and its easy figure.
A stillness greatens, in which

The whole house seems to be thinking,
And then she is at it again with a bunched clamor
Of strokes, and again is silent.   15

I remember the dazed starling
Which was trapped in that very room, two years ago;
How we stole in, lifted a sash

And retreated, not to affright it;
And how for a helpless hour, through the crack of the door,   20
We watched the sleek, wild, dark

And iridescent creature
Batter against the brilliance, drop like a glove
To the hard floor, or the desk-top,

And wait then, humped and bloody,   25
For the wits to try it again; and how our spirits
Rose when, suddenly sure,

It lifted off from a chair-back,
Beating a smooth course for the right window
And clearing the sill of the world.   30

It is always a matter, my darling,
Of life or death, as I had forgotten. I wish
What I wished you before, but harder.

[1971]

Journal Entry

What is your concept of a poet or a writer? Do you think of yourself as a creative person? How do you define creativity?

Textual Considerations

1. Ferlinghetti's poem is based on the simile of the poet as acrobat. Why is it an appropriate comparison for the poem's subject?
2. How does the structure of Ferlinghetti's poem contribute to its meaning?
3. Respond to the concept of the poet as "the super realist" in "Constantly Risking Absurdity." Why does the poet sometimes "not catch" Beauty? Who is the writer in "The Writer"? How does he compare with the poet in "Constantly Risking Absurdity"?
4. The beginning of "The Writer" draws an elaborate comparison between the daughter's writing and a sea voyage. Review the poem and explain each of the sea images.
5. What is the similarity between the daughter's effort to write and the starling's effort to escape? What does the speaker learn from the example of the starling?

Cultural Contexts

1. Discuss the artist's relationship to audience in both poems. What attitude toward himself is the speaker expressing in calling himself "a little charleychaplin man"? Why is he constantly risking absurdity? What is "always a matter, . . . /Of life or death" in "The Writer"? What do both poems suggest about the creative process? Explain the role of community in both texts.
2. Discuss with your group the significance of the allusions to death in both poems. In what sense do artists, writers, and musicians defy death?

DICKINSON

Emily Dickinson

Volcanoes be in Sicily

Volcanoes be in Sicily
And South America
I judge from my Geography—
Volcanos nearer here
A Lava step at any time   5
Am I inclined to climb—
A Crater I may contemplate
Vesuvius at Home.

[c. 1914]

Emily Dickinson

The Soul selects her own society–

The Soul selects her own Society—
Then—shuts the Door—
To her divine Majority—
Present no more—

Unmoved—she notes the Chariots—pausing—   5
At her low Gate—
Unmoved—an Emperor be kneeling
Upon her Mat—

I've known her—from an ample nation—
Choose One—   10
Then—close the Valves of her attention—
Like Stone—

[c. 1862]

Emily Dickinson

Much madness is divinest sense–

Much Madness is divinest Sense—
To a discerning Eye—
Much Sense—the starkest Madness—
'Tis the Majority
In this, as All, prevail—   5
Assent—and you are sane—
Demur—you're straightway dangerous—
And handled with a Chain—

[c. 1862]

Emily Dickinson

Tell all the Truth but tell it slant–

Tell all the Truth but tell it slant—
Success in Circuit lies
Too bright for our infirm Delight
To Truth's superb surprise
As Lightning to the Children eased   5
With explanation kind
The Truth must dazzle gradually
Or every man be blind—

[c. 1868]

Journal Entry

What associations with volcanoes or with madness can you bring to your reading of Dickinson's texts?

Textual Considerations

1. Explain the paradox in the first four lines of "Volcanoes Be in Sicily."
2. Analyze the literal and symbolic significance of volcanoes in the poem.
3. Explain how Dickinson's use of door imagery contributes to the unity and meaning of "The Soul Selects Her Own Society—."
4. What does the poet's use of active verbs imply about the "soul's" anatomy?

5. Analyze Dickinson's use of paradox to enhance meaning in "Much Madness Is Divinest Sense—."
6. Do you agree that the majority decides what is sane or insane?
7. To what extent do you agree with the speaker in "Tell All the Truth but Tell It Slant—"?
8. How do you respond to the speaker's description of truth? Explain the last two lines of "Tell All the Truth but Tell It Slant—."
9. Select one image from each poem and explain how the images enhance meaning. Explain.

Cultural Contexts

1. In 1991, May Sarton, a twentieth-century American poet, described the function of poetry as follows:

> For poetry exists to break through
> to below the level of reason
> where the angels and monsters
> that the amenities keep in the cellar
> may come out to dance,
> to rove and roar,
> growling and singing,
> to bring life back to the enclosed rooms
> where too often we are only
> living and partly living.

   What might Sarton mean by juxtaposing "angels" and "monsters"? What does her choice of verbs suggest about the function of poetry? Why are the rooms "enclosed?" Explain the last two lines. To what extent does Sarton's concept of poetry apply to Dickinson's texts? What is your response to Sarton's description of the role of poetry in people's lives?
2. To what extent do your group members agree with Dickinson that it is dangerous to be a nonconformist? What examples from history or from your own experience can you think of?

DRAMA

Sophocles

Antigone

English version by Dudley Fitts and Robert Fitzgerald

CHARACTERS

ANTIGONE
ISMENE
EURYDICE
CREON
HAIMON
TEIRESIAS
A Sentry
A Messenger
Chorus

SCENE: *Before the palace of* CREON, *King of Thebes. A central double door, and two lateral doors. A platform extends the length of the façade, and from this platform three steps lead down into the "orchestra," or chorus-ground.* TIME: *dawn of the day after the repulse of the Argive army from the assault on Thebes.*

PROLOGUE

(ANTIGONE *and* ISMENE° *enter from the central door of the Palace.*)

ANTIGONE: Ismenê, dear sister,
 You would think that we had already suffered enough
 For the curse on Oedipus:
 I cannot imagine any grief
 That you and I have not gone through. And now—   5
 Have they told you of the new decree of our King Creon?
ISMENE: I have heard nothing: I know
 That two sisters lost two brothers, a double death
 In a single hour; and I know that the Argive army
 Fled in the night; but beyond this, nothing.   10
ANTIGONE: I thought so. And that is why I wanted you

Prologue. S.d. Antigone and Ismene: daughters of Oedipus.

To come out here with me. There is something we must do.

ISMENE: Why do you speak so strangely?

ANTIGONE: Listen, Ismenê:

Creon buried our brother Eteoclês   15
With military honors, gave him a soldier's funeral,
And it was right that he should; but Polyneicês,
Who fought as bravely and died as miserably,—
They say that Creon has sworn
No one shall bury him, no one mourn for him,   20
But his body must lie in the fields, a sweet treasure
For carrion birds to find as they search for food.
That is what they say, and our good Creon is coming here
To announce it publicly; and the penalty—
Stoning to death in the public square!   25
                                                        There it is,
And now you can prove what you are:
A true sister, or a traitor to your family.

ISMENE: Antigonê, you are mad! What could I possibly do?

ANTIGONE: You must decide whether you will help me or not.

ISMENE: I do not understand you. Help you in what?   30

ANTIGONE: Ismenê, I am going to bury him. Will you come?

ISMENE: Bury him! You have just said the new law forbids it.

ANTIGONE: He is my brother. And he is your brother, too.

ISMENE: But think of the danger! Think what Creon will do!

ANTIGONE: Creon is not strong enough to stand in my way.   35

ISMENE: Ah sister!

Oedipus died, everyone hating him
For what his own search brought to light, his eyes
Ripped out by his own hand; and Iocastê died,
His mother and wife at once: she twisted the cords   40
That strangled her life; and our two brothers died,
Each killed by the other's sword. And we are left:
But oh, Antigonê!
Think how much more terrible than these
Our own death would be if we should go against Creon   45
And do what he has forbidden! We are only women,
We cannot fight with men, Antigonê!
The law is strong, we must give in to the law
In this thing, and in worse. I beg the Dead
To forgive me, but I am helpless: I must yield   50
To those in authority. And I think it is dangerous business
To be always meddling.

ANTIGONE: If that is what you think,
I should not want you, even if you asked to come.
You have made your choice, you can be what you want to be.

But I will bury him; and if I must die, 55
I say that this crime is holy: I shall lie down
With him in death, and I shall be as dear
To him as he to me.
     It is the dead,
Not the living, who make the longest demands:
We die for ever . . .
      You may do as you like, 60
Since apparently the laws of the gods mean nothing to you.

ISMENE: They mean a great deal to me; but I have no strength
To break laws that were made for the public good.

ANTIGONE: That must be your excuse, I suppose. But as for me,
I will bury the brother I love.

ISMENE: Antigonê, 65
I am so afraid for you!

ANTIGONE: You need not be:
You have yourself to consider, after all.

ISMENE: But no one must hear of this, you must tell no one!
I will keep it a secret, I promise!

ANTIGONE: Oh tell it! Tell everyone!
Think how they'll hate you when it all comes out 70
If they learn that you knew about it all the time!

ISMENE: So fiery! You should be cold with fear.

ANTIGONE: Perhaps. But I am only doing what I must.

ISMENE: But can you do it? I say that you cannot.

ANTIGONE: Very well: when my strength gives out, I shall do no more. 75

ISMENE: Impossible things should not be tried at all.

ANTIGONE: Go away, Ismenê:
I shall be hating you soon, and the dead will too,
For your words are hateful. Leave me my foolish plan:
I am not afraid of the danger; if it means death, 80
It will not be the worst of deaths—death without honor.

ISMENE: Go then, if you feel that you must.
You are unwise,
But a loyal friend indeed to those who love you.

    (*Exit into the Palace.* ANTIGONE *goes off, L. Enter the* CHORUS.)

PÁRODOS

CHORUS: Now the long blade of the sun, lying   (STROPHE 1)
Level east to west, touches with glory
Thebes of the Seven Gates. Open, unlidded
Eye of golden day! O marching light
Across the eddy and rush of Dircê's stream, 5
Striking the white shields of the enemy

Thrown headlong backward from the blaze of morning!
CHORAGOS: Polyneicês their commander
Roused them with windy phrases,
He the wild eagle screaming   10
Insults above our land,
His wings their shields of snow,
His crest their marshalled helms.
CHORUS: Against our seven gates in a yawning ring   (ANTISTROPHE 1)
The famished spears came onward in the night;   15
But before his jaws were sated with our blood,
Or pinefire took the garland of our towers,
He was thrown back; and as he turned, great Thebes—
No tender victim for his noisy power—
Rose like a dragon behind him, shouting war.   20
CHORAGOS: For God hates utterly
The bray of bragging tongues;
And when he beheld their smiling,
Their swagger of golden helms,
The frown of his thunder blasted   25
Their first man from our walls.
CHORUS: We heard his shout of triumph high in the air   (STROPHE 2)
Turn to a scream; far out in a flaming arc
He fell with his windy torch, and the earth struck him.
And others storming in fury no less than his   30
Found shock of death in the dusty joy of battle.
CHORAGOS: Seven captains at seven gates
Yielded their clanging arms to the god
That bends the battle-line and breaks it.
These two only, brothers in blood,   35
Face to face in matchless rage,
Mirroring each the other's death,
Clashed in long combat.
CHORUS: But now in the beautiful morning of victory   (ANTISTROPHE 2)
Let Thebes of the many chariots sing for joy!   40
With hearts for dancing we'll take leave of war:
Our temples shall be sweet with hymns of praise,
And the long night shall echo with our chorus.

SCENE I

CHORAGOS: But now at last our new King is coming:
Creon of Thebes, Menoikeus' son.
In this auspicious dawn of his reign
What are the new complexities
That shifting Fate has woven for him?   5

What is his counsel? Why has he summoned
The old men to hear him?

(Enter CREON *from the Palace, C. He addresses the* CHORUS *from the top step.)*

CREON: Gentlemen: I have the honor to inform you that our Ship of State, which
recent storms have threatened to destroy, has come safely to harbor at last,
guided by the merciful wisdom of Heaven. I have summoned you here this   10
morning because I know that I can depend upon you: your devotion to King
Laïos was absolute; you never hesitated in your duty to our late ruler Oedipus;
and when Oedipus died, your loyalty was transferred to his children. Unfortunately, as you know, his two sons, the princes Eteoclês and Polyneicês, have
killed each other in battle; and I, as the next in blood, have succeeded to the full   15
power of the throne.

I am aware, of course, that no Ruler can expect complete loyalty from his
subjects until he has been tested in office. Nevertheless, I say to you at the very
outset that I have nothing but contempt for the kind of Governor who is afraid,
for whatever reason, to follow the course that he knows is best for the State;   20
and as for the man who sets private friendship above the public welfare,—I
have no use for him, either. I call God to witness that if I saw my country
headed for ruin, I should not be afraid to speak out plainly; and I need hardly
remind you that I would never have any dealings with an enemy of the people.
No one values friendship more highly than I; but we must remember that   25
friends made at the risk of wrecking our Ship are not real friends at all.

These are my principles, at any rate, and that is why I have made the following decision concerning the sons of Oedipus: Eteoclês, who died as a man
should die, fighting for his country, is to be buried with full military honors,
with all the ceremony that is usual when the greatest heroes die; but his brother   30
Polyneicês, who broke his exile to come back with fire and sword against his
native city and the shrines of his fathers' gods, whose one idea was to spill the
blood of his blood and sell his own people into slavery—Polyneicês, I say, is to
have no burial: no man is to touch him or say the least prayer for him; he shall
lie on the plain, unburied; and the birds and the scavenging dogs can do with   35
him whatever they like.

This is my command, and you can see the wisdom behind it. As long as I am
King, no traitor is going to be honored with the loyal man. But whoever shows
by word and deed that he is on the side of the State,—he shall have my respect
while he is living, and my reverence when he is dead.   40
CHORAGOS: If that is your will, Creon son of Menoikeus,
You have the right to enforce it: we are yours.
CREON: That is my will. Take care that you do your part.
CHORAGOS: We are old men: let the younger ones carry it out.
CREON: I do not mean that: the sentries have been appointed.   45
CHORAGOS: Then what is it that you would have us do?
CREON: You will give no support to whoever breaks this law.
CHORAGOS: Only a crazy man is in love with death!

CREON: And death it is; yet money talks, and the wisest
Have sometimes been known to count a few coins too many.   50

       (*Enter* SENTRY *from L.*)

SENTRY: I'll not say that I'm out of breath from running, King, because every time
    I stopped to think about what I have to tell you, I felt like going back. And all
    the time a voice kept saying, "You fool, don't you know you're walking straight
    into trouble?"; and then another voice: "Yes, but if you let somebody else get
    the news to Creon first, it will be even worse than that for you!" But good sense   55
    won out, at least I hope it was good sense, and here I am with a story that
    makes no sense at all; but I'll tell it anyhow, because, as they say, what's going to
    happen's going to happen, and—
CREON: Come to the point. What have you to say?
SENTRY: I did not do it. I did not see who did it. You must not punish me for what   60
    someone else has done.
CREON: A comprehensive defense! More effective, perhaps,
    If I knew its purpose. Come: what is it?
SENTRY: A dreadful thing . . . I don't know how to put it—
CREON: Out with it!
SENTRY: Well, then;   65
    The dead man—

             Polyneicês—

    (*Pause. The* SENTRY *is overcome, fumbles for words.* CREON *waits impassively.*)

             out there—
                      someone,—
New dust on the slimy flesh!

    (*Pause. No sign from* CREON.)

Someone has given it burial that way, and
Gone . . .

    (*Long pause.* CREON *finally speaks with deadly control:*)

CREON: And the man who dared do this?   70
SENTRY: I swear I
Do not know! You must believe me!
                    Listen:
The ground was dry, not a sign of digging, no,
Not a wheeltrack in the dust, no trace of anyone.
It was when they relieved us this morning: and one of them,   75
The corporal, pointed to it.
              There it was,
The strangest—
        Look:
The body, just mounded over with light dust: you see?
Not buried really, but as if they'd covered it

Just enough for the ghost's peace. And no sign   80
Of dogs or any wild animal that had been there.

And then what a scene there was! Every man of us
Accusing the other: we all proved the other man did it,
We all had proof that we could not have done it.
We were ready to take hot iron in our hands,   85
Walk through fire, swear by all the gods,
It was not I!
I do not know who it was, but it was not I!

> (CREON's *rage has been mounting steadily, but the* SENTRY *is too intent upon his story to notice it*)

And then, when this came to nothing, someone said
A thing that silenced us and made us stare   90
Down at the ground: you had to be told the news,
And one of us had to do it! We threw the dice,
And the bad luck fell to me. So here I am,
No happier to be here than you are to have me:
Nobody likes the man who brings bad news.   95
CHORAGOS: I have been wondering, King: can it be that the gods have done this?
CREON (*Furiously*):   Stop!
  Must you doddering wrecks
  Go out of your heads entirely? "The gods!"
  Intolerable!   100
The gods favor this corpse? Why? How had he served them?
Tried to loot their temples, burn their images,
Yes, and the whole State, and its laws with it!
Is it your senile opinion that the gods love to honor bad men?
A pious thought!—
                  No, from the very beginning   105
There have been those who have whispered together,
Stiff-necked anarchists, putting their heads together,
Scheming against me in alleys. These are the men,
And they have bribed my own guard to do this thing.

Money!   (*Sententiously*)   110
There's nothing in the world so demoralizing as money.
Down go your cities,
Homes gone, men gone, honest hearts corrupted,
Crookedness of all kinds, and all for money!   (*To* SENTRY)
                  But you—!   115
I swear by God and by the throne of God,
The man who has done this thing shall pay for it!
Find that man, bring him here to me, or your death
Will be the least of your problems: I'll string you up

Alive, and there will be certain ways to make you   120
Discover your employer before you die;
And the process may teach you a lesson you seem to have missed:
The dearest profit is sometimes all too dear:
That depends on the source. Do you understand me?
A fortune won is often misfortune.   125
SENTRY: King, may I speak?
CREON: Your very voice distresses me.
SENTRY: Are you sure that it is my voice, and not your conscience?
CREON: By God, he wants to analyze me now!
SENTRY: It is not what I say, but what has been done, that hurts you.
CREON: You talk too much.
SENTRY: Maybe; but I've done nothing.   130
CREON: Sold your soul for some silver: that's all you've done.
SENTRY: How dreadful it is when the right judge judges wrong!
CREON: Your figures of speech
May entertain you now; but unless you bring me the man,
You will get little profit from them in the end.   (*Exit* CREON *into the Palace.*)   135
SENTRY: "Bring me the man"—!
I'd like nothing better than bringing him the man!
But bring him or not, you have seen the last of me here.
At any rate, I am safe!   (*Exit* SENTRY)

ODE I

CHORUS: (STROPHE 1)
Numberless are the world's wonders, but none
More wonderful than man; the stormgray sea
Yields to his prows, the huge crests bear him high;
Earth, holy and inexhaustible, is graven
With shining furrows where his plows have gone   5
Year after year, the timeless labor of stallions.

The lightboned birds and beasts that cling to cover,   (ANTISTROPHE 1)
The lithe fish lighting their reaches of dim water,
All are taken, tamed in the net of his mind;
The lion on the hill, the wild horse windy-maned,   10
Resign to him; and his blunt yoke has broken
The sultry shoulders of the mountain bull.

Words also, and thought as rapid as air,   (STROPHE 2)
He fashions to his good use; statecraft is his,
And his the skill that deflects the arrows of snow,   15
The spears of winter rain: from every wind
He has made himself secure—from all but one:
In the late wind of death he cannot stand.

O clear intelligence, force beyond all measure!   (ANTISTROPHE 2)
O fate of man, working both good and evil!   20
When the laws are kept, how proudly his city stands!
When the laws are broken, what of his city then?
Never may the anárchic man find rest at my hearth,
Never be it said that my thoughts are his thoughts.

SCENE II

(*Re-enter* SENTRY *leading* ANTIGONE.)

CHORAGOS: What does this mean? Surely this captive woman
  Is the Princess, Antigonê. Why should she be taken?
SENTRY: Here is the one who did it! We caught her
  In the very act of burying him.—Where is Creon?
CHORAGOS: Just coming from the house.   5

(*Enter* CREON, *C.*)

CREON: What has happened?
  Why have you come back so soon?
SENTRY: (*Expansively*)   O King,
  A man should never be too sure of anything:
  I would have sworn
  That you'd not see me here again: your anger   10
  Frightened me so, and the things you threatened me with;
  But how could I tell then
  That I'd be able to solve the case so soon?

  No dice-throwing this time: I was only too glad to come!

  Here is this woman. She is the guilty one: 15
  We found her trying to bury him.
  Take her, then; question her; judge her as you will.
  I am through with the whole thing now, and glád óf it.
CREON: But this is Antigonê! Why have you brought her here?
SENTRY: She was burying him, I tell you!
CREON: (*Severely*)   Is this the truth?   20
SENTRY: I saw her with my own eyes. Can I say more?
CREON: The details: come, tell me quickly!
SENTRY: It was like this:
  After those terrible threats of yours, King,
  We went back and brushed the dust away from the body.
  The flesh was soft by now, and stinking,   25
  So we sat on a hill to windward and kept guard.
  No napping this time! We kept each other awake.
  But nothing happened until the white round sun
  Whirled in the center of the round sky over us:

Then, suddenly,   30
A storm of dust roared up from the earth, and the sky
Went out, the plain vanished with all its trees
In the stinging dark. We closed our eyes and endured it.
The whirlwind lasted a long time, but it passed;
And then we looked, and there was Antigonê!   35
I have seen
A mother bird come back to a stripped nest, heard
Her crying bitterly a broken note or two
For the young ones stolen. Just so, when this girl
Found the bare corpse, and all her love's work wasted,   40
She wept, and cried on heaven to damn the hands
That had done this thing.
                         And then she brought more dust
And sprinkled wine three times for her brother's ghost.

We ran and took her at once. She was not afraid,
Not even when we charged her with what she had done.   45
She denied nothing.
                    And this was a comfort to me,
And some uneasiness: for it is a good thing
To escape from death, but it is no great pleasure
To bring death to a friend.
                          Yet I always say
There is nothing so comfortable as your own safe skin!   50
CREON: (*Slowly, dangerously*) And you, Antigonê,
     You with your head hanging,—do you confess this thing?
ANTIGONE: I do. I deny nothing.
CREON (*To* SENTRY):   You may go.   (*Exit* SENTRY)

     (*To* ANTIGONE:)

Tell me, tell me briefly:
Had you heard my proclamation touching this matter?   55
ANTIGONE: It was public. Could I help hearing it?
CREON: And yet you dared defy the law.
ANTIGONE: I dared.
     It was not God's proclamation. That final Justice
     That rules the world below makes no such laws.
     Your edict, King, was strong,   60
     But all your strength is weakness itself against
     The immortal unrecorded laws of God.
     They are not merely now: they were, and shall be,
     Operative for ever, beyond man utterly.

     I knew I must die, even without your decree: 65
     I am only mortal. And if I must die

Now, before it is my time to die,
Surely this is no hardship: can anyone
Living, as I live, with evil all about me,
Think Death less than a friend? This death of mine   70
Is of no importance; but if I had left my brother
Lying in death unburied, I should have suffered.
Now I do not.

               You smile at me. Ah Creon,
Think me a fool, if you like; but it may well be
That a fool convicts me of folly.   75

CHORAGOS: Like father, like daughter: both headstrong, deaf to reason!
    She has never learned to yield.

CREON: She has much to learn.
    The inflexible heart breaks first, the toughest iron
    Cracks first, and the wildest horses bend their necks
    At the pull of the smallest curb.

                     Pride? In a slave?   80
    This girl is guilty of double insolence,
    Breaking the given laws and boasting of it.
    Who is the man here,
    She or I, if this crime goes unpunished?
    Sister's child, or more than sister's child,   85
    Or closer yet in blood—she and her sister
    Win bitter death for this!

       (*To* SERVANTS:)

                Go, some of you,
    Arrest Ismenê. I accuse her equally.
    Bring her: you will find her sniffling in the house there.

    Her mind's a traitor: crimes kept in the dark
    Cry for light, and the guardian brain shudders;   90
    But how much worse than this
    Is brazen boasting of barefaced anarchy!

ANTIGONE: Creon, what more do you want than my death?

CREON: Nothing.
    That gives me everything.

ANTIGONE: Then I beg you: kill me.   95
    This talking is a great weariness: your words
    Are distasteful to me, and I am sure that mine
    Seem so to you. And yet they should not seem so:
    I should have praise and honor for what I have done.
    All these men here would praise me   100
    Were their lips not frozen shut with fear of you.   (*Bitterly*)
    Ah the good fortune of kings,
    Licensed to say and do whatever they please!

CREON: You are alone here in that opinion.

ANTIGONE: No, they are with me. But they keep their tongues in leash. 105

CREON: Maybe. But you are guilty, and they are not.

ANTIGONE: There is no guilt in reverence for the dead.

CREON: But Eteoclês—was he not your brother too?

ANTIGONE: My brother too.

CREON: And you insult his memory?

ANTIGONE (*Softly*): The dead man would not say that I insult it. 110

CREON: He would: for you honor a traitor as much as him.

ANTIGONE: His own brother, traitor or not, and equal in blood.

CREON: He made war on his country. Eteoclês defended it.

ANTIGONE: Nevertheless, there are honors due all the dead.

CREON: But not the same for the wicked as for the just. 115

ANTIGONE: Ah Creon, Creon,
　Which of us can say what the gods hold wicked?

CREON: An enemy is an enemy, even dead.

ANTIGONE: It is my nature to join in love, not hate.

CREON (*Finally losing patience*): Go join him, then; if you must have your love, 120
　Find it in hell!

CHORAGOS: But see, Ismenê comes:

(*Enter* ISMENE, *guarded*)

　Those tears are sisterly, the cloud
　That shadows her eyes rains down gentle sorrow.

CREON: You, too, Ismenê, 125
　Snake in my ordered house, sucking my blood
　Stealthily—and all the time I never knew
　That these two sisters were aiming at my throne!

　　　　　　　　　　　　　　　　Ismenê,
　Do you confess your share in this crime, or deny it?
　Answer me. 130

ISMENE: Yes, if she will let me say so. I am guilty.

ANTIGONE (*Coldly*): No, Ismenê. You have no right to say so.
　You would not help me, and I will not have you help me.

ISMENE: But now I know what you meant; and I am here
　To join you, to take my share of punishment. 135

ANTIGONE: The dead man and the gods who rule the dead
　Know whose act this was. Words are not friends.

ISMENE: Do you refuse me, Antigonê? I want to die with you:
　I too have a duty that I must discharge to the dead.

ANTIGONE: You shall not lessen my death by sharing it. 140

ISMENE: What do I care for life when you are dead?

ANTIGONE: Ask Creon. You're always hanging on his opinions.

ISMENE: You are laughing at me. Why, Antigonê?

ANTIGONE: It's a joyless laughter, Ismenê.

ISMENE: But can I do nothing?
ANTIGONE: Yes. Save yourself. I shall not envy you.   145
    There are others who will praise you; I shall have honor, too.
ISMENE: But we are equally guilty!
ANTIGONE: No more, Ismenê.
    You are alive, but I belong to Death.
CREON (*To the* CHORUS):   Gentlemen, I beg you to observe these girls:
    One has just now lost her mind; the other,   150
    It seems, has never had a mind at all.
ISMENE: Grief teaches the steadiest minds to waver, King.
CREON: Yours certainly did, when you assumed guilt with the guilty!
ISMENE: But how could I go on living without her?
CREON: You are.
    She is already dead.
ISMENE: But your own son's bride!   155
CREON: There are places enough for him to push his plow.
    I want no wicked women for my sons!
ISMENE: O dearest Haimon, how your father wrongs you!
CREON: I've had enough of your childish talk of marriage!
CHORAGOS: Do you really intend to steal this girl from your son?   160
CREON: No; Death will do that for me.
CHORAGOS: Then she must die?
CREON (*Ironically*):   You dazzle me.
                              —But enough of this talk!

          (*To* GUARDS:)

    You, there, take them away and guard them well:
    For they are but women, and even brave men run
    When they see Death coming.   (*Exeunt* ISMENE, ANTIGONE, *and* GUARDS)   165

          ODE II

CHORUS: Fortunate is the man who has never tasted God's vengeance!   (STROPHE 1)
    Where once the anger of heaven has struck, that house is shaken
    For ever: damnation rises behind each child
    Like a wave cresting out of the black northeast,
    When the long darkness under sea roars up   5
    And bursts drumming death upon the whirlwhipped sand.

    I have seen this gathering sorrow from time long past   (ANTISTROPHE 1)
    Loom upon Oedipus' children: generation from generation
    Takes the compulsive rage of the enemy god.
    So lately this last flower of Oedipus' line   10
    Drank the sunlight! but now a passionate word
    And a handful of dust have closed up all its beauty.

What mortal arrogance   (STROPHE 2)
Transcends the wrath of Zeus?
Sleep cannot lull him, nor the effortless long months   15
Of the timeless gods: but he is young for ever,
And his house is the shining day of high Olympos.
    All that is and shall be,
    And all the past, is his.
No pride on earth is free of the curse of heaven.   20

    The straying dreams of men   (ANTISTROPHE 2)
    May bring them ghosts of joy:
But as they drowse, the waking embers burn them;
Or they walk with fixed éyes, as blind men walk.
But the ancient wisdom speaks for our own time: 25
    Fate works most for woe
    With Folly's fairest show.
Man's little pleasure is the spring of sorrow.

SCENE III

CHORAGOS: But here is Haimon, King, the last of all your sons.
    Is it grief for Antigonê that brings him here,
    And bitterness at being robbed of his bride?

    (*Enter* HAIMON)

CREON: We shall soon see, and no need of diviners.
                                                —Son,
    You have heard my final judgment on that girl: 5
    Have you come here hating me, or have you come
    With deference and with love, whatever I do?
HAIMON: I am your son, father. You are my guide.
    You make things clear for me, and I obey you.
    No marriage means more to me than your continuing wisdom.   10
CREON: Good. That is the way to behave: subordinate
    Everything else, my son, to your father's will.
    This is what a man prays for, that he may get
    Sons attentive and dutiful in his house,
    Each hating his father's enemies,   15
    Honoring his father's friends. But if his sons
    Fail him, if they turn out unprofitably,
    What has he fathered but trouble for himself
    And amusement for the malicious?
                                    So you are right
    Not to lose your head over this woman.   20
    Your pleasure with her would soon grow cold, Haimon,
    And then you'd have a hellcat in bed and elsewhere.

Let her find her husband in Hell!
Of all the people in this city, only she
Has had contempt for my law and broken it.   25

Do you want me to show myself weak before the people?
Or to break my sworn word? No, and I will not.
The woman dies.
I suppose she'll plead "family ties." Well, let her.
If I permit my own family to rebel,   30
How shall I earn the world's obedience?
Show me the man who keeps his house in hand,
He's fit for public authority.
                   I'll have no dealings
With law-breakers, critics of the government:
Whoever is chosen to govern should be obeyed—   35
Must be obeyed, in all things, great and small,
Just and unjust! O Haimon,
The man who knows how to obey, and that man only,
Knows how to give commands when the time comes.
You can depend on him, no matter how fast   40
The spears come: he's a good soldier, he'll stick it out.

Anarchy, anarchy! Show me a greater evil!
This is why cities tumble and the great houses rain down,
This is what scatters armies!

No, no: good lives are made so by discipline.   45
We keep the laws then, and the lawmakers,
And no woman shall seduce us. If we must lose,
Let's lose to a man, at least! Is a woman stronger than we?
CHORAGOS: Unless time has rusted my wits,
What you say, King, is said with point and dignity.   50
HAIMON (*Boyishly earnest*):   Father:
Reason is God's crowning gift to man, and you are right
To warn me against losing mine. I cannot say—
I hope that I shall never want to say!—that you
Have reasoned badly. Yet there are other men   55
Who can reason too; and their opinions might be helpful.
You are not in a position to know everything
That people say or do, or what they feel:
Your temper terrifies them—everyone
Will tell you only what you like to hear.   60
But I, at any rate, can listen; and I have heard them
Muttering and whispering in the dark about this girl.
They say no woman has ever, so unreasonably,
Died so shameful a death for a generous act:

"She covered her brother's body. Is this indecent?   65
She kept him from dogs and vultures. Is this a crime?
Death?—She should have all the honor that we can give her!"

This is the way they talk out there in the city.

You must believe me:
Nothing is closer to me than your happiness.   70
What could be closer? Must not any son
Value his father's fortune as his father does his?
I beg you, do not be unchangeable:
Do not believe that you alone can be right.
The man who thinks that,   75
The man who maintains that only he has the power
To reason correctly, the gift to speak, the soul—
A man like that, when you know him, turns out empty.

It is not reason never to yield to reason!

In flood time you can see how some trees bend,   80
And because they bend, even their twigs are safe,
While stubborn trees are torn up, roots and all.
And the same thing happens in sailing:
Make your sheet fast, never slacken,—and over you go,
Head over heels and under: and there's your voyage.   85

Forget you are angry! Let yourself be moved!
I know I am young; but please let me say this:
The ideal condition
Would be, I admit, that men should be right by instinct;
But since we are all too likely to go astray,   90
The reasonable thing is to learn from those who can teach.
CHORAGOS: You will do well to listen to him, King,
   If what he says is sensible. And you, Haimon,
   Must listen to your father.—Both speak well.
CREON: You consider it right for a man of my years and experience   95
   To go to school to a boy?
HAIMON: It is not right
   If I am wrong. But if I am young, and right,
   What does my age matter?
CREON: You think it right to stand up for an anarchist?
HAIMON: Not at all. I pay no respect to criminals.   100
CREON: Then she is not a criminal?
HAIMON: The City would deny it, to a man.
CREON: And the City proposes to teach me how to rule?
HAIMON: Ah. Who is it that's talking like a boy now?

CREON: My voice is the one voice giving orders in this City!   105
HAIMON: It is no City if it takes orders from one voice.
CREON: The State is the King!
HAIMON: Yes, if the State is a desert.   (*Pause*)
CREON: This boy, it seems, has sold out to a woman.
HAIMON: If you are a woman: my concern is only for you.
CREON: So? Your "concern"! In a public brawl with your father!   110
HAIMON: How about you, in a public brawl with justice?
CREON: With justice, when all that I do is within my rights?
HAIMON: You have no right to trample on God's right.
CREON (*Completely out of control*):   Fool, adolescent fool! Taken in by a woman!
HAIMON: You'll never see me taken in by anything vile.   115
CREON: Every word you say is for her!
HAIMON (*Quietly darkly*):   And for you.
   And for me. And for the gods under the earth.
CREON: You'll never marry her while she lives.
HAIMON: Then she must die.—But her death will cause another.
CREON: Another?   120
   Have you lost your senses? Is this an open threat?
HAIMON: There is no threat in speaking to emptiness.
CREON: I swear you'll regret this superior tone of yours!
   You are the empty one!
HAIMON: If you were not my father,
   I'd say you were perverse.   125
CREON: You girlstruck fool, don't play at words with me!
HAIMON: I am sorry. You prefer silence.
CREON: Now, by God—!
   I swear, by all the gods in heaven above us,
   You'll watch it, I swear you shall!

   (*To the* SERVANTS:)

                                 Bring her out!
   Bring the woman out! Let her die before his eyes!   130
   Here, this instant, with her bridegroom beside her!
HAIMON: Not here, no; she will not die here, King.
   And you will never see my face again.
   Go on raving as long as you've a friend to endure you.   (*Exit* HAIMON)
CHORAGOS: Gone, gone.   135
   Creon, a young man in a rage is dangerous!
CREON: Let him do, or dream to do, more than a man can.
   He shall not save these girls from death.
CHORAGOS: These girls?
   You have sentenced them both?
CREON: No, you are right.
   I will not kill the one whose hands are clean.   140
CHORAGOS: But Antigonê?

CREON: (*Somberly*)   I will carry her far away
    Out there in the wilderness, and lock her
    Living in a vault of stone. She shall have food,
    As the custom is, to absolve the State of her death.
    And there let her pray to the gods of hell: 145
    They are her only gods:
    Perhaps they will show her an escape from death
    Or she may learn,
                        though late,
    That piety shown the dead is pity in vain.   (*Exit* CREON)

ODE III

CHORUS: Love, unconquerable   (STROPHE)
    Waster of rich men, keeper
    Of warm lights and all-night vigil
    In the soft face of a girl:
    Sea-wanderer, forest-visitor!   5
    Even the pure Immortals cannot escape you,
    And mortal man, in his one day's dusk,
    Trembles before your glory.

    Surely you swerve upon ruin   (ANTISTROPHE)
    The just man's consenting heart,   10
    As here you have made bright anger
    Strike between father and son—
    And none has conquered but Love!
    A girl's glánce wórking the will of heaven:
    Pleasure to her alone who mocks us,   15
    Merciless Aphroditê.

SCENE IV

CHORAGOS (*As* ANTIGONE *enters guarded*):   But I can no longer stand in awe of this,
    Nor, seeing what I see, keep back my tears.
    Here is Antigonê, passing to that chamber
    Where we all find sleep at last.
ANTIGONE: Look upon me, friends, and pity me   (STROPHE 1) 5
    Turning back at the night's edge to say
    Good-by to the sun that shines for me no longer;
    Now sleepy Death
    Summons me down to Acheron,° that cold shore:
    There is no bridesong there, nor any music.   10
CHORUS: Yet not unpraised, not without a kind of honor,

III.iv. 9. Acheron: river in Hades, the home of the dead.

You walk at last into the underworld;
Untouched by sickness, broken by no sword.
What woman has ever found your way to death?
ANTIGONE: How often I have heard the story of Niobê,°   (ANTISTROPHE 1)   15
Tantalos' wretched daughter, how the stone
Clung fast about her, ivy-close: and they say
The rain falls endlessly
And sifting soft snow; her tears are never done.
I feel the loneliness of her death in mine.   20
CHORUS: But she was born of heaven, and you
Are woman, woman-born. If her death is yours,
A mortal woman's, is this not for you
Glory in our world and in the world beyond?
ANTIGONE: You laugh at me. Ah, friends, friends,   (STROPHE 2)   25
Can you not wait until I am dead? O Thebes,
O men many-charioted, in love with Fortune,
Dear springs of Dircê, sacred Theban grove,
Be witnesses for me, denied all pity,
Unjustly judged! and think a word of love   30
For her whose path turns
Under dark earth, where there are no more tears.
CHORUS: You have passed beyond human daring and come at last
Into a place of stone where Justice sits.
I cannot tell   35
What shape of your father's guilt appears in this.
ANTIGONE: You have touched it at last: that bridal bed   (ANTISTROPHE 2)
Unspeakable, horror of son and mother mingling:
Their crime, infection of all our family!
O Oedipus, father and brother!   40
Your marriage strikes from the grave to murder mine.
I have been a stranger here in my own land:
All my life
The blasphemy of my birth has followed me.
CHORUS: Reverence is a virtue, but strength   45
Lives in established law: that must prevail.
You have made your choice,
Your death is the doing of your conscious hand.
ANTIGONE: Then let me go, since all your words are bitter,   (EPODE)
And the very light of the sun is cold to me.   50
Lead me to my vigil, where I must have
Neither love nor lamentation; no song, but silence.

---

15. Niobe: her several children were slain in punishment for their mother's boastfulness. She was turned into stone on Mount Sipylus, and her tears became the stream of the mountain.

(CREON *interrupts impatiently*)

CREON: If dirges and planned lamentations could put off death,
Men would be singing for ever.

(*To the* SERVANTS:)

                    Take her, go!
You know your orders: take her to the vault   55
And leave her alone there. And if she lives or dies,
That's her affair, not ours: our hands are clean.
ANTIGONE: O tomb, vaulted bride-bed in eternal rock,
Soon I shall be with my own again
Where Persephonê welcomes the thin ghosts underground: 60
And I shall see my father again, and you, mother,
And dearest Polyneicês—
                    dearest indeed
To me, since it was my hand
That washed him clean and poured the ritual wine:
And my reward is death before my time!   65

And yet, as men's hearts know, I have done no wrong,
I have not sinned before God. Or if I have,
I shall know the truth in death. But if the guilt
Lies upon Creon who judged me, then, I pray,
May his punishment equal my own.
CHORAGOS: O passionate heart,   70
Unyielding, tormented still by the same winds!
CREON: Her guards shall have good cause to regret their delaying.
ANTIGONE: Ah! That voice is like the voice of death!
CREON: I can give you no reason to think you are mistaken.
ANTIGONE: Thebes, and you my fathers' gods,   75
And rulers of Thebes, you see me now, the last
Unhappy daughter of a line of kings,
Your kings, led away to death. You will remember
What things I suffer, and at what men's hands,
Because I would not transgress the laws of heaven.   80

(*To the* GUARDS, *simply:*)

Come: let us wait no longer.   (*Exit* ANTIGONE, *L., guarded*)

ODE IV

CHORUS: All Danaê's° beauty was locked away   (STROPHE 1)
   In a brazen cell where the sunlight could not come:
   A small room, still as any grave, enclosed her.
   Yet she was a princess too,
   And Zeus in a rain of gold poured love upon her.   5
   O child, child,
   No power in wealth or war
   Or tough sea-blackened ships
   Can prevail against untiring Destiny!

   And Dryas' son° also, that furious king,   (ANTISTROPHE 1) 10
   Bore the god's prisoning anger for his pride:
   Sealed up by Dionysos in deaf stone,
   His madness died among echoes.
   So at the last he learned what dreadful power
   His tongue had mocked: 15
   For he had profaned the revels,
   And fired the wrath of the nine
   Implacable Sisters° that love the sound of the flute.

   And old men tell a half-remembered tale   (STROPHE 2)
   Of horror done where a dark ledge splits the sea   20
   And a double surf beats on the gráy shóres:
   How a king's new woman, sick
   With hatred for the queen he had imprisoned,
   Ripped out his two sons' eyes with her bloody hands
   While grinning Arês watched the shuttle plunge   25
   Four times: four blind wounds crying for revenge,

   Crying, tears and blood mingled.—Piteously born,   (ANTISTROPHE 2)
   Those sons whose mother was of heavenly birth!
   Her father was the god of the North Wind
   And she was cradled by gales,   30
   She raced with young colts on the glittering hills
   And walked untrammeled in the open light:
   But in her marriage deathless Fate found means
   To build a tomb like yours for all her joy.

Ode IV. 1. Danae: she was locked away to prevent the fulfillment of a prophecy that she would bear a son who would kill her father. Despite this, she was impregnated by Zeus, who came to her in a shower of gold.   **10. Dryas's son:** King Lycurgus, whom Dionysus, the god of wine, caused to be stricken with madness.   **17–18. nine. . . Sisters:** the nine muses who presided over poetry, music, and the arts and sciences.

SCENE V

(*Enter blind* TEIRESIAS, *led by a boy. The opening speeches of* TEIRESIAS *should be in singsong contrast to the realistic lines of* CREON.)

TEIRESIAS: This is the way the blind man comes, Princes, Princes,
   Lock-step, two heads lit by the eyes of one.
CREON: What new thing have you to tell us, old Teiresias?
TEIRESIAS: I have much to tell you: listen to the prophet, Creon.
CREON: I am not aware that I have ever failed to listen.   5
TEIRESIAS: Then you have done wisely, King, and ruled well.
CREON: I admit my debt to you. But what have you to say?
TEIRESIAS: This, Creon: you stand once more on the edge of fate.
CREON: What do you mean? Your words are a kind of dread.
TEIRESIAS: Listen, Creon: 10
   I was sitting in my chair of augury, at the place
   Where the birds gather about me. They were all a-chatter,
   As is their habit, when suddenly I heard
   A strange note in their jangling, a scream, a
   Whirring fury; I knew that they were fighting,   15
   Tearing each other, dying
   In a whirlwind of wings clashing. And I was afraid.
   I began the rites of burnt-offering at the altar,
   But Hephaistos failed me: instead of bright flame,
   There was only the sputtering slime of the fat thigh-flesh   20
   Melting: the entrails dissolved in gray smoke,
   The bare bone burst from the welter. And no blaze!

   This was a sign from heaven. My boy described it,
   Seeing for me as I see for others.

   I tell you, Creon, you yourself have brought   25
   This new calamity upon us. Our hearths and altars
   Are stained with the corruption of dogs and carrion birds
   That glut themselves on the corpse of Oedipus' son.
   The gods are deaf when we pray to them, their fire
   Recoils from our offering, their birds of omen   30
   Have no cry of comfort, for they are gorged
   With the thick blood of the dead.
                  O my son,
   These are no trifles! Think: all men make mistakes,
   But a good man yields when he knows his course is wrong,
   And repairs the evil. The only crime is pride.   35

   Give in to the dead man, then: do not fight with a corpse—
   What glory is it to kill a man who is dead?

Think, I beg you:
It is for your own good that I speak as I do.
You should be able to yield for your own good.   40
CREON: It seems that prophets have made me their especial province.
All my life long
I have been a kind of butt for the dull arrows
Of doddering fortune-tellers!
                         No, Teiresias:
If your birds—if the great eagles of God himself   45
Should carry him stinking bit by bit to heaven,
I would not yield. I am not afraid of pollution:
No man can defile the gods.
                    Do what you will,
Go into business, make money, speculate
In India gold or that synthetic gold from Sardis,   50
Get rich otherwise than by my consent to bury him.
Teiresias, it is a sorry thing when a wise man
Sells his wisdom, lets out his words for hire!
TEIRESIAS: Ah Creon! Is there no man left in the world—
CREON: To do what?—Come, let's have the aphorism!   55
TEIRESIAS: No man who knows that wisdom outweighs any wealth?
CREON: As surely as bribes are baser than any baseness.
TEIRESIAS: You are sick, Creon! You are deathly sick!
CREON: As you say: it is not my place to challenge a prophet.
TEIRESIAS: Yet you have said my prophecy is for sale.   60
CREON: The generation of prophets has always loved gold.
TEIRESIAS: The generation of kings has always loved brass.
CREON: You forget yourself! You are speaking to your King.
TEIRESIAS: I know it. You are a king because of me.
CREON: You have a certain skill; but you have sold out.   65
TEIRESIAS: King, you will drive me to words that—
CREON: Say them, say them!
Only remember: I will not pay you for them.
TEIRESIAS: No, you will find them too costly.
CREON: No doubt. Speak:
Whatever you say, you will not change my will.
TEIRESIAS: Then take this, and take it to heart!   70
The time is not far off when you shall pay back
Corpse for corpse, flesh of your own flesh.
You have thrust the child of this world into living night,
You have kept from the gods below the child that is theirs:
The one in a grave before her death, the other,   75
Dead, denied the grave. This is your crime:
And the Furies and the dark gods of Hell
Are swift with terrible punishment for you.

Do you want to buy me now, Creon?

                                      Not many days,
And your house will be full of men and women weeping,   80
And curses will be hurled at you from far
Cities grieving for sons unburied, left to rot
Before the walls of Thebes.

These are my arrows, Creon: they are all for you.
But come, child: lead me home.   (*To* Boy:)   85
Let him waste his fine anger upon younger men.
Maybe he will learn at last
To control a wiser tongue in a better head.   (*Exit* TEIRESIAS)
CHORAGOS: The old man has gone, King, but his words
    Remain to plague us. I am old, too,   90
    But I cannot remember that he was ever false.
CREON: That is true. . . . It troubles me.
    Oh it is hard to give in! but it is worse
    To risk everything for stubborn pride.
CHORAGOS: Creon: take my advice.
CREON: What shall I do?   95
CHORAGOS: Go quickly: free Antigonê from her vault
    And build a tomb for the body of Polyneicês.
CREON: You would have me do this?
CHORAGOS: Creon, yes!
    And it must be done at once: God moves
    Swiftly to cancel the folly of stubborn men.   100
CREON: It is hard to deny the heart! But I
    Will do it: I will not fight with destiny.
CHORAGOS: You must go yourself, you cannot leave it to others.
CREON: I will go.
         —Bring axes, servants:
    Come with me to the tomb. I buried her, I   105
    Will set her free.
            Oh quickly!
My mind misgives—
The laws of the gods are mighty, and a man must serve them
To the last day of his life!   (*Exit* CREON)

     PÆAN

CHORAGOS: God of many names   (STROPHE 1)
CHORUS: O Iacchos
                son
  of Kadmeian Sémelê
         O born of the Thunder!

Guardian of the West
                Regent
of Eleusis' plain
                O Prince of maenad Thebes
and the Dragon Field by rippling Ismenos: 5
CHORAGOS: God of many names   (ANTISTROPHE 1)
CHORUS: the flame of torches
  flares on our hills
                the nymphs of Iacchos
  dance at the spring of Castalia:

  from the vine-close mountain
                    come ah come in ivy:
  Evohé evohé! sings through the streets of Thebes   10
CHORAGOS: God of many names   (STROPHE 2)
CHORUS: Iacchos of Thebes
  heavenly Child
                of Sémelê bride of the Thunderer!
  The shadow of plague is upon us:
                    come
  with clement feet
               oh come from Parnasos
  down the long slopes
               across the lamenting water   15
CHORAGOS: Iô Fire! Chorister of the throbbing stars!   (ANTISTROPHE 2)
  O purest among the voices of the night!
  Thou son of God, blaze for us!
CHORUS: Come with choric rapture of circling Maenads
  Who cry *Iô Iacche!*
            God of many names!   20

ÉXODOS

(Enter MESSENGER, *L.)*

MESSENGER: Men of the line of Kadmos, you who live
  Near Amphion's citadel:
               I cannot say
Of any condition of human life "This is fixed,
This is clearly good, or bad." Fate raises up,
And Fate casts down the happy and unhappy alike: 5
No man can foretell his Fate.
             Take the case of Creon:
Creon was happy once, as I count happiness:
Victorious in battle, sole governor of the land,
Fortunate father of children nobly born.
And now it has all gone from him! Who can say   10

That a man is still alive when his life's joy fails?
He is a walking dead man. Grant him rich,
Let him live like a king in his great house:
If his pleasure is gone, I would not give
So much as the shadow of smoke for all he owns.   15

CHORAGOS: Your words hint at sorrow: what is your news for us?

MESSENGER: They are dead. The living are guilty of their death.

CHORAGOS: Who is guilty? Who is dead? Speak!

MESSENGER: Haimon.
Haimon is dead; and the hand that killed him
Is his own hand.

CHORAGOS: His father's? or his own?   20

MESSENGER: His own, driven mad by the murder his father had done.

CHORAGOS: Teiresias, Teiresias, how clearly you saw it all!

MESSENGER: This is my news: you must draw what conclusions you can from it.

CHORAGOS: But look: Eurydicê, our Queen:
Has she overheard us?   25

(*Enter* EURYDICE *from the Palace, C.*)

EURYDICE: I have heard something, friends:
As I was unlocking the gate of Pallas' shrine,
For I needed her help today, I heard a voice
Telling of some new sorrow. And I fainted
There at the temple with all my maidens about me.   30
But speak again: whatever it is, I can bear it:
Grief and I are no strangers.

MESSENGER: Dearest Lady,
I will tell you plainly all that I have seen.
I shall not try to comfort you: what is the use,
Since comfort could lie only in what is not true?   35
The truth is always best.

                    I went with Creon
To the outer plain where Polyneicês was lying,
No friend to pity him, his body shredded by dogs.
We made our prayers in that place to Hecatê
And Pluto, that they would be merciful. And we bathed   40
The corpse with holy water, and we brought
Fresh-broken branches to burn what was left of it,
And upon the urn we heaped up a towering barrow
Of the earth of his own land.

                    When we were done, we ran
To the vault where Antigonê lay on her couch of stone.   45
One of the servants had gone ahead,
And while he was yet far off he heard a voice
Grieving within the chamber, and he came back

And told Creon. And as the King went closer,
The air was full of wailing, the words lost,   50
And he begged us to make all haste. "Am I a prophet?"
He said, weeping, "And must I walk this road,
The saddest of all that I have gone before?
My son's voice calls me on. Oh quickly, quickly!
Look through the crevice there, and tell me   55
If it is Haimon, or some deception of the gods!"

We obeyed; and in the cavern's farthest corner
We saw her lying:
She had made a noose of her fine linen veil
And hanged herself. Haimon lay beside her,   60
His arms about her waist, lamenting her,
His love lost under ground, crying out
That his father had stolen her away from him.

When Creon saw him the tears rushed to his eyes
And he called to him: "What have you done, child? Speak to me.   65
What are you thinking that makes your eyes so strange?
O my son, my son, I come to you on my knees!"
But Haimon spat in his face. He said not a word,
Staring—
            And suddenly drew his sword
And lunged. Creon shrank back, the blade missed; and the boy,   70
Desperate against himself, drove it half its length
Into his own side, and fell. And as he died
He gathered Antigonê close in his arms again,
Choking, his blood bright red on her white cheek.
And now he lies dead with the dead, and she is his   75
At last, his bride in the houses of the dead.   (*Exit* EURYDICE *into the Palace*)
CHORAGOS: She has left us without a word. What can this mean?
MESSENGER: It troubles me, too; yet she knows what is best,
    Her grief is too great for public lamentation,
    And doubtless she has gone to her chamber to weep   80
    For her dead son, leading her maidens in his dirge.
CHORAGOS: It may be so: but I fear this deep silence.   (*Pause*)
MESSENGER: I will see what she is doing. I will go in.
                                        (*Exit* MESSENGER *into the Palace*)

            (*Enter* CREON *with attendants, bearing* HAIMON'S *body*)

CHORAGOS: But here is the King himself: oh look at him,
    Bearing his own damnation in his arms.   85
CREON: Nothing you say can touch me any more.
    My own blind heart has brought me

From darkness to final darkness. Here you see
The father murdering, the murdered son—
And all my civic wisdom!   90

Haimon my son, so young, so young to die,
I was the fool, not you; and you died for me.
CHORAGOS: That is the truth; but you were late in learning it.
CREON: This truth is hard to bear. Surely a god
Has crushed me beneath the hugest weight of heaven,   95
And driven me headlong a barbaric way
To trample out the thing I held most dear.

The pains that men will take to come to pain!

(*Enter* MESSENGER *from the Palace*)

MESSENGER: The burden you carry in your hands is heavy,
But it is not all: you will find more in your house.   100
CREON: What burden worse than this shall I find there?
MESSENGER: The Queen is dead.
CREON: O port of death, deaf world,
Is there no pity for me? And you, Angel of evil,
I was dead, and your words are death again.   105
Is it true, boy? Can it be true?
Is my wife dead? Has death bred death?
MESSENGER: You can see for yourself.

(*The doors are opened, and the body of* EURYDICE *is disclosed within.*)

CREON: Oh pity!
All true, all true, and more than I can bear!   110
O my wife, my son!
MESSENGER: She stood before the altar, and her heart
Welcomed the knife her own hand guided,
And a great cry burst from her lips for Megareus dead,
And for Haimon dead, her sons; and her last breath   115
Was a curse for their father, the murderer of her sons.
And she fell, and the dark flowed in through her closing eyes.
CREON: O god, I am sick with fear.
Are there no swords here? Has no one a blow for me?
MESSENGER: Her curse is upon you for the deaths of both.   120
CREON: It is right that it should be. I alone am guilty.
I know it, and I say it. Lead me in,
Quickly, friends.
I have neither life nor substance. Lead me in.
CHORAGOS: You are right, if there can be right in so much wrong.   125

The briefest way is best in a world of sorrow.
CREON: Let it come,
  Let death come quickly, and be kind to me.
  I would not ever see the sun again.
CHORAGOS: All that will come when it will; but we, meanwhile,   130
  Have much to do. Leave the future to itself.
CREON: All my heart was in that prayer!
CHORAGOS: Then do not pray any more: the sky is deaf.
CREON: Lead me away. I have been rash and foolish.
  I have killed my son and my wife.   135
  I look for comfort; my comfort lies here dead.
  Whatever my hands have touched has come to nothing.
  Fate has brought all my pride to a thought of dust.

  (*As* CREON *is being led into the house, the* CHORAGOS *advances and speaks
  directly to the audience*)

CHORAGOS: There is no happiness where there is no wisdom;
  No wisdom but in submission to the gods.   140
  Big words are always punished,
  And proud men in old age learn to be wise.

[441 B.C.]

Journal Entry

What knowledge of Greek history and culture do you bring to your reading of this play?
Should individuals obey the law under any circumstances, or in what cases can you justify expressions of civil disobedience?

Textual Considerations

1. A "foil" is a contrasting character that helps to define another. To what extent is
   Ismene a foil to Antigone? What arguments do the sisters communicate in the opening debate of the play? Which side of the argument do you support?
2. What is the function of the Chorus? Summarize the argument of the *Párodos*, the
   entrance of the chanting Chorus. What does this poetic ode add to the play as a
   whole? Can you explain how a tragic event like the brothers' death in *Antigone* or the
   attacks of September 11, 2001, in the United States have been or eventually will be
   transmuted into poetry, legend, and myth?
3. Read Creon's speech to the Chorus in Scene I and summarize the main principles of
   Creon's political philosophy. Compare Creon's political platform with that of your
   city's mayor, the governor of your state, the president of your country, or any other
   current ruler. Have Creon's principles changed much?
4. What arguments do Creon and Teiresias use against each other? What does their
   debate express about their physical characteristics, their personality traits, and the
   position they occupy as ruler and subject? After careful reading of this debate, do you

understand the position prophets occupied in ancient Greece? What function did Teiresias fulfill in ancient Greek society?

5. What does the debate between Creon and Haimon reveal about their father–son relationship? About their political ideas? About their concern for Antigone? What does Haimon mean when he says that his concern is not only for Antigone but "for you (Creon), / And for me. And for the gods under the earth." Analyze this in view of the Greeks' ideal of individual and social harmony.

Cultural Contexts

1. Debate whether Creon's right to legislate and maintain order versus Antigone's right to bury her brother, follow her conscience, and defend the gods might represent equal dangers to the state. Can you think of two leaders, two nations, or two cultures or civilizations that demonstrate the same inability to negotiate, cooperate with each other, or use a political language? What is your assessment of people's inability to interact, engage in dialogue, or understand each other? Identify the voices of moderation in the play and in your society.
2. Discuss the interplay of gender and power with your group. How do gender relations between Creon and Antigone shape the outcome of Creon's decision about his enemy? Does the fact that Creon's enemy is a woman bother him? What does gender reveal about Creon's real power?

Performance Exercises

PERFORMANCE EXPRESS (45 MINUTES)

Prepare an improvisational and spontaneous dialogue from *Antigone*; Creon's and Haimon's debate would be a good choice. Use classroom props to simulate the set of the palace. Present the dialogue to the whole class.

PERFORMANCE PROJECTS

1. French playwright Jean Anouilh communicates in his reinterpretation of *Antigone*, written in occupied France in 1944, the major struggle of his generation: the war of the French resistance against the Nazi invaders. Discuss what Antigone means for your generation. Then stage a production of one scene, which your group has rewritten and adapted to highlight what you consider one of the major concerns of your generation. You may also think in terms of current conflicts between individual autonomy versus American identity or individual freedom versus public security. Decide on the casting of classmates for the main roles, the size of the chorus, and its choreography.
2. Stage an all-male performance of *Antigone* in which the brothers, Eteoclês and Polyneicês, are cast as the survivors of the House of Oedipus and the sisters, Antigone and Ismene, are referred to as the dead warriors. Rewrite one scene of the play; after staging it, discuss whether your gender-reversal production has changed your classmates' dramatic expectations about the play.

Molière (Jean-Baptiste Poquelin)

Tartuffe[1]

Translated by Richard Wilbur

Pronouncing Glossary

The following list uses common English syllables and stress accents to provide rough equivalents of selected words whose pronunciation may be unfamiliar to the general reader.

Cléante: *clay-ahnt'*	Molière: *moh-lyar'*
Damis: *dah-mee'*	Orante: *oh-rahnt'*
Dorine: *do-reen'*	Orgon: *or-gohnh'*
Elmire: *el-meer'*	Pernelle: *payr-nel'*
Flipote: *flee'-pot*	Tartuffe: *tahr-toof'*
Laurent: *lor'-awn*	Valère: *vah-layr'*
Loyal: *lwah-al'*	Vincennes: *vanh-s*

Preface

Here is a comedy that has excited a good deal of discussion and that has been under attack for a long time; and the persons who are mocked by it have made it plain that they are more powerful in France than all whom my plays have satirized up to this time. Noblemen, ladies of fashion, cuckolds, and doctors all kindly consented to their presentation, which they themselves seemed to enjoy along with everyone else; but hypocrites do not understand banter: they became angry at once, and found it strange that I was bold enough to represent their actions and to care to describe a profession shared by so many good men. This is a crime for which they cannot forgive me, and they have taken up arms against my comedy in a terrible rage. They were careful not to attack it at the point that had wounded them: they are too crafty for that and too clever to reveal their true character. In keeping with their lofty custom, they have used the cause of God to mask their private interests; and *Tartuffe*, they say, is a play that offends piety: it is filled with abominations from beginning to end, and nowhere is there a line that does not deserve to be burned. Every syllable is wicked, the very gestures are criminal, and the slightest glance, turn of the head, or step from right to left conceals mysteries that they are able to explain to my disadvantage. In vain did I submit the play to the criticism of my friends and the scrutiny of the public: all the corrections I could make, the judgment of the king and queen[2] who saw the play, the approval of great princes and ministers of state who honored it with their presence, the opinion of good men who found it worthwhile, all this did not help. They will not let go of their prey, and

---

[1] The first version of *Tartuffe* was performed in 1664 and the second in 1667. When a second edition of the third version was printed in June 1669, Molière added his three petitions to Louis XIV; they follow the preface.   [2] Louis XIV was married to Marie Thérèse of Austria.

every day of the week they have pious zealots abusing me in public and damning me out of charity.

I would care very little about all they might say except that their devices make enemies of men whom I respect and gain the support of genuinely good men, whose faith they know and who, because of the warmth of their piety, readily accept the impressions that others present to them. And it is this which forces me to defend myself. Especially to the truly devout do I wish to vindicate my play, and I beg of them with all my heart not to condemn it before seeing it, to rid themselves of preconceptions, and not aid the cause of men dishonored by their actions.

If one takes the trouble to examine my comedy in good faith, he will surely see that my intentions are innocent throughout, and tend in no way to make fun of what men revere; that I have presented the subject with all the precautions that its delicacy imposes; and that I have used all the art and skill that I could to distinguish clearly the character of the hypocrite from that of the truly devout man. For that purpose I used two whole acts to prepare the appearance of my scoundrel. Never is there a moment's doubt about his character; he is known at once from the qualities I have given him; and from one end of the play to the other, he does not say a word, he does not perform an action which does not depict to the audience the character of a wicked man, and which does not bring out in sharp relief the character of the truly good man which I oppose to it.

I know full well that by way of reply, these gentlemen try to insinuate that it is not the role of the theater to speak of these matters; but with their permission, I ask them on what do they base this fine doctrine. It is a proposition they advance as no more than a supposition, for which they offer not a shred of proof; and surely it would not be difficult to show them that comedy, for the ancients, had its origin in religion and constituted a part of its ceremonies; that our neighbors, the Spaniards, have hardly a single holiday celebration in which a comedy is not a part; and that even here in France, it owes its birth to the efforts of a religious brotherhood who still own the Hôtel de Bourgogne, where the most important mystery plays of our faith were presented;[3] that you can still find comedies printed in gothic letters under the name of a learned doctor[4] of the Sorbonne; and without going so far, in our own day the religious dramas of Pierre Corneille[5] have been performed to the admiration of all France.

If the function of comedy is to correct men's vices, I do not see why any should be exempt. Such a condition in our society would be much more dangerous than the thing itself; and we have seen that the theater is admirably suited to provide correction. The most forceful lines of a serious moral statement are usually less powerful than those of satire; and nothing will reform most men better than the depiction of their faults. It is a vigorous blow to vices to expose them to public laughter. Criti-

---

[3] A reference to the *Confrérie de la Passion et Résurrection de Notre-Seigneur* (Fraternity of the passion and resurrection of our Savior), founded in 1402. The Hôtel de Bourgogne was a theater in rivalry with Molière's.   [4] Probably Maître Jehán Michel, a medical doctor who wrote mystery plays.   [5] Pierre Corneille (1606–1684) and Racine were France's two greatest writers of classic tragedy. The two dramas Molière doubtlessly had in mind were *Polyeucte* (1643) and *Théodore, vierge et martyre* (1645).

cism is taken lightly, but men will not tolerate satire. They are quite willing to be mean, but they never like to be ridiculed.

I have been attacked for having placed words of piety in the mouth of my impostor. Could I avoid doing so in order to represent properly the character of a hypocrite? It seemed to me sufficient to reveal the criminal motives which make him speak as he does, and I have eliminated all ceremonial phrases, which nonetheless he would not have been found using incorrectly. Yet some say that in the fourth act he sets forth a vicious morality; but is not this a morality which everyone has heard again and again? Does my comedy say anything new here? And is there any fear that ideas so thoroughly detested by everyone can make an impression on men's minds; that I make them dangerous by presenting them in the theater; that they acquire authority from the lips of a scoundrel? There is not the slightest suggestion of any of this; and one must either approve the comedy of *Tartuffe* or condemn all comedies in general.

This has indeed been done in a furious way for some time now, and never was the theater so much abused.[6] I cannot deny that there were Church Fathers who condemned comedy; but neither will it be denied me that there were some who looked on it somewhat more favorably. Thus authority, on which censure is supposed to depend, is destroyed by this disagreement; and the only conclusion that can be drawn from this difference of opinion among men enlightened by the same wisdom is that they viewed comedy in different ways, and that some considered it in its purity, while others regarded it in its corruption and confused it with all those wretched performances which have been rightly called performances of filth.

And in fact, since we should talk about things rather than words, and since most misunderstanding comes from including contrary notions in the same word, we need only to remove the veil of ambiguity and look at comedy in itself to see if it warrants condemnation. It will surely be recognized that as it is nothing more than a clever poem which corrects men's faults by means of agreeable lessons, it cannot be condemned without injustice. And if we listened to the voice of ancient times on this matter, it would tell us that its most famous philosophers have praised comedy—they who professed so austere a wisdom and who ceaselessly denounced the vices of their times. It would tell us that Aristotle spent his evenings at the theater[7] and took the trouble to reduce the art of making comedies to rules. It would tell us that some of its greatest and most honored men took pride in writing comedies themselves;[8] and that others did not disdain to recite them in public; that Greece expressed its admiration for this art by means of handsome prizes and magnificent theaters to honor it; and finally, that in Rome this same art also received extraordinary honors; I do not speak of Rome run riot under the license of the emperors, but of disciplined Rome, governed by the wisdom of the consuls, and in the age of the full vigor of Roman dignity.

---

[6] Molière had in mind Nicole's two attacks on the theater: *Visionnaires* (1666) and *Traité de la Comédie* (1667) as well as the prince de Conti's *Traité de la Comédie* (1666).   [7] A reference to Aristotle's *Poetics* (composed between 335 and 322 B.C., the year of his death).   [8] Scipio Africanus Minor (ca. 185–129 B.C., the Roman consul and general responsible for the final destruction of Carthage in 146 B.C., collaborated with Terence (Publius Terentius Afer, ca. 195 or 185–ca. 159 B.C.), a writer of comedies.

I admit that there have been times when comedy became corrupt. And what do men not corrupt every day? There is nothing so innocent that men cannot turn it to crime; nothing so beneficial that its values cannot be reversed; nothing so good in itself that it cannot be put to bad uses. Medical knowledge benefits mankind and is revered as one of our most wonderful possessions; and yet there was a time when it fell into discredit, and was often used to poison men. Philosophy is a gift of Heaven; it has been given to us to bring us to the knowledge of a God by contemplating the wonders of nature; and yet we know that often it has been turned away from its function and has been used openly in support of impiety. Even the holiest of things are not immune from human corruption, and every day we see scoundrels who use and abuse piety, and wickedly make it serve the greatest of crimes. But this does not prevent one from making the necessary distinctions. We do not confuse in the same false inference the goodness of things that are corrupted with the wickedness of the corrupt. The function of an art is always distinguished from its misuse; and as medicine is not forbidden because it was banned in Rome,[9] nor philosophy because it was publicly condemned in Athens,[10] we should not suppress comedy simply because it has been condemned at certain times. This censure was justified then for reasons which no longer apply today; it was limited to what was then seen; and we should not seize on these limits, apply them more rigidly than is necessary, and include in our condemnation the innocent along with the guilty. The comedy that this censure attacked is in no way the comedy that we want to defend. We must be careful not to confuse the one with the other. There may be two persons whose morals may be completely different. They may have no resemblance to one another except in their names, and it would be a terrible injustice to want to condemn Olympia, who is a good woman, because there is also an Olympia who is lewd. Such procedures would make for great confusion everywhere. Everything under the sun would be condemned; now since this rigor is not applied to the countless instances of abuse we see every day, the same should hold for comedy, and those plays should be approved in which instruction and virtue reign supreme.

I know there are some so delicate that they cannot tolerate a comedy, who say that the most decent are the most dangerous, that the passions they present are all the more moving because they are virtuous, and that men's feelings are stirred by these presentations. I do not see what great crime it is to be affected by the sight of a generous passion; and this utter insensitivity to which they would lead us is indeed a high degree of virtue! I wonder if so great a perfection resides within the strength of human nature, and I wonder if it is not better to try to correct and moderate men's passions than to try to suppress them altogether. I grant that there are places better to visit than the theater; and if we want to condemn every single thing that does not bear directly on God and our salvation, it is right that comedy be included, and I should willingly grant that it be condemned along with everything else. But if we admit, as is in fact true, that the exercise of piety will permit interruptions, and

---

[9] Pliny the Elder says that the Romans expelled their doctors at the same time that the Greeks did theirs.
[10] An allusion to Socrates' condemnation to death.

that men need amusement, I maintain that there is none more innocent than comedy. I have dwelled too long on this matter. Let me finish with the words of a great prince on the comedy, *Tartuffe*.[11]

Eight days after it had been banned, a play called *Scaramouche the Hermit*[12] was performed before the court; and the king, on his way out, said to this great prince: "I should really like to know why the persons who make so much noise about Molière's comedy do not say a word about *Scaramouche*." To which the prince replied, "It is because the comedy of *Scaramouche* makes fun of Heaven and religion, which these gentlemen do not care about at all, but that of Molière makes fun of *them*, and that is what they cannot bear."

THE AUTHOR

Jean-Baptiste Poqueline Molière

First Petition[13]

(Presented to the King on the Comedy of Tartuffe)

Sire,

As the duty of comedy is to correct men by amusing them, I believed that in my occupation I could do nothing better than attack the vices of my age by making them ridiculous; and as hypocrisy is undoubtedly one of the most common, most improper, and most dangerous, I thought, Sire, that I would perform a service for all good men of your kingdom if I wrote a comedy which denounced hypocrites and placed in proper view all of the contrived poses of these incredibly virtuous men, all of the concealed villainies of these counterfeit believers who would trap others with a fraudulent piety and a pretended virtue.

I have written this comedy, Sire, with all the care and caution that the delicacy of the subject demands; and so as to maintain all the more properly the admiration and respect due to truly devout men, I have delineated my character as sharply as I could; I have left no room for doubt; I have removed all that might confuse good with evil, and have used for this painting only the specific colors and essential lines that make one instantly recognize a true and brazen hypocrite.

Nevertheless, all my precautions have been to no avail. Others have taken advantage of the delicacy of your feelings on religious matters, and they have been

---

[11] One of Molière's benefactors who liked the play was the prince de Condeé; de Condeé had *Tartuffe* read to him and also privately performed for him.   [12] A troupe of Italian comedians had just performed the licentious farce, in which a hermit dressed as a monk makes love to a married woman, announcing that *questo e per mortificar la carne* ("this is to mortify the flesh").   [13] The first of the three *petitions* or *placets* to Louis XIV concerning the play. On May 12, 1664, *Tartuffe*—or at least the first three acts roughly as they now stand—was performed at Versailles. A cabal unfavorable to Molière, including the archbishop of Paris, Hardouin de Péréfixe, Queen Mother Anne of Austria, certain influential courtiers, and the Brotherhood or Company of the Holy Sacrament (formed in 1627 to enforce morality), arranged that the play be banned and Molière censured.

able to deceive you on the only side of your character which lies open to deception; your respect for holy things. By underhanded means, the Tartuffes have skillfully gained Your Majesty's favor, and the models have succeeded in eliminating the copy, no matter how innocent it may have been and no matter what resemblance was found between them.

Although the suppression of this work was a serious blow for me, my misfortune was nonetheless softened by the way in which Your Majesty explained his attitude on the matter; and I believed, Sire, that Your Majesty removed any cause I had for complaint, as you were kind enough to declare that you found nothing in this comedy that you would forbid me to present in public.

Yet, despite this glorious declaration of the greatest and most enlightened king in the world, despite the approval of the Papal Legate[14] and of most of our churchmen, all of whom, at private readings of my work, agreed with the views of Your Majesty, despite all this, a book has appeared by a certain priest[15] which boldly contradicts all of these noble judgments. Your Majesty expressed himself in vain, and the Papal Legate and churchmen gave their opinion to no avail: sight unseen, my comedy is diabolical, and so is my brain; I am a devil garbed in flesh and disguised as a man,[16] a libertine, a disbeliever who deserves a punishment that will set an example. It is not enough that fire expiate my crime in public, for that would be letting me off too easily: the generous piety of this good man will not stop there; he will not allow me to find any mercy in the sight of God; he demands that I be damned, and that will settle the matter.

This book, Sire, was presented to Your Majesty; and I am sure that you see for yourself how unpleasant it is for me to be exposed daily to the insults of these gentlemen, what harm these abuses will do my reputation if they must be tolerated, and finally, how important it is for me to clear myself of these false charges and let the public know that my comedy is nothing more than what they want it to be. I will not ask, Sire, for what I need for the sake of my reputation and the innocence of my work: enlightened kings such as you do not need to be told what is wished of them; like God, they see what we need and know better than we what they should give us. It is enough for me to place my interests in Your Majesty's hands, and I respectfully await whatever you may care to command.

(August, 1664)

---

[14] Cardinal Legate Chigi, nephew to Pope Alexander VII, heard a reading of *Tartuffe* at Fontainebleau on August 4, 1664.   [15] Pierre Roullé, the curate of St. Barthélémy, who wrote a scathing attack on the play and sent his book to the king.   [16] Molière took some of these phrases from Roullé.

Second Petition[17]

(Presented to the King in His Camp before the City of Lille, in Flanders)

Sire,

It is bold indeed for me to ask a favor of a great monarch in the midst of his glorious victories; but in my present situation, Sire, where will I find protection anywhere but where I seek it, and to whom can I appeal against the authority of the power that crushes me,[18] if not to the source of power and authority, the just dispenser of absolute law, the sovereign judge and master of all?

My comedy, Sire, has not enjoyed the kindnesses of Your Majesty. All to no avail, I produced it under the title of *The Hypocrite* and disguised the principal character as a man of the world; in vain I gave him a little hat, long hair, a wide collar, a sword, and lace clothing,[19] softened the action and carefully eliminated all that I thought might provide even the shadow of grounds for discontent on the part of the famous models of the portrait I wished to present; nothing did any good. The conspiracy of opposition revived even at mere conjecture of what the play would be like. They found a way of persuading those who in all other matters plainly insist that they are not to be deceived. No sooner did my comedy appear than it was struck down by the very power which should impose respect; and all that I could do to save myself from the fury of this tempest was to say that Your Majesty had given me permission to present the play and I did not think it was necessary to ask this permission of others, since only Your Majesty could have refused it.

I have no doubt, Sire, that the men whom I depict in my comedy will employ every means possible to influence Your Majesty, and will use, as they have used already, those truly good men who are all the more easily deceived because they judge of others by themselves.[20] They know how to display all of their aims in the most favorable light; yet, no matter how pious they may seem, it is surely not the interests of God which stir them; they have proven this often enough in the comedies they have allowed to be performed hundreds of times without making the least objection. Those plays attacked only piety and religion, for which they care very little; but this play attacks and makes fun of them, and that is what they cannot bear. They will never forgive me for unmasking their hypocrisy in the eyes of everyone. And I am sure that they will not neglect to tell Your Majesty that people are shocked by my comedy. But the simple truth, Sire, is that all Paris is shocked only by its ban, that the most scrupulous persons have found its presentation worthwhile, and men

---

[17] On August 5, 1667, *Tartuffe* was performed at the Palais-Royal. The opposition—headed by the first president of parliament—brought in the police, and the play was stopped. Since Louis was campaigning in Flanders, friends of Molière brought the second *placet* to Lille. Louis had always been favorable toward the playwright; in August 1665 Molière's company, the *Troupe de Monsieur* (nominally sponsored by Louis's brother Philippe, duc d'Orléans), had become the *Troupe du Roi*.   [18] President de Lanvignon, in charge of the Paris police.   [19] There is evidence that in 1664 Tartuffe played his role dressed in a cassock, thus allying him more directly to the clergy.   [20] Molière apparently did not know that de Lanvignon had been affiliated with the Company of the Holy Sacrament for the previous ten years.

are astounded that individuals of such known integrity should show so great a deference to people whom everyone should abominate and who are so clearly opposed to the true piety which they profess.

I respectfully await the judgment that Your Majesty will deign to pronounce: but it's certain, Sire, that I need not think of writing comedies if the Tartuffes are triumphant, if they thereby seize the right to persecute me more than ever, and find fault with even the most innocent lines that flow from my pen.

Let your goodness, Sire, give me protection against their envenomed rage, and allow me, at your return from so glorious a campaign, to relieve Your Majesty from the fatigue of his conquests, give him innocent pleasures after such noble accomplishments, and make the monarch laugh who makes all Europe tremble!

(August, 1667)

Third Petition

(Presented to the King)

Sire,

A very honest doctor[21] whose patient I have the honor to be, promises and will legally contract to make me live another thirty years if I can obtain a favor for him from Your Majesty. I told him of his promise that I do not deserve so much, and that I should be glad to help him if he will merely agree not to kill me. This favor, Sire, is a post of canon at your royal chapel of Vincennes, made vacant by death.

May I dare to ask for this favor from Your Majesty on the very day of the glorious resurrection of *Tartuffe*, brought back to life by your goodness? By this first favor I have been reconciled with the devout, and the second will reconcile me with the doctors.[22] Undoubtedly this would be too much grace for me at one time, but perhaps it would not be too much for Your Majesty, and I await your answer to my petition with respectful hope.

(February, 1669)

---

[21] A physician friend, M. de Mauvillain, who helped Molière with some of the medical details of *Le Malade imaginaire*.   [22] Doctors are ridiculed to varying degrees in earlier plays of Molière: *Dom Juan, L'Amour médecin,* and *Le Médecin malgré lui.*

CHARACTERS°

MADAME PERNELLE, ORGON's *mother*
ORGON, ELMIRE's *husband*
ELMIRE, ORGON's *wife*
DAMIS, ORGON's *son,* ELMIRE's *stepson*
MARIANE, ORGON's *daughter,* ELMIRE's *stepdaughter, in love with* VALÈRE
VALÈRE, *in love with* MARIANE
CLÉANTE, ORGON's *brother-in-law*
TARTUFFE, *a hypocrite*
DORINE, MARIANE's *lady's-maid*
M. LOYAL, *a bailiff*
A POLICE OFFICER
FLIPOTE, MME. PERNELLE's *maid*

The SCENE *throughout:* ORGON's *house in Paris*

ACT 1

SCENE I°

MADAME PERNELLE *and* FLIPOTE, *her maid,* ELMIRE, MARIANE, DORINE,
DAMIS, CLÉANTE

MADAME PERNELLE: Come, come, Flipote; it's time I left this place.
ELMIRE: I can't keep up, you walk at such a pace.
MADAME PERNELLE: Don't trouble, child; no need to show me out.
   It's not your manners I'm concerned about.
ELMIRE: We merely pay you the respect we owe.   5
   But, Mother, why this hurry? Must you go?
MADAME PERNELLE: I must. This house appals me. No one in it
   Will pay attention for a single minute.
   I offer good advice, but you won't hear it.
   Children, I take my leave much vexed in spirit.   10
   You all break in and chatter on and on.
   It's like a madhouse with the keeper gone.
DORINE: If . . .
MADAME PERNELLE: Girl, you talk too much, and I'm afraid
   You're far too saucy for a lady's-maid.
   You push in everywhere and have your say.   15

Characters: The name Tartuffe has been traced back to an older word associated with liar or charlatan: *truffer,* "to deceive" or "to cheat." Then there was also the Italian actor Tartufo, physically deformed and truffle shaped. Most of the other names are typical of this genre of court comedy and possess rather elegant connotations of pastoral and *bergerie.* Dorine would be a *demoiselle de compagne* and not a mere maid, that is, a female companion to Mariane of roughly the same social status. This in part accounts for the liberties she takes in conversation with Orgon, Madame Pernelle, and others. Her name is short for Théodorine.   **I.i. Scene:** In French drama, the scene changes every time a character enters or exits.

DAMIS: But . . .

MADAME PERNELLE: You, boy, grow more foolish every day.
    To think my grandson should be such a dunce!
    I've said a hundred times, if I've said it once,
    That if you keep the course on which you've started,
    You'll leave your worthy father broken-hearted.   20

MARIANE: I think . . .

MADAME PERNELLE: And you, his sister, seem so pure,
    So shy, so innocent, and so demure.
    But you know what they say about still waters.
    I pity parents with secretive daughters.

ELMIRE: Now, Mother . . .

MADAME PERNELLE: And as for you, child, let me add   25
    That your behavior is extremely bad,
    And a poor example for these children, too.
    Their dear, dead mother did far better than you.
    You're much too free with money, and I'm distressed
    To see you so elaborately dressed.   30
    When it's one's husband that one aims to please,
    One has no need of costly fripperies.

CLÉANTE: Oh, Madam, really . . .

MADAME PERNELLE: You are her brother, Sir,
    And I respect and love you; yet if I were
    My son, this lady's good and pious spouse,   35
    I wouldn't make you welcome in my house.
    You're full of worldly counsels which, I fear,
    Aren't suitable for decent folk to hear.
    I've spoken bluntly, Sir; but it behooves us
    Not to mince words when righteous fervor moves us.   40

DAMIS: Your man Tartuffe is full of holy speeches . . .

MADAME PERNELLE: And practises precisely what he preaches.
    He's a fine man, and should be listened to.
    I will not hear him mocked by fools like you.

DAMIS: Good God! Do you expect me to submit   45
    To the tyranny of that carping hypocrite?
    Must we forgo all joys and satisfactions
    Because that bigot censures all our actions?

DORINE: To hear him talk—and he talks all the time—
    There's nothing one can do that's not a crime.   50
    He rails at everything, your dear Tartuffe.

MADAME PERNELLE: Whatever he reproves deserves reproof.
    He's out to save your souls, and all of you
    Must love him, as my son would have you do.

DAMIS: Ah no, Grandmother, I could never take   55
    To such a rascal, even for my father's sake.
    That's how I feel, and I shall not dissemble.

His every action makes me seethe and tremble
With helpless anger, and I have no doubt
That he and I will shortly have it out.   60
DORINE: Surely it is a shame and a disgrace
To see this man usurp the master's place—
To see this beggar who, when first he came,
Had not a shoe or shoestring to his name
So far forget himself that he behaves   65
As if the house were his, and we his slaves.
MADAME PERNELLE: Well, mark my words, your souls would fare far better
If you obeyed his precepts to the letter.
DORINE: You see him as a saint. I'm far less awed;
In fact, I see right through him. He's a fraud.   70
MADAME PERNELLE: Nonsense!
DORINE: His man Laurent's the same, or worse;
I'd not trust either with a penny purse.
MADAME PERNELLE: I can't say what his servant's morals may be;
His own great goodness I can guarantee.
You all regard him with distaste and fear   75
Because he tells you what you're loath to hear,
Condemns your sins, points out your moral flaws,
And humbly strives to further Heaven's cause.
DORINE: If sin is all that bothers him, why is it
He's so upset when folk drop in to visit?   80
Is Heaven so outraged by a social call
That he must prophesy against us all?
I'll tell you what I think: if you ask me,
He's jealous of my mistress' company.
MADAME PERNELLE: Rubbish!
(*To* ELMIRE.)   He's not alone, child, in complaining   85
Of all of your promiscuous entertaining.
Why, the whole neighborhood's upset, I know,
By all these carriages that come and go,
With crowds of guests parading in and out
And noisy servants loitering about.   90
In all of this, I'm sure there's nothing vicious;
But why give people cause to be suspicious?
CLÉANTE: They need no cause; they'll talk in any case.
Madam, this world would be a joyless place
If, fearing what malicious tongues might say,   95
We locked our doors and turned our friends away.
And even if one did so dreary a thing,
D' you think those tongues would cease their chattering?
One can't fight slander; it's a losing battle;
Let us instead ignore their tittle-tattle.   100
Let's strive to live by conscience clear decrees,

And let the gossips gossip as they please.
DORINE: If there is talk against us, I know the source:
It's Daphne and her little husband, of course.
Those who have greatest cause for guilt and shame   105
Are quickest to besmirch a neighbor's name.
When there's a chance for libel, they never miss it;
When something can be made to seem illicit
They're off at once to spread the joyous news,
Adding to fact what fantasies they choose.   110
By talking up their neighbor's indiscretions
They seek to camouflage their own transgressions,
Hoping that others' innocent affairs
Will lend a hue of innocence to theirs,
Or that their own black guilt will come to seem   115
Part of a general shady color-scheme.
MADAME PERNELLE: All that is quite irrelevant. I doubt
That anyone's more virtuous and devout
Than dear Orante; and I'm informed that she
Condemns your mode of life most vehemently.   120
DORINE: Oh, yes, she's strict, devout, and has no taint
Of worldliness; in short, she seems a saint.
But it was time which taught her that disguise,
She's thus because she can't be otherwise.
So long as her attractions could enthrall,   125
She flounced and flirted and enjoyed it all,
But now that they're no longer what they were
She quits a world which fast is quitting her,
And wears a veil of virtue to conceal
Her bankrupt beauty and her lost appeal.   130
That's what becomes of old coquettes today:
Distressed when all their lovers fall away,
They see no recourse but to play the prude,
And so confer a style on solitude.
Thereafter, they're severe with everyone,   135
Condemning all our actions, pardoning none,
And claiming to be pure, austere, and zealous
When, if the truth were known, they're merely jealous,
And cannot bear to see another know
The pleasures time has forced them to forgo.   140
MADAME PERNELLE: (*Initially to* ELMIRE.)
That sort of talk° is what you like to hear;
Therefore you'd have us all keep still, my dear,

---

141. sort of talk: In the original, a reference to a collection of novels about chivalry found in *La Biblio-thèque bleue* (The blue library), written for children.

While Madam rattles on the livelong day.
Nevertheless, I mean to have my say.
I tell you that you're blest to have Tartuffe   145
Dwelling, as my son's guest, beneath this roof;
That Heaven has sent him to forestall its wrath
By leading you, once more, to the true path;
That all he reprehends is reprehensible,
And that you'd better heed him, and be sensible.   150
These visits, balls, and parties in which you revel
Are nothing but inventions of the Devil.
One never hears a word that's edifying:
Nothing but chaff and foolishness and lying,
As well as vicious gossip in which one's neighbor   155
Is cut to bits with épée, foil, and saber.
People of sense are driven half-insane
At such affairs, where noise and folly reign
And reputations perish thick and fast.
As a wise preacher said on Sunday last,   160
Parties are Towers of Babylon,° because
The guests all babble on with never a pause;
And then he told a story which, I think . . .
(*To* CLÉANTE.) I heard that laugh, Sir, and I saw that wink!
Go find your silly friends and laugh some more!   165
Enough; I'm going; don't show me to the door.
I leave this household much dismayed and vexed;
I cannot say when I shall see you next.

       (*Slapping* FLIPOTE.)

Wake up, don't stand there gaping into space!
I'll slap some sense into that stupid face.   170
Move, move, you slut.

    SCENE II

    CLÉANTE, DORINE

CLÉANTE: I think I'll stay behind;
  I want no further pieces of her mind.
  How that old lady . . .
DORINE: Oh, what wouldn't she say
  If she could hear you speak of her that way!
  She'd thank you for the *lady*, but I'm sure   5
  She'd find the *old* a little premature.
CLÉANTE: My, what a scene she made, and what a din!

---

161. Towers of Babylon: Tower of Babel. Madame Pernelle's malapropism is the cause of Cléante's laughter. **I.ii.**

And how this man Tartuffe has taken her in!
DORINE: Yes, but her son is even worse deceived;
  His folly must be seen to be believed.   10
  In the late troubles,° he played an able part
  And served his king with wise and loyal heart,
  But he's quite lost his senses since he fell
  Beneath Tartuffe's infatuating spell.
  He calls him brother, and loves him as his life,   15
  Preferring him to mother, child, or wife.
  In him and him alone will he confide;
  He's made him his confessor and his guide;
  He pets and pampers him with love more tender
  Than any pretty maiden could engender,   20
  Gives him the place of honor when they dine,
  Delights to see him gorging like a swine,
  Stuffs him with dainties till his guts distend,
  And when he belches, cries "God bless you, friend!"
  In short, he's mad; he worships him; he dotes;   25
  His deeds he marvels at, his words, he quotes,
  Thinking each act a miracle, each word
  Oracular as those that Moses heard.
  Tartuffe, much pleased to find so easy a victim,
  Has in a hundred ways beguiled and tricked him,   30
  Milked him of money, and with his permission
  Established here a sort of Inquisition.
  Even Laurent, his lackey, dares to give
  Us arrogant advice on how to live;
  He sermonizes us in thundering tones   35
  And confiscates our ribbons and colognes.
  Last week he tore a kerchief into pieces
  Because he found it pressed in a *Life of Jesus:*
  He said it was a sin to juxtapose
  Unholy vanities and holy prose.   40

SCENE III

ELMIRE, MARIANE, DAMIS, CLÉANTE, DORINE

ELMIRE (*To* CLÉANTE.):   You did well not to follow; she stood in the door
  And said *verbatim* all she'd said before.
  I saw my husband coming. I think I'd best
  Go upstairs now, and take a little rest.

I.ii. 11. late troubles: A series of political disturbances during the minority of Louis XIV. Specifically these consisted of the *Fronde* ("opposition") of the Parlement (1648–49) and the *Fronde* of the Princes (1650–53). Orgon is depicted as supporting Louis XIV in these outbreaks and their resolution.

CLÉANTE: I'll wait and greet him here; then I must go.   5
  I've really only time to say hello.
DAMIS: Sound him about my sister's wedding, please.
  I think Tartuffe's against it, and that he's
  Been urging Father to withdraw his blessing.
  As you well know, I'd find that most distressing.   10
  Unless my sister and Valère can marry,
  My hopes to wed *his* sister will miscarry,
  And I'm determined . . .
DORINE: He's coming.

SCENE IV

ORGON, CLÉANTE, DORINE

ORGON: Ah, Brother, good-day.
CLÉANTE: Well, welcome back. I'm sorry I can't stay.
  How was the country? Blooming, I trust, and green?
ORGON: Excuse me, Brother; just one moment.
  (*To* DORINE.)   Dorine . . .
  (*To* CLÉANTE.) To put my mind at rest, I always learn   5
  The household news the moment I return.
  (*To* DORINE.) Has all been well, these two days I've been gone?
  How are the family? What's been going on?
DORINE: Your wife, two days ago, had a bad fever,
  And a fierce headache which refused to leave her.   10
ORGON: Ah. And Tartuffe?
DORINE: Tartuffe? Why, he's round and red.
  Bursting with health, and excellently fed.
ORGON: Poor fellow!
DORINE: That night, the mistress was unable
  To take a single bite at the dinner-table.
  Her headache-pains, she said, were simply hellish.   15
ORGON: Ah. And Tartuffe?
DORINE: He ate his meal with relish,
  And zealously devoured in her presence
  A leg of mutton and a brace of pheasants.
ORGON: Poor fellow!
DORINE: Well, the pains continued strong,
  And so she tossed and tossed the whole night long,   20
  Now icy-cold, now burning like a flame.
  We sat beside her bed till morning came.
ORGON: Ah. And Tartuffe?
DORINE: Why, having eaten, he rose
  And sought his room, already in a doze,
  Got into his warm bed, and snored away   25

In perfect peace until the break of day.

ORGON: Poor fellow!

DORINE: After much ado, we talked her
Into dispatching someone for the doctor.
He bled her, and the fever quickly fell.

ORGON: Ah. And Tartuffe?

DORINE: He bore it very well.   30
To keep his cheerfulness at any cost,
And make up for the blood Madame had lost,
He drank, at lunch, four beakers full of port.

ORGON: Poor fellow.

DORINE: Both are doing well, in short.
I'll go and tell Madame that you've expressed   35
Keen sympathy and anxious interest.

SCENE V

ORGON, CLÉANTE

CLÉANTE: That girl was laughing in your face, and though
I've no wish to offend you, even so
I'm bound to say that she had some excuse.
How can you possibly be such a goose?
Are you so dazed by this man's hocus-pocus   5
That all the world, save him, is out of focus?
You've given him clothing, shelter, food, and care;
Why must you also . . .

ORGON: Brother, stop right there.
You do not know the man of whom you speak.

CLÉANTE: I grant you that. But my judgment's not so weak   10
That I can't tell, by his effect on others . . .

ORGON: Ah, when you meet him, you two will be like brothers!
There's been no loftier soul since time began.
He is a man who . . . a man who . . . an excellent man.
To keep his precepts is to be reborn,   15
And view this dunghill of a world with scorn.
Yes, thanks to him I'm a changed man indeed.
Under his tutelage my soul's been freed
From earthly loves, and every human tie:
My mother, children, brother, and wife could die,   20
And I'd not feel a single moment's pain.

CLÉANTE: That's a fine sentiment, Brother; most humane.

ORGON: Oh, had you seen Tartuffe as I first knew him,
Your heart, like mine, would have surrendered to him.
He used to come into our church each day   25
And humbly kneel nearby, and start to pray.

He'd draw the eyes of everybody there
By the deep fervor of his heartfelt prayer;
He'd sigh and weep, and sometimes with a sound
Of rapture he would bend and kiss the ground;   30
And when I rose to go, he'd run before
To offer me holy-water at the door.
His serving-man, no less devout than he,
Informed me of his master's poverty;
I gave him gifts, but in his humbleness   35
He'd beg me every time to give him less.
"Oh, that's too much," he'd cry, "too much by twice!
I don't deserve it. The half, Sir, would suffice."
And when I wouldn't take it back, he'd share
Half of it with the poor, right then and there.   40
At length, Heaven prompted me to take him in
To dwell with us, and free our souls from sin.
He guides our lives, and to protect my honor
Stays by my wife, and keeps an eye upon her;
He tells me whom she sees, and all she does,   45
And seems more jealous than I ever was!
And how austere he is! Why, he can detect
A mortal sin where you would least suspect;
In smallest trifles, he's extremely strict.
Last week, his conscience was severely pricked   50
Because, while praying, he had caught a flea
And killed it, so he felt, too wrathfully.°
CLÉANTE: Good God, man! Have you lost your common sense—
Or is this all some joke at my expense?
How can you stand there and in all sobriety . . .   55
ORGON: Brother, your language savors of impiety.
Too much free-thinking's made your faith unsteady,
And as I've warned you many times already,
'Twill get you into trouble before you're through.
CLÉANTE: So I've been told before by dupes like you: 60
Being blind, you'd have all others blind as well;
The clear-eyed man you call an infidel,
And he who sees through humbug and pretense
Is charged, by you, with want of reverence.
Spare me your warnings, Brother; I have no fear   65
Of speaking out, for you and Heaven to hear,
Against affected zeal and pious knavery.

---

52. **too wrathfully:** In the *Golden Legend (Legenda sanctorum)*, a popular collection of the lives of the
saints written in the 13th century, it is said of St. Marcarius the Elder (died 390) that he dwelt naked in
the desert for six months, a penance he felt appropriate for having killed a flea.

There's true and false in piety, as in bravery,
And just as those whose courage shines the most
In battle, are the least inclined to boast, 70
So those whose hearts are truly pure and lowly
Don't make a flashy show of being holy.
There's a vast difference, so it seems to me,
Between true piety and hypocrisy:
How do you fail to see it, may I ask? 75
Is not a face quite different from a mask?
Cannot sincerity and cunning art,
Reality and semblance, be told apart?
Are scarecrows just like men, and do you hold
That a false coin is just as good as gold? 80
Ah, Brother, man's a strangely fashioned creature
Who seldom is content to follow Nature,
But recklessly pursues his inclination
Beyond the narrow bounds of moderation,
And often, by transgressing Reason's laws, 85
Perverts a lofty aim or noble cause.
A passing observation, but it applies.
ORGON: I see, dear Brother, that you're profoundly wise;
You harbor all the insight of the age.
You are our one clear mind, our only sage, 90
The era's oracle, its Cato° too,
And all mankind are fools compared to you.
CLÉANTE: Brother, I don't pretend to be a sage,
Nor have I all the wisdom of the age.
There's just one insight I would dare to claim: 95
I know that true and false are not the same;
And just as there is nothing I more revere
Than a soul whose faith is steadfast and sincere,
Nothing that I more cherish and admire
Than honest zeal and true religious fire, 100
So there is nothing that I find more base
Than specious piety's dishonest face—
Than these bold mountebanks, these histrios
Whose impious mummeries and hollow shows
Exploit our love of Heaven, and make a jest 105
Of all that men think holiest and best;
These calculating souls who offer prayers
Not to their Maker, but as public wares,
And seek to buy respect and reputation
With lifted eyes and sighs of exaltation; 110

91. Cato: Roman statesman (95–46 B.C.) with an enduring reputation for honesty and incorruptibility.

These charlatans, I say, whose pilgrim souls
Proceed, by way of Heaven, toward earthly goals,
Who weep and pray and swindle and extort,
Who preach the monkish life, but haunt the court,
Who make their zeal the partner of their vice—   115
Such men are vengeful, sly, and cold as ice,
And when there is an enemy to defame
They cloak their spite in fair religion's name,
Their private spleen and malice being made
To seem a high and virtuous crusade,   120
Until, to mankind's reverent applause,
They crucify their foe in Heaven's cause.
Such knaves are all too common; yet, for the wise,
True piety isn't hard to recognize,
And, happily, these present times provide us   125
With bright examples to instruct and guide us.
Consider Ariston and Périandre;
Look at Oronte, Alcidamas, Clitandre°;
Their virtue is acknowledged; who could doubt it?
But you won't hear them beat the drum about it.   130
They're never ostentatious, never vain,
And their religion's moderate and humane;
It's not their way to criticize and chide:
They think censoriousness a mark of pride,
And therefore, letting others preach and rave,   135
They show, by deeds, how Christians should behave.
They think no evil of their fellow man,
But judge of him as kindly as they can.
They don't intrigue and wangle and conspire;
To lead a good life is their one desire;   140
The sinner wakes no rancorous hate in them;
It is the sin alone which they condemn;
Nor do they try to show a fiercer zeal
For Heaven's cause than Heaven itself could feel.
These men I honor, these men I advocate   145
As models for us all to emulate.
Your man is not their sort at all, I fear:
And, while your praise of him is quite sincere,
I think that you've been dreadfully deluded.

ORGON: Now then, dear Brother, is your speech concluded?   150
CLÉANTE: Why, yes.
ORGON: Your servant, Sir.

     (*He turns to go.*)

128. Clitandre: Vaguely Greek and Roman names derived from the elegant literature of the day.

CLÉANTE: No, Brother; wait.
  There's one more matter. You agreed of late
  That young Valère might have your daughter's hand.
ORGON: I did.
CLÉANTE: And set the date, I understand.
ORGON: Quite so.
CLÉANTE: You've now postponed it; is that true?   155
ORGON: No doubt.
CLÉANTE: The match no longer pleases you?
ORGON: Who knows?
CLÉANTE: D'you mean to go back on your word?
ORGON: I won't say that.
CLÉANTE: Has anything occurred
  Which might entitle you to break your pledge?
ORGON: Perhaps.
CLÉANTE: Why must you hem, and haw, and hedge?   160
  The boy asked me to sound you in this affair . . .
ORGON: It's been a pleasure.
CLÉANTE: But what shall I tell Valère?
ORGON: Whatever you like.
CLÉANTE: But what have you decided?
  What are your plans?
ORGON: I plan, Sir, to be guided
  By Heaven's will.
CLÉANTE: Come, Brother, don't talk rot.   165
  You've given Valère your word; will you keep it, or not?
ORGON: Good day.
CLÉANTE: This looks like poor Valère's undoing;
  I'll go and warn him that there's trouble brewing.

ACT II

SCENE I

ORGON, MARIANE

ORGON: Mariane.
MARIANE: Yes, Father?
ORGON: A word with you; come here.
MARIANE: What are you looking for?
ORGON (*Peering into a small closet.*):   Eavesdroppers, dear.
  I'm making sure we shan't be overheard.
  Someone in there could catch our every word.
  Ah, good, we're safe. Now, Mariane, my child,   5
  You're a sweet girl who's tractable and mild,
  Whom I hold dear, and think most highly of.

MARIANE: I'm deeply grateful, Father, for your love.

ORGON: That's well said, Daughter; and you can repay me
  If, in all things, you'll cheerfully obey me.   10

MARIANE: To please you, Sir, is what delights me best.

ORGON: Good, good. Now, what d'you think of Tartuffe, our guest?

MARIANE: I, Sir?

ORGON: Yes. Weigh your answer; think it through.

MARIANE: Oh, dear. I'll say whatever you wish me to.

ORGON: That's wisely said, my Daughter. Say of him, then,   15
  That he's the very worthiest of men,
  And that you're fond of him, and would rejoice
  In being his wife, if that should be my choice.
  Well?

MARIANE: What?

ORGON: What's that?

MARIANE: I . . .

ORGON: Well?

MARIANE: Forgive me, pray.

ORGON: Did you not hear me?

MARIANE: Of *whom*, Sir, must I say   20
  That I am fond of him, and would rejoice
  In being his wife, if that should be your choice?

ORGON: Why, of Tartuffe.

MARIANE: But, Father, that's false, you know.
  Why would you have me say what isn't so?

ORGON: Because I am resolved it shall be true.   25
  That it's my wish should be enough for you.

MARIANE: You can't mean, Father . . .

ORGON: Yes, Tartuffe shall be
  Allied by marriage° to this family,
  And he's to be your husband, is that clear?
  It's a father's privilege . . .   30

SCENE II

DORINE, ORGON, MARIANE

ORGON (*To* DORINE.):   What are you doing in here?
 Is curiosity so fierce a passion
 With you, that you must eavesdrop in this fashion?

DORINE: There's lately been a rumor going about—
 Based on some hunch or chance remark, no doubt—   5

II.i. 28. Allied by marriage: This assertion is important and more than a mere device in the plot of the day. The second *placet* or petition insists that Tartuffe be costumed as a layman, and Orgon's plan for him to marry again asserts Tartuffe's position in the laity. In the 1664 version of the play Tartuffe had been dressed in a cassock suggestive of the priesthood, and Molière was now anxious to avoid any suggestion of this kind.

That you mean Mariane to wed Tartuffe.
I've laughed it off, of course, as just a spoof.
ORGON: You find it so incredible?
DORINE: Yes, I do.
   I won't accept that story, even from you.
ORGON: Well, you'll believe it when the thing is done.   10
DORINE: Yes, yes, of course. Go on and have your fun.
ORGON: I've never been more serious in my life.
DORINE: Ha!
ORGON: Daughter, I mean it; you're to be his wife.
DORINE: No, don't believe your father; it's all a hoax.
ORGON: See here, young woman . . .
DORINE: Come, Sir, no more jokes;   15
   You can't fool us.
ORGON: How dare you talk that way?
DORINE: All right, then; we believe you, sad to say.
   But how a man like you, who looks so wise
   And wears a moustache of such splendid size,
   Can be so foolish as to . . .
ORGON: Silence, please!   20
   My girl, you take too many liberties.
   I'm master here, as you must not forget.
DORINE: Do let's discuss this calmly; don't be upset.
   You can't be serious, Sir, about this plan.
   What should that bigot want with Mariane?   25
   Praying and fasting ought to keep him busy.
   And then, in terms of wealth and rank, what is he?
   Why should a man of property like you
   Pick out a beggar son-in-law?
ORGON: That will do.
   Speak of his poverty with reverence.   30
   His is a pure and saintly indigence
   Which far transcends all worldly pride and pelf.
   He lost his fortune, as he says himself,
   Because he cared for Heaven alone, and so
   Was careless of his interests here below.   35
   I mean to get him out of his present straits
   And help him to recover his estates—
   Which, in his part of the world, have no small fame.
   Poor though he is, he's a gentleman just the same.
DORINE: Yes, so he tells us; and, Sir, it seems to me   40
   Such pride goes very ill with piety.
   A man whose spirit spurns this dungy earth
   Ought not to brag of lands and noble birth;
   Such worldly arrogance will hardly square

With meek devotion and the life of prayer.   45
. . . But this approach, I see, has drawn a blank;
Let's speak, then, of his person, not his rank.
Doesn't it seem to you a trifle grim
To give a girl like her to a man like him?
When two are so ill-suited, can't you see   50
What the sad consequence is bound to be?
A young girl's virtue is imperilled, Sir,
When such a marriage is imposed on her;
For if one's bridegroom isn't to one's taste,
It's hardly an inducement to be chaste,   55
And many a man with horns upon his brow
Has made his wife the thing that she is now.
It's hard to be a faithful wife, in short,
To certain husbands of a certain sort,
And he who gives his daughter to a man she hates   60
Must answer for her sins at Heaven's gates.
Think, Sir, before you play so risky a role.

ORGON: This servant-girl presumes to save my soul!

DORINE: You would do well to ponder what I've said.

ORGON: Daughter, we'll disregard this dunderhead.   65
Just trust your father's judgment. Oh, I'm aware
That I once promised you to young Valère;
But now I hear he gambles, which greatly shocks me;
What's more, I've doubts about his orthodoxy.
His visits to church, I note, are very few.   70

DORINE: Would you have him go at the same hours as you,
And kneel nearby, to be sure of being seen?

ORGON: I can dispense with such remarks, Dorine.
(*To* MARIANE.) Tartuffe, however, is sure of Heaven's blessing,
And that's the only treasure worth possessing.   75
This match will bring you joys beyond all measure;
Your cup will overflow with every pleasure;
You two will interchange your faithful loves
Like two sweet cherubs, or two turtledoves.
No harsh word shall be heard, no frown be seen,   80
And he shall make you happy as a queen.

DORINE: And she'll make him a cuckold, just wait and see.

ORGON: What language!

DORINE: Oh, he's a man of destiny;
He's *made* for horns, and what the stars demand
Your daughter's virtue surely can't withstand.   85

ORGON: Don't interrupt me further. Why can't you learn
That certain things are none of your concern?

DORINE: It's for your own sake that I interfere.

(*She repeatedly interrupts* ORGON *just as he is turning to speak to his daughter.*)

ORGON: Most kind of you. Now, hold your tongue, d'you hear?
DORINE: If I didn't love you . . .
ORGON: Spare me your affection.   90
DORINE: I'll love you, Sir, in spite of your objection.
ORGON: Blast!
DORINE: I can't bear, Sir, for your honor's sake,
   To let you make this ludicrous mistake.
ORGON: You mean to go on talking?
DORINE: If I didn't protest
   This sinful marriage, my conscience couldn't rest.   95
ORGON: If you don't hold your tongue, you little shrew . . .
DORINE: What, lost your temper? A pious man like you?
ORGON: Yes! Yes! You talk and talk. I'm maddened by it.
   Once and for all, I tell you to be quiet.
DORINE: Well, I'll be quiet. But I'll be thinking hard.   100
ORGON: Think all you like, but you had better guard
   That saucy tongue of yours, or I'll . . .
   (*Turning back to* MARIANE.)   Now, child,
   I've weighed this matter fully.
DORINE (*Aside.*):   It drives me wild
   That I can't speak.

      (ORGON *turns his head, and she is silent.*)

ORGON: Tartuffe is no young dandy,
   But, still, his person . . .
DORINE: (*Aside.*) Is as sweet as candy.   105
ORGON: Is such that, even if you shouldn't care
   For his other merits . . .

      (*He turns and stands facing* DORINE, *arms crossed.*)

DORINE: (*Aside.*) They'll make a lovely pair.
   If I were she, no man would marry me
   Against my inclination, and go scot-free.
   He'd learn, before the wedding-day was over,   110
   How readily a wife can find a lover.
ORGON (*To* DORINE.):   It seems you treat my orders as a joke.
DORINE: Why, what's the matter? 'Twas not to you I spoke.
ORGON: What *were* you doing?
DORINE: Talking to myself, that's all.
ORGON: Ah! (*Aside.*) One more bit of impudence and gall,   115
   And I shall give her a good slap in the face.

(He puts himself in position to slap her; DORINE, *whenever he glances at her, stands immobile silent.)*

Daughter, you shall accept, and with good grace,
The husband I've selected . . . Your wedding-day . . .
(To DORINE.) Why don't you talk to yourself?

DORINE: I've nothing to say.

ORGON: Come, just one word.

DORINE: No thank you, Sir. I pass.   120

ORGON: Come, speak; I'm waiting.

DORINE: I'd not be such an ass.

ORGON: *(Turning to* MARIANE.)
In short, dear Daughter, I mean to be obeyed,
And you must bow to the sound choice I've made.

DORINE *(Moving away.)*:   I'd not wed such a monster, even in jest.

*(*ORGON *attempts to slap her, but misses.)*

ORGON: Daughter, that maid of yours is a thorough pest;   125
She makes me sinfully annoyed and nettled.
I can't speak further; my nerves are too unsettled.
She's so upset me by her insolent talk,
I'll calm myself by going for a walk.

SCENE III

DORINE, MARIANE

DORINE *(Returning.)*:   Well, have you lost your tongue, girl? Must I play
Your part, and say the lines you ought to say?
Faced with a fate so hideous and absurd,
Can you not utter one dissenting word?

MARIANE: What good would it do? A father's power is great.   5

DORINE: Resist him now, or it will be too late.

MARIANE: But . . .

DORINE: Tell him one cannot love at a father's whim;
That you shall marry for yourself, not him;
That since it's you who are to be the bride,
It's you, not he, who must be satisfied;   10
And that if his Tartuffe is so sublime,
He's free to marry him at any time.

MARIANE: I've bowed so long to Father's strict control,
I couldn't oppose him now, to save my soul.

DORINE: Come, come, Mariane. Do listen to reason, won't you?   15
Valère has asked your hand. Do you love him, or don't you?

MARIANE: Oh, how unjust of you! What can you mean
By asking such a question, dear Dorine?

You know the depth of my affection for him;
I've told you a hundred times how I adore him.   20
DORINE: I don't believe in everything I hear;
   Who knows if your professions were sincere?
MARIANE: They were, Dorine, and you do me wrong to doubt it;
   Heaven knows that I've been all too frank about it.
DORINE: You love him, then?
MARIANE: Oh, more than I can express.   25
DORINE: And he, I take it, cares for you no less?
MARIANE: I think so.
DORINE: And you both, with equal fire,
   Burn to be married?
MARIANE: That is our one desire.
DORINE: What of Tartuffe, then? What of your father's plan?
MARIANE: I'll kill myself, if I'm forced to wed that man.   30
DORINE: I hadn't thought of that recourse. How splendid!
   Just die, and all your troubles will be ended!
   A fine solution. Oh, it maddens me
   To hear you talk in that self-pitying key.
MARIANE: Dorine, how harsh you are! It's most unfair.   35
   You have no sympathy for my despair.
DORINE: I've none at all for people who talk drivel
   And, faced with difficulties, whine and snivel.
MARIANE: No doubt I'm timid, but it would be wrong . . .
DORINE: True love requires a heart that's firm and strong.   40
MARIANE: I'm strong in my affection for Valère,
   But coping with my father is his affair.
DORINE: But if your father's brain has grown so cracked
   Over his dear Tartuffe that he can retract
   His blessing, though your wedding-day was named,   45
   It's surely not Valère who's to be blamed.
MARIANE: If I defied my father, as you suggest,
   Would it not seem unmaidenly, at best?
   Shall I defend my love at the expense
   Of brazenness and disobedience?   50
   Shall I parade my heart's desires, and flaunt . . .
DORINE: No, I ask nothing of you. Clearly you want
   To be Madame Tartuffe, and I feel bound
   Not to oppose a wish so very sound.
   What right have I to criticize the match?   55
   Indeed, my dear, the man's a brilliant catch.
   Monsieur Tartuffe! Now, there's a man of weight!
   Yes, yes, Monsieur Tartuffe, I'm bound to state,
   Is quite a person; that's not to be denied;
   'Twill be no little thing to be his bride.   60

The world already rings with his renown;
He's a great noble—in his native town;
His ears are red, he has a pink complexion,
And all in all, he'll suit you to perfection.
MARIANE: Dear God!
DORINE: Oh, how triumphant you will feel   65
At having caught a husband so ideal!
MARIANE: Oh, do stop teasing, and use your cleverness
To get me out of this appalling mess.
Advise me, and I'll do whatever you say.
DORINE: Ah no, a dutiful daughter must obey   70
Her father, even if he weds her to an ape.
You've a bright future; why struggle to escape?
Tartuffe will take you back where his family lives,
To a small town aswarm with relatives—
Uncles and cousins whom you'll be charmed to meet.   75
You'll be received at once by the elite,
Calling upon the bailiff's° wife, no less—
Even, perhaps, upon the mayoress,°
Who'll sit you down in the *best* kitchen chair.°
Then, once a year, you'll dance at the village fair   80
To the drone of bagpipes—two of them, in fact—
And see a puppet-show, or an animal act.°
Your husband . . .
MARIANE: Oh, you turn my blood to ice!
Stop torturing me, and give me your advice.
DORINE (*Threatening to go.*):
Your servant, Madam.
MARIANE: Dorine, I beg of you . . .   85
DORINE: No, you deserve it; marriage must go through.
MARIANE: Dorine!
DORINE: No.
MARIANE: Not Tartuffe! You know I think him . . .
DORINE: Tartuffe's your cup of tea, and you shall drink him.
MARIANE: I've always told you everything, and relied . . .
DORINE: No. You deserve to be tartuffified.   90
MARIANE: Well, since you mock me and refuse to care,
I'll henceforth seek my solace in despair:
Despair shall be my counsellor and friend,

II.iii. 77. bailiff's: A high-ranking official in the judiciary, not simply a sheriff's deputy as today.   **78. mayoress:** The wife of a tax collector (*élue*), an important official controlling imports, elected by the Estates General.   **79. kitchen chair:** In elegant society of Molière's day, there was a hierarchy of seats, and the use of each was determined by rank. The seats descended from *fauteuils* to *chaises, perroquets, tabourets,* and *pliants*. Thus Mariane would get the lowest seat in the room.   **82. animal act:** In the original, *fagotin,* literally "a monkey dressed up in a man's clothing."

And help me bring my sorrows to an end.   (*She starts to leave.*)

DORINE: There now, come back; my anger has subsided.   95
    You do deserve some pity, I've decided.

MARIANE: Dorine, if Father makes me undergo
    This dreadful martyrdom, I'll die, I know.

DORINE: Don't fret; it won't be difficult to discover
    Some plan of action . . . But here's Valère, your lover.   100

SCENE IV

VALÈRE, MARIANE, DORINE

VALÈRE: Madam, I've just received some wondrous news
    Regarding which I'd like to hear your views.

MARIANE: What news?

VALÈRE: You're marrying Tartuffe.

MARIANE: I find
    That Father does have such a match in mind.

VALÈRE: Your father, Madam . . .

MARIANE: . . . has just this minute said   5
    That it's Tartuffe he wishes me to wed.

VALÈRE: Can he be serious?

MARIANE: Oh, indeed he can;
    He's clearly set his heart upon the plan.

VALÈRE: And what position do you propose to take,
    Madam?

MARIANE: Why—I don't know.

VALÈRE: For heaven's sake—   10
    You don't know?

MARIANE: No.

VALÈRE: Well, well!

MARIANE: Advise me, do.

VALÈRE: Marry the man. That's my advice to you.

MARIANE: That's your advice?

VALÈRE: Yes.

MARIANE: Truly?

VALÈRE: Oh, absolutely.
    You couldn't choose more wisely, more astutely.

MARIANE: Thanks for this counsel; I'll follow it, of course.   15

VALÈRE: Do, do; I'm sure 'twill cost you no remorse.

MARIANE: To give it didn't cause your heart to break.

VALÈRE: I gave it, Madam, only for your sake.

MARIANE: And it's for your sake that I take it, Sir.

DORINE: (*Withdrawing to the rear of the stage.*)
    Let's see which fool will prove the stubborner.   20

VALÈRE: So! I am nothing to you, and it was flat
   Deception when you . . .
MARIANE: Please, enough of that.
   You've told me plainly that I should agree
   To wed the man my father's chosen for me,
   And since you've deigned to counsel me so wisely,   25
   I promise, Sir, to do as you advise me.
VALÈRE: Ah, no, 'twas not by me that you were swayed.
   No, your decision was already made;
   Though now, to save appearances, you protest
   That you're betraying me at my behest.   30
MARIANE: Just as you say.
VALÈRE: Quite so. And I now see
   That you were never truly in love with me.
MARIANE: Alas, you're free to think so if you choose.
VALÈRE: I choose to think so, and here's a bit of news:
   You've spurned my hand, but I know where to turn   35
   For kinder treatment, as you shall quickly learn.
MARIANE: I'm sure you do. Your noble qualities
   Inspire affection . . .
VALÈRE: Forget my qualities, please.
   They don't inspire you overmuch, I find.
   But there's another lady I have in mind   40
   Whose sweet and generous nature will not scorn
   To compensate me for the loss I've borne.
MARIANE: I'm no great loss, and I'm sure that you'll transfer
   Your heart quite painlessly from me to her.
VALÈRE: I'll do my best to take it in my stride.   45
   The pain I feel at being cast aside
   Time and forgetfulness may put an end to.
   Or if I can't forget, I shall pretend to.
   No self-respecting person is expected
   To go on loving once he's been rejected.   50
MARIANE: Now, that's a fine, high-minded sentiment.
VALÈRE: One to which any sane man would assent.
   Would you prefer it if I pined away
   In hopeless passion till my dying day?
   Am I to yield you to a rival's arms   55
   And not console myself with other charms?
MARIANE: Go then: console yourself; don't hesitate.
   I wish you to; indeed, I cannot wait.
VALÈRE: You wish me to?
MARIANE: Yes.
VALÈRE: That's the final straw.
   Madam, farewell. Your wish shall be my law.   60

(*He starts to leave, and then returns: this repeatedly.*)

MARIANE: Splendid.

VALÈRE (*Coming back again.*):   This breach, remember, is of your making;
It's you who've driven me to the step I'm taking.

MARIANE: Of course.

VALÈRE (*Coming back again.*):   Remember, too, that I am merely
Following your example.

MARIANE: I see that clearly.

VALÈRE: Enough. I'll go and do your bidding, then.   65

MARIANE: Good.

VALÈRE (*Coming back again.*):   You shall never see my face again.

MARIANE: Excellent.

VALÈRE (*Walking to the door, then turning about.*)
                Yes?

MARIANE: What?

VALÈRE: What's that? What did you say?

MARIANE: Nothing. You're dreaming.

VALÈRE: Ah. Well, I'm on my way.
Farewell, Madame.

(*He moves slowly away.*)

MARIANE: Farewell.

DORINE (*To* MARIANE.):   If you ask me,
Both of you are as mad as mad can be.   70
Do stop this nonsense, now. I've only let you
Squabble so long to see where it would get you.
Whoa there, Monsieur Valère!

(*She goes and seizes* VALÈRE *by the arm; he makes a great show of resistance.*)

VALÈRE: What's this, Dorine?

DORINE: Come here.

VALÈRE: No, no, my heart's too full of spleen.
Don't hold me back; her wish must be obeyed.   75

DORINE: Stop!

VALÈRE: It's too late now; my decision's made.

DORINE: Oh, pooh!

MARIANE (*Aside.*):   He hates the sight of me, that's plain.
I'll go, and so deliver him from pain.

DORINE: (*Leaving* VALÈRE, *running after* MARIANE.)
And now *you* run away! Come back.

MARIANE: No, no.   80
Nothing you say will keep me here. Let go!

VALÈRE (*Aside.*):   She cannot bear my presence, I perceive.
To spare her further torment, I shall leave.

DORINE: (*Leaving* MARIANE, *running after* VALÈRE.)
    Again! You'll not escape, Sir; don't you try it.
    Come here, you two. Stop fussing, and be quiet.

    (*She takes* VALÈRE *by the hand, then* MARIANE, *and draws them together.*)

VALÈRE (*To* DORINE.):   What do you want of me?   85
MARIANE (*To* DORINE.):   What is the point of this?
DORINE: We're going to have a little armistice.
    (*To* VALÈRE.) Now, weren't you silly to get so overheated?
VALÈRE: Didn't you see how badly I was treated?
DORINE (*To* MARIANE.):   Aren't you a simpleton, to have lost your head?   90
MARIANE: Didn't you hear the hateful things he said?
DORINE (*To* VALÈRE.):   You're both great fools. Her sole desire, Valère,
    Is to be yours in marriage. To that I'll swear.
    (*To* MARIANE.) He loves you only, and he wants no wife
    But you, Mariane. On that I'll stake my life.   95
MARIANE (*To* VALÈRE.):   Then why you advised me so, I cannot see.
VALÈRE (*To* MARIANE.):   On such a question, why ask advice of *me*?
DORINE: Oh, you're impossible. Give me your hands, you two.
    (*To* VALÈRE.) Yours first.
VALÈRE (*Giving* DORINE *his hand.*):   But why?
DORINE (*To* MARIANE.):   And now a hand from you.   100
MARIANE: (*Also giving* DORINE *her hand.*)
    What are you doing?
DORINE: There: a perfect fit.
    You suit each other better than you'll admit.

    (VALÈRE *and* MARIANE *hold hands for some time without looking at each other.*)

VALÈRE: (*Turning toward* MARIANE.)
    Ah, come, don't be so haughty. Give a man
    A look of kindness, won't you, Mariane?

    (MARIANE *turns toward* VALÈRE *and smiles.*)

DORINE: I tell you, lovers are completely mad!   105
VALÈRE (*To* MARIANE.):   Now come, confess that you were very bad
    To hurt my feelings as you did just now.
    I have a just complaint, you must allow.
MARIANE: *You* must allow that you were most unpleasant . . .
DORINE: Let's table that discussion for the present;   110
    Your father has a plan which must be stopped.
MARIANE: Advise us, then; what means must we adopt?
DORINE: We'll use all manner of means, and all at once.
    (*To* MARIANE.) Your father's addled; he's acting like a dunce.
    Therefore you'd better humor the old fossil.   115
    Pretend to yield to him, be sweet and docile,

And then postpone, as often as necessary,
The day on which you have agreed to marry.
You'll thus gain time, and time will turn the trick.
Sometimes, for instance, you'll be taken sick,   120
And that will seem good reason for delay;
Or some bad omen will make you change the day—
You'll dream of muddy water, or you'll pass
A dead man's hearse, or break a looking-glass.
If all else fails, no man can marry you   125
Unless you take his ring and say "I do."
But now, let's separate. If they should find
Us talking here, our plot might be divined.
(*To* VALÈRE.) Go to your friends, and tell them what's occurred,
And have them urge her father to keep his word.   130
Meanwhile, we'll stir her brother into action,
And get Elmire,° as well, to join our faction.
Good-bye.
VALÈRE (*To* MARIANE.):   Though each of us will do his best,
    It's your true heart on which my hopes shall rest.   135
MARIANE (*To* VALÈRE.):   Regardless of what Father may decide,
    None but Valère shall claim me as his bride.
VALÈRE: Oh, how those words content me! Come what will . . .
DORINE: Oh, lovers, lovers! Their tongues are never still.
    Be off, now.
VALÈRE (*Turning to go, then turning back.*):
    One last word . . .
DORINE: No time to chat: 140
    You leave by this door; and *you* leave by that.

(DORINE *pushes them, by the shoulders, toward opposing doors.*)

ACT III

SCENE I

DAMIS, DORINE

DAMIS: May lightning strike me even as I speak,
    May all men call me cowardly and weak,
    If any fear or scruple holds me back
    From settling things, at once, with that great quack!
DORINE: Now, don't give way to violent emotion.   5
    Your father's merely talked about this notion,

II.iv. 131. Elmire: Orgon's second wife.

And words and deeds are far from being one.
Much that is talked about is never undone.
DAMIS: No, I must stop that scoundrel's machinations;
I'll go and tell him off; I'm out of patience.   10
DORINE: Do calm down and be practical. I had rather
My mistress dealt with him—and with your father.
She has some influence with Tartuffe, I've noted.
He hangs upon her words, seems most devoted,
And may, indeed, be smitten by her charm.   15
Pray Heaven it's true! 'Twould do our cause no harm.
She sent for him, just now, to sound him out
On this affair you're so incensed about;
She'll find out where he stands, and tell him, too,
What dreadful strife and trouble will ensue   20
If he lends countenance to your father's plan.
I couldn't get in to see him, but his man
Says that he's almost finished with his prayers.
Go, now. I'll catch him when he comes downstairs.
DAMIS: I want to hear this conference, and I will.   25
DORINE: No, they must be alone.
DAMIS: Oh, I'll keep still.
DORINE: Not you. I know your temper. You'd start a brawl,
And shout and stamp your foot and spoil it all.
Go on.
DAMIS: I won't; I have a perfect right . . .
DORINE: Lord, you're a nuisance! He's coming; get out of sight.   30

      (DAMIS *conceals himself in a closet at the rear of the stage.*)

SCENE II

TARTUFFE, DORINE

TARTUFFE: (*Observing* DORINE, *and calling to his manservant offstage.*)
Hang up my hair-shirt, put my scourge in place,
And pray, Laurent, for Heaven's perpetual grace.
I'm going to the prison now, to share
My last few coins with the poor wretches there.
DORINE (*Aside.*):   Dear God, what affectation! What a fake!   5
TARTUFFE: You wished to see me?
DORINE: Yes . . .
TARTUFFE: (*Taking a handkerchief from his pocket.*)
                        For mercy's sake,
Please take this handkerchief, before you speak.
DORINE: What?

TARTUFFE: Cover that bosom,° girl. The flesh is weak.
   And unclean thoughts are difficult to control.
   Such sights as that can undermine the soul.   10
DORINE: Your soul, it seems, has very poor defenses,
   And flesh makes quite an impact on your senses.
   It's strange that you're so easily excited;
   My own desires are not so soon ignited,
   And if I saw you naked as a beast,   15
   Not all your hide would tempt me in the least.
TARTUFFE: Girl, speak more modestly; unless you do,
   I shall be forced to take my leave of you.
DORINE: Oh, no, it's I who must be on my way;
   I've just one little message to convey.   20
   Madame is coming down, and begs you, Sir,
   To wait and have a word or two with her.
TARTUFFE: Gladly.
DORINE (*Aside.*):   *That* had a softening effect!
   I think my guess about him was correct.
TARTUFFE: Will she be long?
DORINE: No: that's her step I hear.   25
   Ah, here she is, and I shall disappear.

SCENE III

ELMIRE, TARTUFFE

TARTUFFE: May Heaven, whose infinite goodness we adore,
   Preserve your body and soul forevermore,
   And bless your days, and answer thus the plea
   Of one who is its humblest votary.
ELMIRE: I thank you for that pious wish. But please,   5
   Do take a chair and let's be more at ease.

            (*They sit down.*)

TARTUFFE: I trust that you are once more well and strong?
ELMIRE: Oh, yes: the fever didn't last for long.
TARTUFFE: My prayers are too unworthy, I am sure,
   To have gained from Heaven this most gracious cure;   10
   But lately, Madam, my every supplication
   Has had for object your recuperation.
ELMIRE: You shouldn't have troubled so. I don't deserve it.
TARTUFFE: Your health is priceless, Madam, and to preserve it

---

III.ii. 8. bosom: The Brotherhood of the Holy Sacrament practiced alms-giving to prisoners and kept a careful, censorious check on women's clothing if they deemed it lascivious. Thus Molière's audience would have identified Tartuffe as sympathetic—hypocritically—to the aims of the organization.

I'd gladly give my own, in all sincerity.   15
ELMIRE: Sir, you outdo us all in Christian charity.
  You've been most kind. I count myself your debtor.
TARTUFFE: 'Twas nothing, Madam. I long to serve you better.
ELMIRE: There's a private matter I'm anxious to discuss.
  I'm glad there's no one here to hinder us.   20
TARTUFFE: I too am glad; it floods my heart with bliss
  To find myself alone with you like this.
  For just this chance I've prayed with all my power—
  But prayed in vain, until this happy hour.
ELMIRE: This won't take long, Sir, and I hope you'll be   25
  Entirely frank and unconstrained with me.
TARTUFFE: Indeed, there's nothing I had rather do
  Than bare my inmost heart and soul to you.
  First, let me say that what remarks I've made
  About the constant visits you are paid   30
  Were prompted not by any mean emotion,
  But rather by a pure and deep devotion,
  A fervent zeal . . .
ELMIRE: No need for explanation.
  Your sole concern, I'm sure, was my salvation.
TARTUFFE: (*Taking* ELMIRE's *hand and pressing her fingertips.*)
  Quite so; and such great fervor do I feel . . .
                      35
ELMIRE: Ooh! Please! You're pinching!
TARTUFFE: 'Twas from excess of zeal.
  I never meant to cause you pain, I swear.
  I'd rather . . .

      (*He places his hand on* ELMIRE's *knee.*)

ELMIRE: What can your hand be doing there?
TARTUFFE: Feeling your gown; what soft, fine-woven stuff!
ELMIRE: Please, I'm extremely ticklish. That's enough.   40

      (*She draws her chair away;* TARTUFFE *pulls his after her.*)

TARTUFFE: (*Fondling the lace collar of her gown.*)
  My, my, what lovely lacework on your dress!
  The workmanship's miraculous, no less.
  I've not seen anything to equal it.
ELMIRE: Yes, quite. But let's talk business for a bit.
  They say my husband means to break his word   45
  And give his daughter to you, Sir. Had you heard?
TARTUFFE: He did once mention it. But I confess
  I dream of quite a different happiness.
  It's elsewhere, Madam, that my eyes discern
  The promise of that bliss for which I yearn.   50

ELMIRE: I see: you care for nothing here below.
TARTUFFE: Ah, well—my heart's not made of stone, you know.
ELMIRE: All your desires mount heavenward, I'm sure,
    In scorn of all that's earthly and impure.
TARTUFFE: A love of heavenly beauty does not preclude   55
    A proper love for earthly pulchritude;
    Our senses are quite rightly captivated
    By perfect works our Maker has created.
    Some glory clings to all that Heaven has made;
    In you, all Heaven's marvels are displayed.   60
    On that fair face, such beauties have been lavished,
    The eyes are dazzled and the heart is ravished;
    How could I look on you, O flawless creature,
    And not adore the Author of all Nature,
    Feeling a love both passionate and pure   65
    For you, his triumph of self-portraiture?
    At first, I trembled lest that love should be
    A subtle snare that Hell had laid for me;
    I vowed to flee the sight of you, eschewing
    A rapture that might prove my soul's undoing;   70
    But soon, fair being, I became aware
    That my deep passion could be made to square
    With rectitude, and with my bounden duty.
    I thereupon surrendered to your beauty.
    It is, I know, presumptuous on my part   75
    To bring you this poor offering of my heart,
    And it is not my merit, Heaven knows,
    But your compassion on which my hopes repose.
    You are my peace, my solace, my salvation;
    On you depends my bliss—or desolation;   80
    I bide your judgment and, as you think best,
    I shall be either miserable or blest.
ELMIRE: Your declaration is most gallant, Sir,
    But don't you think it's out of character?
    You'd have done better to restrain your passion   85
    And think before you spoke in such a fashion.
    It ill becomes a pious man like you . . .
TARTUFFE: I may be pious, but I'm human too:
    With your celestial charms before his eyes,
    A man has not the power to be wise.   90
    I know such words sound strangely, coming from me,
    But I'm no angel, nor was meant to be,
    And if you blame my passion, you must needs
    Reproach as well the charms on which it feeds.
    Your loveliness I had no sooner seen   95

Than you became my soul's unrivalled queen;
Before your seraph glance, divinely sweet,
My heart's defenses crumbled in defeat,
And nothing fasting, prayer, or tears might do
Could stay my spirit from adoring you.　　　　　　　　　　　　100
My eyes, my sighs have told you in the past
What now my lips make bold to say at last,
And if, in your great goodness, you will deign
To look upon your slave, and ease his pain,—
If, in compassion for my soul's distress,　　　　　　　　　　105
You'll stoop to comfort my unworthiness,
I'll raise to you, in thanks for that sweet manna,
An endless hymn, an infinite hosanna.
With me, of course, there need be no anxiety,
No fear of scandal or of notoriety.　　　　　　　　　　　　110
These young court gallants, whom all the ladies fancy,
Are vain in speech, in action rash and chancy;
When they succeed in love, the world soon knows it;
No favor's granted them but they disclose it
And by the looseness of their tongues profane　　　　　　　115
The very altar where their hearts have lain.
Men of my sort, however, love discreetly,
And one may trust our reticence completely.
My keen concern for my good name insures
The absolute security of yours;　　　　　　　　　　　　　120
In short, I offer you, my dear Elmire,
Love without scandal, pleasure without fear.
ELMIRE:　I've heard your well-turned speeches to the end,
And what you urge I clearly apprehend.
Aren't you afraid that I may take a notion　　　　　　　　125
To tell my husband of your warm devotion,
And that, supposing he were duly told,
His feelings toward you might grow rather cold?
TARTUFFE:　I know, dear lady, that your exceeding charity
Will lead your heart to pardon my temerity;　　　　　　　130
That you'll excuse my violent affection
As human weakness, human imperfection;
And that—O fairest!—you will bear in mind
That I'm but flesh and blood, and am not blind.
ELMIRE:　Some women might do otherwise, perhaps,　　　　135
But I shall be discreet about your lapse;
I'll tell my husband nothing of what's occurred
If, in return, you'll give your solemn word
To advocate as forcefully as you can
The marriage of Valère and Mariane,　　　　　　　　　　140

Renouncing all desire to dispossess
Another of his rightful happiness,
And. . .

SCENE IV

DAMIS, ELMIRE, TARTUFFE

DAMIS: (*Emerging from the closet where he has been hiding.*)
No! We'll not hush up this vile affair;
I heard it all inside that closet there,
Where Heaven, in order to confound the pride
Of this great rascal, prompted me to hide.
Ah, now I have my long-awaited chance   5
To punish his deceit and arrogance,
And give my father clear and shocking proof
Of the black character of his dear Tartuffe.
ELMIRE: Ah no, Damis; I'll be content if he
Will study to deserve my leniency.   10
I've promised silence—don't make me break my word;
To make a scandal would be too absurd.
Good wives laugh off such trifles, and forget them;
Why should they tell their husbands, and upset them?
DAMIS: You have your reasons for taking such a course,   15
And I have reasons, too, of equal force.
To spare him now would be insanely wrong.
I've swallowed my just wrath for far too long
And watched this insolent bigot bringing strife
And bitterness into our family life.   20
Too long he's meddled in my father's affairs,
Thwarting my marriage-hopes, and poor Valère's.
It's high time that my father was undeceived,
And now I've proof that can't be disbelieved—
Proof that was furnished me by Heaven above.   25
It's too good not to take advantage of.
This is my chance, and I deserve to lose it
If, for one moment, I hesitate to use it.
ELMIRE: Damis . . .
DAMIS: No, I must do what I think right.
Madam, my heart is bursting with delight,   30
And, say whatever you will, I'll not consent
To lose the sweet revenge on which I'm bent.
I'll settle matters without more ado;
And here, most opportunely, is my cue.°

III.iv. 34. cue: In the original stage directions, Tartuffe now reads silently from his breviary—in the
Roman Catholic Church, the book containing the Divine Office for each day, which those in holy orders
are required to recite.

SCENE V

ORGON, DAMIS, TARTUFFE, ELMIRE

DAMIS: Father, I'm glad you've joined us. Let us advise you
  Of some fresh news which doubtless will surprise you.
  You've just now been repaid with interest
  For all your loving-kindness to our guest.
  He's proved his warm and grateful feelings toward you;   5
  It's with a pair of horns he would reward you.
  Yes, I surprised him with your wife, and heard
  His whole adulterous offer, every word.
  She, with her all too gentle disposition,
  Would not have told you of his proposition;   10
  But I shall not make terms with brazen lechery,
  And feel that not to tell you would be treachery.
ELMIRE: And I hold that one's husband's peace of mind
  Should not be spoilt by tattle of this kind.
  One's honor doesn't require it: to be proficient   15
  In keeping men at bay is quite sufficient.
  These are my sentiments, and I wish, Damis,
  That you had heeded me and held your peace.

SCENE VI

ORGON, DAMIS, TARTUFFE

ORGON: Can it be true, this dreadful thing I hear?
TARTUFFE: Yes, Brother, I'm a wicked man, I fear:
  A wretched sinner, all depraved and twisted,
  The greatest villain that has ever existed.
  My life's one heap of crimes, which grows each minute;   5
  There's naught but foulness and corruption in it;
  And I perceive that Heaven, outraged by me,
  Has chosen this occasion to mortify me.
  Charge me with any deed you wish to name;
  I'll not defend myself, but take the blame.   10
  Believe what you are told, and drive Tartuffe
  Like some base criminal from beneath your roof;
  Yes, drive me hence, and with a parting curse:
  I shan't protest, for I deserve far worse.
ORGON (*To* DAMIS.):   Ah, you deceitful boy, how dare you try   15
  To stain his purity with so foul a lie?
DAMIS: What! Are you taken in by such a fluff?
  Did you not hear . . . ?
ORGON: Enough, you rogue, enough!
TARTUFFE: Ah, Brother, let him speak: you're being unjust.

Believe his story; the boy deserves your trust.   20
Why, after all, should you have faith in me?
How can you know what I might do, or be?
Is it on my good actions that you base
Your favor? Do you trust my pious face?   25
Ah, no, don't be deceived by hollow shows;
I'm far, alas, from being what men suppose;
Though the world takes me for a man of worth,
I'm truly the most worthless man on earth.
(*To* DAMIS.) Yes, my dear son, speak out now: call me the chief
Of sinners, a wretch, a murderer, a thief;   30
Load me with all the names men most abhor;
I'll not complain; I've earned them all, and more;
I'll kneel here while you pour them on my head
As a just punishment for the life I've led.
ORGON: (*To* TARTUFFE.)
   This is too much, dear Brother.
   (*To* DAMIS.)   Have you no heart?   35
DAMIS: Are you so hoodwinked by this rascal's art . . . ?
ORGON: Be still, you monster.
   (*To* TARTUFFE.)   Brother, I pray you, rise.
   (*To* DAMIS.) Villain!
DAMIS: But . . .
ORGON: Silence!
DAMIS: Can't you realize . . . ?
ORGON: Just one word more, and I'll tear you limb from limb.
TARTUFFE: In God's name, Brother, don't be harsh with him.   40
   I'd rather far be tortured at the stake
   Than see him bear one scratch for my poor sake.
ORGON: (*To* DAMIS.) Ingrate!
TARTUFFE: If I must beg you, on bended knee,
   To pardon him . . .
ORGON: (*Falling to his knees, addressing* TARTUFFE.)
                    Such goodness cannot be!
   (*To* DAMIS.) Now, *there's* true charity!
DAMIS: What, you . . . ?
ORGON: Villain, be still!   45
   I know your motives; I know you wish him ill:
   Yes, all of you—wife, children, servants, all—
   Conspire against him and desire his fall,
   Employing every shameful trick you can
   To alienate me from this saintly man.   50
   Ah, but the more you seek to drive him away,
   The more I'll do to keep him. Without delay,
   I'll spite this household and confound its pride

    By giving him my daughter as his bride.
DAMIS: You're going to force her to accept his hand?   55
ORGON: Yes, and this very night, d'you understand?
    I shall defy you all, and make it clear
    That I'm the one who gives the orders here.
    Come, wretch, kneel down and clasp his blessed feet,
    And ask his pardon for your black deceit.   60
DAMIS: I ask that swindler's pardon? Why, I'd rather . . .
ORGON: So! You insult him, and defy your father!
    A stick! A stick! (*To* TARTUFFE.) No, no—release me, do.
    (*To* DAMIS.) Out of my house this minute! Be off with you,
    And never dare set foot in it again.   65
DAMIS: Well, I shall go, but . . .
ORGON: Well, go quickly, then.
    I disinherit you; an empty purse
    Is all you'll get from me—except my curse!

SCENE VII

ORGON, TARTUFFE

ORGON: How he blasphemed your goodness! What a son!
TARTUFFE: Forgive him, Lord, as I've already done.
    (*To* ORGON.) You can't know how it hurts when someone tries
    To blacken me in my dear Brother's eyes.
ORGON: Ahh!
TARTUFFE: The mere thought of such ingratitude   5
    Plunges my soul into so dark a mood . . .
    Such horror grips my heart . . . I gasp for breath,
    And cannot speak, and feel myself near death.
ORGON: (*He runs, in tears, to the door through which he has just driven his son.*)
    You blackguard! Why did I spare you? Why did I not
    Break you in little pieces on the spot?   10
    Compose yourself, and don't be hurt, dear friend.
TARTUFFE: These scenes, these dreadful quarrels, have got to end.
    I've much upset your household, and I perceive
    That the best thing will be for me to leave.
ORGON: What are you saying!
TARTUFFE: They're all against me here;   15
    They'd have you think me false and insincere.
ORGON: Ah, what of that? Have I ceased believing in you?
TARTUFFE: Their adverse talk will certainly continue,
    And charges which you now repudiate
    You may find credible at a later date.   20
ORGON: No, Brother, never.

TARTUFFE: Brother, a wife can sway
  Her husband's mind in many a subtle way.
ORGON: No, no.
TARTUFFE: To leave at once is the solution;
  Thus only can I end their persecution.
ORGON: No, no, I'll not allow it; you shall remain.   25
TARTUFFE: Ah, well; 'twill mean much martyrdom and pain,
  But if you wish it . . .
ORGON: Ah!
TARTUFFE: Enough; so be it.
  But one thing must be settled, as I see it.
  For your dear honor, and for our friendship's sake,
  There's one precaution I feel bound to take.   30
  I shall avoid your wife, and keep away . . .
ORGON: No, you shall not, whatever they may say.
  It pleases me to vex them, and for spite
  I'd have them see you with her day and night.
  What's more, I'm going to drive them to despair   35
  By making you my only son and heir;
  This very day, I'll give to you alone
  Clear deed and title to everything I own.
  A dear, good friend and son-in-law-to-be
  Is more than wife, or child, or kin to me.   40
  Will you accept my offer, dearest son?
TARTUFFE: In all things, let the will of Heaven be done.
ORGON: Poor fellow! Come, we'll go draw up the deed.
  Then let them burst with disappointed greed!

ACT IV

SCENE I

CLÉANTE, TARTUFFE

CLÉANTE: Yes, all the town's discussing it, and truly,
  Their comments do not flatter you unduly.
  I'm glad we've met, Sir, and I'll give my view
  Of this sad matter in a word or two.
  As for who's guilty, that I shan't discuss;   5
  Let's say it was Damis who caused the fuss;
  Assuming, then, that you have been ill-used
  By young Damis, and groundlessly accused,
  Ought not a Christian to forgive, and ought
  He not to stifle every vengeful thought?   10
  Should you stand by and watch a father make
  His only son an exile for your sake?

Again I tell you frankly, be advised:
The whole town, high and low, is scandalized;
This quarrel must be mended, and my advice is   15
Not to push matters to a further crisis.
No, sacrifice your wrath to God above,
And help Damis regain his father's love.
TARTUFFE: Alas, for my part I should take great joy
In doing so. I've nothing against the boy.   20
I pardon all, I harbor no resentment;
To serve him would afford me much contentment.
But Heaven's interest will not have it so:
If he comes back, then I shall have to go.
After his conduct—so extreme, so vicious—   25
Our further intercourse would look suspicious.
God knows what people would think! Why, they'd describe
My goodness to him as a sort of bribe;
They'd say that out of guilt I made pretense
Of loving-kindness and benevolence—   30
That, fearing my accuser's tongue, I strove
To buy his silence with a show of love.
CLÉANTE: Your reasoning is badly warped and stretched,
And these excuses, Sir, are most far-fetched.
Why put yourself in charge of Heaven's cause?   35
Does Heaven need our help to enforce its laws?
Leave vengeance to the Lord, Sir; while we live,
Our duty's not to punish, but forgive;
And what the Lord commands, we should obey
Without regard to what the world may say.   40
What! Shall the fear of being misunderstood
Prevent our doing what is right and good?
No, no; let's simply do what Heaven ordains,
And let no other thoughts perplex our brains.
TARTUFFE: Again, Sir, let me say that I've forgiven   45
Damis, and thus obeyed the laws of Heaven;
But I am not commanded by the Bible
To live with one who smears my name with libel.
CLÉANTE: Were you commanded, Sir, to indulge the whim
Of poor Orgon, and to encourage him   50
In suddenly transferring to your name
A large estate to which you have no claim?
TARTUFFE: 'Twould never occur to those who know me best
To think I acted from self-interest.
The treasures of this world I quite despise;   55
Their specious glitter does not charm my eyes;
And if I have resigned myself to taking

The gift which my dear Brother insists on making,
I do so only, as he well understands,
Lest so much wealth fall into wicked hands,   60
Lest those to whom it might descend in time
Turn it to purposes of sin and crime,
And not, as I shall do, make use of it
For Heaven's glory and mankind's benefit.

CLÉANTE: Forget these trumped-up fears. Your argument   65
Is one the rightful heir might well resent;
It *is* a moral burden to inherit
Such wealth, but give Damis a chance to bear it.
And would it not be worse to be accused
Of swindling, than to see that wealth misused?   70
I'm shocked that you allowed Orgon to broach
This matter, and that you feel no self-reproach;
Does true religion teach that lawful heirs
May freely be deprived of what is theirs?
And if the Lord has told you in your heart   75
That you and young Damis must dwell apart,
Would it not be the decent thing to beat
A generous and honorable retreat,
Rather than let the son of the house be sent,
For your convenience, into banishment?   80
Sir, if you wish to prove the honesty
Of your intentions . . .

TARTUFFE: Sir, it is half-past three.
I've certain pious duties to attend to,
And hope my prompt departure won't offend you.

CLÉANTE: (*Alone.*) Damn.

SCENE II

ELMIRE, MARIANE, CLÉANTE, DORINE

DORINE: Stay, Sir, and help Mariane, for Heaven's sake!
She's suffering so, I fear her heart will break.
Her father's plan to marry her off tonight
Has put the poor child in a desperate plight.
I hear him coming. Let's stand together, now,   5
And see if we can't change his mind, somehow,
About this match we all deplore and fear.

SCENE III

ORGON, ELMIRE, MARIANE, CLÉANTE, DORINE

ORGON: Hah! Glad to find you all assembled here.
(*To Mariane.*) This contract, child, contains your happiness,
And what it says I think your heart can guess.
MARIANE: (*Falling to her knees.*)
Sir, by that Heaven which sees me here distressed,
And by whatever else can move your breast,   5
Do not employ a father's power, I pray you,
To crush my heart and force it to obey you,
Nor by your harsh commands oppress me so
That I'll begrudge the duty which I owe—
And do not so embitter and enslave me   10
That I shall hate the very life you gave me.
If my sweet hopes must perish, if you refuse
To give me to the one I've dared to choose,
Spare me at least—I beg you, I implore—
The pain of wedding one whom I abhor;   15
And do not, by a heartless use of force,
Drive me to contemplate some desperate course.
ORGON: (*Feeling himself touched by her.*)
Be firm, my soul. No human weakness, now.
MARIANE: I don't resent your love for him. Allow
Your heart free rein, Sir; give him your property,   20
And if that's not enough, take mine from me;
He's welcome to my money; take it, do,
But don't, I pray, include my person too.
Spare me, I beg you; and let me end the tale
Of my sad days behind a convent veil.   25
ORGON: A convent! Hah! When crossed in their amours,
All lovesick girls have the same thought as yours.
Get up! The more you loathe the man, and dread him,
The more ennobling it will be to wed him.
Marry Tartuffe, and mortify your flesh!   30
Enough; don't start that whimpering afresh.
DORINE: But why . . . ?
ORGON: Be still, there. Speak when you're spoken to.
Not one more bit of impudence out of you.
CLÉANTE: If I may offer a word of counsel here . . .
ORGON: Brother, in counselling you have no peer;   35
All your advice is forceful, sound, and clever;
I don't propose to follow it, however.
ELMIRE: (*To Orgon.*)
I am amazed, and don't know what to say;

Your blindness simply takes my breath away.
You are indeed bewitched, to take no warning   40
From our account of what occurred this morning.
ORGON: Madam, I know a few plain facts, and one
   Is that you're partial to my rascal son;
   Hence, when he sought to make Tartuffe the victim
   Of a base lie, you dared not contradict him.   45
   Ah, but you underplayed your part, my pet;
   You should have looked more angry, more upset.
ELMIRE: When men make overtures, must we reply
   With righteous anger and a battle-cry?
   Must we turn back their amorous advances   50
   With sharp reproaches and with fiery glances?
   Myself, I find such offers merely amusing,
   And make no scenes and fusses in refusing;
   My taste is for good-natured rectitude,
   And I dislike the savage sort of prude   55
   Who guards her virtue with her teeth and claws,
   And tears men's eyes out for the slightest cause:
   The Lord preserve me from such honor as that,
   Which bites and scratches like an alley-cat!
   I've found that a polite and cool rebuff   60
   Discourages a lover quite enough.
ORGON: I know the facts, and I shall not be shaken.
ELMIRE: I marvel at your power to be mistaken.
   Would it, I wonder, carry weight with you
   If I could *show* you that our tale was true?   65
ORGON: Show me?
ELMIRE: Yes.
ORGON: Rot.
ELMIRE: Come, what if I found a way
   To make you see the facts as plain as day?
ORGON: Nonsense.
ELMIRE: Do answer me; don't be absurd.
   I'm not now asking you to trust our word.
   Suppose that from some hiding-place in here   70
   You learned the whole sad truth by eye and ear—
   What would you say of your good friend, after that?
ORGON: Why, I'd say . . . nothing, by Jehoshaphat!
   It can't be true.
ELMIRE: You've been too long deceived,
   And I'm quite tired of being disbelieved.   75
   Come now: let's put my statements to the test,
   And you shall see the truth made manifest.
ORGON: I'll take that challenge. Now do your uttermost.

We'll see how you make good your empty boast.
ELMIRE (*To* DORINE.):   Send him to me.
DORINE: He's crafty; it may be hard   80
   To catch the cunning scoundrel off his guard.
ELMIRE: No, amorous men are gullible. Their conceit
   So blinds them that they're never hard to cheat.
   Have him come down
   (*To* CLÉANTE *and* MARIANE.) Please leave us, for a bit.

SCENE IV

ELMIRE, ORGON

ELMIRE: Pull up this table, and get under it.
ORGON: What?
ELMIRE: It's essential that you be well-hidden.
ORGON: Why there?
ELMIRE: Oh, Heavens! Just do as you are bidden.
   I have my plans; we'll soon see how they fare.
   Under the table, now; and once you're there,   5
   Take care that you are neither seen nor heard.
ORGON: Well, I'll indulge you, since I gave my word
   To see you through this infantile charade.
ELMIRE: Once it is over, you'll be glad we played.

   (*To her husband, who is now under the table.*)

I'm going to act quite strangely, now, and you   10
Must not be shocked at anything I do.
Whatever I may say, you must excuse
As part of that deceit I'm forced to use.
I shall employ sweet speeches in the task
Of making that imposter drop his mask;   15
I'll give encouragement to his bold desires,
And furnish fuel to his amorous fires.
Since it's for your sake, and for his destruction,
That I shall seem to yield to his seduction,
I'll gladly stop whenever you decide.   20
That all your doubts are fully satisfied.
I'll count on you, as soon as you have seen
What sort of man he is, to intervene,
And not expose me to his odious lust
One moment longer than you feel you must.   25
Remember: you're to save me from my plight
Whenever . . . He's coming! Hush! Keep out of sight!

SCENE V

TARTUFFE, ELMIRE, ORGON

TARTUFFE: You wish to have a word with me, I'm told.
ELMIRE: Yes. I've a little secret to unfold.
  Before I speak, however, it would be wise
  To close that door, and look about for spies.

(TARTUFFE *goes to the door, closes it, and returns.*)

  The very last thing that must happen now   5
  Is a repetition of this morning's row.
  I've never been so badly caught off guard.
  Oh, how I feared for you! You saw how hard
  I tried to make that troublesome Damis
  Control his dreadful temper, and hold his peace.   10
  In my confusion, I didn't have the sense
  Simply to contradict his evidence;
  But as it happened, that was for the best,
  And all has worked out in our interest.
  This storm has only bettered your position;   15
  My husband doesn't have the least suspicion,
  And now, in mockery of those who do,
  He bids me be continually with you.
  And that is why, quite fearless of reproof,
  I now can be alone with my Tartuffe,   20
  And why my heart—perhaps too quick to yield—
  Feels free to let its passion be revealed.
TARTUFFE: Madam, your words confuse me. Not long ago,
  You spoke in quite a different style, you know.
ELMIRE: Ah, Sir, if that refusal made you smart,   25
  It's little that you know of woman's heart,
  Or what that heart is trying to convey
  When it resists in such a feeble way!
  Always, at first, our modesty prevents
  The frank avowal of tender sentiments: 30
  However high the passion which inflames us,
  Still, to confess its power somehow shames us.
  Thus we reluct, at first, yet in a tone
  Which tells you that our heart is overthrown,
  That what our lips deny, our pulse confesses,   35
  And that, in time, all noes will turn to yesses.
  I fear my words are all too frank and free,
  And a poor proof of woman's modesty;
  But since I'm started, tell me, if you will—
  Would I have tried to make Damis be still,   40

Would I have listened, calm and unoffended,
Until your lengthy offer of love was ended,
And been so very mild in my reaction,
Had your sweet words not given me satisfaction?
And when I tried to force you to undo   45
The marriage-plans my husband has in view,
What did my urgent pleading signify
If not that I admired you, and that I
Deplored the thought that someone else might own
Part of a heart I wished for mine alone?   50
TARTUFFE: Madam, no happiness is so complete
As when, from lips we love, come words so sweet;
Their nectar floods my every sense, and drains
In honeyed rivulets through all my veins.
To please you is my joy, my only goal;   55
Your love is the restorer of my soul;
And yet I must beg leave, now, to confess
Some lingering doubts as to my happiness.
Might this not be a trick? Might not the catch
Be that you wish me to break off the match   60
With Mariane, and so have feigned to love me?
I shan't quite trust your fond opinion of me
Until the feelings you've expressed so sweetly
Are demonstrated somewhat more concretely,
And you have shown, by certain kind concessions,   65
That I may put my faith in your professions.
ELMIRE: (*She coughs, to warn her husband.*)
Why be in such a hurry? Must my heart
Exhaust its bounty at the very start?
To make that sweet admission cost me dear,
But you'll not be content, it would appear,   70
Unless my store of favors is disbursed
To the last farthing, and at the very first.
TARTUFFE: The less we merit, the less we dare to hope,
And with our doubts, mere words can never cope.
We trust no promised bliss till we receive it;   75
Not till a joy is ours can we believe it.
I, who so little merit your esteem,
Can't credit this fulfillment of my dream,
And shan't believe it, Madam, until I savor
Some palpable assurance of your favor.   80
ELMIRE: My, how tyrannical your love can be,
And how it flusters and perplexes me!
How furiously you take one's heart in hand,
And make your every wish a fierce command!

Come, must you hound and harry me to death?   85
Will you not give me time to catch my breath?
Can it be right to press me with such force,
Give me no quarter, show me no remorse,
And take advantage, by your stern insistence,
Of the fond feelings which weaken my resistance?   90
TARTUFFE: Well, if you look with favor upon my love,
    Why, then, begrudge me some clear proof thereof?
ELMIRE: But how can I consent without offense
    To Heaven, toward which you feel such reverence?
TARTUFFE: If Heaven is all that holds you back, don't worry.   95
    I can remove that hindrance in a hurry.
    Nothing of that sort need obstruct our path.
ELMIRE: Must one not be afraid of Heaven's wrath?
TARTUFFE: Madam, forget such fears, and be my pupil,
    And I shall teach you how to conquer scruple.   100
    Some joys, it's true, are wrong in Heaven's eyes;
    Yet Heaven is not averse to compromise;
    There is a science, lately formulated,
    Whereby one's conscience may be liberated,°
    And any wrongful act you care to mention   105
    May be redeemed by purity of intention.
    I'll teach you, Madam, the secrets of that science;
    Meanwhile, just place on me your full reliance.
    Assuage my keen desires, and feel no dread:
    The sin, if any, shall be on my head.   110

        (ELMIRE *coughs, this time more loudly.*)

You've a bad cough.
ELMIRE: Yes, yes. It's bad indeed.
TARTUFFE: (*Producing a little paper bag.*)
    A bit of licorice may be what you need.
ELMIRE: No, I've a stubborn cold, it seems. I'm sure it
    Will take much more than licorice to cure it.
TARTUFFE: How aggravating.
ELMIRE: Oh, more than I can say.   115
TARTUFFE: If you're still troubled, think of things this way:
    No one shall know our joys, save us alone,
    And there's no evil till the act is known;
    It's scandal, Madam, which makes it an offense,
    And it's no sin to sin in confidence.   120
ELMIRE: (*Having coughed once more.*)
    Well, clearly I must do as you require,

---

104. liberated: Molière created his own footnote to this line: "It is a scoundrel who speaks."

And yield to your importunate desire.
It is apparent, now, that nothing less
Will satisfy you, and so I acquiesce.
To go so far is much against my will;   125
I'm vexed that it should come to this; but still,
Since you are so determined on it, since you
Will not allow mere language to convince you,
And since you ask for concrete evidence, I
See nothing for it, now, but to comply.   130
If this is sinful, if I'm wrong to do it,
So much the worse for him who drove me to it.
The fault can surely not be charged to me.
TARTUFFE: Madam, the fault is mine, if fault there be,
  And . . .
ELMIRE: Open the door a little, and peek out;   135
  I wouldn't want my husband poking about.
TARTUFFE: Why worry about the man? Each day he grows
  More gullible; one can lead him by the nose.
  To find us here would fill him with delight,
  And if he saw the worst, he'd doubt his sight.   140
ELMIRE: Nevertheless, do step out for a minute
  Into the hall, and see that no one's in it.

SCENE VI

ORGON, ELMIRE

ORGON: (*Coming out from under the table.*)
  That man's a perfect monster, I must admit!
  I'm simply stunned. I can't get over it.
ELMIRE: What, coming out so soon? How premature!
  Get back in hiding, and wait until you're sure.
  Stay till the end, and be convinced completely;   5
  We mustn't stop till things are proved concretely.
ORGON: Hell never harbored anything so vicious!
ELMIRE: Tut, don't be hasty. Try to be judicious.
  Wait, and be certain that there's no mistake.
  No jumping to conclusions, for Heaven's sake!   10

        (*She places* ORGON *behind her, as* TARTUFFE *re-enters.*)

SCENE VII

TARTUFFE, ELMIRE, ORGON

TARTUFFE: (*Not seeing* ORGON.)
  Madam, all things have worked out to perfection;

I've given the neighboring rooms a full inspection;
No one's about; and now I may at last . . .
ORGON (*Intercepting him.*):   Hold on, my passionate fellow, not so fast!
I should advise a little more restraint.   5
Well, so you thought you'd fool me, my dear saint!
How soon you wearied of the saintly life—
Wedding my daughter, and coveting my wife!
I've long suspected you, and had a feeling
That soon I'd catch you at your double-dealing.   10
Just now, you've given me evidence galore;
It's quite enough; I have no wish for more.
ELMIRE (*To* TARTUFFE.):   I'm sorry to have treated you so slyly,
But circumstances forced me to be wily.
TARTUFFE: Brother, you can't think . . .
ORGON: No more talk from you;   15
Just leave this household, without more ado.
TARTUFFE: What I intended . . .
ORGON: That seems fairly clear;
Spare me your falsehoods and get out of here.
TARTUFFE: No, I'm the master, and you're the one to go!
This house belongs to me, I'll have you know,   20
And I shall show you that you can't hurt *me*
By this contemptible conspiracy,
That those who cross me know not what they do,
And that I've means to expose and punish you,
Avenge offended Heaven, and make you grieve   25
That ever you dared order me to leave.

SCENE VIII

ELMIRE, ORGON

ELMIRE: What was the point of all that angry chatter?
ORGON: Dear God, I'm worried. This is no laughing matter.
ELMIRE: How so?
ORGON: I fear I understood his drift.
I'm much disturbed about that deed of gift.
ELMIRE: You gave him . . . ?
ORGON: Yes, it's all been drawn and signed.   5
But one thing more is weighing on my mind.
ELMIRE: What's that?
ORGON: I'll tell you; but first let's see if there's
A certain strong-box in his room upstairs.

ACT V

SCENE I

ORGON, CLÉANTE

CLÉANTE: Where are you going so fast?
ORGON: God knows!
CLÉANTE: Then wait;
  Let's have a conference, and deliberate
  On how this situation's to be met.
ORGON: That strong-box has me utterly upset;
  This is the worst of many, many shocks.   5
CLÉANTE: Is there some fearful mystery in that box?
ORGON: My poor friend Argas brought that box to me
  With his own hands, in utmost secrecy;
  'Twas on the very morning of his flight.
  It's full of papers which, if they came to light,   10
  Would ruin him—or such is my impression.
CLÉANTE: Then why did you let it out of your possession?
ORGON: Those papers vexed my conscience, and it seemed best
  To ask the counsel of my pious guest.
  The cunning scoundrel got me to agree   15
  To leave the strong-box in his custody,
  So that, in case of an investigation,
  I could employ a slight equivocation
  And swear I didn't have it, and thereby,
  At no expense to conscience, tell a lie.   20
CLÉANTE: It looks to me as it you're out on a limb.
  Trusting him with that box, and offering him
  That deed of gift, were actions of a kind
  Which scarcely indicate a prudent mind.
  With two such weapons, he has the upper hand,   25
  And since you're vulnerable, as matters stand,
  You erred once more in bringing him to bay.
  You should have acted in some subtler way.
ORGON: Just think of it: behind that fervent face,
  A heart so wicked, and a soul so base!   30
  I took him in, a hungry beggar, and then . . .
  Enough, by God! I'm through with pious men:
  Henceforth I'll hate the whole false brotherhood,
  And persecute them worse than Satan could.
CLÉANTE: Ah, there you go—extravagant as ever!   35
  Why can you not be rational? You never
  Manage to take the middle course, it seems,
  But jump, instead, between absurd extremes.

You've recognized your recent grave mistake
In falling victim to a pious fake;   40
Now, to correct that error, must you embrace
An even greater error in its place,
And judge our worthy neighbors as a whole
By what you've learned of one corrupted soul?
Come, just because one rascal made you swallow   45
A show of zeal which turned out to be hollow,
Shall you conclude that all men are deceivers,
And that, today, there are no true believers?
Let atheists make that foolish inference;
Learn to distinguish virtue from pretense,   50
Be cautious in bestowing admiration,
And cultivate a sober moderation.
Don't humor fraud, but also don't asperse
True piety; the latter fault is worse,
And it is best to err, if err one must,   55
As you have done, upon the side of trust.

Scene II

Damis, Orgon, Cléante

DAMIS: Father, I hear that scoundrel's uttered threats
   Against you; that he pridefully forgets
   How, in his need, he was befriended by you,
   And means to use your gifts to crucify you.
ORGON: It's true, my boy. I'm too distressed for tears.   5
DAMIS: Leave it to me, Sir; let me trim his ears.
   Faced with such insolence, we must not waver.
   I shall rejoice in doing you the favor
   Of cutting short his life, and your distress.
CLÉANTE: What a display of young hotheadedness!   10
   Do learn to moderate your fits of rage.
   In this just kingdom, this enlightened age,
   One does not settle things by violence.

Scene III

Madame Pernelle, Mariane, Elmire, Dorine, Damis, Orgon, Cléante

MADAME PERNELLE: I hear strange tales of very strange events.
ORGON: Yes, strange events which these two eyes beheld.
   The man's ingratitude is unparalleled.
   I save a wretched pauper from starvation,
   House him, and treat him like a blood relation,   5
   Shower him every day with my largesse,

Give him my daughter, and all that I possess;
And meanwhile the unconscionable knave
Tries to induce my wife to misbehave;
And not content with such extreme rascality,   10
Now threatens me with my own liberality,
And aims, by taking base advantage of
The gifts I gave him out of Christian love,
To drive me from my house, a ruined man,
And make me end a pauper, as he began.   15
DORINE: Poor fellow!
MADAME PERNELLE: No, my son, I'll never bring
  Myself to think him guilty of such a thing.
ORGON: How's that?
MADAME PERNELLE: The righteous always were maligned.
ORGON: Speak clearly, Mother. Say what's on your mind.
MADAME PERNELLE: I mean that I can smell a rat, my dear.   20
  You know how everybody hates him, here.
ORGON: That has no bearing on the case at all.
MADAME PERNELLE: I told you a hundred times, when you were small,
  That virtue in this world is hated ever;
  Malicious men may die, but malice never.   25
ORGON: No doubt that's true, but how does it apply?
MADAME PERNELLE: They've turned you against him by a clever lie.
ORGON: I've told you, I was there and saw it done.
MADAME PERNELLE: Ah, slanderers will stop at nothing, Son.
ORGON: Mother, I'll lose my temper . . . For the last time,   30
  I tell you I was witness to the crime.
MADAME PERNELLE: The tongues of spite are busy night and noon,
  And to their venom no man is immune.
ORGON: You're talking nonsense. Can't you realize
  I saw it; saw it; saw it with my eyes?   35
  Saw, do you understand me? Must I shout it
  Into your ears before you'll cease to doubt it?
MADAME PERNELLE: Appearances can deceive, my son. Dear me,
  We cannot always judge by what we see.
ORGON: Drat! Drat!
MADAME PERNELLE: One often interprets things awry;   40
  Good can seem evil to a suspicious eye.
ORGON: Was I to see his pawing at Elmire
  As an act of charity?
MADAME PERNELLE: Till his guilt is clear,
  A man deserves the benefit of the doubt.
  You should have waited, to see how things turned out.   45
ORGON: Great God in Heaven, what more proof did I need?
  Was I to sit there, watching, until he'd . . .

You drive me to the brink of impropriety.

MADAME PERNELLE: No, no, a man of such surpassing piety
Could not do such a thing. You cannot shake me.   50
I don't believe it, and you shall not make me.

ORGON: You vex me so that, if you weren't my mother,
I'd say to you . . . some dreadful thing or other.

DORINE: It's your turn now, Sir, not to be listened to;
You'd not trust us, and now she won't trust you.   55

CLÉANTE: My friends, we're wasting time which should be spent
In facing up to our predicament.
I fear that scoundrel's threats weren't made in sport.

DAMIS: Do you think he'd have the nerve to go to court?

ELMIRE: I'm sure he won't: they'd find it all too crude   60
A case of swindling and ingratitude.

CLÉANTE: Don't be too sure. He won't be at a loss
To give his claims a high and righteous gloss;
And clever rogues with far less valid cause
Have trapped their victims in a web of laws.   65
I say again that to antagonize
A man so strongly armed was most unwise.

ORGON: I know it; but the man's appalling cheek
Outraged me so, I couldn't control my pique.

CLÉANTE: I wish to Heaven that we could devise   70
Some truce between you, or some compromise.

ELMIRE: If I had known what cards he held, I'd not
Have roused his anger by my little plot.

ORGON: (*To* DORINE, *as* M. LOYAL *enters.*)
What is that fellow looking for? Who is he?
Go talk to him—and tell him that I'm busy.   75

SCENE IV

MONSIEUR LOYAL, MADAME PERNELLE, ORGON, DAMIS, MARIANE, DORINE,
ELMIRE, CLÉANTE

MONSIEUR LOYAL: Good day, dear sister. Kindly let me see
Your master.

DORINE: He's involved with company,
And cannot be disturbed just now, I fear.

MONSIEUR LOYAL: I hate to intrude; but what has brought me here
Will not disturb your master, in any event.   5
Indeed, my news will make him most content.

DORINE: Your name?

MONSIEUR LOYAL: Just say that I bring greetings from
Monsieur Tartuffe, on whose behalf I've come.

DORINE (*To* ORGON.):   Sir, he's a very gracious man, and bears

A message from Tartuffe, which, he declares,   10
  Will make you most content.
CLÉANTE: Upon my word,
  I think this man had best be seen, and heard.
ORGON: Perhaps he has some settlement to suggest.
  How shall I treat him? What manner would be best?
CLÉANTE: Control your anger, and if he should mention   15
  Some fair adjustment, give him your full attention.
MONSIEUR LOYAL: Good health to you, good Sir. May Heaven confound
  Your enemies, and may your joys abound.
ORGON (*Aside, to* CLÉANTE.):   A gentle salutation: it confirms
  My guess that he is here to offer terms.   20
MONSIEUR LOYAL: I've always held your family most dear;
  I served your father, Sir, for many a year.
ORGON: Sir, I must ask your pardon; to my shame,
  I cannot now recall your face or name.
MONSIEUR LOYAL: Loyal's my name; I come from Normandy,   25
  And I'm a bailiff, in all modesty.
  For forty years, praise God, it's been my boast
  To serve with honor in that vital post,
  And I am here, Sir, if you will permit
  The liberty, to serve you with this writ . . .   30
ORGON: To—*what?*
MONSIEUR LOYAL: Now, please, Sir, let us have no friction:
  It's nothing but an order of eviction.
  You are to move your goods and family out
  And make way for new occupants, without
  Deferment or delay, and give the keys . . .   35
ORGON: I? Leave this house?
MONSIEUR LOYAL: Why yes, Sir, if you please.
  This house, Sir, from the cellar to the roof,
  Belongs now to the good Monsieur Tartuffe,
  And he is lord and master of your estate
  By virtue of a deed of present date,   40
  Drawn in due form, with clearest legal phrasing. . .
DAMIS: Your insolence is utterly amazing!
MONSIEUR LOYAL: Young man, my business here is not with you
  But with your wise and temperate father, who,
  Like every worthy citizen, stands in awe   45
  Of justice, and would never obstruct the law.
ORGON: But . . .
MONSIEUR LOYAL: Not for a million, Sir, would you rebel
  Against authority; I know that well.
  You'll not make trouble, Sir, or interfere
  With the execution of my duties here.   50

DAMIS: Someone may execute a smart tattoo
On that black jacket° of yours, before you're through.
MONSIEUR LOYAL: Sir, bid your son be silent. I'd much regret
Having to mention such a nasty threat
Of violence, in writing my report.   55
DORINE (*Aside.*):   This man Loyal's a most disloyal sort!
MONSIEUR LOYAL: I love all men of upright character,
And when I agreed to serve these papers, Sir,
It was your feelings that I had in mind.
I couldn't bear to see the case assigned   60
To someone else, who might esteem you less
And so subject you to unpleasantness.
ORGON: What's more unpleasant than telling a man to leave
His house and home?
MONSIEUR LOYAL: You'd like a short reprieve?
If you desire it, Sir, I shall not press you,   65
But wait until tomorrow to dispossess you.
Splendid. I'll come and spend the night here, then,
Most quietly, with half a score of men.
For form's sake, you might bring me, just before
You go to bed, the keys to the front door.   70
My men, I promise, will be on their best
Behavior, and will not disturb your rest.
But bright and early, Sir, you must be quick
And move out all your furniture, every stick:
The men I've chosen are both young and strong,   75
And with their help it shouldn't take you long.
In short, I'll make things pleasant and convenient,
And since I'm being so extremely lenient,
Please show me, Sir, a like consideration,
And give me your entire cooperation.   80
ORGON (*Aside.*):   I may be all but bankrupt, but I vow
I'd give a hundred louis, here and now,
Just for the pleasure of landing one good clout
Right on the end of that complacent snout.
CLÉANTE: Careful; don't make things worse.
DAMIS: My bootsole itches   85
To give that beggar a good kick in the breeches.
DORINE: Monsieur Loyal, I'd love to hear the whack
Of a stout stick across your fine broad back.
MONSIEUR LOYAL: Take care: a woman too may go to jail if
She uses threatening language to a bailiff.   90

V.iv. 52. jacket: In the original, *justaucorps à longues barques,* a close-fitting, long black coat with skirts, the customary dress of a bailiff.

CLÉANTE: Enough, enough, Sir. This must not go on.
  Give me that paper, please, and then begone.
MONSIEUR LOYAL: Well, *au revoir*. God give you all good cheer!
ORGON: May God confound you, and him who sent you here!

SCENE V

ORGON, CLÉANTE, MARIANE, ELMIRE, MADAME PERNELLE, DORINE, DAMIS

ORGON: Now, Mother, was I right or not? This writ
  Should change your notion of Tartuffe a bit.
  Do you perceive his villainy at last?
MADAME PERNELLE: I'm thunderstruck. I'm utterly aghast.
DORINE: Oh, come, be fair. You mustn't take offense   5
  At this new proof of his benevolence.
  He's acting out of selfless love, I know.
  Material things enslave the soul, and so
  He kindly has arranged your liberation
  From all that might endanger your salvation.   10
ORGON: Will you not ever hold your tongue, you dunce?
CLÉANTE: Come, you must take some action, and at once.
ELMIRE: Go tell the world of the low trick he's tried.
  The deed of gift is surely nullified
  By such behavior, and public rage will not   15
  Permit the wretch to carry out his plot.

SCENE VI

VALÈRE, ORGON, CLÉANTE, ELMIRE, MARIANE, MADAME PERNELLE, DAMIS,
DORINE

VALÈRE: Sir, though I hate to bring you more bad news,
  Such is the danger that I cannot choose.
  A friend who is extremely close to me
  And knows my interest in your family
  Has, for my sake, presumed to violate   5
  The secrecy that's due to things of state,
  And sends me word that you are in a plight
  From which your one salvation lies in flight.
  That scoundrel who's imposed upon you so
  Denounced you to the King an hour ago   10
  And, as supporting evidence, displayed
  The strong-box of a certain renegade
  Whose secret papers, so he testified,
  You had disloyally agreed to hide.
  I don't know just what charges may be pressed,   15
  But there's a warrant out for your arrest;

Tartuffe has been instructed, furthermore,
To guide the arresting officer to your door.
CLÉANTE: He's clearly done this to facilitate
His seizure of your house and your estate.   20
ORGON: That man, I must say, is a vicious beast!
VALÈRE: You can't afford to delay, Sir, in the least.
My carriage is outside, to take you hence;
This thousand louis should cover all expense.
Let's lose no time, or you shall be undone;   25
The sole defense, in this case, is to run.
I shall go with you all the way, and place you
In a safe refuge to which they'll never trace you.
ORGON: Alas, dear boy, I wish that I could show you
My gratitude for everything I owe you.   30
But now is not the time; I pray the Lord
That I may live to give you your reward.
Farewell, my dears; be careful . . .
CLÉANTE: Brother, hurry.
We shall take care of things; you needn't worry.

SCENE VII

The OFFICER, TARTUFFE, VALÈRE, ORGON, ELMIRE, MARIANE, MADAME
PERNELLE, DORINE, CLÉANTE, DAMIS

TARTUFFE: Gently, Sir, gently; stay right where you are.
No need for haste; your lodging isn't far.
You're off to prison, by order of the Prince.
ORGON: This is the crowning blow, you wretch; and since
It means my total ruin and defeat,   5
Your villainy is now at last complete.
TARTUFFE: You needn't try to provoke me; it's no use.
Those who serve Heaven must expect abuse.
CLÉANTE: You are indeed most patient, sweet, and blameless.
DORINE: How he exploits the name of Heaven! It's shameless.   10
TARTUFFE: Your taunts and mockeries are all for naught;
To do my duty is my only thought.
MARIANE: Your love of duty is most meritorious,
And what you've done is little short of glorious.
TARTUFFE: All deeds are glorious, Madam, which obey   15
The sovereign prince who sent me here today.
ORGON: I rescued you when you were destitute;
Have you forgotten that, you thankless brute?
TARTUFFE: No, no, I well remember everything;
But my first duty is to serve my King.   20
That obligation is so paramount

That other claims, beside it, do not count;
And for it I would sacrifice my wife,
My family, my friend, or my own life.
ELMIRE: Hypocrite!
DORINE: All that we most revere, he uses   25
To cloak his plots and camouflage his ruses.
CLÉANTE: If it is true that you are animated
By pure and loyal zeal, as you have stated,
Why was this zeal not roused until you'd sought
To make Orgon a cuckold, and been caught?   30
Why weren't you moved to give your evidence
Until your outraged host had driven you hence?
I shan't say that the gift of all his treasure
Ought to have damped your zeal in any measure,
But if he is a traitor, as you declare,   35
How could you condescend to be his heir?
TARTUFFE: (*To the* OFFICER.)
Sir, spare me all this clamor; it's growing shrill.
Please carry out your orders, if you will.
OFFICER°: Yes, I've delayed too long, Sir. Thank you kindly.
You're just the proper person to remind me.   40
Come, you are off to join the other boarders
In the King's prison, according to his orders.
TARTUFFE: Who? I, Sir?
OFFICER: Yes.
TARTUFFE: To prison? This can't be true!
OFFICER: I owe an explanation, but not to you.
(*To* ORGON.) Sir, all is well; rest easy, and be grateful.   45
We serve a Prince to whom all sham is hateful,
A Prince who sees into our inmost hearts,
And can't be fooled by any trickster's arts.
His royal soul, though generous and human,
Views all things with discernment and acumen;   50
His sovereign reason is not lightly swayed,
And all his judgments are discreetly weighed.
He honors righteous men of every kind,
And yet his zeal for virtue is not blind,
Nor does his love of piety numb his wits   55
And make him tolerant of hypocrites.
'Twas hardly likely that this man could cozen
A King who's foiled such liars by the dozen.
With one keen glance, the King perceived the whole

V.vii. 39. Officer: In the original, *un exempt.* He would actually have been a gentleman from the king's personal body-guard with the rank of lieutenant colonel or "master of the camp."

Perverseness and corruption of his soul, 60
And thus high Heaven's justice was displayed:
Betraying you, the rogue stood self-betrayed.
The King soon recognized Tartuffe as one
Notorious by another name, who'd done
So many vicious crimes that one could fill 65
Ten volumes with them, and be writing still.
But to be brief: our sovereign was appalled
By this man's treachery toward you, which he called
The last, worst villainy of a vile career,
And bade me follow the impostor here 70
To see how gross his impudence could be,
And force him to restore your property.
Your private papers, by the King's command,
I hereby seize and give into your hand.
The King, by royal order, invalidates 75
The deed which gave this rascal your estates,
And pardons, furthermore, your grave offense
In harboring an exile's documents.
By these decrees, our Prince rewards you for
Your loyal deeds in the late civil war,° 80
And shows how heartfelt is his satisfaction
In recompensing any worthy action,
How much he prizes merit, and how he makes
More of men's virtues than of their mistakes.

DORINE: Heaven be praised!

MADAME PERNELLE: I breathe again, at last. 85

ELMIRE: We're safe.

MARIANE: I can't believe the danger's past.

ORGON (*To* TARTUFFE.):   Well, traitor, now you see . . .

CLÉANTE: Ah, brother, please
Let's not descend to such indignities.
Leave the poor wretch to his unhappy fate,
And don't say anything to aggravate 90
His present woes; but rather hope that he
Will soon embrace an honest piety,
And mend his ways, and by a true repentance
Move our just King to moderate his sentence.
Meanwhile, go kneel before your sovereign's throne 95
And thank him for the mercies he has shown.

ORGON: Well said: let's go at once and, gladly kneeling,
Express the gratitude which all are feeling.
Then, when that first great duty has been done,

---

80. war: A reference to Orgon's role in supporting the king during the *Frondes*.

We'll turn with pleasure to a second one,   100
And give Valère, whose love has proven so true,
The wedded happiness which is his due.

[1664]

Journal Entry

Do you identify with any of the characters in *Tartuffe*? How do you respond to the topic of individual obsession and religious hypocrisy? Explain.

Textual Considerations

1. What role does Dorine play in *Tartuffe*? Which scenes best illustrate the position she occupies in the Orgon household?
2. Select a few examples that illustrate Tartuffe's voracious appetite for food, sex, and wealth. What do they reveal about his true intentions toward the Orgon family?
3. Describe the relationship between Orgon and Tartuffe. Why do they appear to need each other?
4. Why does Molière delay Tartuffe's appearance until Act III? What dramatic techniques does he use to characterize Tartuffe in Acts I and II?
5. Explain Elmire's reasons for concealing from her husband Tartuffe's sexual advances. What do they reveal about her role as wife?
6. Analyze Tartuffe's speech in Act III, Scene 6. What argument does he use to convince Orgon that he is not a fraud?
7. Explain why Molière's satiric comedy ends with Orgon's romantic promise of "wedded happiness" to Valère.
8. Explain the significance of the role Molière has assigned to the King in Act V.

Cultural Contexts

1. How does Molière satirize the theme of political and religious hypocrisy in *Tartuffe*? How does Molière's satirical tale resonate in today's world?
2. In the preface to *Love's the Best Doctor*, Molière states the need for plays to be performed, not read. Discuss with your group whether the same statement is true of *Tartuffe*. What may be gained by experiencing a performance of the play?

Performance Exercises

PERFORMANCE EXPRESS (45 MINUTES)

Cast one of your classmates in the role of Tartuffe, and ask the others to sit in a wide circle. The student playing the role of Tartuffe should go around the circle addressing all of his classmates, including the ones performing the roles of the other characters in the play. Tartuffe and the whole class should interact, discussing the motives for the characters' behavior in the Orgon household and answering questions from one another. It will be helpful to videotape your performances.

PERFORMANCE PROJECTS

1. Working with your group, present the scene of Tartuffe's seduction of Elmire (Act IV, Scenes 5–7) as Molière wrote it, and then repeat the same scene as a humorous pantomime. Decide on the kind of background music that might be effective for this pantomime, and discuss with your classmates their response to each production.

2. Using the Internet for your sources, conduct research on two classical productions of *Tartuffe*. Read what the reviews say about the scenery and costume design to learn about the manners, fashion, and taste of French polite society in the seventeenth century. Use makeup, music, and costumes that evoke the sophisticated standards of taste of Molière's society. Your goal here is not a costly production of *Tartuffe*, but one that suggests the social reality of Molière's society.

TOPICS FOR DISCUSSION AND WRITING

Writing Topics

1. Examine the images or metaphors of fences, boundaries, or walls in any three texts in Part Five. Consider, for example, walls within families as well as those between or within groups.

2. The limitations of conformity are explored in the poems by Dickinson, Stevens, Williams, and Cummings. Choose images from any three texts that express the speakers' attitudes toward the constraints of predictability and respectability. To what extent do you agree or disagree with their points of view?

3. Many of the texts in Part Five make statements for or against conformity to accepted norms. Using "The Guest" and "A Rose for Emily," analyze the degree to which nonconformity influenced the choices of Daru and Miss Emily. Use evidence from both stories to support your point of view.

4. Compare and contrast the role of the family in "The Metamorphosis," "Eveline," and "The Boarding House." To what extent do members of the family contribute to the autonomy of the protagonists in any of the stories above?

5. Analyze the functions of setting in "Eveline," "The Boarding House," "The Guest," and "Dead Men's Path." What role does the setting play in shaping the protagonists' choices in these stories?

6. Compare and contrast the portrayals of the community in "The Lottery," "The Guest," and "Dead Men's Path." What causes the members of both communities to behave as they do? Are they seeking to decrease or even to destroy the rights of the individual protagonists? Explain.

7. Would it be fair to describe Daru in "The Guest" or Antigone as rebels? Write an analysis of the causes and effects of their rebellion, including your attitude toward it.

8. Analyze the role of the forces of authority in the selections by Olds, Camus, or Sophocles. What positions do they take? How do they enhance or impede the dialogue between our private and communal selves? What did you learn about the relationship between the individual and the law?

9. Discuss the role of tradition, mass psychology, and social pressure in "The Lottery" and "Dead Men's Path." Consider how human beings respond to stereotypes, tradition, and outside pressures and how they balance the clash of the old versus the new and of the autonomous versus the communal self.

10. Discuss images of life and death in the poems by Olds, Wilbur, Yevtushenko, and Ferlinghetti. Consider how form—defined by the diversity of stanzaic patterns, rhythm, tone, and rhymes and other phonic devices—affects meanings and defines the speakers' philosophies of life.

11. Several texts in Part Five portray characters who are particularly unimaginative. What indications of lack of imagination do you find in the texts by Romero, Stevens, Cummings, or Achebe?

12. The issue of alienation of the individual from society emerges in texts by Kafka, Camus, Dickinson, Stevens, and many others. Select three of these texts and write an essay in which you characterize the kind of alienation—physical, psychological, intellectual, social, political, religious, or artistic—that these texts explore.

13. Kafka described "The Metamorphosis" as a story in which "the dream reveals the reality." What does this comment suggest about the underlying psychological significance of Gregor's physical transformation?

14. *Tartuffe* has never been absent from American stages. Use the Internet to read the drama reviews of *Tartuffe*, with which Seattle's Intiman Theatre and New York's Roundabout Theatre opened their 2003 seasons. Compare and contrast the approaches these productions used for *Tartuffe*. What does the popularity of *Tartuffe* tell us about the power of Molière's play to resonate with American audiences?

15. Blake and Wordsworth focus on social problems in nineteenth-century London as well as on the failure of church and state to respond to them. Write an essay focusing on what you consider to be important urban problems in the present. How responsive have contemporary political and religious leaders been in addressing these issues? Limit yourself to two or three issues.

Research Topics

1. Several texts, including *Antigone* and "The Guest," address civil disobedience and the historical right of the individual to engage in social protest. Working with your group, write a documented essay on this issue, consulting at least two of the following sources: Plato's *Crito*, Henry David Thoreau's *On Civil Disobedience*, Martin Luther King Jr's "Letter from a Birmingham Jail," Thomas Jefferson's "Declaration of Independence," and/or Elizabeth Cady Stanton's "Declaration of Sentiments and Resolutions." Given a choice between a society in which individual rights come first and one in which community needs have priority, which would you choose?

2. Write a documented paper explaining why *Tartuffe* was banned from the stage in 1664–1667. Why did Louis XIV's social milieu react so fiercely against Molière's satire of religious hypocrisy? In your opinion, does the play explore issues more threatening than the vices embodied by Tartuffe? Read Molière's preface to *Tartuffe* in Richard Wilbur's translation of the play in this book, and consult other critical sources as well.

3. Access the Nobel Prize speeches by Camus, Faulkner, Gordimer, and Morrison on the Internet, and analyze them. What do they reveal about the speakers' humanitarian, political, and social viewpoints? What do they portray about the speakers themselves and their view of art, literature, and history? How do you respond to these speeches? How do they challenge you as a reader?

FILM ANGLES

INDIVIDUALISM AND COMMUNITY: THE FILM ANGLE

The relationship between the individual and the community is the basis of every society—the heart and pulse of what sustains it. If the relationship is a healthy one, both the individual and the community thrive. If the relationship is inhospitable, both suffer. Literature and art offer countless illustrations of the struggle between the two, sometimes igniting the hope that humanity might learn from its mistakes. Some authors even imagine a Utopia, in which all of society's abuses and errors are corrected and all individuals live in harmony.

The range of literary works that express this theme is wide—from Sophocles' tragedy *Antigone*, in which the individual challenges the authority of the state, to Kafka's "The Metamorphosis," Joyce's "Eveline," and Faulkner's "A Rose For Emily," all of which deal with characters doomed to lead eccentric, insular lives by the patriarchal and social forces that have shaped them. So, too, the range of movies that can be discussed in the context of Part Five is broad and varied.

FILM HISTORY AND GENRE

The extraordinary excitement that motion pictures elicited in the early years of the twentieth century was precisely because, like all new technologies, film generated a Utopian spirit. Filmmakers and critics believed that because film was a more "democratic" art form, as opposed to elitist, it would fulfill the dream of uniting humanity—that since film was a visual language that transcended linguistic barriers and national cultures, it could reach the common ground that all beings share. Film, it was thought, would create a true communal theater of a scope undreamed of by the Greeks or the Elizabethans. Early pioneer filmmakers such as D. W. Griffith and Cecil B. DeMille approached the medium with a messianic spirit, making movies with an aim toward correcting social injustices and transforming the world.

Like other technologies, however, motion pictures also provided opportunities for disseminating propaganda on an unprecedented scale and were used to promote the policies and values of such twentieth-century political tyrants as Lenin, Stalin, and Hitler. For every movie that has advanced the cause of social justice and educated millions on subjects like the Holocaust and civil rights, there are dozens devoted to mindless entertainment and questionable values.

Perhaps no theme is more compelling than that of the heroic individual who struggles valiantly against a formidable opponent. Clearly, the theme is universal, appealing to the rebel in all of us, and it can be discerned in many genres. In the costume epic *Gladiator* (d. Ridley Scott, 2000), the protagonist fights the corruption of the Roman empire at the expense of his own life. In the teenage drama *Rebel Without a Cause* (d. Nicholas Ray, 1955), young people seek in each other the comfort and understanding they do not get from their parents. In the biographical-historical drama *Gandhi* (d. Richard Attenborough, Great Britain, 1982), a public figure rouses millions to fight a colonialist empire. In all cases, the protagonist is one who refuses to compromise personal values or bow to authority, legitimate or not.

Often, the heroic figure is larger than life, suggesting that only such individuals have the charisma and power to make a difference. In John Ford's *Young Mr. Lincoln* (1939), many visual and cinematic motifs in the film emphasize that even Lincoln's idiosyncrasies predestined him for greatness. In the film versions of Jean Anouilh's *Becket* (d. Peter Glenville, 1964) and Robert Bolt's *A Man for All Seasons* (d. Fred Zinneman, 1966), the protagonists—Archbishop Thomas Becket and Chancellor Thomas More, respectively—resist the manipulative autocratic powers of English kings, preferring to die rather than compromise their consciences. In Spike Lee's *Malcolm X* (1992), the protagonist's personal life is virtually sacrificed to his determination to give voice to the needs of an unempowered community.

Movies have also shown ordinary people acting on personal convictions in everyday situations and affecting the course of events. A fledgling senator stands up against political corruption in *Mr. Smith Goes to Washington* (d. Frank Capra, 1939); a housewife and factory worker fight unfair labor practices in *Norma Rae* (d. Martin Ritt, 1979); an office worker pursues the cover-up of environmental pollutions in *Erin Brockovich* (d. Steven Soderbergh, 2000); a writer risks alienating her family in her fight against apartheid in *A World Apart* (d. Chris Menges, 1988); an employee puts his life and family in jeopardy when he gives incriminating evidence against the tobacco industry in *The Insider* (d. Michael Mann, 1999).

Questions to Consider

1. Discuss any film in terms of how it dramatizes the relationship between the individual and the community. Is the individual portrayed as ordinary or extraordinary? If both, how does the film balance the character's human limitations with his or her heroic features? Is the character too good to be true? If so, how does this affect your ability to relate to the character or appreciate the film?
2. In Sophocles' *Antigone*, the heroine defies authority by burying her brother—against King Creon's ruling. Since her action springs from such a strong personal impulse, can it also be seen as an example of civil disobedience? Can you think of a character in a film whose actions are both very personal and of public consequence?

CASE STUDIES

12 Angry Men

The film *12 Angry Men* (d. Sidney Lumet, 1957) is one of the strongest movies ever made about the jury system. A tour de force, with an all-star cast headed by Henry Fonda, the film is frequently shown on television and remains more popular than its remake, which was made for television in 1997. When the film opens, twelve members of a jury are directed by the judge to arrive at a unanimous verdict and decide the fate of a young Hispanic man accused of killing his father; they are told that a guilty verdict automatically means the death penalty. At the initial vote, eleven jurors, convinced that it is an open-and-shut case, find the defendant guilty and consider the holdout member a nuisance whose opposition will only prolong the inevitable verdict. Since the circumstances of the crime point convincingly to the defendant's guilt, it is no easy task to convince anyone that the case is worth discussing, much less that they should change their minds. Nevertheless, as the drama unfolds and the details of the evidence are scrutinized, each juror exposes the weaker aspects of his personality, revealing personal motives and deep-seated prejudices that strongly determine his judgment.

The individual—whose name, Davis, we only learn at the very end—who acts as the catalyst for the reversal of judgment is neither a recalcitrant rebel nor a radical with his own agenda. He is an ordinary man in doubt, an independent thinker who refuses simply to go along with the majority unless he can live with his conscience. He claims to have neither greater insight nor higher moral standards, but it is his insistence that the evidence may be flawed that plants doubt in the others' minds and triggers a more rigorous analysis of the case. In this way, Davis is neither a hero nor a martyr to a cause, but a citizen who reminds others how democracy and the court system should work.

Except for brief scenes in the beginning and end, the entire film is set in a drab and impersonal room in a courthouse in lower Manhattan, where the jury must sit until they reach a decision. This lends an air of authenticity and claustrophobia to the drama, which is appropriate to the experience the men must endure as strangers forced together in an insulated environment. The uncomfortable physical conditions—it is the "hottest day of the year" and the room has a fan that doesn't work—add to the growing tension and confrontational nature of the characters' interactions.

Questions to Consider

1. Why do you think we never learn the names or ethnic identities of the men? Why are they referred to only by their juror numbers?
2. Examine the interaction among the men. Do your first impressions of any of the characters change throughout the film? How and why?
3. Describe Davis's personality. What features stand out? Why does he feel the way he does? Does he seem morally superior to the others? Does the actor convince you that he is an average man? If not, does this affect the impact of the drama?
4. Since the jury ultimately shifts its initial view, its status as a "community" also changes. What is this change? Does the film encourage you to examine further the role of the individual in relation to his or her community?
5. How does the restricted setting affect the overall atmosphere of the film?

The Crucible

Arthur Miller's play *The Crucible*, set in Salem, Massachusetts, in 1692 during the witch trials, was first produced on the stage in 1953. At the time, certain forces of the U.S. government were bent on rooting out Communists who allegedly had infiltrated the U.S. Army and various departments of government. Although the hearings in Washington, under the leadership of Senator Joseph McCarthy, were criticized and lamented by many, even at the time, they created a national hysteria—a paranoid fear of Communism—and destroyed many careers and lives in the process. For this reason, they were, then and now, referred to as a "witch hunt"—a clear reference to witchcraft trials throughout history, including those at Salem. Not coincidentally, therefore, Miller's play was interpreted not just as a dramatization of the historical events of the seventeenth century, but as an allegory about contemporary American life.

The 1996 film version, directed by Nicholas Hytner and with a screenplay by Miller, is an intelligent, well-acted adaptation—compelling evidence that the story has not lost its relevance. It makes it clear that however much we like to imagine our own times as more enlightened than the past, the compulsion to look for scapegoats to conceal our own flaws and hunt down and destroy the "other" in the name of the welfare of the community or the safety of the state is always subject to resurgence.

The drama concerns the havoc wreaked on the town of Salem by a group of young, sexually precocious women, led by Abigail Williams, who claim to be victims of the devil and certain "witches" among various members of the community. Among those accused are Elizabeth, wife of John Proctor, with whom Abigail has had an affair. The drama demonstrates how hysteria rules over reason and how the combination of human corruption and superstition, when backed by authority, leads to tyranny.

Since witchcraft is an "invisible crime"—as Judge Danforth, the Massachusetts authority who must decide the case says—about which only the witch and her victim can testify, there is little that a lawyer can do. Therein lies another resemblance between the play's theme and the McCarthy hearings of the 1950s: The very *accusation* of witchcraft, like that of being a Communist, virtually equaled guilt. There was no recourse but submission. In both cases, the only way to exonerate oneself was to "name" others. Under the absurdity of the circumstances, the challenge to the individual was either to confess to a crime of which he or she was innocent or deny it and be executed. John Proctor, the primary character faced with this dilemma in the film, has every reason to want to live, yet finally refuses to lie and destroy his good name.

Questions to Consider

1. The film, unlike the play, begins with a scene in the forest. What is the significance of this scene? Is it simply one of the more realistic touches films can provide over stage versions of plays, or does it add something important to what we learn later through the dialogue in the play? What is the view of the forest as it is discussed by Miller in one of the commentaries in the play? What did it represent to the Christian community of Salem?

2. Describe John Proctor and Elizabeth Proctor as characters and as individuals who become the primary focus of the drama. What are their strengths and weaknesses? How do these contribute to our impressions of them? Are they an average man and woman or larger-than-life heroes?

3. Many minor characters in *The Crucible* help form the Salem community. Which of these characters reinforce the repressive atmosphere of the community and which of them resist it?

4. Much of the play's and film's impact depends on the credibility of the Abigail Williams character. Do you think she is a convincing figure? Even if several members of the community "believe" her for their own personal reasons, how can we explain the effect she has on Judge Danforth, an outsider who seems intelligent, wise, and not easily manipulated?

5. While the community seems to be a unified force with similar views of witchcraft's threat to security, there is disagreement even among the outside specialists and lawmakers regarding how to arrive at the truth. Who are the contesting figures, and how can we incorporate their views in our general impression of the Salem community?

Research Topics

1. The protagonists of *Gandhi*, *Lawrence of Arabia* (d. David Lean, Great Britain, 1962), *Malcolm X*, *Spartacus* (d. Stanley Kubrick, 1960), and *Gladiator* are involved on a grand scale with momentous historical events. Compare two or three of these films

in terms of how the character balances his personal ambitions or desires with his role as a leader.

2. Violence can be a means of oppression as well as liberation. Both *Spartacus* and *Gladiator*, for example, depict violence as a means of entertainment mandated by the governing authority (ancient Rome in both cases) for the pleasure of its citizens. Bloodshed, dismemberment, and the deaths of the gladiators were essential to the experience. In both films, individual gladiators—Spartacus in the first case, Maximus in the latter—survive only by conforming to the game and biding their time, eventually turning the violence against their oppressors and freeing the enslaved portion of the community. (At one critical moment in the arena, Maximus tells his fellow gladiators that the way to survive is to stay together.) Do the themes of these films indicate that authoritarian states can never be overcome through peaceful means? Do they suggest that violence in itself is a neutral phenomenon, its ethical dimension determined by the purpose it serves? Is the individual ever permitted to use violence against a repressive community? If so, what is the moral basis of this "permission"?

3. Compare the visions of the future in *Blade Runner* (d. Ridley Scott, 1982), *Gattica* (d. Andrew Nicoll, 1997), and *1984* (d. Michael Radford, Great Britain, 1984). Are the societies fantasized in these films an improvement over the ones in existence today? Is the relationship of the individual and the community more or less as it is today? Discuss specific images and scenes in each film to illustrate your answers.

4. In some ways, *American Beauty* (d. Sam Mendes, 1999), *Being There* (d. Hal Ashby, 1979), *Ordinary People* (d. Robert Redford, 1980), and *Pleasantville* (d. Gary Ross, 1998) represent the extremes of a less confrontational relationship between the individual and the community. Each poses questions about the nature of dependency in that relationship and the community's effects on the individual. What are these "extreme" positions, and how does each film treat the question of the individual's role within the community?

5. In some ways, *12 Angry Men* presents a relatively optimistic viewpoint in dramatizing a situation in which individuals are forced to confront their prejudices and rise above them and can make some difference in the way justice is meted out in society. Clearly, this can occur only in a democratic society. Discuss the role of the individual in how the law functions in the societies represented in such films as *City of God* (d. Fernando Meirelles, Brazil/Portugal, 2003), *The Magdalene Sisters* (d. Peter Mullan, Ireland, 2003), *Lagaan: Once Upon a Time in India* (d. Ashutush Gowariker, India, 2002), and *Lumumba* (d. Raoul Peck, France/Belgium/Haiti, 2001).

6. Arthur Miller's play *The Crucible* was first filmed in 1956 in a French/East German co-production directed by Raymond Rouleau with a screenplay by noted existentialist writer Jean-Paul Sartre. Just as Miller wrote the play as an allegory of contemporary America, Sartre adopted it to express sentiments in France following World War II. As a result, there are many differences between this version and the 1996 film, especially the ending. Watch the video of both versions and consider these differences with special attention to (a) which characters are most affected by the changes, (b) whether the changes affect the meaning of the story, and (c) whether the French version violates the spirit of Miller's play.

An Introduction to the Elements of Fiction, Nonfiction, Poetry, and Drama

FICTION

What do we mean by *fiction*? For the novelist Toni Morrison, "fiction, by definition, is distinct from fact. Presumably it's the product of imagination—invention—and it claims the freedom to dispense with 'what really happened' or where it really happened, or when it really happened, and nothing in it needs to be publicly verifiable, although much of it can be verified." Morrison goes on to say, however, that as a storyteller she is less interested in the distinction between fiction and fact than in that between fact and truth, "because facts can exist without human intelligence, but truth cannot." Fiction, then, is concerned with what the novelist William Faulkner calls "the verities and truths of the heart."

Tales, fables, parables, epic poems, and romances, and even the fairy tales you heard as a child, rank among the most ancient modes of fiction, kept alive by the power of the human voice to narrate and transmit the excitement and authenticity of imaginary actions and events. Short stories, however, belong to a more contemporary mode of narrative fiction and gained in recognition through the works of nineteenth-century American and European writers, including Edgar Allan Poe, Mary E. Wilkins Freeman, Anton Chekhov, and Guy de Maupassant.

This appendix introduces several technical terms, such as *character, plot, setting, theme, narrator, style,* and *tone,* that are used to describe the formal elements of a short story. Getting acquainted with these terms will help you to understand how short stories are put together and make it easier for you both to read them and to write about them.

Character

A *character* is a fictional person in a story, and readers' first reactions to him or her are usually based on their subjective capacity to empathize with the character's experiences. A character is often revealed through his or her actions, which provide readers with clues about the character's personality, motives, and expectations. Many stories present a conflict between the protagonist (the story's central character) and the antagonist (the opposing character or force); the conflict is revealed through the author's use of dialogue and narrative. In Alifa Rifaat's story "Another Evening at the Club" (p. 350), for instance, the main character or protagonist, Samia, is in conflict with her husband, the antagonist, because of her inability to liberate herself from his dominating behavior.

Fictional characters are sometimes referred to as *round* or *flat, static* or *dynamic*. A round character is usually more fully developed, challenging readers to analyze the character's motives and evaluate his or her actions. Round characters change, grow, and possess a credible personality, like the mother in Mary E. Wilkins Freeman's short story "The Revolt of 'Mother'" (p. 315). Flat characters, in contrast, usually play a minor role in a story, act predictably, and are often presented as stereotypes. The minister in Freeman's story, for example, is presented as an unimaginative and inflexible individual. In fact, he is in many ways a foil to Mrs. Penn, because he has a totally opposite personality.

Plot

Plot is the arrangement of the events in a story according to a pattern devised by the writer and inferred by the reader. Often the plot develops when characters and situations oppose each other, creating conflicts that grow and eventually reach a climax, the point of highest intensity of the story. After this climactic turning point, the action of the story finally declines, moving toward a resolution of the conflict.

Although the time frame in a story may vary from recapturing an intense, momentary experience to narrating an event that covers a much longer period, the storyteller must focus on what Poe terms the "single effect" as the action of the story moves toward a resolution of the conflict.

"Another Evening at the Club" provides an example of a plot centered on a conflict between Samia and her husband. The action starts to rise in dramatic intensity (*the rising action*) when Samia's loss of her emerald ring destabilizes her relationship with her husband. After this initial exposition, or narrative introduction of characters and situation, the action reaches its crisis (the *climax* of the action) when Samia's husband refuses to exonerate the maid, even though he knows she is innocent. Notice that this external conflict also parallels the internal conflict of the protagonist when she recognizes the degree of the husband's control over her and her inability to oppose him. The action of the story moves toward the resolution of its conflict (*the falling action*) when Samia yields to her husband's authority.

While many writers continue to follow this traditional model of plot development, some authors deviate from it. Liam O'Flaherty, in "The Sniper," for example, and Stephen Crane, in "A Mystery of Heroism," prefer the surprise ending, while Liam O'Flaherty, in "The Sniper," ends his story without a resolution of the protagonist's inner conflict.

Although the typical fictional plot has a beginning, a middle, and an end, authors may also vary their patterns of narration. In "The Sniper," the story's events unfold in the order in which they took place, following a *chronological* development. In "Another Evening at the Club," Rifaat uses *flashbacks*, selecting a few episodes to build a plot that moves backward and forward in time: the action begins in the present with Samia's anguish at her husband's decision to blame the maid for the theft of the ring; then, through the use of flashbacks, the author reports past events that illustrate the position that women like Samia occupy in a patriarchal culture. Rifaat also uses *suspense* or uncertainty, creating a sense of anticipation and curiosity about what the protagonist will do next. Will she defend the servant accused of stealing the ring? How will her husband react when he finds out that the ring was not stolen? Many stories also use *foreshadowing*, providing details and hints about what will happen next. In Mary E. Wilkins Freeman's short story, the title "The Revolt of Mother" functions as a foreshadowing, anticipating the outcome of the story.

Fictional devices such as flashback and foreshadowing do not operate in isolation but rather work together with characterization, setting, point of view, style, and tone to create a unified effect.

Setting

The time, place, and social context of a story constitute its *setting*. In Nathaniel Hawthorne's "Young Goodman Brown," the somber atmosphere that pervades the whole story, including the protagonist's moral despondency, emerges from Hawthorne's representation of a supernatural setting. By situating young Goodman Brown's mysterious journey in a gloomy, dreamlike forest, Hawthorne prepares the reader for Brown's brutal confrontation with "the great power of blackness." Other stories reconstruct historical moments with great precision. The setting of Ernest Gaines's "The Sky Is Gray" transports readers to the American South in the 1940s, while the symbolic narrative of "Young Goodman Brown" describes Salem Village and a New England forest in the seventeenth century. Still others tell of events that could have taken place anywhere and at any time.

As you read a short story, watch for details related to time, place, and social context that reveal the motivation of the protagonist and establish the story's credibility. Pay particular attention to the writer's use of visual imagery aimed at helping you to create mental pictures of the setting and assessing its effects on the characters' actions.

Theme

Theme may be defined as the central or dominant idea of the story reinforced by the interaction of fictional devices such as character, plot, setting, and point of view. The theme is the overall generalization we can make about the story's meaning and significance. Sometimes the theme can be stated in a short phrase. For instance, "the rights of the community versus those of an individual" is one theme that emerges in Achebe's short story "Dead Men's Path." The theme of "The Sky Is Gray" is complex because the story is concerned not only with the relationship between the narrator and his mother but also with the complexity of race relationships in the American South in the 1940s.

To define the theme of a story, look for clues provided by the author such as the title, imagery, symbolism, and dialogue between the characters. A story may evoke a range of meanings. And readers—because of their diverse interests, cultural backgrounds, and expectations—will react individually and produce varied meanings. Meanings should be supported by evidence from the story, however.

Narrator

The voice that narrates a story is not necessarily the writer's; while the author writes the story, the narrator tells it. The *narrator* is a technique that writers use to create a particular point of view from which they will tell the story, present the actions, and shape the readers' responses. Narrators can report external and internal events, but most important, they express the narrative angle that writers use to tell the story.

Narrators that are *omniscient* know everything or almost everything that happens in the story, including what goes on inside the minds of the characters. They are presumed to be *reliable*. In "The Storm" by Kate Chopin, the narrator penetrates the minds of several people: Calixta, the wife who faces the storm at home; Bobinôt, the absent husband, who is especially concerned about his wife's safety; Alcée, Calixta's seducer; and Clarisse, Alcée's wife. By exposing the effect of the storm upon these characters, the omniscient narrator provides glimpses of their different views of life and marriage. By exposing their interior thoughts, the omniscient narrator provides glimpses of a dramatic dialogue between two opposing points of view. Omniscient narrators tend to be objective—emotionally removed from the action—and to use the third-person *he, she, it,* and *they* to create a *third-person* point of view.

First-person narrators report the events from the point of view of the *I*, or first person. A first-person narrator differs from an omniscient narrator because the *I* both participates in the action and communicates a single point of view. This type of narrator usually creates a greater degree of intimacy with the reader, as in "First Confession" (p. 893). The writer's choice of a narrator is important because it determines the *point of view* (or the voice and angle from which the narrator tells the story) and thereby affects the story's tone and meaning.

Unreliable narrators do not possess a full understanding of the events they narrate, and the reader can see more than they do. In "The Sky Is Gray," the reader encounters implications of issues related to race and class that escape the young African American narrator. The narrator's lack of awareness is evident in the dentist's office scene when a college student disagrees with an older preacher about the existence of God and racial viewpoints.

Style and Tone

Style refers to the way writers express themselves. Style depends on *diction* (the writer's choice of vocabulary), *syntax* (grammar and sentence structure), as well as *voice* and *rhythm*. Style reveals the writer's linguistic choices or preferences and therefore is as private and unique as their personalities and identities. Notice the sharp contrast, for example between Kate's Chopin's dramatic use of words and images to infuse them with symbolic significance in "The Storm" and Edith Wharton's straightforward, concise style, created to evoke the rhythm of a colloquial conversation in "Roman Fever." To make their language unique and particular, writers also use other devices, such as the following:

- *Irony* is the discrepancy between what is expected and what actually happens. The title of Franz Kafka's story "The Metamorphosis" is ironic because it reverses the reader's expectations of a positive change from an inferior to a superior state. Verbal irony is the discrepancy between what the words convey and what they actually mean, as in the title of Stephen Crane's "A Mystery of Heroism."
- A *symbol* is something—a word or an object—that stands for an idea beyond a literal meaning. In Elie Wiesel's "The Watch," the watch may function as a symbol of "the soul and memory" of the past.
- A *metaphor* is a figure of speech that compares two dissimilar elements without using *like* or *as:* "The rain was coming down in sheets" ("The Storm"). A *simile* is a comparison using *like* or *as:* "Her lips were as red and moist as pomegranate seed" ("The Storm").

- *Tone* is the manner, mood, or pervading attitude that writers establish for characters, situations, and readers. Authors use a variety of different tones such as intimate or distant, ironic or direct, hostile or sympathetic, formal or casual, humorous or serious, and emotional or objective.

In "First Confession," for example, Frank O'Connor uses humor to communicate his young protagonist's terror, reinforced by his sister's threats of punishment, as he faces his first religious confession. In "Jasmine," Bharati Mukherjee uses irony to portray her protagonist's experiences as an illegal alien in the United States.

That successful creators of short fiction must be involved with the intricacies of their craft is clear, but remember also that their primary purpose is to use language to communicate to you. As the novelist William Faulkner reminds us, in his 1950 Nobel Prize acceptance speech, writers like to tell and retell stories about "love and honor and pity and pride and compassion and sacrifice"—in other words, stories about the lives and experiences of all human beings.

CREATIVE OR LITERARY NONFICTION: THE ESSAY

Creative or literary nonfiction—such as memoirs, personal writing, journalism, and cultural and academic criticism—is often defined as writing that is neither imaginary nor inhabited by fictional characters like the literary offspring of fiction, poetry, and drama. The essay, a creative or literary nonfiction prose, emphasizes writers' tendency toward self-analysis, their casual free flow of thoughts, the range of their personal experiences, and the reliability of their voices.

The history of the essay takes us back to French writer Michel de Montaigne, a retired French magistrate, who in 1570 wrote in a flexible prose discourse a series of personal meditations on subjects like cannibalism, friendship, repentance, physiognomy, and experience. He referred to this informal, casual kind of writing as *"essai,"* from the French word meaning "experiment," "trial," or "attempt." Montaigne's essays first reached England through John Florio's translation in 1580, and since then this creative nonfiction form has been widely used. Joseph Addison (1672–1719) and Sir Richard Steele (1672–1729) excelled in the creation of the "magazine" essay in England, showing how the essay could serve cultural needs and fulfill the moral, social, and political expectations of the average reader. In the twentieth century, the essay form proliferated in the hands of such outstanding essayists as Virginia Woolf and George Orwell. Following Montaigne's personal, digressive writing style, Woolf explored a wide range of subjects related to the position of women, while Orwell exposed in his essays the challenge of political, ideological, and social flaws. Woolf wrote more than 500 literary reviews and essays, creating what rhetorician Thomas J. Farrell has called a "female mode of rhetoric"—a style of writing highlighted by association of ideas, a light tone, and personal experience. Its purpose is to oppose what Woolf viewed as the hierarchical, logical discourse of male literary tradition.

In the United States, the essay reached its great heights in the hands of Ralph Waldo Emerson and Henry David Thoreau, who explored issues related to self-reliance, transcendentalism, and civil disobedience in nineteenth-century New England. The essay then suffered a steady decline when readers in the twentieth century tended to favor creative fiction. In the late 1970s, American essayist E. B. White called attention to the role the essay played as a "second-class citizen" in relation to poetry, fiction, and drama. However, in the 1980s and 1990s, the contemporary American essay—whether formal, informal, or in the guise of personal memoir or criticism—has gained momentum and new literary energy in journals, reviews, and book collections. As Joseph Epstein, noted Chicago essayist says, "Don't spread it around but it's a sweet time to be an essayist." Several features may account for the "rebirth" of the American essay:

1. Essayists use creative literary tools such as symbols, metaphors, and images; they also feel free to use the essay form to express their emotions. Thus, by collapsing the boundaries between fiction and nonfiction, essayists are being accorded the same recognition as writers of fiction.
2. Philosophers, mathematicians, and other professionals have been adopting the personal essay form to combine intimate recollections with factual evidence of scientific discourse.
3. Essayists also use the essay to combine their private and public voices to create texts that possess a sense of journalistic immediacy.

Audiences are especially receptive to the essay form as a personal, informal way of absorbing genuine intimate experience.

Form

In view of the diverse literary possibilities open to the contemporary essay, it is impossible to come up with a precise definition of its form. However, essayists' tentative exploration of a topic, their personal engagement in the process of self-analysis, their use of a nonauthoritative tone and such fictional devises as symbols and metaphors, as well as their intimate address to an audience have emerged as some of the most notable features of essays.

The following classification is based on four fundamental modes of argumentation, which will help you analyze some of the most prominent features of the essays in this book. Notice, however, that any rigid classification of essay type tends to blur because of writers' lively, dynamic use of this creative nonfiction. As Susan Sontag, a prominent essayist on modern culture, has said, "In contrast to poetry and fiction, the nature of the essay is diversity—diversity of level, subject, tone, diction."

Narrative

Narratives essays tend to make a point by creating a sense of personal immediacy in an autobiographical narrative, in which writers disclose their own experiences and their self-discoveries about the way they relate to a specific topic. Narrative essays usually follow a chronological pattern.

Example: Brent Staples's "A Brother's Murder" and May Sarton's "The Rewards of Living a Solitary Life"

Staples's personal incursion into the past narrates the obstacles he encountered to save his brother from the terrifying threats of street life in the inner city. The essay's thesis, "I wanted desperately for him to live," also underscores the tone of urgency with which Staples fashions his biography to persuade the reader of his role as a devoted brother and a remorseful survivor of the dangers of urban street life. By concluding the essay with his own reaction to Blake's death, Staples places his experience into a larger social context: Should society feel guilty about the Blakes of the ghetto?

In contrast, Sarton's biographical narrative about the joys of a solitary life doesn't aim to persuade the reader; rather it reaffirms her enjoyment of the solitary life by committing it to writing. Frederick Douglass's "How I Learned to Read and Write" and Salman Rushdie's "From *Imaginary Lands*" are also examples of memoirs and prose naratives.

Descriptive

Writers use descriptive essays to appeal primarily to the readers' sensory perception of sight, sound, touch, taste, and smell in order to transport them to a visual setting or to create a mental picture.

Example: Plato's "The Allegory of the Cave"

In "The Allegory of the Cave," Plato uses visual images to challenge his listener's imaginary eyes to "see," to "behold" the prisoner in the cave with the same sensory acuteness of his own eyes. Responding to the power of the speaker's description, Glaucon, student listener, also begins to look with the prisoner's eyes as he ascends into sunlight and descends back into the cave. Eventually, Glaucon finally "sees" the allegorical meaning of Plato's argument about the human capacity to understand reality. In "The Allegory of the Cave," descriptions function on the physical level of visual sight, the imaginative level of the mind's eye, and the allegorical level of abstraction.

Expository

Writers use expository essays to analyze, inform, argue, explain and clarify ideas, expose arguments, and propose solutions.

Example: Eric Liu's "A Chinaman's Chance: Reflections on the American Dream"

In this essay, Liu adopts a polemic initial tone to refute the idea that "the American Dream is dead." Throughout the essay, he analyzes and exposes his viewpoint by adding more arguments about immigrant expectations of America. Like a classical rhetorician who relies on the presentation of proofs, Liu wants to "prove" in his expository essay that the immigrants' journey to America is worth it. While Liu's proofs increase his support of his topic, in such references as "my sister called me a 'banana,'" he combines exposition with personal experience. Much of the energy of Liu's essay derives from his effective fusion of analysis and personal viewpoint.

Argumentative

Writers craft persuasive arguments to expose a problem, present evidence, reinforce or refute solutions, and convince the reader about a controversial issue. When writing persuasive essays, they also consider the audience's attitude toward a problem and their possible interpretation of the evidence presented.

Example: Deborah Tannen's "Sex, Lies and Conversation: Why Is It So Hard for Men and Women to Talk to Each Other?" and Virginia Woolf's "Professions for Women."

In these essays, Tannen and Woolf attempt to persuade readers about their theses. Tannen's scientific method reveals the imbalance in gender communication as a sociocultural phenomenon. Her conclusion—"Like charity, successful cross-cultural communication should begin at home"—fully reveals, however, that she uses a rigorous inductive method to reach and persuade her audience.

Woolf, in contrast, organizes her expository essay around two specific points: her conscious murder of the "angel of the house" and her inability to tell "the truth about my own experiences as a body." In the course of her analysis she uses other rhetorical devices, such as comparison and contrast (herself versus the "angel," man versus woman) and cause and effect (the consequences of the angel's death). Like Tannen, however, she also ends with a personal challenge to the audience, whom she dares to answer the questions she has posed to them. Notice that such a challenge also betrays to a great extent the degree of emotional commitment that sustains the rigorous clarity of Woolf's argumentative method.

Rhetorical Strategies

Writers use a host of rhetorical strategies to narrate, to analyze, to argue, and to persuade. If you become familiar with them, they will help you examine and analyze the argumentative possibilities of the essay form. The following texts illustrate some of these rhetorical devices, such as comparison and contrast, cause and effect, and process analysis.

Through comparison and contrast, Bruce Catton, in "Grant and Lee: A Study in Contrasts," builds insightful characterization for his powerful portraits of Grant and Lee. Daniel Meier's memoir, "One Man's Kids," informs the reader about the causes and effects behind his decision to become a first-grade teacher and, at the same time, criticizes society's negative attitude toward grade school teaching as a male profession.

Seth Mydans and Martin Luther King Jr. also use cause and effect. In "Not Just the Inner City: Well-to-Do Join Gangs," Mydans explains the reasons for the growing popularity of gangs in U.S. suburbia, while in "I Have a Dream," King delivers his emotional plea for a shared view of the promises of the American dream through an analysis of the causes and consequences of its failure.

The examples and illustrations that Peter Lyman uses in "The Fraternal Bond as a Joking Relationship" expose his thesis about sexual stereotypes very effectively, while David W. Powell's examples and illustrations in "Vietnam: What I Remember" form a powerful memoir of the antiheroic events he "observed" and "watched" in Vietnam. Reflecting on his attitude toward the AIDS epidemic, Paul Monette's "Borrowed Time" is a most moving memoir that invites readers to assess their own responses to AIDS.

POETRY

What is poetry? The nineteenth-century poet William Wordsworth defines it as "an overflow of powerful feelings." For the contemporary poet Jeffrey Harrison, "Poetry is the lens through which the soul looks at the world, thereby keeping the soul alive." For E. E. Cummings, "Poetry is being, not doing."

Poets, like other artists, regardless of their historical moment, write for a variety of different reasons, but they share an imaginative view of language and a belief in the power of words. Compare, for example, Emily Dickinson's thoughts on words expressed in her poem number 1212:

A word is dead
When it is said,
Some say.
I say it just
Begins to live
That day.

with those of Lawrence Ferlinghetti in his poem "Constantly Risking Absurdity," written a century later:

> the poet like an acrobat
> climbs on rime
> to a high wire of his own making.

Both poets focus on the possibilities and power of words, emphasizing the ability of language to shape and express human experiences. Despite the contradictory claims and concerns with which different generations define poetry, there is some consensus that poetry combines emotional expression, meanings, and experiences through rhythm, images, structural form, and, above all, words.

Voice and Tone

The voice that communicates the feelings, emotions, and meanings of the poem is called the speaker. The speaker's voice is not the voice of the poet but a created voice, or *persona*. Robert Browning, in "My Last Duchess," creates the persona of a Renaissance duke to draw a portrait of his former wife. The speaker's voice, like that of a real person, may change and may express different tones throughout the poem as his or her attitudes vary toward the subject, toward himself or herself, and toward the reader. In "Idle Hands" by Gabriel Spera, the speaker's tone is at first meditative, but in the last lines it becomes angry and polemic.

The Poetic Elements: Images, Simile, Metaphor, Symbol, Personification, Paradox

Notice that the language of poetry is especially rich in creating images that evoke the senses of sight, smell, hearing, taste, and touch. To achieve their purposes, writers use not only language that communicates images literally but also figurative language that compares objects, describes emotions, and appeals to the reader's imagination through figures of speech such as simile, metaphor, symbol, personification, and paradox. To become an effective reader of poetry, you should learn to recognize how these elements reinforce poetic meaning.

Images are words and phrases that communicate sensory experiences and convey moods and emotions. Notice in "To His Coy Mistress," for example, how Andrew Marvell uses visual images such as "The Indian Ganges" and "Deserts of vast eternity" as well as auditory images, like "Time's winged chariot hurrying near," to evoke an exotic view of the romantic urgency of passion and desire.

A *simile* is a direct comparison between two explicit terms, usually introduced by *like* or *as*. In "London, 1802," the patriotic speaker of William Wordsworth's poem compares Milton's soul to a "star" and the "sound" of his voice to the sea: "Thy soul was like a Star . . . Thou hadst a voice whose sound was like the sea." Through these similes, the speaker endows Milton's soul and voice with emblematic naturelike qualities that place him above the "selfish men."

A *metaphor* is an implicit comparison that omits *like* or *as*. Wordsworth ends "London, 1802" with the metaphor of England as "a fen / Of stagnant waters" to criticize the inertia and stagnation in which the country had fallen in the beginning of the nineteenth century. Much of the meaning of this poem depends on the contrast that the speaker, who includes himself among the "selfish men," established between himself and Milton.

A *symbol* is a sign that points to meanings beyond its literal significance. The cross, for instance, is an archetype universally accepted as a symbol of Christianity. In John Keats's

"Bright Star," the "bright star" points beyond the literal meaning the word suggests to function as a symbol that affirms and negates the idealized view of love.

Personification is the attribution of human qualities to animals, ideas, or inanimate things. It is used in these lines from Ralph Waldo Emerson's "Concord Hymn":

> Spirit that made those heroes dare
> To die and leave their children free

A *paradox* is a statement that appears to be contradictory and absurd but displays an element of truth. In Yevgeny Yevtushenko's poem "People," the paradox "We who knew our fathers / in everything, in nothing" suggests our inability to know or understand fully another human being, even a parent.

Types of Poetry: Lyric, Dramatic, and Narrative

A *lyric poem* is usually a short composition depicting the speaker's deepest emotions and feelings. Lyric poems are especially effective in arousing personal participation of readers and in stirring their sensations, feelings, and emotions. Songs, elegies, odes, and sonnets fall into this category.

A *dramatic poem* uses dramatic monologue or dialogue and assumes the presence of another character besides the speaker of the poem. In Robert Browning's "My Last Duchess" and also in Spera's poems "Idle Hands" and "Kindness," the speakers assume the presence of an audience.

A *narrative poem* usually emphasizes action or plot. "Home Burial" by Robert Frost qualifies as a narrative poem in which the action of the story—the loss of a child—creates the obstacle that impairs communication between husband and wife. The narrative is also dramatic because the action emerges though dialogue, not indirectly by description.

The Forms of Poetry

Some poems in this anthology use structural forms long established by literary history and tradition. In fact, for many poets a vision of poetic completion revolves around an idea of poetic structure or the formal beauty of a poetic pattern. Thus, to read a poem effectively and establish a dialogue with its poetic voice, you should be able to recognize some of the elements of poetic form.

Meter is the recurrent pattern of stressed and unstressed syllables in a poetic line. Together with elements such as rhyme and pause, meter determines the rhythm of the poem. One way to identify the metrical pattern of a poem is to mark the accented and unaccented syllables of the poetic line, as in the following example from a sonnet by Shakespeare:

> $\breve{}$ $\acute{}$ $\breve{}$ $\acute{}$ $\breve{}$ $\acute{}$ $\breve{}$ $\acute{}$ $\breve{}$ $\acute{}$
> **My mistress' eyes are nothing like the sun**

Next, divide the line into feet, the basic unit of measurement, according to patterns of accented and unaccented syllables. These are the five most common types of poetic feet.

iamb	($\breve{}$ $\acute{}$)	forget
trochee	($\acute{}$ $\breve{}$)	morning
anapest	($\breve{}$ $\breve{}$ $\acute{}$)	at a house

dactyl   (´ ˘ ˘) separate

spondee (´ ´)   come, now

Shakespeare's line thus marked becomes five feet of iambs:

˘ ´ / ˘ ´ / ˘ ´ / ˘ ´ / ˘ ´ /
My mis / tress' eyes / are no / thing like / the sun /
　　1　　　**2**　　　**3**　　　**4**　　　**5**

Notice that the length of the poetic lines depends on the number of poetic feet they possess, and they are defined by the following terms:

one foot   = monometer
two feet   = dimeter
three feet = trimeter
four feet = tetrameter
five feet = pentameter
six feet   = hexameter

Shakespeare's line "My mistress' eyes are nothing like the sun" is a good example of iambic pentameter, one of the most common patterns in English poetry.

Two other terms you should recognize in relation to meter are *caesura*, a pause or pauses within the poetic line, and *enjambment*, a poetic line that carries its meaning and sound to the next line. The following lines, from the poem "Concord Hymn" by Ralph Waldo Emerson, provide us with a good example of an enjambment followed by a caesura:

Bid Time and Nature gently spare
The shaft we raise to them and thee.

A *stanza* is a group of two or more poetic lines forming the same metrical pattern or a closely similar pattern that is repeated throughout the poem. Most stanzas combine a fixed pattern of poetic lines with a fixed *rhyme scheme*. Thomas Hardy's poem "The Man He Killed" follows the traditional pattern of the *ballad stanza*: a quatrain (four-line stanza).

Had he and I but met
By some old ancient inn,
We should have sat us down to wet
Right many a nipperkin!

Notice that Hardy varies the typical rhyme scheme of the ballad stanza, in which only the second and fourth lines rhyme (which is called an *abcb* scheme), by also rhyming his first and third lines, to create an *abab* scheme.

Conventionally, the English *sonnet* is a poem of fourteen iambic pentameter lines. Immortalized by the fourteenth-century Italian poet Petrarch, the sonnet spread throughout Europe, becoming a major form across many cultures. Through it, sonneteers represented and explored the inward self and public life. Shakespeare and many other English poets used the *abab cdcd efef gg* rhyme scheme, which marks the division of a sonnet into three quatrains (four-line groupings) and a couplet (two rhyming lines). John Keats also uses this Shakespearean sonnet pattern in "Bright Star."

Blank verse is unrhymed iambic pentameter. Because it closely approximates the rhythm of human speech, blank verse was long considered an ideal dramatic medium and was used by Shakespeare in many of his plays.

Free verse is poetry that does not follow a fixed pattern of rhythm, rhyme, and stanzaic arrangements. Like Walt Whitman, many poets have abandoned any kind of poetic structure for free verse, relying instead on a pattern based largely on repetition and parallel grammatical structure. The primary focus of free verse is not the external poetic form but the presence of an internal voice of address. One example is Whitman's "What Is the Grass?"

> What do you think has become of the young and old men?
> And what do you think has become of the women and children?

Most contemporary poets either use free verse or combine traditional and new patterns.

Poetry as Performance: The Sounds of Poetry

Reading a poem aloud is more than encountering actions and situations that the poet's creative imagination reshaped as meanings, rhythms, and emotions; it is an act of oral delivery conveying to the poetic discourse a special kind of situation and point of view comparable to the performance of a play. In fact, in most ancient cultures, and in some contemporary ones, poetry had strong ties to the oral tradition, and it was often meant to be sung and accompanied by musical instruments like the lyre. Although the oral delivery of poetry has been widely replaced by silent reading, reading a poem aloud will allow you to recover the emotional and phonic potential through which poetry expresses its relation to music and to life's dramatic possibilities. You will encounter the poetic voice—the voice that speaks the poem—in the act of expressing the poem's full potentiality.

To form layers of poetic meaning, poets throughout the centuries have explored several phonic devices such as alliteration, repetition, onomatopoeia, assonance, as well as effects of orchestration, the clash of consonants. Here are some of the most common poetic devices.

Alliteration is the repetition of the initial sounds of the words in a poetic line. In "Federico's Ghost," Martín Espada uses alliteration (repetition of the plosive sound {p}) along three poetic lines:

> The pilot understood.
> He circled the plane and sprayed again,
> watching a fine gauze of poison . . .

Repetition refers to the repetition of a single word or phrase; the repetition of a refrain or a specific line or lines in a poem; or the repetition of a slightly changed version of a poetic line.

Onomatopoeia is the use of words that evoke or imitate the sounds they describe, such as *slam*, *murmur*, and *splash*.

DRAMA

Unlike fiction and most poetry, plays are intended to be performed before an audience, making drama primarily a communal art form in which the playwright collaborates with actors, director, and designers of set, lighting, and costume to produce an aural, visual, and social experience. If you are unable to see a performance of the plays included in this book, try to view a video production of *Antigone, Medea, Hamlet,* or *Tartuffe.*

What is the function of drama? Although its purpose and functions have evolved from ancient Greece to the present, according to contemporary playwright Arthur Miller, "all plays we call great, let alone those we call serious, are ultimately involved with some aspects of a single problem. It is this. How may man make of the outside world a home?" Unlike Greek playwrights or Shakespeare, many modern dramatists, like Miller, are most concerned with presenting social issues on stage. In the last decade, for example, several dramas have focused on the suffering and death caused by two contemporary forms of plague, cancer and AIDS, demonstrating the playwright's commitment to exploring the relation between the individual and society and to urging the audience to consider its personal and social commitment.

The Basic Elements of Drama

Characterization

Dramatis personae are the characters in a play. Usually the names of the persons who appear in a play, the dramatic characters, are listed at the beginning, often with a brief description. Read this list carefully to understand who the characters are.

As you read the play, pay attention not only to the dialogue of the characters but also to what the *stage directions* say about their entrances and exits, clothing, tone of voice, facial expressions, gestures, and movements.

As in fiction, the *protagonist*, or main character, of a play opposes the *antagonist*, or the character or other elements that defy his or her stability. In some plays there is a fairly simple contrast, as between Medea and Jason and between Medea and Athenian law; in others, as in *Antigone*, there is a more complex or involved contrast—not just between Antigone and Creon but also between Antigone and Ismene, Creon and Haimon, and religious and civil law. Often, if you recognize different sides of the conflict between a protagonist and an antagonist, you will be able to identify the core of the dramatic action of the play.

It is also important to notice that characters and dramatic action are intrinsically connected. In *Othello*, for instance, dramatic action emerges from Iago's inner motivation and goals to bring about Othello's downfall.

Plot

Plot may be defined as the arrangement of the dramatic action of a play. A typical plot structure follows a pattern of rising and falling action along five major steps: the exposition (or presentation of the dramatic situation), the rising action, the climax, the falling action, and the conclusion. The arrangement of the dramatic action in *Hamlet* may be illustrated by the so-called pyramid pattern, which is not always as symmetrical as the following diagram suggests.

Plot Structure of *Hamlet*				
Exposition	Rising action	Climax	Falling action	Conclusion
Death of old Hamlet	Appearance of ghost	From the play within the play to the killing of Polonius	Ophelia's death	Hamlet's death
Accession of Claudius	Hamlet's promise of revenge		Hamlet's return	
Gertrude's marriage				

To understand how the plot develops, consider the dramatic crisis that follows the major conflict, as well as *subplots*, or secondary lines of action connected with the main plot. In *The*

Conduct of Life, for instance, the crisis involving Olimpia, the servant, reflects and comments on the major conflicts centered on Orlando and Leticia.

One can look at the plot arrangement of Greek plays such as *Antigone* and *Medea* from the point of view of the conventions of *time, place,* and *action* (the three unities). According to these conventions, traditionally attributed to Aristotle and the later dramatic theorists of the Renaissance (although Shakespeare did not observe them), the action of a play should not exceed a period of twenty-four hours (unity of time). Its locale should always remain the same (unity of place), and its actions and incidents should all contribute to the resolution of the plot (unity of action). An analysis of *Antigone* and *Medea* from the viewpoint of these conventions will reveal the dramatic freedom taken in the film versions of these classical plays.

Theme

Theme is the central idea or ideas dramatized in a play. Although you can look for a play's theme in the title, conflict, characters, or scenery, the ideas and the meanings you identify with will depend on your own set of beliefs, assumptions, and experiences. The play *Kiss of the Spider Woman*, for instance, explores what happens when two male characters, a revolutionary and a homosexual, liberate themselves from the oppressive constrictions of their own psyches.

Types of Plays: Tragedy, Comedy, and Tragicomedy

According to Aristotle, whose *Poetics* provides an analysis of the nature of classical drama, *tragedy* is the highest form of literary art. It deals with protagonists who are better than we are because of their engagement in honorable or dignified actions and their capacity to maintain their human dignity when withstanding adversity and suffering. Tragic protagonists are often also somehow connected with the religious and political destiny of their country. *Antigone*, for example, asks deeply religious questions about an individual's responsibility to the laws of God and the laws of the state. Greek and Shakespearean tragedies such as *Antigone, Medea,* and *Hamlet* are centered on the struggle that the protagonists, the *tragic heroes* and *heroines,* conduct against antagonistic forces.

The major event in a tragedy is the downfall that the protagonist suffers as a result of external causes (fate, coincidence), internal causes (ambition, excessive pride or hubris), or some error or frailty for which he or she is at least partially responsible. According to Aristotle, the spectators are purged of the emotions of "pity and fear" as they watch the hero or the heroine fall from greatness and as they witness the self-knowledge that the tragic protagonist gains in the process. The term *catharsis* refers to the emotional process that spectators undergo when they view a tragedy.

For modern playwrights, the protagonists of tragedies are no longer extraordinary beings but ordinary human beings caught in the struggle to shape their identities amid the crude realities of external and internal circumstances. In *Kiss of the Spider Woman*, for instance, Manuel Puig explores the causes and effects of political and sexual violence on Valentin and Molina. In the modern tragedy, the audience is urged to confront the corresponding social issues. Sometimes, in contemporary plays, the audience is also asked to participate in the actual performance of the play, or to construct meanings that determine the conclusion of the play.

In its ancient origins, *comedy* was a type of drama, designed to celebrate the renewal of life. Classical comedies usually dealt with the lives of ordinary people caught in personal and social conflicts, which they attempted to overcome through wit and humor. Unlike classical tragedies, which focus on heroes and heroines who are greater than ordinary human beings, classical comedies such as *Tartuffe* explore the lives of ordinary people facing the realities of love, sex, and class. Tragedies usually lead to a sense of wasted human potential in the death of the protagonist, whereas comedies tend to promote a happy ending through the reestablishment of social norms. Most contemporary plays, however, are tragicomedies combining the hilarious ingredients of comedy with the dramatic overtones of tragedy, as seen in *Picnic on the Battlefield,* Fernando Arrabal's humorous portrayal of the irrationality of war.

Kinds of Theater

Greek theater developed in Athens in connection with religious celebrations in honor of Dionysus, the god of wine and revelry. Athenian drama festivals also gained social and political meaning, becoming an intrinsic part of Athenian cultural life.

Plays such as *Medea* and *Antigone* were performed in large, semicircular amphitheaters like the Theater of Dionysus at Athens, which could hold about seventeen thousand spectators. To cope with the physical conditions of such huge amphitheaters, actors had to look larger than life by wearing masks, padded costumes, elevated shoes, and mouthpieces that amplified their voices. Women's roles were performed by male actors because in Greek culture, as in many other early cultures, performances by women were taboo.

Greek plays such as *Antigone* usually alternate dramatic episodes with choral odes, following a five-part dramatic structure:

Prologue	Parados	Episodia/Stasimon	Exodos
Background information	Chorus, Evaluation of situation	Debates followed by choral odes	Last scene

The *chorus* consisted of a group of about twelve actors (often led by a leader, or *choragos*) who sang and danced in the *orchestra,* an area at the foot of the amphitheater. The chorus served

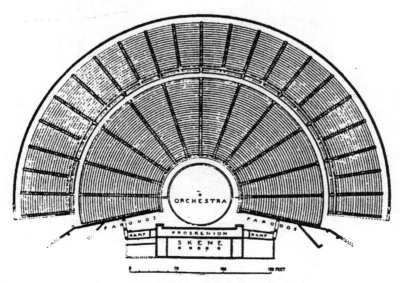

Illustration of the Greek Amphitheater at Epidaurus

several other functions as well: it represented the voice of the community, commented on the events of the play, provided background information about the story, and sometimes participated in the dramatic action. As part of its choreography, the chorus moved from right to left across the orchestra, the "dancing place" of the stage, as they sang the *strophe*, or the choral lyric, of the ode, and from left to right as they sang the *antistrophe*.

When reading a Greek play, keep in mind the following theatrical conventions:

Comic relief is provided by comic speeches or scenes that occur in a serious play. Consider, for example, the relief from dramatic action that the character of the sentry provides in *Antigone*.

Dramatic irony is a double meaning that occurs when the audience possesses foreknowledge of the situation and is therefore better informed than the characters. An effective example of dramatic irony occurs when Creon says after Haimon's death that nothing else could hurt him. However, he speaks this moments before he finds out about his wife's death, of which the audience is already aware.

Elizabethan theater, including Shakespearean theater, refers to plays written during the reign of Queen Elizabeth I of England (1558–1603). Compared to the huge Greek amphitheaters, the Elizabethan playhouse was small, seating a maximum of three thousand spectators. Its stage, as the illustration below shows, protruded into the orchestra so that the audience and actors could enjoy a more intimate theatrical atmosphere. Since Elizabethan theater used little setting, it was the power of Shakespeare's poetic language that stimulated the spectators to exercise their imagination and visualize places like the platform of the watch at the royal castle at Elsinore in *Hamlet*.

Although the text of *Hamlet* shows a series of structural divisions into acts and scenes, in Shakespeare's day *Hamlet* and the other Shakespearean plays were performed without any

Illustration of a Shakespearean Playhouse

intermission. In Elizabethan theater, as in Greek theater, female roles were performed by male actors. The first actresses appeared on the English stage only after the Restoration of Charles II in 1660.

Shakespearean plays employ the theatrical conventions of soliloquy and aside:

A *soliloquy* is a speech delivered by a character who is alone on the stage. Through these speeches, such as Hamlet's famous soliloquy "O, what a rogue and peasant slave am I!" (act 2, scene 2, line 475), actors reveal their thoughts, feelings, inner struggles, and psychological complexity, securing their ties with the audience. The critic Ralph Berry believes that soliloquies permit the actors to establish a special kind of relationship with the audience. It is in his sequence of soliloquies, Berry argues, that Hamlet manages to seduce the audience.

An *aside* is a short speech that a character delivers in an undertone directly to the audience and that is not heard by the other actors on stage. For instance, Hamlet's aside "A little more than kin, and less than kind!" (act 1, scene 2, line 65) invites the audience to share the state of mind he has adopted toward Claudius.

In *neoclassical theater* the elegant and sophisticated dramas of Pierre Corneille (1606–1684), Jean-Baptiste Poquelin Molière (1622–1673), and Jean Racine (1639–1699) established the principles of a new theatrical style. Dating from seventeenth-century France, neoclassical plays of the Golden Age of French drama were performed indoors in a proscenium theater (area located between the curtain and the orchestra) equipped with a raised stage and painted Italianate scenery. Mythological heroic figures and biblical sources became the subject matter of neoclassic tragedies, while the manners, values, and sexual intrigues of the upper and middle classes supplied the subject matter for comedies like Molière's *Tartuffe*.

Neoclassical theater employed several theatrical conventions, most of which were established as rules or formulas by which the Académie française, founded by Cardinal Richelieu in 1637, evaluated the artistic merits of a play. Molière uses many of the fundamental neoclassical conventions, such as the five-act structure, the principles of decorum (conformity to social conventions) and verisimilitude (the appearance of being true or near), and the unities of time, place, and action.

Realistic theater dates from nineteenth-century Europe. One of its purposes was to set the daily reality of middle-class life against antagonistic social conventions. The physical conditions of the picture-frame stage, with its proscenium arch, favored the exhibiting of realistic, lifelike pictures of everyday life. *Kiss of the Spider Woman*, by Manuel Puig, is a good example of a play that relies on the specific conditions of a realistic setting. The prison cell where the protagonists are confined conveys to the audience the degree to which its oppressive, degrading surroundings can influence and dominate human actions.

Theater of the absurd, which has developed in the second half of the twentieth century, portrays human beings as antiheroes caught in a world that is basically irrational, unpredictable, and illogical. Playwright Eugene Ionesco (1912–1994) defined theater of the absurd as "that which has no purpose or goal or objective." Two major techniques of absurdist drama include the lack of logically connected events and the presence of characters whose fragmented language, personalities, and nihilistic attitudes undermine their ability to control their own destiny. *Picnic on the Battlefield*, Fernando Arrabal's absurdist play, provides a good example of a drama whose challenges to a rational view of life verge on the absurd. Instead of constructing a classical plot or creating characters with developed personalities, Arrabal presents one dramatic episode in which the characters Zapo and Zépo are so similar that they are practically interchangeable. Although absurdist theater can be performed on any kind of stage, twentieth-century dramatists prefer a stage with only a few props that are suggestive of a realistic setting or symbolic of the play's meaning.

Late twentieth-century modern experimental theater is here illustrated by playwright Maria Irene Fornes, who in the early 1960s started to develop an unconventional, eclectic theater in Greenwich Village circles. Through her focus on characters as autonomous individuals, Fornes's experimental plays portray human beings who relate to one another through their use of language and struggle for survival in a world beset by the threat of nuclear annihilation, military dictatorship, and ethnic cleansing.

FICTION, POETRY, AND DRAMA AS CULTURAL PRODUCTIONS

As part of your reading experience, *Literature Across Cultures* asks you not only to analyze the formal aspects of literature but also to integrate your study of the literary genres with a cultural focus that attempts to discover connections among literature, film, culture, and society. Such interactions will enable you not only to consider the interpretation of the literary text but to understand also its historical and cultural significance.

In addition to the Cultural Contexts questions after each reading selection in this anthology, the following topics will help you initiate a culturally oriented discussion of literature and film:

1. To examine the relation between the text and its social reality, consider the relation between writers and the cultural and historical issues of their times. Your focus here should be the literary text and its cultural (philosophical, religious, sociohistorical, and political) perspectives.
2. Focus on the physical and social aspects of the setting, attempting to define the tensions and relations between the setting and the speaker.
3. Notice how many plots, especially in fiction, tend to challenge or reinforce the conventional focus concerning the quest for individual identity and the sometimes competing values of the community.
4. When you study characterization, explore private and public attitudes toward race, class, gender, law, economics, and justice.
5. Think about the extent to which social and psychological forces such as heredity, environment, or fate control the action of individuals. Are individuals presented as victims of society? What kinds of responses do they develop to counteract the influence of society?

You may also consider the following topics:

6. The interplay of gender and power.
7. Gender differences.
8. Male gender construction.
9. The male patriarchal psyche and its definition of masculinity.
10. Sex role stereotypes supporting traditional notions of masculine aggression and feminine passivity.
11. The conflict between the individual and the social self.
12. Individuality and community as the core of American character.
13. Individual aspirations and community responsibility.
14. The psychological drama of the individual self.
15. The presence of the self in social, sexual, and cultural contexts.
16. The relation between war and violence.

17. Issues of cultural identity, gender, politics, and class. Their effects on individual and social identity.
18. Individuality and identity as products of a fixed historical era.
19. The forces of tradition and change and their effects on individual and communal lives.
20. The politics of domestic life; the organization of the family; the separation of private and public responsibility.
21. Changing concepts of the role of the family.
22. The politics of domestic life as affected by gender and class.
23. The significance of single-parent households.
24. The nature of mother–daughter, father–daughter, father–son, mother–son relations.
25. The role of the family in validating or manipulating one's sense of self.
26. The ethnic structure of the family and its effects on gender identity and communal relationships.
27. The literary text as a protest against racism or sexism.
28. The relation between war and sexual violence.
29. Immigration and its influence on contemporary culture.
30. The dominant ideology of the text: who has power, who benefits from portrayal of power.
31. The dynamics of male–female relations both within and outside of conventional social roles.
32. Women as creators and shapers of culture and history.
33. Evolving images and representations of women and men.
34. The causes and effects of sexism and domestic violence.
35. The sexual division of labor and its effects on gender relations.
36. Class distinction and class mobility within society; the causes of exclusion from the mainstream.
37. The interplay of class, race, and economics.
38. The causes and effects of segregation and integration.
39. Racial stereotypes, racial differences, and racial dominance; their effects on individuals and group identity.
40. Causes and effects of racial, sexual, and economic oppression.
41. Stereotypes of sexuality and race; the function of color in literary and social contexts.
42. The relation among racism, sexism, and violence; attitudes toward sexual preferences and sexual differences.
43. Concepts of the melting pot versus ethnic identity.
44. The notion of tragedy, moving away from Aristotelian stress on character and tragic flaw toward a concern for the sociopolitical roles of men and women.
45. Causes and effects of sociopolitical order and disorder.
46. AIDS; the discrimination imposed on AIDS victims; the effects of AIDS on the family and on gender relationships.
47. The attempt to understand our individualism and participate in it.
48. How writers situate their work in relation to the collective past.
49. The role that movies have assumed as powerful cultural agents in rewriting the past.
50. Films as articulators of gender roles; films, in which male–female relationships are central to the story, as a reflection of traditional and/or social perspectives on gender roles.
51. Gender, race, sex, violence, and identity as prominent cultural issues in films.

52. How a film that you believe addresses an important issue in contemporary society either endorses the standard criteria of values or questions how standards of behavior are created and applied.
53. Portrayals of World War II and the Vietnam War in film.
54. Literature and film as articulators of male and female experiences of war.
55. The interplay of war and terrorism.
56. Individual freedom and terrorism.
57. Wars of choice and wars of necessity.
58. Patriotism and terrorism.
59. Peacemaking and wars of necessity.
60. It takes two to make peace.
61. Pop culture icons of music, beauty, and filmmaking.
62. The biological foundations of gender differences.
63. The myths and realities of sensuality and sexuality in American, Arab, and Hispanic societies.
64. Memories, recollections, or being witness to the Holocaust.
65. The battle between human conscience and the law of dictatorship.
66. Biracial buddy films.

APPENDIX B

Writing a Research Paper

By this point in your college education, you have likely had experience with academic research. A research paper is your investigation and examination of a chosen subject; in it you locate, evaluate, incorporate, and document the opinions of various experts on the subject. In tackling a research assignment, you may already know a great deal about the topic or you may know nothing at all about it. This does not alter the nature of your investigation, which is to go beyond what you, the researcher, already know on the subject, and present your findings to your reader.

WHAT IS A LITERARY RESEARCH PAPER?

Writing a literary research paper involves gathering and examining evidence in relation to a text, a related group of texts, or an author's body of work. The key difference between research in one of the sciences and a literary research paper is that scientific research aims for *explanation*, whereas humanities research, of which the literary research paper is an example, aims for *understanding*. The objectivity of the sciences is not entirely obtainable in the humanities—you will be exploring opinion and conjecture in a literary research paper more often than you will be dealing with "hard fact." Literary research means not only analyzing a particular work, such as Manuel Puig's *Kiss of the Spider Woman*, but also consulting literary criticism that enhances your understanding of the text within cultural and historical contexts.

Writing a literary research paper involves

- Examining your *primary source* (the text or texts in question) in depth
- Analyzing researched materials (*secondary sources*) relating to your primary source
- Reaching conclusions based on your research and your own opinions.
- Presenting your conclusions in a well-developed paper, supported by valid, fully documented evidence assembled from your research.

What Are Primary and Secondary Sources?

In doing research, you will typically analyze a primary source or sources, and you will utilize secondary sources that put your primary sources in context.

- *Primary Sources:* The focuses of your research—the poems, plays, short stories, or novels you are investigating—are considered *primary* sources. If you were doing research on Walt Whitman, his writings (such as the poem "What Is the Grass?") would be your primary sources.
- *Secondary Sources:* Analytical materials that comment on and interpret primary sources are *secondary* sources. Critical responses to Whitman's "What Is the Grass?," academic analyses of "What Is the Grass?," and any other writings that shed light on "What Is the Grass?" are considered secondary sources for that poem.

Locating Materials

The first thing a student embarking on a research paper should do is consult the library's reference librarian. There are constant updates to library databases, and librarians will have intimate knowledge of the services the library provides and how to best go about gaining access to materials not available on campus. Don't go to the librarian unprepared. Know full well what your assignment is and how long the paper must be, and have at least a general idea of what you want to investigate. The more prepared you are, the more the librarian will be able to assist you. Details on locating research materials can be found in Appendix C.

How to Choose a Topic

Most likely, your instructor will have specific instructions regarding the assignment. If not, do not be afraid to seek more specific guidance.

In an introductory literature course, it is unlikely that you will be studying an author's entire body of work for a research assignment. Most likely, you will focus on text(s) by an assigned author that can be covered in detail in the paper's length (a short story, a related group of poems). However, you often analyze long texts (such as *Hamlet*) and in cases like that you likely will explore a specific aspect or issue in the work you find interesting. You would not be able to write an in-depth analysis of the entire play in ten pages or under.

POTENTIAL GOALS IN LITERARY RESEARCH
- To enhance your and your readers' understanding of a text (such as researching critical responses to Kate Chopin's "The Storm" at the time of its publication).
- To investigate an author's life (such as exploring relations between Franz Kafka's private life and that of the protagonist in "The Metamorphosis").
- To compare and contrast various works by one or more authors (such as investigating shared themes in the works of Charlotte Perkins Gilman and Kate Chopin).

WHAT IS LITERARY CRITICISM?

In literature classes, the secondary sources you locate will generally, though not always, fall under the heading of literary criticism. Literary criticism is the evaluation, analysis, and interpretation of literary works. It is more in-depth than the basic book review you might read in a Sunday paper. Criticism could analyze a specific literary work, a group of works, or an author's writings as a whole; your paper will do the same, employing researched criticism.

CREATING A TOPIC WORTH INVESTIGATING
- Generate a list of observations and questions raised while reading a text. An aspect of a work that interests you might be worth investigating further (a theme, a use of symbolism, an enigmatic character). Even a problem that arose during the reading of a

text might make a good topic; investigating secondary sources that explore the same problem and comparing the authors' viewpoints to your own can make for a compelling research paper.

- Discuss with your instructor aspects of a potential text you find interesting. See if she or he has any advice regarding potential research avenues.
- Pick a topic that you yourself find interesting. Why do you feel this issue deserves exploration? Why might analysis of this topic be enlightening to your readers?
- Do some preliminary reading of secondary sources to gain a general idea of the aspects of the text that seem to be receiving the greatest response from accredited experts.
- Formulate a thesis that you can deal with, given the limited amount of space and time; your paper must present an argument regarding an aspect of a text that is narrow enough to be covered in detail in the space allotted, but not so narrow or lacking in interest that you will have nothing to say.

A thesis for a literary research paper is a sentence that makes an argument about a text or group of texts. It has to fit the pattern of something that needs to be proven and with which others may disagree.

```
Hamlet is not, despite his words to the contrary, feigning
his insanity throughout the play; he is, in fact, quite
insane from the moment he sees the ghost of his murdered
father.
```

The foregoing is an example of an adequate thesis for a literary paper. You would have to support this thesis by focusing on moments throughout the play in which Hamlet "appears" mad and analyze them. In a literary *research* paper, you would also have to scrutinize secondary sources that also investigate Hamlet's madness, and either "argue" with them or use them in support of your argument.

If your assignment topic is to be self-generated, make sure you discuss with the instructor its suitability before moving forward in your research.

ENGAGING IN A DIALOGUE

What does it mean to "argue" with a source? Writing is no less a form of communication than speech; throughout history, arguments have raged on the printed page. A literary research paper is your chance to continue this noble tradition.

- In this kind of assignment, you will generally enter into an academic "dialogue" with the authors of the researched texts. Your responsibility is not only to present their assertions to your readers but to respond to them as well.
- Ideally, your goal is to persuade your readers to accept your thesis as their own. You will do this by offering responses to the primary text supported by evidence obtained from both the primary text and the researched secondary opinions. Note that not all opinions gathered in your research may agree with your personal interpretation. Do not ignore differing opinions. If you can make a solid case to disagree with a published opinion, using textual evidence from both your primary source and other researched criticism, it can be very effective and thought-provoking. If you cannot, it is a warning that your interpretation may be either inaccurate or not fully developed.

- At a minimum, you want to compel your readers' respectful attention. Even if they ultimately disagree with your conclusions, you want them to find your presentation informed, thoughtful, and valid.

INFORMED

You demonstrate mastery of relevant data.

Your use of sources establishes that you are aware of your topic's key issues and of experts' perspectives on them.

Your thesis is backed by thorough knowledge of your subject.

THOUGHTFUL

You examine your sources critically, and you show an awareness of the relation of secondary sources to primary sources and to each other. You do not, for instance, include sources that contradict each other without showing your awareness of the contradiction.

In your selection and employment of sources, you clearly and consistently show understanding of how researched sources relate to your thesis.

VALID

All conclusions must follow sensibly from your presented evidence and arguments.

All supporting ideas and evidence must be organized so that they cohere with and reinforce your thesis.

DRAFTING THE PAPER

Follow the basic rules of effective writing, as discussed in your introductory composition classes.

- Write an introduction that compels the reader to continue. The introduction should also provide the name and author of the primary work(s) and present your thesis statement.
- The body of your paper should develop your thesis, supporting your assertions with evidence compiled from your primary source(s) and from your researched secondary sources. Use *limited* plot summary, only when necessary to clarify a point being made.
- Incorporate all sources smoothly, using clear, precise transitions between your work and theirs, and cite them correctly.
- Write an overall conclusion that brings the paper to a satisfying end.

The "Formula" for a Literary Research Paper

You need to self-generate an opinion (a working thesis) about the work of literature you are studying. You are required to support this with textual evidence.

- *If you think Hamlet truly loves Ophelia, what moments in the play support this interpretation?*

You then need to research literary criticism sources that explore aspects of and issues relevant to your thesis. They may support your ideas, or they may contradict. They may enhance your understanding of the text and may even alter your own opinions, which is perfectly warranted, provided you give them credit in your paper for where they "won you over."

- *If a researched article persuasively convinces you that Hamlet's admiration for Ophelia is fleeting, feel free to adjust your opinion, as long as you discuss in your paper that source's influence.*

If you uncover criticism contradicting your viewpoints, ask yourself if you can find evidence in the text and opinion in other researched sources that supports your argument. This returns us to the idea of engaging in a literary debate. If you can build a strong argument against one of the experts whose criticism you are utilizing, it is certainly justifiable to do so.

- *If you disagree with a critic's viewpoint that Hamlet's love for Ophelia is fleeting, present his or her arguments along with evidence you find in the text that you feel contradicts the critic's reading, as well as any other researched criticism that supports your point of view.*

Taking Notes During the Research Process

To record bibliographic information about your sources, use 4″ × 6″ note cards. Always include the following details:

- Name of author, editor, and/or translator (if any)
- Title of work (including book title as well as article or chapter title, if applicable)
- Edition or volume of work
- Place of publication
- Publishing company
- Date

If you use electronic sources, record all of the foregoing information that is relative, along with the name of the website or subscription service or online database you are utilizing and its web address.

This information is essential to organize the Works Cited list that will appear at the end of your paper.

- When possible, it is best to photocopy the original sources, so that you can highlight, cross out, and comment on the text directly.
- Once you have decided what information is relevant and useful, you should write each useful item on a separate card, noting its page number(s) in the original source.
- Read it over, and then write it in your own words as if explaining it to someone.

A good research paper alternates between direct and indirect quotation, and preparing your note cards in this way (directly copying original wording, and then rewording yourself) will both make you more familiar with the material and give you flexibility in how to present each piece of information.

Organizing Your Information

Once you have collected potentially useful information on note cards, organize it, exploring how material from different sources fits together. A research paper is not an exercise in dutifully summarizing one source on page one, then moving on to the next source on page two, and so on. It involves mixing and matching information related to your thesis.

In investigating Hamlet's relationship with Ophelia, for example, you may have gathered four interesting sources that analyze their first scene together. Three of them agree with your opinion, but one has a very different take on the scene. Your job is to present your research in a logical and stimulating manner. Gather related opinions to validate a point you are making and to prove the thoroughness of your research, but also contrast differing opinions to show your mastery of your research.

Two of your sources may have interesting interpretations of Hamlet's interaction with Ophelia at the "play within a play," whereas a fifth, yet-unused source may offer the most interesting analysis of this segment of the play yet offers little else of value to your debate. The idea is to know your research so well that you can manipulate its presentation, showing true editorial judgment regarding when and how sources are utilized.

Even interesting researched material can sound awkward and plodding if delivered in a "cut and paste" fashion. Your job is to shape the discussion, presenting researched sources in a logical and lively manner that reminds the reader that this manuscript is solely your creation.

HOW TO DOCUMENT USING THE MLA FORMAT

A formal literary research paper involves citing, or documenting, the texts (both primary and secondary) you have employed. Presenting research means incorporating conclusions and ideas not originated by you. You must document all sources of information used, whether you quote the source directly using the exact words of the original author, or indirectly, rewriting the information in your own words. For general knowledge, such as the fact that Nathaniel Hawthorne wrote "Young Goodman Brown" or that Salem is in Massachusetts, you need not attribute such facts to a source. However, when you include information that you would not have known without referring to a particular source, such as the fact that Nathaniel Hawthorne's ancestors were involved in the Salem witch trials, you must credit the source. Therefore it is essential to take notes on all information you gather from your sources.

Once you've researched your sources, chosen the best ones, and organized your materials, there is still the matter of how to present the information properly within the text. The format for parenthetical citation used in this book follows the guidelines that the Modern Language Association of America (MLA) has established for research papers on literary subjects. See the *MLA Handbook for Writers of Research Papers* (sixth edition) for further information.

Both direct quotations and paraphrased information from sources should be cited throughout your manuscript. MLA style dictates that the last name of the author and the page number of the source are given in parentheses at the end of employment of the source. Such citations inform the reader which source is currently being quoted or paraphrased and guide the reader to the Works Cited page at the end of your manuscript, which provides further details regarding the source.

The following citation appearing at the end of a direct quote or paraphrase would alert the reader to the source being used:

```
(Christian 72)
```

Since this presents only the last name of the author and the page number of the source, the reader learns the full detail of the source utilized upon referencing the Works Cited page:

```
Christian, Barbara. Black Women Novelists: The Development
    of a Tradition, 1892-1976. Westport: Greenwood, 1980.
```

Direct Quotation

You should utilize an introductory phrase (or "signal phrase") before quoting a source in the body of your essay. If you mention the author's name in your signal phrase, then only the page number is required in the parenthetical citation at the end of the sentence. For example, if you mentioned Barbara Carlton's name in your sentence before quoting her, you would have to put only the page number (72) in the parenthetical citation. If the quotation is taken from another author's work, you must make note in the parenthetical citation. For example, if you quote Toni Morrison in an interview she gave to Barbara Carlton, you would alert the reader that you are quoting Morrison in your signal phrase, then note Carlton in the citation:

```
As Toni Morrison feels, ". . ." (qtd. in Carlton, 125).
```

If you have read your sources in depth, have organized a basic structure to your paper (following the guidelines for writing a literary essay in the introduction—it is the same basic pattern, only now you are offering opinions beyond your own), and are ready to write a draft that synthesizes your ideas with those of the experts you read, you still have to present the research smoothly.

There should be an organizing principle to your paper that makes the readers feel you are gracefully leading them on an "intellectual journey" to a logical conclusion. You can't just drop research onto a page in a disorganized manner, jerkily leading your reader through detours, down one-way and dead-end streets and to a sudden halt, also known as "The End."

Although you should have a basic idea of essay construction from previous composition classes (and from the discussion of literary essay writing in the introduction to this book), you still might be hesitant about how to present research within the body of your essay.

Signal Phrases

Be sure when you quote to use "signal phrases" that alert the reader that the quote is coming and that put the quotation in context with what preceded it. Just as you need strong transitions between paragraphs in any essay, you need strong transitions when shifting from your thoughts to another writer's. In the following examples of signal phrases, take note of the placement of your punctuation—especially quotation marks and end punctuation.

```
As Sigmund Freud has noted, ". . ." (134).
In the words of Tim O'Brien, ". . ." (qtd. in Lowell, 33).
In the late 1940's, Simone de Beauvoir encouraged her
readers to ". . ." (106).
". . .," suggests Diane Elizabeth Dreher (55).
```

Note that periods go after the citations.

To keep your research paper from sounding repetitive, you should vary the ways in which you present quotations. The following are further examples of signal phrases:

```
X confidently argues
According to X,
In the words of X
X agrees with Y by stating
Another point X makes is that
```

```
. . . suggests X.
X writes
X disagrees, stating
```

Although *says* and *writes* are perfectly acceptable, other verbs provide degrees of meaning that can be utilized in signal phrases: *acknowledge, agree, argue, ask, assert, believe, claim, comment, communicate, confirm, contend, declare, deny, emphasize, endorse, insist, note, observe, point out, propose, refute, reject, report, speculate, suggest, think,* and many others. Spend time finding that *perfect* way to translate your researched author's thoughts.

Short Quotations

A quotation need not always be a complete sentence. Your voice, guiding us to an author's opinion, can be quite effective, as long as you don't mislead the reader into a distortion of the original thought:

```
Among many other things, Barbara Christian suggests the
importance of "practical slave culture without which black
people as an abused race would not have been able to sur-
vive" (72).
```

You can omit words within a quotation if they are not essential to your point and if they slow down the rhythm of your paper. Use an ellipsis (three spaced periods) with brackets around it (to differentiate from an ellipsis in the original source) as identification that something has been deleted:

```
Among many other things, Barbara Christian suggests the
importance of "practical slave culture without which black
people [. . .] would not have been able to survive" (72).
```

Long Quotations

Your paper should not be overburdened with long quotations; with too many long quotations, the paper ceases to be yours—it's as if you are renting space to the authors of the original texts. On occasion, however, long quotations are necessary to present an author's complex theory or to set up a long analysis of the quoted material.

Any quotation of more than three lines should start on a new line and should be indented ten spaces. Since the indented format indicates that the words are taken from a secondary source, quotation marks are not necessary. The parenthetical citation should come two spaces after the period that ends the long quotation.

Note the difference in punctuation from short quotations that appear within the body of your paragraphs, where the parenthetical citation comes before the period ending the sentence.

```
Randall Jarrell demonstrates his enthusiasm for Robert
Frost's poetry when he asserts in Poetry and the Age:
          Frost's virtues are extraordinary. No other
          living poet has written so well about the
```

```
actions of ordinary men; his wonderful dramatic
monologues or dramatic scenes come out of a
knowledge of people that few poets have had,
and they are written in a verse that uses,
sometimes with absolute mastery, the rhythms of
actual speech. (28)
```

Quoting from a Poem

When quoting from poetry, use slash marks to designate the end of a line, and duplicate the exact capitalization and punctuation of the poem. Give the line numbers in parentheses.

```
In "Babiy Yar," Yevgeny Yevtushenko creates images that
stimulate the imagination when he writes, "I, wandering in
Egypt. / I crucified, I, perishing." (7-8).
```

If you are quoting more than a few lines of poetry, begin on a new line and indent ten spaces. Copy the quoted lines exactly. Do not follow the citation of line numbers with a period.

```
In the example below, Martin Espada uses alliteration to
paint a vivid picture of his protagonist in "Cross Plains,
Wisconsin":

          Blue bandana
          across the forehead,
          beard bristling
          like a straw broom
          sleeveless T-shirt
          of the Puerto Rican flag (1-6)
```

Quoting from a Play

When quoting from a play, always give act, scene, and line numbers in Arabic (not Roman) numerals. Brief quotations may be placed within your main text. Start long quotations on a new line, and indent the quotation ten spaces.

```
Hamlet observes Claudius and says, "Now might I do it pat,
now he is praying, / And now I'll do it" (3.3.73-74).

Hamlet initially appears to feel confident that killing
Claudius as the King prays would fulfill his mandate for
revenge:
          Now might I do it pat, now he is praying,
          And now I'll do it. And so he goes to Heaven,
          And so I am revenged. That would be scanned:
```

>   A villain kill my father, and for that
>   I, his sole son, do this same villain send
>   To Heaven. (3.3.73-78)

He sounds as if he is ready to act, but by repeating himself in lines 73 and 74 ("I do it" and "I'll do it") it appears he is not ready, but instead is trying to convince himself to act. Twice repeating in lines 74 and 78 that Claudius will be sent "to Heaven" is another indication that this plan, despite being seemingly "scanned," is not all that it initially appears: he has a creeping awareness that Claudius going to heaven would hardly be a befitting comeuppance.

Note that you return to the left margin to continue the paragraph in which you are utilizing the long quotation. Also note that if you do use a long quotation, you need to comment on it fully; here, the writer covers several lines from the passage quoted to justify the use of the long quote. If the writer were to analyze only lines 73 and 74, she or he would be justified in quoting only those two lines.

When quoting from plays that are not divided into acts, such as *Antigone*, give the scene and line numbers:

>   Creon asks his son Haimon a key question in relation to
>   his decision regarding Antigone: "You have heard my final
>   judgement on that girl: Have you come here hating me, or
>   have you come With difference and with love, whatever I
>   do?" (3.5-8)

Also indicate who is speaking if you are quoting dialogue or a passage in which more than two characters speak:

>   Hamlet, feeling betrayed, is suddenly aggressive
>   toward his love:
>
>   HAMLET. Ha, ha! Are you honest?
>   OPHELIA. My lord?
>   HAMLET. Are you fair?
>   OPHELIA. What means your lordship?
>   HAMLET. That if you be honest and fair, your
>   honesty should admit not discourse to your
>   beauty? (3.1.103-107)
>
>   One sees that Ophelia, despite her betrayal of
>   Hamlet, has no taste for it. When he begins

> questioning her honesty and fairness, she appears
> unsure of how to respond, as if in fact she has
> forgotten that she is currently deceiving him.

Again, note that when you quote, it is your responsibility to comment on the passage. Explain how it relates to the overall point you are trying to make in the paragraph. Don't expect a quotation to explain itself—it is your duty to assume that the reader needs assistance in assimilating the information.

Indirect Quotation: Paraphrasing

Instead of quoting a source directly, you can paraphrase, or give the information in your own words, using roughly the same number of words you found in the source. The key to paraphrasing is to relay the source's information without directly copying the original phrasing.

The following quotation by R.W.B. Lewis, regarding influences on Edith Wharton's *Ethan Frome*, is followed by a paraphrased version.

> A certain Melvillian grandeur went into the configuration
> of her tragically conceived hero. Despite her early
> disclaimers, the spirit of Nathaniel Hawthorne pervades
> the New England landscape of the novella. . . . The role of
> the inquisitive city-born narrator is deployed with a good
> deal of the cunning and artistry of Henry James.

> R.W.B. Lewis notes the influence of Herman Melville,
> Nathaniel Hawthorne, and Henry James on Edith Wharton's
> novel <u>Ethan Frome</u>. The nobility of the hero derives from
> the epic characters of Melville's style with the added
> urban outlook of the Jamesian protagonist. The atmosphere
> is similar to that found in Hawthorne's depiction of New
> England. (309)

The source would be listed in the Works Cited just like a directly quoted source:

> Lewis, R.W.B. <u>Edith Wharton: A Biography</u>. New York:
>   Harper, 1975.

List of Works Cited

The Works Cited list contains information about all the works you referred to or cited in your paper. If you obtained information from a source but ultimately did not use it in the paper, do not list it in the Works Cited list. List only sources cited in the paper.

- The list should appear on a separate page at the end of your paper.
- The heading (Works Cited) should be centered.
- Citations should be listed alphabetically by author, last name first.

- Double-space entries.
- To help readers locate the citations more easily, indent all lines of an entry except the first by ½ inch (or five spaces).

Print and Nonprint Sources

BOOK BY ONE AUTHOR

Allen, Jeffrey Renard. <u>Rails Under My Back</u>. New York: Farrar, 2000.

BOOK BY TWO OR THREE AUTHORS

Gilbert, Sandra M., and Susan Gubar. <u>The Madwoman in the Attic: The Woman Writer and the Nineteenth-Century Literary Imagination</u>. New Haven: Yale UP, 1979.

BOOK BY FOUR OR MORE AUTHORS

Gatto, Joseph, et al. <u>Exploring Visual Design</u>. 2nd ed. Worcester: Davis, 1987.

BOOK WITH AN EDITOR

Gates, Henry Louis, Jr., ed. <u>Classic Slave Narratives</u>. New York: NAL, 1987.

TWO OR MORE BOOKS BY THE SAME AUTHOR

Frye, Northrup. <u>Anatomy of Criticism: Four Essays</u>. Princeton: Princeton UP, 1957.

———. <u>The Myth of Deliverance: Reflections on Shakespeare's Problem Comedies</u>. Toronto: U of Toronto P, 1983.

WORK IN AN ANTHOLOGY OR COLLECTION

Berghahn, Marion. "Images of Africa in the Writings of James Baldwin." <u>James Baldwin</u>. Ed. Harold Bloom. New York: Chelsea, 1986.

MULTIVOLUME WORK

Wimsatt, William K., and Cleanth Brooks. <u>Literary Criticism: A Short History</u>. 2 vols. Chicago: U of Chicago P., 1979.

ARTICLE IN A JOURNAL THAT PAGES EACH ISSUE SEPARATELY

Giles, Ronald K. "Archetype and Irony in <u>The Natural</u>." <u>English Journal</u> 75.4 (1986): 49–54.

ARTICLE IN A JOURNAL THAT USES CONTINUOUS PAGINATION

Ryan, Katy. "Revolutionary Suicide in Toni Morrison's
Fiction." <u>African American Review</u> 34 (2000):
389–412.

ARTICLE IN A NEWSPAPER

Mcdowell, Edwin. "Black Writers Gain Audience and
Visibility in Publishing." <u>New York Times</u> 12 Feb.
1991: C11.

BOOK REVIEW

Gonzales, Ray. Rev. of <u>City of Coughing and Dead
Radiators</u>, by Martín Espada. <u>The Nation</u> 30 Jan.
1994: 131–33.

FILM

<u>Hamlet</u>. Dir. Campbell Scott. Perf. Campbell Scott and
Blair Brown. Artisan Entertainment, 2000.

AUDIOTAPE

<u>The Metamorphosis</u>. Read by James Mason. Audiocassette.
Caedmon/Harper, 1962.

Electronic Sources

Citing electronic sources is an even more involved and complicated process than citing traditional print sources. Many online sources, particularly those of good repute, follow the practices of traditional publishing to some extent. The Works Cited page should list as much of the following information as possible regarding Internet sources:

- Author or editor name
- Title of article or document
- Print publication information, if any
- Name of online site, journal, or database
- Length in pages or paragraphs or section numbers, if given
- Date of online publication and volume or issue number, if applicable
- Date you acquired the information
- URL (Uniform Resource Locater)—the electronic address for the source

The following examples will help you in documenting Internet sources:

ONLINE JOURNAL

Loranger, Carol. "'This Book Spills Off the Page in All
Directions': What Is the Text of Naked Lunch?"

<u>Postmodern Culture</u> 10.1 (1999): 24 pars. 10 Oct. 1998
<http://www.iath.virginia.edu/pmc/current.issue/
10.11oranger.html>.

ABSTRACT OF A JOURNAL ARTICLE

Poovey, M. "Beyond the Current Impasse in Literary
Studies." <u>American Literary History</u> 11.2 354-377.
Abstract. 22 Dec. 2001 <http://www3.oup.co.uk/
alhist/hdb/Volume_11/Issue_02/110354.sgm.abs.html>.

ONLINE MAGAZINE

Offman, Craig. "Book Publishers Don't Check Their
Authors' Facts." <u>Salon</u>. 25 Oct. 1999. 25 Oct. 2002
<http://www.salon.com/books/log/1999/10/25/felon/
index.html>.

ONLINE MAGAZINE, NO AUTHOR LISTED

"Complete Journals of Sylvia Plath Will Be Published."
<u>CNN</u> 14 Oct. 1999. 21 Oct. 2002
<http://www.cnn.com/books/news/9910/14/plath.journals.
ap/index.html>.

GOVERNMENT DOCUMENT

United States. National Endowment of the Arts. <u>NEA
Strategic Plan</u> 1999-2004. 15 Jan. 2003
<http://arts.endow.gov/learn/Strategic/Contents.html>.

ARTICLE IN A REFERENCE DATABASE

"Alice Walker." <u>Britannica Online</u>. Vers. 99.1.1. Mar.
1999. Encyclopaedia Britannica. 21 Sep. 1999
<http://www.eb.com:1754>

Refer to the *MLA Handbook* or your college handbook for a more detailed listing of formats for the Works Cited list. These formats are also available at www.mla.org.

REVISING AND REWRITING

Writing is about rewriting. Especially in something as detailed as an analytical literary research paper, you cannot hope to put together something coherent the evening before the paper is due. Give yourself time to read and reread your primary source, building the case for your thesis. It will take effort to merge your ideas with those of the experts whose opinions you have researched, and again, your final draft should be an informed, valid, and thoughtful defense of your thesis.

Presenting Your Research Paper

A quality presentation is key to a successful research paper. A sloppily presented paper will make the reader suspicious of the diligence of your overall research. The following are some guidelines for the proper presentation of your research paper:

- Use standard 8½″ × 11″ paper and a 12-point font unless otherwise instructed.
- Make multiple print copies of your paper, in case one is misplaced.
- Double-space your document.
- Center the title of your essay. The title should be relevant to your paper's thesis; a "hook" to get a reader's attention, followed by a colon and a more in-depth announcement of your paper's intentions is often an effective choice, though not the only one:

```
"What Dreams May Come": The Afterlife as Explored in
Hamlet
```

or

```
How to Drive a Woman Insane Without Even Trying:
Wallpaper as a Prison in "The Yellow Wallpaper"
```

Both of these titles intrigue the reader while announcing the overall topic of the paper.

- Number every page, except the title page, in the upper right-hand corner.

After finishing your "final draft," ask yourself the following questions:

1. Have I proofread for clarity of presentation?
2. Have I proofread for spelling and punctuation?
3. Are all sources credited?
4. Have I made clear which opinions are mine and which belong to other authors?
5. Does the information I have included relate directly to a clear thesis?
6. Have I cited my sources correctly?
7. Do I have a Works Cited page? Is it correctly formatted?

Sample Research Papers

DeAngeli 1

Patricia DeAngeli
Professor Shaw
English 102
April 8, 2005

"You Can't Put Me Back!" Wallpaper as a
Prison in "The Yellow Wallpaper"

The features of a wall are irrelevant
when papered. Whether smooth and glossy, or
chipped and broken, its appearance is masked
by the paper covering it. Only by peeling
away the layers of paper that "protect" it
can we see what truly lurks beneath. In
Charlotte Perkins Gilman's "The Yellow Wall-
paper," the wallpaper covers the wall beneath
as the expectations of the protagonist's
husband cover her true self. The very
pattern of the wallpaper is representative
of the contradictory and erratic restrictions society placed upon the protagonist
and women in general at the time of the
story's publication, 1899: "when you follow
the lame, uncertain curves for a little
distance they suddenly commit suicide--
plunge off at outrageous angles, destroy
themselves in unheard of contradictions" (371).

Even today, society demands that women
accept their assigned roles and not deviate
from them. Yet to many, such as the protagonist of "The Yellow Wallpaper," such roles
are unfulfilling or meaningless. She is a

[margin annotations:]
Last name:
inch from th
top of each
page

Heading:
double-space
1/2 inch from
the top

Title: center
double-space

DeAngeli 2

wife and mother, which are not inherently
bad roles, but her husband has cast her as
"wife" and "mother," not to mention "housekeeper," defining these roles in their most
traditional, limiting, and degrading definitions. They are empty labels, anyway:
the baby has a nanny, her sister-in-law
Jane keeps the house, and ultimately her
husband treats her more as child than wife.
The one role that she herself desires--
writer--is denied her, as her husband
"hates to have me write a word" (371).

The confining roles assigned her are
what cause her malady, but her husband
instead treats her like a simple invalid,
actually worsening her condition with his
treatment of "a schedule prescription for
each hour of the day" (370). As the
protagonist acknowledges, "[her husband]
hardly lets me stir without special direction" (370). The room he chooses for her,
the nursery, merely reinforces her dependent
status. He expects her to do as she is told
and, in effect, to behave as an invalid and
child. When she tries to discuss her worries
about her illness with him, he lovingly
patronizes her: "Bless her little heart, she
shall be as sick as she pleases!" (375). The
"wallpaper" covering her isn't only the
roles assigned her by a stifling society,

*Brackets
indicate that
words are not
in the original
text*

DeAngeli 3

but the artificial diagnosis her husband
has for her illness; even her despair has a
condescending candy-coated gloss to it,
layered on by her husband.

The protagonist struggles, through
creative expression, to break free of the
roles in which society (labeling her wife/
mother) and her husband (as delicate invalid)
have cast her. However, as she is forbidden
to write, to create, and to occupy her mind
in any meaningful way, she starts to obsess
over the one stimulus found in her confinement: the wallpaper. As Janice Haney-Peritz
suggests, "Ironically, it is precisely
because the narrator is patient enough to
follow some of the doctor's [her husband's]
orders that she finds it necessary to deal
with the yellow wallpaper" (115).

She observes the paper through sight
and scent, which can be taken as a reflection of the oppressive roles society imposed
on women in Gilman's time. The patriarchal
structure shows the limited use women were
allowed to make of themselves in a male-
dominated society. Like the smell the protagonist is obsessed with, women's prescribed
limitations were also encountered everywhere,
permeating every aspect of a woman's life:

> . . . the smell is here. It creeps
> all over the house. I find it

Short citat[ion]
- introduced [by]
  a phrase
- quotation
  marks
- page numb[er]
- the period [at]
  the end

Long citatio[n]
- no quotat[ion]
  marks
- indented [?]
  spaces
- followed b[y]
  period and
  page numb[er]
  in
  parenthes[es]

DeAngeli 4

> hovering in the dining-room,
> skulking in the parlor, hiding in
> the hall, lying in wait for me on
> the stairs. . . . It is not bad--at
> first, and very gentle, but quite
> the subtlest, most enduring odor I
> have ever met. (402)

At first the wallpaper pattern merely irritates the protagonist, much as the behavior of the killing-her-with-kindness husband might appear to the reader. He truly means no harm. But as she begins to study it, she realizes how much it, and (subconsciously, most likely) her husband's limiting condescension is "lying in wait" at every turn. She concludes that something is hidden beneath the design: "I didn't realize for a long time what the thing was that showed behind, that dim sub-pattern, but now I am quite sure it is a woman" (401). She is losing touch with the "real" world most likely because the real world has no use for her and her talents, and she sees her reality plain as day transformed to the "woman" in the wall. "[T]he narrative pauses to suggest that an external reality hitherto objectively perceived and transparently visible can blur and dissolve," opines one writer, "that the firm, knowable texture of a familiar world can be shaken and lost" (Bader 176).

DeAngeli 5

She starts to identify with the woman behind the paper behind the wallpaper, as this fantasy world is the one outlet for a creativity she must keep secret as "[she is] denied this activity by her husband and her brother for fear of it over-stimulating her" (Elliot). The trapped woman who must creep is her. The tragedy of the woman who is "all the time trying to climb through" is hers (378). The futility of her effort is understood at a subconscious level by this woman, hinting that, growing insanity or not, she is all too aware of her own destiny: "But nobody could climb through that pattern--it strangles so" (378).

The protagonist cannot reconcile her husband's kind and gentle treatment of her with the jailer of her perhaps more percep-tive imagination. Once she has escaped from the paper (representing her escape from reality and from her husband's treatment), she seems proud that she is finally rid of her roles and has outwitted her husband. Knowing the smothering effect of the roles placed on a woman (and the paper placed on the wall), she has grown mistrustful of being returned to the prison of social expectations: "I've got out at last . . . in spite of you and Jane. And I've pulled off most of the paper, so you can't put me

Short citat

DeAngeli 6

back!" (381). The narrator is representative of all women of the time, forced to
subvert their true natures, "kept, virtual
prisoners, in their homes, until they
descend into madness based on inactivity
and denial of basic intellectual and
emotional stimulation" (Elliot). It took a
leap into insanity to find her freedom, but
is insanity really a worse path than
imprisonment?

Short citation

DeAngeli 7

Works Cited

Bader, J. "The Dissolving Vision: Realism in
    Jewett, Freeman, and Gilman." <u>American
    Realism: New Essays</u>. Ed. Eric J. Sandquist.
    Baltimore: Johns Hopkins UP, 1982.

Elliot, Kathleen. "Analysis of 'The Yellow
    Wallpaper'." 29 Oct. 2002. 14 Jan. 2003.
    <http://www.lexingtoncatholic.com/faculty
    /elliott/Gilma_1892.htm>

Gilman, Charlotte Perkins. "The Yellow
    Wallpaper." <u>Literature Across Cultures</u>.
    Ed. Sheena Gillespie, Terezinha Fonseca,
    and Carol Sanger. New York: Longman, 2005.

Haney-Peritz, Janice. "Monumental Feminism and
    Literature's Ancestral House: Another Look
    at 'The Yellow Wallpaper'." <u>Women's
    Studies</u> 12 (1986): 113-28.

List of Work
Cited:
- typed on a
  separate
  page
- double-spa
- heading is
  centered a
  typed 1 in
  from the
  of the pa
- in
  alphabati
  order
- after firs
  line all line
  indented
  spaces

Pipolo 1

Isabel Pipolo

Professor Robson

Introduction to Literature

2 December 2005

Antigone: The Woman, the Heroine,
the Role Model

The character of Antigone in Sophocles'
play has many different facets to her. She
can be analyzed either as a woman, as a
heroine, or as a role model. However, upon
closer examination, is it necessary to
unite all these facets to create a unique
character and personality? Or can we say
that if taken separately, any one of these
individual personal traits would be enough
to describe her?

Antigone is not only different from
women in today's society, she's unique
among the Greek society presented in Sophocles' play. She especially contrasts with
the law-abiding Ismene. As Ismene is overwhelmed by Creon's power, she expects
Antigone to behave as a typical woman and
submit to men: "we must be sensible. Remember we are women, / we're not born to contend with men. Then too, / we're underlings,
ruled by much stronger hands, / so we must
submit in this, and things still worse"
(2.74-77). Antigone, however, is independent and believes that she has a right to

Pipolo 2

her own opinion. Moreover, she is willing
to defend them at all costs even if it
means forsaking the roles--traditionally
assigned to women--of marriage and
children.

Thus, while Ismene views her womanhood
in traditional ways, Antigone discovers
strength in her female nature and uses it to
her own advantage. Unlike Ismene, Antigone
is not afraid to defy her king. As the
passage below shows, she values marriage and
children, but she is willing to give them up
for the honor of burying her brother:

> And now he leads me off, a captive
> in his hands, with no part in the
> bridal-song, the bridal-bed, denied
> all joy of marriage, raising
> children--deserted so by loved
> ones, struck by fate, I descend
> alive to the caverns of the dead.
> (2.1008-12).

Unlike Creon's, Antigone's values seem to be
deeply rooted in her duties to the dead
members of her family. She values her
emotional ties to brother Polyneices over
her ties to country and king.

As a woman, too, Antigone resents the
way Creon sexualizes the power hierarchy in
Thebes. As Charles Paul Segal writes in his
essay "Sophocles' Praise of Man and the

Pipolo 3

Conflicts of the <u>Antigone</u>," "Antigone's
struggle is the woman's emotional resistance
to the ordered male reason of the state"
(66). However, the conflict between Antigone
and Creon can go beyond the debate between
a woman and a man. It can be further defined, as Segal mentions, as Creon's
inability to grasp the reasons, the
motives, and the nature of the "woman's
resistance." In such a debate, Antigone
comes out as more "typically female" or at
least as representing the emotional side of
human nature.

Antigone's display of her female nature
in such a rash and unrelenting way can be
better understood when we realize that
Antigone is still a very young, impetuous
woman. Bowra remarks in his book <u>Sophoclean
Tragedy</u> that Antigone "is young, a girl on
the verge of womanhood, not yet married,
with a girl's directness and refusal to
compromise" (90). Because of her age,
Antigone expresses her love for her brother
in a less "rational" way than we might
expect.

Antigone can also be considered a
heroine, not only in the context of the
play but also in a more universal sense.
Even though she is oppressed and stifled by
Creon and his laws, which she considers

Pipolo 4

unjust, she shows a heroic kind of
resilience, courage, and determination to
fight him to the death to defend her own
principles. If we see Creon representing
the "state" in a more general sense, then
Antigone symbolizes the heroic moral claims
of individual conscience.

In the play, Creon is often portrayed
as a blind, stubborn leader who is drunk on
his own power: "The city is the king's--
that's the law!" (1.825). As Rebecca
Bushnell notes in her book Prophesying
Tragedy, "Creon is tyrannical in his belief
in the power of his own voice and his separation of himself from the claims of humanity" (54). He also raises the power of the
city and his rule above the religious traditions of the people. According to the critic
Gerald Else, this empowerment of the state
defied what the Greeks considered the
natural order: "Creon [exalts] the city
above the gods and their laws, thus
subverting the hierarchical order" (12).

Antigone is also portrayed in the play
as an oppressed member of society who
envisions power and glory as the outcome
of her heroic struggle against impossible
odds:

> Give me glory! What greater glory
> could I win than to give my own

Pipolo 5

brother decent burial? These
citizens here would all agree, they
would praise me too if their lips
weren't locked in fear. (2.562-65)

Antigone is a representative of the common
people who are unable to voice their
opinions because of the threat of political
dictatorship. As she rises as a heroic
figure, she becomes an ideal for those who
are not strong enough to stand up on their
own and fight. Because of her strength,
obstinate personality, and moral convictions, she also becomes a role model for
her sister Ismene and for those who believe
she is right.

Even though Antigone has some influence
over Ismene, this is not enough to convince
her sister to defy Creon, his patriarchal
system, and his public policy. By the end
of the play, however, after Ismene has been
convinced of the heroic purpose of Antigone's
madness and is willing to die with her,
Antigone will not let her. She feels that
Ismene would be sharing the glory for a
courageous act in which she had no part:
"Never share my dying, / don't lay claim to
what you never touched. / My death will be
enough" (2.615-17).

Antigone also becomes a role model for
Haimon, her cousin and husband-to-be. In

Pipolo 6

spite of his initial assurance of his
loyalty to his father, Haimon proves that
he and the people of Thebes support
Antigone. He tries to lend his support to
her by discussing the situation with his
father, but he fails to convince Creon of
his error. His support for Antigone
unfailing, he ultimately has no choice:
"Haemon can join [Antigone] only by joining
in her death" (Scodel 50). Haimon's
suicide, in fact, may be seen as his final
act in support of Antigone.

What is most remarkable about
Antigone's influence over Haimon is that
her actions motivate him to challenge his
father's private and public authority. It
is to Antigone that Haimon owes his
loyalty. Not only does Haimon betray his
father to someone else, but he also betrays
him for a woman, which is exactly what
Creon seems to fear throughout. As Segal
remarks in his essay,

> [Creon] sees in Antigone a
> challenge to his whole way of
> living and his basic attitudes
> toward the world. And of course he
> is right, for Antigone's full
> acceptance of her womanly nature,
> her absolute valuation of the bonds
> of blood and affection, is a total
> denial of Creon's obsessively
> masculine rationality. (70)

Pipolo 7

In betraying his father, therefore, and siding with Antigone, Haimon not only breaks his bonds of loyalty to father and family, but breaks them in conjunction with his affirmation of female power. His attitude especially antagonizes his father. The fact that Haimon takes such action against Creon's powerful voice may be considered a sign that Antigone functioned as a role model to him.

The individual traits that make up Antigone's character, portraying her as a woman, a heroine, and a role model, are all important factors in understanding her motivations and what she symbolizes as a whole. None of these categorizations on their own, however, is enough to completely explain her, since she has so many differ-ent sides. Bowra describes her character as a complex one that can be seen from differ-ent perspectives at different times:

> She is a human being, moved by deep affection and capable of true love. . . . She is no embodiment of abstract devotion to duty, no martyr for martyrdom's sake, but a girl of strong character and strong feelings. Her motives are fundamentally simple, but are displayed now in one light, now in another, as her circumstances or her needs vary. (90)

Pipolo 8

However, together with each one of her
individual facets, Antigone also shows a
dark and complex side to her personality. It
is this darkness and complexity, in fact,
that makes her so interesting. She is also
guided by what we might consider some self-
centered, negative drives.

She is inspired by her loyalty to her
family and to the gods, but what really
drives her and what enables her to stand
resolute against Creon's decree is her tragic
inability to negotiate, compromise, or see
any kind of virtue in somebody else's argument. Such personality traits make Antigone
inflexible and unable to relate well to
others. Eventually they lead to her death.
However, they also are what really makes
Antigone different and noticeable in this
play. She is fighting for what she believes
in, and even though she is far from perfect,
she is carrying out her fight her own way.

Therefore, as a whole, we could say
that what Antigone really represents is a
complete human being. She means well when
she defends her individual conscience
against Creon's public policy. However, she
is undone by her own frailties and cannot
overcome them. She becomes a heroine
because she is able to fight for what she
believes in, and in this process, she shows

Pipolo 9

much strength as a woman. She also becomes
a role model for several of the characters
in the play. However, as she cannot and
does not try to meet anyone's expectations
of her, eventually her inability to
compromise causes her undoing.

Pipolo 10

Works Cited

Bowra, C. M. <u>Sophoclean Tragedy</u>. Oxford:
    Oxford UP, 1944.

Bushnell, Rebecca W. <u>Prophesying Tragedy</u>.
    Ithaca: Cornell UP, 1988.

Else, Gerald. <u>The Madness of Antigone</u>.
    Heidelberg: Carl Winter, 1976.

Scodel, Ruth. <u>Sophocles.</u> Boston: Twayne,
    1984.

Segal, Charles Paul. "Sophocles' Praise of
    Man and the Conflicts of the <u>Antigone</u>."
    <u>Sophocles</u>. Ed. Thomas Woodard.
    Englewood Clifts: Prentice Hall, 1966.
    62–85.

Sophocles. <u>Antigone: The Three Theban Plays</u>.
    Trans. Robert Fagles. Middlesex, Eng.:
    Penguin, 1984.

Researching Literary Sources

To write a good research paper, you must first be a good researcher. This means taking full advantage of all resources available to you, including the library, online resources, electronic databases, and texts and discussions provided in class.

- *Spend time in the library:* Not only are libraries the primary source of printed texts, they also provide computer terminals for online access, subscription-only databases, and CD-ROM resources such as *MLA International Bibliography*, which index texts that may relate to your topic.

Note: In an increasingly computerized society, do not make the mistake of limiting yourself to research via computer, even if the library's printed text holdings are cataloged via the computer terminal. Thorough library research should include a check of any traditional card catalogs that still exist in the library; although they will not list the library's most recent acquisitions, they often house a more thorough listing of available older texts. They may be especially helpful if you are researching a text published over fifty years ago.

- *Be realistic:* As discussed in Appendix B, pick a topic that is limited enough in scope so that you can thoroughly explore it in the number of pages required by your instructor. Also, plan your time so that you do not have to rush at the last moment, which will result in sloppy, incomplete research. Research is a rewarding process, but it is also time-consuming. The time you invest will be rewarded.
- *Do not despair:* If your library does not provide everything you need, it is not acceptable to throw your hands in the air and say "It's not my fault that I can't find anything." The effort to obtain all possible high-quality sources will pay back in a much more thorough and effective paper. You may need to make trips to nearby libraries or look into interlibrary loans. Online indexes may reveal interesting resources in other states or even other countries. Ask yourself if there is any way you can obtain a particular text—perhaps electronically. The answer very possibly could be yes, but if not, do not despair. With effort, you should be able to find relevant, readily available materials, regardless of the topic. You cannot rush a research project, but with steady, focused work, you can keep it quite manageable.

RESEARCH RESOURCES

- Talk to a reference librarian at your school library. Be prepared to discuss your specific topic along with your instructor's length/resource requirements.
- Search your library's catalog, which lists books, magazines, and journals that are held either in print or on microfilm by your library.
- Search subscription databases and CD-ROM catalogs for scholarly articles on the topic.
- Search subscription databases for popular articles on the topic (if applicable).
- Search online literary criticism resources.

Too often, a college student's first impulse is to choose quantity of sources over quality, particularly when an instructor has required a minimum number of sources. For example, you may be required to use seven sources regarding the work of Robert Browning. You decide to go online, print the first seven documents that *Yahoo!* returns mentioning Browning's name, and assume the job is well done. Wrong. This method of "research" typically leads to a pieced-together collection of irrelevant, often poorly written, and ultimately useless texts, which are distorted to "fit" your thesis. Researching is not just a matter of gathering information; it includes evaluating a source and analyzing its usefulness.

In all research, it is important to understand indexing—the systems by which librarians and other information specialists categorize information. If you know what categories of information you are looking for, finding the information becomes much easier. For this reason, you need to know a little bit about your paper topic before beginning your research.

For a literary research paper, you will be looking primarily in the categories of *humanities* and *literature*. However, within literature there are further subdivisions of categories:

- Genre (poetry, drama, short fiction, essays, etc.)
- Nationality (American, British, French, etc.)
- Period (the historical time in which the work was written—nineteenth century, medieval, etc.)
- Literary movement (Realism, Naturalism, etc.)

Try to think of your topic in categories. For example, Jane Austen was an eighteenth-century British woman novelist. A study of Jane Austen would require searches using her name, but you might also find useful information in studies of the novel in general, British literature, eighteenth-century literature, and women's literature. In print sources, you will often find bibliographies that lead you to further sources; and on the Internet, you will often find links between these various types of information. Therefore, a page on Jane Austen might have links to pages about eighteenth-century novels in general or to archives of women's literature.

It is not enough for a text to be tangentially related to your topic. It must relate specifically to your thesis and to other researched documents you are utilizing. For example, you may find a fascinating journal article exploring the twentieth-century Freudian interpretation of Hamlet's relationship with Gertrude, his mother. However, if your paper topic is to compare and contrast how Hamlet and Laertes pursue revenge for a father's death, then you may have to discard this fascinating article because it does not relate closely to your area of exploration.

Occasionally, research may feel like searching for a needle in a haystack, but the process need not be so arbitrary. To find articles that relate to your topic, you first should check books and online databases that list sources according to subject and author.

Again, it cannot be stressed enough that your number one tool in pursuing research is the aid of the research librarians at your campus library. They are most aware of what the library holds, what the library does not hold but can access, and major changes to the library's holdings and databases in the recent past. Use them!

The following sections list frequently used reference works and databases, both print and online, in the field of literature. These resources are often good in locating background material and pointing you in the right direction for further sources.

A little research can go a long way. By locating a subject (for example, Leo Tolstoy) in a reference work or database, you will undoubtedly be directed to dozens, if not hundreds or thousands, of potentially useful sources immediately. Upon locating a source or web page dedicated to a subject, you will often find a bibliography (on a web page, not only a bibliography but a collection of links to other websites) that will reveal other closely related sources. You should realize that each source you locate may well be a gateway to another source you were not aware of. You are unlikely to be the first person to investigate a certain topic! Use the works cited in researched sources to locate further resources.

Reference Works

The first step in researching a topic is to know what your topic is: Are you researching poetry? A novel? Two novels with similar themes? By having a clear topic you will be able, with the help of a reference librarian, to know which indexes (both in print and electronically stored) to employ in your search.

A discussion of a poem such as "My Last Duchess" by Robert Browning may be included in a collection of essays on poetry in general or in a book focusing on the work of Browning. How do you locate such an article? One way is to use the *Essay and General Literature Index*, available both in print and online, which is designed to help you find a specific subject that may be "hidden" in chapters or parts of books that are not exclusively focused on your subject. Under *Browning, Robert*, you'll find analyses of his works under the subdivision "About Individual Works." There are indexes and bibliographies that are all-encompassing and others that specialize in subjects such as African American literature of the twentieth century or medieval English literature. Some basic titles and indexes to be aware of in a literature survey course include:

- *MLA International Bibliography of Books and Articles in the Modern Languages and Literatures (1922–)*; also available online and as a CD-ROM, which are more up-to-date.
- *Reader's Guide to Periodical Literature (1900–)*; although this has been superseded by online databases such as *InfoTrac* for modern periodical (magazine, newspaper) articles, it is still a necessary tool for research of older periodical texts.
- *American Literary Scholarship* (1965–)
- *Oxford Companion to Contemporary Authors*; Oxford University Press has published many useful books in this reference series that could be helpful in literary research.
- *Dictionary of Literary Biography*
- *Masterplots* (print and CD-ROM)
- *Magill's Survey of Literature*
- *New Cambridge Bibliography of English Literature*
- *Reader's Guide to Literature in English*
- *Encyclopedia of American Literature*

Note that many of the print-based indexes, such as the aforementioned *Essay and General Literature Index*, increasingly have web and CD-ROM based equivalents that are updated much more frequently.

Your library's computer catalog will list all books it holds; as noted earlier, if a card catalog still exists, cross-reference that as well for older texts. Remember that if you are researching James Joyce, do not search only using his name as a subject. Use it as a keyword as well, and with each source that comes up, see what subject headings it is listed under for hints about subject headings that could prove useful.

Electronic Databases

Electronic databases can lead you to articles in scholarly journals, newspapers and magazines, e-journals, dissertations, and more. Check with your librarian about which services your library provides. Databases that might be useful in literary research include:

- *InfoTrac*
- *Lexis-Nexis Academic Universe*
- *MLA International Bibliography*

Not all databases provide the full text of articles; some may offer abstracts, which are summaries of article content. They will give you the necessary information for you to locate the full article via other means.

Online Sources

The Reliability of Web-Based Information

No one is in charge of the web, and anyone can put up a website. You should examine all your research sources carefully, but examine online sources with extra care. To judge the reliability of a website, it is important to know who created it. Look for links to the website's home page—the opening page of the site—and go there to see who has authored the website and what other types of information are included.

Always consider the purpose of a page you are viewing. Many sites are "democratic," allowing anyone to post a review or comment with no questions asked. A likeable concept, but the point of quality literary research is to research the arguments of *experts* in the subject you are covering, not draw quotations from people who may never have read the texts they are commenting on! Also note that sites such as Amazon.com are in the business of selling products and are unlikely to say negative or controversial things regarding a book they are promoting.

The lines are blurring regarding web addresses and what they signify, but it still holds true that a site ending in .edu is an educational domain. This does not guarantee a web page's quality, however, as students often can put up their own websites on a school server. Still, the majority of serious literary criticism available on the Internet will be found on .edu sites. Use common sense and good judgment in determining an online source's quality. If you are still not sure after a thorough investigation of the site, speak to your instructor or a librarian about the potential source's suitability.

The following sites offer advice for evaluating Internet websites:

University at Albany Libraries: Evaluating Internet Resources
http://library.albany.edu/internet/evaluate.html

Widener University Wolfgram Memorial Library: Evaluating Web Resources
http://www2.widener.edu/Wolfgram-Memorial-Library/
  webevaluation/webeval.htm

Searching Online Sources

With these foregoing warnings taken into account, it holds true that literary research has benefited enormously from the Internet. A great deal of quality information and research on authors and texts can be found with a few keystrokes. The sites listed in the following sections are all serious attempts to gather thoughtful and useful information regarding all aspects of literature. Many provide links to other valuable sites. The number of sites and indexes available via the web are too numerous to list here, and websites are notorious for disappearing without notice or moving to an unannounced address. To locate web sources not listed here try using the following search engines:

- http://www.google.com (the most comprehensive search engine—will also return the most useless and tangential texts)
- http://www.kartoo.com (intriguingly visual in its returns, mapping out sites and showing connections between them)
- http://www.yahoo.com (selective in what it returns—will mostly avoid useless texts but may also overlook quality ones)

Do not use just one search engine; all have strengths and weaknesses. Other engines, such as http://www.altavista.com and http://www.northernlight.com, are very useful as well.

Remember when searching online:

- If you are searching for a proper name, put it in quotation marks. Searching *"James Joyce"* will give you sites that reference only the author; if you type *James* and *Joyce* without quotation marks, you will still get sites related to the author, but you will also get sites that have the (common) names James and Joyce located *anywhere* on the site.
- Check a search engine's "Help" guide for hints on how to search more precisely. Using "and" or "not" often helps limit a search. For example, *"James Joyce"* AND *"Eveline"* will lead you only to websites that reference both Joyce and this story from *The Dubliners*, whereas *"James Joyce"* NOT *"Eveline"* would delete all sites that referenced this story.
- Remember to "bookmark" (save the location to your web browser) every page that seems useful, so that you can find it again later.

Not all search engines use the same format; some prefer a plus sign (+) instead of *AND*. Check each site's guidelines.

Online Encyclopedias

- *Encyclopedia Britannica*
  http://www.eb.com
- *Columbia Encyclopedia*
  http://www.bartleby.com/65/

Online Literary Texts

- *The Bartleby Project*
  http://www.bartleby.com/index.html
- *Project Guttenberg*
  http://promo.net/pg/
- *American Literary Classics*
  http://www.americanliterature.com/
- *American Poetry*
  http://etext.lib.virginia.edu/ampo.html
- *The Internet Poetry Archives* (focusing on modern poets)
  http://www.ibiblio.org/dykki/poetry/index.html
- A library center and poetry archive
  http://www.poetshouse.org/

Literary Criticism Research Sites

- *The Voice of the Shuttle* is an outstanding place to start all research in the humanities.
  http://vos.ucsb.edu/
- Jack Lynch's *American Literature* page at Rutgers University is one of the best Web resources for literary studies.
  http://andromeda.rutgers.edu/~jlynch/Lit/american.html
- Indiana University Libraries at Bloomington sponsors this site, which links to dozens of online journals for literary studies
  http://www.indiana.edu/~libsalc/pwillett/english-www.html
- University of Kentucky houses updated links to online resources
  http://www.uky.edu/Subject/englit.html
- The *Internet Public Library* has a section devoted to literary criticism
  http://www.ipl.org/div/litcrit/
- American literature resources housed at Columbia University
  http://www.columbia.edu/~lmg21/bookmark.htm
- American literature—general resources
  http://bubl.ac.uk/link/a/americanliterature-general.htm
- *Luminarium* is a resource for Middle English literature, renaissance literature, and seventeenth-century literature.
  http://www.luminarium.org/
- University of Kentucky theater web resources
  http://www.uky.edu/Subject/theater.html
- The American Academy of Poets has an outstanding site dedicated to poets
  http://www.poets.org/
- English poetry from the Anglo-Saxon times until the end of the nineteenth century
  http://etext.virginia.edu/epd.html

Author-Based Sites

There are many quality sites related to authors, some hosted by academic institutions and many by fans. They are often excellent as an overview of an author's life and work and usually contain links to other sites of interest. Some examples:

The American Academy of Poets site for Robert Frost contains quality information on Frost and also introduces you to a website that has pages for many important literary figures.

`http://www.poets.org/poets/poets.cfm?prmID=196`
A page for Jamaica Kincaid from the site *Voices from the Gaps: Women Writers of Color*,
    will lead you to pages for other African American female authors
`http://voices.cla.umn.edu/authors/jamaicakincaid.html`
A site that endeavors to be a complete annotated guide to scholarly Shakespearian
    resources on the web
`http://shakespeare.palomar.edu/`

To locate sites such as these, use the search engines listed earlier.

Other Online Sources

There are many online discussions and newsgroups relating to literary topics. *DejaNews*
(`http://www.deja.com`), now controlled by `http://www.google.com`, provides
links to many discussion groups that are worthwhile for stimulating discussion but are not
particularly helpful as research tools, as the discussions are generally unmoderated, unsub-
stantiated, and unfocused. These discussions are worth a look if you are interested in finding
like-minded Ernest J. Gaines fans, for example, but they can be dangerous as a source for
research.

Resource Guidelines

The foregoing sites are just a few of the valuable resources available online, through subscription services, and in your library's holdings. Discuss with your school's reference librar-
ian(s) which holdings and databases you can access.
    Keep in mind these general guidelines as you research literary sources:

- Be aware of whether a reference book contains a critique itself or just provides a list of
  places to find criticism.
- Don't judge a book by its title. Investigate what information can be found in the book
  by checking the table of contents and the index. Also, check to see the date of publication of the book and the information collected in it. If your instructor requires texts
  published in the last ten years, a book published twenty years ago, no matter how
  interesting, is irrelevant to your research.
- Recognize that locating and evaluating sources can be time-consuming! Remember,
  however, that it will save you time later in the process of constructing your paper.
  Locating excellent sources early on will make the actual writing of your paper much
  more engaging and satisfying for both you and your readers.

SAMPLE RESEARCH: JAMES JOYCE

Let us look at some of these research principles in practice. Suppose you are writing a
research paper on James Joyce, the brilliant expatriate Irish author whose works take place in
Dublin, Ireland, portraying his efforts to be free of religious and geographic restrictions. The
search here was done in January, 2003.

Online Library Catalog

By searching the City University of New York (CUNY) online library catalog, using *Joyce
James* as author (last name first per the database's instructions) we located more than
400 texts. If any of these texts seemed useful, we would have to double-check that

Queensborough Community College, the institution from which we were doing the research, held a copy. If not, we would have to investigate the possibility of an *interlibrary loan*, whereby a book is lent between institutions.

Author Search

One book that seemed interesting was an edition of *The Dubliners* edited by Robert E. Scholes and A. Walton Litz, published by Penguin Books in 1996; the online record indicated that it contained criticism, notes, and a bibliography. We noted that the book is held at Queensborough, so this would be a good first step in the research process.

Keyword Search

We then did a keyword search for *James Joyce* and *symbolism*. Many books and articles about Joyce might not directly relate to his use of symbolism. By using these keywords, however, we hoped to find sources that would lead us in the right direction.

We found eight sources available at CUNY under a keyword search in all fields, but none were available at Queensborough. If any of the sources were provocative, we would have to utilize an interlibrary loan, which is not a difficult process but can take some time, and we would have to plan accordingly.

Electronic Databases and Subscription Services

Every college has electronic databases held on CD-ROM. Again, it is best to consult with a reference librarian regarding which databases best suit your research purposes. Utilizing a subscription service available at CUNY, we used *InfoTrac* to access the *MLA International Bibliography*, where we searched for *James Joyce* under the heading "Author as Subject" within journal articles in the English language (we could have, and would have, searched under books and book articles as well). The result was 4009 articles! The first was entitled "See that Straw? That's a Straw: Anti-Semitism and Narrative Form in *Ulysses*," by Neil Levi in the September 2002 edition of *Modernism/Modernity*. By clicking on it, we reached a site that did *not* provide the whole article but gave pertinent information should we wish to locate it. Assuming for the moment that our topic was Joyce's *Dubliners*, this would not be a relevant document for our current search. So we would refine the search by altering our search requirements.

Now we tried *"James Joyce and Dubliners"* under the "Words Anywhere" heading, hoping to find journal articles that dealt at least partially with this work. We also requested documents published only in the last twelve years, as we assumed any new works would refer to older works and ultimately guide us to relevant older sources. We returned five sources, three of which seemed promising upon inspection.

You are not expected to be an expert at this the first time out. Give yourself enough time, and, again, enlist a reference librarian to familiarize you with your school's holdings and to assist you in choosing the best direction to begin your research in.

Online Searches

The first place we searched was Yahoo! The initial search returned directory categories that included *Authors > James Joyce; James Joyce > Ulysses; James Joyce > Dubliners;* and *James Joyce > Works*, which could help us narrow our search (if we were researching *The Dubliners*, one of these above choices would be obvious!) as well as several web sites. The sites we found included:

- *James Joyce Center*, which is the official site of the James Joyce Center, at `http://www.jamesjoyce.ie/home/index.asp`. An excellent introduction to Joyce, it offers a biography, a gallery, and links to several other Irish and Joyce sites that could prove valuable in our research.

At such a point, you may wish to use the links offered on a high-quality site like this, as well as the links found on a search engine, which are more likely to be hit-or-miss. A quality site would be unlikely to put up links it did not think were also of a certain quality. This is another example of how the time spent researching pays off in unexpected ways.

- *Work in Progress*, located at `http://www.2street.com/joyce/` is a fan-run site that contains excellent links to a biographical timeline, maps of Dublin (essential in analysis of *The Dubliners*), digitized audio recordings of Joyce reading from his work, Joyce works on the web, and the like.
- *The James Joyce Resource Center*, located at `http://www.cohums.ohio-state.edu/english/organizations/ijjf/jrc/default.htm`, is a terrific site that offers bibliographies of various criticisms not available on the Internet—a valuable resource if you are having trouble using the subscription databases and library catalogs.

We then clicked on the directory for *James Joyce > Dubliners* and were given a listing of five sites, one of which—`http://www.robotwisdom.com/jaj/dubliners/`—was entitled *Web Resources for Joyce's Dubliners* and provided a good overview of what it promised. Also listed, however, were cites focused on *Ulysses* and *The Dead*, two fine Joyce works that were irrelevant to our *Dubliners* research.

By searching "*James Joyce*" (in quotes, as a phrase—remember, we do not want every site with *James* and *Joyce* appearing on it!) on `http://www.google.com`, we had different results. A more undisciplined, albeit more inclusive search engine, Google returned many of the same sources found on Yahoo! on the first page, but promised 235,000 total results, a little much. Google's far-reaching search capabilities allow you to perform narrowly worded searches more successfully, but often prove overwhelming on more general subjects. When we searched for "*James Joyce*" + "*symbolism*" + "*Eveline*," we came up with a more manageable 176 sites, and although many were irrelevant or poorly written or (alas) offered to take our money for poorly written papers, we did come across some seemingly thoughtful sites, such as `http://members.xoom.virgilio.it/sitotesina/Inglese/joyce.htm`. However, this site offered only a short, unsubstantial paragraph on symbolism in *The Dubliners* and linked only to a home page in Italian! This was not a quality source for a serious investigation of the topic, but with a little more digging we either could find a quality source or deduce that our search strategy was not working and therefore alter it.

This sample research was only a brief outline to remind you that research starts at point zero for everyone, but that with a little effort and discipline, you will quickly "get the scent" and be on the right path toward collecting quality resources for your research. Your main thrust will still be toward the holdings of your library and academic institutions that sponsor subscriber-only information electronically. The Internet is still largely, but not exclusively, a source for background and biographical information on a subject. Proper usage of all available resources will lead to a successful paper.

There is no lack of information available on any author you might research during your higher education career. You should practice researching continually; pick a favorite author and research him or her just for your personal interest. At the very least, use your university's and the Internet's resources to investigate any subject that interests you, whether it is the New York Yankees, oil painting, or Tom Cruise. The more you utilize these resources, the more you will master them. Who knows, if you do a quality research project, you may be cited in a future researcher's work!

Critical Approaches: A Case Study of Hamlet

You probably have noticed that at times your response to a literary text may differ greatly from that of your classmates. Sometimes as you listen to these various voices in your literature class, you may even wonder whether you have all read the same text. Diverse factors such as your personalities, lifestyles, social environments, and experiences may lead you to adopt various kinds of value judgments, and to react differently to the stories, poems, and plays that you read. Like you, literary critics also come up with different responses to and diverse interpretations of the same literary work. Often they also adopt reading strategies that reflect a personal affiliation to various critical theories, such as formalism, psychoanalytic criticism, reader-response criticism, feminist criticism, and the New Historicism.

The following selections highlight five different ways that literary critics have chosen to interpret Shakespeare's *Hamlet*. As you read them, you will discover how each can illuminate your reading of *Hamlet*, making you aware of new ways to delve into its literary complexity. Sigmund Freud once said that the poets and artists of the past had anticipated most of his findings about the unconscious. Freud's thesis may also be applied to *Hamlet*, the literary complexity of which seems to have anticipated the possibilities of various critical interpretations.

Notice that while none of the interpretations in this appendix claims to express an ideal evaluation of *Hamlet*, each will help you to uncover the rich complexity, ambiguity, and suggestiveness of Shakespeare's play.

PSYCHOANALYTIC CRITICISM

What Is the Focus of Psychoanalytic Criticism?

Psychoanalytic criticism takes the methods used to analyze the behavior of people in real-life situations and applies them to the dramatized patterns of human behavior in literature. Overall, it explores some basic assumptions devised by the pioneer of psychoanalysis, Sigmund Freud (1856–1939). Most important among these are Freud's fundamental ideas about the structure of the human psyche, his theory of repression, and the Oedipus complex model that Freud applied to his reading of *Hamlet*.

Freud's Theory of Repression. Freud viewed one part of the human psyche, the *id* or unconscious, as the site of our instincts, or the unconscious part of ourselves that is biologically rooted and is always pressing for some kind of satisfaction. For Freud, the id basically fulfilled the principle of life he called the "pleasure principle." The *ego* or the *"I,"* on the other hand, forms the rational part of the psyche. The ego opposes the id, as well as the *superego* or conscience. In a simplified view, the superego is that part of ourselves that regulates our moral judgment, telling us what is right or wrong. Based on this structural model, Freud developed his theory of *repression.* In his theory, the id becomes the repository of repressed material such as pain, sexual desires, wishes, and fears that the ego and superego tend to censor because of social mores, taboos, and other factors. As Freud viewed it, such repressed forces might eventually be reactivated to emerge either through our creative activities or through our fantasies, dreams, language, slips of the tongue, neuroses, repressed fears, and other sorts of mental conflicts.

The Oedipus Complex. The name Oedipus takes us back to the Greek hero Oedipus who unwittingly kills his father and marries his mother. By *Oedipus Complex* Freud meant to define one of the major repressed wishes of a boy's childhood: his desire to identify with the father and replace him in the affection of the mother. Psychoanalysts who came after Freud constructed a feminine version of the Oedipus complex, called the *Electra Complex.* Named after a Greek legend in which the heroine Electra kills her mother to avenge the death of her father, the Electra Complex describes a girl's unconscious wish to take the mother's place in the affection of the father.

A Psychoanalytic Reading of *Hamlet*

In his analysis of *Hamlet,* which was later amplified by his disciple and biographer Ernest Jones, Freud used his theory of repression and his overall assessment of the Oedipus complex to raise the issue of how Hamlet's strong repressed desire for his mother prevents him from fulfilling the task assigned to him by his father's ghost.

Sigmund Freud

The Interpretation of Dreams

Another of the great creations of tragic poetry, Shakespeare's *Hamlet,* has its roots in the same soil as *Oedipus Rex.* But the changed treatment of the same material reveals the whole difference in the mental life of these two widely separated epochs of civilization: the secular advance of repression in the emotional life of mankind. In the *Oedipus* the child's wishful phantasy that underlies it is brought into the open and realized as it would be in a dream. In *Hamlet* it remains repressed; and—just as in the case of a neurosis—we only learn of its existence from its inhibiting consequences. Strangely enough, the overwhelming effect produced by the more modern tragedy has turned out to be compatible with the fact that people have remained completely in the dark as to the hero's character. The play is built up on Hamlet's hesitations over fulfilling the task of revenge that is assigned to him; but its text offers no reasons or motives for these hesitations and an immense variety of attempts at interpreting them have failed to produce a result. According to the view which was originated by Goethe and is still the prevailing one to-day, Hamlet represents the type of man whose power of direct action is paralysed by an excessive development of his intellect. (He is "sicklied o'er with the pale cast of thought.") According to another view, the dramatist has tried to portray a pathologically irresolute character which might be classed as neurasthenic. The plot of the drama shows us, however, that Hamlet is far from being represented as a person incapable of taking any action. We see him doing so on two occasions: first in a sudden outburst of temper, when he runs his sword through the eavesdropper behind the arras, and secondly in a premeditated and even crafty fashion, when, with all the callousness of a Renaissance prince, he sends the two courtiers to the death that had been planned for himself. What is it, then, that inhibits him in fulfilling the task set him by his father's ghost? The answer, once again, is that it is the peculiar nature of the task. Hamlet is able to do anything—except take vengeance on the man who did away with his father and took that father's place with his mother, the man who shows him the repressed wishes of his own childhood realized. Thus the loathing which should drive him on to revenge is replaced in him by self-reproaches, by scruples of conscience, which remind him that he himself is literally no better than the sinner whom he is to punish.

Freud's psychoanalytic theories have been complemented, disputed, and revised by many of his followers. For instance, Carl Gustav Jung (1875–1961), Freud's student and later opponent, replaced Freud's main focus on sex with a theory of the *collective unconscious*. Unlike Freud, who highlights the individual history of repressed wishes, Jung emphasizes the importance of the collective unconscious, also known as racial memory, or the collective desires of the human race. The French psychoanalyst Jacques Lacan (1901–1981) shifted Freud's view from mental processes to argue that the unconscious is structured like a language.

A Psychosocial Reading of *Hamlet*

Recent psychoanalytic thought, as well as some post-Freudian development in psychoanalysis, has opened up the criticism of *Hamlet* to different approaches. One such approach is known as the psychosocial. Without ignoring the psychosexual implications of the play, a *psychosocial approach* to *Hamlet*, such as the one David Leverenz adopts in his article "The Women in *Hamlet*: An Interpersonal View," emphasizes the role that culture plays in shaping Hamlet's identity. On the basis of such a rationale, Leverenz argues that the real tragedy of *Hamlet* is that Hamlet finally does act. He assumes the aggressive masculine role that the patriarchal structure of power imposes on him, even though he views it as quite meaningless.

David Leverenz

The Women in Hamlet: *An Interpersonal View*

  Hamlet's tragedy is the forced triumph of filial duty over sensitivity to his own heart. To fulfil various fathers' commands, he has to deny his self-awareness, just as Gertrude and Ophelia have done. That denial is equivalent to suicide, as the language of the last act shows. His puritanical cries about whoredom in himself and others, his hysterical outbursts to Ophelia about nunneries and painted women, are the outer shell of a horror at what the nurtured, loving, and well-loved soul has been corrupted to. From a more modern perspective than the play allows, we can sense that the destruction of good mothering is the real issue, at least from Hamlet's point of view.

  Freudians, too many of whom have their own paternal answers to "Who's there," see Hamlet as an unconscious Claudius-Oedipus, or as a man baffled by pre-Oedipal ambivalences about his weak-willed, passionate, fickle mother. While acknowledging Hamlet's parricidal and matricidal impulses, we should see these inchoate feelings as responses, not innate drives. Interpersonal expectations, more than self-contained desires, are what divide Hamlet from himself and conscript him to false social purposes. In this perspective, taken from Harry Stack Sullivan, R. D. Laing, and D. W. Winnicott, Hamlet's supposed delay is a natural reaction to overwhelming interpersonal confusion. His self-preoccupation is paradoxically grounded not so much in himself as in the extraordinary and unremitting array of "mixed signals" that separate role from self, reason from feeling, duty from love.

  Hamlet has no way of unambiguously understanding what anyone says to him. The girl who supposedly loves him inexplicably refuses his attentions. His grieving mother suddenly marries. His dead father, suddenly alive, twice tells him to deny his anger at his mother's shocking change of heart. Two of his best friends "make love to this employment" of snooping against him (V.ii.57). Polonius, Claudius, and the Ghost all manifest themselves as loving fathers, yet expect the worst from their sons and spy on their children, either directly or through messengers. Who is this "uncle-father" and "aunt-mother" (II.ii.366), or this courtier-father, who preach the unity of being true to oneself and others yet are false to everyone, who can "smile, smile, and be a villain" (I.v.108)? Gertrude's inconstancy not only brings on disgust and incestuous feelings, it is also the sign of diseased doubleness in everyone who has accommodated to his or her social role. Usurping Claudius is the symbol of all those "pretenders," who are now trying to bring Hamlet into line. No wonder Hamlet weeps at the sight of a genuine actor—the irony reveals the problem—playing Hecuba's grief. The male expressing a woman's constancy once again mirrors Hamlet's need. And the role, though feigned, at least is openly played. The actor's tears are the play's one unambiguous reflection of the grief Hamlet thought his mother shared with him before the onset of so many multitudinous double-dealings.

  To kill or not to kill cannot be entertained when one is not even sure of existing with any integrity. Being, not desiring or revenging, is the question. Freudians assume that everyone has strong desires blocked by stronger repressions, but contemporary work with schizophrenics reveals the tragic variety of people whose voices are only amalgams of other people's voices, with caustic self-observation or a still more terrifying vacuum as their incessant inward reality. This is Hamlet to a degree, as it is Ophelia completely. As Laing says of her in *The Divided Self,* "in her madness, there is no one there. She is not a person. There is no integral selfhood expressed through her actions or utterances. Incomprehensible statements are said by nothing. She has already died. There is now only a vacuum where there was once a person." Laing misrepresents her state only because there are many voices in Ophelia's madness speaking through her, all making sense, and none of them her own. She becomes the mirror for a madness-inducing world. Hamlet resists these pressures at the cost of a terrifying isolation. Once he thinks his mother has abandoned him, there is nothing and no one to "mirror" his feelings, as Winnicott puts it. Hamlet is utterly alone, beyond the loving semi-understanding of reasonable Horatio or obedient Ophelia.

A world of fathers and sons, ambition and lust, considers grief "unmanly," as Claudius preaches (I.ii.94). Hamlet seems to agree, at least to himself, citing his "whorish" doubts as the cause of his inability to take manly filial action. This female imagery, which reflects the play's male-centered world view, represents a covert homosexual fantasy, according to Freudian interpretation. Certainly Hamlet's idealisations of his father and of Horatio's friendship show a hunger for male closeness. Poisoning in the ear may unconsciously evoke anal intercourse. And the climactic swordplay with Laertes does lead to a brotherly understanding. But these instances of covert homosexual desire are responses to a lack. Poisoning in the ear evokes conscious and unconscious perversity to intimate the perversion of communication, especially between men. The woman in Hamlet is the source of his most acute perceptions about the diseased, disordered patriarchal society that tries to "play upon this pipe" of Hamlet's soul (III.ii.336), even as a ghost returning from the dead.

Reading Contexts

Freud's Text

1. Why, according to Freud, have Shakespeare's readers and critics remained completely in the dark in their attempts to interpret Hamlet's character?
2. Freud mentions that the Hamlet theory developed by the German poet Goethe (1749–1832) still prevailed in his time. Describe Goethe's theory, and summarize the arguments that Freud developed to refute Goethe's romantic interpretation of Hamlet's character. How does Freud's psychoanalytic interpretation differ from Goethe's romantic one?

Leverenz's Text

1. Explain the distinction between Freud's psychosexual interpretation and Leverenz's psychosocial interpretation of *Hamlet*, which highlights the idea that we are creatures of culture.
2. Leverenz argues that "interpersonal expectations, more than self-contained desires, are what divide Hamlet from himself and conscript him to false social purposes." In your opinion, is Leverenz's argument complex enough to explain the Hamlet problem?
3. One of the major arguments running through Leverenz's article supports the idea that Hamlet is manipulated and ultimately controlled by the male roles that patriarchal society imposes on him. Do you agree or disagree with Leverenz?

Psychoanalytic Criticism: Reading References

The reading references in this section include a series of works that, although not directly connected with *Hamlet*, highlight some of the critical ideas that inform the modern reading of *Hamlet*.

Erlich, Avi. *Hamlet's Absent Father*. Princeton: Princeton UP, 1977.

Freud, Sigmund. "The Interpretation of Dreams." *The Standard Edition of the Complete Psychological Works*. Ed. James Strachey. London: Hogarth, 1953–1974.

Kurtzweil, Edith, and William Philips, eds. *Literature and Psychoanalysis*. New York: Columbia UP, 1983.

Lacan, Jacques. "Desire and the Interpretation of Desire in *Hamlet*." *Literature and Psychoanalysis: The Question of Reading: Otherwise*. Ed. Shoshana Felman. Baltimore: Johns Hopkins UP, 1982.

Leverenz, David. "The Women in *Hamlet*: An Interpersonal View." *Hamlet: Contemporary Critical Essays*. Ed. Martin Coyle. New York: St. Martin's, 1992.

Sprengnether, Madelon. *The Spectral Mother: Freud, Feminism and Psychoanalysis*. Ithaca: Cornell UP, 1990.

FORMALISM/NEW CRITICISM

What Is the Focus of Formalism?

Formalism seeks to emphasize the importance of the formal elements of literature or the formal qualities related to the language, form, and content of a literary text. It directly opposes any extrinsic kind of criticism that views the literary text as a product of the author's intentions or as a reflection of ethical and sociocultural forces. In modern formalist criticism, especially in the works of formalist critics known as *New Critics*, literature is alienated and isolated from the actual world, seeking to fulfill the purposes of revealing deeper truths and embodying a unified vision of life in the shaped structure of a work of art.

Formalism flourished from the 1940s to the 1960s. To some extent, the close reading it advocates has remained a major goal not only for formalists but for all readers who rely on formal devices, such as imagery, irony, paradox, symbols, diction, plot, characterization, and narrative techniques, to understand the meanings of a literary text. A formalist reading of poetry can show, for instance, how a poem can integrate an ideal order of form and content by relating its phonic devices (aspects related to sounds, rhythm, and meter) to its images, symbols, and overall mode of poetic construction.

A New Critical Reading of *Hamlet*

Since a major focus of the New Critical method or formalism is the construction of literary craft, formalist critics have explored Shakespeare's use of character, language, and staging to validate the dramatic world of *Hamlet*. In "Hamlet and His Problems," T. S. Eliot applies formalist strategies to argue that feelings and emotions can be viewed as an objective mode of construction and be formally channeled in art. Shakespeare fails in *Hamlet*, Eliot argues, because he is unable to find "an objective correlative" or "a set of objects, a situation, a chain of events which shall be the formula of that *particular* emotion." Thus, as Eliot sees it, emotions and feelings in *Hamlet* exceed the literary form of Shakespeare's tragedy and cannot be expressed in art—they are "in excess of the facts." As to Gertrude, Eliot remarks that she "arouses in Hamlet the feeling which she is incapable of representing."

T. S. Eliot

Hamlet and His Problems

The only way of expressing emotion in the form of art is by finding an "objective correlative": in other words, a set of objects, a situation, a chain of events which shall be the formula of that *particular* emotion; such that when the external facts, which must terminate in sensory experience, are given, the emotion is immediately evoked. If you examine any of Shakespeare's more successful tragedies, you will find this exact equivalence; you will find that the state of mind of Lady Macbeth walking in her sleep has been communicated to you by a skilful accumulation of imagined sensory impressions; the words of Macbeth on hearing of his wife's death strike us as if, given the sequence of events, these words were automatically released by the last event in the series. The artistic "inevitability" lies in this complete adequacy of the external to the emotion; and this is precisely what is deficient in *Hamlet*. Hamlet (the man) is dominated by an emotion which is inexpressible, because it is in *excess* of the facts as they appear. And the supposed identity of Hamlet with his author is genuine to this point: that Hamlet's bafflement at the absence of objective equivalent to his feelings is a prolongation of the bafflement of his creator in the face of his artistic problem. Hamlet is up against the difficulty that his disgust is occasioned by his mother, but that his mother is not an adequate equivalent for it; his disgust envelops and exceeds her. It is thus a feeling which he cannot understand; he cannot objectify it, and it therefore remains to poison life and obstruct action. None of the possible actions can satisfy it; and nothing that Shakespeare can do with the plot can express Hamlet for him. And it must be noticed that the very nature of the *données* of the problem precludes objective equivalence. To have heightened the criminality of Gertrude would have been to provide the formula for a totally different emotion in Hamlet; it is just *because* her character is so negative and insignificant that she arouses in Hamlet the feeling which she is incapable of representing.

Reading Contexts

1. New Criticism or formalism attempts to present a unified vision of a work of art in which every element, such as a word, an image, or a situation, contributes to a formal view of unity. With this in mind, analyze the use that Eliot makes of words such as *deficient*, *excess*, *not adequate*, and *negative* to support his reading of *Hamlet*.
2. According to Hazard Adams, what Eliot really meant by the "objective correlative" is not very clear. Examine Eliot's definition of this concept in the beginning of the first paragraph of his essay, and then decide whether you agree or disagree with Adams.

Formalism / New Criticism: Reading References

Brooks, Cleanth, and Robert Penn Warren. *Understanding Poetry*. New York: Henry Holt, 1938.

Crane, Ronald Salmon. *The Languages of Criticism and the Structure of Poetry*. Toronto: U of Toronto P, 1953.

Eliot, T. S. "Hamlet and His Problems." *Selected Essays*. New York: Harcourt, 1960.

Warren, Austin. *Rage for Order: Essays in Criticism*. Ann Arbor: U of Michigan P, 1948.

READER-RESPONSE CRITICISM
What Is the Focus of Reader-Response Criticism?

Reader-response criticism places much emphasis on the literary experience of individual readers not only as interpreters of texts but as producers of meanings. One of its basic assumptions is that each reading of a text by a single reader will be different because the dynamic and subjective scope of the reader's responses makes each reader react in different ways. Thus, the major focus of reader-response criticism is the diversity and plurality of the reader's interpretive experiences. As individual readers are apt to be influenced by social, communal, cultural, and political values, reader-response criticism also focuses on how women, individuals, and groups, in different social settings and in different time periods, read texts. Some studies show, for instance, how readers can interact with the texts' gaps, ambiguities, and pluralities or use the reading process itself to revise and build up their own expectations as readers.

A Reader-Response Analysis of *Hamlet*

Reader-response criticism can make us understand why we encounter such diverse interpretive responses to our study of *Hamlet*. The critic Norman N. Holland, for instance, explains how three different readers can respond to *Hamlet* and construct the meaning of this play according to their emotional and psychological reactions to the concept of authority. For Holland, as for most reader-response critics, whenever a text threatens the identity of its readers, the readers question, rewrite, and project their feelings on it.

In the following passage, another reader-response critic, Stephen Booth, analyzes *Hamlet* in terms of the audience's response to the play. For Booth, the audience not only is involved in constructing the meaning of *Hamlet* but is also affected when its character and experience are altered and revised by the reading process itself. Thus, at times *Hamlet's* audience is invited to settle its mind, to get information, to develop double and contrary responses to Claudius, while at other times it gets frustrated, finding its focus shifted and its understanding threatened. At least once the audience is taken to the brink of intellectual terror. Most important, according to Booth, the audience never knows what it would have done in Hamlet's situation. Notice how Booth focuses on the position that the audience occupies in shaping the literary experience of act 2 of *Hamlet*.

Stephen Booth

On the Value of Hamlet

The audience sets out into Act II knowing what Hamlet knows, knowing Hamlet's plans, and secure in its superiority to the characters who do not. (Usually an audience is superior to the central characters: it knows that Desdemona is innocent, Othello does not; it knows what it would do when Lear foolishly divides his kingdom; it knows how Birnam Wood came to come to Dunsinane. In *Hamlet*, however, the audience never knows what it would have done in Hamlet's situation; in fact, since the King's successful plot in the duel with Laertes changes Hamlet's situation so that he becomes as much the avenger of his own death as of his father's, the audience never knows what Hamlet would have done. Except for brief periods near the end of the play, the audience never has insight or knowledge superior to Hamlet's or, indeed, different from Hamlet's. Instead of having superiority *to* Hamlet, the audience goes into the second act to share the superiority *of* Hamlet.) The audience knows that Hamlet will play mad, and its expectations are quickly confirmed. Just seventy-five lines into Act II, Ophelia comes in and describes a kind of behavior in Hamlet that sounds like the behavior of a young man of limited theatrical ability who is pretending to be mad (II.i.77–84). Our confidence that this behavior so puzzling to others is well within our grasp is strengthened by the reminder of the ghost, the immediate cause of the promised pretense, in Ophelia's comparison of Hamlet to a creature "loosed out of hell / To speak of horrors."

Before Ophelia's entrance, II.ii has presented an example of the baseness and foolishness of Polonius, the character upon whom both the audience and Hamlet exercise their superiority throughout Act II. Polonius seems base because he is arranging to spy on Laertes. He instructs his spy in ways to use the "bait of falsehood"—to find out directions by indirections (II.i.74). He is so sure that he knows everything, and so sure that his petty scheme is not only foolproof but brilliant, that he is as contemptible mentally as he is morally. The audience laughs at him because he loses his train of thought in pompous byways, so that, eventually, he forgets what he set out to say: "What was I about to say? . . . I was about to say something! Where did I leave?" (II.i.50–51). When Ophelia reports Hamlet's behavior, Polonius takes what is apparently Hamlet's bait: "Mad for thy love?" (II.i.85). He also thinks of (and then spends the rest of the act finding evidence for) a specific cause for Hamlet's madness: he is mad for love of Ophelia. The audience knows (1) Hamlet will pretend madness, (2) Polonius is a fool, and (3) what is actually bothering Hamlet. Through the rest of the act, the audience laughs at Polonius for being fooled by Hamlet. It continues to laugh at Polonius' inability to keep his mind on a track (II.ii.85–130); it also laughs at him for the opposite fault—he has a one-track mind and sees anything and everything as evidence that Hamlet is mad for love (II.ii.173–212; 394–402). Hamlet, whom the audience knows and understands, spends a good part of the rest of the scene making Polonius demonstrate his foolishness.

Reading Contexts

1. What kind of argument is Booth trying to make when he mentions that the audience in *Hamlet* "never knows what it would have done in Hamlet's situation"? Notice that while the formalist or New Critical approach to *Hamlet* privileges character analysis, Booth's overall assumptions privilege the position of the audience.
2. How would you characterize Booth's portrayal of the audience in *Hamlet*? To what extent does the audience in *Hamlet* function as a reflection and a mirror of Hamlet's own frustrations and contradictions? Where do you stand in relation to this reader-response reading of *Hamlet*?

Reader-Response Criticism: Reference Readings

Booth, Stephen. "On the Value of *Hamlet*." *Reinterpretations of Elizabethan Drama*. Ed. Norman Rabkin. New York: Columbia UP, 1969.

Eco, Umberto. *The Role of the Reader*. Bloomington: Indiana UP, 1979.

Iser, Wolfgang. *Prospecting: From Reader Response to Literary Anthropology*. Baltimore: Johns Hopkins UP, 1989.

Suleiman, Susan R., and Inge Crossman, eds. *The Reader in the Text: Essays on Audience and Interpretation*. Princeton: Princeton UP, 1980.

Tompkins, Jane P. "An Introduction to Reader-Response Criticism." *Reader-Response Criticism: From Formalism to Post-Structuralism*. Ed. Jane P. Tompkins. Baltimore: Johns Hopkins UP, 1980.

FEMINIST CRITICISM
What Is the Focus of Feminist Criticism?

Modern *feminist criticism* emerged in the late 1960s and early 1970s out of a sociopolitical movement aimed at the defense of women's rights. It addressed the need women felt to reinterpret literature, to rewrite history, and to change the power structure that has traditionally defined male and female relationships in patriarchal societies. Like Marxist, African American, and the New Historical Criticism, the socially oriented perspective of feminist criticism has spread its voice in many directions. Among other things, it has promoted a reevaluation of the Freudian theory of sexual differences, a reassessment of female and male writing, a revision of the role of gender in literature, and a critique of the oppressive rationale of patriarchal ideology.

In her essay "This Sex Which Is Not One," the feminist critic Luce Irigaray has revised Freud's theory of sex difference, protesting against the view of woman as a biological version of the male model. In following the assumptions of Jacques Lacan, French feminists have also criticized, among other things, the logic of language that associates positive qualities such as those related to creativity, light, logic, and power with masculinity. Many feminists like Hélène Cixous, who tend to draw a relationship between women's writing and women's bodies, have also attempted to create a language or a specific kind of women's writing (*écriture féminine*) that refuses participation in masculine discourse.

Other feminists have promoted a feminist critique of masculine ideology, protesting against the political marginalization women have suffered as blacks, chicanos, Asian Americans, and lesbians. For the feminist critic Catharine R. Stimpson, the defiance of sexual difference, the celebration of sexual difference, and the recognition of differences constitute the three major principles of feminist criticism. Many of the critical efforts of feminists have also been aimed at the study of women's history and the role of women in literary tradition.

Complementing feminism, lesbian and gay criticism, another by-product of a gender-centered approach, has sparked much recent debate in critical circles. One of its main premises, shaped by a feminist viewpoint, ponders whether lesbians and gays read and write the same way or differently from heterosexuals.

A Feminist Reading of *Hamlet*

One of the major contributions that feminist literary criticism has made to our reading of *Hamlet* has been its revisionist affirmation that female characters such as Gertrude and Ophelia possess a narrative of their own or a form of feminine discourse.

Notice in the following passage that Diane Elizabeth Dreher's feminist analysis of *Hamlet* opens new possibilities for an evaluation of Ophelia. By analyzing the forces that shaped Ophelia's identity as a "dominated daughter," Dreher liberates Ophelia from the rigid stereotypes that traditional criticism has ascribed to her. According to Dreher, because of the "fearful domination" that Polonius, Laertes, and Hamlet exercised on Ophelia, which cast her in the role of the "other," Ophelia is unable to grasp the full complexity of her self and resolve the crisis of her identity. As Dreher sees it, Ophelia is defined as a "simpleminded creature" only when evaluated from a male-oriented viewpoint.

Diane Elizabeth Dreher

Dominated Daughters

A feminist analysis of Ophelia's behavior demonstrates that she is not the simpleminded creature she seems. Traditional readings of her character have been as superficial as nineteenth-century productions, which portrayed her as a simple, pretty girl of flowers whose mad scenes were artfully sung and danced. As Helena Faucit realized and dared to play her to a stunned audience in 1844–45, Ophelia actually does go mad. There is pain and struggle beneath that sweet surface. Her misfortune merits not only our pity but our censure of traditional mores that make women repress themselves and behave like automatons.

Contrary to prevailing opinion, Ophelia is more than a simple girl, living in "a world of dumb ideas and feelings." The pity of it is that Ophelia *does* think and feel. A careful examination of the text in I.iii reveals that she loves Hamlet and thinks for herself, but is forced to repress all this at her father's command, conforming to the stifling patriarchal concept of female behavior that subordinates women to their "honor," their procreative function in male society.

Torn between what she feels and what she is told to be, Ophelia is tormented by the crisis of identity. As one critic pointed out long ago, "she is not aware of the nature of her own feelings; they are prematurely developed in their full force before she has strength to bear them." Caught in adolescent uncertainty between childhood and adulthood, she cannot enter the stage of intimacy and adult commitment because she does not yet know who she is. Carol Gilligan has pointed to the difficulties young women have in individuation. Raised with an emphasis on empathy rather than autonomy, girls tend to subordinate their own needs to those of others. Ophelia experiences severe role confusion in which her personal feelings are suppressed in favor of external expectations. . . .

Ophelia has been condemned for letting her father dominate her, for failing to "observe the fundamental responsibilities that hold together an existence." But let us consider the situation from her point of view. As a young woman, she is, first of all, more inclined to defer to the wishes of others than follow her own feelings. Ophelia errs in trusting her father, but she is not the only person in the play who has taken a parent at face value. Hamlet failed to recognize his mother's moral weakness until her marriage to Claudius. Furthermore, reverence for one's parents was expected of Renaissance youth. As Harley Granville-Barker emphasized, "we may call her docility a fault, when, as she is bid, she shuts herself away from Hamlet; but how not to trust to her brother's care for her and her father's wisdom?" Like Othello, Ophelia errs in trusting the wrong moral guide: in his case a friend who had shared dangers on the battlefield, in hers a father to whom convention bound her duty and obedience. Polonius' warning, seconded by her brother's, gains greater credibility. But most significant, her moral guides have not only told her how to behave; they have redefined her entire universe, inculcating in Ophelia a view of human sexuality as nasty and brutish as that which infects Othello. Ophelia sees herself in a world in which sexuality transforms human beings into beasts, with men the predators and women their prey.

Reading Contexts

1. Describe the traditional critical assumptions about Ophelia, and then contrast them with Dreher's. Explain how Dreher collapses the traditional view of Ophelia, offering insights into a new representation of this character.

2. To what extent does Dreher's argument about the rival claims of individuation and external expectations help to explain Ophelia's identity crisis? Where do you stand in relation
to this argument?

Feminist Literary Criticism: Reading References

Abel, Elizabeth, ed. *Writing and Sexual Difference*. Chicago: UP, 1982.

Abelove, Henry, et al., eds. *The Lesbian and Gay Studies Reader*. New York: Routledge,
1993.

Carby, Hazel V. *Reconstructing Womanhood: The Emergence of the Afro-American Woman
Novelist*. New York: Oxford UP, 1987.

de Beauvoir, Simone. *The Second Sex*. Trans. and ed. H. M. Parshley. New York: Knopf,
1953.

Dreher, Diane Elizabeth. *Dominance and Defiance: Fathers and Daughters in Shakespeare*.
Kentucky: U of Kentucky P, 1986.

Showalter, Elaine. "Representing Ophelia: Women, Madness, and the Responsibilities
of Feminist Criticism." *Shakespeare and the Question of Theory*. Ed. Patricia Parker
and Geoffrey Hartman. London: Methuen, 1985.

THE NEW HISTORICISM

What Is the Focus of the New Historicism?

The *New Historicism*, or cultural poetics, may be defined as a form of political criticism
closely related to Marxist criticism. One of its main goals is to focus on the critical study of
power relations, politics, and ideology. For the New Historicist critics, such as Stephen
Greenblatt, who coined the term "New Historical" in the early 1980s, this criticism displaces
the traditional view of history as a discipline committed to an altruistic search for truth and to
a faithful reconstruction of the dates and events of the past. Instead, the New Historicist perspective advocates a focus on a historical dynamic or a view of history in action. Its aim is to
erase the boundaries among disciplines such as literature, history, and the social sciences.
The ideas of the French philosopher and historian Michel Foucault (1926–1984) seem to
inform much of the rationale that New Historicism established for the complex relation
among language, power, and knowledge.

New Historical critics tend to view Shakespeare's plays as political acts reflecting and
shaping the collective codes and beliefs of Shakespeare's times. New Historicists also affirm
the reciprocity between the text and the world, which they attempt to rewrite by showing
how sociopolitical practices and institutions such as the theater can shape and transform cultural meanings. When considering the relation between text and reader, the New Historicists advocate the reciprocity between these two elements, viewing them as dynamic forces
interacting with and responding to each other.

A New Historical Reading of *Hamlet*

Leonard Tennenhouse's reading of *Hamlet* shows Shakespeare's play as a critique of power
relations centered on a struggle for power between Hamlet and Claudius. According to Tennenhouse, the political struggle in *Hamlet* emerges from the clash between two different
claims to the throne of Denmark: Hamlet's, which is based on blood and popular support,
and Claudius's, which is based on his marriage to Gertrude and his use of force.

By approaching Shakespeare's tragedy through the critical lens traditionally applied in the criticism of history plays such as *Richard III*, *Richard II*, and *Henry IV*, Tennenhouse has erased the boundaries that traditional and formalist criticism insisted on establishing between Shakespeare's tragedies and his history plays. In his critique of the play-within-the-play in *Hamlet*, Tennenhouse also shifts the focus from Hamlet's goal of "catch[ing] the conscience of the King" to Hamlet's crime against the state. Tennenhouse also argues that in the play-within-the-play Hamlet fails because the political force he generates amounts to a mere symbolic gesture.

Leonard Tennenhouse

Power in Hamlet

Hamlet rehearses [the] dilemma of a state torn between two competitors, neither of whom can embody the mystical power of blood and land associated with the natural body. Hamlet's claim to power derives from his position as son in a patrilinear system as well as from "popular support." It is this support which Claudius consistently lacks and which, at the same time, prevents him from moving openly against Hamlet. Following the murder of Polonius, for example, Claudius says of Hamlet, "Yet must not we put the strong law on him. / He's lov'd of the distracted multitude . . ." (IV.iii.3–4). But this alone does not guarantee authority. Hamlet is not by nature capable of exercising force. To signal this lack, Shakespeare has given him the speech of Stoical writing, which shifts all action onto a mental plane where any show of force becomes self-inflicted aggression. We find this identification of force with self-assault made explicit in Hamlet's speeches on suicide as well as those in which he berates himself for his inability to act.

In contrast with Hamlet, Claudius's authority comes by way of his marriage to Gertrude. Where he would be second to Hamlet and Hamlet's line in a patrilineal system, the queen's husband and uncle of the king's son occupies the privileged male position in a matrilineal system. Like one of the successful figures from a history play, Claudius overthrew the reigning patriarch. Like one of the successful courtiers in a romantic comedy, he married into the aristocratic community. What is perhaps more important, he has taken the position through the effective use of force. Thus Shakespeare sets in opposition the two claims to authority—the exercise of force and the magic of blood—by means of these two members of the royal family. Because each has a claim, neither Hamlet nor Claudius achieves legitimate control over Denmark. Each one consequently assaults the aristocratic body in attempting to acquire the crown. It is to be expected that Claudius could not legally possess the crown, the matrilinear succession having the weaker claim on British political thinking. Thus the tragedy resides not in his failure but in the impossibility of Hamlet's rising according to Elizabethan strategies of state. This calls the relationship between the metaphysics of patriarchy and the force of law into question.

Reading Contexts

1. Find the sentences that best describe the two rival claims to power that Tennenhouse discusses in his text. Analyze the way these images of power reflect Tennenhouse's political views of *Hamlet*.

2. What conclusions can you draw from Tennenhouse's reading of this scene? Decide whether or not you agree or disagree with Tennenhouse's interpretation of *Hamlet*.

The New Historicism: Reading References

Brook, Thomas. *The New Historicism and Other Old-Fashioned Topics*. Princeton: Princeton UP, 1991.

Greenblatt, Stephen J. *Renaissance Self-Fashioning: From More to Shakespeare*. Chicago: U of Chicago P, 1980.

——, ed. *Representing the English Renaissance*. Berkeley: U of California P, 1988.

Hunt, Lynn, ed. *The New Cultural History*. Berkeley: U of California P, 1989.

Lindenberger, Herbert. "Toward a New History in Literature Studies." *Profession: Selected Articles from the Bulletin of the Association of Departments of English and the Association of Departments of Foreign Languages*. New York: MLA, 1984.

Tennenhouse, Leonard. "Power in *Hamlet*." *Hamlet*. Ed. Martin Coyle. New York: St. Martin's, 1992.

Biographical Endnotes

Achebe, Chinua (b. 1930)

Born in Nigeria, Achebe is considered one of Africa's most accomplished writers. He was educated at the University College of Ibadan and London University, and then took up a career in radio broadcasting. Dismayed with European writers' depiction of African life, he decided that Africans should tell their own stories and proceeded to write his first novel, *Things Fall Apart* (1958). This book has been translated into forty-five languages; has been adapted for stage, television, and radio; has won awards for its author; and is considered a classic in English. The novel's theme reflects Achebe's belief that outside influences eradicate traditional culture and values. When military forces took over Nigeria's government, Achebe left for the United States, taught at the University of Massachusetts, and lectured around the country. "Dead Men's Path" takes up his themes of loss of respect for tradition, and the past versus the present. His latest work includes *The Trouble with Nigeria* (1984), *Anthills of the Savannah* (1988), *Arrow of God* (1989), *A Man of the People* (1989), *Hopes and Impediments: Selected Essays* (1990), *Girls at War; And Other Stories* (1991), *Another Africa* (1998), and *Home and Exile* (2000).

Anderson, Sherwood (1876–1941)

Born in Camden, Ohio, Anderson was a self-educated man who, at the age of thirty-six, left his wife and business to resettle in Chicago and become a writer. His masterpiece, a collection of short stories titled *Winesburg, Ohio* (1919), portrays life in a typical small midwestern town where many inhabitants are frustrated creatively and emotionally. "Hands" is the first story in that collection.

Arrabal, Fernando (b. 1932)

Arrabal, born in Spanish Morocco, lived his early years in Madrid. At the age of twenty-three, finding life in Spain intolerable because of parental problems and the atmosphere of political oppression, he moved to Paris, where he still resides. Tuberculosis sapped his strength and his early works mirror the despair he experienced because of his illness. He regained his health after an operation in 1957, and his plays were soon produced in Paris theaters. He refers to his work as "panic theater" in the tradition of the theater of the absurd. *Picnic on the Battlefield* was written when he was fourteen and is the most frequently performed of his plays. Arrabal's concerns are the horrors of civil war, betrayal, torture, tyranny, and human helplessness in an alien universe. Recent work includes *The Body-Builder's Book of Love: Brevano de Amor de un Halterofilo* (translation by Lorenzo Mans) (1999) and *Porte Disparu* (2000).

Bambara, Toni Cade (1939–1995)

Bambara grew up in New York City, deeply conscious of the inequities of race and class. A graduate of Queens College and City College of New York, she became a social worker, educator, and filmmaker. Her short story collections, such as *Gorilla, My Love* (1972), *The Sea Birds Are Still Alive* (1977), and *The Salt Eaters* (1980), deal particularly with the problems of women in urban environments. With humor and candor, she skillfully portrays the politics and culture of community life.

Behn, Aphra (1640?–1689)

The early details of Behn's life have not been conclusively established, but most historians agree that she and her family probably sailed from England to Surinam in South America in 1663. Her father was to become lieutenant governor but died during the trip. Although she lived in Surinam less than a year, Behn had such vivid impressions of the country that she later incorporated them in a novel, *Oroonoko: or, The Royal Slave* (1688). On her return to England in 1664, she married a wealthy London merchant and became popular at the court of Charles II. Unfortunately, her husband died in 1666, and for reasons unknown she was left an impoverished widow. For a short time she became a spy for Charles II but was not remunerated for her work. In desperation, she turned to writing, an unheard-of female occupation. Her first play *The Forced Marriage; or The Jealous Bridegroom* proved successful and she continued writing plays, featuring sexual promiscuity and amorous intrigues in the mode of the day. Her poems are less coarse than many of those of her contemporaries, but she freely discusses female sexual desires and issues concerning gender roles. Critics charged her with indecency, but she fought back, claiming that she was singled out because of her gender. Never possessing much wealth, she lived in less than healthy conditions, which led to an early death. Behn was honored by burial in Westminster Abbey and has won the admiration of many feminists, including Virginia Woolf.

Blake, William (1757–1827)

Born in Soho, London, Blake was apprenticed to James Basire, engraver to the Society of Antiquaries. His first poems appeared in *Poetical Sketches* in 1783, followed by *Songs of Innocence* (1789), a work in which he seeks to recapture the innocence and joy of childhood by manifesting his faith in human sympathy, integrity, and divine love. However, in his *Book of Thel* and his prose work entitled *The Marriage of Hell* (1790), Blake endorses a fiercely satiric outlook and a revolutionary position against issues such as the disintegration of personality, the abuse of authority, and the religious dogma of eternal punishment. His *Songs of Experience* (1794), centered on his deeper awareness of the state of experience and the mysterious power of evil, also contrasts with the joyful spontaneous assessment of the power of divine love in *Songs of Innocence*.

Today Blake is widely recognized as a great Christian, visionary, and mystical poet. In his own lifetime, however, he had to make a living by giving drawing lessons, working as an engraver, and illustrating books such as *The Divine Comedy*. He also illustrated his own books, some of which he colored by hand after applying a special color-printed process of his own invention.

In most of his works, Blake communicated his disgust for eighteenth-century scientific rationalism: "I will not reason and compare: my business is to create." In works such as *The Book of Los* (1795) and *The Four Zoas* (1797), he created his own mythological figures such as Los (imagination), Urizen (reason), Luvah (passions), and Tharmas (instincts). Blake became a spokesman for a group of intellectual radicals, and a great supporter of the French and American revolutions.

Borowski, Tadeusz (1922–1951)

Born of Polish parents in the Soviet Ukraine, Borowski lived a life of poverty and oppression. When he was four, his father was sent to an Arctic labor camp. Four years later, his mother was sent to Siberia. The family was reunited in Warsaw before World War II. He was eventually arrested by the Gestapo for his political activities and sent to the concentration camp at Auschwitz. There he observed the horror and brutality perpetrated on the victims. He also witnessed prisoners betraying each other in order to survive. Borowski became a hospital orderly to escape extermination. The American forces freed him and his fellow prisoners in 1945. Borowski returned to Warsaw where he wrote short stories based on his experiences. His work has been criticized because he portrays some of the victims who resorted to betrayal and other criminal acts. Ironically, Borowski committed suicide using gas when he was twenty-nine.

Browning, Robert (1812–1889)

Born in England, Browning was a relatively unrecognized poet until his middle age. In fact, for a time he was better known for his dramatic rescue of Elizabeth Barrett from her tyrannical father. The couple had carried on a love affair through poetry and letters until they eloped and escaped to Italy, where they lived until her death in 1861. During his life in Italy, Browning developed his dramatic monologues, in which a person reveals his or her motives and thoughts through speech. Browning researched many subjects of the Italian Renaissance. His most famous work is *The Ring and the Book* (1868–1869), one of the longest poems in English literature.

Camus, Albert (1913–1960)

An Algerian-born French writer of novels, essays, and plays, Camus is identified with the concept of absurdity, the problem of man's desire for a rational universe as compared with the reality of its incoherence. Camus was only ten months old when his father was killed in World War I. Brought up in poverty by his illiterate mother, he fortunately encountered a teacher who encouraged his studies. Subsequently, he earned a scholarship to a lycée (secondary school) where he studied philosophy and read widely. In 1930 he had the first of many attacks of tuberculosis, and in the late 1930s he commenced his lifelong journals and completed his first novel, *A Happy Death*. During World War II, he lived in Paris and was editor of the French Resistance newspaper *Combat*. Throughout his life, he struggled to find a positive solution to the dilemma of the absurd. At the age of 44, he was awarded the Nobel Prize for literature in recognition of his profound humanism.

Some of his most famous works include *The Stranger* (1942, tr. 1946), *The Myth of Sisyphus* (1942, tr. 1955), *The Plague* (1947, tr. 1948), *The Outsider* (1942, tr. 1946), *The Rebel*

(1951, tr. 1953), and *The Fall* (1956, tr. 1957). His final novel, *The First Man*, was published posthumously in 1995. Camus died in an automobile crash in 1960.

Catton, [Charles] Bruce (1899–1978)

After working as a newspaper journalist, Catton entered government service in 1942 and later served as director of information for the U.S. Department of Commerce. During this time he became interested in the Civil War, but it was not until his retirement from public service that he began a career of writing about the war. He produced a prodigious body of work, including *A Stillness at Appomattox* (1953), for which he won the Pulitzer Prize and the National Book Award in 1954. For five years (1954–59) he edited *American Heritage* magazine. His trilogy—*The Coming Fury* (1961), *Terrible Swift Sword* (1963), and *Never Call Retreat* (1965)—was widely acclaimed. "It was not the strategy or political meanings" that interested him, Catton said, but the "almost incomprehensible emotional experience which this war brought to our country." Among his numerous other books are *This Hallowed Ground* (1956), *The Army of the Potomac* (1962), *Grant Takes Command* (1969), and *Waiting for the Morning Train* (1972), a memoir of his boyhood in Michigan.

Chock, Eric (b. 1950)

Chock currently teaches in the Poets in the Schools program in Honolulu, Hawaii. His first book of poems, *Ten Thousand Wishes*, is now out of print. His second book of poems, *Last Days Here*, appeared in 1989. Chock is the editor or co-editor of several anthologies, including *The Best of Bamboo Ridge* (1986), *Small Kid Time Hawaii* (1981), and *Talk Story: An Anthology of Hawaii's Local Writers* (1978). An active member of the literary community, Chock has served on the board of directors of the Hawaii Literary Arts Council and the Honolulu City Commission on Culture and the Arts. His most recent collections include *Growing Up Local* (1998) and *The Best of Honolulu Fiction* (1999).

Chopin, Kate (1851–1904)

Chopin was born in St. Louis, and moved to New Orleans when she married a Louisiana Creole. Her short stories and novels usually take place in that locale. Her last novel, *The Awakening* (1899), found a new audience during the women's movement of the 1960s, not only because it examined a woman's search for personal identity but also for its interest in financial and sexual autonomy.

Cofer, Judith Ortiz (b. 1952)

Cofer was born in Puerto Rico but moved with her family to New Jersey when she was a small child. Her work explores common challenges of the immigrant experience and the difficulties inherent in navigating between the values of her parents and those of the world in which she moves. As a graduate student at Florida Atlantic University she began writing, first, poetry and subsequently prose forms as well. Her 1989 novel, *The Line of the Sun*, received a Pulitzer Prize nomination. She has published many essays as well as a book of stories for young adults, and she has won a number of awards and prizes, including the 1990 Pushcart Prize for nonfiction and the 1994 O. Henry Prize for short stories. Her short story collection, *An Island Like You: Stories of the Barrio* (1995), was named a Best Book of the Year by the American Library Association. Now Franklin Professor of English and Creative

Writing at the University of Georgia, her recent publications are *The Year of Our Revolution: New and Selected Stories and Poems* (1998) and *Woman in Front of the Sun: On Becoming a Writer* (2000).

Crane, Stephen (1871–1900)

Born in Newark, New Jersey, Crane was a journalist, short story writer, novelist, and poet. He is best known for *The Red Badge of Courage* (1895), a realistic study of the mind of a soldier in the Civil War. This classic is remarkable for its accuracy because Crane had not experienced war when he wrote it. Later, as a war correspondent, he covered the Spanish-American War and the Greco-Turkish War. He died of tuberculosis at twenty-eight in self-imposed exile. His war stories reflected his wish to shatter the beliefs of those who saw war as a romantic and idealized experience. Among the best known of his many short stories are "The Open Boat," "The Blue Hotel," and "The Bride Comes to Yellow Sky."

Cruz, Sor (Sister) Juana Inés de la (1651?–1695)

Born in Nepantla, Mexico, to a Spanish father and a Creole mother, Cruz was one of the earliest authors in the Americas. At the age of three, she followed her sister to school and learned to read and write. With the guidance of her learned grandfather, she became educated far beyond many of her contemporaries. Cruz attracted the attention of the royal court in Mexico City, where she became a lady-in-waiting to the viceroy's wife. During those two years, she started writing poetry. Abruptly, at nineteen, she entered a convent. She continued to study and write, but her superiors demanded that she devote herself to church duties. When she refused to comply, and argued that women should not have to submit to men's orders, she was accused of heresy. Sor Juana yielded and gave up her intellectual pursuits. While nursing her sister nuns during a plague in 1695, she contracted the disease and died.

Cummings, E. E. (Edward Estlin) (1894–1962)

A native of Cambridge, Massachusetts, Cummings received both the B.A. and the M.A. from Harvard University, then volunteered as an ambulance driver in France during World War I. There he was imprisoned on a treason charge for three months, which he described in *The Enormous Room* (1922), a prose narrative that won wide acclaim. Beginning with his first volume of poetry, *Tulips and Chimneys* (1923), his work has received both positive and negative attention for its unconventional language and punctuation, most famously his insistence on lowercase letters, even in his name. Cummings's influence on contemporary poetry is not limited to the widespread mimickry of his experiments with line breaks, punctuation, and capitalization. He published many volumes of poetry during his lifetime, including *No Thanks* (1935), *50 Poems* (1940), *1 × 1* (1944), *Xaipe: Seventy-One Poems* (1950), *95 Poems* (1958), *Selected Poems, 1923–1958* (1960). One of the many posthumous collections of his poetry, *Complete Poems: 1904–1962* (1994) contains more than a thousand poems.

Dickey, James (1923–1997)

A World War II veteran born in Atlanta, Dickey's life was in some ways that of a typical mid-twentieth-century American man. He played football in college and upon returning from the war spent several years as an advertising copywriter before becoming a teacher, writer, and eventually poet in residence at the University of South Carolina. His work, fiction as well as poetry, is often brutal—like his famous novel *Deliverance* (1970)—and tends toward narrative. His books include the poetry volumes *Buckdancer's Choice* (1965) and *James Dickey: The Selected Poems* (1998), the novel *To the White Sea* (1993), and *Crux: The Letters of James Dickey*, published in 1998, after his death. Another posthumous collection is *The James Dickey Reader* (1999).

Dickinson, Emily (1830–1886)

Born in Amherst, Massachusetts, Dickinson was educated at schools for females, and then retired to her home. She rarely left it, and saw only family and a few friends during her lifetime. Although she wrote almost two thousand poems, only two were published while she lived. Many of her poems reflect her interest in the dialectic of private and public selves.

Donne, John (1572–1631)

Donne was born Catholic in England during a period of anti-Catholicism so severe that he was prevented from finishing his degree at Oxford. He eventually converted to Anglicanism, but only after spending time as an adventurer, first on the high seas with Sir Walter Raleigh, among others, and then later in London. He studied law, became secretary to a powerful noble, served as a Member of Parliament, and even went to jail briefly for a secret marriage, which ruined his chances for a civil career. Donne and his wife had twelve children; she died at thirty-three after the birth of their youngest. After his conversion to Anglicanism and subsequent ordination at age forty-two, Donne quickly became an extremely influential preacher and the dean of St. Paul's Cathedral in London. He was known as a wit and a man of letters, and although his poems were not published until after he died, more than 130 of his sermons appeared in print during his lifetime. In addition to the sermons and essays he produced in later life, he probably began writing poetry in his twenties, and his manuscripts were widely circulated among his friends. His work—dense and complicated sonnets, elegies, epigrams, and verse letters loaded with paradox, irony, and incongruity—was mostly ignored until the twentieth century. Beginning with his "rediscovery" by T. S. Eliot, Donne had an immense influence on the poetry of the twentieth century.

Douglass, Frederick (1817?–1895)

Douglass was the illegitimate child of a white man and a black slave in Tuckahoe, Maryland. Upon his escape from slavery in 1838, he adopted the last name of Douglass and settled in New Bedford, Massachusetts. He so impressed the Massachusetts Anti-Slavery Society when he spoke before them in 1841 that they hired him. During the next four years, he toured the country, speaking out against slavery. Mobbed and beaten because of his views, he described his experiences in *Narrative of the Life of Frederick Douglass: An American Slave*. After a two-year visit to England, where he earned enough money to buy his freedom, he founded a newspaper, *The North Star*. For seventeen years he edited and wrote eloquent articles advocating the use of black troops during the Civil War and on civil rights for freedmen. Other autobiographical works included *My Bondage and My Freedom* (1855) and *Life and Times of Frederick Douglass* (1881). Abraham Lincoln consulted with him on matters pertaining to slavery. He held various public offices after the war, such as U.S. Marshal for the District of Columbia (1877–81), recorder of deeds for D.C., and U.S. Minister to Haiti (1889–91). Many of Douglass's writings, not available previously, have been collected in *Frederick Douglass: Selected Speeches and Writings* (1999).

Dubus, André (1936–1999)

Born in Lake Charles, Louisiana, and educated in his home state, Dubus became an officer in the U.S. Marine Corps at age twenty-two. After five years, he resigned, resumed his education, and became a teacher of fiction and creative writing at Bradford College in Massachusetts. In 1970, one of his stories was chosen for the annual volume of *Best American Short Stories*. Dubus has written eight short-story collections, including *The Times Are Never So Bad* (1983), *The Last Worthless Evening* (1986), *Collected Stories* (1988), *Dancing After Hours* (1996), and *Meditations from a Movable Chair* (1998). "The Curse" was written while he was convalescing from the loss of his leg in a highway accident. The themes of frailty and fallibility can be noted in Dubus's works. He died of a heart attack in 1999.

Eberhart, Richard (Ghormley) (b. 1904)

Born in Minnesota, Eberhart studied at Dartmouth College as well as Cambridge University. Over the course of a long life, in addition to teaching, he has worked as a businessman, a naval officer, a cultural adviser, and a tutor to the son of the king of Siam. His many books include *Gifts of Being* (1968), *Collected Poems* (1930, 1976, 1988), *Uncollected Poems 1948–1983* (1984), *Maine Poems* (1988), and *New and Selected Poems: 1930–1990* (1990). The governor of New Hampshire, where Eberhart had lived for many years, proclaimed a Richard Eberhart Day in 1982.

Emanuel, James A. (b. 1921)

Born in Alliance, Nebraska, Emanuel was educated at Howard, Northwestern, and Columbia universities, and is professor emeritus at City College of the City University of New York. Poet, biographer, and critic, he has published several volumes of poetry, including *The Treehouse and Other Poems* (1961), *Panther Man* (1970), and *The Broken Bowl: New and Uncollected Poems* (1983). In the last decade, he has written most of his poetry and prose in Europe. Some of his more recent publications include *The Quagmire Effect* (1988), *Whole Grain: Collected Poems, 1958–1989* (1990), *De la rage au coeur* (bilingual, with French translations by Jean Migrenne and Amiot Lenganey) (1992), and *Blues in Black and White*, with Godelieve Simons (1992).

Emerson, Ralph Waldo (1803–1882)

Emerson was born in Boston and graduated from Harvard. He became a minister, but resigned because he could not accept certain doctrines of the church. After traveling in Europe, where he met English philosophers and poets, he formulated the theory of transcendentalism, which stressed the divinity of human kind and relied on intuition to reveal life's truths. Although his prose writings were revolutionary, his poetry followed traditional form and content.

Erdrich, Louise (b. 1954)

A member of the Turtle Mountain Band of Chippewa, Erdrich was born in Minnesota and grew up in North Dakota. After getting her degree in anthropology from Dartmouth College, she taught in North Dakota for a while, then went to Johns Hopkins to study writing. Her work reflects her deep concern with Native American issues, both cultural and political, often depicting reservation life. She has won awards and prizes for both fiction and poetry, including the American Academy of Poets Prize when she was at Dartmouth. Her 1984 novel *Love Medicine* won the National Book Critics Circle Award. Her other novels have won both critical and popular success, establishing her as one of the country's major contemporary writers. They include *The Beet Queen* (1986), *Tracks* (1988), *The Bingo Palace* (1994), and *Tales of Burning Love* (1996), which continue various narrative threads she initiated with *Love Medicine*. *The Antelope Wife* (1998) and *The Last Report on the Miracles at Little No Horse* (2001) are her most recent publications. She has also published two volumes of poetry, *Jacklight* (1984) and *Baptism of Desire* (1989), and has collaborated with her husband, Michael Dorris, on two books: the nonfiction work *Broken Cord* (1989) and the novel *The Crown of Columbus* (1991).

Espada, Martín (b. 1957)

Born in Brooklyn, New York, Espada is considered one of the leading poets of Latino heritage. Educated at the University of Wisconsin and Northeastern University, his work experience encompasses a variety of jobs from bouncer to radio journalist in Nicaragua. At present he is a tenant lawyer in Boston. The themes of his poetry include immigrants, hard work, and poverty. His published works include *The Immigrant Iceboy's Bolero* (1982), *Trumpets from the Islands of Their Eviction* (1987), *Rebellion Is the Circle of a Lover's Hands* (1990), *City of Coughing and Dead Radiators* (1993), *Imagine the Angels of Bread* (1996), *Zapata's Disciple* (1998), and *A Mayan Astronomer in Hell's Kitchen: Poems* (2000).

Euripides (480–406 B.C.)

Born on the Greek island of Salamis, Euripides was a writer of tragedies. Today he is considered as great a dramatist as Sophocles and Aeschylus, although during his lifetime he was not popular. His themes reflected a pessimistic view of life, and his criticism of social matters was not viewed approvingly. He attacked the inequalities of women's status in *Medea*, the emphasis on the glories of war in *The Trojan Women*, and the unjust treatment of illegitimate children in *Hippolytus*. Only nineteen of his eighty or ninety plays exist today, among them *Alcestis*, *Electra*, and *Ion*.

Faulkner, William (1897–1962)

Born in New Albany, Mississippi, Faulkner was raised in the nearby town of Oxford. He attended the University of Mississippi briefly before joining the Canadian Air Force in 1918. In the early 1920s he traveled to New York City, New Orleans, and Europe. *The Marble Faun* (1924), a book of poems, was his first published work. In his third novel, *Sartoris* (1929), he invented the fictional county of Yoknapatawpha (similar to the setting of his Mississippi boyhood) that became the scene for many of his future works. Two recurring themes include the relationship of the past to the present and the disintegration of traditional Southern society. Among his distinguished works are *The Sound and the Fury* (1939), *As I Lay Dying* (1930), *Light In August* (1932), *Sanctuary* (1931) and *Absalom, Absalom!* (1938). His distinguished writing earned him Pulitzer Prizes for *A Fable* (1954) and *The Reivers* (1962), and a Nobel Prize for literature in 1949.

Ferlinghetti, Lawrence (b. 1919)

Poet, playwright, and editor, Ferlinghetti is co-owner of City Lights Books in San Francisco and founder and editor of City Lights Publishing House. He was an important figure in the Beat movement of the 1950s, whose adherents were primarily concerned with rebelling against society and taking strong stands on political issues. In 1994, the city of San Francisco celebrated Ferlinghetti's contributions by naming a street in his honor and followed up that tribute in 1998, crowning him the city's first Poet Laureate. Ferlinghetti writes in the language and speech rhythms of ordinary people, rather than in formal poetic language and structures. In his poem "Constantly Risking Absurdity" (1958), he speculates on the poet's responsibility to society. His latest collection is *These Are My Rivers: New & Selected Poems, 1955–1993* (1993). In 2001 he won the *Los Angeles Times'* Robert Kirsch Award for his body of work.

Forché, Carolyn (b. 1950)

Born in Detroit, Michigan, and educated at Michigan State University, Forché is a poet, journalist, and educator. While a journalist in El Salvador from 1978 to 1980, she reported on human rights conditions for Amnesty International. This experience greatly affected her poetry, and she also lectured extensively on the subject when she returned to the United States. Her poetry collections include *Gathering the Tribes* (1976), *The Country Between Us* (1981), *The Angel of History* (1994), and *Star Quilt* (1998). She is the editor of *Against Forgetting: Twentieth-Century Poetry of Witness* (1993). She teaches at George Mason University in Fairfax, Virginia.

Fornes, Maria Irene (b. 1930)

Born in Cuba, Fornes immigrated to the United States at age fifteen. She lived in Europe as a painter in her twenties, then worked as a textile designer in New York City for a few years before becoming a playwright and director. She has won six Obie awards for her off-Broadway plays, and though she is not well known outside professional circles, she is highly regarded among people who work in theater. Her first major success was the musical *Promenade* (1965). Among her other plays are *Fefu and Her Friends* (1977), *Abingdon Square* (1987), and *Hunger* (1989), and in 1987 she created a musical, *Lovers and Keepers*, with the great Latin percussionist Tito Puente.

Freeman, Mary E. Wilkins (1852–1930)

Freeman, born in Randolph, Maine, is one of the few women of her time who earned her living through writing. When she was fifty years old, she married Dr. Charles Freeman and moved with him to New Jersey, but their marriage failed because of his alcoholism. She specialized in stories of people in remote New England villages, and her characters were often determined individualists, particularly the women who endured despite lack of possibilities and economic security. Her work, which was popular during her lifetime, lost favor after her death but has been revived in the last twenty years. Her best-known works are: *A Humble Romance and Other Stories* (1887) and *A New England Nun and Other Stories* (1891).

Frost, Robert (1874–1963)

Born in San Francisco, Frost moved east with his family when he was a child, and his poems reflect New England life and people. He attended Dartmouth and Harvard for short periods, held a variety of jobs, and tried farming in New Hampshire. During these years, he wrote poetry but was rejected by publishers. Finally, he went to England where his poems were published. On his return to the United States, he met with more success. During his long life, he received four Pulitzer Prizes and many other awards. At President John F. Kennedy's inauguration in 1961, he read his poem "The Gift Outright." In many of his poems, Frost uses nature as the backdrop for his reflections on human behavior. In 1994, the Library of America published the most comprehensive collection of his works in a single volume—*Collected Poems, Prose & Plays* consists of 1,036 pages.

Gaines, Ernest J. (b. 1933)

Born in Louisiana, Gaines spent his childhood working in the fields. When he moved to California, he attended San Francisco College and Stanford University. His work recounts the everyday lives of poor people whose experiences reflect the violence and deprivation of slavery and segregation. "The Sky Is Gray" is from his short story collection *Bloodline* (1968). His many novels include *A Gathering of Old Men* (1983) and *A Lesson before Dying* (1993). Gaines's novel *The Autobiography of Miss Jane Pittman* (1971) was made into a movie. He has been the recipient of a number of awards and prizes, including a John D. and Catherine T. MacArthur Foundation fellowship in 1993; a National Book Critics Circle Award for Fiction in 1993 for *A Lesson Before Dying*; and induction into the Literary Hall of Fame for Writers of African Descent at Chicago State University in 1998. *Conversations with Ernest Gaines*, edited by John Lowe, was published in 1995.

Gillan, Maria Mazziotti

Born in New Jersey, Gillan has taught in a number of colleges. She is presently the director of the Poetry Center of Passaic County Community College in Paterson, New Jersey, and editor of *Footwork: The Paterson Literary Review*. In addition to the many anthologies in which her work appears, she has written six books of poetry, including *Flowers from the Tree of Night* (1981) and *Where I Come From* (1995). With her daughter Jennifer, she has edited *Unsettling America: An Anthology of Contemporary Multicultural Poetry* (1994). *Growing up Ethnic in America* was published in 1999. Her most recent volume of poetry is *Italian Women in Black Dresses* (2002).

Gilman, Charlotte Perkins (1860–1935)

Born in Hartford, Connecticut, and educated at the Rhode Island School of Design, Gilman was a social critic and feminist who wrote prolifically about the necessity of social and sexual equality, particularly about women's need for economic independence. Following a nervous breakdown after the birth of her daughter, Gilman divorced her husband and devoted her time to lecturing and writing about feminist issues. Her nonfiction includes *Women and Economics* (1898) and *The Man-Made World* (1911). Her novels include *Herland* (1915) and *With Her in Ourland* (1916). "The Yellow Wallpaper" (1899) is a fictionalized account of Gilman's own postpartum depression.

Gordimer, Nadine (b. 1923)

Born in Johannesburg, South Africa, and educated at the University of Witwatersrand, Gordimer was one of the few outspoken whites living in South Africa who protested the policy of apartheid (the restrictive laws that governed blacks and those of mixed race). Since her country's dismantling of apartheid in the 1990s, her work—both fiction and nonfiction—has continued to address with depth and nuance the personal and political complications of life in that racially and politically fraught society. She has written many novels and short stories and is the recipient of international awards, including the Nobel Prize for literature in 1991. Some of her recent works include *My Son's Story* (1990), *None to Accompany Me* (1994), *Writing and Being* (1995), *House Gun* (1998), *Living in Hope and History* (1999), and *The Pickup* (2001).

Greenberg, Barbara L. (b. 1932)

Greenberg was born in Boston and received a bachelor's degree from Wellesley College and a master's degree from Simmons College. Living in Massachusetts with her husband and two children, she finds the themes for her short stories, plays, and poems in women's experiences of everyday life. Her published books include *The Spoils of August* (1974), *Fire Drills: Stories* (1982), *The Never-Not Sonnets* (1989), *What Nell Knows* (1997), and a book with Dianne Patterson for teachers, *Art in Chemistry, Chemistry in Art* (1998).

Hardy, Thomas (1860–1928)

Born in Dorset, England, Hardy became an architect but started writing in 1867. The success of one of his novels, *Far from the Madding Crowd* (1874), enabled him to give up architecture for a literary career. After two more successful novels, *Tess of the D'Urbervilles* (1891) and *Jude the Obscure* (1896), he gave up fiction for poetry. A reliance on language close to that of speech, and the subjects of fate, character, and environment (which characterized his novels), continued to permeate his poetry.

Harrison, Jeffrey (b. 1957)

A native of Cincinnati, Ohio, Harrison once told an interviewer that, for him, poetry is "an effort to make sense of the world." He is a contributor to a wide variety of journals, both literary and general. He is the recipient of many prizes and fellowships, and his books include *The Singing Underneath* (1988), *Signs of Arrival* (1996), and, in 2001, *Feeding the Fire*.

Hawthorne, Nathaniel (1804–1864)

A novelist and short story writer, Hawthorne was born in Salem, Massachusetts, and traced his roots to the Puritans. His ancestors were prominent in the seventeenth-century witch trials and in Quaker persecutions. Hawthorne incorporated his sense of guilt into his writing. After graduating from Bowdoin College, he devoted himself to writing for twelve years. He wrote sketches and stories for annuals and newspapers, and in 1837 his first collection of short stories, *Twice-Told Tales*, was published. This collection, along with the works of Edgar Allan Poe, helped establish the American short story as a legitimate literary form. Nine years later, he produced his second series, *Mosses from an Old Manse* (1846). Between the publishing of these two works, it became necessary for Hawthorne to better support his family, and he became a surveyor in the Boston Customs House. He and his wife lived on Brook Farm, an experiment in community living, for a short time but the lifestyle was not to his liking, and he moved to Concord, Massachusetts. There his neighbors included Ralph Waldo Emerson and Henry David Thoreau, the leading Transcendentalists of the nineteenth century. Another move took him back to his birthplace in Salem. Again he served as a surveyor in a customs house, but after his political party was removed from power, he lost his job. His career as a novelist commenced with *The Scarlet Letter* (1850). Financial independence finally allowed him to spend all his time writing, and he wrote *The House of the Seven Gables* (1851) and *The*

Blithedale Romance (1852). When his friend Franklin Pierce became the fourteenth president, Hawthorne was appointed U.S. Consul in Liverpool, England (1853–1857). His last published novel was *The Marble Faun* (1860). In the last years of his life, he wrote infrequently. Four unpublished novels were found among his notes after his death. His use of symbol and allegory influenced Herman Melville, author of *Moby Dick*, and later William Faulkner and Henry James.

Hayden, Robert (1913–1980)

Born and reared in a Detroit ghetto, Hayden not only suffered from the indignities of poverty but was ridiculed because of his poor eyesight. He immersed himself in books and attended Detroit City College and the University of Michigan, where he studied with the poet W. H. Auden. His poetry was not widely appreciated until the 1960s. He was the first African American writer to serve as poetry consultant to the Library of Congress, and was a member of the American Academy and Institute of Arts and Letters. Among his important works are *Heart-Shape in the Dust* (1940), *Angle of Ascent* (1975), and *American Journal* (1979), in which he celebrates the triumphs of his people despite their years of slavery in the American South.

Heaney, Seamus (b. 1939)

Heaney was the first of nine children born on a farm near Belfast in County Derry, Northern Ireland. After local schooling he went to Queen's University in Belfast, where he earned first-class honors with his English degree. His work was first published as he worked toward his teacher's certificate in English at St. Joseph's College, also in Belfast. As a Catholic native of that strife-torn city, Heaney has been called the "laureate of violence." Heaney's poetry demonstrates the national preoccupation with the carnage in Northern Ireland; his work is consistently concerned with memorialization, and he has said that there is no other Heaney besides "the elegiac." He is considered the most important Irish poet since Yeats and, indeed, one of the greatest living poets, a distinction reflected in his many prizes and awards over the years, beginning with an early book of poems, *Death of a Naturalist* (1966), and culminating in the 1995 Nobel for literature. Not just an enormously popular poet, Heaney is an internationally sought-after teacher, having served at Oxford University, the University of California at Berkeley, and Harvard University. His 1999 verse translation of the Old English epic *Beowulf* was a commercial and critical success, and his many volumes of poetry include *Door into the Dark* (1969), *Wintering Out* (1973), *North* (1975), *Field Work* (1976), *Poems 1965–1975* (1980), *Station Island* (1985), *Poems 1966–1987* (1990), *Seeing Things* (1991), *The Spirit Level: Poems* (1996), and *Opened Ground: Selected Poems 1966–1996* (1999). His prose work is collected in *Preoccupations: Selected Prose 1968–1978* (1980) and *The Government of the Tongue: Selected Prose 1978–1987*.

Hogan, Linda (b. 1947)

Hogan was born in Denver of Chickasaw heritage and earned a bachelor's degree from the University of Colorado. Her honors include the Five Civilized Tribes Playwriting Award in 1980 for *A Piece of Moon* and the 1986 Before Columbus Foundation's American Book Award for *Seeing Through the Sun*. Presently, Hogan is an associate professor of American Indian studies at the University of Minnesota. Her poems reflect her interest in preserving the Chickasaw culture. She works as a volunteer with environmental and wildlife groups. Although Hogan published her first novel in 1990, she has been writing poetry since the 1970s.

She was a finalist for the Pulitzer Prize for *Mean Spirit* (1994) as well as for a National Book Critics Circle Award for *The Book of Medicines* (1993). *Dwellings: A Spiritual History of the Living World* (1995) is a book of essays looking at the interconnectedness of nature, religion, and myth. Hogan's work is often concerned with the variety of complicated relationships between humans and the animal kingdom. She was co-editor of both *Between Species: Women and Animals* (1997) and *Intimate Nature: The Bond Between Women and Animals* (1998). She published a novel, *Power*, in 1998, and *The Woman Who Watches Over the World: A Native Memoir*, in 2001.

Hongo, Garrett (b. 1951)

Hongo was born in Hawaii but moved with his family to California at the age of six. He has explored the Asian American experience through poetry and prose and through drama as well—both as a playwright and as the founder and artistic director of a Seattle theater group. A professor of English and creative writing at a number of West Coast universities over the years, he has also served as a jury member of the Pulitzer Prize committee. His volumes of poetry include *Yellow Light* (1982) and *The River of Heaven* (1988), and in 1995 he published *Volcano: A Memoir of Hawaii*.

Hughes, Langston (1902–1967)

One of the most important African American literary figures of the twentieth century, Hughes was born in Missouri and grew up in Lawrence, Kansas, and Cleveland, Ohio, where he graduated from high school, having already begun to write. Enrolled at New York's Columbia University in 1921, he was not permitted to live in the racially restricted dormitories and so took up residence at the nearby Harlem YMCA, where he came across the budding Harlem Renaissance, of which he was to become a major figure. After a few years of international travel and work as a sailor, he graduated from Lincoln University in Pennsylvania and returned to New York City. His first book of poems, *The Weary Blues*, appeared in 1926. Besides poetry, Hughes wrote short stories, novels, plays, scripts for both radio and film, children's books, and works of humor and nonfiction. He also lectured frequently at black universities across the South. Hughes's poetry incorporated the conventions of black spirituals and the blues into more traditional verse forms, and his writing in general was celebratory of black life, artistic expression, and spirituality, in both structure and content. At the same time he addressed the pain, frustration, and loss inherent in the second-class citizenship to which African Americans were relegated. An exceedingly prolific writer, his many books include *Not Without Laughter* (1930), *Dear Lovely Death* (1931), *The Negro Mother* (1931), *The Dream Keeper* (1932), *The Ways of White Folks* (1933), *A New Song* (1938), *One-Way Ticket* (1949), *The Sweet Flypaper of Life* (1955), *Ask Your Mama* (1961), *Simple's Uncle Sam* (1965), and many others.

Jackson, Shirley (1919–1965)

Best known for her macabre gothic fiction, of which *The Lottery* (1949) is the most famous example, Jackson's work often portrays the more sinister tendencies of people and communities. Her novels, such as *The Haunting of Hill House* (1959) and *We Have Always Lived in the Castle* (1962), are psychological thrillers, often with a bizarre ironic twist. She is less widely known for her juvenile fiction and humorous books on family life—collections of short sketches usually first published in women's magazines and widely praised by contemporary critics.

Jarrell, Randall (1914–1965)

A Tennessee native, Jarrell studied at Vanderbilt University, where he received both the B.A. and the M.A. His experience as a combat pilot in World War II informs his early collections of poetry, *Little Friend, Little Friend* (1945) and *Losses* (1948), which are considered to be among the most powerful American war commentaries. After the war he went back to work as a professor, poet, and critic, publishing several collections of verse, including *Selected Poems* (1955) and *The Woman at the Washington Zoo* (1960). He went on to write children's books, including *The Bat Poet* (1964). He was hit and killed by a car in 1965.

Joyce, James (1882–1941)

Born in Dublin, Ireland, the eldest in a family of ten children, Joyce knew a life of poverty and efforts to maintain respectability. He was educated in Jesuit schools, where he was trained in Catholicism and the classics. However, he rebelled against his religion, his country, and his family, and at twenty he left Dublin for a life in Europe as an exile. By teaching languages and doing clerical work, he eked out a living for his common-law wife and their two children. His novel *Ulysses*, written in an innovative style, took seven years to complete. *Finnegans Wake*, his most experimental work, is written in a language he created. He also wrote poems, short stories, and one play. Despite his years of exile, all of his fiction is set in his native Dublin and portrays his attempt to free himself of religious and geographic restrictions.

Kafka, Franz (1883–1924)

Born in Prague, Czechoslovakia, Kafka spent an unhappy life as a victim of anti-Semitism and in a job he detested in an insurance company. His stories, such as "The Metamorphosis," (1915), and his three novels, *The Trial* (1925), *The Castle* (1926), and *Amerika* (1927), reflect his feelings of alienation from the community. When he died of tuberculosis at forty-one, he left his unpublished manuscripts to a friend with instructions that they be destroyed. Instead, the friend edited and published them, thereby establishing the obscure clerk as a world-renowned author.

Keats, John (1795–1821)

Born in London, Keats studied to be a doctor but he never practiced medicine. His early interest in literature and his friendship with poets inspired him to write poetry. Along with Lord Byron and Percy Bysshe Shelley, he established romantic poetry, with its emphasis on emotion and the imagination over reason and intelligence. Idealized love was the subject of many of his poems. At twenty-six, he died of tuberculosis.

Kincaid, Jamaica (b. 1949)

Born Elaine Potter Richardson in St. Johns, Antigua, Kincaid left the island as a teenager for New York City, where she started out as an *au pair* and found herself in 1976 a staff writer for *The New Yorker* magazine. Known for her "clear bitter prose," Kincaid first won wide recognition with the publication of her first two books, *At the Bottom of the River* (1983), in which "Girl" appears, and the novel *Annie John* (1985). In these and other books about life on the Caribbean island of Antigua, Kincaid's language is poetic and rhythmic, rich with imagery and characterization and at the same time almost telegraphic in its simplicity. She also writes essays on gardening for various periodicals, some of which have been collected in *My Garden* (1999). Other recent books include a 1997 memoir about her brother's last years, *My Brother* (1997), the novels *Lucy* (1990) and *The Autobiography of My Mother* (1995), and the book of essays *Talk Stories* (2000).

King, Martin Luther Jr. (1929–1968)

Born in Georgia, King was the son and grandson of Baptist ministers. He was educated at Morehouse College, Crozier Theological Seminary, and Boston University. He was pastor of a Baptist church in Montgomery, Alabama, when Rosa Parks refused to relinquish her seat on a bus to a white person. King, influenced by the teachings of Mahatma Gandhi, led a non-violent bus boycott in 1955 that attracted national attention. This incident led to the U.S. Supreme Court's ruling that Alabama's bus segregation was unconstitutional. King wrote of the experience in *Stride toward Freedom* (1958).

The message of passive resistance spread, and King and his followers organized many protests against segregation and injustice in the South. Although he was arrested, jailed, and stabbed, and his home was bombed, King continued to preach his philosophy and gained respect and admiration all over the world. In 1963, his *Letter from the Birmingham Jail* replied to those who criticized his methods and beliefs. King organized the March on Washington in 1963 and delivered his memorable "I Have a Dream" speech. He was awarded the Noble Peace Prize in 1964—at 35, he was the youngest recipient. King continued to lead protests and coupled his message about segregation with opposition to the Vietnam War. While preparing to march with striking workers in Memphis, Tennessee, in 1968, he was assassinated.

Komunyakaa, Yusef (b. 1947)

Born in Bogalusa, Louisiana, Komunyakaa received the Bronze Star while serving with the U.S. Army in Vietnam from 1965 to 1967 as an information specialist and as editor of a military newspaper. On his return stateside, he went to college and graduate school in the West, but went back to Louisiana to teach in the New Orleans schools at both the elementary and post-secondary levels. The winner of a number of awards, in 1994 he claimed the Pulitzer Prize and the $50,000 Kingsley Tufts Poetry Award for his *Neon Vernacular: New and Selected Poems*. His work weaves together the strands of his life experiences, from Louisiana to Vietnam, dealing variously with war, jazz, culture shock, and the power of American racism in history and the present. Some of his other books include *Copacetic* (1984), *Toys in a Field* (1986), *Dien Cai Dau* (1988), *Thieves of Paradise* (1998), *Talking Dirty to the Gods* (2000), and *Pleasure Dome: New and Collected Poems* (2001).

Lagerkvist, Pär (Fabian) (1891–1974)

This Swedish writer left his homeland as a young man for Paris, where he was intensely affected by the modern art movements of the time—Fauvism, cubism, and naivism. *Anguish* (1916), his early book of poetry, is seen by some as the first expressionistic work in Swedish literature, and its publication established his reputation. Like many of his generation, he was deeply disturbed by World War I, and much of his work is concerned with the meaning of life and the conflict between good and evil. As he got older, his work became less pessimistic and more realistic, although in many ways his thematic concerns were the same. He was basically unknown in the United States until 1951, when he won the Nobel Prize for Literature and the English translation of his novel *Barabbas* appeared. Nine years later the movie adaptation of the book appeared, to wide acclaim. In the meantime he had written *The Eternal Smile and Other Stories* (1954) and *The Marriage Feast and Other Stories* (1955).

Lassell, Michael (b. 1947)

Born in New York City, Lassell has earned degrees from Colgate University, California Institute of the Arts, and the Yale School of Drama. Now living in Los Angeles, he is managing editor of *LA Style* magazine and has worked as a critic, photographer, teacher, and writer. His book *Poems for Lost and Un-Lost Boys* won the Amelia Chapbook Award in 1986. His latest published collections are *Hard Way* (1995), *Flame for the Touch that Matters* (1998), and *Certain Ecstasies* (1999).

Laviera, Tato (b. 1951)

Laviera, born in Puerto Rico, has lived in New York City since 1960. He has taught creative writing at several northeastern universities, including Rutgers. His poetry and drama celebrate the ethnic diversity of New York City, and he often writes in English and Spanish as well as in "Spanglish," a mixture of the two languages used by several bilingual poets. He is deeply committed to preserving the oral traditions of Puerto Rico and the Caribbean, and, although his poetry is published in written form, it is meant to be sung and celebrated by the community. He has written *AmeRican* (1985), *Mainstream Ethics=Etica Corriente* (1988), and *La Carreta Made a U-Turn* (1992).

Lee, Li-Young (b. 1957)

The Lee family's journey began in the early 1950s when they fled China's political turmoil for Indonesia. When anti-Chinese sentiment commenced in their new home, Lee's father was sent to prison. The family escaped to Hong Kong, and Mr. Lee rose to prominence as an evangelical preacher. The author, born in Jakarta, emigrated to America when he was six years old. Mr. Lee became the minister of an all-white Presbyterian church in a small town in western Pennyslvania. The imposing, elusive, God-like figure of his father haunts Lee's work. He is the author of two award-winning volumes of poetry: *Rose* (1986) and *The City in Which I Love You* (1990). *The Winged Seed: A Remembrance* (1995) is an autobiographical work. Lee has taught in several universities including Northwestern and the University of Iowa. His most recent book is *Book of My Nights: Poems* (2001).

Levertov, Denise (1923–1997)

Born in England of Welsh and Jewish parents, Levertov was a nurse in World War II. She married an American writer and moved to the United States in 1948. Her poetic style was influenced by her affiliation with the Black Mountain poets of North Carolina, who advocated verse form that duplicates everyday speech patterns. Some of her poems focus on human relationships; many others express her commitment to social and environmental issues. Among her numerous collections of poetry are *Light Up the Cave* (1981), *A Door in the Hive* (1989), *Evening Train* (1992), and a memoir, *Tesserae: Memories and Suppositions* (1995). The poet Kenneth Rexroth once wrote that she was "the most subtly skillful poet of her generation, the most profound, the most moving."

Liu, Eric (b. 1968)

The son of Taiwanese immigrants, Liu was born in Poughkeepsie, New York. A summa cum laude graduate of Yale University, he founded and edits *The Next Progressive*, a journal of opinion. He was a speechwriter for President Bill Clinton and has been a commentator on MSNBC. Liu edited the anthology *Next: Young American Writers on the New Generation*. His memoir, *The Accidental Asian: Notes of a Native Speaker* (1998) articulates the Asian American experience in defining one's identity. He also speaks eloquently of his father's struggles both in Taiwan and in America.

Lyman, Peter (b. 1940)

Lyman is a university librarian and professor at the School of Information Management and Systems at the University of California, Berkeley. His research interests include the sociology of information, computer literacy, and electronic libraries.

McKay, Claude (1890–1948)

Born on the island of Jamaica to peasant farmers, McKay heard African folk tales when he was a child and came to appreciate his racial heritage. He was encouraged in his literary ambitions by an Englishman through whose efforts two of his poetry collections were published in England. In 1912, he came to the United States to study agriculture. After a few years of school, he left for New York City to become a writer. Although he had experienced discrimination in Jamaica, he was unprepared for the extreme racism he encountered in the United States. McKay channeled his anger into a collection of poetry, *Harlem Shadows* (1922), which heralded the Harlem Renaissance (a period of unprecedented creativity by black writers centered in Harlem). His poetry reflects his concern over the treatment of African Americans in U.S. society. His other works include *Home to Harlem* (1928), *Banjo* (1929), *Songs of Jamaica* (1911), *Constab Ballads* (1912), and *Spring in New Hampshire and Other Poems* (1920).

Marvell, Andrew (1621–1678)

Son of an Anglican clergyman, Marvell entered Cambridge and received his bachelor's degree in 1638. When his father died in 1640, he spent his inheritance on a four-year tour of the Continent. On his return, he tutored the daughter of a Lord General and wrote poems on gardens and country life. For most of his life, Marvell took an active interest in politics and wrote many satirical pamphlets about the controversies of the times. A friend of John Milton, Marvell was influential in saving the poet from prison after the Restoration. During the last twenty years of his life, he was a representative in Parliament. His poetical works were virtually ignored until 1921. T. S. Eliot wrote an essay commemorating Marvell's birth, and interest in his lyric poetry flourished. Other poems include "The Garden," "The Definition of Love," and "A Dialogue between Body and Soul."

Meier, Daniel (b. 1959)

A graduate of Wesleyan University and Harvard Graduate School of Education, Meier now teaches in an elementary school in Boston. His previous published work deals with the art of teaching and other educational issues. His book *Learning in Small Moments: Life in an Urban*

Classroom appeared in 1997 and most recently he published *Scribble Scrabble—Learning to Read and Write: Success with Diverse Teachers, Children, and Families* (2000).

Millay, Edna St. Vincent (1892–1950)

Born in Rockland, Maine, Millay began to write poetry at an early age. Her first poem, "Renascence," was published during her senior year in college. During the 1920s, she lived a bohemian life in Greenwich Village, where she acted in plays and continued to write poetry. Her love sonnets, which advocated sexual and emotional freedom for women, were particularly popular. In 1923, she won the Pulitzer Prize in Poetry for *The Harp-Weaver and Other Poems*. She wrote infrequently during the last years of her life, and she died in relative obscurity.

Mirikitani, Janice (b. 1942)

A third-generation Japanese American, Mirikitani is program director and president of the Corporation at Glide Church/Urban Center, a community organization in California. Her poetry illuminates contemporary urban life and also focuses on the injustices experienced by Japanese Americans who were interned in U.S. camps during World War II. Her published books include *Awake in the River* (1978), *Shedding Silence: Poetry and Prose* (1987), *We, the Dangerous: New and Selected Poems* (1995) and *Love Works* (2001) is the most recent.

Molière, pseudonym of Jean-Baptiste Poquelin (1622–1673)

Educated by Jesuits, Molière was the son of an upholsterer who served the royal household of Louis XIV. In 1643, Molière became an actor and cofounded a theater in Paris for which he wrote his first plays. Failure to make a profit led the theater troupe to tour the provinces for thirteen years, finally returning to the capital when the king granted them a theater. Molière has been called the father of modern French comedy because he broke away from the farces and plots of intrigue popular with his predecessors. His plays reveal the pretensions and hypocrisy of the society he observed around him. Molière's command of dramatic structure, witty verse, and comic ingenuity have established his reputation as supreme in his genre. Many of his characters have become immortal types. His creations include *Les Précieuses ridicules* (*The Ridiculous Snobs*) (1659), *L'École des maris* (*The School for Husbands*) (1661), *Les Fâcheux* (*The Bores*) (1661), and *Le Misanthrope* (*The Misanthrope*) (1666). *Tartuffe* (1664) was opposed by the clergy and banned twice before 1669, but is considered one of Molière's greatest comic achievements. He followed it with another masterpiece, *Le Bourgeois Gentilhomme* (*The Would-Be Gentleman*) (1670). Moliére died suddenly after a severe hemorrhage at the age of 51. The clergy denied him a holy burial.

Monette, Paul (1945–1995)

A writer whose fiction, poetry, and autobiography deal mainly with issues of homosexuality and AIDS, Monette was born in Lawrence, Massachusetts, and attended Yale University. His novels include *Taking Care of Mrs. Carroll* (1978), *The Gold Diggers* (1979), *The Long Shot* (1990), and *Halfway Home* (1991). But he is most remembered for his autobiographical trilogy *Borrowed Time: An AIDS Memoir* (1988), *Becoming a Man: Half a Life Story* (1992), and *Last Watch of the Night: Essays Too Personal and Otherwise* (1994). Monette won the National Book Award for *Becoming a Man*, which tells his experiences of coming to terms with his homosexuality and disclosing it to others. *Borrowed Time* presents an account of the AIDS death of his longtime lover Roger Horwitz. *Last Watch of the Night* was his final published work before his death from AIDS in 1995.

Mora, Pat (b. 1942)

Born in El Paso, Texas, Mora now lives in Cincinnati. She received a bachelor's degree from Texas Western College and a master's degree from the University of Texas at El Paso. Her poetry reflects her Hispanic perspective, and she writes frequently on gender and political issues. Her work has been collected in *Chants* (1984), *Borders* (1986), *Communion* (1991), *Aqua Santa—Holy Water* (1995), and *House of Houses* (1997). Among the most distinguished contemporary Hispanic writers, Mora receives praise for her cultural activism as well as her writing. She has also written many children's books, a book of autobiographical essays, *Nepantla: Essays from the Land in the Middle* (1993), and a memoir in essay form, *House of Houses* (1997). Her most recent volume of poetry for adults is *Aunt Carmen's Book of Practical Saints* (1997).

Morrison, Toni, pseudonym of Chloe Anthony Wofford (b. 1931)

Born in an African American community in Lorain, Ohio, Morrison earned the B.A. in English from the historically black Howard University in Washington, D.C., and the M.A. at Cornell University. Her continuing success as a novelist began in 1970 with the publication of *The Bluest Eye* and proceeded with *Sula* (1973), *Song of Solomon* (1977), and *Tar Baby* (1981). Recognition of her importance broadened when she won the 1987 Pulitzer Prize for Literature with the publication of *Beloved* and continued to grow with *Jazz* (1992) and *Paradise* (1998). Morrison's fiction is brilliantly written, sometimes fantastical, and preoccupied with the quest for self and with the personal and communal repercussions of African American history, which she paints as both searingly painful and profoundly beautiful. Her work has universal artistic and social significance. That importance was acknowledged internationally in 1993 when she was awarded the Nobel Prize for Literature. Her book of essays, *Playing in the Dark: Whiteness and the Literary Imagination* (1992), addresses issues of importance across academic disciplines with a clarity and intellectual certainty rarely to be found in scholarly discussions of race.

Mukherjee, Bharati (b. 1940)

Born in Calcutta, India, Mukherjee has lived in Canada but is now a permanent resident of the United States. She received her doctorate from the University of Iowa and has taught at several academic institutions, including Skidmore College and Columbia University. Her novels include *The Tiger's Daughter* (1972), *The Wire* (1975), *The Middleman and Other Stories* (1988), and *Jasmine* (1989), an expansion of the story appearing in this anthology. Her themes often deal with immigrants adjusting to life in a new society. *The Holder of the World* was published in 1993. *Consuming Desires: Consumption, Culture, and the Pursuit of Happiness* appeared in 1999.

Mydans, Seth (b. 1946)

Mydans is a veteran foreign correspondent who has served in England, the Philippines, Thailand, and the former Soviet Union. He is at present chief correspondent for the *New York Times* Bangkok bureau. He deals here with youth gangs, once the exclusive province of racial and poverty-stricken minorities. Rising in the suburbs are gangs of more affluent youths who see glamour in banding together, carrying guns, and scrawling graffiti.

Niatum, Duane (b. 1938)

Born in Seattle, this Native American poet was educated at the University of Washington and Johns Hopkins University. Niatum has worked as an editor, librarian, and teacher. The Pacific Northwest Writers Conference has awarded him first prize in poetry twice. His books include *Ascending Red Cedar Moon* (1969), *Songs for the Harvester of Dreams* (1982), and *Pieces* (1981). His poems express the disappointments and dreams of his people as they attempt to reconcile their private and communal selves. His most recent collection is *Drawings of the Song Animals: New And Selected Poems* (1991).

O'Brien, Tim (b. 1946)

Born in Austin, Minnesota, and educated at Macalester College and Harvard University, O'Brien was drafted into the army during the Vietnam War. For his service he received the Purple Heart. His war experiences have inspired both fiction and autobiography. *If I Die in a Combat Zone, Box Me Up and Ship Me Home* (1973) and *Northern Lights* (1974) preceded *Going after Cacciato* (1978), which won him the National Book Award. Many critics proclaim *Cacciato* be the finest work written about the Vietnam War. The short story *The Things They Carried* deals with survival, lost innocence, and the war's lasting legacy for good and evil. It was excerpted from a collection of his works, *The Things They Carried* (1990) and was included in *The Best American Short Stories of 1987*. His recent publications include *In the Lake of the Woods* and *Twinkle, Twinkle* (both 1994), *Tomcat in Love* (1998), and *July, July* (2002).

O'Connor, Frank (1903–1966)

O'Connor was born in Cork, Ireland. His real name was Michael O'Donovan. During his imprisonment in Ireland's 1923 civil war, he educated himself by reading Irish literature. He became a director of the Abbey Theatre in Dublin during the Irish Renaissance, a period in the 1920s when the Irish people awakened to the realization of the richness and value of their own culture. Subsequently, he moved to the United States, but his themes remained the Irish-English troubles and a realistic picture of contemporary life in Ireland. Two of his short story collections are *Guests of the Nation* (1931) and *Dutch Interior* (1940). His autobiographical works include *An Only Child* (1960) and *My Father's Son* (1968).

O'Flaherty, Liam (1896–1984)

Born in the Aran Islands off the west coast of Ireland, O'Flaherty was educated for the priesthood but abandoned it and joined the Irish Guard before World War I. He was wounded and discharged in 1918. After completing his education, he traveled for several years, returning to Ireland in 1921 to fight with the Republicans against the Free Staters in the Irish civil war. He was exiled soon after, and while living in England he published his first short story, "The Sniper." His best-known novel, *The Informer* (1925), became an Academy Award-winning film. However, *Famine* (1937), a novel based on the potato famine that claimed more than one million lives in Ireland during the 1840s, is considered his greatest work. Ireland's poor people were often the main characters in his stories.

Olds, Sharon (b. 1942)

Born in San Francisco, Olds, who now resides in New York City, graduated from Stanford University and received a doctorate from Columbia University. She has authored *Satan Says* (1980); *The Dead and the Living* (1984), for which she was awarded a National Book Critics Circle Award in poetry; and *The Gold Cell* (1987). Much of her work expresses her involvement with contemporary social issues and their effects on private and public selves. Her latest works include *The Father* (1992), *The Wellspring* (1996), *Blood, Tin, Straw* (1999), and *The Unswept Room* (2002).

Olsen, Tillie (b. 1913)

Olsen, born in Omaha, Nebraska, was determined to be a writer although she worked at many jobs and raised four children. She began working on her novel *Yonnondio* in the 1920s and finished it in the 1970s. The subjects of her short stories and novels are people who have been denied their chance at creativity because of their sex, race, or class. Olsen's work is often anthologized. *Tell Me a Riddle* (1961) and *Silences* (1978) are among her published works.

Owen, Wilfred (1893–1918)

Born in Shropshire, England, Owen is considered the most famous of the English poets of World War I. He expressed his hatred of war in descriptions of brutality and horror that he experienced on the battlefield. Owen died in action a week before the Armistice. "Above all this book is not concerned with Poetry, the subject of it is War, and the pity of War. The Poetry is in the pity. All a poet can do is warn," he wrote.

Petry, Ann (1908–1997)

Petry's was one of the few African American families in Old Saybrook, Connecticut, where she was born. She earned a pharmacy degree at the University of Connecticut and then went on to Columbia University, where she graduated in 1946. Her first novel, *The Street*, depicting the struggles of a young woman in Harlem, came out in 1946 to great success. She worked in New York as a reporter and editor for various newspapers, while producing novels such as *The Country Place* (1947) and *The Narrows* (1953). A book of short stories, *Miss Muriel and Other Stories*, came out in 1971, just before she left New York to teach English for a few years at the University of Hawaii. Returning to New York, she worked as a teacher and an actress at the American Negro Theatre.

Plato (427–348 B.C.)

A Greek philosopher, teacher, and writer who became actively involved in the politics of the Athenian city-state, Plato vehemently protested the corruption that had permeated Athenian democracy, and the death of his teacher and friend Socrates impelled him to search for an alternative lifestyle. In "The Allegory of the Cave," one of his most famous philosophic dialogues, he talks about the human desire for illusion rather than truth.

Powell, David W.

Powell served as a marine in Vietnam from 1965 to 1967. "Vietnam: What I Remember" is excerpted from Powell's memoir, "Patriotism Revisited," which he submitted to a creative writing class at the University of Arizona in Tucson.

Puig, Manuel (1932–1990)

As a young boy in Argentina, Puig constantly watched North American and European films. He was so obsessed with movies that he wanted to become either a director or a screenwriter. Neither career suited him, and he turned to fiction. His work, however, is saturated with references to films and popular culture. Puig's autobiographical novel, *Betrayed by Rita Hayworth*, was completed in 1965 but wasn't published until three years later. It was translated into English in 1971 and found an appreciative audience in the United States. Life in Argentina became increasingly uncomfortable for Puig when Juan Peron returned to power in 1971. The writer left the country and lived in Mexico, Brazil, and New York.

His subsequent novels, *Heartbreak Tango* (1973) and *The Buenos Aires Affair: A Detective Novel* (1976), were not as popular, but his next novel, *Kiss of the Spider Woman* (1979), gained instant success and was subsequently made into a movie and a Broadway musical. It was recognized as an attack on the political and cultural corruption of Argentina. His novels and plays continue to attract attention from readers and critics alike. He died of a heart attack in 1990.

Rifaat, Alifa (Fatma Abdalla) (b. 1930)

Born in Cairo, Egypt, Rifaat still resides there. She wrote a short story when she was nine, but was punished for doing so. Although opposition to her writing continued in her Muslim family, her first short stories were published in 1955. Obstacles prevented her from writing for fifteen years during her marriage, but she resumed work in 1975 and has published hundreds of stories and a few novels. Themes related to the sexual and emotional problems encountered by married women in the Middle East dominate her fiction. Her collection *Distant View of a Minaret and Other Stories* was published in 1985, and the novel *Girls of Baurdin* came out in 1995.

Roethke, Theodore (1908–1963)

Roethke was born and raised in Saginaw, Michigan, where his father was the owner of a greenhouse. He studied at both the University of Michigan and Harvard University and went on to teach, settling finally at the University of Washington, where he was known as a great teacher. He was said never to have truly recovered from the death of his father when he was only fourteen, and indeed his work often has a mournful tone. His father's influence is also apparent in his frequent use of greenhouse imagery, as well as metaphors of nature. Roethke's work gained important recognition: *The Waking: Poems 1933–1953* won the 1954 Pulitzer Prize. Other honors included Guggenheim Fellowships in 1945 and 1950 as well as both a National Book Award and the Bollingen Prize in 1959 for *Words for the Wind* (1958). Other collections are *The Lost Son and Other Poems* (1948), *Praise to the End* (1951), *The Lost Field* (1964), and *Collected Poems* (1966).

Romero, Leo (b. 1950)

Born in New Mexico, Romero uses his home state as the setting for many of his poems. Educated at the University of New Mexico and New Mexico State University, he is a leading writer of Chicano poetry. His works include *During the Growing Season* (1978), *Celso* (1985), *Desert Nights* (1989), *Going Home Away Indian* (1990), and *Rita & Los Angles* (1995) and its sequel *Michael & Los Angeles* (1998). He has also produced a novel, *Crazy for Fabiola*, and the more recent poetry collections *San Femandez Beat*, *Ravens Are Real*, *The God of Oranges*, and *At Dusk Through the Canyon*.

Roy, Sandip

Born in Calcutta, India, Roy now lives in San Francisco where he edits *Trikone Magazine*. His work has appeared in *India Currents Magazine* and *Christopher Street*, *A Magazine*, as well as in anthologies such as *Queer View Mirror* and *Men on Man 6*.

Rukeyser, Muriel (1913–1980)

Born in New York City, Rukeyser was educated at Vassar College and Columbia University. A journalist as well as a poet, she reported from Spain on the Spanish civil war and was one of the journalists arrested at the Scottsboro Trial in 1931, an important moment in the history of civil rights in the United States. Her poems, published over a period of forty years, reflect her commitment to her Jewish heritage, civil rights, and the antiwar movement. Since her death, two works have been published—*Out of Silence* (1992), and *A Muriel Rukeyser Reader* (1996).

Rushdie, Salman (Ahmed) (b. 1947)

Rushdie was born in Bombay, India, and educated in his homeland and in England. He was an actor and an advertising copywriter before he began his writing career in the 1970s. His first novels received many prestigious awards. Among them are *Grimus* (1975), *Midnight's Children* (1981), *Shame* (1983), and *The Satanic Verses* (1988). The latter work outraged Muslims around the world and was immediately banned in a dozen countries for his alleged blasphemy against Islam. Demonstrations and riots in India, Pakistan, and South Africa showed the depth of feeling against the book. Supporters of Rushdie have pointed out that all the objectionable scenes take place in the dreams of a character who harbors insane delusions and are not necessarily the beliefs of the author. In 1989, Iran's religious leader, Ayatollah Khomeini, issued a death warrant and a $1 million reward to any Muslim who would assassinate the writer. Rushdie lived in hiding for several years but continued to write. Although the bounty on his life has been lifted, he still lives in semi-seclusion. His recent books include *Imaginary Homelands* (1991), *East, West* (1994), *The Moor's Last Sigh* (1996), *The Ground beneath Her Feet* (1999), *Fury* (2001), *Conversations with Salman Rushdie* (edited by Michael Reder, 2000), and *Step Across This Line: Collected Nonfiction 1992–2002* (2002).

Sarton, May (1912–1995)

Born in Belgium, Sarton was brought to the United States at the outbreak of World War I. Her early enthusiasms were poetry and acting. She joined Eva Le Gallienne's repertory theater in New York and later directed her own company. In the 1930s, she began to write poetry while supporting herself with teaching jobs, lecturing, and book reviewing. Sarton's main theme is the effect that love, in all its forms, has on personal relationships. Some of her works are *Encounter in April* (1937), *A Grain of Mustard Seed* (1971), *Collected Poems 1930–1973* (1974), *Halfway to Silence* (1980), and *The Silence Now: New and Uncollected Earlier Poems* (1988).

    Throughout her life she kept journals in which she recorded the events of everyday life. They have been published in *Journal of Solitude* (1973), *At Seventy* (1984), and *Encore: A Journal of the Eightieth Year* (1993).

Chief Seattle (1788–1866)

Chief Seattle was born near the city that now bears his name, and was chief of the Squamish and allied Indian tribes in the 1800s. He saw the influx of settlers that poured into the Pacific Northwest region and, fearing that conflicts could cause wars between them and his tribes, encouraged friendships and trading relations with the newcomers. Seattle managed to maintain peace until 1854, when the governor of the Washington Territories proposed buying two million acres of tribal land. The selection included here is the chief's reply, and it reflects his fears about the future. In the following year, treaty agreements were breached and Seattle chose not to fight in the Yakima War. Instead he consented to relocating his tribes to a reservation. When the city of Seattle was named for him, he objected, believing that after death, his spirit would be troubled each time his name was spoken.

Sexton, Anne (1928–1974)

Born and raised in Newton, Massachusetts, Sexton studied with Robert Lowell at Boston College, going on to work for a year as a fashion model in Boston and then marrying and becoming a suburban housewife. At twenty-eight, she had a nervous breakdown and, having been encouraged by a therapist to write, saw wide success in 1960 with her first book of confessional poetry, *To Bedlam and Part Way Back*. Her second collection, *Live or Die*, won the Pulitzer Prize for 1967, and though she saw poetry as a form of therapy, saying "suicide is the opposite of the poem," she was not able to overcome her troubles, finally succeeding in 1974 after various attempts at taking her own life. A posthumous collection, *The Awful Rowing Toward God* (1975), describes in part the feelings that brought her to that point. Other collections include *All My Pretty Ones* (1962), *Love Poems* (1969), *Transformations* (1971), and *The Death Notebooks* (1974). By no means limited to the contemplation of mental instability and death, her work also examines themes of love, motherhood, and daughterhood. Her work broke through many of the constraints on female poets with wit and style.

Shakespeare, William (1564–1616)

Born in Stratford-on-Avon, England, Shakespeare was a poet and dramatist of the Elizabethan Age. Relatively little is known about his personal life. He received a grammar school education and in 1594 was a member of the Lord Chamberlain's company of actors. By 1597, Shakespeare had written at least a dozen plays, including comedies, histories, and one tragedy. His greatest plays include the tragedies *Julius Caesar* (1600), *Hamlet* (1601), *Othello*

(1604), *King Lear* (1605), and *Macbeth* (1606). He also composed a series of 154 sonnets between 1593 and 1601.

Shelley, Percy Bysshe (1792–1822)

One of the most important of the English Romantic poets, Shelley was a true revolutionary in life as well as work. He was expelled from Oxford in 1811 for a pamphlet he wrote entitled *The Necessity of Atheism*. In the same year he married sixteen-year-old Harriet Westbrook, leaving her just a few years later for Mary Wollstonecraft Godwin, who would later write *Frankenstein* (1818). The pair settled in Italy and were married after Harriet committed suicide in 1816. In company with other Romantics, such as Keats, Byron, and Coleridge, Shelley broke down powerful conventions of social as well as literary behavior in his short life. His short lyric poems, such as "Ode to the West Wind," "To a Skylark," and "Ozymandias," were among his best-known works, but the longer dramatic poem "Prometheus Unbound" and his elegy to Keats, "Adonais," stand high in the Romantic pantheon. He also wrote plays and essays, and was working on a long philosophic poem entitled "The Triumph of Life" when he was drowned in a boating accident at thirty.

Shoaib, Mahwash (b. 1973)

A native of Pakistan, Shoaib is a graduate of the University of Punjab and is currently in the doctoral program in English at the Graduate Center at the City University of New York. She is a poet, a writer, and a translator of poetry from her native Urdu to English. Keenly interested in philosophy as a way of life, she devotes her time to the study of language and literature, writing, and bibliophilia. Her aim is to realize her creative potential in both fiction and poetry.

Song, Cathy (b. 1955)

Song was born in Honolulu. She attended the University of Hawaii, received a bachelor's degree from Wellesley College, and earned a master's degree at Boston University. Her first book, *Picture Bride* (1983), won the Yale Series of Younger Poets Award and was nominated for a National Book Critics Circle Award. Her poems reflect a deep awareness of her Asian heritage and the struggles of her people to find their own voices in contemporary culture. She has also written *Frameless Windows, Squares of Light* (1988), and *School Figures* (1994).

Sophocles (496–406 B.C.)

Born near Athens, Greece, Sophocles was the most popular playwright of his day. He also held posts in the military and political life of Athens. Of the more than one hundred plays that he wrote, only seven survive, among them three about Oedipus and his children, *Oedipus the King, Oedipus at Colonus,* and *Antigone*. Using mythology as the backdrop for his complex exploration of our private and public selves, Sophocles expressed the continuity of human experience.

Soyinka, Wole (b. 1934)

Born in Nigeria, Soyinka, a poet, playwright, novelist, and essayist, was educated in his homeland and in England. Through his efforts, the theater in Nigeria has flourished. For his role in the political life of his country, he was imprisoned. Although denied the chance to write while in jail, he used scraps of cigarette and toilet papers to compose a collection of poems, which was smuggled out and published as *Poems from Prison* (1969). In 1986, he was awarded the Nobel Prize in literature. His themes, social injustice and the preservation of individual freedom, are developed with humor and satire. *The Open Sore of a Continent: A Personal Narrative of the Nigerian Crisis* was published in 1996, and *The Burden of Memory, the Music of Forgiveness* in 1998. *Arms and the Arts—A Continent's Unequal Dialogue* was published in 1999, and *Conversations with Wole Soyinka* (edited by Biodun Jeyifo) appeared in 2001.

Spera, Gabriel (b. 1966)

Spera received the B.A. from Cornell University and the M.F.A. from the University of North Carolina at Greensboro. He works as a technical editor in Los Angeles. His work has appeared in a number of journals and his first collection of poems, *The Standing Wave*, was published in 2003.

Staples, Brent (b. 1951)

Staples is from Chester, Pennsylvania, and has a Ph.D. in psychology from the University of Chicago. He is currently on the editorial board of the *New York Times*, where he writes on culture and politics. His autobiography, *Parallel Time: Growing Up in Black and White*, was published in 1994.

Stevens, Wallace (1879–1955)

Stevens was born in Reading, Pennsylvania, was educated at Harvard University and New York University Law School, and was an insurance executive for most of his life. He published his first book of poems, *Harmonium*, in 1923 at the age of forty-four. Going on to become a vice-president in his company in 1934, he continued to write poetry and became a central figure in twentieth-century American literature. His verse is musical, descriptive, and elegant, often giving weight and shape to abstract concepts. Among his collections of poetry are *Ideas of Order* (1935), *The Man With the Blue Guitar* (1937), *Parts of a World* (1942), *Transport to Summer* (1947), *Auroras of Autumn* (1950), and *Collected Poems* (1954), for which he won both the Pulitzer Prize and the National Book Award. His prose publications include *Notes toward a Supreme Fiction* (1942) and *The Necessary Angel* (1951).

Tannen, Deborah (b. 1945)

Tannen has written many articles and books on linguistics that are easily accessible to the general public. *That's Not What I Meant: How Conversational Style Makes or Breaks Your Relations with Others* (1986), *You Just Don't Understand: Women and Men in Conversation* (1990), *Gender and Discourse* (1994), and *The Argument Culture* (1999) are her most well known works. As a professor of linguistics at Georgetown University, she has also written scholarly works such as *Linguistics in Context* (1988) and *Framing in Discourse* (1993). Her most recent book is *I Only Say This Because I Love You: How the Way We Talk Can Make or Break Family Relationships throughout Our Lives* (2001). She has also published a collection of short stories, *Greek Icons*.

Tapahonso, Luci (b. 1951)

Luci Tapahonso is a Navajo who lives in Albuquerque, New Mexico. Her published work includes *Sáanii Dahataal, the Women Are Singing: Poems and Stories* (1993), *Song for the Direction of North* (1994), *Navajo ABC: A Dine Alphabet Book* (1995), *Blue Horses Rush In: Poems and Stories* (1997), and *Songs of Shiprock Fair* (1999).

Tennyson, Alfred (1st Baron Tennyson, commonly called Alfred, Lord Tennyson) (1809–1892)

Born in Somersby, Lincolnshire, England, Tennyson is considered representative of the Victorian era in his native country. His work encompasses the gamut of lyric, elegaic, dramatic, and epic poetry. His subject matter includes Arthurian legends, classical mythology, and the moral values of the upper classes. Among his best-known poems are "The Lady of Shalott," "In Memoriam," and "Crossing the Bar."

Thomas, Dylan (1914–1953)

Thomas, born in Swansea, Wales, avoided formal education but began to write poems at an early age. By the age of twenty, he was a published poet. His voice impressed audiences who heard him read his works in lecture halls, on radio, and through recordings. His pastoral poems frequently reflect his joy in the frightening but beautiful processes of nature. "Do Not Go Gentle into That Good Night," "And death shall have no dominion," "A Refusal to Mourn Death, by Fire of a Child in London," and "Fern Hill" are among his best-known poems. *Portrait of the Artist As a Young Dog* (1940) recalls his childhood and youth in Wales. *Under Milk Wood* (1954) is an inventive radio play for voices.

Vigil-Piñón, Evangelina (b. 1952)

Vigil-Piñón, a Latina, produced a volume of poetry, *Thirty an' Seen a Lot* (1982), that reflects her explanations of the relation between past and present as it pertains to the preservation of family, myth, culture, and history. The role of the woman as lifegiver, literally as well as metaphorically, is central to her poetic vision. In addition to *The Computer Is Down* (1987), she has contributed to and edited two anthologies: *Woman of Her Word: Hispanic Women Writers* (1983) and *Decade II: An Anniversary Anthology* (1993). She has also written a children's book, *Nalina's Muumuu* (2001), and is a contributor to numerous literary periodicals.

Wagner, Maryfrances Cusumano (b. 1947)

Born in Kansas City, Missouri, Wagner teaches high school English. Like many second generation Italian Americans she learned the language during her adult life. Her poetry reflects her interest in traditional and present day attitudes toward her ethnic heritage. She has written *Bandaged Watermelon and Other Rusty Ducks* (1976) and *Tonight Cicadas Sing* (1981).

Walker, Alice (b. 1944)

Born in Georgia to a family of sharecroppers, Walker was encouraged to excel in school and attended college in Atlanta and New York. Her first volume of poetry was published in 1968. In addition, she has written novels, short stories, and a book of essays. *The Color Purple* (1982) won a Pulitzer Prize and became a successful film. Her fiction examines the role of black women in a world dominated by sexism and racial oppression. Walker was active in the civil rights movement in Mississippi. In addition to *The Color Purple*, her novels include *The Third Life of Grange Copeland* (1973), *Meridian* (1976), and *The Temple of My Familiar* (1989). Her short story collection includes *In Love and Trouble: Stories of Black Women* (1973) and *You Can't Keep a Good Woman Down* (1981). Her collected poetry appears in *Good Night, Willie Lee, I'll See You in the Morning* (1979); *Horses Make a Landscape More Beautiful* (1984); and *Possessing the Secret of Joy* (1992). An autobiography, *The Same River Twice: Honoring the Difficult: A Meditation of Life, Spirit, and the Making of the Film, The Color Purple, Ten Years Later* was published in 1996.

In 1994, the California State Board of Education removed two of Walker's short stories from one of its programs. "Roselily" was one of those banned because it concerned a teenage unwed mother. *Alice Walker Banned* (1996) relates the controversy and includes newspaper articles, letters, and an assessment by Patricia Holt.

Walker's recent nonfiction includes *Anything We Love Can Be Saved: A Writer's Activism* (1997) and *Dreads: Sacred Rites of the Natural Hair Revolution* (with Francesco Mastalia and Alfonse Pagano, 1999). Her latest works of fiction are *By the Light of My Father's Smile* (1998) and *The Way Forward Is with a Broken Heart* (2000).

Wharton, Edith (1862–1937)

Wharton, born in New York City to wealthy and socially prominent parents, married a Boston banker in 1885. However, resenting the restrictions of a society matron, she pursued her own intellectual interests. She wrote novels such as *The House of Mirth* (1902) and *The Custom of the Country* (1913), which probed the emptiness of life in aristocratic New York society. A favorite theme was the rigid code of manners and conventions that denied personal happiness to both men and women. In 1907, she moved permanently to Europe but continued to write books with American settings and themes of the ironies and tragedies of life. *The Age of Innocence* (1920) won a Pulitzer Prize. The Cross of the Legion of Honor was awarded to her for relief work in World War I.

Whitman, Walt (1819–1892)

Born near Huntington, Long Island, in New York, Whitman held a variety of jobs, including office boy, carpenter, printer, schoolteacher, journalist, and editor. In 1855, he published a volume of poems entitled *Leaves of Grass*, but it was unfavorably reviewed because of its radical form and content. During the next thirty-five years, he revised and added to it in nine editions. When his brother was wounded in the Civil War, Whitman went to Virginia to nurse him. He stayed on in Washington, D.C., as a nurse in army hospitals. After the war, he was a clerk in a government office but was fired because *Leaves of Grass* was considered an immoral book. His verse was appreciated in Europe, however, and eventually he received recognition in his own country. "When Lilacs Last in the Dooryard Bloom'd" and "O Captain! My Captain!" commemorated the death of Abraham Lincoln. His war impressions appear in *Drum Taps and Specimen Days*. Some of his war poems reflect a nostalgic or romantic vision of war.

Wiesel, Elie (b. 1928)

Born in Rumania, Wiesel is a survivor of the Nazi concentration camps at Auschwitz and Buchenwald, where his parents and sister were killed. François Mauriac, the French novelist and essayist, urged Wiesel to write of the horrors of the war, and Wiesel produced *Night* in 1956. This memoir-novel recounts his family's death-camp sufferings and his own guilt at surviving. Since then, he has completed twenty-five books on Holocaust themes. Man's inhumanity to man, survival, and injustice are his subjects. In 1986, he was awarded the Nobel Peace Prize. *All Rivers Run to the Sea* (1995) contains his latest reflections on the Holocaust. *Untitled Memoirs* (1988), *And the Sea Is Never Full* (1999), *The Testament* (1999), *The Judges: A Novel* (2002), and *Night: With Related Readings* (2003) are his latest works.

Wilbur, Richard (Purdy) (b. 1921)

A native of New York City, Wilbur earned his B.A. from Amherst College and an M.A. from Harvard, and he served in the U.S. Army in World War II. He has taught English at many Ivy League colleges. His poetry collections include *The Beautiful Changes* (1947), *Ceremony*

(1950), *Things of This World* (Pulitzer and National Book Award, [1956]), *The Beastiary* (1955), *Advice to a Prophet* (1961), *The Poems of Richard Wilbur* (1963), *Walking to Sleep* (1960), and *The Mind Reader* (1971). He has also translated many of Molière's plays into English, including *Tartuffe*, one of the plays in this anthology. His work is collected in *The Poems of Richard Wilbur* (1988), *The Catbird's Songs: Prose Pieces, 1963– 1995* (1997), and his most recent work includes *The Disappearing Alphabet* (illustrated by David Diaz, 1998), *Opposites, More Opposites, and a Few Differences* (2000), and *Mayflies: New Poems and Translations* (2000).

Williams, William Carlos (1883–1963)

For most of his life, Williams lived and practiced medicine in his hometown of Rutherford, New Jersey. His patients' language often inspired his poems, which frequently focused through everyday objects and experiences. Although he lived and worked away from the literary world, he was friends with important writers of his time like Wallace Stevens, Ezra Pound, and H.D. (Hilda Aldington), and he traced his roots to Whitman. His first book, *Poems*, appeared in 1909, followed by *The Tempers* (1913), *Kora in Hell* (1920), *Spring and All* (1923), several volumes of *Collected Poems* (1934, 1950, and 1951), *Journey to Love* (1955), and *Pictures from Breughel and Other Poems* (1963), which won a Pulitzer Prize. In addition to the five-volume epic *Paterson* (1946–1958), Williams wrote *Autobiography* in 1951, several volumes of criticism, and a book of stories, *The Farmer's Daughter* (1961).

Woolf, Virginia (1882–1941)

Born in London, Woolf was reared in an upper-middle-class family dominated by her father, Sir Leslie Stephen, a noted scholar. Because of her delicate health and her father's views on the proper place of women, she was tutored at home and had free access to his extensive library. After her father's death, she and her sister Vanessa hosted gatherings at their home in the Bloomsbury section of London, attracting literary and intellectual figures of the day. Woolf kept diaries from an early age and soon began writing novels and short stories. At first conventional in form, she later wrote in an innovative and distinguished manner in such novels as *Jacob's Room* (1922), *To the Lighthouse* (1927), and *Orlando* (1928). She used stream of consciousness, a form of interior dialogue similar to the technique of her contemporary James Joyce. An absence of conventional plot and action characterized her distinctive style. She and her husband Leonard Woolf, a writer on politics and economics, started the Hogarth Press, and the success of their first ventures in publishing led to a series of works by the best and most original young authors such as T. S. Eliot and E. M. Forster. The first English edition of the works of Sigmund Freud, the originator of psychoanalysis, highlighted their endeavors. A strong advocate of women's rights, Woolf's views are expressed in a group of essays in *A Room of One's Own* (1929) and *Three Guineas* (1938). The essay "Professions for Women" was originally a talk delivered in 1931 to The Women's Service League. During her life, she suffered numerous nervous breakdowns, and in 1941, fearing the onset of another attack and the subsequent treatments, she committed suicide.

Wordsworth, William (1770–1850)

Wordsworth is considered the poet who introduced romanticism to England. Nurtured in the beautiful Lake District of England, Wordsworth experienced a life that led him to revere nature. He was educated at Cambridge University and lived for a short time in France where he became an advocate of the French Revolution. He believed the revolutionaries were interested in improving the life of the common man. On his return to England, he made the acquaintance of Samuel Taylor Coleridge and thus began a close friendship which led to their collaboration on the *Lyrical Ballads* (1798). In his celebrated preface to the second edition of this work, he declared himself a nature poet and one who was committed to democratic equality and the language of the common people. *The Prelude* was completed in 1805 but was not published until his death. His other works include *Poems in Two Volumes* (1807) and *The Excursion* (1814). In his later years, Wordsworth became more conservative in his beliefs and, although he continued to write, little of it is considered equal to his earlier works. In 1843, he was appointed poet laureate.

Wright, James (1927–1980)

Wright was born in Martins Ferry, Ohio, and studied with Theodore Roethke at the University of Washington, where he received the Ph.D. He taught at a number of colleges, finally settling at Hunter College in New York City, where he taught from 1966 until his death from cancer in 1980. A midwesterner who reviled his native soil, his work yet relied for much of its inspiration on that region. His central image was that of a nomadic figure, alone in an overwhelming universe. *The Green Wall*, his first collection, appeared in 1957, followed by *Saint Judas* (1959), *The Lion's Tail and Eyes* (1962), *The Branch Will Not Break* (1963), *Shall We Gather at the River* (1968), and the Pulitzer Prize–winning *Collected Poems* (1971). Later collections include *Moments of the Italian Summer* (1976), *To a Blossoming Pear Tree* (1977), and *This Journey*, which was published posthumously in 1982.

Yamauchi, Wakako (b. 1924)

Yamauchi's parents left Japan and became farmers in Westmoreland, California, where Wakako was born in 1924. The family lived in a community of Japanese immigrants but she went to American public schools. At home the household looked back to Japan for its traditions, values, and rewards, while the children were struggling to become Americans. In 1942, during World War II, she and her family were interned in a "relocation" camp in Arizona. There Yamauchi worked on the camp newspaper and met the writer Hisaye Yamamoto. It was the first time she had "read a writer who spoke about things I knew about. . . the kinds of lives we led before the war. She taught me not to be ashamed or afraid of being Japanese in my writing, in my heart." Several years after her release from camp, Yamauchi started writing stories and plays, many of which deal with tensions between Japanese immigrant parents and their American-born children. They also address the universal elements of human endurance, survival, and strength. Her works have been collected in *Songs My Mother Taught Me: Stories, Plays, and Memoir* (1994).

Yevtushenko, Yevgeny (b. 1933)

Yevtushenko was born in Zima, Siberia, and had his first volume of poetry published when he was nineteen. He became prominent as the leader of the Soviet younger generation in its criticism of his country's policies. "Babiy Yar," his poem condemning the Nazis' murder of ninety-six thousand Jews in the Ukraine, caused consternation because it implied complicity on the part of the Soviet leadership. During the cold-war thaw in the late 1950s, he was allowed to travel to the United States to give poetry readings that attracted large audiences. In recent years, he again gained prominence for his support of Soviet president Mikhail Gorbachev's policy of *glasnost*. Some of his poems celebrate the everyday life of ordinary people. His works include *The Poetry of Yevgeny Yevtushenko* (1981), *Wild Berries* (1989), *Fatal Half Measures: The Cultures of Democracy in the Soviet Union* (1991), and *Don't Die Before You're Dead* (1995). Most recently, he has published *Pre-Morning: A New Book of Poetry in English and Russian* (1995) and *The Best of the Best: A New Book of Poetry in English and Russian* (1999).

Glossary

Abstract   Without physical, tangible existence in itself; a concept as opposed to an object. A "child" is a concrete object that our senses can perceive, but "childishness" is an abstract quality.

Act   A major division of the action of a play, usually subdivided into scenes—smaller units of action with no breaks in place or time.

Alienation   Emotional or intellectual separation from peer groups and/or society.

Allegory   A narrative that has a second meaning in addition to the obvious one. The meaning may be religious, moral, or political. Settings, objects, and events are only representational. Characters are incarnations of abstract ideas, for example, faith, hope, or desire.

Alliteration   Repetition of the same consonant sounds at the beginning of words on the same line or in close proximity—"Stole with soft step its shining archway through," for example.

Allusion   A reference to a familiar mythical, historical, or literary person, place, or thing.

Ambiguity   Intentional uncertainty or lack of clarity about meaning, where more than one meaning is possible.

Ambivalence   The existence of mutually conflicting attitudes or feelings.

Anachronism   Wrongful assignment of an event, person, or scene to a time when it did not exist.

Anecdote   Brief, unadorned narrative of an event or happening. It differs from a short story in that it is shorter, consists of a single episode, and has a simple plot.

Antagonist   The character in a drama, poem, or other fiction who opposes or rivals the protagonist.

Anticlimax   A trivial event immediately following significant events. The reader expects something greater or more serious to occur but finds a less striking event.

Antihero   A protagonist who is deficient in attributes usually attributed to a hero.

Anti-Semitism   Hostility toward Jews as a religious or racial minority group, often accompanied by social, economic, and/or political discrimination.

Apostrophe   A poetic figure of speech in which some abstract quality or personification is addressed, for example, "O ye Fountains, Meadows, Hills and Groves . . ."

Archetype   Primordial images from Jung's "collective unconscious" of the human race, often expressed in myths, religion, dreams, and literature. Can provoke a profound, resonating reader response.

Argumentation   In persuasive essays, a unit of discourse meant to prove a point or to convince; the process of proving or persuading.

Aside   Speech directed to the audience and, by convention, presumed inaudible to other characters on stage.

Assonance   In a line, sentence, or stanza, the repetition of similar vowel sounds, for example, *penitent* and *reticence*.

Atmosphere   The overall mood of a literary work, often created by the setting or landscape.

Audience   A work's intended readership, the author's perception of which directly affects style and tone. As a rule, the more limited or detailed the subject matter, the more specific the audience. An author may write more technically if the intended audience is composed of specialists in the field and may write less technically if the writing is for the general public.

Audio-Visual Montage   The relationship between visual material on the screen and a sound that does not belong to that material, for example, a shot of a woman about to scream accompanied by the loud sound of a train whistle instead of the scream.

Author (film)   The "author" of a film, as opposed to that of a novel or play, is considered to be the director, not the screenwriter, because the director must bring together and integrate all elements of a film, of which the screenplay is only one.

Ballad   A form that originated in the oral folk tradition as an anonymous shared song, usually terse, dramatic, and impersonal. Also, a literary poem deliberately written in the spirit and form of the folk ballad, for example, Keat's "La Belle Dame sans Merci."

Biographical Criticism   Based on the premise that knowledge of an author's life can enhance interpretation of his or her work.

Blank Verse   Unrhymed iambic pentameter. A fluid and common verse form close to the natural rhythms of English speech.

Burlesque   A form of comedy characterized by ridiculous and exaggerated actions.

Caesura   A pause in the meter and rhythm of a line of poetry, indicated in scansion by double straight slashes (//). See also *scansion*.

Camera movement   Can be anything from a brief *pan* or *tilt* of the camera to widen our view of a particular scene, to elaborate *tracking shots* in which the camera moves over a large expanse of space in any direction, e.g., to follow the action in a continuous take rather than breaking it down through editing, to enhance the sense of the reality of a setting, or as directorial commentary on the action.

Canon   A criterion or standard of measurement; the generally accepted list of great works of literature or accepted list of an author's works.

Canto   A division or section of a long poem.

Carpe Diem   Latin for "seize the day," a popular literary theme stressing that life is all too brief and should be enjoyed as it unfolds.

Catharsis   The effect of tragedy in relieving or purging the emotions of an audience. Aristotle explains the theory in his *Poetics*.

Cause and Effect   A type of exposition used primarily to answer the questions "Why did this occur?" and "What will happen next?" The structure of a cause-and-effect essay is a series of events or conditions, the last of which (the effect) cannot occur without the preceding ones (causes). When you write a cause-and-effect essay, it is helpful to keep chronology clearly in mind: Remember, causes always create effects and effects are derived from causes.

Character Type   A standard, recognizable kind of secondary character, often stereotypical in nature and found in many genre films, such as the country bumpkin or the good-hearted prostitute.

Chorus   In Greek drama, a group of performers who comment on the actions or characters in the play.

Classical Hollywood Filmmaking   This term refers to the collection of codes and stylistic conventions (such as *continuity editing* that preserves a logical sense of time and space from shot to shot) used in narrative filmmaking as established by Hollywood during the dominance of the studio system from the 1930s through the 1960s. It is not an evaluative term implying that every movie made in Hollywood during this time is a "classic" in the conventional sense of that word.

Classical Tragedy   Refers to the tragedy of the ancient Greeks and Romans. The rules of tragic composition are derived from Aristotle and Horace.

Climax   The point at which dramatic or narrative action builds to its highest point, and the reader experiences the greatest emotional response.

Collective Unconscious   A foundational Jungian concept stemming from Jung's belief that racially inherited images and ideas persist in individual consciousness, and unconscious motivations are therefore collectively shared as well as personal.

Comedy   A dramatic work intended to engage and amuse the audience with the embarrassments and discomfitures endured by its main characters until a favorable ending is arrived at. High comedy, a comedy of manners and verbal wit, evokes intellectual laughter, and low comedy depends on physical antics, slapstick, or burlesque for humor.

Comedy of Manners   Realistic comedy concerned with the manners, fashion, and conventions of seventeenth-century high society. Usually characterized by witty dialogue, or repartee, and sexual innuendo.

Commedia dell'Arte   Italian low comedy from the mid-sixteenth century in which professional actors playing stock characters, performing in masks, improvised dialogue to fit a given scenario.

Comparison and Contrast   A type of exposition that states or suggests similarities and differences between two or more things. Two types of organization for comparison and contrast essays are point by point and subject by subject.

Complication   The part of the plot in which the conflict between opposing forces is developed.

Composition   The way visual material is organized in a film shot, such as foreground and background, and the arrangement of people and objects within the frame. Composition also includes the way the camera photographs the material—for example, from a high or low angle.

Conceit   A comparison between two very different objects.

Conflict   The struggle between opposing characters that causes tension or suspense.

Connotation   The implication(s) and overtones, qualities, feelings, and ideas that a word suggests. Connotation goes beyond literal meaning or dictionary definition.

Consensus   General agreement and/or collective opinion of a group.

Controlling Image   An image or metaphor that recurs in a literary work and symbolizes the theme, such as the wallpaper in Charlotte Perkins Gilman's "The Yellow Wallpaper."

Convention   Any device, style, or subject matter that has become, through its recurring use, an accepted element of technique.

Couplet   Two successive lines of verse that rhyme.

Cross-cutting   A form of film editing that repeatedly alternates between two or more different actions, often to imply simultaneity. It is commonly used in chase sequences, where the film cuts from shots of the pursuer to shots of the pursued throughout the progress of the chase.

Culture The total pattern of human (learned) behavior embodied in thought, speech, action, and artifacts. It is dependent on the human capacity for learning and transmitting knowledge to succeeding generations through the use of tools, language, and systems of abstract thought.

Deconstructionism A critical method of close textual analysis that explores the ambiguities of language and the many possible readings they suggest.

Definition A type of exposition that explains the meaning of a word or concept by bringing its characteristics into sharp focus. An extended definition explores the feelings and ideas you attach to a word. Extended definitions are suited to words with complex meanings, words that are subject to interpretation, or words that evoke strong reactions. Such definitions are an appropriate basis for organizing exposition. A dictionary definition places a word in a class with similar items but also differentiates it from members of the same class.

Denotation The literal meaning of a word as defined in a dictionary. It is distinct from connotation.

Denouement A French word for the "unknotting" or falling action that follows the climax and leads to the resolution of the plot.

Description A method of paragraph development that conveys sensory experience through one or more of the five senses: sight, hearing, touch, taste, and smell. Description is generally either objective or subjective and can be organized in three broad categories: spatial, chronological, or dramatic.

Diction The writer's choice of words. In proper diction, word choice enhances the expression of the author's ideas; in poor diction, words get in the way of the author's intended meaning.

Discourse Sets of statements that hold together around languages; any statements across culture that organize a mechanism, discipline, or sexuality; the social use of language.

Downstage The area of the stage behind the proscenium, nearest the audience.

Drama The literary form designed for the theater in which actors impersonate the characters and perform the dialogue and action.

Dramatic Irony See *irony*.

Dramatic Monologue A poetic form that presents one character speaking to a silent audience and revealing in the discourse personal temperament and a dramatic situation.

Dramatic Unities See *three unities*.

Editing (film) The process by which individual shots are joined to create meaning and develop the narrative. Editing can be of the "classical" type, following strict rules in order to sustain continuity and logic; or it can be experimental, creating ambiguous or provocative relationships between shots.

Ego According to Freud, the rational and conscious part of the psyche that opposes the id as well as the superego.

Electra Complex Female counterpart of the Oedipus complex. A daughter's unconscious competition with her mother for her father's affection. Based on the Greek myth of Electra and Agamemnon. See also *Oedipus complex*.

Elegy A formal sustained expression of grief about the death of a particular person or the passing of a particular way of life.

Elizabethan Age The English literary period named after Queen Elizabeth, lasting from 1558 until 1642, the year of the closing of the theaters. Notable names of the period include Shakespeare, Sidney, Spencer, and Marlowe.

Epic A long narrative poem, dignified in theme and style with a hero who, through experiences of great adventure, accomplishes important deeds.

Epigram   A witty or clever saying, concisely expressed.

Epigraph   A quotation at the beginning of a work that is related to the theme.

Epilogue   A concluding statement, sometimes in verse, summarizing the themes of the work.

Epiphany   A moment of insight for a character, often the catalyst for a turning point in a narrative or drama.

Episode   An incident in the course of a series of events.

Erotic   Tending to excite sexual pleasure or desire.

Ethnicity   Ethnic quality or affiliation, physical or cultural characteristics that identify an individual with a particular race, religion, or cultural group.

Ethnocentrism   The tendency to judge other cultures by the standards of one's own.

Exclusion   The act of deliberately not including someone or something, or preventing entry into a place or activity.

Existentialism   A twentieth-century philosophy that denies the existence of a transcendent meaning to life and places the burden of justifying existence on individuals.

Exposition   A mode or form of discourse that conveys information, gives directions, or explains an idea that is difficult to understand.

Fable   A simple tale, either in prose or verse, told to illustrate a moral. The subject matter may be drawn from folklore.

Fantasy   An imaginative or fanciful work concerning supernatural or unnatural events or characters.

Farce   A dramatic piece intended to generate laughter through exaggerated or improbable situations.

Feminist Criticism   A mode of analysis, a method of approaching life and politics, rather than a set of political conclusions about the oppression of women; examines representations of the feminine in all literature and often focuses on works written by women.

Figurative Language   Words used to express meaning beyond the literal denotative level.

Figures of Speech   Language that departs from the standard denotation of words to achieve special meaning and effects. See also *metaphor, personification, simile.*

Film Genre   A kind of film, made in Hollywood and elsewhere, that follows established narrative, characterization, and thematic conventions and formulas—such as the melodrama, the western, the horror film, the war film, the musical, the crime or detective film, and science fiction.

Filmic Metaphor   The juxtaposition of two or more shots that establishes a likeness, similarity, or analogy among different elements, for example, a shot of people crowded in a subway during rush hour followed by a shot of sheep being herded into a pen.

Film Noir   A term introduced in the early 1940s to identify a style of Hollywood filmmaking, usually found in crime stories and melodramas, that relies on heavy use of shadows and dark, atmospheric cinematography.

Flashback   A device by which the chronology of events is interrupted by relating events from the past.

Flat Character or Stock Character   A person in a fictional or dramatic work who does not undergo individual development and who often embodies a stereotype.

Foil   A term for any character who, through extreme contrast, intensifies the character of another.

Foot   A unit of stressed and unstressed syllables used in the scansion of poetry. The most common are the iamb, trochee, anapest, and dactyl. The predominant foot in a given line, together with the number of feet in the line, define that line's meter. See also *iambic foot, meter, scansion.*

Foreshadowing   Subtle clues early in the narrative indicating what will happen later in the plot.

Formalist Criticism   A method of criticism in which the formal aspects of literature (such as figurative language and narrative techniques) and literary craft are the touchstones in studying a text.

Framing   The way a film shot is positioned in relation to the four borders of the screen; often used in conjunction with *composition*.

Free Verse   Verse that does not rhyme and uses open speech patterns and forms to create poetry.

Gay and Lesbian Criticism   A critical method that examines the representation of homosexuality in literature.

Gender   Characteristics and roles assigned by family and/or culture to establish preferred patterns of behavior based on sex; sets of social attributions, characteristics, behavior, appearance, dress, expectations, roles, and so on expected of individuals based on gender assignment at birth.

Genre   District categories of literature, such as the play, the short story, the poem, and the novel.

Hero/Heroine   See *tragic hero/heroine*.

Heterocentrism   The tendency to judge or treat as invisible any sexual or affectional relationship that does not conform to the dominant heterosexual or marriage standard.

High Comedy   See *comedy*.

Hubris   Excessive arrogance or pride that results in the downfall of the protagonist.

Hyperbole   Obvious exaggeration or an extravagant statement intended to create a memorable image. A fisherman who brags that the one that got away was "as big as a whale" almost certainly is speaking hyperbolically.

Iambic Foot   A metrical foot in which an unstressed syllable is followed by a stressed syllable, for example, *away*.

Id   According to Freud, the driving force of the unconscious mind that is endowed with energy and is capable of motivating our actions.

Identity   The set of behavioral or personal characteristics by which an individual is recognizable as a member of a group.

Ideology   A system of belief used overtly or covertly to justify or legitimize preferred patterns of behavior.

Imagery   Used in descriptive passages in poetry to convey thematic mood and emotion. In film, a repeated use of related visual material, which accumulates important associations and illuminate some aspect of the story or theme (e.g., many shots of doors or rain or light).

Imperialism   The imposition of the power of one state over the territories of another, normally by military means, in order to exploit subjugated populations to extract economic and political advantages.

Institution   That which is established or accepted in society; an established way of behaving; established procedures and organizations—schools, for example.

Internal Rhyme   Rhyming words that appear within a line of poetry.

Irony   The undermining or contradicting of someone's expectations. Irony may be either verbal or dramatic. Verbal irony arises from a discrepancy, sometimes intentional and sometimes not, between what is said and what is meant, as when a dog jumps forward to bite you, and you say, "What a friendly dog!" Dramatic irony arises from a discrepancy between what someone expects to happen and what does happen, for example, if the dog that seemed so unfriendly to you saved your life.

Jargon   The vocabulary or phrases peculiar to a particular profession or group. It may also mean a language or word incomprehensible to others or garbled.

Journal   A daily written record of ideas, memories, experiences, or dreams. A journal can be used for prewriting and as a source for formal writing.

Literal   The ordinary or primary meaning of a word or expression. Strictly denotative language without imagination or embellishment.

Low Comedy   See *comedy*.

Lyric   A poem, usually brief, that expresses states of mind and emotion. See also *elegy, ode, sonnet*.

Marginalized   Not fully explored or realized.

Melodrama   A play written in a sensational manner, pitting a stereotypical hero and villain against one another in violent, suspenseful, and emotional scenes.

Metaphor   A comparison between unlike things that does not use *as* or *like*, such as "The road is a ribbon of moonlight."

Meter   The measurement establishing the rhythm of a line of poetry. The unit within the line is a foot, each being a set of accented and unaccented syllables. The number of feet in a line is also enumerated in the meter. For example, a line of five iambs is called iambic pentameter. See a specialized dictionary for a detailed explanation of meter. See also *foot*.

Metonymy   A figure of speech in which the name of one object or concept is substituted for that of a related one, for example, using "the bottle" to mean "strong drink" or "The White House" to refer to "the President."

Mise-en-Scène   A French term referring to the way a stage designer organizes the setting, lighting, and character movement in a play. In film, it refers to all visual components of the image: props, set design, color, lighting, organization of space, and character movement in relation to all of the above.

Misogyny   Women-hating; the belief that women are inferior to men mentally, emotionally, and physically.

Mixed Metaphor   An inconsistent and incongruous comparison between two things.

Modernism   A movement of the early twentieth century against the conventions of romantic literary representation. The modernists rejected what they viewed as the flowery and artificial language of Victorian literature and originated new techniques such as stream of consciousness in fiction and free verse in poetry.

Monoculturalism   Pertaining to one culture to the exclusion of all other cultures.

Montage   A form of editing developed by Russian filmmakers of the silent era, determined not by story logic and continuity, but by an idea the filmmaker wishes to suggest through a challenging and provocative juxtaposition of individual shots. In Sergei Eisenstein's *Battleship Potemkin*, the montage of a sword, a cross, and the czar's insignia suggests the collaboration of military, church, and state authorities.

Motif   A recurring character, theme, or situation that appears in many types of literature.

Motive   Whatever prompts a person to act in a particular way.

Multiculturalism   Assimilation of several cultures while allowing each culture to retain its separate identity.

Myth   A traditional or legendary story with roots in folk beliefs.

Narration   A narrative essay is a story with a point; narration is the technique used to tell the story. When writing a narrative essay, pay close attention to point of view, pacing, chronology, and transitions.

Narrative   The art, technique, or process of telling a story.

Narrator The point of view from which the story is told. A first-person narrator is a character, not the author. A third-person narrator refers to an omniscient point of view. See also *omniscient narrator*.

Naturalism A school of writing that tries to show that human fate is controlled by environment and heredity, both of which humans do not understand.

Neoclassicism Eighteenth-century literary theory and practice in theater and poetry with emphasis on tradition, form, and the social position and limitations of humanity. For example, the view that "the proper study of mankind is man."

Neurosis Emotional disturbance due to unresolved unconscious conflicts, typically involving anxiety and depression.

New Criticism An approach to criticism of literature that concentrates on textual criticism without referring to biographical or historical study.

New Historicism A politically oriented school of criticism, focusing on the power relations, ideologies, and political currents implicit in a text. It shares many of the tenets of Marxist criticism.

Ode A lyric poem that expresses exalted or enthusiastic emotion and often commemorates a person or event.

Oedipus Complex A male adult's repressed childhood wishes to identify with his father and to take his father's place in the affections of his mother. See also *Electra complex*.

Off-Screen Anything not seen on screen but whose existence is implied beyond the edges of the film's frame. It can be suggested by a sound, by the glance of a character in an off-screen direction, or by the viewer's preestablished knowledge of what lies in the off-screen space. Off-screen space is effectively used in horror and mystery films to create anxiety or suspense.

Omniscient Narrator A narrator who may reveal the consciousness of varying numbers of the story's characters. Three types of third person narrators are frequently used by writers: *third person omniscient*: thoughts and feelings of any number of characters are revealed; *third person limited omniscient*: only one character's thoughts and feelings are revealed; and *third person objective*: no character's thoughts and feelings are revealed.

Onomatopoeia A word whose pronunciation suggests its meaning, such as *hiss*, *buzz*, or *bang*.

Oppression The conditions and experience of subordination and injustice. Oppression is the condition of being overwhelmed or heavily burdened by another's exercise of wrongful authority or power, for example, the unjust or cruel treatment of subjects or inferiors; the imposition of unreasonable or unjust burdens.

Oxymoron A figure of speech that produces an effect of seeming contradiction, for example, "Make haste slowly."

Parable A short allegorical story designed to convey a truth or a moral lesson.

Paradox A seemingly contradictory statement that, upon examination, contains a truth, for example, "damn with faint praise."

Paraphrase The restatement of a passage using the reader's own words.

Pastoral Any literary work that celebrates the simple rural life or those who live close to nature.

Pathos The power of literature to evoke feelings of pity or compassion in the reader.

Patriarchy A system in which men have all or most of the power and importance in a society or group. The patriarchal system is preserved through marriage and the family; those who promote the system believe that it is rooted in biology rather than in economics or history.

Pentameter A line of poetry that contains five metrical feet.

Persona The mask or voice that the author creates to tell a story.

Personification   An abstract concept or inanimate object that is represented as having human qualities or characteristics. To write that "death rides a pale horse," for example, is to personify death.

Persuasion   The art of moving someone else to act in a desired way or to believe in a chosen idea. Logic and reason are important tools of persuasion. Equally effective may be an appeal either to the emotions or to the ethical sensibilities.

Plagiarism   Using the words or ideas of another writer and representing them as one's original work.

Poetic Justice   The ideal judgment that rewards virtue and punishes evil.

Point of View   The vantage point from which an author writes. For example, in expository writing, an author may adopt a first-person point of view. See also *narrator*.

Point of View Shot   A film shot that is seen from the perspective of a particular character. An entire narrative film may be from the viewpoint of one character, often reinforced by a narrative voice-over.

Postcolonial Criticism   See *New Historicism*.

Postmodernism   Literary and artistic philosophy that rejects all formal constraints. The postmodern artist tends to accept the world as fragmented and incoherent and to represent those characteristics in art, typically in a comic and self-reflexive style.

Projection   The unconscious process of attributing one's own feelings and/or attitudes to others, especially as defense against guilt or feelings of inferiority.

Proscenium Arch   A picture-frame stage.

Protagonist   The main character in a play or story, also called the hero or heroine.

Psyche   The aggregate of the mental components of an individual, including both conscious and unconscious states and often regarded as an entity functioning apart from or independently of the body.

Psychoanalytic Criticism   Criticism using the theories of Freud and other psychologists to analyze human behavior in literature much as it is analyzed in real-life situations.

Pun   A play on words based on the similarity of sound between two words differing in meaning. For example, "Ask for me tomorrow and you will find me a grave man."

Purpose   A writer's reason for writing. A writer's purpose is clarified by his or her answer to the question, "*Why* am I writing?"

Quatrain   A four-line stanza employing various meters and rhyme patterns. The most common stanza in English poetry.

Reader-Response Criticism   Criticism that focuses on the reader's construction of meaning while experiencing a text, taking into account the wide range of responses a given text may produce.

Real Time   The actual concurrence of an action or event with the time it takes to unfold on film. For example, a performance of a dance photographed in a single, uninterrupted, unedited shot preserves the actual time of the dance itself, this adding to the viewer's appreciation of the performance skill of the dancers.

Realism   A literary movement that lasted from approximately the mid-nineteenth century to the early twentieth century in America, England, and France. Realism is characterized by the attempt to truthfully depict the lives of ordinary people through accurate description and psychologically realistic characters.

Refrain   A phrase or verse consisting of one or more lines repeated at intervals in a poem, usually at the end of each stanza.

Repression   The exclusion from consciousness of painful, unpleasant, or unacceptable memories, desires, and impulses.

Resolution   The conclusion to the major and minor subplots of a drama. The ending.

Rhetorical Question   A question not requiring a response. The answer is obvious and is intended to produce an effect.

Rhyme   The repetition of similar or duplicate sounds at regular intervals—often the terminal sounds of the last words of lines of verse. For example, *girl, whirl*.

Rhythm   The pattern of recurrent strong and weak accents and long and short syllables in speech, music, and poetry. Rhythm creates sound patterns and accentuates meaning.

Romanticism   An artistic revolt of the late eighteenth and early nineteenth centuries against the traditional, formal, and orderly ideals of neoclassicism. The writers of this time dropped conventional poetic diction and forms in favor of freer forms and bolder language, and they explored the grotesque, nature, mysticism, and emotional psychology in their art.

Satire   A literary work in poetry or prose in which a subject or person is held up to scorn, derision, or ridicule with the intent of improving a situation.

Scansion   Counting the stresses in a line of poetry in order to establish its metrical pattern.

Scene   An episode that relates one part of a play's story. Acts are usually composed of more than one scene. The term may also refer to the setting of a work.

Script   A written text of a play used in preparation for performance. Includes dialogue, stage directions, and sometimes set, props, music, and lighting instructions.

Setting   The physical environment that is an element of a literary work, which can create atmosphere and mood and is closely related to the action and theme of the work. For example, psychological studies can gain in intensity if set in confined areas.

Sex   The anatomical and physiological characteristics that distinguish males from females. See also *gender*.

Simile   A comparison using *like* or *as*, such as *he ate like a pig; her heart felt as light as a feather*. A simile's effectiveness is determined by the contrast in the objects compared.

Social Class   Those having similar shares of power or wealth, thus forming a stratum in the hierarchy of possessions.

Social Structure   The organized patterns of human behavior in a society.

Soliloquy   A speech by one character in a play or other composition to disclose the speaker's innermost thoughts.

Sonnet   A fourteen-line poem with a set rhyme scheme. There are two main forms: the Italian (Petrarchan) and the English (Shakespearean). The Italian is divided into an eight-line stanza (octave) and a six-line stanza (sestet). The rhyme scheme in the octave is *abba, abba* and the sestet is either *cde, cde* or *cdc, dcd*. The English form has four divisions; three quatrains and a rhymed couplet, *abab, cdcd, efef*, and *gg*.

Stage Directions   Written instructions to the actors and director regarding actions, body movements, and facial expressions during a play.

Stanza   A division in the formal pattern of a poem. Usually indicated by indentations or spaces.

Stream of Consciousness   A technique of writing in which a character's thoughts are presented as they occur in random sequence.

Subjective camera   In general, the sense that what we see is from the vantage point of a particular character. A sustained movement of the subjective camera through several spaces can convey the awkward or erratic moves of a character walking behind it. Used to stress the physical presence of a character or, as in a horror film, the unseen monster.

Subjectivity   The personal element in writing. The more subjective a piece of writing the more likely it is to be focused on the writer's opinions and feelings.

Subplot   A secondary line of action in a play or fiction often parallel with or in opposition to the main plot.

Superego   According to Freud, the part of the unconscious that regulates our moral judgment.

Suspense   Uncertainty or excitement resulting from the reader's anxiety in awaiting a decision or outcome.

Symbol   Any word, image, description, name, character, or action that has a range of meanings and associations beyond its literal meaning. An eagle is a conventional symbol of the United States. It may also suggest freedom, power, or solitude.

Textual Criticism   A form of scholarship that attempts to establish an authentic text in the exact form the author wrote it.

Theatre of the Absurd   A type of twentieth-century avant garde drama that presents the human condition as illogical, irrational, and meaningless. *Picnic on the Battlefield* is a good example of the genre.

Theme   The abstract concept embodied in the structure and imagery of a nondidactic or purely imaginative work.

Theory   A way of making sense of or explaining some social phenomenon.

Thesis   The main idea of an essay or other nonfiction work.

Thesis Statement   The part of an essay that clearly and directly states a writer's meaning—it tells what the essay will be about. A thesis statement should be one sentence long and is usually placed in the introduction.

Three Unities   Based on Aristotle's *Poetics*, the specification that a play's action should occur within one day (unity of time) and in a single locale (unity of place) and should reveal clearly ordered actions and plot incidents moving toward the plot's resolution (unity of action). Later scholars and critics, especially those in the neoclassical tradition, interpreted Aristotle's ideas as rules and established them as standards for drama.

Thrust stage   A stage extending beyond the *proscenium arch*, out to the audience so that patrons can be seated around three sides; similar to the Elizabethan stage.

Tone   An author's attitude toward his or her subject. It may be angry, resigned, humorous, serious, sentimental, mocking, ironic, sarcastic, satrical, reasoning, emotional, or philosophic. One tone may predominate, or many tones may be heard in a work.

Tragedy   Literary and particularly dramatic representations of serious actions that turn out disastrously for the chief character.

Tragic Hero/Heroine   In classical Greek drama, a noble character who possesses a tragic flaw that leads to his or her destruction.

Understatement   An obvious downplaying or underrating. It is the opposite of hyperbole, though either may create a memorable image or an ironic effect. To say that "after they ate the apple, Adam and Eve found life a bit tougher" is to understate their condition.

Unities   Aristotle's rules about action (a play should tell a single story); time (it should happen in a single day); and place (it should occupy a single setting).

Upstage   The area of the performance space farthest away from the audience.

Verse   A general term for a poem, often one with a metrical pattern and rhyme.

Verisimilitude   The appearance or semblance of truth.

Visual motif   Similar to the term imagery, but more inclusive in that it can refer not only to things contained within a shot but to camera angles, framings, and compositions of shots, which, when repeated in another context take on additional meaning. For example, an expressive camera angle and composition in *Letter from an Unknown Woman* evokes the feelings of the female protagonist whose point of view was the initial motive for the shot.

Voice-Over   The technique by which a character's or a narrator's voice is heard over the images as a film progresses. If a film is a first-person narrative, it is used to establish and reinforce the first-person point of view.

Credits

1142

Euripides, *Medea* from *Ten Plays by Euripides,* translated by Moses Hadas and John McLean. Copyright © 1960 by the Estate of Elizabeth C. Hadas. Reprinted by permission of the Estate of Elizabeth C. Hadas.

William Faulkner, "A Rose for Emily" is from *Collected Stories of William Faulkner* by William Faulkner. Copyright © 1930 and renewed © 1958 by William Faulkner. Reprinted by permission of Random House, Inc.

Lawrence Ferlinghetti, "Constantly Risking Absurdity," from *A Coney Island of the Mind* by Lawrence Ferlinghetti. Copyright © 1958 by Lawrence Ferlinghetti. Reprinted by permission of New Directions Publishing Corporation.

Carolyn Forché, "The Visitor," "The Memory of Elena," "As Children Together," and "The Colonel," from *The Country between Us* by Carolyn Forché. Copyright © 1981 by Carolyn Forché. Reprinted by permission of HarperCollins Publishers Inc. "The Colonel" originally appeared in *Women's International Resource Exchange.*

Maria Irene Fornes, *The Conduct of Life* in *Maria Irene Fornes: Plays* by Maria Irene Fornes. Copyright © 1986 by Maria Irene Fornes. Reprinted by permission of PAJ Publications.

Ernest J. Gaines, "The Sky is Gray." Copyright © 1963 by Ernest J. Gaines, from *Bloodline* by Ernest J. Gaines. Used by permission of Doubleday, a division of Random House, Inc.

Maria Mazziotti Gillan, "Public School No. 18: Paterson, New Jersey" is reprinted by permission of the author from *Winter Light,* Chantry Press, 1985.

William Glaberson, "New Twist on Lost Youth: Mall Rats." Copyright © 1992 by the New York Times Co. Reprinted by permission.

Nadine Gordimer, "The Moment Before the Gun Went Off" from *Jump and Other Stories* by Nadine Gordimer. Copyright © 1991 by Felix Licensing, B. V. Reprinted by permission in Farrar, Straus and Giroux, LLC. "Town and Country Lovers, One—City Lovers," and "Town and Country Lovers, Two—Country Lovers," copyright © 1975 by Nadine Gordimer, from *Soldier's Embrace* by Nadine Gordimer. Used by permission of Viking Penguin, a division of Penguin Putnam Inc.

Barbara L. Greenberg, "The Faithful Wife" is reprinted from *Poetry Northwest,* Vol 19, no. 2. Copyright ©1979 by Barbara L. Greenberg. Reprinted by permission of the author.

Notes to *Hamlet* from *The Complete Works of Shakespeare,* 4th ed. by David Bevington. Copyright © 1997 by Addison-Wesley Educational Publishers, Inc. Reprinted by permission of Pearson Education, Inc.

Jeffrey Harrison, "Reflection on the Vietnam War Memorial" by Jeffrey Harrison from *The Singing Underneath* (E.P. Dutton, 1988).

Robert Hayden, "Those Winter Sundays." Copyright © 1966 Robert Hayden, from *Angle of Ascent: New and Selected Poems by Robert Hayden.* Used by permission of Liveright Publishing Corporation. "Frederick Douglass," "Runagate Runagate," and "Tour 5," Copyright © 1962, 1966 by Robert Hayden, from *Collected Poems of Robert Hayden* by Robert Hayden, edited by Frederick Glaysher. Used by permission of Liveright Publishing Corporation.

Seamus Heaney, "Mid-Term Break" from *The Opened Ground: Selected Poems 1966-1996* by Seamus Heaney. Copyright © 1998 by Seamus Heaney. Reprinted by permission of Farrar, Straus and Giroux, LLC.

Linda Hogan, "First Light" from *Savings.* Copyright © 1988 Linda Hogan with the permission of Coffee House Press, Minneapolis, Minnesota.

Garrett Hongo, "Fraternity," from *Volcano: A Memoir of Hawaii* by Garrett Hongo. Copyright © 1995 by Garrett Hongo. Used by permission of Alfred A. Knopf, a division of Random House, Inc.

Langston Huges, "The Negro Speaks of Rivers," "The Weary Blues," "Dream Variations," and "Harlem (A Dream Deferred)," from *The Collected Poems of Langston Hughes* by Langston Hughes. Copyright © 1994 by The Estate of Langston Hughes. Used by permission of Alfred A. Knopf, a division of Random House, Inc.

Shirley Jackson, "The Lottery," from *The Lottery and Other Stories* by Shirley Jackson. Copyright © 1948, 1949 by Shirley Jackson. Copyright renewed © 1976, 1977 by Laurence Hyman, Barry Hyman, Mrs. Sarah Webster and Mrs. Joanne Schnurer. Reprinted by permission of Farrar, Straus and Giroux, LLC.

Randall Jarrell, "The Death of the Ball Turret Gunner" from *The Complete Poems* by Randall Jarrell. Copyright © 1969, renewed ©1997 by Mary von S. Jarrell. Reprinted by permission of Farrar, Straus and Giroux, LLC.

Index of Authors and Titles

Index of First Lines

Index of Terms